T0205727

Communications in Computer and Information Science   1449

More information about this series at http://www.springer.com/series/7899

Haijun Zhang · Zhi Yang · Zhao Zhang · Zhou Wu · Tianyong Hao (Eds.)

Neural Computing for Advanced Applications

Second International Conference, NCAA 2021
Guangzhou, China, August 27–30, 2021
Proceedings

 Springer

Editors
Haijun Zhang ⓘ
Harbin Institute of Technology
Shenzhen, China

Zhi Yang ⓘ
Nanfang College of Sun Yat-sen University
Guangzhou, China

Zhao Zhang ⓘ
Hefei University of Technology
Hefei, China

Zhou Wu ⓘ
Chongqing University
Chongqing, China

Tianyong Hao ⓘ
South China Normal University
Guangzhou, China

ISSN 1865-0929   ISSN 1865-0937 (electronic)
Communications in Computer and Information Science
ISBN 978-981-16-5187-8   ISBN 978-981-16-5188-5 (eBook)
https://doi.org/10.1007/978-981-16-5188-5

This Springer imprint is published by the registered company Springer Nature Singapore Pte Ltd.
The registered company address is: 152 Beach Road, #21-01/04 Gateway East, Singapore 189721, Singapore

Preface

Neural computing and artificial intelligence (AI) have become the hottest topics in recent years. To promote multi-disciplinary development and application of neural computing, a series of NCAA conferences was initiated on the theme of "making academic research more practical", to provide an open platform for academic discussions, industrial showcases, and basic training tutorials. This volume contains the papers accepted at the 2021 International Conference on Neural Computing for Advanced Applications (NCAA 2021). NCAA 2021 was organized by Nanfang College of Sun Yat-sen University, South China Normal University, Harbin Institute of Technology, Chongqing University, and Hefei University of Technology, and it was supported by Springer Nature Group. Due to the impact of COVID-19, the mainstream NCAA 2021 conference was turned into a hybrid event, with online and offline participants, in which people could freely connect to a live broadcast of the keynote speeches and presentations.

This volume collates 54 high-quality papers that were selected for publication from among 144 submissions after double-blinded peer-review, which indicates that the acceptance rate of NCAA 2021 was less than 40%. These papers were categorized into 10 technical tracks: neural network theory and cognitive sciences; machine learning, data mining, data security and privacy protection, and data-driven applications; computational intelligence, nature-inspired optimizers, and their engineering applications; cloud/edge/fog computing, the Internet of Things/Vehicles (IoT/IoV), and their system optimization; control systems, network synchronization, system integration, and industrial artificial intelligence; fuzzy logic, neuro-fuzzy systems, decision making, and their applications in management sciences; computer vision, image processing, and their industrial applications; natural language processing, machine translation, knowledge graphs, and their applications; neural computing-based fault diagnosis, fault forecasting, prognostic management, and system modeling; and spreading dynamics, forecasting, and other intelligent techniques against coronavirus disease (COVID-19).

The authors of each paper in this volume have reported their novel results of computing theory or application. The volume cannot cover all aspects of neural computing and advanced applications, but we hope it will inspire insightful thoughts for readers and researchers. We continue to wish that more secrets of AI will be unveiled, and that academic research will find more practical applications.

June 2021

Haijun Zhang
Zhi Yang
Zhao Zhang
Zhou Wu
Tianyong Hao

Organization

Honorary Chairs

John MacIntyre   University of Sunderland, UK
Tommy W. S. Chow   City University of Hong Kong, Hong Kong

General Chairs

Haijun Zhang   Harbin Institute of Technology, China
Zhi Yang   Nanfang College of Sun Yat-sen University, China
Zhao Zhang   Hefei University of Technology, China
Zhou Wu   Chongqing University, China
Tianyong Hao   South China Normal University, China

Program Co-chairs

Kai Liu   Chongqing University, China
Yu Wang   Xi'an Jiaotong University, China
Weiwei Wu   Southeast University, China
Reza Maleklan   Malmö University, Sweden
Yimin Yang   Lakehead University, Canada

Organizing Committee Co-chairs

Choujun Zhan   Nanfang College of Sun Yat-sen University, China
Mingbo Zhao   Donghua University, China
Shi Cheng   Shaanxi Normal University, China
Zhen Luo   Chongqing University of Posts and Telecommunications, China

Local Arrangement Co-chairs

Likeng Liang   South China Normal University, China
Guo Luo   Nanfang College of Sun Yat-sen University, China

Registration Co-chairs

Jing Zhu   Nanjing University of Aeronautics and Astronautics, China
Bing Li   Wuhan University of Technology, China
Shuqiang Wang   Chinese Academy of Sciences, China

Publication Co-chairs

Jingjing Cao   Wuhan University of Technology, China
Cuili Yang   Beijing University of Technology, China
Qiang Jia   Jiangsu University, China

Publicity Co-chairs

Liang Feng   Chongqing University, China
Xiangping Zhai   Nanjing University of Aeronautics and Astronautics, China
Xianghua Chu   Shenzhen University, China
Penglin Dai   Southwest Jiaotong University, China
Jianghong Ma   City University of Hong Kong
Dong Yang   University of California, Merced, USA

Sponsor Co-chairs

Wangpeng He   Xidian University, China
Bingyi Liu   Wuhan University of Technology, China

NCAA Steering Committee Liaison

Xiaoying Zhong   Harbin Institute of Technology, China

Web Chair

Ziliang Yin   Harbin Institute of Technology, China

Program Committee

Dong Yang   University of California, Merced, USA
Sheng Li   University of Georgia, USA
Jie Qin   Swiss Federal Institute of Technology, Switzerland
Xiaojie Jin   Bytedance AI Lab, USA
Zhao Kang   University of Electronic Science and Technology, China
Xiangyuan Lan   Hong Kong Baptist University, Hong Kong
Peng Zhou   Anhui University, China
Chang Tang   China University of Geosciences, China
Dan Guo   Hefei University of Technology, China
Li Zhang   Soochow University, China
Xiaohang Jin   Zhejiang University of Technology, China
Wei Huang   Zhejiang University of Technology, China
Chao Chen   Chongqing University, China

Jing Zhu	Nanjing University of Aeronautics and Astronautics, China
Weizhi Meng	Technical University of Denmark, Denmark
Wei Wang	Dalian Ocean University, China
Jian Tang	Beijing University of Technology, China
Heng Yue	Northeastern University, China
Yimin Yang	Lakehead University, Canada
Jianghong Ma	City University of Hong Kong, Hong Kong
Jicong Fan	Cornell University, USA
Xin Zhang	Tianjing Normal University, China
Xiaolei Lu	City University of Hong Kong, Hong Kong
Penglin Dai	Southwest Jiaotong University, China
Liang Feng	Chongqing University, China
Xiao Zhang	South-Central University for Nationalities, China
Bingyi Liu	Wuhan University of Technology, China
Cheng Zhan	Southwest University, China
Qiaolin Pu	Chongqing University of Posts and Telecommunications, China
Hao Li	Hong Kong Baptist University, Hong Kong
Junhua Wang	Nanjing University of Aeronautics and Astronautics, China
Yu Wang	Xi'an Jiaotong University, China
BinQiang Chen	Xiamen University, China
Wangpeng He	Xidian University, China
Jing Yuan	University of Shanghai for Science and Technology, China
Huiming Jiang	University of Shanghai for Science and Technology, China
Yizhen Peng	Chongqing University, China
Jiayi Ma	Wuhan University, China
Yuan Gao	Tencent AI Lab, China
Xuesong Tang	Donghua University, China
Weijian Kong	Donghua University, China
Yang Lou	City University of Hong Kong, Hong Kong
Chao Zhang	Shanxi University, China
Yanhui Zhai	Shanxi University, China
Wenxi Liu	Fuzhou University, China
Kan Yang	University of Memphis, USA
Fei Guo	Tianjin University, China
Wenjuan Cui	Chinese Academy of Sciences, China
Wenjun Shen	Shantou University, China
Mengying Zhao	Shandong University, China
Shuqiang Wang	Chinese Academy of Sciences, China
Yanyan Shen	Chinese Academy of Sciences, China
Haitao Wang	China National Institute of Standardization, China
Yuheng Jia	City University of Hong Kong, Hong Kong
Chengrun Yang	Cornell University, USA
Lijun Ding	Cornell University, USA
Zenghui Wang	University of South Africa, South Africa
Xianming Ye	University of Pretoria, South Africa
Reza Maleklan	Malmö University, Sweden

Contents

Machine Learning, Data Mining, Data Security and Privacy Protection, and Data-Driven Applications

Neural Computing-Based Fault Diagnosis, Fault Forecasting, Prognostic Management, and System Modeling

Computational Intelligence, Nature-Inspired Optimizers, and Their Engineering Applications

Fuzzy Logic, Neuro-Fuzzy Systems, Decision Making, and Their Applications in Management Sciences

Control Systems, Network Synchronization, System Integration, and Industrial Artificial Intelligence

Cloud/Edge/Fog Computing, The Internet of Things/Vehicles (IoT/IoV), and Their System Optimization

Spreading Dynamics, Forecasting, and Other Intelligent Techniques Against Coronavirus Disease (COVID-19)

Neural Network Theory, Cognitive Sciences, Neuro-System Hardware Implementations, and NN-Based Engineering Applications

An Optimization Method to Boost the Resilience of Power Networks with High Penetration of Renewable Energies

Bingchun Mu, Xi Zhang$^{(\boxtimes)}$, Xuefei Mao, and Zhen Li

Beijing Institute of Technology, Beijing, China
{3220180635,xizhang,mxf14,zhenli}@bit.edu.cn

Abstract. This paper proposes a new method to enhance the resilience of power systems with high penetrations of renewable energies. Firstly, the resilience enhancement is configured as maintaining as much electric energy to critical loads in a fixed number of post-disaster periods by properly coordinating the available resources. Secondly, an optimal decision-making method is proposed to maximize the power supply of critical loads and to minimize the instability risks considering the randomness of the output power of renewable energies. The power consumption of loads and power generation of generators and spinning reserve ratios of the renewable energy at each period are taken as controllable variables. Constraints include spinning reserve, power flow constraints, power consumption/generation limits. The interior-point method is used to solve the formulated optimization problem. It is found that a balance should be sought between decreasing stability risks and increasing the maintained loads in extreme environments. Numerical simulations verified the effectiveness and superiority of the proposed optimization method in restoring power supply and boosting grid resilience after disasters.

Keywords: Power grid resilience optimization · Renewable energy · Spinning reserve

1 Introduction

1.1 Backgrounds

Power networks are important infrastructures that support almost all kinds of activities in modern society, and their ability to maintain a reliable electricity supply to the consumers under various conditions is crucial to all day-to-day operations of society. Due to the broad geographical coverage and exposure to wild and adverse environments, the power system is subject to various kinds of disturbances. In recent years, the concept of power grid resilience has drawn widespread attention. The resilience of the power system refers to the ability of the power grid to resist interference and restore power promptly in the face of extreme weather such as typhoons, rain, snow, and earthquakes, or man-made attacks such as graphite bombs, high-altitude nuclear magnetic explosions, and computer viruses [1]. Extreme environments will seriously affect the normal operation

© Springer Nature Singapore Pte Ltd. 2021
H. Zhang et al. (Eds.): NCAA 2021, CCIS 1449, pp. 3–16, 2021.
https://doi.org/10.1007/978-981-16-5188-5_1

of the power system, making the system hard to maintain the original connectivity and functions, resulting in a large amount of load that cannot be supplied normally, and seriously endangering economic development and social stability [2].

Motivated by energy and environmental requirements, the power network is going through a drastic change featuring increasing deployment of renewable energies. Differing from traditional power sources, the power outputs of renewable energies are strongly determined by the weather which is random and intermittent. Renewable energy power stations use power electronic equipment to connect to the grid, with zero inertia and low tolerance. While renewable energies bring huge environmental and social benefits, they also bring challenges to the safe operation of the power grid and the recovery of the system after severe damage in extreme environments.

In extreme environments, the components and equipment of the power system are likely to be physically damaged, and it takes a long time to repair them or build new equipment [3]. In this case, making full use of existing available resources to achieve the maximum power supply capacity (the maximum power system sufficiency) as soon as possible, by emergency dispatch and reasonable topology adjustments, is an effective means to improve the resilience of the power system, and it is beneficial to alleviating the negative impact of extreme environments on social stability [4].

In this paper, we study enhancing the resilience of power systems with high penetrations of renewable energies. Firstly, the amount of electric energy maintained to critical loads in a fixed number of periods is identified as an important resilience metric of the power system. Secondly, the decision-making strategy to maximize the power supply of critical loads and to minimize the instability risks by properly coordinating the available resources is formulated as an optimization issue, where controllable variables include the power consumption of loads and power generation of generators and spinning reserve ratios of the renewable energy at each period, and constraints include spinning reserve, power flow constraints, power consumption/generation limits. Simulation results show that the proposed optimization method can effectively restore power supply and boost grid resilience.

1.2 An Insight to Enhance the Grid Resilience

When the power system is affected by extreme environments, its load-supply capacity is reduced. In a short term after the impact of extreme conditions, it is difficult to repair electrical components that are physically damaged. Therefore, after disasters, it is practically feasible to boost the resilience of damaged power grid by making good use of the remaining available resources to maximize the power supply benefit of the damaged power system, which can help alleviate the negative impact of extreme environments on social stability to a great degree.

Under extreme environments, it is hard for the power system to satisfy the power supply requirements of all loads. At this time, to maximize the power supply benefit of the power system, the load should be regarded as a controllable variable, that is, the power consumption of each load is planned by the dispatch center. At the same time, during the special period of insufficient power supply after disasters, the load should also be prioritized. For example, the power supply priority of the government, hospitals, etc. should be higher than the power supply priority of some factories. The weighted sum of the loads serves as the main part of the power supply benefit that is the objective function of the optimization in this paper.

To maintain the safety and stability of the power system, a certain amount of spinning reserve needs to be reserved for the conventional generators to cope with randomness and intermittent in the power system. Under normal circumstances, there are two main sources of randomness and volatility in power systems with high penetrations of renewable energies: load and renewable energy generators. However, in extreme environments, considering that loads could be controlled, the load no longer has the randomness and volatility, which means that the system only needs to plan conventional generators to reserve a certain amount of spinning reserve to balance the fluctuation of the renewable energy generators. The product of the total power generation of renewable energy generators in the system and the spinning reserve ratio during each period serves as the spinning reserve capacity of the system for each period. The amount of the spinning reserve ratio of the system at each time will also affect the power supply capacity of the system in extreme environments. If the spinning reserve ratio is too large, the power of the conventional generators for load supply will be reduced, which will affect the power supply benefit. In contrast, if the ratio is too small, once the actual output of the renewable energy generators is much smaller than the planned output, the planned load power will not be supplied, and even the power system will lose balance and a series of cascading failures will occur, which will deprive the power system in extreme environments.

Therefore, it is necessary to weigh the plan settings of the spinning reserve ratio for each period. The spinning reserve ratio of the system for each period is also an important factor that needs to be considered for flexibility optimization.

2 Establishment of the Optimization Model

2.1 Disposal of the Uncertainty of Renewable Energy Power

In this paper, the time scale of the resilience optimization research of the power system is a short time (a few hours) after disasters, so the uncertainty of the renewable energy output in a short time needs to be considered [5, 6]. Since the current renewable energy power generation is mainly wind power and photovoltaic power generation, and wind power accounts for the highest proportion (about 70%) of renewable energy power, and the short-term forecast error models of wind power and photovoltaic power are similar. The disposal of the uncertainty of renewable energy power in this paper mainly refers to the short-term forecast error model of wind power output.

As renewable energy power generation is affected by weather and other factors, it is random and volatile, and cannot be accurately predicted. The forecast error of renewable energy output is defined as:

$$\tilde{P}_{re}(t) = P_{re}(t) + \Delta P_{re}(t) \tag{1}$$

where $\tilde{P}_{re}(t)$, $P_{re}(t)$ and $\Delta P_{re}(t)$ are respectively the actual value, forecast value, and forecast error of renewable energy power output. According to the statistical characteristics of wind power output forecast errors, they are generally simulated as Gaussian statistical variables [7, 8]. This article refers to the model of wind power output forecast errors and regards the short-term forecast errors of the renewable energy as obeying the Gaussian distribution of $N(0, \sigma_{re}^2)$, whose standard deviation is always got by:

$$\sigma_{re}(t) = K \cdot P_{re}(t) + RE_I/50 \tag{2}$$

where K is the forecast error factor for renewable energy power, which is always 0.2; RE_I is the total installed capacity of renewable energy power supply.

2.2 Optimization Variable

In the optimization model, the controllable variables are composed of the following parts:

- The output of each conventional generator node of each period $P_i(t)$
- The power of each load node of each period $P_l(t)$
- The output of each renewable energy generator node of each period $P_{re}(t)$
- The spinning reserve ratio of the renewable energy of each period $r(t)$

2.3 Objective Function

The objective of the optimization problem of the power system resilience studied in this paper is to get the maximum power supply benefit by supplying power to various loads according to their priority in a short term under extreme environments, through the remaining generation resources, regardless of the cost. In addition to the power supply to loads, the stability of the power system also plays an important role in the evaluation of the benefit. Therefore, due to the randomness of renewable energy power generation, conventional generator nodes are required to provide a certain amount of upward spinning reserve to deal with the situation where the actual output of the renewable energy is lower than the planned output, to avoid causing the failure to supply load as planned power and cascading failure caused by power grid instability. In conclusion, the objective function of the optimization problem is:

$$\max F = \sum_{t=1}^{m} ((P_L(t) - Q(t)) \cdot \Delta t) \tag{3}$$

where $P_L(t)$ is the weighted sum of the power of all load nodes of the period t, $Q(t)$ is the loss rate of the power supply benefit caused by the insufficient actual output of renewable energy power generator nodes and insufficient spinning reserve of the period t, Δt is the duration of a period, which is a quarter in this optimization model.

The specific formula $P_L(t)$ is as follows:

$$P_L(t) = \sum_{l=1}^{L} w_l \cdot P_l(t) \tag{4}$$

where $P_l(t)$ is the planned power of load l during the period t, w_l is the power supply weight factor of the load l. The larger the value, the higher the power supply priority of the load in extreme environments, such as the government and hospitals.

The analysis of $Q(t)$, which is the loss rate of the power supply benefit caused by the insufficient actual output of the renewable energy and insufficient spinning reserve during the period t, is as follow:

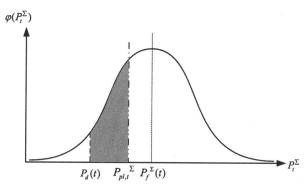

Fig. 1. Probability density distribution of the total output of the renewable energy during the period t

As shown in Fig. 1, assuming that the actual power of renewable energy during the period t obeys the Gaussian distribution, the abscissa P_t^{Σ} is the actual value of the total output of the renewable energy during the period t, and $P_f^{\Sigma}(t)$ is the average value, which is the forecast output during the period t; $P_{pl,t}^{\Sigma}$ is the planned total output of the renewable energy power during the period t. The shaded part in the figure is the range of renewable energy output that can be balanced by the spinning reserve reserved by the system and $P_d(t)$ is the minimum value of the actual total output of the renewable energy allowed by the spinning reserve. Therefore, when the actual output of the renewable energy is less than $P_d(t)$, the spinning reserve is insufficient, resulting in that the power supply to the load node cannot reach the expected amount. Under extreme environmental conditions, failure to supply load as planned power is likely to cause serious economic losses and even cause more serious cascading failures. The specific formula $Q(t)$ is:

$$Q(t) = K_{loss} \cdot \int_0^{P_d(t)} \varphi(P_t^{\Sigma})(P_d(t) - P_t^{\Sigma})dP_t^{\Sigma} \tag{5}$$

where K_{loss} is the benefit loss factor. The larger the value of K_{loss}, the more serious the loss of the power supply benefit caused by insufficient renewable energy output and insufficient spinning reserve. $\varphi(P_t^{\Sigma})$ is the Gaussian distribution function of renewable energy power; $P_d(t)$ is the integral upper limit, which is the minimum value of the actual total output of the renewable energy allowed by the spinning reserve, and it can be calculated by the formula as follow:

$$P_d(\text{t}) = (1 - r(t))(\sum_{re=1}^{RE} P_{re}(t)) \tag{6}$$

where $P_{re}(t)$ is the planner output of the renewable energy generator node re, and RE contains all the renewable energy generator nodes.

In summary, it is clear that the reaction of $P_L(t)$ and $Q(t)$ of each period of the objective function to the change of the spinning reserve ratio of each period is the same, but the changes of the two have opposite effects on the value of the objective function. Therefore, the objective function of the optimization model in this paper will drive the optimization algorithm to find a balance value in the determination of the spinning reserve ratio of each period of the system, so that the system can maximize its power supply capacity while maintaining a certain degree of reliability under extreme environments to achieve the greatest power supply benefit.

2.4 Constraints

Constraints include active power balance constraint (Eq. (7)), spinning reserve constraint (in Eq. (8)), power flow constraint of lines (in Eq. (9)), output constraint of the conventional generator nodes (in Eq. (10)), constraints of the output rate of change of the conventional generator nodes (in Eq. (11) and (12)), load power constraint (in Eq. (13)), and output constraint of renewable energy generator nodes (in Eq. (14)).

$$\sum_{i=1}^{N} P_i(t) + \sum_{re=1}^{RE} P_{re}(t) = \sum_{l=1}^{L} P_l(t) \tag{7}$$

$$\sum_{i=1}^{N} \min(P_{i,\max} - P(t), P_{i,up} * \Delta t) \geq r(t) * \sum_{re=1}^{RE} P_{re}(t) \tag{8}$$

$$-L_{ij,\max} \leq L_{ij}(t) \leq L_{ij,\max} \tag{9}$$

$$P_{i,\min} \leq P_i(t) \leq P_{i,\max} \tag{10}$$

$$P_i(t+1) - P_i(t) \leq \Delta P_{i,up} \tag{11}$$

$$P_i(t) - P_i(t+1) \leq \Delta P_{i,down} \tag{12}$$

$$P_{l,\max} \leq P_l(t) \leq 0 \tag{13}$$

$$0 \leq P_{re}(t) \leq P_{re,f}(t) \tag{14}$$

where $P_{i,\max}$ and $P_{i,\min}$ are respectively the upper limit and lower limit of output of conventional generator node i; $P_i(t)$ is the output of conventional generator node i during the period t; N contains the conventional generator nodes in the system; $\Delta P_{i,up}$ and $\Delta P_{i,down}$ are respectively the maximum upward ramp rate and the maximum downward ramp rate of conventional generator node i; $P_{l,\max}$ is the maximum absorbed power of load node i, which is a negative value; $P_{re,f}(t)$ is the predicted output of the renewable energy power generator node re of the period t.

The spinning reserve constraint is specifically the upward spinning reserve constraint. The principle is that when the actual output of the renewable energy unit cannot reach the planned output, a certain amount of upward spinning reserve is required to make up for the lack of renewable energy output. Corresponding to the upward spinning reserve is the downward spinning reserve. When the actual output of the renewable energy unit is higher than the predicted output, the conventional generators are required to provide a certain amount of downward spinning reserve to offset the overflow of renewable energy output to avoid abandonment of energy. Since the research background of this paper is the power system in extreme environment, considering the load controllable, for the renewable energy generators, to obtain the maximum power supply benefit within a short term, its planned output should be controlled below its forecast output to avoid potential safety hazards of the power grid caused by the upward fluctuation of the output of renewable energy and the burden of the downward spinning reserve. Therefore, the downward spinning reserve is not taken into consideration in this paper.

3   Case Study

3.1   Case Description

The simulations in this paper are based on the IEEE 39-Bus Test Case, as shown in Fig. 2. Node 34, 35, 36, 37, 38 are selected as wind power generator nodes. It is assumed that nodes whose index are 23, 24, 31, 32, 33, 37, 38 are damaged due to extreme environments and are unavailable for the power dispatching center.

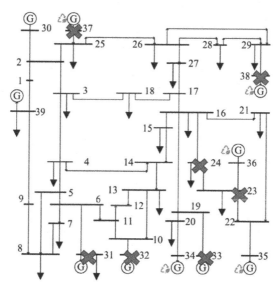

Fig. 2. The power system used in this paper based on the IEEE 39-Bus system (✖ indicates the damaged node; ⚡ indicates the renewable energy generator node)

To improve the efficiency of computation, the simulations in this paper adopt the DC power flow model. The nodes in the system model are divided into three types:

conventional generator nodes, renewable energy generator nodes, and load nodes. The main parameters of conventional generator nodes and load nodes are shown in Table 2 and Table 3 in the appendix.

A set of forecast values of the renewable energy output is drawn up with reference to the actual output data of the renewable energy in a certain place. Since the time scale of the renewable energy ultra-short-term forecast is 4-h and the time resolution is 15-min, the time range studied in this paper is 2-h (8-period) after the disaster. The forecast output values of renewable energy generator nodes are shown in Table 4 in the appendix. The simulation is programmed in Matlab based on the functions provided by Matpower [9].

3.2   Analysis of Results

The benefit loss factor is set to 10, the load priority weight is set to two levels of 1 and 10, and the standard deviation of the short-term forecast error of renewable energy output is set to 0.2 times the output of renewable energy generation. The results of the optimization are as follows.

3.2.1   Results of Optimal Variables

The results of the spinning reserve ratio of each period and the planned power of nodes are shown in Fig. 3.

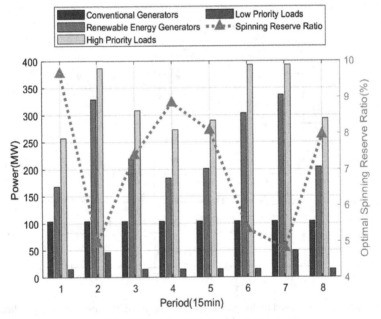

Fig. 3. Results of optimal variables

The relationship between the optimal spinning reserve ratio of each period and the total output of renewable energy generator nodes is shown in Fig. 4.

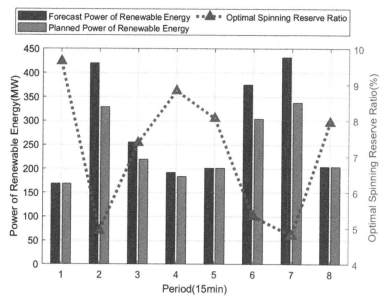

Fig. 4. The relationship between the optimal spinning reserve ratio of each period and the forecast power and planned power of the renewable energy

Through analyzing the results of the optimization variables, we can see that the optimal spinning reserve ratio of each period has an inverse relationship with the renewable energy output of that period, that is, the higher the renewable energy output in a period, the smaller the optimal spinning reserve ratio in that period. The reason is that when the renewable energy output is high during the period, the same reserve ratio means more reserve capacity will be reserved by the conventional generators. Excessive spinning reserve will occupy the scarce conventional generation resources of post-disaster power system, resulting in a decline in the power supply efficiency of the system. Therefore, the optimization method in this paper can flexibly determine the spinning reserve rate of each period when the output of renewable energy fluctuates in different periods in extreme environments, to maximizes the power supply benefit.

Besides, the results show that loads with high priority fluctuate less with the output of renewable energy and have a high degree of satisfaction, while loads with low priority fluctuate more with the output of renewable energy and are almost zero when the output of renewable energy is low.

In extreme environments, to maximize the power supply benefit, the planned output of renewable energy generator nodes is often lower than the forecast output. The reason is that the topology of the post-disaster network is different from that of normal condition, and constraints such as power flow constraint and active power balance constraint restrict the power of each node, including renewable energy generator nodes.

3.2.2 Improvement of Power Supply Benefit

The traditional reserve configuration method is often to set the ratio of reserve to a fixed value, which is usually between 5 and 10%. The optimization method in this article is compared with the traditional reserve configuration with a fixed ratio of 5%. To compare the two methods, and the power supply benefits of each period of the two methods are shown in Fig. 5.

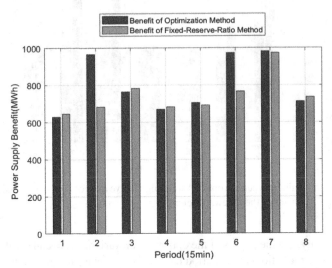

Fig. 5. Power supply benefits of the two methods in each period

As for the total power supply benefit of 8 periods, the total benefit of the optimization method is 6405.471 MWh, while the total benefit of the traditional fixed-reserve-ratio method is 5961.039 MWh. Compared with the traditional method, the method in this paper has significantly improved the power supply benefit by attaining a 7.45% increase in total power supply benefit. However, as for the power supply benefit of some period (such as period 1 and period 3), the optimization method behaves worse than fixed-reserve-ratio method. The reason is that the objective function of the optimization method is the total benefit of all periods, and there are constraints of the output rate of change of the conventional generator nodes (in Eq. (11) and (12)). As a result, the optimization method may try to obtain the optimal total benefit by sacrificing the benefit of some period.

Besides, this paper also set up other simulation experiments to compare the performance differences of the two methods when the power grid has different requirements for stability in extreme environments.

In this paper, the degree of negative impact on the system, caused by the fact that the reserve is insufficient to make up for the insufficient actual output of the renewable energy, is quantified as the index "benefit loss factor", which can be seen in Eq. (5). For different extreme environments and different power systems, the benefit loss caused by the failure to supply load as planned power in the system and the risk caused by the instability of the grid will change with the situation, which is reflected in different benefit loss factors. The result of the calculation case mentioned above is the simulation result when the benefit loss factor is set to 10. To analyze the influence of the benefit loss factor on the optimization result, this paper also draws up 4 other benefit loss factors: 5, 50, 100, and 200, composing 5 groups of data with different benefit loss factors. We compare the optimization results of the optimization method proposed in this paper and the traditional method whose ratio is fixed to 5%, as shown in Table 1.

Table 1. Parameters of conventional power generation nodes

Benefit loss factor	The power supply benefit of the fixed-ratio method (MWh)	The power supply benefit of the optimization method in this paper (MWh)	The average value of the optimal reserve ratio of each period	The percentage of the increase by the optimized ratio method compared with the fixed-ratio method
5	6242.268	6472.302	6.91%	3.68%
10	5961.039	6405.471	7.12%	7.45%
50	5504.943	6007.452	7.59%	9.13%
100	5321.283	5732.577	8.16%	7.73%
200	5130.534	5432.856	8.82%	5.89%

It can be clearly seen from the results that as the benefit loss factor increases, the optimal spinning reserve ratio calculated by the optimization method also increases, and the power supply benefit decreases accordingly. And as the loss factor increasing, the power supply benefit improvement of the optimized reserve ratio method compared with the fixed-reserve-ratio method goes upward firstly and then goes downward, reaching the peak on one value of loss factor.

The greater of the benefit loss factor when the reserve is insufficient means that the negative impact of the failure to supply load as planned power under extreme conditions is more serious, and it also means that the negative impacts caused by the instability of the grid balance are more serious when the pre-planned spinning reserve provided by the system cannot compensate for the actual output of the renewable energy that is seriously lower than the planned output. Both points indicate that the greater the benefit loss factor, the higher the reliability required by the power system in extreme environments, and the system needs to provide more spinning reserve to reduce the possibility of the situation where the reserve is insufficient.

In the optimization method proposed in this paper, the reserve ratio of each period of the system will be flexibly changed according to the importance of the power supply to loads in extreme environments and the system's requirements for stability, obtaining the best short-term power supply benefit after disasters. In contrast, because the traditional reserve configuration method with a fixed reserve ratio is too subjective and lacks flexibility in extreme environments, it is difficult to reasonably balance the system's requirements for power supply and stability during special periods, and it is impossible to obtain the best power supply benefit in the short term after disasters.

4 Conclusion

This paper studies restoring as much amount of power supply to critical loads after disasters addressing the uncertainty of renewable energy output. Considering the priority of different loads and safety risks, the overall power supply benefit of the power system with high penetrations of renewable energies in several post-disaster periods is identified as a resilience indicator of the power system. An optimization model for obtaining maximum power supply benefit is established with the spinning reserve ratio of each period and the power of each node as optimization variables. The objective in the optimization model comprehensively considers the priority difference of each load and the negative impact of the failure to supply load as planned power caused by the insufficient actual output of the renewable energy and insufficient spinning reserve. Simulations on the IEEE 39-Bus Test Case are performed to verify the methods proposed in this paper. The results show that the optimization method proposed can flexibly determine the spinning reserve ratio and the power of each node in extreme environments, realizing the optimal power supply benefit of the power system after disasters. Further experiments show that the optimal spinning reserve ratio of renewable energy will increase when the benefit loss factor is high, and the optimization method proposed in this paper has improved the power supply benefit more significantly in extreme environments, compared with the traditional method about reserve configuration.

Acknowledgements. This paper is supported by Open Fund of State Key Laboratory of Operation and Control of Renewable Energy & Storage Systems (China Electric Power Research Institute) No. NYB51202001596.

Appendix

Table 2. Parameters of conventional generator nodes

Node index	The upper limit of output (MW)	The lower limit of output (MW)	Maximum up rate (MW/h)	Maximum down rate (MW/h)
30	115	35	46	46
31	300	90	120	120
32	313	94	125	125
33	304	91	122	122
39	47	14	19	19

Table 3. Parameters of load nodes

Node index	Weights	Maximum absorbed power (MW)
1	1	59
2	1	4
3	10	193
4	1	300
5	1	0
6	1	26
7	10	140
8	1	313
9	1	4
10	1	27
11	1	0
12	1	5
13	1	0
14	1	0
15	1	192
16	10	197
17	1	0
18	1	95
19	1	20
20	10	417
21	1	164
22	1	10
23	1	148
24	1	185
25	1	142
26	1	83
27	1	169
28	1	123
29	1	182

Table 4. Forecast output during each period of renewable energy generator nodes

Index	Period							
	1	2	3	4	5	6	7	8
34	72	177	99	63	108	213	225	126
35	96	243	156	129	93	162	207	78
36	75	225	108	63	105	195	153	96
37	45	186	135	105	57	156	189	66
38	117	267	189	138	141	222	195	135

References

1. Cooke, D.W.: The Resilience of the Electric Power Delivery System in Response to Terrorism and Natural Disasters: Summary of a Workshop. The National Academies Press, Washington D.C. (2013)
2. Panteli, M., Trakas, D.N., Mancarella, P., et al.: Power systems resilience assessment: hardening and smart operational enhancement strategies. Proc. IEEE **105**(7), 1202–1213 (2017)
3. Zhang, X., Guo, J., Wang, T., et al.: Identifying critical elements to enhance the power grid resilience. In: 2020 IEEE International Symposium on Circuits and Systems (ISCAS), Seville, Spain, pp. 1–5 (2020)
4. Gao, H., Chen, Y., Mei, S., et al.: Resilience-oriented pre-hurricane resource allocation in distribution systems considering electric buses. Proc. IEEE **105**(7), 1214–1233 (2017)
5. Hodge, B., Milligan, M.: Wind power forecasting error distributions over multiple timescales. IEEE Trans. Power Syst. **21**(1), 24–27 (2011)
6. Bludszuweit, H.: Statistical analysis of wind power forecast error. IEEE Trans. Power Syst. **23**(3), 983–991 (2008)
7. Chaiyabut, N., Damrongkulkamjorn, P.: Uncertainty costs of wind power generation considering expected energy not supplied under different spinning reserve lever. In: The Second IASTED International Conference on Power and Energy Systems and Applications, Las Vegas, USA, pp. 1–5 (2012)
8. Bouffard, F., Galiana, F.D.: Stochastic security for operations planning with significant wind power generation. IEEE Trans. Power Syst. **23**(2), 306–316 (2008)
9. Zimmerman, R.D., Murillo-Sanchez, C.E., Thomas, R.J.: MATPOWER: steady-state operations, planning, and analysis tools for power systems research and education. IEEE Trans. Power Syst. **26**(1), 9–12 (2011)

Systematic Analysis of Joint Entity and Relation Extraction Models in Identifying Overlapping Relations

Yuchen Luo[1], Zhenjie Huang[1], Kai Zheng[2(✉)], and Tianyong Hao[1]

[1] School of Computer Science, South China Normal University, Guangzhou, China
{2019022611,2020022962,haoty}@m.scnu.edu.cn
[2] Network Center, South China Normal University, Guangzhou, China
david@scnu.edu.cn

Abstract. Named entity recognition and relation extraction are two fundamental tasks in the domain of natural language processing. Joint entity and relation extraction models have attracted more and more attention due to the performance advantage. However, there are difficulties in identifying overlapping relations among the models. To investigate the differences of structures and performances of joint extraction models, this paper implements a list of state-of-the-art joint extraction models and compares their difference in identifying overlapping relations. Experiment results show that the models by separating entity features and relation features work better than the models with feature fusion in identifying overlapping relations on three publicly available datasets.

Keywords: Named entity recognition · Relation extraction · Overlapping relation · Feature separation

1 Introduction

With the development of natural language processing, research in information extraction has attracted more and more attention. The research of information extraction are usually divided into three main tasks: named entity recognition, relation extraction, and event extraction. Named entity recognition, as the core foundation of other information extraction, aims to identify the mentions that represent named entities from a natural language text and label their locations and types [1]. The main purpose of relation extraction is to extract semantic relation between named entities from natural language text, i.e., to determine the classes of relations between entity pairs in unstructured text based on entity recognition, as well as to form structured data for computation and analysis [2]. After named entity recognition and relation extraction, the extracted entities and relations can be represented in the form of a triple (*Entity 1, Relation, Entity 2*). For example, in the sentence "He was somewhat agitated, so his Keppra was switched to Topiramate", "Agitated" and "Topiramate" are named entities in "Reason" and "Drug" types, respectively. The entities have a certain relation "Reason-Drug". Thus they can be expressed as a triple ("Agitated", "Reason-Drug", "Topiramate").

© Springer Nature Singapore Pte Ltd. 2021
H. Zhang et al. (Eds.): NCAA 2021, CCIS 1449, pp. 17–31, 2021.
https://doi.org/10.1007/978-981-16-5188-5_2

The traditional entity-relation extraction models frequently utilize the pipeline manner, which is performed in two independent steps, named entity recognition and then relation extraction sequentially. The pipeline manner completely separates the named entity recognition and relation extraction tasks, while neglecting the relevant information between the two tasks, leading to an error transfer problem [3]. Unlike the pipeline manner, joint extraction models deal with both named entity recognition and relation extraction tasks simultaneously for solving the error transfer problems. Recent studies have shown that joint learning methods can effectively integrate entity and relation information to obtain better performance in both tasks [4, 5]. However, several joint models, such as SPTree [6] and Novel Tagging [7], although they can improve the performance for solving the error transfer problem, still suffer from the problem of ineffective identifying overlapping relations.

Overlapping relations mean that there are multiple relations in a natural language sentence, and there may be an overlap between multiple relations. Zeng et al. [8] first carefully classified overlapping relations into two types: EntityPairOverlap (EPO) in which two entities are overlapping in two relations, as well as SingleEntityOverlap (SEO) in which only one entity is overlapping in two relations. Despite the increasing number of overlapping relation studies in recent years, identifying overlapping relations is still a difficult problem to overcome for the relation extraction research.

This paper focuses on comparing and analyzing the performance of recent joint extraction models and the capability of identifying overlapping relations. Four state-of-the-art joint extraction models are implemented: Novel Tagging [7], Multi-head [9], Two are better than one [10], and TPLinker [11]. In terms of feature processing, Novel Tagging and TPLinker represent a fusion of entity and relation features based on an annotation scheme, while Multi-head and Two are better than one use a form of feature separation and information interaction between entity and relation features via a specific structure. The models except Novel Tagging are able to identify overlapping relations via different strategies. This paper analyzes these models on the following three datasets: NYT, CoNLL04, and N2C2 2018 (Track2). By comparing the performance of the four models, this paper investigates the differences in identifying overlapping relations, and analyzes the advantages and disadvantages of feature fusion and feature separation strategies. Experiment results show that the joint models with identifying overlapping relation strategies outperform the other models, and the feature separation strategy has better performance than feature fusion in identifying overlapping relations.

The main contributions of this paper are the following three aspects: 1) implemented the four latest joint extraction models and compared the differences of model structures and performance; 2) compared and analyzed the performance of four joint extraction models in identifying overlapping relations on multiple datasets; 3) discovered a new finding that the feature separation strategy has advantage than the feature fusion strategy in identifying overlapping relations.

2 Related Work

In recent years, researchers have proposed many models to extract entities and relations. In terms of traditional pipeline manner, Hoffimann et al. [12] utilized external components and knowledge-based approaches to extract entities and relations, while a large number of researchers [13–16] adopt deep neural network approaches. In terms of joint extraction models, Miwa and Bansal [6] firstly used Bi-LSTM to implement a named entity recognition model, and then combine Bi-TreeLSTM as well as dependency analysis trees to obtain relations between entities, which is the first using neural networks for joint entity and relation extraction. However, this approach needs to rely on external resources, such as the need to perform dependency analysis on sentences in the extraction of entities and relations. To reduce the dependency on external resources, Bekoulis et al. [9] proposed to treat relation extraction as a multi-head selection problem. After identifying entities, this method assumed that each entity might be the head entity of a certain relation, and then recognized relations with all other identified entities. Based on the framework of multi-head recognition, Zhao et al. [17] introduced a feature representation of relative positions of entities and a global optimization function GRC to express overall semantic information of the sentence for improvement. Zhao et al. [18] believed that traditional models treated the tasks of named entity recognition and relation extraction differently, which would lose closely related information between the two tasks. Therefore, they proposed a CMAN framework that could apply feature information to the two tasks. Benefiting from the performance improvement brought by the interactions of the two tasks of named entity recognition and relation extraction, the Two are Better than One proposed by Wang and Lu [10] used sequence and table features to replace entity features and relation features respectively, as well as provided a mechanism to enable sufficient interaction between the two features.

The sequence-to-sequence models are an implementation way in the joint extraction models. These methods treated the entity relation extraction task as a translation-like task, by taking text sequences as input and entity-relation triplet sequences as output. Nayak and Ng [19] designed a new representation of entity-relation triples based on the encoder-decoder structure to solve the task of entity and relation extraction at one time. However, this basic sequence-to-sequence problem is prone to a kind of exposure error, which refers to the use of real data values during training, and the use of prediction at the previous moment as input during testing. There is a deviation issue between the distributions learned during training and during testing. Therefore, Zhang et al. [20] proposed a structure of seq2UMTree to reduce the exposure error, that is, the decoding part was no longer decoded in the form of a sequence but in a tree structure. Sui et al. [21] utilized a non-auto regressive model for decoding and proposed Bipartite Matching Loss to eliminate the dependence on the order of entity-relation triples from original sequence to current sequence. Gupta et al. [22] proposed to use lower triangle part of tables to implement the entity-relation extraction task. The features on diagonal line were used to realize named entity recognition, while the features on off-diagonal line were used to implement the relation extraction. Nevertheless, this model was transformed into a sequence for traversal, so there was still a long-term dependency problem. To overcome this problem, Ma et al. [23] used the form of tensor dot product to extract relations.

Tagging is another type of joint extraction model. The design of this method focused on how to design a reasonable tagging to characterize entities and relations, and how to obtain feature expression of tagging through neural networks. Zheng et al. [7] first proposed a novel tagging method, each word had a corresponding tag. A tag was composed of the position of the entity where a word was located, the type of relation that a word participated in, and whether the relation between words was a head entity or a tail entity. Under this tagging, sequence annotation could be used. The method identified a tag for each word and then combines all identified tags to extract entity relations using the principle of nearest matching. Wang et al. [11] proposed a structure of TPLinker, which constructed a tag of entire sequence for each word. This method marked the words that form entity boundary with current word in the sequence. All entities and relations related to current word was identified via the tags of this sequence.

Although the joint extraction models were considered to be utilized to alleviate the gradient error propagation, many scholars had shown that some joint models mixed the features of entities and the characteristics of relations. The mixture of these two features might brought a negative impact to the performance of the models. Zhong and Chen [24] used a simple pipeline model for entity-relation extraction, and finally achieved SOTA results on several datasets. They believed that the pipeline model could avoid the problem of feature fusion and both tasks could be improved if entity feature was properly integrated into the relation extraction task.

Therefore, this paper compares and analyzes two types of joint extraction models with feature fusion and feature separation strategies, as well as investigates the method differences in identifying overlapping relations.

3   Joint Extraction Model Comparison

The structure of joint extraction models is often complex and diverse and can be divided into two types of strategies according to the way the models handle entity features and relation features: feature fusion and feature separation. Different feature processing strategies can affect the overall performance of the models and the recognition performance of overlapping relation identification. To investigate their differences, this paper implements four latest state-of-the-art models, compares and analyzes their structural feature strategies, and analyzes the traits of the models.

3.1   Model Differences

In terms of model structure, the major difference between the two strategies lies in the way of handling entity features and relation features while separating or mixing the features may leads to different performance the models. The strategy of feature separation makes the two tasks of named entity identification and relation extraction clear, but it may lead to gradient error propagation. The feature-fusion strategy is able to extract triples at once, but ignores the information interaction between the two tasks. Figure 1 shows a common joint extraction framework with the two feature processing strategies.

To investigate the influencing factors of the performance of joint extraction models, this paper conducts a comparison of the four models including Multi-head, Two are Better than One, Novel Tagging, and TPLinker. Table 1 shows the difference and relevance of the four models. The comparison consists of feature processing strategy, the way of information interaction, and the applicability of SEO and EPO. Multi-head and Two are

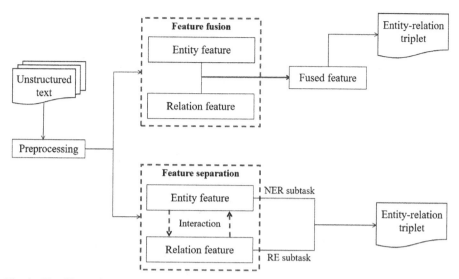

Fig. 1. The illustration of joint extraction framework with feature separation and feature fusion strategies

Better than One are two models based on feature separation strategy. Both models can identify the SEO overlap issue, but cannot identify the EPO overlap issue. Multi-head can only carry out one-direction information exchange, while Two are Better than One can carry out two-direction information exchange. Novel Tagging and TPLinker are two models based on feature fusion strategy. Novel Tagging cannot identify the problem of overlapping relations, while TPLinker can identify the problem of SEO and EPO issues at the same time.

Table 1. Comparison of the four state-of-the-art joint extraction models

Model	Strategy	Interaction	SEO	EPO
Multi-head	Feature separation	One-direction	√	×
Two are better than one	Feature separation	Two-direction	√	×
Novel tagging	Feature fusion	–	×	×
TPLinker	Feature fusion	–	√	√

3.2 Feature Separation Strategy

Feature separation is a strategy to treat entity features and relation features separately in a model. The fact that entities and relations share a complete set of feature representations respectively does not mean that they are unrelated to each other. Through means such as neural network parameter sharing, a model can enhance information interaction between the two features, while the interaction is usually beneficial. Since the two tasks of named entity recognition and relation extraction are related, the performance of a joint model can be improved if information interaction is appropriate.

This paper selects the Multi-head and Two are Better than One models with feature separation strategy. The Multi-head model can only transfer the interactive information of entity features to the relation extraction task in one direction due to its structure limitation. The entity feature information to be transferred is extracted by a Bi-LSTM during named entity recognition. Multi-head regards the task of relation extraction as a multi-head selection problem. The model assumes that any entity may be the head entity of a certain relation, and it is judged whether the relation is established through a Sigmoid function and received entity interaction information. This method can identify situations where there are multiple relations between two entities. Multi-head model consists of five layers: word embedding layer, Bi-LSTM layer, CRF layer, label embedding layer and Sigmoid layer. Word embedding layer maps each token to a word vector using a word2vec model. Bi-LSTM layer encodes information from left to right and right to left by taking the word embedding as input. CRF layer labels the word using a BIO encoding scheme to identify all entity arguments. After that, the label embedding layer maps the entity label of each token to a label vector, and then it concats the label embedding and the output of Bi-LSTM. At last, the Sigmoid layer takes the output of CRF layer to identify for all tokens, the most probable head word of the head entity and the most probable corresponding relation.

Two are Better than One model uses sequence features and table features to replace entity features and relation features respectively. With the four-dimensional features of the table structure, the model can transfer entity features and relation features in both directions. Assuming that the input of each encoding unit in the table structure is the initial input $S0$, the input corresponding to the sequence structure is $Sl\text{-}1$. Xl, i, j is the input of the sequence feature, and $Tl\text{-}1$ is the output of the previous table feature unit. According to the four-dimensional features, l, i, j represents the different directions. The received interactive information is shown in Eq. (1) and (2).

$$T_{l,i,j} = GRU(X_{l,i,j}, T_{l-1,i,j}, T_{l,i-1,j}, T_{l,i,j-1}) \tag{1}$$

$$X_{l,i,j} = ReLU(Linear([S_{l-1,i}; S_{l-1,j}])) \tag{2}$$

The table encoder takes the sequence feature as input, and concat it as a table. The element in row i and column j of the table represents the relations of the i-th word and the j-th word in the sentence. Next the Multi-Dimensional Recurrent Neural Network encodes the table feature and output hidden feature. The structure of sequence encoder is similar to the structure of the encoder of transformer. However the self-attention is replaced with a table-guided attention which converts the table feature to sequence feature.

3.3   Feature Fusion Strategy

Feature fusion refers to a strategy in which the model fuses entity features and relation features in a specific way to form a new feature representation. The models with the strategy can complete the task of joint extraction only by extracting and decoding fused features. However, the models usually lose interactive information between entities and relations. The focus of feature fusion is how to blend entity features and relation features, while tagging is one of the solutions.

Novel Tagging and TPLinker are two feature fusion models based on Tagging schemes. Novel Tagging firstly introduces the Tagging scheme to the joint extraction models. It combines relation features and entity features into joint labels. The compositions of a label are three pieces of information: the position of an entity where a word is located, the type of relation that a word may participate in, and whether a relation where the word is located is a head entity or a tail entity. This means that the entire task can be finally transformed into a sequence labeling task as long as the joint labels are recognized. The model structure of Novel Tagging is an end-to-end model, consisting of an encoder Bi-LSTM and a decoder LSTM. However, Novel Tagging cannot identify the problem of overlapping relations since it binds a pair of entities to a relation.

The TPLinker model constructs a tag about the entire sequence for each word through a handshaking tagging scheme. This kind of tagging marking words that form the boundary of an entity with current word in the sequence, the words that form the beginning of the entity in the same relation with current word, and the words that form the end of the entity in the same relation with current word. All entities and relations related to current word can be identified via tagging of this sequence. Therefore, TPLinker can recognize both SEO and EPO issues. The goal of TPLinker model is to identify the link of each token pair in three types: 1) Entity head to entity tail (EH-to-ET). This link type indicates that the two tokens form a head word and a tail word of the same entity. 2) Subject head to object head (SH-to-OH). This type indicates that two tokens are the start token of a paired subject entity and object entity. 3) Subject tail to object tail (ST-to-OT). Similar to that of subject head to object head, this type indicates the end word of a paired subject entity and object entity. In order to find out all links, TPLinker construct three sequences for each token in a sentence, namely EH-to-ET sequence, SH-to-OH sequence and ST-to-OT sequence. Among these three sequences, all corresponding links with current word are recognized. For convenience of tensor calculation, TPLinker concats SH-to-OH sequences of all tokens in a sentence, as ST-to-OT sequences. Without recognizing entity types, all words in a sentence share the same EH-to-ET sequence. To address the problem of overlapping relation, TPLinker constructs a ST-to-OT sequence and a SH-to-OH sequence for each relation. Thus, TPLinker constructs $2N + 1$ sequences for a sentence if there are N relation types.

However, the above both models obliterate entity features and thus they cannot identify entity types. To address this problem, the TPLinker-plus model adds a module for entity type recognition without changing the original tagging scheme.

4 Results and Analysis

4.1 Datasets

Three publicly available data sets are used including NYT, CoNLL04, and N2C2 2018 (Track2). The NYT dataset was released by Riedel et al. [25] in 2010 containing texts derived from New York Times. Named entities were annotated using the Stanford NER tool and combined with the Freebase knowledge base. The relations between named entity pairs were obtained by linking and referring to the relations in the external Freebase knowledge base combined with a remote supervision method. The CoNLL04 dataset was the data with entity and relation recognition corpora [26]. The N2C2 2018 (Track2) dataset was from the shared track 2 of the 2018 National NLP Clinical Challenges competition. It was oriented to medication and adverse drug events extraction in EHR [27]. Table 2 shows the statistical characteristics of the tree datasets. The NYT dataset has 1297 SEO cases and 978 EPO cases, while the CoNLL04 and N2C2 2018 (Track2) datasets contain only a small number of EPO cases. The SEO overlap cases of N2C2 2018 (Track2) accounts for 68.9%. Thus, the N2C2 2018 (Track2) is unbalanced dataset.

Table 2. The statistical characteristics of the three datasets, where SEO denotes "SingleEntityOverlap" and EPO denotes "EntityPairOverlap"

Dataset	#Normal	#SEO	#EPO	Total
NYT	3266	1297	978	5541
CoNLL04	795	1245	2	2042
N2C2 2018 (Track2)	18583	41195	32	59810

4.2 Evaluation

Three widely used indicators including precision (P), recall (R) and F1 score (F1) are used to measure the performance of each model. The calculation of the indicators are shown in Eq. (3), (4), and (5). True Positive (TP) means that the prediction of a sample is positive and it is actually positive. False Positive (FP) refers to the prediction of a sample is positive but it is actual negative. False Negative (FN) refers to the prediction of a sample is negative but it is actual positive. F1 score is a balanced score of precision and recall.

$$Precision = \frac{TP}{TP + FP} \tag{3}$$

$$Recall = \frac{TP}{TP + FN} \tag{4}$$

$$F_1 - score = \frac{2 * Precision * Recall}{Precision + Recall} \tag{5}$$

The evaluation is based on a strict matching method. Specifically, an entity is considered correct if both the boundary and type of the entity are correct. A relation is considered correct if both the type of the relation and the associating entities are correct.

4.3 Results

Four experiments were conducted to compare the differences of the models. The first experiment compared the performance of each model on the task of named entity recognition. The result is shown in Table 3. Multi-head obtained a F1 score of 0.841 and 0.870 on the CoNLL04 and N2C2 2018 (Track2) datasets, respectively. Two are Better than One model acquired an F1 score of 0.866 on the CoNLL04 dataset, which was higher than that of Multi-head. However, its performance on the N2C2 2018 (Track2) dataset was lower than that of the Multi-head model. The F1 score of TPLinker-plus on the N2C2 2018 (Track2) data was higher than Two are Better than One model but lower than the Multi-head model.

Table 3. The performance comparison of the models on the named entity recognition task

Model	CoNLL04			N2C2 2018 (Track2)		
	P	R	F1	P	R	F1
Multi-head	0.835	0.847	0.841	**0.879**	**0.860**	**0.870**
Two are better than one	**0.860**	**0.871**	**0.866**	0.711	0.759	0.734
Novel tagging	/	/	/	/	/	/
TPLinker-plus	0.662	0.603	0.631	0.799	0.845	0.821

The second experiment compared the performance of each model on the relation extraction task. The result is shown in Table 4. The Multi-head model obtained an F1 score of 0.738 on the N2C2 2018 (Track2) dataset, which was higher than that of the other three models. Two are Better than One obtained an F1 score of 0.690 on the CoNLL04 dataset, which was higher than Multi-head. TPLinker achieved 0.820 and 0.488 F1 values on NYT and N2C2 2018 (Track2) datasets, respectively, which were higher than that of the Novel Tagging model.

Table 4. The performance comparison of the models on the relation extraction task

Model	NYT			CoNLL04			N2C2 2018(Track2)		
	P	R	F1	P	R	F1	P	R	F1
Multi-head	/	/	/	0.679	0.561	0.614	**0.768**	0.710	**0.738**
Two are better than one	/	/	/	**0.750**	**0.639**	**0.690**	0.551	0.544	0.547
Novel tagging	0.451	0.259	0.329	/	/	/	0.412	0.315	0.357
TPLinker	**0.849**	**0.793**	**0.820**	/	/	/	0.348	**0.814**	0.488

The third experiment compared the recognition performance of Multi-head and Two are Better than One models on different entity types on the N2C2 2018 (Track2) dataset. The result is shown in Fig. 2. Among them, the entity types with poor recognition performance were ADE (Adverse drug event), Duration, and Reason. The recognition performance of ADE entities was the worst, and the F1 scores by the two models were less than 40%. The recognition performance of Multi-head model for all entity types was higher than that of the Two are Better than One model.

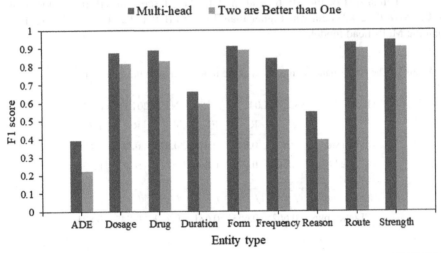

Fig. 2. The recognition performance of two models for different entity types on the N2C2 2018 (Track2) dataset

The fourth experiment compared the extraction of the Multi-head and Two are Better than One models on the N2C2 2018 (Track2) dataset for different relation types. Among them, the relation types with low extraction performance are ADE-Drug, Duration-Drug, and Reason-Drug. The two models both achieved F1 scores lower than 30% on the extraction of the ADE-Drug relation. For the extraction of the Duration-Drug relation, the F1 scores obtained by the Two are Better than One model was nearly 40% lower than that of the Multi-head model, reflecting their significant performance difference. The result is reported as Fig. 3.

4.4 Analysis

In the first experiment, the F1 scores of the Multi-head and TPLinker-plus models were higher on the N2C2 2018 (Track2) dataset than that on the CoNLL04 dataset. It can be seen that for these two models, increasing the amount of data can effectively improve the performance of the named entity recognition task, while both models show strong robustness to sentence length on the task of named entity recognition. In particular, TPLinker-plus improved the F1 score by nearly 20%, and it is speculated that the possible reason is that a large number of sentences without entities in the N2C2 2018 (Track2) dataset acts as negative samples.

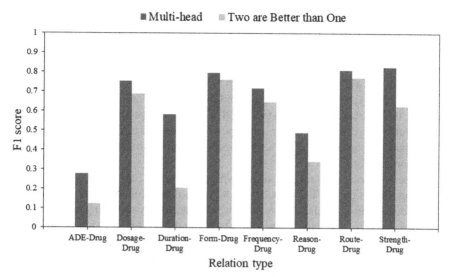

Fig. 3. The extraction performance of the two models for different relation types on the N2C2 2018 (Track2) dataset

In the second experiment, the models that could identify overlapping relations had higher F1 scores than that of the Novel Tagging model, indicating the effectiveness of overlapping relation identification. In the comparison of models with different feature processing strategies, the F1 scores of the Multi-head and Two are Better than One models were higher than those of Novel Tagging and TPLinker models, indicating that the models with feature separation strategies had better performance than that with feature fusion strategy in the task of overlapping relation identification. The interaction information of entity features in the Two are Better than One model had a positive effect on the relation extraction task.

The Multi-head model assumed that any entity could be a head entity of a certain relation for solving the SEO issue. In the experiment, the Multi-head model performed better on the N2C2 2018 (Track2) dataset containing a large number of SEO cases. On the more balanced CoNLL04 dataset, Two are Better than One model with two-direction feature interaction made better use of interaction information than the Multi-head model with one-direction interaction, thus achieving better performance on both tasks. The overall sentence length of the N2C2 2018 (Track2) dataset was longer than that of the CoNLL04 dataset. Two are Better than One model used table feature for entity relation extraction, while the size of table was proportional to the quadratic of the length of sentences. Therefore, the longer the sentences were, the larger the tables were. Longer sentences resulted in a more serious long-term dependency problem when Two are Better than One model traversed tables, which decreased the performance of the model on the N2C2 2018 (Track2) dataset.

In the third and fourth experiments, the entities in ADE type in the N2C2 2018 (Track2) dataset contained complex medical information, and the ADE and Reason entity types had very similar representations. Both were easily confused in the recognition task, resulting in lower recognition performance of both ADE and Reason entities than the others. Improving the recognition performance of ADE and Reason entities had positive implications for the models on the N2C2 2018 (Track2) dataset. In addition, the eight relation types in the dataset were all related to Drug entities, and this specificity leaded to more serious SEO issue. However, both the Multi-head and Two are Better than One model could identify the SEO issue, and most of the relation types were extracted correctly. In the relation extraction task, ADE-Drug, Duration-Drug, and Reason-Drug were the relation types with poor extraction performance. This mainly caused by gradient error propagation problem due to the poor recognition performance of ADE, Duration, and Reason entities.

The performance of the TPLinker model on the N2C2 2018 (Track2) dataset was lower than that on the NYT dataset. It was speculated that this might be caused by the different distributions of relations between the two datasets. After slicing the N2C2 2018 (Track2) dataset into sentences, there were a large number of sentences without relations, and a large number of relations were concentrated on certain sentences. The tagging of the TPLinker model was based on sentence-level annotation. Thus, the exits of different of relations in the sentences had an impact on the performance of the models. To analyze the effect of the number of relations in one sentence to the performance of the TPLinker model, an additional comparison was conducted on the N2C2 2018 (Track2) dataset and the NYT dataset. The two datasets were sliced into testsets containing different numbers of relations in the same sentences for performance comparison. The NYT dataset contained much fewer sentences with multiple relations, thus five relations in the same sentence was utilized, while ten relations in the same sentences were utilized for the N2C2 2018 (Track2). The comparison result is shown in Fig. 4.

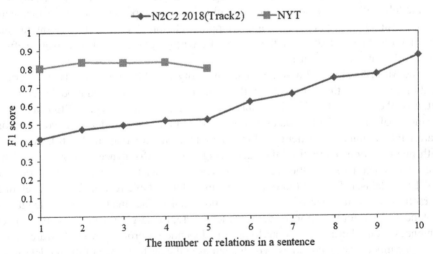

Fig. 4. The performance of TPLinker model for different number of relations in a sentence

For the N2C2 2018 (Track2) dataset, the performance was improving with the increasing of the number of relations. For the NYT dataset, the performance of the

TPLinker model tended to be stable. It indicated that the TPLinker model had advantage on more relations in the same sentences. This showed that the tagging in the model by marking words into sequence could better represent relation information. The sentences with multiple relations in the N2C2 2018 (Track2) dataset were generally long. Different sentence split methods would dramatically affect the sliced sentences thus affecting the performance of the TPLinker model. Thus, appropriate sentence split methods should be paid attention to ensure the performance of the model on long sentences with multiple relations.

5   Conclusions

This paper implemented the latest four joint extraction models and compared the structure and performance differences of the models. Particularly, the performance the four models were evaluated in identifying overlapping relations on three standard datasets. The models with feature separation strategy had better performance than that with feature fusion strategy in the overlapping relation identification task. This indicated the interactions between entity and relation features had positive affect for the joint models. The number of relations in the same sentences had an impact on model performance, thus appropriate sentence split methods were necessary for tagging-based joint extraction models.

Acknowledgements. This work was supported by National Natural Science Foundation of China (No. 61772146) and Natural Science Foundation of Guangdong Province (2021A1515011339).

References

1. Liu, L., Wang, D.: A survey of named entity recognition. Inf. Sci. **37**(3), 329–340 (2018)
2. Xu, K., Feng, Y., Huang, S., Zhao, D.: Semantic relation classification via convolutional neural networks. Comput. Sci. **71**(7), 132–137 (2015)
3. Qi, L., Ji, H.: Incremental joint extraction of entity mentions and relations. In: The 52th Annual Meeting of the Association of Computational Linguistics, pp. 402–412 (2014)
4. Dai, D., Xiao, X., Lyu, Y., Dou, S., Wang, H.: Joint extraction of entities and overlapping relations using position-attentive sequence labeling. In: The AAAI Conference on Artificial Intelligence, vol. 33, no. 01, pp. 6300–6308 (2019)
5. Tan, Z., Zhao, X., Wang, W., Xiao, W.: Jointly extracting multiple triplets with multilayer translation constraints. In: The AAAI Conference on Artificial Intelligence, vol. 33, no. 01, pp. 7080–7087 (2019)
6. Miwa, M., Bansal, M.: End-to-end relation extraction using LSTMs on sequences and tree structures. In: The 54th Annual Meeting of the Association of Computational Linguistics, pp. 1105–1116 (2016)
7. Zheng, S., Wang, F., Bao, H., Zhou, P., Xu, B.: Joint extraction of entities and relations based on a novel tagging scheme. In: The 55th Annual Meeting of the Association of Computational Linguistics, pp. 1227–1236 (2017)
8. Zeng, X., Zeng, D., He, S., Kang, L., Zhao, J.: Extracting relational facts by an end-to-end neural model with copy mechanism. In: The 56th Annual Meeting of the Association of Computational Linguistics, pp. 506–514 (2018)

9. Giannis, B., Johannes, D., Thomas, D., Chris, D.: Joint entity recognition and relation extraction as a multi-head selection problem. Expert Syst. Appl. **114**(Dec), 34–45 (2018)
10. Wang, J., Lu, W.: Two are better than one: Joint entity and relation extraction with table-sequence encoders. In: The 2020 Conference on Empirical Methods in Natural Language Processing, pp. 1706–1721 (2020)
11. Wang,Y., Yu, B., Zhang, Y., Liu, T., Sun, L.: TPLinker: single-stage joint extraction of entities and relations through token pair linking. In: The 28th International Conference on Computational Linguistics, pp. 1572–1582 (2020)
12. Hoffmann, R., Zhang, C., Xiao, L., Zettlemoyer, L. S., Weld, D. S.: Knowledge-based weak supervision for information extraction of overlapping relations. In: The 49th Annual Meeting of the Association of Computational Linguistics, pp. 541–550 (2011)
13. Zeng, D., Liu, K., Lai, S., Zhou, G., Zhao, J.: Relation classification via convolutional deep neural network. In: The 25th International Conference on Computational Linguistics, pp. 2335–2344 (2014)
14. Vu, N.T., Adel, H., Gupta, P., Schütze, H.: Combining recurrent and convolutional neural networks for relation classification. In: The 2016 Conference of the North American Chapter of the Association for Computational Linguistics, pp. 534–539 (2016)
15. Vashishth, S., Joshi, R., Prayaga, S.S., Bhattacharyya, C., Talukdar, P.: RESIDE: improving distantly-supervised neural relation extraction using side information. In: The 2018 Conference on Empirical Methods in Natural Language Processing, pp. 1257–1266 (2018)
16. Nayak, T., Ng, H.T.: Effective attention modeling for neural relation extraction. In: The 23rd Conference on Computational Natural Language Learning (CoNLL), pp. 603–612 (2019)
17. Zhao, T., Yan, Z., Cao, Y., Li, Z.: Entity relative position representation based multi-head selection for joint entity and relation extraction. In: Sun, M., Li, S., Zhang, Y., Liu, Y., He, S., Rao, G. (eds.) CCL 2020. LNCS (LNAI), vol. 12522, pp. 184–198. Springer, Cham (2020). https://doi.org/10.1007/978-3-030-63031-7_14
18. Zhao, S., Hu, M., Cai, Z., Liu, F.: Modeling dense cross-modal interactions for joint entity-relation extraction. In: The 29th International Joint Conference on Artificial Intelligence, pp. 4032–4038 (2020)
19. Nayak, T., Ng, H.T.: Effective modeling of encoder-decoder architecture for joint entity and relation extraction. In: The AAAI Conference on Artificial Intelligence, vol. 34, no. 05, pp. 8528–8535 (2020)
20. Zhang,R.H., Liu, Q., Fan, A.X., Ji, H., Kurohashi, S.: Minimize exposure bias of seq2seq models in joint entity and relation extraction. In: The Association for Computational Linguistics: EMNLP 2020, pp. 236–246 (2020)
21. Sui, D., Chen, Y., Liu, K., Zhao, J., Liu, S.: Joint entity and relation extraction with set prediction networks. CoRR arXiv:2011.01675 (2020)
22. Gupta, P., Schütze, H., Andrassy, B.: Table filling multi-task recurrent neural network for joint entity and relation extraction. In: The 26th International Conference on Computational Linguistics (COLING2016), pp. 2537–2547 (2016)
23. Ma, Y., Hiraoka, T., Okazaki, N.: Named entity recognition and relation extraction using enhanced table filling by Contextualized Representations. CoRR arXiv:2010.07522 (2020)
24. Zhong, Z., Chen, D.: A frustratingly easy approach for joint entity and relation extraction. CoRR arXiv:2010.12812 (2020)
25. Riedel, S., Yao, L., McCallum, A.: Modeling relations and their mentions without labeled text. In: Balcázar, J.L., Bonchi, F., Gionis, A., Sebag, M. (eds.) ECML PKDD 2010. LNCS (LNAI), vol. 6323, pp. 148–163. Springer, Heidelberg (2010). https://doi.org/10.1007/978-3-642-15939-8_10

26. Roth, D., Yih, W.: A linear programming formulation for global inference in natural language tasks. In: The 8th Conference on Computational Natural Language Learning (CoNLL), pp. 1–4 (2010)
27. Sam, H., Kevin, B., Michele, F., Amber, S., Ozlem, U.: 2018 n2c2 shared task on adverse drug events and medication extraction in electronic health records. J. Am. Med. Inform. Assoc. **27**(1), 3–12 (2020)

Abnormality Detection and Identification Algorithm for High-Speed Freight Train Body

Tongcai Liu, Qing Liu$^{(\boxtimes)}$, and Zhiwei Wan

School of Automation, Wuhan University of Technology, Wuhan 430070, China

Abstract. Abnormality detection and identification for high-speed freight train body is an indispensable part of the Train Operation Status Monitoring System. Generally, abnormality detection and data recording are performed manually, which is very prone to cause problems such as false detections, missing detections and recording errors because of lots of freight trains passing through the station simultaneously. In order to tackle these problems, we proposes an Improved-YOLO model, based on the YOLOv4, adding the SE-Block to optimize the feature selection method, switching to Cascade PConv Module and Integrated BN combination instead of PANet for multi-level feature fusion, using random data augmentation to improve the generalization. Meanwhile, model training is assisted by introducing negative sample mechanism. With 4594 positive samples (including freight train body abnormalities) and 5406 negative samples (excluding freight train body abnormalities) collected at the actual station as the train set, and 4705 images of freight train body within 24 h as the test set, the Improved-YOLO has dropped by 18.72% and 7.10% in false detection rate and missing detection rate respectively compared to the original YOLO model and reached 8.95% and 9.38%.

Keywords: Improved-YOLOv4 · Freight train · Abnormality detection · Engineering application

1 Introduction

The development of railroad transport facilitating people and promoting economic growth, a variety of hidden dangers are also in urgent need of investigation and management. Common categories of freight train body abnormalities include shed train door opening, shed train window opening, tanker train cover opening, personnel climbing, foreign objects hanging, tarpaulin floating up, train body damage, cargo spilling. For the security issues of freight trains operation, there are already some safety monitoring systems in use, such as the TFDS (Trouble of moving freight train detection system) [1]. This system is mainly used for monitoring freight trains by setting up highspeed line scan cameras obtain images of both sides of the carriage. And then staff check the trouble of important parts such as bogie, hook buffer structure, sleeper spring, brake beam. Although TFDS can ensure high accuracy, it is extremely inefficient.

Since traditional image processing technology may significantly reduce the labor intensity of staff, the studies on using that for freight train body abnormality detection

H. Zhang et al. (Eds.): NCAA 2021, CCIS 1449, pp. 32–43, 2021.
https://doi.org/10.1007/978-981-16-5188-5_3

and identification are gradually increasing. Weilang Yan proposed an algorithm that can be used to judge if the door or window of shed train is opening in practical engineering application [2]. It can basically judge the state accurately with great lighting conditions, but it is prone to numerous false detections with low brightness.

With the rapid development of deep learning and convolutional neural network, more and more researchers have given the difficult problems in their fields to ask for deep learning algorithms. Wenwei Song proposed an abnormality recognition method for high-speed train body based on the two-stage object detection algorithm Faster R-CNN [3], which transformed the original abnormality recognition task into the detection task of key points on the train body, but the result of the method is not satisfactory [4].

Insufficient light intensity, stains and damages on the train body are very common phenomena in actual engineering conditions. These factors make a plentiful false detections and missing detections in the recognition results. In order to mitigate these problems and achieve the recognition effect required by practical engineering application, we propose the Improved-YOLO model for freight train body abnormality detection and recognition based on the one-stage object detection algorithm YOLOv4 [5]. The Improved-YOLO model optimizes the feature selection mechanism and enhances the mobility between low-level location information and high-level semantic information. It also reuses multi-level statistical data and improves the utilization rate of training samples, and in turn reduces the number of missing detection and false detection.

2 Characterization of Examined Objects and Train Set

In this paper, we need to detect and identify five types of freight train body abnormalities, which are shed train door opening, shed train window opening, tank train top cover opening, personnel climbing and foreign objects hanging. The characteristics of the examined objects are as follows:

- Because the aspect ratio of image is too small and the color of freight train body is in a dark style, it causes the background of freight train body to be mixed with abnormalities mentioned before.
- On the roof of freight train, ponding resulting in reflection makes images overexposed.
- The inherent hardware of freight train body, such as sealant and plastic extrusion, have similar characteristics with foreign objects hanging. They are prone to cause interference during the process of engineering application.
- In the category of foreign objects hanging, it contains many kinds of objects. For example, straw, wooden sticks, wire, bottles, plastic bags and twine. They belong to the same category, but there are different sizes, characteristics and spatial location distribution between them.

Through cooperation with station staff, a total of 4,594 freight train body images containing abnormalities were collected, and the numbers of various types of freight train body abnormalities are shown in Table 1. The comparison and analysis revealed that freight train body abnormalities in the train set have the following characteristics.

Table 1. The number of five types of freight train body abnormalities in the train set

Serial number	Abnormality category	Number of samples
1	Shed train door opening	185
2	Shed train window opening	185
3	Tanker train cover opening	164
4	Personnel climbing	1247
5	Foreign objects hanging	2813
Total		**4594**

- The number of three types of abnormalities, namely shed train door opening, shed train window opening and tanker train cover opening, is much fewer than that of personnel climbing and foreign objects hanging. There exists uneven distribution between the number of categories.
- In the category of tanker train cover opening, with the problem of inconspicuous abnormality features, it is difficult for the algorithm to extract valid features that can be easily distinguished.

3   Abnormality Detection and Identification Based on YOLOv4

The framework of the YOLOv4 model is shown in Fig. 1, which uses CSPDarknet-53 as the feature extraction module, SPPNet [6] as an additional module for the feature extraction module, PANet [7] as the feature fusion module, and YOLO_head as the output module.

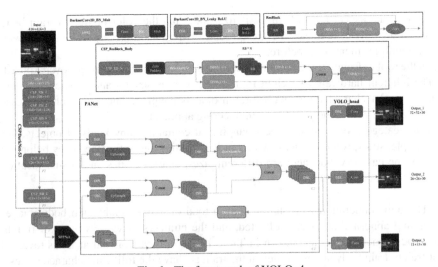

Fig. 1. The framework of YOLOv4

CSPDarknet-53 splits the original stacking method of Darknet53 in YOLOv3 [8] into two parts: the main part continues stacking ResBlock, and the other part adds a shortcut connection, which is directly connected to the final feature map after 1×1 convolution. In this way, CSPDarkNet-53 improves the utilization of low-level features and enhances the gradient during back propagation. The specific connection pattern is shown in the CSP_ResBlock_Body in Fig. 1. SPPNet performs four different scales of max pooling operation (13×13, 9×9, 5×5, 1×1) on the feature map P3 that outputs from the 5th CSP_ResBlock_Body of CSPDarknet-53, which enhances receptive field and adaptability to object deformation. YOLO_head is consistent with YOLOv3. Using full convolution operates the feature maps C1, C2 and C3 that obtained by repeatedly fusing P1, P2 and P3 in PANet. Finally, every YOLO_head outputs the category, confidence and coordinate of predicted objects under the corresponding scale.

Compared with Faster R-CNN, SSD [9] and DetectoRS [10], the YOLOv4 model performs proper compromise between accuracy and speed on the MS COCO dataset. We tried to train the YOLOv4 model on the existing 4594 positive samples and test on 4705 freight train body images collected within 24 h at the station. 16.48% false detection rate and 27.67% missing detection rate are non-ideal so that this model cannot meet the actual engineering application. To realize better performance on the abnormality detection task, the following improvements are made on the training strategy and the YOLOv4 model:

- Perform random data augmentation on the train set to increase the generalization of the model during the process of training.
- Freight train body images without abnormality are tested on the YOLOv4 model which trained on the 4594 positive samples, and then we record false detections to add them to the train set after being made into negative samples.
- Introduce SE-Block for feature extraction module (CSPDarknet-53) to enhance feature learning capability and optimize feature selection method.
- Cascade PConv Module instead of the feature fusion module (PANet) to mine the intrinsic scale correlation and achieve the effect of multi-scale training.
- Introduce Integrated Batch Normalization for new feature fusion module (Cascade PConv Module) to stabilize the gradient flow during training.

4 The Improved-YOLOv4 Model

4.1 Data Augmentation

According to Sect. 2, the number of certain abnormality is relatively few in the train set. The uneven distribution in category easily leads model to overfit and influences final recognition result. Therefore, during the process of training, the samples containing shed train door opening or shed train window opening or tanker train cover opening will be randomly operated once with a probability of 0.5. The data augmentation includes horizontal flip, salt-and-pepper noise and color space transformation. Take the abnormality of shed train window opening from the train set as an example, the comparison between original image and transformed images after data augmentation is shown in Fig. 2.

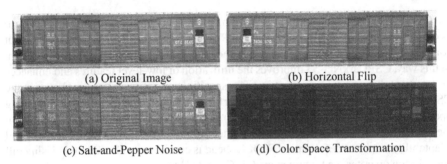

(a) Original Image   (b) Horizontal Flip

(c) Salt-and-Pepper Noise   (d) Color Space Transformation

Fig. 2. Example of data augmentation for abnormality of shed train window opening

4.2 Negative Sample Mechanism

The original YOLOv4 model generates many false detections in freight train body abnormality detection and recognition. Originally, we could increase the size of train set to improve the accuracy of model and thus reduce false detections. Since the percentage of freight train body with abnormality in the actual engineering conditions is very low, we cannot obtain a large number of positive samples in a short time. Therefore, the images of freight train body without abnormality collected in the early stage are sent into the trained YOLOv4 model for identification, and the misidentified images are screened and marked in misidentified areas. Then they will be made into negative samples to be added into the train set for fewer false detections in final result.

4.3 SE_CSPDarknet-53

In a 2-D convolution, the number of channels of the convolution kernel is generally the same as the input feature map, and the calculation results are accumulated by channel, which leads to mixture of the feature relations in the channel dimension and those in the spatial dimension learned by the convolution kernel. To solve this problem, SE-Block [11] relearns the feature relations between channels by "Squeeze", "Excitation" and "Merging" operation after the convolutional computation is completed.

The so-called "Squeeze" is to use the global average pooling to encode each channel and integrate them into a global feature map; the "Excitation" is done by two fully connected layers. The first fully connected layer FC_1 with ReLU complete the function of downscaling and enhancing the nonlinearity of the model, and the second fully connected layer FC_2 with Sigmoid transform parameter distribution to the interval [0, 1]; the "Merging" operation is to multiply channel activations from FC_2 with feature map from a 2-D convolution. The hyperparameter r in FC_1 in Fig. 3 is taken as 16, and the output of FC_2 can be regarded as the weight coefficients of each channel, which makes the model more discriminative for features of different channels.

Given a feature map $F \in \mathbb{R}^{H \times W \times C}$ calculated by a 2-D convolutional operator, firstly a statistic $s \in \mathbb{R}^{C}$ which presents global spatial information is generated by shrinking F

through its spatial dimensions $H \times W$ in " Squeeze " operation. The cth element of s is calculated by Eq. (1).

$$s_c = \frac{1}{H \times W} \sum_{p=1}^{H} \sum_{q=1}^{W} f_c(p, q) \tag{1}$$

where $f_c(p, q)$ is the value of the pth row, q^{th} column and c^{th} channel in the feature map F. Secondly, $k \in \mathbb{R}^C$ which reflect a nonlinear interaction and a non-mutually-exclusive relationship between channels is calculated by two fully connected layers:

$$k = \sigma(W_2 \zeta(W_1 s)) \tag{2}$$

Among them, ζ refers to the ReLU function, σ refers to the Sigmoid function, $W_1 \in \mathbb{R}^{(C/r) \times C}$ and $W_2 \in \mathbb{R}^{C \times (C/r)}$ are the weights of FC_1 and FC_2 respectively. Finally, the cth element of final output is obtained by rescaling F with the activations k:

$$\hat{f}_c = k_c f_c \tag{3}$$

where $\hat{F} = \left[\hat{f}_1, \hat{f}_2, \ldots, \hat{f}_c, \ldots, \hat{f}_C\right], \hat{F} \in \mathbb{R}^{H \times W \times C}$ is the final feature map.

The improvement to CSPDarknet-53 focuses on the ResBlock, and the original Res-Block (RB) and the improved SE-ResBlock (SE-RB) are shown in Fig. 3. The SE-Block is located behind serial convolution of ResBlock and in front of shortcut connection of ResBlock, which enhance the ability of ResBlock to extract feature relationships between channels. Since the number of channels in the shallow layers is too small, only the Res-Block on the 3th, 4th and 5th CSP_ResBlock_Body of CSPDarknet-53 are replaced by the SE-ResBlock. Their stacking method between the modules remains unchanged and constitutes the new feature extraction module SE_CSPDarknet-53 in turn.

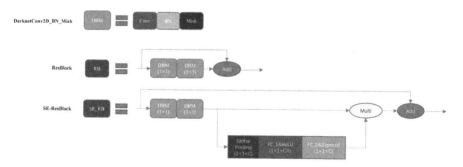

Fig. 3. The structure of ResBlock and SE-ResBlock

4.4 Cascade PConv Module

Pyramid Convolution Module (PConv) [12] is a 3-D convolution approach across spatial and dimensional dimensions, which is capable of aggregating both high and low-dimensional features, as shown in Fig. 4 for implementation. Assuming that A_1, A_2, and

A_3 are the feature maps before fusion, and B_1, B_2, and B_3 are the feature maps after fusion. The scale of feature maps decreases sequentially with the increase of subscript, the calculation is as follows:

$$B_1 = w_1 * A_1 + UpSample\,(w_2 * A_2) \tag{4}$$

$$B_2 = DownSample\,(w_1 * A_1) + (w_2 * A_2) + UpSample\,(w_3 * A_3) \tag{5}$$

$$B_3 = DownSample\,(w_2 * A_2) + w_3 * A_3 \tag{6}$$

Among them, * refers to an ordinary convolution with stride 1 and w_1, w_2, w_3 are three independent 2-D convolution kernels. Up-sampling can be implemented by a bilinear interpolation layer and an ordinary convolution with stride 1. Down-sampling can be implemented by an ordinary convolution with stride 2.

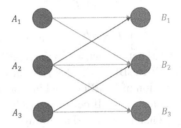

Fig. 4. The structure of Pyramid Convolution. The solid lines with same color indicate that they share the same convolution kernels

Cascade PConv Module replaces the feature fusion module (PANet), and their structures are shown in Fig. 5. Since Cascade PConv Module is able to perform top-down and bottom-up feature fusion simultaneously twice in succession, the new feature fusion approach can facilitate the information flow between high-level semantic features and low-level positional information more effectively compared to PANet. It also facilitates more accurate prediction of abnormality category and coordinates by YOLO_head.

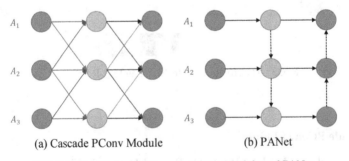

(a) Cascade PConv Module   (b) PANet

Fig. 5. The structure of Cascade PConv Module and PANet

4.5 Integrated Batch Normalization

Take the process of generation to feature map B_2 in Fig. 6 as an example to illustrate the differences between Integrated Batch Normalization and Independent Batch Normalization. When fusing feature pyramids, Independent BN only normalizes the current pyramid level, and each level of BN is independent of each other. Integrated BN performs parameter statistics on all feature maps it aggregates, and only obtains a set of mean and variance. All of pyramid levels share a set of parameters γ and β benefited from Integrated BN, which accelerates the convergence speed of model during the process of training and makes the model trained with small batch size can also get an ideal result.

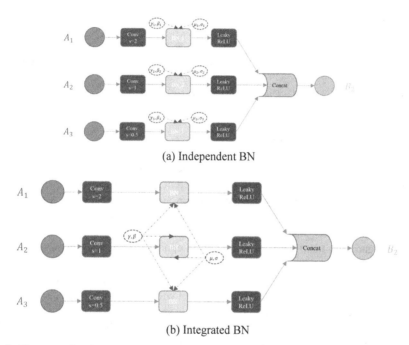

(a) Independent BN

(b) Integrated BN

Fig. 6. The normalization method of Independent BN and Integrated BN. In the case of three 2-D convolution, Independent BN normalizes a certain pyramid level respectively, but Integrated BN normalizes all of pyramid levels simultaneously

4.6 The Framework of Improved-YOLOv4

After the above improvement on YOLOv4, the framework of the Improved-YOLOv4 model is shown in Fig. 7. Due to the space limitation of the canvas, SE-ResBlock does not emerge in the Fig. 7, whose specific structure can refer to the Fig. 3.

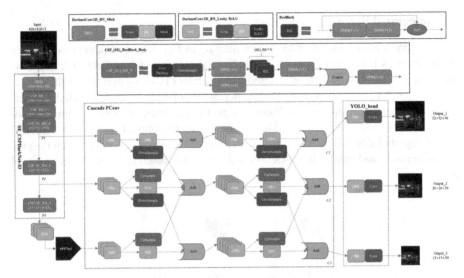

Fig. 7. The framework of Improved-YOLOv4

5   Experiment and Analysis

Under the same parameter settings of input image size, training step, batch size, initial learning rate, and optimizer, the effects of different improvement schemes on freight train body abnormality detection and recognition are tested separately. Among them, the input image size is a 416×416 RGB image, the batch size is 2, the optimizer is Adam, and the weight decay is $2e-5$. 5 epochs are trained on a GeForce GTX 1660Ti 6G using a learning rate of 0.001, followed by 45 epochs using a learning rate of 0.0001.

The training loss curves of the original YOLOv4 model and the Improved-YOLOv4 model are shown in Fig. 8. It is obvious that the value of training loss of the Improved-YOLOv4 model is smaller than the YOLO model with faster convergence speed.

In order to verify whether those improvements are effective, 4705 freight train body images (352 of them exist abnormalities) of a station within 24 h are tested, and the false detection rate and missing detection rate are used as the evaluation criteria to judge the performance of model. The experiment results are shown in Table 2.

From Table 2, it is known that:

- The original YOLOv4 model produces very serious false detections and missing detections in conducting freight train body abnormality detection and identification, and cannot be directly used in industrial sites, where the false detection rate is 27.67% (1302 sheets) and the missing detection rate is 16.48% (58 sheets).
- After using random data augmentation, the 2th group of the model reduced the false detection rate by 1.04% and the missing detection rate by 3.13% compared with the 1th group. It can be seen that data augmentation can increase the generalization of the model to a certain extent, and enable the model to identify those abnormalities that belong to the same category but with slightly different characteristics.

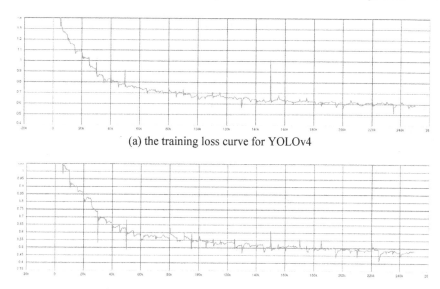

(a) the training loss curve for YOLOv4

(b) the training loss curve for Improved-YOLOv4

Fig. 8. The training loss curves for YOLOv4 and Improved-YOLOv4

Table 2. Comparison of model performance with different improvements

Group	Model	False detection rate	Missing detection rate
1	YOLOv4	27.67%	16.48%
2	YOLOv4 + Data Augmentation	26.63%	13.35%
3	YOLOv4 + Data Augmentation + Negative Sample Mechanism	12.35%	15.63%
4	YOLOv4 + Data Augmentation + Negative Sample Mechanism + SE-Block	11.65%	12.22%
5	YOLOv4 + Data Augmentation + Negative Sample Mechanism + SE-Block + Cascade PConv Module	9.67%	9.66%
6	YOLOv4 + Data Augmentation + Negative Sample Mechanism + SE-Block + Cascade PConv Module + Integrated BN	8.95%	9.38%

– Introducing the negative sample mechanism to the train set makes the false detection rate of the 3th group decreased by 14.28% and the missing detection rate increased by 2.28% compared with the 2th group. The decrease of false detection rate is due to the fact that the regions that are prone to false detection are correctly distinguished by the new category, while the increase of the missing detection rate is due to the fact that the model needs to predict more categories but the feature extraction or feature fusion capability is insufficient.

- In order to strengthen the feature extraction capability of CSPDarknet-53 and optimize the feature extraction method, SE_ResBlock is introduced on the basis of ResBlock. Therefore the 4th group of the model reduced the false detection rate by 0.70% and the missing detection rate by 3.41% compared with the 3th group.
- Based on the 4th group of the model, Cascade PConv Module instead of PANet makes the false detection rate reduced by 1.98% and the missing detection rate reduced by 2.56%. Consecutive simultaneous top-down and bottom-up feature fusion resultes in a substantial reduction in both the false detection rate and the missing detection rate of the model.
- In the Cascade PConv Module, Integrated BN is introduced. This improvement resulted in a 0.72% reduction in the false detection rate and a 0.28% reduction in the missing detection rate for the 6th group of the model. The reduction in the false detection rate and missing detection rate is attributed to stronger parameter statistics of Integrated BN that all pyramid levels share a set of mean, variance and training parameters. While the faster convergence speed allows the Integrated BN-containing model to get closer to the extreme value point for the same training step.

The results of Improved-YOLO to detect freight train body abnormality is shown in Fig. 9.

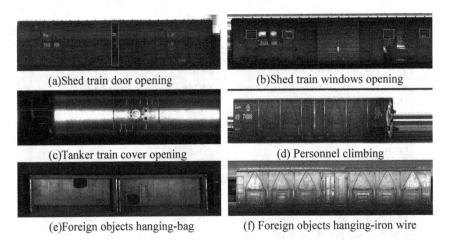

(a)Shed train door opening   (b)Shed train windows opening

(c)Tanker train cover opening   (d) Personnel climbing

(e)Foreign objects hanging-bag   (f) Foreign objects hanging-iron wire

Fig. 9. Results of freight train body abnormality detection with Improved-YOLO

6 Conclusion

The Improved-YOLO model proposed in this paper is based on the YOLOv4 and introduces SE-Block, Cascade PConv Module and Integrated BN to enhance the feature extraction and feature fusion capability of the model for the sample characteristics of body abnormalities in freight trains. While using data augmentation and negative sample mechanism improve the utilization of training samples. In the task of freight train body abnormality detection and identification, the Improved-YOLO model reduces the false detection rate by 18.72% and the missing detection rate by 7.10% compared with the original YOLOv4 model, which achieves 8.95% false detection rate and 9.38% missing detection rate for freight train body abnormality detection and identification. In the future, we will continue contributing to deploy more and more state-of-the-art algorithms of deep learning for engineering application.

References

1. Ying, Z.: Study on the optimization scheme of railroad vehicle operation safety monitoring system (5T system). In: Railway Transportation and Economy, pp. 52–57 (2016)
2. Weilang, Y.: Research on computer vision-based algorithm for railroad shed car door and window opening and closing status detection, pp. 1–80. Wuhan University of Technology (2018)
3. Shaoqing, R., Kaiming, H., Ross, G., Jian, S.: Faster R-CNN: towards real-time object detection with region proposal networks. In: Proceedings of the Advances in Neural Information Processing Systems, pp. 91–99 (2015)
4. Wenwei, S.: Research on the recognition of abnormalities in high-speed rolling stock images based on convolutional neural network, pp. 1–94. Southwest Jiaotong University (2019)
5. Alexey, B., Chien-Yao, W., Hong-Yuan, M.L.: YOLOv4: optimal speed and accuracy of object detection, pp. 1–17. arXiv preprint arXiv:2004.10934v1 (2020)
6. Kaiming, H., Xiangyu, Z., Shaoqing, R., Jian, S.: Spatial pyramid pooling in deep convolutional networks for visual recognition. In: IEEE Transactions on Pattern Analysis and Machine Intelligence (TPAMI), pp. 1904–1916 (2015)
7. Shu, L., Lu, Q., Haifang, Q., Jianping, S., Jiaya, J.: Path aggregation network for instance segmentation. In: Proceedings of the IEEE Conference on Computer Vision and Pattern Recognition (CVPR), pp. 8759–8768 (2018)
8. Joseph, R., Ali, F.: YOLOv3: an incremental improvement. arXiv preprint arXiv:1804.02767, pp. 1–6 (2018)
9. Wei, L., et al.: SSD: single shot multibox detector. In: Proceedings of the European Conference on Computer Vision (ECCV), pp. 21–37 (2016)
10. Siyuan, Q., Liang-Chieh, C., Alan, Y.: DetectoRS: detecting objects with recursive feature pyramid and switchable atrous convolution, pp. 1–12. arXiv preprint arXiv:2006.02334v2 (2020)
11. Jie, H., Li, S., Samuel, A., Gang, S., Enhua, W.: Squeeze-and-excitation networks. In: Proceedings of the IEEE Transactions on Pattern Analysis and Machine Intelligence (TPAMI), pp. 2011–2023 (2020)
12. Xinjiang, W., Shilong, Z., Zhuoran, Y., Litong, F.: Scale-equalizing pyramid convolution for object detection. In: Proceedings of the IEEE Computer Society Conference on Computer Vision and Pattern Recognition (CVPR), pp. 13356–13365 (2020)

Pheromone Based Independent Reinforcement Learning for Multiagent Navigation

Kaige Zhang[1]([✉]), Yaqing Hou[1]([✉]), Hua Yu[1], Wenxuan Zhu[1], Liang Feng[2], and Qiang Zhang[1]([✉])

[1] Dalian University of Technology, Dalian, China
{zhangKaigeyqhf,houyq,yhiccd,zhuwenxuan,zhangq}@dlut.edu.cn
[2] Chongqing University, Chongqing, China
liangf@cqu.edu.cn

Abstract. Multiagent systems (MAS) have been generally applied in numerous applications, including computer networks, robotics, and smart grids due to their flexibility, reliability for complex problem-solving. Communication is an important factor for the multiagent world to stay organized and productive. Previously, most existing studies try to pre-define the communication protocols or adopt additional decision modules for instructing the communication schedule, which induces significant communication cost overhead and cannot generalized to a large collection of agents directly. In this paper, we propose a lightweight communication framework—Pheromone Collaborative Deep Q-Network (PCDQN), which combines deep Q-network with the pheromone-driven stigmergy mechanism. In partially observable environments, this framework exploits the stigmergy as circuitous communication connections among independent reinforcement learning agents. Experiments dependent on the minefield navigation task have shown that PCDQN displays superiority in accomplishing higher learning productivity of multiple agents when contrasted with Deep Q-network (DQN).

Keywords: Multiagent system · Reinforcement learning · Communication · Stigmergy

1 Introduction

Multiagent systems (MAS), as a means to develop complex systems involving numerous agents and a component for coordination of autonomous agents' practices, have gotten enormous consideration in different disciplines, including software engineering, civil engineering, and electrical designing [3]. Typically, it aims to act in complex huge, open, dynamic, and erratic environments. However, it is normally troublesome and sometimes even difficult to appoint the systems a priori at the time of their design and preceding their utilization in such environments. Moreover, the multiagent control task is often too complex to be solved effectively by agents with preprogrammed behaviors. The achievable method to

© Springer Nature Singapore Pte Ltd. 2021
H. Zhang et al. (Eds.): NCAA 2021, CCIS 1449, pp. 44–58, 2021.
https://doi.org/10.1007/978-981-16-5188-5_4

adapt to this trouble is to integrate machine learning techniques in MAS, commonly known as multiagent learning (MAL), which endows individual agents with intelligence to build up the capability of the general system and their own approach.

In MAS, to ideally share assets or to amplify one own's benefit, proper activity coordination is highly concerned by multiple agents. While previous research of agent coordination centred around the off-line design of agent associations, social principles, arrangement conventions, and so forth. But it was perceived that agents operating in open, dynamic environments should have the option to adjust to changing demands and opportunities [14]. The most appropriate technique for this situation in MAL is reinforcement learning (RL) [9], which learns to achieve the given goal by trial-and-error iterations with its environment. As long as the environment that the agent experiences are Markov and the agent is permitted to evaluate adequate actions, it is ensured that the standalone RL algorithm converges to the optimal strategy. Be that as it may, an basic supposition of RL techniques, the dynamics of the environment is not influenced by other agents, is violated in multiagent fields. The desired approach to solve this problem is communication, which permits every agent to autonomously changes its strategy on the basis of its partial observation along with the information received from other agents.

Communication is one of the hallmarks of bio-intelligent, for instance, humans communicate through languages, while social insects using chemicals as their medium of communication. These allow organisms to share information efficiently between individuals and coordinate on shared tasks successfully. It is not surprising, then, that computer scientists have drawn inspiration from investigating the behavior of social insects, to design mechanisms for the communication of the multiagent systems. An especially intriguing assortment of work is stigmergy [6] that exhibits strong robustness in a simple way when mediating interactions between animals such as coordination within insects' activities. In insect societies, stigmergy is often realized via pheromone-based interactions. For instance, ants are equipped for tracking down the briefest way from a food source to their nest by making use of pheromone information. What's more, there exists no central control in an ant colony and environmental changes confronted by a colony are sudden instead of predetermined. When facing inner disturbances and outer difficulties, undertakings are finished in a decentralized way even if some ants fail. In a word, an ant colony, as a kind of MAS exploiting the stigmergic communication, are appropriate for figuring out distributed problems in nature, which dynamically changing, and require working in adaptation to internal failure [1].

Inspired by the stigmergy indirect communication mechanism, this research presents a novel multiagent independent RL method called Pheromone Collaborative Deep Q-Network (PCDQN) to enhance mutual communication in MAL with the assistance of a stigmergy mechanism. Particularly, the proposed method simulates natural pheromone to form a digital pheromone (DP) network in fulfilling its role in stigmergy as the medium of communication indirectly in distributed MAS. The remainder of this paper is mainly organized as follows. In Sect. 2, we describe the concept of reinforcement learning and then present the stigmergy mechanism. Section 3 discusses the details of PCDQN, which is a deep q-network algorithm combined with a stigmergy mechanism for multiagent coordination. Subsequently, the experiment result and analysis of PCDQN are demonstrated on the multiagent navigation problem in Sect. 4. At last, we summarize the whole paper.

2   Background

2.1   Multiagent Systems (MAS) and Reinforcement Learning (RL)

We consider MAS with N agents working coordinately in a partially observed environment, in which coordination is made more difficult by the unpredictable environment and imperfect agents' information. This issue can be displayed as a Decentralized Partially Observable Markov Decision Processes (Dec-POMDPs) [29], denoted by a tuple $\mathcal{G} = <\mathcal{S}, \mathcal{N}, \mathcal{A}, \mathcal{O}, \mathcal{Z}, \mathcal{P}, \mathcal{R}, \gamma>$, where $s \in \mathcal{S}$ means the global state. At each step $t \in \mathbb{Z}^+$, every agent $i \in \mathcal{N} = \{1, \cdots, n\}$ selects its action $a_i \in \mathcal{A}$, where a joint action represented by $\boldsymbol{a} := (a_i)_{i \in \mathcal{N}} \in \mathcal{A}^\mathcal{N}$. Each agent only has access to its local observation $o \in \mathcal{O}$ due to the partially observed environment, which is gained from the observation function $\mathcal{Z}(s, a): \mathcal{S} \times \mathcal{A} \to \mathcal{O}$. The determines $\mathcal{P}(s'|s, \boldsymbol{a}) := \mathcal{S} \times \mathcal{A} \to [0, 1]$ state transition dynamics. Agents aim to optimize the shared goal $\mathcal{R}(s, \boldsymbol{a}): \mathcal{S} \times \mathcal{A}^\mathcal{N} \to \mathbb{R}$, the $\gamma \in [0, 1)$ discounts the future rewards as well.

Q-Learning Algorithm. Reinforcement learning concerns what to do, how to map situations to actions as well as maximize future reward signals. Essentially, it is a closed-loop problem because the current action influences its following state. More specifically, the agent interacts with its environment at every discrete-time step in a time-sequence $t = 0, 1, 2, 3 \cdots$. The agent-environment interaction is shown in Fig. 1.

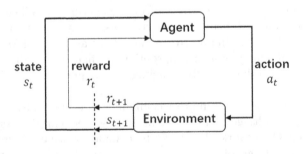

Fig. 1. Interaction of agent-environment.

In RL, the agent in the state s_t selects action a_t depending on policy π and takes the action and then transfers to the next state s_{t+1} with probability $p[s_{t+1}|s_t, a_t]$, meanwhile receives the reward r_t from the environment. The interaction of an agent with its environment is formalized by the Markov decision process (MDP) in RL. MDP is defined as tuple $< S, A, r, P, \gamma >$, where S is the set of states and A denotes a collection of available actions, and also $\gamma \in [0, 1]$ is the discount factor. $P : S \times A \rightarrow S$ is called transition probability function that giving probability distribution over next states based on states and actions, and $r : S \times A \rightarrow \mathbb{R}$ signifies the reward. RL solves the MDP by fitting policy $\pi : S \rightarrow A$ so as to maximize the expected discount return $R_t = \mathbb{E}[\sum_{k=1}^{\infty} \gamma^k r_{k+t}|\pi]$. The policy induces a value function $V^\pi(S) = \mathbb{E}_\pi[R_t|s_t = s]$ and action value function $Q^\pi(s, u) = \mathbb{E}_\pi[R_t|s_t = s, u_t = u]$.

Given state s, action a, reward r and next state s', the optimal action value $Q^*(s, u) = \max_\pi Q^\pi(s, u)$ can be approximated iteratively by the Bellman equation:

$$Q^*(s, u) = \mathbb{E}_{s'}[r + \gamma \max_{u'} Q^*(s', u')|s, u] \tag{1}$$

Q-learning estimates expected reward starting in state s_t, taking action u_t as $Q(s_t, u_t)$. Each $Q(s_t, u_t)$ estimates of the corresponding optimal Q^* function that maps state-action pairs to the discounted sum of future rewards by following the optimal policy subsequently.

Deep Q-Network (DQN). Deep Q-network (DQN) [5] combines standard Q-learning [12] with deep neural networks by approximating the Q-function using a non-linear neural network, in which the Q-function parameterized by weights θ is called Q-network. Typically, using neural to represent the Q-function network will result in unstable or even diverge RL policy. For fear of divergence in neural networks, the standard online Q-learning is modified by DQN in two ways. One is experience replay, that is agent's experiences $e_t = (s_t, u_t, r_t, s_{t+1})$ are stored in a data set $D_t = e_1, \ldots, e_t$ at every step t and are sampled uniformly, $(s, u, r, s') \sim U(D)$, as training examples. The other is target Q network using a separate network for generating the Q-learning targets $r + \gamma \max_{u'} \hat{Q}(s', u'; \theta_i^-)$. In detail, it clones the network Q to obtain a target network $\hat{Q}$ at every C updates and then uses it to generate Q-learning targets for the following C steps.

Through adjusting the parameters θ_i at iteration i, Q-network can be trained to reduce the mean-squared error in the Bellman equation (Eq. 1). For iteration i, Q-learning uses the following loss function to update:

$$L_i(\theta_i) = \mathbb{E}_{s,u,r,s' \sim U(D)}[(r + \gamma \max_{u'} \hat{Q}(S', u'; \theta_i^-) - Q(s, u; \theta_i))^2] \tag{2}$$

in which γ is the discount factor, θ_i denotes the parameters of Q-network and θ_i^- is the parameters of $\hat{Q}$, which used to compute the Q-learning target. The θ_i^- is only updated with θ_i at every C step and held fixed between singular updates.

2.2   The Mechanism of Stigmergy

French zoologist Pierre-Paul Grassé firstly introduced the concept of stigmergy for studying the coordination in social insects. Those insects constitute a complex system to enable them to work together effectively. When returning from food sources, pheromone trails left by ants are a sort of representative application of stigmergy. Other ants in the colony are motivated to walk along on the same road by those pheromone trails. Ants will enhance the pheromone trails and return the nest along trails When discovering the food source. This mechanism creates an efficient pheromone network that bridging the shortest possible routes between the nest and major food sources. This foraging behavior forms a feedback loop in which an ant leaves a pheromone marker which in turn triggers the following action, and then generates another marker, and so forth (see Fig. 2) [4].

Stigmergy [6], as illustrated in Fig. 3, typically encompasses four main components: action, condition, medium, and trace. The most primitive is "action", which is a causal process causing the state of the environment to change. Typically, those actions are performed by independent, goal-oriented agents. The "condition" wherein "action" happens determines the state of the environment, while the "action" indicates the transformation of that state subsequently. The "medium" is another important component of stigmergy, which is regarded as a part of the environment. It goes through changes via "action" and its state creates conditions for those actions in the future. The final component "trace" is the discernible influence made by "action" in the "medium". As a consequence of the action, the trace contains information belonging to the action that caused it.

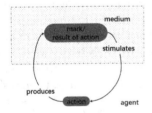

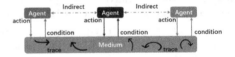

Fig. 2. The stigmergic feedback loop.   **Fig. 3.** The stigmergy mechanism.

3   Method

In this section, we propose Pheromone Collaborative Deep Q-Network (PCDQN) (as shown in Fig. 4), which is composed of modified DQN and stigmergy respectively. Therein, DQN architecture plays a role as the neural system that directs agents' policy to acclimate the environment and learn from interaction to achieve their goal. Further, the stigmergy is introduced as an indirect communication bridge among the independent learning agents when coordinating. In what follows, first comes the modified DQN architecture–Dueling Double Deep Q-network with Prioritized Replay that we have used. Then, we show how to fuse this architecture with stigmergy mechanism eventually.

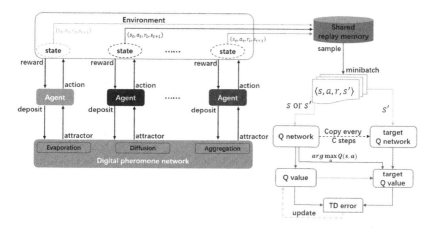

Fig. 4. The framework of Pheromone Collaborative Deep Q-Network (PCDQN).

3.1 Dueling Double Deep Q-Network with Prioritized Replay

We propose a parameter sharing multiagent RL structure called Dueling Double Deep Q-network with Prioritized Replay, which extends the standalone DQN algorithm to multiple agents by sharing the parameters of the policy network among our agents. DQN has been an important milestone in DRL, but several limitations of this algorithm are now known in solving completely real-world applications, such as overestimation bias, data inefficiency, and poor approximation in state-value function. To mitigate the impact of these drawbacks while accelerating the learning performance, we adopt several DQN variants in our implementation for multiagent settings.

DQN Variants. By means of end-to-end reinforcement learning, Deep Q networks (DQN) learn successful policies from high-dimensional images straightly. Although DQN has been well used to solve fully real applications, its has multiple imperfections that can be repaired by integrating different solutions ranging from simple forms to complex corrections.

Double DQN [11] (DDQN) is the first and simplest form of DQN variants. During training process, DDQN reduces the overestimation of Q-values by separating the "greedy" action selection from action evaluation. In another word, the max operator in Eq. (2) is dissociated into two different elements, as represented by the following loss function:

$$L_i(\theta_i) = \mathbb{E}_{s,u,r,s' \sim U(D)}[(r + \gamma \max_{a'} \hat{Q}(S', \arg\max_{a'} Q(s', a'; \theta_i^-); \theta_i^-) - Q(s, u; \theta_i))^2]$$

$$(3)$$

In DQN, the experience replay plays a crucial part. It breaks the sample dependency and improves the utilization of "rare" samples. But in fact, sample data can not be separated completely when taking random samples by experience replay. Concretely speaking, rare or target-related data samples are expected to occur more frequently than redundant ones. Accordingly, a prioritized experience replay technique was proposed by Schaul et al. [8], which prioritizes a sample i on account of its absolute value TD error

$$p_i = |\delta_i| = |r_i + \gamma \max_a Q(s_i, a|\theta_i^-) - Q(s_{i-1}, a_{i-1}|\theta_i)|. \tag{4}$$

Dueling network, a novel network architecture, was designed by Wang et al. [13]. It decouples value and advantage in DQN explicitly by separating the state values estimation and state-related action. The dueling network contains two streams representing the value and advantage functions respectively combined by a mutual feature learning module later. In this architecture, one network figures out the state-value function $V(s|\theta)$ represented by θ, while the other is parameterized by θ' standing for the advantage action function $A(s, a|\theta')$. After that, it is the following formula that aggregates the two networks to figure out the Q-value function:

$$Q(s, a|\theta, \theta') = V(s|\theta) + (A(s, s|\theta') - \frac{1}{|\mathcal{A}|} \sum_{a'} A(s, a'|\theta')) \tag{5}$$

In practice, every variation empowers remarkable enhancement individually. Since they do so by addressing radically different issues and are built on a shared framework, they could plausibly be combined.

Neural Network Architecture. In this subsection, we integrate all the aforementioned optimized extensions: Double Q-learning, Prioritized experience reply, and Dueling networks into a single integrated architect, which we call Dueling Double Deep Q-network with Prioritized Replay. As shown in Fig. 5, the input of the network is an n-dimensional vector containing sensor signal, digital pheromone information, and the serial number of the agent itself. The first hidden layer, consisting of 256 Rectifier Linear Units (ReLu), is fully-connected. This is followed by a dueling architecture consisting of two streams to separately estimate state-value and the advantages of each action. Finally, the last linear layer projects each valid action.

3.2   Digital Pheromones Coordination Mechanism

As a coordination mechanism, stigmergy relies on traces, left by action in the medium, to trigger succeeding activities. In a natural ant colony, ants operate on chemical pheromones—as a form of stigmergy—to encourage deliberate activities. By accumulating deposits from distinctive agents, it fuses information on multiple agents. Over time it evaporates pheromones as well. Inspired by such a mechanism, we develop a kind of digital-analog called digital pheromones that is well suited to the dynamical environment in a distributed way. Such a pheromone structure resides in a network of agents in the environment area. Each agent is adjacent to a limited number of other agents, for which they exchange local

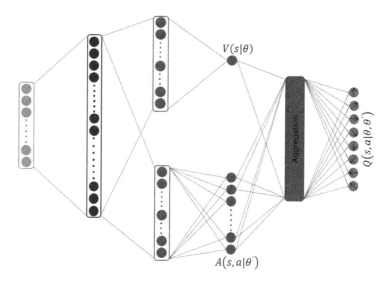

Fig. 5. Schematic illustration of the network architecture.

pheromone information with one another. On account of pheromone is quantitative, conditions detected by agents vary in intensity or extent. Besides, stronger traces inspire more powerful actions generally.

In our setting, we look upon the digital pheromone network as the medium. It is this medium that allows collaboration or correspondence between various activities and hence, potentially, among agents who performing actions. In a limited area, agents are able to sense the amount of pheromone within the digital pheromone network. Here, network nodes, brimming with digital pheromones, are considered as "attractor". It is appealing for the surrounding agents and can provide effective observation about the local state space (see Fig. 6). In a local area, each agent selects an "attractor" to conduct its behavior (i.e., close to "attractor"), independent of several potential agents in its perception range. The probability with which agent k chooses "attractor" j from its current position node i at time step t is defined as follows:

$$
C_{i,j}^k(t) = \begin{cases} \dfrac{D(d_{i,j}^k(t)) \cdot \varepsilon_j(t)}{\sum_{j \in \mathcal{N}_i^k(t)} D(d_{i,j}^k(t)) \cdot \varepsilon_j(t)}, & if\ j \in \mathcal{N}_i^k(t) \\ 0, & others. \end{cases}
\tag{6}
$$

Each agent k chooses the next "attractor" j with the highest probability as follows:

$$
j = \arg\max_{l \in \mathcal{N}_i^k(t)} D(d_{i,l}^k(t)) \cdot \varepsilon_l(t)
\tag{7}
$$

where $d_{i,j}^k(t)$ and $\varepsilon_i(t)$ are, respectively, at time step t, the distance between current node i and the pheromone concentration within "attractor" j. $\mathcal{N}_i^k(t)$ is a group of alternative "attractor" within the perception range of agent k

when situating at node i. What's more, the "attractor" selection rule given by Eq. (6) is called a random-proportional rule [2]. It is inclined to select nodes that contain abundant pheromone as well as connected by shorter paths. In addition, we employ $D(\cdot)$, a monotonous function, to diminish the impact of digital pheromone with increasing inter-distance $d_{i,j}^k(t)$. At the bottom of Fig. 6, the amplitude of response for the interactive influence using pheromone is determined by the inter-distance between agents. The function $D(\cdot)$ solves the ping-pong effect [7] as to enable agents to focus on the "attractor" nearby. In practical terms, $D(\cdot)$, shown below, is represented as the Gaussian function:

$$D(d_{i,j}^k(t)) = a \cdot e^{-\frac{(d_{i,j}^k(t)-b)^2}{2c^2}} \qquad (8)$$

In this formula, a stands for a peak value of 1 and $b = 0$ is averaging. The c, set to 0.25 normally, is the standard deviation preventing the pheromone concentration from varying too much and falling the agent into a local optimum.

When a dynamic change occurs in the environment, some previously generated pheromone trails may lead to a possibly poor solution for the new environment. For this reason, ant colony optimization [2] uses an evaporation-based framework to update pheromone trails and, consequently, they adapt to dynamic change. We are loosely inspired by MAX-MIN Ant System (MMAS), the digital pheromone value of every node j at time step $t + 1$ is updated by applying evaporation as follows:

$$\varepsilon_j(t+1) = (\varepsilon_j(t) + \Delta_{diffuse}) \cdot (1 - \rho), \forall j \notin D \qquad (9)$$

where $\rho \in (0, 1]$ is the evaporation rate, $\Delta_{diffuse}$ is the digital pheromone amount diffused by nearby nodes and D is the region consisting of every agent's target node. In particular, following the principle of linear superposition, $\Delta_{diffuse}$ is the summation of digital pheromone diffused from the four adjoining nodes above, below, to the left, and the right of the node. And the agent k releases the redundant digital pheromone in the medium, creating new conditions for the afterward "attractor" selection, after performing the selected action. By applying the depositing rule of Eq. (10), the digital pheromone concentration is renewed.

$$\varepsilon_j(t+1) = \varepsilon_j(t) + \varepsilon_0, \forall j \in D \qquad (10)$$

where ε_0 is the constant amount of pheromone to be deposited. The lower and upper limits $\varepsilon_{\min}$ and $\varepsilon_{\max}$ of the digital pheromone values are imposed such that $\forall j : \varepsilon_{\min} < \varepsilon_j < \varepsilon_{\max}$.

4   Experiments

In this section, we describe the Minefield Navigation Environment [10] that using to perform our experiments, as well as demonstrate the effectiveness of PCDQN, its superiority for multiagent navigation.

4.1   Minefield Navigation Environment (MNE)

We adopt MNE that is a two-dimensional world with discrete space and time, consisting of n agents and m obstacles. On account of the locality of observation, which restricted to the perception range centered on the unit (see Fig. 7), independent agents only occupy one unit at a time in the MNE. Within a prescribed time frame, agents aim to traverse the MNE to their destinations without hitting a mine. An episode terminates when all agents have either died or arrived at their own target or overrun pre-specified time.

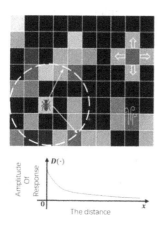

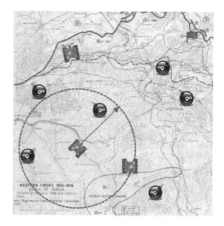

Fig. 6. The digital pheromone network.   **Fig. 7.** The sensing range of the agent.

- **State and Observation:** At each step, every agent receives local observation drawn within their field of sense as well as selects a node in the digital pheromone network as its own "attractor" in the meantime. Among local observation, it encompasses information about obstacles and other agents within a circular area. The observation of each agent comprises the following properties: sensor signal, relative position to its destination, "attractor" location, and its identification number. Relying on eight sonars, every agent has a crude sensory capability with a 360° view. For any direction $i \in [0, 7]$, the perception is defined by $s_i = \left(\frac{1}{d_i} \right)$, wherein d_i represents the interval to the obstacle or to another agent.
- **Action Space:** It is the discrete set consisting of eight actions that allowing to perform by agents. At each time step, the agent can choose one possible action within this set, namely, *move north, move northeast, move east, move southeast, move south, move southwest, move west,* and *move northwest.*

- **Rewards:** Sparse reward problem is the core problem of reinforcement learning in solving practical tasks. Solving the sparse reward problem is conducive to improving the sample efficiency and the quality of optimal policy, and promoting the application of deep reinforcement learning to practical tasks. To cope with this, we adopt reward shaping to figure out a reward depended on whether the agent reaches its goal, hits a mine, collides with others, and so on.

4.2   Effectiveness of PCDQN

We start by measuring the effectiveness of PCDQN on a multiagent collaboration task. Our testbed consists of 4 agents, using a 16×16 environment containing 15 min.

Experimental Setup. By using additional reward features, we shape the primary reward to appropriately encourage or punish interactions, filling the gap of the original sparse reward feature. At each time step t, agent k receives its immediate reward r_t^k defined as follows:

$$r_t^k = \begin{cases} r_{arrive}^k, & \text{if reaching its destination} \\ r_{collision}^k, & \text{if hitting a mine or another} \\ r_{turn}^k + r_{close}^k + r_{stop}^k + r_{range}^k + r_{attractor}^k & \text{otherwise} \end{cases}$$

(11)

where r_{arrive}^k and $r_{collision}^k$ are, respectively, the success reward and failure penalty for agent k. When reaching its destination successfully, it receives the reward $r_arrive^k = +1$. While hitting a mine or another agent, it fails and is penalized by getting points $r_collision^k = 1$. Otherwise, r_t^k is composed of r_{turn}^k, r_{close}^k, r_{stop}^k, r_{range}^k, and $r_{attractor}^k$.

To prevent agents through the minefield in a zigzag way, r_{turn}^k is used to punish agent k for deviating from its previous direction to force it to walk in a straight line. The punishment to agent k who close to obstacles is measured by r_{close}^k as follows:

$$r_{close}^k = -\sigma \cdot \max(s_i), \forall i \in [0, 7]$$

(12)

where $\sigma \in [0, 1]$ determines the importance of sensory signal s_i. The r_{stop}^k is set up to prevent the agent k from being stuck on the edge of the minefield for a long time. When the coordinates of agent at current are the same as the previous moment, a certain penalty will be given to it.

Considering the overall goal, agent k cannot simply focus on its own interests such that r_{range}^k is defined by the sum of the distance between every agent and its destination as follows:

$$r_{range}^k = -\lambda \cdot \sum_{j=1}^{n} \min_{1 \geq i \leq n} \left(dist(i, j) \right)$$

(13)

where $\lambda \in [0,1]$ determines the significance of the total distance, and $dist(i,j)$ means the distance between agent i and destination j for $\forall i,j \in [1,n]$, and n is the total number of agents existing in the minefield. The $r^k_{attractor}$ as the feedback of its "attractor" when the agent k closing to or leaving away it is defined as:

$$r^k_{attractor} = \beta \cdot \left(\frac{1}{d_{k,j}}\right) \tag{14}$$

where $\beta \in [0,1]$ stands for the proportion of pheromone attribute we adopt in r^k_t, and $d_{(k,j)}$ is the distance between agent k and its "attractor" j.

Results. By receiving feedback signals from the environment, agents are able to learn from scratch. We carry out a total of 2000 trials and evaluate training at every 100 intervals. The success rate is identified by the proportion of agents who achieve their goals inside the predefined time steps. While the failure rate can divide into three parts: hit mine, time out, and collision. They are, respectively, categorized by percentage of agents that hit mines, cannot achieve their goals within the max time steps, or collide with others.

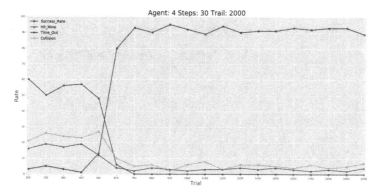

Fig. 8. Success rate and failure (hit mine, time out, and collision) rate of the PCDQN multiagent system averaged at every 100 intervals on the collaboration task.

Figure 8 shows the average success and failure rate of PCDQN. The success rate is highly unstable in the beginning but then increases rapidly after 400 trials. By the end of 700 trials, the multiagent system has achieved more than a 90% success rate. It's because the replay buffer has not yet stored enough experiences to update the policy sufficiently at the beginning. In addition, the training still keeps stable despite the non-stationary of the environment which arises due to the other agents changing their behavior during training. In the meantime, the failure rate decreases as the training progress especially for time out. At the beginning of training, there is a high probability of time out for agents, but after 700 trials, the time out drops to about 0%, indicating that agents have learned to take correct actions when navigating. Besides, we particularly see the benefit of the digital pheromone network. Hit mine and collision also drop significantly after a certain number of rounds of training, indicating that agents have sensed traces left in medium and learned to avoid getting too close to mines and other moving agents in the process of moving.

We perform an ablation experiment to investigate the influence of the digital pheromone network in PCDQN. We analyze the significance of digital pheromone on the mixing framework by comparing it against PCDQN without the digital pheromones coordination mechanism. We calculated curves of the average performance for 2000 trials for each approach on this task and we display the accumulated reward over time in Fig. 9. With the help of digital pheromones, agents converge to a better policy faster. The multiagent system takes about 700 trials to achieve the best performance without the digital pheromones coordination mechanism. In contrast, the PCDQN multiagent system obtains the best success rate around 600 trials. In terms of stability, PCDQN agents maintain relatively more stability after convergence in the later stage of training. To the lack of pheromone guidance (blue curve in Fig. 9), some strong fluctuations will occur due to environmental instability after agents converge to their optimum.

Fig. 9. The accumulated reward curves for PCDQN with (red) and without (blue) the digital pheromones coordination mechanism. (Color figure online)

Figure 10 shows the searched navigation paths in the multiagent collaboration task by using the PCDQN framework in MNE. Every agent has successfully not only planed a safe collision-free path when performing its task but also that path is relatively straight not zigzag. We specifically examine the variation of digital pheromone concentration in the whole environment during the process of trial. And we extract a sample in 2000 trials and display digital pheromone concentration at 2-step intervals within 30 steps shown in Fig. 11. In the beginning, digital pheromone concentration is 0 everywhere. After several time steps, some of the agents reach their goals and release digital pheromone. In the meantime, these digital pheromone diffuses into their surroundings to guide other agents to

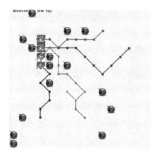

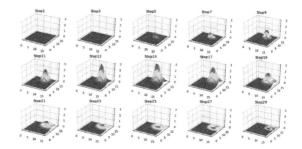

Fig. 10. The searched navigation paths in the MNE.

Fig. 11. The change of digital pheromone concentration during training for a single trial.

achieve their targets faster. Digital pheromone concentration clearly increases as time goes by and achieves its peak at about step 15. At this point, almost all agents reach their destination successfully. After that, digital pheromone gradually evaporates and drops to 0 at the end, which corresponds with the phenomenon observed in the natural ant colony.

5 Conclusion

This paper proposes a PCDQN, a deep multiagent RL method, which allowing to learn decentralized policies and making efficient use of a digital pheromones coordination mechanism. Our results in the multiagent navigation task in the MNE show that PCDQN exhibits excellent performance in respect of stability as well as its learning efficiency, and converges to an optimal policy eventually. In the future, we will investigate the multiagent credit assignment, which produces different rewards for each agent to deduce its own contribution, in turn, make teams achieve their success in more challenging tasks.

Acknowledgement. This work was supported in part by the National Natural Science Foundation of China under Grant 61906032, the NSFC-Liaoning Province United Foundation under Grant U1908214, the Fundamental Research Funds for the Central Universities under grant DUT21TD107, the LiaoNing Revitalization Talents Program, No. XLYC2008017, the National Key Research and Development Program of China under Grant 2018YFC0910500, the National Natural Science Foundation of China under Grant 61976034, and the Liaoning Key Research and Development Program under Grant 2019JH2/10100030.

References

1. Dorigo, M., Bonabeau, E., Theraulaz, G.: Ant algorithms and stigmergy. Futur. Gener. Comput. Syst. **16**(8), 851–871 (2000)
2. Dorigo, M., Gambardella, L.M.: Ant colony system: a cooperative learning approach to the traveling salesman problem. IEEE Trans. Evol. Comput. **1**(1), 53–66 (1997)

3. Dorri, A., Kanhere, S.S., Jurdak, R.: Multi-agent systems: a survey. IEEE Access **6**, 28573–28593 (2018)
4. Heylighen, F.: Stigmergy as a universal coordination mechanism I: definition and components. Cogn. Syst. Res. **38**, 4–13 (2016)
5. Mnih, V., et al.: Human-level control through deep reinforcement learning. Nature **518**(7540), 529–533 (2015)
6. Musil, J., Musil, A., Biffl, S.: Introduction and challenges of environment architectures for collective intelligence systems. In: Weyns, D., Michel, F. (eds.) E4MAS 2014. LNCS (LNAI), vol. 9068, pp. 76–94. Springer, Cham (2015). https://doi.org/10.1007/978-3-319-23850-0_6
7. Naeem, B., Javed, S., Kasi, M.K., Sani, K.A.: Hybrid fuzzy logic engine for ping-pong effect reduction in cognitive radio network. Wireless Pers. Commun. **116**(1), 177–205 (2021)
8. Schaul, T., Quan, J., Antonoglou, I., Silver, D.: Prioritized experience replay. arXiv preprint arXiv:1511.05952 (2015)
9. Sutton, R.S., Barto, A.G.: Reinforcement Learning: An Introductio, 2nd edn. The MIT Press (2018). http://incompleteideas.net/book/the-book-2nd.html
10. Tan, A.H., Lu, N., Xiao, D.: Integrating temporal difference methods and self-organizing neural networks for reinforcement learning with delayed evaluative feedback. IEEE Trans. Neural Networks **19**(2), 230–244 (2008)
11. Van Hasselt, H., Guez, A., Silver, D.: Deep reinforcement learning with double Q-learning. In: Proceedings of the AAAI Conference on Artificial Intelligence, vol. 30 (2016)
12. Vinyals, O., et al.: Alphastar: mastering the real-time strategy game starcraft II. DeepMind Blog **2** (2019)
13. Wang, Z., Schaul, T., Hessel, M., Hasselt, H., Lanctot, M., Freitas, N.: Dueling network architectures for deep reinforcement learning. In: International Conference on Machine Learning, pp. 1995–2003. PMLR (2016)
14. Weiß, G.: Adaptation and learning in multi-agent systems: some remarks and a bibliography. In: Weiß, G., Sen, S. (eds.) IJCAI 1995. LNCS, vol. 1042, pp. 1–21. Springer, Heidelberg (1996). https://doi.org/10.1007/3-540-60923-7_16

A Deep Q-Learning Network Based Reinforcement Strategy for Smart City Taxi Cruising

Zhenyao Hua[1,2,3], Dongyang Li[1,3], and Weian Guo[1,2,3](✉)

[1] School of Information and Electronics Engineering, Tongji University, Shanghai 201804, China
{2032976,guoweian}@tongji.edu.cn
[2] Sino-German College of Applied Sciences, Tongji University, Shanghai 201804, China
[3] Shanghai Institute of Intelligent Science and Technology, Tongji University, Shanghai 200092, China

Abstract. Smart transportation is crucial to citizens' living experience. A high efficiency dispatching system will not only help drivers rise income, but also save the waiting time for passengers. However, drivers' experience-based cruising strategy cannot meet the requirement. By conventional strategies, it is not easy for taxi drivers to find passengers efficiently and will also result in a waste of time and fuel. To address this problem, we construct a model for taxi cruising and taking passengers based on the view of drivers' benefits. By employing real data of taxi orders, we apply a deep-Q-network in the framework of reinforcement learning to find a strategy to reduce the cost in taxi drivers' finding the passengers and improve their earning. Finally, we prove the effect of our strategy by comparing it with a random-walk strategy in different segments of time both in workday and weekend.

Keywords: Taxi cruising strategy · Deep Q-Network · Reinforcement learning · Drivers' benefits

1 Introduction

As an important role in urban transportation network, taxis provide convenient and comfortable services for citizens travelling. However, there still exist many problems in the supply and demand of service between taxis and clients, resulting in the fact that many taxis stay vacant in a large percent of their working time while some clients should wait for a long time to take a taxi. Such cases will cause a large waste of energies and time from both drivers and clients [1]. With the development of information technology, it is possible to apply artificial intelligence in taxis cruising to enhance the service efficiency. In early 1990s, Dial proposed a phone-calling-based system for taxi service [2]. Currently, thanks to the appearance of smart phones and GPS technology, it is very popular to use APPs for booking and calling taxis service. Consequently, lots of transportation network companies appear, such as Didi, Uber and many others. By

H. Zhang et al. (Eds.): NCAA 2021, CCIS 1449, pp. 59–70, 2021.
https://doi.org/10.1007/978-981-16-5188-5_5

building an information platform, both locations of taxi drivers and clients are shared on it to call and response taxis services [3].

In general, taxis cruising strategy much influences drivers' income and clients' waiting time. When a taxi is non-hailing, drivers usually cruise randomly or go to a target area according to drivers' own experiences. However, an inferior taxi dispatching strategy will cause increasing non-hailing time, more costs for taxi drivers and result in a long waiting time for clients [4]. An intelligent and optimized taxi dispatching system will much enhance the efficiency of taxi service. For such issue, during past decades, a few studies tried to discover the pattern of the human drivers' real actions based on taxis trajectories [5–7]. Some researchers used the real time information of the taxis distribution in a city to evaluate the saturation degree of different regions and then schedule the taxis [8–10]. Liu constructed the scheduling model based on three aspects involving clients demands, taxis distribution and routing situation by comparing both real-time data and historical data [11]. Swarm intelligence was also used to realize a more sensible global resources allocation [12, 13]. Markov decision process [14, 15] and Q-learning [16, 17] were investigated in similar studies. However, the current researches focus on the macroscopic view, but lacks of related researches from taxi agents' standpoint for cruising strategy.

To address this problem, in this paper, we contribute the following works. We employ a deep Q-network (DQN) and taxi trajectory data to train a taxi cruising model in order to provide a strategy for the taxi drivers when non-hailing. Based on such strategy, the drivers will have a large probability to increase their income and reduce the waste of both time and fuel.

The remainder of this paper is organized as follows. In Sect. 2, we construct a model for taxi cruising based on the view of drivers' benefits. Section 3 introduces a Q-network in detail and describes the DQN learning procedures. Section 4 conducts experiments and simulations to evaluate the proposed models in different time zones in one day. The proposed strategy is also analyzed and compared with a random-walk strategy. We end this paper in Sect. 5, and present our future work.

2 Problem Description

2.1 Modeling

In general, taxi drivers cruise based on their own experience, for different kinds of purposes, such as total profit or total accounts of service, etc. In addition, some other factors in the real scenarios are also supposed to be considered, which involve the position and total work time of the taxi driver. There also exists uncertainties in clients demands, because in different periods of one day or in different dates, the transportation situations are not similar. Besides, the weather conditions and citizens preferences will also affect the transportation situation so that it is difficult to build an analytical formula for taxis dispatching system just by drivers' experience. Therefore, it is necessary to apply artificial intelligence on such scenarios. In this paper, reinforcement learning is employed to address the problems. In the framework of reinforcement learning, we take taxis as agents, while the taxi service environment is regarded as a learning environment.

The objective of a cruising strategy, shown in (1), is modeled as an optimization problem which maximizes drivers' profit.

$$Maximize : P = \sum_i G_i - \sum_j F_j \tag{1}$$

where P is the total profit of a period in one period of work, G_i is the taken income in the ith order, while F_j is the comsumption of oil fee in the jth driving. In general, a driver will stay in three states which are cruising, picking and carrying. For the cruising state, the driver is cruising and finding customers. Once the driver responses an order, the driver will go into picking state to pick up the clients. During picking state, there is no earning. After the clients get on the taxi, the taximeter begins to count and the driver will be in carrying state.

There are three states defined in the proposed model, which are cruising, picking and carrying. A taxi is initialized in the state of cruising. It always transits through the picking state to the carrying state. When the carrying state is over, it will check whether there is an order immediately to determine whether it transits back to the cruising state or to the picking state (the pattern after the F_3 and F_7). In the Fig. 1, all the three states will cost fees and only the carrying state will bring income.

A typical pattern of the state transition is shown in Fig. 1 from t_0 to t_3. The taxi starts with the cruising state during t_0 and t_1. When it finds an order, the state changes to picking state at t_1 and the state lasts to t_2. When the taxi picks up a passenger at t_2, the state changes to carrying state. Finally, when the taxi finishes an order task at t_3, the state changes back to the cruising. In the bottom two lines in Fig. 1, all the three states will cost fees and only the carrying state will bring income.

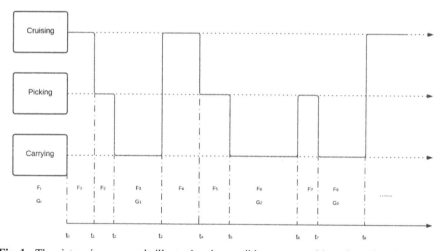

Fig. 1. The picture is an example illustrating the possible states transition of a taxi as time passes.

Considering that a taxi cannot work too much time due to the limitation of fuel, or the service policy of a driver, we split one day into several segments. In addition, for the learning environment, a whole city is divided by N in both north-south direction and east-west direction into grids. Namely, the city area is divided into N * N grids. When a taxi transits to the cruising state it uses the grid index as the function input to determine which grid it goes to, otherwise it is more difficult and consumed in computation. Therefore, the strategy can be defined as follows.

$$T = S(x,y) \tag{2}$$

where S is the strategy function and T is the strategy target when the taxi is in the grid of (x, y). The T is also a two-dimension grid index. Figure 2 is an example where the taxi is in grid (0, 0) and the strategy is to go to grid (2, 2). In a period of time the strategy is the same, and in different periods of time we trained different strategy functions.

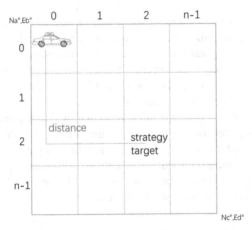

Fig. 2. The picture shows how the considered region is divided into grids and the input and output of the strategy in our model. The distance of two positions is calculated in the form of Manhattan Distance.

In the modelling, some preliminaries and assumptions are made as follows.

1. For a booking order, it includes the GPS position of start position and destination position, the booking time and the price.
2. For a booking order, the transportation process is ignored. The distance travelled is calculated according to Manhattan Distance as shown in Fig. 2.
3. For a grid which contains more than one taxi, they have competition relationship. Only one taxi can response an order with a predefined probability.
4. From start position to destination position, a taxi will not response to any order during the transportation process.

2.2 Brief of Deep Reinforcement Learning

Reinforcement learning (RL), as a powerful tool in machine learning, has been well applied to various implementations, such as workflow scheduling [18], automated radiation adaption in lung cancer [19], stock market forecasting [20], etc. In RL, by iterative interactions with environments, agents will learn an optimized policy for guiding their behaviors. For each interaction, agents are expected to make a smart decision to pursue more rewards [21]. At each time step t, an agent is described by a state s_t from state-space, while it will also select a feasible action a_t from the action-space, following a policy $\pi(a_t|s_t)$. Then the agent receives a reward r_t and transits to the next state s_{t+1}. The process repeats until a predefined termination condition is met. The goal of reinforcement learning is to obtain a policy $\pi(a_t|s_t)$ to maximize the accumulated rewards with a discount factor $\gamma \in [0, 1]$. The accumulated reward is defined in (3):

$$R_t = \sum_{k=0}^{\infty} \gamma^k r_{t+k} \tag{3}$$

where R_t is the accumulated rewards at the t time step, γ is the discount factor and r_{t+k} is the expected reward got at the $t + k$ time step. In this paper, Q-network learning [22] is employed to optimize the policy π. In Q-network, Q is used to depict action value and defined in (4):

$$Q_\pi(s, a) = E(R_t|s_t = s, a_t = a) \tag{4}$$

where the right part is the expected accumulated reward for the selected action a in state s. Then we can get a policy in (5):

$$\pi(s) = \underset{a}{argmax}(Q_\pi(s, a)) \tag{5}$$

where $\pi(s)$ is the policy function to get the selected action a by solving a maximization function. Namely the action a will help the agent get the largest expected accumulated reward in the current Q function. During the process, we employ temporal difference (TD) learning strategy with bootstrapping, as a kernel part, in reinforcement learning to optimize Q function from agents' experience. In this way, the whole learning process will be model-free, online, and fully incremental. According to one time of experience, (st, at, st + 1, rt), the TD error is

$$E_{td} = \left(r_t + \gamma \max_a Q(s_{t+1}, a)\right) - Q(s_t, a_t) \tag{6}$$

and the update rule is

$$Q(s, a) \leftarrow Q(s, a) + \eta E_{td} \tag{7}$$

where η is the learning rate. Q-learning converges to the optimum action-values with probability 1 so long as all actions are repeatedly sampled in all states and the action-values are represented discretely[22].

Considering that there are thousands of grids for a city and the scale of (state, value) pairs are too large, it is not feasible to build a Q-table. Here we use a neural network to represent the Q function and call this deep reinforcement learning. The detail of the network design is introduced in Sect. 3. The input of the neural network is the state and output is the Q-value of every action. The parameters in the neural network is updated through gradient descent as the update rule mentioned above. The Q function may not stay stable when the function is in the form of approximation [23, 24]. To stabilize the learning process, there are still many essential operations [25] like replacing buffer, target network and hyperparameter tuning. To balance the exploration and exploitation, epsilon greedy is used in this paper.

3 Design of DQN

3.1 Network Expressed Strategy

As explained in Sect. 2, the cruising strategy obtained in this paper decides the next position only depends on which grid the taxi is in. We use a neural network to express the strategy and it is also the action value function Q, whose input is the index of grid where the taxi is. The output of neural network is the Q value of every action. Therefore, we can get the strategy output according to formula (3). We do not use the grid number but use a two-dimension index as the input because the adjacent grid may have a consistency of the regular pattern. The structure of the network is shown in Fig. 3.

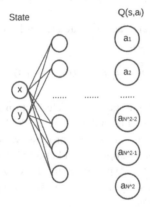

Fig. 3. The picture shows the structure of the network. The leftmost two nodes are the input nodes while the rightmost row of nodes are the output nodes, and others are intermediate nodes.

3.2 Procedure

In the model training procedure, though generally there are many steps in a normal single episode, in this paper every episode has only one step. When the episode begins, the taxi is initialized in a random location in the map with a random working time. Initially, for each taxi, there is no passengers on it, and then the taxi will take an action toward another location block. After that, the environment, namely the dispatching system, will check whether there is an order in that location at that time. If there is not an order, the episode is over. If there exist some orders, the taxi will take one of them and implement the order to move to the destination position. After finish the task, a taxi will repeat cruising, picking and carrying states.

The strategy still aims for the total profit for a whole taxi work time because the temporal difference learning is used and the Q value of the next state is considered. Every Q value means the expected profit at an action for a state in an infinite sequence restrained by the discount factor γ. The episode will be repeated for many times, so the agent may learn much experience from the specific time period.

Figure 4 shows information flow in the training procedure. A taxi interacts with the environment with the information of the orders and maps. The interaction information stored in the replay buffer for further trains. A strategy will be trained iteratively and used in the future policy decision for a taxi.

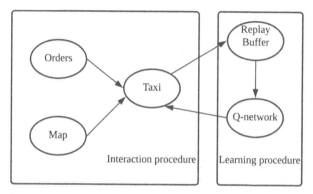

Fig. 4. The picture shows the information flow in the training procedure.

For Q-learning process, state, action and reward are depicted as follows.

1) State: We only use a location to establish the state of a taxi. More precisely, the state of the taxi is of two degrees, the segment number in the east-west direction and in the south-north direction, as shown in Fig. 2. Both of them are integers in the range of 0 to N-1.

2) Action: As described in Sect. 2, an action instructed by the Q network for the taxi is another position described by the block number. For the simplicity, it is the same as the state as a two-dimension integer tuple.

3) Reward: Whenever the taxi runs, it results in a minus reward as a cost of oil. It is calculated by multiplying a factor on the distance. Whenever the taxi takes an order, it results in a positive reward.

The procedure to train a Q-network suitable for a different time is only different in the initialized time of the taxi when the episode begins.

Algorithm 1 provides the pseudo-codes for the learning process, which follows DQN learning process and is adapted for our requirements in the part of interaction with the environment.

4 Experiments and Results

In this section, we conduct experiments to validate the performance of the proposed algorithm. The data is obtained from GAIA Open Dataset provided by DiDi company, which depicts taxis operations in Chengdu City. The dataset includes booking orders in November 2016, which records the cryptographic and anonymous location data of order time, start position and destination position. To eliminate the sporadic data, we sample the data in Chengdu from the west-south corner named Tianfufurong Garden to the east-north corner named Qilong Temple. Based on the information, we calculated the payment price of each order by Ali cloud.

We divide the whole map into 100 grids by N with size of 10. The Q-network is a mapping from a state to the Q value of every action, so the number of input nodes is two and the number of output nodes is 100. We design the number of hidden layer as 3. The number of nodes respectively is set as 20, 80, 160 respectively.

In this experiment, a taxi works for a period of four hours. In the following tables we list four kinds of indices, the total income of the four hours, the total time used to pick up the passengers, the total non-hiring time, and the number of the total orders. We test three models separately trained for three periods of time from 8:00 to 12:00, from 16:00 to 20:00 and from 20:00 to 24:00. For each time period, we conduct the test for 20 times and record the mean value (AVG), the standard deviation (SD).

Regardless of whether it is workday or weekend, we present the comparison results in Table 1. It is obvious that the proposed algorithm marked by "DQN" has much better performance than the random-walk strategy marked by "rand". For the index of income and order number, DQN has improved almost 350% and 220% respectively. The increasement of pick time is relevant to the order number. The non-hiring time also reduces a lot. Besides, the standard deviation reduces significantly only except the order number and pick time during the period of 20:00 to 24:00.

Table 1. Training effect of non-distinguishing workday and weekend compared with a random strategy in three periods of time

		Income		Pick time		Vacant run time		Order num	
		AVG	SD	AVG	SD	AVG	SD	AVG	SD
8:00–12:00	rand	40.68	52.17	722.07	552.0	9842.2	3419.6	4.8	3.19
	DQN	141.79	24.80	1570.7	367.8	3588.1	1298.6	10.6	2.08
16:00–20:00	rand	39.96	56.65	741.64	537.0	9908.7	3480.9	4.55	3.29
	DQN	140.81	22.02	1638.7	417.8	3899.9	1201.7	10.7	2.02
20:00–24:00	rand	22.97	45.67	520.52	356.0	11549	2899.8	3.6	2.43
	DQN	123.20	38.90	1083.3	447.9	4878.9	2730.3	7.8	2.96

Then we train our model specialized only for workday and weekend. We test for corresponding date with the specialized models and list the same kinds of indices respectively in Tables 2 and 3 respectively. The increasement of income are also remarkable and the standard deviations in "DQN" algorithm are smaller than the "rand" strategy. The difference from the results in Table 1 are mainly displayed in the decrease in the standard deviation.

Table 2. Training effect specialized for workday

		Income		Pick time		Vacant run time		Order num	
		AVG	SD	AVG	SD	AVG	SD	AVG	SD
8:00–12:00	rand	37.09	45.19	741.5	570.06	10374	2970.0	4.85	3.13
	DQN	146.09	26.68	1721	438.29	3242.7	1330.6	11.6	2.15
16:00–20:00	rand	30.93	51.13	608.4	378.98	10875	3695.5	4.2	2.46
	DQN	127.03	18.48	1532	371.65	4573.1	1029.7	10.1	1.87
20:00–24:00	rand	12.91	44.30	528.1	307.78	11756	2751.2	3.25	1.89
	DQN	130.22	11.81	1503	368.30	4064.6	1101.5	9.9	1.51

Table 3. Training effect specialized for weekend

		Income		Pick time		Vacant run time		Order num	
		AVG	SD	AVG	SD	AVG	SD	AVG	SD
8:00–12:00	rand	39.22	42.43	756.9	544.40	10089	2871.8	5.05	2.89
	DQN	142.17	20.79	1463	423.8	3470.5	1344.7	9.9	2.30
16:00–20:00	rand	59.78	46.41	915.4	505.69	8643.4	2920.3	6.3	3.12
	DQN	136.33	26.23	1569	305.78	3845.7	1427.6	10.7	1.52
20:00–24:00	rand	34.55	52.83	602.0	478.06	10589	3532	4.15	3.10
	DQN	134.28	25.77	1336	372.94	4160.5	1530.2	9.1	1.81

At last we specifically compare the income in the three tables and list the bar chart. Wee see the income of situation 'all' is almost in the middle of other two situation 'workday' and 'weekend' in all three time periods. It brings small improvement by the workday and weekend specialized training, seeing the income listed in '20–24'. In our experiment, though the improvement between the 'DQN' and 'rand' is remarkable, the train specialized for the workday and weekend have rather less improvement (Fig. 5).

Algorithm 1 DQN for guiding taxis without clients

---
input: replay memory size M, episode times N, discount factor γ, time period for train.

output: Q-network Q(s,a)

1: Initialize replay memory M, evaluation-network Q and target-network $\hat{Q}$;

2: **for** episode $i = 1, ..., N$ **do**

3:     Initialize the taxi at random location and needed time;

4:     take an action according to the state and the greedy policy;

5:     run as the action and record the reward;

6:     **while** order exists **do**

7:         run the taxi to pick the passenger and record the reward;

8:         run as the order and record the reward;

9:     **end while**

10:     store transition(s_i, a_i, r_i, s_{i+1}) into the buffer;

11:     Randomly sample batch size of transitions(s_j, a_j, r_j, s_{j+1});

12:     let input be s_j, target be $r_j + \gamma \max_a \hat{Q}(s_{j+1}, a)$;

13:     update the parameters of Q;

14:     Every C steps reset $\hat{Q} = Q$;

15: **end for**

Fig. 5. The picture contains the algorithm 1.

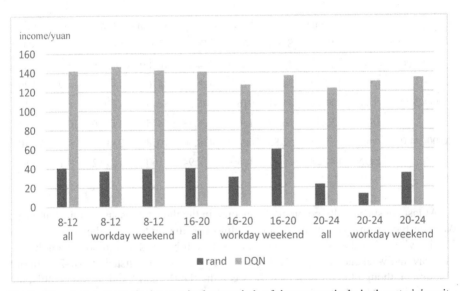

Fig. 6. The picutre shows the income in three periods of time respectively in three training situations. For example, '8–12' is a simplified expression which means the period is from 8:00 to 12:00. And 'all', 'workday', 'weekend' stands for the situation in Tables 1, 2, and 3.

5 Conclusions and Future Work

This paper provides a designed model for the taxi cruising strategy according to an order data set and a method for training the cruising strategy by using DQN strategy. The taxi running model is adjustable to the desired precision and computation consumption by changing the parameter in the model. Then we compare the trained cruising strategy with a random strategy and show the significant improvement.

In our paper, we use the possibility of the orders taken by other taxis to simulate the existence of other taxis, which may cause some degree of inconsistency with the real world about whether there can be an order. And since we only have one taxi in the simulation world, we cannot test the competition situation when many taxis run in a typical trained strategy. It should be considered in the future work about a simulation and new model of multiple taxis.

References

1. Wang, H.: A Practice of Smart City-Intelligent Taxi Dispatch Services with Real-Time Traffic and Customer Information, 1st edn. Beihang University Press, Beijing (2011)
2. Dial, B.: Autonomous dial-a-ride transit introductory overview. Transp. Res. Part C Emerg. Technol. 3(5), 261–275 (1995)
3. Zeng, W., Wu, M., Sun, W., Xie, S.: Comprehensive review of autonomous taxi dispatching systems. Comput. Sci. 47(05), 181–189 (2020)
4. Powell, W., Huang, Y., Bastani, F., Ji, M.: Towards reducing taxicab cruising time using spatio-temporal profitability maps. In: Proceedings of the 12th International Conference on Advances in Spatial and Temporal Databases (SSTD 2011), pp. 242–260. Springer, Heidelberg (2011). https://doi.org/10.1007/978-3-642-22922-0
5. Liu, L., Andris, C., Ratti, C.: Uncovering cabdrivers' behavior patterns from their digital traces. Comput. Environ. Urban Syst. 34(6), 541–548 (2010)
6. Li, B., et al.: Hunting or waiting? Discovering passenger-finding strategies from a large-scale real-world taxi dataset. In: Proceedings of the 2011 IEEE International Conference on Pervasive Computing and Communications Workshops (PERCOM Workshops), pp. 63–68. (2011)
7. Zhang, K., Chen, Y., Nie, Y.M.: Hunting image: taxi search strategy recognition using sparse subspace clustering. Transp. Res. Part C Emerg. Technol. 109, 250–266 (2019)
8. Maciejewski, M., Bischoff, J., Nagel, K.: An assignment-based approach to efficient real-time city-scale taxi dispatching. IEEE Intell. Syst. 31(1), 68–77 (2016)
9. Nourinejad, M., Ramezani, M.: Developing a large-scale taxi dispatching system for urban networks. In: Proceedings of the IEEE 19th International Conference on Intelligent Transportation Systems (ITSC), pp. 441–446. IEEE (2016)
10. Wang, Y., Liang, B., Zheng, W.: The development of a smart taxicab scheduling system: a multi-source fusion perspective. In: Proceedings of the IEEE 16th International Conference on Data Mining (ICDM), pp. 1275–1280. IEEE (2016)
11. Liu, Z., Miwa, T., Zeng, W.: Shared autonomous taxi system and utilization of collected travel-time information. J. Adv. Transport. 2018, 1–13 (2018)
12. Shen, Y., Chen, C., Zhou, Q.: Taxi resource allocation optimization under improved particle swarm optimization algorithm based on multi-chaotic strategy. J. Heilongjiang Univ. Technol. (Comprehens. Ed.) 18(05), 72–76 (2018)
13. Xie, R., Pan, W., Shibasaki, R.: Intelligent taxi dispatching based on artificial fish swarm algorithm. Syst. Eng. Theory Pract. 37(11), 2938–2947 (2017)
14. Verma, T., Varakantham, P., Kraus, S., Lau, H.C.: Augmenting decisions of taxi drivers through reinforcement learning for improving revenues. In: Proceedings of the 27th International Conference on Automated Planning and Scheduling, Pittsburgh, pp. 409–417 (2017)

15. Rong, H., Zhou, X., Yang, C., Shafiq, Z., Liu, A.: The rich and the poor: a Markov decision process approach to optimizing taxi driver revenue efficiency. In: Proceedings of the 25th ACM International on Conference on Information and Knowledge Management, pp. 2329–2334. Association for Computing Machinery, New York (2016)
16. Miyoung, H., Pierre, S., Stéphane, B., Wu, H.: Routing an autonomous taxi with reinforcement learning. In: Proceedings of the 25th ACM International on Conference on Information and Knowledge Management, pp. 2421–2424. Association for Computing Machinery, New York (2016)
17. Shi, D., Ding, J., Sai, E.: Deep Q-network-based route scheduling for TNC vehicles with passengers location differential privacy. IEEE Internet Things J. **6**(5), 7681–7692 (2019)
18. Wang, Y., Liu, H., Zheng, W.: Multi-objective workflow scheduling with deep-Q-network-based multi-agent reinforcement learning. IEEE Access **7**, 39974–39982 (2019)
19. Tseng, H., Luo, Y., Cui, S.: Deep reinforcement learning for automated radiation adaptation in lung cancer. Med. Phys. **44**(12), 6690–6705 (2017)
20. Carta, S., Ferreira, A., Podda, S.: Multi-DQN: an ensemble of deep Q-learning agents for stock market forecasting. Exp. Syst. Appl. **164**, 113820 (2021)
21. Sutton, S., Barto, G.: Reinforcement Learning: An Introduction. 2nd Edn. MIT Press, Cambridge (2018).
22. Watkins, H., Dayan, P.: Q-learning. Mach. Learn. **8**, 279–292 (1992)
23. Leemon, B.: Residual algorithms: reinforcement learning with function approximation. In: Proceedings of the International Conference on Machine Learning (ICML 1995), pp. 30–37. Elsevier, Amsterdam (1995)
24. Justin, B., Andrew, M.: Generalization in reinforcement learning: safely approximating the value function. In: Tesauro, G., Touretzky, D.S., Leen, T.K. (eds.) Advances in Neural Information Processing Systems 7 (NIPS-94), pp. 369–376. MIT Press, Cambridge (1995)
25. Volodymyr, M., et al.: Human-level control through deep reinforcement learning. Nature **518**(7540), 529–533 (2015)

Weighted Average Consensus in Directed Networks of Multi-agents with Time-Varying Delay

Xiang Li[1] and Jing Zhu[1,2(✉)]

[1] College of Automation Engineering, Nanjing University of Aeronautics and Astronautics, Jiangsu 211100, China
drzhujing@nuaa.edu.cn

[2] Institute of Systems Engineering, Macau University of Science and Technology, Macau, China

Abstract. In this paper, we discuss the weighted average consensus problem of multi-agent system in directed networks with fixed topology and time-varying communication delay. By employing the method of linear matrix inequality and constructing a Lyapunov function, we analyze the convergence of the directed network, and get the maximum allowable upper bound of time-varying delay. Finally, the simulation of the fixed topology of multi-agent directed network is carried out to verify the theoretical results.

Keywords: Weighted average consensus · Directed network · Linear matrix inequality · Time-varying delay

1 Introduction

In recent decades, due to the application of multi-agent system in multi-robot formation control [1–5], flocking control [6–8], attitude control of artificial multi-satellite [9, 10] and communication network congestion control, more and more scholars have paid attention to multi-agent distributed control. For a multi-agent system, only when a certain state of each agent is unified, it is possible for the agents to cooperate with each other and complete complex tasks together. Thus, the consensus problem is the key problem. In recent years, the research on consensus of multi-agent systems has achieved richer research results. According to the final convergence state, the consensus problem can be divided into average consensus [11–15], weighted consensus [16–18], maximum consensus [19–21], and so on. The weighted consensus used in this paper is proposed for the first time in [17], the authors first design a distributed weighted control protocol with no delay in the system under a directed communication topology, and analyze the necessary and sufficient conditions for the system to achieve weighted consensus. On the basis of [17, 18] designs linear and nonlinear weighted average consensus controllers respectively for multi-agent systems under the influence of fixed delay, and obtains the algebraic conditions for linear controllers to achieve weighted consensus through theoretical analysis criterion. [22] studies the weighted consensus problem under a fixed,

H. Zhang et al. (Eds.): NCAA 2021, CCIS 1449, pp. 71–82, 2021.
https://doi.org/10.1007/978-981-16-5188-5_6

directed, asymmetric, and unbalanced information switching topology, by changing the classic control protocol, obtains some sufficient conditions for multi-agents to achieve consensus.

Although average consensus is a special kind of weighted consensus, compared with average consensus, there are few researches on weighted average consensus. In practical application, time delay is an unavoidable existence for most systems. The existence of time delay will not only make the control accuracy of the system deviate, but also may make the system unstable. In the actual multi-agent system, according to the different sources of time delay, time delay can be divided into communication time delay [23–25] and input time delay [26–28]. The former is often reflected in the aspects of information sending, information transmission, information receiving, etc., while the latter is reflected in the aspects of processor analyzing, processing data and making decisions as well as agent response control. In complex environment, time delay is not a fixed quantity, but a time-varying quantity. However, the aforementioned literatures only consider the problem of weighted consensus under the influence of no time delay or fixed time delay. Therefore, there are many aspects worth exploring for the research on the weighted consensus of multi-agents under the influence of time-varying delay. Inspired by the existing research results, this paper considers to design a distributed weighted consensus control protocol in a multi-agent system with time-varying delay, and realizes the consensus control of the multi-agent system under this protocol. In this paper, due to the addition of time-varying delay, we introduce linear matrix inequality (LMI) to solve this problem. As a convenient and flexible tool, LMI has been widely used in the study of time-delay systems. Here, by using LMI, we can prove that multi-agents can reach weighted consensus asymptotically when the network graph is a strongly connected graph. Then by using the feasible LMI, we obtain the maximum allowable upper bound of the time-varying delay. In the end, the final numerical simulation also verifies the validity and correctness of the results.

The rest of paper is organized as follows. Section 2 addresses the basic problem of this paper and some preliminary results. The main results are elaborated in Sect. 3 in which the weighted averaged consensus conditions are proposed in terms of linear matrix inequalities. Experiments are conducted in Sect. 4 by MATLAB simulation to show the validation of our proposed consensus conditions. In the end, conclusion is draw in Sect. 5.

2   Problem Statement

In the full paper, A^T represents the transpose of A. $\|\cdot\|$ represents the Euclidean norm. Let $G = (V, E, A)$ be a weighted directed graph, where $V = \{v_1, \ldots, v_n\}$ is called the node set, $E \subseteq V \times V$ is the edge set of the graph, and $A = [a_{ij}]$ is a weighted adjacency matrix that describes the communication relationship between agents, and its elements a_{ij} are all nonnegative. $I = \{1, \cdots, n\}$ represents the set of node index. Each edge is denoted by $e_{ij} = (v_i, v_j) \in E, i, j \in I$. The elements of the weighted adjacency matrix A connected by the edge are positive constants, i.e., $e_{ij} \in E$ if and only if $a_{ij} > 0$. Assuming that all agents do not have self-loops, i.e., $a_{ii} = 0$ for all $i \in I$. Then we denote the set of neighbors of node v_i as $N_i = \{v_j \in V : (v_i, v_j) \in E\}$. Define the out-degree and in-degree of a node respectively as $deg_{out}(v_i) = \sum_{j=1}^{n} a_{ij}$ and $deg_{in}(v_i) = \sum_{j=1}^{n} a_{ji}$ for all $i \in I$. The degree matrix of G is defined as $D = diag\{deg_{out}(v_1), \cdots, deg_{out}(v_n)\}$, Let $L = D - A$ is Laplace matrix of G. In a directed graph, if there exists a directed path connection between any two nodes, then the directed graph is strongly connected. The state value of node v_i is represented by $x_i \in \mathbb{R}$. These state values may represent some physical quantities, such as position, velocity, etc.

Support that the dynamic model of each agent is

$$\dot{x}_i(t) = u_i(t), i \in I \tag{1}$$

In order to achieve weighted consensus of the multi-agent network, consider the following linear control

$$u_i(t) = \frac{1}{b_i} \sum_{v_j \in N_i} a_{ij}(x_j(t) - x_i(t)) \tag{2}$$

where b_i is called weighted factor, which satisfies $\sum_{i=1}^{n} b_i = 1, b_i > 0$ for all $i \in I$.

This paper considers the weighted consensus in a multi-agent system with time-varying communication delay, so the weighted control protocol is designed as follows

$$u_i(t) = \frac{1}{b_i} \sum_{v_j \in N_i} a_{ij}(x_j(t - \tau(t)) - x_i(t - \tau(t))) \tag{3}$$

where $\tau(t)$ is time-varying communication delay.

Under protocol (2), system (1) can be rewritten as

$$\dot{x}_i(t) = \frac{1}{b_i} \sum_{v_j \in N_i} a_{ij}[x_j(t - \tau(t)) - x_i(t - \tau(t))] \tag{4}$$

The matrix form of (4) is

$$\dot{x}(t) = -B_1 L x(t - \tau(t)) \tag{5}$$

where $B_1 = diag\{\frac{1}{b_1}, \cdots, \frac{1}{b_n}\}$.

For the convenience of analysis, we make the following assumptions that time-varying communication delay in (5) satisfies

(A1) $0 \leq \tau(t) \leq h$, $\dot{\tau}(t) \leq d$ for $t \geq 0$, where $h > 0$ and $d \geq 0$ or
(A2) $0 \leq \tau(t) \leq h$ for $t \geq 0$, where $h > 0$. The derivative information of $\tau(t)$ is unknown.

Definition 1 [29]. (Balanced Graph): If the in-degree and out-degree of a node are equal, i.e., $deg_{in}(v_i) = deg_{out}(v_i)$, then we call the node is a balanced node. Further if all nodes of the graph are balanced nodes, i.e.,

$$\sum_{j=1}^{n} a_{ji} = \sum_{j=1}^{n} a_{ij}, \forall i \in I$$

then the graph is a balanced graph.

Lemma 1 [29]. Assuming that G is a connected undirected graph, and its Laplacian matrix is, the eigenvalues of L have a positive real part except for a single eigenvalue at 0.

Lemma 2 [18]. $G = (V, E, A)$ is a directed graph with adjacency matrix $A = [a_{ij}]$. Then the following statements are equivalent

(1) G is a balanced graph.
(2) $\omega = (1, 1, \cdots, 1)^T$ is the eigenvector corresponding to the zero eigenvalue in the Laplacian of G, i.e., $1^T L = 0$.
(3) $\sum_{i=1}^n b_i u_i = 0$, $\forall x \in \mathbb{R}^n$, where

$$u_i(t) = \frac{1}{b_i} \sum_{v_j \in N_i} a_{ij} \left(x_j(t - \tau(t)) - x_i(t - \tau(t)) \right).$$

Lemma 3 [30] (Schur complement). Let A_{11}, A_{12} and A_{22} be given matrices with appropriate dimensions. Then the following statements are equivalent

(1) $A = \begin{bmatrix} A_{11} & A_{12} \\ A_{12}^T & A_{22} \end{bmatrix} < 0.$
(2) $A_{11} < 0$ and $A_{22} - A_{12}^T A_{11}^{-1} A_{12} < 0.$
(3) $A_{22} < 0$ and $A_{11} - A_{12} A_{22}^{-1} A_{12}^T < 0.$

Lemma 4 [31]. For differential vector function $x(t) \in \mathbb{R}^n$ and $n \times n$ constant matrix $P = P^T > 0$, we have the following inequality

$$h^{-1}[x(t) - x(t - \tau(t))]^T P[x(t) - x(t - \tau(t))] \leq \int_{t-\tau(t)}^{t} \dot{x}^T(s) P \dot{x}(s) ds, \ t \geq 0$$

where $\tau(t)$ satisfies (A1) or (A2).

Lemma 5 [32]. For a connected undirected graph G, the following equation holds:

$$\begin{array}{c} min \\ x \neq 0 \\ 1^T x = 0 \end{array} \frac{x^T L x}{x^2} = \lambda_2(L)$$

where $0 = \lambda_1(L) < \lambda_2(L) \leq \cdots \leq \lambda_n(L)$ are eigenvalues of L.

3   Main Results

In this section, we discuss weighted consensus problem in balanced directed networks. We assume $x(t) = \phi(t)$ for $t \leq 0$, where $\phi(t)$ is the initial state. By employing LMI, we prove that when the communication delay $\tau(t)$ satisfies an appropriate upper bound, system (5) can achieve weighted average consensus if the graph G is a strongly connected graph.

Notice that the condition $\sum_{i=1}^{n} b_i u_i = 0$, $\dot{\alpha} = \sum_{i=1}^{n} b_i \dot{x}_i = \sum_{i=1}^{n} b_i u_i = 0$, $\alpha = WAve(x) = \sum_{i=1}^{n} b_i x_i$ is an invariant quantity. [4] proves that α is the decision value of each node. Decompose x as follows:

$$x = \alpha 1 + \delta \tag{6}$$

where $\delta = (\delta_1, \cdots, \delta_n)^T \in \mathbb{R}^n$ is called the disagreement vector, which satisfies $1^T B_2 \delta = 0$ with

$$B_2 = \begin{bmatrix} b_1 & & \\ & \ddots & \\ & & b_{n-1} \\ -b_1 & \cdots & -b_{n-1} \end{bmatrix} \in \mathbb{R}^{n \times (n-1)}$$

According to disagreement dynamics given by

$$\dot{\delta}(t) = -B_1 L \delta(t - \tau(t)) \tag{7}$$

Theorem 1. Assume that the communication time-varying delay in system (5) satisfies (A1) and the topology graph is a strongly connected graph. Then for $0 \le d < 1$, there exists $h > 0$ such that system (5) can achieve weighted consensus. In addition, the allowed delay bound h can be obtained from the LMI below:

$$\Phi = \begin{bmatrix} \Phi_{11} & \Phi_{12} & \Phi_{13} \\ * & \Phi_{22} & \Phi_{23} \\ * & * & \Phi_{33} \end{bmatrix} < 0 \tag{8}$$

where

$$\Phi_{11} = B_2^T \left(-\left(L^T B_1 + B_1 L \right) + dP \right) B_2,$$

$$\Phi_{12} = B_2^T (B_1 L + (1-d)P) B_2,$$

$$\Phi_{13} = B_2^T B_1 L Q,$$

$$\Phi_{22} = B_2^T \left((d-1)P - h^{-1}Q \right) B_2,$$

$$\Phi_{23} = -B_2^T B_1 L Q,$$

$$\Phi_{33} = -h^{-1}Q,$$

P and Q are positive definite matrices of appropriate dimensions.

Proof: Firstly, we prove the feasibility of (8) under assumption (A1). On the other hand, there exists positive definite matrices P and Q of appropriate dimensions such that (8) holds if the topology graph is a strongly connected graph. Choose $P = \varepsilon I_n$ and $Q = I_n$, where $\varepsilon > 0$. By using Schur complement (Lemma 3), (8) is equivalent to

$$
\begin{bmatrix} -B_2^T \left(L^T B_1 + B_1 L \right) B_2 & B_2^T B_1 L B_2 \\ * & -h^{-1} B_2^T Q B_2 \end{bmatrix}
$$
$$
+ \varepsilon \begin{bmatrix} d B_2^T B_2 & (1-d) B_2^T B_2 \\ * & (d-1) B_2^T B_2 \end{bmatrix} + h F^T F < 0 \tag{9}
$$

where $F = -B_2 L^T$. First, since B_1 is symmetric matrix, $\hat{L} = L^T B_1 + B_1 L$ can be regarded as the Laplacian matrix of an undirected graph. It can be seen from the definition of B_2, and according to Lemma 5, $1^T B_2 \delta = 0$, then we can get that

$$
\delta^T B_2^T \hat{L} B_2 \delta = (B_2 \delta)^T \hat{L} (B_2 \delta) \geq \lambda_2 \left(\hat{L} \right) (B_2 \delta)^T (B_2 \delta) > 0,
$$

which implies that

$$
B_2^T \hat{L} B_2 > 0, \text{ i.e., } B_2^T \left(L^T B_1 + B_1 L \right) B_2 > 0.
$$

Obviously, if we choose h_0 and ε_0 sufficiently small, (9) holds when $h \leq h_0$ and $\varepsilon \leq \varepsilon_0$. Thus (8) is solvable for $0 \leq d < 1$ when (A1) holds.

Next, we prove that for $0 \leq d < 1$, system (5) can achieve weighted average consensus asymptotically for $0 \leq \tau(t) \leq h$. Construct the following relevant Lyapunov function:

$$
V(t) = \tilde{\delta}^T(t) \tilde{\delta}(t) + \int_{t-\tau(t)}^t \tilde{\delta}^T(s) P \tilde{\delta}(s) ds + \int_{t-h}^t (s-t+h) \dot{\tilde{\delta}}^T(s) Q \dot{\tilde{\delta}}(s) ds \tag{10}
$$

where P and Q are positive definite matrices, $h > 0$ is a scalar, $\tilde{\delta}(t) = B_2 \delta(t)$.

Then rewrite (7) into the following form

$$
\dot{\delta}(t) = -B_1 L \delta(t) + B_1 L \eta(t) \tag{11}
$$

where $\eta(t) = \delta(t) - \delta(t - \tau(t))$. Then by assumption (A1) and Lemma 4 we can get that

$$
\dot{V}(t) \leq \dot{\tilde{\delta}}^T(t) \tilde{\delta}(t) + \tilde{\delta}^T(t) \dot{\tilde{\delta}}(t) + \tilde{\delta}^T(t) P \tilde{\delta}(t) - (1-d) \tilde{\delta}^T(t - \tau(t)) \tilde{\delta}(t - \tau(t))
$$
$$
+ h \dot{\tilde{\delta}}^T(t) Q \dot{\tilde{\delta}}(t) - h^{-1} \tilde{\eta}^T(t) Q \tilde{\eta}(t) \tag{12}
$$

where $\tilde{\eta}(t) = \tilde{\delta}(t) - \tilde{\delta}(t - \tau(t))$.

Let $\tilde{y}^T(t) = \left(\tilde{\delta}^T(t), \tilde{\eta}^T(t) \right)$, then (12) can be rewritten as

$$
\dot{V}(t) \leq \tilde{y}^T(t) \hat{\Phi} \tilde{y}(t) \tag{13}
$$

where $\hat{\Phi} = \begin{bmatrix} -L^T B_1 - B_1 L + dP + h L^T B_1 Q B_1 L & B_1 L + (1-d)P - h L^T B_1 Q B_1 L \\ * & (d-1)P + h L^T B_1 Q B_1 L - h^{-1} Q \end{bmatrix}$.

According to Lemma 3 (Schur complement), $\hat{\Phi} < 0$ is equivalent to (8).

In [33], it shows that the zero solution of system (7) is asymptotically stable. Hence for $0 \leq d < 1$, system (5) achieves weighted consensus for $0 \leq \tau(t) \leq h$ where h can be obtained from (8). Therefore, the proof is completed.

For the condition that $d \geq 1$ or the derivative information of $\tau(t)$ is unknown, we have the following corollary:

Corollary 1: Assume that the communication time-varying delay in system (5) satisfies (A2) and the topology graph is a strongly connected graph. Then for any $d \geq 1$ or the derivative information of $\tau(t)$ is unknown, there exists appropriate $h > 0$ such that system (5) achieves weighted consensus. In addition, the allowed delay bound h can be obtained from the linear matrix inequality below:

$$\Theta = \begin{bmatrix} \Theta_{11} & \Theta_{12} & \Theta_{13} \\ * & \Theta_{22} & \Theta_{23} \\ * & * & \Theta_{33} \end{bmatrix} < 0 \tag{14}$$

where

$$\Theta_{11} = -B_2^T \left(L^T B_1 + B_1 L \right) B_2,$$

$$\Theta_{12} = B_2^T B_1 L B_2,$$

$$\Theta_{13} = \Phi_{13},$$

$$\Theta_{22} = -h^{-1} B_2^T Q B_2,$$

$$\Theta_{23} = \Phi_{23},$$

$$\Theta_{33} = \Phi_{33},$$

and Q is a positive definite matrix of appropriate dimensions.

The proof of the Corollary 1 is similar to the proof of Theorem 1, we can easily proof this by constructing the following Lyapunov function:

$$V(t) = \tilde{\delta}^T(t) \tilde{\delta}(t) + \int_{t-h}^{t} (s - t + h) \dot{\tilde{\delta}}^T(s) Q \dot{\tilde{\delta}}(s) ds \tag{15}$$

Remark: It should be noted that under the condition that $b_i > 0$, $\sum_{i=1}^{n} b_i = 1$, when choose different weighted factors, b_i the maximum allowable upper bound of the time-varying communication delay obtained from Theorem 1 or Corollary 1 may be different. In addition, it can be found that when we choose $b_i = b_j = \frac{1}{n}$ for all $i, j \in I$, in this case, the weighted average consensus becomes the average consensus and the decision value of multi-agent system is $\alpha = \frac{1}{n} \sum_{i=1}^{n} x_i$.

4 Simulation

In this section, the weights of the graph are all 0–1, that is the elements of the adjacency matrix A of the graph are all 0 or 1.

We give an example where a multi-agent system composed of 5 agents achieves weighted average consensus in a fixed network topology. The initial states of the five agents are $x(0) = (40, 55, 75, 60, 80)^T$ respectively, and the corresponding weighting coefficients are $b = (0.25, 0.2, 0.1, 0.3, 0.15)^T$ respectively. Then the calculated decision value is $\alpha = WAve(x) = \sum_{i=1}^{n} b_i x_i = 58.5$. The network topology is shown in Fig. 1 as a strongly connected balance graph, where we can find the connections among these dynamic multi-agents.

The Eqs. (8) and (15) are solved using the LMI toolbox in MATLAB, and we get h value corresponding to different:

(1) For $d = 0$, i.e., $\tau(t) \equiv h$, we get $h \leq 0.086$; for $d = 0.2$, we can get $h \leq 0.083$; for $d = 0.4$, we can get $h \leq 0.077$; for $d = 0.9$, we can get $h \leq 0.072$. The simulation result of $d = 0$ and $h = 0.086$ also reveals this fact (see Fig. 2).
(2) For the condition that the derivative information of $\tau(t)$ is unknown, we have $h \leq 0.069$.

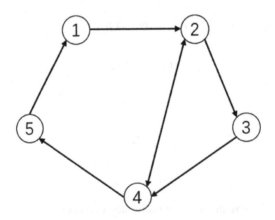

Fig. 1. Strongly connected directed graph.

From Fig. 2 we can find that the nominal system eventually becomes stable after $t = 6$ s, when the delay parameter is equal to 0.086, and the derivate of $\tau(t)$ is 0. Consequently, the validation of our proposed consensus condition is proved.

It can be seen from Fig. 3 that when we choose $\tau(t) = 0.02 \sin(10t) + 0.063$ with $d = 0.2$ and $h = 0.083$, the multi-agent system converges to the decision value in about 1.5 s. It can be seen that Theorem 1 is also valid when the derivative of time-varying communication delay is not zero.

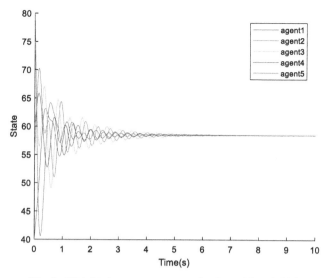

Fig. 2. Weighted consensus on graph when $\tau(t) = 0.086$.

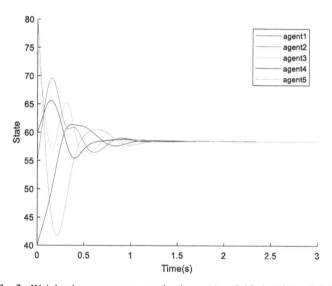

Fig. 3. Weighted consensus on graph when $\tau(t) = 0.02\sin(10t) + 0.063$.

To verify the correctness of Corollary 1 when the derivative of time-varying communication delay in the multi-agent system is unknown, random numbers in the range of 0–0.069 are selected as time-varying delay (see Fig. 5). From Fig. 4, it can be seen that the system converges to the decision value at about 1 s.

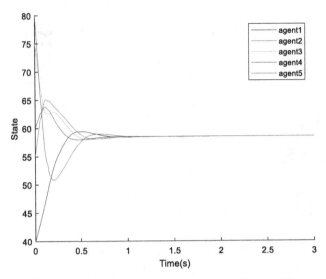

Fig. 4. Weighted consensus on graph when $(t) \leq 0.069$.

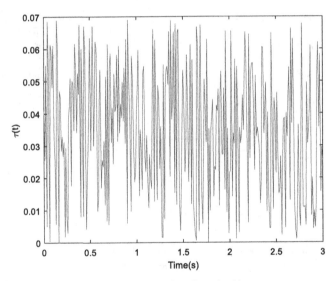

Fig. 5. Randomly selected $\tau(t)$

5 Conclusion

This paper studies the weighted consensus problem of a multi-agent system with time-varying delay when its topological network is directed and strongly connected. By using the method of linear matrix inequality and constructing the relevant Lyapunov function, the sufficient conditions for the multi-agent system to achieve weighted consensus under the two cases of dependence and independence of the delay derivative are respectively given. Finally, a simulation case is used to verify the correctness and validity of the theory.

Acknowledgements. This work was fund by the Science and Technology Development Fund, Macau SAR (File no. 0050/2020/A1).

References

1. Egerstedt, M., Hu, X.: Formation constrained multi-agent control. In: Proceedings IEEE International Conference on Robotics & Automation, pp. 947–951 (2001)
2. Zhang, J., Hu, Q., Jiang, C., Ma, G.: Robust sliding mode attitude synchronization control of satellite formation with communication time-delay. In: Proceedings of the 32nd Chinese Control Conference., Xi'an, China, pp. 7005–7010 (2013)
3. He, L., Hou, Y., Liang, X., Zhang, J., Bai, P.: Time-varying formation tracking control for aircraft swarm with switching directed sympathetic networks. In: 3rd IEEE Information Technology, Networking, Electronic and Automation Control Conference (ITNEC), Chengdu, China, pp. 199–204 (2019)
4. Li, H., Ma, Q., Zhang, J.: Research on formation control technology for multiple flight vehicles based on consensus theory. In: 9th IEEE Joint International Information Technology and Artificial Intelligence Conference (ITAIC), Chongqing, China, pp. 1458–1462 (2020).
5. Dong, X., Zhou, Y., Ren, Z., Zhong, Y.: Time-varying formation tracking for second-order multi-agent systems subjected to switching topologies with application to quadrotor formation flying. IEEE Trans. Ind. Electron. **64**(6), 5014–5024 (2017)
6. Olfati-Saber, R., Fax, J.A., Murray, R.M.: Consensus and cooperation in networked multi-agent systems. Proc. IEEE **95**(1), 215–233 (2007)
7. Cheng, J., Wang, B.: Flocking control of mobile robots via simulated annealing algorithm. In: 39th Chinese Control Conference (CCC), Shenyang, China, pp. 3931–3935 (2020)
8. Li, W., Lin, P., Cai, G., Shang, T.: Multi-aircraft flight control method based on flocking theory. In: 2020 Chinese Automation Congress (CAC), pp. 1843–1848 (2020)
9. Wei, R.: Synchronized multiple spacecraft rotations: a revisit in the context of consensus building. In: American Control Conference IEEE, New York, USA (2007)
10. Mu, W.Q., Liu, R., Yang, X.X., Kamel, E.: Analysis of precision estimation of RF metrology in satellite formation flying. In: 2015 International Conference on Wireless Communications & Signal Processing (WCSP), Nanjing, China, pp. 1–5 (2015)
11. Chen, Y., Qi, D., Zhang, J., Wang, Z., Li, Z.: Study on distributed dynamic average consensus algorithm. In: 7th International Conference on Information, Communication and Networks (ICICN), Macao, China, pp. 225–229 (2019)
12. Xie, W., Ma, B.: Average consensus control of nonlinear uncertain multiagent systems. In: 36th Chinese Control Conference (CCC), Dalian, China, pp. 8299–8303 (2017)
13. Jian, L., Tian, J., Li, L., Li, J., Yang, S.: Continuous-time distributed control algorithm for multi-robot systems dynamic average consensus. In: 2020 Chinese Automation Congress (CAC), Shanghai, China, pp. 6051–6054 (2020)
14. Zhang, J., Gao, Y.: Average consensus in networks of multi-agent with switching topology and time-varying delay. In: 2016 Chinese Control and Decision Conference (CCDC), Yinchuan, China, pp. 71–76 (2016)
15. Jiang, X., Jin, X.Z.: Average consensus problems of a class of multi-agent systems against perturbations. In: 2010 Chinese Control and Decision Conference, Xuzhou, China, pp. 3518–3522 (2010)

16. Shang, Y.: Finite-time weighted average consensus and generalized consensus over a subset. IEEE Access **4**, 2615–2620 (2016)
17. Yu, H., Jian, J.G., Wang, Y.J.: Weighted average consensus for directed networks of multi-agent. Microcomput. Inf. **23**(7), 239–241 (2007)
18. Yu, H., Jian, J.G.: Weighted average-consensus for directed networks of multi-agent with switching topology. In: 27th Chinese Control Conference, Kunming, China, pp. 526–530 (2008)
19. Zhu, J.D.: Maximum consensus speed of second-order multi-agent network systems under a kind of dynamic consensus protocols. In: Proceedings of the 29th Chinese Control Conference, Beijing, China, pp. 796–800 (2010)
20. Venkategowda, N.K.D., Werner, S.: Privacy-preserving distributed maximum consensus. IEEE Signal Process. Lett. **27**, 1839–1843 (2020)
21. Wang, X., He, J., Cheng, P., Chen, J.: Differentially private maximum consensus: design, analysis and impossibility result. IEEE Trans. Netw. Sci. Eng. **6**(4), 928–939 (2019)
22. Liu, W., Deng, F., Liang, J., Yan, X.: Weighted average consensus problem in networks of agents with diverse time-delays. Syst. Eng. Electron. Technol. **25**(6), 1056–1064 (2014)
23. Liu, J., An, B., Wu, H.: Consensus of third-order multi-agent systems with communication delay. In: 2018 Chinese Control and Decision Conference (CCDC), Shenyang, China, pp. 1428–1432 (2018)
24. Liu, C.L., Tian, Y.P.: Consensus of multi-agent system with diverse communication delays. In: 2007 Chinese Control Conference, Zhangjiajie, China, pp. 726–730 (2007)
25. Park, M., Kwon, O., Park, J., Lee, S., Kim, K.: Randomly occurring leader-following consensus criterion for multi-agent systems with communication delay. In: 12th International Conference on Control, Automation and Systems, Jeju, South Korea, pp. 883–886 (2012)
26. Wu, H., An, B., Song, Y.: Consensus of third-order multi-agent systems with fixed topology and input delay. In: 2018 Chinese Control and Decision Conference (CCDC), Shenyang, China, pp. 3879–3883 (2018)
27. Liu, C., Liu, F.: Consensus of multi-agent systems with sampled information and input delay. In: Third International Symposium on Intelligent Information Technology Application, Nanchang, China, pp. 453–457 (2009)
28. Mehra, S., Sahoo, S.R.: Trajectory tracking with input delay in multi-agent system: double integrator case. In: 2016 International Conference on Unmanned Aircraft Systems (ICUAS), Arlington, VA, USA, pp. 387–393 (2016)
29. Olfati-Saber, R., Murray, R.M.: Consensus problems in networks of agents with switching topology and time-delays. IEEE Trans. Autom. Control **49**(9), 1520–1533 (2004)
30. Boyd, B., Ghaoui, L.E., Feron, E., Balakrishnan, V.: Linear Matrix Inequalities in System and Control Theory. SIAM, Philadelphia (1994)
31. Yuan, G.S., Long, W., Xie, G.: Average consensus in networks of dynamic agents with switching topologies and multiple time-varying delays. Syst. Control Lett. **57**(2), 175–183 (2008)
32. Godsil, C., Royle, G.: Algebraic Graph Theory. Springer, New York (2001). https://doi.org/10.1007/978-1-4613-0163-9
33. Hale, J.K., Verduyn Lunel, S.M.: Introduction to Function Differential Equations. Springer, New York (1993). https://doi.org/10.1007/978-1-4612-4342-7

An Improved Echo State Network Model for Spatial-Temporal Energy Consumption Prediction in Public Buildings

Yuyang Sun[1], Ji Xu[2], Ruiqi Jiang[1], and Zhou Wu[1](✉)

[1] College of Automation, Chongqing University, Chongqing 400044, China
{yuyangsun,jiang_ruiqi,zhouwu}@cqu.edu.cn
[2] School of Electrical Engineering and Automation, Wuhan University, Wuhan 430072, China

Abstract. With the continuous development of the global economy and the acceleration of urbanization, the annual energy consumption of buildings also occupies a considerable scale. In order to achieve energy saving and emission reduction in buildings, reasonable energy management for buildings is an important tool to achieve the goal of energy saving and emission reduction. In this paper, an improved Echo State Network method is used to predict building energy consumption. This improved echo state network can not only handle energy consumption data of a single building, but also combine multiple spatially correlated building energy consumption data to further improve the accuracy of energy prediction. The results show that the accuracy of the new model proposed in this paper for building energy consumption prediction is better than that of the classical ESN model and other classical machine learning models, and the model is well suited for end-to-end prediction tasks for multiple buildings. Combined with the clustering algorithm, it can also achieve acceleration for end-to-end prediction tasks.

Keywords: Echo state network · Building energy consumption · End-to-end prediction

1 Introduction

With the continuous development of the global economy and urbanization, the energy demand is constantly growing. Buildings' energy consumption occupies a large property of it [1]. Especially, large public buildings consumption can reach many times of ordinary [2]. In many countries, buildings consume even more than 40% of total energy [3]. Therefore, it is important for decision makers who take charge of energy generation to understand the energy consumption future trends. [4, 5], which means accurate building energy consumption forecasting is essential.

The prediction of energy consumption has been studied by certain researchers [6, 7]. Traditionally, using building energy simulation engines such as DOE-2 and EnergyPlus, the prediction of a building energy consumption can be achieved by using various related information about it. However, various physical information about the building is not easily collected [8], which causes difficulty for prediction.

© Springer Nature Singapore Pte Ltd. 2021
H. Zhang et al. (Eds.): NCAA 2021, CCIS 1449, pp. 83–95, 2021.
https://doi.org/10.1007/978-981-16-5188-5_7

In recent years, neural network methods have been widely used in energy consumption area. Some researchers have improved the energy consumption prediction accuracy by making some improvements on the classical neural network [9, 10]. In [10], the study used an improved extreme gradient boosting tree to predict the different time-scale energy consumption. Pham et al. used random forest to predict the five different buildings energy consumption in single and multiple steps respectively [12]. In [13], the study used the support vector machine to predict the energy consumption of public buildings, and through the trained model and the prediction errors, they had good prediction results and different levels of warnings. There are also researchers who predict the consumption by reinforcement learning methods [14, 15]. Above reference didn't concern about the relationship among different buildings' data.

In this study, a novel Echo State Network (ESN), which is composed by ESN chain and called Chain-structure Echo State Network (CESN), is used to predict the consumption. The CESN model can uses the relationship among the buildings. Thus, it can reach a relatively high prediction accuracy [21]. Moreover, because CESN has the character of fast training, it can also predict the future energy consumption of multiple buildings in a short period of time and achieve end-to-end prediction for multiple buildings.

This paper will then introduce the classical ESN model in Sect. 2 and the CESN model in Sect. 3. Subsequently, we will conduct experiments on building energy consumption prediction using the CESN model in Sect. 4 and show the results of the experiments in Sect. 5. Finally, conclusions are drawn in Sect. 6.

2   Structure of Classical ESN

The CESN model consists of several ESN modules. As shown in Fig. 1, classic ESN likes recurrent neural network, consists of three neural network layers, namely, input layer, reservoir and output layer.

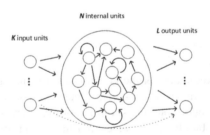

Fig. 1. Classical structure of echo state network (ESN)

The difference between ESN and ordinary recurrent neural network is that when ESN model is trained, only the weight $\mathbf{W}^{out}$ of the output layer is needed to be trained, and the other parameters remain unchanged after random initialization. This means that ESN requires fewer training parameters, so ESN is faster than normal recurrent neural network training. The core of ESN consists of a reservoir in the middle, and as it differs from the hidden layer of a recurrent neural network, it is called a reservoir for discrimination. The reservoir is composed of a structure of neurons with a sparse self-connecting reservoir. The reservoir structure encodes the input dynamic nonlinear signal and maps the original low-dimensional information to the high-dimensional space.

As shown in Fig. 1, ESN contains three neural network layers, among which the hidden layer contains K neurons, the reservoir contains N neurons, and the output layer contains L neurons. The neuron state update function inside the reservoir is as follows:

$$\mathbf{x}(i) = \tanh(\mathbf{W}^{in}\mathbf{u}(i) + \mathbf{W}^{res}\mathbf{x}(i-1)) \tag{1}$$

Where $\mathbf{u}(i) = [u_1(i), u_2(i), \ldots, u_K(i)]$ represents the input data at time i, $\mathbf{x}(i) = [x_1(i), x_2(i), \ldots, x_N(i)]$ represents the state of neurons in the reservoir at time i, $\mathbf{W}^{in} \in \mathbf{R}^{N \times K}$, is the connection weight of ESN input layer to the reservoir, $\mathbf{W}^{res} \in \mathbf{R}^{N \times N}$ is the self-connection matrix between neurons in the reservoir, because the self-connection of neurons in the reservoir is relatively sparse, therefore, $\mathbf{W}^{res}$ is a sparse matrix. $\tanh(*)$ is a activation function, and activation function used in this paper is the hyperbolic tangent function.

In order to make ESN adapt to more complex situations, leaky integrate neurons was also considered in the study [21, 22]. Because the neuron activation function tanh used in this paper have no memory capacity, So there is no direct relationship between the state $x(i)$ of the reservoir neuron at time i and the state $x(i-1)$ at time $i-1$. Therefore, traditional state echo network is more suitable for processing discrete data rather than continuously changing system data. In order to enable ESN to deal with continuously changing time data, the ESN we used is different from traditional ESN, which do not have leaky integrate neurons. So the neural network which we used has better short-term memory ability. In this case, the updating mode of neurons in the reservoir is as follows:

$$\begin{aligned}\mathbf{x}(i) = (1-a)\mathbf{x}(i-1) + a\tanh(\mathbf{W}^{in}\mathbf{u}(i) \\ + \mathbf{W}^{res}\mathbf{x}(i-1))\end{aligned} \tag{2}$$

Where $\mathbf{x}(i-1)$ is the state of reservoir neuron at time $i-1$ and $a \in [0, 1][0, 1]$ is the leaky decay rate. When a is small, the rate of state change of the neuron is slower, which makes the updating frequency of the neural network decrease during training phase.

In the ESN module used in this paper, when the state of reservoir is updated, its output value at time i is calculated as follows:

$$\mathbf{y}(i) = \mathbf{W}^{out}\mathbf{x}(i) \tag{3}$$

Where $\mathbf{W}^{out} \in \mathbf{R}^{L \times N}$ is the connection matrix between the reservoir and the output layer. In order to prevent the over-fitting of ESN model during training phase, we use the ridge regression training algorithm to calculate $\mathbf{W}^{out}$. The calculation method is as follows:

$$(\mathbf{W}^{out})^T = (\mathbf{X}^T\mathbf{X} + \eta\mathbf{E})^{-1}\mathbf{X}^T\mathbf{Y} \tag{4}$$

Where $\mathbf{X} = (\mathbf{x}(1), \mathbf{x}(2), \ldots, \mathbf{x}(l_{tr}))^T$ represents the set of input data vectors, $\mathbf{Y} = (\mathbf{y}(1), \mathbf{y}(2), \ldots, \mathbf{y}(l_{tr}))^T$ represents the set of output data vectors, where l_{tr} represents the length of the training data, $\mathbf{E}$ represents the identity matrix, and η is the regularizing parameter.

3 Chain-Structure Echo State Network

Due to the limited processing ability of classical ESN when dealing with multi-dimensional data, a Chain-structure Echo State Network (CESN) approach is used in this paper, which has been used for solar irradiance prediction in previous work [21]. Its structure is shown in Fig. 2.

From Fig. 2, we can see that CESN is stacked with ESNs. When using the CESN for forecasting, we can define the number of ESNs to be stacked based on the amount of building energy consumption data to be processed. In other words, if we have a total of n different buildings with energy consumption time series, we can use n ESN modules to compose the CESN model.

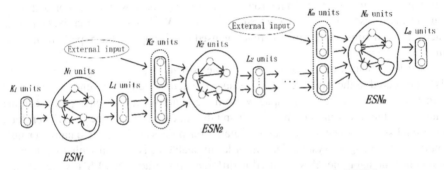

Fig. 2. The structure of chain-structure echo state network (CESN)

Suppose that CESN consists of a total of n ESN modules, namely ESN_1, ESN_2,..., ESN_n, where the input layer of each ESN module has $K_1, K_2, \ldots, K_n$ units and the reservoir has $N_1, N_2, \ldots, N_n$ units, with $L_1, L_2, \ldots, L_n$ units in the output layer, respectively. When building the CESN model, we first need to initialize each neuron state of ESN randomly. After that, when training the CESN model, we need to train each ESN module.

When training the CESN, it is important to note that we need to start training from the first ESN module, i.e., from ESN_1 in Fig. 2. The reason for this is that the input layers of the other ESN modules depend on the output of the previous ESN module, and only the input layer of the first ESN module depends only on the input of external data. In such a training sequence, for the mth ESN module, the update mode of its reservoir at time i is as follows:

$$
\begin{aligned}
\mathbf{x}^{(m)}(i) = (1 - a_m)\mathbf{x}^{(m)}(i-1) \\
+ a_m \tanh(\mathbf{W}_m^{in}\mathbf{I}^{(m)}(i) + \mathbf{W}_m^{res}\mathbf{x}^{(m)}(i-1))
\end{aligned}
\tag{5}
$$

And the output value of this module at time i is calculated as follows:

$$
\mathbf{y}^{(m)}(i) = \mathbf{W}_m^{out}\mathbf{x}^{(m)}(i)
\tag{6}
$$

where $\mathbf{I}^{(m)}(i)$ of Eq. (5) is the input of the mth ESN module of the CESN at time i and has the following value:

$$
\mathbf{I}^{(m)}(i) = \begin{cases} \mathbf{u}^{(1)}(i), & \text{if } m = 1 \\ [\mathbf{u}^{(m)}(i); \mathbf{y}^{(m-1)}(i)], & \text{if } m > 1 \end{cases}
\tag{7}
$$

We can also see from Eq. (7) that the input to the first ESN module is $\mathbf{u}^{(1)}(i)$, i.e., only the input of external data. The inputs of the remaining modules are $[\mathbf{u}^{(m)}(i); \mathbf{y}^{(m-1)}(i)]$, i.e., the input of the mth ESN module has not only the external data $\mathbf{u}^{(m)}(i)$, but also the output data $\mathbf{y}^{(m-1)}(i)$ of the previous ESN module, and by stacking the two left and right to form the new input data, the This data can then be used for the training and output of the ESN module.

Based on the above description, we can summarize the algorithm of the CESN model in the training phase.

Algorithm 1 Training phase of CESN

1: Input: $\mathbf{u}^{(1)}, \mathbf{u}^{(2)}, ..., \mathbf{u}^{(Nu)}$;

2: Output: $\mathbf{W}_1^{out}, \mathbf{W}_2^{out}, ..., \mathbf{W}_{Nu}^{out}$

3: for $m \leftarrow 1$ to Nu

4:   Let matrix $S^{(m)} \in R^{(l_{tr}-N_1-N_2)\times(N_1\times N_2)}$, where $S^{(m)}[i,j] = u^{(m)}[i+j-1]$

5: for $m \leftarrow 1$ to Nu

6:   Initilization:$\{ \mathbf{W}_m^{in}, \mathbf{W}_m^{res}, a_m, K_m, N_R, L_M, \eta \}$;

7:   for $i \leftarrow 1$ to $l_{tr} - N_1 - N_2$

8:     if $m = 1$ then

9:         $\mathbf{I}^{(m)}(i) \leftarrow S^{(m)}[i,0:N_1]$;

10:    else

11:        $\mathbf{I}^{(m)}(i) \leftarrow [S^{(m)}[i,0:N_1]; \mathbf{y}^{(m-1)}(i)]$;

12:    Compute $\mathbf{x}^{(m)}(i)$ as Eq.(5);

13:        $\mathbf{y}^{(m)}(i) \leftarrow S^{(m)}[i,(N_1+1):(N_1+N_2)]$;

14: end

15:    $\mathbf{X}_m \leftarrow [\mathbf{x}^{(m)}(1), \mathbf{x}^{(m)}(2), ..., \mathbf{x}^{(m)}(l_{tr})]$;

16:    $\mathbf{Y}_m \leftarrow [\mathbf{y}^{(m)}(1), \mathbf{y}^{(m)}(2), ..., \mathbf{y}^{(m)}(l_{tr})]$;

17:    $(\mathbf{W}_m^{out})^T \leftarrow (\mathbf{X}_m^T\mathbf{X}+\eta\mathbf{E})^{-1}\mathbf{X}_m^T\mathbf{Y}_m$;

18:    $\mathbf{y}^{(m)}(i) \leftarrow \mathbf{W}_m^{out}\mathbf{I}^{(m)}(i)$;

19:end

---

4 Experiment Design

4.1 Datasets and Model Preparation

The data used in this experiment are derived from publicly available building energy consumption data [23], and we selected historical energy consumption data for 37 of these buildings in this dataset, all of which are from New York, USA. The historical energy consumption data of each building contains data from January 1, 2015 at 5:00 to January 1, 2016 at 4:00 for a total of one year, and the energy consumption data is recorded hourly, so the energy consumption data of each building consists of 8760 pieces of data. Figure 3 shows the data of two buildings from these 37 buildings. Table 1 shows some basic information about the energy consumption data for four buildings of these 37 buildings.

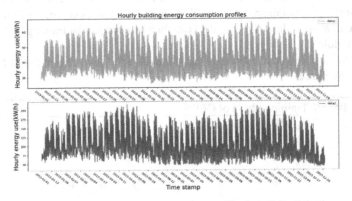

Fig. 3. Historical hourly energy consumption profiles in buildings for one year

Table 1. Some building energy consumption datasets.

Dataset	Building name	Duration	Hourly energy consumption in buildings (kW/h)	
			Mean	Std.
Dataset 1	UnivLab_Preston	12 months	41.418	9.652
Dataset 2	Office_Pam	12 months	105.478	40.210
Dataset 3	UnivClass_Pete	12 months	52.300	15.795
Dataset 4	Office_Pamela	12 months	27.834	11.274

4.2 Spatio-Temporal Forecasting of Hourly Building Energy Consumption

In the CESN model, the output of the final output of the CESN model is the last ESN module output. Therefore, we enter the energy consumption data of the target building into the last ESN module of the CESN model. Before this ESN module, we should have the building energy consumption data that is most relevant to the energy consumption of the target building entered into the previous ESN module, and to accurately describe the correlation between building energy consumption, we quantitatively describe the correlation between two building energy consumption data by means of a correlation coefficient. The correlation coefficient between the two buildings a, b is calculated as follows:

$$\rho(d_a, d_b) = \frac{\text{cov}(d_a, d_b)}{\sigma_{d_a}\sigma_{d_b}} \tag{8}$$

where d_a and d_b represent the historical energy consumption data of building a and building b, respectively, which are one-dimensional time series. $\text{cov}(d_a, d_b)$ represents the covariance between the time series d_a and d_b. σ_{d_a} and σ_{d_b} represent the standard deviation of d_a and d_b, respectively. We selected four buildings from the energy consumption data set of 37 buildings mentioned in the previous section. By means of Eq. (8), we can calculate the correlation between these four building energy consumption data, the results of which are shown in Table 2.

Table 2. Correlation coefficients between buildings two by two

Buidings	UnivLab_Preston	Office_Pam	UnivClass_Pete	Office_Pamela
UnivLab_Preston	1	0.954	0.889	0.876
Office_Pam	0.954	1	0.871	0.853
UnivClass_Pete	0.889	0.871	1	0.844
Office_Pamela	0.876	0.853	0.844	1

In addition, we predict the four buildings in Table 1, respectively. In CESN predicting processing, the consumption data of the target building is input into the last ESN submodule. And the consumption data which has highest relationship to the target building is input into the forward ESN module. Other CESN's inputs are organized by this way.

After determining the way to enter the data, we also need to allocate the training data and forecast data appropriately. In this experiment, we have divided the data equally into four parts according to four seasons. In each season, we used the first 80% of the data for training and the last 20% for testing.

When conducting the experiments, we also need to make some settings for the parameters of the CESN model. In this section of experiments, we use the historical energy consumption data of each building for the previous two hours as input data to predict the energy consumption in the next hour. The number of reservoir neurons for each ESN submodule in the CESN model is 100 and the sparsity of $\mathbf{W}^{res}$ is 0.9. When initializing the neuron weights, set the weights to lie in the interval $[-0.01, 0.01]$. Set the leaky decay rate a to 0.7, and when training each ESN module, the regularization parameter η of its output layer connection weight matrix $\mathbf{W}^{out}$ update was set to 0.001.

To reflect the predictive accuracy of the model, we use root mean square error (RMSE) to describe it, which is calculated as follows:

$$RMSE = \sqrt{\frac{1}{l_{test}} \sum_{i=1}^{l_{test}} (y_{real,i} - y_{measured,i})^2} \qquad (9)$$

where l_{test} denotes the length of the test dataset, in this paper $l_{test} = 438$, $y_{real,i}$ denotes the true energy consumption of the building and $y_{measured,i}$ denotes the predicted value of the model.

4.3   End-to-End Experiments on Buildings Using CESN Model

The longer the length of the CESN model, with the higher prediction accuracy usually, but its training time also grows linearly with its length. To strike a balance between prediction accuracy and prediction speed. We design some experiments to determine the optimal length of the CESN model.

We conducted experiments using energy consumption data from the first season of 37 buildings in the dataset. For example, the building to be predicted is UnivLab_Preston. The data used for training and prediction are also divided in the same way as the experiments described in Sect. 4.2. The prediction error of CESN with a fixed number of ESN submodules is recorded and the results shown in Fig. 3 are obtained.

As can be seen in Fig. 4, the root mean square error of energy consumption decreases as the CESN model continues to lengthen, but when the number of ESN modules in the CESN model reaches 3–4 or more, the mean square error of CESN stops decreasing, at which point the prediction accuracy of the CESN model is close to its limit and does not continue to improve with the lengthening of the CESN model.

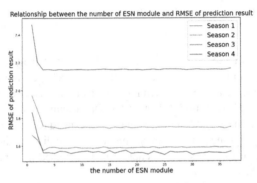

Fig. 4. The number of ESN modules in CESN with daily data versus predicted RMSE

In the end-to-end experiment described above, when the number of buildings reaches 37, in our experiment environment, the time consumed for the whole prediction takes 65.2 s, and its average RMSE of 4 seasons is 1.758. However, when the number of ESN modules in CESN is fixed to 4, in the same experiment environment, the time consumed for the whole prediction only takes 7 s, and its average RMSE of 4 seasons is 1.759, which is close to the 37 buildings' experiment prediction accuracy.

The above analysis tells us that when making energy consumption predictions for many related buildings, it is not necessary to process all the data at once. When predicting the future energy consumption of a particular building, it is only necessary to select the energy consumption data of a limited number of buildings related to it. In this way, the size of the CESN model can be reduced and the prediction speed of CESN can be accelerated without affecting the prediction performance.

The above analysis points out that the CESN model can still maintain a good performance when its size is reduced to a certain level. Besides, we can notice that in the end-to-end prediction processing, the CESN model needs to be retrained once when it faces a new case. If the number of training times of the CESN model in end-to-end prediction can be reduced, the prediction speed can be effectively accelerated. The energy consumption data between different buildings often have certain similarities, and the similarity between some buildings is relatively high. We process the energy consumption data of the four buildings mentioned in Sect. 4.1, as follows, to analyze the similarity between them. The energy consumption data of each building is normalized separately. The Fast Fourier Transform (FFT) is applied and the result is plotted in the figure, shown in Fig. 5.

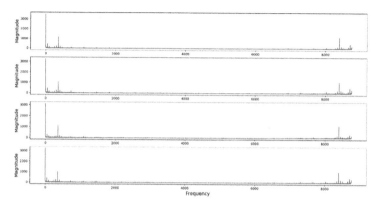

Fig. 5. Energy consumption data in the frequency domain for the four buildings

As can be seen from Fig. 5, the magnitude distribution of the four buildings in the frequency domain is very similar. This means that we can first normalize these 4 buildings and find their clustering center when we make energy consumption predictions for them. Then the CESN model is used to predict the future energy consumption of the cluster center, and finally the prediction result of the cluster center is renormalized according to the energy consumption of the original buildings to obtain the prediction results of the energy consumption of the four buildings respectively. This method takes advantage of the high similarity of energy consumption between certain buildings to reduce the number of model training for end-to-end prediction and accelerate the speed of prediction.

5 Experiment Results

5.1 Experimental Results of Spatio-Temporal Prediction

In the prediction experiments for the CESN model mentioned in Sect. 5.2, we performed the same experiments for all four seasons of data and also used the classical ESN model and the commonly used machine algorithm Support Vector Regression (SVR) and BP neural network for each of the four buildings in turn, and for each model, the experiments were repeated 20 times to obtain the average results of RMSE, and the final results are shown in Table 3.

Table 3. The average results of RMSE of 20 independent experiments for four seasons

Target buildings	Network models	1st season	2nd season	3rd season	4th season
UnivLab_Preston	CESN	**2.153**	1.677	**1.608**	**1.598**
	ESN	2.409	**1.659**	1.650	1.651
	SVR	2.487	1.930	1.961	1.737
	BP	2.814	2.052	1.950	1.708
Office_Pam	CESN	8.961	**8.732**	7.366	8.040
	ESN	**8.858**	8.780	8.581	**7.169**
	SVR	10.951	12.429	10.345	8.097
	BP	10.330	12.276	9.628	8.428
UnivClass_Pete	CESN	**2.944**	**3.210**	**3.541**	**2.707**
	ESN	3.419	3.476	3.587	2.821
	SVR	4.131	4.513	4.477	3.645
	BP	4.409	4.453	4.417	3.597
Office_Pamela	CESN	**3.135**	**2.665**	**3.626**	**2.775**
	ESN	3.172	2.963	4.108	2.877
	SVR	4.210	4.098	4.797	3.410
	BP	4.212	3.939	3.823	3.375

From the experimental results, it can be seen that the prediction accuracy of CESN is better than the classical ESN model and support vector regression in most cases.

5.2 Experimental Results of End-to-End Prediction

With the input of historical data for multiple buildings, the future energy consumption of each building is predicted separately, i.e., the end-to-end prediction is similar for each building as it was for the single building in the experiment above. The model predicts each building with its structure unchanged and the parameters vary with the historical data used for training. Since the CESN model requires few parameters for training, the end-to-end processing of multiple buildings can be maintained at a certain rate even with on-the-fly training, and the predictions for four of the 37 buildings under the first season are shown in Fig. 6 for the end-to-end prediction experiments for the 37 buildings situation. The mean RMSE of the prediction results is 4.743.

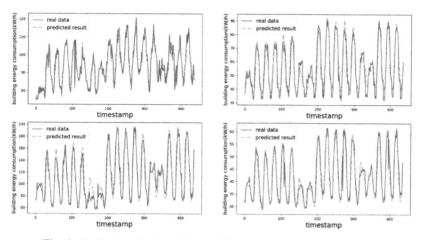

Fig. 6. Predictions for four of the buildings under end-to-end prediction

When using clustering centers instead of the original energy consumption of multiple buildings, the prediction speed is accelerated and still maintains a good accuracy. Here are the prediction results in this case. The mean RMSE of the prediction results is 5.057 (Fig. 7).

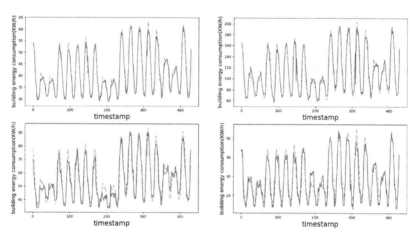

Fig. 7. Predictions for four of these buildings under end-to-end predictions accelerated using clustering center

6 Conclusion

In this paper, a CESN model is proposed to improve the prediction ability of the model by exploiting the correlation between buildings and constructions. Compared with classical machine learning models, such as BP, SVR, and ESN, the prediction accuracy is improved by using the CESN model for prediction. After that, we analyze some internal properties of the CESN model. The prediction performance of the CESN model does not increase all the time with the number of ESN submodules. By limiting the ESN submodules to a certain range, both prediction accuracy and decent prediction speed can be guaranteed. With this feature, we can make the CESN model predict the future energy consumption of multiple buildings continuously in a short period of time and realize the end-to-end prediction task for multiple buildings.

When the CESN model predicts the future energy consumption of a building, the improvement of its prediction accuracy relies on the correlation between the energy consumption data of different buildings. When the correlation between buildings is high enough, the prediction accuracy of the CESN model will be improved accordingly. If the correlation between the energy consumption data of different buildings is not high, it may not have a positive impact on the prediction accuracy of the CESN model. In addition, when the CESN model performs end-to-end prediction for multiple buildings, the prediction speed of the CESN model is guaranteed because the size of the CESN model is limited.

In addition, other methods such as frequency domain analysis can be used to identify certain close relationships between different buildings' energy consumption. The cluster center of these buildings are used to replace the original energy consumption data, thus it can reduce the number of repetitive training of the CESN parameters and accelerate the end-to-end prediction.

In our future work, other characteristic extraction methods and ESN improvement will be considered. This study uses the buildings energy consumption raw data which may have certain noise and can't represent the data features. So it is important to make the data features more prominent. Besides, ESN units are randomly generated, and it is also important to research on ESN pre-training.

References

1. Allouhi, A., El-Fouih, Y., Kousksou, T., Jamil, A., Zeraouli, Y., Mourad, Y.: Energy consumption and efficiency in buildings: current status and future trends. J. Clean. Prod. **109**, 118–130 (2015)
2. Banihashemi, S., Ding, G., Wang, J.: Developing a hybrid model of prediction and classification algorithms for building energy consumption. Energy Procedia **110**, 371–376 (2017)
3. Moga, L., Moga, I.: Building design influence on the energy performance. J. Appl. Eng. Sci. **5**(1), 37–46 (2015)
4. Chang, C., Jing, Z., Zhu, N.: Energy saving effect prediction and post evaluation of air-conditioning system in public buildings. Energy Build. **43**(11), 3243–3249 (2011)
5. Fong, W.K., Matsumoto, H., Lun, Y.F., et al.: System dynamic model for the prediction of urban energy consumption trends (2007)
6. Guo, Y., Wang, J., Chen, H., et al.: Machine learning-based thermal response time ahead energy demand prediction for building heating systems. Appl. Energy **221**, 16–27 (2018)
7. Killian, M., Koze, M.: Ten questions concerning model predictive control for energy efficient building. Build. Environ. **105**, 403–412 (2016)
8. Amasyali, K., El-Gohary, N.M.: A review of data-driven building energy consumption prediction studies. Renew. Sustain. Energy Rev. **81**, 1192–1205 (2018)

9. Luo, X.J., Oyedele, L.O., Ajayi, A.O., et al.: Feature extraction and genetic algorithm enhanced adaptive deep neural network for energy consumption prediction in buildings. Renew. Sustain. Energy Rev. **131**, 109980 (2020)
10. Ruiz, L.G.B., Rueda, R., Cuellar, M.P., et al.: Energy consumption forecasting based on elman neural networks with evolutive optimization. Expert Syst. Appl. **149**(11), 57–68 (2017)
11. Lu, H., Cheng, F., et al.: Short-term prediction of building energy consumption employing an improved extreme gradient boosting model: a case study of an intake tower. Energy **203**, 117756 (2020)
12. Pham, A.-D., Ngo, N.-T., et al.: Prediction energy consumption in multiple buildings using machine learning for improving energy efficiency and sustainability. J. Clean. Prod. **260**, 121082 (2020)
13. Liu, Y., Chen, H., et al.: Energy consumption prediction and diagnosis of public buildings based on support vector machine learning: a case study in China. J. Clean. Prod. **272**, 122542 (2020)
14. Liu, T., Tan, Z., Xu, C., et al.: Study on deep reinforcement learning techniques for building energy consumption forecasting. Energy Build. **208**, 109675.1-109675.14 (2020)
15. Brandi, S., Piscitelli, M.S., Martellacci, M., et al.: Deep reinforcement learning to optimise indoor temperature control and heating energy consumption in buildings. Energy Build. **224**, 110225 (2020)
16. Jaeger, H., Haas, H.: Harnessing nonlinearity: predicting chaotic systems and saving energy in wireless communication. Science **304**(5667), 78–80 (2004)
17. Sun, L., Jin, B., Yang, H., et al.: Unsupervised EEG feature extraction based on echo state network. Inf. Sci. **475**, 1–17 (2019)
18. Lacy, S.E., Smith, S.L., Lones, M.A.: Using echo state networks for classification: a case study in parkinsons disease diagnosis. Artif. Intell. Med. **86**, 53–59 (2018)
19. Chouikhi, N., Ammar, B., Rokbani, N., et al.: PSO-based analysis of echo state network parameters for time series forecasting. Appl. Soft Comput. **55**, 211–225 (2017)
20. Sun, W., Liu, M.: Wind speed forecasting using FEEMD echo state networks with RELM in Hebei, China. Energy Convers. Manag. **114**, 197–208 (2016)
21. Qian, L., Zhou, W., Hz, C.: Spatio-temporal modeling with enhanced flexibility and robustness of solar irradiance prediction: a chain-structure echo state network approach. J. Clean. Prod. **261**, 121151 (2020)
22. Jaeger, H., Lukosevicius, M., Popovici, D., et al.: Optimization and applications of echo state networks with leaky-integrator neurons. Neural Netw. **20**(3), 335–352 (2007)
23. Miller, C., Meggers, F.: The building data genome project: an open, public data set from non-residential building electrical meters. Energy Procedia **122**, 439–444 (2017)

Modeling Data Center Networks with Message Passing Neural Network and Multi-task Learning

Kai Zhang[1]([✉]), Xueyong Xu[2], Chenchen Fu[3], Xiumin Wang[4], and Weiwei Wu[3]([✉])

[1] School of Cyber Science and Engineering, Southeast University, Nanjing 210096, China
kzhang@seu.edu.cn
[2] North Information Control Research Academy Group Co., Ltd., Beijing, China
[3] School of Computer Science and Engineering, Southeast University, Nanjing 210096, China
{101012509,weiweiwu}@seu.edu.cn
[4] School of Computer Science and Engineering,
South China University of Technology (SCUT) , Guangzhou, China

Abstract. Network modeling is a pivotal component to operate network efficiently in future Software Defined Network (SDN) based Data Center Networks. However, obtaining a general network model to produce accurate predictions of key performance metrics such as delay, jitter or packet loss jointly at minimal cost is difficult. To this end, we propose a novel network model based on message passing neural network (MPNN) and multi-task learning, which could unveil the potential connections between network topology, routing and traffic characteristics to produce accurate estimates of per-source/destination mean delay, jitter and packet drop ratio with only one model. Specifically, an extended multi-output architecture is proposed and an elaborate loss function is introduced to facilitate the learning task. In addition, we present the modules of our simulation environment for generating the training samples, which is generic and easy to deploy. Experimental results show that our approach can get better performance compared to the state of the art.

Keywords: Network modeling · Message passing neural network · Multi-task learning · Data center networks

1 Introduction

With the development of the Internet, traffic density has expanded rapidly and the demands for efficient and reliable data centers are gradually increasing. However, how to understand the characteristics of data centers is thought to be the bottleneck in the field of network optimization. The technology involved is so-called "network modeling" [1], in which we try to model real data center networks to simulate and optimize them. Thanks to the rapid development of emerging technologies, such as Software-Defined Networks (SDN) [2], Network Function Virtualization (NFV) [3], and so on, the network could be fully controlled through the SDN controller from a centralized control plane,

© Springer Nature Singapore Pte Ltd. 2021
H. Zhang et al. (Eds.): NCAA 2021, CCIS 1449, pp. 96–112, 2021.
https://doi.org/10.1007/978-981-16-5188-5_8

which may assist in operating the network efficiently and detecting the changes in the network promptly. In this context, a series of optimization objectives are proposed by the network administrators (e.g., minimizing the mean delay or drop ratio) [4]. Then the SDN controllers usually take two steps to satisfy the requirement. Firstly, obtain an accurate network model by certain methods, which reveals the inner connections between network topology, traffic characteristics and routing configuration to predict the routing performance metrics (e.g., end-to-end delay, drop ratio). Secondly, adopt some optimization algorithms to evaluate different configurations sequentially until finding one that accomplish the optimization goals. However, we can only optimize what we are able to model [4]. For example, if we would like to minimize the end-to-end delay for some certain users, we must understand how other network characteristics affect the resulting delay. Therefore, the first step above is more important which is the one this paper would pay attention to.

In the past, numerous studies have been devoted to building network models to predict performance metrics. Many heuristics are mainly based on network calculus [5, 6] or queuing theory [7], which make a strong assumption about the network or flows characteristics thus cannot adapt to the dynamics of network. Moreover, some packet-level simulators such as NS-3 [8] or OMNeT++ [9] are promising to get optimal predictions. However, they could only get the routing performance when the routing paths are already chosen as input. When applied to the routing selection scenario, it may cost much computation time to iterate over all routing configurations thus cannot make decision in short time scales.

With the explosive development of artificial intelligence, deep learning [10] has undoubtedly become one of the hottest topics in recent years. Neural networks are extremely powerful function approximators, which has been proven that three hidden layers are enough for neural networks to achieve super approximation capacity [11]. [12] is the first research that uses neural network to model the delay of a computer network. Although it could predict the delay to some extent, but it ignores the potential characteristics of network topology and cannot generalize to more complex network scenes.

The main challenge in solving this problem is that, the network topology, traffic intensity and routing configuration are intricately intertwined together, which result in the great difficulty to describe this relationship between the network features (e.g., link capacities, bandwidth and so on) and routing performance (i.e., end to end delay, jitter and drop ratio).

The most related research with our work is the state of art, RouteNet [13], which designs a GNN (graph neural network) based optimization algorithm to select the best routing paths for each source-destination traffic demand pair. It could encode variant-length paths into fixed-length embeddings and output accurate predictions with different network topology, traffic intensity and routing configurations. However, it ignores the connections between the key performance metrics (i.e., delay, jitter and drops), which requires to train two models separately to produce the results of target metrics (one for delay and jitter, the other for drops), which may cost more computation time and memory to get the results and do not achieve a real generalization.

To this end, the main contributions of this paper are summarized as follows,

1. We convert the network modeling problem to a multi-task learning process, for which a new feature-shared architecture is introduced to facilitate the learning task;
2. We introduce a weighted loss function to fit into the multi-task prediction task, which could even get better performance than predict them individually;
3. We conduct experimental evaluation on large-scale data center networks, and the training samples are generated within the packet-level simulator OMNeT++ [9]. Experimental results show that our approach can achieve better results compared with the state of art.

The rest of this paper is organized as follows. Section 2 reviews the related work on network modeling and routing optimization. Section 3 describes the background knowledge about this paper. The proposed solution is presented in Sect. 4. And in Sect. 5, the simulation results are presented in detail. Finally, we conclude this paper in Sect. 6.

2 Related Work

In this section, we classify the related researches into two categories, i.e., network modeling and routing optimization.

2.1 Network Modeling

Network modeling is a term that has been proposed a long time ago, yet the study concerned on this field are mainly heuristic. Ciucu et al. [14] proposed a network calculus based approach to get exact network models and solutions. They proved that there is no free lunch in the framework of network calculus and it is a tradeoff between generality and exactness. Giovanni [7] introduced a basic description of current networking technologies and many important tools for network performance analysis based on queuing theory. What's more, Eun [15] proposed a fluid model toward the congestion control, which uses stochastic models to break the tradeoff between the link utilization, buffer size requirement for large systems, thus the congestion control could be more flexible, and the allocation of network resources would be more efficient. Xiong et al. [16] proposed a network performance analysis model based on queuing theory. By separately modeling the packet forwarding of OpenFlow switches and the packet-in message processing of SDN controllers into different queuing systems, the function expression of the packets' average retention time is solved, and the forwarding performance of the packets is evaluated. Compared with the benchmark method, this model can approximate the performance of SDN controllers more accurately. Li et al. [17] proposed a dynamic deployment scheme based on load balancing for the SDN multi-controller system. By transforming the flow requests into a queuing model, they redistributed the switches in different sub-domains and assigned the switches to the most suitable controller, thereby reducing the transmission delay of flows and realizing multi-controller load balancing. Altman et al. [18] aimed at a type of network shared by N non-cooperative users, where each user needs to send flows from a specific source to a destination. By modeling the link cost as a polynomial function, the competitive routing solution of multiple network flows in a shared network is obtained based on the Nash equilibrium theory. However, there is an inherent defect in all heuristics, they build a fixed model or make a strong assumption, which may be not suitable for real network scenarios.

With the rapid development of artificial intelligence, many researches have resorted to the machine learning methods. To improve the QoS of network, Jain et al. [19] proposed an association analysis mechanism, which can be divided into two stages. Firstly, the correlation between each input feature and QoS indicators is measured based on the decision tree algorithm. Secondly, the linear regression algorithm is used for quantitative analysis, and the influence coefficient of each feature on QoS indicators is given exactly. Guided by the linear equations obtained, this method can prevent network congestion and improve the quality of network service. Mestres et al. [12] proposed to apply neural networks to model the delay of a computer network as a function of the input traffic. Plenty of experiments are conducted to explore the factors that affect the resulting delay. Rusek et al. [4, 13] proposed to leverage graph neural network to model the performance metrics with different network topology, traffic intensity and routing configurations, which achieved accurate predictions.

2.2 Routing Optimization

Routing Optimization is a fundamental and yet core problem in the filed of network optimization. The ultimate goal of network modeling is to choose the best routing paths to achieve the optimization goals, which is also called traffic engineering. Traditional routing optimization formulate the problem as a multi-commodity flow problem, then solve the problem approximately through a certain optimization method. Al-Fares et al. [20] proposed Hedera, a scalable, dynamic flow scheduling system, which could adaptively schedule a multi-stage switching fabric to utilize the network resources of aggregation layers efficiently. Considering the high overhead brought by Hedera's centralized detection of elephant flows, Curtis et al. [21] proposed Mahout, which held that the detection of elephant flows should be performed on the terminal host. Specifically, a shim layer was used to detect the socket buffer on the terminal host. When the buffer size exceeds the threshold, the shim layer will mark some packets of the network flow as an elephant flow and send them to the centralized controller. When a marked data packet is received, the controller selects the least congested path for transmission according to the current link utilization, while the other flows are still transmitted by some static routing algorithms (for example ECMP [22]). However, due to the sensitivity of mouse flows to delay, the static routing algorithms may not be able to complete the transmission within the specified time. Wang et al. [23] proposed FDALB, which schedules elephant flows and mouse flows in different ways. Specifically, if the bytes sent by a network flow exceed a certain threshold, it will be marked as an elephant flow. For the mouse flows, they are still transmitted according to the static routing algorithm. As for the elephant flows, they are scheduled through greedy polling instead of assigning to the least congested path. It is worth noting that to adapt to the dynamic changes of flows, once the flow transmission is completed, the above threshold will also be adjusted dynamically. Lin et al. [24] proposed a QoS-aware adaptive algorithm for routing optimization problems in hierarchical SDN networks, which selects paths with better QoS performance for flows according to their types, thereby improving the quality of network service effectively. Leconte et al. [25] introduced an optimization-based framework of network resource allocation. Firstly, they model the resource allocation problem in network slicing as a multi-constrained optimization problem, a distributed ADMM algorithm is proposed to solve the constrained optimization problem iteratively, which complete the problem of dynamic allocation and scheduling of slice resources. In [26], Chen et al. proposed AuTo, a deep reinforcement learning based end-to-end traffic optimization system that can collect network information, learn from past decisions, and perform actions to achieve operator-defined goals.

3 Background

In this section, we first introduce the network modeling problem in communication networks. Then some background knowledge is elaborated for better statement and understanding.

3.1 Problem Setup

We can formulate a computer network as an undirected acyclic graph $G = (V, E, X)$ with node set V and edge set E, where V could be the routers or switches in the network, E represents the physical links connecting the nodes and X is the set of edge/link attributions (e.g., the link capacity, link delay and so on). By default, there is no difference between edges and links unless otherwise specified. And we also call nodes rather than routers/switches more often. Assume that there are N nodes $V = \{v_1, v_2, \ldots v_N\}$ in the graph. We denote an edge from node $v_s \in V$ to node $v_t \in V$ as e_{st}, which forms the set of edges by $E = \{e_{1i}, e_{1j}, \ldots e_{ij}, \ldots, e_{Nj}\}$. For simplification, we instead denote the edges as $L = \{l_1, l_2, \ldots l_M\}$, where M is the number of edges. And $X = \{x_1, x_2, \ldots x_M\}$ corresponds to the vector set of edge attributes.

On the one hand, a path can be represented as a sequence $p = \{v_s, \ldots, v_i, v_j \ldots v_t\}$ in the graph, where v_s is the sourc node and v_t is the destination. On the other hand, the same sequence can be also identified uniquely by the edges/links lying on the path, i.e., $p_i = \{l_{i1}, l_{i2}, \ldots \ldots, l_{i|p_i|}\}$ where $|p_i|$ is the number of links forming the path i. Figure 1 shows that there are two paths in a communication network. Then we can denote path1 as $p_1 = \{l_1, l_3, l_7\}$ and path2 as $p_2 = \{l_6, l_{10}\}$. Furthermore, we denote the set of sequences as $P = \{p_1, \ldots, p_K\}$, which implys that there're K paths in the network.

Before we formulate the problem formally, some key performance metrics for each end-to-end path need be elaborated:

- **Mean delay.** The average time cost among all packets received at destination node, i.e., for each s-t path, sum the total propagation time cost by all packets received, and then average over the number of packets. Note the propagation time is measured end to end, so it may include the transmission delay, queuing delay and so on.
- **Mean jitter.** The average variance of the delay between packets received within each s-t path, i.e., sum the difference of delay among the packets, and then average over the number of packets (more concretely, the number of packets minus one). For example, the first packet could arrive with a 20 ms delay, the second with a 60 ms delay, the third one with a 10 ms delay, then the mean jitter is $(40 + 50)/2 = 45$ ms. Network jitter refers to this fluctuation in latency.

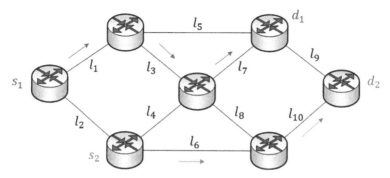

Fig. 1. A diagram of a communication network

- **Drop ratio.** The number of packets sent divided by the number of packets dropped.

The key problem of network modeling is as follows: Given a set of end-to-end paths generated by the network administrator under different traffic intensity (i.e., end-to-end bandwidth), routing configuration and network topology, how can we accurately predict the performance metrics above (i.e., the mean delay, mean jitter and drop ratio).

3.2 Overview of Message Passing Neural Network

Same as the convolution neural network tailored for images, graph neural network (GNN) is dedicated to generalize the convolution operation on graphs. What's more, most of the graph neural networks can be regarded as an implementation of the message passing neural network (MPNN) framework [27]. Particularly, given an input graph G, one of the main purposes of MPNN is to learn the low-dimensional embedding of the nodes. During each message passing iteration in MPNN, the embedding $h_u^{(k)}$ of node u in V is updated by aggregating the features of $u's$ graph neighborhood $\xi(u)$. The update process of message can be formally expressed as follows:

$$h_u^{(k+1)} = UPDATE^{(k)}\left(h_u^{(k)}, AGGREGATE^{(k)}\left(h_v^{(k)}, \forall v \in \xi(u)\right)\right)$$

$$= UPDATE^{(k)}\left(h_u^{(k)}, m_{\xi(u)}^{(k)}\right) \tag{1}$$

where $UPDATE$ and $AGGREGATE$ could be arbitrary differentiable functions (e.g., trainable neural networks) and $m_{\xi(u)}^{(k)}$ is the "message" aggregated from node $u's$ neighborhood $\xi(u)$. What's more, the different superscripts represent different iterations of message passing process.

In conclusion, at each iteration k of the MPNN, the update function UPDATE combines the message $m_{\xi(u)}^{(k)}$ with the previous embedding $h_u^{(k-1)}$ of node u to get the updated embedding $h_u^{(k)}$. The initial embeddings at k = 0 are set to the input features for all nodes, i.e., $h_u^{(0)} = x_u, \forall u \in$ V. After running K iterations of the message passing, the node could collect the information of their K-hop neighborhoods and generate the output of the final layer $h_u^{(K)}$. The final step is usually called READOUT, which typically feeds the final embeddings of all nodes to multilayer neural networks for the downstream machine learning tasks.

3.3 State of the Art Method: RouteNet

The proposed method called RouteNet [13] is the state of art for network modeling task, which leverages message passing neural network to understand the complex network characteristics. Particularly, the method focus on two main entities: paths and links.

The basic idea of RouteNet [13] is the following: the paths and links can be encoded with fixed-dimension embeddings to represent their respective information. Then two assumptions are made: firstly, a path state h_{P_i} depends on the links lying on this path; secondly, a link state h_{l_j} depends on the state of all the paths containing this link. Therefore, there is a circular dependency between the links and the paths, which can be expressed as:

$$h_{P_i} = f\left(h_{l_{i1}}, h_{l_{i2}}, \ldots \ldots, h_{l_{i|P_i|}} \right) \tag{2}$$

$$h_{l_j} = g\left(h_{p_1}, h_{p_2}, \ldots, \ldots, h_{p_m} \right), l_j \in p_i, i = 1, 2, \ldots, m \tag{3}$$

where f and g are implicit functions with the states as hidden variables. Moreover, the hidden states depend on the network characteristics, which are composed of the traffic bandwidths, routing paths and link features.

As the figure below, path1 P_1 sends packets from S1 to D1 and path2 P_2 sends packets from S2 to D2 respectively, so the connectins between paths and links can be summarized as:

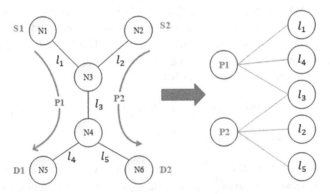

Fig. 2. Connection between links and paths

Similar to the message passing neural network, RouteNet [13] first encodes link state $h_l^{(0)}$ with the link features (i.e., link capacity) and path state $h_p^{(0)}$ with the path features (i.e., end-to-end traffic bandwidths). Then perform the message passing process among the paths and links, which the update rules are respectively:

$$h_p^{(k+1)} = RNN_k\left(h_p^{(k)}, h_l^{(k)} \right), for\ each\ l \in p \tag{4}$$

$$h_l^{(k+1)} = U_k\left(h_l^{(k)}, \sum h_{p_i}^{(k+1)}\right), for\ each\ p_i\ contain\ l \tag{5}$$

where RNN_k and U_k are both Gate recurrent Units (GRU) for each iteration, $h_p^{(k)}$ and $h_p^{(k+1)}$ are the path state of iteration k and k + 1, $h_l^{(k)}$ and $h_l^{(k+1)}$ are the link state of iteration k and k + 1 respectively. After T iterations, the final path embeddings $h_p^{(T)}$ are feeded to the READOUT layers (i.e., deep neural networks) to generate the final outputs.

4   Methods

We mainly discuss our methods in three aspects in this section. Firstly, we will introduce our extended architecture of RouteNet [13]. Secondly, we introduce the loss function to fit into our architecture. Finally, we present the method for generating the training samples to conduct experiments.

Training neural networks is time consuming and needs a lot of computation resources. Moreover, these trained models are typically designed to finish only one particular task. To get various network models in real-world applications, it is natural to convert the prediction tasks of multiple performance metrics to a multi-task learning process. This is more efficient not only in terms of computer memory and inference speed, but also in improving the generalization ability of the model to prevent overfitting.

4.1   The Extended Multi-output Architecture

A multi-task learning architecture usually contains task-shared and task-specific layers [28]. The naïve solution is to output three values directly, which represents the predictions of delay, jitter and drop ratio respectively. However, we find some feature correlations when analyzing the dataset, which inspires us a new design.

Pearson Correlation [29] is a measure of vector similarity, whose output range is $[-1, 1]$, where 0 means no correlation, negative value is negative correlation, and positive value is positive correlation. The definition can be formally expressed by:

$$\rho(X, Y) = \frac{E[(X - u_X)(Y - u_Y)]}{\sigma_X \sigma_Y}$$
$$= \frac{E[(X - u_X)(Y - u_Y)]}{\sqrt{\sum_{i=1}^{n}(X_i - u_X)^2}\sqrt{\sum_{i=1}^{n}(Y_i - u_Y)^2}} \tag{6}$$

We calculate the pearson correlations between all targets, the results are shown as follows:

As we can see from Table 1, there is some strong correlations between these metrics; especially the Pearson correlation of delay and drop ratio is 0.845074, which implies there is a strong correlation among them. (The findings also validate that training a neural network for multiple performance metrics is feasible). Inspired by this observation, we combine the output of task 1 with the output of the shared layer and input to task 2. Similarly, the output of task 2 and the output of the shared layer are also concatenated

Table 1. The Pearson correlations between all metrics

	Delay	Jitter	Drop ratio
Delay	1.00000	**0.427781**	**0.845074**
Jitter	0.427781	1.00000	0.247753
Drop ratio	0.845074	0.247753	1.00000

as the input to task 3, which enhances the input features and assists in generating the predictions of task 3.

The proposed architecture of the multi-task learning process is shown as the figure below.

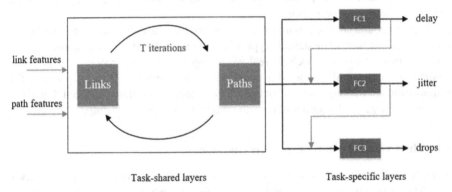

Fig. 3. The extended multi-output architecture

4.2 Loss Function Design

Loss function is critical for training deep neural networks, which is also important in multi-task learning. Because of the differences in training difficulty, easier tasks tend to dominate the training process. In this section, we introduce a loss function to facilitate the learning tasks.

For generating the outputs of per-path performance metrics (i.e., the per-path delay, jitter and drop ratio), RouteNet [13] proposes two generalized probability models to design the loss function. Specifically, to model the delay and jitter, considers that jitter is the variance of delay, the loss function is shown as:

$$l(u_i, \sigma_i) = -n_i \left(\frac{s^2(w_i)}{2\sigma_i^2} + \frac{(\overline{w}_i - u_i)^2}{2\sigma_i^2} + \log(\sigma_i) \right) \tag{7}$$

where n_i is total number of received packets, and u_i and σ_i are the outputs of the neural network, which represent the predictions of delay and jitter respectively. $\overline{w}_i$ and $s^2(w_i)$

are the labels of mean delay and jitter respectively. And the loss function is a variant of mean squared error, which is obtained by maximizing the log-likelihood function of the normal distribution.

Moreover, the loss function for drop ratio is given by:

$$l(p_i) = l_i \log(p_i) + n_i \log(1 - p_i) \tag{8}$$

where l_i is the observed number of packet losses, and p_i is the prediction of drop ratio.

Unlike the complex form of RoutNet [13], we simply denote the loss function of this task as:

$$loss = w_1 * MSE(y_1, \overline{y_1}) + w_2 * MSE(y_2, \overline{y_2}) + w_3 * MSE(y_3, \overline{y_3}) \tag{9}$$

where y_1, y_2, y_3 denote the label of delay, jitter and drop ratio, $\overline{y_1}, \overline{y_2}, \overline{y_3}$ is the predictions of delay, jitter and drop ratio, MSE is the naïve mean square error, which could be expressed by:

$$MSE(y, \overline{y}) = \frac{\sum_{i=1}^{n}(y_i - \overline{y_i})^2}{n} \tag{10}$$

where y_i is the label, $\overline{y_i}$ is the prediction and n is the number of test samples.

However, deciding the best choice for w_1, w_2 and w_3 is time-consuming and tend to get the suboptimal solution. Inspired by [30], we introduce a method to learn the weights automatically. The final loss function of this paper is:

$$loss = \frac{1}{2\sigma_1^2}MSE(y_1, \overline{y_1}) + \frac{1}{2\sigma_2^2}MSE(y_2, \overline{y_2}) + \frac{1}{2\sigma_3^2}MSE(y_3, \overline{y_3}) + \log(\sigma_1\sigma_2\sigma_3) \tag{11}$$

where $\sigma_1, \sigma_2, \sigma_3$ are three trainable parameters of the neural network, which represent the variance of these learning tasks, and the item $\log\sigma_i$ could pevent σ_i from being too large.

4.3 Sample Generation

We generate the training samples for our model with a packet-level simulator using OMNeT++ [9] implemented in C++. The overall framework of simulation environment can be described as the figure below. In addition, there are five modules of the simulation environment:

- Traffic Controller: control the source, destination node and traffic intensity (i.e., packets arrival time distribution);
- Application: control the distribution of packet size and the total simulation time;
- Routing: decide the port of next hop for the packets and whether the packets arrive the destination or exceed their TTLs;
- Node Queue: control the cache queues for each node, when the number of packets exceeds the queue size, packet loss will occur.
- Statistics: collect the statistics of various performance metrics, which used as features and labels for learning task.

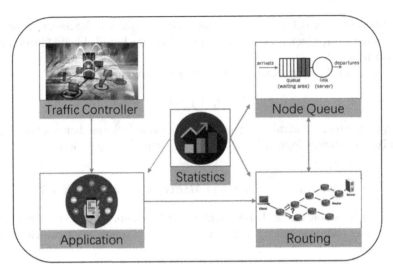

Fig. 4. The block diagram of simulation

The network topology of our simulation is a common fat-tree data center network [31]. The topology could be classified into three layers according to their link capacities: core, aggregate and access layer, which is 500,100 and 10 kbps respectively. In order to ensure the reality of the simulation environment, the flows are generated from the nodes of access layers and sent to the other nodes except the aggregate layers above, which follows:

$$TM(s_i, d_i) = \frac{U(0.1, 1) * U\left(TI_{low}, TI_{high}\right)}{N_{access}}, \forall s_i \in N_{access} \tag{12}$$

where $U(0.1, 1)$ is an uniform distribution in the range $[0.1, 1]$. TI represents a parameter about the traffic intensity which controls the congestion level of the network. $U(TI_{low}, TI_{high})$ is an uniform distribution in the range $\left[TI_{low}, TI_{high}\right]$. N_{access} is the number of access layer nodes. Note that in each simulation, the traffic and packets sent are different and fluctuate within a certain range.

The distribution of packet size follows log-normal distribution [32] with $\mu = 6, \sigma = 1$, which is one kind of the long tail distributions. And the probability density function of packet size is shown below, which describes traffic distribution of real data centers. The arrival times of packets are modeled with an exponential distribution whose mean is related to traffic intensity. The queue size of each node is 32 packets.

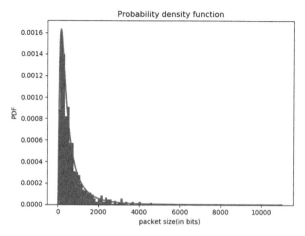

Fig. 5. Long-tail distribution of packet size

5 Experiments

5.1 Experiment Setup

In this section, we carry out several experiments to evaluate the proposed architecture. Specifically, experiments are conducted in the following settings:

- 36 nodes network, which consists of 48 edges, the flows are generated from the 16 nodes of access layer, with 336 source-destination pairs in total.
- 99 nodes network, which consists of 162 edges, the flows are generated from the 54 nodes of access layer, with 702 source-destination pairs in total.
- 36 + 99 nodes network, which is the combination of the above two settings.

Compared Methods. For fair comparison, we compare our method with RouteNet [13] (i.e., the state of the art) with the same parameters settings.

Parameters of Our Model. There are 30,000 samples in each network topology, which consist of 10,080,000 and 21,060,000 end-to-end paths in the 36 nodes and 99 nodes network respectively. The train, evaluation and test set are split into 7:2:1. We execute the training over the samples on the train set, and evaluate the model on the evaluation set. At last, we pick the best model with the least loss to infer the predictions on test set.

In our experiments, we select a size of 32 for both the paths' hidden states h_p and the links' hidden states h_l. The bandwidth of each source-destination path is set as the initial path states x_p and the link capacities are the initial link states x_l. There are three fully connected layers in the READOUT layer. And the number of hidden units in the first two layers and the last layer is 256 and 3 respectively. The number of iteration T is 8, batch size is 16, the dropout rate is equal to 0.5, and the number of training steps for each model is 150,000. What's more, the L2 regularization is used to prevent overfitting and make the model more robust. The total loss function is minimized using an Adam optimizer with an initial learning rate of 0.001. Note that the learning rate is exponential decay every 50000 steps, where the decay rate is 0.9. All the experiments are conducted with a GPU NVidia GeForce GTX TITAN Xp.

5.2 Experiment Results

As shown in Table 2, we evaluate the root mean squared error (RMSE), mean relative error (MRE) of the baseline RouteNet, and our approach in three experiments. It can be seen that, our method has lower values in both RMSE and MRE. Particularly, in the experiment of larger network topology of 99 nodes, our method could get a great improvement on the prediction of jitter, which shows that our method gains about 44.8% than the baseline in MRE.

Table 2. Summary of the evaluation results (RMSE, MRE)

	Delay				Jitter			
	RMSE		MRE		RMSE		MRE	
	RouteNet	Ours	RouteNet	Ours	RouteNet	Ours	RouteNet	Ours
36	0.01884	0.01659	0.03843	0.03514	0.01376	0.01292	0.0393	0.03725
99	0.18096	0.17553	0.04888	0.04881	0.07501	**0.03852**	0.06246	**0.03446**
36 + 99	0.15698	0.14473	0.04715	0.04992	0.08	**0.03275**	0.05851	**0.03625**

In our simulation datasets, there are many cases with zero drops, so we will face the dilemma of zero division when calculating the MRE. Table 3 shows the RMSE and R2 score of the prediction of drop ratio. As we can see, our approach could also get better results in both RMSE and R2 score on drop ratio prediction.

Table 3. Summary of the evaluation results (RMSE, R2 score)

	Drop ratio			
	RMSE		R2 score	
	RouteNet	Ours	RouteNet	Ours
36	0.00186	**0.00145**	0.95998	**0.97585**
99	0.00347	**0.00304**	0.98802	**0.99082**
36 + 99	0.00276	0.00266	0.98951	0.99027

In order to observe the overall distribution of relative error, we choose the experiment of 99 nodes for comparison. Note that we observe the similar results in the 36 + 99 nodes experiment setup.

Figure 6 shows the boxplot of the distribution of relative error, where we can see that the delay and drop ratio are nearly the same. However, we can get more accurate jitter predictions compared to the baseline (i.e., most relative errors are around zero) without any loss of delay and drop ratio prediction. However, we will face division by zero when computing the relative error for drop ratio. Therefore, we only plot the cases where we observed at least one packet dropped. But the cases with zero drop can be also predicted accurately due to the high value of R2 score shown in above table.

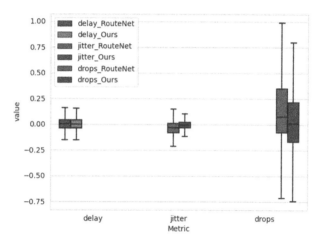

Fig. 6. The relative error distribution of 99 nodes

As shown in Fig. 7, we also present a cumulative distribution function (CDF) of the relative error about delay and jitter. According to the formula:

$$P(a < X \leq b) = F_X(b) - F_X(a) \tag{13}$$

we could get the probability of relative error in any intervals. It can be seen that, our methods get lower prediction errors in both delay and jitter.

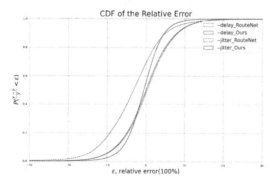

Fig. 7. The cumulative distribution (CDF) of the relative error (delay and jitter)

As we can see from Fig. 8, the CDF of relative error is nearly the same as the baseline, which implies that our approach will not cause any loss on drops prediction with only one model.

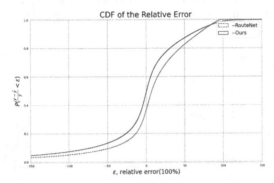

Fig. 8. The cumulative distribution (CDF) of the relative error (drop ratio)

6 Conclusion

In this paper, we propose a novel approach to model the data center networks, which leverages message passing neural network and multi-task learning to produce accurate estimates of per-source/destination mean delay, jitter and packet drop ratio with a unified model. Experimental results show that our approach can get better performance compared to the state of the art. The future research directions include generating more data to make the model applicable to more diverse network scenarios and introducing incremental learning or online learning methods to update the model continuously so that the generalization of the model is further enhanced.

Acknowledgment. The work is supported in part by the national key research and development program of China under grant No. 2019YFB2102200, the Natural Science Foundation of China under Grant No. 61902062 and the Jiangsu Provincial Natural Science Foundation of China under Grant No. BK20190332.

References

1. Mestres, A., Rodriguez-Natal, A., Carner, J., et al.: Knowledge-defined networking. ACM SIGCOMM Comput. Commun. Rev. **47**(3), 2–10 (2017)
2. Kreutz, D., Ramos, F.M.V., Verissimo, P.E., et al.: Software-defined networking: a comprehensive survey. Proc. IEEE **103**(1), 14–76 (2014)
3. Han, B., Gopalakrishnan, V., Ji, L., et al.: Network function virtualization: challenges and opportunities for innovations. IEEE Commun. Mag. **53**(2), 90–97 (2015)
4. Rusek, K., Suárez-Varela, J., Mestres, A., et al.: Unveiling the potential of graph neural networks for network modeling and optimization in SDN. In: Proceedings of the 2019 ACM Symposium on SDN Research, pp. 140–151 (2019)

5. Geyer, F., Bondorf, S.: DeepTMA: predicting effective contention models for network calculus using graph neural networks. In: IEEE INFOCOM 2019-IEEE Conference on Computer Communications, pp. 1009–1017. IEEE (2019)
6. Geyer, F., Bondorf, S.: On the robustness of deep learning-predicted contention models for network calculus. In: 2020 IEEE Symposium on Computers and Communications (ISCC), pp. 1–7. IEEE (2020)
7. Giambene, G.: Queuing Theory and Telecommunications: Networks and Applications. Springer, New York (2005)
8. Carneiro, G.: NS-3: network simulator 3. In: UTM Lab Meeting, vol. 20, pp. 4–5 (2010)
9. András, V.: The OMNeT++ discrete event simulation system. In: ESM 2001 (2001)
10. Goodfellow, I., Bengio, Y., Courville, A., et al.: Deep Learning. MIT Press, Cambridge (2016)
11. Shen, Z., Yang, H., Zhang, S.: Neural network approximation: three hidden layers are enough. arXiv preprint arXiv:2010.14075 (2020)
12. Mestres, A., Alarcón, E., Ji, Y., et al.: Understanding the modeling of computer network delays using neural networks. In: Proceedings of the 2018 Workshop on Big Data Analytics and Machine Learning for Data Communication Networks, pp. 46–52 (2018)
13. Rusek, K., Suárez-Varela, J., Almasan, P., et al.: RouteNet: leveraging graph neural networks for network modeling and optimization in SDN. IEEE J. Sel. Areas Commun. **38**(10), 2260–2270 (2020)
14. Ciucu, F., Schmitt, J.: Perspectives on network calculus: no free lunch, but still good value. In: Proceedings of the ACM SIGCOMM 2012 Conference on Applications, Technologies, Architectures, and Protocols for Computer Communication, pp. 311–322 (2012)
15. Eun, D.Y.: On the limitation of fluid-based approach for internet congestion control. Telecommun. Syst. **34**, 3–11 (2007)
16. Xiong, B., Yang, K., Zhao, J., et al.: Performance evaluation of OpenFlow-based software-defined networks based on queueing model. Comput. Netw. **102**, 172–185 (2016)
17. Li, G., Wang, X., Zhang, Z.: SDN-based load balancing scheme for multi-controller deployment. IEEE Access **7**, 39612–39622 (2019)
18. Altman, E., Basar, T., Jimenez, T., et al.: Competitive routing in networks with polynomial costs. IEEE Trans. Autom. Control **47**(1), 92–96 (2002)
19. Jain, S., Khandelwal, M., Katkar, A., et al.: Applying big data technologies to manage QoS in an SDN. In: 2016 12th International Conference on Network and Service Management (CNSM), pp. 302–306. IEEE (2016)
20. Al-Fares, M., Radhakrishnan, S., Raghavan, B., et al.: Hedera: dynamic flow scheduling for data center networks. In: NSDI 2010, vol. 10, no. (8), pp. 89–92 (2010)
21. Curtis, A.R., Kim, W., Yalagandula, P.: Mahout: low-overhead datacenter traffic management using end-host-based elephant detection. In: 2011 Proceedings IEEE INFOCOM, pp. 1629–1637. IEEE (2011)
22. Chiesa, M., Kindler, G., Schapira, M.: Traffic engineering with equal-cost-multipath: an algorithmic perspective. IEEE/ACM Trans. Netw. **25**(2), 779–792 (2016)
23. Wang, S., Zhang, J., Huang, T., et al.: Fdalb: flow distribution aware load balancing for datacenter networks. In: 2016 IEEE/ACM 24th International Symposium on Quality of Service (IWQoS), pp. 1–2. IEEE (2016)
24. Lin, S.C., Akyildiz, I.F., Wang, P., et al.: QoS-aware adaptive routing in multi-layer hierarchical software defined networks: a reinforcement learning approach. In: 2016 IEEE International Conference on Services Computing (SCC), pp. 25–33. IEEE (2016)
25. Leconte, M., Paschos, G.S., Mertikopoulos, P., et al.: A resource allocation framework for network slicing. In: IEEE INFOCOM 2018-IEEE Conference on Computer Communications, pp. 2177–2185. IEEE (2018)

26. Chen, L., Lingys, J., Chen, K., et al.: Auto: scaling deep reinforcement learning for datacenter-scale automatic traffic optimization. In: Proceedings of the 2018 Conference of the ACM Special Interest Group on Data Communication, pp. 191–205 (2018)
27. Gilmer, J., Schoenholz, S.S., Riley, P.F., et al.: Neural message passing for quantum chemistry. In: International Conference on Machine Learning, pp. 1263–1272. PMLR (2017)
28. Liu, S., Johns, E., Davison, A.J.: End-to-end multi-task learning with attention. In: Proceedings of the IEEE/CVF Conference on Computer Vision and Pattern Recognition, pp. 1871–1880 (2019)
29. Benesty, J., Chen, J., Huang, Y., et al.: Pearson correlation coefficient. In: Noise Reduction in Speech Processing, pp. 1-4. Springer, Heidelberg (2009)
30. Kendall, A., Gal, Y., Cipolla, R.: Multi-task learning using uncertainty to weigh losses for scene geometry and semantics. In: Proceedings of the IEEE Conference on Computer Vision and Pattern Recognition, pp. 7482–7491 (2018)
31. Leiserson, C.E.: Fat-trees: universal networks for hardware-efficient supercomputing. IEEE Trans. Comput. **100**(10), 892–901 (1985)
32. Zhang, J., Yu, F.R., Wang, S., et al.: Load balancing in data center networks: a survey. IEEE Commun. Surv. Tutorials **20**(3), 2324–2352 (2018)

Machine Learning, Data Mining, Data Security and Privacy Protection, and Data-Driven Applications

A Computational Model Based on Neural Network of Visual Cortex with Conceptors for Image Classification

Xiumin Li$^{(\boxtimes)}$, Jie Yu, and Wenqiang Xu

School of Automation, Chongqing University, Chongqing 400044, China
{xmli,wenqiangxu}@cqu.edu.cn, 2015500226@smail.xtu.edu.cn

Abstract. Artificial neural networks, especially for deep learning, has made great progress in image recognition in recent years. However, deep learning neural networks have the disadvantage of biologically implausibility and the excessive consumption of energy because of the non-local transmission of real-valued error signals and weights. With the rapid development of theories and applications in brain science, more and more researchers are paying attention to brain-inspired computational models in recent years. In this paper, we propose a novel computational model for image classification with conceptor networks and two visual cortex neural networks, including the primary visual layer (V1) and the feature orientation layer (V2). We have examined the performance of this model on the MNIST database, ORL face databases and CASIA-3D FaceV1 databases. Our model can achieve the same high classification accuracy with much fewer training samples than the other methods. Our results demonstrate that both of the orientation-selective characteristics of V2 layer and the feature detection of conceptors can provide remarkable contributions for efficient classification with small training samples.

Keywords: Spiking neural network · Conceptors · Image classification · Visual cortex

1 Introduction

Deep learning neural networks have made great progress in the field of machine learning and pattern recognition in recent years [1–6]. Researchers have developed many methods for image recognition, for example, softmax regression [7], support vector machine [8] and deep belief networks [9]. In these methods, convolutional neural networks (CNNs) are one of the most well-known models with efficient feature extraction methods and more often utilized for classification and computer vision tasks.

However, CNNs have the drawbacks of biologically implausibility and the excessive consumption of energy, which are dramatically different from what have been observed in in brain cortex in three main aspects. Firstly, current artificial intelligence focuses on computations in feedforward circuits with linear static units, which are much easier to be mathematically analyzed compared with the spiking neurons which consist of nonlinear

© Springer Nature Singapore Pte Ltd. 2021
H. Zhang et al. (Eds.): NCAA 2021, CCIS 1449, pp. 115–127, 2021.
https://doi.org/10.1007/978-981-16-5188-5_9

dynamical units and recurrently complex connections. Secondly, the non- local transfer of real-valued error signals and weights for CNNs is backpropagation [10], which is a supervised learning process and not commonly observed in the cortex [11]. Thirdly, both training and execution of large-scale CNNs need massive amounts of computational power to perform single tasks. Large number of training data and iteration times are needed to ensure the accuracy, causing excessive power consumption.

For these reasons, there has been a growing interest in spiking neural networks (SNNs) recently. In SNNs, all neurons operate in parallel and only the arrival of spike events triggers processing, i.e. the event-driven signal processing mechanism. It has been known that this non-continuous signal processing mechanism is quite efficient for computational tasks. However, relevant research on the brain-inspired intelligence with computational application of SNN is very limited. With enhanced understanding of the brain mechanisms responsible for image recognition in the visual cortex, some brain-inspired SNNs have been proposed [13–17]. Michael Beyeler et al. [18] present a visually-guided navigation model for robots exploring a real-world environment, based on a spiking neural network simulator (CARLsim) which is an efficient computing platform for large-scale spiking neural networks [19, 20]. They proposed a biologically plausible SNN model and achieved high recognition accuracy in the MNIST database of handwritten digits with only 2000 training samples.

Inspired from the above literature, in this paper, we propose a modified recurrent neural network with reservoir computing, i.e. conceptor network [21, 22] for image classification based on two visual cortex neural networks, including the primary visual layer (V1) and the feature orientation layer (V2). The conceptor network could load and store multiple signals into reservoir and filter the corresponding states via a 'conceptor' component, and finally realize the reconstruction of input which is the basis of achieving high precision classification [22]. It has overcome traditional classifiers failing to model new class of data by default for a supervised learning task. We demonstrate that this model is efficient for MNIST hand-written digit recognition, and face recognitions of the ORL dataset and CASIA-3D FaceV1 dataset. Our model can achieve the same high classification accuracy with much fewer training samples than the other methods.

The remainder of this paper is organized as follows: Sect. 2 induces neuron model and conceptor networks. Section 3 describes network structure and each module in the network structure in detail. Section 4 shows the results of recognition tasks on the MNIST database, ORL face databases and CASIA-3D FaceV1 databases. In Sect. 5, we present both advantages and disadvantages as well as some perspectives of our approach.

2   Methods

2.1   Spiking Neuron Model

Spiking neurons in the visual cortical networks are modeled by using the Izhikevich neuron [23]. The neuron model is a simplified two-dimensional system of ordinary differential equations from the Hodgkin-Huxley type neuron:

$$\frac{dv(t)}{dt} = 0.04v^2(t) + 5v(t) + 140 - u(t) + I_{syn}(t) \tag{1}$$

$$\frac{du(t)}{dt} = a(bv(t) - u(t)) \tag{2}$$

$$v(t)(v > 30) = c, u(t)(v > 30) = u(t) - d \tag{3}$$

where V is the membrane potential, I_{syn} is synaptic current, u is the recovery variable. And a, b, c, d in the above formula are four open parameters which can be set as different values according to different neuron types. In this paper, $a = 0.02$, $b = 0.2$, $c = -65$, $d = 8$.

Synaptic conductance g obeys the exponential decay and changed when presynaptic spikes arrived. It can be described by the following equation:

$$\frac{dg_r(t)}{dt} = \frac{1}{\tau_r} g_r(t) + \omega \sum_i \delta(t - t_i) \tag{4}$$

In Eq. (4), the subscript r denotes the receptor type, τ_r is time constant, ω is the weight of the synapse model. Here δ is the Dirac delta function, t_i is the arrival time of presynaptic spikes. There are four receptor types, that is, AMPA (fast excitation), NMDA (slow excitation), GABA$_a$ (fast inhibition), or GABA$_b$ (slow inhibition). τ_{AMPA} is the fast decay and set as 5 ms, τ_{NMDA} is slow decay and voltage-dependent which is set as 150 ms, τ_{GABAa} is the fast decay and set as 6 ms, τ_{GABAb} is the slow decay and set 150 ms [24, 25]. Rising time of synaptic conductance is simplified as instantaneous for AMPA, NMDA, and GABA$_a$ [24], but for GABA$_b$, its rising time is 10 ms [26]. Synaptic current I_{syn} in Eq. (1) for each neuron is given by:

$$I_{syn} = g_{AMPA}(V - 0) - g_{NMDA} \frac{\left((V + 80)/60\right)^2}{1 + \left((V + 80)/60\right)^2}(V - 0)$$
$$-g_{GABAa}(V + 70) - g_{GABAb}(V + 90) \tag{5}$$

For more details, please refer to the reference [25] and the CARLsim 2.0 release paper [19].

2.2 Conceptors

The conceptor is a neural computing mechanism that may be understood as a filter that characterizes temporal neural activation patterns [22]. Conceptor network can be considered as a modified recurrent network, comprising an input layer, a hidden layer, and an output layer. The hidden layer is composed of N recurrently connected neurons, which is called the dynamical reservoir. The network is driven by several dynamic input models $P^1, P^2, ..., P^j$, where P^j may be a stable or unstable single or multi-dimensional signal. When the neural network is driven by P^j, the active states of the hidden layer form a high-dimensional state space $X^j = (x1^j, x2^j, x3^j, ...xn^j)$. The input signal $P^j(n)$ enters the reservoir through the input weight matrix W_{in}. The states of reservoir network can be described as:

$$x^j(n + 1) = tanh(w * x^j(n) + w_{in}P^j(n + 1) + b) \tag{6}$$

Where x is the state vector of reservoir neurons, $w*$ is the internal connectivity matrix. W_{in} is the N * 1 dimensional input weight connection, and b is a bias term. Due to the hyperbolic tangent (tanh) excitation function, the state vector of the reservoir is limited in the range of $(-1,1)$. Initially, neurons in the reservoir layer are randomly connected. For the reservoir state sequences $x(1)$, $x(2)$,..., $x(L)$, the following cost function can be established:

$$J = \sum_{n=1...L} \frac{\|x(n) - cx(n)\|^2}{L} + \alpha^{-2}\|c\|^2 \tag{7}$$

C is the conceptor machine matrix, which describes the characteristic of the reservoir state space. α is an adjusting parameter for minimizing the objective cost function. The conceptor C can be obtained by using the random gradient descent method. R is correlation matrix and defined as $R = XX^T/L$. During the training stage, the following equation is employed to obtain a preliminary conceptor C for each image j:

$$C(R, \alpha) = R(R + \alpha^{-2}I)^{-1} \tag{8}$$

In (8) R corresponds to the correlation matrix of the jth image class. I refers to the identity matrix. By adjusting the parameter α, we can find an equilibrium where the objective function J in (7) is minimized. A more detailed explanation of the conceptor model can be found in [28].

Here the positive term of the conceptor C_j^+ is used as the decision basis for each recognition class. During the testing stage, image samples of each class were fed into the reservoir states. Similarity between the reservoir states x and each conceptor is calculated in the following way: $h^+ = xC_i^+x$. he output with the largest h^+ value is the classification result.

3   Network Structure

Here we performed all simulations in a large-scale SNN simulator platform CARLsim 2.20 [19]. Our network model consists of four layers, i.e., the input layer (MNIST grayscale images with 28 × 28 pixels), primary visual cortex layer (V1), orientation visual cortex layer (V2), Conceptors and decision layer (output layer). The architecture diagram is shown in Fig. 1. The details of each layer will be explained in the following sections.

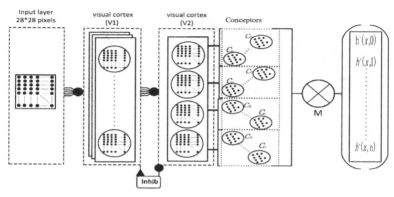

Fig. 1. Architecture of our proposed V1-V2-C model. The network consists of an input layer, V1 complex layer, V2 orientation layer and conceptors layer. Grayscale images are inputs for a feedforward visual cortex network consisting of V1 layer and V2 layer, which are projected to a downstream population of conceptors (output layer).

3.1 Visual Cortex (V1)

The input is the raw pixel value of 28*28 grayscale images and processed at three different spatiotemporal scales r = 0, 1, 2 (i.e. which represents color depth, namely R, G, B). The first scale r = 0 refers to the original input, and the other two scales need successive inputs to the previous scale using a Gaussian kernel function. The V1 layer consists of three banks of spatiotemporal filters which were constructed by using rate-based motion energy model [13]. Since the motion energy model expected movies rather than static images as an input, each image is expanded into videos (20 frames with each duration of 50 ms) and the input images are fed frame-by-frame through V1 layer. Filter responses were then interpreted as the mean firing rates of Poisson spike trains which are the input of V1 spiking neurons. For more details about a complete model description and the selection of model parameters, please refer to [18–20].

3.2 The Orientation Layer (V2)

V2 only consists of spiking neurons which receive the input from V1 spiking neurons. Neurons in the orientation layer V2 respond preferentially to one of the four spatial orientations, i.e. horizontal direction "H", right diagonal "RD", vertical "V" and left diagonal "LD". That is, neurons respond strongly to their preferred input orientations, but weakly to the other orientations. This layer consists of four 28*28 neuron pools, including a total of 3136 neurons corresponding to 28 × 28 pixels in four orientations. The firing rate of V2 neurons encodes the four orientation information for each image. Here, V1 and V2 layers are established by using the CARLSim platform which is available on the website http://www.socsci.uci.edu/jkrichma/CARLsim/. Orientation-selective responses for different digit samples are shown in Fig. 2. Firing rates are color coded ranging from 0 Hz (blue) to 50 Hz (white).

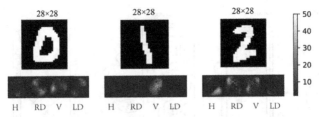

Fig. 2. Orientation-selective responses for different digit samples (28*28). Each image is spatially expanded into four groups of orientation-selective neurons in the V2 layer. Each group of neurons selectively responded to one of four spatial orientations, i.e. horizontal "H," right diagonal "RD," vertical "V" and left diagonal "LD". The color coding of the firing rate ranges from 0 Hz (blue) to 50 Hz (white). (Color figure online)

3.3 Decision Output Layer

Each pool of orientation-selective neurons in V2 are fully connected with N conceptor networks, where N is the number of classification types. For the MNIST dataset, N equals to 10. The number of neurons in the conceptor layers is also set as 10. During the training stage, training samples of each digit are fed into the V1 and V2 orientation layer and explored into four groups of firing rates of the V2 neuron population corresponding to the four orientation information, i.e. horizontal direction "H", right diagonal "RD", vertical "V" and left diagonal "LD". Then, we employ Eq. (8) to obtain four preliminary conceptors C_H, C_{LD}, C_V, C_{RD}. for each digit. These conceptors store the dynamical characteristics of each digit pattern in four orientations, which can be obtained by using the random gradient descent method. During the testing state, similarities h^+ between reservoir states x and each conceptor C in the four orientations are calculated by $h^+ = x^T C_i^+ x$ respectively. The average value h^+ of the four similar-ties for each digit type is calculated as $h^+ = (h_H + h_{LD} + h_V + h_{RD})/4$. The output with the largest h^+ value is the classification result. The notation 'M' shown in Fig. 1 refers to the average calculation.

4 Results

The computational ability of our proposed model on image classification is examined based on the extensively studied MNIST database for handwritten-digits classification, ORL databases and CASIA-3D FaceV1 databases for face recognition. The results of each experiment are shown in the following subsections.

4.1 The MNIST Database

The original MNIST dataset consists of 60,000 training samples of hand-written numerals, and 10,000 for test set. The 28*28 pixel images are fed into the V1 and V2 orientation layer and explored into four groups of firing rates of the V2 neuron population corresponding to the four orientation information. The orientation information is then trained and stored in four conceptors for each digit type. For each testing image, the digital recognition is realized by calculating the largest average similarity between current neuronal states and conceptors. The average similarity of four orientations is obtained by h^+

$= (h_H + h_{LD} + h_V + h_{RD})/4$, output with the largest h^+ is selected as the classification result. The basic idea of this process is that if the reserve pool is driven by the correct digit type, the resulting reserve pool state is located in a linear subsystem of its state space. Figure 3 shows ten digital classification criteria h^+. The brighter the color is, the higher the value is. We can see that the maximum values for each digit are on the diagonal, corresponding to the correct recognition.

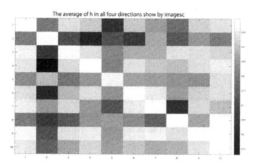

Fig. 3. Ten digital classification results based on the similarity criteria h^+.

Since convolutional neural networks (CNN) are the most well-known models with efficient feature extraction, we specifically compared the computational accuracy of our model and a traditional CNN in the task with different training sample numbers. Here CNN is a 2-layer convolutional neural network, consisting of 32 convolution kernels of size 3×3. Two pooling layers of 2×2 window size, and a fully connected layer of 128 $\times$ 10. Figure 4 presents our V1-V2-C model on digital handwriting recognition. In this experiment, the number of testing samples remain unchanged, namely 1000 datasets. We can see from Fig. 4 that the accuracy of our model increases exponentially and reaches to 90% when the number of training samples is larger than 100. Compared with the traditional 2-layer CNN, our model shows remarkable improvement of recognition performance especially when the number of training samples is very small. Big data of training samples (usually 60,000) as commonly used in CNNs is not necessary for this model, since the computing accuracy keeps stable and has no significant increase when training sample reaches to 500.

The recognition performance of different models on MNIST classification is shown in Table 1. Our model can achieve the same high classification accuracy with much fewer training samples than the other methods. Among these models, our model shows the highest accuracy with the same number of training set and testing set. Our results demonstrate that the original image are expanded into high dimensional information through the processing of orientation-selective V2 layer. Feature extraction of the four orientations provides the main contribution to reduce the training samples. Our results also show that the conceptors are efficient for feature detections to capture the dynamical characteristics of each orientation information, which further improves the recognition performance.

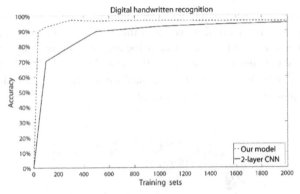

Fig. 4. The comparison of classification accuracy between our model and CNN in the tasks for different number of training samples. The testing sample is 1000. Here CNN is a 2-layer convolutional neural network consisting of 32 convolution kernels of size 3 × 3, two pooling layers of 2 × 2 window size, and a fully connected layer of 128 × 10.

Table 1. The comparison of classification performance with other models for MNIST database.

Model	Architecture	Train	Test	Accuracy
Michael Beyeler et al. [20]	SNN+STDP	2000	1000	92%
Peter U. Diehl et al. [29]	Spiking Deep NN	60,000	10,000	98.6%
redo Spiking Deep NN [29]	Spiking Deep NN	2000	1000	90.5%
PeterOConnor et al. [30]	LIF+event-based	60,000	10,000	94.09%
Yuhuang Huk et al. [31]	Conceptor Network	60,000	10,000	97.49%
redo Conceptor Network [31]	Conceptor Network	2000	1000	92.9%
Our model	V1-V2-C	2000	1000	97.5%
Our mode	V1-V2-C	300	1000	97.3%

4.2 The ORL Face Database

From the above handwritten digit recognition experiment, we can see that our model has very good classification ability. To further verify the computational performance of our model, face recognition is also examined based on the ORL face database. The ORL face database contains 400 facial images of 40 individuals with 10 samples for each person (see Fig. 5). There are variations in facial expressions (open or closed eyes, smiling or non-smiling) and facial details (glasses or no glasses). All images are gray with 256 levels and size of 112*92 pixels. Here the original images are scaled into 28*28 pixels. It can be obtained from http://www.cl.cam.ac.uk/research/dtg/at-tarchive/facedatabase.html.

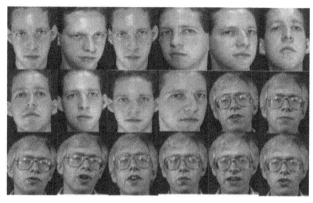

Fig. 5. The ORL face examples. There are variations in facial expressions (open or closed eyes, smiling or non-smiling) and facial details.

Facial expressions (open or closed eyes, smiling or non-smiling) and facial details (glasses or no glasses). All images are gray with 256 levels and size of 112*92 pixels you can get it from http://www.cl.cam.ac.uk/research/dtg/attarchive/facedatabase.html. A schematic diagram of two of them can be seen from Fig. 6.

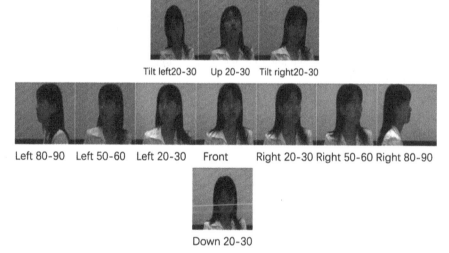

Fig. 6. The CASIA-3D FaceV1 face database.

The comparison of performance with other models for face recognition is shown in Table 2. Here we use the total 400 face images of 40 persons, where 240 samples for training and 160 images for testing. It can be seen that our model can achieve the high accuracy of 95.63%. However, since there are only 10 samples for each person in the ORL database, both training and testing samples are very limited. Therefore, the advantage of our model for small sample recognition is not obvious. Another database for face recognition is used in the following subsection.

Table 2. The comparison of recognition performance with other models for ORL face database.

Model	Method	Train	Test	Accuracy
Yongfeng Qi et al. [32]	(2D)^{2}PCALDA	200	1000	92%
Yongfeng Qi et al. [32]	(2D)^{2}PCALDA	200	10,000	98.6%
Young-Gil Kim et al. [33]	A fusion method based on bidirectional 2DPCA	200	1000	90.5%
Guodong Guo et al. [34]	SVMs	200	10,000	94.09%
Geng Li et al. [35]	1-Level DWT/2DLPP	120	10,000	97.49%
Our model	V1-V2-C	240	1000	97.5%

4.3   The CASIA-3D FaceV1 Database

The CASIA-3D FaceV1 database is collected by the Chinese Academy of Sciences Institute of Automation (CASIA) and can be loaded at http://biometrics.idealtest.org. The face recognition data for test verification come from http://www.nlpr.ia.ac.cn/CN-/folder/folder8.shtml. We use the BMP1-30 dataset of CASIA-3D Face V1 and take its first 10 images for testing. In this database, there are 37–38 samples for each person, containing one 2D color image and one 3D facial triangulated surface. Several image samples are shown in Fig. 6.

Table 3. The comparison of recognition performance with other models for CASIA-3D Face V1 database.

Model	Architecture	Train	Test	Accuracy
Our model	4 Directions	240	100	89%
Our mode	8 Directions	240	100	94%

In this database, we randomly select 10 persons' images for the experiment, where 240 samples for training, 100 samples for testing. Table 3 shows that recognition accuracy of our model is 89%. In order to improve the recognition accuracy, the number of orientations in V2 layer is expanded from 4 directions into 8 directions (that is, select the direction by pi/4 angle). The schematic diagram of digit '0' extended from 4 to 8 directions is shown in Fig. 7. With the same training and testing samples, the recognition accuracy of our model can achieve 94%, which is much higher than the case of 4 directions in V2 layer. Our results indicate that the finer the direction feature extraction in V2 layer, the higher the recognition accuracy can be obtained.

28×28   28×112

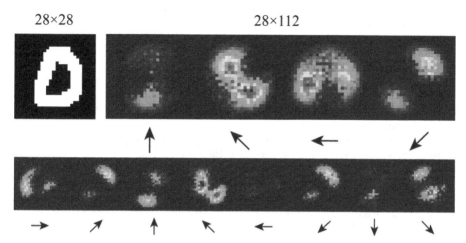

Fig. 7. Image examples and their corresponding orientation-selective responses for digit '0' extended from 4 to 8 directions. Firing rates are color-coded ranging from 0 Hz (blue) to 50 Hz (red).

5   Conclusion

In this paper, we propose a brain-inspired computational model to recognize image by building neural networks with conceptors based on visual cortex V1 and V2 layers. We have examined the performance of this model on the MNIST database, ORL face databases and CASIA-3D FaceV1 databases. Our model can achieve the same high classification accuracy with much fewer training samples than the other methods. Our results demonstrate that both of the orientation-selective characteristics of V2 layer and feature detection of conceptors can provide remarkable contributions for efficient classification with small training samples. In the face recognition experiment of the CASIA-3D FaceV1 database, we also find that recognition accuracy can be obviously improved by increasing the number of directions in the orientation V2 layer. This result indicates that the finer the direction feature extraction in V2 layer, the higher the recognition accuracy can be obtained.

References

1. Ioffe, S., Szegedy, C.: Batch normalization: accelerating deep network training by reducing internal covariate shift. CoRR, vol. abs/1502.03167 (2015)
2. Ng, J.Y.-H., Hausknecht, M., Vijayanarasimhan, S., Vinyals, O., Monga, R., Toderici, G.: Beyond short snippets: deep networks for video classification. CoRR, vol. abs/1503.08909 (2015)

3. Schroff, F., Kalenichenko, D., Philbin, J.: Facenet: a unified embedding for face recognition and clustering. CoRR, vol. abs/1503.03832 (2015)
4. Szegedy, C., et al.: Going deeper with convolutions. CoRR, vol. abs/1409.4842 (2014)
5. Mnih, V., et al.: Human-level control through deep reinforcement learning. Nature **518**(7540), 529–533 (2015)
6. Karpathy, A., Toderici, G., Shetty, S., Leung, T., Sukthankar, R., FeiFei, L.: Large-scale video classification with convolutional neural networks. In: The IEEE Conference on Computer Vision and Pattern Recognition (CVPR) (2014)
7. Bishop, C.: Pattern Recognition and Machine Learning, pp. 140–155. Springer, New York (2006)
8. Chang, C.-C., Lin, C.-J.: Libsvm: a library for support vector machines. ACM Trans. Intel. Syst. Technol. **2**(3), 1–27 (2011)
9. Mohamed, A.-R., Dahl, G.E., Hinton, G.: Acoustic modeling using deep belief networks. IEEE Trans. Audio Speech Language Process. **20**(1), 14–22 (2012)
10. Rumelhart, D.E., Hinton, G.E., Williams, R.J., et al.: Learning representations by back-propagating errors. Cognit. Model. **5**(3), 1 (1988)
11. OReilly, R.C., Munakata, Y.: Computational Explorations in Cognitive Neuroscience: Understanding the Mind by Simulating the Brain. MIT Press, Cambridge (2000)
12. Bogler, C., Bode, S., Haynes, J.D.: Orientation pop-out processing in human visual cortex. Neuroimage **81**(6), 73–80 (2013)
13. Simoncelli, E.P., Heeger, D.J.: A model of neuronal responses in visual area MT. Vis. Res. **38**(5), 743–761 (1998)
14. Miller, C.E., Shapiro, K.L., Luck, S.J.: Electrophysiological measurement of the effect of inter-stimulus competition on early cortical stages of human vision. Neuroimage **105**, 229–237 (2015)
15. Beyeler, M., Richert, M., Dutt, N.D., et al.: Efficient spiking neural network model of pattern motion selectivity in visual cortex. Neuroinformatics **12**(3), 435–454 (2014)
16. Kamitani, Y., Tong, F.: Decoding seen and attended motion directions from activity in the human visual cortex. Curr. Biol. **16**(11), 1096–1102 (2006)
17. Kamitani, Y., Tong, F.: Decoding the visual and subjective contents of the human brain. Nat. Neurosci. **8**(5), 679–685 (2005)
18. Beyeler, M., Oros, N., Dutt, N., et al.: A GPU-accelerated cortical neural network model for visually guided robot navigation. Neural Netw. **72**, 75–87 (2015)
19. Richert, M., Nageswaran, J.M., Dutt, N., et al.: An efficient simulation environment for modeling large-scale cortical processing. Front. Neuroinform. **5**(19), 19 (2011)
20. Beyeler, M., Dutt, N.D., Krichmar, J.L.: Categorization and decision-making in a neurobiologically plausible spiking network using a STDP-like learning rule. Neural Netw. **48**(10), 109–124 (2013)
21. Jaeger, H., Haas, H.: Harnessing nonlinearity: Predicting chaotic systems and saving energy in wireless communication. Science **304**(5667), 78–80 (2004)
22. Jaeger, H.: Using conceptors to manage neural long-term memories for temporal patterns. J. Mach. Learn. Res. **18**(13), 1–43 (2017)
23. Izhikevich, E.M.: Simple model of spiking neurons. IEEE Trans. Neural Netw. **14**, 1569–1572 (2003)
24. Dayan, P., Abbott, L.: Theoretical neuroscience: computational and mathematical modeling of neural systems. Philos. Psychol. **15**(1), 154–155 (2001)
25. Izhikevich, E.M., Gally, J.A., Edelman, G.M.: Spike-timing dynamics of neuronal groups. Cereb. Cortex **14**(8), 933–944 (2004)
26. Koch, C.: Biophysics of Computation: Information Processing in Single Neurons Computational Neuroscience Series. Oxford University Press, Oxford (1999)

27. Jaeger, H.: Controlling recurrent neural networks by conceptors (2014). arXiv:1403.3369
28. Diehl, P.U., Neil, D., Binas, J., et al.: Fast-classifying, high-accuracy spiking deep networks through weight and threshold balancing. In: International Joint Conference on Neural Networks, pp. 1–8. IEEE (2015)
29. Peter, O., Daniel, N., Liu, S.C., et al.: Real-time classification and sensor fusion with a spiking deep belief network. Front. Neurosci. **7**(7), 178 (2013)
30. Hu, Y., Ishwarya, M.S., Chu, K.L.: Classify images with conceptor network. Comput. Sci. (2015)
31. Qi, Y., Zhang, J.: (2D)2PCALDA: An Efficient Approach for Face Recognition. Elsevier Science Inc., Amsterdam (2009)
32. Kim, Y.G., Song, Y.J., Chang, U.D., et al.: Face recognition using a fusion method based on bidirectional 2DPCA. Appl. Math. Comput.. **205**(2), 601–607 (2008)
33. Guo, G., Li, S.Z., Chan, K.: Proceedings of the Face Recognition by Support Vector Machines IEEE International Conference on Automatic Face and Gesture Recognition, 2000, pp. 196–201. IEEE (2002)
34. Li, G., Zhou, B., Su, Y.N.: Face recognition algorithm using two dimensional locality preserving projection in discrete wavelet domain. Open Automat. Contr. Syst. J. **7**(1), 1721–1728 (2015)
35. Braitenberg, V., Schz, A.: Cortex: Statistics and Geometry of Neuronal Connectivity. Springer, Heidelberg (1998)

Smoothed Multi-view Subspace Clustering

Peng Chen[1], Liang Liu[2], Zhengrui Ma[2], and Zhao Kang[2,3](✉)

[1] Jangsu Automation Research Institute, Lianyungang, Jiangsu, China
[2] University of Electronic Science and Technology of China, Chengdu, Sichuan, China
Zkang@uestc.edu.cn
[3] Trusted Cloud Computing and Big Data Key Laboratory of Sichuan Province, Chengdu, Sichuan, China

Abstract. In recent years, multi-view subspace clustering has achieved impressive performance due to the exploitation of complementary information across multiple views. However, multi-view data can be very complicated and are not easy to cluster in real-world applications. Most existing methods operate on raw data and may not obtain the optimal solution. In this work, we propose a novel multi-view clustering method named smoothed multi-view subspace clustering (SMVSC) by employing a novel technique, i.e., graph filtering, to obtain a smooth representation for each view, in which similar data points have similar feature values. Specifically, it retains the graph geometric features through applying a low-pass filter. Consequently, it produces a "clustering-friendly" representation and greatly facilitates the downstream clustering task. Extensive experiments on benchmark datasets validate the superiority of our approach. Analysis shows that graph filtering increases the separability of classes.

Keywords: Multi-view learning · Subspace clustering · Graph filtering · Smooth representation

1 Introduction

As one of the most fundamental tasks in data mining, pattern recognition, and machine learning, clustering has been extensively used as a preprocessing step to facilitate other tasks or a standalone exploratory tool to reveal underlying structure of data [8]. According to their intrinsic similarities, it partitions unlabeled data points into disjoint groups. Nevertheless, clustering performance can be easily affected by many factors, including data representation, feature dimension, and noise [41]. Clustering is still a challenging task though numerous progresses have been made in the past few decades [33,42].

Specifically, there are a number of classical clustering algorithms, including K-means clustering, DBSCAN, agglomerative clustering, spectral clustering. It is well-known that K-Means works best for data evenly distributed around some

© Springer Nature Singapore Pte Ltd. 2021
H. Zhang et al. (Eds.): NCAA 2021, CCIS 1449, pp. 128–140, 2021.
https://doi.org/10.1007/978-981-16-5188-5_10

centroids [20,37], which is hard to satisfy in real-world data. Afterwards, numerous techniques, including kernel trick, principal component analysis, and canonical correlation analysis, are applied to map the raw data to a certain space that better suits K-means. In recent years, spectral clustering has become popular due to its impressive performance and well-defined mathematical framework [24]. Many variants of spectral clustering have been developed in the literature [4]. The performance of such methods heavily depend on the quality of similarity graph [13]. Some recent efforts are made to automatically learn a graph from data [15,30].

During the last decade, subspace clustering (SC) has attracted considerable attention due to its capability in partitioning high dimensional data [22]. It assumes that data lie in or near some low-dimensional subspaces and each data point can be expressed as a linear combination of others from the same subspace. The learned coefficient matrix Z is treated as a similarity graph and then it is fed to a spectral clustering algorithm. Consequently, each cluster corresponds to one subspace [18]. Two seminal subspace clustering models are sparse subspace clustering (SSC) [6] and low-rank representation (LRR) [19]. For Z, SSC enforces ℓ_1-norm to achieve a sparse solution, while LRR applies the nuclear norm to obtain a low-rank representation. To capture non-linear relationships, some kernel-based subspace clustering [14] and deep neural networks based methods have been developed [9,12].

In the era of big data, increasing volume of data are collected from multiple views. For instance, news can be reported in different languages and in the form of texts, images, and videos [10,36]; an image can be represented by different features, e.g., GIST, LBP, Garbor, SIFT, and HoG [3,5]. Therefore, many multiview subspace clustering methods have been proposed to explore the consensus and complementary information across multiple views [32]. For example, [7] learns a graph for each view and let them share a unique cluster indicator matrix; [2] explicitly incorporates the diversity of views; [16] performs information fusion in partition space; [39] performs learning in a latent space. Nevertheless, these methods have a high time complexity. Until recently, a linear algorithm for multi-view subspace clustering was developed by Kang et al. [11,17].

We observe that most of the existing multi-view subspace clustering methods operate on the raw data. In real-world applications, complex high-dimensional data in original data space itself might not satisfy self-expression property so that the data are not be separable into subspaces. Therefore, some studies perform subspace clustering in an alternative representation space instead of the original domain. The motivation is that the data are separable after being projected into a new domain. In particular, there are two categories of methods, i.e., [27] learns a tight-frame for subspace clustering; [9] learn a latent representation via auto-encoders. The former class are shallow techniques which lack high discriminative capability while the later are deep learning approaches which involve large number of parameters and are computationally expensive.

In this paper, we manage to find a smooth representation for multi-view subspace clustering, in which similar samples will have similar representations. Therefore, this representation is "clustering-friendly", i.e., it is easy to cluster. To this end, we preserves the graph geometric features by applying a low-pass filter. Putting it differently, the structure information carried by similarity graph is employed to extract meaningful data representation for clustering. To verify the effectiveness of our approach, we examine it on multi-view model. Notably, the proposed strategy is general enough to integrate with various multi-view subspace clustering models. Extensive experiments and analysis demonstrate our superiority.

The main contributions of this paper are summarized as follows:

- A graph filtering framework for multi-view subspace clustering is developed, which provides a new representation learning strategy.
- Remarkable improvements brought by graph filtering are demonstrated on multi-view datasets.
- Experimental analysis shows that the graph filtering obviously pushes different clusters apart.

2   Preliminaries and Related Work

2.1   Graph Filtering

Given an affinity matrix $W \in \mathbb{R}^{n \times n}$ of an undirected graph G, where $w_{ij} = w_{ji} \geq 0$ and n is the number of nodes, the degree matrix and symmetrically normalized Laplacian can be derived as $D = diag(d_1, \cdots, d_n)$ and $L_s = I - D^{-\frac{1}{2}} W D^{-\frac{1}{2}}$, where $d_i = \sum_{j=1}^{n} w_{ij}$. Since L_s is real-symmetric, it could be eigen-decomposed as $L_s = U \Lambda U^{\top}$, where $U = [u_1, \cdots, u_n]$ is an unitary matrix and the eigenvalues $\Lambda = diag(\lambda_1, \cdots, \lambda_n)$ are sorted in increasing order. The eigenvectors, i.e., $\{u_1, \cdots, u_n\}$, are the Fourier basis associated with the graph G and the corresponding eigenvalues λ_i indicate their frequencies [31].

A *graph signal* is in fact a mapping function f defined on the nodes, i.e., $f = [f(v_1), f(v_2), ..., f(v_n)]^{\top}$. When a feature matrix $X = [x_1, \cdots, x_n]^{\top} \in \mathbb{R}^{n \times m}$ is given in real-world application, each feature dimension can be considered as a signal on the graph nodes. A graph signal is then denoted as a linear combination of the Fourier basis of the graph,

$$f = \sum_{i=1}^{n} c_i u_i = U c, \tag{1}$$

where $c = [c_1, c_2, ..., c_n]^{\top}$ represents the Fourier coefficient and the absolute value of c_i suggests the strength of the basis signal u_i in the graph signal f. Thus, we can measure the smoothness of graph signal f in frequency domain by

$$E_f = \frac{1}{2} \sum_{i,j=1}^{n} w_{ij} \| \frac{f_i}{\sqrt{d_i}} - \frac{f_j}{\sqrt{d_j}} \|_2^2 = f^{\top} L_s f$$

$$= (U c)^{\top} L_s U c = \sum_{i=1}^{n} c_i{}^2 \lambda_i. \tag{2}$$

This formulation shows that smooth signal should have small eigenvalue. Therefore, a smooth signal f mainly contains low-frequency basis signals [40].

In practice, the natural signal is often smooth since the graph signal values change slowly between connected neighbor nodes. If we want to get a smooth signal after filtering, a low-pass graph filter G can be applied. Define $h(\lambda_i)$ as the low-pass frequency response function and its value should decrease when the frequency λ_i increase. Since the eigenvalues of L_s fall into $[0, 2]$, a simple low-pass filter could be designed as $h(\lambda_i) = (1 - \frac{\lambda_i}{2})^k$, where $k > 0$ is an integer capturing the k-hop neighborhood relationship [23]. Then, the filtered $\bar{f}$ could be formulated as

$$\bar{f} = Gf = \sum_{i=1}^{n} h(\lambda_i)c_i u_i = UH(\Lambda)c = UH(\Lambda)U^\top f$$

$$= U(I - \frac{\Lambda}{2})^k U^{-1} f = (I - \frac{L_s}{2})^k f. \tag{3}$$

We can also employ this low-pass filter on X to achieve a smoothed representation $\bar{X}$, i.e.,

$$\bar{X} = (I - \frac{L_s}{2})^k X. \tag{4}$$

For $\bar{X}$, nearby nodes will have very similar feature values in each dimension. Equation (4) can be expanded as following

$$\bar{x}_i^{(0)} = x_i, \quad \bar{x}_i^{(1)} = \frac{1}{2}\left(\bar{x}_i^{(0)} + \sum_j \frac{w_{ij}}{\sqrt{d_i d_j}}\bar{x}_j^{(0)}\right), \cdots,$$

$$\bar{x}_i^{(k)} = \frac{1}{2}\left(\bar{x}_i^{(k-1)} + \sum_j \frac{w_{ij}}{\sqrt{d_i d_j}}\bar{x}_j^{(k-1)}\right).$$

We can see that $\bar{x}_i$, i.e., $\bar{x}_i^k$, is obtained by aggregating the features of its neighbors iteratively. Notably, the j-th point won't contribute anything to $\bar{x}_i$ if they are not connected, i.e., $w_{ij} = 0$. Hence, it incorporates long-distance data relations, which would be beneficial for downstream tasks.

2.2 Multi-view Subspace Clustering

It can be known from the above discussion that numerous subspace clustering studies have been proposed. Let $X \in \mathbb{R}^{n \times m}$ be a set of n data points, and then subspace clustering aims to identify the subspaces by expressing each sample as a linear combination of other samples. The math model can be simplified as

$$\min_Z \|X^\top - X^\top Z\|_F^2 + \alpha R(Z), \tag{5}$$

where $\alpha > 0$ is a trade-off parameter and $R(\cdot)$ is a regularization term. The subspace information is embedded in the coefficient matrix Z. The learned coefficient matrix Z is often regarded as a similarity graph and then it is fed to a spectral clustering algorithm. Following above procedures, a great number of subspace clustering methods have been proposed [21,29].

Recently, multi-view subspace clustering (MVSC) has achieved significant success. Generally, for multi-view data $X = [X^1; \cdots; X^i; \cdots; X^v] \in \mathcal{R}^{\sum_{i=1}^{v} n \times m_i}$, MVSC aims to solve:

$$\min_{\{Z^i\}_{i=1}^v} \sum_{i=1}^{v} \|X^{i\top} - X^i Z^i\|_F^2 + \alpha R(Z^i). \tag{6}$$

Here, Eq. (6) provides different solutions with different forms of R. For example, [35] enforces agreement between pairs of graphs; [2] emphasizes the complementarity of different views. In the case of multiple graphs, [7] assumes that they produce the same clustering result; [2,35] perform spectral clustering on averaged graph.

Nevertheless, most existing subspace clustering methods often operate on the raw data without incorporating the inherent graph structure information contained in the data points. Manifold regularization is a popular way to incorporate graph information [38], but it involves an additional term. In practice, the data might not be easy to partition in the original domain. Therefore, some methods project the data into a new space [27]. Another category of methods are inspired by the success of deep learning and implement subspace clustering with the latent representation learned by auto-encoders [9,28]. The former class of methods are shallow techniques which lack high discriminative capability while the later are deep learning approaches which involve large number of parameters and are computationally expensive.

3   Proposed Methodology

Finding a suitable representation is paramount for the performance of subspace clustering. Based on the cluster assumption, adjacent points are more likely belonging to the same cluster. Putting it differently, points from the same cluster should have similar feature values. Motivated by the theory of graph filtering, we apply a low-pass graph filter on the raw data to achieve a smooth representation, which in turn makes the downstream clustering task easier.

3.1   Smoothed Multi-view Subspace Clustering

For multi-view data, we could apply graph filtering strategy on it. In this paper, we choose the recently proposed large-scale multi-view subspace clustering (LMVSC) [17] model to demonstrate it. This technique can obtain the partitions in $O(n)$ time. Specifically, for each view X^i, rather than learning a $n \times n$ graph, it constructs a smaller matrix $Z^i \in \mathbb{R}^{n \times p}$, which characterizes the relations between p landmarks $\bar{A}^i \in \mathbb{R}^{m_i \times p}$ and the original data $X^i \in \mathbb{R}^{n \times m_i}$. The landmarks are supposed to well represent the whole data samples, which can be obtained by K-means or random sampling. Our proposed smoothed multi-view subspace clustering (SMVSC) can be formulated as

$$\min_{\{Z^i\}_{i=1}^v} \sum_{i=1}^{v} \|\bar{X}^{i\top} - \bar{A}^i (Z^i)^\top\|_F^2 + \alpha \|Z^i\|_F^2. \tag{7}$$

Here, we employ certain graph construction method, e.g., the probabilistic neighbor method [26], to build a graph for each view X^i. Then, for the graph filtering part, we can specify the number of filtering k and a smoothed representation $\bar{X}^i = X^i(I - \frac{L_i}{2})^k$ for each view is obtained. For subspace clustering part, we run K-means on $\bar{X}^i$ and let g cluster centers form $\bar{A}^i$. Equation (7) produces Z^i for each view.

Afterwards, we define $\bar{Z} = [Z^1, \cdots, Z^i, \cdots, Z^v] \in \mathcal{R}^{n \times pv}$. It has been shown that the spectral embedding matrix $Q \in \mathcal{R}^{n \times g}$, i.e., consisting of the g left singular vectors, can be achieved by applying singular value decomposition (SVD) on $\bar{Z}$. Eventually, K-means is implemented on Q to obtain the final partitions. The complete steps for our SMVSC method is summarized in Algorithm 1.

Note that SMVSC algorithm is iteration-free and very efficient. Specifically, the computation of Q costs $\mathcal{O}(p^3 v^3 + 2pvn)$ and the subsequent K-means consumes $\mathcal{O}(ng^2)$. Solving Z^i takes $\mathcal{O}(np^3 v)$. Since $p, v \ll n$, the overall complexity is linear to the sample number.

Algorithm 1. SMVSC algorithm

Input: Multi-view data $X^1, \cdots, X^i, \cdots, X^v \in \mathcal{R}^{\sum_{i=1}^{v} n \times m_i}$
Parameter: filter order k, trade-off parameter α,
anchor number p, cluster number g

1: Build a graph for each view by the probabilistic neighbor method
2: Apply k times graph filter on $X^1, \cdots, X^i, \cdots, X^v$ to obtain the smooth representation $\bar{X}^1, \cdots, \bar{X}^i, \cdots, \bar{X}^v$
3: Run K-means on $\bar{X}^i$ form landmark $\bar{A}^i \in \mathbb{R}^{m_i \times p}$, and calculate $Z^i \in \mathbb{R}^{n \times p}$ by Eq. (7), which is composed of $\bar{Z} \in \mathcal{R}^{n \times pv}$
4: Calculate Q by performing SVD on $\bar{Z}$
5: Achieve the cluster partitions by performing K-means clustering on Q

Output: g partitions

---

4 Multi-view Experiments

In this section, we execute several experiments on multi-view datasets to demonstrate the effectiveness of our approach. The source code is available at https://github.com/EricliuLiang/SMVSC.

4.1 Dataset

Several benchmark datasets, including Handwritten, Caltech-101 and Citeseer are applied. Handwritten contains images of digits 0 to 9. Caltech-101 consists of object images, two subsets of which, i.e., Caltech-7 and Caltech-20 are commonly used in the literature. Citeseer is a citation network, whose nodes represent publications. The statistics information of above datasets are shown in Table 1.

Table 1. Detail information of the multi-view datasets. The feature dimension is shown in parenthesis.

View	Handwritten	Caltech-7/Caltech-20	Citeseer
1	Profile correlations (216)	Gabor (48)	Citation Links (3312)
2	Fourier coefficients (76)	Wavelet moments (40)	Words presence (3703)
3	Karhunen coefficients (64)	CENTRIST (254)	–
4	Morphological (6)	HOG (1984)	–
5	Pixel averages (240)	GIST (512)	–
6	Zernike moments (47)	LBP (928)	–
Data samples	2000	1474/2386	3312
Cluster number	10	7/20	6

4.2 Comparison Methods

To have a convincing comparison between SMVSC and existing methods, we select several recently proposed methods that report the state-of-the-art performance.

- Parameter-Free Auto-Weighted Multiple Graph Learning (AMGL) [25]: it extends spectral clustering to multi-view scenario with a novel weighting mechanism to distinguish the importance of different views.
- Multi-view Low-rank Sparse Subspace Clustering (MLRSSC) [1]: It develops a multi-view low-rank plus sparse subspace clustering algorithm and enforces agreements between representations of the pairs of views or a common centroid.
- Multi-view Subspace Clustering with Intactness-aware Similarity (MSC_IAS) [34]: it constructs the similarity in the intact space by assuming that it has maximum dependence with its corresponding intact space, which is measured by the Hilbert–Schmidt Independence Criterion (HSIC).
- Large-scale Multi-View Subspace Clustering (LMVSC) [17]: it addresses the scalability issue of multi-view subspace clustering method by employing anchor strategy.

4.3 Experimental Setup

As introduced in Sect. 3.1, we first apply probabilistic neighbor method [26] to obtain the low-pass filter and then achieve the smooth representation for each view. For the Handwritten data, the anchor number p is searched from the range $[g, 20, 30, 40, 50, 60, 70, 80, 90, 100]$ and α is searched in $[0.01, 0.1, 1, 10, 100, 1000]$; the Caltech-7, p is searched from the range $[g, 50, 100, 150, 200, 250, 300]$ and α is searched in $[0.001, 0.01, 0.1, 1, 10, 100, 1000]$; the Caltech-20, p is searched from the range $[g, 50, 100, 150, 200, 225, 250]$ and α is searched in $[5, 10, 15, 20, 25, 30, 35, 40, 45, 50]$; the Citeseer, p is searched from the range $[g, 20, 30, 40, 50, 60, 70, 80, 90, 100]$ and α is searched in $[1, 10, 100, 1000, 10000]$.

Clustering performance is evaluated by three commonly used metrics, including accuracy (ACC), normalized mutual information (NMI), and purity (PUR) [16]. Besides clustering performance, we also test the time consumed by these methods based on a computer equipped with a 2.6 GHz Intel Xeon CPU and 64 GB RAM, Matlab R2016a.

Table 2. Clustering performance on multi-view datasets ($k = 1$).

Data	Method	ACC	NMI	PUR	TIME(s)
Handwritten	AMGL [25]	84.60	87.32	87.10	67.58
	MLRSSC [1]	78.90	74.22	83.75	52.44
	MSC_IAS [34]	79.75	77.32	87.55	80.78
	LMVSC [17]	91.65	84.43	91.65	10.55
	SMVSC	**94.30**	**88.95**	**94.30**	8.58
Caltech-7	AMGL [25]	45.18	42.43	46.74	20.12
	MLRSSC [1]	37.31	21.11	41.45	22.26
	MSC_IAS [34]	39.76	24.55	44.44	57.18
	LMVSC [17]	72.66	51.93	75.17	135.79
	SMVSC	**73.54**	**52.04**	**84.87**	236.32
Caltech-20	AMGL [25]	30.13	40.54	31.64	77.63
	MLRSSC [1]	28.21	26.70	30.39	607.28
	MSC_IAS [34]	31.27	31.38	33.74	93.87
	LMVSC [17]	53.06	**52.71**	58.47	342.97
	SMVSC	**56.92**	51.90	**64.42**	447.58
Citeseer	AMGL [25]	16.87	0.23	16.87	449.07
	MLRSSC [1]	25.09	02.67	63.70	106.10
	MSC_IAS [34]	34.11	11.53	**80.76**	191.29
	LMVSC [17]	52.26	**25.71**	54.46	21.33
	SMVSC	**55.40**	25.57	57.27	21.82

4.4 Results

In this experiment, we fix graph filter order $k = 1$, and the experiment results are summarized in Table 2. As we can see, our proposed method SMVSC often achieves the best performance. In particular, SMVSC consistently enhances the accuracy of LMVSC on four datasets. In terms of NMI, our method produces better or comparable results as LMVSC. As for PUR, our proposed method outperforms others for three datasets except the last one. Note that the only difference between SMVSC and LMVSC lies in that SMVSC adopts graph filtering to preprocess the data. Both SMVSC and LMVSC often outperform other techniques by a large margin. This could be explained by their inherent draw-backs. For example, AMGL uses the inversion of loss as the weight for each view, which is too restrictive in practice; MLRSSC imposes both low-rank and sparse constraints, which could lead to conflict solutions; MSC_IAS employs a fixed weight for each view, which fails to explore the heterogeneity in views.

In terms of computation time, our method is also competitive with respect to others. It can be seen that our time fluctuates a lot on different datasets. This could be explained by the fact that our complexity is closely related to the number of anchors and different numbers are used for different datasets. Similarly, LMVSC is also heavily influenced by the number of anchors. These verify the effectiveness and efficiency of SMVSC.

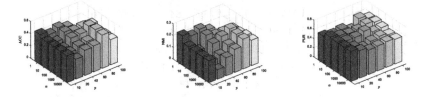

Fig. 1. The influence of parameters α and p for SMVSC on Citeseer dataset.

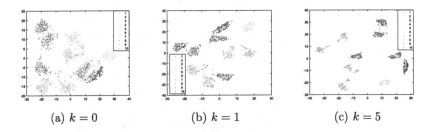

(a) $k = 0$ (b) $k = 1$ (c) $k = 5$

Fig. 2. The visualization of smooth representation in different graph filter order k.

4.5   Parameter Analysis

There are three parameters in our model, including trade-off parameter α, anchor number p, graph filter order k. Taking Citeseer as an example, we show the influence of α and p in Fig. 1. It can be observed that, for a fixed α, the performance can be improved by increasing p to some extent. Nevertheless, the performance deteriorates if p has a too large value. In addition, we can see that it is easy to obtain a good performance with an appropriate p, and so we can achieve reasonable results by fixing p to a small range and tuning α in practice.

Table 3. The influence of graph filter order k on ACC, NMI, PUR for two datasets.

Data	Metric	Unfiltered	$k=1$	$k=2$	$k=3$	$k=4$	$k=5$	$k=6$	$k=7$	$k=8$	$k=9$	$k=10$
Handwritten	ACC	91.65	94.30	93.25	93.30	93.80	95.40	95.35	**95.65**	95.50	95.50	95.35
	NMI	84.43	88.95	87.55	88.14	88.60	90.94	90.90	91.21	91.44	**91.66**	91.52
	PUR	91.65	94.30	93.25	93.30	93.80	95.40	95.35	**95.65**	95.50	95.50	95.35
Caltech-7	ACC	72.66	73.54	**76.79**	72.72	72.11	73.54	72.04	72.11	70.96	72.93	70.01
	NMI	51.93	52.04	**56.06**	50.43	53.85	52.42	53.57	52.57	49.36	53.99	52.01
	PUR	75.17	84.87	83.92	85.27	84.73	**86.02**	82.76	84.12	84.12	85.34	79.71

Table 3 summarizes the clustering results of Handwritten and Caltech-7 datasets under different graph filter order k, fixed α and p. As previously discussed, when k increases, the features of adjacent nodes will be more similar. Nevertheless, if k is too large, it will result in over-smoothing, i.e., the features of nodes from different clusters will be mixed and lead to indistinguishable. Therefore, a too large k will negatively destroy the clustering performance. Specifically, we could observe that the clustering performance keeps increasing till k equals 7 for Handwritten, and k reaches 2 for Caltech-7. Moreover, the reported clustering performance on two datasets are much better than that in Table 2. From this perspective, we can also improve clustering performance in other multi-view datasets by choosing an appropriate graph filter order. On the other hand, LMVSC, which doesn't employ graph filtering, generates clustering performance 0.9165, 0.8443, 0.9165 on Handwritten, 0.7266, 0.5193, 0.7517 on Caltech-7, in terms of accuracy, NMI, purity, respectively. They are inferior to our performance.

To clearly see the effect of graph filtering, we apply t-SNE on Handwritten to observe the evolution process of representation $\bar{X}$ in Fig. 2. It can be seen that the smooth representation displays a clear cluster structure when filter order increases. Furthermore, we can see that the distance between clusters become larger when k increases. Hence, graph filtering could increases the separability of clusters. As a result, the grouping property of smooth representation reduce the difficult of separating the data points into disjoint subspaces.

5   Conclusion

In this paper, we propose to perform multi-view subspace clustering in a smooth representation realized by a graph filtering technique. The proposed strategy is general enough to integrate with various multi-view subspace clustering models. In particular, through a low-pass filter, the new data representation becomes more separable and is easy to cluster. Consequently, the smooth representation can boost the clustering performance. Extensive experiments on multi-view data validate the superiority of our approach. Experimental analysis shows that graph filtering can increase the separability of clusters, which also explain why it improves clustering performance.

Acknowledgments. This paper was in part supported by Grants from the Natural Science Foundation of China (Nos. U19A2059, 61806045), the National Key R&D Program of China (Nos. 2018AAA0100204, 2018YFC0807500), the Sichuan Science and Technology Program (No. 2020YFS0057), the Fundamental Research Fund for the Central Universities under Project ZYGX2019Z015, the Ministry of Science and Technology of Sichuan Province Program (Nos. 2018GZDZX0048, 20ZDYF0343, 2018GZDZX0014, 2018GZDZX0034).

References

1. Brbić, M., Kopriva, I.: Multi-view low-rank sparse subspace clustering. Pattern Recogn. **73**, 247–258 (2018)
2. Cao, X., Zhang, C., Fu, H., Liu, S., Zhang, H.: Diversity-induced multi-view subspace clustering. In: Proceedings of the IEEE Conference on Computer Vision and Pattern Recognition, pp. 586–594 (2015)
3. Chen, M.S., Huang, L., Wang, C.D., Huang, D.: Multi-view clustering in latent embedding space. In: Proceedings of AAAI Conference on Artificial Intelligence, vol. 34, pp. 3513–3520 (2020)
4. Chen, X., Chen, R., Wu, Q., Fang, Y., Nie, F., Huang, J.Z.: LABIN: balanced min cut for large-scale data. IEEE Trans. Neural Netw. Learn. Syst. **31**(3), 725–736 (2019)
5. Chen, Y., Xiao, X., Zhou, Y.: Jointly learning kernel representation tensor and affinity matrix for multi-view clustering. IEEE Trans. Multimedia **22**(8), 1985–1997 (2019)
6. Elhamifar, E., Vidal, R.: Sparse subspace clustering: algorithm, theory, and applications. IEEE Trans. Pattern Anal. Mach. Intell. **35**(11), 2765–2781 (2013)
7. Gao, H., Nie, F., Li, X., Huang, H.: Multi-view subspace clustering. In: Proceedings of the IEEE International Conference on Computer Vision, pp. 4238–4246 (2015)
8. Jain, A.K.: Data clustering: 50 years beyond k-means. Pattern Recogn. Lett. **31**(8), 651–666 (2010)
9. Ji, P., Zhang, T., Li, H., Salzmann, M., Reid, I.: Deep subspace clustering networks. In: Advances in Neural Information Processing Systems, pp. 24–33 (2017)
10. Kang, Z., et al.: Multiple partitions aligned clustering. In: Proceedings of the 28th International Joint Conference on Artificial Intelligence, pp. 2701–2707. AAAI Press (2019)
11. Kang, Z., Lin, Z., Zhu, X., Xu, W.: Structured graph learning for scalable subspace clustering: from single-view to multi-view. IEEE Trans. Cybern. (2021). https://doi.org/10.1109/TCYB.2021.3061660
12. Kang, Z., Lu, X., Liang, J., Bai, K., Xu, Z.: Relation-guided representation learning. Neural Netw. **131**, 93–102 (2020)
13. Kang, Z., Pan, H., Hoi, S.C., Xu, Z.: Robust graph learning from noisy data. IEEE Trans. Cybern. **50**(5), 1833–1843 (2020)
14. Kang, Z., et al.: Structured graph learning for clustering and semi-supervised classification. Pattern Recogn. **110**, 107627 (2021)
15. Kang, Z., Peng, C., Cheng, Q., Xu, Z.: Unified spectral clustering with optimal graph. In: Proceedings of the AAAI Conference on Artificial Intelligence, vol. 32 (2018)
16. Kang, Z., et al.: Partition level multiview subspace clustering. Neural Netw. **122**, 279–288 (2020)

17. Kang, Z., Zhou, W., Zhao, Z., Shao, J., Han, M., Xu, Z.: Large-scale multi-view subspace clustering in linear time. In: Proceedings of the AAAI Conference on Artificial Intelligence, vol. 34, pp. 4412–4419 (2020)
18. Li, Z., Liu, J., Tang, J., Lu, H.: Robust structured subspace learning for data representation. IEEE Trans. Pattern Anal. Mach. Intell. **37**(10), 2085–2098 (2015)
19. Liu, G., Lin, Z., Yan, S., Sun, J., Yu, Y., Ma, Y.: Robust recovery of subspace structures by low-rank representation. IEEE Trans. Pattern Anal. Mach. Intell. **35**(1), 171–184 (2012)
20. Liu, Y., et al.: Nearly optimal risk bounds for kernel k-means. In: ICML (2020)
21. Lu, C., Feng, J., Lin, Z., Mei, T., Yan, S.: Subspace clustering by block diagonal representation. IEEE Trans. Pattern Anal. Mach. Intell. **41**(2), 487–501 (2018)
22. Lv, J., Kang, Z., Lu, X., Xu, Z.: Pseudo-supervised deep subspace clustering. IEEE Trans. Image Process. **30**, 5252–5263 (2021)
23. Ma, Z., Kang, Z., Luo, G., Tian, L., Chen, W.: Towards clustering-friendly representations: subspace clustering via graph filtering. In: Proceedings of the 28th ACM International Conference on Multimedia, pp. 3081–3089 (2020)
24. Ng, A.Y., Jordan, M.I., Weiss, Y.: On spectral clustering: analysis and an algorithm. In: Advances in Neural Information Processing Systems, pp. 849–856 (2002)
25. Nie, F., Li, J., Li, X.: Parameter-free auto-weighted multiple graph learning: a framework for multiview clustering and semi-supervised classification. In: International Joint Conference on Artificial Intelligence, pp. 1881–1887 (2016)
26. Nie, F., Wang, X., Jordan, M.I., Huang, H.: The constrained Laplacian rank algorithm for graph-based clustering. In: Proceedings of the Thirtieth AAAI Conference on Artificial Intelligence, AAAI 2016, pp. 1969–1976. AAAI Press (2016)
27. Patel, V.M., Van Nguyen, H., Vidal, R.: Latent space sparse and low-rank subspace clustering. IEEE J. Sel. Top. Sig. Process. **9**(4), 691–701 (2015)
28. Peng, X., Xiao, S., Feng, J., Yau, W.Y., Yi, Z.: Deep subspace clustering with sparsity prior. In: IJCAI, pp. 1925–1931 (2016)
29. Peng, X., Yi, Z., Tang, H.: Robust subspace clustering via thresholding ridge regression. In: Twenty-Ninth AAAI Conference on Artificial Intelligence, vol. 29 (2015)
30. Ren, Z., Sun, Q.: Simultaneous global and local graph structure preserving for multiple kernel clustering. IEEE Trans. Neural Netw. Learn. Syst. **32**, 1839–1851 (2020)
31. Shuman, D.I., Narang, S.K., Frossard, P., Ortega, A., Vandergheynst, P.: The emerging field of signal processing on graphs: extending high-dimensional data analysis to networks and other irregular domains. IEEE Sig. Process. Mag. **30**(3), 83–98 (2013)
32. Tan, J., Shi, Y., Yang, Z., Wen, C., Lin, L.: Unsupervised multi-view clustering by squeezing hybrid knowledge from cross view and each view. IEEE Trans. Multimedia 1–1 (2020). https://doi.org/10.1109/TMM.2020.3019683
33. Wang, J., Wang, X., Yu, G., Domeniconi, C., Yu, Z., Zhang, Z.: Discovering multiple co-clusterings with matrix factorization. IEEE Trans. Cybern. PP(99), 1–12 (2019)
34. Wang, X., Lei, Z., Guo, X., Zhang, C., Shi, H., Li, S.Z.: Multi-view subspace clustering with intactness-aware similarity. Pattern Recogn. **88**, 50–63 (2019)
35. Wang, Y., Zhang, W., Wu, L., Lin, X., Fang, M., Pan, S.: Iterative views agreement: an iterative low-rank based structured optimization method to multi-view spectral clustering (2016)
36. Wen, J., et al.: Adaptive graph completion based incomplete multi-view clustering. IEEE Trans. Multimedia PP(99), 1–1 (2020)

37. Yang, B., Fu, X., Sidiropoulos, N.D., Hong, M.: Towards k-means-friendly spaces: simultaneous deep learning and clustering. In: Proceedings of the 34th International Conference on Machine Learning, vol. 70, pp. 3861–3870. JMLR.org (2017)

38. Zhai, H., Zhang, H., Zhang, L., Li, P.: Laplacian-regularized low-rank subspace clustering for hyperspectral image band selection. IEEE Trans. Geosci. Remote Sens. **57**(3), 1723–1740 (2018)

39. Zhang, C., et al.: Generalized latent multi-view subspace clustering. IEEE Trans. Pattern Anal. Mach. Intell. **42**(1), 86–99 (2018)

40. Zhang, X., Liu, H., Li, Q., Wu, X.M.: Attributed graph clustering via adaptive graph convolution. In: the 28th International Joint Conference on Artificial Intelligence (2019)

41. Zhang, Z., et al.: Flexible auto-weighted local-coordinate concept factorization: a robust framework for unsupervised clustering. IEEE Trans. Knowl. Data Eng. (2019)

42. Zhou, P., Du, L., Liu, X., Shen, Y.D., Fan, M., Li, X.: Self-paced clustering ensemble. IEEE Trans. Neural Netw. Learn. Syst. (2020)

Sample Reduction Using ℓ_1-Norm Twin Bounded Support Vector Machine

Xiaohan Zheng[1], Li Zhang[1,2](✉), and Leilei Yan[1]

[1] School of Computer Science and Technology, Joint International Research Laboratory of Machine Learning and Neuromorphic Computing, Soochow University, Suzhou 215006, China
{20184227056,20204027001}@stu.suda.edu.cn
[2] Provincial Key Laboratory for Computer Information Processing Technology, Soochow University, Suzhou 215006, China
zhangliml@suda.edu.cn

Abstract. Twin support machine (TSVM) has a lower time complexity than support vector machine (SVM), but it has a poor ability to perform sample reduction. In order to improve the ability of TSVM to reduce sample, we propose an ℓ_1-norm twin bounded support machine (ℓ_1-TBSVM) inspired by the sparsity of ℓ_1-norm in feature space. The objective function of ℓ_1-TBSVM contains the hinge loss and the ℓ_1-norm terms, both which can induce sparsity. We solve the primal programming problems of ℓ_1-TBSVM to prevent the disappearance of sparsity and avoid the situation that the inverse of matrix does not exist. Thus, ℓ_1-TBSVM has a good sparsity, or a good ability to reduce sample. Experimental results on synthetic and UCI datasets indicate that ℓ_1-TBSVM has a good ability to perform sample reduction and simultaneously enhances the classification performance.

Keywords: Support vector machine · Twin support vector machine · ℓ_1-norm regularization · Sparsity · Sample reduction

1 Introduction

As a technique of data processing, sample reduction has been widely used in practical applications [9,13]. Since sample reduction can make the storage of data simple and the test of data fast, it is specially important for large-scale or high-dimensional data to find valuable samples. Support vector machine (SVM) was proposed based on the statistical learning theory [2,3,19], which is a famous learner and has the ability to reduce data. The aim of SVM is to find an optimal separating hyperplane by maximizing the margin between two classes and minimizing the empirical risk. The sparsity of model coefficients in SVM directly reflects the ability to reduce sample. A sparse learner stands for a better generalization performance and a lower computational efficiency [6,8]. To enhance the sparsity of SVM, some versions of ℓ_1-norm SVM were proposed [1,21,25].

© Springer Nature Singapore Pte Ltd. 2021
H. Zhang et al. (Eds.): NCAA 2021, CCIS 1449, pp. 141–153, 2021.
https://doi.org/10.1007/978-981-16-5188-5_11

Since SVM has an issue of computational complexity, many improved methods have been proposed. On the basis of SVM, Mangasarian and Wild [12] proposed a generalized eigenvalue proximal support vector machine (GEPSVM). GEPSVM divides a large two-class problem into two relatively small problems, and obtains two non-parallel hyperplanes by solving the classical generalized eigenvalue problems, which are easy to be solved. Inspired by SVM and GEPSVM, Jayadeva et al. [10] proposed twin support vector machine (TSVM). Similar to GEPSVM, TSVM also constructs two non-parallel hyperplanes for two classes. Different from SVM solving a single large quadratic programming problem (QPP), TSVM requires to solve two smaller QPPs, which results a lower computational complexity than SVM. Many variants of TSVM have been designed, such as twin bounded support vector machine (TBSVM) [16], twin parametric support vector machine (TPMSVM) [15], v-TSVM [20] and least squares twin support vector machine (LS-TSVM) [11]. The above TSVM-like algorithms have the issue of weak ability to perform sample reduction. Although some of these algorithms have the term of hinge loss, they find solutions in the dual form that may cause the disappearance of sparsity [14].

In order to improve the ability of TSVM to perform sample reduction, some variants of TSVM have been proposed. For example, Tian et al. [18] presented a sparse non-parallel support vector machine (SNSVM), which uses two loss functions: the ϵ-insensitive quadratic loss and the soft margin quadratic loss. However, SNSVM does not consider feature reduction, and finds the solution in the dual space that leads to a weak sparsity. In [14], Peng proposed a sparse twin support vector machine (STSVM). The objective function of STSVM is totally identical to TBSVM that has a weak sparsity. Fortunately, STSVM employs a back-fitting strategy to iteratively and simultaneously add a support vector, and searches an optimal solution in the primal space. The sparsity of STSVM can be guaranteed by setting a larger stopping parameter. However, it is not easy for STSVM to finely control this parameter. A new linear programming twin support vector machines (NLPTSVM) was proposed in [17]. The ℓ_1-norm improves the robustness and sparsity of NLPTSVM. The ability of NLPTSVM to reduce samples is validated by experimental results in [17]. Gao et al. [7] proposed an ℓ_1-norm least square twin support vector machine (ℓ_1-LSTSVM) by introducing the ℓ_1-norm into LS-TSVM. Further, an ℓ_p-norm least square twin support vector machine (ℓ_p-LSTSVM) was proposed by using an adaptive learning procedure with the ℓ_p-norm $(0 < p < 1)$ [24]. However, the computational complexity of ℓ_p-LSTSVM is high for determining the optimal p.

To solve the issue of lacking sparsity in TSVM or TBSVM, and provide an alternative method for sample reduction, this paper proposes an ℓ_1-norm twin bounded support vector machine (ℓ_1-TBSVM) by introducing the ℓ_1-norm into TBSVM. Similar to TBSVM, ℓ_1-TBSVM consists of three terms, including minimizing the distance between samples in the positive (or negative) class and the corresponding hyperplane for the positive (or negative) class, minimizing the hinge loss, and minimizing the ℓ_1-norm about model coefficients. The last two terms can induce sparsity. To avoid the ill-condition in some situation and prevent the disappearance of sparsity, ℓ_1-TBSVM is trained by solving a pair of

QPPs in the primal space instead of the dual space. By utilizing the kernel function, sample reduction can be achieved. Extensive experiments are conducted on synthetic and UCI data sets.

The rest of this paper is organized as follows. Section 2 proposes ℓ_1-TBSVM. Numerical experiments are given to demonstrate the ability to perform sample reduction and the classification performance of ℓ_1-TBSVM in Sect. 3. Finally, we conclude this paper in Sect. 4.

2 ℓ_1-TBSVM

In this section, we describe the formulations, solutions and property analysis for ℓ_1-TBSVM, respectively. For a binary classification task, assuming we have a set of n training samples X that is divided into two subsets X_1 and X_2 for positive and negative classes, respectively. Let $\boldsymbol{X}_1 = [\boldsymbol{x}_{11}, ..., \boldsymbol{x}_{1n_1}]^T \in \mathbb{R}^{n_1 \times m}$ be the positive sample matrix and $\boldsymbol{X}_2 = [\boldsymbol{x}_{21}, ..., \boldsymbol{x}_{2n_2}]^T \in \mathbb{R}^{n_2 \times m}$ be the negative sample matrix, where $\boldsymbol{x}_{ji} \in \mathbb{R}^m$, n_1 and n_2 are the number of positive and negative samples respectively, $n = n_1 + n_2$, and m is the number of features, the superscript T is the transpose of a vector or matrix. Without loss of generality, let y_{ji} denote the label of $\boldsymbol{x}_{ji}$, where $y_{1i} = 1$ and $y_{2i} = -1$.

2.1   Formulations

Given the training set of X, we map the elements in this set into a feature space by a nonlinear mapping $\phi(\cdot)$:

$$\boldsymbol{x} = [x_1, x_2, \cdots, x_m]^T \in \mathbb{R}^m \to \phi(\boldsymbol{x}) = [\phi_1(\boldsymbol{x}), \phi_2(\boldsymbol{x}), \cdots, \phi_D(\boldsymbol{x})]^T \in \mathbb{R}^D \quad (1)$$

where $\phi_j(\boldsymbol{x})$, $j = 1, \cdots, D$ are nonlinear functions, the dimension of the input space and the feature space are m and D, respectively. Zhang et al. gave a kind of kernel empirical mapping [23]. For any $\boldsymbol{x}_i$, its image in the feature space has the form:

$$\phi(\boldsymbol{x}_i) = [k(\boldsymbol{x}_i, \boldsymbol{x}_1), ..., k(\boldsymbol{x}_i, \boldsymbol{x}_n)]^T = k(\cdot, \boldsymbol{x}_i) \in \mathbb{R}^n \quad (2)$$

where $k(\cdot, \cdot)$ is a kernel function, which is symmetric. Generally, the Mercer kernel is common used one that is not only symmetric, but also positive semi-definite [19].

In the feature space, the positive-class sample matrix can be represented as

$$\boldsymbol{K}_1 = [\phi(\boldsymbol{x}_{11}), ..., \phi(\boldsymbol{x}_{1n_1})]^T \in \mathbb{R}^{n_1 \times n} \quad (3)$$

and the negative-class sample matrix is

$$\boldsymbol{K}_2 = [\phi(\boldsymbol{x}_{21}), ..., \phi(\boldsymbol{x}_{2n_2})]^T \in \mathbb{R}^{n_2 \times n} \quad (4)$$

where $\phi(\boldsymbol{x}_{ji}) = [k(\boldsymbol{x}_{ji}, \boldsymbol{x}_1), \cdots, k(\boldsymbol{x}_{ji}, \boldsymbol{x}_n)]^T$.

For a binary problem, ℓ_1-TBSVM is to find two hypothesis functions in the feature space:

$$f_1(\boldsymbol{x}) = \boldsymbol{w}_1^T \phi(\boldsymbol{x}) + b_1 \quad (5)$$

and

$$f_2(\boldsymbol{x}) = \boldsymbol{w}_2^T \phi(\boldsymbol{x}) + b_2 \quad (6)$$

where $\boldsymbol{w}_1 \in \mathbb{R}^n$ and $\boldsymbol{w}_2 \in \mathbb{R}^n$ are the weight vectors for the positive-class and negative-class hypothesis functions in the feature space, respectively, b_1 and b_2

are thresholds of hypothesis functions in the feature space. To find $\boldsymbol{w}_1$, $\boldsymbol{w}_2$, b_1 and b_2, ℓ_1-TBSVM solves the following optimization problems:

$$\min_{w_1, b_1, \xi_2} \quad \frac{1}{2}\|\boldsymbol{K}_1\boldsymbol{w}_1 + \boldsymbol{e}_1 b_1\|_2^2 + C_1\left(\|\boldsymbol{w}_1\|_1 + \|b_1\|_1\right) + C_2\boldsymbol{e}_2^T\boldsymbol{\xi}_2 \tag{7}$$
$$\text{s.t.} \quad -(\boldsymbol{K}_2\boldsymbol{w}_1 + \boldsymbol{e}_2 b_1) + \boldsymbol{\xi}_2 \geq \boldsymbol{e}_2, \quad \boldsymbol{\xi}_2 \geq \boldsymbol{0}_{n_2}$$

and

$$\min_{w_2, b_2, \xi_1} \quad \frac{1}{2}\|\boldsymbol{K}_2\boldsymbol{w}_2 + \boldsymbol{e}_2 b_2\|_2^2 + C_3(\|\boldsymbol{w}_2\|_1 + \|b_2\|_1) + C_4\boldsymbol{e}_1^T\boldsymbol{\xi}_1 \tag{8}$$
$$\text{s.t.} \quad (\boldsymbol{K}_1\boldsymbol{w}_2 + \boldsymbol{e}_1 b_2) + \boldsymbol{\xi}_1 \geq \boldsymbol{e}_1, \quad \boldsymbol{\xi}_1 \geq \boldsymbol{0}_{n_1}$$

Next, we use two positive vectors to represent $\boldsymbol{w}_1$, and two positive variables to represent b_1 in (7). Namely, $\boldsymbol{w}_1 = \boldsymbol{\beta}_+^* - \boldsymbol{\beta}_+$ and $b_1 = \gamma_+^* - \gamma_+$, where $\boldsymbol{\beta}_+^* \geq \boldsymbol{0}_n$, $\boldsymbol{\beta}_+ \geq \boldsymbol{0}_n$, $\gamma_+^* \geq 0, \gamma_+ \geq 0$. Finally, (7) can be rewritten as in matrix:

$$\min_{\alpha} \quad \frac{1}{2}\boldsymbol{\alpha}^T\boldsymbol{Q}\boldsymbol{\alpha} + \boldsymbol{\zeta}_1^T\boldsymbol{\alpha} \tag{9}$$
$$\text{s.t.} \quad \boldsymbol{P}\boldsymbol{\alpha} \geq \boldsymbol{e}_2, \quad \boldsymbol{\alpha} \geq \boldsymbol{0}_{(2n+2+n_2)}$$

where $\boldsymbol{\alpha} = \begin{bmatrix} \boldsymbol{\beta}_+^{*T} & \boldsymbol{\beta}_+^T & \gamma_+^* & \gamma_+ & \boldsymbol{\xi}_2^T \end{bmatrix}^T \in \mathbb{R}^{(2n+2+n_2)}$, $\boldsymbol{\zeta}_1 = \begin{bmatrix} C_1\boldsymbol{1}_n^T & C_1\boldsymbol{1}_n^T & C_1 & C_1 \\ \end{bmatrix}$ $C_2\boldsymbol{e}_2^T]^T \in \mathbb{R}^{(2n+2+n_2)}$, $\boldsymbol{P} = \begin{bmatrix} -\boldsymbol{K}_2 & \boldsymbol{K}_2 & -\boldsymbol{e}_2 & \boldsymbol{e}_2 & \boldsymbol{I}_{n_2 \times n_2} \end{bmatrix} \in \mathbb{R}^{n_2 \times (2n+2+n_2)}$, and

$$\boldsymbol{Q} = \begin{bmatrix} \boldsymbol{Q}_1 & \boldsymbol{O}_{(2n+2) \times n_2} \\ \boldsymbol{O}_{n_2 \times (2n+2)} & \boldsymbol{O}_{n_2 \times n_2} \end{bmatrix} \in \mathbb{R}^{(2n+2+n_2) \times (2n+2+n_2)}$$

with

$$\boldsymbol{Q} = \begin{bmatrix} \boldsymbol{K}_1^T\boldsymbol{K}_1 & -\boldsymbol{K}_1^T\boldsymbol{K}_1 & 0.5\boldsymbol{K}_1^T\boldsymbol{e}_1 & -0.5\boldsymbol{K}_1^T\boldsymbol{e}_1 \\ -\boldsymbol{K}_1^T\boldsymbol{K}_1 & \boldsymbol{K}_1^T\boldsymbol{K}_1 & -0.5\boldsymbol{K}_1^T\boldsymbol{e}_1 & 0.5\boldsymbol{K}_1^T\boldsymbol{e}_1 \\ 0.5\boldsymbol{e}_1^T\boldsymbol{K}_1 & -0.5\boldsymbol{e}_1^T\boldsymbol{K}_1 & \boldsymbol{e}_1^T\boldsymbol{e}_1 & -\boldsymbol{e}_1^T\boldsymbol{e}_1 \\ -0.5\boldsymbol{e}_1^T\boldsymbol{K}_1 & 0.5\boldsymbol{e}_1^T\boldsymbol{K}_1 & -\boldsymbol{e}_1^T\boldsymbol{e}_1 & \boldsymbol{e}_1^T\boldsymbol{e}_1 \end{bmatrix} \in \mathbb{R}^{(2n+2) \times (2n+2)}$$

By introducing $\boldsymbol{w}_2 = \boldsymbol{\beta}_-^* - \boldsymbol{\beta}_-$ and $b_2 = \gamma_-^* - \gamma_-$, where $\boldsymbol{\beta}_-^* \geq \boldsymbol{0}_n$, $\boldsymbol{\beta}_- \geq \boldsymbol{0}_n$, $\gamma_-^* \geq 0, \gamma_- \geq 0$, (8) can be rewritten as:

$$\min_{\delta} \quad \frac{1}{2}\boldsymbol{\delta}^T\boldsymbol{G}\boldsymbol{\delta} + \boldsymbol{\zeta}_2^T\boldsymbol{\delta} \tag{10}$$
$$\text{s.t.} \quad \boldsymbol{H}\boldsymbol{\delta} \geq \boldsymbol{e}_1, \quad \boldsymbol{\delta} \geq \boldsymbol{0}_{(2n+2+n_1)}$$

where $\boldsymbol{\delta} = \begin{bmatrix} \boldsymbol{\beta}_-^{*T} & \boldsymbol{\beta}_-^{*T} & \gamma_-^* & \gamma_- & \boldsymbol{\xi}_1^T \end{bmatrix} \in \mathbb{R}^{(2n+2+n_1)}$, $\boldsymbol{\zeta}_2 = \begin{bmatrix} C_3\boldsymbol{1}_n^T & C_3\boldsymbol{1}_n^T & C_3 & C_3 \\ \end{bmatrix}$ $C_4\boldsymbol{e}_1^T]^T \in \mathbb{R}^{(2n+2+n_1)}$, $\boldsymbol{H} = \begin{bmatrix} \boldsymbol{K}_1 & -\boldsymbol{K}_1 & \boldsymbol{e}_1 & -\boldsymbol{e}_1 & \boldsymbol{I}_{n_1 \times n_1} \end{bmatrix} \in \mathbb{R}^{n_1 \times (2n+2+n_1)}$ and

$$\boldsymbol{G} = \begin{bmatrix} \boldsymbol{G}_1 & \boldsymbol{O}_{(2n+2) \times n_1} \\ \boldsymbol{O}_{n_1 \times (2n+2)} & \boldsymbol{O}_{n_1 \times n_1} \end{bmatrix} \in \mathbb{R}^{(2n+2+n_1) \times (2n+2+n_1)}$$

with

$$G = \begin{bmatrix} K_2^T K_2 & -X_2^T K_2 & 0.5K_2^T e_2 & -0.5K_2^T e_2 \\ -K_2^T K_2 & X_2^T K_2 & -0.5K_2^T e_2 & 0.5K_2^T e_2 \\ 0.5e_2^T K_2 & -0.5e_2^T K_2 & e_2^T e_2 & -e_2^T e_2 \\ -0.5e_2^T K_2 & 0.5e_2^T K_2 & -e_2^T e_2 & e_2^T e_2 \end{bmatrix} \in \mathbb{R}^{(2n+2)\times(2n+2)}$$

2.2 Solutions and Property Analysis

The hypothesis functions (5) and (6) can be obtained by solving (9) and (10), respectively. The computational complexity of ℓ_1-TBSVM is $O((2n+2+n_2)^3 + (2n+2+n_1)^3)$. Then we can have the positive-class hyperplane $H_1:f_1(x) = 0$ and the negative-class hyperplane $H_2:f_2(x) = 0$. For a given x, let $\rho(x)$ be its distance difference from H_1 to H_2.

For a new sample x, its distance difference from H_1 to H_2 is

$$\rho(x) = |f_2(x)| - |f_1(x)| \tag{11}$$

which can predict the label information for x. Namely,

$$\hat{y} = \begin{cases} +1, & if \ \rho(x) > 0 \\ -1, & otherwise \end{cases} \tag{12}$$

where $\hat{y}$ is the estimated label for x. We can obtain a hyperplane where $\rho(x) = 0$ for $\forall x$, which is obviously the separating hyperplane $H : |f_2(x)| - |f_1(x)| = 0$.

In the following, we illustrate hypersurfaces obtained by ℓ_1-TBSVM as shown in Fig. 1, where 50 positive samples denoted by symbols "*" and 50 negative samples denoted by "×". Figure 1(a) shows the positive-class hypersurface $H_1:f_1(x) = 0$ and the hypersurface $f_1(x) = -1$ where negative samples with losses that are circled and sparse vectors are squared. There are two marked negative samples x_{21}, x_{22}, and the corresponding losses of them have the relations: $\xi_{21} > \xi_{22} > 0$. Certainly, x_{21} is the closest to H_1 and has the greatest loss. Those negative samples lying between H_1 and $f_1(x) = -1$ have losses, and the negative ones with $f_1(x) < -1$ have no loss. In addition, there are four sparse vectors, which is to say that these four vectors are enough for constructing H_1. The negative-class hypersurface H_2 and the hypersurface $f_2(x) = 1$ are given in Fig. 1(b), where positive samples with losses that are circled and sparse vectors are squared. There are also two marked positive samples x_{11}, x_{12}, and the corresponding losses of them have the relations: $\xi_{11} = \xi_{12} = 0$. Since there are no positive samples locating between H_2 and $f_2(x) = 1$, all positive samples are lossless. Moreover, to construct H_2, we need more sparse vectors. Figure 1(c) shows hypersurfaces H_1, H_2 and the separating hypersurface H.

In fact, sample reduction in the original space is identical to feature reduction in the feature space. In other words, sample reduction in ℓ_1-TBSVM means that the dimension of images in the feature space is reduced. The definition of sample reduction is given below.

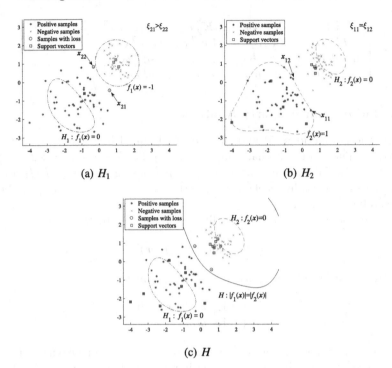

Fig. 1. Hypersurfaces obtained by ℓ_1-TBSVM

Definition 1. *Let* $X = \{(\boldsymbol{x}_i, y_i)\}_{i=1}^n$ *be a set of training samples with* $\boldsymbol{x}_i \in \mathbb{R}^m$, *and* $f(\boldsymbol{x}) = \boldsymbol{w}^T \phi(\boldsymbol{x}) + b$ *be the hypothesis function with* $\phi(\boldsymbol{x}) = \boldsymbol{k}(\cdot, \boldsymbol{x})$. *If* $\boldsymbol{w}$ *is sparse, then the set* X *can be reduced to* $X' = \{(\boldsymbol{x}_i, y_i)|w_i \neq 0, i = 1, \cdots, n\}$ *with* $|X'| = n'$, *where* $n' < n$ *and* $\boldsymbol{x}_i \in X'$ *is a sparse vector, which is called sample reduction.*

3   Numerical Experiments

We carry out experiments to evaluate the performance of ℓ_1-TBSVM. One artificial and 12 real-world datasets have been used to validate our method from sample reduction and classification performance. All experiments are performed on a personal computer with operation system Windows 10, 3.0 GHZ Intel Core and 8 G bytes of memory.

3.1   Artificial Dataset

This section adopts an artificial dataset named Dataset 1 to analyzes the ability of ℓ_1-TBSVM to perform sample reduction, and define the degree of sample reduction (DSR) to measure this ability that can be described as:

$$DSR = \left(1 - \frac{||\boldsymbol{w}_1||_0 + ||\boldsymbol{w}_2||_0}{length(\boldsymbol{w}_1) + length(\boldsymbol{w}_2)}\right) \times 100\% \qquad (13)$$

where $\|\cdot\|_0$ is the ℓ_0-norm, and $length(\cdot)$ is to find the number of elements in vector $\cdot$. Note that the greater DSR is, the better the sparsity is.

Figure 2 shows the data distribution of Dataset 1, where the noise samples lie between two-class normal samples. Dataset 1 consists of 1000 samples (500 positive and 500 negative samples) which have two features. In Dataset 1, the first 40 samples (20 positive and 20 negative samples) are normal ones and the others (480 positive and 480 negative samples) are noise ones. The valid positive samples are drawn from the uniform distribution with $[-1, 0] \times [-1, 0]$, and the valid negative samples are drawn from the uniform distribution with $[0, 1] \times [0, 1]$. The noise samples are drawn from the Gaussian distribution with a mean $[0, 0]^T$ and a covariance matrix $0.01\boldsymbol{I}$, where $\boldsymbol{I} \in \mathbb{R}^2$ is the identify matrix.

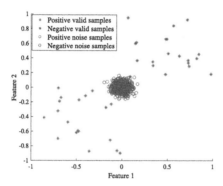

Fig. 2. Data distribution of Dataset 1.

We validate the ability of ℓ_1-TBSVM to reduce samples on Dataset 1, and use the Gaussian kernel function:

$$k(\boldsymbol{x}, \boldsymbol{x}') = \exp(\|\boldsymbol{x} - \boldsymbol{x}'\|^2 / 2\sigma^2) \tag{14}$$

where $\sigma > 0$ is the kernel parameter and can be determined by the median method described in [22].

Empirically, we set the regularization parameters $C_i = 0.1, i = 1, \cdots, 4$. The values of weight vectors $\boldsymbol{w}_1$ and $\boldsymbol{w}_2$ are shown in Fig. 3, where the dotted line is the division between the normal samples and the noise ones. From these Fig. 3, it can be seen that weight values corresponding to the noise samples are almost zero. In this case, ℓ_1-TBSVM can be thought of as sample reduction which ignores or narrows the effect of samples with small or even zero weights on the classification performance. According to (13), we can compute DSR and obtain $DSR = 99.35\%$, which implies that ℓ_1-TBSVM has a good sample reduction performance.

3.2   UCI Datasets

In this section, we compare the performance of ℓ_1-TBSVM and the related methods including SVM [2], TSVM [10], TBSVM [16], ℓ_p-LSTSVM [24], SNSVM [18],

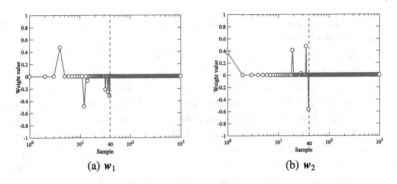

Fig. 3. The values of w_1 and w_2 for the ℓ_1-TBSVM on Dataset 1.

STSVM [14] and NLPTSVM [17]. Thus, we conduct experiments on 12 UCI datasets, which are all from the UCI machine learning repository [4]. Table 1 shows the details of these datasets. Five-fold cross validation is used here to obtain the average accuracy [5]. In other words, we repeat 5 time experiments on the partitioned datasets. In each partition, regularization parameters in all algorithms are determined by applying the grid search method on the training sets and searching in the set $\{2^{-3}, ..., 2^3\}$.

Table 1. The details of UCI datasets

Date Set	#Sample (#Class 1, #Class −1)	#Feature	# Class
Australian	690 (307, 383)	14	2
Breast	277 (81, 196)	9	2
Bupa	345 (145, 200)	6	2
Diabetes	768 (500, 268)	8	2
German	1000 (300, 700)	24	2
Heart	270 (150, 120)	13	2
Pima	768 (500, 268)	8	2
Sonar	208 (97, 111)	60	2
Tic_tac_toe	958 (332, 626)	9	2
Vote	435 (267, 168)	16	2
Wdbc	569 (212, 357)	30	2
Wpbc	194 (46, 148)	33	2

We still use the Gaussian kernel function for all learning algorithms, where the kernel parameter σ is determined by the median method in [22]. Table 2 lists the average five fold cross-validation results of these methods, and Table 3 shows the average of DSR. Observation on Table 2 indicates that ℓ_1-TBSVM has the best classification accuracy on six out of 12 datasets, and both SVM and SNSVM obtain the best classification accuracy on three out of 12 datasets, respectively. Similar to the linear case, observation on Table 3 also implies that ℓ_1-TBSVM has a medium DSR, which is smaller than that of NLPTSVM and greater than those of TBSVM, TSVM, and SNSVM. According to Tables 2 and 3, we know that proper sparsity can provide better classification performance.

In order to intuitively compare the performance of algorithms on sample reduction, we add 50 noise samples to each dataset. Each feature variable of these 50 noise samples obeys the Gaussian distribution with zero mean and 0.01 variance. Tables 4 and 5 show the accuracy and DSR of these algorithms in this case, respectively. Our method still performs well on eight out of 12 datasets based on results in Table 4. Since DSR in Table 5 does not increase on all datasets based on Table 3, these algorithms are not so robust to noise samples in all cases.

Figures 4 and 5 show the weight vectors w_1 and w_2 obtained by ℓ_1-TBSVM, NLPTSVM, ℓ_p-LSTSVM, SNSVM, TBSVM and TSVM on the Wpbc dataset, where the error threshold is 10^{-8}, and the dashed lines are the boundaries between the original samples of datasets and the added noise samples. Observation on Figs. 4 and 5 clearly indicate that ℓ_1-TBSVM and NLPTSVM have a better weight sparsity, that is, the two methods have a better performance on sample reduction. Compared with these two methods, the weights of the other four methods are not very satisfactory.

Table 2. Mean and standard deviation of test accuracy (%) on UCI datasets

Datasets	SVM	TBSVM	TSVM	ℓ_p-LSTSVM	NLPTSVM	SNSVM	STSVM	ℓ_1-TBSVM
Australian	86.52 ± 2.79	82.60 ± 2.98	82.32 ± 3.93	86.66 ± 2.79	87.97 ± 1.33	86.95 ± 3.82	77.50 ± 9.99	**88.70 ± 2.62**
Breast	73.31 ± 5.18	67.54 ± 3.64	65.71 ± 4.17	74.39 ± 2.41	73.65 ± 5.53	74.39 ± 3.02	72.93 ± 3.54	**75.45 ± 0.91**
Bupa	70.43 ± 3.92	57.68 ± 10.06	58.84 ± 4.87	67.83 ± 1.89	69.28 ± 6.75	70.43 ± 2.83	63.48 ± 5.16	**73.62 ± 2.15**
Diabetes	76.30 ± 1.19	69.66 ± 2.53	69.92 ± 1.06	76.30 ± 0.60	73.44 ± 2.91	74.87 ± 1.63	66.80 ± 3.25	**76.43 ± 2.04**
German	76.60 ± 1.17	72.30 ± 2.49	72.10 ± 3.49	73.90 ± 2.01	75.40 ± 3.09	**76.60 ± 2.10**	62.00 ± 14.17	76.00 ± 0.79
Heart	80.37 ± 3.10	81.11 ± 1.55	82.22 ± 3.10	80.74 ± 4.26	83.33 ± 2.27	81.48 ± 2.62	65.56 ± 10.77	**84.07 ± 2.48**
Pima	**75.00 ± 0.68**	69.01 ± 3.09	68.23 ± 2.47	74.74 ± 2.17	75.13 ± 2.00	75.13 ± 2.18	53.11 ± 16.84	76.56 ± 2.18
Sonar	86.04 ± 6.36	86.08 ± 6.89	85.61 ± 8.72	85.08 ± 6.54	84.58 ± 7.29	**88.00 ± 6.14**	71.16 ± 8.09	87.07 ± 6.15
Tic_tac_toe	**99.48 ± 0.37**	90.50 ± 3.85	91.02 ± 1.77	98.95 ± 0.98	98.22 ± 1.41	97.91 ± 1.05	75.57 ± 2.75	92.90 ± 2.00
Vote	**93.57 ± 1.91**	91.49 ± 4.31	92.86 ± 3.34	93.12 ± 2.87	91.96 ± 1.62	92.20 ± 2.15	77.66 ± 7.41	93.34 ± 2.85
Wdbc	98.07 ± 1.57	94.72 ± 1.67	96.30 ± 0.76	**98.07 ± 1.31**	97.36 ± 1.40	**98.07 ± 0.97**	80.34 ± 7.03	97.53 ± 0.76
Wpbc	76.84 ± 2.84	78.39 ± 3.65	77.35 ± 4.06	77.86 ± 5.17	74.30 ± 4.24	76.39 ± 6.21	67.40 ± 17.33	**78.43 ± 5.48**

Table 3. DSR (%) on UCI datasets

Datasets	SVM	TBSVM	TSVM	ℓ_p-LSTSVM	NLPTSVM	SNSVM	STSVM	ℓ_1-TBSVM
Australian	10.56 ± 23.21	0.00 ± 0.00	0.00 ± 0.00	0.00 ± 0.00	**92.99 ± 1.70**	0.00 ± 0.00	63.77 ± 3.84	6.86 ± 10.87
Breast	5.60 ± 6.23	0.00 ± 0.00	0.00 ± 0.00	0.00 ± 0.00	**81.80 ± 11.45**	0.00 ± 0.00	60.10 ± 0.00	37.12 ± 27.28
Bupa	20.87 ± 10.95	0.00 ± 0.00	0.00 ± 0.00	0.00 ± 0.00	**94.06 ± 3.66**	0.00 ± 0.00	27.54 ± 0.00	16.99 ± 19.01
Diabetes	7.85 ± 17.55	0.00 ± 0.00	0.00 ± 0.00	0.00 ± 0.00	**95.13 ± 0.75**	0.00 ± 0.00	68.91 ± 2.00	24.86 ± 22.27
German	24.58 ± 5.51	0.00 ± 0.00	0.00 ± 0.00	0.00 ± 0.00	**88.30 ± 7.19**	0.00 ± 0.00	75.00 ± 0.00	0.01 ± 0.01
Heart	14.07 ± 19.42	0.00 ± 0.00	0.00 ± 0.00	0.00 ± 0.00	**74.91 ± 7.34**	0.00 ± 0.00	13.43 ± 6.31	57.45 ± 25.26
Pima	8.59 ± 11.92	0.00 ± 0.00	0.00 ± 0.00	0.00 ± 0.00	**85.89 ± 1.86**	0.00 ± 0.00	67.45 ± 0.00	15.91 ± 15.14
Sonar	20.36 ± 4.12	0.00 ± 0.00	0.00 ± 0.00	0.00 ± 0.00	**49.28 ± 4.07**	0.00 ± 0.00	25.26 ± 14.40	21.10 ± 16.43
Tic_tac_toe	43.92 ± 15.67	0.00 ± 0.00	0.00 ± 0.00	0.00 ± 0.00	66.74 ± 5.13	0.00 ± 0.00	**73.90 ± 0.00**	0.01 ± 0.02
Vote	52.66 ± 29.72	0.00 ± 0.00	0.00 ± 0.00	0.00 ± 0.00	**65.42 ± 7.06**	0.00 ± 0.00	43.22 ± 1.46	0.11 ± 0.26
Wdbc	60.88 ± 17.39	0.00 ± 0.00	0.00 ± 0.00	0.00 ± 0.00	**72.56 ± 2.92**	0.00 ± 0.00	56.06 ± 0.11	13.00 ± 12.04
Wpbc	19.36 ± 11.08	0.00 ± 0.00	0.00 ± 0.00	0.00 ± 0.00	**83.71 ± 2.94**	0.00 ± 0.00	32.56 ± 28.89	29.94 ± 5.84

Table 4. Mean and standard deviation of test accuracy (%) on UCI datasets with 50 noise samples

Datasets	SVM	TBSVM	TSVM	ℓ_p-LSTSVM	NLPTSVM	SNSVM	STSVM	ℓ_1-TBSVM
Australian	87.10 ± 3.51	82.60 ± 3.94	83.48 ± 3.47	86.08 ± 1.41	87.10 ± 2.92	87.83 ± 2.55	79.71 ± 5.12	**87.97 ± 3.61**
Breast	**74.72 ± 5.00**	70.40 ± 2.37	70.06 ± 2.63	73.32 ± 3.97	71.10 ± 2.45	71.15 ± 4.30	59.49 ± 15.48	74.37 ± 4.47
Bupa	68.99 ± 3.01	56.81 ± 7.49	58.26 ± 6.75	69.28 ± 2.38	69.57 ± 7.03	73.33 ± 1.65	60.00 ± 8.85	**73.62 ± 3.30**
Diabetes	75.78 ± 1.39	68.48 ± 4.43	68.09 ± 6.02	76.69 ± 1.08	75.00 ± 1.55	76.04 ± 2.41	70.06 ± 3.14	**76.82 ± 1.07**
German	**77.10 ± 1.71**	69.40 ± 3.42	70.70 ± 3.42	74.50 ± 1.17	75.40 ± 2.36	76.40 ± 1.47	65.60 ± 10.68	76.60 ± 3.07
Heart	81.48 ± 2.62	75.19 ± 4.26	73.70 ± 4.42	80.00 ± 2.03	82.59 ± 4.26	82.96 ± 2.75	66.30 ± 6.47	**85.56 ± 1.55**
Pima	76.04 ± 1.09	68.10 ± 3.17	68.75 ± 3.58	75.13 ± 1.98	75.14 ± 2.34	76.17 ± 3.08	65.86 ± 12.35	**76.56 ± 12.27**
Sonar	85.57 ± 7.52	85.03 ± 7.66	84.10 ± 6.66	85.07 ± 6.82	84.58 ± 8.06	86.50 ± 7.88	67.28 ± 8.29	**86.58 ± 7.10**
Tic_tac_toe	**97.19 ± 1.35**	79.43 ± 1.93	81.21 ± 2.27	87.58 ± 4.63	84.76 ± 1.79	89.04 ± 2.32	75.37 ± 1.56	88.31 ± 1.93
Vote	91.50 ± 3.41	87.13 ± 6.05	88.29 ± 4.80	**93.57 ± 2.08**	90.82 ± 3.96	92.20 ± 3.01	77.42 ± 8.00	92.41 ± 1.78
Wdbc	97.71 ± 1.35	95.60 ± 2.26	96.65 ± 1.47	97.89 ± 1.47	97.54 ± 1.14	97.19 ± 0.74	83.17 ± 10.40	**98.23 ± 1.77**
Wpbc	77.95 ± 7.71	78.41 ± 4.30	78.43 ± 4.56	78.90 ± 4.00	68.17 ± 7.55	78.43 ± 5.15	74.26 ± 5.85	**79.41 ± 2.88**

Table 5. The DSR (%) on UCI datasets with 50 noise samples

Datasets	SVM	TBSVM	TSVM	ℓ_p-LSTSVM	NLPTSVM	SNSVM	STSVM	ℓ_1-TBSVM
Australian	27.58 ± 25.30	0.00 ± 0.00	0.00 ± 0.00	0.00 ± 0.00	**90.07 ± 5.82**	0.00 ± 0.00	66.78 ± 0.00	6.82 ± 9.38
Breast	5.96 ± 12.10	0.00 ± 0.00	0.00 ± 0.00	0.00 ± 0.00	**88.84 ± 5.48**	0.00 ± 0.00	35.85 ± 0.00	12.25 ± 15.37
Bupa	20.92 ± 0.67	0.00 ± 0.00	0.00 ± 0.00	0.00 ± 0.00	**90.25 ± 6.59**	0.00 ± 0.00	56.07 ± 0.00	0.53 ± 0.23
Diabetes	8.00 ± 17.80	0.00 ± 0.00	0.00 ± 0.00	0.00 ± 0.00	**95.41 ± 1.43**	0.00 ± 0.00	77.60 ± 0.00	0.54 ± 0.26
German	21.93 ± 12.37	0.00 ± 0.00	0.00 ± 0.00	0.00 ± 0.00	**91.69 ± 4.55**	0.00 ± 0.00	76.47 ± 0.00	19.54 ± 26.42
Heart	19.25 ± 17.44	0.00 ± 0.00	0.00 ± 0.00	0.00 ± 0.00	**77.37 ± 3.75**	0.00 ± 0.00	36.17 ± 0.00	34.44 ± 19.54
Pima	16.55 ± 9.69	0.00 ± 0.00	0.00 ± 0.00	0.00 ± 0.00	**87.12 ± 3.42**	0.00 ± 0.00	69.90 ± 0.00	1.72 ± 1.57
Sonar	17.19 ± 2.33	0.00 ± 0.00	0.00 ± 0.00	0.00 ± 0.00	**61.05 ± 4.48**	0.00 ± 0.00	26.78 ± 0.00	15.20 ± 9.81
Tic_tac_toe	35.54 ± 11.48	0.00 ± 0.00	0.00 ± 0.00	0.00 ± 0.00	**78.81 ± 1.49**	0.00 ± 0.00	0.00 ± 0.00	0.13 ± 0.12
Vote	42.94 ± 21.10	0.00 ± 0.00	0.00 ± 0.00	0.00 ± 0.00	**64.42 ± 4.32**	0.00 ± 0.00	13.75 ± 0.00	1.38 ± 1.20
Wdbc	61.09 ± 5.88	0.00 ± 0.00	0.00 ± 0.00	0.00 ± 0.00	**75.64 ± 3.12**	0.00 ± 0.00	60.41 ± 0.00	12.12 ± 16.01
Wpbc	18.91 ± 5.13	0.00 ± 0.00	0.00 ± 0.00	0.00 ± 0.00	**87.55 ± 9.87**	0.00 ± 0.00	60.39 ± 0.00	31.68 ± 5.67

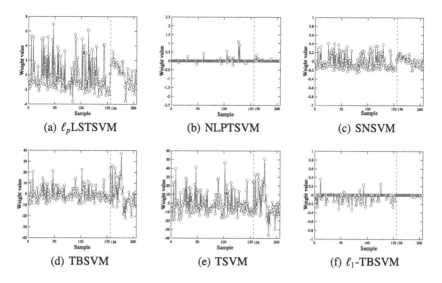

(a) ℓ_pLSTSVM   (b) NLPTSVM   (c) SNSVM

(d) TBSVM   (e) TSVM   (f) ℓ_1-TBSVM

Fig. 4. Weight vector w_1 obtained by TSVM-like methods on Wpbc with 50 noise samples

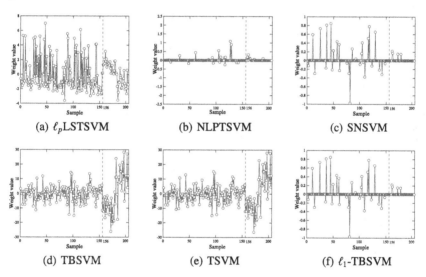

(a) ℓ_pLSTSVM   (b) NLPTSVM   (c) SNSVM

(d) TBSVM   (e) TSVM   (f) ℓ_1-TBSVM

Fig. 5. Weight vector w_2 obtained by TSVM-like methods on Wpbc with 50 noise samples

In conclusion, we made the following observations.

– Situation 1: datasets without noise samples. In Situation 1, ℓ_1-TBSVM is superior to other methods on seven out of twelve datasets, followed by SNSVM, ℓ_p-LSTSVM and SVM.

– Situation 2: datasets with 50 noise samples. In Situation 2, ℓ_1-TBSVM is superior to other methods on eight out of twelve datasets, followed by ℓ_p-LSTSVM, SVM and SNSVM.
– Unlike NLPTSVM, ℓ_1-TBSVM does not one-sidedly focus on sparsity, disregarding classification performance. Compared with other TSVM-like algorithms except for NLPTSVM, the ability of ℓ_1-TBSVM to reduce sample is rather strong.

4   Conclusion

For binary classification tasks, we propose a novel ℓ_1-TBSVM algorithm. The main merit of ℓ_1-TBSVM is that it has a good performance on sample reduction, which is due to introducing the ℓ_1-norm and the hinge loss function in feature space, and finding solutions in the primal space where it can avoid the ill-condition in some situation. Extensive experiments are conducted. On an artificial dataset, we validate the ability of ℓ_1-TBSVM to reduce sample. On UCI datasets, we demonstrate the superiority of ℓ_1-TBSVM in classification performance.

Although ℓ_1-TBSVM performs well in experiments, ℓ_1-TBSVM would still suffer from high computational complexity when dealing with large-scale datasets. Thus, how to improve the training efficiency of ℓ_1-TBSVM is an issue that needs to be solved. Moreover, we only construct ℓ_1-TBSVM for the binary classification problems instead of multi-class classification problems or regression problems.

Acknowledgment. This work was supported in part by the Natural Science Foundation of the Jiangsu Higher Education Institutions of China under Grant No. 19KJA550002, by the Six Talent Peak Project of Jiangsu Province of China under Grant No. XYDXX-054, by the Priority Academic Program Development of Jiangsu Higher Education Institutions, and by the Collaborative Innovation Center of Novel Software Technology and Industrialization.

References

1. Bi, J., Bennett, K.P., Embrechts, M., Breneman, C.M., Song, M.: Dimensionality reduction via sparse support vector machines. J. Mach. Learn. Res. **3**, 1229–1243 (2003)
2. Cortes, C., Vapnik, V.: Support vector networks. Mach. Learn. **20**(3), 273–297 (1995)
3. Cristianini, N., Shawe-Taylor, J.: An Introduction to Support Vector Machines and Other Kernel-Based Learning Methods. Cambridge University, Cambridge (2000)
4. Dheeru, D., Karra Taniskidou, E.: UCI machine learning repository (2017). http://archive.ics.uci.edu/ml
5. Duda, R.O., Hart, P.E., Stork, D.G.: Pattern Classification, 2nd edn. Wiley, New York (2001)
6. Floyd, S., Warmuth, M.: Sample compression, learnability, and the Vapnik-Chervonenkis dimension. Mach. Learn. **21**(3), 269–304 (1995)

7. Gao, S., Ye, Q., Ye, N.: 1-norm least squares twin support vector machines. Neurocomputing **74**(17), 3590–3597 (2011)
8. Graepel, T., Herbrich, R., Shawe-Taylor, J., Holloway, R.: Generalisation error bounds for sparse linear classifiers. In: Proceedings of the Thirteenth Annual Conference on Computational Learning Theory, pp. 298–303 (2000)
9. Huffener, F., Niedermeier, R., Wernicke, S.: Techniques for practical fixed-parameter algorithms. Comput. J. **51**(1), 7–25 (2008)
10. Jayadeva, Khemchandani, R., Chandra, S.: Twin support vector machine for pattern classification. IEEE Trans. Pattern Anal. Mach. Intell. **29**(5), 905–910 (2007)
11. Kumar, M.A., Gopall, M.: Least squares twin support vector machine for pattern classification. Expert Syst. Appl. **36**, 7535–7543 (2009)
12. Mangasarian, O.L., Wild, E.: Multisurface proximal support vector machine classification via generalized eigenvalues. IEEE Trans. Pattern Anal. Mach. Intell. **28**(1), 69–74 (2006)
13. Niedermeier, R.: Invitation to Fixed-Parameter Algorithms. Oxford University Press, Oxford (2006)
14. Peng, X.: Building sparse twin support vector machine classifiers in primal space. Inf. Sci. **181**(18), 3967–3980 (2011)
15. Peng, X.: TPSVM: a novel twin parametric-margin support vector machine for pattern recognition. Pattern Recogn. **44**, 2678–2692 (2011)
16. Shao, Y., Zhang, C., Wang, X., Deng, N.: Improvements on twin support vector machine. IEEE Trans. Neural Netw. **22**(6), 962–968 (2011)
17. Tanveer, M.: Robust and sparse linear programming twin support vector machines. Cogn. Comput. **7**(1), 137–149 (2015)
18. Tian, Y., Ju, X., Qi, Z.: Efficient sparse nonparallel support vector machines for classification. Neural Comput. Appl. **24**(5), 1089–1099 (2014)
19. Vapnik, V.N.: The Nature of Statistical Learning Theory. Springer, New York (2000). https://doi.org/10.1007/978-1-4757-3264-1
20. Xu, Y., Wang, L., Zhong, P.: A rough margin-based v-twin support vector machine. Neural Comput. Appl. **21**, 1307–1317 (2012)
21. Zhang, L., Zhou, W.: On the sparseness of 1-norm support vector machines. Neural Netw. **23**(3), 373–385 (2010)
22. Zhang, L., et al.: Kernel sparse representation-based classifier. IEEE Trans. Sig. Process. **60**(4), 1684–1695 (2012)
23. Zhang, L., Zhou, W., Jiao, L.: Hidden space support vector machine. IEEE Trans. Neural Netw. **15**(6), 1424–1434 (2004)
24. Zhang, Z., Zhen, L., Deng, N., Tan, J.: Sparse least square twin support vector machine with adaptive norm. Appl. Intell. **41**(4), 1097–1107 (2014)
25. Zhou, W., Zhang, L., Jiao, L.: Linear programming support vector machines. Pattern Recogn. **35**(12), 2927–2936 (2002)

Spreading Dynamics Analysis for Railway Networks

Xingtang Wu[1,2](✉), Mingkun Yang[2], Hongwei Wang[3], Hairong Dong[2](✉)(iD), Jinhu Lü[1], and Haifeng Song[2]

[1] School of Automation Science and Electrical Engineering,
Beihang University, Beijing 100191, China
[2] The State Key Laboratory of Rail Traffic Control and Safety,
Beijing Jiaotong University, Beijing 100044, China
wuxingtang@bjtu.edu.cn
[3] National Research Center of Railway Safety Assessment Beijing Jiaotong
University, Beijing 100044, China

Abstract. The 2019 Coronavirus Disease (COVID-19), with the characteristics of rapid onset, strong infectivity, fast transmission and wide susceptibility, has quickly swept China since its appearance in Wuhan, Hubei province. COVID-19 spreads among people mainly by movement and close contact. Railway plays an important role in transport people national-wide as its essential role in public transportation, which conduced to the spreading of COVID-19 from Hubei province to other provinces in some sense. Inspired by this, this paper collected the data of Trains with Infectors (TwI) reported by the national health commission of the People's Republic of China. Then the spreading of COVID-19 via railway network with the concept of complex network is analyzed. Results show that nodes with higher centrality tends to provide more TwI, and the closure of Wuhan railway station significantly prevents the spreading of COVID-19.

Keywords: COVID-19 · Railway network · Complex network

1 Introduction

In December 2019, the Coronavirus Disease (COVID-19) was noticed in Wuhan, China, followed by a large-scale outbreak throughout the whole country. The COVID-19 has the characteristics of rapid onset, strong infectivity, fast transmission and wide susceptibility, *etc.* By March 19, 2020, a total of 81,262 people had been infected and 3,250 had died according to the statistics from National Health Commission of China [6]. Figure 1(a) shows the trend of the epidemic in Hubei Province from the end of January to the end of March. Recently, COVID-19 attacks Italy, Spain, the United States, and many other countries, resulting in a large-scale spreading and infection. As of April 9th, 2021, the cumulative number of confirmed cases in the world exceeded 13 billion, and the cumulative number of deaths exceeded 2 billion, as shown in Fig. 1(b)

© Springer Nature Singapore Pte Ltd. 2021
H. Zhang et al. (Eds.): NCAA 2021, CCIS 1449, pp. 154–165, 2021.
https://doi.org/10.1007/978-981-16-5188-5_12

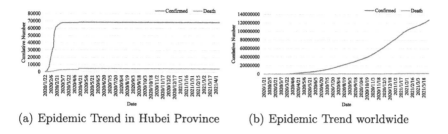

(a) Epidemic Trend in Hubei Province   (b) Epidemic Trend worldwide

Fig. 1. Basic statistics of the TwI data

COVID-19 spreads among people mainly by movement and close contact. Since the outbreak of COVID-19, a large number of researches have appeared to study the issue of virus spread and control strategy. By extensively analyzing the confirmed cases, the fundamental statistical characteristic of the infectors with age, gender, as well as the geographical-temporal spread distribution are studied in [7]. In the study of Chinazzi *et al.* [1], they applied the disease transmission model to define the virus spread problem and studied the impact of travel restriction on disease transmission. According to the real-time mobility data and the historical mobility data in Wuhan, Kraemer *et al.* [4] clarified the influence of imported cases on virus spread in cities among China and demonstrated the good effects of the control measures taking by the Chinese government. Zheng *et al.* [11] examined the impacts of transportation on spreading COVID-19 among cities and indicated that the transmission risk level was strongly relevant to the connectivity and distance among cities. Zhao *et al.* [10] studied the relationship between public transportation and the number of imported cases. Results showed that the railway played a more important role in transmitting virus than air transportation and road traffic. Du *et al.* [2] estimated the probability of COVID-19 spread from Wuhan to other cities in China. Prem *et al.* [5] proposed a model to verify the effectiveness of the implemented distance control measures on controlling the spread of COVID-19. Tian *et al.* [8] analyzed the data of confirmed cases, human movement, and government control measures. Then conclusions were drawn that the interventions of government were very effective in delaying the outbreak of the virus and reducing the incidence of cases. To assess the border control measures, Wells *et al.* [9] focused on the role of the airport travel network in spreading COVID-19, and their results indicated that the control measures are effective but not sufficient in stopping the global transmission of COVID-19. Iacus *et al.* [3] proposed a method to estimate the passenger number transported by airplane from mainland China to the other countries using the historical data, which could be applied to all other countries in the same way.

Railway, as an essential part of national-wide public transportation, plays an important role in transport people. By the end of 2019, China's total railway mileage had exceeded 139,000 km, forming a huge *Rail Transit Network* (RTN) covering most cities in the country, and the cumulative turnover of rail-

Fig. 2. Accumulative flow graph of the trains with infectors, where the red dot denotes the start of the train, and the green dot denotes the terminal of the train. (Color figure online)

way passengers nationwide were more than 12,3000 billion person/km. In order to prevent the spreading of COVID-19, the Chinese government isolated Wuhan since January 23th, 2020 to cut down the contact between Wuhan (a main source of infection) and other cities in China. Under the travel restriction, all train stopping in Wuhan has ceased operation. However, it was reported that 5,000,000 people across the country from Wuhan before the closure of Wuhan as the date was closed to the lunar year of China. A large part of travellers (including infectors and incubation people) would chose rail transportation as Wuhan was a hub of RTN, helping the spreading of COVID-19 nationwide. According to the national health commission of the People's Republic of China's statistics, a total of 1136 infectors travelling by train was reported, resulting in numerous people was quaranteed. However, current research seldomly analyzed the relationship of railway network and the spread of COVID-19.

In order to reveal the spreading characteristic of COVID-19 by RTN, this paper proposes an analytical method from a complex network perspective based on the infectors travelling data and the RTN data. Specifically the spreading of COVID-19 versus the topology characteristic of the CHR network is revealed, and the evolutionary law of the TwI is studied. The reminder of this paper is organized as follows. Section 2 gives a brief description of the collected data. The spreading characteristics of COVID-19 via RTN is studied in Sect. 3, and Sect. 4 concluded this work.

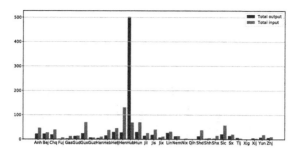

(a) The basic statistics of TwI data before the closure of Wuhan

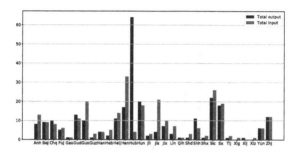

(b) The basic statistics of TwI data Afetre the closure of Wuhan

Fig. 3. Basic statistics of the TwI data

2 Data Set

In order to analyze the spreading characteristic of COVID-19 by RTN, this paper collects and organizes the data of infectors travelling by railway. A total of 1136 records were collected from the national health commission of the People's Republic of China official website. A infector's record included the travel date, the train index, the start and terminal of the train, carriage number, and the description of the patient. The date of those records ranged from December 27th, 2019 to February 8th, 2020, a total of 43 days. Figure 2 shows the cumulative flow graph of those data. It can be seen that trains with infectors are mainly originated from Hubei province. Besides, the stops of all related trains were obtained from the 'www.12306.com'.

In order to make the data more statistically significant, all the data were treated in a macro perspective, i.e., the route of a train was represented by the province to which the station belongs. For example, the start and the terminal of train $G420$ were Ningbo station and Beijing south station in the original data set, respectively; after the data processing, the start and the terminal of train $G420$ were Zhejiang province and Beijing, respectively. Specifically, if a train passed through Hubei province, then Hubei province was treated as the source of the

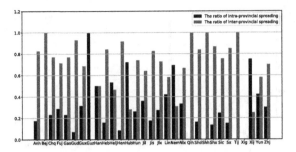

(a) The ratio of intra-province spreading and inter-province spreading before the closure of Wuhan

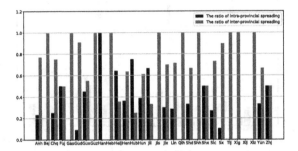

(b) The ratio of intra-province spreading and inter-province spreading after the closure of Wuhan

Fig. 4. The ratio of intra-province spreading and inter-province spreading

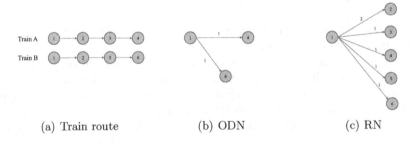

(a) Train route   (b) ODN   (c) RN

Fig. 5. Network modeling example

train, the route between the original province and Hubei province was deleted. The reason is as follows. The start of the train indicated the transmission source of COVID-19, if the *Train with Infector*(TwI) passed through Hubei province, it was reasonable to believe that the infectors boarded the train from Hubei as Hubei province was the center of disease outbreak. So the section between the original province and Hubei province was not affected by the TwI.

After the data pre-processing, the basic statistics of the TwI data is shown in Fig. 3. Figure 3(a) and Fig. 3(b) show the total number of input and output TwIs for each province. It can be seen that Hubei Province was the main TwI source among all the provinces before and after the closure of Wuhan. The number of TwI originated from Hubei province decreased by 87% after the closure of Wuhan station. Besides the average number of input TwI in each province has also been reduced by 68% after the closure of Wuhan station. Figure 4(a) and Fig. 4(b) show the ratio of intra-province spreading and inter-province spreading for each province. The proportion of TwI spreading within the province is 28.19%, while the proportion of TwI spreading between provinces is 71.09%. Basic conclusions can be drawn that the closure of Wuhan station has a significant improvement in suppressing the spreading of COVID-19, while it has no direct impact on the proportion of intra-provincial and inter-provincial transmission.

The passenger volume of the China's High-speed Railway (CHR) accounts for 64.1% of the total railway passenger volume in 2019, so the CHR network is extracted as a typical railway structure to analyze the relationship between the railway network and the spreading of infectors via railway. The CHR network contains XX stations and 108 lines (including side lines).

3 COVID-19 Spreading Characteristics via Rail Network

3.1 Network Modeling

In this paper, three network are considered, namely *CHR Network* (CHRN), Original-Destination Network (ODN), and *Radiation Network*(RN). The CHRN was an un-directed and un-weighted network, which referred to the network consisted of the railway tracks and stations. A node referred to a station, and if there was a track between two stations, there was an edge between the two corresponding nodes. The ODN and RN are established based on the TwI data. For the ODN, a province was treated as a node, and there was an edge between two nodes if a node was the original of a train and another node was the terminal of the train. The weight of the edge was the number of trains that connecting two nodes, and the direction of any edges equaled to the train's forward direction. For the RN, a province was treated as a node, and there was an edge between the original of the train and the following nodes in the train route. The weight of the edge equaled to the number of trains between the two nodes, and the direction of the edge equaled to the train direction. An example was shown for illustration. Assume that there were two trains A and B, the route of train A was $1 \rightarrow 2 \rightarrow 3 \rightarrow 4$, and the route of train B was $1 \rightarrow 2 \rightarrow 5 \rightarrow 6$, then the ODN and RN were shown in Fig. 5(b) and Fig. 5(c), respectively. A network could be fully represented by an adjacency matrix A, whose element a_{ij} equals to the weight of the edge if there exists an edge between node i and node j, and equals 0 otherwise.

3.2   Basic Characteristics of the CHR Network

In this section, the topological characteristic of the CHRN is analyzed. Firstly, the characteristic path length of the CHRN is studied. The characteristic path length is defined as the average shortest path length of the network, i.e.,

$$L = \frac{\sum_i \sum_j d_{ij}}{N(N-1)}, \tag{1}$$

where d_{ij} is the shortest path length between node i and j. The characteristic path length reveals the connectivity of a network. Then the node centrality is studied to evaluate the relative importance of Wuhan in the CHRN network. The Betweenness Centrality is widely used matrix and it is defined as:

$$B(i) = \sum_{j,k} \frac{n_{jk}(i)}{n_{jk}} \tag{2}$$

where n_{jk} denotes the number of shortest path between node j and node k, and $n_{jk}(i)$ denotes that number of shortest path between node j and node k that pass through node i. A high value of betweenness centrality of a node indicates that this station has a higher impact on the network global performance. The betweenness centrality value for Wuhan station is 70075, ranking third among all nodes. The large value of betweenness of Wuhan station shows its high importance level. Besides the characteristic path length for CHRN before and after the closure of Wuhan are 37 and 52, respectively. It can be seen that the closure of wuhan increased the characteristic path length of the CHRN network by 41%, which significantly helps the suppressing of COVID-19 via CHRN.

3.3   Spreading Characteristics Analysis

First, we verified the spreading of COVID-19 from Hubei province via rail network with ODN network. A series of ODNs were established based on the daily TwI data. Then the variation of node strength was studied. The node strength is a very basic but powerful parameter for weighted network structure characteristic. The strength of a node i is defined as the sum of weights of all edges that connected to node i. For directed networks, the strength of node was divided into in-strength and out-strength, i.e.

$$S^{\text{in}}(i) = \sum_j a_{ji}, \tag{3}$$

$$S^{\text{out}}(i) = \sum_j a_{ij}, \tag{4}$$

The out-strength of a node in ODN indicated the number of TwI that started from this node. Figure 6 showed the out-strength variation of Wuhan over time. It was shown that the out-strength followed the Gaussian distribution with parameter (a, b, c). By the day January 23th, 2020, the number of Iwt reached the maximum value, then started to decreased with time. This figure verified that the closure of Wuhan significantly helped to prevent the spreading of COVID-19 via RTN.

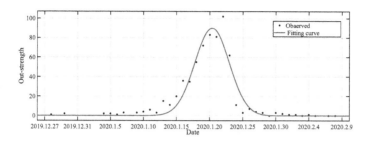

Fig. 6. Distribution of Hubei province out-strength for ODN over time

Then the correlation between node strength and the closeness of ODN was studied. The node strength could directly unfold the number of trains that started from this province, and the closeness centrality could quantify the centrality of a node in the sense of distance to all other nodes. The closeness was defined as follows, i.e.,

$$CC(i) = \frac{n-1}{\sum_{i \neq j} d_{ij}} \tag{5}$$

In a ODN, the shortest path length between two nodes indicated the minimum number of trains that connecting two province. A higher value of $CC(i)$ means the shorter distance of the node i from all other nodes, thus indicating the higher importance of the node. Figure 7 showed the correlation between the two parameters. It could be seen that these two variables were positively and linearly correlated. The correlation between the two parameters manifested that provinces closer to other provinces via ODN tended to provide more TwIs.

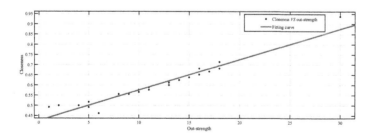

Fig. 7. Correlation between out-strength and closeness centrality in ODN

Next, the node temporal distribution of in-strength and out-strength in RN were analyzed. The in-strength of a node showed the number of provinces that

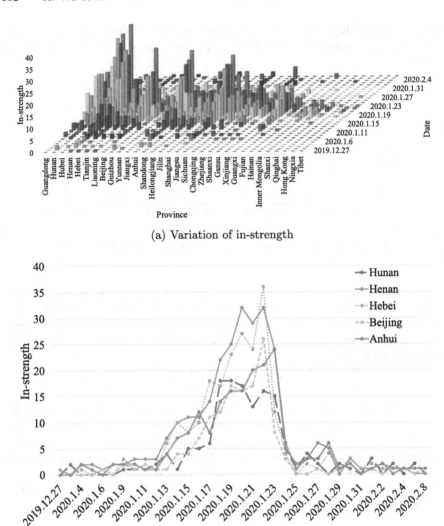

(a) Variation of in-strength

(b) Variation of in-strength for 5 province

Fig. 8. Node in-strength variation for RN over time

providing TwIs to this province, and the out-strength of a node showed the number of provinces that was potentially affected by this province. Figure 8 and Fig. 9 showed the variation of node in-strength and out-strength over time, respectively. From Fig. 8 we can see that Hunan province, Henan province, Hebei province, Beijing, and Anhui province are the five top affected provinces, besides the peak period of TwIs' input of each province is concentrated between January 10 and January 23. Based on Fig. 9, we can see that Hubei province is main source

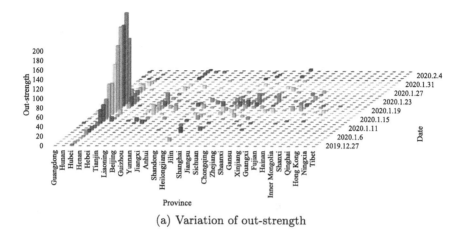

(a) Variation of out-strength

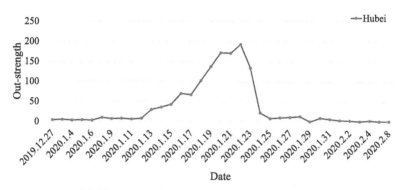

(b) Variation of out-strength for Hubei province

Fig. 9. Node out-strength variation for RN over time

of TwIs. The number of TwIs that provided by Hubei province is much higher than other provinces. In order to explicitly show the radiation by Hubei Province of each province, Fig. 10 shows the in-strength distribution from Hubei province for every provinces. We can still see that Hunan province, Henan province, Hebei province, Beijing, and Anhui province are the five top affected provinces. Based on Fig. 10(a) and Fig. 10, conclusions can be drawn that the imported infectors of most provinces are from Hubei province, and spread among other provinces are rare. Besides, both figures indicate the important role of the closure of Wuhan in suppressing TwIs transmission.

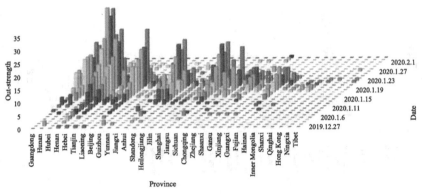

(a) Variation of in-strength from Hubei province

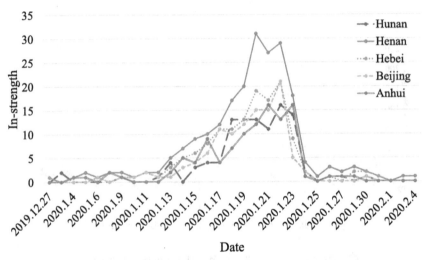

(b) Variation of in-strength from Hubei province for 5 province

Fig. 10. Node in-strength variation from Hubei province for RN over time

4   Conclusion

The 2019 Coronavirus Disease (COVID-19) outbreaked since it was noticed in Wuhan, China in December 2019. The disease was rapidly sweeping the world due to its rapid onset, strong contagion, rapid spread, and strong susceptibility. Studying the spreading characteristics of COVID-19 in order to prevent further spreading is a worldwide problem. The railway is an essential part of the national-wide public transportation due to its advantages of high velocity, large capacity, et al. In order to unfold how the COVID-19 spread via the railway network in China, the reported *Train with Infectors* (TwI) data was collected to analyze the spreading characteristics. Three networks named China's *High-speed*

Rail Network(CHRN), *Original-Destination Network* (ODN) and *Radiation Network* (RN) were constructed with the concept of complex network. Then the characteristic of the three network were studied. Specifically the node strength variation and the correlation between the node strength and the node centrality were revealed. Related conclusions can help other countries to further prevent the spread of the epidemic through railways.

Acknowledgements. This work is supported by National Natural Science Foundation of China (No. U1834211 and No. 61925302).

References

1. Chinazzi, M., et al.: The effect of travel restrictions on the spread of the 2019 novel coronavirus (COVID-19) outbreak. Science **368**(6489), 395–400 (2020)
2. Du, Z., et al.: Risk for transportation of coronavirus disease from Wuhan to other cities in China. Emerging Infect. Dis. **26**(5), 1049 (2020)
3. Iacus, S.M., Natale, F., Vespe, M.: Flight restrictions from china during the COVID-2019 coronavirus outbreak. arXiv preprint arXiv:2003.03686 (2020)
4. Kraemer, M.U., et al.: The effect of human mobility and control measures on the COVID-19 epidemic in China. Science **368**(6490), 493–497 (2020)
5. Prem, K., et al.: The effect of control strategies to reduce social mixing on outcomes of the COVID-19 epidemic in Wuhan, China: a modelling study. Lancet Public Health **5**(5), 261–270 (2020)
6. Sohrabi, C., et al.: World health organization declares global emergency: a review of the 2019 novel coronavirus (COVID-19). Int. J. Surg. **76**, 71–76 (2020)
7. Surveillances, V.: The epidemiological characteristics of an outbreak of 2019 novel coronavirus diseases (COVID-19)-China, 2020. China CDC Weekly **2**(8), 113–122 (2020)
8. Tian, H., et al.: An investigation of transmission control measures during the first 50 days of the COVID-19 epidemic in China. Science **368**(6491), 638–642 (2020)
9. Wells, C.R., et al.: Impact of international travel and border control measures on the global spread of the novel 2019 coronavirus outbreak. Proc. Natl. Acad. Sci. **117**(13), 7504–7509 (2020)
10. Zhao, S., et al.: The association between domestic train transportation and novel coronavirus (2019-nCoV) outbreak in china from 2019 to 2020: a data-driven correlational report. Travel Med. Infect. Dis. **33**, 101568 (2020)
11. Zheng, R., Xu, Y., Wang, W., Ning, G., Bi, Y.: Spatial transmission of COVID-19 via public and private transportation in China. Travel Med. Infect. Dis. **34**, 101626 (2020)

Learning to Collocate Fashion Items from Heterogeneous Network Using Structural and Textual Features

Qiong Yu, Wenjian Xu, Yingji Wu, and Haijun Zhang$^{(\boxtimes)}$

Department of Computer Science, Harbin Institute of Technology, Shenzhen, China
`hjzhang@hit.edu.cn`

Abstract. This research presents a new framework for collocating fashion items from heterogeneous network using structural and textual features. Specifically, we construct a fashion heterogenous network, and extract structural features of fashion items from the heterogenous network by utilizing a GATNE model. Then we propose a fashion collocation model based on the fusion of structural and textual features. Given item pairs, their textual features achieved by a Siamese network and structural features achieved by the GATNE model in advance are fused to generate new features. Our framework was examined on a large-scaled clothing item set. The experiment results demonstrate that our proposed framework is effective in the task of fashion collocation.

Keywords: Fashion collocation · GATNE model · Siamese network · Feature fusion

1 Introduction

With the rapid development of e-commerce, more and more people are accustomed to buying clothes online. In recent years, there exist extensive studies about clothing classification, attribute prediction, clothing retrieval, fashion collocation and other issues in the field of fashion learning. However, very few researchers construct fashion heterogeneous network and use network representation learning methods to solve problems in the field of fashion.

Most of extant studies on fashion collocation were carried out by using item images and texts. Veit *et al.* [1] introduced a method by embedding clothing images into a style-compatible space. They utilized a Siamese Convolutional Neural Network (CNN) architecture to extract visual features. Likewise, Zhang *et al.* [2] presented a new framework for matching clothes by using a Siamese Long-short Term Memory (LSTM) architecture to extract textual features. In the actual dressing scene, there exist certain specific relationships between fashion items, such as similarity relationships and allocation relationships. Existing studies tend to focus on individual fashion items or outfits. However, fashion items and their relationships cannot be treated as a whole, and a fashion heterogeneous network has not been explored. Moreover, in the past few decades,

H. Zhang et al. (Eds.): NCAA 2021, CCIS 1449, pp. 166–180, 2021.
https://doi.org/10.1007/978-981-16-5188-5_13

many researchers in other fields have been carried out in heterogenous network representation learning. For example, Cen *et al.* [3] proposed a GATNE model to embed attributed multiplex heterogeneous network. The approach has been successfully deployed and evaluated on Alibaba's recommendation system with excellent scalability and effectiveness. However, there are few studies on heterogeneous network in the fashion field. Therefore, constructing a fashion heterogeneous network to make full use of the relationships between fashion items and the information of fashion items themselves is of important practical significance.

In this research, we construct a fashion heterogeneous network with similar and matching relationships and learn to collocate fashion items from heterogenous network using structural and textual features. We extract structural features of fashion items from heterogenous network by using the GATNE model [3]. Moreover, we further propose a fashion collocation model which fuses structural and textual features of fashion items. Specifically, the contributions of this paper are summarized into twofold: 1) we introduce a fashion heterogenous network, in which nodes represent fashion items and two kinds of edges represent similar and matching relationships between fashion items; and 2) we propose an approach to collocating fashion items from heterogenous network using structural and textual features. By fusing structural and textual features, we improve the performance of fashion collocation.

The remainder of this article is organized as follows. Section 2 briefly reviews the related work. The proposed framework to collocate fashion items from heterogenous network using structural and textual features is introduced in Sect. 3. Section 4 describes the verification experiment. This article concludes with future work propositions in Sect. 5.

2   Related Work

In this section, we review related state-of-the-arts for network embedding, heterogeneous network embedding, and fashion collocation.

1) Network Embedding: In order to transform network from original network space to vector space, the commonly used models include matrix factorization, random walk, deep neural networks and their variations. Singular value decomposition [4] and non-negative matrix factorization [5] are representative methods of matrix factorization. Representative methods of random walk include Deep-Walk [6] and node2vec [7], etc. Deep neural networks are used to embed complex networks, whose representative methods include SDNE [8], SDAE [9], SiNE [10], etc. In addition, these three models are not mutually exclusive, and their combinations can produce new solutions.

2) Heterogeneous Network Embedding: Most heterogeneous network embedding methods are based on homogeneous network representation learning. The goal of heterogeneous network embedding is to map different types of nodes and edges to latent space. Many heterogeneous network embedding methods are based on skip-gram framework. PTE [11] projects heterogenous network into multiple homogenous networks. It defines the proximity of vertices in each homogeneous network by assuming that vertices with similar neighbors are similar with each other and their representations in low-dimensional space are close. Based on this assumption, PTE applies skip-gram framework to each homogeneous network and jointly optimizes all embedding representations. Metapath2vec [12] introduces a random walk strategy based on meta-path to construct the heterogeneous neighborhood of a node and then uses skip-gram models to learn node embeddings. Subsequently, meta-path is utilized to construct heterogeneous context to learn representation vectors for different downstream tasks in many methods, such as HIN2vec [13], GATNE [3], TamEm [14], NeRank [15] and HeteSpaceyWalk [16]. In addition to skip-gram-based methods, there exist other heterogeneous network embedding methods, including label propagation, factorization, and generative adversarial networks-based methods.

3) Fashion Collocation: Most of extant studies on fashion collocation are carried out by using two types of features: images and texts. Siamese network appears to be an effective method in fashion collocation. Veit *et al.* [1] proposed a learning framework which can learn a feature transformation from clothing images into a latent space that expresses compatibility. Pairs of items that are either compatible or incompatible are input into Siamese CNN architecture. Zhang *et al.* [2] proposed a learning framework which extracts textual features of clothes. After obtaining textual features of clothes through Siamese LSTM architecture, a compatibility matrix was used to integrate feature embeddings into style-compatible space. In addition to seeking for clothes matching among existing clothes, some researchers were devoted to generating collocated clothes. Liu *et al.* [17] presented a multi-discriminator cGAN framework for the task of generating collocation clothing images. An Attribute-GAN framework was proposed to learn a map from collocation clothing pairs, and a CA-GAN framework was proposed to implement clothing image translation.

4) Features of Our Model: There exist several studies focusing on fashion collocation. For example, the works in [1] and [2] both used Siamese network to extract features of fashion items. The difference lies in that the method in [1] utilized Siamese CNN to extract visual features, while the method in [2] utilized Siamese LSTM to extract textual features. Our model is also based on Siamese network, but our model utilizes structural features of fashion items. We construct a fashion heterogeneous network, in which nodes represent fashion items and two kinds of edges represent similar and matching relationships between fashion items. We then extract structural features of fashion items from heterogenous network and fuse structural and textual features in Siamese network. In this way, we not only use paired items, but also consider the features of fashion items in the whole heterogenous network.

3   Fashion Collocation Based on Heterogenous Network

3.1   Overview of Our Framework

The goal of fashion collocation task can be formulated as follows. Given two fashion items, our proposed model returns their compatibility. For clarity, our framework is shown in Fig. 1, which illustrates the basic flow of our approach. First, GATNE [3] is employed to extract structural features, and Siamese network is used to extract textual features. Then we fuse fashion items' structural and textual features to generate new features. Finally, the compatibility of two fashion items is calculated accordingly.

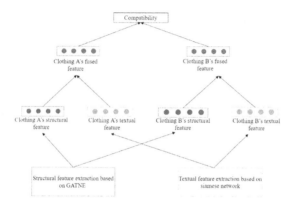

Fig. 1. The overview of the proposed fashion collocation framework.

3.2   Network Construction

Fashion heterogeneous network is aimed to fully model fashion data from a network perspective. It contains two important elements, i.e., fashion items and relationships between fashion items. Fashion items are represented as $V = \{v_1, v_2, \ldots, v_m\}$, where m denotes the number of fashion items. Relationships between fashion items are represented as $R = \{s, p\}$, where s denotes similar relationships and p denotes matching relationships. Fashion items have two attributes, i.e., categories and textual descriptions. Categories are represented as $T = \{t_1, t_2, \ldots, t_n\}$, where n denotes the number of categories. Textual descriptions are represented as $L = \{l_1, l_2, \ldots, l_n\}$ where m denotes the number of fashion items.

Fashion heterogeneous network is showed in Fig. 2. The main elements of the network include nodes, relationships, and node attributes. In fashion heterogeneous network, nodes represent clothing; edges represent relationships between fashion items, including similar relationships and matching relationships; and node attributes include categories and textual descriptions of fashion items.

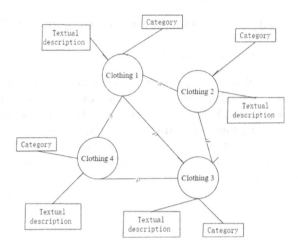

Fig. 2. Fashion heterogeneous network.

3.3 Structural Feature Extraction

We use GATNE [3] to model fashion heterogenous network and obtain the vectorized representations of fashion items under various relationships. The vectorized representations of fashion items under the matching relationship are treated as structural features of fashion items. Then we use structure features of two fashion items to calculate a cosine similarity, which is regarded as compatibility.

GATNE [3] includes two kinds of models, GATNE-T and GATNE-I. The overall embedding of a certain node v_i on each edge type r includes base embedding and edge embedding. The base embedding is shared between different edge types. GATNE-T only uses network structure information while GATNE-I considers both structure information and node attributes. In this paper, we use GATNE-T to extract structural features of fashion items. The fashion collocation process base on GATNE-T model is as follows. First, we initialize parameters of GATNE model; second, we generate random walks on each edge type r as P_r relationships; then, we generate training samples $\{(v_i, v_j, r)\}$ from random walks P_r on each edge type r; at last, we sample L negative samples and train GATNE model. In the training process, the vectorized representations of fashion items under the matching relationships are treated as the structural feature. After each training epoch, we use validation set to evaluate the model's performance. For a sample in validation set, we use cosine similarity to calculate the compatibility of two fashion items. We calculate all samples' compatibility in the validation set and calculate an AUC(area under curve). If AUC decreases, the training process is stopped. At this time, the vectorized representations of fashion items under the matching relationships are the final structural feature of fashion items.

3.4   Textual Feature Extraction

Siamese network encodes two sentences of different lengths into vectors of same length to calculate the similarity of the two sentences [18]. We extend it to the compatibility of sentences and apply it to the problem of fashion collocation.

Word segmentation is used to obtain words of a piece of clothing's description text. First, we count occurrences of words in the training set and add the words with more than 2 occurrences to dictionary. The number of words in the final dictionary is 25,052. Each word is represented by a 300-dimensional vector, which is stored in a dictionary matrix. A row of the dictionary matrix represents a word. The number of rows of the dictionary matrix is 25,052, which is equal to the number of words in the dictionary. The number of columns of the dictionary matrix is 300, which is equal to the dimension of word vector. We set the length of sentence to 30. The description text of a piece of clothing is represented as a matrix with 30 rows and 300 columns. The dictionary matrix is initialized randomly and participates the model training.

The fashion text collocation model based on Siamese network is shown in Fig. 3. The vectorized representations of the description texts of two fashion items are input to the model. Through two stacked LSTM structures, we get the textual features x_a and x_b. The stacked LSTM in our implementation contains 3 layers, and the two stacked LSTM structures do not share parameters with each other. After obtaining the textual features of two fashion items, we use Euclidean distance to calculate compatibility of two fashion items. In the model, stacked LSTM can be replaced with Bidirectional LSTM or CNN, etc. Besides, we can get better experimental result if left and right networks do not share parameters with each other.

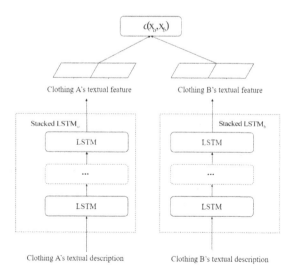

Fig. 3. Fashion text collocation model based on Siamese network.

3.5   Feature Fusion

The process of fusing the structural features and textual features of clothing includes two steps. First, we use GATNE [3] to model fashion heterogenous network. The vectorized representations of fashion items under the matching relationships are regarded as structural feature of fashion items. Subsequently, the structural features of fashion items are integrated into the clothing text collocation model based on Siamese network. Structural and textual features are fused accordingly. Aiming at addressing the key issue on how to integrate structural feature with text feature, we propose a fashion collocation model based on the fusion of structural and textual features, as shown in Fig. 4.

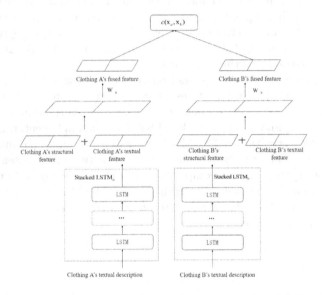

Fig. 4. Fashion collocation model based on the fusion of structural and textual features.

We take the fashion collocation model using stacked LSTM as an example to introduce the main idea of feature fusion. The difference between the fusion model and the fashion text collocation model based on Siamese network is mainly reflected in the part after stacked LSTM. First, structural feature obtained by GATNE and textual feature obtained by stacked LSTM are spliced together. Subsequently, the spliced feature is multiplied by a transformation matrix W to map the feature to a specific dimension. The product is regarded as the final clothing feature. Then, we use fused features to calculate compatibility of two fashion items. Supposing the structural features of clothing A and B are e_a and e_b, and the textual features are t_a and t_b, the fused features are defined by:

$$x_a = concat\,(e_a, t_a)\,W_a \tag{1}$$

$$x_b = concat\,(e_b, t_b)\,W_b \tag{2}$$

In the fashion collocation model based on the fusion of structural feature and text feature, stacked LSTM can be replaced with Bidirectional LSTM or CNN. In addition, the left and right networks do not share parameters with each other.

After feature fusion, we calculate the distance between two fashion items and then obtain compatibility. The smaller the distance between two fashion items is, the greater the compatibility appears to be. Methods for calculating distance between fashion items include Manhattan distance, Euclidean distance, cosine distance, etc. Supposing the textual features of two fashion items are t_i and t_j, the structural features are x_i and x_j, the distance and the compatibility are defined as follows. For Manhattan distance, the distance $d(x_i, x_j)$ and the compatibility $c(x_i, x_j)$ are defined as follows:

$$d(x_i, x_j) = \|x_i - x_j\|_1,\tag{3}$$

$$c(x_i, x_j) = \exp\left(-\|x_i - x_j\|_1\right).\tag{4}$$

For Euclidean distance, the distance $d(x_i, x_j)$ and the compatibility $c(x_i, x_j)$ are defined as follows:

$$d(x_i, x_j) = \frac{\|x_i - x_j\|_2}{\|t_i\|_2 + \|t_j\|_2},\tag{5}$$

$$c(x_i, x_j) = 1 - \frac{\|x_i - x_j\|_2}{\|t_i\|_2 + \|t_j\|_2}.\tag{6}$$

For cosine distance, the distance $d(x_i, x_j)$ and the compatibility $c(x_i, x_j)$ are defined as follows:

$$d(x_i, x_j) = 1 - \cos(\theta) = 1 - \frac{\|x_i \cdot x_j\|_2}{\|x_i\|_2 \cdot \|x_j\|_2},\tag{7}$$

$$c(x_i, x_j) = \frac{\|x_i \cdot x_j\|_2}{\|x_i\|_2 \cdot \|x_j\|_2}.\tag{8}$$

We can calculate a collocation sample's loss by using its compatibility and true label. In the fashion collocation model based on the fusion of structural and textual features, we use contrastive loss function. The contrastive loss function is defined in the following form:

$$L(x_i, x_j) = y_{ij} d^2(x_i, x_j) + (1 - y_{ij})\left(\max\left(m - d(x_i, x_j), 0\right)\right)^2,\tag{9}$$

where y_{ij} denotes the label of a sample. Here, $y_{ij} = 1$ represents positive sample and $y_{ij} = 0$ represents negative sample. The contrastive loss is composed of terms for the positive sample and negative sample. For positive sample, the greater the distance between two fashion items, the greater the loss. For negative sample, if the distance between two fashion items is smaller than m, the sample will be penalized. Otherwise, the loss is equal to 0.

4 Experiment

4.1 Dataset

The dataset used in this paper comes from a large online electronic mall. The original dataset contains 127,024 fashion items. In order to construct fashion heterogenous network, we need to consider the relationships between fashion items, including matching relationships and similar relationships. We extract the attribute "complete_looks" and get multiple outfits related to one item. In every outfit, any two items are regarded as a compatible pair. A total of 330,827 matching pairs are obtained, and these matching pairs contain 76,172 items. We extract the attribute "similar_items" of the 76,172 items. For each item, its attribute "similar_items" includes many items. One of these items and current item are similar. A total of 330,829 similar pairs are obtained. The statistics of the dataset can be found in Table 1. Then, we construct a fashion collocation dataset. For collocation samples, its data format is shown in Table 2.

Table 1. The statistics of the dataset.

Attribute	Number
Nodes	76172
Node types	47
Edge types	2
Similar edges	330829
Matching edges	330827

Table 2. Data format of collocation samples.

Attribute	Value
Clothing A's ID	6180
Clothing B's ID	6179
Clothing A's text	Allen Schwartz ivory steph wide leg pant - trousers high concealed fly side pockets plain
Clothing B's text	Furla Pervinca Babylon envelope - clutch zip mobile phone pocket plain
Whether to match 0/1	1

For the collocation model that only uses structural features, its dataset includes training set, validation set and testing set. All of 317,385 similar relationships are stored in training set. The matching relationships are divided into training set, validation set and testing set according to the ratio 8:1:1. In the training set, there are 317,385 similar pairs and 264,663 matching pairs. In the validation set, there are matching positive samples and negative samples, the numbers of which are both equal to 33,082. The ratio of positive and negative samples is 1:1. The numbers of matching positive samples and negative samples in the testing set are the same as the validation set.

For the collocation model that only uses textual features, its dataset includes training set and testing set. In the training set, the ratio of matching positive and negative samples is 1:10. Besides, the positive samples are the sum of positive samples in the training set and the validation set of the collocation model that only uses structural features. The total number of positive samples is 297,745. In the testing set, the ratio of positive and negative samples is 1:1. The positive samples are the same as the positive samples in the testing set of the collocation model that only use structural features. The numbers of positive samples and negative samples are all equal to 33,082. In addition, the dataset also contains text description information of fashion items.

For the fashion collocation model based on the fusion of structural and textual features, its dataset is equivalent to the sum of the above two models' datasets. We use GATNE [3] model to get the structural features of fashion items. Then, the structural features are regarded as a part of dataset of the fusion model. So, the dataset of fusion model is composed of the structural features output by GATNE and the dataset of textual collocation model.

4.2   Experiment Settings

The parameters are mostly related to the GATNE model [3]. The settings of various parameters are shown in Table 3. In these parameters, dimension, edge-dim and att-dim represent the dimension of node vectors, the dimension of node features on an edge type and the dimension of self-attention mechanism, respectively. Besides, walk-length represents the length of random walk, window-size represents the size of window while generating samples using random walks, and negative-samples represents the number of negative samples generated for each positive sample. In addition, neighbor-samples represents the number of aggregate neighbors. The above parameters are related to the GATNE model. Moreover, hidden-units denotes the number of hidden layer units in the LSTM part and fused-dimension denotes the dimension of fused features.

During the training process, the batch size was set to 512. Moreover, we used Adam optimizer to update the parameters of model and the learning rate was initialized to 0.001. We used a validation set to control whether the model training ends. After every training epoch, if AUC of the validation set decreases, the training will stop. Our experiment was performed on a machine with a two-way Geforce GTX 1080 GPU with 12-GB memory. AUC was adopted to quantify the performance of different models [19, 20]. This metric is produced by the ROC. Moreover, we also adopted F1-score to evaluate models.

4.3   Results and Comparison

We compared the experimental results of three kinds of fashion collocation models. The heterogeneous network representation model, GATNE [3], only used

Table 3. The parameters of our model.

Parameters	Value
Dimension	200
Edge-dim	100
Att-dim	20
Walk-length	10
Window-size	5
Negative-samples	10
Neighbor-samples	30
Hidden-units	256
Fused-dimension	200

structural features. The fashion text collocation model based on Siamese network only used textual features. The fashion collocation model based on the fusion of structural and textual features used both structural features and textual features.

Table 4. Quantitative results of AUC and F1-score delivered by compared models.

Fashion collocation models	AUC	F1-score
GATNE	0.8577	0.7891
Siamese-CNN	0.9047	0.8338
Siamese-BiLSTM	0.9403	0.8752
Siamese-StackedLSTM	0.9424	0.8815
GATNE-CNN (ours)	0.9741	0.9193
GATNE-BiLSTM (ours)	0.9670	0.9066
GATNE-StackedLSTM (ours)	**0.9803**	**0.9317**

Table 4 illustrates the comparative results of different methods in terms of AUC and F1-score. GATNE represents the fashion collocation network that only uses structural feature. Siamese-CNN, Siamese-BiLSTM and Siamese-StackedLSTM are three fashion text collocation models based on Siamese network which contains CNN, Bi-LSTM and stacked LSTM, respectively. GATNE-CNN, GATNE-BiLSTM, GATNE-StackedLSTM are three fashion collocation models based on the fusion of structural and textual features.

It is observed that our proposed fashion collocation model based on the fusion of structural and textual features outperforms fashion text collocation models based on Siamese network. We regard the structural features as external features and textual features as internal features. The experimental results show that structural feature and textual feature can be complementary to each other.

By fusing structural feature and textual feature, the features of fashion items can be better represented. Moreover, GATNE-CNN, GATNE-BiLSTM and GATNE-StackedLSTM produce better results than Siamese-CNN, Siamese-BiLSTM and Siamese-StackedLSTM, respectively. Among three fashion text collocation models, feature fusion brings the largest improvement for Siamese-CNN. Besides, GATNE delivers worst performance, because it is not sufficiently to only use structural features to collocate fashion items. The AUC and F1-score of various fashion text collocation models based on Siamese network are higher than that of the fashion collocation model based on GATNE. This indicates that textual features are more useful than structural features in the task of fashion collocation. Among three fashion text collocation models based on Siamese network, Siamese-BiLSTM and Siamese-StackedLSTM produce similar results. Therefore, stacked LSTM and Bi-LSTM have similar modeling capabilities for text descriptions of fashion items. Siamese-BiLSTM and Siamese-StackedLSTM deliver better performance than Siamese-CNN. It suggests that recurrent neural networks model textual features better than convolutional neural networks.

4.4   Parametric Study

We calculate the distance between two fashion items in specific ways and then obtain compatibility. Three distance calculation methods are introduced in Sect. 3.5, including Manhattan distance, Euclidean distance, and cosine distance. We used these three methods to experiment in Siamese-StackedLSTM model and GATNE-StackedLSTM model. The performance of three methods to calculate distance between fashion items is shown in Fig. 5. The AUC result of Euclidean distance exhibits the best in three methods to calculate distance between fashion items. In addition, the result of cosine distance is also promising. Cosine distance plays an important role in calculating the distance between fashion items on both Siamese-StackedLSTM model and GATNE-StackedLSTM model. Manhattan distance is only available in the fashion text collocation model based on Siamese network. In the fashion collocation model based on the fusion of structural and textual features, the AUC of Manhattan distance is 0.5. At this time, the fashion collocation model has no effect. Therefore, Manhattan distance is not suitable for calculating the distance between fashion items in the fashion collocation model based on the fusion of structural and textual features. We adopted Euclidean distance in both the fashion text collocation model based on Siamese network and the fashion collocation model based on the fusion of structural and textual features.

We also evaluated the influence of whether parameters are shared in the Siamese network on the experimental results. We set parameters in Siamese-StackedLSTM and GATNE-StackedLSTM to be shared and unshared. Table 5 summarizes the AUC results. In Siamese-StackedLSTM model, whether to share parameters has a greater impact on the experimental results. The AUC result of unshared parameters is 4.01% higher than that of shared parameters. In GATNE-StackedLSTM model, there is slight difference between the AUC results of shared and unshared parameters. In this paper, the fashion text collocation model based

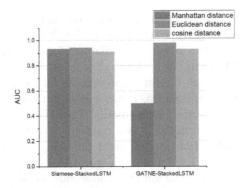

Fig. 5. ROC curves of compared models.

Table 5. AUC result of whether to share parameters.

	Siamese-StackedLSTM	GATNE-StackedLSTM
Share parameters	0.9023	0.9847
Not share parameters	0.9424	0.9803

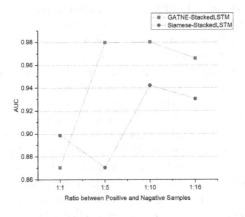

Fig. 6. The performance of different ratios between positive and negative samples.

on Siamese network and the fashion collocation model based on the fusion of structural and textual features do not share parameters.

In the training process of the fashion text collocation model based on Siamese network and the fashion collocation model based on the fusion of structural and textual features, positive and negative samples are input to models. The ratio of positive item pairs against negative item pairs has impact on the performance of models. We used Siamese-StackedLSTM and GATNE-StackedLSTM to investigate different ratios, including 1:1, 1:5, 1:10, and 1:16. Figure 6 summarizes the results over the two models. With the ratio increases, the AUC result shows a rise at first and becomes decreased finally. When the ratio is 1:10, two models both achieve high AUC results.

5 Conclusion

In this paper, we introduced a new framework to collocate fashion items from heterogenous network using structural and textual features. Specifically, we constructed a fashion heterogenous network, in which fashion items are regarded as nodes and similar and matching relationships are regarded as edges. Moreover, we proposed a fashion collocation model based on the fusion of structural and textual features. Experimental results demonstrate that our proposed model achieves significantly better performance in terms of evaluation metrics such as AUC and F1-score, compared to fashion text collocation model based on GATNE model and fashion text collocation model based on Siamese network. Moreover, the proposed method is not only applicable to fashion collocation, but also can be extended to other fields. In future work, it is possible to add more kinds of elements to fashion heterogenous network.

Acknowledgements. This work was supported in part by the National Natural Science Foundation of China under Grant no. 61972112 and no. 61832004, the Guangdong Basic and Applied Basic Research Foundation under Grant no. 2021B1515020088, and the HITSZ-J&A Joint Laboratory of Digital Design and Intelligent Fabrication under Grant no. HITSZ-J&A-2021A01.

References

1. Veit, A., Kovacs, B., Bell, S., McAuley, J., Bala, K., Belongie, S.: Learning visual clothing style with heterogeneous dyadic co-occurrences. In: Proceedings of the IEEE International Conference on Computer Vision, pp. 4642–4650 (2015)
2. Zhang, H., Huang, W., Liu, L., Chow, T.W.: Learning to match clothing from textual feature-based compatible relationships. IEEE Trans. Ind. Inf. **16**(11), 6750–6759 (2019)
3. Cen, Y., Zou, X., Zhang, J., Yang, H., Zhou, J., Tang, J.: Representation learning for attributed multiplex heterogeneous network. In: Proceedings of the 25th ACM SIGKDD International Conference on Knowledge Discovery & Data Mining, pp. 1358–1368 (2019)
4. Ou, M., Cui, P., Pei, J., Zhang, Z., Zhu, W.: Asymmetric transitivity preserving graph embedding. In: Proceedings of the 22nd ACM SIGKDD International Conference on Knowledge Discovery and Data Mining, pp. 1105–1114 (2016)
5. Wang, X., Cui, P., Wang, J., Pei, J., Zhu, W., Yang, S.: Community preserving network embedding. In: Proceedings of the AAAI Conference on Artificial Intelligence, vol. 31 (2017)
6. Perozzi, B., Al-Rfou, R., Skiena, S.: DeepWalk: online learning of social representations. In: Proceedings of the 20th ACM SIGKDD International Conference on Knowledge Discovery and Data Mining, pp. 701–710 (2014)
7. Grover, A., Leskovec, J.: node2vec: scalable feature learning for networks. In: Proceedings of the 22nd ACM SIGKDD International Conference on Knowledge Discovery and Data Mining, pp. 855–864 (2016)
8. Wang, D., Cui, P., Zhu, W.: Structural deep network embedding. In: Proceedings of the 22nd ACM SIGKDD International Conference on Knowledge Discovery and Data Mining, pp. 1225–1234 (2016)

9. Cao, S., Lu, W., Xu, Q.: Deep neural networks for learning graph representations. In: Proceedings of the AAAI Conference on Artificial Intelligence, vol. 30 (2016)

10. Wang, S., Tang, J., Aggarwal, C., Chang, Y., Liu, H.: Signed network embedding in social media. In: Proceedings of the 2017 SIAM International Conference on Data Mining, pp. 327–335. SIAM (2017)

11. Tang, J., Qu, M., Mei, Q.: PTE: predictive text embedding through large-scale heterogeneous text networks. In: Proceedings of the 21th ACM SIGKDD International Conference on Knowledge Discovery and Data Mining, pp. 1165–1174 (2015)

12. Dong, Y., Chawla, N.V., Swami, A.: Metapath2vec: scalable representation learning for heterogeneous networks. In: Proceedings of the 23rd ACM SIGKDD International Conference on Knowledge Discovery and Data Mining, pp. 135–144 (2017)

13. Fu, T.y., Lee, W.C., Lei, Z.: HIN2Vec: explore meta-paths in heterogeneous information networks for representation learning. In: Proceedings of the 2017 ACM on Conference on Information and Knowledge Management, pp. 1797–1806 (2017)

14. Park, C., Kim, D., Zhu, Q., Han, J., Yu, H.: Task-guided pair embedding in heterogeneous network. In: Proceedings of the 28th ACM International Conference on Information and Knowledge Management, pp. 489–498 (2019)

15. Li, Z., Jiang, J.Y., Sun, Y., Wang, W.: Personalized question routing via heterogeneous network embedding. In: Proceedings of the AAAI Conference on Artificial Intelligence, vol. 33, pp. 192–199 (2019)

16. He, Y., Song, Y., Li, J., Ji, C., Peng, J., Peng, H.: HeteSpaceyWalk: a heterogeneous spacey random walk for heterogeneous information network embedding. In: Proceedings of the 28th ACM International Conference on Information and Knowledge Management, pp. 639–648 (2019)

17. Liu, L., Zhang, H., Xu, X., Zhang, Z., Yan, S.: Collocating clothes with generative adversarial networks cosupervised by categories and attributes: a multidiscriminator framework. IEEE Trans. Neural Netw. Learn. Syst. **31**(9), 3540–3554 (2019)

18. Mueller, J., Thyagarajan, A.: Siamese recurrent architectures for learning sentence similarity. In: Proceedings of the AAAI Conference on Artificial Intelligence, vol. 30 (2016)

19. Li, Y., Cao, L., Zhu, J., Luo, J.: Mining fashion outfit composition using an end-to-end deep learning approach on set data. IEEE Trans. Multimedia **19**(8), 1946–1955 (2017)

20. Huang, J., Ling, C.X.: Using AUC and accuracy in evaluating learning algorithms. IEEE Trans. Knowl. Data Eng. **17**(3), 299–310 (2005)

Building Energy Performance Certificate Labelling Classification Based on Explainable Artificial Intelligence

Thamsanqa Tsoka[1]([✉]), Xianming Ye[1], YangQuan Chen[2], Dunwei Gong[3], and Xiaohua Xia[1]

[1] Department of Electrical Electronic and Computer Engineering, University of Pretoria, Pretoria 0002, South Africa
thamsanqa.tsoka@tuks.co.za, xianming.ye@up.ac.za, xxia@up.ac.za
[2] Mechanical Engineering Department, University of California, Merced, CA 95340, USA
ychen53@ucmerced.edu
[3] School of Information and Control Engineering, China University of Mining and Technology, Xuzhou 221116, China

Abstract. In this study, the machine learning based classification approach is aptly applied to classify the building energy performance certificate (EPC) rating levels instead of applying the traditional approach of direct measurements of the annual building energy consumption and its effective floor areas. Accurately acquired EPC ratings deliver a successful building EPC programme which enables future regulatory actions for the buildings nationwide. Historical data and experiences from the countries who have implemented the building EPC programme can help to accelerate the development of such a programme in the developing countries like South Africa. With these concerns, an artificial neural network (ANN) classification model together with the explainable artificial intelligence (XAI) tools are adopted in this study to obtain the building EPC rating levels. In this study, an ANN model is trained from the historical registry of the building EPC best practices in Lombardy, Italy. The ANN classification model is calibrated and validated with optimal number of neurons. Results show that probability of detection for the 'G' labelled buildings is 0.9655 with a precision of 0.8547. In addition, the Local Interpretable Model-Agnostic Explanation (LIME) is adopted to explain the inherent properties of the identified ANN classification model. The LIME XAI shows that opaque surface and average U values for walls are the most influential features on the EPC rating classification while the degree day feature has the least influence during the ANN based EPC rating classification process.

Keywords: Building EPC · ANN · Artificial intelligence · XAI · Machine learning

© Springer Nature Singapore Pte Ltd. 2021
H. Zhang et al. (Eds.): NCAA 2021, CCIS 1449, pp. 181–196, 2021.
https://doi.org/10.1007/978-981-16-5188-5_14

1   Introduction

The building sector accounts for about 40% of the global energy use [25] and an estimated value of 36% of all the carbon dioxide (CO_2) emissions [5]. In an attempt to alleviate the energy problems encountered by buildings, building energy performance certificate (EPC) programmes have been widely adopted in many countries such as Australia, Italy, Germany, United Kingdom and France [11,17]. Building energy performance certificates were made compulsory for all European Union member states through the implementation of the Energy Performance of Building Directive in 2002 [17,18]. The building EPC programme is one of the most valuable policy instruments to track buildings' energy performance, which will enable building owners, managers, and tenants to thoroughly assess the energy performance of buildings. It can consequently aid in determining energy efficiency interventions for lower energy consumption, less green house gas emission and minimum operation cost of buildings. To determine the building EPC rating, the key performance indicator is the effective building energy intensity, which is a ratio between the annual total kWh energy consumption and the effective floor areas [23]. The annual building energy usage can either be acquired through energy models or direct measurements [20]. Energy models can be derived from both computer simulation and data driven methods. Due to the complexity and critical skill requirements to build computer simulation models of building energy systems, numerous data driven energy models are built using historical building energy system operational data. These data driven models include but are not limited to the multivariate regression splines (MARS), Kriging (KG), radial basis function (RBF), support vector machines (SVM), and artificial neural networks (ANN) [4].

Machine Learning (ML) algorithms are techniques that have been developed with the ability to predict future data, or execute various decisions under uncertainty through pre-determined patterns in the data [10]. There are three types of machine learning techniques namely unsupervised, supervised and reinforcement learning. Supervised learning is executed through the analysis of labelled input and output pairs to determine and construct a relationship from the inputs to outputs. Supervised learning goes through a series of corrections (training) trying to reduce the error between the models predicted output and the actual expected output. Regression and classification are two common practices of supervised learning. The regression process predicts actual values taken from the input of the training data while the classification process determines the group the input data is ascribed to from the known categories given by the output of the training data [10,15]. The classification can suffer from several practical limitations. Firstly, classes not included in the training dataset will not be detected. The second pitfall is data bias, which should be minimised in order for the ML algorithms to yield good performances. Thirdly, tremendous amounts of historical data are required to train the model. For the purposes of classifying the building EPC rating into the correct category, instead of using the direct measurement approaches, these three practical limitations are carefully avoided during the implementation process.

The most common input data used in building energy performance forecasting problems are occupancy, meteorological, and temporal data. These are major factors that aid in machine learning models to acquire enough information to create models [10]. The Certificazione Energitica degli edifici(CENED) online database covers sufficient building characteristics data records to enable the machine learning classification approach.

Systems using AI have become sophisticated to the point that very little human interaction is required in their deployment and design. For AI applications in critical areas such as law or medicine, one needs to understand the internal functioning mechanisms of the AI models [1,12]. Many AI machine learning algorithms such as deep neural networks are considered complex black box models, which are not transparent and their internal functioning mechanisms are unclear. Obviously to enable the AI model applications in critical areas, interpretability of these models is required. For this purpose, the so called Explainable AI (XAI) has attracted tremendous research activities. Through XAI, the model becomes robust. Discovery of elements that can negatively influence the prediction and guarantee objectivity in decision making are determined through appropriate tools [3]. XAI produces explainable models containing good prediction accuracy and allowing people to trust, understand and handle the new AI systems. XAI is greatly influenced by the psychology of explanation in the Social Sciences field [19]. In this study, we developed an ANN model that predicts energy classification with the aid of Local Interpretable Model-Agnostic Explanation (LIME). The LIME aids in determining the extent to which an input feature has for the energy classification. There is a greater insight and understanding brought about by LIME through the model operation and post modelling. When feature engineering is incorporated into XAI on an ML model, management of effective input parameters and dimensions is attainable [1,3].

The South African building EPC program can benefit from historical data and experiences of countries who have implemented these practices. The program aims to rate and determine the energy performance of buildings from an existing standard that compares the energy amount used by a certain building with reference to intensity set in the SANS 10400-XA standard [22]. It is set to be applied to buildings occupied or owned by the government and later rolled out to all categories of buildings. The South African building EPC labelling (rating levels) system spans from A-G with 'A' depicting a highly efficient building and 'G' symbolising the worst efficiency level to be acquired by a building [9]. This concept of using ML ANN classification with XAI principles for energy labelling purposes is ideal for the South African building EPC. The ANN model is complex and difficult to use however, it performs predictions in a reasonable amount of time, is robust, and is relatively accurate [2,25]. ANNs have been used in various building energy estimation and forecasting of lighting, cooling/heating loads and overall building energy consumption [2,14]. Its inputs vary between measured and calculated information which aids in the options of data to be acquired to determine the most optimal model. One of the parameters required by the South African building EPC is the evaluated annual net energy consumption in kilowatt hours per square meter per year [9]. The acquisition of that parameter needs detailed yearly energy consumption data which requires the effective area and yearly energy consumption of that effective area, which can prove costly as energy auditors are required. Biases and inaccuracies arise when energy consumption data is unavailable, as energy consumption estimations are required. However, ANNs are considered hybrid based approaches as energy use information can be acquired through measurement and calculation based approaches. The cost of implementation is determined by the information given to the models therefore it can be limited by choosing and determining the most important and minimal information [24]. So, a reduction in the time required for assessment can be achieved through the implementation of input features not measured and acquired over a year. The ML ANN model is meant to aid the already available measuring and energy labelling principles that exist. As a result, it can be implemented as a verification process. New building EPC development becomes a possibility through this procedure as the evaluated annual net energy consumption in kilowatt hours per square meter per year may be bypassed. This study presents the use of machine learning approaches to determine an energy class of a building by using technical and human influenced factors. An ANN model is developed for the classification process. Input features are also derived from practical and significant building characteristics. The results of the ANN model need to be inferred and explained to the parties involved and therefore, the XAI tools are implemented. XAI tools also explain the elements that guarantee objectivity and negative influence for the prediction. This should assist building tenants, owners, managers and energy auditors in knowing the factors that mainly contribute to the building EPC rating level and further improve the EPC rating levels (labels). In the following, Sect. 2 presents the problem formulation. Modeling of the ANN system with feature selection, training, testing, evaluation and explanation of the building EPC labelling model is presented in Sect. 3. Section 4 is the case study. Section 5 covers the results and discussions with XAI analysis. The study ends with a conclusion in Sect. 6.

2   Problem Formulation

This study aims to address following research problems.

- Develop an accurate and robust ANN model that is able to classify the existing buildings into different building EPC rating levels, i.e., A-G.
- Using the XAI tools to explain the rational of the developed ANN model, in order to identify the key features and determinants of the EPC rating level classification principle. The AI explanation will facilitate the model construction efforts with the guidance of most relevant features to be included during the modelling process.
- Based on the identified key features that contribute to the building EPC rating levels, proper energy efficiency interventions can be adopted to improve the building EPC rating level in supporting the practice of building energy efficiency.

3   Methodology

The research methodology is briefly illustrated in Fig. 1. Historical building characteristics and operational data are obtained and processed to be ready for the ANN model development. The data pre-processing procedures including the removal of defective data is considered feature engineering. The features are used in the ANN model training and development. Before applying the ANN model for the building EPC rating level classification, the ANN model structure is optimised and the model coefficients are identified. Detailed ANN modelling procedures are introduced in Sect. 3.1, during which the model accuracy is analysed with model validations. In order to further improve the ANN model robustness, usefulness, and accuracy, the XAI tools are applied to explain the ANN model's internal operating mechanism and result analysis [16]. In this study, the LIME XAI tool is selected for preliminary explanation investigations of the proposed ANN model.

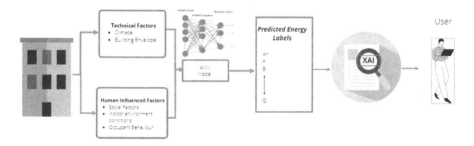

Fig. 1. The procedures of applying the machine learning approach for building EPC classification

3.1   ANN Modelling

The ANN is derived from the concept of a biological neuron in a brain. The ANN models are divided into three layers namely the input, output, and hidden layers. Figure 1 shows the interconnections of the inputs, outputs, and the layers. The neurons from one layer are connected to the next adjacent layers. A neuron is made of two parts namely the transfer and activation functions. The calculated values are propagated to the next layer by the transfer function while the output values are estimated through the weight and bias values in the activation function [6,8,14].

The input features include both the human influenced and technical factors. The social factors that fall under human influenced refer to operations and maintenance, occupant behaviour and indoor environment conditions. The technical specifications are the building envelope, building appliances, and climate conditions. These parameters are used to train the building EPC classification model. The determination of the influence of each input parameter is important, which is known as causal strength. The varied input values will give different output values and the calculated causal strengths will make a generalised ANN model that is more reliable, which will, in turn, be able to indicate and analyse the variations in building stock and determine their EPC labels [6].

A typical ANN model can be described as

$$y = f_x \left(\sum_{i=1}^{n} (w_i X_i + b) \right), \tag{1}$$

where y is the output of the model. The input data, depicted by X_i, is multiplied by the weights w_i. b is the bias or threshold value which is a dummy weight value related to the neuron. The transfer function f_x can be selected either as a step, sigmoid, rectified linear or hyperbolic function [6].

In this classification model, the optimal transfer function for the hidden layers is a rectified linear function and for the output layer the use of the softmax function is the most ideal. The rectified linear function returns zeros for all negative inputs and returns the actual value for all positive inputs. The function takes the form

$$h(a) = \begin{cases} 0, & \text{if } x =< 0, \\ a, & \text{if } x > 0 \end{cases} \tag{2}$$

where $h(a)$ is the transfer function and a is the input weights and bias values. The softmax function is one that takes N real values from the previous layer and normalises them into N real values that add up to 1. These input values tend to be values that are an un-normalised score of the input values being of a certain class. The transformation turns the scores into values between 0 and 1 which results in probability values. The probability value is directly proportional to the input value and remains between 0 and 1. This function therefore scales output value scores of a deep neural network into normalised probability distribution. It works well for multi-class classifiers when the classes are mutually exclusive [13]. It takes the form of

$$\sigma(\vec{y})_i = \frac{e^{x_i}}{\sum_{c=1}^{N} e^{x_c}} \tag{3}$$

where $\vec{y}$ is the input vector to the softmax function, made up of $(y_0, \ldots, y_N)$, while x_i is the input values from the previous layer, e^{x_i} is the exponential applied to the input vector, which retains all values greater than one and the bottom term gives the output vector summation, which is the normalisation term and determines the probability distribution.

Basic Analysis and Feature Determination. As described in Fig. 1 the input features where derived from the technical factors category. Therefore, average U-value of walls, roof, basement and windows, opaque surface, glazed surface, net volume and net surface area are considered building envelope features. The heating degree days is considered to be a climate feature. Numerous feature engineering techniques and filters applied on these input features were adopted from studies on the same dataset [7,14].

For the case study, we used the building characteristics and operational data of residential buildings from Lombardy, Italy. The data from the CENED website was imbalanced as depicted by Fig. 2. It shows that 'G' rated buildings represent 52.03% of the data. 'A+' and 'A' labelled buildings account for 0.57% and 3.35% of buildings in the database, respectively. After data cleaning and implementing filters derived from previous studies [7,14] on the same database, there was about 207 325 data points remaining of these about 107 876 were of buildings rated 'G'. These filters remove data that is inconsistent with expected values. Input data for neural networks needs to be reliable and void of defective data. If these data criteria are not attained, the errors in the weights given to each neuron will be propagated from one layer to the next which affects the accuracy of the model [14]. Table 1 represents the conditions of the filters applied to the dataset.

Table 1. Filtered parameters from the CENED database [6,14]

Filtered parameter	Filter restrictions	Unit
Net Floor Area	$50 <$ input	m^2
Glass opaque surface ratio	$0 <$ input < 0.9	–
Net Volume	$130 <$ input	m^3
U-value of walls, roof and floor	$0.15 <$ input < 3	W/m^2K
U-value of windows	$0.8 <$ input < 6	W/m^2K
Glazed Surface	$1 <$ input	m^2

Energy Performance Labels Distribution

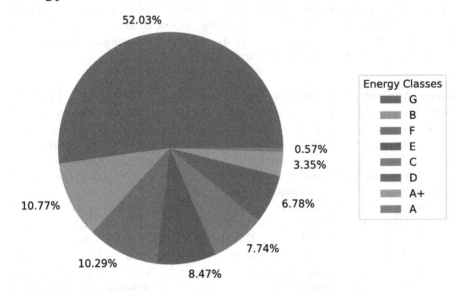

Fig. 2. Building EPC percentage distribution of the labels

3.2   Model Training, Test, and Evaluation

A summary of the ANN model characteristics is given in Table 2. The parameters were modified accordingly for EPC building classification. In order to prevent over-fitting, the data are split into three parts. The first group was the testing set, which is 20% of the original data. The remaining data was further split into training and validation dataset in an 80/20 split. The training process does not make use of the test dataset. The test dataset is used for the evaluation of the developed ANN model. The performance evaluation is conducted through accuracy measures such as probability of detection, precision, and overall accuracy. A confusion matrix and XAI tools are also implemented for the evaluation.

Table 2. The building EPC ANN classification model characteristics

Factors	Value
Features	9
First Layer Neurons	16
Second Layer Neurons	32
Output Layer	8
Test sample	0.2
Validation sample	0.16
Training sample	0.64
Epochs	60

The equations Eqs. (4)–(6) introduce the performance indicators in terms of accuracy, precision, and sensitivity of the ANN model training. The equation for accuracy illustrates the total percentage of total samples correctly classified by the model and is depicted by Eq. (4).

$$Accuracy = \frac{CP + CN}{CP + CN + WP + WN},\tag{4}$$

where the following abbreviations have been used: CP (Correct Positives) represents the number of correctly predicted classes, WP (Wrong Positives) represents incorrectly predicted classes, CN (Correct Negatives) represents correctly predicted classes that were not the class being analysed, and WN (Wrong Negatives) represents incorrectly predicted classes that where thought to be not of the class being analysed. Precision and Probability of Detection take the forms:

$$Precision = \frac{CP}{CP + WP}\tag{5}$$

$$Probability\ of\ Detection\ (Sensitivity) = \frac{CP}{CP + WN}.\tag{6}$$

Eqs. (5)–(6) are the formulas to evaluate the ANN model for precision and sensitivity, respectively. The precision is the percentage of correct classes that were truly correct while sensitivity is the percentage of correct classes that were correctly predicted as true by the model.

3.3 Explanation of the Building EPC Labelling Classification Model

Local Interpretable Model-Agnostic Explanation (LIME). Local Interpretable Model-agnostic Explanations (LIME) is a procedure to create an approximation model that makes the process model agnostic [21]. This process is done locally with the end result being a globally understood machine learning model [16]. The process was introduced in order to explain the black-box model and its prediction or classification results better. The explanation takes the form of:

$$\xi(z) = \underset{g \in G}{\operatorname{argmin}}\, L(f, g, \pi_z) + \Omega(g)\tag{7}$$

where the explanation model is defined as $g \in G$ with G being a group of interpretable models that include falling rule lists, linear models, and decision trees. The resulting $g \in G$ model may not necessarily be the easiest to explain therefore a complexity factor is determined and represented by $\Omega(g)$. This factor can be the amount of non-zero weights in a linear model or the tree depth in decision trees and the idea is to keep it as low as possible to be interpretable by humans. In classification, the black-box model being explained tends to output probabilities of z belonging to a certain class. These probabilities are depicted by $f(z)$. The proximity measure, π_z, establishes the locality around z and determines its neighbourhood size at an instance of w to z. The operation to determine how well the g explains the black-box model f is done by $L(f, g, \pi_z)$ which is minimised to get the best interpretation. The local models produced by LIME estimate f globally [1,16].

3.4 Model Improvement and Optimisation

LIME is applied to improve the overall performance of the initially established ANN classification model by determining the feature importance. Moreover, it is to make the classification process understandable to the user and aid the developer in making necessary improvements. The result would be the exclusion of features that negatively or have little impact on the model and the provision of better inputs. The analysis of the results gives rise to the identification of features that may be addressed to improve the rating of the building. The prediction results allow for the understanding of why the model classified a particular building in that manner. This further allows for the development of better feature selection and understanding.

4   Case Study

4.1   Data Description and Processing

The Italian Lombardy Region building EPC open source database, with various buildings recorded values from the CENED software, was adopted to develop the building EPC classification model. The online database is used to extract features that will determine a minimalist approach to certify and classify building EPC rating levels. Figure 1 shows the main input parameters to be used in classifying the buildings into different EPC labels.

Residential buildings are selected as they represent the largest group in the dataset labelled by the code E.1(1). Moreover, filters were then applied to features such as thermal conductivity categories and zero entries were removed.

5   Results and Discussions

5.1   Trained Model Analysis

The ANN model was trained using the 9 input features, with 7 extracted from the database and the other 2 (opaque surface, glazed surface) as the hybrid inputs. The ANN classification model gives an accuracy of 70.12% for the trained dataset as depicted by Fig. 3, which shows the model simulation with regards to the classification accuracy trends over epochs. The optimal amount of epochs was determined in-order to attain the optimal amount of time to reach the highest possible accuracy for the model.

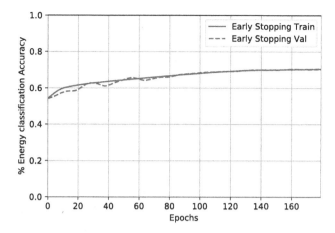

Fig. 3. Training performance of the model based on epochs and classification accuracy

This section analyses the effectiveness of the proposed approach in determining the building energy EPC labelling. This ANN ML method was implemented on the Python 3.7 platform. The XAI tools enable explainability through feature importance determination and their effects on the output for this black-box ML model, making it usable for building EPC labelling.

The confusion matrix in Fig. 4 is a representation of the predicted label by the model against the actual label given by the test dataset. It summarises the results of the derived model on the unseen test dataset. Accuracy on the test data is 69.93% which is close to the training accuracy of 70.12% which shows a good performing model with good fitting. The building EPC rating level classifications that were correctly predicted as true by the ANN model are represented in the main diagonal of the confusion matrix. Moreover, the total number of the buildings in each different class from the test data is derived by adding the values of each row. Equations (5)–(6) are used to indicate the performance of the model on the classification of each class. The results are summarised in Table 3. The group label 'A' represents the smallest group of buildings with 0.54%. It is inferred that the zero precision and detection probabilities are as a result of the low representation in the training and test datasets. However, 'G' accounting for 52.26%, has the highest sensitivity (0.9655) and possible correct prediction (0.8547) by the model followed by groups 'B' and 'E', respectively.

Table 3 depicts the probability of detection of each energy class. It is noted that the original dataset has unequal entries for building EPC rating level distributions as can be seen in Fig. 2. The confusion matrix indicates that it is able to accurately and reliably detect and classify the highly popularised data.

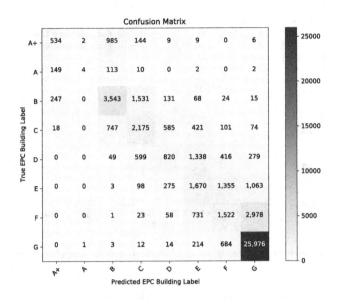

Fig. 4. Comparison of declared energy class and predicted energy class through a
Confusion matrix

Table 3. Summary of model performance

Energy class	Probability of detection	Precision	Number of labels	Percentage of labels
A+	0.3162	0.5633	1689	3.26%
A	0.0143	0.5714	280	0.54%
B	0.6373	0.6508	5559	10.73%
C	0.5278	0.4736	4121	7.95%
D	0.2342	0.4334	3501	6.75%
E	0.3741	0.3750	4464	8.61%
F	0.2865	0.3710	5313	10.25%
G	0.9655	0.8547	26904	51.91%

5.2   LIME XAI Results

LIME is used for local explainability and when it is applied to the building EPC
classifier for individual predictions and explanations, the most influential features are determined as depicted in Figs. 5 and 6. Each figure has three parts
with the left part showing the class prediction probability for the buildings under
investigation, the middle part shows an evaluation of the features effect on the
prediction, and the bottom part is a table with the feature names in the order
of influence and their values. The most influential features for building classification in Fig. 5 are the opaque surface and net surface area with degree day and

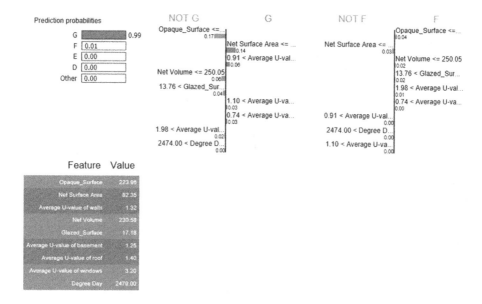

Fig. 5. LIME explanations for correct building classification

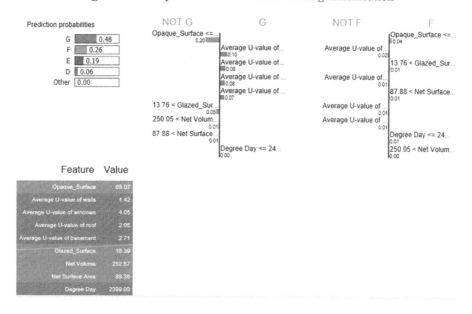

Fig. 6. LIME explanations for incorrect building classifications

average U value of windows having the least significance. Each feature either contributes positively or negatively to the prediction and this is depicted in the explanations, e.g., opaque surface pushes the prediction of the building towards not being in that class (negative effect). The average U value of walls induces a positive effect that the building belongs to that class. The local explanations of a correct prediction and an incorrect prediction are depicted in Figs. 5 and 6, respectively. The predicted class in Fig. 5 is 'G' which is the correct prediction with a probability of 0.99 with 'F' being the second prediction with a 0.01 probability. This explanation shows that an increase in opaque surfaces and a decrease in the average U values of walls would improve the class rating of the building under investigation. The predicted class in Fig. 6 is 'G' which is the incorrect prediction with a probability of 0.48. Features such as average U value of windows, walls, roof and basement had a great positive impact on the prediction while opaque surface area had a significant negative impact. However the next highest prediction which is correct is class 'F' at 0.26. In Class 'Fs' prediction the features influences have the inverse effect to that of the prediction that it is a class 'G'. However, the features influence is very low as can be seen by the weight values assigned to them.

6   Conclusion

This study presents an ANN model that was used to determine the energy performance certificate labels of buildings. The implementation of LIME, an XAI tool, on the ANN model aided in the explanation and understanding of the results of the various predictions given by the model. The XAI tools are a great contribution to the building EPC labelling as they fast track the rating process with great transparency for the parties involved.

The building industry and building assessors are expecting fast, less expensive, efficient, robust, and accurate measures for building energy performance assessments. The ANN model can be used to predict the expected energy use and their relevant building EPC labels. Therefore, machine learning tools can serve as an alternative assessment strategy, especially when historical building specifications and operational data are available, and proper XAI tools are applicable to explain the rational of the machine learning based models.

Acknowledgement. This research is supported by National Natural Science Foundation of China (Grant no.: 61803162), the National Research Foundation Competitive Support for Unrated Researchers (CSUR) programme with grant no.: 116309, and Royal Academy of Engineering Transforming Systems through Partnership 2019/2020 grant scheme with reference no.: TSP1020.

References

1. Adadi, A., Berrada, M.: Peeking inside the black-box: a survey on explainable artificial intelligence (XAI). IEEE Access **6**, 52138–52160 (2018)
2. Amasyali, K., El-Gohary, N.M.: A review of data-driven building energy consumption prediction studies. Renew. Sustain. Energy Rev. **81**, 1192–1205 (2018)
3. Arrieta, A.B., et al.: Explainable artificial intelligence (XAI): concepts, taxonomies, opportunities and challenges toward responsible AI. Inf. Fusion **58**, 82–115 (2020)

4. Ascione, F., Bianco, N., De Stasio, C., Mauro, G.M., Vanoli, G.P.: Artificial neural networks to predict energy performance and retrofit scenarios for any member of a building category: a novel approach. Energy **118**, 999–1017 (2017)

5. Bagheri, F., Mokarizadeh, V., Jabbar, M.: Developing energy performance label for office buildings in Iran. Energy Build. **61**, 116–124 (2013)

6. Buratti, C., Barbanera, M., Palladino, D.: An original tool for checking energy performance and certification of buildings by means of artificial neural networks. Appl. Energy **120**, 125–132 (2014)

7. Dall'O', G., Sarto, L., Sanna, N., Tonetti, V., Ventura, M.: On the use of an energy certification database to create indicators for energy planning purposes: application in northern Italy. Energy Policy **85**, 207–217 (2015)

8. Dayhoff, J.E.: Neural Network Architectures: An Introduction. Van Nostrand Reinhold Co. (1990)

9. Fan, Y., Xia, X.: An optimization model for building envelope retrofit considering energy performance certificate. In: 2017 36th Chinese Control Conference (CCC), pp. 2750–2755. IEEE (2017)

10. Fathi, S., Srinivasan, R., Fenner, A., Fathi, S.: Machine learning applications in urban building energy performance forecasting: a systematic review. Renew. Sustain. Energy Rev. **133**, 110287 (2020)

11. Fossati, M., Scalco, V.A., Linczuk, V.C.C., Lamberts, R.: Building energy efficiency: an overview of the Brazilian residential labeling scheme. Renew. Sustain. Energy Rev. **65**, 1216–1231 (2016)

12. Goodman, B., Flaxman, S.: European union regulations on algorithmic decision-making and a "right to explanation". AI Mag. **38**(3), 50–57 (2017)

13. Ketkar, N., Santana, E.: Deep Learning with Python, vol. 1. Springer, Cham (2017)

14. Khayatian, F., Sarto, L., Dall'O', G.: Application of neural networks for evaluating energy performance certificates of residential buildings. Energy Build. **125**, 45–54 (2016)

15. Kim, P.: Matlab deep learning. With machine learning. Neural Netw. Artif. Intell. **130**, 21 (2017)

16. Kuzlu, M., Cali, U., Sharma, V., Güler, Ö.: Gaining insight into solar photovoltaic power generation forecasting utilizing explainable artificial intelligence tools. IEEE Access **8**, 187814–187823 (2020)

17. Li, Y., Kubicki, S., Guerriero, A., Rezgui, Y.: Review of building energy performance certification schemes towards future improvement. Renew. Sustain. Energy Rev. **113**, 109244 (2019)

18. Mattoni, B., Guattari, C., Evangelisti, L., Bisegna, F., Gori, P., Asdrubali, F.: Critical review and methodological approach to evaluate the differences among international green building rating tools. Renew. Sustain. Energy Rev. **82**, 950–960 (2018)

19. Miller, T.: Explanation in artificial intelligence: insights from the social sciences. Artif. Intell. **267**, 1–38 (2019)

20. Pérez-Lombard, L., Ortiz, J., González, R., Maestre, I.R.: A review of benchmarking, rating and labelling concepts within the framework of building energy certification schemes. Energy Build. **41**(3), 272–278 (2009)

21. Ribeiro, M.T., Singh, S., Guestrin, C.: "Why should I trust you?" explaining the predictions of any classifier. In: Proceedings of the 22nd ACM SIGKDD International Conference on Knowledge Discovery and Data Mining, pp. 1135–1144 (2016)

22. The Application of the National Building Regulations Part XA: Energy Usage in Buildings (1 ed.). SANS10400-XA, South African Bureau of Standards (2011)

23. Wang, S., Yan, C., Xiao, F.: Quantitative energy performance assessment methods for existing buildings. Energy Build. **55**, 873–888 (2012)
24. Yezioro, A., Dong, B., Leite, F.: An applied artificial intelligence approach towards assessing building performance simulation tools. Energy Build. **40**(4), 612–620 (2008)
25. Zhao, H.X., Magoulès, F.: A review on the prediction of building energy consumption. Renew. Sustain. Energy Rev. **16**(6), 3586–3592 (2012)

Cross Languages One-Versus-All Speech Emotion Classifier

Xiangrui Liu[1,4], Junchi Bin[2], and Huakang Li[1,3,4(✉)]

[1] Key Laboratory of Urban Land Resources Monitoring and Simulation,
Ministry of Natural Resources, Shenzhen, China
Huakang.Li@xjtlu.edu.cn
[2] School of Engineering, University of British Columbia, Kelowna, Canada
junchi.bin@ubc.ca
[3] School of Artificial Intelligence and Advanced Computing,
Xi'an Jiaotong-Liverpool University, Suzhou, China
[4] Suzhou Privacy Technology Co. Ltd., Suzhou, China

Abstract. Speech emotion recognition (SER) is a task that cannot be accomplished solely depending on linguistic models due to the presence of figures of speech. For a more accurate prediction of emotions, researchers adopted acoustic modelling. The complexity of SER can be attributed to a variety of acoustic features, the similarities among certain emotions, etc. In this paper, we proposed a framework named Cross Languages One-Versus-All Speech Emotion Classifier (CLOVASEC) that identifies speeches' emotions for both Chinese and English. Acoustic features were preprocessed by Synthetic Minority Oversampling Technique (SMOTE) to diminish the impact of an imbalanced dataset then by Principal component analysis (PCA) to reduce the dimension. The features were fed into a classifier that was made up of eight sub-classifiers and each sub-classifier was tasked to differentiate one class from the other seven classes. The framework outperformed regular classifiers significantly on The Chinese Natural Audio-Visual Emotion Database (CHEAVD) and an English dataset from Deng.

Keywords: Speech emotion recognition · Multi-languages · Acoustic modelling · Deep learning · Multiplicative attention

1 Introduction

Researchers have spent years of study in the field of artificial intelligence (AI) and emotion recognition has always been a popular topic as researchers believed that emotion technology may lead to social and personal interaction transformation [19]. Speech, body gesture, and facial expression etc. are the cues of the body emotional phenomena [4,12,29]. Much attention has been paid to textual recognition, for example, Deep Speech 1 from Baidu achieved a 16% error on the Switchboard 2000 Hub5 dataset without the need for a phoneme dictionary and Wav2Vec from Facebook achieved a 2.43% word error rate on the nov92 test set, etc.

© Springer Nature Singapore Pte Ltd. 2021
H. Zhang et al. (Eds.): NCAA 2021, CCIS 1449, pp. 197–210, 2021.
https://doi.org/10.1007/978-981-16-5188-5_15

However, the linguistic models tend to be restricted to a single language which may not be perfectly capable for modern society as globalization has made more and more people bilingual and they may mix up different languages when they are speaking. In this situation, a linguistic model appears to be incapable. Moreover, pure text may be insufficient for people to fully express their sentiments especially when the content involves irony and sarcasm. For example, a sentence like "You think this is funny?" could be a question or a reproach. A computer might not be capable to identify the sentiment within the sentence based on a linguistic model. To identify one's emotion more accurately, recognizing speech emotion is an important research direction in emotion detection and recognition naturally [9,20].

Most researchers approached SER by using Hidden Markov Model (HMM) in the early time. Later, the advent of better models such as Convolutional Neural Network (CNN) and Recurrent Neural Network (RNN) has shifted the methods of tackling multi-class SER tasks. The imbalanced datasets, similarities among sentiments and insufficient understanding of acoustic features have been challenges to SER for a long time. This paper proposed a classifier built upon sub-classifiers to identify eight different emotions: neutral, happy, angry, sad, worried, anxious, surprise and disgust. Acoustic features were extracted and then processed using Principal component analysis (PCA) and Synthetic Minority Oversampling Technique (SMOTE) to train eight binary classifiers with each classifier differentiating one class from the other seven classes. A SoftMax function is then applied to the eight classifiers to arrive at the prediction with the highest confidence level.

The main contributions of the paper are listed as follow:

- To address imbalanced data, SMOTE technique is adopted to the proposed method. The experimental results suggest its effectiveness on an imbalanced speech dataset.
- The proposed method achieved satisfactory performance on acoustic signals from different languages.
- To reduce the computational complexity, PCA is implemented and tuned for combining various acoustic features such as MFCC, energy features, etc.

The rest of the paper is organized as follows. Section 1 summarizes SER related work. Section 2 will introduce the proposed CLOVASEC framework in details. Section 3 presents the experimental results of the proposed framework. Finally, Sect. 4 presents the conclusion.

2   Related Work

At the early time, researchers frequently used HMM for SER. For example, Schuller et al. [23] and Nwe et al. [22] conducted the SER model training using HMM and both teams had good results. Later, there are studies using deep learning to achieve SER. It is shown that most of the SER related machine learning were conducted using either Long Short Term Memory (LSTM) or CNN

[3,18,21,28]. Ming et al. [6] and Feng et al. [10] proposed bimodal systems, that ensembled the predictions from a linguistic model and an acoustic model, achieving 72.05% unweighted accuracy (UA) and 69.67% UA on the IEMOCAP dataset respectively. Shen et al. [24] had a similar bimodal framework but they used an attention network to make interactions between text and audio at a fine-granular level and achieved 76.4% UA on the IEMOCAP dataset. Su et al. [25] presented a gated recurrent unit network with a graph attention mechanism (GA-GRU) that had 63.8% UA on the IEMOCAP and 57.47% UA on the MSP-IMPROV datasets. Latif et al. [15] utilized Generative Adversarial Networks to improve SER in a cross-corpus setting. Fujioka et al. [11] introduced a framework that involved dynamic sample contribution weight estimation and labels correction, improving a BLSTM with an attention baseline by 1.9% on the IEMOCAP dataset. Chiba et al. [7] proposed a feature segmentation and multi-stream processing method to an attention-based BLSTM network which obtained 73.4% accuracy on the JTES database. Issa et al. [14] introduced a new architecture, worked on the raw sound files and outperformed the current best frameworks for the RAVDESS dataset. Zhang et al. [30] ensembled four systems into a system that outperformed the baseline of MEC2017 [17].

3   Methodology

3.1   Overall Structure

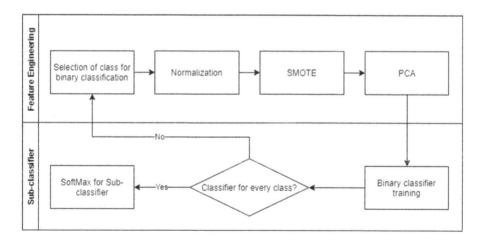

Fig. 1. Flowchart of the CLOVERSEC framework

Figure 1 illustrates the overall flowchart of the proposed CLOVASEC framework. Achieving SER using acoustic features, there will be two goals. They are obtaining and selecting the useful features [18,28] and develop a classifier that can perform effective training on the features. For the classifier to be useful in real scenarios, a well-designed and stable architecture should be implemented. This section introduces how features were extracted, the pre-processing techniques applied, the One-Versus-All classification schema and the models used in the framework.

3.2 Feature Extraction

Extraction of acoustic features was done with a modified pyAudioAnalysis library [27]. The library could extract 34 features and another 102 related features. The first 34 features are shown in Table 1, they are the mean values within a defined window. 35th to 68th features are the derivative of the first 34 features; 69th to 102nd features are the standard deviation of the first 34 features within a window; the last 34 features are the standard deviation of the 35th to 68th features within a window. Modifications were made to the codes so the library could output 3-dimensional arrays in terms of (batch, step, feature). Given the audio files have different length, to make the data aligned, we padded the data with zeros.

3.3 Feature Engineering

Standardization. The features contained values that can be different from a magnitude up to 100 times. Hence, batch standardization should be applied to the data. X refers to the vector of a feature and it is standardization by dividing the difference between X and mean of X by the standard deviation of X.

$$X standardized = \frac{X - \mu}{\sigma} \tag{1}$$

Synthetic Minority Oversampling Technique (SMOTE). Imbalanced data is a common problem that existed in machine learning and often the minority classes are what we interested in. Due to the nature of the most standard algorithm, training using imbalanced data will lead to unfavourable prediction performance for the minority classes [31]. The classification structure and datasets we used were very imbalanced, so to deal with the imbalance problem, we introduced SMOTE to over-sampling. SMOTE is experimental proven to be useful in improving the accuracy of classifiers with minority classes [5].

Principal Component Analysis (PCA). To reduce the computational power required while retaining essential information for machine learning, the PCA technique was used. The choice of PCA was provided with the basis that it reduces data of high dimensional vectors into lower ones while retaining a maximal amount of variance [13]. It is a multivariate statistical technique that many scientific disciplines use [1].

Table 1. The summary of acoustic features

Feature ID	Feature name	Description
1	Zero-Crossing Rate	The rate of sign-changes of the signal during the duration of a particular frame
2	Energy	The sum of squares of the signal values, normalized by the respective frame length
3	Entropy of Energy	The entropy of sub-frames' normalized energies. It can be interpreted as a measure of abrupt changes
4	Spectral Centroid	The centre of gravity of the spectrum
5	Spectral Spread	The second central moment of the spectrum
6	Spectral Entropy	The entropy of the normalized spectral energies for a set of sub-frames
7	Spectral Flux	The squared difference between the normalized magnitudes of the spectra of the two successive frames
8	Spectral Roll-offs	The frequency below which 90% of the magnitude distribution of the spectrum is concentrated
9–21	MFCCs	Mel Frequency Cepstral Coefficients form a cepstral representation where the frequency bands are not linear but distributed according to the mel-scale
22–32	Chroma Vector	A 12-element representation of the spectral energy where the bins represent the 12 equal-tempered pitch classes of western-type music (semitone spacing)
33	Chroma Deviation	The standard deviation of the 12 chroma coefficients

Model. RNN is a type of neural network, specializing in processing sequential information. We chose RNN to work on SER because the features were extracted in a time-series manner. LSTM was specifically chosen because it is a type of RNN that is good for long sequence data processing as compared to the conventional RNN. LSTM also avoids the problem of vanishing gradient as it has extra cells for internal recurrence other than the outer recurrence of RNN [2].

A LSTM network consists of various gates that helps the network to carry the early information to later part of the cells. With refer to Fig. 2, a LSTM unit is made up of three gates, they are forget gate(f), input gate(i) and output gate(o). The forget gate in charge of what information to keep from last hidden state, the input gate determines if any information to update and the output gate determines the next hidden state. The output of a cell will be fed to the next cell, so the previous information is used for text prediction.

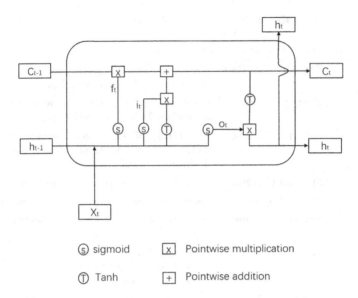

$\textcircled{s}$ sigmoid $\boxed{\text{x}}$ Pointwise multiplication

$\textcircled{T}$ Tanh $\boxed{\text{+}}$ Pointwise addition

Fig. 2. Structure of a LSTM unit

$$i_t = \sigma(W_i[h_{t-1}, X_t] + b_i) \tag{2}$$

$$f_t = \sigma(W_f[h_{t-1}, X_t] + b_f) \tag{3}$$

$$o_t = \sigma(W_o[h_{t-1}, X_t] + b_o) \tag{4}$$

Purely depending on an LSTM network was insufficient for SER because a speech recording may contain multiple sentences accompanied by several periods of silence. Therefore, a self-attention mechanism was introduced to the model. In addition to the LSTM unit, the self-attention based LSTM network contains context vector C as shown in the Fig. 3. A context vector carried all previous hidden states with different weights applied to them, and it is fed into next LSTM unit with a concatenation with the input vector to produce the output. Therefore, a self-attention mechanism allows the network to focus on the features and meaningful part of the data so it can accurately determine the emotions involved.

$$
\begin{aligned}
c_1 &= h_1 \\
c_2 &= align(h_1, h_2)h_1 + align(h_2, h_2)h_2 \\
c_3 &= align(h_1, h_3)h_1 + align(h_2, h_3)h_2 + align(h_3, h_3)h_3 \\
c_i &= align(h_1, h_i)h_1 + align(h_2, h_i)h_2 + ... + align(h_i, h_i)h_i
\end{aligned}
\tag{5}
$$

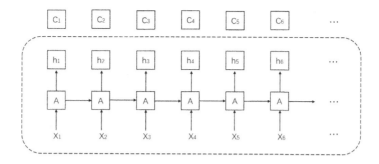

Fig. 3. Overview of an attention based LSTM network

One-Versus-All Classification. Building up a good acoustic model can be challenging as the emotions involved in a speech depends on both frequency features and time-series features. Also, certain classes possessed very similar characteristics which can be tricky for a computer to differentiate the differences among them. Hence, it requires a very complicated network with a well-preprocessed dataset to come up with a stable and accurate multi-class classifier.

Therefore, we proposed to perform a One-Versus-All Classification way to create a speech emotion classifier. Figure 5 illustrates the structure of the combined classifier and Fig. 4 shows the structure a self-attention based BiLSTM binary classifier. Eight binary classifiers for eight different classes were created respectively. The binary classifiers are trained to distinguish a class from the other seven classes. The processed acoustic feature will be fed into the eight sub-classifiers and a SoftMax layer is then applied to the eight predictions to finalize the prediction with the highest confidence level.

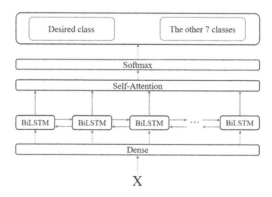

Fig. 4. Overview of an attention based BiLSTM binary sub-classifier

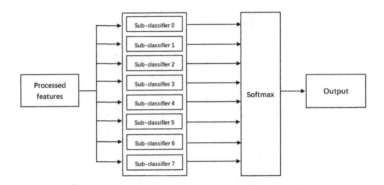

Fig. 5. Overview of the One-Versus-All classification.

4   Experimental Results

4.1   Experimental Setup

The proposed framework was trained using the Chinese Natural Emotional Audio-visual Database(CHEAVD) [16] and evaluated on two datasets, CHEAVD and Deng's dataset [8]. The summary of the datasets is shown in Table 2 The experiment was carried out on a computer with 128 GB RAM and an Nvidia Titan Xp with a graphic RAM size of 12 GB. The training sets had 20% of them split out as validation sets. The optimizer used was Adam with a batch size of 256. With the early stopping technique, the attention models usually stopped around 5 epochs to reach their best performance.

Table 2. The summary of datasets

Class	CHEAVD		Deng's	
	Training set	Testing set	Training set	Testing set
Neutral	1401	200	554	75
Angry	884	128	292	35
Happy	828	119	363	58
Worried	567	81	200	25
Sad	462	67	230	36
Anxious	457	66	133	22
Surprise	175	25	66	10
Disgust	144	21	61	5

4.2   Results of Feature Engineering

The audio files have different length, so a histogram and a boxplot of the length were plotted to visualize the distribution. Figure 6 indicates that audios were clustered around 2.0s with a 3rd percentile lies below 3.0s. Therefore, extraction of features using a window of 0.1s for 50 steps would cover most of the information for the samples of CHEAVD.

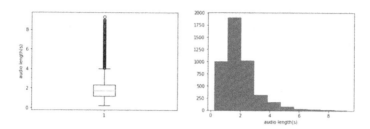

Fig. 6. The boxplot and histogram of CHEAVD audios' length

Macro Average Precision (MAP) and Macro Average Recall (MAR) were the criteria for evaluations. Table 3 shows the effects of SMOTE and PCA on the performance of the classifier over the CHEAVD testing set. When SMOTE and PCA were absent from the framework, the framework had a high accuracy but a very low recall. This observation can be explained by the structure of the dataset. Classes in CHEAVD were highly imbalanced. For its testing set, the total samples of sad, anxious, surprise and disgust only made up about 25% of the testing set. The high accuracy was attributed to the classification of classes with more samples such as neutral and angry. Therefore, the MAR was as low as 15.3%. The application of SMOTE might have lower the overall accuracy but it significantly improved recall, making the system much more stable.

We further adopted PCA on features starting from 130 dimensions with 10 lesser each time. It was found that feeding the model with features that were reduced to 20 had almost no impact on the stability of the system. This can be explained by the types of features extracted for the experiment. Most of the 136 features were related, for instance, the mean of a feature or the standard deviation of a feature over a window region. Also, it was possible that many features extracted could be compressed for an efficient classifier. Besides, compressed representations are also beneficial to reduce the computational cost in both training and inference.

4.3   Framework Evaluation

Table 4 presents the performance of different framework over the CHEAVD original testing set. The bidirectional Gated Recurrent Unit (BiGRU) and bidirectional LSTM network (BiLSTM) was the most basic system implemented and

Table 3. The evaluation of feature engineering techniques

Technique	MAP(%)	MAR(%)
None	58.5	15.3
SMOTE	52.9	49.9
SMOTE+PCA	52.1	51.0

had the worst performance. Applying a self-attention mechanism to the BiGRU and the BiLSTM only increased the MAP and MAR by a little amount, but they were still much lower than the baseline. Zhang's ensembled system [30] had better performance than the baseline but they all had a similar problem as MAR is much lower than MAP leading to an unstable system. The CLOVASEC outperformed other frameworks in both MAP and MAR, especially a higher MAR makes the system more stable.

It was also observed that the classes with a lower number of samples tend to be classified as classes with a higher number of samples. This is also one of the reasons that constrain the performance of the framework. Only 319 out of 4719 samples from the training set are 'surprise' and 'disgust'. The samples were insufficient to train a model that can classify different emotions very accurately. Moreover, there is a wide range of acoustic features for SER but it is yet to know which type is the best for SER [9, 26].

Table 4. The evaluation of different systems on CHEAVD original testing set

SER system	MAP (%)	MAR (%)
BaseLine [17]	39.2	25.3
BiGRU	17.0	18.0
BiGRU+attention	19.0	18.0
BiLSTM	21.0	20.0
BiLSTM+attention	35.0	21.0
Zhang's System [30]	44.4	28.0
CLOVASEC	53.5	56.5

The trained models were later directly applied to Deng's testing set and yielded decent results shown in Table 5. Interestingly, the performance of BiLSTM and BiLSTM with self-attention improved for the English testing set. This might be explained by the difference between the structure of the two datasets. Deng's testing set has a much smaller sample size as compared to CLOVASEC. A smaller testing set contributed to the improvements as minority classes were very limited in samples. For CLOVASEC the drop in MAP and MAR were expected as the models have put more weight in minority classes as compared to the other two systems. Different languages have different ways to express emotions. For example, Mandarin has four pitched tones for each word regardless of the context whereas, English words tones are somehow based on the emotions involved. Hence, such a direct application outcome was accepted. The limitation of our system is that it still has difficulty in handling imbalanced datasets especially when the imbalanced property is significant. Furthermore, it was observed that the feature extraction process was slow.

Table 5. The performance of systems on Deng's testing set

SER system	MAP (%)	MAR (%)
BiLSTM	31.0	26.0
BiLSTM+self-attention	34.0	31.0
CLOVASEC	49.6	48.9

5   Conclusion

In this paper, we presented a multi-classifier fusion framework named CLO-VASEC by splitting eight different classes into eight binary classifiers. Acoustic data was processed by SMOTE to improve the minority classes accuracy. Features were later processed by PCA to reduce the input parameters to the model, increasing the model efficiency. An LSTM network with a self-attention mechanism was used in the framework, it took advantage of LSTM over long-term dependencies information and the self-attention layer allows the machine to learn the import part of the features to generate a stable and accurate model. The framework had a decent and stable performance in both Chinese and English speeches.

To improve the framework, we will evaluate the framework on other languages such as Spanish. Also, pursuing highly accurate emotion recognition, sorely depending on acoustic models is insufficient. We have a few approaches in mind for future research. We will try to work in the direction of acoustic differences between genders and acoustic similarities among emotions. Also, we are looking to include facial recognition and linguistic emotion recognition into the framework for better accuracies. Moreover, we believed that the imbalanced data was one of the most significant factors that affect the performance of our framework. SMOTE was not good enough to deal with the imbalance problem so we may utilize generative adversarial networks to simulate more data for minority classes so the datasets can be balanced. Lastly, we may have a framework to classify each sentence within an audio recording instead of having a whole speech as the input. This is because a speech may not possess a consistent emotion throughout the whole speech.

Acknowledgement. This work was supported by the Six-Talent Peaks Project of Jiangsu Province (XYDXX-204), the Open Fund of Key Laboratory of Urban Land Resources Monitoring and Simulation, Ministry of Natural Resources (KF-2019-04-011, KF-2019-04-065), and Angel Project of Suzhou City science and technology (Grant No. CYTS2018233).

References

1. Abdi, H., Williams, L.J.: Principal component analysis. Wiley Interdiscip. Rev. Comput. Stat. **2**(4), 433–459 (2010). https://doi.org/10.1002/wics.101
2. Akçay, M.B., Oğuz, K.: Speech emotion recognition: emotional models, databases, features, preprocessing methods, supporting modalities, and classifiers. Speech Commun. **116**, 56–76 (2020). https://doi.org/10.1016/j.specom.2019.12.001
3. Badshah, A.M., Ahmad, J., Rahim, N., Baik, S.W.: Speech emotion recognition from spectrograms with deep convolutional neural network. In: 2017 International Conference on Platform Technology and Service, PlatCon 2017 - Proceedings, pp. 3–7 (2017). https://doi.org/10.1109/PlatCon.2017.7883728
4. Bong, S.Z., Wan, K., Murugappan, M., Ibrahim, N.M., Rajamanickam, Y., Mohamad, K.: Implementation of wavelet packet transform and non linear analysis for emotion classification in stroke patient using brain signals. Biomed. Signal Process. Control **36**, 102–112 (2017). https://doi.org/10.1016/j.bspc.2017.03.016
5. Chawla, N.V., Bowyer, K.W., Hall, L.O., Kegelmeyer, W.P.: SMOTE: synthetic minority over-sampling technique nitesh. J. Artif. Intell. Res. **16**(2), 321–357 (2002). https://doi.org/10.1613/jair.953
6. Chen, M., Zhao, X.: A multi-scale fusion framework for bimodal speech emotion recognition. In: Proceedings of the Annual Conference of the International Speech Communication Association, INTERSPEECH 2020-October, pp. 374–378 (2020). https://doi.org/10.21437/Interspeech.2020-3156
7. Chiba, Y., Nose, T., Ito, A.: Multi-stream attention-based BLSTM with feature segmentation for speech emotion recognition. In: Proceedings of the Annual Conference of the International Speech Communication Association, INTERSPEECH 2020-October, pp. 3301–3305 (2020). https://doi.org/10.21437/Interspeech.2020-1199
8. Deng, J., Zhang, Z., Marchi, E., Schuller, B.: Sparse autoencoder-based feature transfer learning for speech emotion recognition. In: Proceedings - 2013 Humaine Association Conference on Affective Computing and Intelligent Interaction, ACII 2013, pp. 511–516 (2013). https://doi.org/10.1109/ACII.2013.90
9. El Ayadi, M., Kamel, M.S., Karray, F.: Survey on speech emotion recognition: features, classification schemes, and databases. Pattern Recogn. **44**(3), 572–587 (2011). https://doi.org/10.1016/j.patcog.2010.09.020
10. Feng, H., Ueno, S., Kawahara, T.: End-to-end speech emotion recognition combined with acoustic-to-word ASR model. In: Proceedings of the Annual Conference of the International Speech Communication Association, INTERSPEECH 2020-October, pp. 501–505 (2020). https://doi.org/10.21437/Interspeech.2020-1180
11. Fujioka, T., Homma, T., Nagamatsu, K.: Meta-learning for speech emotion recognition considering ambiguity of emotion labels. In: Proceedings of the Annual Conference of the International Speech Communication Association, INTERSPEECH 2020-October, pp. 2332–2336 (2020). https://doi.org/10.21437/Interspeech.2020-1082

12. Gunes, H., Piccardi, M.: Bi-modal emotion recognition from expressive face and body gestures. J. Netw. Comput. Appl. **30**(4), 1334–1345 (2007). https://doi.org/10.1016/j.jnca.2006.09.007

13. Ilin, A., Raiko, T.: Practical approaches to principal component analysis in the presence of missing values. J. Mach. Learn. Res. **11**, 1957–2000 (2010)

14. Issa, D., Demirci, M.F., Yazici, A.: Speech emotion recognition with deep convolutional neural networks. Biomed. Signal Process. Control **59**, 101894 (2020). https://doi.org/10.1016/j.bspc.2020.101894

15. Latif, S., Asim, M., Rana, R., Khalifa, S., Jurdak, R., Schuller, B.W.: Augmenting Generative Adversarial Networks for Speech Emotion Recognition. arXiv, pp. 521–525 (2020)

16. Li, Y., Tao, J., Chao, L., Bao, W., Liu, Y.: CHEAVD: a Chinese natural emotional audio-visual database. J. Ambient Intell. Humanized Comput. **8**(6), 913–924 (2017). https://doi.org/10.1007/s12652-016-0406-z

17. Li, Y., Tao, J., Technology, I., Jiang, D., Shan, S., Jia, J.: MEC 2017: Multimodal Emotion Recognition Challenge (2018)

18. Lim, W., Jang, D., Lee, T.: Speech emotion recognition using convolutional and recurrent neural networks. In: 2016 Asia-Pacific Signal and Information Processing Association Annual Summit and Conference, APSIPA 2016, pp. 3–6 (2017). https://doi.org/10.1109/APSIPA.2016.7820699

19. Mayer, J.D.: Emotional intelligence. Imagination Cogn. Pers. **9**(3), 185–211 (1989). https://doi.org/10.2190/DUGG-P24E-52WK-6CDG

20. Nardelli, M., Valenza, G., Greco, A., Lanata, A., Scilingo, E.P.: Recognizing emotions induced by affective sounds through heart rate variability. IEEE Trans. Affect. Comput. **6**(4), 385–394 (2015). https://doi.org/10.1109/TAFFC.2015.2432810

21. Niu, Y., Zou, D., Niu, Y., He, Z., Tan, H.: Improvement on speech emotionrecognition based on deep convolutional neural networks.pdf (2018). https://doi.org/10.1145/3194452.3194460

22. Nwe, T.L., Foo, S.W., De Silva, L.C.: Speech emotion recognition using hidden Markov models. Speech Commun. **41**(4), 603–623 (2003). https://doi.org/10.1016/S0167-6393(03)00099-2

23. Schuller, B., Rigoll, G., Lang, M.: Hidden Markov model-based speech emotion recognition. In: Proceedings - IEEE International Conference on Multimedia and Expo 1, pp. I401–I404 (2003). https://doi.org/10.1109/ICME.2003.1220939

24. Shen, G., et al.: WISE: word-level interaction-based multimodal fusion for speech emotion recognition. In: Proceedings of the Annual Conference of the International Speech Communication Association, INTERSPEECH 2020-October, pp. 369–373 (2020). https://doi.org/10.21437/Interspeech.2020-3131

25. Su, B.H., Chang, C.M., Lin, Y.S., Lee, C.C.: Improving speech emotion recognition using graph attentive Bi-directional gated recurrent unit network. In: Proceedings of the Annual Conference of the International Speech Communication Association, INTERSPEECH 2020-October, pp. 506–510 (2020). https://doi.org/10.21437/Interspeech

26. Sun, Y., Wen, G., Wang, J.: Weighted spectral features based on local Hu moments for speech emotion recognition. Biomed. Signal Process. Control **18**, 80–90 (2015). https://doi.org/10.1016/j.bspc.2014.10.008

27. Theodoros, G.: A Python library for audio feature extraction, classification, segmentation and applications. https://github.com/tyiannak/pyAudioAnalysis

28. Trigeorgis, G., et al.: Adieu features? End-to-end speech emotion recognition using a deep convolutional recurrent network. In: ICASSP, IEEE International Conference on Acoustics, Speech and Signal Processing - Proceedings 2016-May, pp. 5200–5204 (2016). https://doi.org/10.1109/ICASSP.2016.7472669
29. Yuvaraj, R., et al.: Detection of emotions in Parkinson's disease using higher order spectral features from brain's electrical activity. Biomed. Signal Process. Control **14**(1), 108–116 (2014). https://doi.org/10.1016/j.bspc.2014.07.005
30. Zhang, X., Xu, M., Zheng, T.F.: Ensemble system for multimodal emotion recognition challenge. In: 2018 1st Asian Conference on Affective Computing and Intelligent Interaction, ACII Asia 2018 (MEC 2017), pp. 7–12 (2018). https://doi.org/10.1109/ACIIAsia.2018.8470352
31. Zhu, T., Lin, Y., Liu, Y.: Synthetic minority oversampling technique for multi-class imbalance problems. Pattern Recogn. **72**, 327–340 (2017). https://doi.org/10.1016/j.patcog.2017.07.024

A Hybrid Machine Learning Approach for Customer Loyalty Prediction

Hiu Fai Lee[✉] and Ming Jiang

School of Computer Science, Faculty of Technology, University of Sunderland, London, UK
bh46lu@student.sunderland.ac.uk, ming.jiang@sunderland.ac.uk

Abstract. Customer loyalty prediction is one of the most common applications of machine learning in Customer Relationship Management (CRM). Many research studies have tried to compare the effectiveness of different machine learning techniques applied for the model development. Also due to the simplicity and effectiveness, customer purchase behavioral attributes, such as, Recency, Frequency, and Monetary Value (RFM) are commonly used for predicting the customer lifetime value as a measure of loyalty. However, since RFM focuses on the purchase behaviours of customers only, it often overlooks the effect of other important factors to loyalty such as customer satisfaction and product experience. In this paper, a two-stage hybrid machine learning approach is designed to address this. Firstly, both unsupervised clustering and supervised classification model are used in the predication model building in order to realize the possible incremental value of hybrid model combining two learning techniques. Secondly, the proposed model is trained with behavourial RFM attributes and attitudinal factors such as customer satisfaction and product attributes, in order to better capture the influencing factors to loyalty.

Keywords: K-means clustering · Unsupervised learning · Classification · Supervised learning · Customer relationship management · Loyalty prediction

1 Introduction

Customer loyalty was a well discussed marketing concept and had received high level of attention from many businesses since 1980s. Many companies had developed customer relationship management programs with the objective to enhance customer loyalty [1] from marketing point of view. There is also a proven relationship between customer loyalty and company performance across industries namely banking, hotel and retail [2, 3].

Customer loyalty is generally defined as the intention of repurchasing products and services [4]. Bose and Rao [5] suggested that loyalty is the customer's commitment to do business with a particular organization which effects in repeat purchases of goods and services of that organization consistently in future. Apart from the behavioural consequence of loyalty in a form of purchases, loyalty could also result in recommending the goods and services to friends and associates. Besides the behavioural approach of defining loyalty, there is also the attitudinal approach. Attitudinal approach describes

© Springer Nature Singapore Pte Ltd. 2021
H. Zhang et al. (Eds.): NCAA 2021, CCIS 1449, pp. 211–226, 2021.
https://doi.org/10.1007/978-981-16-5188-5_16

loyalty in forms of consumer attitudes, preferences and dispositions towards brands which explain the motives leading to the repurchase behaviours [6, 7].

Because of the difficulty of collecting large-scale attitudinal data, most empirical research papers focus on the behavioural approach which defines loyalty as a propensity to repurchase a brand [8, 9]. Since loyalty is reflected in a form repurchase or a propensity to buy a brand in behavioural approach, loyalty could then be measured quantitatively with customer lifetime value (CLV), which is calculated as a sum of the present value of all profits generated from a customer's future purchases over a full life of relationship with a company [10, 11]. Recent empirical studies supported the relationship between loyalty and CLV. Studies by Zhang, Dixit and Friedmann [11] and Chen et al. [13] supported the hypothesis that customer loyalty was positively correlated with customer lifetime value by proving customer revenue and customer retention were driven by customer loyalty.

To measure CLV, we can estimate the revenue generated from future purchases by using prediction techniques. The most common one according to Gupta et al. [14] is RFM model. RFM model is an effective tool for determining high potential customers by exploring the quantitative characteristics of customers. RFM model was widely used by marketers for customer segmentation, customer loyalty and response prediction [15–17]. The three components of RFM are called recency, frequency and monetary [18]. Recency represents the time interval between now and last transaction time of a customer; Frequency represents the number of transactions a customer made in a period of time; Monetary indicates the total amount of spending of a customer made in a period of time.

However, RFM models could be too simplistic and fail to capture the effect of attitudinal and other industry specific factors to customer loyalty. One factor that is believed to be directly or indirectly related to customer loyalty is customer satisfaction. Customer satisfaction refers to customer feelings or customer reaction to the state of fulfilment of their expectation and needs through the services or products [19, 20]. There are many empirical studies have proven the positive relationship between satisfaction and loyalty in banking and even B2B industries [19, 21]. Some research studies used category or product purchasing data in customer segmentation model to capture the industry specific characteristics. For example, in a recent study, Brito et al. [22] had segmented the shirt customers for an online fashion retailer based on style, colors and fabric. Heilman and Bowman [23] had shown in the study of baby product industry that segmentation could be developed by considering purchase behaviour in multiple categories together.

2 Related Work

There are three approaches of using RFM being discussed in past researches. The first and most common one is simple RFM model. Described by Gupta et al. [14], the simple RFM model predicts the lifetime value with the three RFM components in equal weighting. The second method called weighted RFM model, in which different weightings are applied to frequency, recency and monetary factor [24, 25].

The third approach which is called extended RFM model which predicts the lifetime value using RFM attributes together with additional parameters. Examples of these additional parameters were time since first purchase and churn probability [16]. More recently, Sarvari, Ustundag and Takci [26] applied customer segmentation in fast food chain using RFM accompanied with demographics data.

To my best knowledge, the scope and methodology design of this work has a very comprehensive approach and can generate research contributions to fashion industry, which is a largely under-researched industry. Table 1 summaries the machine learning techniques and studied industries in recent loyalty prediction researches as comparison [27–41].

Table 1. Summary of methodologies used in related studies

Topic	Authors	Year	Industry	Market	Data Mining / Machine Learning Techniques used						
					K-Means Clustering	Logistic Regression	Decision Tree	Random Forest	Boosted Model	SVM	Neural Network
LightGBM: an Effective Decision Tree Gradient Boosting Method to Predict Customer Loyalty in the Finance Industry	Machado, M.R., Karray, S. and de Sousa, I.T.	2019	Financial	South America					Y		
Application of Machine Learning for Churn Prediction Based on Transactional Data (RFM Analysis)	Aleksandrova, Y	2018	Building materials	Bulgaria		Y		Y	Y	Y	Y
ustomer segmentation by using RFM model and clustering methods: a case study in retail industry	Doğan, O., Aygin, E. and Bulut, Z.A.	2018	Retail	Turkey	Y						
Implementation of Clustering Technique Based RFM Analysis for Customer Behaviour in Online Transactions	Sheshasaayee, A. and Logeshwari, L.	2018	Online retail	NA	Y						
Oversampling Techniques for Bankruptcy Prediction: Novel Features from a Transaction Dataset	Le, T. et al	2018	Banking	NA			Y	Y		Y	
Promotion Recommendation Method and System Based on Random Forest	Hu, W.H. et al	2018	Telecom	Taiwan				Y			
Clustering and Profiling of Customers Using RFM For Customer Relationship Management Recommendations	Maryani, I. and Riana, D.	2017	Industrial	Indonesia	Y		Y				
RFM approach for telecom insolvency modeling	Zabkowski, T.S.	2016	Telecom	Poland		Y	Y				
Combining RFM model and clustering techniques for customer value analysis of a company selling online	Daoud, R.A. et al	2015	Online retail	Morocco	Y						
A decision-making framework for precision marketing	You, Z. et al	2015	Retail	China	Y	Y					
A Novel Approach for Providing the Customer Churn Prediction Model using Enhanced Boosted Trees Technique in Cloud Computing	Kaur, K. and Vashisht, S.	2015	Retail	NA					Y		
Applying data mining with a new model on customer relationship management systems: a case of airline industry in Taiwan	Chiang, W.Y.	2014	Airline	Taiwan			Y				
Data accuracy's impact on segmentation performance: Benchmarking RFM analysis, logistic regression, and decision trees.	Coussement, K., Van den Bossche, F.A. and De Bock	2014	Retail	NA	Y	Y	Y				
Data mining for the online retail industry: A case study of RFM model-based customer segmentation using data mining	Chen, D., Sain, S.L. and Guo, K.	2012	Online retail	UK	Y		Y				
Segmentation of telecom customers based on customer value by decision tree model	Han, S.H., Lu, S.X. and Leung, S.C.	2012	Telecom	China			Y				
An LTV model and customer segmentation based on customer value: a case study on the wireless telecommunication industry	Hwang, H., Jung, T., & Suh, E.	2004	Telecom	Korea		Y	Y				Y

3   Research Method

This section aims to introduce the proposed research method for predicting the loyalty of customers. The research method first involves the application of K-means clustering using RFM, then passed along the clustering results from first-stage to a classification model built from different learning techniques.

3.1 K-Means Clustering

Clustering is the automatic process of grouping data of similar attributes into same group. K-means clustering is a very well-known algorithms that has been used extensively in various business applications, one of which is customer segmentation. It works by automatically partitioning a dataset into k groups with the rule of nearest means, which assigns data sample to the cluster with the closest centroid "Mean" [42]. To select the right number of clusters (K value), CH Index is used to compare the validity of different K values. The method is invented by Calinski & Harabasz in 1974 based on the relationship between "the sum of distances within cluster" and "sum of distances between clusters". The CH Index formula is displayed in Eq. (1), where N is the number of observations, K is the number of clusters, and $BCSM$ and $WCSM$ are the between- and within-cluster sums of squares, respectively. According to CH Index, the correct number of clusters is determined by the K value that can maximize CH Index.

$$trace(BCSM)/trace(WCSM) \times (N - k)/(k - 1) \tag{1}$$

3.2 Classification Models for Prediction

Classification method is deployed in the second stage to build the prediction model using the K-means clustering results and other customer features. Contrast to the unsupervised nature of clustering, classification is a supervised learning technique to identify which "class" an observation should belong to, based on a training set of data containing observations with known "class" membership [43]. The learning techniques used for classification are described in the following section.

Decision Tree: Decision tree learning is among the most popular learning technique for classification model. Decision tree learning method uses a tree-based model that starts from splitting data samples based on values of attributes (represented in the branches) until the "decision" about all data samples' target values are decided [44]. In classification problem, the target values are set of discrete class labels and the decision tree is called "classification tree".

Logistic Regression: Regression is a statistical analysis concerned with describing the relationship between a dependent variable and one or more explanatory variables. There are two key categories of regression models, one is linear regression model and one is logistic regression model. The key distinguishing factor of two models is the target (dependent) variable. When the target variable is a continuous set of values, linear regression should be employed, while logistic regression should be used if target variable is a set of categorical values.

Random Forest: The random forest is an ensemble tree method, an aggregation scheme of many individual decision trees. Due to its popularity and its good empirical performance, Breiman's random forest is one of the most used algorithms, and is often directly called "random forest" [45]. In the random forest model, the training data are sampled randomly to create multiple randomized trees, so that different classification results would be obtained from the multiple randomized trees [46]. The final classification result will be the one with most votes (weighted or unweighted) from randomized decision trees. The scheme of an un-weighted random forest algorithm in illustrated in Fig. 1.

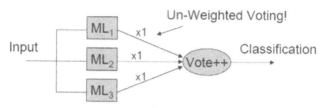

Fig. 1. Scheme of un-weighted random forest algorithm

Boosted Model: Boosted model is also an ensemble tree method but it is different to random forest in the way trees are built and combining results. In boosted model [47], the model works in a forward stage-wise manner that each tree is built once at a time, with the next tree is built with an emphasis of mis-labelled samples based on the previous tree. The mislabelled samples from previous tree are called weak learner, and by adding weighting to weak learners in next tree, it enhances the training of the model towards those previously mis-modelled.

3.3 Design of Two-Stage Model

In the paper, the research method of the prediction model involves two stages of machine learning process. The goal is to improve the overall model performance from a simple one-stage machine learning model. The model also mirrors the extend RFM approach by using RFM attributes and expanded with industry specific product variables. The first stage of the process is to cluster all observations with K-Means clustering using RFM attributes. The resulting cluster label from first stage, along with customer satisfaction variable and product purchase variables, will form a new dataset as the inputs to the classification model in second stage. The new dataset will split into trained and test data in 50%/50% split. More details will be discussed in Sect. 4.

4   Data

4.1 Dataset

The data we use are obtained from a fashion retailer from Europe. The dataset integrates the enterprise customer transaction data and satisfaction survey data obtained across 4 years from January 2016 to December 2019. There are 32,123 rows of data capturing transaction data of customers who made first transaction between Jan to Mar 2016 and are from Greater China region including China, Hong Kong and Taiwan. The transaction database stores the historical purchase records of all customers which including customer details, purchased stores, products, transaction date, sales amount etc. While the satisfaction survey database contains the responses of survey conducted by the company regarding their satisfaction level towards the shopping experience.

4.2 Feature Selection and Engineering

The 4-year period of dataset is split into two periods, of which the first period contains the transaction data of 1st year and 2nd year; and the second period contains those of 3rd year and 4th year. The purpose is to use the RFM variables of first 2 years' period to predict the "customer lifetime value" in the form of the next 2 years' total spending value. The following feature engineering is performed before data analysis.

CLV Classifier: The outcome of classification is to identify customers of top 10% CLV in the "future" period. A new classifier "Second 2 Year-Top 10% spend" is derived based on total spend value in the second 2-years' period.

RFM Attributes: The last purchase date is transformed to the number of months from the last purchase as "Recency"; the number of transactions made under the same customer ID is aggregated as "Frequency"; the total spend under same customer ID is regarded as "Monetary". Values are normalized for K-means clustering.

Product Variables: For each customer ID, product category bought most by value is regarded as "Top spend category", while product category bought in the very first transaction is "First purchase category". Figure 2 summarizes the variables trained in the model after feature engineering, and their corresponding data timeframe, while Table 2 describes the data type and meaning of each variable.

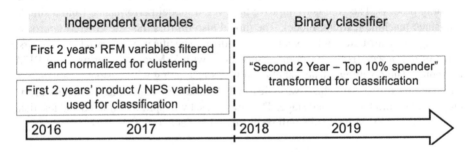

Fig. 2. Independent variables and classifiers for modelling

Table 2. Data type and description of the variables from dataset

Variable name	Data type	Description; typical value
ID	Nominal	Customer ID; unique integral number
Cust Market Code	Nominal	Residence location of customer; HK
First Transaction month	Nominal	First transaction date in YYYY-MM; 2016-03
First Purchase category	Nominal	Category purchased in first transaction; MENS
Top spend category	Nominal	Category purchased most in value; ACC
First 2 Year – Freq	Numeric	Number of transactions in the first 2 years: 10
First 2 Year – Spend	Numeric	Total spent amount in GBP in the first 2 years; 8,999
First 2 Year – Recency	Nominal	Last transaction month in the first 2 years; 05-2017
Second 2 Year – Freq	Numeric	Number of transactions in the second 2-year; 10
Second 2 Year – Spend	Numeric	Total spent amount in GBP in the second 2-year; 8,999
Second 2 Year – Recency	Nominal	Last transaction month in the second 2-year; 10-2019
Net Promoter Score	Numeric	10-point-scale rating for brand recommendation

4.3 Data Analysis Process

The application of clustering and classification modelling are performed in following flow (Fig. 3) using an analytics software called Alteryx Designer.

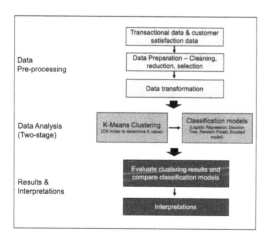

Fig. 3. Workflow of the research methodology

1. Clustering all observations into different clusters based on RFM variables using K-Means algorithm
2. Based on the K-Means clustering result, select the one (or more) cluster with the highest RFM values

3. Split by 50%/50% the samples of the selected cluster into train and test datasets
4. Run the training dataset in 4 different classification method: Boosted Model, Logistic Regression, Decision Tree and Random Forest
5. Select the variable "Second 2 year - Top 10" as the target classifier, and "Net Promoter Score", "Top spend category" and "First purchase category" as the independent variables
6. Run the testing set of data on the 4 models
7. Select the best performing model as the final prediction model by evaluating model performance matrices

4.4 K-Means Clustering

The very first step of K-Means clustering is to determine the number of clusters ie. K value using Calinski & Harabasz Index (CH Index). Figure 4 shows that CH Index is maximized at 4-cluster K-Means, so in this work K value of 4 is selected.

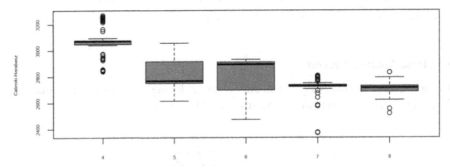

Fig. 4. CH Indices of different value of K (Number of clusters)

The cluster with high RFM values will be selected for next stage classification modelling. This is a very important step of the data analysis design as the selection will affect the subsequent prediction outcomes. From Table 3 and 4, Cluster 4 represents a very exclusive group of high quality customers. They have the highest average spend in the first two years, with average spending 4 times higher than cluster 1 and cluster 3 customers respectively.

Cluster 4 customers' average purchase frequency value at 6.74 times, 6.48 times and 6.50 times in China, Hong Kong and Taiwan respectively, compared to 2.5 to 3.4 times of other clusters. This is no surprise that the average numbers of month since last purchase is lowest for cluster 4 with an average cluster 4 customer last purchased 6–7 months ago. Accordingly, data samples of cluster 4 are selected for the next stage of classification model building.

Table 3. Summary report of K-Means clustering results

Cluster	Size	Avg distance	Max distance	Separation
1	2530	0.623778	2.922327	0.889225
2	1709	0.889329	2.306257	0.858437
3	671	1.117244	3.614569	0.873628
4	568	1.770384	9.383968	1.301326

Table 4. Average of RFM variables of 4 clusters

Cluster	Location	Avg frequency	Avg recency	Avg spend
1	CN	2.49	21.44	1155.87
	HK	2.38	21.76	1143.98
	TW	2.72	21.32	1085.89
2	CN	2.77	7.64	1682.96
	HK	2.62	7.68	1652.28
	TW	2.75	7.6	1575.89
3	CN	3.39	16.63	3829.6
	HK	2.13	16.49	3980.9
	TW	3.22	15.8	3936.05
4	CN	6.74	7.14	4856.95
	HK	6.48	6.24	5993.23
	TW	6.5	6.74	4840.02

4.5   Building Classification Models

The next stage of data analysis is to develop a classification model that could identify the customers from Cluster 4 who would be top 10% of customers in the "future" ie. 3rd/4th year. Classification method is supervised learning method used to model the fit of Cluster 4 data samples to the target parameter "Second 2 year - Top 10% spend". Based on some previous studies, product preference and brand satisfaction are perceived to have an influence to the lifetime value, so variables "Top spending category", "First purchase category" and "Net Promoter Score" are modelled to fit the target parameter.

In the experiment, 568 data samples from cluster 4 are used to build the classification models, with a split of 70%/30% training and testing data. According to Dobbin and Simon [48], the rule of setting the split between training and testing data set is to minimize mean squared error with respect to full dataset, and their study has suggested 40–80% allocation of training data.

4.6 Model Evaluation Techniques

This section describes the different evaluation techniques selected for the loyalty prediction objective.

Confusion Matrix: For the case of focusing on customers who are top 10% spender in next 2 year, the model aims to maximize the number of positive observations and the accuracy rate of a positive class prediction i.e. "Precision" and "recall" are used.

Lift Chart: The lift chart can be used to compare visually the improvement different prediction models deliver against a random guess (without a model) on different proportion of data population [49].

ROC Curve: ROC curve is regarded as one of the most important evaluation methods for a binary classification model [50, 51]. It is drawn by plotting the true positive rate (precision) against the false positive rate at various thresholds. The ROC curve represents a trade-off between true positive rate and false positive rate in model learning. The area under the ROC curve (AUR) is used to measure of quality of a classification model where a random model has a AUR of 0.5 and a perfect model has a AUR of 1.

5 Experimental Results and Discussions

5.1 Model Performance Review

Table 5 shows the distribution of the target variable "Second 2 Year – Top 10% spend" in each cluster, where we can use it as a baseline reference for model performance assessment. From Table 5, 29% of the customers from cluster 4 are the top 10% spender in the second 2 years' period, this suggests that clustering technique has produced 3 times better prediction than a "random pick". This 29% ratio is then used as an important referencing baseline for the model performance review in second stage.

Table 5. Distribution of Y/N attributes of "Top 10% Spend" by cluster

Cluster	Total		Top 10% Spend (Y)		Top 10% Spend (N)	
	Customers	%	Customers	%	Customers	%
1	2530	100	95	4	2435	96
2	1709	100	230	13	1479	87
3	671	100	84	13	587	87
4	568	100	162	29	406	71
All	5478	100	570	10	4907	90

Table 6. Confusion matrices of 4 classification models

Confusion matric of boosted model			Confusion matric of decision tree		
	Actual_0	Actual_1		Actual_0	Actual_1
Predicted_0	166	39	Predicted_0	171	39
Predicted_1	30	49	Predicted_1	25	49
Confusion matric of logistic regression			Confusion matric of random forest		
	Actual_0	Actual_1		Actual_0	Actual_1
Predicted_0	173	44	Predicted_0	173	53
Predicted_1	23	44	Predicted_1	23	35

Table 7. Three measures calculated from confusion matrices

	Accuracy	#	Precision	#	Recall	#
Boosted model	0.757	3rd	0.6203	3rd	0.5568	1st
Decision tree	0.7746	1st	0.6622	1st	0.5568	1st
Logistic regression	0.7324	4th	0.6034	4th	0.5	3rd
Random forest	0.7641	2nd	0.6567	2nd	0.3977	4th

Confusion Matrix Results: After the 4 classification models have been trained, they are then tested with the test dataset on Alteryx Designer to obtain unbiased results for model evaluation (Table 6). Next, the confusion matrix results of each model are then used to calculate the overall model accuracy, precision and recall (Table 7) to evaluate the model performance.

Based on the confusion matrix results, the decision tree model produces the best prediction result with consistently the highest score in accuracy, precision and recall. It has an accuracy of 77.5% overall, a precision of 66.2% and recall rate of 55.7%. Random forest, a variation of decision tree technique, followed closely in terms of accuracy and precision scores at 76.4% and 65.7% respectively, however the model has much lower recall at 39.8% only.

Lift Curve: Another evaluation technique is lift curve (Fig. 5) which compares the lift score of the models at different proportion of data observations. The graph suggests that beyond 40% proportion of data observations, decision tree model starts to produce the most superior lift score than other models do.

ROC Curve: ROC curves are plotted in Fig. 6 to select the model with highest AUC (area under the curve) where it minimizes the false positive rate at any given true positive

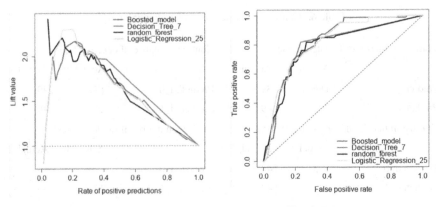

Fig. 5. Lift chart   **Fig. 6.** ROC curve

rate. Decision tree outperforms other 3 models at true positive rate between 70%–83% with lowest false positive rate at the same time. When a higher true positive rate is required over 83%, the boosted model then generally performs the best among 4 models.

5.2 Decision Tree Formulation

In order to interpret the influence of the product preference and satisfaction towards customer loyalty, the best performing model i.e. decision tree model was illustrated in Fig. 7 so that we could interpret the 3 key decision rules of the tree.

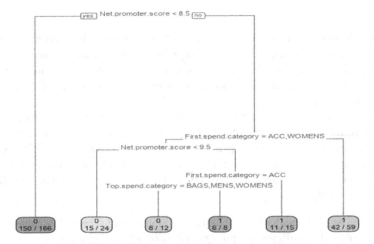

Fig. 7. Illustration of decision tree model

Branch "NPS < 8.5" (NO): The tree model suggests customer satisfaction towards brand is most important to the loyalty. NPS which indicates the likelihood of brand recommendation is the first branch from the root. For customers with NPS is 8.5 or above, 61% of them are "top 10% spender", while if NPS is below 8.5, 91% are not "top 10% spenders" eventually.

Branch "First Spend Category = ACC, WOMENS" (NO): As the tree extended further, "First spend category" is then used to classify customers. The branch "First spend category = ACC, WOMENS" suggests that for customers who with NPS > 8.5 and purchased MENSWEARS/BAGS (Not purchased ACC, WOMENS) at the first purchase, 71% of them would eventually in top 10% spenders.

Branch "Top Spend Category = BAGS, MENS, WOMENS" (NO): "Top spend category" is used only towards very end of the tree to classify a very exclusive group of customers who have NPS score > 9.5 and purchased accessories at the first purchase into "Top 10% spenders".

6 Conclusion and Future Work

The proposed hybrid approach has demonstrated both unsupervised technique (K-means clustering) and supervised technique (classification models) could be constructed in a two-stage model to enhance the prediction results. The values of customer-centric business intelligence have been proven to be instrumental to a fashion brand by applying RFM, customer product preference and customer satisfaction data. Besides the prediction model has the ability of identifying potential loyal customers to optimize marketing and CRM investment, the model features of the two-stage prediction model have also provided important insights of drivers towards loyalty.

While this work has successfully developed a two-stage loyalty prediction model with accuracy rate over 77%, yet a few possible future works could further be accomplished. For example, test the prediction model in other markets given the accessibility to other market data. A different prediction models could be applied to analyse customers with 1-time purchase in first period and from cluster 2 & 3. The current methodology is designed to model only customers who have purchased 2 times or above so that the RFM model can model the "variations in frequency and recency value" of data samples. A Deep Learning model based analysis of RFM in various application including lifetime value model [52] and credit scoring model in banking [53] would be further explored in the future.

References

1. Pitta, D., Franzak, F., Fowler, D.: A strategic approach to building online customer loyalty: integrating customer profitability tiers. J. Consum. Mark. **23**(7), 421–429 (2006)
2. Liu, C., Wang, T.Y.: A study on the effect of service quality on customer loyalty and corporate performance in financial industry. Probl. Perspect. Manag. **15**(2), 355–363 (2017)
3. Ramanathan, U., Subramanian, N., Yu, W., et al.: Impact of customer loyalty and service operations on customer behaviour and firm performance: empirical evidence from UK retail sector. Prod. Plan. Control **28**(6–8), 478–488 (2017)

4. Pi, W.P., Huang, H.H.: Effects of promotion on relationship quality and customer loyalty in the airline industry: the relationship marketing approach. Afr. J. Bus. Manag. **5**(11), 4403–4414 (2011)
5. Bose, S., Rao, V.G.: Perceived benefits of customer loyalty programs: validating the scale in the Indian context. Manag. Mark. **6**(4) (2011)
6. Antonios, J.: Understanding the effects of customer education on customer loyalty. Bus. Leadersh. Rev. **8**(1), 1–15 (2011)
7. Cheng, S.-I.: Comparisons of competing models between attitudinal loyalty and behavioral loyalty. Int. J. Bus. Soc. Sci. **2**(10), 149–166 (2011)
8. Trinh, G.T., Anesbury, Z.W., Driesener, C.: Has behavioural loyalty to online supermarkets declined? Australas. Mark. J. (AMJ) **25**(4), 326–333 (2017)
9. Liu, M.T., Liu, Y., Mo, Z., Zhao, Z., Zhu, Z.: How CSR influences customer behavioural loyalty in the Chinese hotel industry. Asia Pacific J. Mark. Logist. **32**(1), 1–22 (2019)
10. Gupta, S., Lehmann, D.R., Stuart, J.A.: Valuing customers. J. Mark. Res. **41**(1), 7–18 (2004)
11. Rust, R.T., Lemon, K.N., Zeithaml, V.A.: Return on marketing: using customer equity to focus marketing strategy. J. Mark. **68**(1), 109–127 (2004)
12. Zhang, J.Q., Dixit, A., Friedmann, R.: Customer loyalty and lifetime value: an empirical investigation of consumer packaged goods. J. Mark. Theory Pract. **18**(2), 127–140 (2010)
13. Chen, D., Sain, S.L., Guo, K.: Data mining for the online retail industry: A case study of RFM model-based customer segmentation using data mining. J. Database Mark. Customer Strategy Manag. **19**(3), 197–208 (2012)
14. Gupta, S., Hanssens, D., Hardie, B., et al.: Modeling customer lifetime value. J. Serv. Res. **9**(2), 139–155 (2006)
15. Song, M., Zhao, X., Haihong, E., et al.: Statistics-based CRM approach via time series segmenting RFM on large scale data. Knowl.-Based Syst. **132**, 21–29 (2017)
16. Cheng, C.H., Chen, Y.S.: Classifying the segmentation of customer value via RFM model and RS theory. Expert Syst. Appl. **36**(3), 4176–4184 (2009)
17. Coussement, K., De Bock, K.W.: Customer churn prediction in the online gambling industry: the beneficial effect of ensemble learning. J. Bus. Res. **66**(9), 1629–1636 (2013)
18. Yeh, I.C., Yang, K.J., Ting, T.M.: Knowledge discovery on RFM model using Bernoulli sequence. Expert Syst. Appl. **36**(3), 5866–5871 (2009)
19. Hallowell, R.: The relationships of customer satisfaction, customer loyalty, and profitability: an empirical study. Int. J. Service Ind. Manag. (1996)
20. Oliver, R.L.: Customer satisfaction research. In: The Handbook of Marketing Research: Uses, Misuses, and Future Advances, vol. 1 (2006)
21. Chandrashekaran, M., Rotte, K., Tax, S.S., et al.: Satisfaction strength and customer loyalty. J. Mark. Res. **44**(1), 153–163 (2007)
22. Brito, P.Q., Soares, C., Almeida, S., et al.: Customer segmentation in a large database of an online customized fashion business. Robot. Comput.-Integr. Manuf. **36**, 93–100 (2015)
23. Heilman, C.M., Bowman, D.: Segmenting consumers using multiple-category purchase data. Int. J. Res. Mark. **19**(3), 225–252 (2002)
24. Stone, B.: Successful Direct Marketing Methods, pp. 29–35. NTC Business Books, Lincolnwood (1995)
25. Shen, C.C., Chuang, H.M.: A study on the applications of data mining techniques to enhance customer lifetime value. WSEAS Trans. Inf. Sci. Appl. **6**(2), 319–328 (2009)
26. Sarvari, P.A., Ustundag, A., Takci, H.: Performance evaluation of different customer segmentation approaches based on RFM and demographics analysis. Kybernetes **45**(7), 1129–1157 (2016)
27. Machado, M.R., Karray, S., de Sousa, I.T.: LightGBM: an effective decision tree gradient boosting method to predict customer loyalty in the finance industry. In: 2019 14th International Conference on Computer Science & Education, pp. 1111–1116. IEEE (2019)

28. Aleksandrova, Y.: Application of machine learning for churn prediction based on transactional data (RFM analysis). In: 2018 International Multidisciplinary Scientific Geoconference SGEM 2018: Conference Proceedings, vol. 18, no. 2, pp. 125–132 (2018)
29. Doğan, O., Ayçin, E., Bulut, Z.A.: Customer segmentation by using RFM model and clustering methods: a case study in retail industry. Int. J. Contemp. Econ. Adm. Sci. **8**(1), 1–19 (2018)
30. Sheshasaayee, A., Logeshwari, L.: Implementation of clustering technique based RFM analysis for customer behaviour in online transactions. In: 2018 2nd International Conference on Trends in Electronics and Informatics, pp. 1166–1170. IEEE (2018)
31. Le, T., Lee, M.Y., Park, J.R., et al.: Oversampling techniques for bankruptcy prediction: novel features from a transaction dataset. Symmetry **10**(4), 79 (2018)
32. Hu, W.H., Tang, S.H., Chen, Y.C., et al.: Promotion recommendation method and system based on random forest. In: Proceedings of the 5th Multidisciplinary International Social Networks Conference, pp. 1–5 (2018)
33. Maryani, I., Riana, D.: Clustering and profiling of customers using RFM for customer relationship management recommendations. In: 2017 5th International Conference on Cyber and IT Service Management (CITSM), pp. 1–6. IEEE (2017)
34. Zabkowski, T.S.: RFM approach for telecom insolvency modeling. Kybernetes **45**(5), 815–827 (2016)
35. Daoud, R.A., Amine, A., Bouikhalene, B., et al.: Combining RFM model and clustering techniques for customer value analysis of a company selling online. In: 2015 IEEE/ACS 12th International Conference of Computer Systems and Applications (AICCSA), pp.1–6. IEEE (2015)
36. You, Z., Si, Y.W., Zhang, D., et al.: A decision-making framework for precision marketing. Expert Syst. Appl. **42**(7), 3357–3367 (2015)
37. Kaur, K., Vashisht, S.: A novel approach for providing the customer churn prediction model using enhanced boosted trees technique in cloud computing. Int. J. Comput. Appl. **114**(7), 1–7 (2015)
38. Chiang, W.Y.: Applying data mining with a new model on customer relationship management systems: a case of airline industry in Taiwan. Transp. Lett. **6**(2), 89–97 (2014)
39. Coussement, K., Van den Bossche, F.A., De Bock, K.W.: Data accuracy's impact on segmentation performance: benchmarking RFM analysis, logistic regression, and decision trees. J. Bus. Res. **67**(1), 2751–2758 (2014)
40. Han, S.H., Shui Xiu, L., Leung, S.C.H.: Segmentation of telecom customers based on customer value by decision tree model. Expert Syst. Appl. **39**(4), 3964–3973 (2012)
41. Hwang, H., Jung, T., Suh, E.: An LTV model and customer segmentation based on customer value: a case study on the wireless telecommunication industry. Expert Syst. Appl. **26**(2), 181–188 (2004)
42. Zalaghi, Z., Varzi, Y.: Measuring customer loyalty using an extended RFM and clustering technique. Manag. Sci. Lett. **4**(5), 905–912 (2014)
43. Alpaydın, E.: Introduction to Machine Learning. MIT Press, Cambridge (2020)
44. Wu, X., Kumar, V., Quinlan, J.R., et al.: Top 10 algorithms in data mining. Knowl. Inf. Syst. **14**(1), 1–37 (2008)
45. Scornet, E.: Tuning parameters in random forests. In: ESAIM: Proceedings and Surveys, vol. 60, pp.144–162 (2017)
46. Livingston, F.: Implementation of Breiman's random forest machine learning algorithm. ECE591Q Machine Learning Journal Paper, pp. 1–13 (2005)
47. Schapire, R.E.: The boosting approach to machine learning: an overview. In: Denison, D.D., Hansen, M.H., Holmes, C.C., Mallick, B., Yu, B. (eds.) Nonlinear estimation and classification, pp. 149–171. Springer, New York (2003). https://doi.org/10.1007/978-0-387-215 79-2_9

48. Dobbin, K.K., Simon, R.M.: Optimally splitting cases for training and testing high dimensional classifiers. BMC Med. Genomics **4**(1), 1–8 (2011)
49. Jaffery, T., Liu, S.X.: Measuring campaign performance by using cumulative gain and lift chart. In: SAS Global Forum, p. 196 (2009)
50. Vuk, M., Curk, T.: ROC curve, lift chart and calibration plot. Metodoloski zvezki **3**(1), 89 (2006)
51. Ferri, C., Flach, P., Hernández-Orallo, J.: Learning decision trees using the area under the ROC curve. In: ICML, vol. 2, pp. 139–146 (2002)
52. Tkachenko, Y.: Autonomous CRM control via CLV approximation with deep reinforcement learning in discrete and continuous action space. arXiv:1504.01840 (2015)
53. Alborzi, M., Khanbabaei, M.: Using data mining and neural networks techniques to propose a new hybrid customer behaviour analysis and credit scoring model in banking services based on a developed RFM analysis method. Int. J. Bus. Inf. Syst. **23**(1), 1–22 (2016)

LDA-Enhanced Federated Learning for Image Classification with Missing Modality

Xiaoyan Sun[✉] and Xinhao Wang

School of Information and Control Engineering, China University of Mining and Technology, Xuzhou 221116, Jiangsu, China

Abstract. In practical pattern recognition, e.g., image classification or recognition, the problem of missing modality, i.e., new patterns never trained by a learner pop up, can cause a dramatic decrease on the recognition accuracy. Existing algorithms as few-shot learning (FSL) and zero-shot learning (ZSL) have not sufficiently used information from other users or clients. If patterns or knowledge from other sources can be utilized as much as possible, the damage of missing modality is expected to be reduced. Privacy protection must be considered when trying to fetch information from other users. Motivated by these, an enhanced federated learning with linear discriminant analysis (LDA) is developed here. The data of each user is regarded as a client, and the features of each client are first extracted with neural network-based classification. These features are uploaded to the central server and then aggregated with LDA as a central classification to possibly achieve all patterns' features. The trained LDA is then downloaded to the client to fulfill the pattern recognition. The proposed algorithm is applied to an image classification, and the experimental results demonstrate its efficiency in dealing with pattern recognition with missing modality.

Keywords: Federated learning · Missing modality · Image classification · LDA

1 Introduction

In recent years, machine learning has achieved great success in research and has been applied in many fields, especially after the emergence of powerful computing devices (such as GPU and distributed platform), standard and practical large data sets (such as ImageNet-1000 [1]) and advanced model algorithms (such as convolutional neural network CNN [2], long and short time memory neural network LSTM [3], graph neural network GNN [4], etc.), artificial intelligence has developed rapidly in deep learning and has beaten human beings in many fields [5]. Most of the above adopt supervised learning method in training a model, in which there still exist some limitations. For example, in supervised learning-based classification, each class needs enough labeled samples to train the learner, and the classifier can only classify the class instance covered by the training data and cannot process the samples never seen before, which often occur in practical applications [6–8], i.e., existing machine learning is weak when suffering pattern recognition with missing modality.

© Springer Nature Singapore Pte Ltd. 2021
H. Zhang et al. (Eds.): NCAA 2021, CCIS 1449, pp. 227–241, 2021.
https://doi.org/10.1007/978-981-16-5188-5_17

Researchers have proposed some methods as FSL and ZSL to solve pattern recognition with some unknown patterns or modality. FSL often uses a training set with very few labeled samples in each class to train a model, and then takes the model to predict the labels for each test sample. The purpose of ZSL is to classify the samples of classes with labels that have never appeared [6]. FSL and ZSL have become a rapidly developing field in machine learning, and been widely used in machine vision [9, 10], natural language processing [11, 12], pervasive computing [13], etc. However, FSL and ZSL have some defects and challenges. For example, FSL only has strong applicability in data with strong correlation. Most of the ZSL research is just on paper, providing theoretical support for other fields. Therefore, it is necessary to find a new stable and reliable method to solve the missing modality problem.

If a trained machine learning model is regarded as a person, then different persons (models) have different knowledge and can recognize quite different patterns. The knowledge of one person can be a great help to the others. This may be similar to transfer learning. However, transfer learning also greatly depends on the similar distributions among the sources and targets. In practice, every person has his/her own advantage in dealing with different tasks. Therefore, methods using knowledge from different sources with discriminated features will be more powerful for recognizing problems with missing modality. However, privacy protection is the most difficult barrier when we want to share more information from others. Federated learning, proposed by Google in 2017, is a good choice for our problem since it possibly and flexibly share knowledge from different users by effectively preventing privacy leakage [14]. The existing federated learning [15, 16] has not been applied to solve pattern recognition with missing modality.

Motivated by these, we here put forward an improved federated learning by effectively fusing the different features of different clients (patterns) to improve the recognition capability of the client with missing modality. In our algorithm, features of the data on each client will be first extracted with convolution neural network (CNN). Then, these features and parameters of the CNN will be uploaded to the central server to fulfill the aggregation. The aggregated parameters corresponding to the features and DCNN are further downloaded to each client. Such a process is iterated until the termination condition is met. In FL, lower communication cost is always expected. To this end, linear discriminant analysis (LDA), powerful for both dimensions decrease and classification is used on the central server to process the feature fusion. Our algorithm aims at training a stable, high precision and fast convergence sharing model with a small communication cost and ensuring client privacy. This model can help lightweight clients identify new modes using other clients' data features, and for heavy clients, it can also complement and complete its own model to improve the corresponding accuracy.

Under the conditions of different network depths and different data complexity, we compared the results of our method with traditional FL and traditional CNN. The results show that the proposed method is more stable, with faster convergence speed, higher convergence precision and higher initial precision.

The remaining structure of this paper is as follows. The related work, particularly on federal learning and modality missing, is briefly reviewed in Sect. 2. Section 3 addresses the detail process of the algorithm and the overall framework of the model. The experimental results and corresponding analysis on the MINIST and CIFAR datasets are demonstrated in Sect. 4. The conclusion is then followed.

2 Related Work

2.1 Federated Learning

The traditional FL framework consists of two important components: Central Aggregation and Local Model Training. The local training model is trained according to the data stored in the client, and only local model parameters are sent to the server. The server trains the data to aggregate the central aggregation model without sharing the local data. Besides, the traditional FL process includes communication rounds, in which the client has different levels of participation depending on the communication state. For example, a classic FL process is as follows: Suppose the training sample data for the k-th client is recorded as P_k, the corresponding local training model parameter matrix is denoted as ω^k, where $k \in S$, S refers to a participating subset of m clients. Only clients of that subset in each communication round can download parameters in the central model as initial parameters of the local model. After the local training, the client sends the updated model parameter matrix back to the central server, which aggregates the parameter matrix and updates the central model after receiving the parameter matrix of each client, that is $\omega = \text{Agg}(\omega^k)$ [17].

2.2 Pattern Recognition with Missing Modality

Pattern recognition with missing modality is quite general in daily life, a great challenge in the machine learning, and the commonly used solutions to this problem are FSL and ZSL. For example, the FSL is used for the task of evaluating the performance of a new drug [18], which attempts to predict whether a new molecule is toxic or not, resulting in a modal deletion due to the lack of functional modalities for the corresponding molecular structure. The accuracy of correct predictions can be improved by limited functional modality analysis of new molecules and integration of many similar molecular functional modalities as priori knowledge analysis.

ZSL is used to solve missing modality, i.e., the modality that has never been seen before or can be understood is predicted to identify new modes. Based on the idea of ZSL [19], Alina Kuznetsova et al. proposed a metric learning method for joint class prediction and posture prediction. Using partially annotated dataset PASCAL3D+, they proved that the learning metrics can be extended to new unlabeled posture classes, thus classifying unknown posture instances. It can be seen that the overall ideas of FSL and ZSL are similar, they are all trained and learned with highly correlated prior knowledge, and then used the integrated new knowledge they learned to identify and classify the unknown modality. However, once the new modality is not strongly or even unrelated to the prior knowledge, this method is difficult to implement.

3 Proposed Method

3.1 Framework

In view of the limitations of the previous algorithm to solve pattern recognition with missing modality, an LDA enhanced federated learning is proposed here. The framework of our algorithm is shown in Fig. 1. In each communication round, the proposed FL consists of two stages, i.e., offline training stage and online communication one.

In the t-th communication round, the local client receives the model parameters ω_t of its CNN from the server (in the initial, random model parameters will be downloaded from the central server to each client), and the SGD is used to train the local data set offline. After several iterated training, the local model converges and the updated model parameter of the k-th client ω_t^k can be obtained. The corresponding image feature P_t^k extracted by CNN at the last iteration is also collected. At last, P_t^k and ω_t^k are uploaded to the central server for aggregation.

After the central server gets all ω_t^k and P_t^k of all participated clients, they are respectively aggregated and updated. For ω_t^k, FedAvg algorithm [3] as shown in Formula (1) is used, where n_k represents the data size of the k-th client. After aggregation and update, the obtained global model will be transmitted back to each client. The features P_t^k will be simultaneously fused by LDA, which will be explained in detail in the following.

$$\omega_t \leftarrow \sum_{k=1}^{K} \frac{n_k}{n} \omega_t \text{ where } n = \sum_{k=1}^{K} n_k \tag{1}$$

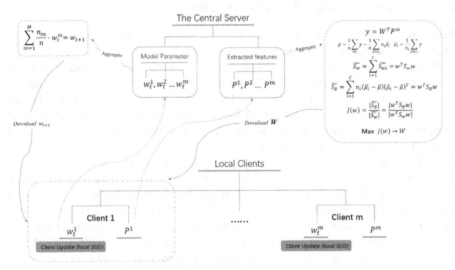

Fig. 1. Framework of improved federated learning algorithm for missing modality.

3.2 LDA-Based Features Aggregation

LDA is a classical linear learning method, which was first used in binary classification problems, and then it is often used in the treatment of multiple classification problems. Its idea is to project samples into a dimensional space given a set of training samples, so that the projection points of similar samples are as close as possible, and the projection points of different samples are as far away as possible. When the new sample is classified, it is projected into the same dimensional space, and then the category of the new sample is determined according to the position of the projection points.

In our model, it is assumed that there are C types of data in all clients, and the dimension of each type of data p is K-dimension, so the basis vector of K-dimension is needed as projection, and the basis vector (projection matrix) is denoted as $W = [w_1 | w_2 | \dots | w_K]$, and the result of sample points after projection is expressed as $Y = [y_1, y_2, \dots, y_K]$. The following formula can be obtained:

$$Y = W^T p \tag{2}$$

Supposed that the mean of the features of the i-th class is μ_i, and that of all the uploaded features is μ, then we have:

$$\mu_i = \frac{1}{n_i} \sum_{p \in c_i} p$$

$$\mu = \frac{1}{n} \sum_{\forall p} p = \frac{1}{n} \sum_{p \in c_i} n_i \mu_i \tag{3}$$

Denote he inter-class hash degree of C is S_w and that of the intra-class is S_B, and they are calculated as:

$$S_w = \sum_{i=1}^{C} S_{w_i} \text{ where } S_{w_i} = \sum_{p \in c_i} (p - \mu_i)(p - \mu_i)^T \tag{4}$$

$$S_B = \sum_{i=1}^{C} n_i(\mu_i - \mu)(\mu_i - \mu)^T \tag{5}$$

The above is the formula before the projection, so it is easy to get the global mean $\tilde{\mu}$, inter-class hash degree $\tilde{S_w}$ and intra-class hash degree $\tilde{S_B}$ after the projection:

$$\tilde{\mu} = \frac{1}{n} \sum_{y \in c_i} n_i \tilde{\mu_l} \text{ where } \tilde{\mu_l} = \frac{1}{n_i} \sum_{y \in c_i} y \tag{6}$$

$$\tilde{S_w} = \sum_{i=1}^{C} \tilde{S_{w_l}} = w^T S_w w \tag{7}$$

$$\tilde{S_{w_l}} = \sum_{y \in c_i} (y - \tilde{\mu_l})(y - \tilde{\mu_l})^T \tag{8}$$

$$\tilde{S_B} = \sum_{i=1}^{C} n_i(\tilde{\mu_l} - \tilde{\mu})(\tilde{\mu_i} - \tilde{\mu})^T = w^T S_B w \tag{9}$$

The measurement formula $J(w)$ can be obtained as follows:

$$J(w) = \frac{|\tilde{S_B}|}{|\tilde{S_w}|} = \frac{|w^T S_B w|}{|w^T S_w w|} \tag{10}$$

The problem ultimately comes down to finding the maximum value of $J(w)$. Its geometric meaning is that the projected sample points are the farthest from each other and the inner sample points are the closest from each other, so that the original sample points can be clearly separated after projection. There are many solutions to find the maximum $J(w)$. The common solution is to derive the fixed denominator after it is 1.

$$S_w^{-1} S_B w_i = \lambda w_i \tag{11}$$

The solution of the matrix equation is its eigenvalues. First, the eigenvalue of $S_w^{-1} S_B$ is calculated, and then the matrix W composed of the first K eigenvectors can be obtained. Finally, the classifier obtained by LDA for feature training of all clients is the scatter graph projected by W. At this point, the second stage is completed by transmitting the updated global model and classifier back.

Compared with the classic FL framework, this algorithm mainly improves the client-side CNN network structure, splitting the previous CNN network into two parts: a CNN subnet and a classifier. The CNN subnet is used to extract image features, and the traditional classifier (generally a fully connected network) is replaced by the projection matrix W trained by the server-side LDA. On the one hand, because LDA is trained with the characteristics of global clients, the W implies the characteristics of other clients. On the other hand, because in the process of uploading, the more complex fully connected network is discarded and the lighter image feature matrix is uploaded. Therefore, after a communication round, each client can recognize the characteristics of other clients while ensuring data security and low communication costs. Figure 2 further shows the feature extraction and classification in the client. Clearly, the classifier here denoted by W getting from the central server has more knowledge than the client itself, and will help to recognize new patterns never been seen before.

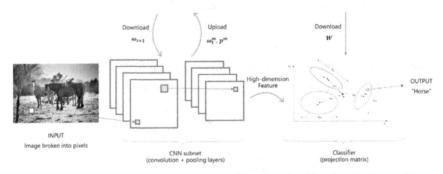

Fig. 2. Client flow chart of improved federated learning algorithm for missing modality

4 Experiments

Two datasets, MNIST and CIFAR-10, are applied here to illustrate the effectiveness of our method. Because the complexity of the data is different, CNNs with different structures are used to extract the corresponding features. In data processing, both datasets have three levels of clients: lightweight client with Alice ID, medium client with Bob ID, and heavy client with Charlie ID. Each client has four types of labels, and the ratio of training set to test set is 6:1. Taking MNIST as an example, to test whether lightweight user Alice can identify missing modalities through this method, we set the test set of Alice with missing modalities, as shown in Table 1.

The compared algorithms of the two datasets are as follows: our algorithm, i.e., FL + LDA, traditional FL with CNN and full connected network as classifier, and a CNN model that does not use FL. The traditional FL framework and FL + LDA framework both use FedAvg algorithm [14] for parameter aggregation. The CNN model that is trained independently has a recognition rate of 0 for missing modes and is treated as a reference algorithm.

Some CNN parameters of the two datasets are as follows: The learning rate of MINST dataset is set to 0.01, batch size is set to 40, and a total of 50 iterations are performed. And the CIFAR-10's learning rate is set to 0.001, batch size and iteration are set to 40 and 250 respectively.

Table 1. Segmentation of MNIST and CIAR-10 datasets

Label	0	1	2	3	4	5	6	7	8	9
Alice	√	√	√	√						
Bob				√	√	√	√			
Charlie							√	√	√	√
Test					√	√	√	√	√	√

4.1 Results on the MNIST Dataset

The MNIST dataset consists of ten handwritten Arabic numerals, each corresponding to a gray scale picture of 28 * 28 pixels. The dataset has 70,000 pictures and is divided into 60,000 for training and 10,000 for testing. In data processing, for experimental convenience, we manually classify pictures according to labels. The training set is divided into 10 groups and the test set into 10 groups. And the data is assigned to different clients according to Table 1.

In the MNIST experiment, we divide the data into three groups for comparison: (I) Alice: Bob: Charlie = 2: 10: 15. (II) Alice: Bob: Charlie = 2: 109: 159. (III) Alice: Bob: Charlie = 2: 109: 159.Among them, (I) and (II) the slope of Non-IID is changed with the same amount of data, (II) and (III) the total amount of data is changed with the same slope of Non-IID. Three sets of data distribution are generated according to the above method, and the corresponding column chart is shown in Fig. 3. The simulation results are shown in Fig. 4 (I) (II) (III).

234 X. Sun and X. Wang

MNIST

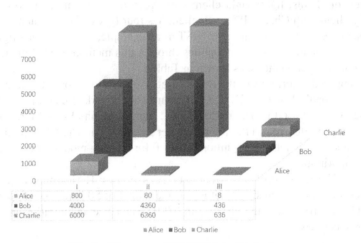

	I	II	III
▪ Alice	800	80	8
▪ Bob	4000	4360	436
▪ Charlie	6000	6360	636

▪ Alice ▪ Bob ▪ Charlie

Fig. 3. Histogram of MNIST data distribution

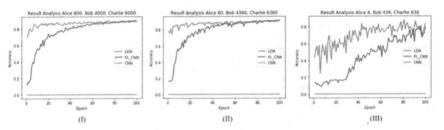

Fig. 4. Simulation results of three comparison algorithms on MINIST dataset

From (I) (II) (III) in Fig. 4, it can be seen that the traditional FL has some effect on decreasing the loss values, but the FL + LDA model has a higher starting accuracy, faster convergence speed and stronger stability during training. The following is a detailed discussion of the experimental indicators. As shown in Fig. 4, (I) (II) (III) image curves are both steadily rising and convergent, then there are three performance indicators used in the MNIST experiment.

1) t: The number of rounds required for the central model to reach a specific accuracy τ, reflecting the convergence rate and communication cost of the model.
2) φ: The reciprocal of the standard deviation of the precision of the central model after reaching a certain precision τ, reflecting the stability of the model.
3) $\overline{Acc}$ and Acc_{max}: The former is the mean of all accuracy after the number of rounds t is reached, and the latter is the global optimal accuracy after all the rounds end, reflecting the overall performance of the model. The better algorithm corresponds to fewer communication rounds, greater stability, higher average and optimal accuracy. In the performance index calculation, τ is set to 70.0%.

Table 2 gives the experimental results on variable slope, and the best results are bolded. From these results, we can see that from the longitudinal point of view, when the total data scale is fixed, from number I to number II, the model stability φ decreases slightly with the increase of slope of Non-IID, whether FL + LDA or FL framework, especially in FL + LDA framework, but in exchange for the increase of average accuracy $\overline{Acc}$ and optimal accuracy Acc_{max}, both increase by about 1%. Horizontal comparison shows that for the same set of data, the FL + LDA model converges faster, reaches a given accuracy basically in the beginning, and the stability is greater than 30, but the FL framework does not exceed 20, indicating that the model has been improved after adding LDA.

Table 2. MNIST experiment on non-IID slope

Number	Data distribution	Model	t	φ	$\overline{Acc}(Acc_{max})$
I	Alice 800: Bob 4000: Charlie 6000 = 2: 10: 15	FL + LDA	**2**	**37.0**	**86.8% (90.2%)**
		FL	20	19.5	83.6% **(90.2%)**
		CNN	/	/	0
II	Alice 80: Bob 4360: Charlie 6360 = 2: 109: 159	FL + LDA	**1**	**32.4**	**87.9% (91.8%)**
		FL	18	18.3	85.5% (91.6%)
		CNN	/	/	0

Table 3. MNIST experiments on data scale

Number	Data distribution	Model	t	φ	$\overline{Acc}(Acc_{max})$
II	Alice 80: Bob 4360: Charlie 6360 = 2: 109: 159	FL + LDA	**1**	**32.4**	**87.9% (91.8%)**
		FL	18	18.3	85.5% (91.6%)
		CNN	/	/	0
III	Alice 8: Bob 436: Charlie 636 = 2: 109: 159	FL + LDA	**30**	17.7	**75.9% (87.8%)**
		FL	85	**19.8**	73.1% (79.4%)
		CNN	/	/	0

Table 3 investigates the impact of data scale on the model framework. Looking lengthwise, it can be seen that when the Non-IID slope is fixed, the model convergence rate decreases dramatically from large datasets numbered II to small datasets numbered III, especially the FL framework is more strongly affected. The model stability φ has a significant decrease in the FL + LDA framework. On the contrary, the FL framework has not changed significantly and has been slightly improved. Besides, the stability of the FL + LDA framework is more sensitive to the data scale. For the average accuracy, the decrease of data scale has a greater impact on it, the average accuracy has decreased by about 12 percentage points, and the overall model performance has decreased. Lateral comparison shows that FL + LDA is superior to FL in both convergence speed and average accuracy, especially for small-scale data distribution of number III. When LDA is added to the FL framework, the number of rounds t decreases from 85 to 30, and the convergence speed improves significantly, thus effectively reducing the communication cost of the FL framework.

4.2 Results on the CIFAR-10 Dataset

CIFAR-10 is a collection of color image data that is close to universal objects. It contains 10 categories of RGB color pictures, each of which has a size of 32 * 32 and 6,000 images in each category. There are 60,000 images in each category, of which 50,000 are training and 10,000 are testing. As with the MNIST experiment, we also pre-grouped these pictures according to labels, with a training set of 10 * 5000 and a test set of 10 * 1000.

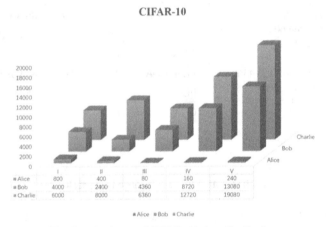

Fig. 5. Histogram of CIFAR-10 data distribution

In the CIFAR-10 experiment, because the data set was more complex, we divided the data into five groups for comparison: (I) Alice: Bob: Charlie = 2: 10: 15. (II) Alice: Bob: Charlie = 1: 6: 20. (III) Alice: Bob: Charlie = 2: 109: 159. (IV) Alice: Bob: Charlie = 2: 109: 159. (V) Alice: Bob: Charlie = 2: 109: 159.The first three groups (I) (II) (III) change the slope of Non-IID with the same amount of data, while the last three groups (III) (IV) (V) change the total amount of data with the same slope of Non-IID. The five groups of data distribution generated by the above methods are shown in Fig. 5 and the experimental results are shown in Fig. 6 and 7.

From the experimental simulation figures given in Figs. 6 and 7, compared with Fig. 4 of the MNIST experiment, we can see that the model stability trained on the CIFAR-10 dataset is worse than that on the MINIST dataset, but the FL + LDA framework is more stable than the FL framework. The training process is divided into two stages: the first 50 communication rounds model is considered to be an ascending period, and the last 50 communication rounds model converges gradually and is considered to be a stationary period, then the three performance indicators of the model here are redefined:

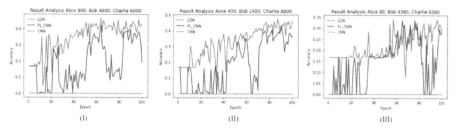

Fig. 6. CIFAR-10 simulation experiment on Non-IID slope

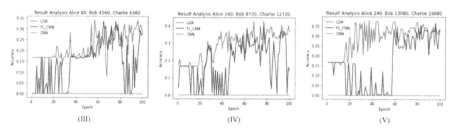

Fig. 7. CIFAR-10 simulation experiment on data scale

(1) t: The number of rounds required for the central model to reach a specific accuracy τ, reflecting the convergence rate of the model.

(2) φ: Reciprocal of all standard deviations of accuracy for 50 communication rounds after the central model, reflecting the stability of the model.

(3) $\overline{Acc}$ **and** Acc_{max}: The former is the mean value of all the precisions in the stationary period of the central model, and the latter is the global optimal precisions after all the communication wheels are finished In the performance index calculation, τ is set to 30.0%.

The experimental results of data scale and Non-IID slope are shown in Table 4 and Table 5.

Table 4 studies the influence of Non-IID slope on the model framework. Longitudinal observation shows that the slope gradually increases from I to III, among which the slope changes between I and II are not obvious, while the changes between III, II and I are significant. From the comparison of t, it can be inferred that the number of communication rounds gradually increases with the aggravation of the Non-IID slope. For the stability index φ, the stability of FL + LDA model decreases significantly with the increase of Non-IID gradient, while the variation trend of FL model is not obvious and fluctuates in a small range. It can be concluded that from the comparison of performance index $\overline{Acc}$ and Acc_{max} that the changes of A and B caused by Non-IID slope fluctuated between 1% and 2% without a significant upward and downward trend, but comparing I, III, II and III, $\overline{Acc}$ and Acc_{max} decrease significantly when the Non-IID slope increase sharply. Lateral comparison shows that the convergence speed, stability and accuracy of FL model are significantly improved after LDA is added, especially for Non-IID data distribution with small slope (such as I).

Table 4. CIFAR-10 experiment on non-IID slope

Number	Data distribution	Model	t	φ	$\overline{Acc}(Acc_{max})$
I	Alice 800: Bob 4000: Charlie 6000 = 2: 10: 15	FL + LDA	12	32.11	41.1% (0.465)
		FL	46	9.79	27.1%(0.423)
		CNN	/	/	0
II	Alice 400: Bob 2400: Charlie 8000 = 1: 6: 20	FL + LDA	24	23.77	40.4% (0.478)
		FL	52	8.95	29.5%(0.437)
		CNN	/	/	0
III	Alice 80: Bob 4360: Charlie 6360 = 2: 109: 159	FL + LDA	54	17.85	26.5% (0.341)
		FL	65	10.62	20.0%(0.338)
		CNN	/	/	0

Based on the above observations, we can draw the following four conclusions: 1) The convergence rate of FL + LDA model and FL model is negatively correlated with the Non-IID slope. 2) The stability of FL + LDA model decreases significantly with the increase of Non-IID slope. The trend of stability of FL model is not obvious with the increase of Non-IID slope, and the fluctuation is small. The sensitivity of FL model to Non-IID slope is lower than that of FL + LDA model. 3) FL + LDA and FL model accuracy are negatively correlated with Non-IID slope, but the fluctuation range of accuracy is smaller when Non-IID slope change is small and larger when Non-IID slope change is large. 4) On CIFAR-10 dataset, FL + LDA is more complicated than traditional FL frameworks in terms of convergence speed, stability and accuracy, but FL + LDA frameworks are more sensitive to Non-IID slope than FL frameworks.

Table 5. CIFAR-10 experiment on data scale

Number	Data distribution	Model	t	φ	$\overline{Acc}(Acc_{max})$
III	Alice 80: Bob 4360: Charlie 6360 = 2: 109: 159	FL + LDA	54	17.85	26.5% (0.341)
		FL	65	10.62	20.0%(0.338)
		CNN	/	/	0
IV	Alice 160: Bob 8720: Charlie 12720 = 2: 109: 159	FL + LDA	27	24.15	34.0% (0.426)
		FL	53	11.05	26.1%(0.425)
		CNN	/	/	0
V	Alice 240: Bob 13080: Charlie 19080 = 2: 109: 159	FL + LDA	20	32.10	34.5% (0.378)
		FL	59	9.50	26.7%(0.366)
		CNN	/	/	0

Table 5 investigates the impact of data scale on the model framework. Longitudinally, the data scale from III to V increases gradually. The multiplier relationship is that the data scale of V is three times larger than that of III and IV is two times larger than that of III. Comparing the performance index t, we can see that the number of rounds decreases with the increase of data scale. Comparing φ shows that the stability of the model increases with the increase of data scale, while comparing $\overline{Acc}(Acc_{max})$ shows that the prediction accuracy of the model increases with the increase of data scale. Looking at the table horizontally, the model performance is improved significantly after FL is added to LDA. In addition, it can be clearly observed that FL + LDA model and FL model have greater changes under the same data distribution conditions, that is, FL + LDA model is more sensitive to data scale.

Based on the above observations, we can draw the following four conclusions: 1) There is a positive correlation between the convergence rate of FL + LDA model and FL model and the amount of data. 2) There is a positive correlation between FL + LDA model and the stability of the FL model and the amount of data. The stability of the FL model does not change significantly with the increase of the amount of data, and the fluctuation is small. The sensitivity of the FL model to the amount of data is lower than that of the FL + LDA model. 3) There is a positive correlation between FL + LDA and FL model accuracy and data quantity. 4) On CIFAR-10 dataset, FL + LDA performs better than traditional FL framework in terms of convergence speed, stability and accuracy, but FL + LDA framework is more sensitive to data scale than FL framework.

In addition, comparing FSL model with FL + LDA model in CIFAR dataset, we find that they have each advantages and deficiencies. Donghyun Yoo et al. used ResNet-18 network as a pre-training network to train CIFAR-100 dataset and migrated to CIFAR-10 dataset for FSL. The results show that with its optimal algorithm, the accuracy of nearly 10,000 iterations to 1-shot reaches 35.95%, and 60.30% to 10-shot after 300 iterations [20]. Minseop Park et al. also migrated to CIAFAR-10 using CIFAR-100, with an optimal classification accuracy of 45.87% for 5-shots after 600 iterations. Although the accuracy of using FSL can be as high as 60.30% [21], the network complexity used in training is high, the number of iterations is large, the convergence rate is slow, and the idea of migrating learning used cannot guarantee the security of personal privacy in practice, which can be well improved by FL + LDA.

In summary, he performance of the proposed algorithm can reduce the needed communication rounds under the same accuracy, indicating that the communication cost is effectively reduced. The recognition accuracy of our algorithm has significant improvement, showing that the FL-based algorithm is effective in dealing with classification with missing modality.

5 Conclusion

In this paper, a model of FL enhanced with LDA is proposed to solve the real pattern recognition problems with missing modality without using few-shot learning and zero-shot learning. At the same time, this paper confirms that the traditional FL framework can also solve such problems to some extent, but due to the Non-IID data distribution in reality, the traditional FL framework will have problems such as slow convergence, instability and low overall accuracy. Experiments on two datasets with different complexity, MNIST and CIAR-10, demonstrate that the overall performance of the model is significantly improved after LDA is improved. The model also has some drawbacks, which require encryption protection when features and labels are extracted and uploaded to the central server, which consumes computing resources. For local clients, its new mode can only be a subset of the global one, that is, it cannot be recognized by other clients. We will develop new algorithm ideas to solve these two shortcomings in the future work.

Acknowledgement. This work is partially supported by National Natural Science Foundation of China with Grant No. 61876184.

References

1. Jia, D., Wei, D., Socher, R., Li, L.J., Kai, L., Li, F.F.: ImageNet: a large-scale hierarchical image database. In: Proceedings of IEEE Computer Vision & Pattern Recognition, pp. 248–255 (2009)
2. Abdel-Hamid, O., Mohamed, A.R., Jiang, H., Deng, L., Penn, G., Yu, D.: Convolutional neural networks for speech recognition. IEEE/ACM Trans. Audio Speech Lang. Process. (TASLP) **22**(10), 1533–1545 (2014)
3. Graves, A., Schmidhuber, J.: Framewise phoneme classification with bidirectional LSTM and other neural network architectures. Neural Netw. **18**(5–6), 602–610 (2005)
4. He, X., Liu, Q., Yang, Y.: MV-GNN: multi-view graph neural network for compression artifacts reduction. IEEE Trans. Image Process. **29**, 6829–6840 (2020). https://doi.org/10.1109/TIP.2020.2994412
5. Wang, F.Y., Zhang, J.J., Zheng, X., Xiao, W., Yang, L.: Where does AlphaGo go: from church-turing thesis to AlphaGo thesis and beyond. Acta Automatica Sinica **3**(2), 113–120 (2016)
6. Wang, W., Zheng, V.W., Yu, H., Miao, C.: A survey of zero-shot learning: settings, methods, and applications. ACM Trans. Intell. Syst. **10**(2), 13.11–13.37 (2019)
7. Long, Y., Liu, L., Shao, L., Shen, F., Ding, G., Han, J.: From zero-shot learning to conventional supervised classification: unseen visual data synthesis, pp. 6165–6174. IEEE Computer Society (2017)
8. Ke, S.R., Hoang, T., Yong-Jin, L., Jenq-Neng, H., Jang-Hee, Y., Kyoung-Ho, C.: A review on video-based human activity recognition. Computers **2**(2), 88–131 (2013)
9. Gan, C., Yang, Y., Zhu, L., Zhao, D., Zhuang, Y.: Recognizing an action using its name: a knowledge-based approach. Int. J. Comput. Vision **120**(1), 61–77 (2016). https://doi.org/10.1007/s11263-016-0893-6
10. Tsai, R.Y.: A versatile camera calibration technique for high-accuracy 3D machine vision metrology using off-the-shelf TV cameras and lenses. IEEE J. Robot. Autom. **3**(4), 323–344 (2003)
11. Berger, A.L.: A maximum entropy approach to natural language processing. Comput. Linguist. **22**(1), 39–71 (1996)
12. Teller, V.: Speech and Language Processing: An Introduction to Natural Language Processing, Computational Linguistics, and Speech Recognition. Daniel Jurafsky and James H. Martin (University of Colorado, Boulder) Prentice Hall, Upper Saddle River. Prentice Hall ser', Computational Linguistics 26(4), 638–641 (2000)

13. Satyanarayanan, M.: Pervasive computing: vision and challenges. IEEE Pers. Commun. **8**(4), 10–17 (2002)
14. Mcmahan, H.B., Moore, E., Ramage, D., Hampson, S., Arcas, B.: Communication-efficient learning of deep networks from decentralized data. In: Artificial Intelligence and Statistics, pp. 1273–1282 (2017)
15. Konen, J., Mcmahan, B., Ramage, D.: Federated Optimization: Distributed Optimization Beyond the Datacenter. Mathematics, pp. 1–5 (2015)
16. Brisimi, T.S., Chen, R., Mela, T., Olshevsky, A., Ioannis, C., Paschalidis, W.S.: Federated learning of predictive models from federated Electronic Health Records. Int. J. Med. Inform. **112**, 59–67 (2018)
17. Hu, Y., Sun, X., Chen, Y., Lu, Z.: Model and feature aggregation based federated learning for multi-sensor time series trend following. In: Rojas, I., Joya, G., Catala, A. (eds.) IWANN 2019. LNCS, vol. 11506, pp. 233–246. Springer, Cham (2019). https://doi.org/10.1007/978-3-030-20521-8_20
18. Altae-Tran, H., Ramsundar, B., Pappu, A.S., Pande, V.: Low data drug discovery with one-shot learning. In: Book Low Data Drug Discovery with One-Shot Learning, pp. 263–274 (2016)
19. Kuznetsova, A., Hwang, S.J., Rosenhahn, B., Sigal, L.: Exploiting view-specific appearance similarities across classes for zero-shot pose prediction: a metric learning approach. In: Proceedings of Proceedings of the Thirtieth AAAI Conference on Artificial Intelligence, pp. 3523–3529 (2016)
20. Yoo, D., Fan, H., Boddeti, V.N., Kitani, K.M.: Efficient k-shot learning with regularized deep networks. In: Book Efficient K-Shot Learning with Regularized Deep Networks, arXiv:1710.02277 (2017)
21. Park, M., Kim, J., Kim, S., Liu, Y., Choi, S.: MxML: mixture of meta-learners for few-shot classification. In: Book MxML: Mixture of Meta-Learners for Few-Shot Classification, arXiv:1904.05658 (2019)

A Data Enhancement Method for Gene Expression Profile Based on Improved WGAN-GP

Shaojun Zhu and Fei Han[✉]

School of Computer Science and Information Engineering, Jiangsu University,
Zhenjiang 212013, China
Hanfei@ujs.edu.cn

Abstract. A large number of gene expression profile datasets mainly exist in the fields of biological information and gene microarrays. Traditional classification approaches are hard to gain a good performance in the gene expression profile data, due to the characteristics of high dimensionality and small sample size of gene expression profile datasets. In fact, as a data a augmentation technology, Wasserstein generative adversarial network based on gradient penalty (WGAN-GP) with conditional generative adversarial network (CWGAN-GP) can generate specified label samples in a simple fully connected network and is beneficial to improve the performance of the classification model. However, this data enhancement method generates the samples with low diversity and distribution uncertainty and decrease the classification accuracy. Therefore, this paper proposes a conditional Wasserstein generative adversarial network based on the gene expression datasets (Gene-CWGAN). Gene-CWGAN adopts a datasets division strategy based on the data distribution to help the model maintain the distribution of realistic samples. Subsequently, Gene-CWGAN enhances the diversity and quality of generated samples by removing the activation function of the output layer and adding constraint penalty items. Finally, Gene-CWGAN is compared with CGAN and CWGAN-GP on Colon, Leukemia2 and SRBCT verified to effectively improve the diversity and distribution stability of generated samples.

Keywords: Gene expression profile · Data enhancement · WGAN-GP · Generate sample diversity · Generate sample distribution stability

1 Introduction

Gene expression profile dataset is a multi classification dataset related to diseases or human physiological status. The use of gene expression profile can be used for early diagnosis of disease and help to develop the best treatment plan. However, gene expression profile dataset is a kind of high-dimensional and small sample dataset, which has the characteristics of high dimension and small sample size [1]. Traditional machine learning classification methods are prone to problems such as low prediction accuracy, inability to identify small samples, and model overfitting and poor stability.

© Springer Nature Singapore Pte Ltd. 2021
H. Zhang et al. (Eds.): NCAA 2021, CCIS 1449, pp. 242–254, 2021.
https://doi.org/10.1007/978-981-16-5188-5_18

At present, there are a lot of researches on feature selection method combined with classifier to classify high-dimensional data [2–4]. However, feature selection is hard to search the optimal feature subset. Data enhancement technology alleviates the problem of high dimension and small sample from the perspective of increasing sample size, and can effectively improve the performance of classification model.

In the field of computer vision, the dataset can be expanded by scaling, clipping, rotating, and adding noise [5]. In the field of sound signal, the information can be expanded through different sampling rates [6]. However, for the original datasets such as gene expression profiles, image processing method are not reliable. Generation adversarial network (GAN) [7] builds a deep learning framework to capture the distribution information of real samples. However, the generation process is too free to generate the required samples. Based on this, Mirza et al. [8] proposed a CGAN model, which introduced label constraints on the basis of GAN to enable the network to generate images with specified labels. Wang et al. [9] improved the ability to capture complex sparse features in OCT images based on the CGAN model. Chen et al. [10] proposed a SpeakerGAN based on CGAN model for data enhancement in speaker recognition task. Although CGAN can generate images with specified tags, CGAN does not solve the problems of gradient disappearance and mode collapse.

WGAN [11] showed that the gradient disappearance and modal collapse of the original GAN were caused by Jensen-Shannon (JS) divergence, and proposed Wasserstein distance instead of JS divergence to solve the problem. However, in order to satisfy the Lipschitz continuity condition, WGAN adopts the strategy of gradient clipping, which makes the network training difficult. Based on this, WGAN-GP [12] proposed gradient penalty instead of gradient clipping to ensure Lipschitz continuity, which solved the problem that WGAN model was difficult to train and made the WGAN-GP model perform well in the simplest full-connection layer network. Gao et al. [13] implemented data enhancement in fault diagnosis on the basis of WGAN-GP model and improved fault diagnosis accuracy. Luo et al. [14] used the WGAN-GP model to generate super-resolution images of satellite cloud images and achieved good results.

The above methods have good performance in data enhancement of image data [15–17], but the effect of direct application in gene expression profile dataset is not good, there are two problems. First, the generated samples are concentrated in the area with dense distribution of real samples, resulting in insufficient diversity of the generated samples. Second, the distribution of samples generated in multiple independent experiments is unstable, which leads to the classification accuracy of the classification model fluctuates greatly.

Based on this, this paper proposes a Gene-CWGAN method for gene expression profile data enhancement. Firstly, in order to be able to generate a sample of the specified label, label constraints are introduced in WGAN-GP. Secondly, in order to stably generate the distribution of samples, a data set partition strategy based on data distribution is proposed to make the training set distribution of the model close to the real sample distribution. Finally, in order to solve the problem of insufficient diversity of generated samples, the activation function of the output layer of the generated model is removed, and a constraint penalty term is proposed to change the strong constraint into the weak constraint, which expands the learning space of the model and improves the diversity of generated samples.

2 Preliminaries

2.1 Conditional Generative Adversarial Networks

Conditional generative adversarial network (CGAN) is based on generative adversarial network (GAN) to add label information and make use of the powerful learning ability of neural network to generate samples with specified labels (Fig. 1).

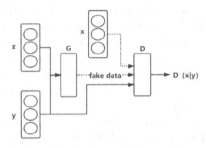

Fig. 1. Conditional generated adversarial network

Generating model G makes the generated sample distribution as close to the real sample distribution as possible by capturing the real sample distribution. The purpose of discriminant model D is to distinguish the real sample distribution and the generated sample distribution. When the input sample is a real sample, the output is close to 1, otherwise the output is close to 0. Equation (1) is the loss function $V(D, G)$ of conditional generative adversarial network.

$$\min_{G} \max_{D} V(D, G) = E_{x \sim p_{data}(x)}[\log D(x|y)] + E_{z \sim p_{z(z)}}[\log(1 - D(G(z|y)|y))] \quad (1)$$

2.2 Wasserstein Generative Adversarial Network Based on Gradient Penalty

In order to overcome the training instability caused by gradient clipping in Wasserstein generative adversarial network (WGAN), WGAN-GP proposed to replace gradient clipping with gradient penalty to prevent gradient explosion. The gradient penalty is defined as:

$$GP = E_{\hat{x} \sim P_{\hat{x}}}[(||\nabla_{\hat{x}} D(\hat{x})||_2 - 1)^2] \quad (2)$$

where GP is the gradient penalty term, $P_{\hat{x}}$ is a distribution between the true distribution and the generated distribution, $\hat{x}$ is a sample from the distribution $P_{\hat{x}}$, $\nabla_{\hat{x}} D(\hat{x})$ is the gradient of discriminator, $E_{\hat{x} \sim P_{\hat{x}}}$ is the calculated mean of sample $\hat{x}$. Compared with WGAN, WGAN-GP has faster convergence speed, easier training and better quality of generated samples.

The tag constraint is introduced into WGAN-GP to form WGAN-GP based on conditional constraint (CWGAN-GP), which can generate samples with specified tags. The loss function $loss_G$ of the generation model and the loss function $loss_D$ of the discriminant model change into:

$$loss_G = -E_{z \sim p(z)}[D(G(z|y)|y)] \tag{3}$$

$$loss_D = E_{z \sim p(z)}[D[G(z|y)|y]] - E_{x \sim p(x)}[D(x|y)] + \lambda E_{\hat{x} \sim p(\hat{x})}[(||\nabla_{\hat{x}} D(\hat{x}|y)||_2 - 1)^2] \tag{4}$$

3   The Proposed Method

The CWGAN-GP model can generate high quality samples with specified labels. However, when the gene expression profile was enhanced, the sample diversity was insufficient and the distribution was unstable. To solve these problems, a Gene-CWGAN method was proposed to generate gene expression profile data. Gene-CWGAN proposes a data set partitioning strategy based on sample distribution and a constraint penalty item on the basis of CWGAN-GP.

3.1   Dataset Partition

In order to generate the sample distribution stably, the distribution of the training set must be as consistent as possible with the distribution of the original data set. Commonly used methods of dividing data sets according to label proportions may miss samples at the edge of distribution. The distribution of the training set is inconsistent with that of the original data set, which makes the sample distribution generated by the model unstable.

In order to make the distribution of training set as consistent as possible with the distribution of original data set, this paper proposes a strategy to divide data set based on data distribution. Firstly, the discrete values of each type of samples are calculated and the matrix of the discrete values is constructed by using Eq. (5):

$$a_{i,j}^c = \sqrt{\sum (x_i^c - x_j^c)^2} \tag{5}$$

where $a_{i,j}^c$ represents the discrete value of sample x_i^c relative to sample x_j^c, and c is the sample category. Then, the average of the dispersion of each sample relative to other samples in the same category is calculated as the dispersion degree of the sample through Eq. (6):

$$S_i^c = E(\sum_{j=1}^{n_c} a_{i,j}^c) \tag{6}$$

where n_c is the number of samples in class c, S_i^c is the degree of dispersion of sample x_i^c in class c, E is the mean of this expression. The high degree of dispersion of the sample indicates that the sample is at the edge of the sample distribution of the same class and needs to be learned by the model.

In order to ensure the uniformity of the distribution of selected samples, the selection process should be controlled to avoid all the selected samples being at the edge or all concentrated together. The test set V_1 is selected as Eq. (7):

$$V_1 = \underset{c \in V_c}{U} [e_{n_c \times p_{test}}(O_c)] \qquad (7)$$

where V_c is a collection of all categories, O_c is the set of $2 \times n_c \times p_{test}$ samples of low dispersion degree in category c, p_{test} is the ratio of the test set to be selected, $e_{n_c \times p_{test}}$ is a random selection of $n_c \times p_{test}$ samples from O_c, and U is the set of samples selected from all categories. Assuming that the set of all samples is V, then the training set V_2 is expressed as follows:

$$V_2 = V - V_1 \qquad (8)$$

Through Eqs. (5), (6), (7) and (8), the samples at the edge of distribution can be divided into the training set to ensure that the distribution of the training set is as consistent as possible with the distribution of the real samples.

3.2 Constraint Penalty Term

Due to the small amount of high-dimensional sample data, the actual value range of each dimension is not clear. Therefore, z-score standardization method was selected.

Because the output layer of the CWGAN-GP model generator uses the tanh activation function, the output range is forcedly limited. However, the value range of the real sample dimension is unknown. Therefore, the existence of tanh activation function will limit the diversity of generated samples.

In this paper, z-score standardization was adopted and tanh activation function was removed. In order to constrain the model learning space and improve the sample quality, a constraint space is defined. When the generated sample exceeds the constraint space, the generator is penalized.

The upper bound of the constraint space as α times of the maximum component value max_dim of each component of all samples in the training set, and the lower bound of the constraint space as α times of the minimum component value max_dim of each component of all samples in the training set. When the sample is generated, the penalty for the generator appears as follows:

$$F_1[G(z|y) - a * max\_dim] = \begin{cases} 0 & G(z|y) - a * max\_dim \leq 0 \\ G(z|y) - a * max\_dim & G(z|y) - a * max\_dim > 0 \end{cases} \qquad (9)$$

$$F_2[G(z|y) - a * max\_dim] = \begin{cases} 0 & G(z|y) - a * max\_dim \geq 0 \\ a * max\_dim - G(z|y) & G(z|y) - a * max\_dim < 0 \end{cases} \qquad (10)$$

where $G(z|y)$ is the simple generated. Equations (9) and (10) show that the generator will be punished when the generated samples exceed the constraint space. Gene-CWGAN's generator loss $loss_G$ and discriminator loss $loss_D$ are respectively Eq. (11) and Eq. (12).

$$loss_G = -E_{z \sim p(z)}[D(G(z|y)|y)] + \mu E_{z \sim p(z)}(F_1 + F_2) \qquad (11)$$

$$loss_D = E_{z\sim p(z)}[D(G(z|y)|y)] - E_{x\sim p(x)}[D(x|y)] + \lambda E_{\hat{x}\sim p(\hat{x})}[(||\nabla_{\hat{x}}D(\hat{x}|y)||_2)^2] \quad (12)$$

where μ is the penalty term coefficient, E is the mathematical expectation, F_1 is the penalty given by the generated samples exceeding the upper bound of the constraint space, and F_2 is the penalty given by the generated samples exceeding the lower bound of the constraint space.

3.3 The Steps of the Proposed Method

In this paper, some useful techniques are used in the training of generating confrontation model. In order to accelerate the convergence speed of the model, only one type of samples is trained in each iteration. In order to prevent over-fitting of the model, small batch sample technique is used for training.

Algorithm parameter: α , threshold parameter. λ ,gradient penalty coefficient. lr ,optimizer learning rate. m ,small batch sample size. *epoch* ,number of training iterations. Each iteration of the generator, the number of iterations of the discriminator is n .

---

1. Divide the model training set according to equations (5), (6), (7), (8)
2. Use z-score standardized training set
3. The constraint space is defined according to the threshold parameter α
4. Initialize the discriminator parameter w_0 , initialize the generator parameter θ_0
5. *for* $e = 0,...,epoch$ *do*
6. $c = e\%label\_size$
7.   A batch sample is selected from the real data labeled c
8.   Sample $\{z_c^i\}_{i=1}^m \sim P_z, z_c^i$ is random vector picked from a prior distribution
9.   *for* $i = 0,...,n$ *do*
10. $loss_d = \frac{1}{m}\sum_{i=1}^m [f_w(x_c^i) - f_w(G(z_c^i))] + \frac{1}{m}\sum_{i=1}^m [\lambda f_w(x_c^i)]$
11. $w \leftarrow w + \text{RMSProp}(w, \nabla_w loss_d, lr)$
12.   *end for*
13. $loss_g = -\frac{1}{m}\sum_{i=1}^m D[f_\theta(z_c^i)] + \frac{\mu}{m}\sum_{i=1}^m (f_1 + f_2)$, f_1 and f_2 are the differentials of the upper and lower bounds of the constrained space
14. $\theta \leftarrow \theta + \text{RMSProp}(\theta, \nabla_\theta loss_g, lr)$
15. *end for*

---

4 Experiments and Discussion

4.1 Datasets and Algorithm Parameters Setting

The datasets of Colon, Leukemia2 and SRBCT [18] are used in this experiment. Table 1 shows the details of the experimental datasets.

Table 1. The experimental datasets.

	Dimension	Number of samples	Number of categories	Number of samples by category
Colon	2000	62	2	22, 40
Leukemia2	11225	72	3	28, 24, 20
SRBCT	2308	83	4	29, 11, 18, 25

In the experiment of generating sample diversity, CGAN and CWGAN-GP are used as comparison algorithms. In the stability experiment of generating samples, MLP algorithm, KNN algorithm and decision tree algorithm (DT) were used as classifiers, and a random forest based (RFFS) feature selection algorithm [19] was added as a comparative experiment.

In this experiment, all generators adopt a fully connected network structure with 2 hidden layers. The number of output nodes in each layer is 512 and 1024 respectively. All the discriminators adopt the fully connected network structure with 4 hidden layers. The number of output nodes in each layer is 512, 128, 128 and 128 (Table 2).

Table 2. Important parameters of the experiment.

Experimental parameters	Parameter value
Training iterations *epoch*	10000
The update times of discriminator in one iteration n	2
Small batch sample size m	10 (SRBCT is 5)
Optimizer learning rate *learning_rate*	0.0002
Test set ratio p_{test}	0.2
Gradient penalty coefficient λ	10
Threshold parameters α	1.2
Penalty coefficient of constraint penalty term μ	10

RFFS reduces the dimension number of the dataset to 0.1 times of the original dimension, and sets the number of trees in the random forest to 15000. MLP classifier adopts fully connected network structure with two hidden layers. The maximum depth of decision tree classifier is 3.

4.2   Wasserstein Distance Index

In order to evaluate the performance of the model, Wasserstein distance index is used to evaluate the performance of CWGAN-GP and Gene-CWGAN. The Wasserstein distance index can reflect the difference between the two distributions. The smaller the Wasserstein distance index, the better the model performance.

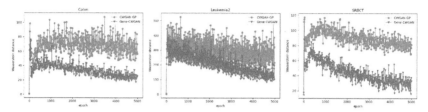

Fig. 2. Comparison of Wasserstein distance between CWGAN-GP and Gene-CWGAN.

As shown in Fig. 2, the sample distribution generated by the Gene-CWGAN model is closer to the real sample distribution than the original CWGAN-GP model. The results show that Gene-CWGAN has better performance.

4.3   Diversity Comparison on the Generated Sample with Different Methods

In order to reflect the diversity of samples generated by the generation model, the generated samples and real samples are visualized. For ease of presentation, this paper only shows the dimension values of the first 20 dimensions of each sample. In the figure, the red line represents the actual sample and the yellow line represents the generated sample.

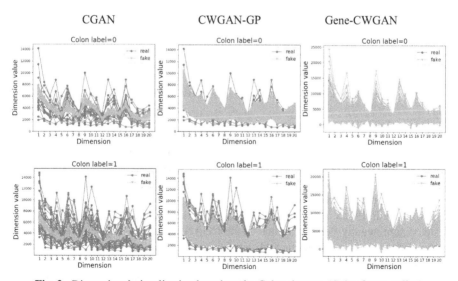

Fig. 3. Dimensional visualization based on the Colon dataset. (Color figure online)

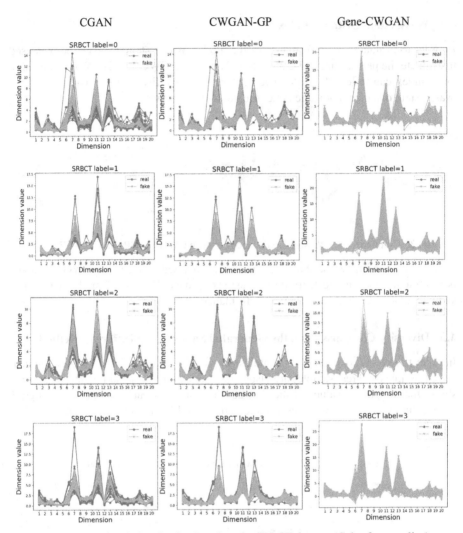

Fig. 4. Dimensional visualization based on the SRBCT dataset. (Color figure online)

Figure 3 and Fig. 4 show the experimental results of the three algorithms on different datasets. The left column shows the dimensional visualization of samples generated based on CGAN model and real samples, the middle column shows the experimental results based on the CWGAN-GP model, and the right column shows the experimental results based on the Gene-CWGAN model.

As shown in Fig. 3 and Fig. 4, the sample diversity generated by the CWGAN-GP model is significantly better than that of the CGAN model, but the samples generated are limited to the areas where the real samples are densely distributed. In this paper, by eliminating the tanh activation function in the output layer of the generated model and introducing the constraint penalty term, the model can learn antagonistically in the edge region of the real sample distribution and increase the diversity of the generated samples. As can be seen from the right column figure, the Gene-CWGAN model is superior to the CWGAN-GP model in generating sample diversity.

4.4 Stability Comparison on the Generated Sample Distribution Stability with Different Methods

In order to verify the distribution stability of the samples generated by the model, the generated samples were used as the training set of the classifier, and then the trained classification model was used to classify the test set. Through five independent experiments, the accuracy and standard deviation of the classification results were taken as the indexes of the stability of the sample distribution. In this part, CGAN, CWGAN-GP and random forest-based feature selection algorithm (RFFS) are used as comparative experiments, and MLP, KNN and decision tree algorithm (DT) are used as classifiers.

Table 3. The classification results based on the Colon dataset.

	MLP	KNN	DT
	mean ± std	mean ± std	mean ± std
/	76.92% ± 15.38%	72.31% ± 11.66%	81.53% ± 6.88%
RFFS	83.07% ± 6.44%	81.53% ± 6.88%	81.53% ± 8.77%
CGAN	46.15% ± 17.54%	41.53% ± **3.76%**	43.07% ± 13.41%
CWGAN-GP	72.30% ± 6.15%	78.46% ± 5.76%	73.84% ± 16.57%
Gene-CWGAN	89.23% ± **4.21%**	**81.54%** ± 4.21%	**86.15% ±6.44%**

Table 4. The classification results based on the Leukemia2 dataset.

	MLP	KNN	DT
	mean ± std	mean ± std	mean ± std
/	86.67% ± 6.67%	74.67% ± 9.89%	88.0% ± 7.30%
RFFS	95.99% ± 3.65%	85.36% ± 5.96%	82.66% ± 5.96%
CGAN	33.33% ± 14.60%	20.0% ± 7.30%	20.0% ± 14.60%
CWGAN-GP	83.67% ± 13.98%	**90.67%** ± 6.79%	69.33% ± 18.67%
Gene-CWGAN	**98.76% ±3.26%**	82.77% ± **5.33%**	**89.33% ±3.65%**

Table 5. The classification results based on the SRBCT dataset.

	MLP	KNN	DT
	mean ± std	mean ± std	mean ± std
/	87.06% ± 9.67%	69.41% ± 11.31%	82.35% ± 5.88%
RFFS	97.64% ± 2.46%	94.72% ± 4.36%	77.64% ± 22.16%
CGAN	27.06% ± 13.72%	30.59% ± 15.96%	10.59% ± 11.41%
CWGAN-GP	92.94% ± 6.86%	83.53% ± 11.41%	83.53% ± 9.41%
Gene-CWGAN	**98.82% ±1.21%**	**95.29% ±2.63%**	**92.94% ±6.44%**

Tables 3, 4 and 5 show the mean and standard deviation of the classification results of each algorithm on different datasets. As shown in Tables 3, 4 and 5, when the classifier is only used to classify the data set, the accuracy is low and the standard deviation is high, which is due to the poor performance of the classification model due to the small sample size. RFFS algorithm does not solve the classification problem under the condition of high dimension and small sample.

The accuracy and standard deviation of the CGAN model are relatively the worst, because the gradient disappears during the training of the CGAN model. CWGAN-GP solves the problem of gradient disappearance and improves the quality of samples generated. However, the standard deviation of the classification results did not significantly decrease, which was because the model's unstable fitting to the sample distribution eventually led to unstable classification accuracy.

Gene-CWGAN adopts a new data set partitioning method proposed in this paper to enable the model to learn the training set distribution close to the real sample distribution. Experimental results show that the stability and accuracy of the generated sample distribution are improved.

4.5 Selection of the Threshold Parameter

The value of the constraint penalty item threshold parameter α affects the adversarial learning of Gene-CWGAN at the edge of the true distribution. If the threshold parameter α is too small, the diversity of generated samples will decrease. If the threshold parameter α is too large, the quality of the generated samples will be reduced.

The 1-NN index can reflect the performance of the model from the closeness of the distribution of the generated sample to the distribution of the real sample. The closer the accuracy of the 1-NN index is to 50%, the closer the distribution of the generated samples is to the real sample distribution, the better the model performance. This paper uses the 1-NN index to evaluate the performance of Gene-CWGAN on each dataset when the constraint threshold parameter α takes values 0.8, 1.0, 1.2, 1.4, and 1.6, as shown in Table 6.

As shown in Table 6, 1-NN index first decreased and then increased on the three data sets. When the constraint threshold α is around 1.2, the 1-NN index is the lowest,

Table 6. Results of 1-NN index based on different threshold parameters α.

	1-NN accuracy				
	$\alpha = 0.8$	$\alpha = 1.0$	$\alpha = 1.2$	$\alpha = 1.4$	$\alpha = 1.6$
Colon	56.04%	55.64%	**54.03%**	54.63%	57.09%
Leukemia2	53.98%	52.25%	**51.39%**	53.29%	53.88%
SRBCT	58.43%	54.81%	**53.01%**	55.42%	56.02%

indicating that the sample distribution generated by Gene-CWGAN is closest to the real sample distribution. Therefore, the threshold parameter α is set to 1.2 in this study.

5 Conclusions

Aiming at the classification problem of gene expression profile data, this paper adopted the idea of data enhancement and proposed the Gene-CWGAN method. This method used a new data set division method to ensure that the training set distribution as close as possible to the real sample distribution under the condition of small samples, which improved the stability of the generated sample distribution. In order to solve the problem of insufficient diversity of generated samples, Gene-CWGAN removed the activation function of the output layer of the generated model, and introduced a constraint penalty term by defining the constraint space, which expands the learning area of the model, improved the diversity of generated samples, and ensured the quality of generated samples.

Acknowledgments. This work was supported by National Natural Science Foundation of China under Grant nos. 61976108 and 61572241.

References

1. Shah, S.H., Iqbal, M.J., Ahmad, I., Khan, S., Rodrigues, J.J.P.C.: Optimized gene selection and classification of cancer from microarray gene expression data using deep learning. Neural Comput. Appl. 1–12 (2020)
2. Aduviri, R., Matos, D., Villanueva, E.: Feature selection algorithm recommendation for gene expression data through gradient boosting and neural network metamodels. In: Proceedings of 2018 IEEE International Conference on Bioinformatics and Biomedicine (BIBM), pp. 2726–2728 (2018)
3. Yuan, J., Li, K.: The fault diagnosis model for railway system based on an improved feature selection method. In: Proceedings of 2019 IEEE 9th International Conference on Electronics Information and Emergency Communication (ICEIEC), pp. 1–4 (2019)
4. Fang, F., Lv, Q.Q., Wang, M.S., Yang, X.H., Zhou, Q.G., Zhou, R.: A hybrid feature selection algorithm applied to high-dimensional imbalanced small-sample data classification. In: Proceedings of 2019 Asia-Pacific Signal and Information Processing Association Annual Summit and Conference (APSIPA ASC), pp. 41–46 (2019)

5. Roth, H.R., et al.: Anatomy-specific classification of medical images using deep convolutional nets. In: Proceedings of 2015 IEEE 12th International Symposium on Biomedical Imaging (ISBI), pp. 101–104 (2015)
6. Omer, D.: Classification of heart sounds with re-sampled energy method. In: Proceedings of 2018 26th Signal Processing and Communications Applications Conference (SIU), pp. 1–4 (2018)
7. Goodfellow, I.J., et al.: Generative adversarial nets. In: Proceedings of Advances in Neural Information Processing Systems (NIPS), pp. 2672–2680 (2014)
8. Mirza, M., Simon, O.: Conditional generative adversarial nets. arXiv e-prints, arXiv:1411.1784 (2014)
9. Wang, M., et al.: Semi-supervised capsule cGAN for speckle noise reduction in retinal OCT images. IEEE Trans. Med. Imaging **40**(4), 1168–1183 (2021)
10. Chen, L.Y., Liu, Y.F., Xiao, W.D., Wang, Y.X., Xie, H.Y.: SpeakerGAN: speaker identification with conditional generative adversarial network. Neurocomputing **418**(22), 211–220 (2020)
11. Martin, A., Soumith, C., Léon, B.: Wasserstein generative adversarial networks. In: Proceedings of Proceedings of the 34th International Conference on Machine Learning (ICML), pp. 214–223 (2017)
12. Gulrajani, I., Ahmed, F., Arjovsky, M., Dumoulin, V., Courville, A.: Improved training of wasserstein GANs. In: Proceedings of Advances in Neural Information Processing Systems (NIPS), pp. 5767–5777 (2017)
13. Gao, X., Deng, F., Yue, X.H.: Data augmentation in fault diagnosis based on the Wasserstein generative adversarial network with gradient penalty. Neurocomputing **396**, 487–494 (2020)
14. Luo, Y.Y., Lu, H.G., Jia, N.: Super-resolution algorithm of satellite cloud image based on WGAN-GP. In: Proceedings of 2019 International Conference on Meteorology Observations (ICMO), pp. 1–4 (2019)
15. Huang, Z.X., et al.: Considering anatomical prior information for low-dose CT image enhancement using attribute-augmented wasserstein generative adversarial networks. Neurocomputing **428**(7), 104–115 (2021)
16. Liu, D.Y., Huang, X.P., Zhan, W.F., Ai, L.F., Zheng, X., Cheng, S.L.: View synthesis-based light field image compression using a generative adversarial network. Inf. Sci. **545**(4), 118–131 (2021)
17. Jiang, Y.F., Chen, H., Loew, M., Ko, H.: COVID-19 CT image synthesis with a conditional generative adversarial network. IEEE J. Biomed. Health Inform. **25**(2), 441–452 (2021)
18. Zhu, Z.X., Ong, Y.S., Dash, M.: Markov blanket-embedded genetic algorithm for gene selection. Pattern Recogn. **40**(11), 3236–3248 (2007)
19. Genuer, R., Poggi, J.M., Tuleau-Malot, C.: Variable selection using random forests. Pattern Recogn. Lett. **31**(14), 2225–2236 (2010)

Examining and Predicting Teacher Professional Development by Machine Learning Methods

Xin Zhang[1] and Yueyuan Kang[2(✉)]

[1] Tianjin Key Laboratory of Wireless Mobile Communications and Power Transmission, Tianjin Normal University, Tianjin 300387, China
ecemark@tjnu.edu.cn
[2] Faculty of Education, Tianjin Normal University, Tianjin 300387, China

Abstract. Core quality and ability development analysis is important for evaluating and deepening the professional development of teachers. It is also useful for improving the quality of education and promotes the growth of the next generation. This research tries to investigate how prominent teachers regulate their professional development. The research also attempts to provide suggestions about current professional status of teachers. The answer to these questions will help teachers to better comprehend how teachers develop. To perform factor analysis for teacher professional development, we develop a set of questionnaire scheme, and collected a certain number of samples through the survey. Professional development is transformed to a classification problem. This study applies machine learning (ML) methods to identify significant attributes that prominent teachers shown in class education, and predict the level of teacher professional development. Eight ML methods are taken to classify the samples. Hyperparameter optimization is performed to improve prediction accuracy. The simulation results show that the ensemble method, support vector machine and artificial neural network are the top three ML methods for the problem. Hyperparameter optimization does not show great impact on the performance of the ensemble and support vector machine methods. The accuracy can reach above 85% by tuning the artificial neural network method through hyperparameter optimization. This study provides an important basis for the future intelligent analysis of teacher professional development.

Keywords: Classification · Education · Machine learning · Teacher professional development

1 Introduction

At present, artificial intelligence in education (AIED) has been widely discussed and studied. In the field of teaching, the future development directions of AIED have been widely recognized [1]. AIED plays a role in promoting students' individual learning; AIED is used to promote students' understanding; AIED would make a breakthrough in the evaluation of open-ended questions and practical ability. For example, artificial intelligence (AI) can fully combine online network with offline classroom, and launch

© Springer Nature Singapore Pte Ltd. 2021
H. Zhang et al. (Eds.): NCAA 2021, CCIS 1449, pp. 255–269, 2021.
https://doi.org/10.1007/978-981-16-5188-5_19

online teaching assistants by evaluating the different needs and academic achievements of different students. Education in the era of AI uses the student behavior analysis and big data to help managers analyze students' behavior, explore the guidance methods of different student behavior patterns, and further help teachers to study the characteristics of various types of students. Moreover, AIED could also be used to evaluate teachers. It is better to formulate different education management modes, and truly implement the dialectical education method to shorten the distance between teachers and students. Therefore, AI can be used to collect and analyze knowledge about teacher professional development. Moreover, AIED is useful to assist the researches of teacher professional development, teacher evaluation as well as student evaluation.

Day believes that the factors affecting teacher professional development include: the stage of teacher professional development, the life history of teachers, the quality of teachers themselves, the characteristics of professional development activities themselves, and the influence of the background of teacher professional activities even outside the school [2]. Kelchtermans, an American scholar, thinks that teacher professional development is the result of the interaction between individual teachers and situations, and divides the factors that affect teacher professional development into three categories: the first is teacher personal characteristics, such as personal life background, existing concepts and orientations on education issues, etc.; The second is the characteristics of the direct social environment in which teacher professional life occurs, such as school culture orientation; the third is the characteristics of measures aimed at promoting teacher professional development, such as teacher policy and teacher management system [3].

To realize AIED, machine learning (ML) methods are inevitable to perform prediction. For example, artificial neural network (ANN) is used to determine the page viewing level of students [4]. An intelligent tutorial system was developed based on ANN, which is a popular ML method. In the ANN method, two hidden layers are used including 20 and 30 neurons, respectively. Although some related works have been done about ML methods in education, teacher professional development has seldom been studied in the literature. To our best knowledge, we are the first to apply ML methods to predict teacher professional development.

This paper attempts to develop a framework for core quality and ability development for teachers. Moreover, the framework is reflected by a questionnaire scheme to perform influencing factor analysis. Furthermore, ML methods are used to solve teach professional development problem. The contributions of the paper are as follows:

(1) A set of questionnaire scheme is developed to perform teacher professional development, and a certain number of samples is collected through the survey.
(2) The collected samples of teacher professional development are transformed to classification problem, artificial neural network is applied to identify significant attributes.
(3) Eight ML methods are taken for study to classify the collected samples. A comparative study of these methods is reported in the paper.
(4) Hyperparameter optimization is used to tune ML methods for teacher professional development problem. The simulation results show that the accuracy rate can reach above 85%.

The paper is organized as follows. Section 2 summarizes the related works. Section 3 presents the proposed questionnaire scheme. Section 4 presents the classification problem and introduces eight ML methods and hyperparameter optimization method. Simulations are presented in Sect. 5. Section 6 concludes the paper.

2 Related Works

Related works about teacher professional development and ML methods in education are summarized in this section.

Based on teacher professional development, Qiu studied burnout of high school teachers in China [5]. Teaching work and teacher developing have put too much stress on high school teachers. It is concluded that teacher professional development is an alternative to relieve job burnout of teachers.

A high-stakes evaluation system was designed in 2011 to reform teacher labor market and partially to remove ineffective teachers. The scholars examined the features of minimally effective and ineffective teachers [6]. The results show that male and novice teachers are tend to be labeled as ineffective. For analyzing and understanding teaching practices in physical education, observation method was used to describe the teaching practices of two non-specialized teachers [7]. One subject of the research is public, while the other subject is private. The results show that physical education is useful for teacher education.

Student performance prediction is an important research topic because it can help teachers prevent students from dropping out before the final examination and identify students who need additional help. To predict the difficult students, the scholars analyzed the data recorded by a technology enhanced learning (TEL) system called digital electronics education and design suite (DEEDS) using ML methods. Machine learning methods include ANN [4], support vector machine (SVM), logistic regression, etc. [8]. DEEDS allows students to solve different difficulties of digital design exercises while recording input data. Then, the data of the previous session is used to train ML methods, and tests the data of the coming session. In [8], k-fold cross validation is carried out, and the receiver performance is calculated to evaluate the performance of the model. The results show that ANN and SVM have higher accuracy than other algorithms. ANN and SVM can be easily integrated into the TEL system. Therefore, the author expects the teacher to report on the improved students' performance in subsequent conversations.

ANN is used as a cognitive and developmental model [9]. It also takes the famous Piaget development task as an example to show that ANN is an ideal tool to simulate cognitive development and scientific learning because of its deep interaction. Any learning environment may lead to multiple perceptions even if the perceptual and descriptive language is limited by culture different learning and learning results. The basic model used by science educators for learning and development should be changed. ANN is used to determine whether the teaching model is suitable for students' learning or development [9].

Based on various international reports, the application of AIED is one of the emerging fields in educational technology. AIED is summarized through systematic review in [10]. 146 articles between 2007 and 2018 were included in the final review [10]. The descriptive results show that most of the subjects involved in AIED papers come from computer science and science, technology, engineering, mathematics (STEM). Quantitative method is the most commonly used method in empirical research. The results show that AIED has four applications in academic support services, institutional and administrative services: (1) analysis and prediction; (2) evaluation and assessment; (3) adaptive system and personalization; (4) intelligent tutoring system.

For the construction of smart campus, teaching performance evaluation is an important part. In [11], the scholars discussed the salient features of smart campus and proposed an architecture model. Principal component analysis method is used to determine six principal components. An improved TOPSIS algorithm is able to provide good teaching performance evaluation while avoiding the subjectivity issue of traditional evaluation method [11].

Permanent education is an essential requirement for adults who would like to take some training need [12]. The scholars studied the factors about digital competence of permanent education teachers in Andalusia, Spain. The results show that low digital competence could be affected by degree, teaching experience and professional category [12].

In STEM education, it is a challenge for teachers to predict students' line of actions, which are ill-defined problems [13]. In [13], sequential pattern mining techniques are used to help teachers to improve prediction. The results show that machine prediction is more accurate than expert prediction. A recommendation system is possible to provide adaptive guidance in STEM education [13].

3   The Proposed Questionnaire Scheme

This section first defines the core qualities and ability development for teacher professional development. Then, it presents the proposed questionnaire scheme.

Previous studies have shown that most scholars study the influencing factors of teacher development from both external and internal factors. However, there is little research on the influence factors for the outstanding teachers' core qualities and ability development. Thus, we focus on the analysis of the influencing factors of the core qualities and ability development of excellent teachers.

Definition 1 (Core Qualities). Core qualities of teachers are defined as the professional cultivation which is developed in the process of accepting and participating in teacher education, engaging in education and teaching and devoting themselves to teaching and research, so that they can adapt to the needs of social development and teacher professional requirements.

Definition 2 (Ability Development). Ability development are defined as the key ability that teachers form and develop in the process of accepting and participating in teacher education, engaging in education and teaching and devoting themselves to teaching and research, which can adapt to the needs of social development and teachers' occupation, and promote their own professional development.

Among the numerous influencing factors, what are the more important significant factors? What are the magnitude and importance of these significant factors? Both questions are solved according to the relevant theories and research results on the influencing factors of teacher professional development in the literature. We construct a theoretical model and influencing factor framework based on analyzing connotation and structural elements of teachers' core qualities and ability development. Connotation refers to the quality and cultivation of teachers. Structural elements refer to political literacy, moral literacy, cultural literacy and educational spirit of teachers.

In this paper, the questionnaire scheme is developed for teacher professional development problem. The influencing factor questionnaire is compiled according to the theoretical framework. Moreover, the questionnaire is pre-tested and revised again after consulting opinions of experts in education. During pre-test, a collection of 50 questions is used. Based on exploratory factor analysis, confirmatory factor analysis and expert consultation, the number of questions is reduced to 43.

The proposed questionnaire scheme is comprised of three main dimensional factors as shown in Fig. 1. They are policy factors, organizational culture factors and individual factors. Policy factors contain five sub-dimensional factors. The policy factors include teacher status policy, teacher treatment policy, teacher rights and obligations policy, teacher education policy and teacher management policy. Organizational culture factors contain four sub-dimensional factors. The organizational culture factors include material culture, behavior culture, system culture and spiritual culture. Individual factors also contain four sub-dimensional factors. The individual factors include subject consciousness, individual practice activity, professional happiness and individual experience.

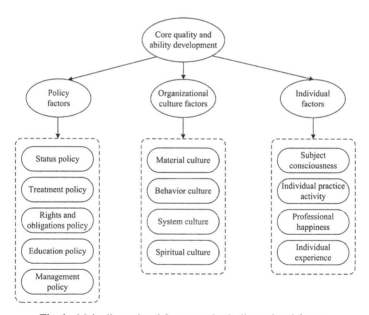

Fig. 1. Main dimensional factors and sub-dimensional factors.

The survey objects include prominent teachers and ordinary teachers. Ordinary teachers are in-service teachers engaged in elementary and secondary education in China. Prominent teachers are generally those who have certain teaching achievements and contributions such as national excellent teachers, advanced teachers of national teachers and models of the whole country, subject leaders, famous teachers, backbone teachers, teaching experts etc. They can be used as research objects of prominent teachers.

After performing the questionnaire survey in China, we have collected 1960 valid samples. Among the samples, the number of prominent teachers is 548, while the number of ordinary teachers is 1412. The ratio of prominent teachers to ordinary teachers is about 3:7.

A previous version of the influencing factor framework and questionnaire survey has been published in Chinese [14]. In this paper, teacher professional development is transformed to binary classification problem. Moreover, we apply ML methods to identify significant attributes and perform prediction for teacher professional development. Furthermore, hyperparameter optimization method is used to improve prediction accuracy.

4   Classification Problem and Machine Learning Methods

This section presents the classification problem, introduces eight ML methods and hyperparameter optimization scheme.

4.1   Classification Problem

We transform the teacher professional development problem to a binary classification problem. Classification is a central problem in ML. Generally, we have a data set consisting of a number of samples. Each sample is comprised of input variables $\mathbf{x}$ and an output variable y. For binary classification, an output variable y can only be true (1) or false (0). For teacher professional development problem, we set "prominent" as the output variable. If a teacher is a prominent teacher, then its corresponding y is true; otherwise, its y is false.

There are 43 factors associated with teacher professional development, which results an observed $\mathbf{x}$ of size 43. All input variables are associated with policy factors, organizational culture factors and individual factors. Each input variable is transformed to discrete numerical values as shown in Table 1.

Table 1. The transformation of input variables to discrete numerical values

Input variable	Very small effect	Small effect	Moderate effect	Great effect	Very great effect
x_i	1	2	3	4	5

As can be seen in Table 1 each input variable is transformed to discrete numeric with five values. Thus, the input variables in the problem are discrete. Based on the transformation, teacher professional development problem becomes binary classification problem, which can then be handled by ML methods.

The target of the problem is to train a model of existing data samples, and then make a decision for a new input variables **x**, where the output variable y is unknown. The goal of ML methods is to build a function to minimize some cost function such that the error rate is also minimized between the estimated output variables and ground-truth output variables. Mathematically, it is:

$$f^* = \arg\min_f \frac{1}{N} \sum_{i=1}^{N} L(f(x_i), y_i) \tag{1}$$

where f stands for an ML method, N is the number of data samples, L is loss function which could be root mean squared error (RMSE) or accuracy rate.

4.2 Machine Learning Methods

This paper takes 8 ML methods for study. Typical ML methods are discriminant analysis (DA), Naïve bayes (NB), decision tree (DT), k-nearest neighbor (kNN), SVM, ANN, and ensemble method (ENS) [15]. DA method includes linear DA (LDA) and quadratic DA (QDA). Thus, there are eight methods in this study.

The LDA method was proposed by Fisher in 1936. It was only used to binary classification problem until being generalized to multiclass classification problem by Rao in 1948. The LDA method is still popular in classification problem [16].

The QDA method is the same as the LDA method except that covariance matrix could be different for each class. It is a probabilistic parametric classification method. The QDA method is also effective for classification problem [17].

The NB methods refer to a set of supervised learning algorithms based on modeling input variables by Bayes's theorem. It generally assumes conditional independence between every pair of input variables. The NB method is also effective for classification problem [18].

The DT method is a tree structure shown as a flow chart. It falls in the category of supervised learning and could make decisions based on previous knowledge or experience. The DT method is one of the most popular ML methods [19].

The kNN method is one of the most basic yet essential ML methods. It is non-parametric as no assumptions are made about data distributions. The kNN method is widely used in pattern recognition and data mining [20].

The SVM method belongs to the category of supervised learning. It was developed by Vapnik and his colleagues in 1990s. The SVM method is initially for binary classification yet is soon extended to multiclass classification problems. The SVM method is still popular for classification problems [21].

The ANN method is also known as neural network for simplicity. It was inspired by neurons of animal brains. The ANN method is one of the main ML tools. It is intended to replicate problem-solving manner like biological brains. The ANN method is also popular for classification problems [22].

The ENS method combines several basic techniques to produce a more powerful method than each method alone. It is comprised of a finite number of basic techniques.

For example, the ENS method is an ensemble of decision tree techniques [23]. The bootstrap aggregating of the ENS method is implemented with random forest.

Thus, there are eight ML methods, which are commonly used for solving classification problems.

4.3 Hyperparameter Optimization Scheme

Generally, an ML method consists of one or more than one hyperparameters, which are used to control learning process of an ML method. Hyperparameter optimization refers to choosing a set of optimal hyperparameters for an ML method. Hyperparameter optimization can also be seen as fine-tuning parameters of an ML method such that it achieves the largest prediction accuracy.

Mathematically, hyperparameter optimization is [24]:

$$x^* = \arg\min_x f(x) \tag{2}$$

where x is hyperparameters, the objective is to minimize function $f(x)$. Function $f(x)$ can be any ML method. As the complex property of ML methods and data sets, it is unpractical to obtain optimal hyperparameters. In general, near-optimal hyperparameters could meet the requirements in applications.

There are six kinds of method for choosing hyperparameters. They are grid search method, random search method, gradient-based methods, Bayesian optimization methods, multifidelity optimization methods, metaheuristic algorithms [24]. It is concluded that Bayesian optimization methods are recommended for small hyperparameter search space, while particle swarm optimization (PSO) algorithm is recommended for large hyperparameter search space.

Note that the number and the configuration search space of hyperparameters is small in this paper, thus, we use Bayesian optimization methods to perform hyperparameter optimization. Specifically, Bayesian optimization hybrid with hyperband (BOHB) is used in this paper. BOHB is able to keep the advantages of Bayesian optimization and hyperband, while it also avoids the shortcomings of both methods [25]. The computational complexity of the BOHB method is $O(N\log N)$.

Note that metaheuristic algorithms are effective for hyperparameter optimization [24]; hence we also use a metaheuristic algorithm to perform hyperparameter optimization. The artificial bee colony (ABC) algorithm is taken for study. On the one hand, the ABC algorithm shows comparable performance with genetic algorithm and PSO for numerical optimization [26]. On the other hand, the ABC algorithm is able to solve problems with micro-population size [27]. Hyperparameter optimization could be time-consuming as the search space becoming larger. This causes users prefer to reduce the number of function evaluations. Micro-population size is suitable for such cases. Thus, we choose the ABC algorithm to perform hyperparameter optimization.

5 Simulation Results

This section presents the simulation results by applying eight ML methods to the teacher professional development problem. The results are reported and discussed.

5.1 Identification of Significant Attributes

As shown in Fig. 1, the candidate attributes are summarized to three main dimensional factors. Each main dimension is comprised of several sub-dimensional factors. The ANN method is applied to identify significant attributes that prominent teachers shown in class education. The ANN method consists of an input layer, a hidden layer and an output layer. The hidden layer is comprised of 50 neurons. A ten-fold cross validation is set in the simulation.

The results are shown in Table 2. For policy factors, teacher status policy is the attribute reaching the highest accuracy rate 72.45% among the five factors. For organizational culture factors, spiritual culture is the attribute reaching the highest accuracy rate 72.35% among the four sub-dimensional factors. For individual factors, individual practice activity is the attributes reaching the highest accuracy 72.24% among the four sub-dimensional factors.

Table 2. The simulation results of the ANN method for identifying significant attributes

Main dimension	Sub-dimension	Accuracy (%)
Policy factors	**Teacher status policy**	**72.45**
	Teacher treatment policy	72.09
	Teacher rights and obligations policy	72.04
	Teacher education policy	72.35
	Teacher management policy	71.94
Organizational culture factors	Material culture	72.09
	Behavior culture	70.92
	System culture	71.17
	Spiritual culture	**72.35**
Individual factors	Subject consciousness	72.19
	Individual practice activity	**72.24**
	Professional happiness	72.04
	Individual experience	72.09

Based on the simulation, the most significant attributes are teacher status policy, spiritual culture and individual practice activity. These attributes cause difference between prominent teachers and ordinary teachers.

5.2 The Effect of Eight ML Methods

In the simulation, we would not do fine-tuning of the eight ML methods, while we attempt to identify which is suitable for our problem without fine-tuning. A ten-fold cross validation is used to obtain a reliable performance of methods. During cross validation,

90% samples are used as training set, while the remaining are used as test set. Accuracy rate is used to measure the performance of methods.

The results are shown in Fig. 2. In the figure, the eight methods are aligned following the descending order of error rate. It can be seen that the DT method is the worst one among the eight methods. The DT, KNN and QDA have much larger error rate than the remaining methods. The LDA, ENS, NB, SVM, and ANN methods have close error rate between 25% and 30%. The ANN method attains the best performance among the eight methods. The error rate of ANN is 27.14% by ten-fold cross validation.

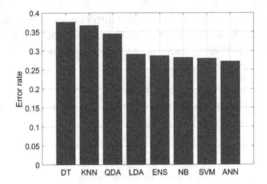

Fig. 2. The effect of eight machine learning methods.

Based on the simulation results, we attempt to improve the ENS, NB, SVM and ANN methods for solving the problem. For the NB method, four techniques are tried to model data distribution. They are kernel smoothing, multinomial distribution, multivariate multinomial distribution, and normal distribution. It turns out that the NB method with kernel smoothing outperforms the others. Thus, it is unable to reduce error rate of the NB method by different data distribution. In the next, we focus on improving the ENS, SVM and ANN methods.

5.3   The Effect of Tuning ENS

The ENS method can be implemented by different ensemble aggregation method. The following methods are used: adaptive boosting (ENS-AB), linear programming boosting (ENS-LPB), random under sampling boosting (ENS-RUB), random subspace (ENS-RS), and totally corrective boosting (ENS-TCB). ENS-RF stands for the ENS method introduced in Sect. 4.2. Hence, there are six different ensemble methods. The simulation results are shown in Fig. 3.

From Fig. 3, the ENS-LPB method is the worst among the six ensemble methods. The ENS-RF method is the second best, and the ENS-RS method shows the best performance in terms of error rate. The error rate of the ENS-RS method is 27.96%. It can be seen that the performance of the ensemble method can be improved by proper ensemble aggregation method. However, the best error rate of the ensemble method is still worse than that of the ANN method (27.14%).

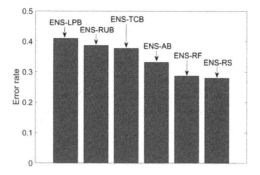

Fig. 3. The effect of six ensemble methods.

5.4 The Effect of Tuning SVM

The SVM method can use different kernel functions. Gaussians, linear and polynomial are three commonly used kernel functions. For the hyperparemters of the SVM method, the bound is set to $[10^{-3}, 10^3]$, and the kernel scale are also set to the same range.

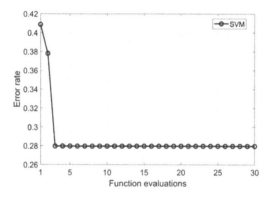

Fig. 4. The effect of tuning hyperparameters of the SVM method.

From Fig. 4, the optimization process is terminated after 30 function evaluations. Hyperparamter optimization of the SVM method quickly converges after 3 function evolutions. The best error rate is 27.96%, which is the same as that of the SVM method in Sect. 5.1. It is observed that both Gaussian kernel and linear kernel can reach the best error rate. Based on the hyperparameter optimization, the performance of the SVM method cannot be improved.

5.5 The Effect of Tuning ANN

The ANN method has many variants. We take cascade learning vector quantization ANN (ANN-LVQ) and feedforward ANN (ANN-CF). For the hyperparemters of the ANN method, the number of hidden layers is set to [1, 3], and the size of hidden layer is set to [10, 200]. The hyperparameter optimization of the ANN method is named as ANN-Hyper. ANN-FF stands for the ANN method introduced in Sect. 4.2. Hence, there are four different ANN methods. The simulation results are shown in Fig. 5.

From Fig. 5, the ANN-FF method is the worst among the four ANN methods. The ENS-CF method is the second best, and the ANN-Hyper method shows the best performance in terms of error rate. The error rate of the ANN-Hyper method is 18.11%. It can be seen that the performance of the ANN method can be improved by properly choosing hyperparameters.

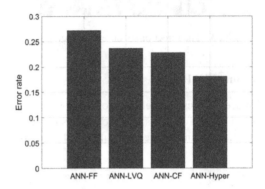

Fig. 5. The effect of tuning hyperparameters of the ANN method.

Based on the above analysis, the best error rate for teacher evaluation problem is 18.11%. Hence, the accuracy rate is 81.89%, which is attained by the ANN-Hyper method. Moreover, Hyperparameter optimization of the ENS method shows some improvement for teacher evaluation problem. Hyperparameter optimization of the SVM method does not show improvement for the problem. Hyperparameter optimization of the ANN method shows great improvement for teacher evaluation problem.

5.6   Applying the ABC Algorithm to Tune ANN

As shown in Sect. 5.4, hyperparameter optimization can improve the effectiveness of the ANN method. It is reported that metaheuristic algorithms are also useful to perform hyperparameter optimization [24]. In this subsection, we apply the ABC algorithm to perform hyperparameter optimization for the ANN method. The method is abbreviated as ANN-ABC. The simulation setting is shown in Table 3.

It can be seen from Table 3 that the number of hidden layers varies from 1 to 3. The number of neurons per layer varies from 10 to 200. Considering these two hyperparameters, the search space is 191^3. In general, "tansig" is a commonly used transfer function. To avoid the scalable issue, initial training weights are randomly created between -0.5 and 0.5. Levenberg-Marquardt is a commonly used training method. For the ABC algorithm, the population size is set to 10, which is smaller than 30 as in [25]. The number of stagnation limit is set to 5. The algorithm is terminated until 100 iterations.

Table 3. The simulation setting of the ANN-ABC method

Parameter	Value
Number of hidden layers	{1, 2, 3}
Number of neurons per layer	[10, 200]
Transfer function	{logsig, tansig, softmax}
Initial weight	random
Number of epochs	100
Training function	Levenberg-Marquardt
Population size	10
Limit	5
Number of iterations	100

In the simulation, the number of hidden layers and the number of neurons per layer are tuned, while the others are fixed. The transfer function is "tansig" as commonly used in the literature. For the ANN-ABC method, the four decision variables are encoded as integer variables. Thus, the hyperparameter optimization is an integer programming problem. The hyperparameter optimization result is shown in Fig. 6. Seen from the figure, the initial error rate is about 29%. Error rate gradually decreases with the number of iterations. Finally, the error rate is 14.34% which is attained at 94 iterations. The accuracy rate of the ANN-ABC method is 85.66%.

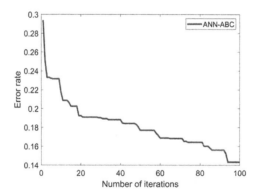

Fig. 6. The convergence curve of the ANN-ABC method.

To sum up, the best accuracy rate is 85.66%, which is attained by the ANN-ABC method. ML methods are useful for teacher professional development problem. It is highly suggested that users could apply ML methods in similar problems. Ensemble method and hyperparameter optimization are good choices for such classification problems. Although hyperparameter optimization could greatly improve prediction accuracy, it also takes a lot of training time to find good hyperparameters. Seen from Fig. 6, the convergence curve of the ANN-ABC method is slow. The method does not show convergence until it is terminated. More powerful hyperparameter optimization methods are required for such problem.

6 Conclusion

In this paper, a questionnaire scheme is developed to perform factor analysis for teacher professional development, and a certain number of samples have been collected through questionnaire survey. Teacher professional development has been transformed to a classification problem. Eight ML methods are then used to analyze the sample data. Based on simulation results, we then tune the ENS, SVM and ANN methods for solving teacher professional development problem. The simulation results show that the accuracy rate can reach above 85% by tuning the performance of the ANN method; whereas accuracy rate does not show great impact on the performance of the ENS and SVM methods. Hyperparameter optimization is shown very useful to improve prediction accuracy. This study provides an important basis for the future intelligent analysis of teacher professional development.

This paper focuses on using ML methods for teacher professional development problem. Among the eight ML methods, the ANN method deserves further study based on its performance. The number of hidden layers in hyperparameter optimization is limited to 3. We attempt to study deep neural network for the problem in future. Moreover, we also attempt to develop new models for teacher professional development problem, which could completely grade teachers and provide suggestions for schools and policy makers.

Acknowledgments. This paper was supported in part by the National Natural Science Foundation of China (Project No. 61901301), in part by the key project of the National Social Science Foundation of China (Project No. AFA70008), and in part by the Tianjin Higher Education Creative Team Funds Program.

References

1. UNESCO: Artificial Intelligence in Education Challenges and Opportunities for Sustainable Development. UNESCO Working Papers on Education Policy, No. 7 (2019)
2. Glatthorn, A.: Teacher development. In: International Encyclopedia of Teaching and Teacher Education, pp. 412–422. Elsevier, Oxford (1995)
3. Kelchtermans, G., Ballet, K.: The micropolitics of teacher induction. A narrative-biographical study on teacher socialization. Teach. Teacher Educ. **18**, 105–120 (2002)
4. Karacı, A., Arıcı, N.: Determining students' level of page viewing in intelligent tutorial systems with artificial neural network. Neural Comput. Appl. **24**(3–4), 675–684 (2012). https://doi.org/10.1007/s00521-012-1284-8
5. Qiu, H.: Research on the burnout of high school teachers based on teacher professional development. Open J. Soc. Sci. **6**, 219–229 (2018)
6. Drake, S., Auletto, A., Cowen, J.M.: Grading teachers race and gender differences in low evaluation ratings and teacher employment outcomes. Am. Educ. Res. J. **56**(5), 1800–1833 (2019)

7. Bennour, N.: Teaching practices and student action in physical education classes perspectives for teacher education. Creat. Educ. **6**, 934–944 (2015)
8. Hussain, M., Zhu, W., Zhang, W., Abidi, S.M.R., Ali, S.: Using machine learning to predict student difficulties from learning session data. Artif. Intell. Rev. **52**(1), 381–407 (2019)
9. Roth, W.-M.: Artificial neural networks for modeling knowing and learning in science. J. Res. Sci. Teach. **37**, 63–80 (2000)
10. Zawacki-Richter, O., Marín, V.I., Bond, M., Gouverneur, F.: Systematic review of research on artificial intelligence applications in higher education-where are the educators. Int. J. Educ. Technol. High. Educ. **16**, 39 (2019)
11. Xu, X., Wang, Y., Yu, S.: Teaching performance evaluation in smart campus. IEEE Access **6**, 77754–77766 (2018)
12. Hinojo-Lucena, F., Aznar-Díaz, I., Cáceres-Reche, M., et al.: Factors influencing the development of digital competence in teachers: analysis of the teaching staff of permanent education centres. IEEE Access **7**, 178744–178752 (2019)
13. Norm Lien, Y.-C., Wu, W.-J., Lu, Y.-L.: How well do teachers predict students' actions in solving an ill-defined problem in STEM education: a solution using sequential pattern mining. IEEE Access **8**, 134976–134986 (2020)
14. Kang, Y.-Y., Li, J.: Research on the factors of core qualities and ability development of teachers: an empirical investigation based on questionaires nationwide. Contemp. Teacher Educ. **12**(4), 17–24 (2019). (in Chinese)
15. Mitchell, T.: Machine Learning. McGraw-Hill Education, New York (1997)
16. Al-Dulaimi, K., et al.: Benchmarking HEp-2 specimen cells classification using linear discriminant analysis on higher order spectra features of cell shape. Pattern Recogn. Lett. **125**, 534–541 (2019)
17. Laiadi, O., et al.: Tensor cross-view quadratic discriminant analysis for kinship verification in the wild. Neurocomputing **377**, 286–300 (2020)
18. Yu, L., Jiang, L., Wang, D., Zhang, L.: Toward naive Bayes with attribute value weighting. Neural Comput. Appl. **31**(10), 5699–5713 (2019)
19. Cai, Y., Zhang, H., Sun, S., Wang, X., He, Q.: Axiomatic fuzzy set theory-based fuzzy oblique decision tree with dynamic mining fuzzy rules. Neural Comput. Appl. **32**(15), 11621–11636 (2020)
20. Gallego, A.-J., et al.: Clustering-based k-nearest neighbor classification for large-scale data with neural codes representation. Pattern Recogn. **74**, 531–543 (2018)
21. Zhu, Y., Zheng, Y.: Traffic identification and traffic analysis based on support vector machine. Neural Comput. Appl. **32**(7), 1903–1911 (2020)
22. Wang, X., Wang, B.: Research on prediction of environmental aerosol and PM2.5 based on artificial neural network. Neural Comput. Appl. **31**(12), 8217–8227 (2019)
23. Abpeykar, S., Ghatee, M.: An ensemble of RBF neural networks in decision tree structure with knowledge transferring to accelerate multi-classification. Neural Comput. Appl. **31**(11), 7131–7151 (2019)
24. Yang, L., Shami, A.: On hyperparameter optimization of machine learning algorithms: Theory and practice. Neurocomputing **415**, 295–316 (2020)
25. Falkner, S., Klein, A., Hutter, F.: BOHB: Robust and efficient hyperparameter optimization at scale. In: Proceedings of the 35th International Conference on Machine Learning (ICML), pp. 2323–2341 (2018)
26. Karaboga, D., Basturk, B.: On the performance of artificial bee colony (ABC) algorithm. Appl. Soft Comput. **8**, 687–697 (2008)
27. Zhang, X., Zhang, X., Gu, C.: A micro-artificial bee colony based multicast routing in vehicular ad hoc networks. Ad Hoc Netw. **58**, 213–221 (2017)

Neural Computing-Based Fault Diagnosis, Fault Forecasting, Prognostic Management, and System Modeling

A Hybrid Approach to Risk Analysis for Critical Failures of Machinery Spaces on Unmanned Ships by Fuzzy AHP

Junzhong Bao[1], Zhijie Bian[1], Zixuan Yu[1], Thammawan Phanphichit[2],
Guoyou Wang[3], and Yuanzi Zhou[1(✉)]

[1] Navigation College, Dalian Maritime University, Dalian 116026, China
`baojunzhong@dlmu.edu.cn`
[2] Faculty of Maritime Studies, Kasetsart University, Si Racha, Chonburi 20230, Thailand
`thammawan.p@ku.th`
[3] Marine Engineering College, Dalian Maritime University, Dalian 116026, China
`wgy@dlmu.edu.cn`

Abstract. This paper proposes a fuzzy evaluation approach that combines fuzzy AHP and fuzzy synthetic evaluation to conduct risk analysis of unmanned ships. In our proposal, a hierarchy of key failures of machinery spaces onboard unmanned ships is constructed based on a literature review and expert consultation. Experts are also invited to contribute their judgement on pairwise comparison of failures in the hierarchy and to evaluate the occurrence of each failure on the lowest tier of the hierarchy so that the Frequency Index of hazards can be obtained by fuzzy synthetic evaluation. In mapping experts' uncertainty in making their judgements, Z-numbers are introduced to depict experts' reliability in doing pairwise comparison. Finally, three critical failures of machinery spaces onboard ships are rated as higher levels of risk, and thus four risk control options are put forward to reduce the frequency of failure occurrences.

Keywords: Unmanned ships · Machinery spaces · Critical failures · Z-number · Fuzzy AHP

1 Introduction

Progress is being made in the design and development of unmanned cargo ships, as well as rule-making stage [1]. The rules surrounding the testing and eventual deployment of unmanned ships are similarly in-progress. Various sources have put forward a variety of terms to classify these ships. Widely used terminology includes intelligent ships, autonomous ships and Maritime Autonomous Surface Ships (MASS) [2]. According to the International Maritime Organization (IMO), MASS refers to ships that can operate with varying levels of human intervention. This definition was put forward provisionally only for use in the IMO's study of MASS rule applicability. To ensure that MASS operation safety levels are the same as that of conventional vessels, the IMO has studied the possible application of existing regulations to MASS, and has released the Interim Guidelines for MASS Trials as a means of mitigating the operational risks of MASS

© Springer Nature Singapore Pte Ltd. 2021
H. Zhang et al. (Eds.): NCAA 2021, CCIS 1449, pp. 273–287, 2021.
https://doi.org/10.1007/978-981-16-5188-5_20

during trials [3]. There are also diversified classifications for MASS ships, mainly based on the degree of control exercised by a human operator and the degree of autonomy of the ship's equipment [4]. The IMO proposed four classifications, namely ships with automated processes and decision support with human controllers onboard, remotely controlled ships with seafarers on board, remotely controlled ships without seafarers on board, and fully autonomous ships [1]. Ships in the latter two degrees, which may be remotely controlled or supervised by operators or completely automated, are referred to as unmanned ships [5].

Some classification societies have published rules for unmanned ships, providing requirements for risk assessment during the design and operation of such ships [5–8]. Many efforts have been made to address the risks of unmanned ships, mainly focusing on four aspects: classification of failures, hazard identification, risk level measurement and risk control measures [6, 9–12]. ABS [7] requires that FMECA (Functional Failure Modes, Effects and Criticality Analysis) be applied to systematically identify potential hazards and assess risks of unmanned ships in relation to the application of intelligence functions. According to DNV-GL [6], when assessing risk for remote-controlled or autonomous ships, failures of rotating machinery, mechanical components, electrical functions of all systems, power distribution and associated control systems should all be considered. Bureau Veritas (BV) [5] carried out unmanned ship risk analysis in five steps: formalization of the ship risk model, hazard identification, risk index calculation, risk assessment and risk control plans. During risk level measurement and risk analysis, impacts to humans, ships and the environment were considered. BV also used a risk matrix to calculate the risk index and ranked the risks for unmanned ships. CCS [8] released Guidelines for Intelligent Ships 2020, asserting that risk assessment methods like Failure Mode and Effect Analysis (FMEA) should be used for thorough identification of hazards and the analysis of risks in relation to design of intelligent navigation systems in all navigation scenarios. In addition, some studies sought to conduct risk assessment unmanned ship operations [5, 13]. Remotely controlled ships may be inherently different from conventional vessels in the areas of navigation, power generation, fuel management, cargo conditioning and fire safety. It is necessary to identify the high-level system hazards during MASS's design and development stage. Mitigation of such system hazards may be achieved by introducing redundancy to certain safety-critical subsystems [14].

Risk assessment of unmanned ships is still in its initial stage. Previous studies mainly focused on exploration of risk assessment methods. Wróbel et al. [15] determined unmanned ships' incident factors via brainstorming and established a Bayesian belief Network for the accident assessment of unmanned ships as per the interaction of different risk factors. In his later writings, Wróbel [16] further used the STPA (System-Theoretic Process Analysis) method to develop a model applicable to risk assessment and analyzed interactions between all the system components to identify potential hazards safely. Thieme et al. [4] further held that some of the existing risk modes and basic frameworks for traditional ships could provide a reference for the development of the risk modes of unmanned ships, considering problems regarding software, control algorithms, and man-machine interaction. Fan et al. [17] proposed a risk analysis framework for MASS based on operational procedures, e.g. voyage plan, berthing and unberthing, and influence factors, e.g. human, environment and technology. In addition to these the previous studies of the risk analysis framework, some scholars have instead focused on the risk of potential hazards on unmanned ships. Wróbel [13] made a qualitative analysis of 100 marine incident reports and evaluated whether the introduction of unmanned ships could change the frequency and severity of the incident results based on a What-if framework. He found that the use of unmanned ships could reduce navigational incidents like collision and grounding, but might lead to more serous non-navigational incidents like fire and hull damage arising from structural failure when compared to conventional ships. Rødseth et al. [18] proposed a relational graph of the unmanned ship operational environment and developed a risk assessment framework. They provided problem-solving methods based on risk-control elements and proposed risk-based structural design approaches [19]. It is noted that most of the studies reviewed focus on the practicability of techniques for risk analysis, as well as on generating roadmaps for risk analyses onboard unmanned ships. There is a lack of studies assessing hazards in machinery spaces, which are urgently needed given the fact that engine failures onboard ships are major contributory factors of ship accidents [20].

Since there is a lack of historical accident data available for use in the risk analysis of unmanned ships, when performing a risk assessment, comparing the risks of the conventional ships is recommended [21]. The main contributions of this study include: firstly, a risk analysis scheme is designed to assess critical failures in machinery spaces on unmanned cargo ships from an operational perspective. Secondly, we apply Fuzzy AHP integrated with Z-numbers to expert pair-wise comparison as a means of weighting the risk factors, rendering measurable the reliability of expert judgements. Thirdly, we move a step forward by presenting a practical path forward in the field of unmanned ship risk analysis (Compared with previous studies mainly focusing on theoretical study or framework research). Finally, this paper provides recommendations for risk control of unmanned ships and analyses the validity of various Risk Control Options (RCOs).

The remainder of this paper proceeds as follows. Section 2 explains some basic concepts and definitions about Triangular Fuzzy Numbers and Z-numbers. Subsequently, Sects. 3 and 4 lays out the methodology and calculation process as applied in this study. Finally, Sect. 5 discusses and analyses the ranking results of the failures and their corresponding effective RCOs and Sect. 6 presents the conclusion and a discussion of future work.

2 Preliminaries

The traditional Analysis Hierarchy Process (AHP) was first introduced by Saaty [22]. AHP is a broadly applied multi-criteria decision-making method used to determine the weights of criteria and priorities of alternatives in a structured manner based on pairwise comparison. However, due to the subjective judgments involved in the comparison process, AHP has the potential to be imprecise. Its shortcomings in depicting the uncertainty and vagueness present in human judgments are highlighted in a study by Kang et al. [23]. Fuzzy AHP in contrast shows greater efficiency in dealing with imprecise numerical quantities and decision makers' subjective preferences than the classical AHP method [24–26]. In the process of judging the relative importance of each pair of factors in the same hierarchy, the decision maker, there exists a real uncertainty regarding that specific judgement. Fuzzy AHP, however, also poorly depicts the reliability of decision makers' judgements. To map the reliability level of human judgements, Zadeh [27] proposed the notion of a Z-number, within which there is both a fuzzy restriction and an embedded measurement of reliability or uncertainty. Some fundamental theories are reviewed in the following section, including fuzzy sets, triangular fuzzy numbers and Z-numbers.

2.1 Fuzzy Sets and Triangular Fuzzy Numbers

A fuzzy set A is defined on a universe X may be given as:

$$A = \{(x, \mu_A(x)) | x \in X\}$$

Where $\mu_A(x) : X \rightarrow [0,1]$ is the membership function A. The membership value $\mu_A(x)$ describes the degree of belongingness of $x \in X$ in A [23, 24, 28].

A triangular fuzzy number $\tilde{A}$ can be defined by a triplet (l_1, m_1, u_1). Fuzzy numbers are standard fuzzy sets defined on the set of real numbers, whose α-cuts for all $\alpha \in [0, 1]$ are closed intervals of real numbers. The membership function of a triangular fuzzy number $\tilde{A}$ is $\mu_{\tilde{A}}(x) : R \rightarrow [0, 1]$ and can be represented by the expression presented in Fig. 1 [23, 26].

$$\mu_{\tilde{A}}(x) = \begin{cases} \frac{(x-1)}{(m-1)}, & x \in [l, m] \\ \frac{(u-x)}{(u-m)}, & x \in [m, u] \\ 0 & otherwise \end{cases} \quad (1)$$

Where $l < m < u$.

In the triplet $\tilde{A}$, the parameter 'm' gives the maximal grade of $\mu_{\tilde{A}}(x)$, and the parameters 'l' and 'u' are the lower and upper bounds which limit the field of the possible evaluation.

Define two triangular fuzzy numbers $\tilde{A}$ and $\tilde{B}$ by the triplets $\tilde{A} = (l_1, m_1, u_1)$ and $\tilde{B} = (l_2, m_2, u_2)$ [26, 29]. There are various operations are performed on triangular fuzzy numbers presented in [26], three important operations applied in this study are illustrated in [30]. Then

- Addition:

$$\tilde{A} + \tilde{B} = (l_1, m_1, u_1) + (l_2, m_2, u_2) = (l_1 + l_2, m_1 + m_2, u_1 + u_2) \quad (2)$$

- Multiplication:

$$\tilde{A} * \tilde{B} \approx (l_1, m_1, u_1) * (l_2, m_2, u_2) = (l_1 * l_2, m_1 * m_2, u_1 * u_2) \quad (3)$$

- Inverse:

$$(l_1, m_1, u_1)^{-1} \approx (1/u_1, 1/m_1, 1/l_1) \quad (4)$$

Where $\approx$ represents approximately equal to.

Tables 1 and 2 give information on fuzzy importance scales with triangular fuzzy numbers (TFN), reliability linguistic terms, corresponding Z-numbers and α.

Table 1. Fuzzy importance scale with TFN [31, 32].

Linguistic scale	Fuzzy triangle numbers	Fuzzy triangle numbers (reciprocal)
Equally important (EI)	(1, 1, 1)	(1, 1, 1)
Slightly more important (SMI)	(2/3, 1, 3/2)	(2/3, 1, 3/2)
Much more important (MMI)	(3/2, 2, 5/2)	(2/5, 1/2, 2/3)
Very much more important (VMMI)	(5/2, 3, 7/2)	(2/7, 1/3, 2/5)
Extremely more important (EMI)	(7/2, 4, 9/2)	(2/9, 1/4, 2/7)

Table 2. Reliability linguistic terms and their corresponding Z-numbers & α [23].

Linguistic terms	Fuzzy triangle numbers	α
Very-low (VL)	(0, 0, 0.25)	0.083
Low (L)	(0, 0.25, 0.5)	0.25
Medium (M)	(0.25, 0.5, 0.75)	0.5
High (H)	(0.5, 0.75, 1)	0.75

2.2 Z-numbers

In order to solve the problem that many decisions are based on uncertain information, Zadeh [27] proposed the concept of a Z-number for uncertain, imprecise and/or incomplete information, namely Z-number, which is an ordered pair of fuzzy numbers $(\widetilde{A},\widetilde{B})$. The first component $(\widetilde{A})$ plays the role of a fuzzy restriction and represents the information about an uncertain variable, while the second $(\widetilde{B})$ is a reliability of $\widetilde{A}$ and can represent its degree of an idea of certainty or probability [23, 24]. Z-numbers are better able to numerically describe uncertain or limited human knowledge expressed in linguistic terms than traditional or classical triangle Fuzzy Numbers. In its two components, it describes both restraint and reliability. For example, in risk analysis, if the frequency of loss is high, with a confidence of very likely, it can be presented as a Z-number thus: $Z = (high, very\ likely)$.

3 Methodology

Based on the Z-number and Fuzzy set theories, this paper extends the traditional AHP method to solve the uncertainty arising from expert judgement in the risk analysis of

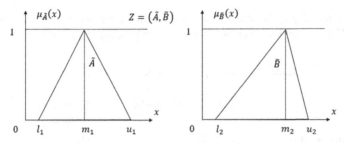

Fig. 1. Z-Numbers and triangular fuzzy numbers.

unmanned ships and thus obtain a more reliable weight for each of the failures identified. The proposed steps are as follows.

Step 1. Constructing a Fuzzy Decision-Making Matrix

Let the matrix M be the decision making matrix, m is the basic element of this matrix, where $m_{ij} = Z_{ij}(\tilde{A}, \tilde{B})$, $i = 1, ..., m$; $j = 1, ..., n$, and $Z_{ij}(\tilde{A}, \tilde{B})$ is the evaluation of the j th criteria for the i th selection. $\tilde{A}$ and $\tilde{B}$ are the constraint and reliability, respectively, of a Z-number.

First, a hierarchy is established, then a pairwise comparison evaluation takes place. All the criteria on the same level of the hierarchy are compared to each criteria on the preceding (upper) level. A pairwise comparison is performed by using Fuzzy linguistic terms on the 0–10 scale described by the triangular fuzzy numbers in Table 1. Here the fuzzy comparison matrix is defined as $\tilde{M}$.

$$\tilde{M} = \begin{pmatrix} 1 & \cdots & \tilde{m}_{1n} \\ \vdots & \ddots & \vdots \\ \tilde{m}_{n1} & \cdots & 1 \end{pmatrix}$$

Where $\tilde{m}_{ij} = \left(m_{ij}^L, m_{ij}^M, m_{ij}^U \right)$ is the relative importance of each criteria in pair-wise comparison and the numbers m_{ij}^L, m_{ij}^M, m_{ij}^U are the minimum value, most plausible value and maximum value of the triangular fuzzy pair wise comparison matrix, which is then broken into crisp matrices formed by taking the minimum values, most plausible values & maximum values from the triangular fuzzy numbers.

Step 2. Converting a Z-number to a Regular Fuzzy Number

Assume a Z-number $Z(\tilde{A}, \tilde{B})$. Let $\{\tilde{A} = (x, \mu_{\tilde{A}}) | x \in [0, 1], \tilde{B} = (x, \mu_{\tilde{B}}) | x \in [0, 1]\}$, $\mu_{\tilde{A}}$ is a triangular membership function and $\mu_{\tilde{B}}$ is a triangular membership function [33]. First, the second component (reliability) is converted into a crisp number using Eq. (5).

$$\alpha = \frac{\int x\mu_B dx}{\int \mu_B dx} \tag{5}$$

Where, the symbolic $\int$ represents an algebraic integration.

Then, the weight of the second component (reliability) is multiplied into the first component (restriction). The final weighted Z-number can be denoted as $\widetilde{Z}^\alpha = \left\{ (x, \mu_{\widetilde{A}^\alpha}) | \mu_{\widetilde{A}^\alpha}(x) = \alpha \mu_{\widetilde{A}}(x), x \in [0, 1] \right\}$.

Step 3. Aggregating the Decision Makers' Preferences
The pairwise comparison matrices of decision makers' preferences are aggregated by using Buckley's fuzzy geometric mean method [33], denoted as Eq. (6).

$$\widetilde{a}_{ij} = \left(\widetilde{a}_{ij}^1 \times \widetilde{a}_{ij}^2 \times \dots \times \widetilde{a}_{ij}^k \right)^{1/k} \tag{6}$$

Where k is the number of decision makers and $i = 1, 2, ..., n; j = 1, 2, ..., n$.

Step 4. Weighting the Evaluation Criteria
After aggregating experts' fuzzy judgment matrix, the fuzzy weight of each criterion (w_i) is yielded by the Eqs. (7) and (8) [24]. w_i is a triangular fuzzy number, i.e. $w_i = (l, m, u)$. Subsequently, the defuzzied weight of each criterion (w_i^*) is obtained via the Eq. (9).

$$w_i = \frac{r_i}{\sum_{i=1}^n r_i} \tag{7}$$

$$r_i = \left(\prod_{j=1}^n a_{ij} \right)^{1/n} \tag{8}$$

$$w_i^* = 1/3 * [(u_{w_i} - l_{w_i}) + (m_{w_i} - l_{w_i})] + l_{w_i} \tag{9}$$

Step 5. Implementing Fuzzy Synthetic Evaluation
Fuzzy synthetic evaluation (FSE), known as a fuzzy evaluation method, is based on a fuzzy set theory first introduced by Zadeh [28]. FSE is capable of combining qualitative and quantitative fuzzy reasoning, transforming qualitative evaluations into quantitative ones according to the membership degree theory of fuzzy mathematics. FSE is therefore a potential mathematical tool for handling fuzzy, uncertain and imprecise preference information in judgements provided by decision makers in an evaluation process [34]. FSE is applied in this study to obtain the frequency index of critical failures, since the observation of occurrence of each failure in machinery spaces onboard ships are estimated by experienced marine chief engineers and such observations are inherently vague and uncertain. The operation of FSE are as follows [34]:

Firstly, the set of evaluation factors is determined. It is represented as a vector $U = \{u_1, u_2, \dots, u_n\}$, and the set of appraisal grades which is represented as a vector $V = \{v_1, v_2, \dots, v_m\}$. A fuzzy evaluation matrix (R) is then established to map the membership degree of each evaluated factor to the V set. Matrix R is denoted in Eq. (10).

$$R = \begin{matrix} & \begin{matrix} V_1 & \cdots & V_m \end{matrix} \\ \begin{matrix} U_1 \\ \vdots \\ U_n \end{matrix} & \begin{bmatrix} r_{11} & \cdots & r_{1m} \\ \vdots & \ddots & \vdots \\ r_{n1} & \cdots & r_{nm} \end{bmatrix} \end{matrix} \tag{10}$$

Where, $r_{ij}(i = 1, 2, ..., n; j = 1, 2, ..., m)$ represents the fuzzy membership degree of an appraisal factor u_i to a grade v_j, $r_{ij} \in [0,1]$.

Secondly, Secondly, fuzzy evaluation set J is obtained by Eq. (11).

$$J = W \circ R = (r_1, r_2, ..., r_n) \tag{11}$$

Where, W is the weight matrix of factor u_i, $i = 1, 2, ..., n$. '$\circ$' is a weighted arithmetic mean operator, and $(r_{i1}, ..., r_{im})$ represents the evaluation set of individual factors u_i.

Thirdly, evaluation results are produced. These results are expressed as the comprehensive evaluation score P, which is obtained based on E and J, which can be used to define the results.

$$P = J \times E = \sum_{i=1}^{n} r_i \times E \tag{12}$$

Where, E is the set of index value of appraisal grades $e_j, j = 1, 2, ..., m$.

4 Case Study

In the case study, the authors explore the possibility of black-outs, steering gear failures and fires in unattended machinery spaces inside unmanned ships (See Table 4). Due to the lack of historical data regarding key failures in machinery spaces onboard unmanned ships, introducing expert evaluation is likely to be a suitable means to parameterize risk models [35, 36]. Since as of now there have been no unmanned cargo ships in operation, to facilitate this study, the following hypotheses are made: the first is that unmanned ships consume traditional fuels, and the second is that the UMS are introduced onboard unmanned ships are fully unmanned, with no maintenance work or watchkeeping going on during a few successive voyages for a limited time (150 h). In the questionnaire used in this study, both hypotheses were provided as a precondition to the experts who were then asked to evaluate the frequency of key failure occurrences in the engine room on board an unmanned ship.

4.1 Risk Measurement

Widely used marine risk analysis techniques include Fault Tree Analysis (FTA), Event Tree Analysis (ETA), FMEA and FSE. FSE can be used for solving problems in which evaluation factors are fuzzy or non-deterministic and it is difficult to quantify qualitative indicators. It can be used for ranking and grading factors based on their scores. Currently, unmanned vessels are on the stage of design and development, and it is hard to employ risk analysis based on statistical data of ship accidents. Expert judgement is therefore an essential means to provide estimation of the frequency and severity of hazards in machinery spaces on unmanned vessels, making FSE an ideal tool to assess the risk level of unmanned vessel operations. According to the risk index (RI) provided in IMO's Guidelines for Formal Safety Assessment [37]:

$$RI = FI + SI \tag{13}$$

Where *FI* refers to a logarithmic probability/frequency index, measured at the rate of ships affected per year, and *SI* refers to a logarithmic severity index, measured in equivalent fatalities. The scales of *FI* given in Table 3 are referred to by experts in making judgements regarding the frequency of occurrence of critical failure modes on unmanned vessels. *SI* given in [37] is of reference to a panel of experts to evaluate the severity of potential hazards. According to Eq. (13), therefore, the risk levels of critical failures of machinery spaces on unmanned vessels can be assessed.

Table 3. Frequency Index [5, 37].

FI	Frequency	Definition	Frequency (per ship year)
6	Common	Likely to occur once per year on one ship	1
5	Reasonably	Likely to occur once per year in a fleet of 10 ships	0.1
4	Possible	Likely to occur once per year in a fleet of 100 ships	0.01
3	Remote	Likely to occur once per year in a fleet of 1000 ships	0.001
2	Unlikely	Likely to occur once per year in a fleet of 10,000 ships	0.0001

4.2   Analysis of Risk of Black-Outs

In this section, we use the Black-outs critical failure category as an illustration of the calculation process, and then list the calculation results of other two critical failures.

Step 1. Constructing a Fuzzy Decision-Making Matrix with Z-numbers and Converting Z-numbers to Regular Fuzzy Numbers. Based on Eq. (5) and the criteria given in Tables 1 and 2, the fuzzy pairwise comparison matrices after the conversion process are depicted in below.

$DM\,1 =$

$$\begin{bmatrix} (0.958, 0.958, 0.958) & (0.866, 0.866, 0.866) & (0.638, 0.958, 1.436) & (2.394, 2.873, 3.352) \\ (0.866, 0.866, 0.866) & (0.958, 0.958, 0.958) & (0.866, 0.866, 0.866) & (0.471, 0.707, 1.061) \\ (0.638, 0.958, 1.436) & (0.866, 0.866, 0.866) & (0.958, 0.958, 0.958) & (0.866, 0.866, 0.866) \\ (0.274, 0.319, 0.383) & (0.471, 0.707, 1.061) & (0.866, 0.866, 0.866) & (0.958, 0.958, 0.958) \end{bmatrix}$$

$DM\,2 =$

$$\begin{bmatrix} (0.958, 0.958, 0.958) & (0.577, 0.866, 1.299) & (1.436, 1.915, 2.394) & (0.638, 0.958, 1.436) \\ (0.577, 0.866, 1.299) & (0.958, 0.958, 0.958) & (2.394, 2.873, 3.352) & (0.638, 0.958, 1.436) \\ (0.383, 0.479, 0.638) & (0.274, 0.319, 0.383) & (0.958, 0.958, 0.958) & (0.638, 0.958, 1.436) \\ (0.638, 0.958, 1.436) & (0.638, 0.958, 1.436) & (0.638, 0.958, 1.436) & (0.958, 0.958, 0.958) \end{bmatrix}$$

$DM3 =$

$$\begin{bmatrix} (0.958, 0.958, 0.958) & (0.638, 0.958, 1.436) & (0.638, 0.958, 1.436) & (0.638, 0.958, 1.436) \\ (0.638, 0.958, 1.436) & (0.958, 0.958, 0.958) & (0.638, 0.958, 1.436) & (0.638, 0.958, 1.436) \\ (0.638, 0.958, 1.436) & (0.638, 0.958, 1.436) & (0.958, 0.958, 0.958) & (0.638, 0.958, 1.436) \\ (0.638, 0.958, 1.436) & (0.638, 0.958, 1.436) & (0.638, 0.958, 1.436) & (0.958, 0.958, 0.958) \end{bmatrix}$$

Step 2. Weighting the Evaluation Criteria. Based on Eq. (6), the aggregated pairwise comparison matrix is presented in below.

Table 4. Hierarchical structure of failures for machinery spaces on unmanned vessels.

Criterion	Primary sub-criterion	Secondary sub-criterion
Black-outs (0.31)	Fuel features and quality (0.3)	Excessive water contents (0.29)
		Contaminated fuel oil (0.27)
		Excessive or insufficient heating (0.21)
		Change over between light and heavy fuel oils (0.23)
	Generator engine failure (0.36)	Low pressure or high temperature of lubricating oil, or high temperature of cooling water (0.31)
		Seize of high pressure pump and fuel injector (0.31)
		Black-out caused by mechanical failure of generator engines (0.38)
	Electrical equipment failure (0.34)	Voltage regulator failure (0.22)
		Air circuit breaker tripped due to phase loss, under-voltages or excess current (0.3)
		Power management system (PMS) failure (0.25)
		Fan and oil system automatically shut off due to false fire alarm (0.23)
Steering gear failure (0.16)	Remote control system failure (0.26)	Power failure (0.33)
		Blown fuse (0.15)
		Poor relay contact connection or loose link between relay terminals and link cables (0.23)
		Electrical components defects (0.29)
	Nonfunctional main oil pump (0.27)	Pump system damaged (0.55)
		Low hydraulic oil level (0.22)
		Suction pipes choked (0.23)

(continued)

Table 4. (*continued*)

Criterion	Primary sub-criterion	Secondary sub-criterion
	Component failure in control system (0.21)	Solenoid valve spool stuck (0.38)
		Solenoid valve spring broken (0.38)
		Internal leak in relief valve (0.24)
	System operational fault (0.26)	Response delay or software system malfunction (0.41)
		Standby steering gear inoperative (0.59)
Fires in machinery spaces (0.53)	Electrical equipment failure (motors, heaters, relay) (0.17)	Short-circuit (0.31)
		Overload (0.2)
		Poor relay contact connection or loose link between relay terminals and link cables (0.16)
		Electrical arcs (0.17)
		Lighting or static electricity (0.16)
	Oil leakage (Hot surface effect) (0.21)	Fuel oil splashes, leaks or spills (0.43)
		Lube oil splashes, leaks or spills (0.32)
		Oil tank leaks (0.25)
	Ventilating and cooling system failure (0.14)	Machinery explosion resulting from high temperature (0.61)
		Spontaneous ignition of stores due to high temperature (0.39)
	Machinery explosion or spontaneous ignition (0.48)	Poor lubrication of moving parts (0.35)
		Bearings damaged (0.34)
		Exhaust gas boiler collapsed partly due to improper cleaning (0.31)

Aggregated =

$$
\begin{bmatrix}
(0.958, 0.958, 0.958) & (0.683, 0.896, 1.174) & (0.837, 1.207, 1.703) & (0.992, 1.381, 0.683) \\
(0.683, 0.896, 1.174) & (0.958, 0.958, 0.958) & (1.098, 1.336, 1.610) & (0.577, 0.866, 1.298) \\
(0.538, 0.760, 1.096) & (0.533, 0.642, 0.781) & (0.958, 0.958, 0.958) & (0.707, 0.926, 1.214) \\
(0.481, 0.664, 0.925) & (0.577, 0.866, 1.298) & (0.707, 0.926, 1.214) & (0.958, 0.958, 0.958)
\end{bmatrix}
$$

The weight of criterion is yielded by Eqs. (7)–(9), and the results are depicted as below.

$$w_1^* = 0.286; w_2^* = 0.260; w_3^* = 0.212; w_4^* = 0.222$$

Normalized as below:

$$W_1 = 0.29; W_2 = 0.27; W_3 = 0.21; W_4 = 0.23$$

Step 3. Carrying Out Fuzzy Synthetic Evaluation. Thirty-five senior experts were invited to provide their judgement on the possibility of critical failures occurring if existing PUMS were to be left purely unmanned on unmanned vessels. Five expert judgement sheets are withdrawn due to the extreme opinions they present. The statistical results are used to calculate R_a, and the aggregated frequency of Black-outs is presented in below.

$$P_a = J_a \times E = W_a \times R_a \times E$$

$$= \begin{pmatrix} 0.087 \\ 0.081 \\ 0.063 \\ 0.069 \\ 0.112 \\ 0.112 \\ 0.137 \\ 0.075 \\ 0.102 \\ 0.085 \\ 0.078 \end{pmatrix}^T \times \begin{vmatrix} 0.233 & 0.333 & 0.267 & 0.167 & 0 \\ 0.2 & 0.433 & 0.167 & 0.2 & 0 \\ 0.1 & 0.2 & 0.233 & 0.333 & 0.133 \\ 0.133 & 0.567 & 0.067 & 0.167 & 0.067 \\ 0.167 & 0.433 & 0.167 & 0.2 & 0.033 \\ 0.2 & 0.333 & 0.233 & 0.2 & 0.033 \\ 0.133 & 0.4 & 0.233 & 0.233 & 0 \\ 0.033 & 0.267 & 0.333 & 0.333 & 0.033 \\ 0.067 & 0.3 & 0.233 & 0.3 & 0.1 \\ 0.1 & 0.167 & 0.3 & 0.333 & 0.1 \\ 0.1 & 0.067 & 0.333 & 0.333 & 0.167 \end{vmatrix} \times \begin{pmatrix} 6 \\ 5 \\ 4 \\ 3 \\ 2 \end{pmatrix} = 4.241$$

The P_a of Black-outs is yielded as per Eqs. (11) and (12). The results of P_i for three critical failures (Black-outs, Steering gear and Fires) respectively and the aggregated frequency of the critical failures are presented in Table 5.

Table 5. The results of fuzzy synthetic evaluation.

Criterion	Fuzzy evaluation set (J_i)	Set of value of appraisal grades (E^T)	Score $(P_i = J_i \times E)$
Black-outs	(0.137, 0.326, 0.233, 0.250, 0.055)	(6, 5, 4, 3, 2)	4.241
Steering gear	(0.037, 0.154, 0.275, 0.378, 0.115)	(6, 5, 4, 3, 2)	3.540
Fires	(0.079, 0.179, 0.317, 0.289, 0.136)	(6, 5, 4, 3, 2)	3.775
Aggregated results	(0.090, 0.221, 0.284, 0.291, 0.114)	(6, 5, 4, 3, 2)	3.882

5 Discussion and Recommendations

Assuming that traditional fuel oil continues to be used for ship propulsion, three critical hazards for machinery spaces on unmanned ships are expected to have a frequency index (FI) reaching 3.88 (almost equal to the frequency of Possible in Table 3), which is equivalent to an occurrence rate of once per year per fleet of 100 ships (Table 3). Assuming such hazards do occur, they may cause collisions, grounding and sinking [5, 6]. Experts assessing the influence of these hazards believes that the SI rating could be as high as 3 (the level of Severe), which is equivalent to more than one fatality in a single accident. The Scales of the SI and RI are shown in [37]. It is believed that the RI for critical hazards for machinery spaces on unmanned spaces rise to nearly 7 as per Eq. (13), placing the risk level in the marginal between the unacceptable zone and as low as reasonably practicable (ALARP) in the RI matrix [37]. Thus, RCOs should be taken to reduce or mitigate the possibility of potential hazards.

The panel of experts brainstormed four suggested RCOs. For ships using traditional fuel and electric propulsion technology on short voyages, the provision of sufficient batteries which can ensure the short-time temporary power supply (UPS) for more than 45 s (RCO1) can significantly mitigate the risk level of black-outs failure. RCO1 however, may not effectively reduce the frequency of steering gear failures and machinery spaces fires. In the case of ships using traditional fuels and electric propulsion technology on long routes, one able seafarer engineer, one Electro-technical Officer and one marine engineer (of second engineer or higher rank) can be manned onboard (RCO2). Under this manning scheme, fire-fighting can be executed immediately upon the outbreak of a fire so that the fire can be contained. For ships using traditional fuel and electric propulsion technology on long routes, an additional generator (RCO3) can also effectively reduce the black-out risk on board. For ships sailing both routes, converting unmanned ships' propulsion systems to use non-conventional fuels (such as Pure electric power system) (RCO4) can greatly reduce the risks of three types of key failure, which can be an effective means to reduce the possibility of fire and significantly reduce the possibility of a rotating machinery failure.

6 Conclusion

In this paper, an UMS using traditional fuels and no maintenance work or watchkeeping going on during a few successive voyages for a limited time (150 h) is defined as a scenario to conduct the survey, aiming at evaluation of the risk level of critical failures on board unmanned ships. A fuzzy synthetic evaluation approach, which integrates Fuzzy AHP with fuzzy synthetic evaluation, is proposed as a method to conduct a risk analysis for critical failures in machinery spaces on unmanned ships. Meanwhile, Z-numbers are utilized to measure experts' reliability in performing pairwise comparison for weighting hazards. In addition, a hierarchy of key failures on machinery spaces onboard ships is constructed to facilitate the study.

References

1. International Maritime Organization (IMO): Regulatory Scoping Exercise for the Use of Maritime Autonomous Surface Ships (MASS). MSC 102/5 (2020)
2. IMO: Regulatory Scoping Exercise for the Use of Maritime Autonomous Surface Ships (MASS) Comments on Document MSC 100/5. MSC 100/5/7 (2018)

3. IMO: Interim Guidelines for Mass Trials. MSC.1/Circ.1604[C] (2019)
4. Thieme, C.A., Utne, I.B., Haugen, S.: Assessing ship risk model applicability to marine autonomous surface ships. Ocean Eng. **165**, 140–154 (2018)
5. Bureau Veritas (BV): Guidelines for Autonomous Shipping. Guidance Note NI 641 DT R01 E (2019)
6. Det Norske Veritas-Germanischer Lloyd (DNV-GL): Autonomous and Remotely Operated Ship (2018)
7. American Bureau of Shipping (ABS): Guide for Smart Functions for Marine Vessels and Offshore Units (2019)
8. China Classification Society (CCS): Guidelines for Autonomous Cargo Ships (2018)
9. Nippon Kaiji Kyokai (NK): Guidelines for Concept Design of Automated Operation Autonomous Operation of Ships (2019)
10. MARITIME U.K.: An Industry Code of Practice: Maritime Autonomous Surface Ships up to 24 Metres in Length (2017)
11. ABS: Smart Functions for Marine Vessels and Offshore Vessels and Offshore Units (2019)
12. Ramos, M.A., Utne, I.B., Mosleh, A.: Collision avoidance on maritime autonomous surface ships: operators' tasks and human failure events. Saf. Sci. **116**, 33–44 (2019)
13. Wróbel, K., Montewka, J., Kujala, P.: Towards the assessment of potential impact of unmanned vessels on maritime transportation safety. Reliab. Eng. Syst. Saf. **165**, 155–169 (2017)
14. Wróbel, K., Montewka, J., Kujala, P.: System-theoretic approach to safety of remotely-controlled merchant vessel. Ocean Eng. **152**, 334–345 (2018)
15. Wrobel, K., Krata, P., Montewka, J., Hinz, T.: Towards the development of a risk model for unmanned vessels design and operations. TransNav:, Int. J. Marine Navigat. Saf. Sea Transport. **10**(2), 267–274 (2016)
16. Wróbel, K., Montewka, J., Kujala, P.: Towards the development of a system-theoretic model for safety assessment of autonomous merchant vessels. Reliab. Eng. Syst. Saf. **178**, 209–224 (2018)
17. Fan, C., Wróbel, K., Montewka, J., Gil, M., Wan, C., Zhang, D.A.: Framework to identify factors influencing navigational risk for Maritime Autonomous Surface Ships. Ocean Eng. **202**, 107188 (2020)
18. Hoem, Å.S.: The present and future of risk assessment of MASS: a literature review. In: Proceedings of the 29th European Safety and Reliability Conference (ESREL), Hannover, Germany, pp. 22–26 (2019)
19. Rødseth, Ø.J., Burmeister, H.-C.: Risk assessment for an unmanned merchant ship. TransNav: Int. J. Marine Navigat. Saf. Sea Transport. **9**(3), 357–364 (2015)
20. Allianz: Safety and Shipping Review 2019. Munich (2019)
21. NK: Guidelines for Automated/Autonomous Operation of Ships ~Design Development, Installation and Operation of Automated Operation Systems/Remote Operation Systems (2020)
22. Saaty, T.L.: The Analytic Hierarchy Process, Planning, Priority Setting, Resource Allocation. McGraw-Hill, New York (1980)
23. Kang, B., Wei, D., Li, Y., Deng, Y.: Decision making using Z-numbers under uncertain environment. J. Comput. Inform. Syst. **8**(7), 2807–2814 (2012)
24. Azadeh, A., Saberi, M., Atashbar, N.Z., Chang, E., Pazhoheshfar, P.: Z-AHP: a Z-number extension of fuzzy analytical hierarchy process. In: Proceedings of the 2013 7th IEEE International Conference on Digital Ecosystems and Technologies (DEST), pp. 141–147 (2013)
25. Deng, H.: Comparing and ranking fuzzy numbers using ideal solutions. Appl. Math. Model. **38**(5–6), 1638–1646 (2014)
26. Chang, D.Y.: Applications of the extent analysis method on fuzzy AHP. Eur. J. Oper. Res. **95**(3), 649–655 (1996)

27. Zadeh, L.A.: A note on Z-numbers. Inf. Sci. **181**(14), 2923–2932 (2011)
28. Zadeh, L.A.: Fuzzy sets. Inf. Control **8**, 338–353 (1965)
29. Zadeh, L.A.: The concept of a linguistic variable and its application to approximate reasoning I. Informat. Sci. **8**(3), 199–249 (1975)
30. Chou, C.C.: The canonical representation of multiplication operation on triangular fuzzy numbers. Comput. Math. Appl. **45**(10–11), 1601–1610 (2003)
31. Srichetta, P., Thurachon, W.: Applying fuzzy analytic hierarchy process to evaluate and select product of notebook computers. Int. J. Model. Optimiz. **2**(2), 168 (2012)
32. Zheng, G., Zhu, N., Tian, Z., Chen, Y., Sun, B.: Application of a trapezoidal fuzzy AHP method for work safety evaluation and early warning rating of hot and humid environments. Saf. Sci. **50**(2), 228–239 (2012)
33. Buckley, J.J.: Fuzzy hierarchical analysis. Fuzzy Sets Syst. **17**(3), 233–247 (1985)
34. Zhou, R., Chan, A.H.: Using a fuzzy comprehensive evaluation method to determine product usability: a proposed theoretical framework. Work **56**(1), 9–19 (2017)
35. Bao, J., Zhou, Y., Li, R.: Competitive advantage assessment for container shipping liners using a novel hybrid method with intuitionistic fuzzy linguistic variables. Neural Comput. Appl. (2021). https://doi.org/10.1007/s00521-021-05718-z
36. Wu, J., Wang, L., Li, L.: 2-Dimensional interval neutrosophic linguistic numbers and their utilization in group decision making. In: Zhang, H., Zhang, Z., Wu, Z., Hao, T. (eds.) Neural Computing for Advanced Applications, NCAA 2020, Communications in Computer and Information Science, vol. 1265, pp. 234–246. Springer, Singapore (2020)
37. IMO: Revised Guidelines for Formal Safety Assessment (FSA) for Use in the IMO Rule-Making Process. MSC-MEPC.2/Circ.12 (2013)

A New Health Indicator Construction Approach and Its Application in Remaining Useful Life Prediction of Bearings

Huiming Jiang[1]([✉]), Jinhai Luo[1], Yunfei Shao[2], Qianxi Ma[1], and Honghai Pan[1]

[1] School of Mechanical Engineering, University of Shanghai for Science and Technology,
516 Jun Gong Road, Shanghai 200093, China
hmjiang@usst.edu.cn
[2] COMAC Shanghai Aircraft Manufacturing Co., Ltd., 919 Shangfei Road, Shanghai
201324, China

Abstract. A good health index (HI) plays an important role in improving the reliability and accuracy of the prediction of remaining useful life (RUL) of rolling bearings. In order to better integrate degradation information contained in high-dimensional features, construct HIs with a good trendability and obtain satisfactory RUL prediction effect, this paper proposes a HI construction method based on spectral clustering and trendability enhancement strategy. Firstly, 28-dimensional time–frequency features are extracted. Secondly, the features are clustered based on the spectral clustering method. Thirdly, the sensitive feature set of degradation process is constructed based on the trendability optimization. Finally, based on the calculation of trendability indicators of sensitive feature set, HIs based on the trendability enhancement strategy are calculated, and its performance can be verified through RUL prediction based on Support Vector Regression (SVR). The vibration data set of XJTU-SY bearing accelerated degradation test was used to evaluate the proposed method. The experimental results showed that the HIs constructed by this method have good accuracy in RUL prediction, and have better trendability and predictability compared with Root Mean Square (RMS) indicators and HIs obtained based on traditional k-means clustering.

Keywords: Health indicator · Remaining useful life · Spectral clustering · Trendability

1 Introduction

Rolling bearings are widely used in various rotating machinery and equipment and are prone to failure. Bearing failure may cause equipment damage, cause economic losses and even endanger the lives of personnel [1]. Therefore, the research of the key technology of the RUL prediction of rolling bearings, to achieve early warning of failure, and then develop maintenance plans, can maximize the service life of the equipment and significantly increase the economic benefits. At present, many researchers roughly divide the key technology methods into two categories in the articles about RUL prediction of

© Springer Nature Singapore Pte Ltd. 2021
H. Zhang et al. (Eds.): NCAA 2021, CCIS 1449, pp. 288–302, 2021.
https://doi.org/10.1007/978-981-16-5188-5_21

rolling bearings. One is the data-driven method, the other is the model-driven method [2]. Because the data-driven method has the characteristics of simple calculation and easy data acquisition through sensors, it is becoming more and more popular in current research and applications [3, 4]. RUL prediction of bearings is generally composed of three key technical procedures, which are feature extraction, HI construction, and RUL prediction [5].

The construction of HI plays a key role in RUL prediction, and its quality directly affects the accuracy of RUL prediction. Constructing a suitable HI can simplify predictive modeling and get more accurate predictive results [1]. Many different HI construction approaches have been proposed [6]. RMS is the most widely HI in the RUL prediction of machinery. Li et al. [7, 8] used kurtosis to select the first predicting time and used RMS to predict the RUL of rolling bearings. Yang et al. [9] introduced scale parameters to unify different types of fault thresholds, select sensitive features from many domain parameters to construct HI, and predict RUL through particle filters. Wang et al. [10] used an improved relevance vector machine (RVM) to predict the degradation process from failure to failure. Chen et al. [11] used a feature selection method based on the correlation of variants to select features that can accurately describe the degradation process, and then used the features selected by auto-associative kernel regression (AAKR) to perform RUL prediction. With the development of deep learning, many deep network architectures are introduced in the HI construction, such as long short-term memory (LSTM) [12] and convolutional neural networks (CNNs) [13] and so on. The deep learning method used to construct HI can automatically learn the deeply hidden features, realizing end-to-end deep feature extraction without human intervention. However, the deep learning method generally has the disadvantages of time-consuming and without clear physical meaning.

Clustering, as an unsupervised classification method, is widely used in bearing fault diagnosis [14] and performance degradation assessment [15]. Liu et al. [16] proposed a discrete hidden Markov model (DHMM) fault diagnosis strategy based on k-means clustering for fault diagnosis of the fuel cell. Baraldi et al. [17] developed a diagnostic system based on the hierarchical structure of K-Nearest Neighbors (KNN). Zhang et al. [18] proposed a tailored diagnostic framework based on an adaptive clustering for fault diagnosis of aero-engine bearing. Conventional clustering algorithms are suitable to find globular clusters, which can't find the non-convex clusters. At present, the spectral clustering method has been widely used because it can find clusters of arbitrary shapes and the solution is globally optimal. Xiong et al. [19] applied spectral clustering to near-infrared spectral analysis, which effectively improved the prediction performance of the model. Gao et al. [20] applied spectral clustering to ship maneuvering behavior pattern recognition, which effectively improved the efficiency of abnormal behavior detection. Spectral clustering can be utilized to cluster high-dimensional features based on the shape of life curves.

With the in-depth study of fault mechanisms and the development of signal feature extraction methods, abundant time–frequency feature extraction methods provide a better theoretical basis for the construction of health indicators. However, how to use the existing rich time–frequency feature extraction methods to better integrate the degradation information contained in the high-dimensional feature and construct the health indicator with good trendability to obtain the satisfactory life prediction results still attract much attention. Different from applications of clustering algorithms in diagnosis and performance degradation assessment, this paper utilizes spectral clustering to reduce the redundancy and enhance the trendability of high-dimensional features simultaneously. A new health indicator construction approach based on spectral clustering and tendability enhancement strategy is proposed. Firstly, features are extracted by time–frequency analysis techniques. Secondly, for the shape diversity of the degradation curves of different features during the lifetime, the clustering of features is realized based on the spectral clustering method. Thirdly, based on the trendability indicator, sensitive features are selected to form the degradation process sensitive feature set. Finally, based on the calculation of trendability indicators of sensitive feature set, health indicators based on the trendability enhancement strategy are calculated, and its performance can be verified through RUL prediction based on Support Vector Regression (SVR). The effectiveness and performance of the proposed method are proved by XJTU-SY rolling bearing accelerated life test data set. HIs based on the proposed approach show better tendability through the whole lifetime and better consistency with degradation trendency, and the RUL prediction based on the obtained HIs shows excellent performance.

2 Theory Background

2.1 Spectral Clustering

Different from the traditional clustering algorithms like k-means, the spectral clustering algorithm is based on spectral graph theory. Spectral clustering takes samples as vertices and the similarity between samples as the weight of vertex connection edge, transforming the clustering problem into the partition problem of an undirected graph with weight. It can find clusters of arbitrary shapes and converge to the global optimal solution [21], which is superior to the traditional clustering method [22]. Time–frequency domain features of bearings during the whole lifetime show different trendabilities and shapes from each other, which are closely related to degradation information. The spectral clustering algorithm can cluster characteristic curves of the same trendability and shape and help to find the degradation sensitive feature set, preserving high dimensional feature richness and reducing information redundancy simultaneously.

For the sample data $\{x_1, x_2, ..., x_n\}$, each data point x_i can be represented as a vertex v_i. Let $G = (\mathbf{V}, \mathbf{E})$ be an undirected graph with a vertex set $\mathbf{V} = \{v_1, v_2, ..., v_n\}$[23]. Assume that the graph G is weighted. The edges between two vertex v_i and vertex v_j have a non-negative weight $w_{ij} \geq 0$. Then a weighted adjacency matrix of the graph can be obtained as follows

$$\mathbf{W} = \{w_{ij}\}(i, j = 1, ..., n) \tag{1}$$

As G is undirected, $w_{ij} = w_{ji}$. If $w_{ij} = 0$, it means that the vertices v_i and v_j are not connected by any edge. Then W($\cdot$, $\cdot$) defines the relations of two not necessarily disjoint sets A,B $\subset$ V.

$$\mathbf{W}(A, B) := \sum_{i \in A, j \in B} w_{ij} \tag{2}$$

In this paper, the weighted adjacency matrix W of the graph is calculated as follows

$$w_{ij} = \exp\left(-\frac{||x_i - x_j||_2^2}{2\sigma^2}\right) \tag{3}$$

The goal of spectral clustering is to cut the graph $G = (V,E)$ into k subgraphs with no connection which can be defined as follows:

$$cut(A_1, A_2, ..., A_k) = \frac{1}{2}\sum_{i=1}^{k} W(A_i, \overline{A}_i) \tag{4}$$

where the set of each subgraph point is defined as $A_1, A_2,.. A_k$, and they satisfy $A_i \cap A_j = \emptyset$, and $A_1 \cup A_2 \cup ... \cup A_k = V$.

In this paper, NCut technique is utilized to solve the cutting graph problem [23]. Based on NCut technique, the problem described in Eq. (3) can be rewritten as

$$\underbrace{\arg\min}_{F} tr(\mathbf{Y}^T \mathbf{D}^{-\frac{1}{2}} \mathbf{L}_{sym} \mathbf{D}^{-\frac{1}{2}} \mathbf{Y})\ s.t.\ \mathbf{Y}^T\mathbf{Y} = \mathbf{I} \tag{5}$$

where the degree matrix D is defined as the diagonal matrix with the degrees $d_1, d_2, ..., d_n$ on the diagonal, and $d_i = \sum_{j=1}^{n} w_{ij}$. L_{sym} is the normalized graph Laplacian matrix defined as

$$\mathbf{L}_{sym} = \mathbf{I} - \mathbf{D}^{-\frac{1}{2}}\mathbf{W}\mathbf{D}^{-\frac{1}{2}} \tag{6}$$

Equation (6) is a standard trace minimization problem. The first k smallest eigenvectors of the matrix L_{sym} form the solution Y. In this paper, the parameter k is determined according to the contribution degree of eigenvalues arranged from small to large Laplace matrix, and the threshold value is set as 0.01. All sampling points of the same category will be projected from the high-dimensional feature space to the low-dimensional feature space (i.e., $x_i \rightarrow y_i$), which enables us to obtain the final clustering result based on the simple clustering method after the feature transformation. This paper adopts the k-means method. In the k-means algorithm, the cluster number is determined based on the inflection point adaptively of the distance ratio graph between classes and within classes.

2.2 Trendability

Trendability is an important indicator to measure the change of variables with time [24]. If the variable changes randomly over time or is constant, the trendability indicator is 0. In most cases, the variable increases or decreases with time, and its indicator is between ± 1. The RUL prediction method can use historical data to predict the future direction of HI and estimate the RUL. So features with strong trendability are more suitable for HIs construction in RUL prediction [25]. The trendability of HIs directly affects the final prediction results [26]. Trendability indicator measures the trendability level of features. The larger the absolute value of this indicator is, the better the corresponding characteristic trendability is, and the more favorable it is to predict the RUL. Based on the results of spectral clustering, the features with similar trendabilities (shapes) are grouped into a cluster. In order to obtain more suitable health indicators for RUL prediction, the trendability is utilized for feature optimization and enhancement. The straight forward formula is given in Eq. (7).

$$T = \frac{\sum\limits_{i=1}^{N} (t_i - \bar{t})(x_i - \bar{x})}{\sqrt{\sum\limits_{i=1}^{N} (t_i - \bar{t})^2 \sum\limits_{i=1}^{N} (x_i - \bar{x})^2}} \tag{7}$$

where N is the data length, t_i and x_i are the values of the i-th time and feature, and $\bar{t}, \bar{x}$ are the averages of time and feature, respectively.

3 Health Indicators Construction Based on Spectral Clustering and Trendability Enhancement Strategy

The performance of the industrial system will gradually decline with the extension of the operating time. Many condition monitoring systems are pro-posed such as CBM (condition based monitoring) and PHM (prognostics and health management). However, the gathered data is highly disturbed by environmental issues and noise, etc. How to transform raw sensory data into features for degradation process prognostics is very challenging. The extracted features can be seen as a kind of health indicator. At present, many researchers have proposed a variety of feature extraction techniques. However, the forms of feature curves during the whole life can be various. Because raw sensory data exhibit rich degradation information with many kinds of disturbing information, it is quite difficult to obtain effective features with strong trendability to reflect the degradation process. Secondly, some traditional features like RMS or Kurtosis, lack of stable change tendency with degradation process until a few time before failure. Consequently, it's difficult to perform accurate RUL prediction promptly to plan maintenance tasks in this situation. According to this, a new health indicator construction approach based on spectral clustering and trendability enhancement strategy is proposed in this paper. The main steps of the proposed method are described as follows.

3.1 Feature Extraction

In engineering applications, time-domain features are usually used to characterize the operating state of the bearing. As a generalization of the wavelet transform, wavelet packet transform has been widely used in signal processing, and its node energy distribution is related to the running state of the bearing. Therefore, the energy and energy entropy of the wavelet packet decomposition node are extracted as features to describe the operating state of the bearing. Two trigonometric features of the standard deviation of inverse hyperbolic cosine (Std-IHC) and standard deviation of inverse hyperbolic sine

(Std-HIS) are adopted. It is proved in reference [25] that they have better monotonic-ity and trendability than traditional features. Finally, 28 commonly used features are extracted shown in Table 1.

Table 1. 28-dimensional features.

Feature Type	Feature	
Time-domain features	F1: Std	F6: Crest factor
	F2: peak-to-peak value	F7: Impulse factor
	F3: Mean-absolute	F8: Skewness factor
	F4: Root-mean-square value	F9: Kurtosis value
	F5: Shape factor	F10: Entropy
Time-frequency features	F11–F18: Wavelet packet energy	
	F19–F26: Wavelet packet energy entropy	
Trigonometric features	F27: Std-IHC	
	F28: Std-HIS	

3.2 Feature Clustering Based on Spectral Clustering

After feature extraction, 28-dimensional feature sets are prepared. Spectral clustering is utilized to cluster the features with similar shapes and trendabilities during the whole lifetime. The features of different clusters contain different bearing deg-radation infor-mation, but the degradation information contained in the features of the same cluster has a certain redundancy, so further feature optimization is further needed.

3.3 Sensitive Feature Selection Based on Trendability Optimization

After spectral clustering, features with different shapes and trendabilities during the whole lifetime are separated from others. To fuse the degradation information in different feature clusters and reduce the information redundancy of similar features at the same time, the trendability indicator is used to optimize the features in each category. In this paper, the feature with the biggest trendability indicator is selected from each cluster. Then a degradation sensitive feature set is established with less redundancy and rich degradation information simultaneously.

3.4 Health Indicator Construction

To obtain a good bearing degradation health indicator, all the selected features are weighted and fused to further enhance the feature trendability while retaining the richness of information. Finally, a new health indicator construction method based on spectral clustering and trendability weighted fusion is proposed. For convenience, this indicator is recorded as HI-SCTWF for short. The weight vector W is defined as:

$$W_i = \frac{T_i}{\sum\limits_{i=1}^{K} |T_i|} (i = 1, 2, ..., K) \tag{8}$$

where T_i is the trend value of the i-th feature, and K is the total number of features.

Then, calculate the HI-SCTWF based on the Manhattan distance between the normal state and the current state, as shown below:

$$HI_t = \sum_{i=1}^{K} \left(w_i \times \left| F_{i,t} - V_i \right| \right)(t = 1, 2, ..., m) \tag{9}$$

where

$$V_i = \frac{1}{p} \sum_{t=1}^{p} F_{i,t}(i = 1, 2, ..., K) \tag{10}$$

where p is the number of normal space dimension, $F_{i,t}$ is t-th feature sample point of the i-th cluster. And the flow chart of the new HI construction approach proposed in this paper is shown in Fig. 1.

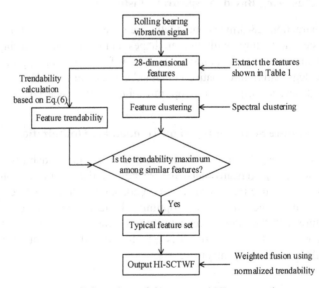

Fig. 1. The overall flow chart of the proposed HI construction approach

4   Case Study

The third part describes in detail the construction strategy of health indicators proposed in this paper. As mentioned above, a good health indicator plays a crucial role in the prediction of the RUL of bearings. Therefore, in this section, the proposed health indicators are constructed using run-to-failure data obtained from the accelerated degradation tests of the rolling bearings, and the SVR is used for RUL prediction to demonstrate the effectiveness of the proposed health indicator construction method.

4.1   Data Description

This article adopts the XJTU-SY data set of the accelerated life test for rolling bearings [27]. The accelerated life testing test rig for bearings is shown in Fig. 2. The accelerated life test can be performed on the bearings by the test rig to obtain the degradation data of the bearings during the whole service life. The bearing type used for the test is LDK URE204, and a total of 15 bearings were tested under three different operating conditions, as shown in Table 2. Photos of the rolling bearings under normal and degraded conditions are shown in Fig. 3. It can be seen that the failure forms of the bearings used for testing include inner ring wear, outer ring wear, and outer ring fracture. Two acceleration sensors, model PCB 352C33, were mounted on the bearing housing of the tested bearing to collect vibration data from bearing operation to failure, with one sensor placed in the horizontal direction and one in the vertical direction. During the test, the sampling frequency was 25.6 kHz, the sampling duration was 1.28 s, and the data was collected once every minute. When the vibration signal amplitude exceeds 20 g, the rolling bearing is considered to have failed, and the data acquisition is stopped at this time. Because the load is loaded in the horizontal direction during the test, the acceleration sensor installed in the horizontal direction of the tested bearing can obtain more degradation information, so the vibration signal in the horizontal direction is selected to estimate the RUL of the tested bearing.

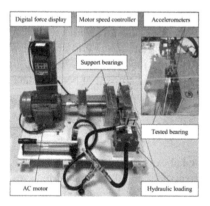

Fig. 2. Bearing testbed

Table 2. Operating conditions of the bearings

Operating condition	Radial force (kN)	Rotating speed (rpm)	Bearing dataset
Condition1	12	2100	Bearing1-1 Bearing1-2 Bearing1-3 Bearing1-4 Bearing1-5
Condition2	11	2250	Bearing2-1 Bearing2-2 Bearing2-3 Bearing2-4 Bearing2-5
Condition3	10	2400	Bearing3-1 Bearing3-2 Bearing3-3 Bearing3-4 Bearing3-5

(a)   (b)   (c)   (d)

Fig. 3. Photos of tested bearings. (a) Normal bearing. (b) Inner race wear. (c) Outer race wear. (d) Outer race fracture

Data sets of Bearing 1–1 and Bearing 1–3 are utilized to verify the effectiveness of the proposed method. Specifically, Bearing 1–3 is used to learn the construction parameters of HI-SCTWF, and Bearing 1–1 is used to test and verify the correctness of the method. Figure 4 shows the horizontal vibration signals of Bearing 1–3 and Bearing 1–1. It can be seen that the whole bearing degradation process consists of two distinct stages, namely: normal operation stage and degradation stage. During the normal operation of the bearing, the generated vibration signals are only random fluctuations with a small amplitude, so it is difficult to obtain information about the running state degradation of the tested bearing. When the bearing runs for a while, it enters the degradation stage. The amplitude of the vibration signal generated by the bearing will increase significantly, and will further increase with the increase of the running time. The vibration signal obtained at this stage contains a large amount of bearing state degradation information. Therefore, when the tested bearing runs to the degraded stage, start RUL prediction.

4.2 Construction of HI-SCTWF

Using the method mentioned above, 28-dimensional original features are extracted from two groups of data respectively. Among the extracted features, some features may have high similarity, which means that the degradation information contained in them is redundant. These characteristics need to be grouped according to their characteristics. The spectral clustering was used to cluster the 28-dimensional data extracted from Bearing 1–3 vibration signals. As cluster number is an important preset parameter in spectral clustering, it plays a crucial role in the final clustering effect and indirectly affects the

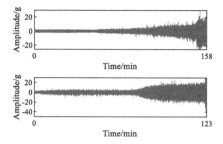

Fig. 4. Vibration signals Bearing 1–3 (above) and Bearing 1–1 (below)

effectiveness of the final constructed health indicators. In this paper, the ratio of between-class distance and within-class distance is used to determine the final cluster number, when this ratio is the largest, the number of clusters is considered to be the optimal value.

It can be seen from Fig. 5 that when the number of clusters is 7, the ratio of inter-class distance after clustering is the largest. Therefore, the number of clusters for the spectral clustering is set to 7. Figure 6 shows the feature clustering results of Bearing 1–3 after spectral clustering, you can see, almost in the same cluster characteristic curve overlapping, that they contain the degradation information is similar, also it can be seen at the same time, some characteristics of the serious stage of failure is sensitive, some features can reflect the early failure of the information, some characteristics and even cannot reflect the status. However, none of these features alone reflects all the information about the degradation process. After the spectral clustering, dimensionality reduction is achieved while more degeneration information is retained. Therefore, only the features with the greatest trendability in the same cluster need to be selected for weighted fusion, and the health indicator after fusion can represent the bearing degradation process. In particular, in this paper, the number p of the normal space in formula 8 is set to 60. Figure 7(a) shows the health indicator chart of Bearing 1–3 in feature-weighted fusion. After obtaining the HI-SCTWF of training Bearing 1–3, the same parameters are used to construct HI-SCTWF on the intercept data of test Bearing 1–1. Figure 7(b) shows the feature-weighted fusion indicator of Bearing 1–1 with the same parameters.

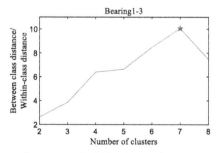

Fig. 5. The ratio of distances between and within classes after spectral clustering of Bearing 1–3

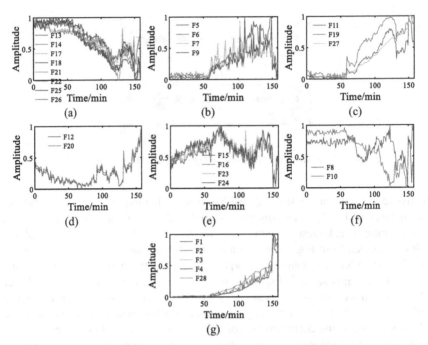

Fig. 6. Feature clustering results of Bearing 1–3 after spectral clustering (a) cluster 1 (b) cluster 2 (c) cluster 3 (d) cluster 4 (e) cluster 5 (f) cluster 6 (g) cluster 7.

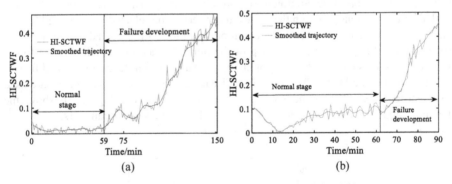

Fig. 7. HI-SCTWF results of Bearing 1–3(a) and 1–1(b)

By comparing Figs. 6 and 7, it can be seen that the comprehensive degradation index contains more degradation information than the original features, and the comprehensive degradation index can more effectively reflect the degradation process of bearings. At the same time, the composite degradation indicator is better and more predictable than any of the original characteristics, as can be seen from the comparison between Fig. 6(g) and Fig. 7(a). On the whole, the features in Fig. 6(g) are the most predictable of all the features, but it is clear that the new HI constructed at the end is more predictable. The degradation indicator of the test bearing is clearly divided into two stages. In the normal stage, its fluctuation is small, which means that the bearing is operating in a normal state. With the increase of running time, the HI curve gradually increases until complete failure. This is also evident in Fig. 7(b), which illustrates this, the feature-weighted fusion degradation indicator model trained by Bearing 1–3 can be well applied to Bearing 1–1.

4.3 Remaining Useful Life Prediction

SVR is a supervised machine learning technology based on the principle of structural risk minimization (SRM). Due to its excellent generalization performance, SVR has been widely used in regression and classification [28]. SVR was used to fit and predict the fusion degradation indicators of Bearing 1–3 and 1–1. The predicted results are shown in Fig. 8(a) and (b). The actual life of training bearing is 150 min, the predicted result is 141 min, and the relative error is −6%. The actual life of test Bearing 1–1 is 90 min, the predicted result is 87 min, and the relative error is −3.3%. The prediction results show that even the simplest prediction method can accurately predict the RUL of bearings according to the health indicators constructed in this paper. The rationality and effectiveness of the health index constructed by the method proposed in this paper are substantiated.

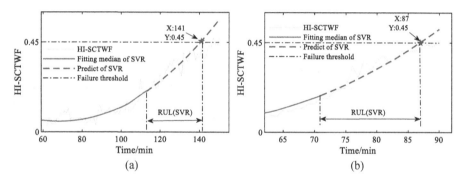

Fig. 8. RUL estimation results using new HI and SVR prognostics approaches (a) Bearing 1–3 (b) Bearing 1–1

4.4 Comparison of Different Health Indicators

To further verify the effectiveness of the health index construction method proposed in this paper, the final HI-SCTWF constructed by Bearing 1–3 is compared with the commonly used degradation characteristic index Root-mean-square value (RMS), as shown in Fig. 9(a). It can be seen from the diagram that HI-SCTWF and RMS have a common starting point of degradation, indicating that the constructed HI-SCTWF effectively characterizes the beginning of bearing degradation. However, it is obvious that the RMS index has a sudden change at the last moment of degradation, while HI-SCTWF always maintains the same degradation trendability, indicating that HI-SCTWF has better predictability of RUL than RMS. Furthermore, HI-SCTWF is compared with the health indicators based on k-means clustering (HI-KMTWF), as shown in Fig. 9(b). Similarly, the two indicators have the same starting point of degradation, but the health indicators based on k-means clustering have a sudden change at the last minute. Obviously, the predictability of the health indicators based on the proposed method is better than that of the health indicators based on k-means clustering.

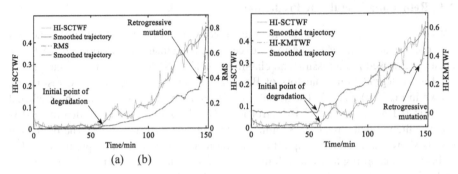

Fig. 9. Comparison of different health indicators (a) Comparison between HI-SCTWF and RMS (b) Comparison between HI-SCTWF and HI-KMTWF

5   Conclusions

Accurate RUL prediction highly depends on the accurate HI that can indicate bearing degradation. In this paper, a new Health Indicator construction approach is proposed and applied in RUL prediction of bearings. Firstly, features are extracted based on signal processing techniques in the time–frequency domain. Secondly, for the shape diversity of the degradation curves of different features during the lifetime, the clustering of features is realized based on the spectral clustering method. Thirdly, based on the trendability indicator, the degradation sensitive features are chosen to constitute the degradation process sensitive feature set. Finally, based on the calculation of trendability indicators of sensitive feature set, health indicators based on the trendability enhancement strategy are calculated, and its performance can be verified through RUL prediction based on SVR. The experimental results show that, compared with the commonly used degradation feature RMS and the health index based on the traditional clustering method (k-means), the health index based on the proposed method can not only fully reflect the degradation process of rolling bearings, but also has a good trendability and can predict the RUL of rolling bearings more effectively.

Acknowledgements. This research was financially supported by National Natural Science Foundation of China (No. 52005335), Shanghai Sailing Program (No. 18YF1417800).

References

1. Lei, Y., Li, N., Guo, L., et al.: Machinery health prognostics: A systematic review from data acquisition to RUL prediction. Mech. Syst. Signal Process. **104**, 799–834 (2018)

2. El-Thalji, I., Jantunen, E.: A summary of fault modelling and predictive health monitoring of rolling element bearings. Mech. Syst. Signal Process. **60–61**, 252–272 (2015)
3. Kumar, A., Kumar, R.: Role of signal processing, modeling and decision making in the diagnosis of rolling element bearing defect: a review. J. Nondestruct. Eval. **38**(1), 5 (2019)
4. Ali, J.B., Chebel-Morello, B., Saidi, L., et al.: Accurate bearing remaining useful life prediction based on Weibull distribution and artificial neural network. Mech. Syst. Signal Process. **56–57**, 150–172 (2015)
5. Rai, A., Kim, J.M.: A novel health indicator based on the Lyapunov exponent, a probabilistic self-organizing map, and the Gini-Simpson index for calculating the RUL of bearings. Measurement **164**, 108002 (2020)
6. Zhu, J., Nostrand, T., Spiegel, C., et al.: Survey of condition indicators for condition monitoring systems. In: Annual Conference of the Prognostic and Health Management Society, vol. 1–13 (2014)
7. Li, N., Lei, Y., Lin, J., et al.: An improved exponential model for predicting remaining useful life of rolling element bearings. IEEE Trans. Industr. Electron. **62**(12), 7762–7773 (2015)
8. Lei, Y., Li, N., Lin, J.: A new method based on stochastic process models for machine remaining useful life prediction. IEEE Trans. Instrum. Meas. **65**(12), 2671–2684 (2016)
9. Yang, H., Sun, Z., Jiang, G., et al.: Remaining useful life prediction for machinery by establishing scaled-corrected health indicators. Measurement **163**, 108035 (2020)
10. Wang, X., Jiang, B., Lu, N.: Adaptive relevant vector machine based RUL prediction under uncertain conditions. ISA Trans. **87**, 217–224 (2019)
11. Chen, C., Xu, T., Wang, G., et al.: Railway turnout system RUL prediction based on feature fusion and genetic programming. Measurement **151**, 107162 (2020)
12. Che, C., Wang, H., Fu, Q., et al.: Combining multiple deep learning algorithms for prognostic and health management of aircraft. Aerosp. Sci. Technol. **94**, 105423 (2019)
13. Li, X., Zhang, W., Ding, Q.: Deep learning-based remaining useful life estimation of bearings using multi-scale feature extraction. Reliab. Eng. Syst. Saf. **182**, 208–218 (2019)
14. Li, H., Wang, W., Huang, P., et al.: Fault diagnosis of rolling bearing using symmetrized dot pattern and density-based clustering. Measurement **152**, 107293 (2020)
15. Yousefi, N., Coit, D.W., Song, S.: Reliability analysis of systems considering clusters of dependent degrading components. Reliab. Eng. Syst. Saf. **202**, 107005 (2020)
16. Liu, J., Li, Q., Chen, W., et al.: A discrete hidden Markov model fault diagnosis strategy based on K-means clustering dedicated to PEM fuel cell systems of tramways. Int. J. Hydrogen Energy **43**(27), 12428–12441 (2018)
17. Baraldi, P., Cannarile, F., Maio, F.D., et al.: Hierarchical k-nearest neighbours classification and binary differential evolution for fault diagnostics of automotive bearings operating under variable conditions. Eng. Appl. Artif. Intell. **56**, 1–13 (2016)
18. Zhang, H., Chen, X., Zhang, X., et al.: Aero-engine bearing fault detection: a clustering low-rank approach. Mech. Syst. Sig. Process. **138**, 106529 (2020)
19. Xiong, Y., Zhang, R., Zhang, F., et al.: A spectra partition algorithm based on spectral clustering for interval variable selection. Infrared Phys. Technol. **105**, 103259 (2020)
20. Gao, M., Shi, G.Y.: Ship-handling behavior pattern recognition using AIS sub-trajectory clustering analysis based on the T-SNE and spectral clustering algorithms. Ocean Eng. **205**, 106919 (2020)
21. Tong, T., Gan, J., Wen, G.: One-step spectral clustering based on self-paced learning. Pattern Recogn. Lett. **135**, 8–14 (2020)
22. Zhu, X., Li, X., Zhang, S.: Graph PCA hashing for similarity search. IEEE Trans Multimedia **19**(9), 2033–2044 (2017)
23. Luxburg, U.V.: A tutorial on spectral clustering. Stat. Comput. **17**(4), 395–416 (2007)

24. Li, N., Lei, Y., Liu, Z., et al.: A particle filtering-based approach for remaining useful life predication of rolling element bearings. In: 2014 International Conference on Prognostics and Health Management, pp. 1–8 (2014)
25. Javed, K., Gouriveau, R., Zerhouni, N., et al.: A feature extraction procedure based on trigonometric functions and cumulative descriptors to enhance prognostics modeling. In: 2013 IEEE Conference on Prognostics and Health Management (PHM), pp. 1–7 (2013)
26. Zhang, B., Zhang, L., Xu, J.: Degradation feature selection for remaining useful life prediction of rolling element bearings. Qual. Reliab. Eng. Int. 32(2), 547–554 (2016)
27. Wang, B., Lei, Y., Li, N., et al.: A hybrid prognostics approach for estimating remaining useful life of rolling element bearings. IEEE Trans. Reliab. 69(1), 401–412 (2020)
28. Ahmad, M.S., Adnan, S.M., Zaidi, S., et al.: A novel support vector regression (SVR) model for the prediction of splice strength of the unconfined beam specimens. Constr. Build. Mater. 248, 118475 (2020)

An Improved Reinforcement Learning for Security-Constrained Economic Dispatch of Battery Energy Storage in Microgrids

Zhongyi Zha, Bo Wang$^{(\boxtimes)}$, Huijin Fan, and Lei Liu

Key Laboratory of Ministry of Education for Image Processing and Intelligent Control, Artificial Intelligence and Automation School, Huazhong University of Science and Technology, Wuhan 430074, China
{m202072829,wb8517,ehjfan,liulei}@hust.edu.cn

Abstract. Battery energy storage systems are widely used in microgrids integrated with volatile energy resources for their ability in peak load shifting. Security constrained economic dispatch over the system's lifecycle is a constrained multi-period stochastic optimization problem, which is intractable. We propose an improved actor-critic-based reinforcement learning combined with a protection layer security control method for this issue, where the distributional critic net is applied to estimate the expected total reward value of a period more accurately, and the policy net with a mask action layer is used to make secure and real-time decision. Additionally, we propose a protection layer to assist the policy net as a secondary control to prevent the unsafe state of microgrids due to the trial-and-error learning of reinforcement learning. Numerical test results show the proposed algorithm can perform better than the conventional economic dispatch and other reinforcement learning algorithms while guaranteeing safe operation.

Keywords: Energy storage · Microgrid · Reinforcement learning · Security constrained economic dispatch · Renewable energy resources

1 Introduction

Due to the rapid depletion of fossil fuels and increased greenhouse gas emissions of conventional generators (CGs), renewable energy resources (RERs) have been widely deployed in microgrids [8,21]. However, with the increasing penetration of RERs into the power system network in recent years, there have been serious concerns over the reliable and satisfactory operation of the power systems [4]. To coordinate the power fluctuations in microgrids caused by the significantly volatile RERs such as wind and photovoltaic (WPV) and electric vehicles (EVs), the energy storage systems (ESSs) and conventional generators (CGs) are needed to overcome these uncertain problems [24]. As simple and efficient ESSs, battery energy storage systems (BESSs) are widely used in microgrids to balance the

H. Zhang et al. (Eds.): NCAA 2021, CCIS 1449, pp. 303–318, 2021.
https://doi.org/10.1007/978-981-16-5188-5_22

power, shave peaks and mitigate the impacts due to the variability and inter-mittency of RERs [6, 11, 15]. Furthermore, Peer to peer (P2P) energy trading allows the BESSs to be discharged in high price periods and charged in low price periods to increase the electricity revenue, namelt econom dispatch [5, 23]. As a result, the security-constrained economic dispatch of BESSs is a key chal-lenge in smart microgrids.

The security-constrained economic dispatch of BESSs aims to minimize the operation cost and ensure the safe operation of the microgrid in the lifecycle of BESSs. The dynamic dispatch of BESSs can be considered as a constrained Markov decision process and modeled as a multi-period stochastic optimiza-tion problem (MSOP) [18]. The conventional method to solve the MSOP is the stochastic programming, which is based on Monte Carlo simulation com-bined with methods of optimization to maximize or minimize the expected value of the objective function [1]. The computational complexity of the stochastic programming method increases exponentially when the number of the scenario of MSOP increases, resulting in huge computational burden. Furthermore, the charging and discharging behavior of the BESSs influence not only the opera-tional costs, but also the life span of the system. In [10], the lifecycle degrada-tion cost of BESSs is simplified to a linear function of the Depth of Discharge (DOD), whereas such a linear approximation method can lead to misestima-tion of the life span, underestimation of the operation cost, and security issues in microgrids. Therefore, the security-constrained economic dispatch that accu-rately models the lifecycle degradation costs of BESSs is a nonconvex and com-putational MSOP.

The Alpha Zero [19] and Alpha Star [20] have manifested the power of rein-forcement learning (RL) as a model-free machine learning method for decision making in complicated environment. Different from the conventional mathemat-ical programming methods, the RL algorithm uses the trial-and-error learning to find the optimal strategy without incorporating detailed on-site information. Besides, the strong representation ability of neural networks helps the deep rein-forcement learning (DRL) algorithm to deal with uncertain problems in random environments. Considering the ability of the actor-critic-based RL algorithm in addressing decision-making tasks of continuous action space, we apply a distri-butional critic net to estimate the cumulative reward value more accurately [22]. A major problem of the RL-based agent in economic dispatch is that the unsafe state of the microgrid can be caused by the trial-and-error learning process. Domain knowledge is a kind of embedded method and has been proved to be effective in combination with RL [3, 7]. The rule-based domain knowledge is numerically expressed through the probabilistic soft logic to ensure the safe operation of microgrids with the RL algorithm [18]. However, due to the unpre-dictability of RERs in the microgrid, the embedding of domain knowledge can not guarantee the security in future states. As a result, this paper not only pro-poses a mask action layer based on domain knowledge to ensure the feasibility of the current action but also a protection layer to conduct secondary control when identifying an omen of unsafe operation of the microgrid. The contributions are summarized as follows.

1. We propose an improved actor-critic-based RL algorithm to solve the uncertainty and real-time decision in the dynamic dispatch problem of BESSs, which is hard for the traditional mathematical method.
2. Domain-knowledge-based rules and secondary control are embedded to guarantee safe operation when applying the RL-based agent as an intelligent controller.
3. We study how the threshold, namely, unsafe-state threshold, in the proposed secondary control and the weights of reward values in RL influence the performance. Several numerical results prove that the proposed algorithm is adaptive and robust.

The remainder of the paper is organized as follows. Section 2 provides the modeling process of MSOP and how to transform it into the environment of the RL algorithm. The improved RL algorithm is introduced in Sect. 3. Experimental comparisons and numerical test results are given in Sect. 4, and Sect. 5 concludes the whole paper.

2   Optimization Problem Modeling

Figure 1(a) shows a simplified model of a grid-connected microgrid integrating BESS and RERs. P_R represents the volatile and intermittent power of RERs, which is the sum of various RER components. P_L and P_D represent the load and distribution grid power respectively. P_B represents the power of BESS, which is the decision variable of the problem. The active power of these components is marked with a positive power flow direction in the figure.

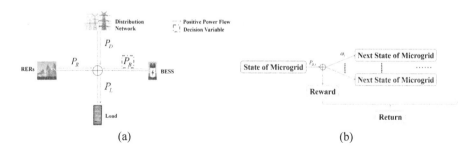

(a)   (b)

Fig. 1. Simplified model of microgrid (a) and MDP for economic dispatch of BESS (b)

2.1   Problem Description

Let t denote the time index. The economic dispatch of BESS can be modeled as a Markov decision process(MDP) (see Fig. 1(b)). Let Q_t denote the power state of each non-dispatchable resource in the microgrid and w_t denote a stochastic factor for the probability in each state over a planning horizon. A scenario $w_t^{t+n} \in \Omega \equiv \Omega_t \times \Omega_{t+1} \times \cdots \times \Omega_{t+n}$ represents a realization of the stochastic process. Let r_t denote the goodness of $P_{B,t}$ in Q_t, and the return over a planning horizon is the objective function of r_t. The Markov decision process is modeled as follows.

$$\mathbb{S} = Q = P_D \times P_R \times P_L \tag{1}$$

$$\delta : \mathbb{S} \times P_B \times \Omega \to \mathbb{S} \iff Q_{t+1} = \delta(Q_t, P_{B,t}, w_t) \tag{2}$$

$$R : \mathbb{S} \times P_B \to \mathbb{R} \iff r_t = R(Q_t, P_{B,t}) \tag{3}$$

The uncertainties of $P_{R,t}, P_{L,t}$ are modeled as shown below.

$$P_{R,t} = max(\overline{P}_{R,t} + \Delta\xi_{PV} + \Delta\xi_{WT}, 0)$$
$$P_{L,t} = \overline{P}_{L,t} + \Delta\xi_L$$
$$\Delta\xi \sim N(\mu_\xi, \sigma_\xi) \tag{4}$$

The objective function is formulated as follows, where $\gamma \in [0,1]$ is the discount factor.

$$f = \max_{P_B} R(Q_t, P_{B,t}) + \gamma \mathbb{E}_{w_t}[\max_{P_B} R(\hat{Q}_{t+1}, P_{B,t+1}) +$$

$$\gamma \mathbb{E}_{w_{t+1}|w_t}[\max_{P_B} R(\hat{Q}_{t+2}, P_{B,t+2}) + \cdots +$$

$$\gamma \mathbb{E}_{w_{t+n-2}|w_{t+n-3}}[\max_{P_B} R(\hat{Q}_{t+n-1}, P_{B,t+n-2})]\cdots]] \tag{5}$$

Considering the power constraints in the microgrid, the model is transformed into a constrained Markov decision-making process. The main constraints are as follows.

$$P_{L,t} = P_{D,t} + P_{R,t} + P_{B,t} \tag{6}$$

$$P_{D,t}^{min} \leqslant P_{D,t} = P_{L,t} - (P_{R,t} + P_{B,t}) \leqslant P_{D,t}^{max} \tag{7}$$

$$P_B^{min} \leqslant P_{B,t} \leqslant P_B^{max} \tag{8}$$

$$SOC^{min} \leqslant SOC_t = SOC_{t-1}(1 - \sigma) - \eta \frac{P_{B,t}T}{C_a V} \leqslant SOC^{max} \tag{9}$$

Let σ, η denote the battery self-discharge rate and battery charging or discharging efficiency respectively, and $C_a V$ the capacity of the battery. The battery state of charge(SOC) is formulated as (9).

Constraints (6)-(9) formulate the constraints of P_B in the Markov decision process for the dynamic dispatch of BESS. To obtain the optimal security-constrained economic dispatch, the challenge is how to solve this intricate MSOP.

2.2   Modeling for Reinforcement Learning

Reinforcement learning is a model-free machine learning method, that is, for the above MSOP, the state transition function δ is unnecessary to be identified. The first step is to transform MSOP into the RL algorithm model (i.e., the state, action, and reward).

State. In the Markov process model, the state Q_t is considered as the power of non-dispatchable components. Considering that the state of the RL model is the input of the neural network, it must be adjusted to fit the learning of the neural network.

In [14], DeepMind suggested four frames of the game as input to the neural network, and the input should include notable features of the environment as much as possible. Therefore, the state is modeled as follows:

$$Ob_t = (P_{D,t}, P_{R,t}, P_{L,t}, SOC_t, P_{D,t}^{set}, c_t) \tag{10}$$

$$S_t = (Ob_{t-3}, Ob_{t-2}, Ob_{t-1}, Ob_t)^T \tag{11}$$

In (10), in addition to the variables from (6)-(9), we introduce $P_{D,t}^{set}$ that denotes the targeted grid power that is expected to maintain at, and c_t the time-of-use tariff (TOU). Ob_t represents the observation of the microgrid at time t. The input vector of the neural network is S_t, which is composed of four consecutive observations.

Action. The action of the RL model is the charging and discharging power of the BESS.

$$a_t = P_{B,t} \tag{12}$$

Reward. The reward value of the RL model indicates the aim of the task in the environment. It is a kind of Markov reward process described by (3). Considering the security-constraints during economic dispatch, the reward value consists of three parts as follows:

$$r_t = \underbrace{a_1 r_{c,t}}_{revenue} + \underbrace{a_2 r_{f,t}}_{fluctuation} + \underbrace{a_3 r_{d,t}}_{degradation} \tag{13}$$

where a_1, a_2, a_3 are the weights of the different parts. r_c is the electricity revenue generated by leveraging the TOU tariff. Given $[x]_+ = max(x, 0)$, r_c is formulated as follows:

$$r_{c,t} = \begin{cases} c_t P_{B,t} T, P_{B,t} \geq 0 \\ -c_t [P_{D,t} - P_{L,t}]_+ T, P_{B,t} \leq 0 \end{cases} \tag{14}$$

r_f is the penalty for the fluctuation of the distribution grid.

$$r_{f,t} = -\left| P_{D,t} - P_{D,t}^{set} \right| \tag{15}$$

r_d is the degradation cost of the BESS due to lifecycle degradation [18]. The kinetic battery model [9,13] treats the battery as a "two tank" system and is assumed in this study to find the relationship between life-cycle throughput and SOC of the BESS. The relationship between throughput (ϑ_{life}), cycles to failure (N) and DOD ($DOD + SOC = 1$) of batteries are depicted in [10] and can be fitted as following non-convex mathematical model [10,12]:

$$N(DOD) = N(DOD = 0.8) \times e^{\rho(0.8 - DOD)} \tag{16}$$

$$\vartheta_{life} = N \times DOD \times \frac{C_a V}{1000} \tag{17}$$

where ρ is an empirical parameter and can be identified from the two points of the actual experimental curve. From (16),(17), the relationship between life-cycle throughput and SOC of the BESS is formulated as follows:

$$\vartheta_{life,t} = N_{0.8} \times e^{\rho SOC_t}(1 - SOC_t) \times \frac{C_a V}{1000} \tag{18}$$

At each charging and discharging moment, the degradation of BESS is measured by $\frac{|P_{B,t}T|}{2\vartheta_{life,t}}$. let C denote the investment cost of BESS and the aim is to extend the life span of BESS, which is related to $-r_d$, so r_d is formulatet as follows:

$$r_{d,t} = -\frac{|P_{B,t}T|}{2\vartheta_{life,t}}C \tag{19}$$

3   Proposed Algorithm

RL algorithm based on the actor-critic framework can effectively solve the continuous action space problem and make decisions in real-time. The key challenge to achieve a smart RL agent is the design of policy function and value function. Considering the neural network as an efficient representation function to deal with uncertainty, the state in the RL environment is applied as the input of a one-dimensional convolution neural network (CNN) to extract features, and two neural networks(i.e., policy net and critic net) with the same structure are applied as an approximation of policy function and value function(see Fig. 2). The distributional critic net method is applied in the improved actor-critic algorithm to estimate the total reward value more accurately [22]. Moreover, due to the trial-and-error learning method of RL, the mask action layer with domain knowledge-based rules is connected to the policy net output to ensure the current safe operation, and the protection layer as a secondary control method is proposed to guarantee the future safe operation.

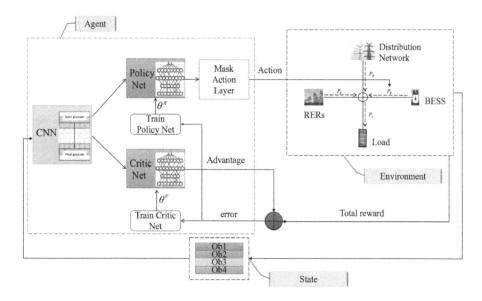

Fig. 2. Simplified block diagram of the proposed reinforcement learning scheme.

3.1 Policy Net with Domain-Knowledge-Based Rules

Actor-critic algorithm for Markov decision processes is a kind of machine learning method. After $n+1$ steps of agent interaction with RL environment, a trajectory $\tau = (s_t, a_t, r_t, s_{t+1}, a_{t+1}, r_{t+1}, \cdots s_{t+n}, a_{t+n}, r_{t+n}) \in \Gamma$ is generated. Let $\Theta = \theta^\pi \times \theta^V$ denote the parameters of the neural networks (i.e., policy net with CNN and critic net with CNN), policy net π gives the probability of the trajectory as follows:

$$p(\tau) = \prod_{i=0}^{n} p_{\theta^\pi}(a_{t+i} \mid s_{t+i}) = \prod_{i=0}^{n} \pi_{\theta^\pi}(a_{t+i} \mid s_{t+i}) \qquad (20)$$

The performance of τ is computed as $R_{\theta^\pi}(\tau) = \sum_{i=0}^{n} \gamma^i r_{t+i}$. Thus the optimal goal of the policy net is : $\theta^\pi = \arg \max_{\theta^\pi} \mathbb{E}_{\tau \sim \Gamma}(R_{\theta^\pi}(\tau))$. Based on Expectation Maximization(EM) Algorithm [16], the gradient of policy net in each episode is formulated as follows:

$$\nabla \mathbb{E}_{\tau \sim \Gamma}(R_{\theta^\pi}(\tau)) \approx \frac{1}{M} \sum_{m=1}^{M} \sum_{i=0}^{n} R_{\theta^\pi}(\tau_{t+i}^m) \nabla log(p_{\theta^\pi}(a_{t+i}^m \mid s_{t+i}^m)) \qquad (21)$$

where $R_{\theta^\pi}(\tau_{t+i}^m)$ is a cumulative reward value (return) obtained from a sampling trajectory. Obviously, this value is an unbiased estimation of $\mathbb{E}_{\tau \sim \Gamma}(R_{\theta^\pi}(\tau))$ but with great variance. Therefore, the critic net V_{θ^V} is added to mitigate the variance and $R_{\theta^\pi}(\tau_{t+i}^m)$ is replaced with advantage function A_t, which represent the deviation between the total reward value and the base value of the current policy, in order to train the policy net more efficiently.

$$\mathbb{E}_{\tau \sim \Gamma}(R_{\theta^\pi}(\tau_t)) \approx V_{\theta^V}(s_t) \tag{22}$$

$$A_t^{(n)} = r_t + \gamma r_{t+1} + \cdots + \gamma^n V_{\theta^V}(s_{t+n}) - V_{\theta^V}(s_t) \tag{23}$$

In [17], Shulman et al. verified the increase of $n+1$ steps led to the decrease of the bias of $A_t^{(n+1)}$ but the increase of variance. To balance the bias and variance, they proposed General Advantage Estimation (GAE) as follows:

$$A_t^{GAE(\lambda,\gamma,n)} = (1-\lambda) \sum_{i=1}^{n} \lambda^{i-1} A_t^{(i)} \tag{24}$$

where $\lambda \in (0,1)$ represents the balancing process of variance and bias.

$\pi_{\theta^\pi}(\cdot \mid s_t) \in [0,1]^k$ is a discrete probability distribution of charging or discharging action with the range of P_B^{min} and P_B^{max} according to the disptach problem (8) of BESSs. k is the output dimension of the critic net and is set to 500 to approximate continuous action. At time t, the agent performs a_t by sampling a_t according to the $\pi_{\theta^\pi}(\cdot \mid s_t)$.

$$P_{B,t} = a_t \sim \pi_{\theta^\pi}(\cdot \mid s_t) \tag{25}$$

However, not all $P_{B,t}$ can satisfy the constraints (7) and (9) at the same time. So we propose a mask action layer with domain knowledge based rules to make feasible explorations. Let $\Phi_{A,t}$ and $\Phi_{B,t}$ denote the sets of actions P_B satisfying (7) and (9) at s_t. Based on domain knowledge, we set two hard rules and one soft rule according to constraint(7) and (9) as follows:

$$\begin{cases} \phi_{h,1}(a_t) = I_{\Phi_{A,t}}(a_t \mid s_t) \\ \phi_{h,2}(a_t) = I_{\Phi_{B,t}}(a_t \mid s_t) \\ \phi_{s,1}(a_t) = e^{-\frac{|P_{D,t}-P_{D,t}^{set}|}{P_{D,t}^{set}}} \end{cases} \tag{26}$$

where $I_A(x)$ is indicator function. Based on these mapping functions, we propose two hard mask action layers (Ψ_A, Ψ_B) and one soft mask action layer (Ψ_C). The mapping relation of hard mask action layer is $\phi_h : P_B \rightarrow \{0,1\}^k$, and that of soft mask action layer is $\phi_s : P_B \rightarrow [0,1]^k$. They have the same size as $\pi_{\theta^\pi}(\cdot \mid s_t)$. In Fig. 2, it is connected after $\pi_{\theta^\pi}(\cdot \mid s_t)$ to generate a set of feasible actions $\mathbb{A}_f$ as follows:

$$\mathbb{A}_{f,t} = \pi_{\theta^\pi}(\cdot \mid s_t) \odot \Psi_{A,t} \odot \Psi_{B,t} \odot \Psi_{C,t} \tag{27}$$

$$P_{B,t} = a_{f,t} \sim \mathbb{A}_{f,t}(\cdot \mid s_t) \tag{28}$$

Let α denote the learning rate, the law for training the policy net is formulated as follows:

$$g_\pi = \frac{1}{M} \sum_{m=1}^{M} \sum_{i=0}^{n} A_{t+i}^{GAE(\lambda,\gamma,n+1)} \nabla_{\theta^\pi} \log\left(\frac{\pi_{\theta^\pi}(a_{f,t+i}^m \mid s_{t+i}^m)}{\sum \mathbb{A}_{f,t}}\right) \tag{29}$$

$$\theta^\pi \leftarrow \theta^\pi + \alpha g_\pi \tag{30}$$

3.2   Distributional Critic Net

The policy net directly determines the performance of the agent. From (29), it indicates that the advantage value A^{GAE} influences the updating direction of the policy net. (23) and (24) show A^{GAE} has a linear relationship with the output $V_{\theta^V}(s_t)$ of the critic net. As a result, the performance of the agent greatly depends on the predictive ability of the critic net, i.e., (22).

The traditional method applies the least square error as the loss function, but this method does not consider the consistency of statistical information. However, if the statistics of each case are collected to obtain the maximum likelihood estimation, the computation is quite large. When using the empirical method to estimate the probability, if the number of samples accounts for a large proportion of the total, the update rate of new probability will be smaller when the new samples come. This is consistent with the concept that the larger the value is, the smaller the derivative is in the softmax classification function. Therefore, we propose a distributional critic net to retain statistical information.

In the distributional critic net, the output $e(R_t \mid s_t)$ of the network is a probability distribution about the return value and each probability of the return value at s_t is $e(R_t^j \mid s_t)$, so $V_{\theta^V}(s_t) = \frac{\sum_{j=1}^{l} e(R_t^j \mid s_t)}{l}$, where l is the size of the output. In order to avoid the empirical method with huge storage to describe the probability distribution, we transform the sampling return value into the probability distribution $\widehat{e}(r_t)$ and calculate the Kullback-Leibler divergence between it and $e(R_t^m \mid s_t)$ as follows:

$$
\widehat{e}(R_t) = \begin{cases} R_t - [R_t] & , R = [R_t] + 1 \\ 1 - (R_t - [R_t]) & , R = [R_t] \\ 0 & , otherwise \end{cases} \tag{31}
$$

$$
g_V = \frac{1}{M} \sum_{m=1}^{M} \sum_{i=0}^{n} \nabla_{\theta^V} \sum_{j=1}^{l} \widehat{e}^m(R_{t+i}^j) \frac{\widehat{e}^m(R_{t+i}^j)}{e_{\theta^V}^m(R_{t+i}^j)} \tag{32}
$$

$$
\theta^V \leftarrow \theta^V - \alpha g_V \tag{33}
$$

3.3   Protection Layer Control Method

The feasible action set $\mathbb{A}_{f,t}$ gives all the feasible actions of the agent at a certain time. However, due to the intermittence and uncertainty of RERs, $\mathbb{A}_{f,t}$ may be empty set ϕ, i.e., the unsafe state of microgrid after continuous feasible action (Fig. 3). To prevent the agent from making the microgrid in an unsafe state, we propose a secondary control method to replace the agent based on the RL algorithm when the microgrid is in a potentially unsafe state.

In the dynamic dispatch problem of BESSs, the sizing problem of BESSs has a great impact on the safe operation of the microgrid and should be considerd [2]. The BESSs with large capacity can effectively deal with the intermittent and uncertainty of RERs, at the cost of huge capital investment, and vice versa. Therefore, the state of charge (SOC) of BESS is used to reflect the potential unsafe state of the microgrid. When SOC exceeds the threshold, the agent applies the secondary control method based on protection layer control to dispatch the BESS as follows:

$$P_{B,t} = \begin{cases} max\Phi_{A,t} \cap \Phi_{B,t} \ , SOC_t > SOC_{threshold,max} \\ min\Phi_{A,t} \cap \Phi_{B,t} \ , SOC_t < SOC_{threshold,min} \end{cases} \tag{34}$$

Equation (34) describes the dispatch rules in the potential unsafe state. The agent chooses the feasible action according to (7) and (9) to maximize the charging or discharging power to escape from the potential unsafe state. In a reasonable threshold setting range, the agent can securely dispatch the BESS to ensure the safe operation of the microgrid.

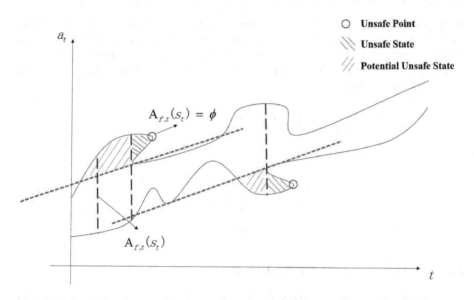

Fig. 3. The potential insecurity caused by the intermittence and uncertainty of renewable energy resources.

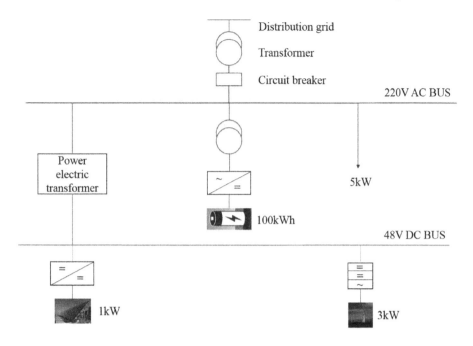

Distribution grid

Transformer

Circuit breaker

220V AC BUS

Power electric transformer

5kW

100kWh

48V DC BUS

1kW

3kW

Fig. 4. Description of the hybrid AC/DC microgrid.

4 Case Study

A microgrid system based on HOMER PRO simulation is provided to conduct case studies [9]. In Subsection A, the energy, load, and storage system in the microgrid are introduced in detail. In Subsection B, various experiments are conducted to verify in detail the performance of the proposed algorithm.

4.1 System Description

Figure 4 represents the hybrid solar–wind system with battery storage. The system mainly consists of photovoltaic (PV), wind turbine (WT), BESS, inverter, and other accessory devices and distribution cables. The rated output power of PV and WT are 3 kW and 1 kW, respectively. The average annual power of the residential load is 5 kW. Weather data including humidity, temperature, wind, and light intensity are provided by HOMER and collected in Wuhan, Hubei Province, China.

The BESS is a 100 kWh lead-acid battery pack and battery parameters are shown in Table 1. In this paper, the main research problem is the dynamic dispatch problem of BESSs and the sizing optimization problem of BESSs is not considered, so the capacity of the BESS is selected as 100 kWh in all case studies refer to [18]. The TOU tariffs are referenced from the actual tariffs in China(i.e. 1.02/kWh from 8:00–22:00; 0.51/kWh for the rest).

Table 1. Battery parameters

Symbol	Quantity	Value
σ	Battery self-discharge rate	4×10^{-5}
η	Battery charging/Discharging efficiency	0.9
$C_a V$	Capacity of the battery	100 kWh
SOC^{min}	Minimum state of charge	0.0
SOC^{max}	Maximum state of charge	1.0
P_B^{min}	Minimum power of the battery	-10 kW
P_B^{max}	Maximum power of the battery	10 kW
ρ	Empirical parameter in the $\vartheta_{life,t}$ function	1.5
$N_{0.8}$	Cycles to failure when $DOD = 0.8$	3000
C	Investment cost of the BESS	2×10^5

4.2 Numerical Results

We apply the agent based on the improved RL algorithm to deal with the problem of intelligent dynamic dispatch of the BESS in the microgrid described in section A. We set the power supply of the distributed grid $P_{D,t}^{set}$ to the median of the residential load power every month, and the planning period is set as one month, that is, $n = 720$. Then we conduct 3 numerical studies as follows. In each study, we fix the policy net and pre-train the critic net for 200 episodes to initial the critic net.

Firstly, we test the influence of different discount coefficients (γ, λ) of GAE method on the agent based on the distributional critic net method to find out the better strategy. Figure 5 shows performance of different discount factors (γ, λ) over a planning period. Figure 5(a) describes the score $(\sum_{t=1}^{720} r_t)$ in 1000 training episodes. We select four γ values(0.9,0.8,0.7,0.6) and four λ values(0.95,0.9,0.85,0.8) for 16 experiments refer to [17]. In Fig. 5(b), the heat graph shows the performance of the agents under each discount coefficient and lighter color indicates better performance. In the heat graph, the results show that when γ value is 0.6 to 0.7 and λ value is 0.9 to 0.95 in (24), the agent can better balance the bias and variance of the return value in the dispatch problem of BESS in this microgrid system. In this dispatch problem, we set the planning period to 720, that is, one month. The experimental results also show that the discount coefficient factors (γ, λ) in GAE method can influence the performance of the agent for different periodic policy problems and we can find a better strategy by adjusting the discount coefficient.

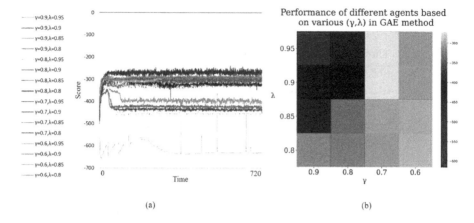

(a)   (b)

Fig. 5. Performance of different discount factors (γ, λ) based agents over a planning period.

Secondly, we study the threshold value in the protection layer control method to find a better threshold value under the protection layer control method to ensure that the agent can achieve security economic dispatch in the microgrid system. Table 2 shows the number of completing security control of the BESS in the microgrid system and the performance of the agents over a period during 1000 training episodes under different threshold settings($SOC_{threshold,max}, SOC_{threshold,min}$) in the protection layer control method. The results in Table 2 show that the threshold setting can guarantee the agent to securely dispatch the BESS over a dispatch period. The wider the threshold range, the agent can apply the RL method to perform dispatching, but it is easier to make the microgrid into an unsafe state. The narrow threshold range makes the agent get out of the potential dangerous state as soon as possible. However, because of the use of regular control, the performance of the agent is reduced. Therefore, the protection layer control method can ensure the safe operation of the microgrid based on RL, and reasonable selection can maintain the performance of the agent. In our experiments, we choose the threshold of (0.7,0.3) to ensure the security-constrained dispatch of the agent. Figure 6 describes the power curves of the components in the microgrid system over a part-time period with thresholds of (0.7, 0.3) and (0.85, 0.15). In the power curve with the threshold value of (0.85,0.15), it can be seen that the SOC of the BESS is always close to SOC^{min} or SOC^{max}, but the agent can not recognize this state, which may lead to an unsafe state due to the uncertainty of RERs. Although the protection layer control method can partly solve this problem, the method to identify the potential unsafe state and the control method is regular dispatch methods, which make the agent not achieve the optimal control. The problem will be studied in the future.

Table 2. Number of completing security control and the best performance over a period

Threshold value	Number	Percentage	Best performance
(0.6,0.4)	1000	100%	−354.2
(0.65,0.35)	1000	100%	−311.66
(0.7,0.3)	1000	100%	−250.3
(0.8,0.2)	761	76.1%	−245.3
(0.85,0.15)	15	1.5%	−241.2

Finally, we compare the performance of agents based on the proposed algorithm, regular dispatch method, random dispatch method, and traditional AC algorithm under the same hyperparameters and mask action layer and protection layer control method are used to all algorithm to ensure the safe operation of the microgrid. We apply the agent which is trained after 1000 episodes to the microgrid system and take the average value of 100 experimental results as the performance of each agent to reduce the variance of the experiment. In Fig. 7, the performance of four different methods based agents is depicted in four colors. $R_c = \Sigma_{t=1}^{720} r_{c,t}$ represents the total revenue of microgrid, $R_f = \Sigma_{t=1}^{720} r_{f,t}$ represents the sum of the absolute difference between the power supply and the expected power supply of the distributed power grid (i.e., the degree of fluctuation of the distributed power grid), $R_d = \Sigma_{t=1}^{720} r_{d,t}$ represents the degradation cost of the BESS during a dispatch period, and $R = R_c + R_f + R_f$ represents the comprehensive performance. The regular dispatch method can achieve no fluctuation dispatch, but it causes great degradation to the BESS and can not achieve the economic dispatch of high price battery discharging and low price charging. The agent based on the random dispatch method is the same structure as the proposed method except that it does not update the policy net and the rest. The agent based on the traditional AC method achieves only 9% performance improvement than the random dispatch method while the agent based on the proposed method greatly improves by 35%.

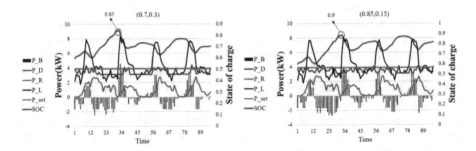

Fig. 6. The power of the components in the microgrid system and SOC of the BESS over a part-time period with thresholds of (0.7, 0.3) and (0.85, 0.15).

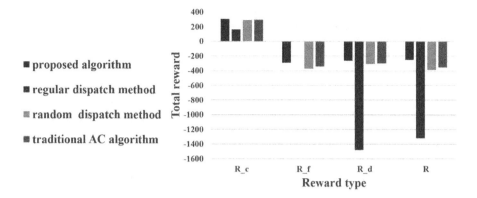

Fig. 7. Performance of different method based agents over a planning period.

5   Conclusion

In this paper, we propose an improved AC algorithm for security-constrained economic dispatch of the BESS in the microgrid system, to ensure the safe operation of the microgrid and achieve economic and energy saving at the same time. The results show that the agent based on the proposed method can earn 20% higher performance than the traditional method, and it can ensure the 100% safe operation of the microgrid in investigated cases. In the future, we will apply the RL algorithm to more complex microgrid systems. For our proposed protection layer control method, we will study a more intelligent method to predict and identify the potential unsafe state of the microgrid to avoid the empty feasible action set of the agent. Additionally, for the weights setting of the reward value, we will study a better and reasonable group of weights of reward value combined with the multi-objective optimization to make the agent perform better.

Acknowledgement. This research is surpported by state grid corporation of China headquarters science and technology project (grant number: 5100-202099522A-0-0-00)

References

1. Birge, J.R., Louveaux, F.: Introduction to Stochastic Programming. Springer Science & Business Media (2011). 10.1007/978-1-4614-0237-4
2. Carpinelli, G., Fazio, D., Rita, A., Khormali, S., Mottola, F.: Optimal sizing of battery storage systems for industrial applications when uncertainties exist. Energies **7**, 130–149 (2014)
3. Christiano, P.F., Leike, J., Brown, T., Martic, M., Legg, S., Amodei, D.: Deep reinforcement learning from human preferences. Adv. Neural Inform. Process. Syst. **30**, 4299–4307 (2017)
4. Divya, K., Østergaard, J.: Battery energy storage technology for power systems–an overview. Electr. Power Syst. Res. **79**(4), 511–520 (2009)

5. Eseye, A.T., Lehtonen, M., Tukia, T., Uimonen, S., Millar, R.J.: Optimal energy trading for renewable energy integrated building microgrids containing electric vehicles and energy storage batteries. IEEE Access **7**, 106092–106101 (2019)
6. Hill, C.A., Such, M.C., Chen, D., Gonzalez, J., Grady, W.M.: Battery energy storage for enabling integration of distributed solar power generation. IEEE Trans. Smart Grid **3**(2), 850–857 (2012)
7. Huang, J., Wu, F., Precup, D., Cai, Y.: Learning safe policies with expert guidance. In: Advances in Neural Information Processing Systems, pp. 9105–9114 (2018)
8. Keirstead, J., Jennings, M., Sivakumar, A.: A review of urban energy system models: approaches, challenges and opportunities. Renew. Sustain. Energy Rev. **16**(6), 3847–3866 (2012)
9. Lambert, T., Gilman, P., Lilienthal, P.: Micropower system modeling with homer. Integr. Altern. Sour. Energy **1**(1), 379–385 (2006)
10. Liu, C., Wang, X., Wu, X., Guo, J.: Economic scheduling model of microgrid considering the lifetime of batteries. IET Gener. Trans. Distrib. **11**(3), 759–767 (2017)
11. Luo, X., Wang, J., Dooner, M., Clarke, J.: Overview of current development in electrical energy storage technologies and the application potential in power system operation. Appl. Energ. **137**, 511–536 (2015)
12. Ma, T., Yang, H., Lu, L.: A feasibility study of a stand-alone hybrid solar-wind-battery system for a remote island. Appl. Energ. **121**, 149–158 (2014)
13. Manwell, J.F., McGowan, J.G.: Lead acid battery storage model for hybrid energy systems. Solar Energ. **50**(5), 399–405 (1993)
14. Mnih, V., Kavukcuoglu, K., Silver, D., Graves, A., Antonoglou, I., Wierstra, D., Riedmiller, M.: Playing atari with deep reinforcement learning. arXiv preprint arXiv:1312.5602 (2013)
15. Nair, N.K.C., Garimella, N.: Battery energy storage systems: assessment for small-scale renewable energy integration. Energ. Build. **42**(11), 2124–2130 (2010)
16. Nechyba, M.: Maximum-likelihood estimation for mixture models: the em algorithm. EEL6935 Fall (2001)
17. Schulman, J., Moritz, P., Levine, S., Jordan, M., Abbeel, P.: High-dimensional continuous control using generalized advantage estimation. arXiv preprint arXiv:1506.02438 (2015)
18. Shang, Y., et al.: Stochastic dispatch of energy storage in microgrids: an augmented reinforcement learning approach. Appl. Energ. **261**, 114423 (2020)
19. Silver, D., et al.: Mastering the game of go without human knowledge. Nature **550**(7676), 354–359 (2017)
20. Vinyals, O., et al.: Grandmaster level in starcraft ii using multi-agent reinforcement learning. Nature **575**(7782), 350–354 (2019)
21. Wu, J., Yan, J., Jia, H., Hatziargyriou, N., Djilali, N., Sun, H.: Integrated energy systems. Appl. Energ. **167**, 155–157 (2016)
22. Zha, Z.Y., Wang, B., Tang, X.S.: Evaluate, explain, and explore the state more exactly: an improved actor-critic algorithm for complex environment. Neural Comput. Appl. **4**, 1–12 (2021)
23. Zhang, C., Wu, J., Zhou, Y., Cheng, M., Long, C.: Peer-to-peer energy trading in a microgrid. Appl. Energ. **220**, 1–12 (2018)
24. Zia, M.F., Elbouchikhi, E., Benbouzid, M.: Microgrids energy management systems: a critical review on methods, solutions, and prospects. Appl. Energ. **222**, 1033–1055 (2018)

Self-supervised Learning Advance Fault Diagnosis of Rotating Machinery

Baoming Zhang[1], Yongfang Mao[1(✉)], Xin Chen[1], Yi Chai[1], and Zhenli Yang[2]

[1] Chongqing University, Chongqing 400044, China
{baomingzhang,yfm,201813021035,chaiyi}@cqu.edu.cn
[2] Chongqing Special Equipment Inspection and Research Institute, Chongqing 401121, China

Abstract. Although the approach of using a large number of unlabeled data in self-supervised pre-training and followed by a supervised fine-tuning has achieved success in image recognition, it has received limited attention in fault diagnosis and analysis. On one hand, due to the weakness of early features and various unseen failure modes, it is quite hard to get the label of collecting data. On the other hand, under the strong noise environment, the representation of time and frequency features of original vibration signals is important to improve the performance of fault diagnosis. To construct more information of positive pairs for self-supervised learning, a self-supervised fault detection approach named WT-MICLe for mechanical systems is presented in this paper based on Wavelet Transform (WT), Multi-Instance Contrastive Learning (MICLe), and Residual Neural Network (ResNet). To begin with, WT is applied to extracting features from original signals. Then, visual representations are constructed for self-supervised learning by using MICLe. We present the proposed self-supervised method for fault diagnosis based on contrastive learning. The experiment is implemented to assess the effectiveness of the approach. With a few labeled data, the results overall have shown that the proposed self-supervised approach for fault diagnosis is robust.

Keywords: Self-supervised learning · Contrastive learning · Wavelet transform · Fault diagnosis

1 Introduction

In machine learning, learning from limited labeled data is a problem, which is especially important for fault diagnosis and fault data analysis. Without human supervision is a long-term problem in learning effective visual representations, and most mainstream approaches fall into the generative model or discriminative model.

(1) Generative approaches learn to generate at the pixel level in the input space [1–3], but pixels generation is expensive in computation and not necessary for representation learning.
(2) Discriminative approaches learn representations by using objective functions which are similar to methods used for supervised learning. However, training networks

© Springer Nature Singapore Pte Ltd. 2021
H. Zhang et al. (Eds.): NCAA 2021, CCIS 1449, pp. 319–332, 2021.
https://doi.org/10.1007/978-981-16-5188-5_23

perform pretext tasks where both the inputs and labels are derived from an unlabeled dataset. Many such approaches are based on pretext tasks from heuristics [4, 5]. They may limit the ability for learning general representations.

Based on contrastive learning, discriminative approaches have recently shown great promise and achieve state-of-the-art results in image recognition [6–8]. Especially when labeled samples are scarce, two common approaches always conduct to learn from limited labeled data:

(1) Pretraining on large labeled datasets, such as ImageNet or CIFAR-10, by using supervised approaches.
(2) Using contrastive learning to conduct self-supervised pretraining [9, 10] on unlabeled data, and applying supervised fine-tuning on the target labeled dataset after pretraining.

Compared with supervised approaches, self-supervised approaches are attractive because they enable the use of unlabeled domain-specific data and learn more relevant representations during pretraining. Contrastive self-supervised approaches, such as discrimination [11], contrastive predictive coding (CPC) [12], Deep info Max [13], Momentum Contrast (MoCo) [14], Pretext-invariant representations (PIRL) [15], these methoda are used to achieve classification accuracy by making use of end-to-end supervised training. Specifically, one can pretrain in a task-agnostic followed by fine-tuning on the task-specific way [9, 16]. Chen et al. [10] show that with little loss on the accuracy, the origin encoder can be distilled into a smaller model. Recently, these methods have been applied to improve label efficiency for semi-supervised learning.

Nowadays, the most generally used approaches for fault diagnosis can be classified into analytic model-based, knowledge-based, and data-driven methods. The rapid progress of artificial intelligence accelerates the development of fault diagnosis techniques [17–19]. Because of lacking annotation to the failure data, it's quite hard for the general approaches to extract fault features and achieve high accuracy of fault diagnosis. To construct more informative positive pairs for self-supervised learning and solve the aforementioned problems, we apply wavelet transform (WT), multi-instance contrastive learning (MICLe) [20] as the failure detection method for rotating machinery in this paper. In our proposed approach, WT is employed for extracting two-dimension (2-D) time-frequency features from one-dimension (1-D) original signals. MICLe, which uses multiple images of the faults (bearing damages), is used to leverage the potential availability of multiple images per failure condition.

In this paper, we study self-supervised learning on bearing signal classification tasks. In order to descript the varieties of bearing damages and the interaction of different causes and conditions, the six main damages are categorized as follows: fatigue, wear, corrosion, electrical erosion, plastic deformation, and fracture and cracking. Each damage can exist at the inner and outer ring (IR & OR) of the ball bearing [19] (Fig. 1).

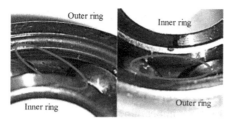

Fig. 1. Indentation at the raceway of the outer ring and small pitting at the raceway of the inner ring

2 Methods

2.1 Wavelet Transform for Data Pre-processing

Compared with 1-D signal, images are 2-D data matrix will carry and represent more powerful information because of the more complex structure distributions. In general, traditional 1-D analysis always faces difficulty in getting the original pattern of failure states. Compared with 1-D signals, images are relatively easy for researchers to learn information, so using 2-D images to represent feature information will be more appropriate [21, 22].

Various approaches have been employed to get time-frequency (T-F) images, such as Wigner-Vile distribution, short-time Fourier transform, and wavelet transform. With the increase of frequency, the sampling interval in the time domain descends. However, the size of windows of short-time Fourier transform has to be fixed, and Wigner-Vile distribution can lead to the cross item problem. Consequently, we apply wavelet transform to extract features from 1-D signals because of its ability to extracting time–frequency features at different scales or resolutions from non-periodic and transient signals. A general wavelet transform can representations as follows:

$$W_\varphi(a, b) = \frac{1}{\sqrt{a}} \int x(t)\varphi^*\left(\frac{t - b}{a}\right)dt, \ a > 0 \tag{1}$$

where $x(t)$ is the given time series, $\varphi(\cdot)$ represents the mother of wavelet, $\varphi^*(\cdot)$ is the complex conjugate of $\varphi(\cdot)$, a is the scaling factor, and b is the translation factor to confirm its location [23].

The selection of wavelet basis function (WBF) is straightly relevant to the quality of data processing and feature extraction. To process signals more appropriately, choosing wavelet basis function (WBF) is the most important thing. Generally, we consider multiple properties to select basis function, such as orthogonal, compact support, and symmetry [24]. When wavelet transform is used to process impulsive signals, it expresses as a convolution of signal and WBF. If the waveform of data is similar to the shape of the selected WBF, the signal will be amplified, and vice versa. Thus, the more similarities between the waveform of WBF and the shape of the impulsive signal, the more fault features can be extracted. The signal at the fault point usually appears as an impulse signal. The similarity between WBF and impulsive signal can be expressed as follows:

$$\delta = \sum_{i=1}^{k} \alpha_i \frac{m_i^2}{s_i} \tag{2}$$

Where δ is the similarity coefficient, s_i represents the area of the absolute value of each peak in WBF, and k is the number of peaks after making the absolute value of WBF.

Table 1. The similarity coefficient δ of four common used WBF

Wavelet basis function	Morlet	Coif5	dbN	Meyer
Similarity coefficient δ	7.2148	6.3298	7.4970	6.6082

As Table 1 shows, although dbN is the greatest basis function, the basis function is not symmetric, and it doesn't have an explicit analytic equation and appropriate smoothness. Moreover, the time-frequency analysis of dbN wavelet is not convenient as well. Compared with dbN, Morlet is the cosine signal with square exponential attenuation, which indicates an explicit analytic equation. It has good smoothness, limited support length, and symmetric curve. Consequently, Morlet is more reasonable and effective to extract feature information of signals than other basic functions. Therefore, we choose Morlet as the wavelet basis function when using wavelet transform.

The schematic diagram of the processing approach is indicated in Fig. 2.

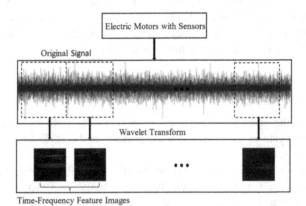

Fig. 2. The schematic diagram of processing original data

2.2 Self-supervised Pretraining

A Simple Framework for Contrastive Learning. After processing the 1-D original signal information to 2-D images, we employ a simple framework for contrastive learning

(SimCLR) [9], which is based on contrastive learning to learn visual representations on unlabeled images. SimCLR learns representations by maximizing agreement between different augmentations of the same data via a contrastive loss in the latent space [25].

(1) A stochastic data augmentation is used to transform any given data at random and result in two correlated views of the same data as a positive pair.
(2) A neural network-based encoder $f(\cdot)$ extracts representations from augmented examples [26].

We randomly use N samples as the minibatch and define the contrastive prediction task on pairs of augmenting examples. Then the other $2(N\text{-}1)$ augmented examples are set as negative examples. These examples derive from the same minibatch.

The ℓ_2 normalized between u and v (i.e. cosine similarity) is given as follows:

$$\text{sim}(u, v) = \frac{u^\top v}{\|u\|\|v\|} \tag{3}$$

Each image transforms to x_i and x_j, which are augmented in different ways, to obtain different correlated views. These two augmented images are encoded by neural network-based encoder $f(\cdot)$. Then the representations are transformed again with a non-linear transformation network $g(\cdot)$ (an MLP construct combined with ReLU), and yielding (z_i, z_j) is used for the contrastive loss. The framework is illustrated in Fig. 3.

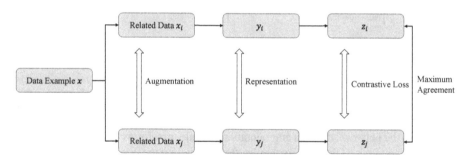

Fig. 3. A simple framework for contrastive learning of visual representations

The contrastive loss function between a pair of positive examples (i, j) with a minibatch of encoded example is defined as follows:

$$\ell_{i,j} = -\log \frac{\exp\left(\text{sim}(z_i, z_j)/\tau\right)}{\sum\limits_{k=1}^{2N} \mathbb{F}_{[k \neq i]} \exp(\text{sim}(z_i, z_k)/\tau)} \tag{4}$$

Where $\mathbb{F}_{[k \neq i]} \in \{0, 1\}$ is an indicator function evaluating to 1 if and only if $k \neq i$ and τ denote a temperature parameter [11, 27].

Multi-instance Contrastive Learning based on Wavelet Transform. In fault diagnosis and analysis, it's general to utilize multiple samples of the same failure to improve classification accuracy and robustness. Such samples are transformed from different data views or at different time points. When multiple time–frequency images are available as part of the training dataset, we propose to learn features from not only different augmentations of the same data [6], but also different time points of the same fault. By integrating WT-MICLe with wavelet transform, a new self-supervised failure detection approach, named WT-MICLe.

For learning general representations by conducting unsupervised pretraining, irrelevant or approximate datasets are used in a task-agnostic way for the first time. Then an additional self-supervised pretraining is conducted in a task-specific way. The self-supervised method WT-MICLe is used to construct more informative positive pairs if multiple data of each condition are available. To the end, using a few labeled data for fine-tuning for further improving predictive performance. This procedure is illustrated in Fig. 4.

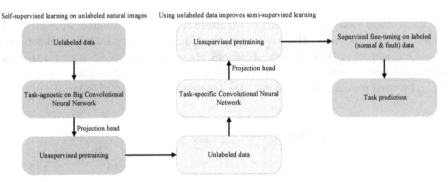

Fig. 4. The self-supervised learning framework leverage unlabeled data in task-agnostic and task-specific way

To train the network, the data augmentation module transforms any given samples in two correlated views of the same example after conducting the positive and the negative samples with standard SimCLR. Each image is augmented twice to create two views of the same example. After pretraining, we conduct another self-supervised learning stage: the positive samples are constructed by drawing two augmentations from two different time points of the same fault, as shown in Fig. 5. In this case, the features of images contributing to each positive pair are distinct. In WT-MICLe, we use N pairs of related images as a minibatch. By using contrastive loss, learning representations from leveraging multiple images can be more robust to the change of sampling points. Moreover, multi-instance contrastive learning can improve accuracy and achieve state-of-the-art results in fault diagnosis.

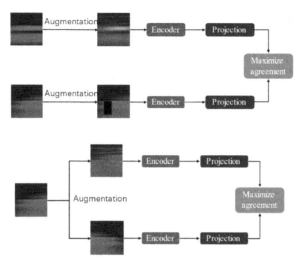

Fig. 5. An illustration of self-supervised pretraining for fault diagnosis on single and multiple images

Figure 6 shows the summary of the proposed approach, which comprises the following steps. After the data pre-processing, we perform' self-supervised pretraining on unlabeled images to learn general representations. For contrastive learning, we use the ImageNet ILSVRC-2012 dataset [28] and ball-bearing dataset from Case Western Reserve University (CWRU) to complete the first pre-training steps. All the 1-D signals transform to T-F images. Then we conduct another training step by using WT-MICLe. These task-specific images are bearing vibration datasets from Paderborn University. Finally, we perform supervised fine-tuning with a few labeled images.

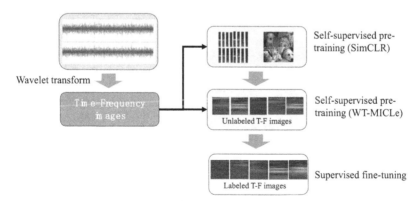

Fig. 6. Flowchart of the proposed approach

3 Experiment Setup and Results

3.1 Self-supervised Pretraining

To assess the effect of self-supervised pretraining by using large and wide neural networks, we use ResNet-50 with three different hidden layer widths (multipliers of $1\times$, $2\times$, $4\times$) as the base encoder networks [9]. Compared with SGD/Momentum optimizer, we follow Chen et al. and use LARS optimizer to stabilize training. Generally, self-supervised learning can benefit from the pretraining on a large unlabeled dataset. We conduct control tests as follows: the first set conduct pretraining on ImageNet as unlabeled images, and the next combine ImageNet and the CWRU ball-bearing datasets for pretraining to compare the influence of different datasets. To investigate the robustness and accuracy of the model, we adopt the WT-MICLe and SimCLR respectively as the self-supervised methods.

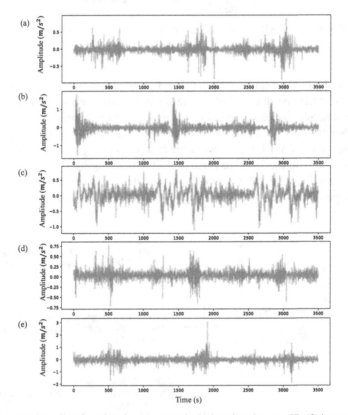

Fig. 7. Time-varying vibration signals: (a) normal, (b) bearing-damage IR (fatigue:pitting), (c) bearing-damage IR (Plastic deform: indentations) (d) bearing-damage OR (fatigue: pitting) (e) bearing-damage OR (Plastic deform: indentations)

After pretraining, we use the bearing vibration datasets from Paderborn University (PBU) [19] for fine-tuning and further task-specific training. Figure 7 shows the time-varying vibration signals with different cases. We train with learning rate in $\{0.01, 0.1, 0.3. 0.5, 1.0\}$, temperature in $\{0.1, 0.5, 1.0\}$, and batch size in $\{16, 32, 64, 128\}$. In addition, We refer to linear evaluation results under single or composition of transformations, and single transformation is insufficient to learn representation [9]. Considering the structure and content of 2-D images in the time–frequency domain, we randomly use these compositions of augmentations: random color distortions, random color jitter (strength $= 0.5$), random color drop, rotate (with $90°, 180°, 270°$ respectively). To some extent, the Gaussian blur may change the local texture variations and other areas of interest, so we do not use it as a way to apply augmentation.

3.2 Supervised Fine-Tuning

After pretraining, we train the model end-to-end fine-tuning and use the weights of pretraining network as the initialization for the downstream supervised task dataset. Following the approach by Chen et al. [9, 10], we train with a batch size of 128 by using SGD and set Nesterov momentum with a momentum parameter of 0.9. We also resize the dataset images to 64×64 during the fine-tuning stage and apply the same data augmentations during fine-tuning. By using 1% or 10% of the labeled sample, we simply fine-tune the whole base network [29]. To identify the best hyperparameters for fine-tuning, the performance of classification models is measured by top-1 accuracy (%) and area under the curve (AUC) under different scenarios. We follow the identical publicly available ResNet models pretrained on ImageNet with cross-entropy loss as the supervised baseline.

3.3 Experimental Results

In this section, we evaluate the benefit of self-supervised pretraining with contrastive learning. Compared with SimCLR, we conduct WT-MICLe for self-supervised pretraining. After that, to investigate the influence of label efficiency, we use the label fractions ranging from 10% to 80% for training datasets.

Performance of the Proposed Self-supervised Method. We use architectures with varying capacities (i.e. Resnet-50, Resnet-50 ($2\times$), Resnet-50 ($4\times$)) as the base network, and then investigate these possible networks for self-supervised pretraining. We use ImageNet and PBU datasets to conduct the efficiency of self-supervised methods without labeled data. Figure 8 shows that the performance of Resnet-50 with different hidden layer widths. Because contrastive learning always benefits from bigger models, the bigger model has a better outcome compared with the smaller one. Considering the calculation of time and accuracy of classification, we decide to use Resnet-5 ($4\times$) as the based network and test other influence factors.

Next, we evaluate transfer learning performance and the influence of different pretraining datasets. We adopt different datasets for self-supervised pretraining in the first step and do not have fine-tuning step: (1) using CWRU bearing datasets only, (2) initializing pretraining with both ImageNet and CWRU datasets, (3) using ImageNet only.

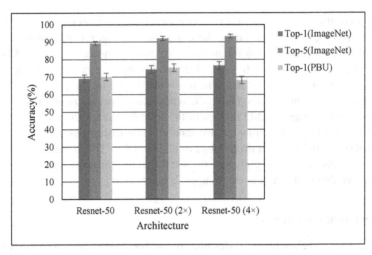

Fig. 8. Self-supervised learning of linear classification with different based networks

Figure 9 suggests that the performance and classification model under measured by top-1 accuracy (%) and area under the curve (AUC). We compare the results in the linear evaluation. Also, one of the ImageNet pre-training models has been made by supervised pretraining to prove transfer performance on downstream tasks [2, 30]. A pretraining on ILSVRC-2012 called Big Transfer (BiT) is used to evaluate a supervised baseline, due to its transfer performance. The results suggest that when using unlabeled correlated data (CWRU) for pretraining, the best performance can be achieved. Then we evaluate whether utilizing WT-MICLe is beneficial to self-supervised pretraining. The WT-MICLe and SimCLR model is used in the second step for task-specific pretraining. Both of these self-supervised methods are better than the supervised ones for the classification improving about 2.2% in top-1 accuracy, and the self-supervised method is better at about 0.4% in mean AUC.

We conduct this experiment to investigate the robustness of self-supervised pretraining models. Self-supervised pretraining models can generalize better to distribution shifts and representations. We also note that without a domain dataset for pretraining and only use ImageNet for self-supervised pretraining. The model performance is worse in this setting even compared with supervised cases. Moreover, we notice that the performance which both use ImageNet and correlated datasets (CWRU bearing damage data) has almost the same outcome compared with using field-correlated datasets only. The accuracy obtained by fine-tuning the self-supervised model can be improved. Because generalization under distribution shift is very important to fault diagnosis, the improvement in the distribution shift due to self-supervised pretraining can be explored and used in further work.

Furthermore, we notice that WT-MICLe surpasses the performance of the accuracy and mean AUC over the original SimCLR when testing PBU bearing dataset after pretraining. By using WT-MICLe, the outcome increases about 0.8% in top-1 accuracy and about 0.7% in mean AUC compared with SimCLR. We observe that the same trends

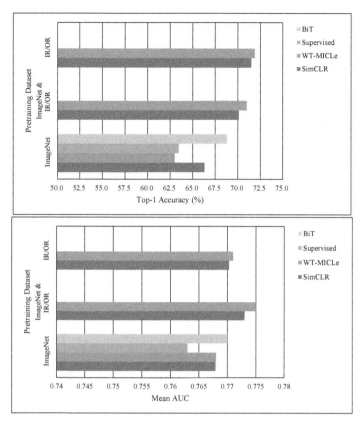

Fig. 9. The influence of pretraining with different datasets (Top-1 accuracy & Mean AUC)

suggest the robustness of the self-supervised representations and the proposed approach is consistent across different tasks.

Label Efficiency of Self-supervised Model. For different base networks, pre-trained followed fine-tuning is better than training from scratch. On one hand, to investigate the label efficiency of selected self-supervised models, we use the same fine-tuning process and base neural network. We also conduct this experiment with a supervised ImageNet pre-trained model. On the other hand, by using different label fractions (1% and range from 10% to 90%) for both training datasets. As shown in Fig. 10, the performance varies using the different fractions of datasets. We note that self-supervised pretraining with both ImageNet and the in-domain datasets is beneficial for representations. Pretraining using self-supervised methods can significantly improve the accuracy by about 10%, and self-supervised methods outperform the supervised ones by about 25%. Then, with the help of more labeled data to access fine-tuning, the accuracy of classification can improve a lot. Moreover, these results show that WT-MICLe model benefits larger from the labeled data and more robust when fine-tuning with the same fraction of labeled examples. The proposed method is better by about 5% accuracy over the SimCLR.

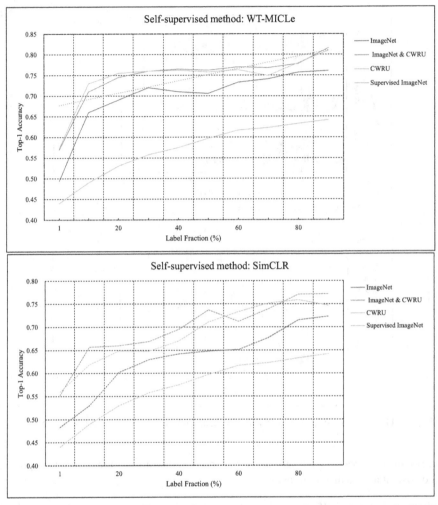

Fig. 10. Top-1 accuracy for fault classification with WT-MICLe, SimCLR, and supervised model with different pretraining datasets and varied sizes of label fraction

4 Conclusion

This paper investigates an alternative approach on scarce labeled data based on the self-supervised method. Combining with wavelet transform and based networks for detection, an intelligent failure detection approach named WT-MICLe is presented. The paper proposes the use of wavelet transform to process the original vibration data to enhance the information of data. Also, we apply this self-supervised model in the fault-diagnosis area to reach a good performance of fault representation, and we find that self-supervised pretraining outperforms supervised pretraining. After the pretraining step, using labeled data for further fine-tuning is necessary. Employing proper data augmentations for self-supervised learning can further improve the classificational ability. Another research is the transferability of self-supervised learning. Sometimes pretraining on the natural dataset is not necessary, it still needs to distinct under different scenarios. We hope this paper can provide an approach in fault diagnosis and analysis when labeled data and unlabeled data are imbalanced.

Acknowledgements. This paper is partially supported by the National Key Research and Development Project (2019YFB2006603), the National Science Foundation of China (Grant No. U2034209), and the technological innovation and application Demonstration Program of Chongqing Science and Technology Commission (Grant No. cstc2020jscx-msxmX0177).

References

1. Bossard, L., Guillaumin, M., Van Gool, L.: Food-101 – mining discriminative components with random forests. In: Fleet, D., Pajdla, T., Schiele, B., Tuytelaars, T. (eds.) Computer Vision – ECCV 2014. Lecture Notes in Computer Science, vol. 8694, pp. 446–461. Springer, Cham (2014). https://doi.org/10.1007/978-3-319-10599-4_29
2. Mahajan, D., Girshick, R., Ramanathan, V., He, K., Paluri, M., Li, Y., Bharambe, A., van der Maaten, L.: Exploring the limits of weakly supervised pretraining. In: Ferrari, V., Hebert, M., Sminchisescu, C., Weiss, Y. (eds.) Computer Vision – ECCV 2018. Lecture Notes in Computer Science, vol. 11206, pp. 185–201. Springer, Cham (2018). https://doi.org/10.1007/978-3-030-01216-8_12
3. Diplaros, A., Vlassis, N., Gevers, T.: A spatially constrained generative model and an EM algorithm for image segmentation. IEEE Trans. Neural Netw. **18**, 798–808 (2007)
4. Doersch, C., Gupta, A., Efros, A.A.: Unsupervised visual representation learning by context prediction. In: IEEE International Conference on Computer Vision (ICCV), pp. 1422–1430 (2015)
5. Zhang, R., Isola, P., Efros, A.A.: Colorful image colorization. In: Leibe, B., Matas, J., Sebe, N., Welling, M. (eds.) Computer Vision – ECCV 2016. Lecture Notes in Computer Science, vol. 9907, pp. 649–666. Springer, Cham (2016). https://doi.org/10.1007/978-3-319-46487-9_40
6. Bachman, P., Hjelm, R.D., Buchwalter, W.: Learning Representations by Maximizing Mutual Information Across Views (2019)
7. Hadsell, R., Chopra, S., LeCun, Y.: Dimensionality reduction by learning an invariant mapping. In: 2006 IEEE Computer Society Conference on Computer Vision and Pattern Recognition (CVPR 2006), pp. 1735–1742 (2006)
8. Dosovitskiy, A., Fischer, P., Springenberg, J.T., Riedmiller, M., Brox, T.: Discriminative unsupervised feature learning with exemplar convolutional neural networks. IEEE Trans. Pattern Anal. Mach. Intell. **38**, 1734–1747 (2016)
9. Chen, T., Kornblith, S., Norouzi, M., Hinton, G.J.A.E.-P.: A simple framework for contrastive learning of visual representations (2020). arXiv:2002.05709
10. Chen, T., Kornblith, S., Swersky, K., Norouzi, M., Hinton, G.J.A.E.-P.: Big self-supervised models are strong semi-supervised learners (2020). arXiv:2006.10029
11. Wu, Z., Xiong, Y., Yu, S.X., Lin, D.: Unsupervised feature learning via non-parametric instance discrimination. In: 2018 IEEE/CVF Conference on Computer Vision and Pattern Recognition, pp. 3733–3742 (2018)
12. Hjelm, R.D., et al.: Learning deep representations by mutual information estimation and maximization (2019)

13. Hjelm, R.D., Fedorov, A., Lavoie-Marchildon, S., Grewal, K., Trischler, A., Bengio, Y.: Learning deep representations by mutual information estimation and maximization (2018)
14. He, K., Fan, H., Wu, Y., Xie, S., Girshick, R.: Momentum contrast for unsupervised visual representation learning. In: 2020 IEEE/CVF Conference on Computer Vision and Pattern Recognition (CVPR), pp. 9726–9735 (2020)
15. Misra, I., Maaten, L.v.d.: Self-supervised learning of pretext-invariant representations. In: 2020 IEEE/CVF Conference on Computer Vision and Pattern Recognition (CVPR), pp. 6706–6716 (2020)
16. Hénaff, O.J., et al.: Data-efficient image recognition with contrastive predictive coding (2019). arXiv:1905.09272
17. Shao, S., McAleer, S., Yan, R., Baldi, P.: Highly accurate machine fault diagnosis using deep transfer learning. IEEE Trans. Industr. Inf. **15**, 2446–2455 (2019)
18. Cheng, Y., Zhu, H., Wu, J., Shao, X.: Machine health monitoring using adaptive kernel spectral clustering and deep long short-term memory recurrent neural networks. IEEE Trans. Industr. Inf. **15**, 987–997 (2019)
19. Lessmeier, C., Kimotho, J.K., Zimmer, D., Sextro, W.: Condition monitoring of bearing damage in electromechanical drive systems by using motor current signals of electric motors: a benchmark data set for data-driven classification. In: European Conference of the Prognostics and Health Management Society (2016)
20. Azizi, S., et al.: Big self-supervised models advance medical image classification (2021). arXiv:2101.05224
21. Chen, R., Huang, X., Yang, L., Xu, X., Zhang, X., Zhang, Y.J.C.I.I.: Intelligent fault diagnosis method of planetary gearboxes based on convolution neural network and discrete wavelet transform. 106, 48–59 (2019)
22. Long, W., Li, X., Liang, G., Zhang, Y.J.I.T.o.I.E.: A New Convolutional Neural Network Based Data-Driven Fault Diagnosis Method. p. 1 (2017)
23. Huang, L., Wang, J.J.N.: Forecasting energy fluctuation model by wavelet decomposition and stochastic recurrent wavelet neural network. Neuro Computing **309**, 70–82 (2018)
24. Chen, Z.X.J.M.S., Technology: The Selection of Wavelet Base in Malfunction Diagnosis (2005)
25. Becker, S., Hinton, G.E.J.N.: Self-organizing neural network that discovers surfaces in random-dot stereograms . Nature **355**, 161 (1992)
26. He, K., Zhang, X., Ren, S., Sun, J.: Deep residual learning for image recognition. In: 2016 IEEE Conference on Computer Vision and Pattern Recognition (CVPR), pp. 770–778 (2016)
27. Sohn, K.: Improved deep metric learning with multi-class N-pair loss objective (2016)
28. Russakovsky, O., Deng, J., Su, H., Krause, J., Satheesh, S., Ma, S., Huang, Z., Karpathy, A., Khosla, A., Bernstein, M., Berg, A.C., Fei-Fei, L.: ImageNet large scale visual recognition challenge. Int. J. Comput. Vision **115**, 211–252 (2015)
29. Beyer, L., Zhai, X., Oliver, A., Kolesnikov, A.: S4L: self-supervised semi-supervised learning. In: 2019 IEEE/CVF International Conference on Computer Vision (ICCV), pp. 1476–1485 (2019)
30. Kolesnikov, A., et al.: Big Transfer (BiT): General Visual Representation Learning (2019). arXiv:1912.11370

A Method for Imbalanced Fault Diagnosis Based on Self-attention Generative Adversarial Network

Xin Chen[1], Yongfang Mao[1(✉)], Baoming Zhang[1], Yi Chai[1], and Zhenli Yang[2]

[1] Chongqing University, Chongqing 400044, China
{201813021035,yfm,baomingzhang,chaiyi}@cqu.edu.cn
[2] Chongqing Special Equipment Inspection and Research Institute, Chongqing 401121, China

Abstract. In the real industrial scenario, the rotating machinery generally works in a normal state, and the sensor can only collect fault signals when the mechanical equipment fails in a few cases. This leads to the problem of data imbalance in fault diagnosis, i.e., the number of normal samples far exceeds the number of fault samples. In this case, the performance of the data-driven fault diagnosis classifier will significantly decrease, leading to misdiagnosis and missed diagnosis. To solve the above problem, we propose a novel method called WT-SAGAN-CNN based on wavelet transform and self-attention generative adversarial networks, which can generate high-quality fault samples to achieve data balance. This method uses continuous wavelet transform (CWT) to convert the one-dimensional signals into images. Then uses the self-attention generative adversarial networks (SAGAN) to generate fault images and stops training until the generative adversarial networks reach the Nash equilibrium. The convolutional neural networks are used as the fault diagnosis classifier, mix the generated images into the imbalanced dataset, and input them into the classifier for training. Experiment shows that the proposed model can generate samples similar to real samples, and as the generated samples continue to be added to the imbalanced dataset, the accuracy of the fault diagnosis classifier has also been significantly improved.

Keywords: Fault diagnosis · Self-attention GAN · Rotating machinery

1 Introduction

For a long time, the fault diagnosis of rotating machinery has been the key to ensuring the reliability of industrial production processes [1]. Some key components have a huge impact on the performance of the equipment, such as bearings, gears, etc. [2]. If faults occur and are not dealt with in time, it will cause huge economic losses.

In recent years, deep learning [3] has been widely used in the field of fault diagnosis [4]. Commonly used models include multi-layer perceptron (MLP) [5], convolutional neural network (CNN) [6], long short-term memory network (LSTM) [7], etc. Xia et al. [8] proposed a fault diagnosis method based on the multi-sensor deep convolutional network for rotating machinery. Zhu et al. [9] proposed an intelligent fault diagnosis method for bearings based on a capsule neural network.

© Springer Nature Singapore Pte Ltd. 2021
H. Zhang et al. (Eds.): NCAA 2021, CCIS 1449, pp. 333–346, 2021.
https://doi.org/10.1007/978-981-16-5188-5_24

In the actual industrial scenario, bearings work under normal operating conditions most of the time, fault samples are not easy to obtain, resulting in a serious imbalance in the collected data. In this case, there will be a higher misdiagnosis accuracy of the data-driven fault diagnosis model. The generative adversarial network proposed by Ian Goodfellow [10] has achieved great success in the field of image generation and data augment, provides a new method for us to solve the fault diagnosis data imbalance. Derived models of GAN including DCGAN [11], WGAN [12], WGAN-GP [13], etc.

Many scholars have proposed a series of solutions to the problem of data imbalance in fault diagnosis based on GAN. Lin et al. [14] proposed to augment the dataset based on GAN to improve the performance of the fault diagnosis model of microcrack defect. Zareapoor et al. [15] proposed to combine oversampling technique with GAN to solve the data imbalance problem of industrial plant failure detection. Gao et al. [16] applied WGAN-GP to data imbalance to augment data in the industrial chemical process.

These methods have achieved good fault diagnosis results, but they are lacking in the stability of GAN training and the criteria for judging the quality of the generated pictures.

To address the problem of bearing data imbalance, this paper proposes a method called WT-SAGAN-CNN, based on self-attention GAN, which can generate high-quality fault samples to augment the original bearing imbalanced dataset and use augmented dataset to train fault diagnosis classifier. The main contributions of this paper are as follows:

1) Adding self-attention mechanism to improve GAN, which is called SAGAN, can generate fault samples to solve the problem of bearing fault data imbalance.
2) The spectral normalization theory is introduced to stabilize the training of GAN, and it is applied to each layer of the generator and discriminator.
3) To verify the performance of the generated fault samples in the bearing imbalanced fault diagnosis, the generated samples are added to the training set for training and conduct the comparison experiment with the unimproved method according to diagnosis accuracy.

2   Theoretical Background

2.1   Continuous Wavelet Transform

Grossman et al. [17] proposed continuous wavelet transform (CWT), by performing CWT on the signal, projecting the one-dimensional signal onto a two-dimensional plane. The noise of the vibration signals is converted into the image background and can retain most of the fault information.

For any function $f(t)$ in $L^2(R)$ space, its CWT is defined as:

$$CWT(a, \tau) = \left[f(t), \psi_{a,\tau}(t) \right] = \frac{1}{\sqrt{a}} \int f(t) \psi \left(\frac{t - \tau}{a} \right) dt \qquad (1)$$

$$\psi_{a,\tau}(t) = \frac{1}{\sqrt{a}} \psi \left(\frac{t - \tau}{a} \right), a, \tau \in \mathbf{R}, a > 0 \qquad (2)$$

Where a is the scale factor, τ is the translation factor, $\psi_{a,\tau}(t)$ is the wavelet basis function.

2.2 Generative Adversarial Networks

Generative adversarial network (GAN) mainly contains two parts: the generator and discriminator. The generator tries to learn the data distribution from the real sample and then uses the generated samples to deceive the discriminator. The role of the discriminator is to judge the true and false of the input images. GAN architecture is shown in Fig. 1.

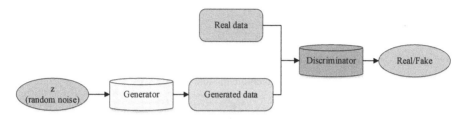

Fig. 1. The architecture of GAN

The optimization goal of GAN:

$$\min_{G} \max_{D} V(G, D) = E_{x \in P_{data}(x)}\big[\log D(x)\big] + E_{z \in P_z(z)}\big[\log(1 - D(G(z)))\big] \quad (3)$$

where G is generator and D is discriminator, $V(G, D)$ is the objective function, x is real data, subject to the real data distribution $P_{data}(x)$, z is random noise signal, subject to the random noise distribution $P_z(z)$, $E(*)$ is mean value functions. The purpose of the discriminator is to maximize $\log D(x)$ as much as possible to increase the probability of judging the real sample as true; at the same time, The purpose of the generator is to minimize the term $\log(1-D(G(z)))$ to increase the probability of the generated sample $D(G(z))$ as a real sample as much as possible, optimize and update the parameters until the Nash equilibrium is reached.

2.3 Self-attention Mechanism Module

Han Zhang, Ian Goodfellow et al. [18] proposed self-attention generative adversarial networks. Convolution has a weak ability to build relationships between distant regions in images. Therefore, introduce the self-attention module to the GAN framework, making generative adversarial networks strengthen the relationships to the distant regions in images.

From Fig. 2, it can be seen that the feature maps of the previous layer x are first converted into two feature spaces f, g, where $f(x) = W_f(x)$, $g(x) = W_g(x)$

$$\beta_{j,i} = \frac{\exp(s_{ij})}{\sum\limits_{1}^{N} \exp(s_{ij})} \quad (4)$$

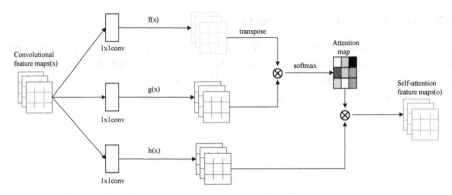

Fig. 2. Self-attention module of SAGAN

where $s_{ij} = f(x_i)^T g(x_j)$, $\beta_{j,i}$ is the calculated attention value, which indicates the extent of attention the model pays to the *ith* position when synthesizing the *jth* region.

$$o_j = v(\sum_{1}^{N} \beta_{j,i} h(x_i)), \ h(x_i) = W_h x_i, \ v(x_i) = W_v x_i \tag{5}$$

In the above formula, W_g, W_f, W_h, W_v are learnable weight matrices and are all convolution kernels with a convolution size of 1.

The final output is:

$$y_i = \gamma o_i + x_i \tag{6}$$

where γ is a learnable parameter, which is initialized to 0. The reason for introducing γ is to allow the neural network to first rely on the information in the local neighborhood and then gradually assign more weight to the information of non-local evidence.

2.4 Spectral Normalization

Miyato T, Kataoka T, Koyama M et al. [19] first proposed to apply spectral normalization to the discriminator to improve the stability of GAN training. The main idea is to add the Lipschitz constraint to the parameters of the discriminator and divide the parameters of each layer of the network by the spectral norm of the matrix of this layer, the formula is as follows:

$$\overline{W}_{SN}(W) = \frac{W}{\sigma(W)} \tag{7}$$

where W represents weight, and $\sigma(W)$ represents the 2-norm of weight. In SAGAN, spectral normalization is applied to each layer of the discriminator and generator. It can significantly reduce the computational cost of training, increase the computational speed, and show more stable training behavior during training.

2.5 Frechet Inception Distance

We evaluated the quality of the generated pictures from the two aspects: the authenticity and diversity of the samples. There are several evaluation methods: including Inception Score, FID score, etc.

FID score is a measure of the distance between the distribution of generated images and real images proposed by Martin Heusel et al. [20]:

$$d^2((m, C), (m_\omega, C_\omega)) = ||m - m_\omega||_2^2 + Tr(C + C_\omega - 2(CC_\omega)^{1/2}) \tag{8}$$

where m and m_ω are the vectors of length 2048 that use InceptionV3 network to extract features from real and generated images dataset to generate an N*2048 matrix, and then take the average of each column. C and C_ω are the covariance matrices of m and m_ω. Tr is the trace of the matrix. The FID score is calculated by Eq. (8). The lower the FID score, the closer the distance of the two distributions. It can be considered that the lower FID score indicates the higher quality of the generated image.

In practice, FID has relatively good robustness to noise, and the computational complexity of FID is not high. Compared with Inception Score, FID score is more flexible and reasonable. So we choose FID score as our evaluation method.

3 System Framework

First, wavelet transform is performed on the original vibration bearing signal, and the complex Morlet wavelet is used as the wavelet basis function. After the transformation,

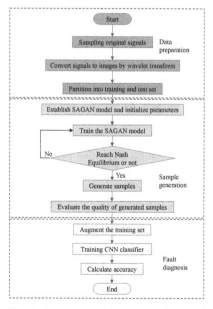

Fig. 3. Flowchart of the proposed method

two-dimensional images are obtained. Then input images into SAGAN and generate a large number of fault sample images. Subsequently, mixed the generated fault sample data into the original fault sample data, and finally, the input augmented dataset to CNN classifier for fault diagnosis (Fig. 3).

3.1 Data Preparation

This paper uses the sliding window to sample one-dimensional vibration signals. The window length is M. Each time the window moves backward by N, M length of data are taken each time for performing wavelet transform, and take the absolute value of the wavelet transformation's result. Then save the matrix and convert it to an RGB image (Fig. 4).

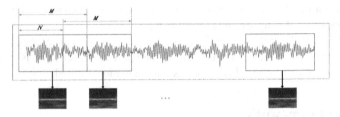

Fig. 4. Schematic diagram of sliding window sampling

Since there are fewer fault signals in actual situations, to sample more pictures and obtain more fault information, this article sets the moving length to be smaller than the window length, that is, $N < M$. In this experiment, sets $N = 256$, $M = 512$.

3.2 The Architecture of the Generator and Discriminator

The following figure shows the architecture of the SAGAN generator, the purpose is to convert the noise into an image through the generator. The input is a 100-dimensional noise vector sampled from a normal distribution, which is reshaped into a (100, 1, 1) three-dimensional feature maps form. The first three deconvolution layers have 512, 256, and 128 filters, and the size of the deconvolution kernel is both 4 × 4. Note that spectral normalization and batch normalization are added before and after each deconvolution layer to avoid gradient disappearance and stable training. As shown in the figure, the output after the first convolution is 512*4*4, and the output after the second convolution is 128*16*16, and then after the first attention module, the output size has not changed, the specific parameters are shown in Fig. 5, and the final output is a generated image with the shape of 3*64*64.

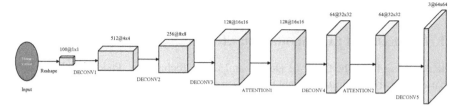

Fig. 5. The architecture of the generator

The architecture of the discriminator is almost symmetric with the generator. The purpose is to judge the input images are true or false. The input is the RGB images with the length and width of 64, and the output value is between 0 and 1, where 0 means the picture is false, and 1 means the picture is true. The picture first passes through three convolutional layers and then outputs a picture of (256, 8, 8), and then passes through the attention module without changing the size. Also note that as with the generator, spectral normalization and batch normalization are applied before and after each convolutional layer (Fig. 6).

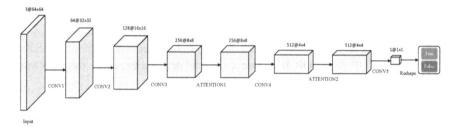

Fig. 6. The architecture of the discriminator

3.3 Fault Diagnosis Classifier

We use CNN as the classifier of fault diagnosis. The architecture of the classifier is shown in Fig. 7.

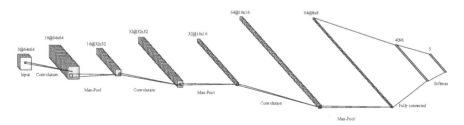

Fig. 7. The architecture of the CNN classifier

4 Case Study and Experiment Result

4.1 Introduction of Experimental Datasets

The dataset is from the Chair of Design and Drive Technology, Paderborn University, we use the bearing vibration signal that was measured and sampled for 4 s at a sampling frequency of 64 kHz, with a total of approximately 256,000 points. There are three states of the bearing: healthy, inner ring failure, and outer ring failure. These damages are caused by artificial or accelerated lifetime tests, as shown in Fig. 8.

EDM   drilling   electric engraver

Fig. 8. Damages in bearings

The selected bearing information is shown in Table 1, Normal represents the normal samples, IR-A and IR-B represent artificial damage and accelerated test inner ring failure respectively, and OR-A and OR-B represent artificial damage and accelerated test outer ring failure respectively.

Table 1. The information of bearings

	KI03	KI04	KA01	KA04	K004
Damage Class	IR-A	IR-B	OR-A	OR-B	Normal
Class label	0	1	2	3	4
Extent of Damages	1	1	1	1	–
Damage method	Artificial	Accelerated	Artificial	Accelerated	–

The bearing vibration signal waveform is shown in Fig. 9.

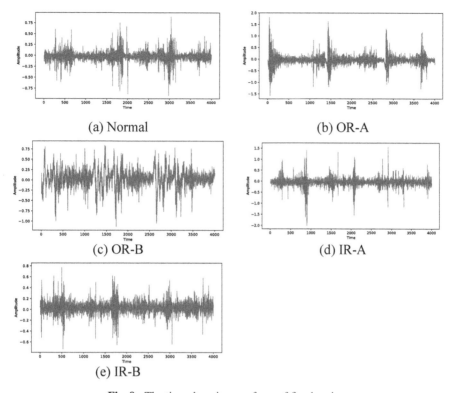

Fig. 9. The time-domain waveform of five bearings

4.2   Images Generation

In the experiment, wavelet transform is performed on the one-dimensional signals of the normal, inner fault, and outer fault to generate a two-dimensional picture. Part of the transformed picture is shown in Fig. 10. In this paper, we select the complex Morlet wavelet as the wavelet basis function, its bandwidth is 3, and the center frequency is 3.

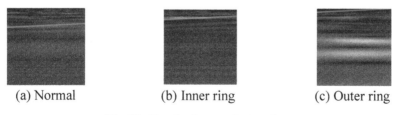

Fig. 10. Signals after wavelet transform

Then input the transformed image into the SAGAN for training (Table 2).

Table 2. Hyperparameters of SAGAN

Training iterations	Batch size	Learning rate	Adam parameters
1500	64	0.00005	beta 1 = 0.5, beta 2 = 0.999

Figure 11 is the loss value curve of SAGAN. The horizontal axis and the vertical axis represent the number of training and the loss value respectively, and the blue curve is the generator loss value, and the orange curve is the discriminator loss value. It can be seen that the discriminator has some oscillations at the beginning, and after 200 iterations, the loss value gradually converges to about 0. The generator oscillates very badly at first, and it gradually converges to a certain value after 500 iterations. Both the generator and the discriminator are convergent, indicating that the model is well trained.

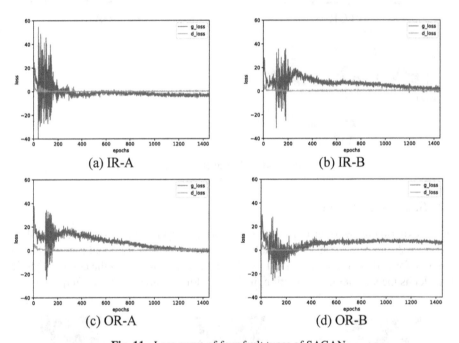

(a) IR-A

(b) IR-B

(c) OR-A

(d) OR-B

Fig. 11. Loss curve of four fault types of SAGAN

We select a batch of the fault real images and generated images for comparison (Fig. 12).

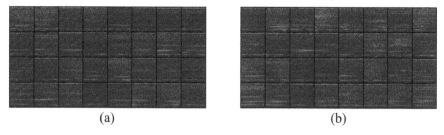

(a)   (b)

Fig. 12. Real images(a) and generated images(b)

FID score is introduced to evaluate the quality of generated images. Figure 13 shows the changes in the FID value of the four types of faults while training epochs increase. It can be seen that as the training epoch increases, the value of the FID score gradually decreases and stabilizes after 800 iterations. At last, the fid score value is already very low, indicating the quality of the generated images is relatively high.

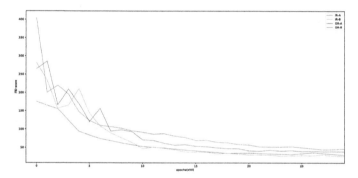

Fig. 13. FID score curve of training

4.3 Fault Diagnosis Classification

We define the imbalance ratio as follows:

$$\text{imbalance ratio} = \frac{N_{minority}}{N_{majority}} \qquad (9)$$

where $N_{minority}$ and $N_{majority}$ represent the number of samples of minority and majority class. The imbalance ratio value is between 0 and 1.

Set the imbalance ratio of 1:100 as the original imbalanced dataset, divide this dataset into a training set and a test set. Then add generated images to the training set. Set three imbalance ratios, and record their accuracy and compare with the original imbalanced dataset. Table 3 shows the data sets of several imbalance ratios:

Table 3. The information of datasets

Imbalance ratio	Label				
	0	1	2	3	4
1:100	8	8	8	8	800
1:20	40	40	40	40	800
1:5	160	160	160	160	800
1:1	800	800	800	800	800
Test set	200	200	200	200	200

The hyperparameters of classifier: batch size is 64, the learning rate of Adam optimizer is 0.001, $\beta_1 = 0.9$, $\beta_2 = 0.999$.

The confusion matrix is used to represent the classification results of the test set, and we can see from Fig. 14 that the number of correctly diagnosed, missed diagnosed, and misdiagnosed samples.

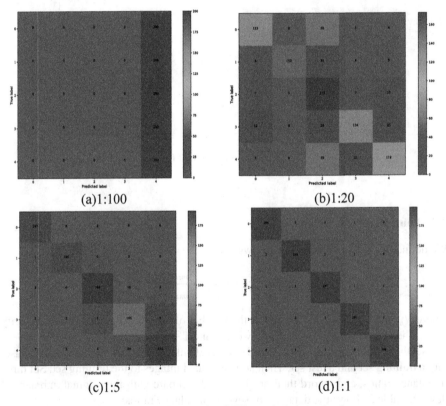

(a)1:100   (b)1:20

(c)1:5   (d)1:1

Fig. 14. Confusion matrix of different imbalanced ratios

It can be seen from Fig. 14, the imbalance ratio of the original imbalanced dataset is 1:100, and the classifier will mistakenly judge the minority samples of all categories as the majority category. This classifier is invalid because it will judge all the input to be the normal class, and the fault will not be detected in time and accurately. When the imbalance ratio is 1:20, the minority class is judged to be correct samples significantly increase. When the imbalance ratio is 1:5, most samples of the minority sample class can be classified correctly. And finally, the training set reaches the balance, only a very small number of fault samples is classified incorrectly.

To verify the effectiveness of the experiment, we compare the accuracy of fault diagnosis based on the SAGAN model with the DCGAN and the original GAN model. The comparison results are shown in Fig. 15.

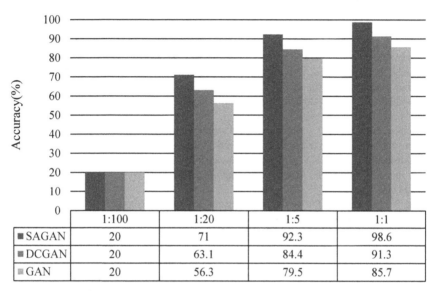

	1:100	1:20	1:5	1:1
■ SAGAN	20	71	92.3	98.6
■ DCGAN	20	63.1	84.4	91.3
▪ GAN	20	56.3	79.5	85.7

Fig. 15. Comparative experiment with DCGAN and GAN

From Fig. 15, it can be seen that besides the original imbalanced dataset, the accuracy of fault diagnosis based on the SAGAN is higher than the other two methods.

5 Conclusion

This paper proposes a new model WT-SAGAN-CNN, based on the self-attention generative adversarial networks. It has a good effect on the rolling bearing imbalanced dataset. This model makes use of the strong abilities of CNN and SAGAN in data feature learning and data generation. Experiment shows that the proposed model can significantly improve the accuracy of the fault diagnosis classifier.

Acknowledgment. The paper is supported by the National Natural Science Foundation of China (Grant No. U2034209) and the technological innovation and application Demonstration Program of Chongqing Science and Technology Commission (Grant No. cstc2020jscx-msxmX0177).

References

1. Cerrada, M., Sánchez, R.V., Li, C.: A review on data-driven fault severity assessment in rolling bearings. Mech. Syst. Signal Process. **99**, 169–196 (2018)
2. Rai, A., Upadhyay, S.H.: A review on signal processing techniques utilized in the fault diagnosis of rolling element bearings. Tribol. Int. **96**, 289–306 (2016)
3. Lecun, Y., Bengio, Y., Hinton, G.E.: Deep learning. Nature **521**(7553), 436–444 (2015)
4. Duan, L., Xie, M., Wang, J.: Deep learning enabled intelligent fault diagnosis: overview and applications. J. Intell. Fuzz. Syst. **35**, 5771–5784 (2018)
5. Gardner, M.W., Dorling, S.: Artificial neural networks (the multilayer perceptron)—a review of applications in the atmospheric sciences. Atmos. Environ. **32**(14–15), 2627–2636 (1998)
6. Krizhevsky, A., Sutskever, I., Hinton, G.E.: ImageNet classification with deep convolutional neural networks. Adv. Neural. Inf. Process. Syst. **25**, 1097–1105 (2012)
7. Hochreiter, S., Schmidhuber, J.: Long short-term memory. Neural Comput. **9**, 1735–1780 (1997)
8. Xia, M., Li, T., Xu, L.: Fault diagnosis for rotating machinery using multiple sensors and convolutional neural networks. IEEE/ASME Trans. Mechatron. **23**(1), 101–110 (2018)
9. Zhu, Z., Peng, G., Chen, Y.: A convolutional neural network based on a capsule network with strong generalization for bearing fault diagnosis. Neurocomputing **323**, 62–75 (2019)
10. Goodfellow, I., Pouget-Abadie, J., Mirza, M.: Generative adversarial nets (2014). arXiv:1406.2661
11. Radford, A., Metz, L., Chintala, S.: Unsupervised representation learning with deep convolutional generative adversarial networks (2015). arXiv:1511.06434
12. Arjovsky, M., Chintala, S., Bottou, L.: Wasserstein gan (2017). arXiv:1701.07875
13. Gulrajani, I., Ahmed, F., Arjovsky, M.: Improved training of Wasserstein gans (2017). arXiv:1704.00028
14. Lin, S., He, Z., Sun, L.: Defect enhancement generative adversarial network for enlarging data set of microcrack defect. IEEE Access **7**, 148413–148423 (2019)
15. Zareapoor, M., Shamsolmoali, P., Yang, J.: Oversampling adversarial network for class-imbalanced fault diagnosis. Mech. Syst. Signal Process. **149**, 107175 (2021)
16. Gao, X., Deng, F., Yue, X.: Data augmentation in fault diagnosis based on the Wasserstein generative adversarial network with gradient penalty. Neurocomputing **396**, 487–494 (2020)
17. Grossmann, A., Morlet, J.: Decomposition of hardy functions into square integrable wavelets of constant shape. SIAM J. Math. Anal. **15**(4), 723–736 (1984)
18. Zhang, H., Goodfellow, I., Metaxas, D.: Self-attention generative adversarial networks (2018). arXiv:1805.08318
19. Miyato, T., Kataoka, T., Koyama, M.: Spectral normalization for generative adversarial networks (2018). arXiv:1802.05957
20. Heusel, M., Ramsauer, H., Unterthiner, T.: Gans trained by a two time-scale update rule converge to a local nash equilibrium (2017). arXiv:1706.08500

Self-supervised Contrastive Representation Learning for Machinery Fault Diagnosis

Yadong Wei, Xiaoman Cai, Jianyu Long, Zhe Yang$^{(\boxtimes)}$, and Chuan Li

Dongguan University of Technology, Dongguan 523808, China
{longjy,yangz,chuanli}@dgut.edu.cn

Abstract. Supervised deep learning methods have been widely applied in the field of machinery fault diagnosis in recent years, which learns quite well the mapping relationship between the monitoring data and the corresponding labels. In many practical industrial applications, however, the monitoring data are unlabeled due to the requirement of expert knowledge and a large amount of labor, which limits the use of supervised methods for fault diagnosis. In view of this problem, in this work a self-supervised representation learning method named contrastive predicting coding (CPC) is employed to automatically extract high-quality features from one-dimensional machinery monitoring signals without the requirement of labels. The method is validated on a benchmark dataset for bearing fault diagnosis, and the quality of extracted features of different classes is quantitatively evaluated. The results show that features extracted by the CPC method are more representative than those obtained by autoencoders and statistics.

Keywords: Contrastive predicting coding · Fault diagnosis · Deep learning · Self-supervised representation learning

1 Introduction

In modern industry, a large number of machines are employed for commercial production. In order to ensure the safe and effective operation of machinery, efficient fault diagnosis methods are indispensable for detecting the machine failure and classifying its cause.

Machine learning methods, such as support vector machine [1–3] and artificial neural network [4–7], have been extensively applied for machinery fault diagnosis. Since these methods rely on the extraction of hand-crafted statistical features which may not be optimal for fault diagnosis which is a classification task, in recent years, deep learning-based fault diagnosis methods have been widely studied [9]. Deep learning methods can adaptively extract useful features from data through multiple nonlinear transformations and achieve excellent performance for fault diagnosis. Deep learning methods include Autoencoder [11], RNN [19], CNN [21], Echo State Network [22] etc. However, most of the fault diagnosis methods belong to the field of supervised learning, which assumes the label of data, e.g. the type of fault, is available for building a data-driven model. In practice, the labeling of monitoring data relies on expert knowledge in a specific field

© Springer Nature Singapore Pte Ltd. 2021
H. Zhang et al. (Eds.): NCAA 2021, CCIS 1449, pp. 347–359, 2021.
https://doi.org/10.1007/978-981-16-5188-5_25

and is very labor-intensive, hindering the preparation of labeled datasets in the industry. For this situation, self-supervised learning methods are expected to automatically mine the data categories by extracting representative features from data without the help of labels. Autoencoder [10–12] is one of the most classic self-supervised methods, which is a symmetrical neural network composed of two parts: an encoder network and a decoder network. The input data of autoencoder will first pass through the encoder network, and the encoder network will convert the input high-dimensional data into low-dimensional features. Then these low-dimensional features are fed to the decoder network to reconstruct the input data. Although autoencoder can extract features from data with minimal loss of information, there is no guarantee that the features extracted by the autoencoder are representative.

Recently, a novel class of self-supervised learning methods, named contrastive learning, has attracted a great of attention. They have been successfully applied for extracting semantically similar representations from the latent classes of text and images [13, 14]. One of the contrastive learning methods, Momentum Contrast (MoCo), is utilized for building large and consistent dictionaries in natural language processing in [15]. In [16], a contrastive learning method is used for image captioning, which explicitly encourages distinctiveness while maintaining the overall quality of the generated captions. Contrastively-trained Structured World Models (C-SWMs) [17] are able to learn abstract state representations from environmental observations.

In this work, we consider a contrastive learning method Contrastive Predicting Coding (CPC) [18] for self-supervised representation learning of machinery monitoring data, given its capability of processing one-dimensional data. The goal of CPC is to train a feature extractor so that it can perform similar coding on similar data while making the coding of different types of data as different as possible. Its key idea is to perform a contrast loss in the latent feature space of a positive sample and multiple negative samples, to maximize the distinguishability of representation of the positive sample from different expanded views of comparison, and each sample in the dataset is considered as the positive sample in turn. To the best of our knowledge, CPC has never been studied for problems in the field of fault diagnosis.

In the actual production process, the data collected on the industrial site is often unlabeled, and it is difficult to be used for fault diagnosis. The purpose of our paper is to study whether the self-supervised method CPC can extract effective features for fault diagnosis, without the information of labels. A benchmark bearing fault diagnosis dataset is employed to evaluate the performance of CPC. First, the CPC method is trained using bearing vibration signals collected under different conditions. Then the feature extractor is used to encode the one-dimensional vibration signal to verify its effectiveness. The obtained results are compared with other classic methods.

The following of this paper is organized as follows. Section 2 introduces the methods used in the experiment. Section 3 describes the process of the experiment and the comparison of the experimental results obtained by each method. The conclusion is drawn in Sect. 4.

2 Method Definition

In this Section, we will briefly introduce the CPC method, and the other two feature extraction methods used for comparison, including autoencoder and statistical features. We focus on the feature extraction of one-dimensional vibration signal which is commonly used for health condition monitoring of machines. Furthermore, two metrics, intra class distance and inter class distance, are introduced to measure the quality of the extracted features.

2.1 Contrastive Predicting Coding

Model Structure

Figure 1 shows the structure of the CPC model [18]. *Genc* is a feature extractor that extracts the representative features z_t from a one-dimensional data sample x_t, i.e. $z_t = Genc(x_t)$. The features of $z_{\leq t}$ are used as the input of an autoregressive model *Gar*, which learns the context latent representation c_t. Then the output of *Gar*, c_t, is used to predict $z_{>t}$. In the application of fault diagnosis, the input data is a one-dimensional vibration signal, where $x_{t-3:t+4}$ represents consecutive vibration signal samples, and $z_{t-3:t+4}$ are features extracted by *Genc*. *Gar* learns context c_t from $z_{t-3:t}$. Then c_t is used to predict $z_{t+1:t+4}$. If the prediction is accurate, it means that our feature extractor *Genc* has extracted representative features.

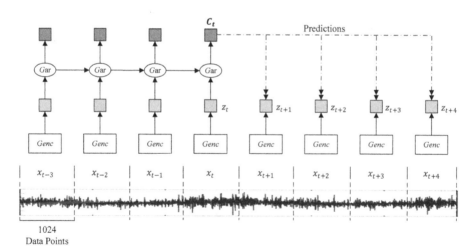

Fig. 1. Contrastive predicting coding structure

Through predicting future information, the model encodes data x using learned nonlinear mappings to context c, which is a compact distributed vector representation. The mutual information of the original data sample x and c is defined as:

$$I(x; c) = \sum_{x,c} p(x, c) log \frac{p(x|c)}{p(x)} \qquad (1)$$

By maximizing the mutual information between the original data and the coding representations, it is possible to extract the common latent variables of the input data samples.

This model preserves the mutual information between x_{t+k} and c_t by establishing a density ratio f:

$$f_k(x_{t+k}, c_t) \propto \frac{P(x_{t+k}|c_t)}{P(x_{t+k})} \tag{2}$$

where $\propto$ means proportional to. The CPC uses a simple logarithmic bilinear model for f:

$$f_k(x_{t+k}, c_t) = \exp(z_{t+k}^T W_k c_t) \tag{3}$$

where $W_k^T c_t$ means that for each step k, a linear transformer W_k is used for prediction. By using density ratio $f(x_{t+k}, c_t)$ to infer the accuracy of z_{t+k} prediction, the model can be liberated from the high-dimensional distribution of x_{t_k}.

In this work, a 1-Dimensional Convolutional Neural Network (1D-CNN) and a Gate Recurrent Unit (GRU) are used as the feature extractor $Genc$ and autoregressive model Gar, respectively. Please refer to [24] and [25] for details of 1D-CNN and GRU, respectively. It is also possible to replace them with other types of neural network models. The parameters of the feature extractor and autoregressive model are shown in Tables 2 and 3.

Loss Function

The infoNCE function is used in the training of the feature extractor and the autoregressive model to optimize them together. For a set of N data samples $X = \{x_1, \ldots, x_N\}$, including one positive sample from $p(x_{t+k}|c_t)$ and $N - 1$ negative samples randomly selected from $p(x_{t+k})$. The loss function to be optimized is:

$$\mathcal{L}_N = -E_X (\log \frac{f_k(x_{t+k}, c_t)}{\sum_{x_j \in X} f_k(x_j, c_t)}) \tag{4}$$

Equation 4 is to calculate the classification cross entropy of correctly classified samples, where $\frac{f_x}{\sum_X f_k}$ is the prediction of the model. Define $p(d = i|X, c_t)$ as the best probability of this loss, where $d = i$ means that the sample x_i is a positive sample. The probability that the sample x_i is from the conditional distribution $p(x_{t+k}|c_t)$ can be written as:

$$p(d = i|X, c_t) = \frac{p(x_i|c_t)\prod_{l \neq i} p(x_l)}{\sum_{j=1}^{N} p(x_j|c_t)\prod_{l \neq j} p(x_l)} = \frac{\frac{p(x_i|c_t)}{p(x_i)}}{\sum_{j=1}^{N} \frac{p(x_j|c_t)}{p(x_j)}} \tag{5}$$

Therefore, the optimal value of $f_k(x_{t+k}, c_t)$ in Eq. 4 is proportional to $\frac{p(x_{t+k}|c_t)}{p(x_{t+k})}$, and has nothing to do with the choice of $N - 1$ negative samples.

The mutual information between the variable c_t and x_{t+k} can be evaluated as follows:

$$I(x_{t+k}, c_t) \geq log(N) - \mathcal{L}_N \tag{6}$$

It can be seen from Eq. 6 that the lower bound of mutual information is maximized while minimizing the loss $\mathcal{L}_N$.

2.2 Autoencoder

Autoencoder [10] is an unsupervised neural network, which consists of two parts: encoder network and decoder network. Its structure is shown in Fig. 2. The input data input of autoencoder will first pass through the encoder network. The encoder network converts the input high-dimensional data into low-dimensional feature. These low-dimensional features are then fed into the decoder network to reconstruct the input data.

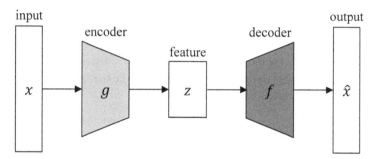

Fig. 2. Autoencoder structure

In Fig. 2 the encoder network is defined as g, and the input one-dimensional vibration data sample is defined as x, so we can get:

$$z = g(x) \tag{7}$$

where z is the low-dimensional feature to be encoded.

The decoder network is defined as g^*, which remaps the low-dimensional feature z to the reconstruction $\hat{x}$:

$$\hat{x} = g^*(z) \tag{8}$$

The purpose of training autoencoder is to minimize the error between input data x and its reconstruction $\hat{x}$, which can be written as:

$$\frac{1}{N} \sum_{i=1}^{N} \left(x_i - \hat{x}_i \right)^2 \tag{9}$$

where N is the number of samples in $X = \{x_1, \ldots, x_N\}$.

2.3 Statistical Features

Traditionally, the most common way of feature extraction from vibration signal is to calculate statistical metrics [23], such as the origin and central moments, of vibration data samples. The k-th order origin moment and central moment on the data sample x are calculated as $E(x^k)$ and $E(x - E(x))^k$, respectively.

In this paper, with respect to a one-dimensional vibration data sample x, the 2nd to the 7th order central moments and the first 7 orders of origin moments are computed as its statistical feature:

$$[E(x - E(x))^2, E(x - E(x))^3, \ldots, E(x - E(x))^7, E(x), E(x^2), \ldots, E(x^7)] \qquad (10)$$

where the 1st order central moment is not used since it is zero by definition.

2.4 Evaluation Metrics

Intra Class Distance

The intra class distance is the mean squared distance between each possible combination of two samples of the same class. Let $x_1^{(i)}, x_2^{(i)}, \ldots, x_{N_i}^{(i)}$ be the samples in the class Ω_i. The intra class distance within the class is as follows:

$$D_{intra}(\Omega_i) = \frac{1}{N_i N_i} \sum_{k=1}^{N_i} \sum_{l=1}^{N_i} d\left(x_k^{(i)}, x_l^{(i)}\right) \qquad (11)$$

Inter Class Distance

The inter class distance is the mean squared distance between two classes. The distance between Ω_i class and Ω_j is:

$$D_{inter}\left(\Omega_i, \Omega_j\right) = \frac{1}{N_i N_j} \sum_{k=1}^{N_i} \sum_{l=1}^{N_i} d\left(x_k^{(i)}, x_l^{(j)}\right) \qquad (12)$$

The $d(x, y)$ used in Eq. 11 and Eq. 12 calculates the Euclidean distance between two samples:

$$d(x, y) = \|x - y\|_2 \qquad (13)$$

3 Experimental Evaluation

The performance of feature extraction of CPC for one-dimensional vibration signals is evaluated and compared with those of autoencoder and statistical features. In the first analysis, the extracted features are qualitatively visualized using t-SNE (t-distributed Stochastic Neighbor Embedding) dimensionality reduction, and then quantitatively evaluated by computing the intra class distance and the inter class distance based on labels of the data. The second analysis performs k-means clustering on the extracted features to investigate whether the data of the same label could be correctly clustered together.

Table 1. Dataset description

Fault type	Fault diameter	Approx. motor speed (rpm)	Label
N	None	1797	0
BF	0.007″		1
	0.014″		2
	0.021″		3
IRF	0.007″		4
	0.014″		5
	0.021″		6
ORF	0.007″		7
	0.014″		8
	0.021″		9

3.1 Dataset

A benchmark dataset provided by the Case Western Reserve University (CWRU) for bearing fault diagnosis is used in this work. The drive-end bearing vibration acceleration signals were collected from a motor-driven mechanical system under the constant load (Motor Load (HP) is 0), with the sampling frequency of 12 kHz. Various types of bearing fault were considered during the experiment, including (1) Normal (N), (2) Outer race fault (ORF), (3) Inner race fault (IRF), (4) Ball fault (BF). The detailed information is as follows (Table 1):

The one-dimensional vibration signal was divided into samples, each contains 1024 data points, without overlapping. In total 1105 samples are obtained from the dataset.

3.2 Model Training

All the experiments were carried out under Ubuntu 20.04 and Keras 2.2.2 environment, running on a computer with an Intel Xeon E5-2680 v3, TITAN V, and 16G RAM.

Contrastive Predicting Coding

For the CPC model, parameters of the feature extractor $Genc$ are shown in Table 2. It is composed of 4 identical one-dimensional convolutional layers, in which the dimension of filters is 64, the kernel_size is 3, and the strides is 2. BatchNormalization is employed after each convolutional layer, with LeakyReLU as the activation function. A Dense layer with linear activation function is added to reduce the dimension of the flattened features, followed also by a BatchNormalization layer. Finally, a Dense layer reduces the dimension of feature to 16. The autoregressive model used in this article is GRU [19], and its parameters are shown in Table 3.

During model training, each batch of data contains 1 positive sequence and $N - 1$ negative sequences. The positive sequence contains 8 consecutive samples, and the

Table 2. Feature extractor parameters

Layers	Category	Parameters	Activation
1	Conv1D	F = 64, KS = 3, S = 2	linear
	Batch normalization	None	LeakyReLU
2	Conv1D	F = 64, KS = 3, S = 2	linear
	Batch normalization	None	LeakyReLU
3	Conv1D	F = 64, KS = 3, S = 2	linear
	Batch normalization	None	LeakyReLU
4	Conv1D	F = 64, KS = 3, S = 2	linear
	Batch normalization	None	LeakyReLU
5	Flatten	None	None
6	Dense	Units = 256	linear
	Batch normalization	None	LeakyReLU
7	Dense	Units = 16	linear

Remarks: F = filters; KS = kernel_size; S = strides

Table 3. GRU parameters

Layers	Category	Parameters	Activation
1	GRU	Units=256	None

autoregressive model uses features learned from the first 4 samples to predict those of the last 4 samples. Based on the positive samples, the negative samples are generated by replacing the last 4 samples of the positive sequence using data samples randomly selected in the dataset. Fourier transform was performed for all the data samples and the Fourier coefficients were used as the input of the feature extractor.

As shown in Fig. 1, in the training process, the first 4 samples in a sentence are sequentially input to the encoder $Genc$, and their output is used as input to train the autoregressive model (GRU) in turn. The output of GRU will be used to predict the features of the last 4 samples given by the feature extractor $Genc$.

The training of CPC model uses the Adam optimizer [20], its learning rate is set to 1e-3, and the number of training epochs is 100.

Autoencoder

For the Autoencoder model, Fourier coefficients of data samples are used as the input. The parameters and structure of the Autoencoder model are shown in Table 4. The Encoder consists of 6 Dense layers, and the numbers of neurons are [512, 256, 128, 64, 32, 16]. Decoder is also composed of 6 Dense layers, and the number of neurons are [32, 64, 128, 256, 512, 512]. Except for the last layer of Decoder which uses sigmoid activation function, all other layers use Relu activation function. The maximum training epoch is 100, and the learning rate is 1e-3. Adam is used as the optimizer.

Table 4. Autoencoder parameters

Layers	Category	Parameters	Activation
Encoder	Dense	Units = 512	Relu
	Dense	Units = 256	Relu
	Dense	Units = 128	Relu
	Dense	Units = 64	Relu
	Dense	Units = 32	Relu
	Dense	Units = 16	Relu
Decoder	Dense	Units = 32	Relu
	Dense	Units = 64	Relu
	Dense	Units = 128	Relu
	Dense	Units = 256	Relu
	Dense	Units = 512	Relu
	Dense	Units = 512	Sigmoid

3.3 Evaluation Using Dimensionality Reduction

After completing the training of the Contrastive Predicting Coding model, the Autoencoder model and the calculation of the statistical features, in this Section, their performance of feature extraction is first visually compared by performing t-SNE to reduce the dimensionality of the extracted features. Then, the quantitative comparison using the intra class distance and the inter class distance is reported by assuming the true labels of the data samples are known.

Visualization

- After the training of the CPC model, the feature extractor $Genc$ is used to perform feature extraction on the data samples. Then the 16-dimensional features extracted by $Genc$ are projected to two dimensions by t-SNE, as shown in Fig. 3(a).
- After training the Autoencoder model, the Encoder model is used to perform feature extraction. Then the 16-dimensional feature extracted by the Encoder is projected to two dimensions by t-SNE, as shown in Fig. 3(b).
- Perform t-SNE dimensionality reduction on the calculated 13-dimensional statistical feature vector (Sect. 2.3), and the two-dimensional projection map is shown in Fig. 3(c).

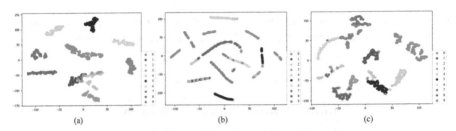

Fig. 3. Two-dimensional projection using t-SNE

Intra Class Distance and Inter Class Distance

The intra class distance and the inter class distance are calculated according to the real label of the data and the two-dimensional feature projection shown in Fig. 3. Table 5 reports the mean and standard deviation of intra class distances of all the 10 classes, and those of inter class distances of all the possible combinations of two classes.

Table 5. Intra class distance and inter class distance

	Statistical features	Autoencoder	Contrastive predicting coding
m-intra-D	24.61790601	56.34504745	21.28349128
usd-intra-D	11.92090304	25.9831751	6.739976173
m-inter-D	106.3398492	97.20098184	132.5177268
usd-inter-D	38.29549121	28.05794659	48.14294552

Remarks: m-intra-D: The mean of intra class distance; usd-intra-D: Unbiased standard deviation of intra class distance; m-inter-D: The mean of inter class distance; usd-inter-D: Unbiased standard deviation of inter class distance

3.4 Evaluation Using Clustering

The k-means clustering is used to cluster the features provided by CPC, autoencoder and statistical features to 10 categories, since we already know there are 10 classes in the dataset, to compare the pros and cons of each method.

- The result of clustering features provided by the feature extractor $Genc$ of CPC is shown in Fig. 4(a). Inspired by the confusion matrix used for measuring the performance of classification tasks, the x-axis is the real data class and the y-axis is the clustered category, therefore, the matrix shows the distribution of classes in each clustered category
- The result of clustering features provided by the encoder of autoencoder is shown in Fig. 4(b).
- The result of clustering the calculated statistical features is shown in Fig. 4(c).

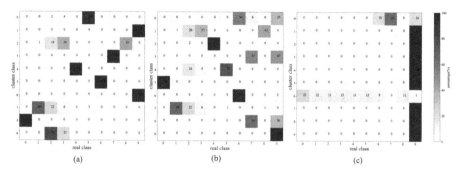

Fig. 4. Confusion matrix-like clustering results: (a) CPC; (b) autoencoder; (c) statistical feature

To quantitatively evaluate the performance of clustering, for each clustered category, the true label with the largest proportion is selected as its clustered label. Based on the clustered labels, we compute the proportion of correctly clustered samples, i.e. the samples whose true label matches the clustered label. The results are shown in the following table (Table 6):

Table 6. Clustering accuracy

	CPC	Autoencoder	Statistical features
Accuracy	0.828959276	0.726696833	0.333031674

3.5 Discussion of Results

Analysis Using Dimensionality Reduction
In order to show the advantages of CPC in reducing the dimensionality of the extracted features. We use t-SNE to perform dimensionality reduction and visualize the data after dimensionality reduction. The results are shown in Fig. 3 and Table 5.

It can be seen from Fig. 3(a) that 7 of the classes can be completely distinguished. The visualization of Fig. 3(b) obtained by using Autoencoder shows that it cannot effectively aggregate the classes, and its cluster shape is curve-like. In Fig. 3(c), there are many mixed classes, only two classes are identified without overlapping.

In Table 5, the average value of the intra class distance obtained by the CPC is 21.28. The average value of the intra class distance of the Autoencoder and statistical features are 56.34 and 24.61, respectively. The mean of inter class distance of CPC, autoencoder and statistical features are 132.51, 92.2, and 106.33. The average value of the intra class distance of CPC is less than the other two comparison methods, and the average value of the intra class distance is greater than the other two methods. It can be seen that the feature extractor trained by CPC can extract better features from the one-dimensional vibration signal.

Cluster Analysis

In Fig. 4(a), using the features extracted by the feature extractor of CPC to perform 10-class k-means clustering, 7 different classes are distinguished with high accuracy. Figure 4(b) shows that only 4 of 10 clusters are distinguished with high accuracy using the features extracted by the Encoder of Autoencoder, and in the remaining clustered categories the classes are highly mixed. In Fig. 4(c), for the result obtained using statistical features, it can be seen that 8 classes are mixed into the sixth clusters, and the real class cannot be distinguished. With respect to the accuracy, the use of CPC obtains 82.89%, larger than 72.66% of Autoencoder, and the accuracy obtained by using the statistical features is only 33.30%.

4 Summary

In this paper, the advanced self-supervised learning method CPC is employed to extract representative features from one-dimensional vibration signal to discover different categories in the dataset. The results are compared with autoencoder, a classic self-supervised learning method, and hand-crafted features extracted using statistical metrics, through t-SNE dimensionality reduction and clustering. The experimental results show that, compared with the autoencoder and statistical features, the feature extractor trained by the CPC can extract more representative features from the one-dimensional vibration signal, making it more effective for many actual industrial applications where the true label of data is not available. The feature extractor used in CPC is 1D-CNN. For the case where there are multiple signals in the monitoring data, each signal can be regarded as a different channel of 1D-CNN input. Therefore, the CPC method is also suitable for the scenario of multiple signals. In the future, we plan to further expand CPC to make it more suitable for the application of fault diagnosis.

Acknowledgements. This research is partially supported by the National Natural Science Foundation of China (52005103, 71801046, 51775112, 51975121), the Guangdong Basic and Applied Basic Research Foundation (2020A1515110139, 2019B1515120095), the Chongqing Natural Science Foundation (cstc2019jcyj-zdxmX0013), and the Intelligent Manufacturing PHM Innovation Team Program (2018KCXTD029, TDYB2019010).

References

1. Chuan, L., Cabrera, D., Sancho, F., Cerrada, M., Sánchez, R., Estupinan, E.: From fault detection to one-class severity discrimination of 3D printers with one-class support vector machine. ISA Trans. **110**, 357–367 (2021)
2. Dongying, H., Na, Z., Peiming, S.: Gear fault feature extraction and diagnosis method under different load excitation based on EMD, PSO-SVM and fractal box dimension. J. Mech. Sci. Technol. **33**(2), 487–494 (2019)

3. Shangjun, M., Bo, C., Zhaowei, S., Geng, L.: Scattering transform and LSPTSVM based fault diagnosis of rotating machinery. Mech. Syst. Signal Process. **104**, 155–170 (2018)
4. Samanta, B.: Gear fault detection using artificial neural networks and support vector machines with genetic algorithms. Mech. Syst. Signal Process. **18**(3), 625–644 (2004)
5. Dongming, X., Jiakai, D., Xuejun, L., Liangpei, H.: Gear fault diagnosis based on kurtosis criterion VMD and SOM neural network. Appl. Sci. **9**(24), 5424 (2019)
6. Moshen, K., Gang, C., Yusong, P., Yong, L.: Research of planetary gear fault diagnosis based on permutation entropy of CEEMDAN and ANFIS. Sensors **18**(3), 782 (2018)
7. Zhixin, Y., Xianbo, W., Pakkin, W.: Single and simultaneous fault diagnosis with application to a multistage gearbox: a versatile dual-ELM network approach. IEEE Trans. Industr. Inf. **14**(12), 5245–5255 (2018)
8. Lei, Y., Wenjie, F., Zongwen, L., Ying, L., Miao, F., Jin, W.: A fault diagnosis model for rotating machinery using VWC and MSFLA-SVM based on vibration signal analysis. Shock Vibr. 2019 (2019)
9. Kolar, D., Lisjak, D., Pająk, M., Pavković, D.: Fault diagnosis of rotary machines using deep convolutional neural network with wide three axis vibration signal input. Sensors **20**(14), 4017 (2020)
10. Hinton, G., Salakhutdinov, R.: Reducing the dimensionality of data with neural networks. Science **313**(5786), 504–507 (2006)
11. Ng, A.: Sparse autoencoder. CS294A Lect. Notes **72**(2011), 1–19 (2011)
12. Chengyuan, L., Weichen, C., Jiunwei, L., Dawran, L.: Autoencoder for words. Neurocomputing **139**, 84–96 (2014)
13. Ting, C., Kornblith, S., Norouzi, M., Hinton, G.: A simple framework for contrastive learning of visual representations. In: Proceedings of International Conference on Machine Learning. PMLR (2020)
14. Arora, S., Khandeparkar, H., Khodak, M., Plevrakis, O., Saunshi, N.: A theoretical analysis of contrastive unsupervised representation learning (2019). arXiv:1902.09229
15. Kaiming, H., Haoqi, F., Yuxin, W., Saining, X., Girshick, R.: Momentum contrast for unsupervised visual representation learning. In: Proceedings of the IEEE/CVF Conference on Computer Vision and Pattern Recognition, pp. 9729–9738 (2020)
16. Bo, D., Dahua, L.: Contrastive learning for image captioning (2017). arXiv:1710.02534
17. Kipf, T., van der Pol, E., Welling, M.: Contrastive learning of structured world models (2019). arXiv:1911.12247
18. Oord, A., Yazhe, L., Vinyals, O.: Representation learning with contrastive predictive coding (2018). arXiv:1807.03748
19. Cho, K., et al.: Learning phrase representations using RNN encoder-decoder for statistical machine translation (2014). arXiv:1406.1078
20. KingaD, A.: A methodforstochasticoptimization. In: Anon. InternationalConferenceon Learning Representations. ICLR, SanDego (2015)
21. Sainath, T., Mohamed, A., Kingsbury, B., Ramabhadran, B.: Deep convolutional neural networks for LVCSR. IEEE. In: Proceedings of 2013 IEEE international conference on acoustics, speech and signal processing, pp. 8614–8618. IEEE (2013)
22. Jianyu, L., Shaohui, Z., Chuan, L.: Evolving deep echo state networks for intelligent fault diagnosis. IEEE Trans. Industr. Inf. **16**(7), 4928–4937 (2019)
23. Jegadeeshwaran, R., Sugumaran, V.: Fault diagnosis of automobile hydraulic brake system using statistical features and support vector machines. Mech. Syst. Signal Process. **52**, 436–446 (2015)
24. Shumei, C., Jianbo, Y., Shijin, W.: One-dimensional convolutional auto-encoder-based feature learning for fault diagnosis of multivariate processes. J. Process Control **87**, 54–67 (2020)
25. Fangfang, Y., Weihua, L., Chuan, L., Qiang, M.: State-of-charge estimation of lithium-ion batteries based on gated recurrent neural network. Energy **175**, 66–75 (2019)

SGWnet: An Interpretable Convolutional Neural Network for Mechanical Fault Intelligent Diagnosis

Jing Yuan[✉], Shuwei Cao, Gangxing Ren, Huiming Jiang, and Qian Zhao

School of Mechanical Engineering, University of Shanghai for Science and Technology, 516 Jun Gong Road, Shanghai 200093, China
yuanjing@usst.edu.cn

Abstract. Deep learning and neural network have great advantages in the field of mechanical fault diagnosis. Mechanical fault diagnosis is stepping into the era of big data and artificial intelligence. CNN (Convolutional Neural Network) is popular in fault pattern recognition due to its powerful nonlinear mapping and feature learning ability, and the signal features extracted by the first layer of CNN influence the performance of the entire network. Therefore, a new one-dimensional convolutional neural network (SGWnet) is proposed in this paper. The first layer of SGWnet is the second-generation wavelet convolution in signal processing, which greatly increases the feature extraction ability of the neural network for the original signal. The interpretability of the second generation wavelet layer in SGWnet is explored in this paper. Meanwhile, CWRU bearing fault data is used to validated the effectiveness of the method.

Keywords: Deep learning · CNN · Signal processing · Second generation wavelet · Interpretability

1 Introduction

With the rapid development of science and technology, more and more large and intelligent mechanical equipment and complex systems are the key to maintain the operation of the country and society. Once the mechanical equipment breaks down, it will cause casualties and property losses, which highlights the importance of mechanical fault diagnosis technology.

Deep learning method has a natural diagnostic advantage for non-stationary signals. After collected by sensors, the non-stationary signals are directly put into the intelligent framework of deep learning for feature extraction and accurate identification. For example, Bruin et.al has designed a long and short term memory of neural network to monitor and identify faults on railway lines, which can achieve 99.7% accuracy [1]. Zhang et.al proposes a method of deep learning for identification of fault type of the rotating machinery based on recursive neural network, which is not only more accurate in diagnosis results, but also robust to noise [2].

© Springer Nature Singapore Pte Ltd. 2021
H. Zhang et al. (Eds.): NCAA 2021, CCIS 1449, pp. 360–374, 2021.
https://doi.org/10.1007/978-981-16-5188-5_26

As an important part of deep learning, CNN is widely used in mechanical fault diagnosis for its strong nonlinear mapping and features. For one-dimensional convolutional neural network (1D-CNN), in view of the shortcomings of single scale and size of the traditional one-dimensional convolutional layer, Cao et.al designed a one-dimensional convolutional neural network with multi-scale convolutional layer (MSK) and the ELU activation function, which has high accuracy and strong robustness in fault diagnosis under strong noise environment [3]. Wei et.al proposed a one-dimensional convolutional neural network (WD-CNN) with a wide one-layer kernel to solve the poor performance of most deep learning models under noise interference which has a higher fault recognition degree and better anti-interference performance in strong noise environment [4]. Chen et al. designed a 1D-CNN which can directly process the original signal, and this model achieved very high accuracy on the data set of bearing fault identification [5]. The above examples show that CNN is not only widely used in fault diagnosis, but also has a very high recognition rate for fault mode and fault degree.

Although CNN has made such brilliant achievements in the field of fault diagnosis, there are few explorations on the interpretability of Convolutional layer. It is well known that shallow convolution of convolutional neural networks is easy to extract more obvious features from the original data, while deep convolution is always more sensitive to high-dimensional nonlinear features. Alekseev and Bobe proposed an interpretable CNN named Gabornet which framework adopts Gabor wavelet as the convolution kernel of neural network, so that the convolution combination is interpretable [6]. Grezmak et.al proposed an interpretable neural network based on hierarchical correlation propagation for gearbox fault diagnosis. Sun et.al proposed an interpretable convolutional neural network for industrial production intelligent diagnosis. The first layer of the network is replaced by continuous wavelet in signal processing, which makes the network have clearer physical meaning and diagnostic performance [7].

The second generation wavelet (SGW) has many excellent properties in mechanical fault processing: SGW break the traditional convention that the wavelet can only be constructed in the frequency domain; the algorithm of the second generation wavelet transform is simple and fast; the second-generation wavelet transform itself is the process of convolution. If the general CNN convolution is replaced by the second-generation wavelet kernel convolution, the features extracted from the input signal through the first layer of the convolutional neural network will be more obvious, which is beneficial to the training and performance of the network. Therefore, a new interpretable CNN (named SGWnet) is proposed in this paper. The first layer of the network is the second generation wavelet transform layer, i.e. the ordinary convolutional kernel is replaced by the second generation wavelet transform convolution. The second-generation wavelet convolution layer has the following characteristics:

1. Since the second generation wavelet transform has split, predict and update operations, the first layer of the network is the complex convolution layer.
2. If the features extracted from the first convolution layer of CNN are clear, it will be helpful for the fault diagnosis performance of the neural network. Therefore, the decomposition times of the second generation wavelet convolution layer are chosen as three times, that is, the second generation wavelet transform is carried out three times. In this way, the signal output by the second-generation wavelet transform

convolution layer could reduce the high-frequency noise-component, and the low-frequency effective information which is really helpful to the network performance would be retained and highlighted.

3. We will add the mathematical restrictions to the second-generation wavelet convolution kernel, which will not only meet the second-generation wavelet conditions in the signal processing field, but also enable the input signal to extract more vivid and clear features when passing through the second-generation wavelet layer. Meanwhile, this paper will facilitate the exploration of the physical significance of the second-generation wavelet layer.

The rest of the thesis is arranged as follows. Section 2 describes the theoretical basis of CNN and the second generation wavelet. Section 3 introduces the core method of this paper, which is to replace the ordinary convolution layer with the second generation wavelet. Section 4 uses the simulation data to verify the performance of the model and explore the interpretability of the second-generation wavelet convolution layer. The final section is the conclusion of this paper.

2 Theoretical Basis

2.1 Second Generation Wavelet Transform

Sweldens proposed a lifting framework that is different from the first generation of wavelet transform, namely the second generation of wavelet transform. The second generation wavelet transform consists of three parts: split, predict and update. Figure 1 show the schematic diagram of the second generation wavelet transform.

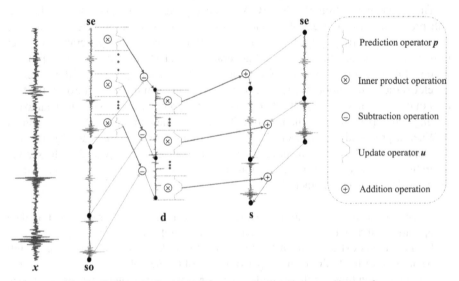

Fig. 1. Schematic diagram of the second generation wavelet transform

Split. Input signal x is splitted into se (sequence of odd samples) and so (even samples), as shown in Eq. 1 and 2.

$$se(n) = x(2n) \tag{1}$$

$$so(n) = x(2n+1) \tag{2}$$

Predict. The adjacent even samples are used to predict the odd samples, and the predict error is the detail signal (d), as shown in Eq. 3.

$$d = so - P(se) \tag{3}$$

where $P(\bullet)$ is a convolution mode. In the edge convolution, this paper adopts the zero-filling mode.

Update. The approximation signal s is obtained by updating even sample on the basis of detail signal d, as shown in Eq. 4.

$$s = se + U(d) \tag{4}$$

where the convolution operation of $U(\bullet)$ is opposite to the zero filling method of the convolution of $P(\bullet)$ on the left and right sides of the signal. Figure 1 shows the schematic diagram of the second generation wavelet transform.

2.2 Estimation Method of Predictor and Updater Coefficients Based on Equivalent Filter

Claypoole et.al proposes a method to solve the prediction operator p and update operator u in the second generation wavelet transform [9]. When the length of p and p of a standard second generation wavelet is determined, its size is determined accordingly. Suppose that the number of prediction p is N, $p = [p_1, p_2, \cdots, p_N]$. When decomposed by the second generation wavelet, the relation between the equivalent high-pass filter coefficient $\tilde{g}$ and the predictor p is expressed as Eq. 5.

$$\tilde{g} = [-p_1, 0, -p_2, 0, \cdots, -p_{N/2}, 1, -P_{N/2+1}, \cdots, 0, p_N] \tag{5}$$

Jawerth and Sweldens has shown that the order of the predictive polynomial is the same as the vanishing distance of the wavelet [10]. Similarly, the equivalent high-pass filter $\tilde{g}$ also has the same vanishing distance, as shown in Eq. 6.

$$\sum_{r=-N+1}^{N-1} r^q \tilde{g}_r = 0, 0 \leq q < N \tag{6}$$

From Eq. 6, the coefficient of the prediction operation p can be calculated. The sequence of coefficients of updating operation u can be obtained by this method [11].

2.3 CNN

Convolution layer. The convolution layer acts as a feature extractor. The input signals are scanned by some specific size convolution checks to form the eigenmatrix. The advantages of the convolutional layer lie in the powerful feature extraction ability and the sharing ability of the convolutional kernel. Compared with the general neural network layer, the computational amount and parameters of the convolutional layer are much less, which is also the main reason why the convolutional neural network is widely used in the field of image recognition and feature extraction.

$$h_j^l = f(w_j^l * x^{(l-1)} + b_j^l) \tag{7}$$

In Eq. 7, w_j^l represent the weight of the j-th convolution kernel at the l layer. b_j^l is the deviation corresponding to the j-th of the l layer. x is the input signal and h is the output signal. f is nonlinear activation function. The function of activation function is that the output signal of the convolutional layer is processed by nonlinear function, which enhances the nonlinear fitting ability of the neural network. For example, the expression for relu is shown as Eq. 8.

$$f(x) = \max(0, x) \tag{8}$$

Pooling layer. The pooling layer reduces the dimension of the data and also extracts the signal features. In the case of convolutional neural network with or without a pooling layer, the accuracy gap is very large, so pooling layer is an essential part of CNN as well as the convolutional layer. There are three types of pooling: maximum pooling, average pooling, and random pooling. In order to highlight the signal characteristics, this paper adopts maximum pooling, as shown in Eq. 9.

$$y^{l+1} = down(h_j^l) + b^{l+1} \tag{9}$$

3 Methods of the Paper

3.1 Combination of Second Generation Wavelet and Convolutional Neural Network

Global operation process of second-generation wavelet convolution kernel based on subdivision prediction update. The second generation wavelet convolution kernel is decomposed by cubic second generation wavelet transform, namely, the process of cubic split, predict and update. It is assumed that the k-th split, predict and decomposition process is being carried out. The k-th second generation wavelet decomposition process is shown in Eqs. 10–13.

$$so_i^k(n) = x_i^{k-1}(2n + 1) \tag{10}$$

$$se_i^k(n) = x_i^{k-1}(2n) \tag{11}$$

where, x_i^{k-1} is the i-th output signal of the k-1-st second generation wavelet transform, and se_i^k and so_i^k are the i-th even sample sequence and odd sample sequence of the k-st second generation wavelet transform.

$$d_i^k = f(so_i^k - g_1(se_i^k, p_i^k)) \tag{12}$$

Equation 12 is the prediction process, and p is the second-generation wavelet prediction operator. g_1 is a convolution with complementing zero at the edge, that is, in order to make the signal length after convolution the same as that before convolution, zero filling operation is carried out on the left and right side of se_i^k. The number of zeros filling depends on the length of p_i^k. d_i^k is the detail signal.

$$s_i^k = f(se_i^k + g_1(d_i^k, u_i^k)) \tag{13}$$

Equation 13 is the updating process, and u is the second-generation wavelet updating operator.

Constraints on the Prediction p
In order to make the signal decomposed by convolution layer with the second generation wavelet kernel (sgwlayer) conform to the law of the second generation wavelet transform, constraint processing of p is needed here. According to Eq. (6), the determination of the second-generation wavelet predictor p is related to the number of coefficients N. Suppose

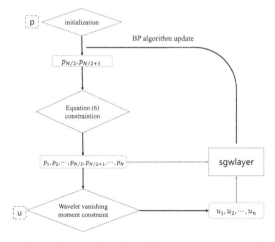

Fig. 2. Specific constraints of convolution kernel in the second generation wavelet kernel of convolution layer

$p = [p_1, p_2, \cdots, p_{N/2}, p_{N/2+1}, \cdots, p_N]$. Here, a predictor with polynomial order N (the number of which is also N) is set to have only $N - 2$ order vanishing distance, and the remaining 2 order vanishing distance is randomly initialized by neural network and trained to update, which is the scale adaptive constraint of the second generation wavelet. The specific operation is shown in Fig. 2.

Obviously, the solution of p_i in Fig. 1 becomes a constrained least squares problem. When $p_{N/2}$ and $p_{N/2+1}$ are determined, p is also determined. When the predictive operator p is determined, the value of u can be determined by same operation.

3.2 Framework and Parameters of SGWnet

The structure of the one-dimensional convolutional neural network whose convolution kernel are based on the second-generation wavelet as proposed in this paper is shown in Fig. 3, and the detailed parameters are shown in Table 1.

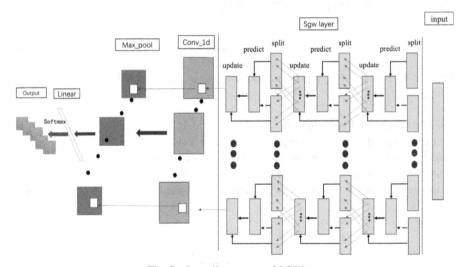

Fig. 3. Overall structure of SGWnet.

Figure 2 describes the general structure of SGWnet neural network framework. Table 1 is a detailed introduction to each layer of SGWnet and the number of parameters it contains. It can be seen from the table that the number of parameters contained in sgwlayer is very small compared with other layers, which is conducive to the training of neural network.

Table 1. Details of SGWnet network parameters.

Layer	Output	Parameters
sgwlayer	$1 \times 6 \times 128$	12
Conv_1d	$1 \times 10 \times 124$	310
Conv_1d	$1 \times 16 \times 100$	4016
Maxpool_1d	$1 \times 16 \times 16$	0
Linear	1×72	18,504
Linear	1×4	292

4 Simulation Experiment

4.1 Simulation Experiment Based on Inner Product Matching Principle

In order to explore whether the first layer convolution kernel of SGWnet extracts signal features in the same way as the second generation wavelet transform, this paper designs a kind of simulation data to verify the interpretability of SGWnet convolution kernel. The simulation data consists of standard (10,10) second-generation wavelets, db2 and db10 wavelets (as shown in Fig. 4). On the basis of each wavelet, a high-frequency sinusoidal signal y is superimposed to generate experimental signals, y is shown in Eq. 8. Numerous wavelet and noise signals are connected in series, and then sample label signals of the same length are intercepted at random positions. The number of data points per sample is 1024. Figure 5 shows one of the label sample signals after noise.

$$y = 0.5\sin(100t), t = 1, 2, 3, \cdots, 1024 \tag{14}$$

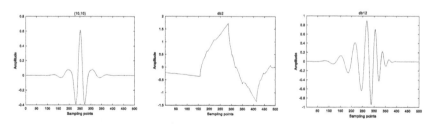

Fig. 4. Shape diagram of (10,10) second generation wavelet, db2 and db10 wavelet

Since the signal features extracted by the first layer of CNN have a great impact on the diagnostic performance of the whole network, the second generation wavelet transform of three times is carried out in the first layer of SGWnet framework. Figure 6 shows the graph of the input signal after three second-generation wavelet transforms.

As can be seen from Fig. 6, signal features after three-layer decomposition are more obvious than those of the first and second decomposition. At this time, high-frequency

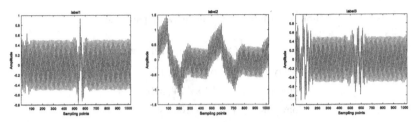

Fig. 5. Label signal with high-frequency sinusoidal noise

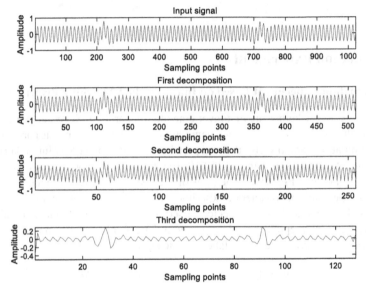

Fig. 6. A (10,10) second generation wavelet denoised signal and three-level approximation signal

sinusoidal noise is basically filtered by SGWnet. Therefore, the second generation wavelet layer of SGWnet is split, predict and update at three times in total.

The training data volume of each sample label is 50 and the test data volume is 30, so the total number of simulation data samples is 240, among which the training and test samples are 150 and 90 respectively. After 40 rounds of training, the accuracy rate of SGWnet neural network on the test set reached 98.9%.

Before training, the second-generation wavelet kernel convolution in the sgwlayer is graphically chaotic due to the initialization of the neural network (represented by the line segment in green color in the Fig. 7). After a period of training, the second-generation wavelet convolution will gradually become the standard (10,10) second-generation wavelet graph (represented by the red line segment in the Fig. 7). Standard second-generation wavelet has been widely used in signal processing and feature extraction due to its advantages., which indicates that the process of extracting signal features of SGWnet by sgwlayer is the same as that of the second-generation wavelet transform. The principle of SGWnet second generation wavelet layer can be explained by the inner product matching principle in signal processing. The principle of inner product matching refers to the inner product between signals x and y, and the size of the inner product result represents the similarity between signals x and y. The larger the inner product result is, the higher the similarity of x and y data structure is, and vice versa. The second generation wavelet transform based on the steps of split, predict and update is also a kind of internal machine transform. In the forward and backward transmission process of sgwlayer, the convolution kernel of the second generation wavelet will gradually find the component most similar to the input signal. In the training data, we add (10,10) second generation wavelet and high frequency noise. Since the predict and update length of sgwlayer's second generation wavelet convolution kernel is also set to 10, following the inner product matching principle, the second generation wavelet convolution kernel from the initial scattered state will be approach to the waveforms of (10,10) wavelet.

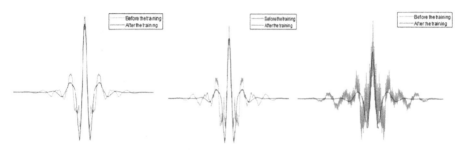

Fig. 7. Kernel variation diagram of the second generation wavelet of SGWnet's first convolutional layer

This paper uses the training signal composed of (10,10) standard second generation wavelet to explore the interpretability of sgwlayer, that is, whether sgwlayer will follow the inner product matching principle in signal processing in the operation of neural network. The results show that the second generation wavelet convolution kernel in sgwlayer will gradually learn (10,10) wavelet from the scattered state of neural network initialization, so as to match waveforms of (10,10) wavelet.

4.2 Validation of CWRU Dataset

CWRU bearing fault data sets were collected on the drive end bearing and fan end bearing respectively[i]. The test bed consists of a motor, a torque sensor/encoder, and a force meter, as shown in Fig. 8. The shaft bearings runs at a constant speed at from 1730 to 1797 rpm, corresponding to the motor load (0HP–3HP). Bearing fault types include roller, inner ring and outer ring faults, and four types of faults with diameters of 0.007, 0.014, 0.021 and 0.028 inches are manufactured under each type of fault. Sampling frequency of sensor is 12 kHz and 48 kHz. Among them, the acquisition signal sampling frequency of the bearing sensor at the drive end is 12 kHz and 48 kHz, and the sampling frequency of the bearing at the fan end is 12 kHz.

Fig. 8. Case western storage bearing test rig (Case Western Reserve University (CWRU))

The bearing signal data were established on the basis of CWRU data set. The driving end bearing with a fault diameter of 0.014 inches was selected. The inner ring (IF), outer ring (OF) and roller (RF) fault signals are obtained under the motor load of 1–3HP, respectively, while the normal bearing signals (NC) are collected under the state without any motor load. Table 2 shows the types of bearing signals collected. Figure 9 shows the signals under the four labels.

Table 2. Bearing signal types selected from CWUR

Workload	NC	IF	RF	OF
0HP	✓			
1HP		✓		
2HP			✓	
3HP				✓

The total number of samples in the bearing signal data set is 400. The training and test samples are divided in a ratio of 1:1. After 35 rounds of training, the mean correct recognition rate of SGWnet on the test set is 99.375%.

In order to explore the performance of, the first convolutional layer in SGWnet, we loosen the restrictions of predict operators and update operators and make it a common convolutional layer and form a neural network framework corresponding to SGWnet, which named CNN with ordinary layer. After the training of CWRU data set, the mean accuracy of CNN with ordinary layer on the test set were 92.125%, respectively. Figure 10 shows the loss changes of the two neural network frameworks in the training process.

As can be seen from Fig. 10, SGWnet loss declines more slowly in the training process compared with CNN with ordinary layer, indicating that SGWnet updates weight parameters greatly in the back propagation.

When we use the T-SNE technique to visualize the output of the last layer of the neural network, as shown in Fig. 11, the distribution of the original data through the last layer of SGWnet is very clear. There is no overlap between the data of each tag.

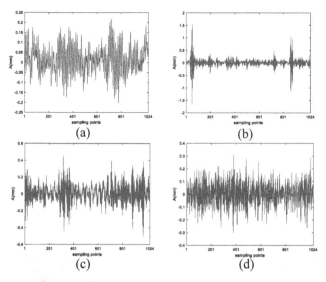

Fig. 9. Bearing signals of four labels. Where (a) is NC, (b) is IF, (c) is RF and (d) is OF

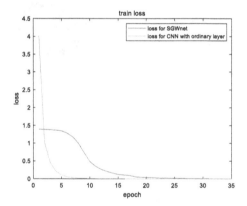

Fig. 10. Variation diagram of train loss

However, In the last layer of CNN with ordinary layer, the IF data tag overlaps with the OF data tag. This is one of the surface reasons why the diagnosis rate of CNN with ordinary layer is not as good as SGWnet. The deep reason is that the first layer of CNN with ordinary layer does not extract clear and effective features like SGWnet.

Figure 12 shows the confusion matrix of SGWnet and CNN with ordinary layer on the test set, indicating that the diagnostic accuracy of SGWnet on the CWUR bearing data set is better than that of CNN with ordinary layer.

This paper also selects two fault signal diagnosis models. The process that the signal is transformed by Fourier transform and then passed through support vector machine

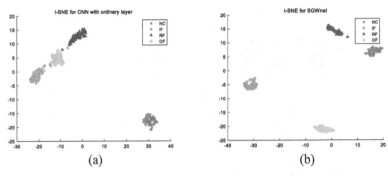

(a)   (b)

Fig. 11. T-SNE visualization of the last layer of CNN. (a) is the last visualization result of CNN with ordinary layer, and (b) is the last visualization result of SGWnet

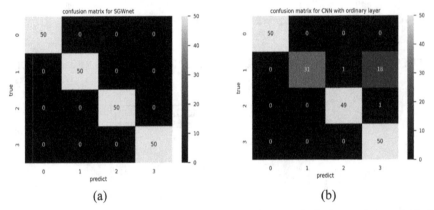

(a)   (b)

Fig. 12. The confusion matrix of the two neural network frameworks in the test data set. (a) is the confusion matrix of SGWnet in test set, (b) is the confusion matrix of CNN with ordinary layer in test set.

(SVM) and Multi-layer Perceptron (MLP) are called FFT_SVM and FFT_MLP, respectively. In addition, the 1D-CNN mainstream deep learning fault diagnosis model in reference 7 is selected here for comparison with the above methods. Table 3 shows the recognition rate of bearing test data by various methods. It can be seen that CNN, which does not limit the second generation wavelet, has the lowest diagnostic rate for fault signals. The traditional signal diagnosis model FFT_SVM has 95% recognition rate for fault signals, while the diagnostic rates of FFT_MLP proposed in this paper has reached 100%. 1D-CNN also has a 99.675% diagnostic rate for bearing data sets with four types of faults.

The comparison of the above results shows that SGWnet has a high recognition rate for bearing fault data sets. These indicate the rationality of SGWnet design and the scientific nature of the method proposed in this paper.

Table 3. Diagnostic accuracy of various diagnostic methods for CWUR **dataset**

Method	Mean accuracy(%)
CNN with ordinary layer	90.5
FFT_SVM	95
FFT_MLP	100
SGWnet	99.125
1D-CNN	99.675

5   Conclusion

In this paper, a new interpretable convolutional neural network (SGWnet) is proposed. The first layer of the neural network is the second generation wavelet convolution layer (sgwlayer), which includes split, predict and update. At the same time, we also limit the vanishing moment of the second generation wavelet convolution. Through a group of simulation data, the graphic changes of the second-generation wavelet convolution in the SGWLayer before and after training can be clearly seen, thus the physical significance of the second-generation wavelet convolution in the sgwlayer can be obtained. The feasibility and effectiveness of SGWnet for CWRU fault bearing data are verified by high diagnosis rate of SGWnet. Meanwhile, it is found that whether the sgwlayer constrains the vanishing moment of p and u operator has a great influence on the diagnostic performance of SGWnet, which also demonstrates the superiority of sgwlayer constraining p and u operator in feature extraction. The comparative experiments show that SGWnet has strong ability of feature extraction and fault signal recognition.

Acknowledgements. This research is sponsored by National Natural Science Foundations of China (No. 51975377 and 52005335), Shanghai Sailing Program (No. 18YF1417800) and Shanghai Aerospace Science and Technology Innovation Fund (SAST2019-100). The work is also partly supported by the Shanghai Special Funds for Industrial Transformation, Upgrading and Development (No. GYQJ-2019-1-03), and Key Laboratory of Vibration and Control of Aero-Propulsion System Ministry of Education, Northeastern University (VCAME201907). (Corresponding author: Jing Yuan.)

References

1. Bruin, T., Verbert, K., Babuka, R.: Railway track circuit fault diagnosis using recurrent neural networks. IEEE Trans. Neural Netw. Learsn. Syst. **28**(3), 523–533 (2016)
2. Zhang, Y., Zhou, T., Huang, X., et al.: Fault diagnosis of rotating machinery based on recurrent neural networks. Measurement **171**, 108774 (2020)
3. Cao, J., He, Z., Wang, J., et al.: An antinoise fault diagnosis method based on multiscale 1DCNN. Shock Vib. **7**, 1–10 (2020)
4. Zhang, W., Peng, G., Li, C., et al.: A new deep learning model for fault diagnosis with good anti-noise and domain adaptation ability on raw vibration signals. Sensors **17**(3), 425 (2017)

5. Chen, C., Liu, Z., Yang, G., et.al.: An improved fault diagnosis using 1D-convolutional neural network model. Electronics **10**, 1–59 (2021)
6. Alekseev, A., Bobe, A.: GaborNet: gabor filters with learnable parameters in deep convolutional neural network. Artificial Neural Networks (2019)
7. Grezmak, J., Wang, P., Sun, C., et.al.: Explainable convolutional neural network for gearbox fault diagnosis. In: Procedia CIRP, pp. 476–481(2019)
8. Li, T., et al.: WaveletKernelNet: An Interpretable Deep Neural Network for Industrial Intelligent Diagnosis (2019)
9. Claypoole, R.L., Baraniuk, R.G., Nowak, R.D.: Adaptive wavelet transforms via lifting. In: IEEE International Conference on Acoustics, Speech and Signal Processing, pp, 1513–1516 (1998)
10. Jawerth, B., Sweldens, W.: An overview of wavelet based multiresulotion analysis (1994)
11. Case Western Reserve University. Bearing Data Center [M/OL]. http://csegroupscaseedu/bearingdatacenter/

GFU-Net: A Deep Learning Approach for Automatic Metal Crack Detection

Yanchao Zhang[1], Xiangdong Li[1], Jingbo Qiu[2(✉)], Xiangping Zhai[2],
and Mingqiang Wei[2]

[1] Jiangsu Special Equipment Safety Supervision and Inspection Institute,
Nanjing 210036, China
[2] Nanjing University of Aeronautics and Astronautics, Nanjing 211106, China
{qiujingbo,blueicezhaixp,mqwei}@nuaa.edu.cn

Abstract. Crack is a common type of metal indication defects, which brings great hidden dangers to safety of hoisting machinery in use. Automatic metal crack detection methods could be practical in less expensive and high efficiency. In this paper, an encoder-decoder convolutional neural network is proposed, called GFU-Net, which can automatically predict pixel-level crack segmentation by end-to-end method. GFU-Net introduces the guide transformer module on U-Net's base to strengthen the fusion between corresponding features and applies the Deeply-Supervised Net (DSN), which places features of each convolutional stage under the integrated straight supervision. The experiments show that our work outperforms all other models we test in this article and detects metal cracks from low-contrast images effectively and explicitly.

Keywords: U-Net · Metal defect detection · Crack segmentation · Deep learning

1 Introduction

Crack is a main performance of surface defect in metal. Under the action of stress, some weak parts of the complete metal will be partially broken. In practical applications, various tiny cracks are unavoidable in metal parts. However, with the gradual growth of cracks, the metal is easily broken. During the use of hoisting machinery, the failure of metal equipment often brings catastrophic consequences. Non-destructive testing for cracks is a key to evaluate the safety status of hoisting machinery. It also can prevent the occurrence of fracture and accidents. Traditional manual cracks detection is mainly performed through the observation of human eyes, which is considerably tedious, time-consuming and subjective. Therefore, automatic detection method has gradually become a trend, which greatly enhances the work efficiency and lower the consumption.

Image processing technology has applied in crack detection area in the past decades, mainly divided into statistical method [16,22,25,29,35], spectral method [19,30,36], model-based method el. Statistical methods use some easily

H. Zhang et al. (Eds.): NCAA 2021, CCIS 1449, pp. 375–388, 2021.
https://doi.org/10.1007/978-981-16-5188-5_27

obtained attributes, such as anisotropy, regularity of distribution and other features for crack detection. Obviously, this method is susceptible to noise, because it is performed in pixel domain. In the spectral method, they utilize the transform domain operation to find a better solution to separate the background. However, it lacks effective use of local information and has a bottleneck on promiscuous defects. In general, the detection results of image processing technology are very sensitive to environmental factors, which make the application of these methods in real life limited.

At the same time, surface cracks have various characteristics which are difficult to solve. First of all, The low contrast between the crack and the surrounding environment makes it difficult to distinguish. Secondly, cracks on the surface usually only occupy a few pixels in the image. Thirdly, Shadows, uneven lighting and other defects such as stains, fray, blowhole in the image make accurate detection a challenge. With the rapid improvement of deep-learning, several works [11,31,33] applied this technique for crack detection naturally. Deep learning completes various tasks by extracting the abstract features and overcome the drawbacks of image processing technology. For crack detect task, object recognition can be divided into three categories: classification, detection and segmentation. This method achieves a great outcome on crack detection when interfered by background noise, but it can not keep more detailed information about the crack.

In summary, how to extract metal cracks under the background of complex noise and retain the details of the cracks is a compelling question to be answered. We propose an end-to-end metal crack detection model, named Guiding Feature U-Net(GFU-Net), which uses the encoder-decoder architecture to achieve precise crack detection. We construct a guide transformer, which can guide the feature map in the encoding network to correct the decoding process. To gain consequential features about crack segmentation, DSN [20] was applied to supervise every side-output layer simultaneously. It is efficient and automatic. We also use the Ghost bottleneck to replace the traditional convolutional layers which will reduce the computation. All the applications make extracting crack results more accurate. This method abandons the limitations of traditional crack detection and extraction technology, and can automatically detect cracks in the image, with high segmentation accuracy, and has high practical application value.

2   Related Work

In this section, two parts are divided to introduce crack detection methods. One is the traditional image processing method in computer vision field. Then, deep learning-based crack detection works are reviewed to compare with traditional approaches.

2.1   Traditional Crack Detection Methods

Because the color of the crack in captured picture is darker than the surrounding pixels, threshold segmentation based on pixel intensity difference is the most direct way to obtain the crack results. NDHM (Neighboring Difference Histogram Method) [22] constructs an objective function to maximize the divergence between crack and background. [16,25,28,29,35] adopted multi-step threshold segmentation technology. Firstly, preprocessing is used to remove most of the noise influence, and then the initial crack candidate region is obtained by improved threshold segmentation method. Finally, morphological operations and other refinements refine the accuracy of cracks region. However, this method cannot completely avoid the noise interference caused by the stains, spots and uneven illumination, and does not perform well during test phase.

To increase preciseness and integrity, the methods based on wavelet transforms were introduced to generate crack localities and regions. Through this way, [36] decomposed the images into different frequency sub-bands. The high frequency sub-band converted from interference and noise is called detail, and the low frequency sub-band converted from background is called approximation. [30] realizes crack segmentation based on wavelet transform, which overcomes the background noise. [19] proved that it is possible to identify features of the occluded crack through two-dimensional spatial wavelet transform. Still and all, due to the anisotropy of wavelet, out crack images with high curvature or low continuity were failed to deal with.

There are some similarities between crack detection and edge detection due to the width of crack is relatively narrow. Canny [3] algorithm is a typical representative, which calculates the intensity and direction of the gradient to determine the range of edge. [32,34] are upgraded versions of [3], which use adaptive filtering algorithms to achieve complete and rich edge details. [2] can automatically set endpoints and integrate both photometric and geometric characteristic. MPS [1] analyzes images from both local and global perspectives. It selects significant pixels as endpoints to limit minimum path and choose their lowest costs. [37] introduced a geodesic shadow-removal algorithm to reduce the influence of background. Then, the MSTs (minimum spanning trees) is used to describe possible path between crack seeds generated from crack probability map. [23] is extended on the basis of F* algorithm, so there is no need to set key points in advance, and local space is set to speed up. The choice and location of endpoints influence achievements of crack detection results, and most algorithms must manually set seed points. In addition, when processing large-size crack images, the algorithm is inefficient.

2.2 Deep Learning-Based Methods

Deep learning has been widely applied to surface defect detection in recent years. [18] introduced CNN (convolutional neural networks), it can automatically extract features into computer vision to solve classification problems. Thus, CNN architecture is widely used in defect detection. A deep framework of CNN built up by [4] detects cracks in concrete and metal surfaces. The results of this method were less influenced by the noise generated by extensively changeable real-world conditions. [14] proposed an end-to-end defect inspection system through fusing multilevel features which can provide detailed defect status. TLU-Net [10] uses pre-trained ResNet [13] and DenseNet [15] to construct the U-net [26] structure, which verifies the effectiveness of transfer learning in surface defect work. You only look once (YOLO) [27] network defines the task of target detection as a regression problem, which reduce detection time consumption and be applied in real-time scenes. [21] developed the YOLO network, which is completely consists by convolutional layers. An end-to-end architecture to the surface defects detection of flat metal is proposed.

However, the model mentioned above can only be a rough positioning of multiple defects. With the development of technology, defect detection needs to provide more complete details, and segmentation methods have been gradually introduced into this field.

Fully Convolutional Network(FCN) [24] proposed by Long el can perform pixel-level segmentation of input images of any size directly, which improves the accuracy and efficiency of image segmentation. SegNet [5] take advantage of pooling indices to reduce the loss of effective features, and improve the results. With the introduction of DeepLab [5–8] series, the segmentation field has reached a new height. The addition of the atrous convolution makes the module enlarge the receptive field and obtain richer information. DeepLab V3+ [8] regards the structure of DeepLab V3 [7] as an encoder, and adds a decoder to obtain better results at the edge of the segmentation. At the same time, it applies depthwise separable convolution [9] in Atrous Spatial Pyramid Pooling (ASPP). As a result, decoder structure greatly reduces the amount of parameters while maintaining performance. In [11], two kinds of self-attention mechanisms are integrated and the distinguishing ability of feature representations is enhanced by establishing rich contextual relevance for local features. On the basis of HED [31,33] adds a pyramid module that can integrate contextual information with low-level, and uses an adaptive hierarchical structure to force network to concentrate on difficult samples. [28] combined deep CNNs and skeleton extraction to effectively and qualitatively detect weak micro-scratches.

In general, deep learning based methods generate can avoid the influence of background noise compared with traditional methods. Nonetheless, exploration on accurate results for robust crack detection was still needed.

3   Methods

3.1   Overview of Proposed Method

We define crack detection task as a binary classification in a pixel-level. That is, the model predicts the input image and divides it into the foreground and background of cracks. GFU-Net is based on the architecture of encoder and decoder, which overall framework shown in the Fig. 1. The encoding network and the decoding network are almost symmetrical.

Deep convolutional neural network has the property of hierarchical learning, it can learn multi-scale convolution features in the form of an increasingly larger and larger receptive field at the down-sampling layer. There are five different scales in this network structure, corresponding to the down-sampling layer. So

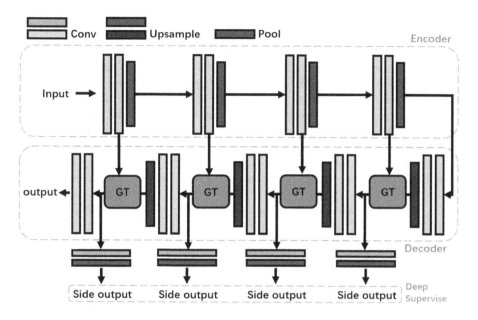

Fig. 1. The architecture of GFU-Net

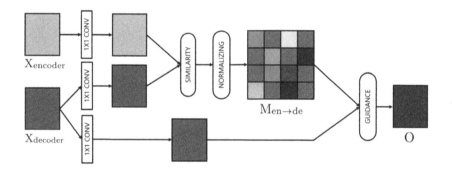

Fig. 2. An illustration of guide transformer.

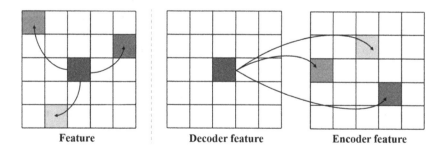

Fig. 3. (left) self-attention, (right) guide-attention.

as to take advantage of the sparsity and continuity of each scale features, we introduced a guide transformer module to establish contact between encoding and decoding network. In Fig. 1, we can see that the last convolutional layer of each scale in the encoder is connected to the corresponding guide transformer in the decoder. Cross-layer fusion uses a series of operations to deal with the convolution features of the connection. Inspired by [12], we replace the convolutional layers and downsampling layers with the Ghost bottleneck in the encode network. The Ghost module, generating more feature maps from cheap operations, is the main component of the Ghost bottleneck. It uses less computational costs and improves performance. Finally, a side network is used for deep supervised learning and supervises directly for features generated from each convolutional stage.

In our pipeline, when input a crack image, the first step is to extract features at different levels in the encoder, and then through to the decoder to restore the original size of the image by hierarchical upsampling. The corresponding level uses the guide transformer for feature fusion, so that the decoding process can exploit the extracted information and find the direct correspondence between the features. Another point is that the feature map of each size will undergo a loss operation to form a deep supervised network. Finally, all reshaped feature maps are fused together through a concat operation, and a crack prediction map is generated through a 1×1 convolutional kernel, and then calculate a final cross entropy loss with mask.

3.2 Guide Transformer

Due to the sharp shape, the retained underlying detailed information of edge features which preformed down-sampling is very limited. Decoder compresses and extracts the abstract features after encoding, and selects some features that are effective for the specific task to restore and reconstruct, and then obtains the corresponding output results. In the decoding process, it is easy to cause feature reconstruction failure or poor results.

In order to improve training efficiency and retain more crack details, the feature map in the encoding process is introduced to "guide" the decoding feature map, emphasizing the importance of some features. Inspired by the attention mechanism, we designed a "Guide Transformer" for feature fusion between the encoder and the decoder. That is to say, the features extracted by the encoder are used to "instruct" the decoder to perform up-sampling to obtain the corresponding feature map, increase the training details of the decoder network, and improve information use efficiency.

As shown in the Fig. 3, the left part is a non-local network. The self-attention mechanism is used to aggregate the aggregation of global information and get rid of the limitation of the local receptive field in the convolutional network. The picture on the right is our work that captures the relationship between the corresponding feature maps. For each pixel in the picture on the left, the "Guide Transformer" will calculate the similarity from the picture on the right, and then make corresponding adjustments. In the self-attention mechanism, a feature map of $H \times W \times C$ shape is first reshaped to $HW \times C$, and then the relationship between any two positions in a map is calculated by matrix multiplication. In this paper, we denote the feature map in the encoder of the input guide transformer as $X_{encoder}$, the feature map in the decoder as $X_{decoder}$, and the output feature map as $\widetilde{X}$. First put $X_{encoder}$ and $X_{decoder}$ into 1×1 convolution. Special $X_{encoder}$ generates a query graph Q after convolution. At the same time, $X_{decoder}$ is fed into another 1×1 convolution to generate key feature K, and then reshape to $H \times C \times W$. Then Q and K are matrix multiplied, and finally through a softmax layer, guide map $M_{en \to de}$ is obtained. Through matrix multiplication, the guide transformer can effectively perform feature encoding on the relationship between any two positions in the input feature map. Then, B generates the response feature map, V through the convolution of 1×1 convolution, and he will further multiply it with $M_{en \to de}$ to generate the output feature O. The specific formula is shown below.

$$\widetilde{X}_i = F_{mul}\left(F_{norm}\left(F_{sim}\left(q_i, k_j\right)\right), v_j\right) \tag{1}$$

Among them, $q_i \in Q^{H \times W \times C}$, $k_j \in K^{H \times W \times C}$, $v_j \in V^{H \times W \times C}$. F_{sim} represents matrix multiplication to calculate the similarity of any position in the two feature maps, F_{norm} represents the normalization function *sigmoid*, F_{mul} represents matrix multiplication, the weight enhancement function, and the encoding feature guide information into the decoding feature and $\widetilde{X}_i$ is the i th feature position in the transformed feature map $\widetilde{X}$. The complete structure is shown in the Fig. 2.

3.3 Data Augmentation

In this paper, we performed data augmentation to enrich the training set. It has been proven that data augmentation is a significant method in deep learning networks [18,31]. In the detection of metal surface cracks, since there is less training data, this method is needed to reduce overfitting. We choose the dataset provided by [17], and select metal crack pictures as base dataset. There are 57 photos of metal cracks and corresponding pixel-level crack masks in this sub-dataset. We select 38 train images randomly and the remaining 19 images make up the test set. We flipped, blurred, and adjusted the brightness and contrast of the training images, so the data set was augmented by 6 times. Due to the inconsistency of image size of the picture, we preprocessed the image by tile filling, adjusted resize it to 608×384 in the training stage. Finally, we trained on a dataset consists of raw data and augmented data.

4 Experiments

4.1 Experimental Setting

Training Details. In the network setting, we apply batch normalization layer, which can improve the convergence speed, after the convolutional layer of whole network. During the training process, the initial learning rate is set to 1e−3

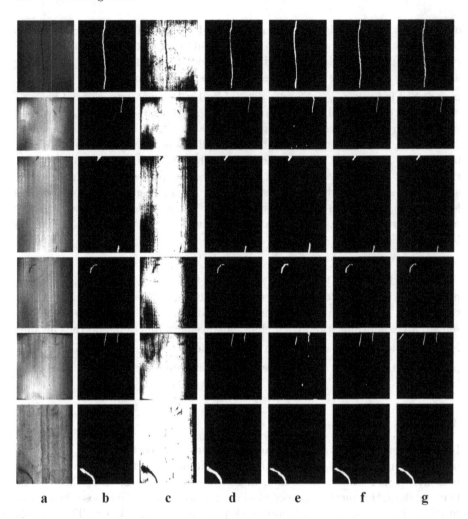

Fig. 4. Several samples with cracks in various scenes. The columns are: (a) original image, (b) ground truth, (c), (d) U-Net, (e) U^2-Net (f) DeepCrack and (g) Ours.

for the first 200 times, 1e−4 for the last 200 times. The momentum and weight decay are set to 0.9 and 0.0005 respectively. We employed the stochastic gradient descent method (SGD) to update the parameters of network. Our proposed network learns from scratch which means that it trained without utilizing any pre-trained models. The experimental code is carried out in the PyTorch and runs on the NVIDIA 2080Ti GPU.

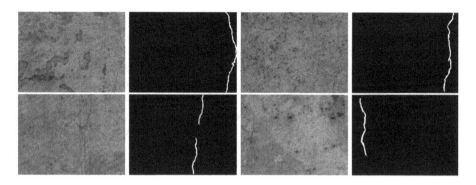

Fig. 5. Several samples from NUAACrack-2000

Evaluation Metrics. The common metrics of semantic segmentation evaluations include Pixel accuracy, Category pixel accuracy, Intersection over Union, etc. To evaluate our work, we introduce Mean Pixel Accuracy (MPA) and Mean Intersection over Union(MIoU) as the final evaluation metrics.

TP (true positive), TN (true negative), FP (false positive), FN (false negative) are common concepts in segmentation tasks. TP and TN respectively indicate that positive and negative samples are correctly classified. FP and FN mean that positive and negative samples classified incorrectly, respectively. Assuming that the original sample contain positive samples and negative samples, and there are $k + 1$ categories in total. It means that the number of pixels of category i is predicted as the number of category j. The calculation method is shown below.

Mean Pixel Accuracy. The average value obtained by adding the summation of pixels' number in each category to the ratio of the summation of pixels' number in each category.

$$MPA = \frac{1}{k+1} \sum_{i=0}^{k} \frac{P_{ii}}{\sum\limits_{j=0}^{k} P_{ij}} \tag{2}$$

Mean Intersection over Union. It is the ratio of the predicted result of the model to the true value of a certain category, and the average cross ratio is to calculate the value of the ratio of cross and sum for each category, and then sum it up.

$$MIoU = \frac{1}{k+1} \sum_{i=0}^{k} \frac{P_{ii}}{\sum\limits_{j=0}^{k} P_{ij} + \sum\limits_{j=0}^{k} P_{ji} - P_{ii}} \tag{3}$$

In the above formula, P_{ii} represents the number of correct classification results, i.e. TN or TP. P_{ij} indicates that the positive sample was misjudged, i.e. FP. P_{ji} means that the negative sample was misjudged, i.e. FN.

In order to objectively evaluate the effect of crack extraction, MPA and MIoU are used as the quantitative evaluation criteria in this paper. 1. In the task of fracture extraction, the overall proportion of fractures is small, the prediction effect of the model is poor, and a higher PA can be obtained, resulting in no significant difference between different model indexes. 2. CPA and IoU are mainly targeted at a certain kind of quantitative indicators. In this task, it is very important to divide both the background and the foreground correctly. MPA and MIoU can be used to measure two indexes simultaneously.

Table 1. Ablation study

GM	GT	MPA	MIoU
		0.9102	0.7194
✓		0.9272	0.7154
	✓	0.9299	0.7229
✓	✓	**0.9416**	**0.7359**

4.2 Ablation Study

An ablation experiment was conducted to verify the performance of Ghost module and Guide transformer. The comparison results are shown in the Table 1. GM represents Ghost module and GT represents Guide transformer. We apply the U-Net as the baseline.

We investigate the performance of encoder consists of Ghost module. As shown in Table 2, it outperforms baseline and greatly improves MPA while keeping MIoU basically unchanged. Through the results, Guide transformer can improve both MPA and MIoU indicators. It means that the feature maps in the encoder can guide the image up-sampling process of the decoder, so that the network can recover more image details and improve the segmentation and recognition capabilities of the network. By using these two methods at the same time, network capabilities have been greatly improved. Not only has strong robustness to background noise, but also can completely extract the crack shape, which is beneficial to the processing of the next task.

Table 2. Quantitative evaluation of different methods on [17]

Methods	MPA	MIoU
U-Net	0.9102	0.7194
DeepCrack	0.9352	0.7160
U^2-Net	0.8910	0.6932
Ours	**0.9416**	**0.7359**

Table 3. Quantitative evaluation of different methods on NUAACrack-2000

Methods	MPA	MIoU
U-Net	0.8222	0.6458
DeepCrack	0.8290	0.6548
U^2-Net	0.8313	0.6569
Ours	**0.8387**	**0.6858**

4.3 Evaluations

We compared our networks with four common crack detection algorithms: Otsu threshold segmentation algorithm, DeepCrack, U-Net and U^2-Net. The first one is the traditional detection method, the latter three are the machine learning method. U-Net is the backbone of our work. Compared with this method, it can show the effectiveness of our work. U^2-Net and DeepCrack are both comparative methods, which show striking results in the field of salient object detection and path crack detection, which are similar to this task. Figure 4 shows several samples with cracks in various scenes.

Compared with traditional methods: In the comparison of the segmentation results of the Otsu algorithm, it can be seen that the algorithm is greatly affected by the uneven illumination and large black blocks will be produced in the shadow area, which is a major shortcoming of the traditional method. Since the machine learning algorithm extracts cracks by abstracting the high-dimensional features of the target, it is less affected by the non-target pixels of the original image, the experimental results of the algorithm proposed in this paper can avoid the interference of noise points to a greater extent.

Compared with deep learning methods: Our method achieve striking improvement of performance. The comparison results with machine learning algorithms are shown in Table 2. As shown, our network achieves the best performance in the evaluation metrics. Compared with the second-performing model, our model's MPA has improved to 94.16%, and the MIoU has increased to 73.59%. As showed in Fig. 2 , we can see the white dots appearing next to the crack image, which indicates that Unet, DeepCrack and U^2-Net produce false detection. At the same time, many details are lost in the results of U^2-Net crack detection, and the detected crack area is much larger than the ground truth.

The results of the U-Net network contain many breakpoints, but the continuity of the cracks is very important in the crack detection task.

To further verify the effectiveness of the GFU-Net, we tested it on an undisclosed data set named NUAACrack-2000. This data set contains 2000 pictures of tunnel crack and corresponding crack labeling masks. Training set and testing set has 1400 and 600 pictures respectively. The Fig. 5 shows several examples in NUAACrack-2000. The quantitative evaluation of each method is shown on the Table 3. Compared with other deep learning network, GFU-Net has obtained the state-of-the-art results.

As a result, the deep learning method can eliminate the influence of uneven illumination, but it cannot avoid the influence of noise similar to cracks on the background. The algorithm presented in this paper for avoiding noise interference is superior to the classical methods in image segmentation. Moreover, the performance of our algorithm for containing crack integrity and details of edges is also superior to other algorithms for crack extraction based on deep learning methods.

5   Conclusion

In this paper, GFU-Net was proposed for metal surface crack detection in an end-to-end way. It uses the encoder-decoder structure to gain precise crack pixel-segmentation. The feature map of the encoding part can correct the decoding process by using the guide transformer. In the encoder, Ghost module is used instead of convolution layer, which reduces the computation and improve the accuracy. The extensive experimental results display that GFU-Net achieves state-of-the-art performance, and has better robustness in terms of background noise.

In future research, we hope to delve into more effective feature fusion methods. Because of the lack of training data, more effective methods of data enhancement are worthy of further study to solve the imbalance between positive and negative samples.

References

1. Amhaz, R., Chambon, S., Idier, J., Baltazart, V.: Automatic crack detection on 2d pavement images: An algorithm based on minimal path selection. IEEE Trans. Intell. Transp. Syst. (2015)
2. Amhaz, R., Chambon, S., Idier, J., Baltazart, V.: A new minimal path selection algorithm for automatic crack detection on pavement images. In: 2014 IEEE International Conference on Image Processing (ICIP), pp. 788–792. IEEE (2014)
3. Canny, J.: A computational approach to edge detection. IEEE Trans. Pattern Anal. Mach. Intell. **PAMI-8**(6), 679–698 (1986)
4. Cha, Y.J., Choi, W., Büyüköztürk, O.: Deep learning-based crack damage detection using convolutional neural networks. Comput. Aided Civ. Infrastruct. Eng. 32(5), 361–378 (2017)

5. Chen, L.C., Papandreou, G., Kokkinos, I., Murphy, K., Yuille, A.L.: Semantic image segmentation with deep convolutional nets and fully connected CRFs. arXiv preprint arXiv:1412.7062 (2014)
6. Chen, L.C., Papandreou, G., Kokkinos, I., Murphy, K., Yuille, A.L.: DeepLab: semantic image segmentation with deep convolutional nets, atrous convolution, and fully connected CRFs. IEEE Trans. Pattern Anal. Mach. Intell. 40(4), 834–848 (2017)
7. Chen, L.C., Papandreou, G., Schroff, F., Adam, H.: Rethinking atrous convolution for semantic image segmentation. arXiv preprint arXiv:1706.05587 (2017)
8. Chen, L.C., Zhu, Y., Papandreou, G., Schroff, F., Adam, H.: Encoder-decoder with atrous separable convolution for semantic image segmentation. In: Ferrari, V., Hebert, M., Sminchisescu, C., Weiss, Y. (eds.) Computer Vision – ECCV 2020. LNCS, vol. 11211, pp. 801–818 (2018). https://doi.org/10.1007/978-3-030-01234-2_49
9. Chollet, F.: Xception: deep learning with depthwise separable convolutions. In: Proceedings of the IEEE Conference on Computer Vision and Pattern Recognition, pp. 1251–1258 (2017)
10. Damacharla, P., Ringenberg, J., Javaid, A.Y., et al.: TLU-NET: a deep learning approach for automatic steel surface defect detection. arXiv preprint arXiv:2101.06915 (2021)
11. Fu, J., et al.: Dual attention network for scene segmentation. In: Proceedings of the IEEE/CVF Conference on Computer Vision and Pattern Recognition, pp. 3146–3154 (2019)
12. Han, K., Wang, Y., Tian, Q., Guo, J., Xu, C., Xu, C.: GhostNet: more features from cheap operations. In: Proceedings of the IEEE/CVF Conference on Computer Vision and Pattern Recognition, pp. 1580–1589 (2020)
13. He, K., Zhang, X., Ren, S., Sun, J.: Deep residual learning for image recognition. In: Proceedings of the IEEE Conference on Computer Vision and Pattern Recognition, pp. 770–778 (2016)
14. He, Y., Song, K., Meng, Q., Yan, Y.: An end-to-end steel surface defect detection approach via fusing multiple hierarchical features. IEEE Trans. Instrum. Meas. 69(4), 1493–1504 (2019)
15. Huang, G., Liu, Z., Van Der Maaten, L., Weinberger, K.Q.: Densely connected convolutional networks. In: Proceedings of the IEEE Conference on Computer Vision and Pattern Recognition, pp. 4700–4708 (2017)
16. Huang, W., Zhang, N.: A novel road crack detection and identification method using digital image processing techniques. In: 2012 7th International Conference on Computing and Convergence Technology (ICCCT), pp. 397–400. IEEE (2012)
17. Huang, Y., Qiu, C., Yuan, K.: Surface defect saliency of magnetic tile. Vis. Comput. 36(1), 85–96 (2020)
18. Krizhevsky, A., Sutskever, I., Hinton, G.E.: ImageNet classification with deep convolutional neural networks. Adv. Neural Inf. Process. Syst. **25**, 1097–1105 (2012)
19. Lam, H.F., Yin, T.: Application of two-dimensional spatial wavelet transform in the detection of an obstructed crack on a thin plate. Struct. Control Health Monitor. 19(2), 260–277 (2012)
20. Lee, C.Y., Xie, S., Gallagher, P., Zhang, Z., Tu, Z.: Deeply-supervised nets. In: Artificial Intelligence and Statistics, pp. 562–570. PMLR (2015)
21. Li, J., Su, Z., Geng, J., Yin, Y.: Real-time detection of steel strip surface defects based on improved yolo detection network. IFAC-PapersOnLine **51**(21), 76–81 (2018)

22. Li, Q., Liu, X.: Novel approach to pavement image segmentation based on neighboring difference histogram method. IEEE Computer Society (2008)
23. Li, Q., Zou, Q., Zhang, D., Mao, Q.: Fosa: F* seed-growing approach for crack-line detection from pavement images. Image Vis. Comput. 29(12), 861–872 (2011)
24. Long, J., Shelhamer, E., Darrell, T.: Fully convolutional networks for semantic segmentation. In: Proceedings of the IEEE Conference on Computer Vision and Pattern Recognition, pp. 3431–3440 (2015)
25. Peng, L., Chao, W., Shuangmiao, L., Baocai, F.: Research on crack detection method of airport runway based on twice-threshold segmentation. In: 2015 Fifth International Conference on Instrumentation and Measurement, Computer, Communication and Control (IMCCC), pp. 1716–1720. IEEE (2015)
26. Ronneberger, O., Fischer, P., Brox, T.: U-net: convolutional networks for biomedical image segmentation. In: Navab, N., Hornegger, J., Wells, W., Frangi, A. (eds.) Medical Image Computing and Computer-Assisted Intervention – MICCAI 2015. MICCAI 2015. LNCS, vol. 9351, pp. 234–241. Springer, Cham (2015). https://doi.org/10.1007/978-3-319-24574-4_28
27. Shafiee, M.J., Chywl, B., Li, F., Wong, A.: Fast yolo: a fast you only look once system for real-time embedded object detection in video. J. Comput. Vis. Imaging Syst. 3(1) (2017)
28. Song, L., Lin, W., Yang, Y.G., Zhu, X., Guo, Q., Xi, J.: Weak micro-scratch detection based on deep convolutional neural network. IEEE Access 7, 27547–27554 (2019)
29. Sun, Y., Salari, E., Chou, E.: Automated pavement distress detection using advanced image processing techniques. In: 2009 IEEE International Conference on Electro/Information Technology, pp. 373–377. IEEE (2009)
30. Wu, S., Liu, Y.: A segment algorithm for crack detection. In: 2012 IEEE Symposium on Electrical & Electronics Engineering (EEESYM), pp. 674–677. IEEE (2012)
31. Xie, S., Tu, Z.: Holistically-nested edge detection. Int. J. Comput. Vis. 125(1–3), 3–18 (2015)
32. Xuan, L., Hong, Z.: An improved canny edge detection algorithm. In: 2017 8th IEEE International Conference on Software Engineering and Service Science (ICSESS), pp. 275–278. IEEE (2017)
33. Yang, F., Zhang, L., Yu, S., Prokhorov, D., Mei, X., Ling, H.: Feature pyramid and hierarchical boosting network for pavement crack detection. IEEE Trans. Intell. Transp. Syst. 21(4), 1525–1535 (2019)
34. Yuan, L., Xu, X.: Adaptive image edge detection algorithm based on canny operator. In: 2015 4th International Conference on Advanced Information Technology and Sensor Application (AITS), pp. 28–31. IEEE (2015)
35. Zhang, D., Li, Q., Chen, Y., Cao, M., He, L., Zhang, B.: An efficient and reliable coarse-to-fine approach for asphalt pavement crack detection. Image Vis. Comput. 57, 130–146 (2017)
36. Zhou, J., Huang, P.S., Chiang, F.P.: Wavelet-based pavement distress detection and evaluation. Opt. Eng. 45(2) (2006)
37. Zou, Q., Cao, Y., Li, Q., Mao, Q., Wang, S.: CrackTree: automatic crack detection from pavement images. Pattern Recogn. Lett. 33(3), 227–238 (2012)

Computational Intelligence, Nature-Inspired Optimizers, and Their Engineering Applications

An Improved Cluster Load Balancing Scheduling Algorithm

Wei Fu$^{(\boxtimes)}$ and Xunhang Cui

Chongqing University of Posts and Telecommunications, Chongwen Road.2,
CHN, Chongqing, China
`fuwei@cqupt.edu.cn`, `s180301034@stu.cqupt.edu.cn`

Abstract. People's lives and work are closely connected to the network, and network activities take up an increasingly large portion of their daily lives, generating large amounts of data. This large amount of data puts tremendous pressure on server clusters, which leads to resource allocation problems. Existing load-balancing algorithms take simple factors into account and do not take into account the server load and the resource consumption of the request. This paper proposes a PSO-GA (Particle Swarm Optimization-Genetic Algorithm) based LVS (Linux Virtual Server) cluster load-balancing scheduling algorithm to quantify the different scheduling options by constructing a resource balance model and an adaptation function. The PSO-GA algorithm is used to solve the adaptation function to obtain the optimal weights. The load balancer schedules requests according to the weights to achieve Linux virtual server cluster load balancing.

Keywords: Load balancing · Resource balance model · Particle swarm optimization

1 Introduction

With the development of big data and cloud computing, a great amount of network data, and geometric form of explosive growth, which brings enormous pressure on the network hardware and software facilities, servers appear overload, congestion, downtime and other problems.

From the perspective of technology development, network bandwidth is growing much faster than processor performance, so customer access to the site performance bottlenecks often appear in the server side [1]. In order to solve this problem, two solutions have gradually formed on the path of exploration: the first is to continue to maintain a single server state, constantly upgrading its hardware to achieve performance improvements, such servers are expensive, and when a large number of requests appear in a short period of time, it is difficult to rely on a single server to better complete the task; the second is the use of clustering technology, server clusters are made up of multiple independent Servers are connected together by certain software or hardware to provide services to customers. In the technical terminology, the individual servers within the cluster can be called nodes, and the internal nodes are not perceptible to the customers

© Springer Nature Singapore Pte Ltd. 2021
H. Zhang et al. (Eds.): NCAA 2021, CCIS 1449, pp. 391–402, 2021.
https://doi.org/10.1007/978-981-16-5188-5_28

[2]. In addition, it is important to note that the number of servers in a cluster can be increased if the cluster is unable to cope with the current access pressures. In summary, server clustering has the advantages of stability, reliability and scalability, which is why many websites use parallel or distributed technology to build server clusters.

2   Related Work

In the early days, the Symmetrical Multi-Processing (SMP) cluster system was developed to improve computer performance at a lower cost, to facilitate the expansion of computers, and to simplify the development of computational science applications [3]. The number of CPUs increased and the linearity of the SMP system became worse and worse, until the advent of clustering technology later out of this predicament. Cluster technology is a computer technology that arises in response to heavy computing tasks, and consists of two or more homogeneous or heterogeneous computers connected together by certain software or hardware methods to provide services to the outside world as a whole [4]. When a node fails, the cluster system can detect the node through the heartbeat line, and the node's tasks are smoothly transferred to other nodes, and then removed from the cluster to ensure the availability of the cluster, the process is called failover.

The first server clusters can be traced back to National Computer Security Association (NCSA) "NCSA Scalable Web Server Cluster". Later, with Cisco, SUN, IBM, Microsoft and other companies in the field of server clustering efforts, the research results of the cluster system have been rapidly expanded [5].

3   Algorithmic Implementation

3.1   Scheduling Algorithm Model and Overall Process

This paper proposes a PSO-GA based load balancing scheduling algorithm for LVS clusters to address the deficiencies of current LVS cluster load balancing scheduling algorithms. In this paper, the load balancing scheduling algorithm considers the following factors: the number of physical indicators that measure node load, real-time load information of nodes, the number of nodes, the number of request tasks, and the consumption of each resource by the request tasks. In this paper, we use four metrics: CPU usage, memory usage, network bandwidth usage, and disk IO usage to measure the real-time load of server nodes. In order to get the optimal weights for each round of request scheduling, the cluster is guaranteed to be load balanced. The PSO-GA based LVS cluster load balancing scheduling algorithm model is shown in Fig. 1, Minimization with Genetic Algorithm in Fig. 2.

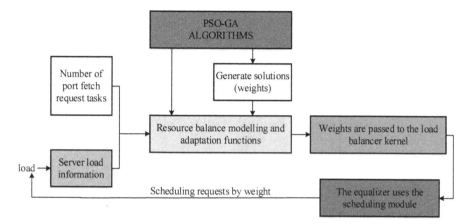

Fig. 1. Scheduling algorithm model

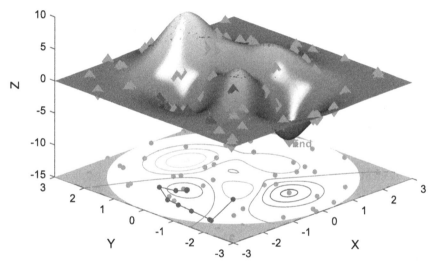

Fig. 2. Minimization with genetic algorithm

3.2 Measurement of Server Node Load

Physical metrics commonly used to measure server performance are generally CPU frequency (GHz), memory capacity (GB), network bandwidth (MB/s), and disk IO rate (MB/s). It is not appropriate to determine the performance of a node by directly comparing the measured values of two nodes, so this paper uses the ratio of the real-time load of a resource of a node to its maximum load capacity as a way to measure its degree of load according to Eq. (1). In this paper, the load ratio of CPU, memory, network bandwidth, and disk IO is used to measure the load status of a server node, so that the comparison is the percentage value. Then the current load condition of the server node S_i can be expressed as follows Eq. (1).

$$(p_{cpu}(S_i) \; p_{mem}(S_i) \; p_{band}(S_i) \; p_{io}(S_i))$$ (1)

The current load profile of n server nodes can be expressed as Eq. (2).

$$\begin{pmatrix} p_{cpu}(S_1) \; p_{mem}(S_1) \; p_{band}(S_1) \; p_{io}(S_1) \\ p_{cpu}(S_2) \; p_{mem}(S_2) \; p_{band}(S_2) \; p_{io}(S_2) \\ \vdots \qquad \vdots \qquad \vdots \qquad \vdots \\ p_{cpu}(S_n) \; p_{mem}(S_n) \; p_{band}(S_n) \; p_{io}(S_n) \end{pmatrix}$$ (2)

3.3 Resource Balance Modelling

1. Value of each resource consumption request
   When considering a cluster as a heterogeneous cluster, n servers can be classified into class j ($j \leq n$), a certain number of request tasks are the same load for each node, but the degree of load they exhibit on each node is different and can be expressed Eq. (3).

$$\begin{pmatrix} N_{cpu,1} \; N_{mem,1} \; N_{band,1} \; N_{io,1} \\ N_{cpu,2} \; N_{mem,2} \; N_{band,2} \; N_{io,2} \\ \vdots \qquad \vdots \qquad \vdots \qquad \vdots \\ N_{cpu,j} \; N_{mem,j} \; N_{band,j} \; N_{io,j} \end{pmatrix}$$ (3)

The elements in the formula are also in percentage form. For example, to process the same number of requests, 200 M of memory is required on node 1, which has 2000 M of memory, or 10%, and 200 M of memory is also required on node 2, which has 4000 M of memory, but with 5%.

2. Resource balance model
   In an LVS cluster, the load balancer schedules requests according to the weights of each node, so for a cluster with n server nodes, their weights can be expressed (already normalized) as $(x_1, x_2, \ldots, x_n)$, When m requests need to be scheduled, it means that the number of requests to be processed by each node is $(mx_1 \; mx_2 \cdots mx_n)$, For node S_i (belongs to the class j server denoted by k_i), the number of requests to be processed is the number of requests mx_i, then the resources to be consumed by each can be expressed as $(N_{cpu,k_i} \times m\frac{x_i}{R} \; N_{mem,k_i} \times m\frac{x_i}{R} \; N_{band,k_i} \times m\frac{x_i}{R} \; N_{io,k_i} \times m\frac{x_i}{R})$, $k_i \in [1,j]$, When node S_i processes off the allocated requests, the load factor for each of its resources will become Eq. (4).

$$\begin{aligned} &(p'_{cpu}(s_i) \; p'_{mem}(s_i) \; p'_{band}(s_i) \; p'_{io}(s_i)) \\ &= (p_{cpu}(s_i) \; p_{mem}(s_i) \; p_{band}(s_i) \; p_{io}(s_i)) \\ &+ \left(N_{cpu,k_i} \times m\frac{x_i}{R} N_{mem,k_i} \times m\frac{x_i}{R} N_{bank,k_i} \times m\frac{x_i}{R} N_{io,k_i} \times m\frac{x_i}{R}\right) \end{aligned}$$ (4)

The load factor for each resource across the cluster can be expressed as Eq. (5).

$$\begin{pmatrix} p'_{cpu}(S_1) \ p'_{mem}(S_1) \ p'_{band}(S_1) \ p'_{io}(S_1) \\ p'_{cpu}(S_2) \ p'_{mem}(S_2) \ p'_{band}(S_2) \ p'_{io}(S_2) \\ \vdots \qquad \vdots \qquad \vdots \qquad \vdots \\ p'_{cpu}(S_n) \ p'_{mem}(S_n) \ p'_{band}(S_n) \ p'_{io}(S_n) \end{pmatrix} \tag{5}$$

The degree of equilibrium can be measured by the mean-squared deviation σ. Therefore, the mean of each resource utilization rate is obtained first and then the mean-squared deviation is calculated. The average utilization rate of each resource in the cluster can be expressed as $\left(\overline{p'_{cpu}} \ \overline{p'_{mem}} \ \overline{p'_{band}} \ \overline{p'_{io}} \right)$ which $\overline{p'_{cpu}} = \frac{1}{n} \sum_{i=1}^{n} p'_{cpu}(S_i)$, The mean variance of the utilization rate of each resource in the cluster can be expressed as $\left(\sigma_{cpu} \ \sigma_{mem} \ \sigma_{band} \ \sigma_{io} \right)$ with Eq. (6). According to Kersey's inequality $\sum_{i=1}^{n} a_i^2 \sum_{i=1}^{n} b_i^2 \geq \left(\sum_{i=1}^{n} a_i b_i \right)^2, a_i, b_i \in R$, further analysis showed that Eq. (7–9).

$$\sigma_{cpu} = \sqrt{\frac{\sum_{i=1}^{n} \left(p'_{cpu}(S_i) - \overline{p'_{cpu}} \right)^2}{n}} \tag{6}$$

$$\sum_{i=1}^{n} \left(p'_{cpu}(S_i) - \overline{p'_{cpu}} \right)^2 \geq \frac{1}{n} \left(\sum_{i=1}^{n} \left(p'_{cpu}(S_i) - \overline{p'_{cpu}} \right) \right)^2 \tag{7}$$

$$\sum_{i=1}^{n} \left(p'_{cpu}(S_i) - \overline{p'_{cpu}} \right)^2 \geq \frac{1}{n} \left(\sum_{i=1}^{n} \left(p'_{cpu}(S_i) - \overline{p'_{cpu}} \right) \right)^2 \tag{8}$$

$$\sigma_{cpu} \geq \frac{1}{n} \sum_{i=1}^{n} \left| p'_{cpu}(S_i) - \overline{p'_{cpu}} \right| \tag{9}$$

if and only if $p'_{cpu}(S_1)=p'_{cpu}(S_2)=\cdots=p'_{cpu}(S_n)=\cdots=p'_{cpu}(S_n)$, σ_{cpu} gets the minimum value. The model shows that the cluster is most balanced when each server has the same resource load factor, which is consistent with the idea of "more work for more energy".

The model suggests that the average variance of resource utilization should be smaller if the cluster is to be balanced, so nodes with smaller load factors should allocate more requests, and nodes with larger load factors should allocate fewer requests. In this way, the nodes with large differences in load rates can be averaged out to ease the cluster load skew and achieve load balancing.

3.4 Design of the Adaptation Function

The resource balancing model has already shown that different scheduling schemes affect the cluster load to different degrees, so this section will design a function to quantify the magnitude of this effect. The adaptation function designed in this paper is a summary of the resource equilibrium model described above, where the smaller the mean variance of resource utilization, the more balanced the load distribution of the cluster, meaning that requests are always allocated to nodes with low load, as adjusted by the equilibrium model. In other words, nodes with more ample remaining performance should allocate more requests [6]. The degree of load balancing of a cluster is expressed as $Q = a\sigma_{cpu} + b\sigma_{mem} + c\sigma_{band} + d\sigma_{io}$, The adaptability function is designed to $F(X) = \frac{a}{\sigma_{cpu}} + \frac{b}{\sigma_{mem}} + \frac{c}{\sigma_{band}} + \frac{d}{\sigma_{io}}$, $F(X)$ is a continuous function on $(x_1, x_2, \ldots, x_n)$, The larger the value of the function indicates that the corresponding scheduling scheme makes the utilization of the resources of the cluster the smaller the mean variance, the more balanced the load of the cluster. The best solution is the optimal weight, which is the request for the optimal scheduling scheme, and the weight indicates that the residual nature of each node can bear the proportion of the request, so the more sufficient residual performance of the node must bear a relatively large number of requests [7]. If the requests are scheduled according to this weight, the impact on the current load of the cluster is minimal.

4   Simulation

In this paper, a router is used to connect the LVS cluster to the client to build a small LAN, and the load balancers in the cluster as well as the server nodes are all Linux virtual machines based on Ubuntu 16.04, using scheduling algorithms to implement the framework. In this section, five functional modules are written on the built LVS cluster: a load information collection module, a communication module, a PSO-GA computation module, a scheduling module, and a weight transfer module. The load information collection module implements node load information collection, the communication module implements load information sending and receiving, the PSO-GA calculation module implements weight calculation, the scheduling module implements weight call, and the weight transfer module implements weight transfer from user space to kernel space [8]. The metrics consist of CPU usage, memory usage, network bandwidth usage, and disk IO usage.

4.1   Test Environment

This article uses a router to connect the LVS cluster to the clients, building a small LAN with a load balancer and server nodes using a Linux virtual machine based on Ubuntu 16.04. The load balancer has two addresses, the virtual address (VIP) 192.168.47.120 is used as the address for client access and 192.168.47.129 is used as the address to connect to the internal real server (RIP). The hardware configuration for this experiment is shown in Table 1 and the software configuration is shown in Table 2.

Table 1. Test environment hardware configuration table

Name	RAM	CPU	Systems	IP
Load Balancer	2 GB	I5-8500	Ubuntu16.04	192.168.47.120(VIP)
				192.168.47.129(RIP)
Real Server 1	2 GB	I5-8500	Ubuntu16.04	192.168.47.130
Real Server 2	4 GB	I5-8500	Ubuntu16.04	192.168.47.131
Real Server 3	4 GB	I5-8500	Ubuntu16.04	192.168.47.132
Client machines	4 GB	Pentium-G645	Windows7	192.168.47.110

Table 2. Test environment software configuration table

Name	Versions
VMware Workstation	15.0
Java jdk	1.8.0
Tomcat	8.5.56

4.2 Response Delay

In the experiments of this paper, the comparison is chosen between the traditional Weighted Least Connected (WLC) algorithm, the load balancing algorithm proposed in the literature [9], and the load balancing algorithm under the GA optimization approach.

The reason for this phenomenon is because the load balancing algorithm in this paper with the GA optimization approach is inherently more complex than the other two algorithms and requires more computer resources, which explains why the WLC algorithm with the literature [10] performs best when the amount of concurrency is small. And when the concurrency continues to increase, the load balancing algorithm in this paper shows some advantages because the algorithm in this paper is able to compute better request scheduling schemes, which brings greater net benefits compared to the other three algorithms. The reason for the poor performance of the load balancing algorithm is that it is not only computationally complex, but also does not yield the optimal weights after complex computation, which simply put is not only complex but also useless. Figure 3 shows a comparison of cluster response delay for different load balancing algorithms, with the horizontal coordinate being the number of requests and the vertical coordinate being the response delay value.

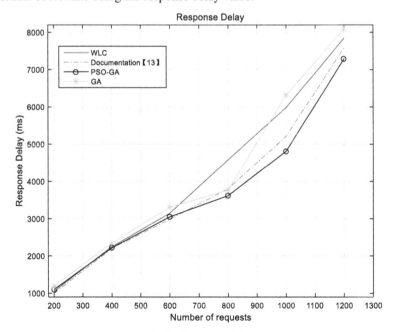

Fig. 3. Response delay

4.3 Throughput

Figure 4 shows a comparison of cluster throughput for different load balancing algorithms, with the horizontal coordinate being the number of requests and the vertical coordinate being the throughput value.

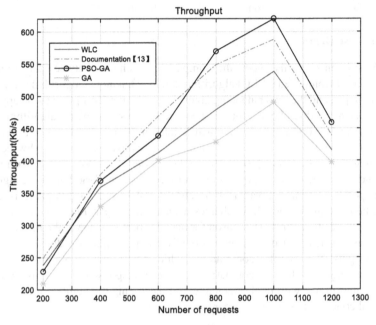

Fig. 4. Throughput

Theoretically, there are two main reasons for this, first, when the number of concurrent requests is small, the additional computational effort of this paper's load balancing algorithm is larger compared to the other three algorithms, and the impact on the cluster throughput is greater; second, the WLC algorithm skew the cluster load more than this paper's algorithm when the number of requests increases. It is only when the number of concurrent requests is large that this paper's algorithm has a better scheduling scheme, which brings a net benefit greater than that brought by the scheduling schemes of several other algorithms, and thus this paper's algorithm shows the overall advantage when the number of concurrent requests is large.

4.4 Request Error Rate

While server clusters have performance limits, the goal of load balancing algorithms is to make the actual results as close to the theoretical limits as possible, using hardware resources as much as possible [12]. Figure 5 shows the statistical results of four load balancing algorithms for different concurrency levels in terms of request error rates.

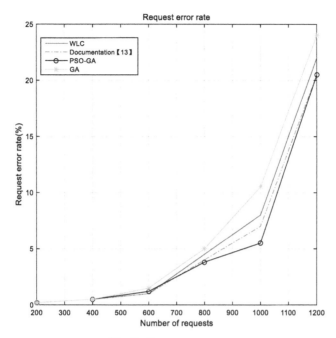

Fig. 5. Request error rate

In this paper, the load balancing algorithm has the slowest increase in the request error rate, and when the number of concurrent requests is less than 600, the difference between this algorithm and the algorithm in the literature [13] is about 2%. When the number of concurrent requests reaches 1000, the gap between the four algorithms is more obvious. As the number of concurrent requests continues to rise and reaches 1200, the request error rate of the four algorithms suddenly rises from less than 10% to about 20%, and the gap between the four begins to narrow, so it can be judged that the number of concurrent requests has reached or exceeded the cluster limit, indicating that the server cluster built in this paper can withstand the limit of concurrency in the 1000–1200. If the load continues to increase, it can be expected that the request error rate of the four algorithms will continue to rise sharply and that the gap between them may disappear.

4.5 Mean Variance in Resource Utilization

In a Linux system, the occupancy of each resource can be recorded through the node logs, and since the cluster contains three nodes, this paper calculates the mean variance of the cluster's resource occupancy, and the mean variance can reflect the degree of balance of the cluster in terms of resource utilization [14–17], as shown in Fig. 6.

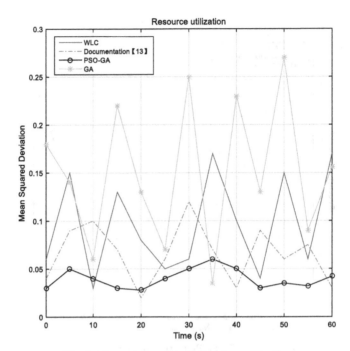

Fig. 6. Request error rate & Resource utilization

The load balancing algorithm proposed in this paper makes the resource utilization of the cluster more uniform and achieves the purpose of load balancing, while the load balancing algorithm under the GA optimization method performs the worst in terms of resource balancing, which confirms the above statement that it is both complex and inaccurate, resulting in a large amount of resource waste.

In summary, the load balancing algorithm proposed in this paper has its own advantages and disadvantages with the algorithms of WLC and literature [13], and the algorithm of literature [13] performs best when the number of concurrent requests is small, and the load balancing algorithm of this paper performs best when the number of concurrent requests exceeds 600. the WLC algorithm and the algorithm of literature [13] respond faster thanks to their own low complexity, while the algorithm of this paper performs best due to the high complexity of the Therefore, it performs poorly when the number of concurrent requests is small because of its high complexity.

However, when the number of concurrent requests is large, it does not perform as well as this paper's algorithm because several other algorithms do not have as good a scheduling scheme as this paper's algorithm, which results in some load skewing of the server cluster. In other words, this paper's algorithm sacrifices a bit of computation time but is able to calculate better weights to determine a better request scheduling scheme. As for the load balancing algorithm under GA optimization, it performs poorly in all the metrics, which confirms the simulation results in Sect. 3 that the load balancing algorithm under GA optimization not only fails to calculate the optimal scheduling scheme, but also has high complexity. In terms of resource utilization, the load balancing algorithm in this paper uses a more accurate resource balancing model, which makes the cluster more evenly distributed in terms of resource utilization and ensures a more balanced cluster load.

5 Summary

In this paper, the Linux virtual server cluster technology belongs to the class of cluster technology, which is also relatively mature in development. In this paper, we present a load balancing algorithm for LVS clusters, which is based on the PSO-GA.

This paper presents a PSO-GA based load balancing scheduling algorithm for LVS cluster, which quantifies the impact of different scheduling schemes on the current load balancing of the cluster by constructing a resource balancing model and an adaptation function, and then solves the adaptation function using the PSO-GA optimization algorithm to obtain the optimal scheduling scheme. Achieve cluster load balancing.

The test results show that the load balancing algorithm proposed in this paper does not perform well in terms of both cluster response delay and throughput when concurrency is small, but it is better than the load balancing algorithm under the GA optimization approach due to its own complexity which is higher than the WLC algorithm and the load balancing algorithm from the literature [13].

The algorithm has a lower overhead, faster response, and better results. The load balancing algorithm in this paper performs better than the other three load balancing algorithms in terms of throughput, response latency, and request error rate. It is also more balanced in terms of resource utilization.

References

1. Kumar, P., Kumar, R.: Issues and challenges of load balancing techniques in cloud computing. ACM Comput. Surv. **51**(6), 1–35 (2019)
2. Padole, M., Shah, A.: Comparative study of scheduling algorithms in heterogeneous distributed computing systems. In: Advanced Computing and Communication Technologies, Singapore, pp. 111–122 (2018)
3. Johnston, W.E.: Rationale and strategy for a 21st century scientific computing architecture: the case for using commercial symmetric multiprocessors as supercomputers. Int. J. High Speed Comput. **9**(3), 191–222 (1997)
4. Weissman, B., van de Laar, E.: SQL Server Big Data Cluster, pp. 11–31. Apress, Germany (2019)
5. Eric, D.K., Michelle, B., Robert, M.: A scalable HTTP server: the NCSA prototype. Comput. Netw. ISDN Syst. **27**(2), 155–164 (1994)
6. Samolej, S., Szmuc, T.: HTCPNs–based modelling and evaluation of dynamic computer cluster reconfiguration. Lect. Notes Comput. Sci. **7054**, 97–108 (2009)
7. Weizheng, R., Wenkai, C., Yansong, C.: Dynamic balance strategy of high concurrent Web cluster based on docker container. Lop Conf. **466**(1), 012011 (2018)
8. Hai, X., Kim, K., Youn, H.: Dynamic load balancing of software-defined networking based on genetic-ant colony optimization. Sensors **19**(2), 311 (2019)
9. Hsiao, H.C., Hao, L., Chen, S.T., et al.: Load balance with imperfect information in structured peer-to-peer systems. IEEE Trans. Parallel Distrib. Syst. **22**(4), 634–649 (2011)

10. Nick, R.: Load Balancing with HAproxy: Open-Source Technology for Better Scalability, Redundancy and Availability in Your IT Infrastructure, pp. 27–52. Independently published, New York (2016)

11. Xin, Z., Lili, J., Xin, F.: A dynamic feedback-based load balancing methodology. Int. J. Mod. Educ. Comput. Sci. **12**(9), 57–65 (2017)

12. Aruna, M., Bhanu, D., Karthik, S.: An improved load balanced metaheuristic scheduling in cloud. Clust. Comput. **22**(1), 1–9 (2019)

13. Xiaolong, W., Zhaohui, J.: Load balancing algorithm based on LVS cluster in cloud environment. Comput. Eng. Sci. **38**(11), 2172–2176 (2016)

14. Ruijie, L., Haitao, X., Meng, L.: Resource allocation in edge-computing based wireless networks based on differential game and feedback control. Comput. Materials Continua **64**(02), 961–972 (2020)

15. Jena, U.K., Das, P.K., Kabat, M.R.: Hybridization of meta-heuristic algorithm for load balancing in cloud computing environment. J. King Saud Univ.- Comput. Inform. Sci. **32**(3), 267–277 (2020)

16. Ruixia, T., Xiongfeng, Z.: A load balancing strategy based on the combination of static and dynamic. In: Second International Workshop on Database Technology and Applications, pp. 1–4. Proceedings IEEE, Hubei (2010)

17. Rathore, N.: Performance of hybrid load balancing algorithm in distributed Web server system. Wireless Pers. Commun. **101**(4), 1233–1246 (2018)

An Improved Cloud Particles Optimizer
for Function Optimization

Wei Li[1,2](✉), Haonan Luo[1], Junqing Yuan[1], Zhou Lei[1], and Lei Wang[2]

[1] School of Computer Science and Engineering,
Xi'an University of Technology, Xi'an 710048, China
`liwei@xaut.edu.cn`
[2] Shaanxi Key Laboratory for Network Computing and Security Technology,
Xi'an 710048, China

Abstract. Evolutionary algorithm is a popular and effective method in optimization field. As one of the optimization algorithms, cloud particles optimizer (CPEA) has shown to be effective in solving problems with different characteristics. However, due to the powerful local search ability, premature convergence is a significant disadvantage of CPEA optimizer. To alleviate this problem, an improved cloud particles optimizer named ICPEA is proposed. In ICPEA, the fluid operation is designed to explore the evolution direction, while the solid operation is employed to improve the exploitation efficiency. Moreover, the dynamical selection strategies of control parameters are employed to cope with premature convergence issues. In order to demonstrate the effectiveness of ICPEA, CEC2014 test suites are used for simulating. The experimental results affirm that ICPEA is a competitive optimizer compared to CPEA algorithm and several state-of-the-art optimizers.

Keywords: Cloud particles optimizer · State change · Exploration-exploitation · Global optimization

1 Introduction

In the real world, there are many optimization problems with complex structure and large scale. Generally, these problems have the characteristics of non-separable, multimodality and discontinuity. It is a big challenge for traditional optimization methods to find a better solution in a given time. Then, many nature-inspired optimization algorithms are developed and demonstrated to be effective in handling different kinds of problems in the real world, including scheduling [1, 2], large scale optimization [3, 4], constrained problems [5], training problems [6], clustering [7], economic problems [8], and function optimization[9, 10].

Currently, many optimization methods have been developed to solve complex problems. The design of most algorithms is inspired by nature, such as biological evolutionary process, natural phenomena and social behavior of different animals. The popular algorithms include genetic algorithm (GA) [11], covariance matrix adaptation algorithm

© Springer Nature Singapore Pte Ltd. 2021
H. Zhang et al. (Eds.): NCAA 2021, CCIS 1449, pp. 403–416, 2021.
https://doi.org/10.1007/978-981-16-5188-5_29

(CMA-ES) [12], artificial bee colony (ABC) [13], differential evolution (DE) [14], simulated annealing (SA) [15], particle swarm optimization (PSO) [16], teaching-learning-based optimization (TLBO) [17], the non-revisiting stochastic search (NrSS) and its variants [18], and whale optimization algorithm (WOA) [19]. The common characteristic of these optimization algorithms is to generate high quality solutions by employing a series of improvements during their optimization process [20]. For example, some optimization algorithms strive to combine local search with exact algorithms including branch-and bound and branch-and-cut [21].

CPEA [22] is designed by imitating the state change of cloud in nature. In CPEA, cloud particles are divided into three forms: gaseous form, liquid form and solid form. The population consists of N D-dimensional cloud particles. First, cloud particles are generated in gaseous form. If the population finds a better solution than its parent at a given number of iterations, the cloud particles will condense gradually from gaseous form to liquid form. If the population finds the region of the promising solution, the cloud particles will condense from liquid form to solid form. Although having some potential for solving optimization problems, CPEA may easily suffer from premature convergence. The cause for this shortcoming is the elite strategy used in CPEA. If the seeds, that is the best particles, are local optima, CPEA is easy to fall into premature convergence because all the cloud particles follow the seeds. Therefore, it is a key problem to adjust the relationship between exploration and exploitation [23]. According to this idea, this paper proposed an improved cloud particles evolution algorithm to improve CPEA performance.

This paper mainly does the following work.

1) In order to simplify the original CPEA algorithm, two states, namely the fluid state and solid state, are employed in ICPEA instead of three states in CPEA. Fluid state focus on exploration, while solid state focus on exploitation.

2) The dynamic selection strategy of control parameters is employed to avoid the proposed algorithm becoming very explorative in fluid state or greedy in solid state. Moreover, the population size is continually decreased to achieve rapid convergence.

The remainder of this paper is organized as follows. First, the original CPEA is reviewed. Then, ICPEA algorithm is described in detail. Next, experiments on the CEC2014 test suits are used to verify the effectiveness of ICPEA algorithm. Finally, the conclusion and the future work are described.

2 Related Work

In CPEA, the cloud particles have three forms: gaseous form, liquid form and solid form. The population is divided into NP subpopulation. At each generation, each subpopulation selects a cloud particle, which has the best fitness in the subpopulation, as the nucleus or the seed. The offspring is generated by the nuclei, which guide the population to explore and exploit the promising areas. The detail of CPEA can be found in [22].

2.1 Cloud Gaseous Phase

CPEA algorithm divides the whole population into NP subpopulation. The population has three control parameters Ex, En and He [24]. Expectation, denoted as Ex, can be regarded as the distribution center of the population. Entropy, denoted as En, is the search range. Hyper-entropy, denoted as He, is used to determine the dispersion degree of En. At each generation, Ex is the cloud particle, which has the best fitness. The population is updated as follows:

$$\mathbf{P}_i = \mathcal{N}(\mathbf{Ex}_i, \mathcal{N}(\mathbf{En}_i, \mathbf{He}_i)) \tag{1}$$

$$\mathbf{En}_i = \frac{|\mathbf{Ex}_i|}{\sqrt{G}} \tag{2}$$

$$\mathbf{He}_i = \frac{|\mathbf{En}_i|}{cd} \tag{3}$$

where $i = 1, \cdots, NP$. $\mathcal{N}$ denotes the normal distribution. G denotes the generation. cd is the condensation factor.

2.2 Cloud Liquid Phase

In order to improve the exploitation ability, En is updated based on the best particle which contains useful information. The updating rule of En is defined as follows:

$$En_i^j = \begin{cases} \frac{Ex_i^j}{e^{\sqrt{NP}}} & if \ \left|Ex_i^j\right| > 1 \\ \frac{Ex_i^j}{\sqrt{NP}} & if \ 0.1 < \left|Ex_i^j\right| < 1 \ j = 1, 2, \cdots, D \\ Ex_i^j & otherwise \end{cases} \tag{4}$$

where $i = 1, \cdots, NP$. $|\bullet|$ is the absolute value function. $\lceil \bullet \rceil$ stands for the rounding up function.

2.3 Cloud Solid Phase

In the cloud solid phase, the solidification operation is defined as follows:

$$En_i^j = \begin{cases} \frac{Ex_i^j}{SF} & if \ \left|Ex_i^j\right| > \frac{1}{NP \times e^{\sqrt{NP}}} \\ Ex_i^j & otherwise \end{cases} \tag{5}$$

$$He_i^j = \frac{En_i^j}{NP \times e^{\lceil \sqrt{NP} \rceil}} \tag{6}$$

where $i = 1, \ldots, NP, j = 1, \ldots, D$. SF is the solidification factor.

3   Improved Cloud Particles Optimizer

As mentioned earlier, CPEA utilizes several best particles to guide the population to explore and exploit at each generation. Experimental results suggest that CPEA has better exploitation, however, the global search ability is low [22]. The reason is that the inferior cloud particles which may be potentially good particles are deleted at each generation. Then, CPEA is more prone to local convergence phenomena because of rapid loss of diversity. In order to solve the relationship between exploration and exploitation during the evolution process, an improved CPEA optimizer (ICPEA) is proposed in this paper.

According to the mobility of the matter, the optimization process in ICPEA is divided into two states, namely fluid state and solid state. The proposed method works in this way: firstly, the cloud particles are generated randomly. Then ICPEA employs fluid operation to guide the cloud particles to explore in the search space. In the iterative process, if the cloud particles constantly find a better solution than their parents, the cloud particles change from fluid form to solid form. Finally, the solid operation is employed to guide the particles to exploit in the decision space.

3.1   Fluid Operation

At first the cloud particles are distributed randomly in the decision space. A cloud particle stands for a feasible solution of the optimization problem. The population is defined by

$$\mathbf{P}_{i,G} = \left(p_{i,G}^1, p_{i,G}^2, \cdots, p_{i,G}^D\right) i = 1, \cdots, N \tag{7}$$

where N denotes the population size. D is defined in Table 1.

The primary task of the fluid operation is to explore the area where better particles may be existed. In general, better particles may guide the evolution direction and result fast convergence. However, due to poorer population diversity, premature convergence is also prone to occur. Conversely, inferior particles may provide helpful information for population diversity [25]. Inspired by this idea, the archive mechanism is introduced to preserve a certain number of inferior particles produced in the previous generation, so as to keep the population diversity. Better particles and inferior particles are simultaneously utilized to explore in the decision space. The fluid operation is designed as

$$\mathbf{V}_{i,G} = \mathbf{P}_{i,G} + lf_{i,G} \times \left(\mathbf{Pbest}_{i,G} - \mathbf{P}_{i,G} + \mathbf{P}_{r1,G} - \mathbf{P}_{r2,G}\right) \tag{8}$$

where $Pbest_{i,G}$ denotes the ith randomly selected cloud particle from the best $N \times t$ ($t \in [0,1]$) particles at generation G. $r1$ and $r2$ are randomly selected integers ($r1, r2 \in [1, N]$), and $r1 \neq r2 \neq i$. $\mathbf{P}_{r2,G}$ is selected from $\mathbf{P} \cup \mathbf{A}$. $\mathbf{P}$ is the current population, and $\mathbf{A}$ is the external archive. The external archive size should less than the specified size, otherwise, some cloud particles are discarded randomly. $lf_{i,G}$ is a liquefaction factor.

3.2 Solid Operation

In solid state, the algorithm will pay more attention to the exploitation in order to achieve the global optimal. Therefore, the superior particles $P_{best,G}$, which is closer to the region where the global solution is located, are devoted to the task of exploitation. The solid operation on the cloud particles is defined as follows.

$$C = \{c_i | \mathcal{N}(En, He), i = 1, \ldots, N\} \tag{9}$$

$$V = \left\{v_{i,G} | \mathcal{N}(\mathbf{Pbest}_{i,G}, c_i), c_i \in C, i = 1, \ldots, N\right\} \tag{10}$$

where $Pbest_{i,G}$ is selected as the same way in Eq. (8). N denotes the current population size. $\mathcal{N}(En, He)$ represents the normal distribution. En and He are the mean value and variance of random variables which obey normal distribution, respectively.

3.3 Control Parameters Selection Mechanism

The liquefaction factor and solidification factor are two important parameters in ICPEA algorithm. Research in [26] shows that the crossover operation in DE can control the population diversity. Generally, large values of the crossover rate may improve the population diversity. Inspired by this idea, the crossover factor CR is used in ICPEA algorithm to improve the search ability of the population. Accordingly, a novel adaptive control parameters method on liquefaction factor and crossover factor is designed to adjust the relationship of the exploration and exploitation in the optimization process. At the beginning, the algorithm employs the fluid operation. The liquefaction factor $lf_{i,G}$ of each particle $P_{i,G}$ at generation G is calculated as follows:

$$Ex_i = f_0 + \frac{1}{D} \tag{11}$$

$$En_i = \frac{tan(1 + log(f_0))}{\pi^2} \tag{12}$$

$$He_i = \frac{\mathbf{En}_i}{\sqrt{MaxFES}} \tag{13}$$

$$lf_{i,G} = rand_1 \times (rand_2 \times He_i + En_i) + Ex_i \tag{14}$$

where D is defined in Table 1. $rand_1$ and $rand_2$ are random numbers which are selected from the range $(0,1)$. f_0 is initialized to be 0.5.

The crossover factor $CR_{i,G}$ of each particle at generation G is calculated by

$$Ex_i = \cos(cr_0) + 1/D \tag{15}$$

$$En_i = 1 - Ex_i \tag{16}$$

$$He_i = \frac{En_i}{\sqrt{MaxFES}} \tag{17}$$

$$CR_{i,G} = rand_1 \times (rand_2 \times He_i + En_i) + Ex_i \tag{18}$$

where cr_0 is initialized to be 0.5.

Generally, the population size will affect the convergence of the algorithm. Then, a linear reduction method of the population size [27] is utilized to enhance the convergence rate of ICPEA algorithm. For each iteration, the current population size N is updated by

$$N = \begin{cases} N - 2 & \text{if } N > N' \\ N & \text{otherwise} \end{cases} \tag{19}$$

$$N' = N_0 - \frac{N_0}{MaxFES} \times FES \tag{20}$$

where *MaxFES* and *FES* are defined in Table 1. N_0 is the population size of the first generation.

Algorithm 1 shows the procedure of ICPEA.

Algorithm 1 The procedure of ICPEA

1: Initialize D, N, N_0; Archive $\mathbf{A}=\varphi$;
2: Generate population $\mathbf{P}$
3: Initialize control parameters according to (11) $\sim$ (18)
4: state = 0
5: **while** the termination criteria are not reached **do**
6:   **if** state = = 0 **then**
7:     Generate new cloud particles $\mathbf{V}$ according to (8)
8:   **else**
9:     Generate new cloud particles $\mathbf{V}$ according to (9) and (10)
10:   **endif**
11:   **for** i =1 to N **do**
12:     **for** j =1 to D **do**
13:       **if** $rand > CR_i$ && $j \neq j_{rand}$ **then**
14:         $\mathbf{V}_{i,j} = \mathbf{P}_{i,j}$
15:       **endif**
16:     **endfor**
17:   **endfor**
18:   **for** i =1 to N **do**
19:     **if** $f(\mathbf{V}_{i,G}) < f(\mathbf{P}_{i,G})$ **then**
20:       $\mathbf{P}_{i,G} \rightarrow \mathbf{A}$; $\mathbf{P}_{i,G+1} = \mathbf{V}_{i,G}$
21:     **endif**
22:   **endfor**
23:   Update the population size according to (19) and (20)
24:   Update the control parameters according to (11) $\sim$ (18)
25: **endwhile**

---

4   Experiments and Discussions

4.1   General Experimental Setting

For a comprehensive evaluation of ICPEA, 30 test problems from *CEC2014* [28] test suits are used to evaluate the performance of ICPEA. Details of experimental settings are given in Table 1.

Table 1. Details of experimental settings

CPU	Celoron 3.40 GHz
Application Software	Matlab R2009b
Dimension	$D = 30$
MaxFES	Maximum number of function evaluations
FES	Current number of function evaluations
Termination Criterion	*MaxFES*
Solution error measure (SEM) [29]	$F(x) - F(x^*)$
$F(x)$	Best fitness value found by an algorithm
$F(x^*)$	Real global optimization value
Wilcoxon's rank-sum test [26]	5% significance level
−	ICPEA is worse than the compared algorithm
†	ICPEA is better than the compared algorithm
=	ICPEA is similar to the compared algorithm

The performance of each algorithm is evaluated by the mean value of SEM. The error will be treated as 0 when SEM is less than 10^{-8}.

In this part, ICPEA is compared with TLBO, Jaya, BBO, DE, JADE, CoDE and CPEA. For ICPEA, The population size N is set to $12 \times D$. The archive size is set to $1.5 \times N$. The parameters of TLBO, Jaya, BBO, DE, JADE, CoDE and CPEA are the same as those used in the corresponding references.

4.2   Comparison of ICPEA with Other Optimization Algorithms

In this section, ICPEA is compared with TLBO (teaching-learning-based algorithm), Jaya [30], BBO (biogeography-based algorithm) [31], DE (differential evolution), JADE (adaptive DE with external archive) [25], CoDE (composite DE) [26] and CPEA (cloud evolution particles algorithm). The statistical results are shown in Tables 2, 3, 4 and 5.

1) *Unimodal problems F_1-F_3*: The experimental results are given in Table 2. It is clear that ICPEA can achieve the optimal results on problems F_1- F_3. DE can also achieve the optimal results on unimodal problems except F_1. ICPEA outperforms TLBO,

Jaya, BBO, DE, JADE, CoDE and CPEA on 3, 3, 3, 1, 2, 3, 3 test problems, respectively. The reason that ICPEA has the better performance on unimodal problems may be a large variation on the control parameters, which are helpful in guiding the search direction.

Table 2. Experimental results on F_1-F_3 obtained by TLBO, Jaya, BBO, DE, JADE, CoDE, CPEA and ICPEA

F	TLBO	Jaya	BBO	DE	JADE	CoDE	CPEA	ICPEA
F_1	5.10e+05†	6.56e+07†	1.74e+07†	6.76e+04†	595†	3.40e+04†	5.28e+05†	0
F_2	26.6†	6.13e+09†	4.50e+06†	0=	0=	5.62†	6970†	0
F_3	673†	5.50e+04†	7220†	0=	2.24e−03†	1.55e−04†	1.41e+04†	0
†	3	3	3	1	2	3	3	\
−	0	0	0	0	0	0	0	\
=	0	0	0	2	1	0	0	\

Table 3. Experimental results on F_4- F_{16} obtained by TLBO, Jaya, BBO, DE, JADE, CoDE, CPEA and ICPEA

F	TLBO	Jaya	BBO	DE	JADE	CoDE	CPEA	ICPEA
F_4	58.3†	382†	123†	0.10†	0 =	24.6†	25.5†	0
F_5	20.9†	20.9†	20.1†	20.9†	20.2†	20.6†	20=	20
F_6	11.9†	33.7†	12.7†	0.33†	9.49†	20.7†	5.42†	0
F_7	2.86e−02†	15.3†	1.02†	0=	0=	8.22e−05†	6.81e−03†	0
F_8	56†	218†	0.663−	132†	0−	19†	51†	8.95
F_9	59.5†	245†	55.9†	178†	25.4†	136†	61†	23.2
F_{10}	1510†	5310†	3.51−	5460†	5.55e−03−	745†	2160†	32.3
F_{11}	6470†	6850†	1940−	6770†	1630−	4860†	2220†	222.0
F_{12}	2.49†	2.49†	0.222−	2.38†	0.261−	0.986†	2.79e−02−	0.31
F_{13}	0.413†	1.34†	0.51†	0.354†	0.211=	0.461†	0.32†	0.20
F_{14}	0.238†	8.03†	0.40†	0.266†	0.243†	0.284†	0.47†	0.19
F_{15}	10.3†	36.4†	13.7†	15.2†	3.13=	13.4†	3.54†	3.05
F_{16}	11.7†	12.9†	9.36−	12.4†	9.26−	11.5†	11†	10.1
†	13	13	8	12	4	13	10	\
−	0	0	5	0	5	0	1	\
=	0	0	0	1	4	0	2	\

2) *Simple multimodal problems F_4-F_{16}*: Table 3 indicates that ICPEA performs better than other seven algorithms on F_4, F_5, F_6, F_9, F_{13}, F_{14} and F_{15}. ICPEA performs better than TLBO, Jaya, BBO, DE, JADE, CoDE and CPEA on 13, 13, 8, 12, 4, 13 and 10 problems respectively.

3) *Hybrid problems F_{17}-F_{22}*: Table 4 shows that ICPEA beats the compared algorithm on F_{17}-F_{21}. ICPEA performs better than TLBO, Jaya, BBO, DE, JADE, CoDE and CPEA on 6, 6, 6, 5, 5, 6 and 6 problems respectively. ICPEA can perform well on these hybrid problems because it takes advantage of the inferior particles information. However, ICPEA did not find the real global optimization value. The reason is that the landscape of the hybrid problems is quite complex. Accordingly, the result obtained by the optimization algorithms is still far from the ideal results.

Table 4. Experimental results on F_{17}- F_{22} obtained by TLBO, Jaya, BBO, DE, JADE, CoDE, CPEA and ICPEA

F	TLBO	Jaya	BBO	DE	JADE	CoDE	CPEA	ICPEA
F_{17}	1.76e+05†	3.80e+06†	2.49e+06†	1420†	1.72e+04†	1480†	4.45e+04†	849
F_{18}	3240†	1.90e+07†	3820†	51.6†	114†	51.4†	2.46e+04†	42.8
F_{19}	13.4†	33.2†	30.2†	4.46†	4.71†	7.17†	9.69†	3.14
F_{20}	988†	6350†	8870†	32.3†	2910†	31.9†	5100†	11.4
F_{21}	7.00e+04†	8.42e+05†	9.08e+05†	650†	5710=	743†	4.34e+04†	413
F_{22}	2410†	577†	480†	47−	149†	126†	192†	97
†	6	6	6	5	5	6	6	\
−	0	0	0	1	0	0	0	\
=	0	0	0	0	1	0	0	\

(4) *Composite problems F_{23}-F_{30}*: The composite problems is of great challenge to optimization algorithms. Table 5 indicates that ICPEA works better than TLBO, Jaya, BBO, DE, JADE, CoDE and CPEA on 4, 8, 7, 2, 4, 3, 6 test problems, respectively.

In order to accurately evaluate the performance of each algorithm, KEEL software [32] is utilized to conduct the multiple-problem Wilcoxon's test according to the PR values. Table 6 and Table 7 show that ICPEA provides higher R + values than R− values compared with TLBO, Jaya, BBO, DE, JADE, CoDE and CPEA. The p values of TLBO, Jaya, BBO, DE, JADE, CoDE and CPEA are less than 0.05, which indicates that ICPEA has a strong competitiveness in the compared algorithms. Moreover, each algorithm is ranked by the Friedman test according to its mean fitness. Table 7 indicates that the overall ranking sequences for all algorithms are ICPEA, JADE, DE, CoDE, CPEA, TLBO, BBO and Jaya. To sum up, it can be stated that ICPEA has significantly better performance in solving CEC2014 benchmark problems.

Table 5. Experimental results on F_{23}- F_{30} obtained by TLBO, Jaya, BBO, DE, JADE, CoDE, CPEA and ICPEA

F	TLBO	Jaya	BBO	DE	JADE	CoDE	CPEA	ICPEA
F_{23}	315=	339†	316†	315=	315=	315=	315=	315
F_{24}	200−	229†	223†	219†	225†	225†	223†	203
F_{25}	200−	220†	208†	202=	204†	202†	206†	202
F_{26}	100=	104†	100=	100=	100=	100=	100=	100
F_{27}	542†	1060†	579†	342†	328=	400†	464†	300
F_{28}	1090†	1250†	921†	805−	796−	941†	877†	840
F_{29}	2.50e+06†	3.45e+06†	1870†	651=	754†	556=	6.35e+05†	716
F_{30}	5260†	1.42e+04†	6210†	616−	1820†	1190†	5240†	1320
†	4	8	7	2	4	3	6	\
−	2	0	0	2	1	0	0	\
=	2	0	1	4	3	5	2	\

Table 6. Results of ICPEA algorithm on the Wilcoxon test

VS	R^+	R^-	Exact P–values	Asymptotic P-value
TLBO	445.5	19.5	≥ 0.2	0.000011
Jaya	465.0	0.0	≥ 0.2	0.000002
BBO	388.0	47.0	≥ 0.2	0.000218
DE	365.5	99.5	≥ 0.2	0.006035
JADE	332.0	103.0	≥ 0.2	0.012895
CoDE	386.5	48.5	≥ 0.2	0.000247
CPEA	453.0	12.0	≥ 0.2	0.000005

Table 7. Average ranking of different algorithms on the Friedman test

Algorithm	Ranking
ICPEA	2.0167
TLBO	5.1
Jaya	7.8167
BBO	5.6
DE	3.7667
JADE	2.95
CoDE	4.0333
CPEA	4.7167

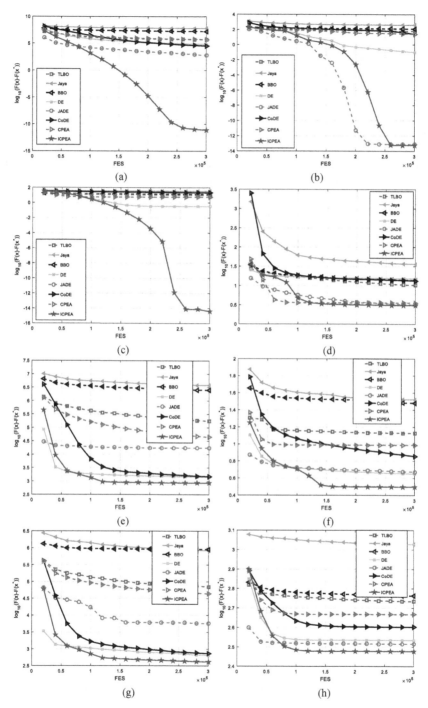

Fig. 1. Results of the mean function error values obtained from TLBO, Jaya, BBO, DE, JADE, CoDE, CPEA and ICPEA versus the number of *FES* on eight representative problems with $D = 30$. (a) F_1. (b) F_4. (c) F_6. (d) F_{15}. (e) F_{17}. (f) F_{19}. (g) F_{21}. (h) F_{27}.

The convergence curves of TLBO, Jaya, BBO, DE, JADE, CoDE, CPEA and ICPEA on eight representative optimization problems according to the mean errors (in logarithmic scale) are plotted in Fig. 1. Figure 1 shows that ICPEA converges faster than the compared algorithms on most optimization problems.

ICPEA can achieve better experimental results mainly because of the utilization of different evolutionary strategies, the dynamical selection of control parameters and the decreasing mechanism of population size. With the fluid operation, on one hand, the superior cloud particles which provide a better direction for the evolution are used to enhance the search ability of ICPEA. On the other hand, the inferior cloud particles which are useful for exploration are used to promote the population diversity. Hence, the cooperation of the superior cloud particles and the inferior cloud particles can effectively trade off the relationship of exploration and exploitation during the evolution process, and then ICPEA can find the region with the optimal solution with a higher probability. With the solid operation, the superior particles, which have good exploitation ability, attract other particles to make exploitation. Moreover, the inferior particles are also used to avoid fast convergence which may lead to a tendency toward local minima entrapment. In addition, ICPEA employs different control parameters for each cloud particle to promote exploration and exploitation simultaneously. The change of the population size also affects the relationship of exploration and exploitation during the evolutionary process.

5   Conclusion

In order to enhance the exploration ability of CPEA, this paper develops an improved cloud particles evolution algorithm, namely ICPEA. Firstly, the cooperation of the superior particles and the inferior particles can effectively adjust the relationship of exploration and exploitation during the iterative process. Then, different control parameters for each cloud particle are designed to further improve the search ability of ICPEA. Finally, the proposed ICPEA is utilized to solve CEC2014 test suits. The experimental results indicate that ICPEA performs better on most optimization problems. Accordingly, the proposed ICPEA algorithm is competitive.

Future work will concentrate on developing effective topological structures to extend the ICPEA algorithm to solve real world problems or large scale optimization problems.

Acknowledgments. This research is partly supported by the Doctoral Foundation of Xi'an University of Technology under Grant 112–451116017, the National Natural Science Foundation of China under Project Code under Grant 61803301, and the National Natural Science Foundation of China under Project Code under Grant 61773314.

References

1. Tian, G.D., Ren, Y.P., Zhou, M.C.: Dual-objective scheduling of rescue vehicles to distinguish forest fires via differential evolution and particle swarm optimization combined algorithm. IEEE Trans. Intell. Transp. Syst. **99**, 1–13 (2016). https://doi.org/10.1109/TITS.2015.250 5323

2. Pan, Z., Lei, D., Wang, L.: A knowledge-based two-population optimization algorithm for distributed energy-efficient parallel machines scheduling. IEEE Trans. Cybern. 1–13(2020). https://doi.org/10.1109/TCYB.2020.3026571

3. Segura, C., CoelloCoello, C.A., Hernández-Díaz, A.G.: Improving the vector generation strategy of differential evolution for large-scale optimization. Inf. Sci. **323**, 106–129 (2015). https://doi.org/10.1016/j.ins.2015.06.029

4. Zhao, S.Z., Liang, J.J., Suganthan, P.N., Tasgetiren, M.F.: Dynamic multi-swarm particle swarm optimizer with local search for large scale global optimization. In: IEEE World Congress on Computational Intelligence, pp. 3845–3852 (2008). https://doi.org/10.1109/CEC.2008.4631320

5. Liu, B., Zhang, Q.F., Fernandez, F.V., Gielen, G.G.E.: An efficient evolutionary algorithm for chance-constrained bi-objective stochastic optimization. IEEE Trans. Evol. Comput. **17**(6), 786–796 (2013). https://doi.org/10.1109/TEVC.2013.2244898

6. Shou-Hsiung, C., Shyi-Ming, C., Wen-Shan, J.: Fuzzy time series forecasting based on fuzzy logical relationships and similarity measures. Inf. Sci. **327**, 272–287 (2016). https://doi.org/10.1016/j.ins.2015.08.024

7. Das, S., Abraham, A., Konar, A.: Automatic clustering using an improved differential evolution algorithm. IEEE Trans. Syst. Man Cybern. Part A **38**(1), 218–236 (2008). https://doi.org/10.1109/TSMCA.2007.909595

8. Zaman, M.F., Elsayed, S.M., Ray, T., Sarker, R.A.: Evolutionary algorithms for dynamic economic dispatch problems. IEEE Trans. Power Syst. **31**(2), 1486–1495 (2016). https://doi.org/10.1109/TPWRS.2015.2428714

9. Liang, J.J., Qin, A.K., Suganthan, P.N., Baskar, S.: Comprehensive learning particle swarm optimizer for global optimization of multimodal functions. IEEE Trans. Evol. Comput. **10**(3), 281–295 (2006). https://doi.org/10.1109/TEVC.2005.857610

10. CarrenoJara, E.: Multi-objective optimization by using evolutionary algorithms: the p-optimality criteria. IEEE Trans. Evol. Comput. **18**(2), 167–179 (2014). https://doi.org/10.1109/TEVC.2013.2243455

11. Koza, J.R.: Genetic Programming: On the Programming of Computers by Means of Natural Selection. MIT Press, Cambridge, MA (1992)

12. Hansen, N., Ostermeier, A.: Completely derandomized self-adaptation in evolution strategies. Evol. Comput. **9**, 159–195 (2001). https://doi.org/10.1162/106365601750190398

13. Basturk, B., Karaboga, D.: An artifical bee colony(ABC) algorithm for numeric function optimization. In: Proceedings of the IEEE Swarm Intelligence Symposium, pp. 12–14, Indianapolis (2006)

14. Storn, R., Price, K.V.: Differential evolution-a simple and efficient heuristic for global optimization over continuous spaces. J. Global Optim. **11**(4), 341–359 (1997). https://doi.org/10.1023/A:1008202821328

15. Kirkpatrick, S., GelattJr, C.D., Vecchi, M.P.: Optimization by simulated annealing. Science **220**(4598), 671–680 (1983)

16. Eberhart, R., Shi, Y.: Particle swarm optimization: developments, applications and resources. In: Proceedings of IEEE Congress on Evolutionary Computation, pp. 81–86 (2001). https://doi.org/10.1109/CEC.2001.934374

17. Rao, R.V., Savsani, V.J., Vakharia, D.P.: Teaching-learning-based optimization: a novel method for constrained mechanical design optimization problems. Comput. Aided Des. **43**(3), 303–315 (2011). https://doi.org/10.1016/j.cad.2010.12.015

18. Lou, Y., Yuen, S.Y., Chen, G.: Non-revisiting stochastic search revisited: results, perspectives, and future directions. Swarm Evol. Comput. **61**(100828), 1–13 (2021). https://doi.org/10.1016/J.SWEVO.2020.100828

19. Mirjalili, S., Lewis, A.: The whale optimization algorithm. Adv. Eng. Softw. **95**, 51–67 (2016). https://doi.org/10.1016/j.advengsoft.2016.01.008

20. Michalewicz, Z.: Quo vadis, evolutionary computation? on a growing gap between theory and practice. In: Advances in Computational Intelligence, 7311, Lecture Notes in Computer Science, pp. 98–121 (2012). https://doi.org/10.1007/978-3-642-30687-7_6

21. Sörensen, K.: Metaheuristics-the metaphor exposed. Int. Trans. Oper. Res. 22(1), 3–18 (2013)

22. Li, W., Wang, L., Jiang, Q.Y., Hei, X.H., Wang, B.: Cloud particles evolution algorithm. Math. Prob. Eng. 2015(434831), 1–21 (2015). https://doi.org/10.1155/2015/434831

23. Awadallah, M.A., Al-Betar, M.A., Bolaji, A.L., Alsukhni, E.M., Al-Zoubi, H.: Natural selection methods for artificial bee colony with new versions of onlooker bee. Soft. Comput. 23(15), 6455–6494 (2018). https://doi.org/10.1007/s00500-018-3299-2

24. Li, D.Y.: Uncertainty in knowledge representation engineering sciences, 2(10), 73–79 (2000)

25. Zhang, J.Q., Sanderson, A.C.: JADE: adaptive differential evolution with optional external archive. IEEE Trans. Evol. Comput. 13(5), 945–957 (2009). https://doi.org/10.1109/TEVC.2009.2014613

26. Wang, Y., Cai, Z.X., Zhang, Q.F.: Differential evolution with composite trial vector generation strategies and control parameters. IEEE Trans. Evol. Comput. 15(1), 55–66 (2011). https://doi.org/10.1109/TEVC.2010.2087271

27. Tanabe, R., Fukunaga, A.S.: Improving the search performance of SHADE using linear population size reduction. In: 2014 IEEE Congress on Evolutionary Computation, Beijing, pp. 1–8 (2014). https://doi.org/10.1109/CEC.2014.6900380

28. Liang, J.J., Qu, B.Y., Suganthan, P.N.: Problem Definitions and Evaluation Criteria for the CEC 2014 Special Session and Competition on Single Objective Real-Parameter Numerical Optimization. Zhengzhou University and Nanyang Technological University, Tech. Rep (2013)

29. Suganthan, P.N., et al.: Problem definitions and evaluation criteria for the CEC2005 special session on real-parameter optimization (2005). http://www.ntu.edu.sg/home/EPNSugan

30. Rao, R.V.: Jaya: a simple and new optimization algorithm for solving constrained and unconstrained optimization problems. Int. J. Ind. Eng. Comput. 7, 19–34 (2016). https://doi.org/10.5267/j.ijiec.2015.8.004

31. Simon, D.: Biogeography-based optimization. IEEE Trans. Evol. Comput. 12(6), 702–713 (2008)

32. Alcalá-Fdez, J., et al.: KEEL: a software tool to assess evolutionary algorithms to data mining problems. Soft. Comput. 13(3), 307–318 (2009). https://doi.org/10.1007/s00500-008-0323-y

Resource Allocation and Trajectory Optimization for UAV Assisted Mobile Edge Computing Systems with Energy Harvesting

Hao Wang[1,2], Yanyan Shen[1(✉)], Shan Wu[2], and Shuqiang Wang[1]

[1] Shenzhen Institute of Advanced Technology, Chinese Academy of Sciences, Shenzhen 518055, China
{wanghao,yy.shen,sq.wang}@siat.ac.cn
[2] Wuhan Research Institute of Posts and Telecommunications, Wuhan 430074, China

Abstract. An unmanned aerial vehicle (UAV) aided wireless powered mobile edge computing (MEC) system is considered in this paper. Different from most existing works that only consider the information transmission assisted by the UAV, in the studied model, the UAV can not only act as an information relay to help the mobile users (MUs) to offload their computation tasks to the MEC server, but also broadcast energy to MUs. This is significant in situations where the target area is experiencing communications and power outage due to an emergency such as an earthquake. The objective of the paper is to maximize the sum of the MU's complete task-input bits by jointly optimizing the time allocation, the UAV's energy transmit power, and the UAV's trajectory under a given time duration. The problem is formulated as an optimization problem, which is nonconvex and difficult to solve directly. To solve this problem, a block coordinate descending algorithm is proposed, which solves two sub-problems iteratively until convergence. Simulation results indicate that the trajectories of the UAV rely highly on the positions of the MUs and the MEC server, and the proposed algorithm has superior performance comparing with two benchmark algorithms under different conditions.

Keywords: UAV communication · Mobile edge computing · Trajectory design · Wireless power transfer

1 Introduction

With the rapid progression of IoT technology, various types of IoT devices, such as, smart home, wearable device, monitoring equipment, keep increasing. However, some IoT devices cannot be equipped with high-performance processors due to their own physical space constraints, so they have weak computing capacity or even lack computing capacity. Fortunately, mobile edge computing (MEC) technologies have brought opportunities to solve the above problems. In MEC, edge nodes, such as base stations and user equipment with high computing capability, can be served as computing servers [5,10]. IoT devices can

© Springer Nature Singapore Pte Ltd. 2021
H. Zhang et al. (Eds.): NCAA 2021, CCIS 1449, pp. 417–431, 2021.
https://doi.org/10.1007/978-981-16-5188-5_30

offload computationally intensive tasks such as VR and image processing to mobile edge computing servers instead of remote cloud servers. Therefore, many advantages such as high transmission rate, low latency, low cost can be provided by the MEC. On the other hand, because of the advantage of high mobility and flexibility [9], unmanned aerial vehicle (UAV) has been combined with wireless communications techniques [7]. UAVs have been applied in various scenarios in wireless communications, such as, remote sensing, military communication, emergency communication in disaster areas [1,6,17]. In UAV communications, two users whose communication channel is blocked can be connected with the help of a UAV, which is served as a mobile relay and can efficiently increase the communication coverage [3]. To assist local resource limited users to utilize the remote computing resources, UAV relay transmission can give a new possible solution [14,15]. Therefore, the new design of UAVs assisted mobile computing gives new opportunities to tackle the challenge issues in wireless communication and computation.

There have been some works in the area of UAV assisted MEC. Specifically, Du et al. in [2] investigated the UAV's energy minimization problem in an MEC system, where both the UAV's hovering energy and computation energy are considered. Zhou et al. in [20] studied UAV-assisted MEC systems from the aspect of security, where the offloading bits from the UAV to the AP can be obtained by a potential evaesdropper through a wiretap channel. Jeong et al. in [4] studied the joint optimization of the UAV's path and location allocation in a MEC system, in which cloudlet installed on the UAV was deployed to provide MUs with the opportunity to offload tasks. Zhang et al. in [16] established a model that the UAV can both calculate and forward information to a remote base station, and this work minimizes the energy consumption of the drone by optimizing time slot allocation, bit allocation, power allocation, and UAV's trajectory. Yuan et al. in [12] proposed a model that both UAV and sensor nodes can perform edge computing. By optimizing the CPU frequency of the UAV, the amount of offloading bits of the sensor node, the energy power emitted by the drone and the trajectory planning, the UAV's energy consumption minimization problem was studied. Liu et al. in [12] creatively proposed a multi-base station model under FDMA condition to perform UAV-assisted edge computing. UAVs can autonomously choose which base station to offload data to. These above works only consider the information transmission by UAVs. Recently, due to the energy scarcity of the mobile users (MUs), UAVs have also be used for wireless energy transmission to MUs. Zhou et al. in [19] studied an edge computing network driven by UAV-enabled wireless energy transmission. Without the consideration of the propulsion energy of UAV, the achievable computing rate is maximized under the limitation of wireless energy transmission. In [18], Zhou et al. investigated a scenario where a UAV provides both energy supply and computing offloading services to users, and the UAV's energy consumption minimization problem was analyzed. However, only the propulsion energy of the UAV is considered in the energy consumption model.

Based on the above analysis, we find that most of the existing works investigate a network scenario where the UAV serves as an information relay to help MUs' bits offloading. Different from these works, we consider a network model where the UAV can not only transmit the bits from MUs to the MEC server for remote computation service but also transfer energy to MUs. In some application scenarios, for example, smart farms, and disaster areas, MUs are often far away from the power source or cannot be charged, so MUs are often inconvenient to charge. Wireless power transfer (WPT) technology brings opportunities to solve the above problems. WPT uses radio frequency technology to transfer energy through electromagnetic fields or electromagnetic waves, eliminating the cost of wiring. Specially, the authors of [19] only consider the UAV's WPT energy. An inaccurate formula of the UAV's propulsion energy is used in [18]. Different from [18] and [19], our work considers a more precise formula of the UAV's propulsion energy consumption. Therefore, our proposed model is more practical, as compared with the existing works.

2 System Model and Problem Formulation

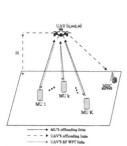

Fig. 1. System model

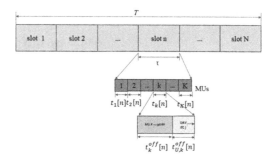

Fig. 2. Time allocation

An UAV based MEC system as described in Fig. 1 is taken into account. It includes k ground mobile users (MUs), a UAV and a ground MEC server. The set of MUs is denoted by $\mathcal{K}$, i.e., $\mathcal{K} = \{1, 2, ..., K\}$. Each MU k, $k \in \mathcal{K}$ has a fixed position s_k, where $s_k = \{x_k, y_k\}^T$, and x_k and y_k are the coordinates of the x-axis and y-axis, respectively. The MEC server is also located at a fixed position that is expressed by $s_0 = \{x_0, y_0\}^T$. MUs have a large amount of data that need to be computed, but they do not have computational capacities, thus they need to transmit their data to MEC server for computing. Due to the signal blockage and shadowing, the MUs cannot directly establish wireless communications links with the MEC server. To help the edge computing process, the UAV is deployed as a mobile relay. Since the MUs are energy limited, the UAV is also served as an energy supplier to transmit energy to MUs by WPT. In this scenario, a 3D wireless communication network is build.

2.1 UAV's Trajectory Model

We utilize the 2-D Euclidean coordinate method to show the positions of MUs, and the MEC server. The total task completion time T second(s) is equally divided into N time slots, each of which has a time duration of $\tau = T/N$. It is assumed that τ is set to be so small that the location of the UAV seems to be invariant during each time slot τ. Let $\mathcal{N} = \{1, ..., N\}$ denote the set of the N time slots. It is assumed that during the flying period, the UAV flies at an invariant altitude, H, hence the UAV's location can be expressed as a 2-D Euclidean coordinate. In time slot n, let $\mathbf{q}[n]$ denote the UAV's horizontal location, where $\mathbf{q}[n] = \{q_x[n], q_y[n]\}$, and $q_x[n]$ and $q_y[n]$ are the coordinates of the x-axis and y-axis, respectively. Let $\mathbf{q}_I = (x_I, y_I)^T$ and $\mathbf{q}_F = (x_F, y_F)^T$ denote the UAV's initial and final horizontal locations, respectively. The UAV's maximum speed is preset as V_{max} satisfying $V_{max} \geq \|\mathbf{q}_F - \mathbf{q}_I\|/T$, which is used to insure that there exists at least one feasible trajectory of the UAV. The UAV's speed cannot be above the maximum speed limit, according to the Federal Aviation Administration rule, which can be expressed by

$$\|\mathbf{v}[n]\| = \frac{1}{\tau}\|\mathbf{q}[n] - \mathbf{q}[n-1]\| \leq V_{max} \quad 2 \leq n \leq N. \tag{1}$$

The constraints on the UAV's initial and final position can be given by

$$\mathbf{q}[0] = \mathbf{q}_I, \mathbf{q}[N] = \mathbf{q}_F. \tag{2}$$

2.2 Communication Channel Model

In UAV assisted networks, since the UAV usually flies at a relatively high altitude, the line of sight (LoS) links can be regarded to be much dominant comparing with shadowing and small-scale fading. As a result, the channel gain from MU k to the UAV at time slot n can be described by the free-space path loss model,[1]

$$h_k[n] = \frac{h_0}{d_k^2[\mathbf{q}[n]]} = \frac{h_0}{\|\mathbf{q}[n] - s_k\|^2 + H^2}, \forall n, k, \tag{3}$$

where h_0 represents the receiver's power at the reference distance of 1 m when the transmission power is 1 W, d_k^2 denotes the square of the distance from MU k to the UAV, and $\|.\|$ refers to a vector's Euclidean norm. Similarly, the channel gain between the UAV and the MEC server at time slot n can be described as

$$h_{EC}[n] = \frac{h_0}{d_{EC}^2[\mathbf{q}[n]]} = \frac{h_0}{\|\mathbf{q}[n] - s_0\|^2 + H^2}, \forall n, \tag{4}$$

where d_{EC}^2 denotes the square of the distance from the UAV to the MEC server.

---

[1] For simplicity, $\forall n$ and $\forall k$ denote $\forall n \in \mathcal{N}$ and $\forall k \in \mathcal{K}$, respectively.

2.3 Energy Consumption and MUs' Task-Input Model

Time-division multiple access (TDMA) protocol is adopted for MUs' data offloading, thus interferences among them can be ignored. To facilitate the data offloading of all K MUs, each slot $n \in \mathcal{N}$ is further divided into K durations, where the k-th duration $t_k[n] \in [0, \tau]$ for $k \in \mathcal{K}$ is allocated to MU k, as shown in Fig. 2. The sum of the durations satisfies the following constraint

$$\sum_{k=1}^{K} t_k[n] \leq \tau, \forall n. \tag{5}$$

$t_k[n]$ can be further divided as $t_k^{off}[n]$ and $t_{U,k}^{off}[n]$, where $t_k^{off}[n]$ and $t_{U,k}^{off}[n]$, $k \in \mathcal{K}$, denote the time MU k spends transmitting data to the UAV and the time the UAV spends transmitting data to the MEC server, respectively. As the amount of data sending back after the MEC server's computation is very small, the time the MEC server spends sending the computed data to the UAV and the UAV spends forwarding the data to the MUs can be ignored. Moreover, based on the UAV trajectory model and channel gain model, the task-input data from MU k to the UAV at time slot n and the energy consumption of MU k can be expressed respectively by

$$L_k^{UL}[n] = t_k^{off}[n] B \log_2(1 + \frac{h_k[n] P_k^{off}}{\sigma^2}), \forall n, k, \tag{6}$$

$$E_k^{off}[n] = P_k^{off} t_k^{off}[n], \forall n, k, \tag{7}$$

where P_k^{off} is MU k's transmission power, and σ^2 represents the additive white Gaussian noise's variance with zero mean. $t_k^{off}[n] \in [0, t_k[n]]$ denotes the time allocation for data offloading from MU k to the UAV at time slot n.

Similarly, let $P_{U,k}^{off}$ and $t_{U,k}^{off}[n] \in [0, t_k[n]]$ refer to the transmit power of the UAV and the time allocation for UAV relaying MU k's data to the MEC server at time slot n, respectively. The data transmission rate from the UAV to the MEC server at time slot n can be given by

$$L_k^{DL}[n] = t_{U,k}^{off}[n] B \log_2(1 + \frac{h_{EC}[n] P_{U,k}^{off}}{\sigma^2}) \quad \forall n, k. \tag{8}$$

And the UAV's energy consumption for offloading MU k's bits to the MEC server at time slot n is given by

$$E_{U,k}^{off}[n] = P_{U,k}^{off} t_{U,k}^{off}[n] \quad \forall n, k. \tag{9}$$

The time allocations for MU k at time slot n satisfy

$$t_k^{off}[n] + t_{U,k}^{off}[n] \leq t_k[n], \forall n, k, \tag{10}$$

which ensures that no interference exists among MUs during the data offloading process due to the adopted TDMA protocol.

The offload bits from the UAV to the MEC server cannot be higher than the offload bits from MU k to the UAV, which creates the information-causality constraint

$$\sum_{i=2}^{n} L_k^{DL}[i] \leq \sum_{i=1}^{n-1} L_k^{UL}[i]. \tag{11}$$

The energy consumption of each MU comes from its harvested energy from the UAV through WPT. Let $P_U[n]$ denote the UAV's energy transmission power at time slot n, the UAV's energy consumption for WPT can be expressed as

$$E_U^{WPT}[n] = P_U[n]\tau \quad \forall n. \tag{12}$$

$$\widetilde{E}_k[n] = \eta_k h_k[n] P_U[n]\tau \quad \forall k,n, \tag{13}$$

where $\eta_k \in (0,1]$ is MU k's energy conversion efficiency.

Because the UAV is flying with a constant speed within a given time slot, the flying trajectory in the time slot is indeed a straight-and-level line, and the UAV's propulsion energy consumption at time slot n can be obtained as

$$E_U^{prop}[n] = \begin{cases} 0, & n = 1, \\ \tau(\zeta_1 \|\mathbf{v}[n]\|^3 + \frac{\zeta_2}{\|\mathbf{v}[n]\|}), & 2 \leq n \leq N, \end{cases} \tag{14}$$

where ζ_1 and ζ_2 are some fixed parameters related to specifications of the UAV. Therefore, the total energy consumption of MU k in time slot n is

$$E_k[n] = E_k^{off}[n] \quad \forall k,n. \tag{15}$$

MU k's energy consumption must be less than its harvested energy, thus we have

$$\sum_{i=1}^{n} E_k[i] \leq \sum_{i=1}^{n} \widetilde{E}_k[i] \quad \forall n,k. \tag{16}$$

The available energy of the UAV is restricted due to the limited capacity of the onboard battery. Generally, the power consumption of the UAV consists of the flying power, the power for wireless energy transmission, and the power for offloading the input-bits of MUs to the MEC server. Therefore, the energy constraint of the UAV can be given by

$$\sum_{n=2}^{N} E_U^{prop}[n] + \sum_{k=1}^{K} \sum_{n=1}^{N} E_{U,k}^{off}[n] + \sum_{n=1}^{N} E_U^{WPT}[n] \leq E, \tag{17}$$

where E represents the UAV's maximum battery capacity.

2.4   Problem Formulation

In the considered model, the UAV's trajectory $\mathbf{Q} \triangleq \{\mathbf{q}[n], \forall n\}$, the energy transmit power of the UAV $\mathbf{P} \triangleq \{P_U[n], \forall n\}$, and the time allocation

$\mathbf{t} \triangleq \{t_k[n], t_k^{off}[n], t_{U,k}^{off}[n], \forall n\}$ at each time slot, will be jointly optimized to maximize the throughput of MUs. Mathematically, the problem can be formulated as

$$\max_{\{\mathbf{Q},\mathbf{P},\mathbf{t}\}} \sum_{k=1}^{K} (\sum_{n=1}^{N} L_k^{UL}[n] + \sum_{n=1}^{N} L_k^{DL}[n]) \tag{18a}$$

$$s.t. \quad \sum_{k=1}^{K} t_k[n] \leq \tau, \forall k, n \tag{18b}$$

$$t_k^{off}[n] + t_{U,k}^{off}[n] \leq t_k[n], \forall k, n \tag{18c}$$

$$\sum_{i=1}^{n} L_k^{DL}[i] \leq \sum_{i=1}^{n} L_k^{UL}[i], \forall k, n \tag{18d}$$

$$\sum_{n=1}^{N} L_k^{UL}[n] = \sum_{n=1}^{N} L_k^{DL}[n], \forall k \tag{18e}$$

$$L_k^{UL}[n] \geq 0, \forall k, n \tag{18f}$$

$$L_k^{DL}[n] \geq 0, \forall k, n \tag{18g}$$

$$\sum_{n=2}^{N} E_U^{prop}[n] + \sum_{k=1}^{K} \sum_{n=1}^{N} E_{U,k}^{off}[n] + \sum_{n=1}^{N} E_U^{WPT}[n] \leq E, \forall n \tag{18h}$$

$$\sum_{i=1}^{n} E_k[i] \leq \eta_k \tau \sum_{i=1}^{n} h_k[i] P_U[i], \forall k, n \tag{18i}$$

$$\mathbf{q}[1] = \mathbf{q}_I, \mathbf{q}[N] = \mathbf{q}_F \tag{18j}$$

$$\|\mathbf{q}[n] - \mathbf{q}[n-1]\| \leq V_{max}\tau, 2 \leq n \leq N. \tag{18k}$$

In problem (18), the constraints (18b), (18c) are time constraints. (18b) requires the sum of time allocated to each MU at time slot n cannot exceed the time slot's duration τ, while (18c) guarantees the time for transmitting data from MU k to the UAV and time for transmitting data from the UAV to the MEC server cannot exceed the time allocated to MU k at time slot n. (18d) is the information-causality constraint. (18e) indicates that all the input data from each MU k must be totaly transmitted to the MEC server. (18f) and (18g) reflects that the transmitted data from the MU k to the UAV and from the UAV to the MEC server cannot be negative. (18h) and (18i) are the energy constraints for the UAV and the MU k, respectively. Constraints (18j) refer to the constraints of the initial and final locations of the UAV. And (18k) is UAV's maximal flying rate constraint.

3 Problem Transformation and Solution

Problem (18) is not a convex problem, since its objective function (18a), and constraints (18d), (18e), (18f), (18g), (18h), (18i) construct a non-convex set.

The time allocation variables in **t** are strongly coupled with the trajectory of the UAV **Q** in $L_k^{DL}[n]$ and $L_k^{UL}[n]$. To address these issues, we propose a block coordinate descending (BCD) algorithm to optimize two subproblems P1 and P2 iteratively.

3.1 Optimization of the UAV's Transmission Power and Time Allocation

When the trajectory of the UAV is given, problem (18) becomes a joint time allocation and transmission power allocation subproblem P1, which is given by

$$\max_{\{P_U[n],t_k[n],t_k^{off}[n],t_{U,k}^{off}[n]\}} \sum_{k=1}^{K}\left(\sum_{n=1}^{N} L_k^{UL}[n] + \sum_{n=1}^{N} L_k^{DL}[n]\right) \tag{19a}$$

$$(18b),(18c),(18d),(18e),(18f),(18g),(18h),(18i). \tag{19b}$$

Since the objective function and constraints are linear, it becomes a convex problem.

3.2 Optimization of the Trajectory of the UAV

Under fixed time allocation **t** and the UAV's energy transmission power **p**, problem (18) reduces to optimize the trajectory of the UAV. The trajectory optimization subproblem can be written as

$$\max_{\{\mathbf{q}[n]\}} \sum_{k=1}^{K}\left(\sum_{n=1}^{N} L_k^{UL}[n] + \sum_{n=1}^{N} L_k^{DL}[n]\right) \tag{20a}$$

$$(18d),(18e),(18f),(18g),(18h),(18i),(18j),(18k) \tag{20b}$$

Problem (20) is a non-convex optimization problem because it has a non-concave objective function and a non-convex constraint set. Generally, non-convex problems are quite difficult to solve. Hence, we will transform it to a convex problem by applying various approximation techniques.

In the objective function, both $L_k^{UL}[n]$ and $L_k^{DL}[n]$ can be approximated by their concave lower bounds, which are denoted as $\check{L}_k^{UL}[n]$ and $\check{L}_k^{DL}[n]$. By taking the first order Taylor expansion, the lower bounds $\check{L}_k^{UL}[n]$ and $\check{L}_k^{DL}[n]$ at a given point $\mathbf{q}^{(l)}[n]$ can be expressed as

$$\check{L}_k^{UL}[n]$$

$$= t_k^{off(l)}[n]B\left\{\log_2\left(1 + \frac{P_k^{off}h_0/\sigma^2}{d_k^2(\mathbf{q}^{(l)}[n])}\right) - \frac{p_k^{off}h_0}{\sigma^2\ln 2}\frac{\|\mathbf{q}[n]-s_k\|^2 - \|\mathbf{q}^{(l)}[n]-s_k\|^2}{d_k^2(\mathbf{q}^{(l)}[n])(d_k^2(\mathbf{q}^{(l)}[n]) + \frac{p_k^{off}h_0}{\sigma^2})}\right\}, \tag{21}$$

$$\check{L}_k^{DL}[n]$$

$$= t_{U,k}^{off(l)}[n]B\left\{\log_2\left(1 + \frac{P_{U,k}^{off}h_0/\sigma^2}{d_k^2(\mathbf{q}^{(l)}[n])}\right) - \frac{p_{U,k}^{off}h_0}{\sigma^2\ln 2}\frac{\|\mathbf{q}[n]-s_0\|^2 - \|\mathbf{q}^{(l)}[n]-s_0\|^2}{d_k^2(\mathbf{q}^{(l)}[n])(d_k^2(\mathbf{q}^{(l)}[n]) + \frac{p_{U,k}^{off}h_0}{\sigma^2})}\right\} \tag{22}$$

In order to approximate the constraint (18d), we first derive the convex upper bounds of $L_k^{UL}[n]$ and $L_k^{DL}[n]$, respectively. Based on the fact that $\|\mathbf{q}[n] - s_k\|^2 \geq \|\mathbf{q}^{(l)}[n] - s_k\|^2 + 2(\mathbf{q}^{(l)}[n] - s_k)^T(\mathbf{q}[n] - \mathbf{q}^{(l)}[n])$, their upper bounds are given by,

$$\hat{L}_k^{UL}[n] = t_k^{off(l)}[n]B\log_2(1 + \frac{P_k^{off}h_0/\sigma^2}{d_k^2(\mathbf{q}^{(l)}[n]) + 2(\mathbf{q}^{(l)}[n] - s_k)^T(\mathbf{q}[n] - \mathbf{q}^{(l)}[n])}),\tag{23}$$

$$\hat{L}_k^{DL}[n] = t_{U,k}^{off(l)}[n]B\log_2(1 + \frac{P_{U,k}^{off}h_0/\sigma^2}{d_k^2(\mathbf{q}^{(l)}[n]) + 2(\mathbf{q}^{(l)}[n] - s_0)^T(\mathbf{q}[n] - \mathbf{q}^{(l)}[n])}).\tag{24}$$

Based on the lower and upper bounds, constraint (18d) can be transformed to

$$\sum_{i=1}^{n} \hat{L}_k^{DL}[i] \leq \sum_{i=1}^{n} \check{L}_k^{UL}[i].\tag{25}$$

And the equality constraint (18e) can be reformulated as two inequalities

$$\sum_{n=1}^{N} \check{L}_k^{DL}[n] \geq \sum_{n=1}^{N} \hat{L}_k^{UL}[n], \sum_{n=1}^{N} \hat{L}_k^{DL}[n] \leq \sum_{n=1}^{N} \check{L}_k^{UL}[n].\tag{26}$$

Constraints (18f) and (18g) can be transformed to

$$\check{L}_k^{UL}[n] \geq 0, \check{L}_k^{DL}[n] \geq 0.\tag{27}$$

We notice that, the propulsion energy consumption of the UAV $E_U^{prop}[n]$ given in (14) is not a convex function about $\mathbf{q}$, which causes the left hand side of constraint (18h) not convex. To solve the problem, the convex upper bound of $E_U^{prop}[n]$ is introduced as

$$\hat{E}_U^{prop}[n] = \tau(\zeta_1\|\mathbf{v}[n]\|^3 + \frac{\zeta_2}{w[n]}),\tag{28}$$

where $w[n]$ is an auxiliary variable we introduced, and it satisfies $\|\mathbf{v}[n]\| \geq w[n]$. This indicates $\|\mathbf{q}[n] - \mathbf{q}[n-1]\|^2 \geq w^2[n]\tau^2$. Taking the first order Taylor expansion at a given point $\mathbf{q}^{(l)}[n]$ to the left hand side, we have $\forall 2 \leq n \leq N$,

$$w^2[n]\tau^2 + 2(\mathbf{q}^{(l)}[n] - \mathbf{q}^{(l)}[n-1])^T(\mathbf{q}[n] - \mathbf{q}[n-1]) - \|\mathbf{q}^{(l)}[n] - \mathbf{q}^{(l)}[n-1]\|^2 \leq 0.\tag{29}$$

By replacing $E_U^{prop}[n]$ with $\hat{E}_U^{prop}[n]$, (18h) is changed to be

$$\sum_{n=2}^{N} \hat{E}_U^{prop}[n] + \sum_{k=1}^{K}\sum_{n=1}^{N} E_{U,k}^{off}[n] + \sum_{n=1}^{N} E_U^{WPT}[n] \leq E, \forall n.\tag{30}$$

The right hand side of constraint (18i) is also not convex, because $h_k[i]$ is not convex. We can use its concave lower bound

$$\check{h}_k[i] = h_0\frac{d_k^2(\mathbf{q}^{(l)}[i]) + \|\mathbf{q}^{(l)}[i] - s_k\|^2 - \|\mathbf{q}[i] - s_k\|^2}{d_k^4(\mathbf{q}^{(l)}[i])}\tag{31}$$

to approximate it, thus the constraint (18i) becomes

$$\sum_{i=1}^{n} E_k[i] \leq \eta_k \tau \sum_{i=1}^{n} \check{h}_k[i] P_U^{(l)}[i], \forall k, n. \tag{32}$$

Now, the trajectory optimization subproblem (**p2**) can be described as follows

$$\max_{\{q[n], R, w[n]\}} R \tag{33a}$$

$$\sum_{k=1}^{K} (\sum_{n=1}^{N} \check{L}_k^{UL}[n] + \sum_{n=1}^{N} \check{L}_k^{DL}[n]) \geq R \tag{33b}$$

$$(18j), (18k), (25), (26), (27), (29), (30), (32). \tag{33c}$$

All the constraints are either linear constraints or in the forms of "convex $\geq$ concave", "concave $\geq$ constant" or "convex $\leq$ constant". As a result, it is convex.

3.3 Overall Algorithm

We summarize the BCD algorithm in Algorithm 1, where the complete task-input bit maximization problem (18) is solved. Algorithm 1 is an iterative algorithm. Firstly, an initial feasible trajectory of the UAV $q^{(l)}[n]$ is given, which should guarantee the trajectory of the UAV satisfies (18h), (18j), (18k). Then, with the given point, we can transform problem **p1** into a linear problem, which can be easily solved. With the solution of **p1**, the solution of **p2** and the objective function $J(l)$ can be obtained by solving a convex problem. Comparing the objective functions $J(l)$ and $J(l-1)$, if their difference is smaller than the precision threshold, the algorithm will stop, and the obtained solution is the final solution, otherwise, the algorithm proceeds.

Algorithm 1. The algorithm for resource allocation and UAV's trajectory optimization

---

1.**input**:give an initial point $q^l[n]$, set the iteration number $l = 0$, and set the small precision threshold ϵ.
2.**repeat**
3.Set $l = l + 1$,
4.Solve problem **p1**, get its solution $P_U^*[n], t_k^*[n], t_k^{off*}[n], t_{U,k}^{off*}[n]$,
5.Replace $q^{(l-1)}[n]$ by $q^{(l)}[n]$, set $P_U^{(l)}[n] = P_U^*[n], t_k^{(l)}[n] = t_k^*[n], t_k^{off(l)}[n] = t_k^{off*}[n]$, $t_{U,k}^{off(l)}[n] = t_{U,k}^{off*}[n]$, and solve problem **P2**,
6.Get the solution $q^{(l)}[n] = q[n]^*$,
7.Get the objective function R^* and let$J(l) = R^*$,
8.**until** $|J(l) - J(l-1)| < \epsilon$.
9.**output**:$q^{(l)}[n], P_U^{(l)}[n], t_k^{(l)}[n], t_{U,k}^{off(l)}[n], J(l)$

Since Algorithm 1 is an iterative algorithm, its total computational complexity depends on the number of iterations and the computational complexity of solving convex problems p1 and p2 in each iteration. Because **P1** and **P2** have $N + 3KN$ and $2N$ variables, respectively, their corresponding computational complexities are $(N + 3N)^3$ and $(2N)^3$ [8]. Therefore, Algorithm 1's computational complexity is $O(Lite((N + 3N)^3 + (2N)^3))$, where $Lite$ is the required number of iterations for convergence.

4   Numerical Simulation Results

Table 1. Simulation parameters

Parameter	Symbol	Value
MUs' number	K	5
Time slots' number	N	60
Task completion time	T	5 s
System bandwidth	B	400 MHz
The channel power gain at a reference distance of $d_0 = 1\,m$	h_0	-30 dB
The noise power	N_0	-60 dBm
The UAV's flying altitude	H	10 m
UAV's maximal speed limit	V_{max}	20 m/s
The energy conversion efficiency	η_k	0.8
Parameters related to the propulsion energy consumption of the fixed-wing UAV [11,13]	(ζ_1, ζ_2)	(0.00614, 15.976)
The tolerant thresholds	ϵ	10^{-2}

In this section, numerical simulations are concluded to verify the performance of the proposed algorithm. In the simulation model, there are $K = 4$ or 5 MUs that are randomly generated within a 8×8 m^2 area. The system parameters are shown in Table 1 unless otherwise specified. In addition, the proposed algorithm is compared with two benchmarks schemes, Equal Time Allocation scheme and Square Trajectory scheme, which are introduced in the following.

- Equal Time Allocation scheme: It only optimizes the power allocation $P_U[n]$ and the trajectory $\mathbf{q}[n]$, since the time allocation for all MUs is equally distributed, i.e., $t_k[n], t_k^{off}[n]$, and $t_{u,k}^{off}[n]$;
- Square Trajectory scheme: It only optimizes time allocation, i.e., $t_k[n], t_k^{off}[n]$, $t_{U,k}^{off}[n]$ and power allocation, i.e., $P_U[n]$, since the UAV flies through a fixed square trajectory.

4.1   Trajectory of the UAV

In this section, the trajectories of the UAV under different numbers of MUs and MEC server's different positions are given. In Fig. 3 and Fig. 4, there are 4 MUs

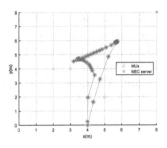

Fig. 3. Trajectory of the UAV (4 MUs)

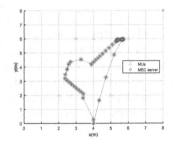

Fig. 4. Trajectory of the UAV (5 MUs)

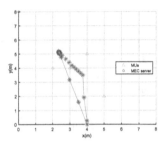

Fig. 5. Trajectory of the UAV (4 MUs)

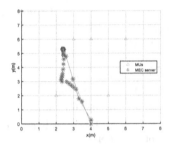

Fig. 6. Trajectory of the UAV (5 MUs)

and 5 MUs that are served in a 8 m × 8 m central area with random locations, respectively. All the MUs are homogeneous. And initial and final locations of the UAV are $\mathbf{q}_I = (4, 4/15)$, and $\mathbf{q}_F = (4, 0)$. Figure 3 and Fig. 4 depict the different trajectories of the UAV when the locations of MUs change. When the location of the MEC server changes, the UAV's trajectory also changes, which are described in Fig. 5 and Fig. 6 for 4MUs and 5MUs, respectively.These figures indicate that the UAV will fly closer to the MUs and the MEC server to gain better performance, because the channel gains between the UAV and the MUs and that between the UAV and the MEC server become much more better as their distances are closer. The UAV tends to spend more longer time staying near to the MU that has the closed distance to the MEC server, because this operation can enhance the channel gain between the UAV to the MU and that between the UAV to the MEC server, and thus can increase the complete task input bits more efficiently.

4.2 Performance Comparison

The performance comparison of the proposed algorithm with two benchmark schemes is conducted by simulations under different conditions.

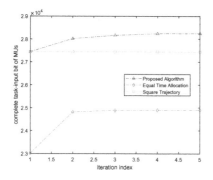

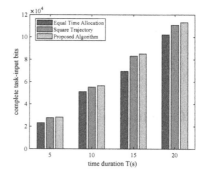

Fig. 7. Convergence of different algorithms (5 MUs)

Fig. 8. The complete task-input bits comparison under different time durations (5 MUs)

The convergence performance is shown in Fig. 7. It can see from Fig. 7 that our proposed algorithm and the Equal Time division algorithm can reach to converge in a few iterations. As the UAV has a fixed trajectory in the Square Trajectory Scheme, the resource allocation problem then becomes a linear problem. For the linear problem, its solution can be obtained directly without the requirement of iterations, thus the completed task input bits do not change. Figure 7 clearly reveals that the complete task input bits of the proposed algorithm is significantly higher than those of the other two algorithms.

The effect of time duration T on the complete task-input bits of MUs is shown in Fig. 8. As it is shown in Fig. 8, the complete task-input bits of all algorithms keep increasing as T becomes larger. This is because with the growth of T, MUs and the UAV can transmit more data. It also shows that the proposed algorithm achieves the highest task-input bits under different values of T. Figure 9 shows the complete task-input bits versus the number of time slots. As the number of

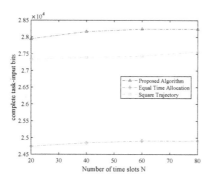

Fig. 9. The complete task-input bits comparison under different numbers of time slots (5 MUs)

time slots N increases, the performance of all algorithms is enhanced. This is because as N increases the time slot duration becomes even smaller, the UAV's trajectory and resource optimization become more accurate. And it also reveals that the algorithm we proposed has the best performance under different values of N.

5 Conclusion

An UAV based MEC model is investigated, where the UAV not only acts as an information relay to help the MUs offload their computation tasks to the MEC, but also serves as an energy provider to transmits energy to the MUs. The complete task-input bits maximization problem is studied, by jointly optimizing time allocation, energy power transmission, and the UAV's trajectory under a given time duration. To address the formulated non-convex optimization problem, we propose a BCD algorithm. Simulation results show the trajectory of the UAV under different network settings and they also indicate the proposed algorithm achieves much higher task input bits comparing with two benchmark schemes.

In our future work, an UAV-assisted MEC model with multiple MEC servers will be investigated. Under this circumstance, a more practical air-to-ground channel model consisting of both LoS and NLoS with probabilities will be used. In addition, experimental results will also be carried out as parts of the future works.

Acknowledgement. This work is partly supported by the Natural Science Foundation of Guangdong Province under grant 2021A1515011856, and the National Natural Science Foundation of China under grant U1801261.

References

1. Baek, H., Lim, J.: Design of future UAV-relay tactical data link for reliable UAV control and situational awareness. IEEE Commun. Mag. **56**(10), 144–150 (2018)
2. Du, Y., Wang, K., Yang, K., Zhang, G.: Energy-efficient resource allocation in UAV based MEC system for IoT devices. In: 2018 IEEE Global Communications Conference (GLOBECOM), pp. 1–6 (2018). https://doi.org/10.1109/GLOCOM.2018.8647789
3. Fan, L., Zhao, N., Lei, X., Chen, Q., Yang, N., Karagiannidis, G.K.: Outage probability and optimal cache placement for multiple amplify-and-forward relay networks. IEEE Trans. Veh. Technol. **67**(12), 12373–12378 (2018)
4. Jeong, S., Simeone, O., Kang, J.: Mobile edge computing via a UAV-mounted cloudlet: optimization of bit allocation and path planning. IEEE Trans. Veh. Technol. **67**(3), 2049–2063 (2018)
5. Liu, L., Chang, Z., Guo, X., Mao, S., Ristaniemi, T.: Multiobjective optimization for computation offloading in fog computing. IEEE Internet Things J. **5**(1), 283–294 (2018)
6. Mao, Y., You, C., Zhang, J., Huang, K., Letaief, K.B.: A survey on mobile edge computing: the communication perspective. IEEE Commun. Surv. Tutor. **19**(4), 2322–2358 (2017)

7. Nan, C., et al.: Air-ground integrated mobile edge networks: architecture, challenges and opportunities. IEEE Commun. Mag. **56**(8), 26–32 (2018)
8. Boyd, S., Boyd, S.P., Vandenberghe, L.: Convex Optimization. Cambridge University Press, Cambridge (2004)
9. She, C., Liu, C., Quek, T.Q.S., Yang, C., Li, Y.: Ultra-reliable and low-latency communications in unmanned aerial vehicle communication systems. IEEE Trans. Commun. **67**(5), 3768–3781 (2019). https://doi.org/10.1109/TCOMM.2019.2896184
10. Tao, X., Ota, K., Dong, M., Qi, H., Li, K.: Performance guaranteed computation offloading for mobile-edge cloud computing. IEEE Wirel. Commun. Lett. **6**(6), 774–777 (2017)
11. Hu, X., Wong, K., Yang, K., Zheng, Z.: UAV-assisted relaying and edge computing: scheduling and trajectory optimization. IEEE Trans. Wirel. Commun. **18**(10), 4738–4752 (2019). https://doi.org/10.1109/TWC.2019.2928539
12. Liu, Y., Xiong, K., Ni, Q., Fan, P., Ben, K.: UAV-assisted wireless powered cooperative mobile edge computing: joint offloading, CPU control, and trajectory optimization. IEEE Internet Things J. **7**(4), 2777–2790 (2019)
13. Zeng, Y., Zhang, R.: Energy-efficient UAV communication with trajectory optimization. IEEE Trans. Wirel. Commun. **16**(6), 3747–3760 (2017). https://doi.org/10.1109/TWC.2017.2688328
14. Zeng, Y., Zhang, R., Lim, T.J.: Throughput maximization for UAV-enabled mobile relaying systems. IEEE Trans. Commun. **64**(12), 4983–4996 (2016)
15. Zhang, S., Zhang, H., He, Q., Bian, K., Song, L.: Joint trajectory and power optimization for UAV relay networks. IEEE Commun. Lett. **22**(1), 161–164 (2018)
16. Zhang, T., Xu, Y., Loo, J., Yang, D., Xiao, L.: Joint computation and communication design for UAV-assisted mobile edge computing in IoT. IEEE Trans. Ind. Inform. **16**(8), 5505–5516 (2020)
17. Zhao, N., et al.: UAV-assisted emergency networks in disasters. IEEE Wirel. Commun. **26**(1), 45–51 (2019)
18. Zhou, F., Wu, Y., Sun, H., Chu, Z.: UAV-enabled mobile edge computing: offloading optimization and trajectory design. In: 2018 IEEE International Conference on Communications (ICC), pp. 1–6 (2018). https://doi.org/10.1109/ICC.2018.8422277
19. Zhou, F., Wu, Y., Hu, R.Q., Yi, Q.: Computation rate maximization in UAV-enabled wireless powered mobile-edge computing systems. IEEE J. Sel. Areas Commun. **36**(9), 1927–1941 (2018)
20. Zhou, Y., et al.: Secure communications for UAV-enabled mobile edge computing systems. IEEE Trans. Commun. **68**(1), 376–388 (2020)

Meta-feature Extraction for Multi-objective Optimization Problems

Xianghua Chu[1,2], Jiayun Wang[1], Shuxiang Li[1], Linya Huang[1], Qiu He[3], Guodan Bao[4], and Wei Zhao[1(✉)]

[1] College of Management, Shenzhen University, Shenzhen, China
x.chu@szu.edu.cn
[2] Institute of Big Data Intelligent Management and Decision, Shenzhen University, Shenzhen, China
[3] d'Overbroeck's, Oxford OX2 7PL, UK
helen0411@yeah.net
[4] Bethany School, Curtisden Green, Cranbrook TN17 1LB, UK

Abstract. Selecting the appropriate meta-features to represent the optimization problems was studied previously. However, the research on the extraction of meta-features for multi-objective problems is lacking. In this paper, a set of meta-features including a unique meta-feature based on Pareto front shape and the combination of meta-features are proposed for the multi-objective optimization problems (MOPs). 25 multi-objective benchmark functions and K-NN algorithm are adopted to realize the algorithm recommendation for MOPs. Experimental results show that the meta-features based on Pareto front can properly represent multi-objective problems and obtain better recommendation performance. The algorithm recommendation accuracy is improved once the combination of meta-features is considered.

Keywords: Meta-feature · Meta-learning · Multi-objective optimization problems · Evolutionary algorithms

1 Introduction

Multi-objective optimization problems (MOPs) refer to the problems with several objectives to be optimized simultaneously, which widely exist in many fields such as mathematics, physics, engineering and business [1]. Typically, an MOP [2,3] can be modeled as follows:

$$minF(x) = (f_1(x), f_2(x), f_3(x), \cdots, f_n(x)) \tag{1}$$

$$subject\ to : x \in \Omega \tag{2}$$

where x is a decision vector, Ω refers to the feasible search region, R^n is the objective space, $F(x) : \Omega \to R^n$ is an m-dimensional objective vector. Since the optimization of one objective often leads to the deterioration of at least one other objective, the optimal solution set x^* is a set of tradeoff solutions

H. Zhang et al. (Eds.): NCAA 2021, CCIS 1449, pp. 432–445, 2021.
https://doi.org/10.1007/978-981-16-5188-5_31

called Pareto optimal solution, where the set of $F(x^*)$ is Pareto front (PF) [4]. Usually, decision makers require an approximation to the PF, so they can select a final solution from the solution set according to her/his preference. Therefore, a number of advanced algorithms have been developed for finding a set of solutions to approximate the PF in a single run. Evolutionary algorithm (EA) is a random search algorithm which simulates biological natural selection and evolution. EA has been proven to be helpful for MOP [5], as they process a set of solutions in parallel, eventually exploiting similarities of solutions by crossover [6]. Various multi-objective evolutionary algorithms (MOEAs) based on different evolutionary mechanisms were constantly designed and applied to solve MOPs successfully, such as decomposition-based MOEA/D [7], NSGA-III [8], domination-based NSGA-II [9], SPEA2 [10] and index-based IBEA [11], EMOEA.

It is known that MOPs have different characteristics [12], while MOEAs perform different search biases [13]. For example, the domination-based NSGA-II, SPEA2 have effective performance when dealing with MOPs with two or three objectives, but the efficiency decreases significantly in tackling many-objective optimization problems (MaOPs). For a complex new MOP instance, one approach is to train the meta-model using a meta-learning (ML) [14] algorithm and adaptively recommend appropriate algorithms for the problem. However, the recommendation process requires prior knowledge about the problem's characteristics and corresponding algorithm performance, which have huge impact on the accuracy of algorithmic recommendation system.

Although many ML literatures have proposed and proved the effectiveness of meta-features [13] for optimization problems, such as meta-features, statistical meta-features and information theoretic meta-features [15,16], no literatures have proposed a set of effective meta-features for MOPs to help algorithm recommendation. Therefore, in this paper, we propose a new set of meta-features for MOPs, which is consist of two components. One is a unique meta-feature based on the shape and properties of the Pareto front, the other is a meta-feature combination based on the target space including common meta-features from statistical features, and geometric measurement features. The proposed meta-feature set is used for the recommendation algorithm for MOPs. Finally, we verify that meta-feature based on Pareto front can represent MOPs and realize algorithm recommendation, and the accuracy of algorithm recommendation will be improved if we consider both meta-features.

This paper is organized as follows: Sect. 2 introduces the background of the meta-features and Pareto front geometrical features of MOPs. Section 3 presents the meta-feature combination proposed in this paper. Section 4 shows the experimental process, setup and result analysis. Section 5 makes conclusions.

2   Related Background

2.1   Meta-feature

Meta-features are a set of data to characterize problem properties and their relations with algorithm performance [14]. Identifying the appropriate set of meta-features is a key challenge and a crucial step for meta-learning task. Limited literatures [17,18] have proposed the formal definition of meta-feature for single objective optimization problem. Meta-features are defined as a function $f : D \to R_k$, calculated by a set of k values extracted from a dataset D. The function f detailed as

$$f(D) = \sigma(m(D, h_m), h_s) \tag{3}$$

According to this function, we can know that the extraction of meta-features is divided into two steps. The first step $m : D \to R'_k$ is a characterization measure [18], it extracts useful fitness information values from a dataset D, the second step $\sigma : R'_k \to R_k$ is a summarization function [18], such as mean, minimum, maximum, skewness and so on.

In the field of single objective optimization, the extraction technology of meta-features is very mature. So far, several types of meta-features are proposed to characterize problem, including simple meta-features, statistical meta-features, information theoretic meta-features [15,16], model based meta-features [16,19] , landmarking meta-features [20], and so on. However, the focus of the research is still to choose a set of meta-features suitable for a certain kind of problem, so that the algorithm recommendation effect of meta-learning is the best. Many literatures have successfully extracted meta-features and developed the algorithm recommendation model for the single objective optimization problem. Fabio Pinto et al. [21] presented a framework to systematically generate meta-features which are more informative than the non-systematic ones. Adriano Rivolli et al. [17,18] proposed a tool MFE to solve the problem that the meta-learning experiment is difficult to reproduce. Jorge Kanda et al. [13] studied the four groups of meta-features of TSP problem, such as the edge and vertex measures, the result shows a good solution with a well meta-feature set, though TSP problem under the different scene; Xianghua Chu et al. [12] proposed an adaptive algorithm recommendation system (ARM) based on meta-learning, which extracted three meta-features, including statistical features, geometric measurement features and landscape features, to represent the target space, and the experimental results showed high recommendation accuracy.

In spite of the technology and application of meta-feature extraction for single objective optimization problem are very mature at present, the technique of feature extraction may not be suitable for multi-objective problems, because MOPs have more complex characteristics. The optimal solution of the MOP is not one, but a Pareto solution set composed of many solutions. Therefore, it is very important to understand the problem from the perspective of Pareto fronts and Pareto solutions. The existing research on the characteristics of multi-objective optimization problems focuses on the construction of benchmark functions and the description of some characteristics of these functions [5,22].

The purpose is to test the multi-objective algorithm on standard test functions with various characteristics. Different algorithms have different performance in solving multi-objective problems with different characteristics. The current research on the characteristics of multi-objective problems only stops at the description of language, No literatures describe the systematic meta-feature extraction and meta-model construction method of MOP. Nevertheless, some studies [22] have shown that the performance of decomposition-based MOEA is closely related to the shape of the Pareto front, indicating that there is also a mapping between the performance of MOEA and some properties specific to MOP. In this paper, we propose the Pareto geometric features peculiar to MOPs as meta-features besides the traditional ones.

2.2   Pareto Front Geometrical Features of MOPs

Different from the Pareto optimal front of the single objective problem is a single point, the Pareto optimal front of the MOPs is a plane mapped by the Pareto optimal solution set, which can have a wide variety of geometric shapes.

The geometrical features of MOPs' Pareto Front include convex, concave, mixed, degenerate, connected [5]. A convex front is one that covers its convex hull. A convex front is a front that is covered by its convex hull. The linear front is both convex and concave. A front is mixed if the front has connected subsets that contain at least two of the three properties strictly convex, strictly concave and linear. A degenerate front is one that the dimension of it is one dimension less than that of the objective space, for instance, a front that is a point in a two objective problem is degenerate.

In this paper, we name the Pareto front geometric feature of MOPs using in ML as PF-based meta-feature, which is used to represent a unique meta-feature of multi-objective problems in the meta-learning task.

3   Proposed Meta-features for MOPs

In order to comprehensively capture the characteristics of the problem and highlight the characteristics of the solution space of the MOPs, we consider two kinds of meta-features: the first one is the target space-based features applied in meta-learning studies [12,23] including statistical features and geometric measurement features. The aim is to characterize the fitness space of MOPs. The other one is a proposed new meta-feature based on the Pareto front to characterize the shape and properties of the Pareto front of MOPs.

3.1   Target Space-Based Features

As we all know, the algorithm carries out random search in the objective space of the optimization problem and approaches the optimal solution step by step according to the specified mechanism. Therefore, the distribution of the objective space can provide important information about the most appropriate search strategy for a particular space. Consistent with the single-objective problem, the objective function of the MOPs also has statistical characteristics that can be used to describe each objective space, so we consider the statistical features which can provide the statistical information of the problem's target space and are relatively simple to be extracted. We take N data points as a sample, the characterization measure is fitness value $f(x_i)$, which is calculated by the correspondent objective function $f(x)$ at the point i. Table 1 shows a set of summarization function that can almost comprehensively capture the statistical characteristics of MOPs' objective space. The mean of fitness value reflects the average level of it, and represents the average height of fitness space to a certain extent. The standard deviation of fitness values evaluates the degree to which the fitness value deviates from the mean and the bumpiness of the surface. Skewness and kurtosis of fitness values evaluates the symmetry of the surface and its flatness relative to the normal distribution.

Table 1. Meta-features based on objective space statistical information.

Meta-feature	Description
$\bar{f} = \frac{1}{N} \sum_{i=1}^{N} f_i$	Mean of fitness values
$SD(f) = \sqrt{\frac{1}{N-1} \sum_{i=1}^{N} (f_i - \bar{f})^2}$	Standard deviation of fitness values
$\gamma_1(f(x)) = E\left\{ \left[(f_i - \bar{f})/Std.(f_i) \right]^3 \right\}$	Skewness of fitness values
$\gamma_2(f(x)) = E\left[(f_i - \bar{f})^4 \right] / (E\left[(f_i - \bar{f})^2 \right])^2$	Kurtosis of fitness values
$\nabla f = lg(abs(max(f_i) - min(f_i)))$	Altitude of search space
$Q_1 = 25\% quartile\ of\ response\ values$	The lower quartile of fitness values
$Q_2 = 50\% quartile\ of\ response\ values$	The median quartile of fitness values
$Q_3 = 75\% quartile\ of\ response\ values$	The upper quartile of fitness values

However, simple statistical features may not be able to capture important problem surfaces characteristics which are very complex, so we consider another set of meta-features that can also describe the objective space surfaces characteristics, the geometric measurement features. We uses the gradient value G_i of the ith data point as the characterization measure, G_i is calculated as:

$$G_i = f(x_i) - f(x_i + \Delta x_i), i = 1, \cdots, N \qquad (4)$$

In this equation, x_i refers to the position of the point i in D dimension, $f(x_i)$ is the fitness value and Δx_i is 1% of the domain of the function. As is shown in the Table 2, we select 5 summarization functions [12] to extract meta-features, including the gradient-based features and outlier ratio. The first meta-feature mean of gradient of fitness surface evaluates the steepness and roughness of the fitness surface based on its rate of change around the sampled data points. The standard deviation of gradient of fitness surface evaluates the changes in the rate of change of sample data. Max of gradient of fitness surface is a measure of the maximum degree of surface mutation. The outlier ratio evaluated by the Grubbs Test measures the percentage of extreme values in all response values.

Table 2. Meta-features based on objective space surfaces characteristics.

Meta-feature	Description
$\overline{\lvert G \rvert} = \frac{1}{N}\sum_{i=1}^{N} \lvert G_i \rvert$	Mean of gradient of fitness surface
$M(\lvert G \rvert)$	Median of gradient of fitness surface
$SD(\lvert G \rvert) = \sqrt{\frac{1}{N-1}\sum_{i=1}^{N}(\lvert G_i \rvert - \overline{\lvert G \rvert})^2}$	Standard deviation of gradient of fitness surface
$\lvert G \rvert_{max} = max\{\lvert G_1 \rvert, \lvert G_2 \rvert, \cdots, \lvert G_N \rvert\}$	Max of gradient of fitness surface
OR	Outlier ratio

3.2 PF-Based Features

The meta-features from the previous section are the features of MOPs' objective space. However, for MOPs, the shape and properties of the Pareto front are also ever-changing and can provide important information for the recommendation of the optimal solution algorithm [23]. Unfortunately, the mapping of the Pareto front can be one-to-one or many-to-one, and the complexity of Pareto front increases with the increase of targets. So it's difficult to extract features from a point of information in the Pareto front. In another way, we can select the classification attribute as the feature of the Pareto front.

The meta-feature is extracted through One-Hot Encoding. Firstly, we determine the feature types of the MOPs' PF, and then the features are transformed into digital features by the One-Hot Encoding. The reason for this method is that it can extend the discrete feature value to Euclidean space, and the code composed of several discrete features corresponds to a point in Euclidean space, so it will be more reasonable to calculate the distance between features. Meta-features based on Pareto front geometrical characteristics are shown in Table 3, the shapes of the Pareto front include concave, convex, linear and mixed. The continuity of the Pareto front indicates whether the Pareto front is disconnected, and the dimensional consistency of Pareto front mapping reveals whether degenerate solutions are exist in the Pareto front.

Table 3. Meta-features based on Pareto front Geometrical characteristics.

Meta-feature	Description
SPF	The shapes of Pareto front
CPF	The continuity of the Pareto front
$DCPF$	The dimensional consistency of Pareto front mapping

4 Experimental Validation and Results

4.1 Experimental Process

To verify the two types of meta-features we used can well capture the characteristics of MOPs, we apply the framework of adaptive recommendation system from Chu's study [12], which has been proved that it can provide better ranking success rate and optimization problem efficiency in the case of extracting the features based on the target space and using the K-NN learning algorithm to learn. Figure 1 shows this framework.

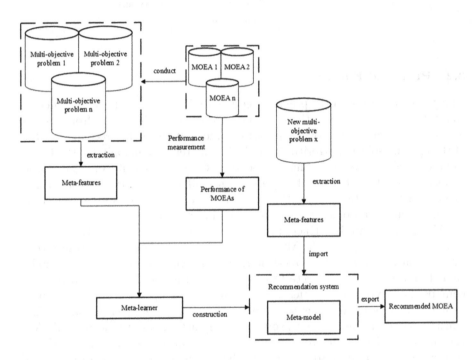

Fig. 1. Adaptive recommendation system framework.

In this study, the problem repository is composed of four problem suites with 25 benchmark functions: DTLZ1-9, WFG1-8, ZDT1-6 and MW1-2. Six representative MOEAs of three types, MOEA/D, NSGA-III, NSGA-II, SPEA2, eMOEA, and IBEA were selected as the algorithm repository. The performance of the MOEAs we selected is measured by the algorithm ideal ranking for each multi-objective benchmark function. The algorithm ideal ranking of a multi-objective benchmark function is determined by the average result of Inverted Generational Distance (IGD), which is a performance indicator obtained by each algorithm runs 10 times on this problem. The smaller the value of IGD, the higher the ranking. Since the more meta-features extracted does not mean the better effect, the combination of meta-features is considered in this paper. Firstly, we test the PF-based meta-feature separately, and use the meta-classifier to train meta-model which can recommend the best algorithm ranking for a new problem. Then the recommendation results of its combination with target space-based meta-features in the Sect. 3 are studied. Besides, we also consider the influence of the combination of meta-features on the recommendation results of different problem dimensions (30-dimension, 40-dimension and 50-dimension). Spearman's rank correlation coefficient (SRCC) and hit ratio are used as indexes to evaluate the performance of the meta-model by leave-one-out cross validation method. SRCC can evaluates the consistency between the recommended ranking and the ideal ranking. The hit ratio can measure the percentage of exact matches between the ideal and recommended best performance in all problems.

Since K-NN has shown its high efficiency in algorithm selection problems [12,13], we choose KNN algorithm for training meta-model. K-NN is based on some distance measurement to find the k examples closest to the target in the training set, and uses "voting method" to classify the new examples based on the type of k nearest neighbor examples. Many literatures [12,13] show that K = 3 has the best effect, so 3-NN is finally selected for classification prediction.

4.2 Experimental Setup

To ensure fairness and unbiased, the following measures are taken in this paper:

1) All the experiments are implemented in MATLAB 2017b with Intel Core i7 2.6 GHz and 16.0 GB RAM.
2) the parameter setting of the MOEAs is the default in the PlatEMO [25].
3) The sample size of the benchmark function is set as 1000, the objective number of each benchmark function is set as 2.
4) The population number and number of iterations of each algorithm are set to 100 and 10,000 respectively, and each algorithm runs 10 times independently.
5) The ideal ranking of algorithm performance of the six algorithms on 25 benchmark functions is obtained through experiments on the PlatEMO [25].

4.3 Experimental Results and Evaluation

In this paper, we obtained the ideal ranking of 6 MOEAs for each MOP benchmark function of 30 dimensions, 40 dimensions and 50 dimensions respectively to measure MOEAs performance. Take the 50-dimensional result in Table 4 as an example, the optimal algorithm data of each benchmark function is indicated in bold. For experimental results from 50-dimension, NSGA-II algorithm has the best performance for benchmark functions DTLZ 2, 3, 5, 6, 9, WFG 4, 5, 6, 7, 8 and ZDT 2, which may be related to the feature that their Pareto fronts are convex and continuous. For the test problems DTLZ 1, DTLZ 8 and WFG 3, where the Pareto front shape is linear and continuous, the MOEAS based on decomposition have the best performance. According to the data, many such relationships can be found, which further indicates that the Pareto front shape can provide information about the optimal performance algorithm.

Table 4. IGD of the six MOEAs on 25 benchmark functions for 50-dimension.

Benchmark function	MOEAD	NSGA-II	NSGA-III	IBEA	SPEA2	eMOEA
DTLZ1	1.3820e+2	1.3419e+2	2.4903e+2	**1.2311e+2**	1.2921e+2	1.7297e+2
DTLZ2	2.8348e−2	**1.7646e−2**	3.5810e−2	2.5657e−2	2.1053e−2	9.0678e−2
DTLZ3	3.7114e+2	**3.3828e+2**	6.2927e+2	3.6210e+2	3.4927e+2	5.3858e+2
DTLZ4	5.2775e−1	3.0988e−1	**4.1815e−2**	3.8568e−1	9.4148e−2	2.8794e−1
DTLZ5	3.0556e−2	**1.7965e−2**	3.4749e−2	2.5436e−2	2.0218e−2	1.0335e−1
DTLZ6	1.6959e+1	**8.8287e+0**	1.0816e+1	9.0258e+0	1.0243e+1	1.5907e+1
DTLZ7	8.1595e−1	7.8510e−2	2.0468e−1	**5.7889e−2**	1.2362e−1	7.2861e−1
DTLZ8	NaN (NaN)	1.6596e−1	**1.5116e−1**	NaN (NaN)	NaN (NaN)	NaN (NaN)
DTLZ9	1.6629e+1	**6.4314e+0**	7.7523e+0	7.1369e+0	7.2025e+0	1.1439e+1
WFG1	1.5047e+0	1.0463e+0	1.1879e+0	**9.4770e−1**	1.0947e+0	1.2010e+0
WFG2	3.1789e−1	**1.0846e−1**	1.1682e−1	1.1242e−1	1.1807e−1	1.9480e−1
WFG3	2.9008e−1	1.1325e−1	1.4112e−1	**9.6788e−2**	1.2120e−1	1.5086e−1
WFG4	2.4521e−1	**8.2535e−2**	9.3848e−2	9.4766e−2	8.5879e−2	1.4315e−1
WFG5	1.6671e−1	**5.5367e−2**	6.8498e−2	6.7162e−2	5.9289e−2	1.0669e−1
WFG6	2.3195e−1	**8.8982e−2**	1.1974e−1	9.9508e−2	1.0070e−1	1.3485e−1
WFG7	3.7602e−1	**4.2815e−2**	6.0185e−2	5.9616e−2	4.6995e−2	1.0329e−1
WFG8	2.6282e−1	**1.2818e−1**	1.4241e−1	1.3408e−1	1.3208e−1	1.7850e−1
ZDT1	4.8669e−1	5.0774e−2	1.0124e−1	**3.1166e−2**	5.7299e−2	1.6325e−1
ZDT2	6.8341e−1	**9.1844e−2**	2.2581e−1	4.6176e−1	9.4580e−2	1.2176e+0
ZDT3	4.8648e−1	5.5911e−2	9.4073e−2	**2.6406e−2**	7.2564e−2	1.6750e−1
ZDT4	7.6528e+1	6.1339e+1	8.2208e+1	6.7255e+1	**5.4032e+1**	2.0289e+2
ZDT5	1.0041e+1	2.3197e−1	5.3910e−1	2.8128e+0	**1.6152e−1**	6.8829e−1
ZDT6	3.7091e+0	3.0061e+0	3.9115e+0	**2.7027e+0**	3.4060e+0	5.2363e+0
MW1	NaN (NaN)	NaN (NaN)	NaN (NaN)	NaN (NaN)	NaN (NaN)	NaN (NaN)
MW2	5.5339e−1	3.7704e−1	5.0171e−1	3.6892e−1	**1.7557e−1**	9.6832e−1

First, PF-based features are used to extract meta-features from multi-objective benchmark functions to help build the meta-model, Table 5 lists the average SRCC and hit ratio for three different problem dimensions. SRCC [26] is a metric used to assess the consistency between a recommended ranking and a real ranking. SRCC is defined as:

$$\rho_i = 1 - 6 \left[\left(\sum_{i=1}^{N} d_{i,a}^2 \right) / (N/(N^2 - 1)) \right] \tag{5}$$

where $d_{i,a}$ is the Manhattan distance between the recommended rank and ideal rank of algorithms a; N is the number of algorithms. If ρ is equal to 1, that means the results are very consistent, the prediction is more accurate. Hit ratio is the ratio between the number of correctly predicted labels in test cases and the number of all test cases. The best result is shown in bold. From the experimental results, the overall average recommendation accuracy is more than 60%, indicating that the MOEAs recommendation method based on Pareto front features has achieved initial success. In Table 5, the highest SRCC 72% occurred in algorithm recommendation for 40-dimensional problems, and the highest hit ratio 76% also occurred in algorithm recommendation for 40-dimensional problems, that is, 19 optimal algorithms could be selected from 25 benchmark functions.

Table 5. The SRCC and hit ratio results of using only PF-based features

Performance indicators	30-D	40-D	50-D
SRCC	0.62 ± 0.04	**0.72 ± 0.02**	0.67 ± 0.03
Hit ratio	0.60 ± 0.02	**0.76 ± 0.02**	0.68 ± 0.02

Table 6. The SRCC and hit ratio results of using two types of features

Performance indicators	30-D	40-D	50-D
SRCC	0.62 ± 0.03	0.72 ± 0.02	**0.74 ± 0.02**
Hit ratio	0.64 ± 0.02	**0.76 ± 0.02**	0.72 ± 0.02

In addition to Pareto-based features, whether combining other features, such as those based on target space, can contribute to the improvement of accuracy remains to be studied. Therefore, we used the target space-based features in the Sect. 3 combined with PF-based features to extract meta-features for the multi-objective benchmark function. The results are shown in Table 6, its overall average recommendation accuracy is also over 60%. Figure 2 shows the line chart

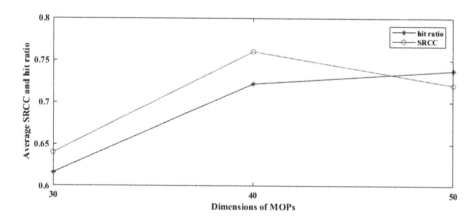

Fig. 2. The performance of the recommendation using three types of features in three dimensions.

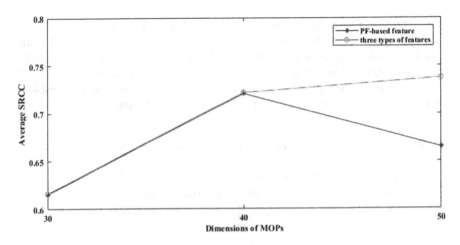

Fig. 3. SRCC values under different meta-features.

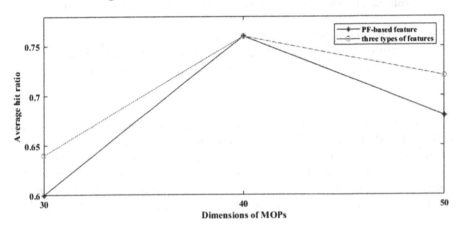

Fig. 4. Hit ratio values under different meta-features.

of average SRCC and hit ratio values under different dimensions. It can be seen that the change of problem dimension will affect the final recommendation result of the problem, and this influence may be positive.

In Fig. 3, when the dimensions are in 30 and 40 dimensions, the combination of Pareto-based features and other problem features as meta-features will not have much impact on the final prediction accuracy, but for 50 dimensions, it improves the prediction accuracy. In Fig. 4, the combined meta-features help improve the hit ratio of the predicted problem. In general, although the Pareto-based meta-features can produce better results for problem recommendation, the combined meta-features perform better than the Pareto-based meta-features alone, which indicates that the Pareto-based and the target space-based meta-features should be considered simultaneously when extracting features for multi-objective problems.

5   Conclusion

Meta-feature extraction is a challenging frontier topic in algorithm selection and recommendation. Its goal is to select the features that can represent the problem and map them with the algorithm performance that can solve the problem, so as to improve the accuracy of recommendation. In the research of single-objective problem, feature extraction and algorithm recommendation have been very mature, and there is no systematic literature to extract features and recommend appropriate algorithms for MOPs. In this paper, we propose a unique meta-feature based on Pareto shape and properties for MOPs, carry out experiment on 25 multi-objective benchmark functions and use K-NN algorithm to realize the algorithm recommendation of extracting PF-based features for MOPs. In the experimental process, we also considered the combination of features based on PF and target space.

The contributions of this paper summarized as follows: 1) We introduce the meta-learning of machine learning field to the algorithm selection of multi-objective problem, which expands the new perspective of solving multi-objective problems; 2) We verify that the shape of the Pareto fronts can provide effective information for the algorithm recommendation of multi-objective problems; 3) We propose the PF-based features peculiar to MOPs for meta-learning processes, which can reduce the space-time complexity of feature extraction under the premise of no significant reduction in recommendation accuracy; 3) The result of our experiment proves that PF-based meta-features can represent MOPs and realize algorithm recommendation. Simultaneously, if the combination of PF-based meta-features and target space-based meta-features is considered, the accuracy of algorithm recommendation will be improved, indicating that the combination of those features can more comprehensively characterize the features of MOPs. This provides more possibilities for multi-objective feature extraction engineering field.

Although the prospect of feature extraction for multi-objective problems is good at present, there is still room for progress. For example, the target space of the MOP also has some features that the single-objective problem does not have, such as multimodal, deceptive. How to represent these features and whether they can be used to extract meta-features remains to be studied.

Acknowledgements. This work was partially supported by the National Natural Science Foundation of China (Grant No. 71971142 and 71701079).

References

1. Li, K., Wang, R., Zhang, T.: Evolutionary many-objective optimization: a comparative study of the state-of-the-art. IEEE Access **6**, 26194–26214 (2018)
2. Ma, X., Yang, J., Wu, N.: A comparative study on decomposition-based multi-objective evolutionary algorithms for many-objective optimization. In: 2016 IEEE Congress on Evolutionary Computation (CEC), pp. 2477–2483 (2016)

3. Wang, R., Zhou, Z., Ishibuchi, H.: Localized weighted sum method for many-objective optimization. IEEE Trans. Evol. Comput. **22**(1), 3–18 (2018)
4. Tanabe, R., Ishibuchi, H.: A review of evolutionary multimodal multiobjective optimization. IEEE Trans. Evol. Comput. **24**(1), 193–200 (2020)
5. Huband, S., Hingston, P., Barone, L.: A review of multiobjective test problems and a scalable test problem toolkit. IEEE Trans. Evol. Comput. **10**(5), 477–506 (2006)
6. Zitzler, E., Thiele, L.: An evolutionary algorithm for multiobjective optimization: the strength pareto approach. TIK-report, vol. 43 (1998)
7. Zhang, Q., Li, H.: MOEA/D: a multiobjective evolutionary algorithm based on decomposition. IEEE Trans. Evol. Comput. **11**(6), 712–731 (2007)
8. Deb, K., Jain, H.: An evolutionary many-objective optimization algorithm using reference-point-based nondominated sorting approach, part I: solving problems with box constraints. IEEE Trans. Evol. Comput. **18**(4), 577–601 (2013)
9. Deb, K., Pratap, A., Agarwal, S.: A fast and elitist multiobjective genetic algorithm: NSGA-II. IEEE Trans. Evol. Comput. **6**(2), 182–197 (2002)
10. Zitzler, E., Laumanns, M., Thiele, L.: SPEA2: improving the strength Pareto evolutionary algorithm. TIK-report, vol. 103 (2001)
11. Zitzler, E., Künzli, S.: Indicator-based selection in multiobjective search. In: Yao, X., et al. (eds.) PPSN 2004. LNCS, vol. 3242, pp. 832–842. Springer, Heidelberg (2004). https://doi.org/10.1007/978-3-540-30217-9_84
12. Chu, X., Cai, F., Cui, C.: Adaptive recommendation model using meta-learning for population-based algorithms. Inf. Sci. **476**, 192–210 (2019)
13. Kanda, J., De Carvalho, A., Hruschka, E.: Meta-learning to select the best meta-heuristic for the traveling salesman problem: a comparison of meta-features. Neurocomputing **205**, 393–406 (2016)
14. Brazdil, P., Carrier, C.G., Soares, C.: Metalearning: Applications to Data Mining. Springer, Heidelberg (2008). https://doi.org/10.1007/978-3-540-73263-1
15. Peng, Y., Flach, P.A., Soares, C., Brazdil, P.: Improved dataset characterisation for meta-learning. In: Lange, S., Satoh, K., Smith, C.H. (eds.) DS 2002. LNCS, vol. 2534, pp. 141–152. Springer, Heidelberg (2002). https://doi.org/10.1007/3-540-36182-0_14
16. Vilalta, R., Giraud-Carrier, C.G., Brazdil, P.: Using meta-learning to support data mining. Int. J. Comput. Sci. Appl. **1**(1), 31–45 (2004)
17. Alcobaca, E., Siqueira, F., Rivolli, A.: MFE: towards reproducible meta-feature extraction. J. Mach. Learn. Res. **21**, 1–5 (2020)
18. Rivolli, A., Garcia, L. P., Soares, C.: Towards reproducible empirical research in meta-learning, pp. 32–52 (2018)
19. Reif, M., Shafait, F., Goldstein, M., Breuel, T., Dengel, A.: Automatic classifier selection for non-experts. Pattern Anal. Appl. **17**(1), 83–96 (2012). https://doi.org/10.1007/s10044-012-0280-z
20. Balte, A., Pise, N., Kulkarni, P.: Meta-learning with landmarking: a survey. Int. J. Comput. Appl. **105**, 8 (2014)
21. Pinto, F., Soares, C., Mendes-Moreira, J.: Towards automatic generation of metafeatures. In: Bailey, J., Khan, L., Washio, T., Dobbie, G., Huang, J.Z., Wang, R. (eds.) PAKDD 2016. LNCS (LNAI), vol. 9651, pp. 215–226. Springer, Cham (2016). https://doi.org/10.1007/978-3-319-31753-3_18
22. Bossek, J.: smoof: single-and multi-objective optimization test functions. R J. **9**(1), 103 (2017)
23. Ishibuchi, H., Setoguchi, Y., Masuda, H.: Performance of decomposition-based many-objective algorithms strongly depends on pareto front shapes. IEEE Trans. Evol. Comput. **21**(2), 169–190 (2017)

24. Cui, C., Hu, M.Q., Weir, J.D.: A recommendation system for meta-modeling: a meta-learning based approach. Expert Syst. Appl. **46**, 33–44 (2016)
25. Tian, Y., Cheng, R., Zhang, X.: PlatEMO: a MATLAB platform for evolutionary multi-objective optimization [educational forum]. IEEE Comput. Intell. Mag. **12**(4), 73–87 (2017)
26. Neave, H., Worthington, P.: Distribution-free tests. Contemp. Sociol. **19**(3), 137–153 (1990)

Feed Formula Optimization Based on Improved Tabu Search Algorithm

Xuecong Zhang[1], Haolang Shen[2(✉)], and Zujian Wu[2]

[1] College of Information Science and Technology, Jinan University, Guangzhou, China
cong200124@stu2018.jnu.edu.cn
[2] Jinan University – University of Birmingham Joint Institute, Jinan University,
Guangzhou, China
shenhaolang2018054918@stu2018.jnu.edu.cn, zujian.wu@jnu.edu.cn

Abstract. The profitability of the livestock industry largely depends on cost-effective feed formula as feed accounts for a large proportion of production costs. Recently, it is one of research hotspots that investigation on how to scientifically formulate livestock feed reducing the cost. In this work, an Improved Tabu Search (ITS) algorithm is proposed to study the pig feed formula optimization method. The proposed ITS algorithm focuses on combination of the tabu search algorithm and intelligent optimization algorithms, which can obtain advantages of global and local optimization search from traditional optimization algorithms. The experimental results show that the ITS algorithm can achieve higher precision search and performs better than other optimization algorithms.

Keywords: Feed formulation model · Tabu search algorithm · Intelligent optimization algorithms · Linear programming

1 Introduction

The cost of feed significantly contributes to the profitability of livestock industry and has been estimated to constitute 60–80% of the total costs of livestock production [1]. While the demands of meat are rising up with continuous variation of the environment, it is important and necessary to find out how to reduce the cost of feed in terms of satisfying the nutritional demand. Therefore, in current livestock industry, study of scientific formulation on feeding is one of key research topics to achieve effective feeding with consideration of nutritional needs of livestock and reduced costs.

This work aims at the problem of pig feed formula optimization, which is a combinatorial optimization problem in essence. Different kinds of raw materials are scientifically used and the amount of these materials are adjusted according to nutrition requirements of feeding pigs. The formula requires to reduce the cost as much as possible under the condition of meeting the minimum nutrition demands. Meanwhile, in order to ensure the nutrition balance, the upper and lower limits of each raw material should be defined. In the formulation development of pig feed, due to the diversity of nutrients in raw materials and the complexity of nutritional indicators required by animals, there are many

© Springer Nature Singapore Pte Ltd. 2021
H. Zhang et al. (Eds.): NCAA 2021, CCIS 1449, pp. 446–457, 2021.
https://doi.org/10.1007/978-981-16-5188-5_32

constraints when solving the objectives of balancing nutrition and controlling materials amount. In order to meet the constraints, it is necessary to reduce the cost, and the time complexity, search range and precision of the results. Therefore, pig feed formula is much more difficult to be investigated under these constraints.

In this work, a feed formula optimization algorithm is proposed based on the existing solution, and it was proved that the proposed algorithm can not only be nested to other algorithms to achieve re-optimization results, but also can control the accuracy of optimization results by setting parameters. From the results and analysis, the proposed algorithm involving combination between the tabu search and intelligent optimization algorithms can improve the traditional tabu search algorithm by shortening the tabu list, canceling the amnesty strategy and changing the neighborhood moving rules. Therefore, the proposed algorithm can be carried out to approach fast and large-scale search in a more complex solution space.

The rest of this work is organized as follows. In Sect. 2, the related work about the feed formula optimization problems and tabu search algorithm are introduced and summarized. In Sect. 3, the feed formula optimization problem is reformulated and then the improved tabu search algorithm is described for feed formula problem in details. In Sect. 4, experiments are carried out for solving the optimization problem. Then, the superiority of the proposed algorithm is verified by comparative experiments, and the newly designed formula is optimized according to China's feed nutrition table. Furthermore, the parameter settings and the experimental results are analyzed in details. The results show that the validation of the proposed algorithm on the optimization ability, time complexity and portability. In Sect. 5, we summarize the current research results and further work in near future is discussed and presented.

2 Related Work

2.1 Feed Formula Optimization Problem

Feed formula problems has been widely studied because of its practical meanings and various kinds of applied algorithms and methods. Uyeh et al. [1] modified the conventional problem formulation with a tolerance parameter and solved the problem with differential evolution. Pratiksha Saxena and Yaman Parasher [2] used artificial neutral network (ANN) to train three objective functions in order to find the most optimal percentage of price, nutrient and water. Uyeh et al. [3] formulated a multi-objective feed formulation problem comprising of two objects, minimizing feed cost and minimizing deviation from the specified requirements. Non-Dominated Sorting Based Genetic Algorithm-II (NSGA-II) was adopted in solving this feed formulation problems. Zhang and Wang [4] set a multi-objective mathematical model for feed formula optimal problem and proposed a new MOPSO-based feed formula optimal method. Tatjana V. Sibalija [5] showed comprehensive and critical analysis of PSO usage. The PSO specific parameters are discussed in detailed according to different problem types. A global selection method of particle and a dominance-principle were presented. Tozer and Stokes [6] examines the potential to use multiple objective programming to reduce nutrient excretion from dairy cows. Xiong et al. [7] introduced a dual model on an original linear programming to obtain those shadow prices of resources and then used the shadow prices to optimize the feed formulation. Zhang [8] proposed a novel hybrid genetic algorithm (HGA) for the feed formula problem. Also, the HGA was shown to have a good performance by comparing it with other 6 feed formulation methods in using different kind of algorithms. Wang and Adam Sobeyb [9] took a comparison between Genetic Algorithm (GA) and other state-of- art algorithms in evolutionary computation, which showed the importance of GA in composite optimization. Huang et al. [10] introduced fuzzy linear programming into the software of optimizing feed formula and a satisfying result was obtained. In the work of Yang et al. [11], an algorithm is presented to solve multi-objective linear programming problems and show its application to planting structure optimization. A new and efficient combinatorial optimization algorithm based on the simulated annealing algorithm is proposed and applied to the feed formula design by Chan [12].

2.2 Tabu Search Algorithm

Tabu search (TS) algorithm was first introduced by Prof. Fred Glover [13] in about 1986 and he improved it in 1990. From then on, tabu search algorithm is applied to solve many practical problems and widely researched by scientists. The TS algorithm is a kind of meta heuristic random search algorithm. It starts from an initial feasible solution, selects a series of specific search directions (moves) as a trial, and selects the moves which generating the value of a specific objective function changes the most. Chang et al. [14] proposed a parallel iterative solution-based tabu search algorithm to solve the obnoxious p-median problem. The proposed algorithm combines a delete-add compound move instead of a typical time-consuming swap move to improve neighborhood exploration, and a solution-based tabu search procedure to strictly prevent visited solutions from being revisited. Liu et al. [15] proposed a two-phase tabu search consisting of a traditional tabu search and a solution-based tabu search. The two-phase tabu search algorithm was aimed to solve the maximum diversity problem (MDP) and the algorithm performs well in both solution quality and computational efficiency. Lee and Ozsen [16] introduced a tabu search heuristic with novel indirect-cost analysis concept, in order to the integrated location-inventory problem. The indirect cost is a ratio used to evaluate candidate facilities, along with direct cost, changes in the objective function value. The works mentioned above show that the tabu search algorithm can be applied to various problems. In this work we will propose an improved tabu search algorithm to solve the feed formula optimization problem and the details will be presented in next section.

3   Improved Tabu Search Algorithm for Feed Formula Optimization Problem

3.1   Feed Formula Optimization Problem

In this work, the problem of pig feed formula was studied to reduce the cost under the conditions of meeting the nutritional needs and dosage restrictions. At the same time, two kinds of feed are optimized: one group is the same as the feed configuration in the literature [8], which shows the advantages of the algorithm; another group is to select and prepare raw materials according to the Chinese feed composition and nutritional value table, which not only explains the meaning of the algorithm, but also realizes the localization of raw material formulation.

First of all, the aim of optimizing pig feed formula is to achieve cost reduction when the conditions are met. Therefore, the unit price of each raw material $[c_1, c_2, \ldots, c_m]$ needs to be determined. According to previous research in academics and industry, we determined the pig nutrient requirements, and obtained the raw materials and their nutrient contents by consulting the Chinese feed composition and nutritional value table, and selected the appropriate raw materials according to the formula design requirements. Finally, we calculate the demand of various feed by carrying out the algorithm, and determine the feed formula.

With m kinds of raw materials and N kinds of feed nutrient requirements, we can construct a matrix $P(a_{ij})$ of $n \times m$, where $i = 1, 2, \ldots n; j = 1, 2, \ldots, m$. Assuming that the feed cost is E, the objective function in the pig feed model can be defined as follows:

$$\min E = c_1 x_1 + c_2 x_2 + \ldots + c_m x_m \tag{1}$$

where $x_i (i = 1, \ldots m)$ is the content of each raw material in the formula.

Since we are studying the formula of the 100 Kg pig feed, we can get the following results:

$$x_1 + x_2 + \ldots + x_m = 100 \tag{2}$$

The constraint conditions of pig feed can be described by the following inequality equations:

$$\begin{cases} a_{11}x_1 + a_{12}x_2 + \ldots + a_{1m}x_m \geq b_1 \\ \qquad \vdots \\ a_{n1}x_1 + a_{n2}x_2 + \ldots + a_{nm}x_m \geq b_n \\ \qquad x_i > 0 (i = 1, \ldots, m) \end{cases} \tag{3}$$

where, a_{ij} is the amount of the j nutrient of the ith raw material; b_j is the minimum standard of nutrients required by pigs.

3.2 Improved Tabu Search Algorithm

Inspired by the main ideas of tabu search algorithm [13], we apply the improved algorithm commonly to the feed formula research. Details of our improved tabu search algorithm in the feed formula research model are shown as follows.

The core point of tabu search algorithm is to realize global search and local search through tabu table. Firstly, the parameters of the algorithm are set to generate the initial solution x, and the empty tabu table is set. However, the initial solutions of the traditional tabu search algorithm are generated randomly, which will lead to the instability of the algorithm results and the low degree of optimization. Therefore, in this work we use the traditional algorithm to optimize the problem first, and then use the obtained results as the initial solution for further optimization. After that, whether the termination condition is met can be determined. Usually, the number of runs or the threshold value that the result reaches will be set as the termination conditions. If the threshold value is reached, the result will be output, otherwise the operation will continue. Then, according to the neighborhood moving rule, the result X is moved in the previous step.

In this work, only the values of two variables in X are changed each time because the total proportion of ingredients up to 100% should be kept. Also, since there are multiple variable values in X, when the values of neighborhood change are the same, there will be a set of new solutions X in a round of neighborhood movement. Substituting all the solutions into the constraint conditions and judging whether the corresponding neighborhood movement rules are in the tabu list, then removing those unsatisfied. By substituting all feasible solutions into the objective function, the optimal solution is obtained, and the fitness value of the objective function, the optimal solution and the neighborhood movement corresponding to the optimal solution will be recorded. Moreover, the corresponding movement is put into the tabu list, and the neighborhood movement are reused after the specified generations (in this work, since the sum of variables in X is restricted, and the neighborhood movement is also an increase or decrease operation, so it is not involved in amnesty rule and there is no need to elaborate here).

Finally, the optimal solution, the fitness value of the objective function and the corresponding algebra are all updated, then the step of judging the termination condition is carried out. Therefore, the traditional algorithm has been used to obtain the optimization results. Set $X = [x_1, x_2, \ldots, x_m]$, and the corresponding feed cost is f. Then the search precision is set as $W = [w_1, w_2, \ldots, w_p]$. The number of runs is K. The x, f, W and K are input to the algorithm.

Next, w_1 is firstly used to search the precision and judging whether K' is less than K. If true, it will continue to run; Otherwise, the loop will end and X and the corresponding f will be output. Within the loops, the neighborhood for X is moved, and the neighborhood move rule is for the element X in x_i and x_j $(i, j = 1, 2, \ldots, m)$ respectively $+w_1$ and $-w_1$ operations, because each element has the possibility of $+w_1$ or $-w_1$. Therefore, the corresponding X may have $m \times (m-1)$ changes (for example:$[x_1, x_2, \ldots, x_i + w_1, \ldots, x_j - w_1, \ldots, x_m]$). Then moving all of the above neighbourhood w matrices $W_t = [\ldots, +w_1, \ldots, -w_1, \ldots]$.

Compared with the neighborhood moving matrix in tabu table T, if the neighborhood mobility matrix of tabu table T plus the neighborhood mobility matrix of a comparison equals 0, then the solution X corresponding to the current neighborhood mobility matrix is eliminated (this can avoid the situation that the optimal value of the previous step cannot jump out because of the local optimization in the previous step). Then, the remaining X are substituted into the constraint condition, the unsatisfied solution is eliminated.

Furthermore, the remaining X are substituted into the objective function. The current optimal solution is obtained by comparison, the feed cost f and the current optimal solution X are recorded and updated. The neighborhood movement matrix corresponding to current X is updated to the tabu table, and setting $K' = K' + 1$, and then it will return to the step of loop judgment. If the loop ends, the precision will continue to be w_2 until the completion of w_p precision search. Finally, the optimization results X and the corresponding feed cost f are output (Fig. 1).

The flowchart of the proposed ITS algorithm is shown as follows:

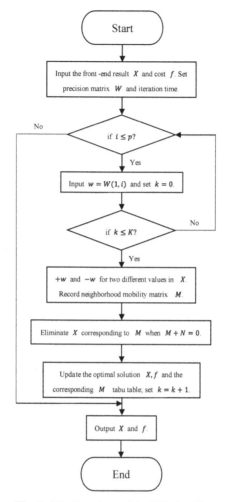

Fig. 1. The flowchart of the ITS algorithm

4 Experiments

In order to evaluate the performance of the ITS algorithm, two study cases are investigated by reusing data from previous work by Zhang [8] on Chinese Journal of Animal Nutrition, *Chinese feed composition and nutritional value table* [20], and *Nutrient Requirement of Swine* [21]. The results of ITS algorithm application are compared with corresponding methodologies from the literature based on the same material. At the same time, this experiment also designs a set of pig feed formula by using the Chinese feed nutrient composition table, and optimizes it by using the ITS algorithm. The experiment is carried out on the hardware platform of the i7-8550u 1.80 GHz CPU and the software MATLAB (version R2017a).

4.1 Comparison Between the ITS Algorithm with Intelligent Optimization Algorithms

In the first experiment, we compare the optimization result of ITS with seven different feed formula optimization methods using different algorithms: general linear programming (LP), goal programming (GP), fuzzy linear programming (FLP), stochastic programming (SP), simulated annealing algorithm (SAA), general genetic algorithm (GA) and hybrid genetic algorithm (HGA). The algorithms used to solve the feed formulation are mainly divided into two streams. One includes various programming methods such as LP, GP [17], FLP [11], SP [18]. The other mainly includes different kinds of intelligent optimization algorithms such as SA [19] and GA. Based on the data and the experimental results provided by Zhang [8], the experimental results are summarized as Table 1 Also the ingredients nutrient levels of pig feed and the nutrient standard is given in Table 2.

This experiment shows that the ITS has the best performance in terms of minimizing the total cost in pig feed formulation comparing to other methods involved in different kinds of algorithms.

Table 1. Comparison of cost calculated by different algorithms in experiment 1.

Ingredients	Price (Yuan/kg)	Amount of usage (%)							
		LP	GP	FLP	SP	SAA	GA	HGA	ITS
Corn	1.65	65.00	68.00	64.91	65.00	55.00	55.00	70.00	73.50
Rice bran meal	1.50	10.36	9.48	13.05	7.67	9.07	—	7.73	6.55
Soybean meal	2.65	22.16	19.81	20.02	23.99	16.62	42.71	19.74	16.51
Rapeseed meal	2.00	—	—	0.23	—	7.84	—	—	—
Cottonseed meal	2.10	—	—	0.18	—	6.15	—	—	—
Coconut oil	8.00	—	0.20	0.08	—	3.00	—	—	—
Limestone	0.12	0.90	0.91	0.08	0.47	0.90	0.73	0.92	1.81
CaHPO$_4$	1.65	0.28	0.30	0.09	1.57	0.12	0.26	0.31	0.33
Lys	10.20	—	—	0.06	—	—	—	—	—
Premix	6.00	1.00	1.00	1.00	1.00	1.00	1.00	1.00	1.00
NaCl	0.86	0.30	0.30	0.30	0.30	0.30	0.30	0.30	0.30
Price (Yuan/t)	—	1883.4	1873.4	1883.4	1912.3	2075.4	2107.0	1862.9	1818.7

Table 2. Ingredients formulation and nutrient level of pig feed.

Nutrient Levels	Ingredients (%)									
	Corn	Rice bran meal	Soybean meal	Rapeseed meal	Cottonse ed meal	Coconut oil	Lime- stone	CaHPO$_4$	Lys	Minimum Requirement
Digestive Energy (Mcal/kg)	14.27	11.55	16.96	10.59	9.42	36.82	—	—	—	14.23
Crude protein	8.70	15.10	49.90	38.60	47.00	—	—	—	—	15.50
Ca	0.02	0.15	0.40	0.65	0.25	—	35.00	24.00	—	0.50
Available phosphorus	0.12	0.24	0.19	0.35	0.38	—	—	16.00	—	0.19
Lys	0.24	0.72	3.13	1.30	2.13	—	—	—	78.80	0.75
Met	0.18	0.28	0.72	0.63	0.56	—	—	—	—	0.20

4.2 Comparison Between Algorithms Using Innovative Feed Formula

In this experiment, pig feed formula optimization problem is investigated. The data is collected from *Chinese feed composition and nutritional value table (30th edition, 2019)* [20] and *Nutrient Requirement of Swine* [21]. Then nine ingredients are selected to formulate the pig feed: corn, wheat bran, rice bran, soybean cake, fish meal, rapeseed cake, casein, salt and corn oil.

The amount used for each ingredient is defined as x_i ($i = 1, \ldots, 9$). Then the objective function is given by:

$$\min f = c_i x_i \tag{4}$$

where c_i is the cost of each ingredient per unit.

We also have:

$$\sum_{i=1}^{9} x_i = 100 \tag{5}$$

The ingredients nutrient levels, price of each ingredient and the usage constrains are summarized in Table 3, which can form the constrains in this experiment.

Table 3. Nutrient level, usage constrains and market price of pig feed (%).

	Corn	Wheat bran	Rice bran	Soybean cake	Fish meal	Rapeseed cake	Casein	Salt	Corn oil	Minimum Requirement
Digestive Energy	3.44	2.24	3.02	3.44	3	2.88	4.13	0	8.75	3.40
Crude protein	9.4	15.7	14.5	41.8	60.2	35.7	88.9	0	0	15.5
Arginine	0.38	1	1.2	2.53	3.57	1.82	3.13	0	0	0.39
Histidine	0.23	0.41	0.44	1.1	1.71	0.83	2.57	0	0	0.29
Isoleucine	0.26	0.51	0.71	1.57	2.68	1.24	4.49	0	0	0.45
Leucine	1.03	0.96	1.13	2.75	4.8	2.26	8.24	0	0	0.85
Lysine	0.26	0.63	0.84	2.43	4.72	1.33	6.87	0	0	0.85
Methionine	0.19	0.23	0.28	0.6	1.64	0.6	2.52	0	0	0.24
Phenylalanine	0.43	0.62	0.71	1.79	2.35	1.35	4.49	0	0	0.51
Threonine	0.31	0.5	0.54	1.44	2.57	1.4	3.77	0	0	0.52
Tryptophan	0.08	0.25	0.16	0.64	0.7	0.42	1.33	0	0	0.15
Valine	0.4	0.71	0.91	1.7	3.17	1.62	5.81	0	0	0.55
Na	0.01	0.07	0.07	0.02	0.97	0.02	0.01	39.5	0	0.10
K	0.29	1.19	1.73	1.77	1.1	1.34	0.01	0	0	0.19
Consumption	44–55	10–20	0–15	0–10	0–5	3–5	0–3	0–3	0–7	---
Price	1.54	1.06	1.2	2.3	4.6	1.4	43	0.86	6	---

After the formulation of the problem, we first use linear programming (LP) and enumeration method (EM) to solve the problem, and then re-optimize the result by ITS.

4.3 Analysis of the ITS Algorithm

Two experiments are carried out with different feed formulas and different algorithms in this work. These two experiments are given the nutritional index of each raw material and the nutritional standard of the actual feed. On the premise of satisfying nutrition, the problem is transformed into a single objective optimization problem to solve the cost. Analysis of the experiments focuses on experiment related to comparison between the ITS algorithm and classic optimization algorithms. Enumeration method and linear programming are used to solve the problems, respectively, and then the results are passed into the application of the ITS algorithm. While in the loop search, we directly search $x_1, \ldots, x_9$, for example: $for\ X1 = 44 : 55$, is the restriction to x_1. At the same time, *check* function and *obj* functions are designed to check whether the X satisfies the restriction condition and defining the objective feed cost function. For linear programming, *linprog* function is called and inputting corresponding parameters to solve the problem. In the enumeration method, only integers are searched and rough solutions can be found in both experiments. If the integer solution cannot be found, it can be solved by shortening the search step length appropriately, but that will increase the time complexity. The linear programming method is superior to the enumeration method both in results and speed when searching the initial solutions. However, when the problem becomes more complex or in other situations, the enumeration method is better than the linear programming method in countability, comprehensiveness and easy modification.

According to the proposed ITS algorithm, X and f are firstly inputted, and the search precision matrix $W = [0.5, 0.1, 0.05, 0.01]$ is set. According to repeated experiments, the ITS can achieve the convergence when $k = 40$. By searching the elements in X twice, we assign positive and negative values to the precision in W, and ensure that the values of the same element will not be assigned twice. Thus, defining the neighborhood moving matrix and realizing the search movement of the solution by $X = X + W$ is appropriate. Through repeated experiments, we determine that the tabu table has a row number of 1 (but if the problem is more complex or high-precision algorithm search has been used, we can consider increasing the length of the tabu table), that is, a matrix of 1×9 is set to N, and if $X + N = 0$, then X is eliminated. In fact, the tabu table ensures that the search process will not fall into the previous local optimization. Similarly, the *check* and *obj* functions are also defined to realize the constraint and objective solution. In this work, in order to avoid the case that a certain element is 0 during searching process, the amount of each component should be greater than 0.1% is set.

Furthermore, we can generally observe the approximate position of the solution obtained by the front-end algorithm. When the conditions are complex, the feasible solution of the algorithm usually does not differ greatly. Therefore, in the design of the search algorithm, some conditional restriction can be reduced, which can achieve efficient search for feasible solutions. For example, in this experiment, when we solve the problem, the amount of salt is small, but the price is high. According to the feasible results, we find that it is impossible to reach the limit of 3%, so we don't need to define $x_8 \le 3$.

In the experiment, we find that if we extend the precision matrix W to a Cyclic precision matrix, such as $[0.5, 0.1, 0.05, 0.01, 0.005, \ldots, 0.5, 0.1, 0.05, 0.01, 0.005]$, the local optimization of the current search can be jumped out and search again. After several experiments, it is determined that convergence can be achieved when the internal precision cycle $w = 8$. We call this procedure to be Cycle Precision Iteration (CPI).

4.4 Analysis of the Experiment Results

In Sect. 4.1, the same data and constraints are reused from Zhang's works [8], and the running results with those in that work are compared. The results are shown in Table 4. The results show that the ITS has the best optimization performance among several kinds of traditional or intelligent optimization algorithms. Similarly, the ITS is used to optimize the new formula proposed in Sect. 4.2. The results are collated and given in Table 5. The corresponding cost and running time are as follows:

Table 4. Cost and running time of each algorithm

	Cost	Running time
EM	2.2124	63.1693 s
LP	2.1941	0.0179 s
EM + ITS	2.0866	1.9856 s
LP + ITS	2.0898	1.8266 s
ITS with CPI	1.8567	11.847 s

Table 5. Feed formula calculated by different algorithms (%)

	Corn	wheat bran	rice bran	Soybean cake	fish meal	Rapeseed cake	casein	Salt	Corn oil
EM	52	10	15	9	4	4	1	1	4
LP	50.8	10	15	10	3.2	5	1	1	4
EM +ITS	51.611	11.425	15	8.64	4.229	4.475	0.71	0.1	3.81
LP +ITS	49.484	12.406	14.998	9.959	3.342	4.952	0.751	0.103	4.005
ITS with CPI	49.911	11.714	15	9.717	4.468	4.999	0.101	0.076	4.014

It shows that the optimization effect of this algorithm is feasible after the complexity of the problem increases. Moreover, the cost is greatly reduced by using the cycle precision iteration.

In summary, after investigation of two experiments, we can find that the proposed ITS algorithm in this work is better than the methods in the literature, and it can be confirmed that the ITS algorithm is not only aiming at the result optimization, but also requires less restricted factors, and it is better in both the running time and the final optimization ability.

5 Conclusions

In this work, the classic tabu search algorithm is introduced and improved for the study of feed formula optimization. The superiority of the proposed algorithm is proved by application of the comparative experiments in two case studies with detailed verification on simulation results. We integrate the traditional algorithm into the whole framework of the algorithm, solve the problem through the traditional algorithm, and then put the results into the improved tabu search algorithm to achieve the re-optimization results. At the same time, when designing the improved algorithm, a new neighborhood moving rule and shortening the tabu table are proposed. In the experiment, it can be found that different precision search has a great influence on the results, so the cycle precision iteration is put forward. Also, it can be found that because of the large gap between the elements and the constraints in the partial solution, by simplifying the code according to some restriction, the results still meet the requirements. In the selection of feed formula, the nutrients of pig feed in China [21] is used, which is more in line with the actual situation.

Acknowledgements. This work was supported by the National Natural Science Foundation of China (NO. 61602209), Jinan University Funding (NO. JG2020145) and National College Students' Innovation and Entrepreneurship Training Program (NO. 202110559016).

References

1. Uyeh, D.D., et al.: Interactive livestock feed ration optimization using evolutionary algorithms. Comput. Electron. Agric. **155**, 1–11 (2018)
2. Saxena, P., Parasher, Y.: Application of Artificial Neural Network (ANN) for Animal Diet Formulation Modeling. Proc. Comput. Sci. **152**, 261–266 (2019)
3. Uyeh, D.D., et al.: Precision animal feed formulation: An evolutionary multi-objective approach. Anim. Feed Sci. Technol. **256**, 114211 (2019)
4. Zhang, J.X., Wang, G.P.: Feed formula optimization method based on multi-objective particle swarm optimization algorithm. In: 2010 2nd International Workshop on Intelligent Systems and Applications. Wuhan, pp. 1–3 (2010)
5. Tatjana, V.S.: Particle swarm optimisation in designing parameters of manufacturing processes: A review (2008–2018). Appl. Soft Comput. **84**, 105743 (2019)
6. Tozer, P.R., Stokes, J.R.: A multi-objective programming approach to feed ration balancing and nutrient management. Agric. Syst. **67**(3), 201–215 (2001)
7. Xiong, B.H., Luo, Q.Y., Pang, Z.H.: Application of dual model to animal feed formulation optimizing system. Agric. Sci. China **2**(4), 463–468 (2003)
8. Zhang, Y.Y.: A new procedure used for feed formulation: hybrid genetic algorithm. Chinese J. Anim. Nutr. **21**(5), 703–710 (2009)
9. Wang, Z.Z., Sobey, A.: A comparative review between Genetic Algorithm use in composite optimization and the state-of-the-art in evolutionary computation. Compos. Struct. **233**, 111739 (2020)
10. Huang, H.Y., Xiong, X.A., Wei, M.X.: Application of fuzzy linear programming to the software of optimizing feed formula. Trans. Chinese Soc. Agric. Eng. **3**, 107–110 (2000)
11. Yang, G.Q., Li, X., Huo, L.J., Liu, Q.: A solving approach for fuzzy multi-objective linear fractional programming and application to an agricultural planting structure optimization problem. Chaos, Solitons Fractals **141**, 110352 (2020)

12. Chan, S.X., Li, C.H., Wang, Y.Y.: Feeding prescription design with simulated annealing algorithm. J. Xiamen Univ. Nat. Sci. **6**, 1319 (2001)
13. Glover, F.W., Laguna, M.: Tabu Search, Springer, US, ISBN: 978–1–4615–6089–0(1997)
14. Chang, J., Wang, L., Hao, J.K., Wang, Y.: Parallel iterative solution-based tabu search for the obnoxious p-median problem. Comput. Oper. Res. **127**, 105155 (2021)
15. Liu, X., Chen, J., Wang, M., Wang, Y., Su, Z., Lü, Z.: A two-phase tabu search based evolutionary algorithm for the maximum diversity problem. Discrete Optim. 100613 (2020)
16. Lee, K., Ozsen, L.: Tabu search heuristic for the network design model with lead time and safety stock considerations. Comput. Indus. Eng. **148**, 106717 (2020)
17. Md Sharif, U., Musa, M., Md Al-Amin, K., Ali, A.: Goal programming tactic for uncertain multi-objective transportation problem using fuzzy linear membership function. Alexandria Eng. J. **60**(2), 2525–2533 (2021)
18. Hassanpour, A., Roghanian, E.: A two-stage stochastic programming approach for non-cooperative generation maintenance scheduling model design. Int. J. Electr. Power Energ. Syst. **126**, 106584 (2021)
19. Viet-Phu, T., Giang, T.T., Van-Khanh, H., Pham, N.V.H., Akio, Y., Hoai-Nam, T.: Evolutionary simulated annealing for fuel loading optimization of VVER-1000 reactor. Ann. Nucl. Energ. **151**, 107938 (2021)
20. Chinese feed composition and nutritional value table, China Feed-database information Network Center (2019)
21. Nutrient requirement of swine, the 11th (ed.). National Research Council (2012)

Adaptive Methods of Differential Evolution Multi-objective Optimization Algorithm Based on Decomposition

Kun Bian[1], Yifei Sun[1(✉)], Shi Cheng[2], Zhuo Liu[1], and Xin Sun[1]

[1] School of Physics and Information Technology, Shaanxi Normal University, Xi'an 710119,
China
{biankun,yifeis}@snnu.edu.cn
[2] School of Computer Science, Shaanxi Normal University, Xi'an 710119, China
cheng@snnu.edu.cn

Abstract. Decomposition-based algorithms e.g., multi-objective evolutionary algorithm based on decomposition (MOEA/D) has been proved as an effective and useful solution in a variety of multi-objective optimization problems (MOPs). On the basis of MOEA/D, the MOEA/D-DE replaces the simulated binary crossover (SBX) operator, which is used to enhance the diversity of the solutions, into differential evolution (DE) operator. However, the amplification factor and the crossover probability are fixed in MOEA/D-DE, which would lead to a low convergence rate and be more likely to fall into local optimum. To overcome such prematurity problem, this paper proposes three different adaptive operators in DE to adjust the parameter settings adaptively, including crossover probability and amplification factor. This paper also designs a changeable parameter η in the proposed algorithms. Several experiments are set to explore how the η would affect the convergence of the proposed algorithms. These adaptive algorithms are tested on many benchmark problems in comparison to MOEA/D-DE. The experimental results illustrate that the three proposed adaptive algorithms have better performance on the most benchmark problems.

Keywords: Multi-objective optimization · Adaptive decomposition · Differential evolutionary algorithms

1 Introduction

In the fields like industrial production and scientific research etc., the solutions for many practical problems are considered as a type of multi-objective optimization according to many researches [14]. And there are many challenges in (MOPs) which means there is still room for improvement. A MOP, which is the main objective in this paper, is illustrated as follows:

$$\begin{cases} min \ F(x) = (f_1(\mathbf{x}), \ldots, f_m(\mathbf{x})) \\ subject \ to \ x \in \Omega \end{cases} \tag{1}$$

© Springer Nature Singapore Pte Ltd. 2021
H. Zhang et al. (Eds.): NCAA 2021, CCIS 1449, pp. 458–472, 2021.
https://doi.org/10.1007/978-981-16-5188-5_33

Where $x = (x_1,...,x_n)$ is a decision vector from the search space Ω (n is the number of decision variables), and $f_1(x), \ldots, f_m(x)$ are m objective functions. As these objectives conflict with one another, the algorithm will generate no single optimal solution, which is the output of single objective optimization, but a group of solutions under the restriction of the balance of the m objective functions $f_1(x), \ldots, f_m(x)$, which means any amelioration in one solution will impair at least one other solution. Such one group of solutions are Pareto optimal solutions (PS). the image of PS in the objective space is defined as the Pareto optimal front (PF). Decision makers can select the probable solutions from a set of PF [1].

The effectiveness of solving MOPs by multi-objective evolutionary algorithms (MOEAs) has been demonstrated. These MOEAs can be classified into three categories by various selection ways [2]: (1) decomposition-based algorithms, e.g., multi-objective evolutionary algorithms based decomposition (MOEA/D) [3] and multiple single objective Pareto sampling (MSOPS) [4]; (2) Pareto-dominance-based algorithms, e.g., the nondominated sorting genetic algorithm (NSGA-II) [5], multi-objective genetic algorithm (MOGA) [6], strength Pareto evolutionary algorithm (SPEA) [7] and SPEA2 [8], niched Pareto genetic algorithm (NPGA) [9] and the Pareto envelope-based selection algorithm for multi-objective optimization (PESA) [10] and PESA-II [11]; (3) performance indicator-based algorithms, e.g., approximated hypervolume-based evolutionary algorithm (HypE) [12] and indicator-based evolutionary algorithm (IBEA) [13]. Decomposition-based MOEAs are becoming one of the most popular algorithms during these years. It's an essential way to combine decomposition with scalarization in the conventional multi-objective optimization. MOEA/D, a representative decomposition-based algorithm, uses a scalarizing approach to divide a MOP into many sub-problems with different weights. It also uses the coefficient method based on population search to solve these sub-problems [14]. Li [15] designed a DE operator in MOEA/D-DE to solve variant MOPs. Baatar [22] designed an adaptive parameter in A-NRDE to solve MOPs. Recently, Zhan [23] proposed an adaptive distributed differential evolution (ADDE) to tackle the difficulties of strategies' selections and parameters' settings. And Wang [24] used a niching method in AED in solving some optimization problems.

In this study, we design three methods to adjust the parameter settings of DE adaptively, and experimental results illustrate that comparing with MOEA/D-DE, these proposed methods have advantages on most of the test functions.

There is the organization of this paper: we expound some basic knowledge in Sect. 2 and elaborate three adaptive algorithms in Sect. 3. Experimental research and results analysis are detailed in Sect. 4. The conclusions of this paper and some future works are presented in Sect. 5.

2 Background

2.1 Basic Definitions

There are some basic definitions in multi-objective problems described as follows:

Definition 1: if y is Pareto dominated by x, then denoted as $x \prec y$, if $\forall i \in \{1, 2, \ldots, m\}, f_i(x) \le f_i(y)$ and $f_j(x) < f_j(y)$ for at least one index $j \in \{1, 2, \ldots, m\}$.

Definition 2: A solution $x^* \in \Omega$ is Pareto optimal if and only if $\nexists x \in \Omega$ such that $x \prec x^*$.

Definition 3: The Pareto set (PS) is described as the set of all Pareto optimal solutions, The set of all Pareto optimal vectors, PF = $\{F(x) \in R^m | x \in PS\}$, is called PF.

2.2 MOEA/D

A MOP can be divided into many sub-problems in the form of single-objective optimization by MOEA/D. Every sub-problem is optimized by different weighted aggregation [16]. The neighborhood of each sub-problem is depended on several weighted vectors which are close to the sub-problem in distance. MOEA/D adopts a group of N uniformly distributed weight vectors, where N represents the number of sub-problems. With the information of the neighborhood, every sub-problem is optimized at the same time. There are many different editions of MOEA/D. Our algorithms are based upon MOEA/D-DE, which is an enhanced edition of MOEA/D. We adopt the Tchebycheff method to aggregate the function:

$$ming^{te}\left(x|\lambda, z^*\right) = \max_{1 \le i \le m} \left\{\lambda_i | f_i(x) - z_i^*\right\} \tag{2}$$

where z^* represents the ideal point which is the point with minimum value in the i th objective. The more details can be found in [3] and [15].

2.3 Differential Evolutionary Algorithms

Kenneth Price and Rainer Storn proposed a variety of variation forms of differential evolution (DE) algorithms [25] We describe the different DE algorithms as a form of DE/ X/Y/Z [26]

X represents the selection of the basis vector (the individual vector to be mutated) in the mutation operation, 'rand' represents an individual which is chosen at random from the race and 'best' represents the individual which has the best performance. Y represents the number of different vectors. Z stands for crossover, the Binomail experiment described as 'bino' is usually used for crossover operation. There are some frequently used algorithms described as follows:

$$\text{DE/rand/1/bin:} \cdot v_i = x_{r_1} + F \times \left(x_{r_2} - x_{r_3}\right) \tag{3}$$

$$\text{DE/best/1/bin:} \cdot v_i = x_{best} + F \times \left(x_{r_2} - x_{r_3}\right) \tag{4}$$

$$\text{DE/rand/2/bin:} \cdot v_i = x_{r_1} + F \times \left(x_{r_2} - x_{r_3}\right) + F \times \left(x_{r_4} - x_{r_5}\right) \tag{5}$$

$$\text{DE/best/2/bin:} \cdot v_i = x_{best} + F \times \left(x_{r_2} - x_{r_3} \right) + F \times \left(x_{r_4} - x_{r_5} \right) \tag{6}$$

Where r_1, r_2, r_3, r_4, r_5 are randomly-selected distinct integers from the set $\{1, 2, ..., N\}$, and r_{best} is the individual which has the best performance. F is an amplification factor, which expands the different vector.

3 Proposed Algorithms

3.1 DE in MOEA/D

Li [15] replaces SBX [17] operator in MOEA/D by the DE/rand/1/bin operator and proposed MOEA/D-DE. The algorithm adopts three randomly-selected individuals r_1, r_2 and r_3 to generate the new solution from the neighborhood P:

$$y_k' = \begin{cases} x_k^{r_1} + F \times \left(x_k^{r_2} - x_k^{r_3} \right) & rand < CR \\ x_k^{r_1} & rand > CR \end{cases} \tag{7}$$

Where CR is the parameter which controls the rate of crossover and F represents the amplification factor. and *rand* represents a random number whose numerical value is between 0 and 1.

The polynomial mutation in DE is described as follows:

$$y_k = \begin{cases} y_k' + \delta_k \times (b_k - a_k) & \text{with probability } p_m \\ y_k & \text{with probability } 1 - p_m \end{cases} \tag{8}$$

$$\delta_k = \begin{cases} (2 \times rand)^{\frac{1}{\omega+1}} - 1 & rand < 0.5 \\ 1 - (2 - 2 \times rand)^{\frac{1}{\omega+1}} & otherwise \end{cases} \tag{9}$$

Where the distribution index ω and the mutation probability p_m are two parameters in the algorithm. a_k represents the lower boundary and b_k is the upper boundary.

3.2 Adaptive Operators

Contrast of other algorithms and MOEA/D-DE shows MOEA/D-DE lower time complexity and fast convergence speed [18]. However, there are weak points such as rough race dispersion and inefficient local search capability of the race in MOEA/D-DE. To overcome these shortcomings, we design three adaptive operators in MOEA/D-DE.

In DE, we encode the crossover probability (CR) and the amplification factor (F) evolved with the increase of iterations. The traditional differential evolutionary (DE) algorithm is to keep the F and CR fixed in value, which will converge slowly and be difficult to search for the global optimal solution as a result of premature convergence [18]. So, we design three adaptive operators to adjust the values of F and CR dynamically.

The first method uses linear variation named MOEA/D-DE-LAD:

$$CR = CR_0 + \eta * \left(\frac{gen}{maxGen}\right) \tag{10}$$

$$F = F_0 - \eta * \left(\frac{gen}{maxGen}\right) \tag{11}$$

The second method uses power function transformation called MOEA/D-DE-PAD:

$$CR = CR_0 + \eta * \left(\frac{gen}{maxGen}\right)^2 \tag{12}$$

$$F = F_0 - \eta * \left(\frac{gen}{maxGen}\right)^2 \tag{13}$$

The third method uses exponential transformation named MOEA/D-DE-EAD:

$$CR = \eta^{\left(1 - \frac{gen}{maxGen}\right)} \tag{14}$$

$$F = \eta^{\left(\frac{gen}{maxGen}\right)} \tag{15}$$

Compared with the traditional DE, these three methods use different strategies to adjust the values of CR and F dynamically. The values of CR and F will change by the generations. η is an artificial parameter changed from 0.1, 0.2 to 0.9 with the step 0.1. We will discuss how the values of η would influence the three proposed algorithms in the following text.

Algorithm 1: Adaptive operators

Input: Current generation: gen, Maximum generation: $maxGen$, Three individuals: r_1, r_2, r_3

Output: the new solution y'

while $gen < maxGen$

  case LAD:

  $$CR = CR_0 + \eta * \left(\frac{gen}{maxGen}\right)$$
  $$F = F_0 - \eta * \left(\frac{gen}{maxGen}\right)$$

  case PAD:

  $$CR = CR_0 + \eta * \left(\frac{gen}{maxGen}\right)^2$$
  $$F = F_0 - \eta * \left(\frac{gen}{maxGen}\right)^2$$

  case EAD:

  $$CR = \eta^{\left(1 - \frac{gen}{maxGen}\right)}$$
  $$F = \eta^{\left(\frac{gen}{maxGen}\right)}$$

end

Generate a new solution y' :

$$y' = \begin{cases} x_{r_1} + F \times (x_{r_2} - x_{r_3}) & rand < CR \\ x_{r_1} & rand > CR \end{cases}$$

The impressions of η on the proposed algorithms will be discussed in the following text detailly. When $\eta = 0.5$, the values of CR and F among three strategies are described as follows.

As shown in the Fig. 1, the three methods use different strategies to adjust the values of CR and F. The values of CR are increased by the generations. On the contrary, the values of F are decreased. When $\eta = 0.5$, the values of CR in MOEA/D-DE-LAD is always bigger than other two methods, and the values of F in MOEA/D-DE-EAD is the minimum among three methods during the evolutionary.

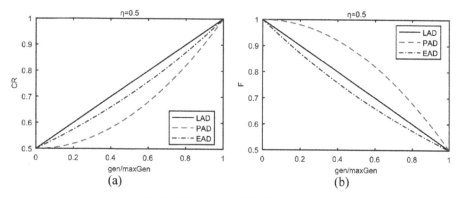

Fig. 1. The values of (a) CR and (b) F

3.3 The Framework of the Proposed Algorithms

We use the different adaptive DE operators to generate the new solutions in MOEA/D. CR and F will change by the increase of generations so as to accelerate the pace of converging to the optimal solution. More details can be found from the following text:

Algorithm 2: Adaptive operators in MOEA/D

Input: The number of populations: N, The number of the weight vectors from neighborhood: T, The maximum generation: $maxGen$.
Output: Optimal solutions.

Step1: Initialization:

Step 1.1: Generate N weight vectors $\lambda^1, \lambda^2, \ldots, \lambda^N$ from objective space evenly;

Step 1.2: Calculate the distances between every pair of the weighted vectors. On the basis of the distances, find T closest weight vectors $\lambda^{i_1}, \ldots, \lambda^{i_T}$ from λ^i as the neighborhood of λ^i. For every $i = 1, \ldots, N$, there are $B(i) = (i_1, \ldots, i_T)$;

Step 1.3: Initialize $z = (z_1, \ldots, z_m)^T$, where $z_j = \min_{1 \leq i \leq N} f_j(x^i)$ is the value which is minimum from objective space;

Step 2: Update:

Step 2.1: For $i = 1, \ldots, N$, select the value of *rand* from 0 to 1 randomly. And set

$$P = \begin{cases} B(i) & if\ rand < \delta, \\ \{1, \ldots, N\} & otherwise. \end{cases} \tag{16}$$

Step 2.2: Generate a new solution y' from $x^{r_1}, x^{r_2}, x^{r_3}$ by an adaptive DE operator shown above, where r_1, r_2, r_3 are three randomly-selected indexes from P, and use the polynomial mutation operator to generate a new solution y.

Step 2.3: If a dimension in y is beyond the search boundary, instead it of the value which is chosen from the value which are within the boundary at random;

Step 2.4: Update the ideal point z : for each $j = 1, \ldots, m$, if $z_j > f_j(y)$, then set $z_j = f_j(y)$;

Step 2.5: Update the solutions: if $g(y|\lambda^j, z) \leq g(x^j|\lambda^j, z)$, then set $x^j = y$.

Step 3: Determine the termination situation:

The algorithm will be stopped and output $\{x^1, \ldots, x^N\}$ and optimal solutions $\{F(x^1), \ldots, F(x^N)\}$ if it reaches the termination condition. If not, move to Step 2.

4   Experimental Research and Results Analysis

4.1   Benchmark Problems

In this section, on the purpose of testing the performance of the proposed algorithms in solving multi-objective optimization problems, the ZDT [19] test function set including ZDT1, ZDT2, ZDT3, ZDT4 and ZDT6 and DTLZ [20] test function set including DTLZ1, DTLZ2, DTLZ3 and DTLZ4 are adopted in experiments.

4.2   Parameter Settings

The settings of the parameters in four algorithms are described as follows:

Parameter	Value	Description
N-2	100	2-Objective
N-3	200	3-Objective
F	0.5	Amplication factor
CR	0.9	Crossover rate
F_0	1.0	Initial value of F
CR_0	0.5	Initial value of CR

Each algorithm is run for 30 times on each test problem, each run is for 30000 function evaluations for 2-objective problem and 60000 evaluations for 3-objective problem.

F and CR are fixed parameters set in MOEA/D-DE. F_0 is the initial value of F, and CR_0 is the initial value of CR are the parameters set in the proposed algorithms. The probability of mutation and its corresponding distribution index are set as $p_m = \frac{1}{n}$ and $\eta_m = 20$.

All the experiments are test on the computer (AMD Ryzen 5 – 4600H CPU (3.0 GHz) 16G RAM Windows 10 systems).

4.3 Performance Metrics

(1) IGD-Metric The reverse generation distance (IGD) [21] is adopted to evaluate the quality of one solution set P in the experiments set in this paper. Assuming that P^* is the true Pareto front, P is the practical Pareto front found by an algorithm. The distance between P^* and P is defined as follows:

$$IGD(P^*, P) = \frac{\sum_{v \in p^*} d(v, P)}{|P^*|} \tag{17}$$

Where $d(v, P)$ is the minimum distance between the point v and P. The algorithms with solutions of smaller values of IGD will be considered having better performance.

(2) HV-Metrics The HV-Metrics evaluates the MOEA performance by calculating the super-volume value of the space between the non-dominant solution set and the reference point. The HV-Metrics can be defined as:

$$HV = \lambda \left(\bigcup_{i=1}^{|S|} v_i \right) \tag{18}$$

Where λ stands for the Lebesgue measure, which is used to measure volume. v_i represents the super-volume of reference points and non-dominant individuals. $|S|$ is the number of nondominant solution sets. The value of HV can comprehensively reflect the convergence and distribution breadth of the solution set. The solutions with higher values of HV are closer to the global Pareto optimal solution. And the algorithms with such solutions are considered having better performance.

4.4 Experiments Analysis

In this paper, the three proposed algorithms: MOEA/D-DE-LAD denoted as LAD, MOEA/D-DE-PAD denoted as PAD and MOEA/D-DE-EAD denoted as EAD are compared with MOEA/D-DE. In every test function, the four algorithms are set to run thirty times using the same setting of environment parameters on independent.

We firstly set different values of η to see how IGD and HV would change, and then we run these proposed algorithms on more test functions with probable η compared with MOEA/D-DE to see which one performs better on these test functions. The probable value of η was decided by the IGD and HV values that most algorithms get best on these test functions. The more details can be found as follows.

To explore the influence of the change of η parameter on the values of IGD and HV, we set η = [0.1, 0.2, ..., 0.9], and see how IGD and HV would change on the 2-objective test functions and 3-objective test functions. The values of η will influence the values of *CR* and *F* changed by generations so as to get different values of IGD and HV. The results of related experiments are shown in the following Figures.

From the Fig. 2, we can know that:

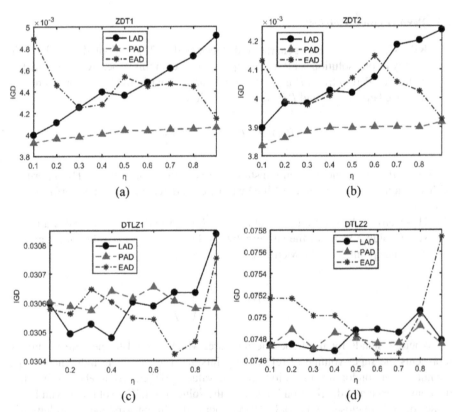

Fig. 2. The values of IGD changed by η

(1) On ZDT1 and ZDT2, the IGD values of LAD and PAD increases as η increases. However, LAD has a sharper increase than PAD. On these two test problems, PAD performs best among the three algorithms. When $\eta = 0.1$, the IGD values of LAD and PAD are minimum. The values of IGD in EAD is minimum when $\eta = 0.9$. For these 2-objective problems, PAD keeps a lower value than the other two algorithms.

(2) On test function DTLZ1 and DTLZ2 test problem, there are no obvious relationships between IGD and η. When $\eta = 0.7$, EAD has the best performance in comparison compared with LAD and PAD. For 3-objective problems, there are much more complex possibility than 2-objective problem. The IGD values are more susceptible to the values of η. We need other methods to test the algorithms.

(3) The IGD values of EAD are complicated and changeable and there are no obvious patterns compared with LAD and PAD. Moreover, in 2-objective test problems LAD and PAD changed more regularly than in 3-objective problems.

From the Fig. 3, we could know that:

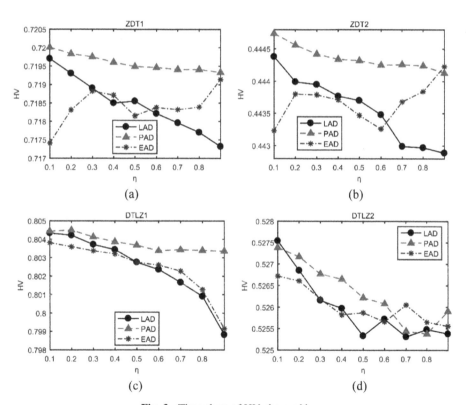

Fig. 3. The values of HV changed by η

(1) The values of HV in LAD and PAD decrease as η increases on ZDT1, ZDT2 and DTLZ1 test functions. On DTLZ2, the overall trends of LAD and PAD are

downward. When η = 0.1, the HV values of LAD and PAD are maximum. LAD and PAD changed more regular than EAD on these test functions.

(2) On ZDT1 and ZDT2, the values of HV in EAD are flexible, there is no obvious pattern on the 2-objective test problems. When η = 0.9, the values of HV are the maximum.

(3) On test function DTLZ1 and DTLZ2 test problem, the HV values of EAD are downward as η changes. The HV values are maximum when η is 0.1. Moreover, in 3-objective test problems EAD changed more regularly than in 2-objective problems.

From the figures shown in this paper, the values of IGD and HV would dynamically change by η. These algorithms perform better on those test functions with η = 0.1, so we set η = 0.1 in these proposed algorithms. We run these algorithms and MOEA/D-DE on ZDT series test problems. The performance of the four algorithms on 2-objective test functions are shown in the figure. In the following text, the True PF is the real Pareto front of the test functions. According to the comparison with the True PF, we can inform that which algorithm performs better among these proposed algorithms.

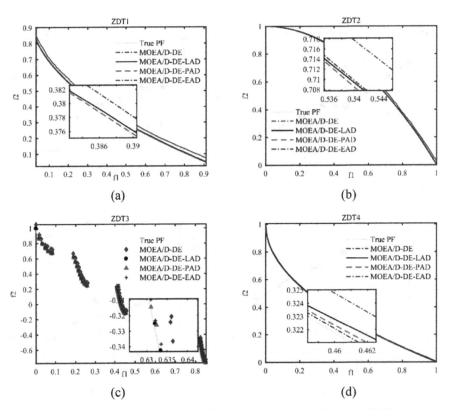

Fig. 4. Attainment surfaces for (a) ZDT1, (b) ZDT2, (c) ZDT3, (d) ZDT4

As shown in the Fig. 4, compared with MOEA/D-DE, the proposed algorithms have better performance on these test functions. On ZDT1, PAD almost converges to the

PF completely. LAD has the best convergence performance on ZDT2. On ZDT3, the proposed algorithms are approximate. Besides, EAD has the best performance among four algorithms on ZDT4. The PFs of three proposed algorithms are much more closer than MOEA/D-DE to the real PF. On these 2-objective test problems, using adaptive strategies can make the distance between the PF of the algorithms and the real PF much closer.

For 2-objective, we made the figures which obtain the comparison of the True PF and the PF of the four algorithms and we can distinguish which algorithm is better from the figures easily. However, for 3-objective, it is uneasy to recognize which performs better from the comparisons of the four algorithms in one figure. Besides, the performance metrics can analyze the performance of algorithm from various aspects. So we select IGD and HV as criterions to judge which performs better on these test functions.

To further explore the performance of these four algorithms on the test problems, we made the statistics of IGD and HV in the tables.

It can be seen from the Table 1 that:

Table 1. IGD metric (mean/std) results

Problem	MOEA/D-DE	MOEA/D-DE-LAD	MOEA/D-DE-PAD	MOEA/D-DE-EAD
ZDT1	1.3148e-2 (3.39e-3)	3.9948e-3 (4.49e-5)	**3.9238e-3 (2.09e-5)**	4.8875e-3 (3.08e-4)
ZDT2	8.5105e-3 (2.11e-3)	3.8976e-3 (3.99e-5)	**3.8352e-3 (1.22e-5)**	4.1308e-3 (1.06e-4)
ZDT3	1.7491e-2 (4.73e-3)	1.0911e-2 (3.45e-5)	1.0912e-2 (2.85e-5)	**1.0799e-2 (7.83e-5)**
ZDT4	1.8778e-1 (1.58e-1)	8.1790e-3 (4.15e-3)	**5.6242e-3 (5.83e-4)**	1.4027e-2 (1.93e-2)
ZDT6	**3.1147e-3 (1.62e-5)**	3.1189e-3 (1.66e-5)	3.1220e-3 (1.52e-5)	8.5842e-3 (1.80e-2)
DTLZ1	3.0854e-2 (5.15e-4)	3.0598e-2 (1.41e-4)	3.0604e-2 (1.58e-4)	**3.0579e-2 (1.26e-4)**
DTLZ2	7.5061e-2 (6.13e-4)	7.4740e-2 (3.27e-4)	**7.4733e-2 (3.14e-4)**	7.5170e-2 (4.48e-4)
DTLZ3	2.6452e-1 (4.20e-1)	7.5338e-2 (1.41e-3)	7.4498e-2 (7.52e-4)	4.1221e-1 (5.96e-1)
DTLZ4	1.1675e-1 (6.70e-2)	7.5895e-2 (8.73e-4)	7.5531e-2 (8.33e-4)	7.7210e-2 (6.94e-3)

(1) Comparing with other algorithms, PAD performs better on the ZDT1, ZDT2, ZDT4, DTLZ2, DTLZ3 and DTLZ4 test problems. PAD has huge advantages than MOEA/D-DE on these test functions except ZDT6 and DTLZ1.

(2) On test functions ZDT3 and DTLZ1, EAD performs best. LAD and PAD perform better than MOEA/D-DE. EAD has tiny advantages than LAD and PAD.

(3) MOEA/D-DE has the best performance on ZDT6 test problem. The IGD values of LAD and PAD are close to MOEA/D-DE on ZDT6. The IGD value of EAD is biggest among these four algorithms.

(4) Compared with MOEA/D-DE, the proposed algorithms have better performance on most test functions. Besides, PAD has better advantages than LAD and EAD on six test functions and only performs worse on three of nine functions. Still, on these test problems which PAD has not best performance, PAD has advantages than MOEA/D-DE except on ZDT6.

From the Table 2, the following results are observed:

Table 2. HV metric (mean/std) results

Problem	MOEA/D-DE	MOEA/D-DE-LAD	MOEA/D-DE-PAD	MOEA/D-DE-EAD
ZDT1	7.0542e-1 (4.39e-3)	7.1970e-1 (1.76e-4)	**7.2001e-1 (9.40e-5)**	7.1741e-1 (6.21e-4)
ZDT2	4.3311e-1 (4.38e-3)	4.4438e-1 (1.98e-4)	**4.4474e-1 (8.20e-5)**	4.4323e-1 (4.10e-4)
ZDT3	5.9565e-1 (6.14e-3)	5.9803e-1 (1.25e-4)	5.9802e-1 (1.09e-4)	**5.9857e-1 (4.03e-4)**
ZDT4	5.0235e-1 (1.57e-1)	7.1262e-1 (6.02e-3)	**7.1646e-1 (9.37e-4)**	7.0274e-1 (3.09e-2)
ZDT6	**3.8868e-1 (3.53e-4)**	3.8865e-1 (3.54e-4)	3.8863e-1 (3.26e-4)	3.8139e-1 (2.38e-2)
DTLZ1	7.9954e-1 (4.20e-3)	8.0434e-1 (4.25e-4)	**8.0444e-1 (5.08e-4)**	8.0382e-1 (5.68e-4)
DTLZ2	5.2575e-1 (1.21e-3)	**5.2754e-1 (1.00e-3)**	5.2738e-1 (1.09e-3)	5.2672e-1 (7.98e-4)
DTLZ3	4.1994e-1 (1.93e-1)	5.2825e-1 (2.98e-3)	**5.2847e-1 (1.81e-3)**	3.6518e-1 (2.27e-1)
DTLZ4	5.2134e-1 (2.15e-2)	**5.3208e-1 (2.04e-3)**	5.3051e-1 (1.92e-3)	5.3067e-1 (3.12e-3)

(1) PAD performs best on ZDT1, ZDT2, ZDT4, DTLZ1 and DTLZ3 test problems and has huge advantages than MOEA/D-DE on these test problems.
(2) Comparing with the proposed algorithms, MOEA/D-DE has the best performance on ZDT6. However, the HV values of LAD and PAD are so closed to MOEA/D-DE.
(3) On DTLZ2 and DTLZ4 test problems, LAD has the maximum HV values. And on ZDT3, EAD performs best.
(4) These three proposed algorithms have better performance on most test functions except on ZDT6 test problem. Moreover, PAD has better advantages than LAD and EAD on five of nine test problems.

From the two tables shown above, the proposed three algorithms have advantages on most of the test functions. MOEA/D-DE only has best values of IGD and HV on ZDT6, however LAD and PAD are close to it on ZDT6. From the results shown in the tables, PAD has advantages than LAD and EAD and these proposed adaptive strategies are effective on these test problems.

5 Conclusion

MOEA/D and MOEA/D-DE have been demonstrated effective and useful in solving MOPs. However, the parameters are fixed which would affect the convergence of the algorithm. This paper proposes three algorithms using different self-adaptive DE operators to automatically adjust the setting of parameters CR and F in different problems based on MOEA/D-DE. We run these three algorithms and MOEA/D-DE on some 2-objective test problems and 3-objective test functions. Comparing with the fixed values of CR and F in MOEA/D-DE, the adaptive operators can help the algorithms converge faster on most of the test functions. Besides, we also design a parameter η changed from 0.1, 0.2 to 0.9 with the step 0.1 to study how the values of CR and F affect the effectiveness of these proposed algorithms. The IGD and HV values in LAD and PAD varied more regularly than EAD overall. The experiments have demonstrated that the adaptive strategies have effectiveness on the 2-objective and 3-objective test functions. Moreover, PAD has better performance than LAD and EAD from the tables of IGD and HV values.

However, there are still some problems to be solved e.g., for many real-world problems, the effectiveness of the adaptive methods needs to be proved. So we need run these adaptive algorithms on more complex problems to identify the effectiveness.

For the further study, firstly, we need to use these three adaptive strategies to run more complex test functions to identify if the PAD method still has advantages than LAD and EAD. Secondly, we would like to use niching technologies in population to accelerate the pace of converging to the optimal solution in the three adaptive algorithms. Thirdly, we would like to apply these proposed algorithms to practical problems like community detection and recommendation system etc.

Acknowledgement. This work was supported by the National Natural Science Foundation of China (Grant No. 61703256, 61806119), Natural Science Basic Research Plan in Shaanxi Province of China (Program No. 2017JQ6070)and the Fundamental Research Funds for the Central Universities (Program No. GK201803020).

References

1. Mardle, S., Miettinen, K.: Nonlinear multiobjective optimization. J. Oper. Res. Soci. **51**(2), 246 (1999)
2. Wang, R., Fleming, P.J., Purshouse, R.C.: General framework for localised multi-objective evolutionary algorithms. Info. Sci. **258**(3), 29–53 (2014)
3. Zhang, Q., Li, H.: MOEA/D: a multiobjective evolutionary algorithm based on decomposition. IEEE Trans. Evol. Comput. **11**(6), 712–731 (2008)
4. Hughes, E.J.: Multiple single objective Pareto sampling. In: The 2003 Congress on Evolutionary Computation, vol. 4, pp. 2678–2684. CEC, Australia (2003)
5. Deb, K., Pratap, A., Agarwal, S., Meyarivan, T.: A fast and elitist multiobjective genetic algorithm: NSGA-II. IEEE Trans. Evol. Comput. **6**(2), 182–197 (2002)
6. Fonseca, C.M., Fleming, P.J.: Multiobjective optimization and multiple constraint handling with evolutionary algorithms I.A unified formulation. IEEE Trans. Syst. Man Cybern. part a: Syst. Humans, **28**(1), 26–37 (1998)
7. Zitzler, E., Thiele, L.: Multiobjective evolutionary algorithms: a comparative case study and the strength Pareto approach. IEEE Trans. Evol. Comput. **3**(4), 257–271 (1999)
8. Bleuler, S., Brack, M., Thiele, L., Zitzler, E.: Multiobjective genetic programming: reducing bloat using SPEA2. In: Proceedings of the 2001 Congress on Evolutionary Computation, vol. 1, pp. 536–543 IEEE, South Korea (2001)
9. Horn, J., Nafpliotis, N., Goldberg, D.E.: A niched Pareto genetic algorithm for multiobjective optimization. In: Proceedings of the First IEEE Conference on Evolutionary Computation. IEEE World Congress on Computational Intelligence, vol. 1, pp. 82–87. IEEE, Orlando (1994)
10. Corne, D.W., Knowles, J.D., Oates, M.J.: The Pareto Envelope-Based Selection Algorithm for Multiobjective Optimization. In: Schoenauer, M., et al. (eds.) PPSN 2000. LNCS, vol. 1917, pp. 839–848. Springer, Heidelberg (2000). https://doi.org/10.1007/3-540-45356-3_82

11. Corne, D.W., Jerram, N.R., Knowles, J.D., Oates, M.J.: PESA-II:Region-based selection in evolutionary multiobjective optimization. In: Proceedings of the 3rd Annual Conference on Genetic and Evolutionary Compution, pp. 283–290 (2001)

12. Bader, J., Zitzler, E.: HypE: an algorithm for fast hypervolume-based many-objective optimization. Evol. Comput. **19**(1), 45–76 (2011)

13. Zitzler, E., Künzli, S.: Indicator-Based Selection in Multiobjective Search. In: Yao, X., et al. (eds.) PPSN 2004. LNCS, vol. 3242, pp. 832–842. Springer, Heidelberg (2004). https://doi.org/10.1007/978-3-540-30217-9_84

14. Wang, R., Zhou, Z., Ishibuchi, H.: Localized weighted sum method for many-objective optimization. IEEE Trans. Evol. Comput. **22**(1), 3–18 (2018)

15. Li, H., Zhang, Q.F.: Multiobjective optimization problems with complicated Pareto sets, MOEA/D and NSGA-II. IEEE Trans. Evol. Comput. **13**(2), 284–302 (2009)

16. Gonçalves, R.A., Almeida, C.P.D., Kuk, J.N.: MOEA/D with adaptive operator selection for the environmental/economic dispatch problem.In: 2015 Latin America Congress on Computational Intelligence, pp. 1–6. IEEE, Curitiba, Brazil (2015)

17. Deb, K.: Multi-Objective Optimization Using Evolutionary Algorithms. John Wiley & Sons, Chichester, U.K. (2001)

18. Han, J., He, M., Wang, X.: Improvement of differential evolution multiobjective optimization algorithm based on decomposition. J. Phy. Conf. Ser. **1213**(3), 7 (2019)

19. Zitzler, E., Deb, K., Thiele, L.: Comparison of multiobjective evolutionary algorithms: empirical results. Evol. Comput. **8**(2), 173–195 (2000)

20. Deb, K., Thiele, L., Laumanns, M.: Evolutionary Multiobjective Optimization. Scalable test problems for evolutionary multi-objective optimization Evolutionary Multiobjective Optimization. Springer, London (2006)

21. Deb, K., Jain, H.: An evolutionary many-objective optimization algorithm using reference-point-based nondominated sorting approach, part i: solving problems with box constraints. IEEE Trans. Evolut. Comput. **18**(4), 577–601 (2014)

22. Baatar, N., Jeong, K., Koh, C.: Adaptive parameter controlling non-dominated ranking differential evolution for multi-objective optimization of electromagnetic problems. IEEE Trans. Magn. **50**(2), 709–712 (2014)

23. Zhan, Z.H., Wang, Z.J., Jin, H., Zhang, J.: Adaptive distributed differential evolution. IEEE Trans. Cybern. **50**(11), 4633–4647 (2020)

24. Wang, Z.J., Zhou, Y.R., Zhang, J.: Adaptive estimation distribution distributed differential evolution for multimodal optimization problems. IEEE Trans. Cybern. (2020)

25. Storn, R., Price, K.: Differential evolution: a simple and efficient heuristic for global optimization over continuous spaces. J. Global Optim. **11**(4), 341–359 (1997)

26. Price, K.V.: Differential evolution: a fast and simple numerical optimizer. In: Proceedings of North American Fuzzy Information Processing, pp. 524–527. Berkeley, USA (1996)

Population Diversity Guided Dimension Perturbation for Artificial Bee Colony Algorithm

Tao Zeng, Tingyu Ye, Luqi Zhang, Minyang Xu, Hui Wang[(✉)], and Min Hu

School of Information Engineering,
Nanchang Institute of Technology, Nanchang 330099, China
huiwang@nit.edu.cn

Abstract. In the original artificial bee colony (ABC), only one dimension of the solution is updated each time and this leads to little differences between the offspring and the parent solution. Then, it affects the convergence speed. In order to accelerate the convergence speed, we can update multiple dimensions of the solution at the same time, and the information of the global optimal solution can be used for guidance. However, using these two methods will reduce the population diversity at the initial stage. This is not conducive to search of multimodal functions. In this paper, a population diversity guided dimension perturbation for artificial bee colony algorithm (called PDDPABC) is proposed, in which population diversity is used to control the number of dimension perturbations. Then, it can maintain a certain population diversity, and does not affect the convergence speed. In order to verify the performance of PDDPABC, we tested its performance on 22 classic problems and CEC 2013 benchmark set. Compared with several other ABC variants, our approach can achieve better results.

Keywords: Artificial bee colony algorithm · Dimension perturbation · Population diversity · Optimization

1 Introduction

In production activities, people often encounter a variety of optimization problems. However, traditional mathematical approaches can't address some of the optimization problems. Inspired by the wisdom of nature and human beings, computational intelligence algorithms have been proposed. Computational intelligence algorithms include evolutionary algorithm [1,2], differential evolution algorithm [3], genetic algorithm [4,5], artificial bee colony [6–9], grey wolf [10], multi-group flower pollination [11], and binary symbiotic organism search [12]. Because of its wide applicability, good global search ability, and no need of strict mathematical derivation for the problem to be solved, computational intelligence algorithm has been paid more and more attention.

© Springer Nature Singapore Pte Ltd. 2021
H. Zhang et al. (Eds.): NCAA 2021, CCIS 1449, pp. 473–485, 2021.
https://doi.org/10.1007/978-981-16-5188-5_34

ABC benefits from a simple algorithm structure and few parameters in contrast to other computational intelligence algorithms [13]. But it also has some shortcomings. For example, at the later stage of the iteration, the selection probability will not work. For two solutions with small function values, their fitness values are equal to 1 and the selection probability is the same. Then, it is impossible to tell the good from the bad of the solution. Wang et al. [14] designed a ring topology, using neighborhood selection in the topology to replace the probability selection. Cui et al. [15] modified the probability selection formula and calculated the selection probability by using the fitness ranking information of each solution. The higher the fitness ranking, the higher the probability of choosing a solution. Furthermore, the exploration ability of ABC is strong, but the exploitation ability is weak. Many scholars boosted the efficiency of ABC by improving exploitation capability. In [16], the efficiency of ABC is improved by applying the information of global best individual. Xue et al. [17] designed several search strategies for adaptive selection to enhance exploitation capacity of ABC. Inspired by the differential evolutionary algorithm, Gao et al. [18] designed two novel search strategies. To get trade-off between exploration and exploitation, Cui et al. [19] designed different search strategies for different search stage. In scout bee phase, the stochastic initialization can assist the individuals escape from the local optimum, but it may affect convergence speed. Wang et al. [20] used the opposition-based learning, the Cauchy disturbance and Eq. (1) to produce three offsprings, then choose the best individual among the three new offsprings to replace the abandon solution.

A population diversity guided dimension perturbation for ABC is proposed to improve search efficiency of ABC. This method controls the frequency of the dimension disturbance through the population diversity, so that the population diversity can be maintained at the beginning of search, meanwhile, convergence rate can be speed up during the final stage of the search. 22 classic benchmark problems with dimensions 30 and 100 is used to verify the efficiency of PDDPABC. Additionally, PDDPABC is also tested on more complex CEC 2013 benchmark problems with dimension 30.

The remaining framework of this paper is described below: the second section presents original ABC, then PDDPABC is introduced in third part, the fourth part shows experiments designed, and summary is given in fifth part.

2   Artificial Bee Colony Algorithm

There are four stages in original ABC: 1) population initialization stage; 2) employed bee stage; 3) onlooker bee stage; 4) scout bee stage.

(1) Initialization stage
   Suppose the population size is SN, each individual $X_i = \{x_{i,1}, x_{i,2}, ..., x_{i,D}\}$ has D dimensions. Each dimension of each individual is initialized by the following formula:

$$x_{i,j} = x_{min,j} + rand(0,1) \cdot (x_{max,j} - x_{min,j}) \tag{1}$$

where $i = \{1, 2, \cdots, Sn\}$, $j = \{1, 2, \cdots, D\}$, x_{min}, x_{max} are lower and upper bounds for independent variable respectively, $rand(0, 1)$ is a stochastic value within $[0, 1]$.

(2) Employed bee stage

Each individual $X_i(i = 1, 2, \cdots, SN)$ uses following formula to perform a neighborhood search on the randomly selected j-th dimension and produce an offspring V_i:

$$v_{i,j} = x_{i,j} + \phi_{i,j} \cdot (x_{i,j} - x_{k,j}) \tag{2}$$

where j is randomly chosen in $\{1, 2, \cdots, D\}$, k is randomly chosen from $\{1, 2, \cdots, Sn\}$,and $i \neq k$, $\phi_{i,j}$ is a random number in the range of $[0,1]$. If offspring is greater than it's parent individual, then parent individual is replaced by it's offspring.

(3) Onlooker bee stage

Selection probability is generated based on fitness value of each individual, and then SN solutions is selected for further search by roulette, and the new solution is updated by Eq. (2). Different from the employed bee phase, better solutions have more chances to be updated. The calculation formula of the fitness value is as follows:

$$fit(X_i) = \begin{cases} \frac{1}{1+f(X_i)}, & \text{if } f(X_i) \geq 0 \\ 1 + |f(X_i)|, & \text{if } f(X_i) < 0 \end{cases} \tag{3}$$

where $f(X_i)$ is the function value of i-th individual. The selection probability of the i-th individual is as follows:

$$p_i = \frac{fit(X_i)}{\sum_{i=1}^{SN} fit(X_i)} \tag{4}$$

(4) Scout bee stage

Scout bee judges whether the solution needs to be reinitialized according to the number of consecutive unupdated times $trial_i$ of each solution X_i. If $trial_i$ exceeds the threshold $limit$, the current individual will be reinitialized with Eq. (1), then $trial_i$ will reset to 0. The main aim of this stage is to protect ABC from trapping in a local optimum.

3   Proposed Approach

Within this section, population diversity guided dimension perturbation for ABC (PDDPABC) is presented. In PDDPABC, there are two main modifications. Firstly, an improved neighborhood search strategy is applied to substitute original search strategy Eq. (2). In contrast with the strong exploration of Eq. (2), the new strategy prefers to exploitation. This can improve the solution accuracy and speed up convergence. Then, population diversity guided dimension perturbation is proposed. By monitoring the population diversity, the frequency of dimension perturbation is dynamically adjusted to balance exploitation and exploration.

Equation (2) is replaced by the following strategy [21]:

$$V_{i,j} = x_{best,j} + \phi_{i,j} \cdot (x_{best,j} - x_{k,j}) \tag{5}$$

where $i = \{1, 2, \cdots, SN\}$, j is a random number in $\{1, 2, \cdots, D\}$, and the numerical value of k is stochastically chosen from $\{1, 2, \cdots, SN\}$ $(i \neq k)$, the stochastic number $\phi_{i,j}$ is within $[0,1]$, and X_{best} is the best solution of the population found currently. The above strategy is taken from our previous work [21]. Based on the guidance of X_{best}, ABC can make the population more quickly converge to the current best solution.

Each individual in ABC updates only one dimension at a time. The updated solution V is little different from the original solution X, which will decelerate the rate of convergence. To solve this problem, an individual can be simultaneously updated for multiple dimensions. Wang et al. [22] manipulated the number of dimension perturbations adaptively with a parameter MR. If offspring V is greater than parent individual X, more dimensions will be disturbed to improve exploitation capacity as well as to accelerate convergence. Otherwise, the number of dimension perturbations will be reduced. Yu et al. [23] designed a formula that controls the number of dimension perturbations to decrease with search process. The author thinks that a larger number of dimension perturbations can make a big difference between offspring V and parent individual X, and speed up the search, while a smaller number of dimension perturbations can narrow the difference between parent individual and offspring, which is beneficial to find a more accurate solution and is suitable for the end of the iteration.

The difference between updated solution V and original solution X becomes larger as the number of dimension perturbations rises. Based on the above point of view, in order to make this difference to be more conducive to search, this paper uses Eq. (5) for neighborhood search, which uses the global best individual to direct the search. Then, if the number of dimension perturbations is increased, each solution will move closer to the current optimal individual. However, for the multimodal problem, if a larger number of dimension perturbations is used during the beginning of iteration, each solution will approach to the best individual found currently, which will reduce population diversity and make algorithm easily trap in local optimum at the beginning.

To tackle above problems, this paper uses two parameters, population diversity and iteration period, to judge whether the number of dimensional perturbations needs to be increased. The population density is defined below:

$$diversity = \frac{1}{Sn \cdot d_{\max}} \sqrt{\sum_{i=1}^{Sn} (x_{ij} - \overline{x}_j)^2} \tag{6}$$

Algorithm 1: Proposed Approach (PDDPABC)

```
 1  Randomly generate SN solutions by Eq. (1) and calculate their function value;
 2  set trialᵢ = 0 and flag = False;
 3  while FEs < MaxFEs do
 4  │  Calculate population diversity by Eq. (6);
 5  │  if diversity > m and iteration < n then
 6  │  │  flag = False;
 7  │  end
 8  │  else
 9  │  │  flag = True;
10  │  end
11  │  for i = 1 to SN do
12  │  │  if flag then
13  │  │  │  Calculate the solution Vᵢ according to Eq. (5);
14  │  │  end
15  │  │  else
16  │  │  │  Calculate the solution Vᵢ according to Eq. (5) and Eq. (10);
17  │  │  end
18  │  │  Calculate f(Vᵢ);
19  │  │  FEs++;
20  │  │  if f(Vᵢ) < f(Xᵢ) then
21  │  │  │  Upadte Xᵢ by Vᵢ and set trialᵢ = 0;
22  │  │  end
23  │  │  else
24  │  │  │  trialᵢ + +;
25  │  │  end
26  │  end
27  │  Calculate population diversity by Eq. (6);
28  │  if diversity > m and iteration < n then
29  │  │  flag = False;
30  │  end
31  │  else
32  │  │  flag = True;
33  │  end
34  │  Calculate the probability pᵢ by Eq. (4);
35  │  Set i = 1 and count = 1;
36  │  while count <= SN do
37  │  │  if rand(0, 1) < pᵢ then
38  │  │  │  count = count + 1;
39  │  │  │  if flag then
40  │  │  │  │  Calculate the solution Vᵢ according to Eq. (5);
41  │  │  │  end
42  │  │  │  else
43  │  │  │  │  Calculate the solution Vᵢ according to Eq. (5) and Eq. (10);
44  │  │  │  end
45  │  │  │  Calculate f(Vᵢ);
46  │  │  │  FEs++;
47  │  │  │  if f(Vᵢ) < f(Xᵢ) then
48  │  │  │  │  Update Xᵢ by Vᵢ and set trialᵢ = 0;
49  │  │  │  end
50  │  │  │  else
51  │  │  │  │  trialᵢ + +;
52  │  │  │  end
53  │  │  end
54  │  │  i = (i + 1)%SN;
55  │  end
56  │  if max {trialᵢ} > limit then
57  │  │  Initialize Xᵢ according to Eq. (1);
58  │  │  Calculate the function value, FEs + + and reset trialᵢ = 0;
59  │  end
60  end
```

where SN is population size, $j = \{1, 2, \cdots, D\}$, $\overline{x}_j$ is the central location of j-th dimension for all individuals, and d_{max} is the distance between the two solutions that are farthest apart in the population. $\overline{x}_j$ and d_{max} are defined by

$$\overline{x}_j = \frac{1}{Sn} \sum_{i=1}^{Sn} x_{ij} \tag{7}$$

$$d_{\max} = \max\{\sqrt{\sum_{j=1}^{D}(d_{i,j} - d_{k,j})^2}\} \tag{8}$$

where $i = \{1, 2, \cdots, Sn\}$, $k = \{1, 2, \cdots, Sn\}$, and $i \neq k$. The result obtained by Eq. (6) is a normalized value, which is obtained by dividing the average distance from all solutions to the center position by the two most distant solutions in the population.

Considering the above issues, the goal of this paper is to maintain a certain level of population diversity during preliminary stage of the search, and not to affect convergence rate at the end of the search. Therefore, thresholds m and n are set in this paper to control population diversity and iteration period respectively. If the population density is greater than m and the number of iterations is less than n, then only one dimension is changed; otherwise, $randint(2, D/2)$ dimensions are changed, and $randint(2, D/2)$ is a random integer in $[2, D/2]$. According to the characteristics of Eq. 5, if the number of dimension perturbations is too large, this individual will quickly approach to the current optimal solution, which will easily trap in local optimum. When the number of dimension perturbations is small, the solution will have a small improvement and the convergence speed will be slow. So we set the upper limit of dimension perturbation as $D/2$. The perturbation of a single dimension prevents the solution from approaching the optimal solution too quickly, as well as maintaining the diversity of the initial population. Multiple dimension perturbations can speed up convergence rate. The number of dimension perturbations k can be described by following equation:

$$k = \begin{cases} 1, \text{if } diversity > m \text{ and } iteration < n \\ randint(2, \frac{D}{2}), \text{ otherwise} \end{cases} \tag{9}$$

Then, we randomly select k different integers in $[1, D]$ and store them in the set S, where S stores the specific dimensions that need to be disturbed. For example, when D is 10 and k is 3, $S = \{2, 5, 7\}$ is obtained. It means that the neighborhood search is performed on the second, fifth, and seventh dimensions of the current solution. The dimensions in the new solution V_i are updated as follows:

$$V_{i,j}^* = \begin{cases} x_{i,j}, & \text{if } j \text{ not in } S \\ V_{i,j}, & \text{if } j \text{ in } S \end{cases} \tag{10}$$

where $j = \{1, 2, \cdots, D\}$, S is a set of k different integers which are randomly selected within $[1, D]$, k is calculated by Eq. (9), $V_{i,j}$ is calculated by Eq. (2),

4 Experimental Study

4.1 Experimental Design and Parameter Selection

To evaluate performance of PDDPABC, two experiments based on different test problems were designed. The first experiment tests the performance of PDDPABC on 22 classic test problems [30], when dimension is 30 and 100. The second experiment verifies the capability of PDDPABC on CEC 2013 test problems set with dimension 30 [31]. The 22 classic benchmark problems are described in [6].

For all experiments, population size $SN = 50$. $MaxFES$ indicates the maximum number of evaluations, $MaxFES$ is set to $5000 \cdot D$, and the parameter m in Eq. (9) is 0.1. The parameter n is $\frac{MaxFEs}{300}$ based on empirical studies. $limit$ is set to 100 in the first experiment, and in the second experiment, $limit = SN \cdot D$. For each set of benchmark functions, we ran 30 times and recorded the mean value.

4.2 Results on Classic Benchmark Problems

On 22 classic benchmark problems, we chose ABC, EABC [24], GABC [16], MEABC [21], MABC [25] to compare with PDDPABC. Table 1 presents the test results of 22 classic test problems of the algorithm in 30 dimensions, and the final row of the table shows the comparison results. PDDPABC performed better than ABC on 19 problems, only on f_{10} did ABC perform better, and on the remaining two problems, both algorithms achieved the same accuracy. PDDPABC performed better on 8 problems compared to EABC, for 10 problems the two algorithms performed equally, and only for the remaining 4 problems did PDDPABC perform slightly worse. PDDPABC performed worse than GABC only on f_{10} and was able to achieve better results on 14 problems, while the performance of both algorithms was the same on the remaining 7 problems. MEABC performed worse on 8 problems than PDDPABC, for 11 problems, both could get the same accuracy, and for the remaining 3 problems, it was slightly better than PDDPABC. PDDPABC was able to achieve better results on 13 problems than MABC, and on the remaining 9 problems, both can reach the same accuracy.

Table 2 lists the results of each algorithm in 22 classic benchmark problems in 100 dimensions. Compared with the results on $D = 30$, there is just little difference. When the dimension increases from 30 to 100, the effect of the algorithm does not become worse. ABC achieved better results than PDDPABC only on f_{10}, and ABC performed worse than PDDPABC on 20 test problems, with the two algorithms achieving the same results on f_{21}. Compared to PDDPABC, EABC performed slightly better on only 3 test problems and worse on 9, with the two algorithms achieving the same effect on the remaining 10 problems.

Table 1. Results on 22 classic problems for $D = 30$.

Problem	ABC	EABC	GABC	MEABC	MABC	PDDPABC
f_1	8.32E−16	3.92E−58	5.16E−16	2.34E−40	4.68E−26	**7.91E−97**
f_2	4.62E−08	5.93E−53	6.72E−16	5.17E−37	4.25E−23	**3.42E−95**
f_3	6.94E−16	5.90E−60	3.69E−16	6.74E−41	2.85E−41	**6.81E−100**
f_4	2.73E−14	8.37E−63	4.73E−17	5.42E−90	2.86E−52	**7.42E− 204**
f_5	2.79E−10	4.24E−31	5.46E−15	3.86E−21	7.56E−14	**7.61E−62**
f_6	3.59E+01	1.21E+00	1.53E+01	4.38E+00	9.80E+00	**1.09E+00**
f_7	**0.00E+00**	**0.00E+00**	**0.00E+00**	**0.00E+00**	**0.00E+00**	**0.00E+00**
f_8	1.43E−22	**7.18E−66**	9.10E−24	**7.18E−66**	**7.18E−66**	**7.18E−66**
f_9	1.91E−01	1.68E−02	1.09E−01	3.86E−02	4.73E−02	**7.78E−03**
f_{10}	1.57E−01	5.96E−01	**7.06E−02**	3.29E−01	6.34E−01	6.24E−01
f_{11}	4.26E−14	**0.00E+00**	**0.00E+00**	**0.00E+00**	**0.00E+00**	**0.00E+00**
f_{12}	9.24E−03	**0.00E+00**	**0.00E+00**	**0.00E+00**	**0.00E+00**	**0.00E+00**
f_{13}	8.13E−14	**0.00E+00**	2.43E−16	**0.00E+00**	**0.00E+00**	**0.00E+00**
f_{14}	**−1.25E+04**	**−1.26E+04**	**−1.26E+04**	**−1.26E+04**	**−1.26E+04**	**−1.26E+04**
f_{15}	7.54E−05	**2.87E−14**	2.42E−10	3.34E−14	4.63E−11	3.15E−14
f_{16}	7.64E−16	**1.57E−32**	5.67E−16	**1.57E−32**	2.01E−27	**1.57E−32**
f_{17}	3.68E−15	**1.35E−32**	5.67E−16	**1.35E−32**	3.37E−26	5.18E−32
f_{18}	1.53E−06	1.34E−16	4.63E−07	**1.17E−21**	4.56E−13	2.14E−16
f_{19}	2.04E−13	9.72E−12	9.54E−16	**1.35E−31**	4.61E−26	**1.35E−31**
f_{20}	−2.93E+01	**0.00E+00**	**0.00E+00**	**0.00E+00**	**0.00E+00**	**0.00E+00**
f_{21}	**−7.83E+01**	**−7.83E+01**	**−7.83E+01**	**−7.83E+01**	**−7.83E+01**	**−7.83E+01**
f_{22}	−2.93E+01	**−2.96E+01**	−2.95E+01	**−2.96E+01**	**−2.96E+01**	**−2.96E+01**
w/t/l	19/2/1	8/10/4	14/7/1	8/11/3	13/9/0	-/-/-

PDDPABC was worse to GABC for only one problem, and on four problems the two algorithms performed equally well, PDDPABC was better on the remaining 17 problems. MEABC was inferior to PDDPABC on 6 problems, the two algorithms were able to achieve the same accuracy for 11 problems, and for the remaining problems, MEABC achieved better results. Out of the 22 problems, MABC had no better results than PDDPABC, on 14 problems, MABC had worse results, the two algorithms obtain the identical results on remaining 8 functions.

Table 3 records the results of Friedman test on 6 different ABC algorithms [32–34]. As you notice from the table that PDDPABC has the smallest mean ranking values in both 30 and 100 dimensions. This shows that PDDPABC can obtain better results than comparison variants. Table 4 lists results of each comparison algorithm for Wilcoxon test. The results show that PDDPABC is significantly better than ABC, GABC and MABC in 30 and 100 dimension.

Figure 1 illustrates convergence curves of PDDPABC and five comparison algorithms for test problems f_1, f_2, f_5, and f_9 ($D = 30$). From the figure, we can see that PDDPABC has the fastest convergence speed among the compared algorithms.

Table 2. Results on 22 classic problems for $D = 100$.

Problem	ABC	EABC	GABC	MEABC	MABC	PDDPABC
f_1	8.15E−15	1.35E−54	3.24E−15	2.52E−36	1.63E−22	**6.25E−77**
f_2	2.75E−06	8.14E−49	3.07E−15	4.48E−33	4.48E−19	**6.72E−77**
f_3	5.24E−15	3.58E−55	3.23E−15	7.84E−37	5.86E−23	**1.76E−78**
f_4	1.22E−08	8.22E−101	4.75E−11	4.03E−87	2.33E−52	**1.09E−199**
f_5	1.29E−09	1.16E−28	6.82E−15	2.44E−19	3.62E−12	**2.18E−47**
f_6	8.82E+01	**2.63E+01**	8.55E+01	3.98E+01	5.16E+01	4.32E+01
f_7	1.28E+00	0.00E+00	0.00E+00	0.00E+00	0.00E+00	0.00E+00
f_8	5.14E−40	**7.12E−218**	6.33E−45	**7.12E−218**	**7.12E−218**	**7.12E−218**
f_9	1.51E+00	9.88E−02	7.37E−01	1.83E−01	2.20E−01	**4.30E−02**
f_{10}	**1.74E−01**	8.94E+00	3.18E−01	1.13E+00	4.65E+00	1.68E+00
f_{11}	1.43E−11	0.00E+00	7.11E−15	0.00E+00	0.00E+00	0.00E+00
f_{12}	9.75E+00	0.00E+00	1.93E+00	0.00E+00	0.00E+00	0.00E+00
f_{13}	2.48E−14	0.00E+00	3.18E−15	0.00E+00	0.00E+00	0.00E+00
f_{14}	−4.12E+04	−4.19E+04	−4.19E+04	−4.19E+04	−4.19E+04	−4.19E+04
f_{15}	5.24E−05	**1.18E−13**	2.75E−07	3.16E−13	5.27E−07	6.12E−13
f_{16}	7.57E−15	1.80E−11	3.23E−15	**4.71E−33**	1.76E−24	5.10E−33
f_{17}	1.42E−13	1.35E−32	3.31E−15	**1.35E−32**	6.86E−23	1.35E−32
f_{18}	7.65E−04	3.35E−16	2.96E−05	**2.04E−16**	1.52E−10	5.77E−15
f_{19}	9.67E−12	6.47E−14	1.22E−14	**1.35E−31**	1.43E−23	**1.35E−31**
f_{20}	2.92E+00	0.00E+00	0.00E+00	0.00E+00	0.00E+00	0.00E+00
f_{21}	−7.83E+01	−7.83E+01	−7.83E+01	−7.83E+01	−7.83E+01	−7.83E+01
f_{22}	−9.72E+01	−9.95E+01	−9.82E+01	−9.95E+01	−9.94E+01	−9.95E+01
w/t/l	20/1/1	9/10/3	17/4/1	6/11/5	14/8/0	

Table 3. Friedman test for different ABC variants.

	$D = 30$ Mean ranking	$D = 100$ Mean ranking
ABC	5.55	5.61
EABC	2.66	2.68
GABC	4.14	4.43
MEABC	2.73	2.48
MABC	3.64	3.59
PDDPABC	**2.3**	**2.2**

Table 4. Wilcoxon test for different ABC algorithms compared with PDDPABC.

	D = 30 ρ value	D = 100 ρ value
ABC	**0.001**	**0.001**
EABC	0.53	0.308
GABC	**0.009**	**0.001**
MEABC	0.328	0.534
MABC	**0.001**	**0.001**

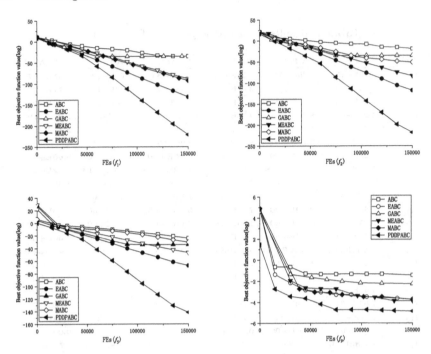

Fig. 1. Convergence curves of six algorithms on f_1, f_2, f_5, and f_9 ($D = 30$).

4.3   Results on CEC 2013 Benchmark Problems

Different ABC variants is tested by CEC 2013 test problems with $D = 30$, and the results is showed in Table 5. The algorithms involved in the comparison include NABC [26], O-ABC [27], MABC$_{SF}$ [28], IABC [29], MABC [28]. Compared with PDDPABC, NABC performed worse on 14 problems, and on 3 problems, the performance of the two algorithms was the same, and on the remaining 11 problems, NABC performed better. O-ABC did not perform as well as PDDPABC on 20 problems, and only outperformed PDDPABC on 3 problems. For the remaining 4 problems, the two algorithms could achieve the same accuracy. PDDPABC performed better on 19 problems than MABC$_{SF}$, slightly worse on 5 problems, and the two algorithms performed equally on the remaining 5 problems. Compared with PDDPABC, IABC performed worse on 18 problems and better on 6 problems, and the two algorithms performed equally on the remaining 4 problems. The effect of MABC was inferior to PDDPABC on 21 problems, and only for 4 problems could it produce better effect. For the remaining 3 problems, the accuracy of the two algorithms was consistent.

Table 5. Results on the CEC 2013 benchmark set for $D = 30$.

Problem	NABC	O-ABC	MABC$_{SF}$	IABC	MABC	PDDPABC
F_1	0.00E+00	0.00E+00	0.00E+00	0.00E+00	0.00E+00	0.00E+00
F_2	1.59E+07	1.64E+07	**5.57E+05**	2.13E+07	6.89E+07	1.54E+07
F_3	5.01E+08	1.66E+09	7.48E+07	4.53E+09	3.35E+09	**8.65E+06**
F_4	7.00E+04	7.63E+04	1.04E+05	4.69E+04	8.06E+04	**3.68E+04**
F_5	0.00E+00	0.00E+00	0.00E+00	0.00E+00	0.00E+00	0.00E+00
F_6	1.93E+01	2.03E+01	**1.45E+01**	3.59E+01	1.76E+01	1.69E+01
F_7	1.05E+02	1.23E+02	1.66E+02	9.64E+01	9.79E+01	**7.30E+01**
F_8	**2.09E+01**	2.10E+01	2.10E+01	**2.09E+01**	**2.09E+01**	2.10E+01
F_9	**2.88E+01**	3.27E+01	3.68E+01	2.92E+01	3.43E+01	3.04E+01
F_{10}	2.99E+00	5.33E+00	**1.03E−01**	2.25E+00	6.22E−01	1.14E+00
F_{11}	0.00E+00	0.00E+00	1.15E+02	0.00E+00	9.60E+01	0.00E+00
F_{12}	1.34E+02	3.06E+02	1.72E+02	2.84E+02	2.28E+02	**1.33E+02**
F_{13}	**1.72E+02**	3.28E+02	2.93E+02	2.83E+02	2.25E+02	1.93E+02
F_{14}	**6.35E−02**	2.09E+01	3.80E+03	9.08E+01	4.14E+03	3.15E−01
F_{15}	4.33E+03	4.92E+03	4.10E+03	5.00E+03	7.37E+03	**4.02E+03**
F_{16}	1.97E+00	2.09E+00	**1.52E+00**	2.20E+00	2.43E+00	1.52E+00
F_{17}	**3.04E+01**	3.11E+01	2.39E+02	3.08E+01	1.43E+02	3.06E+01
F_{18}	1.85E+02	3.46E+02	2.55E+02	3.30E+02	2.52E+02	**1.83E+02**
F_{19}	**2.71E−01**	1.16E+00	1.42E+01	2.75E+00	1.33E+01	5.32E−01
F_{20}	1.39E+01	1.47E+01	1.50E+01	1.30E+01	1.38E+01	**1.22E+01**
F_{21}	3.32E+02	2.28E+02	2.34E+02	3.28E+02	2.61E+02	**2.00E+02**
F_{22}	9.88E+01	1.31E+02	4.96E+03	**1.23E+02**	4.68E+03	2.18E+02
F_{23}	5.08E+03	5.49E+03	5.14E+03	5.82E+03	7.86E+03	**5.03E+03**
F_{24}	2.82E+02	2.92E+02	3.02E+02	**2.53E+02**	2.87E+02	4.99E+02
F_{25}	2.93E+02	3.25E+02	3.09E+02	**2.63E+02**	2.94E+02	6.26E+02
F_{26}	2.01E+02	2.01E+02	2.67E+02	**2.00E+02**	2.08E+02	**2.00E+02**
F_{27}	**4.00E+02**	4.01E+02	1.28E+03	8.71E+02	1.12E+03	5.40E+02
F_{28}	2.96E+02	3.06E+02	9.95E+02	**2.80E+02**	3.00E+02	3.00E+02
w/t/l	14/3/11	20/4/4	19/4/5	18/4/6	21/3/4	-/-/-

5   Conclusion

This paper proposes a population diversity guided dimension perturbation for artificial bee colony algorithm (called PDDPABC) to improve the performance of ABC. We design a equation for population diversity, and use it to manipulate the number of dimension perturbations. With the combination of Eq. 5 and Eq. 9, the algorithm can maintain a certain population diversity and ensure a faster convergence speed.

The performance of PDDPABC is verified by the experiment in the fourth part. The experiment is mainly divided into two parts. The first part tests the performance of PDDPABC on 22 classic test functions when dimension is 30 and 100. The second part of the experiment evaluates the performance of PDDPABC on CEC 2013 benchmark set with $D = 30$. Results of PDDPABC is compared it with five other different ABC variants. Experimental results show that PDDPABC can achieve greater results than other contrast algorithms on most test problems.

In this paper, three parameters are introduced: population diversity, iteration period and the number of dimension perturbations. The first two parameters are fixed values, and the latter one is a random value. How to adaptively select the appropriate parameters for different problems will be investigated in the future work.

References

1. Liu, N.X., Pan, J.S., Sun, C.L., Chu, S.C.: An efficient surrogate-assisted quasi-affine transformation evolutionary algorithm for expensive optimization problems. Knowl.-Based Syst. **209**, 106418 (2020)
2. Du, Z.G., Pan, J.S., Chu, S.C., Luo, H.J., Hu, P.: Quasi-affine transformation evolutionary algorithm with communication schemes for application of RSSI in wireless sensor networks. IEEE Access **8**, 8583–8594 (2020)
3. Pan, J.S., Liu, N., Chu, S.C.: A hybrid differential evolution algorithm and its application in unmanned combat aerial vehicle path planning. IEEE Access **8**, 17691–17712 (2020)
4. Tavakkoli-Moghaddam, R., Safari, J., Sassani, F.: Reliability optimization of series-parallel systems with a choice of redundancy strategies using a genetic algorithm. Reliab. Eng. Syst. Saf. **93**(4), 550–556 (2008)
5. Long, Q.: A constraint handling technique for constrained multi-objective genetic algorithm. Swarm Evol. Comput. **15**, 66–79 (2014)
6. Xiao, S.Y., Wang, W.J., Wang, H., Zhou, X.Y.: A new artificial bee colony based on multiple search strategies and dimension selection. IEEE Access **7**, 133982–133995 (2019)
7. Wang, H., Wang, W.: A new multi-strategy ensemble artificial bee colony algorithm for water demand prediction. In: Peng, H., Deng, C., Wu, Z., Liu, Y. (eds.) ISICA 2018. CCIS, vol. 986, pp. 63–70. Springer, Singapore (2019). https://doi.org/10.1007/978-981-13-6473-0_6
8. Wang, H., et al.: Multi-strategy and dimension perturbation ensemble of artificial bee colony. In: IEEE Congress on Evolutionary Computation, pp. 697–704 (2019)
9. Wang, H., Wang, W., Cui, Z.: A new artificial bee colony algorithm for solving large-scale optimization problems. In: Vaidya, J., Li, J. (eds.) ICA3PP 2018. LNCS, vol. 11335, pp. 329–337. Springer, Cham (2018). https://doi.org/10.1007/978-3-030-05054-2_26
10. Hu, P., Pan, J.S., Chu, S.C.: Improved binary grey wolf optimizer and its application for feature selection. Knowl.-Based Syst. **195**, 105746 (2020)
11. Pan, J.S., Zhuang, J., Luo, H., Chu, S.C.: Multi-group flower pollination algorithm based on novel communication strategies. J. Internet Technol. **22**, 257–269 (2021)
12. Du, Z.G., Pan, J.S., Chu, S.C., Chiu, Y.J.: Improved binary symbiotic organism search algorithm with transfer functions for feature selection. IEEE Access **8**, 225730–225744 (2020)
13. Karaboga, D., Basturk, B.: A powerful and efficient algorithm for numerical function optimization: artificial bee colony (ABC) algorithm. J. Global Optim. **39**(3), 459–471 (2007). https://doi.org/10.1007/s10898-007-9149-x
14. Wang, H., Wang, W., Xiao, S., Cui, Z., Zhou, X.: Improving artificial bee colony algorithm using a new neighborhood selection mechanism. Inf. Sci. **527**, 227–240 (2020)

15. Cui, L., et al.: A ranking-based adaptive artificial bee colony algorithm for global numerical optimization. Inf. Sci. **417**, 169–185 (2017)
16. Zhu, G., Kwong, S.: Gbest-guided artificial bee colony algorithm for numerical function optimization. Appl. Math. Comput. **217**(7), 3166–3173 (2010)
17. Xue, Y., Jiang, J., Zhao, B., Ma, T.: A self-adaptive artificial bee colony algorithm based on global best for global optimization. Soft. Comput. **22**(9), 2935–2952 (2018). https://doi.org/10.1007/s00500-017-2547-1
18. Gao, W., Liu, S.: Improved artificial bee colony algorithm for global optimization. Inf. Process. Lett. **111**(17), 871–882 (2011)
19. Cui, L., et al.: A novel artificial bee colony algorithm with depth-first search framework and elite-guided search equation. Inf. Sci. **367–368**, 1012–1044 (2016)
20. Wang, H., Wang, W., Zhou, X., Zhao, J., Xu, M.: Artificial bee colony algorithm based on knowledge fusion. Complex Intell. Syst. **7**(3), 1139–1152 (2021)
21. Wang, H., Wu, Z., Rahnamayan, S., Sun, H., Liu, Y., Pan, J.S.: Multi-strategy ensemble artificial bee colony algorithm. Inf. Sci. **279**, 587–603 (2014)
22. Wang, H., et al.: Multi-strategy and dimension perturbation ensemble of artificial bee colony. In: IEEE Congress on Evolutionary Computation (CEC 2019), pp. 697–704. IEEE, Wellington (2019)
23. Yu, G., Zhou, H., Wang, H.: Improving artificial bee colony algorithm using a dynamic reduction strategy for dimension perturbation. Math. Probl. Eng. **2019**, 3419410 (2019)
24. Gao, W., Liu, S., Huang, L.: Enhancing artificial bee colony algorithm using more information-based search equations. Inf. Sci. **270**, 112–133 (2014)
25. Gao, W.F., Liu, S.Y.: A modified artificial bee colony algorithm. Comput. Oper. Res. **39**(3), 687–697 (2012)
26. Xu, Y., Ping, F., Ling, Y.: A simple and efficient artificial bee colony algorithm. Math. Probl. Eng. **2013**, 526315 (2013)
27. Sharma, T.K., Gupta, P.: Opposition learning based phases in artificial bee colony. Int. J. Syst. Assur. Eng. Manag. **9**(1), 1–12 (2018). https://doi.org/10.1007/s13198-016-0545-9
28. Akay, B., Karaboga, D.: A modified artificial bee colony algorithm for real-parameter optimization. Inf. Sci. **192**, 120–142 (2012)
29. Cao, Y., Lu, Y., Pan, X., Sun, N.: An improved global best guided artificial bee colony algorithm for continuous optimization problems. Cluster Comput. **22**(2), 3011–3019 (2019). https://doi.org/10.1007/s10586-018-1817-8
30. Xiao, S., Wang, W., Wang, H., Zhou, X.: A new artificial bee colony based on multiple search strategies and dimension selection. IEEE Access **7**, 133982–133995 (2019)
31. Liang, J.J., Qu, B.Y., Suganthan, P.N.: Problem definitions and evaluation criteria for the CEC 2013 special session on real-parameter optimization. Technical report, Computational Intelligence Laboratory, Zhengzhou University (2013)
32. Wang, H., Rahnamayan, S., Sun, H., Omran, M.G.H.: Gaussian bare-bones differential evolution. IEEE Trans. Cybern. **43**(2), 634–647 (2013)
33. Wang, H., Wu, Z.J., Rahnamayan, S., Liu, Y., Ventresca, M.: Enhancing particle swarm optimization using generalized opposition-based learning. Inf. Sci. **181**(20), 4699–4714 (2011)
34. Xiao, S., et al.: An improved artificial bee colony algorithm based on elite strategy and dimension learning. Mathematics **7**(3), 289 (2019)

Artificial Bee Colony Algorithm with an Adaptive Search Manner

Tingyu Ye, Tao Zeng, Luqi Zhang, Minyang Xu, Hui Wang[✉], and Min Hu

School of Information Engineering, Nanchang Institute of Technology,
Nanchang 330099, China
huiwang@nit.edu.cn, minhu73@sina.com

Abstract. Artificial bee colony (ABC) can effectively solve some complex optimization problems. However, its convergence speed is slow and its exploitation capacity is insufficient at the last search stage. In order to solve these problems, this paper proposes a modified ABC with an adaptive search manner (called ASMABC). There are two important search manners: exploration and exploitation. A suitable search manner is beneficial for the search. Then, an evaluating indicator is designed to relate the current search status. An explorative search strategy and another exploitative search strategy are selected to build a strategy pool. According to the evaluating indicator, an adaptive method is used to determine which kind of search manner is suitable for the current search. To verify the performance of ASMABC, 22 complex problems are tested. Experiment result shows that ASMABC achieves competitive performance when contrasted with four different ABC variants.

Keywords: Artificial bee colony algorithm · Adaptive search manner · Evaluating indicator · Strategy pool

1 Introduction

For some time in the past, different intelligence optimization algorithms are proposed. Most of them showed good performance in solving complex optimization problems, There are some representative algorithms, such as evolution algorithm [1,2], differential evolution algorithm [3], ant colony optimization [4,5], firefly algorithm [6,7], particle swarm optimization [8,9], artificial bee colony [10–15], grey wolf optimizer [16], pigeon-inspired optimization [17], and flower pollination algorithm [18]. Among those algorithms, ABC become a popular algorithm because of its simple structure and few parameters.

There are also some shortcomings in ABC algorithm, for instance, falling into stagnation easily and slowing convergence speed. To solve the above problems, many researchers proposed different improved ABCs. Cui et al. [19] put forward a improved ABC, in which elite individuals were used to pilot the search. Zhou et al. [20] introduced a new ABC algorithm on the basic of multi-elite guidance. Different elite-guided search strategies were used for different bees.

© Springer Nature Singapore Pte Ltd. 2021
H. Zhang et al. (Eds.): NCAA 2021, CCIS 1449, pp. 486–497, 2021.
https://doi.org/10.1007/978-981-16-5188-5_35

Gao et al. [21] proposed a modified ABC, in which the search equation was improved by using more information from the search process. In [22], a novel search formula on the basic of Gaussian distribution was constructed. Unlike the original probability selection in ABC, Wang et al. [23] devised a selection mode based on neighborhood. Cui et al. [24] propped an improved ABC, in which a novel selection mechanism based on ranking was utilized.

To strengthen effect of ABC algorithm, a new artificial bee colony algorithm is proposed based on an adaptive search manner (called ASMABC) in this paper. In ASMABC, there are two different search strategies in a strategy pool. Then, a new evaluating indicator is designed to resolve the current search manner. This indicator can change with the iteration period to balance exploration capability and exploitation capability. According to the evaluating indicator, an adaptive method is designed. In the experiment part, ASMABC is tested in 22 test problems. Representations of ASMABC is contrasted with the primeval ABC and three various modified ABCs. Finally, experimental results show that ASMABC is effectual on most test functions.

The next part of this paper is as below. The second part introduces the original ABC algorithm. The third part introduces the improvement ABCs of other researchers. The fourth section introduces ASMABC in detail. The fifth section is experiment and analysis. Finally, conclusion is showed in the sixth section.

2   The Original Artificial Bee Colony Algorithm

At present, artificial bee colony algorithm is a popular optimization algorithm. The whole process of ABC is divided into the following stages: initialization, employed bee stage, onlooker bee stage and scout bee stage. And the whole colony is divided into the following categories: employed bee, onlooker bee and scout bee. Different bees undertake different tasks to assure the orderly implementation of the algorithm. The major flow of the algorithm is gave as below.

1. Initialization stage: in the certain space, the population is generated, the generation formula is as follows.

$$x_{i,j} = Min_j + rand \cdot (Max_j - Min_j) \qquad (1)$$

where Min_j and Max_j are the bounds of a given space, and $rand$ is a random number between 0 and 1.

2. Employed bee stage: The work of employed bees are to search for different honey (food) source, and judge whether there is a better one around the current food source. If there is a better food source, the current food source will be replaced. The search formula is as below.

$$v_{i,j} = x_{i,j} + \phi_{i,j} \cdot (x_{i,j} - x_{k,j}) \qquad (2)$$

where X_i is the current food source, X_k is chose randomly in the swarm $(i \neq k)$, and $\phi_{i,j} \in [-1, 1]$ is a random number.

3. Onlooker bee stage: the task of onlooker bee is also searching the honey source. But different from the stage of employed bee, they choose the honey source by the probability P_i. The calculation formula of P_i is as follows.

$$p_i = \frac{fit(X_i)}{\sum_{i=1}^{SN} fit(X_i)} \qquad (3)$$

where $fit(X_i)$ represents the fitness value of the current honey source. Fitness value is the standard to evaluate the honey source. If the fitness value of the food source is larger, then its quality is better. The formula of fitness value is as follows.

$$fit(X_i) = \begin{cases} \frac{1}{1+f(X_i)}, & \text{if } f(X_i) \geq 0 \\ 1 + |f(X_i)|, & \text{if } f(X_i) < 0 \end{cases} \qquad (4)$$

where $f(X_i)$ is the value of the objective function. Through this selection method, the higher the fitness of the food source, the greater the probability of its being selected. It is often followed by bees to search many times, and the search formula is Eq. (2).

4. Scout bee stage: the work of the scout bee is to updated the honey sources that have been searched for many times but have not been updated. The initialization formula is the same as Eq. (1).

3   ABC with Adaptive Search Manner (ASMABC)

In ABC and other swarm algorithms, there are two important search manners: exploration and exploitation. How to balance them can greatly influence the performance. To tackle this problem, many scholars proposed different improved strategies. Multi-strategy ensemble learning is an effective method. A pool of search strategies is built and each search strategy has distinct search manner. During the search manner, distinct search strategies survive together throughout the search process and contend to produce offspring. However, it is difficult to judge which kind of search manner (strategy) is instrumental in the current search.

In this paper, a modified ABC with an adaptive search manner (called ASMABC) is proposed. The main contribution of ASMABC includes: 1) an explorative search strategy and another exploitative search strategy are used to establish a strategy pool; 2) an evaluating indicator is designed to relate the search status; and 3) an adaptive method is used to determine which kind of search manner is chosen for the current search.

3.1   Strategy Pool

Exploration and exploitation ability have a significant influence on the performance of ABC. A recent study showed that multi-strategy technique is helpful to balance them. Wang et al. [25] designed a strategy pool consisting of three different search strategies. Xiao et al. [12] put forward an modified ABC on the

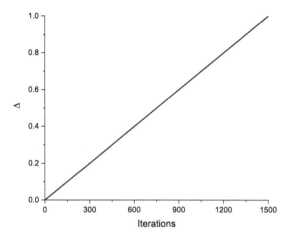

Fig. 1. The change of Δ in the search process.

basic of dual strategy pool, in which each strategy pool has three search strategies. Similarly, three search strategies on the basic of Gaussian distribution was used to constitute a strategy pool [26]. In our work, a strategy pool is also built and it has an explorative search strategy and an exploitative search strategy. The strategy pool is defined as follows.

$$SP(t) = \begin{cases} \text{Eq. (6)} \\ \text{Eq. (7)} \end{cases} \tag{5}$$

$$v_{i,j} = x_{i,j} + \phi_{i,j}(x_{i,j} - x_{k,j}) + \psi_{i,j}(x_{best,j} - x_{i,j}) \tag{6}$$

$$v_{i,j} = x_{best,j} + \phi_{i,j}(x_{best,j} - x_{k,j}) \tag{7}$$

where $SP(t)$ is a strategy pool, X_{best} is the best solution, and the weighting factor $\phi_{i,j} \in [-1,1]$ and $\psi_{i,j} \in [0,1.5]$ are two random values.

The strategy pool is composed of two search strategies. The first search strategy is taken from [27], it is composed of random information and the global best information. Although this is a global search strategy, it can search in a good direction because of the global best information. So it is skilled in exploration search. The other search strategy is derived from our previous work [25]. In Eq. (7), the current solution is guided by the global best solution. A better solution can be found around the best solution. So it does well in exploitation search.

3.2   Adaptive Search Manner

As mentioned before, though several multiple search strategies were used to strengthen the optimization capacity of ABC, it is still difficult to judge which

---

Algorithm 1: Proposed approach (ASMABC)

```
1  Generate SN solutions X_i randomly;
2  Calculate each f(X_i), and set FEs = SN and trial_i = 0;
3  while FEs ≤ MAXFES do
4  │   Choose a search strategy S(t) (Eq. (6) or Eq. (7)) according to Eq. (9);
   │   /* Employed bee search                                              */
5  │   for each X_i in the swarm do
6  │   │   Produce V_i by the strategy S(t);
7  │   │   Calculate f(V_i) and set FEs++;
8  │   │   if f(V_i) < f(X_i) then
9  │   │   │   Update X_i by V_i, and set trial_i = 0;
10 │   │   end
11 │   │   else
12 │   │   │   trial_i = trial_i + 1;
13 │   │   end
14 │   end
   │   /* Onlooker bee search                                             */
15 │   for each X_i in the swarm do
16 │   │   Generate V_i by the strategy S(t);
17 │   │   Calculate f(V_i) and set FEs++;
18 │   │   if f(V_i) < f(X_i) then
19 │   │   │   Update X_i by V_i and set trial_i = 0;
20 │   │   end
21 │   │   else
22 │   │   │   trial_i = trial_i + 1;
23 │   │   end
24 │   end
   │   /* Scout bee search                                                */
25 │   if max{trial_i} > limit then
26 │   │   Generate X_i by Eq. (1);
27 │   │   Set FEs + + and trial_i = 0;
28 │   end
29 end
```

---

kind of search manner (exploration or exploitation) is suitable for the current search. We think a large search space should be searched early in the iteration. And local search should be preferred more as the population continues to converge. According to the above analysis, an adaptive search manner is designed in this section. Firstly, an evaluating indicator Δ is defined to relate the current search status.

$$\Delta = \frac{Iter}{MaxIter} \tag{8}$$

where $Iter$ is the current number of iterations and $MaxIter$ is the maximum number of iterations. The changes of Δ is shown in Fig. 1. It can be seen that Δ varies from 0 to 1 and it changes with the growth of the iteration period obviously. Based on the performance, an adaptive selection manner is described as follows.

$$S(t) = \begin{cases} \text{Exploration search (Eq. (6)), if } \Delta < rand(0,1) \\ \text{Exploitation search (Eq. (7)), otherwise} \end{cases} \tag{9}$$

where $S(t)$ represents the current search manner and it is analyzed as below.

- $\Delta < rand(0,1)$: For this case, $S(t) =$ Eq. (6). It means the exploration search is selected for the current search manner. At the initial search stage, Δ is small and $\Delta < rand(0, 1)$ is easily satisfied. The search prefers to exploration. It is helpful to enhance the global search and avoid falling into minima.

– $\Delta \geq rand(0, 1)$: For this case, $S(t) =$ Eq. (7). It means the exploitation search is selected for the current search manner. With increasing of iterations, Δ becomes large and $\Delta \geq rand(0, 1)$ is easily satisfied. The search gradually prefers to exploitation. This is beneficial for find more accurate solutions.

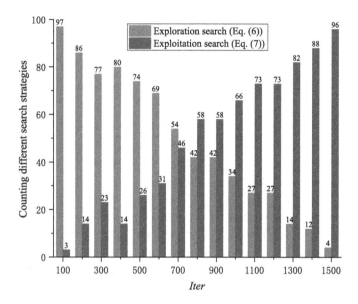

Fig. 2. Comparison of exploration search (Eq. (6)) and exploitation search (Eq. (7)) during the search process.

To clearly illustrate how does our approach work, the Sphere problem is considered as an example. In the experiment, $MaxIter$, SN and $limit$ are set to 1500, 50, and 100, respectively. At each iteration, a strategy is chosen from the strategy pool by Eq. (9). Then, the number of each selected search strategy is counted every 100 iterations. If a strategy is chosen many times, it means the current search period prefers to exploration search or exploitation search. Figure 2 gives the comparison of exploration search (Eq. (6)) and exploitation search (Eq. (7)) during the search process. At the initial search stage, the exploration search dominates the search. From $iter = 1$ to 100, the exploration search is chosen in 97 times, while the exploitation search only occurs in 3 times. As the iteration increases, the search gradually prefers to the exploitation search. The exploitation search strategy is selected more times. From $iter = 1301$ to 1400, the exploitation search is selected in 88 times, while the exploration search only occurs in 12 times. The above dynamic changes of different search manners can be suitable for different optimization problems. It confirms that our approach ASMABC can select search strategy adaptively by monitoring the indicator Δ.

This paper mainly proposes three improvements in ASMABC. First, the strategy pool is built based on two distinct search strategies. Then, an evaluating indicator Δ is built. It changes according the current iteration period. Finally, an appropriate search strategy is chose by an novel adaptive mode from the strategy pool. The major steps of ASMABC are shown in Algorithm 1, where FEs is the number of function evaluations and $MAXFES$ is the maximum value of FEs. Compared with the standard ABC, ASMABC can choose the search manner adaptively, and make use of different search strategies to accelerate the convergence speed.

Table 1. Comparison results for $D = 30$.

Problem	ABC	GABC	MABC	MEABC	ASMABC
f_1	8.67E−16	3.65E−16	8.23E−26	2.67E−40	**1.69E−52**
f_2	2.92E−08	7.12E−16	3.56E−23	7.23E−37	**3.56E−45**
f_3	6.56E−16	2.18E−16	7.48E−41	9.82E−41	**4.49E−50**
f_4	5.19E−14	7.54E−17	2.61E−52	4.29E−90	**9.04E−111**
f_5	2.49E−10	2.70E−15	3.31E−14	2.71E−21	**4.99E−25**
f_6	4.61E+01	1.51E+01	1.19E+01	**4.57E+00**	1.39E+01
f_7	**0.00E+00**	**0.00E+00**	**0.00E+00**	**0.00E+00**	**0.00E+00**
f_8	3.45E−22	7.19E−24	**7.18E−66**	**7.18E−66**	**7.18E−66**
f_9	1.95E−01	1.14E−01	4.92E−02	3.84E−02	**2.81E−02**
f_{10}	1.39E−01	6.93E−02	6.22E−01	3.12E−01	**4.79E−02**
f_{11}	3.18E−14	**0.00E+00**	**0.00E+00**	**0.00E+00**	**0.00E+00**
f_{12}	5.27E−03	**0.00E+00**	**0.00E+00**	**0.00E+00**	**0.00E+00**
f_{13}	5.78E−14	3.57E−16	**0.00E+00**	**0.00E+00**	**0.00E+00**
f_{14}	4.61E+01	**0.00E+00**	**0.00E+00**	**0.00E+00**	**0.00E+00**
f_{15}	6.32E−05	3.16E−10	9.25E−11	3.26E−14	**3.24E−14**
f_{16}	4.57E−16	4.84E−16	5.36E−27	**1.57E−32**	**1.57E−32**
f_{17}	1.47E−15	3.56E−16	7.73E−26	**1.35E−32**	**1.35E−32**
f_{18}	3.12E−06	3.67E−07	6.23E−13	**1.09E−21**	6.10E−16
f_{19}	3.32E−13	5.73E−16	5.62E−26	**1.35E−31**	**1.35E−31**
f_{20}	3.19E−01	**0.00E+00**	**0.00E+00**	**0.00E+00**	**0.00E+00**
f_{21}	**0.00E+00**	**0.00E+00**	**0.00E+00**	**0.00E+00**	**0.00E+00**
f_{22}	−2.93E+01	**−2.96E+01**	**−2.96E+01**	**−2.96E+01**	−2.96E+01

4   Experimental Study

In this section, 22 classic problems are tested to verify the effectiveness of ASMABC [28–31]. These problems are described in [23]. In the experiment,

$MAXFES$, $limit$ and SN are set to $5000 * D$, 100, 100 respectively. To performance of ASMABC, four different ABC algorithms are used for comparison, including the standard ABC [11], GABC [27], MABC [32], and MEABC [25].

Table 2. Comparison results for $D = 100$.

Problem	ABC	GABC	MABC	MEABC	ASMABC
(f_1)	7.43E−15	4.71E−15	2.11E−22	5.43E−36	**1.94E−48**
(f_2)	6.10E−06	2.13E−15	3.09E−19	1.15E−33	**1.23E−42**
(f_3)	9.15E−15	2.76E−15	2.45E−23	1.23E−37	**4.80E−46**
(f_4)	2.41E−08	3.12E−11	7.45E−53	7.63E−85	**1.49E−95**
(f_5)	8.35E−09	8.11E−15	4.23E−12	3.21E−19	**9.09E−27**
(f_6)	7.92E+01	8.72E+01	4.84E+01	**3.64E+01**	8.51E+01
(f_7)	2.41E+00	**0.00E+00**	**0.00E+00**	**0.00E+00**	**0.00E+00**
(f_8)	4.45E−40	5.21E−45	**7.12E−218**	**7.12E−218**	**7.12E−218**
(f_9)	1.67E+00	8.23E−01	3.40E−01	4.62E−01	**2.51E−01**
(f_{10})	2.32E−01	4.75E−01	5.21E+00	1.23E+00	**1.65E−01**
(f_{11})	3.76E−11	6.67E−15	**0.00E+00**	**0.00E+00**	**0.00E+00**
(f_{12})	9.95E+00	2.56E+00	**0.00E+00**	**0.00E+00**	**0.00E+00**
(f_{13})	9.32E−14	4.11E−15	**0.00E+00**	**0.00E+00**	**0.00E+00**
(f_{14})	8.12E−04	**0.00E+00**	**0.00E+00**	**0.00E+00**	**0.00E+00**
(f_{15})	4.12E−05	3.56E−07	6.32E−07	7.42E−13	**6.43E−14**
(f_{16})	8.53E−15	4.26E−15	4.62E−24	**4.71E−33**	**4.71E−33**
(f_{17})	9.43E−12	1.26E−15	6.34E−23	**1.35E−32**	**1.35E−32**
(f_{18})	8.23E−04	1.23E−05	4.12E−10	2.04E−16	**1.24E−21**
(f_{19})	8.89E−11	2.67E−14	4.73E−23	**1.35E−31**	**1.35E−31**
(f_{20})	3.12E+00	**0.00E+00**	**0.00E+00**	**0.00E+00**	**0.00E+00**
(f_{21})	**0.00E+00**	**0.00E+00**	**0.00E+00**	**0.00E+00**	**0.00E+00**
(f_{22})	−9.72E+01	−9.82E+01	−9.94E+01	**−9.95E+01**	**−9.95E+01**

In Table 1, the comparison results of ASMABC are showed when D = 30. It is evident that results of ASMABC is better than other ABC algorithms. ASMABC displays better than the standard ABC in almost all test problems. Compared with GABC, ASMABC is superior on 15 problems. They are equal on the rest problems. Contrasted with MABC, ASMABC get better results on 13 problems. They are equal on other problems. MEABC performs better than ASMABC on 2 problems, but ASMABC is better on 8 problems. In Fig. 3, the variety process of five ABC algorithms on some problems is shown.

In Table 2, the comparison results of ASMABC are showed when D = 100. It can be seen that when the increase of dimension D, the effect of ASMABC is not greatly affected. ASMABC is better than the original ABC on all test

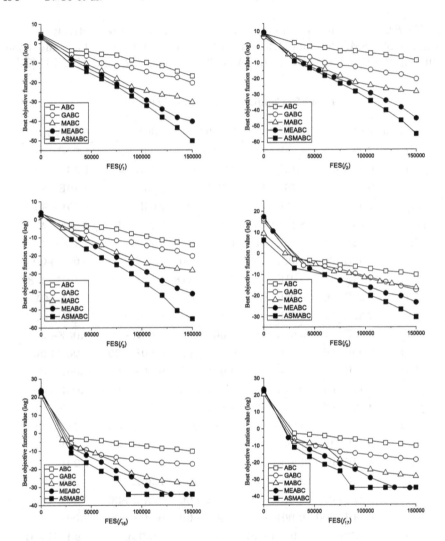

Fig. 3. Convergence curves of five ABC algorithms on f_1, f_2, f_3, f_5, f_{16} and f_{17}.

problems expect f_{21}. Compared with GABC, ASMABC is superior on 17 problems. They are equal on the other problems. Contrasted with MABC, ASMABC demonstrates better on 13 problems. And they are equal on the rest problems. MEABC performs better than ASMABC on 1 problems, but ASMABC is superior on 9 problems. Variation in the iterative process of five ABCs is showed in Figs. 3. It shows the original ABC and four modified ABCs on 6 problems (f_1, f_2, f_3, f_5, f_{16} and f_{17}). Obviously, performance of ASMABC the most effective compare with other four ABCs.

For more comprehensive verification performance of ASMABC, Friedman and Wilcoxon are tested to compare five ABC algorithms on 22 test problems. Form Table 3, it shows the mean ranking of all ABC algorithms being contrasted. It evidently indicate that ASMABC get the best effect. Table 4 exhibits the p-values of five ABC algorithms. Obviously, ASMABC is better than other ABCs.

Table 3. Results for the Friedman test.

	$D = 30$	$D = 100$
ABC	4.73	5.48
GABC	3.43	4.43
MABC	2.84	3.61
MEABC	2.18	2.52
ASMABC	**1.82**	**1.75**

Table 4. Results for the Wilcoxon test.

	$D = 30$	$D = 100$
ABC	**8.90E−05**	**6.64E−04**
GABC	**6.55E−04**	**1.96E−04**
MABC	**2.31E−02**	**1.16E−02**
MEABC	2.85E−01	7.40E−01

5   Conclusion

To improve the shortcomings of ABC algorithm, this paper proposes a new ABC variant called ASMABC. In ASMABC, a strategy pool is built by two different search strategies. Then, an evaluating indicator is designed to relate the current search status. According to the evaluating indicator, a suitable strategy is selected from the strategy pool by an adaptive mechanism. In order to prove the effect of ASMABC, 22 benchmark functions are carried out.

The results prove that ASMABC is better than the standard ABC, GABC, MABC, and MEABC. The performance of ASMABC is not seriously affected for the dimension scale test. From the convergence characteristics, ASMABC converges faster than four other algorithms on most problems. The evaluating indicator Δ is designed according to population information. By monitoring Δ, ASMABC can dynamically adjust the current search strategy. The design of Δ can be further improved, and this work will be investigated in the future.

References

1. Liu, N.S., Pan, J.S., Sun, C.L., Chu, S.C.: An efficient surrogate-assisted quasi-affine transformation evolutionary algorithm for expensive optimization problems. Knowl.-Based Syst. **209**, 106418 (2020)
2. Du, Z.G., Pan, J.S., Chu, S.C., Luo, H.J., Hu, P.: Quasi-affine transformation evolutionary algorithm with communication schemes for application of RSSI in wireless sensor networks. IEEE Access **8**, 8583–8594 (2020)
3. Pan, J.S., Liu, N.S., Chu, S.C.: A hybrid differential evolution algorithm and its application in unmanned combat aerial vehicle path planning. IEEE Access **8**, 17691–17712 (2020)
4. Asghari, S., Navimipour, N.J.: Cloud service composition using an inverted ant colony optimisation algorithm. Int. J. Bio-Inspired Comput. **13**(4), 257–268 (2019)
5. Mohammadi, R., Javidan, R., Keshtgari, M.: An intelligent traffic engineering method for video surveillance systems over software defined networks using ant colony optimization. Int. J. Bio-Inspired Comput. **12**(3), 173–185 (2018)
6. Wang, H., Wang, W.J., Cui, Z.H., Zhou, X.Y., Zhao, J., Li, Y.: A new dynamic firefly algorithm for demand estimation of water resources. Inf. Sci. **438**, 95–106 (2018)
7. Wang, H., Wang, W.J., Sun, H., Rahnamayan, S.: Firefly algorithm with random attraction. Int. J. Bio-Inspired Comput. **8**(1), 33–41 (2016)
8. Wang, F., Zhang, H., Li, K.S., Lin, Z.Y., Yang, J., Shen, X.L.: A hybrid particle swarm optimization algorithm using adaptive learning strategy. Inf. Sci. **436–437**, 162–177 (2018)
9. Wang, H., Sun, H., Li, C., Rahnamayan, S., Pan, J.S.: Diversity enhanced particle swarm optimization with neighborhood search. Inf. Sci. **223**, 119–135 (2013)
10. Amiri, E., Dehkordi, M.N.: Dynamic data clustering by combining improved discrete artificial bee colony algorithm with fuzzy logic. Int. J. Bio-Inspired Comput. **12**(3), 164–172 (2018)
11. Karaboga, D.: An idea based on honey bee swarm for numerical optimization, Technical Report-TR06. Erciyes University, Engineering Faculty, Computer engineering Department (2005)
12. Xiao, S.Y., Wang, W.J., Wang, H., Zhou, X.Y.: A new artificial bee colony based on multiple search strategies and dimension selection. IEEE Access **7**, 133982–133995 (2019)
13. Wang, H., Wang, W.: A new multi-strategy ensemble artificial bee colony algorithm for water demand prediction. In: Peng, H., Deng, C., Wu, Z., Liu, Y. (eds.) ISICA 2018. CCIS, vol. 986, pp. 63–70. Springer, Singapore (2019). https://doi.org/10.1007/978-981-13-6473-0_6
14. Wang, H., et al.: Multi-strategy and dimension perturbation ensemble of artificial bee colony. In: IEEE Congress on Evolutionary Computation (CEC 2019), pp. 697–704 (2019)
15. Wang, H., Wang, W., Cui, Z.: A new artificial bee colony algorithm for solving large-scale optimization problems. In: Vaidya, J., Li, J. (eds.) ICA3PP 2018. LNCS, vol. 11335, pp. 329–337. Springer, Cham (2018). https://doi.org/10.1007/978-3-030-05054-2_26
16. Hu, P., Pan, J.S., Chu, S.C.: Improved binary grey wolf optimizer and its application for feature selection. Knowl.-Based Syst. **195**(11), 105746 (2020)
17. Tian, A.Q., Chu, S.C., Pan, J.S., Cui, H., Zheng, W.M.: A compact pigeon-inspired optimization for maximum short-term generation mode in cascade hydroelectric power station. Sustainability **12**(3), 767 (2020)

18. Pan, J.S., Zhuang, J.W., Luo, H., Chu, S.C.: Multi-group flower pollination algorithm based on novel communication strategies. J. Internet Technol. **22**(2), 257–269 (2021)
19. Cui, L.Z., et al.: A novel artificial bee colony algorithm with depth-first search framework and elite-guided search equation. Inf. Sci. **367**, 1012–1044 (2016)
20. Zhou, X.Y., Lu, J.X., Huang, J.H., Zhong, M.S., Wang, M.W.: Enhancing artificial bee colony algorithm with multi-elite guidance. Inf. Sci. **543**, 242–258 (2021)
21. Gao, W.F., Liu, S.Y., Huang, L.L.: Enhancing artificial bee colony algorithm using more information-based search equations. Inf. Sci. **270**, 112–133 (2014)
22. Zhou, X., et al.: Gaussian bare-bones artificial bee colony algorithm. Soft. Comput. **20**(3), 907–924 (2016). https://doi.org/10.1007/s00500-014-1549-5
23. Wang, H., Wang, W.J., Xiao, S.Y., Cui, Z.H., Xu, M.Y., Zhou, X.Y.: Improving artificial Bee colony algorithm using a new neighborhood selection mechanism. Inf. Sci. **527**, 227–240 (2020)
24. Cui, L.Z., et al.: A ranking based adaptive artificial bee colony algorithm for global numerical optimization. Inf. Sci. **417**, 169–185 (2017)
25. Wang, H., Wu, Z.J., Rahnamayan, S., Sun, H., Liu, Y., Pan, J.: Multi-strategy ensemble artificial bee colony algorithm. Inf. Sci. **27**, 587–603 (2014)
26. Gao, W.F., Huang, L.L., Liu, S.Y., Chan, F.T.S., Dai, C., Shan, X.: Artificial bee colony algorithm with multiple search strategies. Appl. Math. Comput. **271**, 269–287 (2015)
27. Zhu, G., Kwong, S.: Gbest-guided artificial bee colony algorithm for numerical function optimization. Appl. Math. Comput. **217**(7), 3166–3173 (2010)
28. Wang, H., Rahnamayan, S., Sun, H., Omran, M.G.H.: Gaussian bare-bones differential evolution. IEEE Trans. Cybern. **43**(2), 634–647 (2013)
29. Wang, H., Wu, Z.J., Rahnamayan, S., Liu, Y., Ventresca, M.: Enhancing particle swarm optimization using generalized opposition-based learning. Inf. Sci. **181**(20), 4699–4714 (2011)
30. Xiao, S., et al.: An improved artificial bee colony algorithm based on elite strategy and dimension learning. Mathematics **7**(3), 289 (2019)
31. Xiao, S., Wang, H., Wang, W., Huang, Z., Zhou, X., Xu, M.: Artificial bee colony algorithm based on adaptive neighborhood search and Gaussian perturbation. Appl. Soft Comput. **100**, 106955 (2021)
32. Gao, W.F., Liu, S.Y.: A modified artificial bee colony algorithm. Comput. Oper. Res. **39**, 687–697 (2012)

Fuzzy Logic, Neuro-Fuzzy Systems, Decision Making, and Their Applications in Management Sciences

Active Learning Method Based on Axiomatic Fuzzy Sets and Cost-Sensitive Classification

Yifei Liu[1,2], Jiayi Guo[1], Shufan Li[1], and Lidong Wang[1(✉)]

[1] School of Science, Dalian Maritime University, Dalian, China
ldwang@dlmu.edu.cn
[2] Chifeng Erzhong International Experimental School, Chifeng, China

Abstract. Active learning has long been a research topic of machine learning. It aims to train a competitive classifier with a limited amount of labels. We design a novel approach in the study, which we refer to as active learning based on axiomatic fuzzy sets (AFS) and cost-sensitive classification. The classifier-based axiomatic fuzzy sets is employed as the benchmark classifier. The training data is transformed into some semantic rules for guiding the unlabeled instances to obtain class labels. To further improve the model's classification accuracy in terms of the test instances, the cost-sensitive method and mutual k-nearest neighbors are employed to select important instances, and these instances are put into the training set until all test instances have been labeled. Thirteen UCI data sets are used in the experimental study. The results suggest that our designed method keeps a well semantic description for classifier. Additionally, the practicality and effectiveness of this method are verified in misclassification and total teacher costs.

Keywords: Active learning · Axiomatic fuzzy sets · Semantic interpretation · Cost-sensitive

1 Introduction

Classification is an essential data mining technique used to identify group membership of data samples in knowledge discovery and pattern recognition. Due to regarding classification as a supervised learning process, we need to obtain the collected instances' labels by applying classical algorithms. We can easily obtain a large amount of unlabeled data, however many classic classification algorithms cannot be directly used in practice. One intuitive way to deal with this is to label the unlabeled instances. The accuracy of labelling is a direct factor affecting the quality of problem-solving. However, labeling these instances is a somewhat burdensome and expensive task in many practical applications of classification problems. The performance of the classifier may be promoted by only labeling the key instances instead of all instances and submitting them to the training set. Active learning [1] is an effective method for such issues, which can

© Springer Nature Singapore Pte Ltd. 2021
H. Zhang et al. (Eds.): NCAA 2021, CCIS 1449, pp. 501–515, 2021.
https://doi.org/10.1007/978-981-16-5188-5_36

effectively reduce the cost of building a high-performance classifier by selecting and marking the unlabeled instances that deserve to be learned actively.

Active learning covers two parts: learning (training) engine and selection strategy. The learning engine produces a baseline classifier with sound performance on the labeled instances which use supervised learning algorithms. The selection strategy is responsible for running the instance selection algorithms to select the unlabeled instances and add them to the training set after labeling them by experts. After several iterations, The performance of the classifier is gradually improved with several iterations when the predetermined conditions meet the process terminate.

The core issue of active learning is selection strategy. For selection algorithms, they can be divided into two types: stream-based and pool-based. In stream-based active learning, unlabeled instances are submitted to the selection strategy one by one in order, and the selection strategy enforces decision rights whether to label the currently offered instances in processes. If not, it will be discarded. Pool-based active learning keeps a pool of instances which is going to be labeled by using the selection strategy [2]. Query-by-committee approaches [3] build some randomly selected classifiers to comprise a committee and then choose the pool instances with the most significant divergence in prediction. Uncertainty sampling [4] often uses information entropy as a measure of information content in one instance. It selects the instance with the most considerable information entropy whose classification can not be determined using the current classifier.

Cost-sensitive learning [5] has caused tremendous repercussions of the fields of machine learning and data mining. Turney divides the costs in practical applications into nine types: misclassification costs, testing costs, teacher costs, intervention costs, computational costs, and so on. Cost-sensitive active learning [6] focuses on minimizing the total cost in developing classifier with active learning process. In cost-sensitive active learning, the primary objective is to keep balance between the misclassification costs with teacher costs which are paid for label queries [7].

The contribution of this study is to design an active learning method based on AFS (axiomatic fuzzy sets) and cost-sensitive active learning. AFS classifier is employed as the benchmark classifier so that each instance can acquire the correspondingly semantic description. To make full use of the unlabeled instances for training the designed model, the test instances certain conditions are added to the training set (training instance region); then the key instances are identified by the selection strategy and submitted to the training set (critical instance region); and the unlabeled instances continue to be tested as test instances (delayed instance region) until those are labeled. In the iteration process, the fuzzy description (fuzzy rule) of the instances will change according to the increase of training instances.

The remaining arrangements are as follows: Sect. 2 introduces relevant details and applications of AFS theory and cost-sensitive. In Sect. 3, a novel active learning classifier is designed by incorporating AFS fuzzy description and cost-sensitive. In Sect. 4, the experiment on iris data is conducted as an illustrative example, and the comparison between the proposed method and other classification methods are examined. Finally, Sect. 5 draws concluding remarks.

2   Preliminaries

For the sake of completeness of the designed active learning method, we recall the related definitions and theorems of AFS theory [8], cost-sensitive decision system [9], and mutual k-nearest neighbors [10–12].

2.1   AFS Algebra

Axiomatic fuzzy set (AFS) theory was coined by Liu [8], which offers a new way of determining membership functions and corresponding logical operations. Due to the capacity of generating sound semantic descriptions for data collection, AFS theory has witnessed great success in various fields, such as credit analysis [13], financial analysis [14,15], pattern recognition [16], etc. AFS classifier [17] aims on classifying the unlabeled instances by generating fuzzy semantic rules from training data.

Performs of the AFS framework depend heavily on its excellent lattice value representations and operation of fuzzy concepts by introducing AFS structure and AFS algebras. In the following Example 2.1, the description of televisions is employed to serve as an example of how AFS algebra can be defined and used.

Example 2.1: Let $U = \{u_1, u_2, u_3\}$ be a collection of three televisions. Each television is described by five features with numeric data (screen size, screen resolution and price), boolean value (speech recognition system) and order relation (dynamic response). The detailed information is displayed in Table 1.

Table 1. Information of TV.

u	Features				
	Screen size	Screen resolution	Speech recognition	Price	Dynamic response
u_1	55	1366 * 768	0	3869	1
u_2	65	1280 * 720	1	5069	3
u_3	75	1920 * 1080	1	9899	2

Let M be a collection of semantic terms (concepts) predefined on five features, including m_1 ("television with large size of screen"), m_2 ("television with high screen resolution"), m_3 ("television with sound speech recognition system"), m_4 ("television with reasonable price"), m_5 ("television with fast dynamic response"). For example, $\alpha = m_1 m_4 + m_2$ can be interpreted as "television with larger screen and reasonable price" or "television with high screen resolution". In AFS theory, each single semantic term, such as $m_i \in \{m_1, m_2, \cdots, m_5\}$ is simple concepts, and the logical expressions of simple concepts are regarded as complex concepts.

Complex concepts can be formed by "and" and "or" operation of simple concepts, which denote the set of all complex concepts as EM^*:

$$EM^* = \{\sum_{k \in K}(\prod_{m \in A_k} m) \mid A_k \subseteq M, \ K \text{ is any no empty indexing set}\}. \tag{1}$$

For $\sum_{k \in K}(\prod_{m \in A_k} m) \in EM^*$, $\prod_{m \in A_k} m$ denotes a complex concept generated from some simple concepts $m \in A_k$ under the operation "$\wedge$", $\sum_{k \in K}(\prod_{m \in A_k} m)$ is the disjunction of $\prod_{m \in A_k} m$ under the operation "$\vee$".

Definition 1 [18]. *Let M be a nonempty set. A binary relation $\mathcal{R}$ is defined on EM^*. For any $\sum_{j \in J}(\prod_{m \in A_j} m)$, $\sum_{k \in K}(\prod_{m \in B_k} m) \in EM^*$,*

$$[\sum_{j \in J}(\prod_{m \in A_j} m)]\mathcal{R}[\sum_{k \in K}(\prod_{m \in B_k} m)] \Longleftrightarrow$$
$$(i)\forall A_j(j \in J), \exists B_h(h \in K) \text{ such that } A_j \supseteq B_h; \tag{2}$$
$$(ii)\forall B_k(k \in K), \exists A_i(i \in J) \text{ such that } B_k \supseteq A_i.$$

In the above Definition 1, we can observe that $\mathcal{R}$ is an equivalence relation. Thus, $EM^*/\mathcal{R}$ is a quotient set, denoted as EM. $\sum_{j \in J}(\prod_{m \in A_j} m) = \sum_{k \in K}(\prod_{m \in B_k} m)$ indicates that $\sum_{j \in J}(\prod_{m \in A_j} m)$ and $\sum_{k \in K}(\prod_{m \in B_k} m)$ are equivalent under $\mathcal{R}$, for example $\beta = m_1 m_2 + m_1 m_2 m_3 + m_2 m_5 \in EM$ and $\gamma = m_1 m_2 + m_2 m_5 \in EM$ are equivalent in Example 2.1.

Theorem 1 [18]. *Let M be a nonempty set. The triple $(EM, \vee, \wedge)$ forms a completely distributive lattice under the following binary operations "$\vee$" and "$\wedge$": for any $\sum_{j \in J}(\prod_{m \in A_j} m)$, $\sum_{k \in K}(\prod_{m \in B_k} m) \in EM$,*

$$[\sum_{j \in J}(\prod_{m \in A_j} m)] \vee [\sum_{k \in K}(\prod_{m \in B_k} m)] = \sum_{i \in J \sqcup K}(\prod_{m \in C_i} m), \tag{3}$$

$$[\sum_{j \in J}(\prod_{m \in A_j} m)] \wedge [\sum_{k \in K}(\prod_{m \in B_k} m)] = \sum_{j \in J, k \in K}(\prod_{m \in A_j \sqcup B_k} m). \tag{4}$$

where for any $i \in J \sqcup K$, $C_i = A_i$ if $i \in J$, and $C_i = B_i$ if $i \in K$.

From Example 2.1, $\alpha = m_1 m_2 + m_3 m_5$ and $\beta = m_2 m_4$, by using Definition 1 and Theorem 1, we have (i) $\alpha \vee \beta = m_1 m_2 + m_3 m_5 + m_2 m_4$; (ii) $\alpha \wedge \beta = m_1 m_2 m_4 + m_2 m_3 m_4 m_5$.

2.2 AFS Membership Function

Liu proposed a method for generating the membership function which takes full advantage of the fusion of data distribution and subjective weight information [19].

Definition 2 [19]. *Assume that the probability measure space is* $(\Omega, \mathcal{F}, \mathcal{P})$, *where* $\Omega = R^n$, *$\mathcal{F}$ is all set of Borel sets in* Ω, *and* $\mathcal{P}$ *is the normal probability distribution. M denotes the set of simple concepts on* Ω, *and* ρ_α *is the corresponding weight function of* $\alpha \in M$. *For* $\zeta = \sum_{i \in I} (\prod_{m \in A_i} m)$, *it coherence membership function is defined as follows:*

$$\mu_\xi(x) = \sup_{i \in I} \prod_{\alpha \in A_i} \frac{\int_{A_i^\tau(x)} \rho_\alpha(t) d\mathcal{P}(t)}{\int_\Omega \rho_\alpha(t) d\mathcal{P}(t)}, \quad \forall x \in \Omega \tag{5}$$

where $A \subseteq M$, $A^\tau(x) = \{y \mid y \in \Omega, \tau(x,y) \supseteq A\}$, $\tau(x,y) = \{m \mid m \in M, x \leq_m y\}$.

2.3   Neighbor and Mutual Nearest Neighbor

Definition 3 [20]. *Let U be a collection of instances, $U_l \subseteq U$ be a set of the labeled instances, ξ_x represents the semantic description of the instance x. The set of k-nearest neighbors is defined as $NN^k(x)$ that satisfying the following relationships for any $x \in U - U_l$:*
1) $NN^k(x) \subseteq U_l$;
2) $|NN^k(x)| = k$;
3) $\forall y_1 \in NN^k(x)$ and $y_2 \in U_l - NN^k(x)$, $\mu_{\xi_x}(y_1) \geq \mu_{\xi_x}(y_2)$.
where $\mu_{\xi_x}(y_i)$ is membership degree of the instance y_i belonging to the description ξ_x.

In the traditional KNN method, the nearest neighbor of the instance is a one-way relationship. In fact, the information contained in the instances is mutual [21,22], so it need to identify whether the instance x and its neighbor are each other's nearest neighbors or not.

Definition 4 [12]. *Given the training instance $y_i \in U_l$ ($1 \leq i \leq N$) and the test instance x, y_i is regarded as a mutual nearest neighbor of the test instance x if the condition is satisfied:*

$$x \in NN^k(y_i) \vee y_i \in NN^k(x), \ 1 \leq i \leq N \tag{6}$$

where $NN^k(y_i)$ and $NN^k(x)$ are the neighborhood information of y_i and x, respectively.

2.4   Cost-Sensitive Decision System

Definition 5 [9]. *A cost-sensitive decision system is regarded as a 7-tuple:*

$$CS = (U, A_c, A_d, V, I, m_c, t_c) \tag{7}$$

where U denotes universe, A_c is the collection of conditional features and A_d represents the collection of class features, $V = \{V_a | a \in A_c \cup A_d\}$ is the collection of feature values, $I = \{I_a | a \in A_c \cup A_d\}$ denotes an information function, m_c represents the misclassification cost function, and t_c is the teacher costs.

In practice, it's expensive to determine the real class label of an instance. In active learning, the teacher cost t_c is the cost of obtaining the class label of an instance with experts judgement. In the study, the cost of asking a teacher to classify an instance is assumed to be the same for all instances. The misclassification cost is the weight of mistakenly allocating a class label to an instance.

2.5　Misclassification Cost Matrix

Suppose there are C classes. The misclassification cost is the cost of giving an instance with class label j when its actual class label is i. Let $cost(i, j)$, $(i, j \in 1, \cdots, C)$ denotes the cost of misclassifying an instance belonging to the i-th class to the j-th class $(cost(i, i) = 0)$. Table 2 lists a misclassification cost matrix, where the $cost(1, 2) = 60$ indicates the cost of misclassifying an instance belonging to class 1 to class 2 is 60.

Table 2. Misclassification cost matrix.

Prediction	Actual	
	Class 1	Class 2
Class 1	0	40
Class 2	60	0

2.6　Select Critical Instances

In this study, we select critical instances with cost-sensitive methods. We calculate the misclassification cost of the instances and arrange them in ascending order to select one or some critical instances to be added to the training instances. The misclassification cost associated with predicting $d(x)$ as l is defined as [9]:

$$m_c(x, NN^k(x), l) = \frac{\sum_{u \in NN^k(x)} cost(d(u), l)}{|NN^k(x)|} \tag{8}$$

where $cost(d(u), l)$ is determined according to Table 2, $|NN^k(x)|$ is the number of instances in $NN^k(x)$. The misclassification cost of instances is calculated and arranged in ascending order. The critical instances are one or several instances with the minimum misclassification cost.

3　The Designed Method

In this study, we design a novel active learning classification method by integrating AFS theory, mutual k-nearest neighbors and cost-sensitive strategy, named as CS-AFS-KNN-mul. The procedure of the designed method is portrayed in Fig. 1.

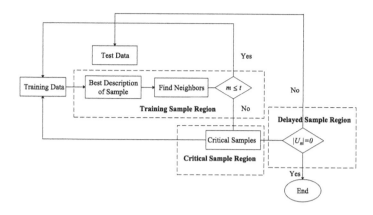

Fig. 1. The general structure of the designed classifier.

First, an AFS classifier is used to obtain three regions of test instances: training instance region (TS Region), critical instance region (CS Region), and delayed instance region (DS Region). TS Region contains the instances satisfying the condition that the misclassification cost is no more than the teacher cost, CS Region contains the instances manually labeled by the expert (automatic mechanism), and DS Region contains the delayed instances. Second, the labeled instances in TS Region and CS Region are put in the training set, and the process continues until all test instances are labeled. In this study, if the misclassification cost is no more than the teacher cost, the instance can be considered to be classified correctly. The corresponding procedure is exhibited in Algorithm 1.

In the training process (TS Region), we utilize AFS theory to generate the best semantic description of the instance through simple concepts predefined on each feature. The specific process of forming fuzzy description of training instances is shown in Algorithm 2. By Algorithm 2, all training instances can be equipped with the corresponding semantic description.

The membership degree of training instance $x_p \in X$ for simple concept $m_q \in M$ is calculated, where $\mu_\nu(x_p)$ in (9) indicates that x_p belongs to the maximum membership degree in the simple concept. In (10), $B_{x_p}^\varepsilon$ is a collection of selecting simple concepts, by which some complex concepts can be further obtained under the AFS logic operations and parameters θ_1, θ_2, then the optimal description of instances is generated under certain conditions.

In the testing stage, as (13), $T(y_i)$ represents the set of membership degrees of instance y_i belonging to the training instance description. According to (6), the mutual neighbors of the test instance are determined. The more instances the mutual neighbors contains, the more representative the selected neighbors are. For k neighbor instances of y_i, the misclassification cost of them is calculated by (8). The class label of instance is assigned by (15).

Algorithm 1. The description of instances

Require:

$X = \{x_p \in \mathbb{R}^d\}_{p=1}^n$: the training set with n instances.

$C = \{X_{\omega_1}, X_{\omega_2}, \cdots, X_{\omega_m}\}$, i.e., m class set.

$M = \{m_1, m_2, \cdots, m_l\}$: simple concept set.

$\varepsilon, \theta_1, \theta_2$: parameters.

Ensure: The descriptions ξ_x for training instances.

  step 1: Calculate the membership $\mu_{m_q}(x_p)$ of x_p belonging to each simple concept $m_q \in M$. Let

$$\mu_\vartheta(x_p) = \arg \max_{1 \leq q \leq l} \mu_{m_q}(x_p) \tag{9}$$

  step 2: Generate the fuzzy description of training set: $\xi_X = \{\xi_{x_p}\}_{p=1}^n$,

    for $x_p \in X$ **do**

$$B_{x_p}^\varepsilon = \{m_q \in M | \mu_{m_q}(x_p) \geq \mu_\vartheta(x_p) - \varepsilon\} \tag{10}$$

    for $x_p \in X_{\omega_i}, \forall y \in X - X_{\omega_i}$,

$$\Lambda_{x_p}^\varepsilon = \{\gamma | \gamma = \prod_{m \in H} m, H \subseteq B_{x_p}^\varepsilon; \ \mu_\gamma(x_p) \geq \theta_1; \ \mu_\gamma(y) < \theta_2\} \tag{11}$$

$$\xi_{x_p} = \arg \max_{\xi \in \Lambda_{x_p}^\varepsilon} \{\mu_\xi(x_p)\} \tag{12}$$

    end for

Generally, critical instances are selected and manually labeled by experts in active learning, the class labels obtained are accurate. In this study, the class labels of critical instances are obtained through (15), and the class labels obtained may not always be accurate. It takes human and material resources (cost) to carry out the instances of expert labels. The method in this paper reduces this cost, and the classification obtained through experimental verification has better performance, and the received categories have sound interpretability.

In the classification process of this study, we select a small part of instances as the training set (5-fold experiment, choose one fold as the training instances, and the rest is referred as the test instances). In each iteration, we add the predicted instances and selected key instances to the training set, update the rules, and continue to train the classifier. For active learning, we should not only pay attention to the classification performance of classifier, but also consider the cost of classification instances. We expect the total cost to be minimal, that is, $|U_{teacher}| \times t + \sum_{x \in U_{predict}} cost(c(x), d(x))$ to be minimal, where $|U_{teacher}| \times t$ is the total teacher cost and $\sum_{x \in U_{predict}} cost(c(x), d(x))$ is the total misclassification cost.

Algorithm 2. The designed classifier

Require:

$U_l = \{x_p \in \mathbb{R}^d\}_{p=1}^n$: the collection of n training instances.

$C = \{X_{\omega_1}, X_{\omega_2}, \cdots, X_{\omega_m}\}$: the data set with m categories.

$CS = (U, C, D, V, I, mis, t)$: a cost-sensitive decision system.

mis : the cost of misclassification.

t: teacher cost.

k : the size of neighborhood.

Ensure: The label of the test instance $y_i \in U_n$.

step 1: The fuzzy description ξ_{x_p} of the instance x_p is formed by using Algorithm 1.

step 2: For the test instance y_i, its membership degree belonging to the description of the training instances ξ_{x_p} is realized by (5). $T(y_i)$ is the group of membership degree.

$$T(y_i) = \{\mu_{\xi_{x_p}}(y_i)\}_{p=1}^n \qquad (13)$$

step 3: Search k mutual nearest neighbors of y according to (6), denote:

$$NN^k(y_i) = \{x_j\}_{j=1}^k \qquad (14)$$

step 4: For k mutual neighbor instances of y_i, the misclassification cost of them is calculated by formula (8).

    Repeat

    for each $NN^k(y_i)$ **do**

      if $mis(x, NN^k(y_i), l) \le t$ **then**

        label y_i with $d(y_i)$, $U_l = U_l \cup \{y_i\}$

$$d(y_i) = arg \min_{l \in D} mis(x, NN^k(y_i), l). \qquad (15)$$

      endif

    endfor

    Then find the critical instance by (8) and (11).

    Until $|U_n| = 0$.

4   Experiments

For examining the effectiveness of the designed method, some experiments are conducted on 13 data sets for comparing the designed method with AFS [17], F-DT (Fuzzy decision tree [23]) and AFS-DT (AFS decision tree [24]) classifier. The experimental data sets are collected from the UCI Machine Learning Repository [25], whose description information is listed in Table 3. The designed method is also compared with CS-AFS-KNN (AFS-KNN [20] incorporated with active learning) and CS-KNN [9] in terms of total misclassification cost and classification accuracy.

Table 3. Description of datasets.

Dataset	Domain	Sample size	Features	Classes
Abalone	Life	4177	8	3
Balance	Sociology	625	4	3
Bloods	Business	748	4	2
Breast(Prognostic)	Life	638	9	2
German	Finance	1000	20	2
Ionosphere	Physics	351	34	2
Iris	Botany	150	4	3
Seeds	Biology	210	7	3
Sonar	Physics	208	60	2
Vehicle	Traffic	946	18	4
WDBC	Life	569	30	2
Wine	Physics	178	13	3
WPBC	Life	194	34	2

4.1 Case Study

To briefly illustrate the designed method's procedure, we take the *Wisconsin Breast Cancer Diagnostic* data (cancer data) as an example. The cancer data set includes binary classes with 683 instances: *benign* and *malignant*. The first category (*benign*) includes 444 instances, and the second category (*malignant*) contains 273 instances. Each sample is described by using 9 features. In the 5-fold cross-validation experiment, 137 instances (class 1: 89, class 2: 48) are selected as the training set, and the remainder samples servers as the test objects. On each feature $f_i \in F$, we predefine 4 simple concepts: "small", "large" and their negation, that is, $M = \{m_{ij} | 1 \leq i \leq 9, 1 \leq j \leq 2\}$, where m_{i1}, m_{i2}, m_{i3} and m_{i4} are fuzzy concepts of "small", "large", "not small" and "not large" on feature f_i. The cost matrix is defines as Table 2, and the teacher cost takes $t = 10$.

By utilizing Definition 2, we can determine the membership of each simple concept and further generate the descriptions of instances by Algorithm 1. The obtained semantic descriptions for instances x_i ($i = 1, 2, \cdots, 137$) are shown as follows.

$$C_1 : \zeta_{x_1} = m_{21}m_{51}, \zeta_{x_2} = m_{14}m_{21}, \cdots, \zeta_{x_{88}} = m_{11}m_{31}, \zeta_{x_{89}} = m_{11}m_{31};$$
$$C_2 : \zeta_{x_{90}} = m_{13}m_{62}, \zeta_{x_{91}} = m_{42}m_{62}, \cdots, \zeta_{x_{136}} = m_{12}m_{22}, \zeta_{x_{137}} = m_{22}m_{42}.$$

For the test samples y_j ($j = 1, 2, \cdots, 546$), we compute the membership degrees of y_j that belongs to the description of x_i, and find k mutual nearest samples of y_j by (6). For example, when $k = 3$, $NN^3(y_1) = \{x_{96}, x_{93}, x_{103}\}; \cdots;$ $NN^3(y_{356}) = \{x_{98}, \cdots x_{120}, x_{137}\}; \cdots; NN^3(y_{546}) = \{x_{120}, x_{132}, x_{137}\}.$

The misclassification cost of these samples y_j ($j = 1, 2, \cdots, 546$) is calculated by (8) and (15). For example, the misclassification cost of sample y_1 is 0

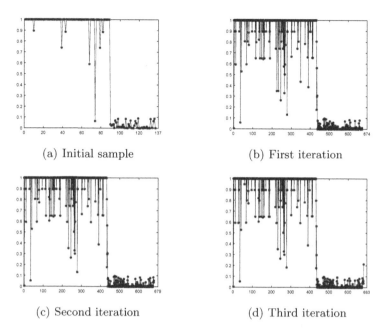

(a) Initial sample   (b) First iteration

(c) Second iteration   (d) Third iteration

Fig. 2. The membership of each class description of class 1 in each iteration (the number of training samples is 137, 674, 679, 683, respectively).

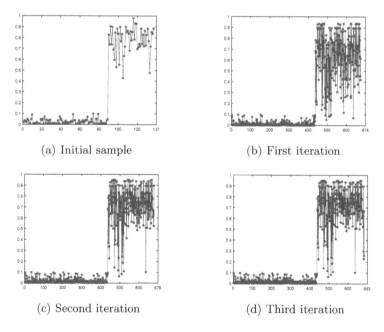

(a) Initial sample   (b) First iteration

(c) Second iteration   (d) Third iteration

Fig. 3. The membership of each class description of class 2 in each iteration (the number of training samples is 137, 674, 679, 683, respectively).

(the misclassification cost of y_1 belonging to the first category is 0, and the misclassification cost of y_1 belonging to the second category is 60), less than the teacher cost. In this case, we classify the sample y_1 into the first category, and add y_1 to the set of U_l. However, if the misclassification cost of a sample is more than the teacher cost, then it is added to CS Region. In this case, the critical sample $y_3, y_{32}, y_{370}, y_{375}, y_{480}, y_{498}, y_{539}$ (the misclassification cost is 20) are identified from the remaining samples. This process is repeated until all samples have been labeled, and this will create the variation of fuzzy rule description of different classes. Figure 2 and Fig. 3 show the membership grade of fuzzy description for each iteration for class 1 and class 2 respectively.

4.2   Experiment Results

Here the effectiveness is examined together with the comparative analysis between the proposed method and other pertinent algorithms (CS-AFS-KNN, CS-KNN [9], AFS [17], F-DT [23], AFS-DT [24]). The comparison results concerning the classification accuracies on different datasets are reported in Table 4 and Table 5. Table 4 exhibits the experimental comparisons between few classification methods with cost-sensitive and the designed methods in this study, and Table 5 shows the experimental results of AFS, F-DT and AFS-DT classification method by incorporating cost-sensitive strategy. Although the performance of CS-AFS-KNN-mul is not always the best, experimental results illustrate that this

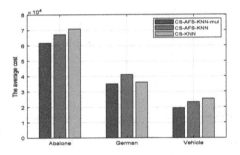

Fig. 4. Comparison of the average misclassification cost in 3 data sets.

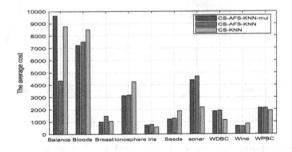

Fig. 5. Comparison of the average misclassification cost in 8 data sets.

Table 4. Comparison with the experimental results of other three methods.

Dataset	Cost	AFS	F-DT	AFS-DT	CS-AFS-KNN-MUL
Abalone	70: 30	0.6973	0.7065	0.7066	**0.7076**
Balance	40: 60	0.7575	0.6725	0.7042	**0.8384**
Blood	40: 60	0.7040	**0.7647**	0.7610	0.7569
Breast	60: 40	0.9597	0.9304	0.9381	**0.9608**
Ionosphere	40: 60	0.8605	0.7877	0.8013	**0.9004**
Iris	50: 50	0.9096	0.9096	**0.9437**	0.9222
German	40: 60	0.6386	**0.6946**	0.6641	0.6430
Seed	50: 50	0.8725	0.8677	0.8354	**0.8725**
Sonar	40: 60	0.4711	0.6935	0.6996	**0.7675**
Vehicle	40: 60	**0.5952**	0.5085	0.5244	0.5336
WDBC	60: 40	0.9138	0.9187	0.9052	**0.9235**
Wine	50: 50	0.9197	0.8469	0.8694	**0.9338**
WPBC	60: 40	0.6931	0.7010	0.6826	**0.7885**

Table 5. Comparison with two cost-sensitive classification methods.

Dataset	Cost	CS-AFS-KNN	CS-KNN	CS-AFS-KNN-MUL
Abalone	70: 30	0.6948	0.6920	**0.7076**
Balance	40: 60	**0.8899**	0.6216	0.8384
Blood	40: 60	0.7522	0.6970	**0.7569**
Breast	60: 40	0.9597	0.9534	**0.9608**
Ionosphere	40: 60	0.8996	0.8612	**0.9004**
Iris	50: 50	0.9119	**0.9489**	0.9222
German	40: 60	0.6350	0.6071	**0.6430**
Seed	50: 50	0.8651	0.8021	**0.8725**
Sonar	40: 60	0.7385	**0.8241**	0.7675
Vehicle	40: 60	0.4623	0.3907	**0.5336**
WDBC	60: 40	0.9169	0.9217	**0.9235**
Wine	50: 50	0.9338	0.9197	**0.9338**
WPBC	60: 40	0.7606	0.7646	**0.7885**

method has some advantages in terms of accuracy and class semantic description. Moreover, Fig. 4 and Fig. 5 show the comparison experiment of the average misclassification cost of 11 data sets in the other three methods. We can observe that the misclassification cost obtained by CS-AFS-KNN-mul is less than those of CS-KNN and CS-AFS-KNN on Abalone, Bloods, Breast, German, Ionosphere, Seeds and Vehicle data.

5   Conclusions

In this study, an active learning classification method based on cost-sensitive, mutual k-nearest neighbors and axiomatic fuzzy set theory is designed. The AFS classification method is employed as the benchmark classifier for generating semantic description for each class. According to the semantic rules, the unlabeled instances are added to the training set or selected as key instances that labeled by the expert's judgement. The experiment results indicate that the designed method outperforms CS-KNN and CS-AFS-KNN active learning methods in terms of the average cost. At the same time, our method can also achieve better classification accuracy by comparing with AFS, F-DT, AFS-DT, CS-KNN, and CS-AFS-KNN. Moreover, the designed method offers semantic interpretations to understand the classifier easily because of each instance's description. This study extends the active learning method, but how to simplify the fuzzy class description for reducing the complexity for large-scale datasets in terms of the number of features or samples is desired to study in the future.

Acknowledgements. This work is supported by the university-industry collaborative education program (No. 201902139012), and the innovation and entrepreneurship training program for college students (No. 202010151583).

References

1. Settles, B.: Active learning. In: Synthesis Lectures on Artificial Intelligence and Machine Learning, pp. 1–114 (2012)
2. Seung, H.S., Opper, M., Sompolinsky, H.: Query by committee. In: Proceedings of the ACM Workshop on Computational Learning Theory, pp. 287–294 (1992)
3. Cai, D., He, X.F.: Manifold adaptive experimental design for text categorization. IEEE Trans. Knowl. Data Eng. **24**(4), 707–719 (2012)
4. Ling, C.X., Sheng, V.S.: Cost-sensitive learning. In: Sammut, C., Webb, G.I. (eds.) Encyclopedia of Machine Learning and Data Mining, pp. 231–235. Springer, Boston (2017). https://doi.org/10.1007/978-0-387-30164-8_181
5. He, Y.-W., Zhang, H.-R., Min, F.: A teacher-cost-sensitive decision-theoretic rough set model. In: Ciucci, D., Wang, G., Mitra, S., Wu, W.-Z. (eds.) RSKT 2015. LNCS (LNAI), vol. 9436, pp. 275–285. Springer, Cham (2015). https://doi.org/10.1007/978-3-319-25754-9_25
6. Margineantu, D.D.: Active cost-sensitive learning. In: International Joint Conference on Artificial Intelligence, pp. 1622–1623 (2005)
7. Wu, Y.X., Min, X.Y., Min, F., Wang, M.: Cost-sensitive active learning with a label uniform distribution model. Int. J. Approximate Reasoning **105**, 49–65 (2019)
8. Liu, X.D.: The fuzzy sets and systems based on AFS structure, EI algebra and EII algebra. Fuzzy Sets Syst. **95**(2), 179–188 (1998)
9. Min, F., Liu, F.L., Wen, L.Y., Zhang, Z.H.: Tri-partition cost-sensitive active learning through kNN. Soft. Comput. **23**, 1557–1572 (2019)
10. Gou, J.P., Zhan, Y.Z., Rao, Y.B., Shen, X.J., Wang, X., Wu, H.: Improved pseudo nearest neighbor classification. Knowl. Based Syst. **70**, 361–375 (2014)

11. Gou, J.P., Ma, H.X., Ou, W.H., Zeng, S.N., Rao, Y.B., Yang, H.B.: A generalized mean distance-based k-nearest neighbor classifier. Expert Syst. Appl. **115**, 356–372 (2019)
12. Pan, Z.B., Wang, Y.D., Ku, W.P.: A new general nearest neighbor classification based on the mutual neighborhood information. Knowl. Based Syst. **121**, 142–152 (2017)
13. Liu, X., Liu, W.: Credit rating analysis with AFS fuzzy logic. In: Wang, L., Chen, K., Ong, Y.S. (eds.) ICNC 2005. LNCS, vol. 3612, pp. 1198–1204. Springer, Heidelberg (2005). https://doi.org/10.1007/11539902_152
14. Guo, H.Y., Pedrycz, W., Liu, X.D.: Fuzzy time series forecasting based on axiomatic fuzzy set theory. Neural Comput. Appl. **31**, 3921–3932 (2019)
15. Wang, W.N., Liu, X.D.: Fuzzy forecasting based on automatic clustering and axiomatic fuzzy set classification. Inf. Sci. **294**, 78–94 (2015)
16. Ren, Y., Li, Q.L., Liu, W.Q., Li, L.: Semantic facial descriptor extraction via axiomatic fuzzy set. Neurocomputing **171**, 1462–1474 (2016)
17. Liu, X.D., Liu, W.Q.: The framework of axiomatics fuzzy sets based fuzzy classifiers. J. Ind. Manag. Optim. **4**(3), 581–609 (2008)
18. Liu, X.D., Chai, T.Y., Wang, W., Liu, W.Q.: Approaches to the representations and logic operations of fuzzy concepts in the framework of axiomatic fuzzy set theory I, II. Inf. Sci. **177**(4), 1007–1026 (2007)
19. Liu, X.D.: The development of AFS theory under probability theory. Int. J. Inf. Syst. Sci. **3**(2), 326–348 (2007)
20. Liu, Y.F., Wang, X., Wang, L.D.: AFSKNN: classification method based on k-nearest neighbors and axiomatic fuzzy sets. In: 2019 IEEE 14th International Conference on Intelligent Systems and Knowledge Engineering (ISKE), pp. 1229–1234 (2019)
21. Ros, F., Guillaume, S.: Munec: a mutual neighbor-based clustering algorithm. Inf. Sci. **486**, 148–170 (2019)
22. Yang, K., Cai, Y., Cai, Z.W., Xie, H.R., Wong, T.L., Chan, W.H.: Top K representative: a method to select representative samples based on k-nearest neighbors. Int. J. Mach. Learn. Cybern. **10**(8), 2119–2129 (2017)
23. Yuan, Y., Shaw, M.J.: Induction of fuzzy decision trees. Fuzzy Sets Syst. **69**, 125–139 (1995)
24. Liu, X.D., Feng, X.H., Pedrycz, W.: Extraction of fuzzy rules from fuzzy decision trees: an axiomatic fuzzy sets (AFS) approach. Data Knowl. Eng. **84**, 1–25 (2013)
25. Dua, D., Graff, C.: UCI machine learning repository. University of California, School of Information and Computer Science, CA (2019). http://archive.ics.uci.edu/ml.Irvine

An Extended TODIM Method Based on Interval-Valued Pythagorean Hesitant Fuzzy Sets and Its Utilization in Green Shipping

Xueqin Liu[1], Junzhong Bao[2], Yanli Meng[3], and Lidong Wang[1(✉)]

[1] School of Science, Dalian Maritime University, Dalian, China
ldwang@dlmu.edu.cn
[2] Navigation College, Dalian Maritime University, Dalian, China
[3] School of Economics and Management, Beihang University, Beijing, China
yanlimeng@buaa.edu.cn

Abstract. With the proposal of a green shipping development strategy, the sustainable development of container ships has become a hot issue for shipping companies. In this study, an extended TODIM method is offered within interval-valued Pythagorean hesitant fuzzy sets and is used to select the ideal container ship. The Pythagorean hesitant fuzzy sets presented in the form of intervals can retain experts' uncertainty and hesitance to the greatest extent and reflect experts' approval and disapproval of container ships. The cosine similarity measure among interval-valued Pythagorean hesitant fuzzy sets is defined for measuring the similarity of any two alternatives. Finally, the evaluation of container ships in terms of the shipping economy, resource, and environmental factors is reported to support the reliability and validity of the designed evaluation method.

Keywords: Interval-valued Pythagorean hesitant fuzzy sets · Cosine similarity measure · TODIM method · Green shipping

1 Introduction

Green shipping is responded to sustainable development requirements, requiring shipping companies to coordinate shipping interests and the environment during operations. In practice, shipbuilding and large trade nation, experts and scholars appeal for speeding up green shipping development strategies [1]. This requires that modern shipping combines sustainable development with economic benefits based on careful consideration of shipping, economy, resource, and environment. Due to the greater significance of container transportation in shipping, it is necessary to evaluate and select the most satisfactory container ship before transport [2]. In the evaluation process, experts or managers from various fields are usually invited to form an evaluation group for offering personal comments on the predetermined alternatives under multiple attributes affecting container

© Springer Nature Singapore Pte Ltd. 2021
H. Zhang et al. (Eds.): NCAA 2021, CCIS 1449, pp. 516–529, 2021.
https://doi.org/10.1007/978-981-16-5188-5_37

ships. For this reason, this evaluation problem can be treated as a multi-attribute group decision-making problem (MAGDM). Because of the evaluation environment's complexity, the uncertainty involved during the evaluation is inevitable. Choosing the description of uncertainty and an appropriate evaluation model to solve this problem is drawing more attention.

MAGDM helps us make decisions by employing certain model established on evaluation information, thereby selecting the ideal ones. Fuzzy sets and their extensions lay a foundation for the development of MAGDM in the complex evaluation environment. Zadeh [3] proposed the fuzzy set theory, which employs membership functions to indicate uncertain information that cannot be quantitatively described. On this basis, the intuitionistic fuzzy set (IFS) [4] is proposed, which can more accurately represent and deal with inaccurate and fuzzy information in certain evaluation problems. However, IFS is subject to the condition that the sum of membership value and non-membership value is not greater than 1. Yager [5,6] proposed the Pythagorean fuzzy sets (PFSs), which has a wide range of applications and is suitable for situations where the sum of the membership value's squares and the non-membership value's squares is not greater than 1. It further expanded the application scope of fuzzy theory compared with IFS. Subsequently, Liu et al. [7] proposed the Pythagorean hesitant fuzzy sets (PHFSs) combining PFS with hesitation fuzzy sets, which can effectively depict experts' hesitation on determining the membership and non-membership degree and reflect the uncertainty of expert preferences. Furthermore, owing to the complexity of practical matters, it is difficult for experts to quantify their opinions accurately with a precise value. Zhang et al. [8] proposed the interval-valued Pythagorean hesitant fuzzy sets (IVPHFSs) to acquire better storage of information and improve its flexibility and applicability, which allowed each alternative's preference values equipped with several possible pairs of interval-valued Pythagorean fuzzy elements. This method not only takes the experts' uncertainty into account but also pays attention to their hesitation so that the results are consistent with their opinions to the greatest extent.

For solving practical decision-making problems, many classical methods are further developed under an uncertain environment, including TOPSIS [9–11], VIKOR [12], ELECTRE [13,14], PROMETHEE [15], etc. The TODIM method, coined by Gomes [16,17] based on the prospect theory, can fully reflect experts' risk preferences and minimize potential risks to help them achieve more satisfactory results. Establishing the dominance function of each alternative over other alternatives based on the prospect theory's value function is the core idea of the TODIM method, which can identify the suitable alternative according to the obtained dominance degree. For instance, Mirnezami [18] designed a novel TODIM approach based on the type-2 fuzzy extension to select the best scenario. Zhang [19] applied the TODIM method based on PHFS to assess the quality of service of airlines.

In some practices, it is more reasonable to determine evaluation preferences in the form of intervals. This study extends the TODIM method to the uncertain context with interval-valued Pythagorean hesitant fuzzy terms for expressing and processing complex evaluation information. Considering experts' hesitations and risk attitude in the evaluation process, an interval-valued Pythagorean hesitant fuzzy TODIM method is designed to solve the selection of container ships in the MAGDM environment. The advantages of the designed method are summarized as follows:

- The cosine similarity measure IVPHFS is defined to calculate the relevance degree between alternatives, which can reflect the differences of the alternatives.
- An extended TODIM method is designed under the IVPHFS context, which takes the risk preferences of expert panels into full consideration in the selection of container ships under multiple attributes.

The paper is structured as follows. Section 2 summarizes the IVPHFS and the classical TODIM method. In Sect. 3, the cosine similarity measure of IVPHFS is defined, and their related properties are demonstrated. Section 4 designs an interval-valued Pythagorean hesitant fuzzy TODIM method. Consequently, the proposed method is applied to solve the operation alternatives of container ships and illustrates the practicability and feasibility in Sect. 5. Finally, the conclusion is presented in Sect. 6.

2   Preliminaries

This section summarizes basic definitions of the IVPHFS and briefly reviews the classical TODIM method.

2.1   Interval-Valued Pythagorean Hesitant Fuzzy Sets

Definition 1. [8]. *An interval-valued Pythagorean hesitant fuzzy set (IVPHFS) $\tilde{\mathscr{P}}$ on U can be expressed by*

$$\tilde{\mathscr{P}} = \left\{ \left\langle x, \left(\tilde{\mu}_{\mathscr{P}}(x), \tilde{\nu}_{\mathscr{P}}(x) \right) \right\rangle \middle| x \in U \right\},$$

where $\tilde{\mu}_{\mathscr{P}}(x)$ and $\tilde{\nu}_{\mathscr{P}}(x)$ are the possible membership degree and non-membership values of $\tilde{\mathscr{P}}$ at x respectively, $\tilde{\mu}_{\mathscr{P}}(x) = [\mu_{\mathscr{P}}^-(x), \mu_{\mathscr{P}}^+(x)] \in D[0,1]$, $\tilde{\nu}_{\mathscr{P}}(x) = [\nu_{\mathscr{P}}^-(x), \nu_{\mathscr{P}}^+(x)] \in D[0,1]$, $\left(\left(\mu_{\mathscr{P}}^+(x) \right)^2 + \left(\nu_{\mathscr{P}}^+(x) \right)^2 \right) \leq 1$. The possible hesitation degree $\tilde{\pi}_{\mathscr{P}}(x) = \sqrt{1 - \left(\tilde{\mu}_{\mathscr{P}}(x) \right)^2 - \left(\tilde{\nu}_{\mathscr{P}}(x) \right)^2}$ and $\tilde{\pi}_{\mathscr{P}}(x) = [\pi_{\mathscr{P}}^-(x), \pi_{\mathscr{P}}^+(x)] \in D[0,1]$.

To facilitate comparing the fuzzy elements of the IVPHFS, the function of score and accuracy [8] can be used for comparison. The score function is the average of the difference between the possible membership and non-membership degree interval. By contrast, the accuracy function indicates the entire accuracy degree of fuzzy elements.

Definition 2. *Let* $\mathscr{P} = \left\{ \langle \widetilde{\mu}_{\mathscr{P}}(x), \widetilde{\nu}_{\mathscr{P}}(x) \rangle \big| \widetilde{\mu}_{\mathscr{P}}(x) = [\mu^-, \mu^+], \widetilde{\nu}_{\mathscr{P}}(x) = [\nu^-, \nu^+] \right\}$
be an IPHFE. The score function and accuracy function is defined as follows:

$$
\begin{aligned}
S(\mathscr{P}) &= \frac{1}{2p} \sum_{\langle \widetilde{\mu}, \widetilde{\nu} \rangle \in \mathscr{P}} (\widetilde{\mu}_{\mathscr{P}}^2 - \widetilde{\nu}_{\mathscr{P}}^2) \\
&= \left[\frac{1}{2p} \sum_{\langle \widetilde{\mu}, \widetilde{\nu} \rangle \in \mathscr{P}} ((\mu^-)^2 - (\nu^+)^2), \frac{1}{2p} \sum_{\langle \widetilde{\mu}, \widetilde{\nu} \rangle \in \mathscr{P}} ((\mu^+)^2 - (\nu^-)^2) \right], \\
H(\mathscr{P}) &= \frac{1}{2p} \sum_{\langle \widetilde{\mu}, \widetilde{\nu} \rangle \in \mathscr{P}} (\widetilde{\mu}_{\mathscr{P}}^2 + \widetilde{\nu}_{\mathscr{P}}^2) \\
&= \left[\frac{1}{2p} \sum_{\langle \widetilde{\mu}, \widetilde{\nu} \rangle \in \mathscr{P}} ((\mu^-)^2 + (\nu^+)^2), \frac{1}{2p} \sum_{\langle \widetilde{\mu}, \widetilde{\nu} \rangle \in \mathscr{P}} ((\mu^+)^2 + (\nu^-)^2) \right],
\end{aligned}
\tag{1}
$$

where p represents the number of the possible interval-valued Pythagorean fuzzy numbers (IVPFNs), and the larger p is, the more hesitant degree of the experts' preference is.

The score and accuracy function can be used to compare the priorities between any two IVPHFEs.

Theorem 1. [8] *Let* $\mathscr{P}_1$ *and* $\mathscr{P}_2$ *be two IVPHFEs,*

(1) when $Q\big(S(\mathscr{P}_1) > S(\mathscr{P}_2)\big) < 0.5$, $\mathscr{P}_1 \prec \mathscr{P}_2$;
(2) when $Q\big(S(\mathscr{P}_1) > S(\mathscr{P}_2)\big) = 0.5$,
    (a) if $Q\big(H(\mathscr{P}_1) > H(\mathscr{P}_2)\big) < 0.5$, *then we can obtain* $\mathscr{P}_1 \prec \mathscr{P}_2$;
    (b) if $Q\big(H(\mathscr{P}_1) > H(\mathscr{P}_2)\big) = 0.5$, *then we can obtain* $\mathscr{P}_1 = \mathscr{P}_2$.

where $Q\big(S(\mathscr{P}_1), S(\mathscr{P}_2)\big) = \max\left\{ 1 - \max\left\{ \frac{S(\mathscr{P}_1)^+ - S(\mathscr{P}_2)^-}{l\big(S(\mathscr{P}_2)\big) + l\big(S(\mathscr{P}_1)\big)}, 0 \right\}, 0 \right\}$ *is derived from the possibility degree* [20] *and* $l\big(S(\mathscr{P})\big) = S(\mathscr{P})^+ - S(\mathscr{P})^-$.

2.2 The Classical TODIM Method

The TODIM method is an effective decision-making tool based on prospect theory, which is used to handle MAGDM problems and capture experts' psychological behavior in the actual evaluation process. By constructing the prospect value function, the degree of dominance of each alternative over the others can be measured, and then its ranking can be determined based on the overall dominance of entire alternatives. The basic steps of the classical TODIM method [21] can be summarized as follows:

Step 1: Collect evaluation matrices and determine the weights of attributes.
Step 2: Determine alternative's dominance degree under individual attribute.
Step 3: Obtain the overall dominance of each alternative under all attributes.
Step 4: Compute each alternative's overall prospect value and rank them on this basis.

3   Cosine Similarity Measure of Interval-Valued Pythagorean Hesitant Fuzzy Sets

In some studies of the TODIM method [22,23], the Euclidean distance measure is usually used when calculating the dominance of the alternative to obtain the difference degree between them, and the Euclidean distance measure focuses on the absolute difference in numerical features. Compared with the Euclidean distance measure, the cosine similarity measure pays more attention to the dimensional difference. The cosine similarity measure uses the cosine value of the angle between two vectors in the vector space to reflect the difference between them. The IVPHFS also considers both the membership and non-membership characteristics, which fully reflects the difference of the alternatives. In view of this, we define the cosine similarity measure of IVPHFS and examine their properties based on the above definitions and the properties of the cosine function for subsequent operations.

Definition 3. *Let* $\mathscr{P}_1 = \left\{ \langle \tilde{\mu}_{\mathscr{P}_1}, \tilde{\nu}_{\mathscr{P}_1} \rangle \big| \tilde{\mu}_{\mathscr{P}_1} = [\mu^-_{\mathscr{P}_1}, \mu^+_{\mathscr{P}_1}], \tilde{\nu}_{\mathscr{P}_1} = [\nu^-_{\mathscr{P}_1}, \nu^+_{\mathscr{P}_1}] \right\}$ *and* $\mathscr{P}_2 = \left\{ \langle \tilde{\mu}_{\mathscr{P}_2}, \tilde{\nu}_{\mathscr{P}_2} \rangle \big| \tilde{\mu}_{\mathscr{P}_2} = [\mu^-_{\mathscr{P}_2}, \mu^+_{\mathscr{P}_2}], \tilde{\nu}_{\mathscr{P}_2} = [\nu^-_{\mathscr{P}_2}, \nu^+_{\mathscr{P}_2}] \right\}$ *are any two IVPHFEs. The cosine similarity measure for* $\mathscr{P}_1$ *and* $\mathscr{P}_2$ *is defined as follows:*

$$\cos(\mathscr{P}_1, \mathscr{P}_2) = \frac{\sum_{i=1}^{p} \sum_{j=1}^{q} \frac{1}{p \times q} [\mu^-_{\mathscr{P}_1,i} \mu^-_{\mathscr{P}_2,j} + \nu^-_{\mathscr{P}_1,i} \nu^-_{\mathscr{P}_2,j} + \mu^+_{\mathscr{P}_1,i} \mu^+_{\mathscr{P}_2,j} + \nu^+_{\mathscr{P}_1,i} \nu^+_{\mathscr{P}_2,j}]}{\sqrt{\sum_{i=1}^{p} \frac{1}{p^2} \left((\mu^-_{\mathscr{P}_1,i})^2 + (\mu^+_{\mathscr{P}_1,i})^2 + (\nu^-_{\mathscr{P}_1,i})^2 + (\nu^+_{\mathscr{P}_1,i})^2 \right)}}$$

$$\times \frac{1}{\sqrt{\sum_{j=1}^{q} \frac{1}{q^2} \left((\mu^-_{\mathscr{P}_2,j})^2 + (\mu^+_{\mathscr{P}_2,j})^2 + (\nu^-_{\mathscr{P}_2,j})^2 + (\nu^+_{\mathscr{P}_2,j})^2 \right)}},$$

$$(2)$$

where p *and* q *denote the number of possible IVPFNs in element* $\mathscr{P}_1$ *and* $\mathscr{P}_2$.

Obviously, when $\cos(\mathscr{P}_1, \mathscr{P}_2) = 1$, it indicates that fuzzy element $\mathscr{P}_1$ is as important as fuzzy element $\mathscr{P}_2$. When $\cos(\mathscr{P}_1, \mathscr{P}_2)$ is less than 1, it manifests a difference between two fuzzy elements where the smaller the value is, the more significant the difference is. The cosine similarity measure can calculate the similarity of any two IVPHFEs from vectors perspectively, reducing the normalization of the data and facilitating the selection of alternatives. Based on the cosine similarity measure of IVPHFS, some properties can be obtained as follows.

Property 1: (Reflexivity). When $\mathscr{P}_1 = \mathscr{P}_2$, we can obtain $\cos(\mathscr{P}_1, \mathscr{P}_2) = 1$; similarly, when $\cos(\mathscr{P}_1, \mathscr{P}_2) = 1$, if and only if $\mathscr{P}_1 = \mathscr{P}_2$.

Proof.

$$\cos(\mathscr{P}_1, \mathscr{P}_2) = \cos(\mathscr{P}_1, \mathscr{P}_1)$$

$$= \frac{\sum_{i=1}^{p}\sum_{i=1}^{p}\frac{1}{p\times p}[\mu^-_{\mathscr{P}_{1,i}}\mu^-_{\mathscr{P}_{1,i}} + \nu^-_{\mathscr{P}_{1,i}}\nu^-_{\mathscr{P}_{1,i}} + \mu^+_{\mathscr{P}_{1,i}}\mu^+_{\mathscr{P}_{1,i}} + \nu^+_{\mathscr{P}_{1,i}}\nu^+_{\mathscr{P}_{1,i}}]}{\sqrt{\sum_{i=1}^{p}\frac{1}{p^2}((\mu^-_{\mathscr{P}_{1,i}})^2 + (\mu^+_{\mathscr{P}_{1,i}})^2 + (\nu^-_{\mathscr{P}_{1,i}})^2 + (\nu^+_{\mathscr{P}_{1,i}})^2)}}$$

$$\times \frac{1}{\sqrt{\sum_{i=1}^{p}\frac{1}{p^2}((\mu^-_{\mathscr{P}_{1,i}})^2 + (\mu^+_{\mathscr{P}_{1,i}})^2 + (\nu^-_{\mathscr{P}_{1,i}})^2 + (\nu^+_{\mathscr{P}_{1,i}})^2)}}$$

$$= \frac{\sum_{i=1}^{p}\frac{1}{p^2}[\mu^-_{\mathscr{P}_{1,i}}\mu^-_{\mathscr{P}_{1,i}} + \nu^-_{\mathscr{P}_{1,i}}\nu^-_{\mathscr{P}_{1,i}} + \mu^+_{\mathscr{P}_{1,i}}\mu^+_{\mathscr{P}_{1,i}} + \nu^+_{\mathscr{P}_{1,i}}\nu^+_{\mathscr{P}_{1,i}}]}{\sum_{i=1}^{p}\frac{1}{p^2}((\mu^-_{\mathscr{P}_{1,i}})^2 + (\mu^+_{\mathscr{P}_{1,i}})^2 + (\nu^-_{\mathscr{P}_{1,i}})^2 + (\nu^+_{\mathscr{P}_{1,i}})^2)}$$

$$= 1.$$

Property 2: (Boundedness). For the cosine similarity measure between any two IVPHFEs, its range conforms to the property of cosine function and lies between $[0, 1]$, that is, for any $\mathscr{P}_1, \mathscr{P}_2$, then $0 \leq \cos(\mathscr{P}_1, \mathscr{P}_2) \leq 1$.

Property 3: (Commutativity). For any two IVPHFEs, $\mathscr{P}_1$ and $\mathscr{P}_2$, there is $\cos(\mathscr{P}_1, \mathscr{P}_2) = \cos(\mathscr{P}_2, \mathscr{P}_1)$.

Proof.

$$\cos(\mathscr{P}_1, \mathscr{P}_2) = \frac{\sum_{i=1}^{p}\sum_{j=1}^{q}\frac{1}{p\times q}[\mu^-_{\mathscr{P}_{1,i}}\mu^-_{\mathscr{P}_{2,j}} + \nu^-_{\mathscr{P}_{1,i}}\nu^-_{\mathscr{P}_{2,j}} + \mu^+_{\mathscr{P}_{1,i}}\mu^+_{\mathscr{P}_{2,j}} + \nu^+_{\mathscr{P}_{1,i}}\nu^+_{\mathscr{P}_{2,j}}]}{\sqrt{\sum_{i=1}^{p}\frac{1}{p^2}((\mu^-_{\mathscr{P}_{1,i}})^2 + (\mu^+_{\mathscr{P}_{1,i}})^2 + (\nu^-_{\mathscr{P}_{1,i}})^2 + (\nu^+_{\mathscr{P}_{1,i}})^2)}}$$

$$\times \frac{1}{\sqrt{\sum_{j=1}^{q}\frac{1}{q^2}((\mu^-_{\mathscr{P}_{2,j}})^2 + (\mu^+_{\mathscr{P}_{2,j}})^2 + (\nu^-_{\mathscr{P}_{2,j}})^2 + (\nu^+_{\mathscr{P}_{2,j}})^2)}}$$

$$= \cos(\mathscr{P}_2, \mathscr{P}_1).$$

4 Solving Multi-attribute Group Decision-Making Problem Based on Extended TODIM Method

Based on the classical TODIM method and cosine similarity measure, in this section, an interval-valued Pythagorean hesitant fuzzy TODIM method is designed to handle the MAGDM issue, and the introduction of its steps is given in detail.

4.1　The Extended TODIM Method

In the classical TODIM method [24], any two alternatives' dominance degree is measured by using the evaluation values of their comparison in the preference matrix. Based on the preference matrix in the form of IVPHFSs (which determines evaluation values for alternatives from the perspectives of approval and disapproval), we use the cosine similarity measure to improve the classical TODIM method. It can have a better performance in the similarity differences among the alternatives.

Here, to facilitate the subsequent description, suppose n alternatives $X = \{x_1, x_2, \ldots, x_n\}$, m attributes $C = \{c_1, c_2, \ldots, c_m\}$, and $E = \{e_1, e_2, \ldots, e_d\}$ is a finite set of d experts. Evaluation matrices of alternatives under individual attribute are provided in the form of IVPHFSs, that is, $\boldsymbol{P}^{(l)} = [\mathscr{P}_{i,k}]_{n \times m}^{(l)}$ denotes the opinion of each expert e_l. The dominance of alternative x_i for each alternative x_j under attribute c_k based on the cosine similarity measure is defined as below:

$$\phi_k(x_i, x_j) = \begin{cases} \sqrt{w_{c_k} \cdot \cos_{c_k}(\mathscr{P}_{i,k}, \mathscr{P}_{j,k})}, & \text{if } \mathscr{P}_{i,k} > \mathscr{P}_{j,k}, \\ 0, & \text{if } \mathscr{P}_{i,k} = \mathscr{P}_{j,k}, \\ -\frac{1}{\theta}\sqrt{w_{c_k} \cdot \cos_{c_k}(\mathscr{P}_{i,k}, \mathscr{P}_{j,k})}, & \text{otherwise,} \end{cases} \tag{3}$$

where w_{c_k} presents the weight of attribute c_k and θ is the predefined attenuation coefficient. The value θ can reflect the expert's risk psychology, the smaller the value, indicating that the expert pays more attention to the inadequacy of the alternative during the selection process. Correspondingly, we can consider three situations including the gain, neutrality, and loss of the alternative x_i when choosing the alternative x_i and x_j. For example, when the attenuation coefficient θ is 1, it reflects the expert's risk-neutral behavior; that is, the importance of the gain and loss of choosing the alternative x_i or x_j is equal.

The magnitude relationship of the evaluation values $\mathscr{P}_{i,k}$ and $\mathscr{P}_{j,k}$ between alternatives x_i and x_j can be calculated by Definition 1. The function $\cos_{c_k}^{(l)}(\mathscr{P}_{i,k}, \mathscr{P}_{j,k})$ represents the cosine similarity measure between any two alternatives x_i and x_j under attribute c_k, and w_k denotes the weight of attribute c_k. Because $\mathscr{P}_{i,k} > \mathscr{P}_{j,k}$ denotes that alternative x_i is better than alternative x_j under attribute c_k, $\phi_k(x_i, x_j)$ indicates a benefit value for alternative x_i under the attribute c_k. On the contrary, when $\mathscr{P}_{i,k} < \mathscr{P}_{j,k}$, $\phi_k(x_i, x_j)$ denotes a benefit value for alternative x_j under the attribute c_k. Then, considering the sum of the beneficial values for alternative x_i over other alternatives, the overall dominance of alternative x_i is defined as follows:

$$\delta^{(l)}(x_i, x_j) = \sum_{k=1}^{m} \phi_k^{(l)}(x_i, x_j). \tag{4}$$

In the sequel, we employ the improved TODIM method to settle practical MAGDM problems and the operation steps are described in detail below.

4.2 Operation Steps of the Designed Method

Step 1: In complex evaluation environments, to reflect the hesitation of experts and the degree of approval or disapproval of the alternatives better, experts are suggested to give preference matrices in the form of IVPHFSs.

$$\boldsymbol{P}^{(l)} = [\mathscr{P}_{i,k}]_{n \times m}^{(l)} = \left[\langle [\mu_{\mathscr{P}_k}^-(x_i), \mu_{\mathscr{P}_k}^+(x_i)], [\nu_{\mathscr{P}_k}^-(x_i), \nu_{\mathscr{P}_k}^+(x_i)] \rangle \right]_{n \times m}^{(l)},$$

$$l = 1, 2, \ldots, d, \ \ k = 1, 2, \ldots, m, \ \ i = 1, 2, \ldots, n,$$

where $\mathscr{P}_{i,k}$ is the preference value of the ith alternative under the kth attribute. Based on Theorem 1, comparative relationship matrix $\boldsymbol{Q}_{c_k}^{(l)} = (Q_{ij})_{n \times n}^{(l)}$ can be obtained by IVPHFEs, which expresses the magnitude of any two alternatives under the same attribute.

In addition, the attributes' weights can be obtained in the form of a reciprocal matrix by comparison in advance and then calculated by the geometric mean method (GM) [25], denoted as $\boldsymbol{w}_c = (w_{c_1}, w_{c_2}, \ldots, w_{c_m})$.

Step 2: The cosine similarity measure matrix $\mathbf{cos}_{c_k}^{(l)}$ of each expert for alternatives under attributes can be calculated by Eq. (2), where $\cos(\mathscr{P}_{i,k}, \mathscr{P}_{j,k})$ represents the cosine similarity measure between alternative x_i and alternative x_j under the attribute c_k. There are n alternatives and m attributes; m symmetric matrices of $n \times n$ dimensions can be obtained.

Step 3: The comparative value of the dominance degree $\phi_k^{(l)}(x_i, x_j)$ of each expert e_l to alternative x_i and x_j under attribute c_k is obtained by using Eq. (3). Then, based on Eq. (4), the dominance matrix $\boldsymbol{\delta}^{(l)}$ among alternatives under all attributes for each expert e_l can be computed as follows:

$$\boldsymbol{\delta}^{(l)} = \begin{pmatrix} 0 & \delta_{12} & \cdots & \delta_{1n} \\ \delta_{21} & 0 & \cdots & \delta_{2n} \\ \vdots & \vdots & \ddots & \vdots \\ \delta_{n1} & \delta_{n2} & \cdots & 0 \end{pmatrix}^{(l)},$$

where $\delta_{ij} = -\delta_{ji}$, and when this value δ_{ij} is higher, it indicates that the greater the difference in the degree of dominance between the two alternatives is, the better the corresponding alternative x_i is.

Step 4: Considering the experts' different weights, it is essential to summarize all experts' opinions to form an aggregation matrix $\bar{\boldsymbol{\delta}} = (\bar{\delta}_{ij})_{n \times m}$ to obtain the overall evaluation results of alternatives. In this regard, we use the goal programming method to obtain the aggregation matrix, which is obtained by minimizing the differences between the aggregation matrix and the corresponding terms in the dominance matrix of alternatives obtained by experts.

$$\min \sum_{l=1}^{d} \omega_l \left(\bar{\delta}(x_i, x_j) - \delta^{(l)}(x_i, x_j) \right)^2$$

$$\begin{cases} \bar{\delta}(x_i, x_j) \leq \max_{l} \left(\delta^{(l)}(x_i, x_j) \right), \\ \bar{\delta}(x_i, x_j) \geq \min_{l} \left(\delta^{(l)}(x_i, x_j) \right), \ l = 1, 2, \ldots, d, \end{cases} \tag{5}$$

where ω_l represents the weight of expert d_l and $\sum_{l=1}^{d} \omega_l = 1$. For constraints, the purpose is to ensure that the obtained optimization results comply with the experts' opinions to a certain extent; that is, each term in the matrix is within the range of the corresponding preference values given by the expert.

Step 5: Calculate each alternative's overall prospect value, which is shown as follows:

$$\varepsilon_i = \frac{\sum_{j=1}^{n} \bar{\delta}(x_i, x_j) - \min_{i} \sum_{j=1}^{n} \bar{\delta}(x_i, x_j)}{\max_{i} \sum_{j=1}^{n} \bar{\delta}(x_i, x_j) - \min_{i} \sum_{j=1}^{n} \bar{\delta}(x_i, x_j)}, \ i = 1, 2, \ldots, n. \tag{6}$$

Finally, we can rank the alternatives based on their overall prospect values ε_i, and then pick on the ideal one.

5   Numerical Study

To illustrate the designed evaluation method, an application example is described in this section. Under the green shipping development strategy requirements, a shipping company proposes four different alternatives for the operation of container ships, which are denoted as $X = \{x_1, x_2, x_3, x_4\}$. Many experts from different industries are invited to form groups based on different industries, and then form an evaluation team, $E = \{e_1, e_2, e_3\}$, with prioritization relation $e_1 = e_2 = e_3$. Group e_1 is composed of five captains with rich navigation experience, group e_2 is five senior PSC inspectors with rich work experience, and group e_3 is five ship business supervisors. Experts need to evaluate according to three fuzzy attributes: c_1 represents the better shipping economy, that is income situation; c_2 denotes the abundant shipping resource, that is transportation technology capability; c_3 is the favorable shipping environment, that is environmental protection ability. Based on the above information, experts give their evaluation preferences of these container ships.

This section is divided into three parts. The first part uses the proposed method to rank the container ships and finds the ideal one. The second part compares the above results with the improved TODIM method based on Euclidean distance and proves the feasibility of this method. Finally, in the TODIM method, sensitivity analysis is performed on the attenuation coefficient θ to obtain its influence on the ranking of the alternatives.

Table 1. The evaluation preference matrix $\boldsymbol{P}^{(1)}$ from group e_1.

e_1	c_1	c_2	c_3
x_1	$\{\langle[0.4,0.5],[0.3,0.5]\rangle\}$	$\{\langle[0.2,0.3],[0.6,0.8]\rangle\}$	$\{\langle[0.6,0.8],[0.1,0.3]\rangle,$ $\langle[0.6,0.7],[0.3,0.3]\rangle,$ $\langle[0.7,0.9],[0.1,0.1]\rangle\}$
x_2	$\{\langle[0.1,0.1],[0.8,0.9]\rangle$ $\langle[0.2,0.4],[0.5,0.6]\rangle\}$	$\{\langle[0.4,0.5],[0.5,0.5]\rangle$ $\langle[0.6,0.7],[0.1,0.2]\rangle$ $\langle[0.6,0.7],[0.1,0.3]\rangle\}$	$\{\langle[0.8,0.9],[0.1,0.2]\rangle\}$
x_3	$\{\langle[0.2,0.3],[0.6,0.6]\rangle\}$	$\{\langle[0.8,0.9],[0.1,0.1]\rangle$ $\langle[0.3,0.4],[0.5,0.6]\rangle\}$	$\{\langle[0.3,0.5],[0.4,0.4]\rangle\}$
x_4	$\{\langle[0.1,0.4],[0.6,0.7]\rangle\}$	$\{\langle[0.3,0.4],[0.5,0.6]\rangle$ $\langle[0.2,0.3],[0.6,0.6]\rangle\}$	$\{\langle[0.6,0.8],[0.2,0.3]\rangle\}$

Table 2. The evaluation preference matrix $\boldsymbol{P}^{(2)}$ from group e_2.

e_2	c_1	c_2	c_3
x_1	$\{\langle[0.7,0.9],[0.1,0.2]\rangle,$ $\langle[0.7,0.8],[0.1,0.2]\rangle,$ $\langle[0.6,0.8],[0.1,0.1]\rangle\}$	$\{\langle[0.4,0.6],[0.3,0.5]\rangle$ $\langle[0.5,0.7],[0.2,0.3]\rangle\}$	$\{\langle[0.9,0.9],[0.1,0.2]\rangle\}$
x_2	$\{\langle[0.7,0.8],[0.1,0.2]\rangle\}$	$\{\langle[0.8,0.9],[0.1,0.3]\rangle\}$	$\{\langle[0.5,0.8],[0.2,0.3]\rangle$ $\langle[0.6,0.8],[0.1,0.2]\rangle\}$
x_3	$\{\langle[0.2,0.3],[0.5,0.6]\rangle$ $\langle[0.3,0.3],[0.6,0.7]\rangle\}$	$\{\langle[0.6,0.8],[0.2,0.3]\rangle\}$	$\{\langle[0.4,0.5],[0.5,0.6]\rangle\}$
x_4	$\{\langle[0.6,0.7],[0.2,0.2]\rangle\}$	$\{\langle[0.6,0.7],[0.2,0.3]\rangle$ $\langle[0.5,0.6],[0.3,0.3]\rangle\}$	$\{\langle[0.1,0.3],[0.6,0.7]\rangle,$ $\langle[0.2,0.2],[0.7,0.8]\rangle,$ $\langle[0.3,0.4],[0.6,0.6]\rangle\}$

Table 3. The evaluation preference matrix $\boldsymbol{P}^{(3)}$ from group e_3.

e_3	c_1	c_2	c_3
x_1	$\{\langle[0.3,0.5],[0.4,0.5]\rangle$ $\langle[0.4,0.4],[0.5,0.5]\rangle\}$	$\{\langle[0.2,0.3],[0.5,0.6]\rangle$ $\langle[0.1,0.2],[0.8,0.9]\rangle\}$	$\{\langle[0.7,0.8],[0.2,0.2]\rangle,$ $\langle[0.9,0.9],[0.1,0.1]\rangle,$ $\langle[0.8,0.9],[0.1,0.2]\rangle\}$
x_2	$\{\langle[0.4,0.6],[0.3,0.4]\rangle$ $\langle[0.4,0.5],[0.5,0.5]\rangle\}$	$\{\langle[0.1,0.3],[0.6,0.9]\rangle\}$	$\{\langle[0.7,0.8],[0.2,0.3]\rangle\}$
x_3	$\{\langle[0.8,0.9],[0.1,0.1]\rangle$ $\langle[0.5,0.7],[0.1,0.2]\rangle\}$	$\{\langle[0.3,0.6],[0.4,0.4]\rangle,$ $\langle[0.4,0.5],[0.4,0.5]\rangle,$ $\langle[0.3,0.5],[0.4,0.5]\rangle\}$	$\{\langle[0.5,0.6],[0.3,0.4]\rangle$ $\langle[0.3,0.4],[0.5,0.6]\rangle\}$
x_4	$\{\langle[0.6,0.7],[0.3,0.4]\rangle\}$	$\{\langle[0.4,0.6],[0.3,0.5]\rangle\}$	$\{\langle[0.3,0.5],[0.5,0.5]\rangle\}$

5.1 Ranking Evaluation Results of Container Ships

Step 1: The three groups of team evaluate the container ships based on three attributes, and use the IVPHFS to give preference matrices $\boldsymbol{P}^{(l)} = (\mathscr{P}_{i,k})_{4\times3}^{(l)}$ in Tables 1, 2 and 3. In order to facilitate the subsequent solution using the improved TODIM method, comparative relationship matrices $\boldsymbol{Q}_{c_k}^{(l)} = (Q_{ij})_{4\times4}^{(l)}$ between any two IVPHFSs can be calculated by Definition 1. For example, we can get the comparative relationship matrix $\boldsymbol{Q}_{c_3}^{(1)}$ for Table 1 under the attribute c_3, as follows:

$$
\boldsymbol{Q}_{c_3}^{(1)} = \begin{pmatrix} 0.5000 & 0.0213 & 1 & 0.5667 \\ 0.9787 & 0.5000 & 1 & 1 \\ 0 & 0 & 0.5000 & 0 \\ 0.4333 & 0 & 1 & 0.5000 \end{pmatrix}.
$$

Obviously, it can be observed that since $0.0213 < 0.5000$, the alternative $x_1 \prec x_2$ under attribute c_3. Based on the GM method, the weights of attributes are $w_1 = 0.1998$, $w_2 = 0.1168$, $w_3 = 0.6833$ in advance.

Step 2: We calculate the cosine similarity measure between any two alternatives under the same attribute for Tables 1, 2 and 3. Such as under the attribute c_1, the cosine similarity measure matrix in Table 1 is shown as follows:

$$
\boldsymbol{\cos}_{c_1}^{(1)} = \begin{pmatrix} 1 & 0.8428 & 0.8892 & 0.8004 \\ 0.8428 & 1 & 0.9909 & 0.9859 \\ 0.8892 & 0.9909 & 1 & 0.9880 \\ 0.8804 & 0.9859 & 0.9880 & 1 \end{pmatrix}.
$$

Step 3: By using the improved TODIM method in which the attenuation coefficient θ is set to 1, the comprehensive evaluation dominance matrices among alternatives under all attributes by each group are obtained as follows:

$$
\boldsymbol{\delta}^{(1)} = \begin{pmatrix} 0 & -0.7031 & 0.9657 & 0.9054 \\ 0.7031 & 0 & -0.0308 & 0.6824 \\ -0.9657 & 0.0308 & 0 & -0.0845 \\ -0.9054 & -0.6824 & 0.0845 & 0 \end{pmatrix},
$$

$$
\boldsymbol{\delta}^{(2)} = \begin{pmatrix} 0 & 0.0424 & 0.7651 & 0.6895 \\ -0.0424 & 0 & 1.4343 & 1.4264 \\ -0.7651 & -1.4343 & 0 & 0.7810 \\ -0.6895 & -1.4264 & -0.7810 & 0 \end{pmatrix},
$$

$$
\boldsymbol{\delta}^{(3)} = \begin{pmatrix} 0 & 0.7177 & 0.0392 & -0.0213 \\ -0.7177 & 0 & 0.0530 & 0.0071 \\ -0.0392 & -0.0530 & 0 & 0.9169 \\ 0.0213 & -0.0071 & -0.9169 & 0 \end{pmatrix}.
$$

Step 4: Next, considering the weights of groups, a collective comprehensive evaluation dominance matrix $\bar{\boldsymbol{\delta}}$ is obtained by using Eq. (4).

$$
\bar{\boldsymbol{\delta}} = \begin{pmatrix} 0 & 0.0190 & 0.5900 & 0.5245 \\ -0.0190 & 0 & 0.4855 & 0.7053 \\ -0.5900 & -0.4855 & 0 & 0.5378 \\ -0.5245 & -0.7053 & -0.5378 & 0 \end{pmatrix}.
$$

Step 5: Finally, the final priority degree of alternatives is obtained from Eq.(6) as follows:

$$
\varepsilon_1 = 0.9870, \varepsilon_2 = 1, \varepsilon_3 = 0.4184, \varepsilon_4 = 0.
$$

Obviously, the ranking of container ships is $x_2 \succ x_1 \succ x_3 \succ x_4$, that is, the alternative x_2 is the ideal alternative for all experts. In this regard, under the requirements of the green shipping development strategy and integration of the various experts' opinions, it is better to choose container ship x_2, which can better meet the coordinated development of the shipping economy and environment.

5.2   Experimental Verification

In the improved TODIM method from the cosine similarity measure of IVPHFS, the selection of alternatives is determined by the two characteristics of membership and non-membership degree, that is, the degree of approval and disapproval of the alternatives. In addition, a TODIM approach [22] is proposed to give the dominance degree values of alternatives by considering the Euclidean distance between fuzzy sets, as shown below:

$$\phi_k(x_i, x_j) = \begin{cases} \sqrt{w_k d(b_{ik}, b_{jk})}, & \text{if } b_{ik} > b_{jk}, \\ 0, & b_{ik} = b_{jk}, \\ -\frac{1}{\theta}\sqrt{w_k d(b_{ik}, b_{jk})}, & \text{otherwise.} \end{cases} \tag{7}$$

Compared with cosine distance, Euclidean distance emphasizes the absolute value of evaluation given by the experts to obtain the final results, while cosine distance pays attention to the given values' dimension and obtains final results by considering the value of each dimension. For this, we define the Euclidean distance between IVPHFSs as follows and use this approach to handle the above problem.

$$d_{c_k}^{(l)}(\mathscr{P}_i, \mathscr{P}_j)$$
$$= \sqrt{(\mu_{\mathscr{P}_1}^- - \mu_{\mathscr{P}_2}^-)^2 + (\mu_{\mathscr{P}_1}^+ - \mu_{\mathscr{P}_2}^+)^2 + (\nu_{\mathscr{P}_1}^- - \nu_{\mathscr{P}_2}^-)^2 + (\nu_{\mathscr{P}_1}^+ - \nu_{\mathscr{P}_2}^+)^2}, \tag{8}$$

where $\mu_{\mathscr{P}_{1,2}}^{\pm} = \frac{1}{p}\sum_{i=1}^{p}\mu_{\mathscr{P}_{1,2},i}^{\pm}$, $\nu_{\mathscr{P}_{1,2}}^{\pm} = \frac{1}{p}\sum_{i=1}^{p}\mu_{\mathscr{P}_{1,2},i}^{\pm}$, p and q respectively represent the number of possible IVPFNs.

Further, when it is applied to solve the above problem, the results are as follows:

$$\varepsilon_1 = 0.9785, \varepsilon_2 = 1, \varepsilon_3 = 0.2075, \varepsilon_4 = 0.$$

The ranking of container ships is $x_2 \succ x_1 \succ x_3 \succ x_4$. We can obtain that the alternatives ranking obtained by the Euclidean distance is the same as that obtained by the cosine similarity measure, which shows that it is feasible to improve the TODIM method through the cosine similarity measure. When the corresponding evaluation values take multiple features into account, we can use the cosine similarity measure to determine similarity among alternatives so that the evaluation values can be better processed in the calculation process for reducing the error caused by merely considering the numerical values. In this regard, we can expand the improved TODIM method with cosine similarity measure to handle MAGDM problems.

5.3   Sensitivity Analysis

In the extended TODIM method, the value of attenuation coefficient θ may affect the ranking of alternatives. So, we analyse the influence of attenuation coefficient θ between 0 and 2 on the ranking of alternatives in the sensitivity analysis. We obtain that when $\theta \leq 0.9755$, that is, experts neglect the shortcomings of the alternatives, alternative x_1 is the ideal alternative; when $\theta > 0.9755$, that is, experts care about the shortcomings of the alternatives, alternative x_2 is the ideal alternative. It can be seen that as experts' psychological state changes, the alternatives' ranking and the selection of the ideal ones will change accordingly. Therefore, experts should select an appropriate coefficient θ in advance to process the alternatives according to their risk attitudes.

6   Conclusion

In this study, under the green shipping development strategy requirements, we propose an extended TODIM method based on the interval-valued Pythagorean hesitant fuzzy environment to solve the selection of container ship operation alternatives in the MAGDM problem. The IVPHFS is used to express the experts' opinions by considering their hesitation and uncertainty, which can better preserve the experts' opinions and make the results conform to their real ideas. And by defining the cosine similarity measure to improve the TODIM method, the similarity between alternatives can better reflect the two dimensions of experts' approval and disapproval. The proposed method can effectively guide the operators of shipping companies to select a more appropriate container ship satisfying the green shipping requirements.

The future study focuses on improving the proposed method by combining a feedback mechanism to adjust the evaluation results so that all experts can approve the final results when a tiny minority of experts disagree.

Acknowledgements. This work was supported by the Science and technology project of the science and technology department of Henan province (No. 212102210149).

References

1. Pike, K., Butt, N., Johnsn, D.: Global sustainable shipping initiatives: Audit and overview.   http://awsassets.Panda.Org/downloads/sustainable_shipping_initiativ es_report_1.pdf. Accessed 16 Mar 2016
2. Lirn, T., Lin, H., Shang, K.: Green shipping management capability and firm performance in the container shipping industry. Marit. Policy Manag. 41(2), 159–175 (2014)
3. Zadeh, L.A.: Fuzzy sets. Inf. Control. 8(3), 338–353 (1965)
4. Atanassov, K.T.: Intuitionistic fuzzy sets. Fuzzy Sets Syst. 20(1), 87–96 (1986)
5. Yager, R.R.: Pythagorean fuzzy subsets. In: Proceeding of the Joint IFSA World Congress and NAFIPS Annual Meeting, Edmonton, Canada, pp. 57–61 (2013)
6. Yager, R.R., Abbasov, A.M.: Pythagorean membership grades, complex numbers, and decision making. Int. J. Intell. Syst. 28(5), 436–452 (2013)

7. Liu, W.F., He, X.: Pythagorean hesitant fuzzy set. Fuzzy Syst. Math. **30**(4), 107–115 (2016)
8. Zhang, M.Y., Zheng, T.T., Zheng, W.R.: Interval-valued Pythagorean hesitant fuzzy set and its application to multi-attribute group decision making. Complexity **2020**(12), 1–26 (2020)
9. Zavadskas, E.K., Mardani, A., Turskis, Z.: Development of TOPSIS method to solve complicated decision-making problems-an overview on developments from 2000 to 2015. Int. J. Inf. Technol. Decis. Making **15**(3), 645–682 (2016)
10. Lei, F., Wei, G., Gao, H.: TOPSIS method for developing supplier selection with probabilistic linguistic information. Int. J. Fuzzy Syst. **22**(3), 749–759 (2020)
11. Akram, M., Adeel, A.: TOPSIS approach for MAGDM based on interval-valued hesitant fuzzy N-soft environment. Int. J. Fuzzy Syst. **21**(3), 993–1009 (2019)
12. Kumar, A., Aswin, A., Gupta, H.: Evaluating green performance of the airports using hybrid BWM and VIKOR methodology. Tour. Manag. **76**(2), 103941.1–103941.16 (2020)
13. Akram, M., Ilyas, F., Garg, H.: Multi-criteria group decision making based on ELECTRE I method in Pythagorean fuzzy information. Soft Comput. **24**(5), 3425–3453 (2020)
14. Hashemi, S.S., Hajiagha, S.H.R., Zavadskas, E.K.: Multicriteria group decision making with ELECTRE III method based on interval-valued intuitionistic fuzzy information. Appl. Math. Modell. **40**(2), 1554–1564 (2016)
15. Makan, A., Fadili, A.: Sustainability assessment of large-scale composting technologies using PROMETHEE method. J. Clean. Prod. **261**, 121244 (2020)
16. Gomes, L., Lima, M.: TODIM: basics and application to multicriteria ranking of projects with environmental impacts. Found. Comput. Decis. Sci. **16**(4), 113–127 (1992)
17. Gomes, L., Lima, M.: From modeling individual preferences to multicriteria ranking of discrete alternatives: a look at prospect theory and the additive difference model. Found. Comput. Decis. Sci. **17**(3), 171–184 (1992)
18. Mirnezami, S.A., Mousavi, S.M., Mohagheghi, V.: An innovative interval type-2 fuzzy approach for multi-scenario multi-project cash flow evaluation considering TODIM and critical chain with an application to energy sector. Neural Comput. Appl. (2020). https://doi.org/10.1007/s00521-020-05095-z
19. Zhang, Y., Yang, W.: Hesitation Pythagorean fuzzy TODIM approach. Fuzzy Syst. Math. **34**(2), 85–92 (2020)
20. Dawood, H.: Theories of interval arithmetic: Mathematical foundations and applications. LAP Lambert Academic Publishing, Saarbrücken, Germany (2011)
21. Zindani, D., Maity, S.R., Bhowmik, S.: A material selection approach using the TODIM (TOmada de Decisao Interativa Multicriterio) method and its analysis. Int. J. Mater. Res. **108**(5), 345–354 (2017)
22. Divya, Z., Saikat, R.M., Sumit, B.: Complex interval-valued intuitionistic fuzzy TODIM approach and its application to group decision making. J. Ambient Intell. Human. Comput. (2020). https://doi.org/10.1007/s12652-020-02308-0
23. Geng, Y., Liu, P., Teng, F.: Pythagorean fuzzy uncertain linguistic TODIM method and their application to multiple criteria group decision making. J. Intell. Fuzzy Syst. **33**(6), 3383–3395 (2017)
24. Luiz, F.A., Luís, A.D.: An application of the TODIM method to the multicriteria rental evaluation of residential properties. Eur. J. Oper. Res. **193**(1), 204–211 (2009)
25. Barzilai, J.: Deriving weights from pairwise comparison matrices. J. Oper. Res. Soc. **48**(12), 1226–1232 (1997)

Control Systems, Network Synchronization, System Integration, and Industrial Artificial Intelligence

Linear Time-Varying Model Predictive Control for Trajectory-Tracking of a Wheeled Mobile Robot

Juntao Wei and Bing Zhu$^{(\boxtimes)}$

The Seventh Research Division, Beihang University,
Beijing 100191, People's Republic of China
{sy1903120,zhubing}@buaa.edu.cn

Abstract. In this paper, a linear time-varying model predictive control (MPC) is proposed for the wheeled mobile robot to track the reference trajectory. The nonlinear model subject to the non-holonomic constraint is linearized and discretized into a linear time-varying model, such that the time-varying MPC can be applied. The MPC algorithm is processed with the linear time-varying model. Recursive feasibility and closed-loop stability are proved in the framework of time-varying systems, while the control inputs (linear and angular velocities) are proved to be bounded within their constraints. A simulation example is provided to support the theoretical result.

Keywords: Model predictive control · Trajectory tracking · Non-holonomic systems

1 Introduction

Motion control problem are basically divided into three types: point stabilization, path following and trajectory tracking. The aim of trajectory tracking is to design the controller, such that the closed-loop system is capable of tracking the time-varying reference position. Trajectory tracking is a fundamental research area in robotics [1]. Wheeled mobile robot is a typical type of non-holonomic systems. Its wheels are with pure rolling and non-slipping in lateral direction, and it is proved to be completely controllable [2]. Although the kinematics model of the wheeled mobile robot appears simple, the existence of non-holonomic constraints brings challenge in its controller design. According to Brockett's theorem [3], non-holonomic systems cannot be stabilized by linear time-invariant feedback law. However, it was proved that asymptotic stabilization can be achieved by using time-varying feedback control [4], discontinuous time-invariant feedback control [5] or hybrid control [6], and some nonlinear control methods such as state feedback linearization [7] and sliding mode [8]. Most of them rarely take the constraints on inputs or states into account, which has crucial impact on performance and stability [9].

© Springer Nature Singapore Pte Ltd. 2021
H. Zhang et al. (Eds.): NCAA 2021, CCIS 1449, pp. 533–544, 2021.
https://doi.org/10.1007/978-981-16-5188-5_38

Model Predictive Control (MPC) is an technique which achieves optimal control sequence to minimizing the objective function at each time step. It has the advantage of handling the constraints on inputs and states. At each sampling instant, the plant model with constraints is used to predict future control and state sequences in predictive horizon online based on the current state, and only the first element of the control sequence is applied to the system. MPC can be applied to the trajectory tracking control of non-holonomic systems. It is shown in [10] that if a local stabilizing feedback controller exists in the terminal state region, by adding a terminal state penalty to the optimized objective function, the closed-loop system achieves asymptotic stability. In [11], it is shown that the possibility of applying NMPC to solve problems of trajectory tracking and point stabilization. It is proposed in [12] an approach to choose terminal state penalty and local stabilizing feedback control law to gain terminal state region based on linear matrix inequality (LMI) and norm-bounded linear differential inclusion (LDI) of nonlinear system. However, for systems with fast and nonlinear dynamics, the NMPC scheme leads to programming non-convex problem and a great deal of decision variables to be solved, resulting in considerable greater computational effort than linear MPC in online optimization [13]. In [14], an approximated NMPC is designed based on Taylor approximation to overcome difficulty of nonlinear optimization.

The aim of this paper is to design a linear MPC for the nonlinear wheeled mobile robot, such that the computational burden of the nonlinear MPC can be avoided. The model of the wheeled mobile robot is nonlinear, and it can be linearized into a linear time-varying model, provided that the reference trajectory is continuously differentiable and bounded. Consequently, the proposed MPC is linear time-varying, with control constraints on the linear and angular velocities, and a terminal constraint to ensure its stability. The main contribution of this paper include that: 1) the linear time-varying MPC ensures that tracking errors of the nonlinear closed-loop system are locally uniformly asymptotically stable around the reference trajectory, and 2) the recursive feasibility and the closed-loop stability is proved within the framework of time-varying systems. Theoretical results are supported by a simulation example.

2   Problem Formulation

2.1   Kinematic Model of the Wheeled Mobile Robot

The wheeled mobile robot is a typical nonlinear system subject to the non-holonomic constraint. It has two rear wheels and one front wheel, as is displayed in Fig. 1. The rear wheels rotates with independent rates, i.e., ω_l and ω_r, generating the translational velocity $v = r(\omega_r + \omega_l)/2$ and the angular velocity $\omega = r(\omega_r - \omega_l)/l$ of the mobile robot, where r denotes the radius of the rear wheels, and l denotes the distance between the two rear wheels. Without loss of generality, v and ω are regarded as the control inputs in this paper.

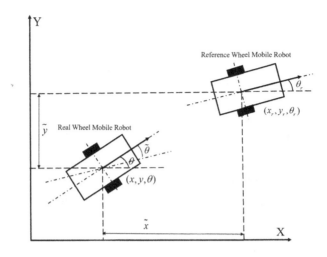

Fig. 1. Global coordinate system of real WMR and reference WMR

The kinematic model of the wheeled mobile robot can be given by

$$\dot{\mathbf{q}} = \begin{bmatrix} \dot{x} \\ \dot{y} \\ \dot{\theta} \end{bmatrix} = \begin{bmatrix} \cos\theta & 0 \\ \sin\theta & 0 \\ 0 & 1 \end{bmatrix} \begin{bmatrix} v \\ \omega \end{bmatrix} = f(\mathbf{q}, \mathbf{u}) \tag{1}$$

where $\mathbf{q} = \begin{bmatrix} x & y & \theta \end{bmatrix}^T$ describes the position and orientation with respect to the inertial reference frame; and $\mathbf{u} = \begin{bmatrix} v & \omega \end{bmatrix}^T$ denotes the control input, including the translational velocity and the angular velocity.

The wheeled mobile robot is subject to the nonholonomic constraint [15] :

$$\dot{y}(t)\cos(\theta(t)) - \dot{x}(t)\sin(\theta(t)) = 0 \tag{2}$$

indicating that there is no side-slip in its motion.

It is supposed that the control inputs are subject to actuator saturation, namely

$$|v| \leq \overline{v}, \quad |\omega| \leq \overline{\omega} \tag{3}$$

where $\overline{v} > 0$ and $\overline{\omega} > 0$ are constants.

2.2 Control Objective

In this paper, we consider the problem of trajectory tracking, where the wheeled mobile robot, subject to control constraints (3), is required to track a uniformly bounded time-varying trajectory given by $[x_r(t) \ y_r(t)]^T$, i.e.,

$$\lim_{t \to +\infty} |x(t) - x_r(t)| = 0, \quad \lim_{t \to +\infty} |y(t) - y_r(t)| = 0. \tag{4}$$

where x_r and y_r are uniformly bounded. Here, the trajectory $[x_r(t) \ y_r(t)]^T$ is supposed to be continuously differentiable, such that it can be tracked by nonholonomic systems.

For nonholonomic system, the reference translational velocity is required not converge to zero, i.e., the reference trajectory should be persistently excited, otherwise the asymptotic stability will be lost [16].

3 Linear Time-Varying MPC for the Wheeled Mobile Robot

3.1 Linearization and Discretization

Based on the reference trajectory, the reference translational velocity and angular velocity can be calculated by:

$$v_r(t) = \sqrt{\dot{x}_r(t)^2 + \dot{y}_r(t)^2}$$

$$\theta_r(t) = \arctan 2\left(\dot{y}_r(t), \dot{x}_r(t)\right)$$

$$\omega_r(t) = \dot{\theta}_r(t) = \frac{\ddot{y}_r(t)\dot{x}_r(t) - \dot{y}_r(t)\ddot{x}_r(t)}{\dot{x}_r^2(t) + \dot{y}_r^2(t)}$$

Let $\tilde{\mathbf{q}} = \mathbf{q} - \mathbf{q}_r$, where $\mathbf{q}_r = [x_r(t), y_r(t), \theta_r(t)]^T$, such that

$$\dot{\mathbf{q}}_r = f(\mathbf{q}_r, \mathbf{u}_r), \tag{5}$$

where $\mathbf{u}_r = [v_r, \omega_r]^T$. It follows that

$$\dot{\tilde{\mathbf{q}}} = f(\mathbf{q}, \mathbf{u}) - f(\mathbf{q}_r, \mathbf{u}_r), \tag{6}$$

where it can be seen that f is continuously differentiable with respect to all its arguments. Consequently, in the neighborhood of the reference trajectory, the nonlinear model (6) can be linearized by

$$\dot{\tilde{\mathbf{q}}} = \mathbf{A}(t)\tilde{\mathbf{q}} + \mathbf{B}(t)\tilde{\mathbf{u}}, \tag{7}$$

where $\tilde{\mathbf{u}} = \mathbf{u} - \mathbf{u}_r$, and

$$\mathbf{A}(t) = \left.\frac{\partial f}{\partial \mathbf{q}}\right|_{\mathbf{q}=\mathbf{q}_r}, \quad \mathbf{B}(t) = \left.\frac{\partial f}{\partial \mathbf{u}}\right|_{\mathbf{u}=\mathbf{u}_r}. \tag{8}$$

If the sampling interval T is chosen small enough, it is appropriate to apply Euler discretization to obtain the time-varying linear discrete-time model:

$$\tilde{\mathbf{q}}(k + 1) = \mathbf{F}(k)\tilde{\mathbf{q}}(k) + \mathbf{G}(k)\tilde{\mathbf{u}}(k) \tag{9}$$

where

$$\mathbf{F}(k) = \begin{bmatrix} 1 & 0 & -v_r(k)\sin\theta_r(k)T \\ 0 & 1 & v_r(k)\cos\theta_r(k)T \\ 0 & 0 & 1 \end{bmatrix}$$

$$\mathbf{G}(k) = \begin{bmatrix} \cos\theta_r(k)T & 0 \\ \sin\theta_r(k)T & 0 \\ 0 & T \end{bmatrix}$$

where k denotes the sampling time. It can be seen that $\mathbf{G}(k)$ and $\mathbf{H}(k)$ are uniformly bounded, if the reference trajectory is uniformly bounded.

3.2   Linear Time-Varying MPC Design

Prediction. The prediction is processed by using the discrete-time linearized model (9).

Define the predictive error series and the predictive control series by

$$\overline{\mathbf{q}}(k+1) = \begin{bmatrix} \tilde{\mathbf{q}}(k+1 \mid k) \\ \tilde{\mathbf{q}}(k+2 \mid k) \\ \vdots \\ \tilde{\mathbf{q}}(k+N \mid k) \end{bmatrix}, \quad \overline{\mathbf{u}}(k) = \begin{bmatrix} \tilde{\mathbf{u}}(k \mid k) \\ \tilde{\mathbf{u}}(k+1 \mid k) \\ \vdots \\ \tilde{\mathbf{u}}(k+N-1 \mid k) \end{bmatrix}$$

where $\tilde{\mathbf{q}}(k+j \mid k)$ and $\tilde{\mathbf{u}}(k+j \mid k)$ are the jth-step forward predictive error and control input at time instant k, respectively.

It then follows that the prediction can be calculated by

$$\overline{\mathbf{q}}(k+1) = \overline{\mathbf{A}}(k)\tilde{\mathbf{q}}(k \mid k) + \overline{\mathbf{B}}(k)\overline{\mathbf{u}}(k) \tag{10}$$

where

$$\overline{\mathbf{A}}(k) = \begin{bmatrix} \mathbf{F}(k \mid k) \\ \mathbf{F}(k+1 \mid k)\mathbf{F}(k \mid k) \\ \vdots \\ \prod_{i=0}^{N-2} \mathbf{F}(k+i \mid k) \\ \prod_{i=0}^{N-1} \mathbf{F}(k+i \mid k) \end{bmatrix} \tag{11}$$

and

$$\overline{\mathbf{B}}(k) = \begin{bmatrix} \mathbf{G}(k \mid k) & 0 & \cdots & 0 \\ \mathbf{F}(k+1 \mid k)\mathbf{G}(k \mid k) & \mathbf{G}(k+1 \mid k) & \cdots & 0 \\ \vdots & \vdots & \ddots & \vdots \\ \prod_{i=1}^{N-2} \mathbf{F}(k+i \mid k)\mathbf{G}(k \mid k) & \prod_{i=2}^{N-2} \mathbf{F}(k+i \mid k)\mathbf{G}(k+1 \mid k) & \cdots & 0 \\ \prod_{i=1}^{N-1} \mathbf{F}(k+i \mid k)\mathbf{G}(k \mid k) & \prod_{i=2}^{N-1} \mathbf{F}(k+i \mid k)\mathbf{G}(k+1 \mid k) & \cdots & \mathbf{G}(k+N-1 \mid k) \end{bmatrix} \tag{12}$$

It is clear that matrices $\overline{\mathbf{A}}(k)$ and $\overline{\mathbf{B}}(k)$ are uniformly bounded.

Cost Function. The cost function to be minimized can be constructed by a quadratic function of the states and control inputs:

$$J(k) = \sum_{j=0}^{N-1} \left[\tilde{\mathbf{q}}^T(k+j \mid k)\mathbf{Q}\tilde{\mathbf{q}}(k+j \mid k) + \tilde{\mathbf{u}}^T(k+j \mid k)\mathbf{R}\tilde{\mathbf{u}}(k+j \mid k) \right]$$
$$+ \tilde{\mathbf{q}}^T(k+N \mid k)\mathbf{P}\tilde{\mathbf{q}}(k+N \mid k) \tag{13}$$

where N is the predictive horizon, and the control horizon is assigned equal to the predictive horizon; $\mathbf{Q}$ and $\mathbf{R}$ are the positive definite weighting matrices.

Substituting (10) into the above cost function yields that

$$J(k) = \overline{\mathbf{q}}^T(k+1)\overline{\mathbf{Q}}\overline{\mathbf{q}}(k+1) + \overline{\mathbf{u}}^T(k)\overline{\mathbf{R}}\overline{\mathbf{u}}(k) + \tilde{\mathbf{q}}^T(k \mid k)\mathbf{P}\tilde{\mathbf{q}}(k \mid k) \tag{14}$$

where

$$\overline{\mathbf{Q}} = \begin{bmatrix} \mathbf{Q} & 0 & \cdots & 0 \\ 0 & \mathbf{Q} & \cdots & 0 \\ \vdots & \vdots & \ddots & \vdots \\ 0 & 0 & \cdots & \mathbf{Q} \end{bmatrix} \quad \text{and } \overline{\mathbf{R}} = \begin{bmatrix} \mathbf{R} & 0 & \cdots & 0 \\ 0 & \mathbf{R} & \cdots & 0 \\ \vdots & \vdots & \ddots & \vdots \\ 0 & 0 & \cdots & \mathbf{R} \end{bmatrix} \tag{15}$$

The const function (14) can be further rewritten by

$$J(k) = \frac{1}{2}\overline{\mathbf{u}}^T(k)\mathbf{H}(k)\overline{\mathbf{u}}(k) + \mathbf{f}^T(k)\overline{\mathbf{u}}(k) + \mathbf{d}(k) \tag{16}$$

where

$$\mathbf{H}(k) = 2\left(\overline{\mathbf{B}}(k)^T\overline{\mathbf{Q}}\overline{\mathbf{B}}(k) + \overline{\mathbf{R}}\right)$$

$$\mathbf{f}(k) = 2\overline{\mathbf{B}}^T(k)\overline{\mathbf{Q}}\overline{\mathbf{A}}(k)\tilde{\mathbf{q}}(k \mid k)$$

$$\mathbf{d}(k) = \tilde{\mathbf{q}}^T(k \mid k)(\overline{\mathbf{A}}^T(k)\overline{\mathbf{Q}}\overline{\mathbf{A}}(k) + \mathbf{Q})\tilde{\mathbf{q}}(k \mid k)$$

Since $\mathbf{d}(k)$ depends only on the current error $\tilde{\mathbf{q}}(k|k) = \tilde{\mathbf{q}}(k)$, and does not explicitly contain $\overline{\mathbf{u}}(k)$, minimizing $J(k)$ in (16) is equivalent to minimizing the following cost function

$$J(k) = \frac{1}{2}\overline{\mathbf{u}}^T(k)\mathbf{H}(k)\overline{\mathbf{u}}(k) + \mathbf{f}^T(k)\overline{\mathbf{u}}(k) \tag{17}$$

Constraints. It follows from (3) that predictive tracking errors and control inputs are subject to the following constraints:

$$\mathbf{u}_{\min} - \mathbf{u}_r(k+j) \leq \tilde{\mathbf{u}}(k+j \mid k) \leq \mathbf{u}_{\max} - \mathbf{u}_r(k+j), \quad j \in [0, N-1] \tag{18}$$

where $\mathbf{u}_{\min} = [-\overline{v}, -\overline{\omega}]^T$, and $\mathbf{u}_{\max} = [\overline{v}, \overline{\omega}]^T$. The terminal equation constraint is designed by

$$\tilde{\mathbf{q}}(k+N \mid k) = \mathbf{0} \tag{19}$$

which forces the predicted system state to reach zero at the end the prediction horizon and ensures the closed-loop stability.

Optimization. In the proposed time-varying MPC, the optimization is formulated as follows:

$$\overline{\mathbf{u}}^*(k) = \arg\min_{\overline{\mathbf{u}}(k)}\{J(k)\} \tag{20}$$

subject to discrete-time linear model (9) and constraints (18)–(19), where the cost function $J(k)$ is constructed by (17).

Receding Horizon Implementation. The optimization is implemented in receding horizon scheme:

$$\mathbf{u}(k)^* = \left[I_{n_u \times n_u} \; \mathbf{0} \cdots \mathbf{0}\right]_{1 \times m} \overline{\mathbf{u}}(k)^* + \mathbf{u}_r(k) \tag{21}$$

in each sampling time instant k.

4   Stability Analysis on the Closed-Loop System

Proposition 1. *Suppose that the optimization* (20) *is feasible at* $k = 0$, *then it is feasible at all future time, and the trajectory tracking error of the closed-loop system is uniformly asymptotically stable.*

Proof of Recursive Feasibility. At time instant k, suppose that the optimal solution of the optimization (20) is given by:

$$\overline{\mathbf{u}}(k)^* = \{\tilde{\mathbf{u}}^*(k \mid k), \tilde{\mathbf{u}}^*(k+1 \mid k), \cdots, \tilde{\mathbf{u}}^*(k+N-1 \mid k)\}$$

And the associated optimal predictive states are

$$\overline{\mathbf{q}}(k)^* = \{\tilde{\mathbf{q}}^*(k+1 \mid k), \tilde{\mathbf{q}}^*(k+2 \mid k), \cdots, \tilde{\mathbf{q}}^*(k+N-1 \mid k), 0\}$$

where the zero state at the end of the optimal predictive state series is resulted from the terminal constraint (19).

Suppose that the MPC is implemented by (21). Then, it holds that

$$\tilde{\mathbf{q}}(k+1) = \tilde{\mathbf{q}}^*(k+1 \mid k)$$

At the next time instant $k + 1$, a feasible (not necessarily optimal) solution to the optimization (20) can be assigned by shifting the optimal solution at time k:

$$\overline{\mathbf{u}}(k+1) = \begin{bmatrix} \tilde{\mathbf{u}}(k+1 \mid k+1) \\ \tilde{\mathbf{u}}(k+2 \mid k+1) \\ \vdots \\ \tilde{\mathbf{u}}(k+N-1 \mid k+1) \\ \tilde{\mathbf{u}}(k+N \mid k+1) \end{bmatrix} = \begin{bmatrix} \tilde{\mathbf{u}}^*(k+1 \mid k) \\ \tilde{\mathbf{u}}^*(k+2 \mid k) \\ \vdots \\ \tilde{\mathbf{u}}^*(k+N-1 \mid k) \\ 0 \end{bmatrix} \qquad (22)$$

and the associated optimal predictive states are

$$\overline{\mathbf{q}}(k+1) = \begin{bmatrix} \tilde{\mathbf{q}}(k+2 \mid k+1) \\ \tilde{\mathbf{q}}(k+3 \mid k+1) \\ \vdots \\ \tilde{\mathbf{q}}(k+N \mid k+1) \\ \tilde{\mathbf{q}}(k+N+1 \mid k+1) \end{bmatrix} = \begin{bmatrix} \tilde{\mathbf{q}}^*(k+2 \mid k) \\ \tilde{\mathbf{q}}^*(k+3 \mid k) \\ \vdots \\ \tilde{\mathbf{q}}^*(k+N-1 \mid k) \\ 0 \\ 0 \end{bmatrix} \qquad (23)$$

indicating that there exists at least a solution to (20), such that the control constraint (18) and the terminal constraint (19) are still satisfied. It implies that, if the optimization (20) is feasible at $k = 0$, then it will be feasible at all future times, and this completes the proof of recursive feasibility.

Proof of Closed-Loop Stability. Select the (time-dependent) Lyapunov candidate $V(\tilde{\mathbf{q}}(k), k)$ equal to the optimal cost function $J^*(k)$ at time instant k:

$$V(\tilde{\mathbf{q}}(k)) = J^*(k) = \|\tilde{\mathbf{q}}(k)\|_{\mathbf{Q}}^2 + \min\left\{ \sum_{i=1}^{N} \left(\|\tilde{\mathbf{q}}(k+i \mid k)\|_{\mathbf{Q}}^2 + \|\tilde{\mathbf{u}}(k+i-1 \mid k)\|_{\mathbf{R}}^2 \right) \right\} \tag{24}$$

where it can be seen that $V(0) = 0$, and $V(\tilde{\mathbf{q}}(k)) > 0$ for all $\tilde{\mathbf{q}}(k) \neq 0$. Moreover, it is clear that

$$V(\tilde{\mathbf{q}}(k), k) \geq \|\tilde{\mathbf{q}}(k)\|_{\mathbf{Q}}^2 \tag{25}$$

indicating that $V(\tilde{\mathbf{q}}(k), k)$ is positive definite.

Since $\mathbf{F}(k)$ and $\mathbf{G}(k)$ are uniformly bounded, and the control $\mathbf{u}$ is bounded, then it follows from (16) that there exists some constant $\alpha > 0$, such that

$$V(\tilde{\mathbf{q}}(k), k) \leq \alpha \|\tilde{\mathbf{q}}(k)\|_{\mathbf{Q}}^2 \tag{26}$$

indicating that $V(\tilde{\mathbf{q}}(k), k)$ is decrescent.

It follows from (22) and (23) that the associated (not necessarily optimal) cost function $J(k+1)$ at time $k+1$ can be calculated by

$$J(k+1) = J^*(k) - \|\tilde{\mathbf{q}}^*(k \mid k)\|_{\mathbf{Q}}^2 - \|\tilde{\mathbf{u}}^*(k \mid k)\|_{\mathbf{R}}^2$$

and

$$\begin{aligned} V(k+1) - V(k) =& J^*(k+1) - J^*(k) \leq J(k+1) - J^*(k) \\ \leq& -\|\tilde{\mathbf{q}}^*(k \mid k)\|_{\mathbf{Q}}^2 - \|\tilde{\mathbf{u}}^*(k \mid k)\|_{\mathbf{R}}^2 \\ \leq& -\|\tilde{\mathbf{q}}^*(k \mid k)\|_{\mathbf{Q}}^2 \end{aligned} \tag{27}$$

indicating the variation of $V(\tilde{\mathbf{q}}(k))$ is negative definite.

It follows from (25), (26) and (27) that the closed-loop linearized system is uniformly asymptotically stable.

The original nonlinear model can be regarded as the linearized model plus a vanishing disturbance (which vanishes at $\tilde{\mathbf{q}} = 0$), and it is straightforward to prove that the tracking error of the closed-loop nonlinear system is locally uniformly asymptotically stable around the reference trajectory.

5   Simulation

In this section, a simulation example is provided to test the performance of the proposed time-varying MPC. The wheeled mobile robot is required to follow a circular trajectory given by

$$\begin{cases} x_r(t) = 4\sin(0.5t) \\ y_r(t) = 4\cos(0.5t - \pi) + 4 \end{cases}$$

The reference the reference tangential velocity and angular velocities are calculated by $v_r(t) = 2m/s$, $\omega_r(t) = 0.5$ rad/s. The initial configuration of the

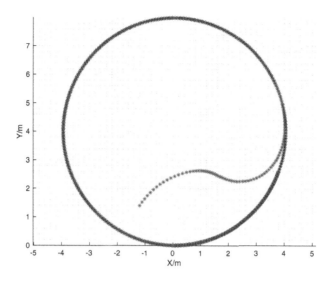

Fig. 2. Trajectory-tracking performance of the closed-loop system in the X-Y plane: reference trajectory (blue) and actual trajectory (red) (Color figure online)

robot and the reference robot at time $k = 0$ are $(x_0, y_0, \theta_0) = \left(0, 0, \frac{\pi}{3}\right)$ and $(x_{r0}, y_{r0}, \theta_{r0}) = (0, 0, 0)$. The control constraints are given by

$$-1 \text{ m/s} \leq \tilde{v} \leq 1 \text{ m/s}$$
$$-\frac{\pi}{2} \text{ rad/s} \leq \tilde{\omega} \leq \frac{\pi}{2} \text{ rad/s}$$

and it follows that constraints on the tangential velocity and angular velocities are:

$$1 \, m/s \leq v \leq 3 \, m/s \tag{28}$$

$$-\frac{\pi}{2} + 0.5 \text{ rad } /s \leq w \leq \frac{\pi}{2} + 0.5 \text{ rad } /s \tag{29}$$

The sampling interval is set by $T = 0.01$ s. The weighting matrices used are assigned by $\mathbf{Q} = \text{diag}(1, 1, 0.5)$ and $\mathbf{R} = 0.1\mathbf{I}_{2\times 2}$. The prediction horizon is chosen by $N = 20$.

Simulation results are displayed in Figs. 2–5. The two-dimensional representation of trajectory tracking is illustrated by Fig. 2, where it is shown that the closed-loop system actuated by the proposed time-varying MPC is capable of tracking the circular trajectory. It can be indicated from Fig. 3 that tracking performances are acceptable, since the tracking errors resulted from initial states converge with short and smooth transient processes. The linear velocity and the angular velocity are shown in Fig. 4, where it can be witnessed that they are well-bounded within their bounds given by (28) and (29). Tracking errors are the feedback parts of the linear velocity and the angular velocity are depicted in

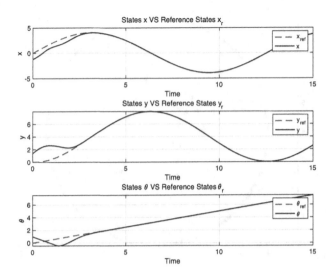

Fig. 3. The position and attitude of the closed-loop system with the proposed time-varying MPC: they track the reference trajectory with short transient processes.

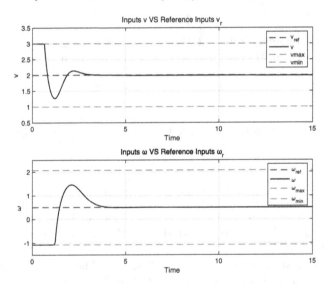

Fig. 4. Control inputs (The linear velocity and the angular velocity): they are bounded by their constraints.

Fig. 5, where it can be seen that the transient process is very short, and there exist almost no steady state tracking errors. Overall, it can be claimed that the performances of the closed-loop system with the proposed time-varying MPC are satisfactory.

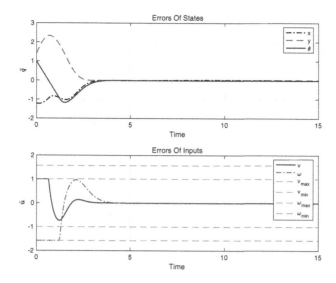

Fig. 5. Tracking errors and the feedback parts of the control inputs: the transient process is short and there exists almost no steady-state errors.

6   Conclusion

In this paper, a time-varying linear MPC is proposed for the wheeled mobile robot to track the reference trajectory. The nonlinear model is linearized and discretized into a linear time-varying model, such that the time-varying MPC can be applied. The prediction and optimization are processed with the time-varying linear model, and the control is implemented in a receding horizon scheme. It is proved that, in the framework of time-varying systems, the tracking error of the closed-loop system with the proposed time-varying MPC is uniformly asymptotically stable, while the control inputs (linear and angular velocities) are bounded within their constraints. A simulation example is provided to support the theoretical result.

Acknowledgement. This work was supported by National Natural Science Foundation of China under grants 62073015 and 61703018.

References

1. Kanjanawaniskul, K.F.: Motion control of a wheeled mobile robot using model predictive control: a survey. Asia-Pacific J. Sci. Technol. **17**(5), 811–837 (2012)
2. Kolmanovsky, I., Mcclamroch, N.H.: Developments in nonholonomic control problems. IEEE Control Syst. **15**(6), 20–36 (1995)
3. Brockett, R.: Asymptotic stability and feedback stabilization. Differ. Geom. Control Theor. **27**(1), 181–191 (1983)

4. Godhavn, J.M., Egeland, O.: A Lyapunov approach to exponential stabilization of nonholonomic systems in power form. IEEE Trans. Autom. Control **42**(7), 1028–1032 (1997)
5. Sontag, E.D.: Stability and feedback stabilization. Mathematics of Complexity and Dynamical Systems, pp. 1639–1652 (2011)
6. Panagou, D., Kyriakopoulos, K.J.: Dynamic positioning for an underactuated marine vehicle using hybrid control. Int. J. Control **87**(2), 264–280 (2014)
7. Michaek, M., Kozowski, K.: Vector-field-orientation feedback control method for a differentially driven vehicle. IEEE Trans. Control Syst. Technol. **18**(1), 45–65 (2009)
8. Chwa, D.K., Seo, J.H., Kim, P., et al.: Sliding-mode tracking control of nonholonomic wheeled mobile robots in polar coordinates. IEEE Trans. Control Syst. Technol. **12**(4), 637–644 (2004)
9. Indiveri, G., Paulus, J., Plöger, P.G.: Motion control of swedish wheeled mobile robots in the presence of actuator saturation. In: Lakemeyer, G., Sklar, E., Sorrenti, D.G., Takahashi, T. (eds.) RoboCup 2006. LNCS (LNAI), vol. 4434, pp. 35–46. Springer, Heidelberg (2007). https://doi.org/10.1007/978-3-540-74024-7_4
10. Mayne, D.Q., Rawlings, J.B.: Constrained model predictive control: stability and optimality. Automatica **36**(6), 789–814 (2000)
11. Gu, D., Hu, H.: Receding horizon tracking control of wheeled mobile robots. IEEE Trans. Control Syst. Technol. **14**(4), 743–749 (2006)
12. Yu, S., Chen, H., Zhang, P., et al.: An LMI optimization approach for enlarging the terminal region of MPC for nonlinear systems. Acta Autom. Sinica **34**(7), 798–804 (2008)
13. Nascimento, T.P., Moreira, A.P., Conceição, A.: Multi-robot nonlinear model predictive formation control: moving target and target absence. Robot. Auton. Syst. **61**(12), 1502–1515 (2013)
14. Hedjar, R., Alsulaiman, M., Almutib, K.: Approximated nonlinear predictive control for trajectory tracking of a wheeled mobile robot. In: First International Conference on Robot, Vision and Signal Processing, F. (eds.) Conference 2011, pp. 296–299. Kaohsiung, Taiwan (2011)
15. Guechi, E.H., Lauber, J., DAmbrine, M., et al.: Output feedback controller design of a unicycle-type mobile robot with delayed measurements. IET Control Theor. Appl. **6**(5), 726–733 (2012)
16. Thuilot, B.D., Andrea-Novel, B., Micaelli, A.: Modeling and feedback control of mobile robots equipped with several steering wheels. IEEE Trans. Robot. Autom. **12**(3), 375–390 (1996)

A Traffic Light Control System Based on Reinforcement Learning and Adaptive Timing

Pengchun Wu[1], Bin Song[1], Xinhai Chen[2], and Bingyi Liu[1(✉)]

[1] School of Computer Science and Technology, Wuhan University of Technology, Wuhan, China
{wpc,bsong,byliu}@whut.edu.cn
[2] Chongqing Engineering Research Center of Research and Testing for Automated Driving System and Intelligent Connected Vehicle, Chongqing, China
cjchenxinhai@cmhk.com

Abstract. Intelligent traffic light control is a key approach to improve the efficiency of transportation system. However, existing intelligent traffic light control methods usually only adjust phase with fixed duration or just adjust duration in a fixed phase circle. In actual scenarios with complicated and dynamic traffic flow, these methods cannot give the optimal phase and duration corresponding to the current situation because of their restricted traffic control mode, which limits the potential to further improve the efficiency of traffic transportation. For this sake, we propose a novel traffic light control system that achieves completely dynamic control. The system is able to efficiently adjust both phase and duration via deep reinforcement learning and adaptive timing. Among them, the reinforcement learning model is specially used for phase decision and the adaptive timing algorithm used for duration decision is designed for effective utilization of green time in each phase. We test our system in different traffic flows and explore the relationship between optimal duration and traffic flow. We also verify the superb performance of our traffic light control system in a whole-day traffic scene.

Keywords: Traffic light control · Completely dynamic control · Deep reinforcement learning · Adaptive timing · Effective utilization of green time

1 Introduction

Good traffic conditions, as the basis of urban economic activities, play a very important role in urban development, people's production and living standards. However, traffic congestion has the opposite effect. Therefore, how to improve the efficiency of traffic management and reduce traffic congestion receives much concern. The intersection is the bottleneck of traffic congestion, where multiple vehicle flows meet. Vehicles in different flows need to be coordinated to pass

© Springer Nature Singapore Pte Ltd. 2021
H. Zhang et al. (Eds.): NCAA 2021, CCIS 1449, pp. 545–559, 2021.
https://doi.org/10.1007/978-981-16-5188-5_39

quickly and orderly, which is mainly done by traffic light. Therefore, the traffic light control of intersections is crucial for traffic congestion control and traffic efficiency improvement [1, 2].

Traditional traffic light control methods set a fixed phase sequence in a circle, and its signal timing is either the same or set according to historical traffic volume data [3]. However, due to the randomness of vehicle arrival, these fixed programs cannot adapt to the dynamic changes of complex traffic.

With the usage of detecting facilities such as loop detectors and camera detectors, traffic information like the number of incoming vehicles can be gathered, thus many actuated control systems are proposed one after another [4,5]. Some optimization methods, such as fuzzy logic and genetic algorithm, are also applied in this field. In recent years, with the development of Vehicular Ad-Hoc Networks (VANETs) and Internet of Things (IoT) techniques, real-time intelligent traffic light control becomes possible due to plenty of traffic information collected all the time [5,6].

In 2016, AlphaGo came as a famous deep reinforcement learning application [7]. After that, deep reinforcement learning was also used as a novel method for traffic light control [8–10]. Deep reinforcement learning is very suitable for dynamic control of traffic lights to achieve long-term goals such as minimizing the average waiting time, traveling time, and so on. However, recent deep reinforcement learning methods only dynamically control the phase of traffic light and set fixed and equal duration, which cannot keep appropriate due to the uneven and constantly changing traffic flow distribution at intersections. Sometimes the preset fixed duration exceeds the time required for sparse traffic flow, and sometimes it is significantly less than that for dense traffic flow. Although several methods try to solve this problem by setting minor duration, it is very likely to incur new challenges including difficulty in model training well as frequent phase conversion that lefts very little time for drivers to react and slow down.

All aforementioned approaches achieve the partial traffic light control mode rather than a complete one, Which means the dynamic selection of both phase and duration. If the optimal phase and corresponding duration are selected by the complete traffic light control at each step, the traffic efficiency of intersections will reach the maximum.

According to the idea above, we have conducted some important work in the paper and the main contributions are listed as follows.

- We give an completely dynamic traffic light control mode, which is more efficient than any single control in scenarios with complicated and dynamic traffic flow.
- In the light of the completely dynamic control mode, we propose a novel control system that achieves whole decision-making of traffic light. The system combines reinforcement learning with adaptive timing, which makes our system dynamically select both appropriate phase and duration according to the real-time traffic situation. Specially, we make phase decision based on deep reinforcement learning, i.e. Advantage Actor-Critic (A2C), which is able to

select the most appropriate phase at each step. Then we analyze the concept of effective green time and find the effective utilization of green time is highly correlated with minimization of time loss. We hence design a new adaptive timing algorithm to adjust the optimal phase length from the perspective of reducing loss of green time.

– We conduct experiments on both synthetic and real-world data. The experimental results show its feasibility and superiority in different traffic flows and a whole day flow. We also explore the positive correlation between the optimal phase length and traffic flow through experiments, which means dynamic timing along with change of traffic flow is quite rational.

The rest of this paper is organized as follows. Section 2 presents the literature review. The specific system and method are shown in Sect. 3. The experimental results are shown in Sect. 4. Finally, the paper is concluded in Sect. 5.

2   Related Work

As a result of the stochastic characteristics of vehicle arrival in time and direction, conventional fixed-time systems with pre-set phase sequence and duration are quite ineffective for traffic light control.

Therefore, some adaptive methods adopt dynamic timing to improve traffic efficiency. Pei Chi Hsieh et al. optimize the phase length based on genetic algorithm [11]. C. Tang et al. collect real-time traffic information based on fog computing system, and then calculate the optimal duration by genetic algorithm [12]. These methods improve traffic efficiency to a certain extent.

Other methods are more than timing optimization. Based on a type of clustering algorithm, Shen et al. optimize the phase combination, that is, traffic flows in different directions are divided into rational phases. Besides, the time of a whole traffic light cycle is split into segments to maximize the utilization of green time via the bilevel programming model. However, the total cycle time is still fixed [13]. In [14], both phase sequence and phase duration are optimized by fuzzy logic model. The author compares the effects of single timing optimization, single optimization of phase sequence, and comprehensive optimization of the two. But its comprehensive optimization scheme effect is not ideal in phase control, which makes its performance is not even significantly better than that of the fixed-time method. In [15], the authors think that traffic flow is the key factor to adjust phase lengths, which is similar to our ideal. But the traffic flow is only evaluated by queue length. Furthermore, they don't consider dynamic phase adjustment and just find the need for a separated left lane in high-density traffic flow.

In the past, reinforcement learning was only used for dynamic phase selection, but the duration was preset. Recently, some studies using reinforcement learning for traffic light control also realize the necessity of dynamic timing. In [9], Li et al. analyze the variation of phase duration ratio with traffic flow in each direction in their experiment. The experimental results show that the heavier the traffic flow, the longer the duration. In [16], Liang et al. also point out that fixed-length interval setting in previous reinforcement learning methods does not work well in many scenes. Therefore, the action is designed as four phases' durations in a whole circle. But this kind of action is not very flexible that no phase duration can be adjusted until the end of the whole light circle. It may bring about a nonadjustable interval that incurs considerable inefficiency, especially when the traffic flow is unstable. In addition, the method is unable to make flexible phase decisions. In [17], Zhao et al. also realize the importance of dynamic timing, but they have no good idea to achieve it that their method does not function well. These studies all realize the limitation of single traffic control and some of them explore the combination of phase control and duration adjustment. But their ideas are still rough and inflexible that fail to achieve the super effect of integrated control. Our system combines reinforcement learning with adaptive timing based on maximum utilization of green time, which is more reasonable in duration adjustment, shows the superiority of integrated control in complicated and dynamic traffic flows.

3   Method

3.1   Proposed Traffic Light Control System

We focus on main intersections in urban areas and only consider the incoming vehicles. In this scenario, we assume that all vehicles are equipped with a DSRC communication module. Within a certain range, all vehicles close to the intersection would send their real-time information such as speed, location to our traffic signal system through the vehicular wireless network [6].

For the above scenario, our traffic light control system is designed with three modules: a receiver, a phase controller, as well as an adaptive timing controller. The receiver collects and processes real-time information from vehicles. The phase controller is actually a reinforcement learning model, i.e. A2C model that determines which phase is optimal at the current time step. The adaptive timing controller is used to dynamically adjust the current phase length.

More precisely, the receiver processes all incoming vehicle information into vector representation of intersection state and inputs it into the phase controller to make a reasonable phase decision. Next, the adaptive timing controller detects the current green light utilization in real-time and judges whether to terminate the phase in advance. The scenario is shown in Fig. 1.

3.2   Agent Design

State. State is required to capture the situation of intersection accurately for reasonable and accurate control from the reinforcement learning model. Specifically, the traffic situation in four incoming directions within 400 m of the intersection is extracted to make up the state. We divide each entry road into two parts because each road with incoming traffic flow consists of multiple lanes, in which straight and right turn lanes and left-turn lanes are calculated separately because they are affected by different phases. Straight and right turns are

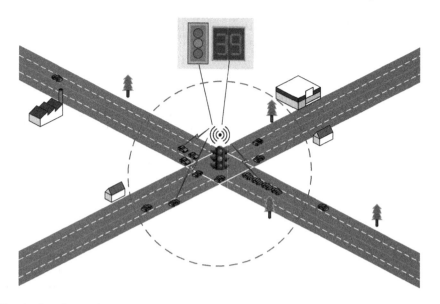

Fig. 1. Our focused scenario and proposed traffic light control system (Color figure online)

allowed in one phase, and left turn is allowed in another phase. Next, we segment lanes in each part. More precisely, the lane of 400 m is divided into 9 distinct segments, and then the number of vehicles in each segment is calculated.

In Table 1, the sequence and length of segments are shown in detail. The closer to the intersection, the smaller the segment length.

Table 1. The sequence and length of segments for each lane

Segment	1	2	3	4	5	6	7	8	9
length	7	7	7	7	12	20	40	60	240
Distance	0–7	7–14	14–21	21–28	28–40	40–60	60–100	100–160	160–400

As a consequence, the state is a 72-dimension vector that consists of 8 set of lanes with 9 segments.

Action. In our model, the reinforcement learning agent is in control of traffic light phase and its action space is 4 because there are 4 phases in our context.

Reward. Immediate reward is the key to guiding the training of reinforcement learning model to achieve the maximum optimization goal. In the problem of traffic light control, the most important goal is to improve the efficiency of vehicles, reduce the waiting time of vehicles and avoid congestion. In our setting,

Reward is the difference between the waiting time of two adjacent steps, which is in common use due to its high correlation with the optimization goal and easy implementation. The reward at time step t is calculated by the following equation:

$$r_t = W_t - W_{t+1} \tag{1}$$

W_{t+1} represents the total waiting time of all vehicles in incoming directions at the current time, W_t is that at the previous time step. If via the traffic lights control, a large number of vehicles pass the intersection smoothly, and leading to the number of vehicles in line reduce, the total waiting time of vehicles will be dramatically reduced, in other words, the agent will easily get greater rewards. It worth mentioned that only negative reward is calculated.

3.3   A2C Algorithm

The reason why we choose A2C algorithm is that it has stronger learning ability and robustness than Q-learning algorithm in our traffic light control scenarios.

A2C algorithm is based on policy gradient method, which is different from Q-learning [18,19]. This kind of method directly learns the optimal policy in the interaction with environment. A2C algorithm has two structures: actor and critic. The actor interacts with the environment, that is, observing the environment and selecting an action to perform. And then the critic evaluates the actor's choice of action, i.e. how good or bad it is. In the synchronous learning process, the critic's evaluation of action becomes more and more accurate. Under the guidance of critic, the actor also understands what the optimal action is in different states.

In fact, the critic is an evaluation function of state value and it is often approximated by neural network. The actor is an policy function, which is also represented by neural network.

The update formula of critic is as follows:

$$A^\pi (s_t, a_t) \approx r (a_t, s_t) + \gamma V_\emptyset^\pi (s_{t+1}) - V_\emptyset^\pi (s_t) \tag{2}$$

$$\emptyset \leftarrow \emptyset + \alpha A^\pi (s_t, a_t) \nabla_\emptyset V^\pi (s_t, a_t) \tag{3}$$

Where $A^\pi (s_t, a_t)$ is the advantage function, α is the learning rate, and $\emptyset$ is the critic network parameter.

At each step, the policy network parameter θ is updated by:

$$\theta \leftarrow \theta + \beta \nabla_\theta \log \pi_\theta(a \mid s) A^\pi(s, a) \tag{4}$$

Where β is the learning rate of policy network.

The more intuitive structure and training process can be seen in Fig. 2.

3.4   Adaptive Timing Algorithm

We believe that the optimal phase duration means the most effective utilization of green time. Figure 3.a shows the full utilization of green time. All vehicles

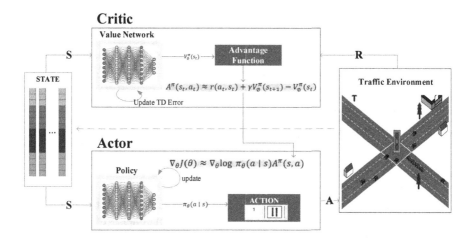

Fig. 2. The intuitive structure and training process of A2C

directly cross the intersection at saturation speed without waiting, and current phase just ends when the last vehicle passes the stop line. However, this ideal situation is very unlikely to happen. Due to the conflict of traffic flows in different directions, vehicles often have to stop and wait. On the other hand, the saturation flow will not last forever. Therefore, the loss of green time is inevitable in an actual situation, and what we can do is to reduce the time loss as much as possible.

Lost time refers to the time that is not effectively used by traffic flow in the phase, including start-up lost time and end-up lost time. When vehicles in the queue start to cross the stop line continuously, they should have an acceleration process from zero to saturation speed, causing a time loss just called start-up lost time. At the end of the phase, the vehicle closest to the intersection cannot pass the stop line in the remaining time, resulting in an end-up lost time.

In each phase, the adaptive timing controller ensures the effective utilization of green time. If loss of time is detected, it will terminate the current phase ahead of time. The specific process is as follows.

Firstly, we set a big time limit, recorded as T_{max}, in order to avoid the infinite continuation of the phase. Then we introduce the concept of departure headway that means the time difference of arriving at the stop line between the current vehicle and the previous one. For saturated traffic flow, each vehicle has the same headway, which is called saturated headway.

At the beginning of the phase, the headway of the vehicles in the fleet keeps a small value, which is equal to the saturated headway. When most vehicles passing through the intersection, it is likely to enter the end of the current phase. At that time, it is necessary to compare the minimum headway h_{rear} in the green direction with phase remaining time $t_{remaining}$.

$$h_{\text{rear}} > t_{\text{remaining}} > threshold_1 \qquad (5)$$

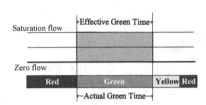 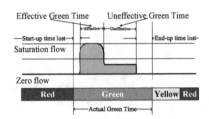

(a) The full utilization of green time   (b) All types of time loss in a phase

Fig. 3. Two utilization cases of green time (Color figure online)

If satisfied inequality above, that is, the last vehicle cannot reach the intersection before the yellow light is on, the adaptive timing controller will terminate the current phase. Additionally, $t_{remaining}$ must be greater than a certain value for the sake of safety, namely, $threshold_1$, which gives drivers time to react and slow down.

But when there are few queuing vehicles, most vehicles pass through the intersection at the very beginning of the phase, and the traffic flow is soon unsaturated, which means the headway of rear vehicles may be large. In this case, the utilization of green light time will be reduced rapidly, which is regarded as inefficient green light time as shown in Fig. 3.b. It is especially true if a large number of vehicles queue up in directions of red light. At that time, the current phase will be terminated if the minimum headway in current release lanes is greater than the threshold, i.e. $threshold_1$

$$h_{\min,g} > threshold_1 \tag{6}$$

However, if there are no vehicles arriving at the intersection in all directions of red light, it is necessary to compare the minimum headway $h_{\min,r}$ in red directions with minimum headway $h_{\min,g}$ in the green direction.

$$h_{\min,g} - h_{\min,r} > threshold_2 \tag{7}$$

When inequality above is satisfied, vehicles in red directions will arrive at the intersection some time earlier than vehicles in the green direction. In this case, the adaptive timing controller will terminate the current phase in advance, which reduces the start-up time loss of vehicles in next green direction to a certain extent. This is because the fleet can keep a certain speed and directly pass through the intersection without stopping, which is more efficient than the fleet starting from zero. Of course, if all directions of red light have no vehicle waiting or approaching, there is no need for phase conversion.

In addition, in some special situations such as congestion, the starting speed of vehicles may be very small, and its headway is greater than the threshold. To avoid frequent phase switching caused by wrong judgment, the adaptive timing controller also counts the number of vehicles within D_g meters from the intersection.

The specific decision procedure is presented in Algorithm 1.

Algorithm 1. Adaptive Timing Algorithm

1: The current phase begins after A2C model makes phase decision;
2: Set $t_{remaining} = T_{max}$;
3: **while** $t_{remaining} > 0$ **do**
4:    Continue a second for current phase and then collect traffic information;
5:    $t_{remaining} = t_{remaining} - 1$
6:    **if** $h_{min,g} > threshold_1$ and no vehicle within D_g of the intersection **then**
7:       **if** $h_{min,g} - h_{min,r} > threshold_2$ **then**
8:          Terminate current phase;
9:       **end if**
10:   **end if**
11:   **if** $h_{rear} > t_{remaining} > threshold_1$ **then**
12:      Terminate current phase;
13:   **end if**
14: **end while**

---

4   Experiment

4.1   Experiment Setting and Parameter Setting

The experiments are conducted on an open source and microcosmic traffic simulator SUMO (Simulation of Urban Mobility) [20]. SUMO supports custom road network and route data of vehicles. Besides, it provides precise and flexible traffic control, and a large number of real-time statistical data for analysis via TraCI interface. Hence it is very suitable for the development of traffic control model.

The simulation is performed in a single intersection scenario. Specifically, the intersection links to four perpendicular roads with length of 500 m. And each road has four lanes: a rightmost lane, two through lanes in the middle and a left inner one that only allows left turns. The rightmost one allows both straight and right turn. The design speed of all lanes is 13.89 m/s, that is 50 km/s. However, the actual speed of vehicles can reach 60 km/s. Moreover, the maximum acceleration and minimum deceleration of each vehicle are $1 \, m/s^2$ and $4.5 \, m/s^2$, respectively.

This intersection environment simulates main urban intersections. Compared with the real-world scene, it is simplified, but it can effectively verify the feasibility of our proposed method. In addition, the research of more intersection types and more phase control can be further conducted based on it.

There are several parameters of the adaptive timing algorithm should be set before experiment. Among them, T_{max} is 30 s, D_g is 15 m, both $threshold_1$ and $threshold_2$ are 3 s. These parameters are set based on both efficiency and safety. Besides, the parameter group has been proved effective in the following experiments.

4.2   Evaluation Metric

Average Waiting Time. Vehicle waiting time is calculated when the vehicle speed is below 0.1 m/s. The average waiting time refers to the average waiting time of all vehicles passing through the intersection. In addition, it is the main indicator we use in the training and testing phase.

Average Stops. Vehicle stops refer to the number of times vehicle speed is less than $0.1\,\mathrm{m/s}$. hence this indicator represents mean stops of all vehicles.

Average Speed. Speed refers to the average speed of the vehicle to complete the route. This indicator represents the average value of all vehicle speeds.

Average Phase Duration. The indicator refers to mean green phase duration in the whole simulation time.

The Number of Phases. This index represents the number of phase transitions in the whole simulation time. The larger the value is, the more frequent the phase switching is.

4.3   Compared Methods

Fixed-Time Control (FT) [3]. This method presets the phase sequence and duration so that its phases change periodically.

Self-Organizing Traffic Light Control (SOTL) [4]. This adaptive traffic light control method has no fixed phase length. It decides whether to switch over to the next phase according to real-time traffic information, including the number of vehicles in the green direction and that in the red direction.

Deep Q-Learning Network for Traffic Light Control (DQN). This method fits the action value through deep neural network. For DQN, the action with the greatest action value will be chosen in the testing stage. It is mentioned that we train DQN model under different duration settings and find the one with 10-second duration is the best.

Double Dueling Deep Q-Network for Traffic Light Circle Control (3DQN) [16]. This method uses 3DQN structure with prioritized experience replay to achieve traffic light circle control. Moreover, its state is an image extracted from the position and speed of vehicles at an intersection.

Adaptive Timing (AT). Here, adaptive timing is used to dynamically adjust phase duration for a fixed phase sequence that cannot be changed.

A2C for Traffic Light Control (A2C). A2C model here is applied to make phase decision. However, each phase duration is preset as the same value 15 s and cannot be dynamically adjusted.

Our proposed method achieves the entire dynamic control of traffic lights via the combination of AT and A2C, i.e. A2C&AT. Hence, we want to verify whether their combination is better than their respective performance.

4.4 Performance on Synthetic Data

In order to evaluate the performance and stability of each method in different traffic flows, we generated 12 synthetic route data to simulate the situation of sparse and dense traffic flow. Their traffic flow rates vary from 0.2 veh/s to 1.3 veh/s, with the interval of 0.1 veh/s.

Figure 4.a–f shows the performance as well as phase conversion of each method in different traffic flows. With the increase of vehicle flow rate, the efficiency of traffic control decreases for each method. Obviously, with the increase of incoming vehicles, their average waiting time and time loss get inevitably larger, and the average speed of vehicles decreases correspondingly. However, our method has good performance in all traffic flow rates among all methods. Besides, our method makes the traffic efficiency decrease very slowly, and AT method has similar performance. It can be seen that the effect of adaptive timing is quite obvious that it adapts well to the change of traffic flow and gives more reasonable phase duration, thereby reducing lots of time loss. In addition, since our method also controls the phase dynamically by A2C model compared with AT, its average waiting time and average time loss are further reduced.

However, when the vehicle flow rate becomes larger, the performance of A2C&AT and AT method is very close. The reason may be that the difference of traffic density in each direction is small due to uniformly generation of vehicles, which render slight effect of phase selection. But in term of average stops and average speed of vehicles, our method is still the best. Figure 4.c–d shows the number of phase adjustment and average phase duration of each method in different traffic flow rates. It can be seen that the number of phase adjustment of our method and AT method decreases gradually. Accordingly, their average phase duration becomes longer. 3DQN has a similar trend, although its performance is weaker than our method and AT method. That means the phase adjustment of our method is quite reasonable. It also shows that the larger the traffic flow rate is, the longer the optimal phase duration is, which is in a dynamic changing process.

4.5 Performance of a Whole Day

In this subsection, the real-world traffic flow from Luxemburg sumo traffic (LuST) is used for the experiment. We extract complete flow data of one day in a certain intersection (12408) in Luxemburg to conduct the experiment [21]. In the intersection, its average vehicle flow rate is 0.266 veh/s, which is relatively sparse. Specifically, the overall traffic flow rate is high at 7–9 a.m. and 17–18

Table 2. Detailed experimental results in a whole day

Method	Waiting time							Stops						
	Mean	Std	Min	25%	50%	75%	Max	Mean	Std	Min	25%	50%	75%	Max
FT	29.72	25.86	0	2	27	52	153	0.976	0.62	0	1	1	1	4
SOTL	22.62	24.97	0	1	15	37	130	0.90	0.63	0	1	1	1	4
DQN	16.36	25.46	0	1	9	22	444	0.96	0.71	0	1	1	1	9
3DQN	14.62	14.75	0	1	12	23	144	0.99	0.65	0	1	1	1	4
A2C	15.55	20.5	0	1	9	24	478	0.91	0.63	0	1	1	1	4
AT	6.79	8.15	0	0	4	11	63	0.81	0.62	0	0	1	1	3
A2C& AT	4.81	8.53	0	0	1	6	150	0.66	0.63	0	0	1	1	3
Method	Time loss							Speed						
	Mean	Std	Min	25%	50%	75%	Max	Mean	Std	Min	25%	50%	75%	Max
FT	41.44	27.66	3.1	15.3	40.0	64.1	187.2	8.56	2.62	2.4	6.4	8.0	10.7	16.3
SOTL	33.50	26.02	2.8	10.2	28.3	48.7	141.9	9.24	2.54	3.1	7.2	9.1	11.3	16.3
DQN	27.84	28.48	2.9	11.2	20.6	34.2	463.6	9.79	2.30	1.3	8.3	10.0	11.4	16.8
3DQN	26.00	17.4	3.0	13.0	24.0	34.6	174.0	9.73	2.02	2.7	8.3	9.6	11.1	16.3
A2C	26.51	21.64	2.6	11.0	21.8	36.2	490.8	9.79	2.18	1.5	8.3	9.8	11.4	16.8
AT	17.10	9.68	2.7	8.9	16.0	22.6	76.9	10.70	1.64	5.0	9.6	10.7	11.8	17.1
A2C& AT	14.6	9.9	2.9	7.62	12.0	18.4	161.7	11.08	1.63	2.8	10.1	11.1	12.2	16.9

p.m., and low in early morning and late night. In other time periods, the traffic flow rate fluctuates from 0.2 to 0.4 veh/s, as shown in Fig. 5.a.

We compare the performance of several methods by waiting time, stops, time loss and speed of vehicles and our proposed method gets the best results in all indicators. According to Table 2, our proposed method is obviously superior to other baselines. Not only the average waiting time is greatly reduced, but also the standard deviation is rather small. Of all the vehicles, 25% do not need to wait at all, 50% only need to wait within 1 s, and 75% only need to wait within 6 s. The only disadvantage is that the maximum waiting time is not as good as AT and SOTL. The reinforcement learning method, no matter A2C or DQN, is obviously better than the traditional FT method. In terms of average waiting time, DQN is 55% of FT, A2C is 52.3% of FT, and their standard deviations also decrease to a certain extent. The disadvantage is that a few vehicles wait too long, up to 400 s. As for 3DQN, it has better performance than A2C and DQN due to its special design.

Furthermore, the performance of AT is even better than that of reinforcement learning methods, which shows the superiority of our adaptive timing algorithm. By the A2C model selecting the optimal phase, A2C&AT can further reduce the average waiting time to the minimum, which is the only 16.2% of FT, 21.2% of SOTL, 29.4% of DQN, 32.9% of 3DQN, and 70.8% of pure AT method. In terms of time loss, we can also get similar comparison results. In terms of the number of stops, our method makes the average stops the least, only 0.658, far better than A2C and AT. Moreover, over 25% of vehicles do not need to stop and wait at the intersection. More precisely, the actual percentage is 43% and

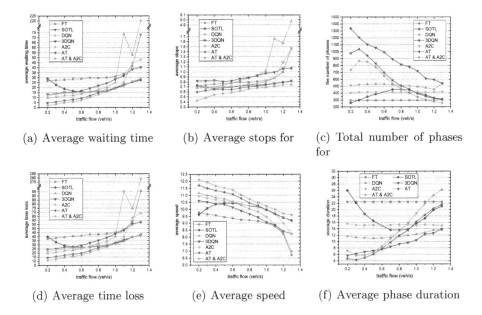

(a) Average waiting time

(b) Average stops for

(c) Total number of phases for

(d) Average time loss

(e) Average speed

(f) Average phase duration

Fig. 4. Experimental results for all methods in different traffic flows

far superior to other methods (A2C is 24.4%, DQN is 23.5%, 3DQN is 19.3%, FT is 19.6%, SOTL is 24.86%, and AT is 30.4%). Our proposed method also maximizes the average speed of vehicles, which means greater traffic throughput and higher traffic efficiency at the intersection.

According to the above analysis, single phase decision based on A2C or single duration decision based on AT algorithm can greatly improve traffic efficiency. By combining A2C method with AT, however, our method conducts both phase selection and duration adjustment to further improve traffic efficiency.

Since the traffic flow rate fluctuates all day with obvious peaks and troughs, we count the average phase duration per hour and its corresponding average waiting time to observe the adaptability of each method to traffic flow changes.

As can be seen from the Fig. 5.b–c, the traffic flow is quite small at 0–4 a.m., and the average duration of each method is large, but the average waiting time is very different. Among them, our proposed method makes the average waiting time near zero, which is far superior to other methods.

In other time periods, the average green time of DQN, 3DQN, and A2C changes slightly while that of FT does not change at all. The average phase duration of our method is similar to the change of vehicle flow rate so that its average waiting time per hour is minimum with slight fluctuation. AT method with fixed phase sequence also shows this similarity. It is worth noting that compared with A2C&AT, AT method has more phase transitions, but its performance is relatively poor. We can infer the positive effect of phase selection by A2C, that is, choosing a more reasonable phase every time step helps to reduce the frequent phase conversion.

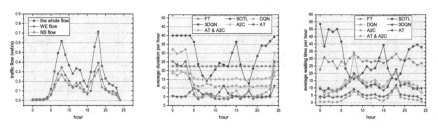

(a) The traffic flow in a whole day (b) Average duration per hour (c) Average waiting time per hour

Fig. 5. Experimental results at different hours of a day

5   Conclusion

In this paper, we propose a novel traffic light control system based on reinforcement learning and adaptive timing according to the idea of dynamically adjusting both phase and duration. In our system, the most suitable phase is judged by the A2C model and the most effective duration by adaptive timing. We conduct extensive experiments using both synthetic and real-world traffic data and demonstrate the superior performance of our proposed method over others. Besides, we explore the relationship between optimal duration and traffic flow that the best duration would climb accordingly with the increase of traffic flow.

We are also aware of several limitations of the current approach. First of all, A2C may make a wrong phase decision in some cases that the application of other better reinforcement learning models can reduce the mistake. Secondly, our experiments can be carried out at different kinds of intersections and multiple intersections to further verify the performance of our proposed method. In addition, we also hope to apply our method to more complex intersection conditions with pedestrians and bicycles. We expect to study further in these mentioned directions to make our method more applicable to real traffic scenarios.

Acknowledgments. This work was supported by Open Project of Chongqing Vehicle Test & Research Institute (No. 20AKC18) and Sanya Science and Education Innovation Park of Wuhan University of Technology (No. 2020KF0055).

References

1. Jin, J., Ma, X., Kosonen, I.: An intelligent control system for traffic lights with simulation-based evaluation. Control Eng. Pract. **58**, 24–33 (2017)
2. Xiong, Z., Sheng, H., Rong, W., Cooper, D.E.: Intelligent transportation systems for smart cities: a progress review. Sci. China Inf. Sci. **55**(12), 2908–2914 (2012). https://doi.org/10.1007/s11432-012-4725-1
3. Miller, A.J.: Settings for fixed-cycle traffic signals. J. Oper. Res. Soc. **14**(4), 373–386 (1963)

4. Cools, S.B., Gershenson, C., D'Hooghe, B.: Self-organizing traffic lights: a realistic simulation. In: Prokopenko, M. (ed.) Advances in Applied Self-Organizing Systems. Advanced Information and Knowledge Processing., pp. 45–55. Springer, London (2013). https://doi.org/10.1007/978-1-4471-5113-5_3
5. Pandit, K., Ghosal, D., Zhang, H.M., Chuah, C.N.: Adaptive traffic signal control with vehicular ad hoc networks. IEEE Trans. Veh. Technol. **62**(4), 1459–1471 (2013)
6. Zhang, R., Ishikawa, A., Wang, W., Striner, B., Tonguz, O.: Using reinforcement learning with partial vehicle detection for intelligent traffic signal control. IEEE Trans. Intell. Transp. Syst., 1–12 (2020). https://doi.org/10.1109/TITS.2019.2958859
7. Silver, D., et al.: Mastering the game of Go with deep neural networks and tree search. Nature **529**(7587), 484–489 (2016)
8. Li, L., Lv, Y., Wang, F.Y.: Traffic signal timing via deep reinforcement learning. IEEE/CAA J. Autom. Sin. **3**(3), 247–254 (2016)
9. Wei, H., Zheng, G., Yao, H., Li, Z.: Intellilight: a reinforcement learning approach for intelligent traffic light control. In: Proceedings of the 24th ACM SIGKDD International Conference on Knowledge Discovery & Data Mining, pp. 2496–2505 (2018)
10. Wei, H., et al.: Colight: learning network-level cooperation for traffic signal control. In: Proceedings of the 28th ACM International Conference on Information and Knowledge Management, pp. 1913–1922 (2019)
11. Hsieh, P.C., Chen, Y.R., Wu, W.H., Hsiung, P.A.: Timing optimization and control for smart traffic. In: 2014 IEEE International Conference on Internet of Things (iThings), and IEEE Green Computing and Communications (GreenCom) and IEEE Cyber, Physical and Social Computing (CPSCom), pp. 9–16. IEEE (2014)
12. Tang, C., Xia, S., Zhu, C., Wei, X.: Phase timing optimization for smart traffic control based on fog computing. IEEE Access **7**, 84217–84228 (2019)
13. Shen, G., Zhu, X., Xu, W., Tang, L., Kong, X.: Research on phase combination and signal timing based on improved k-medoids algorithm for intersection signal control. Wirel. Commun. Mob. Comput. **2020** (2020)
14. Vogel, A., Oremović, I., Šimić, R., Ivanjko, E.: Fuzzy traffic light control based on phase urgency. In: 2019 International Symposium ELMAR, pp. 9–14. IEEE (2019)
15. Yi-Fei, W., Zheng, G.: Research on polling based traffic signal control strategy with fuzzy control. In: 2018 IEEE 4th International Conference on Computer and Communications (ICCC), pp. 500–504. IEEE (2018)
16. Liang, X., Du, X., Wang, G., Han, Z.: A deep reinforcement learning network for traffic light cycle control. IEEE Trans. Veh. Technol. **68**(2), 1243–1253 (2019)
17. Zhao, C., Hu, X., Wang, G.: Pdlight: a deep reinforcement learning traffic light control algorithm with pressure and dynamic light duration. arXiv preprint arXiv:2009.13711 (2020)
18. Sutton, R.S., McAllester, D.A., Singh, S.P., Mansour, Y., et al.: Policy gradient methods for reinforcement learning with function approximation. In: NIPs, vol. 99, pp. 1057–1063. Citeseer (1999)
19. Mnih, V., et al.: Asynchronous methods for deep reinforcement learning. In: International Conference on Machine Learning, pp. 1928–1937. PMLR (2016)
20. Lopez, P.A., et al.: Microscopic traffic simulation using sumo. In: 2018 21st International Conference on Intelligent Transportation Systems (ITSC), pp. 2575–2582. IEEE (2018)
21. Codecá, L., Frank, R., Faye, S., Engel, T.: Luxembourg sumo traffic (lust) scenario: traffic demand evaluation. IEEE Intell. Transp. Syst. Mag. **9**(2), 52–63 (2017)

Computer Vision, Image Processing, and Their Industrial Applications

A Transformer-Based Decoupled Attention Network for Text Recognition in Shopping Receipt Images

Lang Ren, Haibin Zhou, Jiaqi Chen, Lujiao Shao, Yingji Wu,
and Haijun Zhang[✉]

Department of Computer Science, Harbin Institute of Technology, Shenzhen, China
`hjzhang@hit.edu.cn`

Abstract. Optical character recognition (OCR) of shopping receipts plays an important role in smart business and personal financial management. Many challenging issues remain in current OCR systems for text recognition of shopping receipts captured by mobile phones. This research constructs a multi-task model by integrating saliency object detection as a branch task, which enables us to filter out irrelevant text instances by detecting the outline of a shopping receipt. Moreover, the developed model utilized a deformable convolution so as to learning visual information more effectively. On the other hand, to deal with attention drift of text recognition, we propose a transformer-based decoupled attention network, which is able to decouple the attention and prediction processes in attention mechanism. This mechanism can not only increase prediction accuracy, but also increase the inference speed. Extensive experimental results on a large-scale real-life dataset exhibit the effectiveness of our proposed method.

Keywords: Shopping receipt · Optical character recognition · Text detection · Text recognition · Saliency object detection

1 Introduction

Optical character recognition (OCR) is one of the mainstream tasks in the field of computer vision. OCR has a wide range of applications in practice, such as image-text retrieval [1], plate recognition [31] and ID card identification [30], etc. As a main container of information in human society, text is ubiquitous in various visual tasks. As a result, accurate text recognition turns out to be very crucial in many real-life applications.

Acutally, OCR of shopping receipts plays an important role in smart commerce [32], which is an application scenario suitable for a lot of machine learning algorithms. For shopping malls, one of basic tasks is to know the consumption information of a customer. In practice, although the merchants know the information of shopping receipts, it is difficult to obtain such information for shopping malls due to various commercial reasons. However, the key consumption

H. Zhang et al. (Eds.): NCAA 2021, CCIS 1449, pp. 563–577, 2021.
https://doi.org/10.1007/978-981-16-5188-5_40

information plays an important role on the formulation of business strategies of shopping malls and certain new commercial applications. For example, in order to attract more users, shopping malls usually return some cupons, which largely rely on accurate recognition of user's consumption information.

Most of mainstream methods [4,6,8,10,13] of text detection work on street images. Although they work well on shopping receipt images, these methods cannot distinguish text instances inside and outside a receipt's boundary, resulting in extra errors for subsequent tasks, such as text recognition. This paper proposes a multi-task method that performs text detection and saliency object detection [34] jointly, which can filter out the text instances outside a receipt. In addition, this model adopts deformable convolution [33], aiming at handling text instances with complex outlines in shopping receipt images. On the other hand, one of extant key issues of text recognition lies in the attention drift in attention mechanism [24]. To overcome this, we propose a transformer-based decoupled attention network, which can not only decouple the attention process and prediction process, but also increase the speed of model inference.

The remaining sections of this paper are organized as follows. Section 2 introduces text detection and text recognition methods related to this work. Section 3 presents the proposed multi-task text detection model and the transformer-based decoupled attention text recognition model, respectively. Experimental verifications have been conducted and covered in Sect. 4. Section 5 concludes the paper with suggestions for future work.

2   Related Work

The purpose of OCR is to obtain content and position of text instances from images. This technology can be divided into two tasks: text detection and text recognition. With the rise of neural network modeling technology, both of them based on neural network models have become the mainstream methods.

2.1   Text Detection

In general, text detection methods can be divided into three categories: regression-based methods, component-based methods and semantic segmentation-based methods. Regression-based methods are usually constructed on the framework of object detection methods, and perform regression on the basis of bounding boxes. Rotational region convolutional neural network (R2CNN) [1] uses suitable ratio of bounding boxes to deal with the large aspect ratio problem of text instances. Similarly, in order to solve the problem of different aspect ratios, feature enhancement network [3] introduces a weighted sum method, in which the importance of different text boxes is determined according to confidence scores, and the final coordinates of text boxes are obtained by a weighted sum. Textboxes [4] uses the idea of single shot multiBox detector(SSD) [5] to predict text boxes of different sizes based on different feature maps. Efficient and accurate scene text detector(EAST) [6] directly infers pixel-level quadrangles of text candidates without anchor mechanism.

Component-based methods compose parts of a text instance into the whole text instance. Text in an image has global homogeneity and locality in comparison to other objects [7]. Homogeneity and locality indicate that any part of a text instance remains the nature of the text. Human beings can recognize that it belongs to a text without seeing the whole text instance. Detecting text in a natural image with connectionist text proposal network(CTPN) [8] uses a modified framework of Faster RCNN [9] to extract horizontal text components with a fixed-size width for easily connecting dense text components and generating horizontal text lines. Detecting oriented text in natural images by linking segments(SegLink) [10] decomposes every text instance into two detectable elements, namely segment and link, where the link indicates that a pair of adjacent segments belong to the same word. Character region awareness for text detection(CRAFT) [11] detects the text area by exploring each character and affinity between characters. TextDragon [12] firstly detects the local area of the text, and then groups them according to their geometric relations.

Semantic segmentation-based methods predict at the pixel level. The aim of pixel-level text detection method is to use an end-to-end network to predict a dense feature map with the same size of an input image. Each pixel in the map indicates whether the pixel belongs to the text region or not, and then the pixels predicted as the text region are aggregated into the output text instances by postprocessing. Pixellink [13] not only predicts the feature map, but also predicts the connections between two pixels. Pixel-Anchor [14] proposes an integrated training method by combining target detection and semantic segmentation. Pixel aggregation network(PAN) [15] predicts the kernel of text instances which actually is shrunken text instance, and predicts the relationship between pixels and kernels. Progressive scale expansion network(PSENet) [16] reports a progressive fusion method, which aims at predicting n feature maps with different scales, and then fuses text instances of different scales by breadth-first search method to get the final result. Real-time scene text detection with differentiable binarization(DB) [17] proposes a differentiable binary method to predict the boundary of text instances while predicting the feature graph, so as to addressing dense texts.

2.2   Text Recognition

Traditional text recognition works at the character level. It can be divided into three steps: data preprocessing, character segmentation and character prediction. The accuracy of recognition heavily depends on the effect of character segmentation. Due to the complexity of the scene and the irregularity of character arrangements, the recognition rate is limited. With the development of deep learning technology, researchers have tried to use deep learning techniques to learn the features by variable-length prediction. At present, there exist two kinds of methods to deal with the problem of variable-length prediction. One is on the basis of connectionist temporal classification (CTC) loss function, and the other relies on attention mechanism.

The essence of CTC-based method is to optimize the conditional probability $P(L|Y)$, where Y represents the predicted label and L represents the ground-truth label. Convolutional recurrent neural network (CRNN) [18] proposes to superimpose RNN network on CNN to better learn intersection information of text instance. Gao et al. [19] proposed to use stacked deeper CNN directly, instead of RNN for recognition, which can ensure good accuracy and faster reasoning speed. Duc et al. [20] used memory enhanced neural network to further enhance the capability of CTC model in addressing long text instances. Yin et al. [21] proposed a character model that slides on the text line, and the detection process and recognition process are completed in a forward propagation.

Attention mechanism [22] is firstly proposed in the area of machine translation, and has been used in many other fields. Lee et al. [23] proposed a model using RNN for sequence modeling and attention mechanism for sequence predication. Cheng et al. [24] found that extant attention-based methods cannot address the problem of attention drift. They proposed an extra attention-supervised branch to deal with the problem. Bai et al. [25] proposed edit probability (EP) to tackle the attention alignment problem. Different from the general attention-based model using maximum likelihood estimation, this method generates strings by evaluating an input image as the output sequence of conditional probability distribution. In order to improve the efficiency of attention mechanism, Liu et al. [26] proposed a binary constraint to train the encoder.

3   Our Method

3.1   Overview of Our Framework

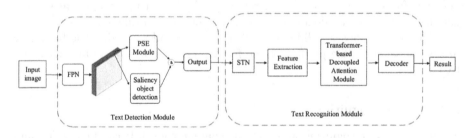

Fig. 1. Framework of our method

The overall framework of our method is shown in Fig. 1, which contains text detection module and text recognition module. In text detection module, given an input image, it is firstly fed into FPN [36] to extract visual information with several feature maps. Parts of convolution layer of FPN are replaced by deformable convolution [33]. Then, $N-1$ feature maps are fed into PSE module to generate output text instances. One feature map is fed into a saliency object detection branch [34] to generate the receipt outline. Subsequently, the receipt outline is utilized to perform position wise and operation such that those irrelavant text instances can be filtered out. For text recognition module, input text instance is firstly fed into STN [27] rectification module to rectify the tilt and perspective problem. Then, it is fed to feature extraction network. As a result, a sequence of feature vector is generated. The feature sequence is then sent to an attention branch with a transformer [35] to learn attention information. Here, it is directly sent to the attention module as the key and value of attention mechanism at the same time. In order to make better use of the information in sequences, the decoder is also composed of transformer blocks.

3.2   Multi-task Text Detection Model

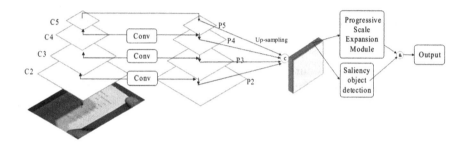

Fig. 2. The framework of text detection model

The framework of the multi-task text detection is shown as Fig. 2. The augmented input images are firstly fed into feature extraction network, which is built on the FPN [36] and ResNet [37] used as backbone. Assume that C_2, C_3, C_4, C_5 are the feature maps of different sizes in down-sampling process. C_5 is considered as the first feature map of up-sampling. P_4 is generated by the addition of C_4 mapped by convolution layer and up-sampled P_5. P_3 and P_2 are generated in the same way.

Deformable convolution [33] layer is adopted to replace the convolution layer of the first module in each forward down-sampling process, so that the model can learn visual information better to predict text instance outline more accurately. The shape of convolution kernel is fixed as rectangle, which makes convolution module pay more attention to objects with complex shape. In order to adjust the shape of convolution kernel, the deformable convolution adds an extra convolution layer to the original convolution position, which can output offset of the original convolution kernel. With the offset, deformable convolution can retain more visual information, which makes it more suitable for complex outline of text instances in hard cases. For a pixel in normal convolution, the calculation process is shown in the form of:

$$y(p_0) = \sum_{P_n \in R} w(p_n) \cdot (p_0 + p_n), \tag{1}$$

where P_N is an enumeration of the positions listed in a regular grid. For deformable convolution, learned offsets are added to the original convolution kernel. For a pixel p_0, the calculation is formulated as:

$$y(p_0) = \sum_{P_n \in R} w(p_n) \cdot x(p_0 + p_n + \Delta p_n), \tag{2}$$

Feature extraction network outputs N feature maps. The first $N - 1$ feature maps are utilized to predict text instances used by PSE module [16]. The reason for use $N - 1$ feature maps lies in dealing with the problem of distinguishing close text instances. Among these feature maps, the first one corresponds to the smallest text instance, which is used to determine the number of text instances and the center area of the text instances. Text pixels of other feature maps are aggregated to smaller one based on breadth-first principle. Text instances with few pixels will be filtered out.

The last feature map of model output corresponds to the output of saliency object detection branch, which is the predicted outline of the receipt. The output feature map is mapped to the probability space by a sigmoid function, and then is transformed into a binary graph by a threshold. The binary graph is used to filter out extra text instances outside the receipt by bitwise and operation with all other feature maps.

Saliency Object Detection Branch. The purpose of text detection is to extract the location and outline of text instances in shopping receipt images. However, many shopping receipt images contain complex backgrounds which may degrade the performance of subsequent applications. For example, Some shopping receipts even include more than two receipts, which will affect the performance of subsequent applications. Moreover, shopping receipt data usually come from mobile phone camera, resulting in many challenges such as perspective transformation, curling, bending, wrinkle, occlusion, shadow, and so on. If these problems can be rectified in advance, the recognition accuracy will be greatly increased. Saliency object detection which can detect the outline of shopping receipt makes it possible. In our application, shopping receipt is the most informative object in an image. Therefore, the detection of receipt outline can be constructed as a saliency object detection problem. In this task, the saliency object is a shopping receipt.

As shown in Fig. 3, shopping receipts are firstly fed into a feature extraction network. After feature fusion, $N - 1$ feature maps are used to generate text instances, and one feature map is used to obtain receipt outline. Binary image of receipt outline is generated by mapping the feature map to a probability space.

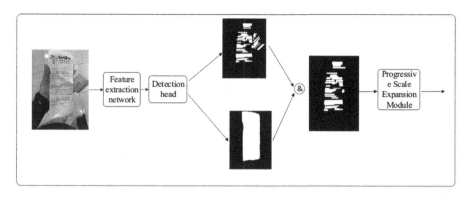

Fig. 3. The process of filtering out extra text instances by saliency objection detection

Then, the binary image conducts pixel wise and operation with all $N-1$ feature maps used to generate text instances. Extra text instances can be filtered out by the operation.

Loss Function. There are two optimization goals of the loss function design. First, the model should be able to predict the text instances of different scales as accurately as possible. Secondly, it should be able to accurately predict the saliency area of an input image, which is the outline of the shopping receipt. The loss function is constructed as follows:

$$L = \alpha L_c + \beta L_s + \gamma L_m, \tag{3}$$

where L_c represents the complete text instance loss function, L_s epresents the loss function of different scaled text instances, while L_m represents the loss function of saliency object detection. In addition, α, β, γ are super parameters, which were set at 0.7, 0.3 and 0.5, respectively, in our experiment. It is noticed that the number of text pixels is much smaller than the non-text pixels in shopping receipt images. If we adopt commonly used binary cross entropy loss, the target of the task cannot be well described due to the imbalance of categories. In the proposed model, a dice loss is used. Dice index is calculated as follows:

$$D\left(S_i, G_i\right) = \frac{2\sum_{x,y}\left(S_{i,x,y} * G_{i,x,y}\right)}{\sum_{x,y} S_{i,x,y}^2 + \sum_{x,y} G_{i,x,y}^2}, \tag{4}$$

where $S_{i,x,y}$ and $G_{i,x,y}$ are the prediction value S_i and the ground truth G_i of coordinate (x,y), respectively. Therefore, the calculation of l_c is formulated in the form of:

$$L_c = 1 - D\left(S_n, G_n\right). \tag{5}$$

L_s, representing the loss function of different scaled text instances, is the average of different scaled text instance losses:

$$L_s = 1 - \frac{\sum_{i=1}^{n-1} D\left(S_i \cdot W, G_i \cdot W\right)}{n-1}, \tag{6}$$

$$W_{x,y} = \begin{cases} 1, \ if S_{n,x,y} \geq 0.5 \\ 0, \ otherwise \end{cases}, \tag{7}$$

where W is the mask used to filter non-text pixels in a predicted image, and $S_{n,x,y}$ is pixel value of S_n in position (x, y). L_m is Lovasz loss [28] for saliency object detection, which is a smooth implementation of IoU (intersection-over-union). The implementation in binary segmentation is described as follows:

$$loss(F) = \overline{\Delta_{J_1}}(m(F)), \tag{8}$$

where Δ_{J_1} is Jaccard loss encoding a submodular loss, $\overline{\Delta}$ is the tight convex closure of Δ, and F is the output score. More details can be referred to [28].

3.3 Transformer-Based Decoupled Attention Network

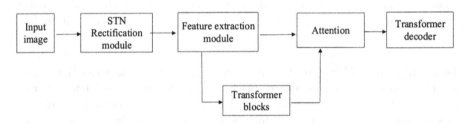

Fig. 4. The structure of transformer-based decoupled attention network

The structure of the transformer-based decoupled attention network is shown in Fig. 4. The input image is firstly fed into the STN [27] rectification network to correct the tilt and perspective problem. The network does not need extra supervised information to learn the parameter for rectifying an input image. For an input image, the module assumes two lines of pixels as the real position of control points, and two lines of pixel positions are inferred by control point leaning network. The map between the original image and rectified image is calculated by the two control point sets. The rectification process can be completed when conducting the map of each pixel in an input image.

The feature extraction network of the text recognition model is constructed according to the characteristics of shopping receipts. Different from a common feature extraction network, the objective of feature extraction in text recognition is not to get a series of feature maps, but to get a sequence of vectors. In order to achieve this goal, text instances need to be compressed into one dimension. The length of a compressed sequence is one fourth of the width of an input image, and the dimension of each vector in the sequence is the number of output channels of the last layer convolution network. Due to good characteristics of avoiding model degradation, Resnet is adopted as the backbone of feature extraction network. The first component in each down-sampling layer does not use the pooling operation, but an extra convolution layer is added at the end of each layer for better preserving the information of an image.

The feature sequence is then sent to an attention branch with transformer to learn attention information, and is directly sent to the attention module as the key and value of attention mechanism at the same time. In order to make better use of the information in sequences, the decoder is also composed of transformer blocks. The difference lies in that it is only used to better learn the relationship between sequences. Due to the attention mechanism assuming that the model has completed the alignment operation, it is sufficient to train each element in the output sequence by multi-classification loss function. In this method, cross entropy loss is used for training.

Transformer-Based Decoupled Attention Network. Wang *et al.* [29] claimed that the problem of attention drift exists because the general attention method puts the alignment and prediction tasks in the same structure, corresponding to the same batch of parameters. They proposed an alignment module based on convolution layer, which can calculate the weight information of attention in parallel. In this paper, transformer is utilized to construct attention mechanism. The parallel characteristics of transformer make it meet the paradigm of decoupled attention mechanism. Its structure is shown in Fig. 5. On one hand, a feature sequence is directly fed into the attention module as the key and value of attention mechanism. On the other hand, it is encoded by the embedding layer and sent to the transformer branch to learn the attention weight of each element in the output sequence. The self-attention structure of transformer can carry out the attention process in parallel. For an input sequence of self-attention module, each element in the input sequence plays the role of query, key and value at the same time. The vector representing the information of an element in the output sequence is mapped to query, key and value through different full connection layers. Therefore, different from the general attention mechanism which needs to obtain the corresponding weight of each element one by one, transformer can accelerate this process. The output sequence of transformer is mapped to the same size of output sequence, and then the features learned from feature extraction network are multiplied by matrix to obtain the corresponding features of each element in the sequence. In order to make better use of the information between feature sequences, the decoder is also composed of transformer blocks.

The advantage of transformer-based decoupled attention mechanism is described as follows. First, transformer is used to learn the attention weight information of each element in the sequence. Due to its parallel characteristics, transformer can decouple both the attention process and prediction process so as to improving the efficacy of the model. Second, transformer can capture the global dependencies between the elements of an input sequence. Finally, due to the parallel computing characteristics of transformer, the inference speed of the model can be largely improved in comparison to a common attention mechanism method.

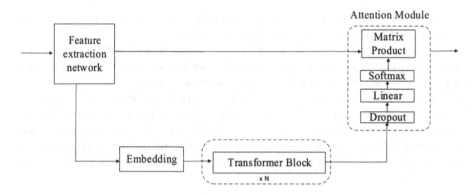

Fig. 5. Transformer-based decoupled attention module

Loss Function. The attention mechanism assumes that the attention branch can learn the weight of each element in an output sequence, which means that the model has completed the alignment operation in prediction. By matrix multiplication of the weight and the learned feature sequence, the feature information corresponding to each element in an output sequence can be obtained, and the sequence learning task is transformed into multi-classification learning for each element. Cross entropy loss function is employed to conduct the training process as shown in the form of:

$$Loss = -\sum_{t=1}^{T} \log P\left(g_t \mid I, \theta\right),\tag{9}$$

where T is the length of the sequence, t is the t-th frame in the sequence, g_t is the ground truth of the t-th frame, I is an input image, and θ is the parameter of the model.

4   Experiment

4.1   Experiments on Multi-task Text Detection Model

Fig. 6. Samples of text detection

Text Detection Dataset. We constructed a large-scale text detection dataset, which contains 9,845 images and 52,6351 text instances in total. Some examples are shown in Fig. 6. It is easy to find out that the shapes of text instances are quite diverse, and the shapes of receipts are usually irregular too. All text annotations in this paper adopt polygon annotation. For evaluation, we used three commonly adopted metrics in text detection, i.e., precision, recall and F1-score, to quantitatively evaluate the performance of our method.

Comparative Results. In this paper, 8,845 images were utilized as the training dataset, and 1000 images were regarded as the validation dataset. There are three mechanisms that need to be verified, including the multi-task training framework, deformable convolution, and data enhancement.

Table 1 shows the results of using saliency branch for multi-task training in comparison to that without using saliency branch. It can be found that precision, recall and F1-score are improved by 1.8%, 0.4% and 1.1%, respectively, compared with no saliency branch. Table 1 also shows the comparison before and after using deformable convolution. It can be found that, compared with the normal convolution, precision, recall and F1-score are improved by 1.5%, 0.5% and 1.0%, respectively.

Table 1. Comparative results using saliency branch

Model	Precision(%)	Recall(%)	F1-score(%)
Without saliency branch	79.4	81.6	80.5
With saliency branch	81.2	82.0	81.6
Normal convolution	79.4	81.6	80.5
Deformable convolution	80.9	82.1	81.5

In order to compare the mechanisms proposed in this paper, Table 2 summarizes all of ablation results. Among them, basic model is the model without any extra mechanism. Proposed model uses all mechanisms including saliency branch and deformable convolution. As shown in the table, the best precision, recall and F1-score are 82.7%, 83.8%, and 83.2%, respectively.

Table 2. Comparation of the proposed mechanism

Model	Accuracy(%)	Recall(%)	F1-score(%)
Basic model	75.4	76.3	75.8
Saliency branch	81.2	82.0	81.6
Deformable convolution	80.9	82.1	81.5
Proposed model	82.7	83.8	83.2

In order to further verify the effectiveness of the proposed method, this paper compares the proposed model with other commonly used text detection methods, as shown in Table 3. Among them, EAST which is usually regarded as benchmark model of text detection is the first model to use semantic segmentation for text detection,. PAN and DB are representative works published in recent years. It can be found that the F1-score of our model is 5.2%, 5.8% and 2.3% higher than that of EAST, PAN and DB, respectively. Although the precision is 2.5% lower than that of PAN, the recall is 12.9% higher than the model.

Table 3. Comparation between proposed model and other methods

Model	Accuracy(%)	Recall(%)	F1-score(%)
EAST [6]	79.2	77.1	78.1
PAN [15]	**85.2**	70.9	77.4
DB [17]	81.7	80.0	80.9
Proposed model	82.7	**83.8**	**83.2**

4.2 Experiment on Transformer-Based Decoupled Attention Network

Text Recognition Dataset. Text recognition dataset in this paper is also a self-built dataset. The text recognition dataset consists of text instances and their contents which contains 611,814 text instances. The samples are shown in Fig. 7. Compared with other computer vision tasks, text recognition task requires an extra dictionary, in which the key and the value are character label and digital label, respectively. For English text recognition, character labels are upper and lower case English letters and common English punctuation. For Chinese text recognition tasks, the alphabet should include all 92 printable characters in ASCII code, Chinese characters appearing in all text instances, and common Chinese character set. In addition, for different recognition algorithms, different functional characters need to be added to the alphabet. For the method based on CTC loss function, we need an extra character representing "blank", which indicates that the element in an output sequence does not predict any characters. For attention-based methods, two functional characters "BOS" and "EOS" are often added. "BOS" represents the beginning of a sequence and "EOS" represents the end of a sequence.

Fig. 7. Samples of text recognition

Comparative Results. We took 550,632 text instances as training dataset and 10,000 text instances as valid dataset. In order to ensure the accuracy of the experimental results, all of experiments in this paper chose the same hyper parameters. The batch size is 64, the optimizer is adadelta, the learning rate is 1.0, and the attenuation index is 0.95. For comparison, we used two evaluation metrics for text recognition: accuracy and normalized edit distance (norm ED).

The comparison between the proposed model and other text recognition models is listed in Table 4. ResNet-CTC and ResNet-BiLSTM-CTC are based on CTC loss function, while ResNet-BiLSTM-Attn is based on attention mechanism. It can be seen that the accuracy of proposed model is 6.5% and 2.2% higher than that of two CTC-based models, respectively, and the norm-ED is 2.4% and 0.7% higher than that of two CTC-based models, respectively. Compared with the ResNet-BiLSTM-Attn using attention mechanism, the proposed model achieves 0.6% and 0.4% gain with respect to accuracy and normal-ED, respectively. Moreover, the reference speed of our model is 1.9 times faster than that of ResNet-BiLSTM-Attn.

Table 4. Comparison of proposed model and other models

Model	Accuracy(%)	Norm-ED(%)	FPS
ResNet-CTC(Gao [19])	73.8	92.4	**131.6**
ResNet-BiLSTM-CTC(CRNN [18])	78.1	94.1	101.1
ResNet-BiLSTM-Attn(Aster [27] without STN)	79.7	94.4	39.9
Proposed(without STN)	80.3	94.8	75.2
Proposed(with STN)	**81.2**	**95.2**	68.5

5   Conclusions

This paper explored the problems of both text detection and text recognition. For text detection, to filter out the extra text instances, a multi-task model fused by text detection and saliency object detection is proposed. The method outperforms other state-of-art models in shopping receipt images. In order to address the drift problem in attention mechanism of text recognition models, a transformer-based decoupled attention text recognition network is proposed. The transformer-based decoupled attention text recognition model exhibits promising results in comparison to other methods, and its inference speed has been highly improved. In the future, this paper will explore image-level rectification methods to correct shopping receipt images, and try to apply the super-resolution method to the text recognition task.

Acknowledgements. This work was supported in part by the National Natural Science Foundation of China under Grant no. 61972112 and no. 61832004, the Guangdong Basic and Applied Basic Research Foundation under Grant no. 2021B1515020088, and the HITSZ-J&A Joint Laboratory of Digital Design and Intelligent Fabrication under Grant no. HITSZ-J&A-2021A01.

References

1. Mithun, N.C., et al.: Webly supervised joint embedding for cross-modal image-text retrieval. In: Proceedings of the 26th ACM International Conference on Multimedia (2018)
2. Jiang, Y., Zhu, X., Wang, X., et al.: R2CNN: rotational region cnn for orientation robust scene text detection (2017). arXiv:170609579
3. Zhang, S., Liu, Y., Jin, L., et al.: Feature enhancement network: a refined scene text detector (2017). arXiv:171104249
4. Liao, M., et al.: Textboxes: a fast text detector with a single deep neural network. In: Proceedings of the AAAI Conference on Artificial Intelligence, vol. 31, no. 1 (2017)
5. Liu, W., et al.: SSD: single shot multibox detector. In: European Conference on Computer Vision. Springer, Cham (2016)
6. Zhou, X., et al.: East: an efficient and accurate scene text detector. In: Proceedings of the IEEE Conference on Computer Vision and Pattern Recognition (2017)
7. Long, S., He, X., Yao, C.: Scene text detection and recognition: the deep learning era. Int. J. Comput. Vis. **129**, 1–24 (2020)
8. Tian, Z., et al.: Detecting text in natural image with connectionist text proposal network. In: European Conference on Computer Vision. Springer, Cham (2016)
9. Ren, S., He, K., Girshick, R., et al.: Faster R-CNN: towards real-time object detection with region proposal networks. In: Advances in Neural Information Processing Systems, pp. 91–99 (2015)
10. Shi, B., Bai, X., Belongie, S.: Detecting oriented text in natural images by linking segments. In: Proceedings of the IEEE Conference on Computer Vision and Pattern Recognition, pp. 2550–2558 (2017)
11. Baek, Y., et al.: Character region awareness for text detection. In: Proceedings of the IEEE Conference on Computer Vision and Pattern Recognition (2019)
12. Feng, W., et al.: Textdragon: an end-to-end framework for arbitrary shaped text spotting. In: Proceedings of the IEEE International Conference on Computer Vision (2019)
13. Deng, D., Liu, H., Li, X., et al.: Pixellink: detecting scene text via instance segmentation (2018). arXiv:180101315
14. Li, Y., Yu, Y., Li, Z., et al.: Pixel-anchor: a fast oriented scene text detector with combined networks (2018). arXiv:181107432
15. Wang, W., Xie, E., Song, X., et al.: Efficient and accurate arbitrary-shaped text detection with pixel aggregation network. In: Proceedings of the IEEE International Conference on Computer Vision, pp. 8440–8449 (2019)
16. Wang, W., Xie, E., Li, X., et al.: Shape robust text detection with progressive scale expansion network. In: Proceedings of the IEEE Conference on Computer Vision and Pattern Recognition, pp. 9336–9345 (2019)
17. Liao, M., Wan, Z., Yao, C., et al.: Real-time scene text detection with differentiable binarization. In: AAAI Conference on Artificial Intelligence, pp. 11474–11481 (2020)
18. Shi, B., Bai, X., Yao, C.: An end-to-end trainable neural network for image-based sequence recognition and its application to scene text recognition. IEEE Trans. Pattern Anal. Mach. Intell. **39**(11) 2298–2304 (2016)
19. Gao, Y., Chen, Y., Wang, J., et al.: Reading scene text with attention convolutional sequence modeling (2017). arXiv:170904303

20. Nguyen, D., Tran, N., Le, H.: Improving long handwritten text line recognition with convolutional multi-way associative memory (2019). arXiv:191101577
21. Yin, F., Wu. Y.-C., Zhang, X.-Y., et al.: Scene text recognition with sliding convolutional character models (2017). arXiv:170901727
22. Bahdanau, D., Cho, K., Bengio, Y.: Neural machine translation by jointly learning to align and translate. In: International Conference on Learning Representations (2015)
23. Lee, C.-Y., Osindero, S.: Recursive recurrent nets with attention modeling for OCR in the wild. In: Proceedings of the IEEE Conference on Computer Vision and Pattern Recognition, pp. 2231–2239 (2016)
24. Cheng, Z., Bai, F., Xu, Y., et al.: Focusing attention: towards accurate text recognition in natural images. In: Proceedings of the IEEE Conference on Computer Vision and Pattern Recognition, pp. 5076–5084 (2017)
25. Bai, F., Cheng, Z., Niu, Y., et al.: Edit probability for scene text recognition. In: Proceedings of the IEEE Conference on Computer Vision and Pattern Recognition, pp. 1508–1516 (2018)
26. Liu, Z., Lin, G., Yang, S., et al.: Learning markov clustering networks for scene text detection. In: Proceedings of the IEEE Conference on Computer Vision and Pattern Recognition (2018)
27. Shi, B., Yang, M., Wang, X., et al.: Aster: an attentional scene text recognizer with flexible rectification. IEEE Trans. Pattern Anal. Mach. Intell. **41**(9), 2035–2048 (2018)
28. Berman, M., Amal, R.T., Blaschko, M.B.: The lovász-softmax loss: a tractable surrogate for the optimization of the intersection-over-union measure in neural networks. In: Proceedings of the IEEE Conference on Computer Vision and Pattern Recognition (2018)
29. Wang, T., Zhu, Y., Jin, L., et al.: Decoupled attention network for text recognition. In: AAAI Conference on Artificial Intelligence, pp. 12216–12224 (2020)
30. Ryan, M., Hanafiah, N.,: An examination of character recognition on ID card using template matching approach. Procedia Comput. Sci. **59**, 520–529 (2015)
31. Chang, S.-L., et al.: Automatic license plate recognition. IEEE Trans. Intell. Transp. Syst. **5**(1), 42–53 (2004)
32. Maes, P.: Smart commerce: the future of intelligent agents in cyberspace. J. Interact. Mark. **13**(3) 66–76 (1999)
33. Dai, J., et al.: Deformable convolutional networks. In: Proceedings of the IEEE International Conference on Computer Vision (2017)
34. Ji, Y., Haijun, Z., Wu, Q.J.: Salient object detection via multi-scale attention CNN. Neurocomputing **322** 130–140 (2018)
35. Vaswani, A., et al.: Attention is all you need. In: Advances in Neural Information Processing Systems (2017)
36. Lin, T.-Y., et al.: Feature pyramid networks for object detection. In: Proceedings of the IEEE Conference on Computer Vision and Pattern Recognition (2017)
37. He, K., et al.: Deep residual learning for image recognition. In: Proceedings of the IEEE Conference on Computer Vision and Pattern Recognition (2016)

Interactive Clothes Image Retrieval via Multi-modal Feature Fusion of Image Representation and Natural Language Feedback

Xianrui Li[1], Yu Rong[1], Mingbo Zhao[1(✉)], and Jicong Fan[2,3(✉)]

[1] Donghua University, Shanghai, China
180910526@mail.dhu.edu.cn, mzhao4@dhu.edu.cn
[2] The Chinese University of Hong Kong, Shenzhen, China
fanjicong@cuhk.edu.cn
[3] Shenzhen Research Institute of Big Data, Shenzhen, China

Abstract. Clothes image retrieval is an element task that has attracted research interests during the past decades. While in most case that single retrieval cannot achieve the best retrieval performance, we consider to develop an interactive image retrieval system for fashion outfit search, where we utilize the natural language feedback provided by the user to grasp compound and more specific details for clothes attributes. In detail, our model is divided into two parts: feature fusion part and similarity metric learning part. The fusion module is used for combining the feature vectors of the modified description and the feature vectors of the image part. It is then optimized in an end-to-end method via a matching objective, where we have adopted contractive learning strategy to learn the similarity metric. Extensive simulations have been conducted. The simulation results show that the compared with other complex multi-model proposed in recent years, our work improves the model performance while keeping the model simple in architecture.

Keywords: Interactive image retrieval · Feature fusion · Fasion AI

1 Introduction

Fashion industry is an element industry that is closely associated with social, cultural, and economic applications since there are a huge amount of data of clothes emerged in different e-commerce platform. On the other hand, clothes also plays a key role to enhance peoples' daily life, as proper outfit can greatly improve personal quality and beauty. As a result, how to meet user' requirement of purchase is of great importance to improve user's feeling and to increase the sales of clothes. Merited from recently developed technology, namely deep learning [13, 19, 25, 28, 33], has been widely used in extensive applications of fashion due

H. Zhang et al. (Eds.): NCAA 2021, CCIS 1449, pp. 578–589, 2021.
https://doi.org/10.1007/978-981-16-5188-5_41

to the strong feature extraction ability . Such applications include clothes detection [6,22], clothes parsing [8,18,37], clothes compatibility learning [4,10,21,39], clothes image retrieval [23,36,38], clothes virtual try on [11,31,35,40], et al.

It should be noted that in the real world, there are increasing clothes images generated in Internet or e-commerce platform. To deal with such large-scale database, clothes image retrieval is an element technique that has attracted research interests during the past few years. The goal of clothes image retrieval is to search the most relevant images provided the query image via the extracted features of image. Therefore, a key element is how to extract the feature of clothes image that can characterize the semantic concepts of the original data so that the "semantic gap" can be narrowed. To solve this problem, some works employ deep structure composed of multiple non-linear transformations, where the underlying embedding semantic information of images could be better grasped [6,23,36].

While the above models have achieved satisfied retrieval performance in some clothes image retrieval system, one problem is that most of them cannot obtain the best results only in one retrieval procedure. Therefore, the utilization of relevance feedbacks is also good for handle the "semantic gap", as user's high-level perception can capture some key discriminative or side information to further enhance the performance of image retrieval. This can also be confronted in clothes image retrieval. In practice, the user first gives some key attributes of certain clothes. However, since there are quite many clothes have satisfied the key attributes, the retrieval clothes cannot directly match the meets of user. Then, the user can provide more attribute feedback information as supplement information to the retrieval image. As a result, the natural language relative feedback combined with original retrieval image feature can be fused as a new around retrieval so that the retrieval performance can be further enhanced.

In this paper, motivated by the above work, we consider to develop an interactive image retrieval system for fashion outfit search, where we utilize the natural language feedback provided by the user to grasp compound and more specific details for clothes attributes. In detail, we consider a practical case where queries are formulated as an input clothes image plus a text string that describes some desired modification to the clothes. Our goal is to search the most relevant clothes image given the queries of above multi-modal feature fusion. Our model can be divided into two parts: feature fusion procedure and similarity metric learning procedure. The feature fusion part includes three components: Semantic Extraction Module, Image Extraction Module and Fusion Module. The Semantic Extraction Module encodes the modified description and converts it into feature vectors through the attention mechanism, the image extraction module is responsible for encoding the reference image and converting it into feature vectors through the CNN network. And the fusion module is used for combining the feature vectors of the modified description and the feature vectors of the image part. All the components are jointly optimized in an end-to-end method via a matching objective, where we have adopted contractive learning strategy to learn the similarity metric.

2   Proposed Method

As mentioned above, multi-modal image retrieval is a very challenging task. Therefore in this section, we propose a novel model to combine image and natural language features for fashion image retrieval. Figure present an overview of our model. The advanced model includes three components: Semantic Extraction Module, Image Extraction Module and Fusion Module. The Semantic Extraction Module encodes the modified description and converts it into feature vectors through the attention mechanism, the image extraction module is responsible for encoding the reference image and converting it into feature vectors through the CNN network. And the fusion module is used for combining the feature vectors of the modified description and the feature vectors of the image part. All of the components are jointly optimised in an end-to-end method via a matching objective. All the modules outlined above will be described in detail in Sect. 2.1, Sect. 2.2, Sect. 2.3, and Sect. 2.4 (Fig. 1).

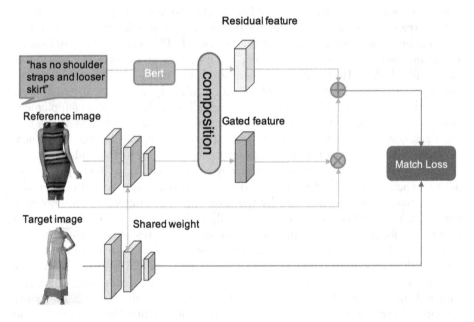

Fig. 1. An overview of our model

2.1   Semantic Extraction Module

Text Representation. Natural language serves as a import bridge to discriminate two different images. In the section, we extract the feature vectors of the modified text using modern transformer architecture [29]. Recently the transformer architecture has been seen in many Natural Language Processing (NLP) tasks and it achieved significant performance compared with other sequence to sequence model [15]. However, many transformer-like models contain millions of parameters and require an abundance of computing power. It is hard to train and apply on downstream tasks. Taking these into account, we take advantage of knowledge distillation [2,14] technique to compact large model. Fig. 2 shows BERT [5], a popular natural language processing model today, which has reached top levels in several language-based tasks since its emergence. As we can see from the figure, BERT consists of multiple Transformer [29] Encoders stacked on top of each other, each transformer encoder is structured as shown in the right half of the figure, containing a self-attention layer and a feed-forward network layer. Each sub-layer in each encoder has a residual connection around it, and is followed by a layer-normalization step. This model is simple in structure and powerful in performance, but the downside is that the training and inference time is much longer than the traditional network like the LSTM [15], with 110 million parameters included in the BERT.

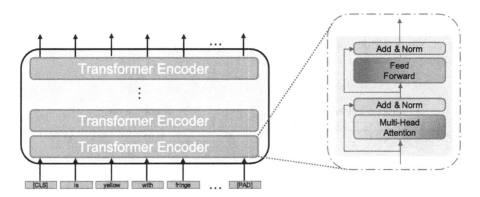

Fig. 2. A simple diagram of BERT. The BERT is basically a trained Transformer Encoder stack.

Knowledge Distillation. Knowledge distillation is a common model compression method that enables a set of light and small models, often called student models, to approximate the performance of a large and heavy model that called teacher models. In our experiment, we use DistilBERT [27] as our Semantic Extraction Module. DistilBERT is the student model that has the similar architecture to the teacher model, which is called BERT, where the *token-type embedding* and the *pooler* are removed, the number of layers is reduced from 12 to 6. The linear layer and layer normalisation are not modified because they have been highly optimized, so no modification is done.

To best utilize the common dimensionality between teacher and students networks, the DistilBERT model was directly initialized using the weights of the BERT model by taking one layer out of two. In the training part, the DistilBERT uses the same training data and training strategy as the original BERT model, but without using the next sentence objective.

In order for the student model to reach the performance of the teacher model as much as possible, we need the student model to mimic the output distribution of the teacher model, and for this purpose three loss functions are introduced. First, the student models uses distillation loss over the soft target during training: $L_{ce} = \sum_i t_i * log(s_i)$, where t_i represents the teacher's output distribution. However, directly using the *softmax* output results of the teacher model is not a efficient way, because the network trained well could have a very high confidence in the correct answer, while the prediction probability for other answers similar to the correct answer will be quite low. This can lead to difficulties in communicating similar data information learned by the teacher model to the student model. Therefore, [14] proposed a *softmax-temperature*: $p_i = \frac{exp(z_i/T)}{\sum_j z_j/T}$, where T controls the degree of smoothing of the output and z_i is the output distribution before *softmax* of the model. Students and teachers use the same T parameters during training, while at inference, T is set to 1 to revert to a standard *softmax*. In addition, L_{mlm} is used as the *masked language modeling loss* function for supervised training. Also adding *cosine embedding loss L_{cos}* helps align the directions of hidden states vectors in the student and the teacher model. The training process is shown in the Fig. 5 (Fig. 3).

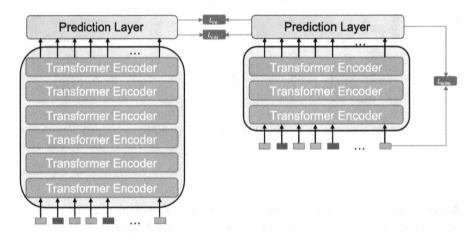

Fig. 3. An overview of knowledge distillation training process. The left half is the teacher model and the right half is the student model. The gray squares are the masked tokens. The training part uses three loss functions to train the student model.

2.2   Image Extraction Module

Image Representation. To encapsulate the visual contents into discriminative representations, we use a standard convolutional neural network(CNN) as the image extraction module. As it is known to all that a CNN has the ability to learn various visual concepts [34] from a image, we use ResNet [12] to extract features that can describe and modify by natural language.

Transfer Learning. As datasets become larger, *Transfer Learning* on smaller datasets is becoming more popular. Using a pre-trained model for a task different from what it was originally trained for is known as *transfer learning* [16]. With this advanced technology, the model have been carefully trained to be good at general tasks. In detail, for Image Extraction Module, the pre-trained model has the ability to encode general concepts, such as discriminating colors, texture and edges, which is much useful in fashion retrieval. Furthermore, for our task, considering the size of the fashion retrieval datasets [1,32] are much smaller than some well-known datasets [7,22,26] that are ideal places to train general models, using transfer learning is a smart choice to avoid annoying situation like insufficient data and overfit model.

2.3   Fusion Module

Many experiments on multimodel learning [20,24] are investigating a variety of methods of feature fusion. Fusion part is responsible for combining image and text features from Semantic Extraction Module and Image Extraction Module part. Following [30], we use Text Image Residual Gating(TIRG) as our Fusion Module:

$$\phi_{xt}^{rg} = w_g f_{gate}(\phi_x, \phi_t) + w_r f_{res}(\phi_x, \phi_t),$$

where f_{gate}, f_{res} denote gating and residual features, and w_g, w_r are learnable weights. In detail

$$f_{gate}(\phi_x, \phi_t) = \sigma(W_{g2} * RELU(W_{g1} * [\phi_x, phi_t]) \odot \phi_x)$$

$$f_{res}(\phi_x, \phi_t) = W_{r2} * RELU(W_{r1} * ([\phi_x, phi_t]))$$

where σ is the *sigmoid* function, $\odot$ is the dot product, and $*$ denotes the 2d convolution with batch normalization. w_{g1} and W_{g2} are 3×3 convolutions. Unlike other methods that constructing target features from zero, the main function of the TIRG is to modify the output features of the Image Extraction Module by the output features of the Semantic Extraction Module.

2.4   Matching Objective Module

The training objective is to learn an embedding space that make the modified features of the candidate image closer to the feature of the target image. In our experiment, we use the classication loss function, cross-entropy loss, for the task. Specifically, a set of images containing one positive sample and K-1 negative samples is selected at training time, and the *softmax* crossentropy loss is used:

$$L = \frac{-1}{MB} \sum_{i=1}^{B} \sum_{m=1}^{M} log \frac{exp(\kappa(\psi_i, \phi_i^+)}{\sum_{\phi_j \in N_i^m} exp\kappa(\psi_i, \phi_i)},$$

where ψ_i is the feature extracted by the fusion module and ϕ_i^+ is the feature of the target image. B is the batch size size and M is the number of times each batch is compared. κ is a similarity kernel and N_i^m is every possible set (Fig. 4).

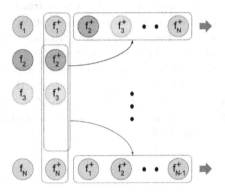

Fig. 4. An overview of matching objective module.

3   Simulations

3.1   Dataset

In this section, we will conduct experiments on the Fashion-IQ [32] dataset, a natural language interaction-based image fashion retrieval dataset, which contains a total of 77,648 publicly available images collected from Amazon. It include three subcategories: *Dresses, Tops&Tees* and *Shirts*. For each image pair, a candidate image, a target image and two descriptions of the difference between the candidate image and the target image are included.

3.2   Experimental Parameters

As it is known to all that Transfer Learning approaches in Computer Vision(CV) and Natural Language Processing(NLP) with large-scale pre-trained models are prevalent in all kinds of tasks. Benefiting from the diversity and complexity of data from large datasets, pre-trained models can usually extract the desired data features. In our experiments, we utilize the pre-trained DistilBERT as the initial Semantic Extraction Module. DistilBERT, a general purpose lightweight pre-trained model of language representation, is a distilled version of BERT, and it is pre-trained on the English Wikipedia and Toronto Book Corpus [41] dataset. Compared to BERT, it is 40% smaller and 60% faster, while retaining 97% language understanding capabilities. And we use the ResNet-50 [12] model, pre-trained based on the ImageNet [26] Dataset, as the initial Image Extraction Module. The pre-trained model can effectively extract the low-level feature information, such as edge information and texture information contained in the image, as well as abstract feature. The output size of Image Extraction Module is 512, as the same as the output size of Semantic Extraction Module. By, default, the batch size is set to 32, and we use Adam [17] optimiser with initial learning rate of 1×10^{-4}. We train the task for 85 epochs and a learning strategy of decreasing the learning rate by a factor of 10 every 40 rounds.

3.3 Results

Quantitative Analysis. Table 1 shows the performance on the test split of our model and the compared models. It is notable that TIRG is proposed originally for image retrieval with attribute-like text feedback. So in our experiments, we implement existing methods named TIRG*, which uses the same CNN architecture as our model and one-layer LSTM with 1024 hidden units for a fair comparison.

Table 1. Quantitative results of image retrieval on FashionIQ. Avg: averaged R@10/50 computed over three categories. R@K means recal at rank k.

Method	Dress		Shirt		Tops& Tees		Avg	
	R@10	R@50	R@10	R@50	R@10	R@50	R@10	R@50
Guo [9]	6.25	20.26	3.86	13.95	3.03	12.34	4.38	15.52
TIRG	8.10	23.27	11.06	28.08	7.71	23.44	8.96	24.93
Wu [32]	12.45	35.21	11.05	28.99	11.24	30.45	11.58	31.55
JVSM [3]	10.70	25.9	12.0	27.1	13.0	26.9	11.9	26.63
TIRG*	14.87	34.66	18.26	37.89	19.08	39.62	17.40	37.39
Ours	**22.07**	**46.85**	**18.15**	**41.31**	**23.97**	**48.65**	**21.35**	**45.6**

Qualitative Analysis. Figure 5 presents our qualitative results on FashionIQ. From the Fig. 5, we can see that the model understands semantic information well. First, it could accurately grasp figurative information, such as color, outline, texture. Moreover, we are surprised to find that our model could learn abstract concept, like style, feeling, and mood. Beside, we also find that in most cases, the top k targets that our model finds are not only able to accurately reflect the semantic information, but also able to preserve the original parts of the

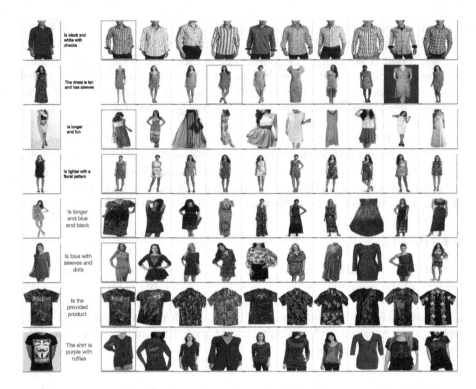

Fig. 5. Qualitative results of image search with natural language text feedback on FashionIQ.

reference pictures as much as possible. This phenomenon is in line with our philosophy of designing models, because we only want the model to modify the content mentioned in the semantics without moving the other features. So at the beginning of the design, we discarded the idea of generating target features directly.

4   Conclusion

In our work, we proposed a novel and simple method to solve the challenging task of image search with natural language description. The model fully benefits from the most advanced concepts and methods in today's deep learning filed, combining cutting-edge research on multi-modal fusion, attention mechanisms, model distillation, unsupervised learning, etc., with significant performance improvements compared to previous approaches. We make full use of the prior knowledge brought by pre-trained models, while inspired by residual networks [12], and use residual connections to fuse features of multiple modalities. Overall, compared with other complex multi-model proposed in recent years, our work improves the model performance while keeping the model simple in architecture.

Acknowledgement. This work is partially supported by National Key Research and Development Program of China (2019YFC1521300), partially supported by National Natural Science Foundation of China (61971121), partially supported by the Fundamental Research Funds for the Central Universities of China and partially supported by the T00120210002 of Shenzhen Research Institute of Big Data.

References

1. Berg, T.L., Berg, A.C., Shih, J.: Automatic attribute discovery and characterization from noisy web data. In: European Conference on Computer Vision. pp. 663–676. Springer (2010)
2. Buciluundefined, C., Caruana, R., Niculescu-Mizil, A.: Model compression. In: Proceedings of the 12th ACM SIGKDD International Conference on Knowledge Discovery and Data Mining, pp. 535–541. KDD 2006, Association for Computing Machinery, New York (2006). https://doi.org/10.1145/1150402.1150464
3. Chen, Y., Gong, S., Bazzani, L.: Image search with text feedback by visiolinguistic attention learning. In: Proceedings of the IEEE/CVF Conference on Computer Vision and Pattern Recognition, pp. 3001–3011 (2020)
4. Cui, Z., Li, Z., Wu, S., Zhang, X.Y., Wang, L.: Dressing as a whole: Outfit compatibility learning based on node-wise graph neural networks. In: The World Wide Web Conference, pp. 307–317 (2019)
5. Devlin, J., Chang, M.W., Lee, K., Toutanova, K.: Bert: pre-training of deep bidirectional transformers for language understanding (2019)
6. Ge, Y., Zhang, R., Wang, X., Tang, X., Luo, P.: Deepfashion2: a versatile benchmark for detection, pose estimation, segmentation and re-identification of clothing images. In: Proceedings of the IEEE/CVF Conference on Computer Vision and Pattern Recognition, pp. 5337–5345 (2019)
7. Ge, Y., Zhang, R., Wu, L., Wang, X., Tang, X., Luo, P.: A versatile benchmark for detection, pose estimation, segmentation and re-identification of clothing images. In: CVPR (2019)
8. Gong, K., Liang, X., Zhang, D., Shen, X., Lin, L.: Look into person: self-supervised structure-sensitive learning and a new benchmark for human parsing. In: Proceedings of the IEEE Conference on Computer Vision and Pattern Recognition, pp. 932–940 (2017)
9. Guo, X., Wu, H., Cheng, Y., Rennie, S., Tesauro, G., Feris, R.S.: Dialog-based interactive image retrieval (2018). arXiv:1805.00145
10. Han, X., Wu, Z., Jiang, Y.G., Davis, L.S.: Learning fashion compatibility with bidirectional lstms. In: Proceedings of the 25th ACM International Conference on Multimedia, pp. 1078–1086 (2017)
11. Han, X., Wu, Z., Wu, Z., Yu, R., Davis, L.S.: Viton: An image-based virtual try-on network. In: Proceedings of the IEEE Conference on Computer Vision and Pattern Recognition, pp. 7543–7552 (2018)
12. He, K., Zhang, X., Ren, S., Sun, J.: Deep residual learning for image recognition (2015)
13. He, K., Zhang, X., Ren, S., Sun, J.: Deep residual learning for image recognition. In: Proceedings of the IEEE conference on computer vision and pattern recognition, pp. 770–778 (2016)
14. Hinton, G., Vinyals, O., Dean, J.: Distilling the knowledge in a neural network (2015)

15. Hochreiter, S., Schmidhuber, J.: Long short-term memory. Neural Comput. **9**(8), 1735–1780 (1997)
16. Howard, J., Gugger, S.: Deep Learning for Coders with Fastai and Pytorch: AI Applications Without a PhD. O'Reilly Media, Incorporated (2020). https://books.google.no/books?id=xd6LxgEACAAJ
17. Kingma, D.P., Ba, J.: Adam: A method for stochastic optimization (2017)
18. Li, J., Zhao, J., Wei, Y., Lang, C., Li, Y., Sim, T., Yan, S., Feng, J.: Multiple-human parsing in the wild (2017). arXiv:1705.07206
19. Li, Q., Wu, Z., Zhang, H.: Spatio-temporal modeling with enhanced flexibility and robustness of solar irradiance prediction: a chain-structure echo state network approach. J. Cleaner Prod. **261**, 121–151 (2020)
20. Li, X., Ye, Z., Zhang, Z., Zhao, M.: Clothes image caption generation with attribute detection and visual attention model. Pattern Recognit. Lett. **141**, 68–74 (2021). https://doi.org/10.1016/j.patrec.2020.12.001, https://www.sciencedirect.com/science/article/pii/S0167865520304281
21. Liu, L., Zhang, H., Xu, X., Zhang, Z., Yan, S.: Collocating clothes with generative adversarial networks cosupervised by categories and attributes: a multidiscriminator framework. IEEE Trans. Neural Netw. Learn. Syst. (2019)
22. Liu, Z., Luo, P., Qiu, S., Wang, X., Tang, X.: Deepfashion: powering robust clothes recognition and retrieval with rich annotations. In: Proceedings of IEEE Conference on Computer Vision and Pattern Recognition (CVPR), June 2016
23. Liu, Z., Yan, S., Luo, P., Wang, X., Tang, X.: Fashion landmark detection in the wild. In: European Conference on Computer Vision (ECCV), October 2016
24. Lu, J., Goswami, V., Rohrbach, M., Parikh, D., Lee, S.: 12-in-1: Multi-task vision and language representation learning. In: 2020 IEEE/CVF Conference on Computer Vision and Pattern Recognition (CVPR), pp. 10434–10443 (2020). https://doi.org/10.1109/CVPR42600.2020.01045
25. Redmon, J., Farhadi, A.: Yolov3: an incremental improvement (2018). arXiv:1804.02767
26. Russakovsky, O., et al.: ImageNet large scale visual recognition challenge. Int. J. Comput. Vis. (IJCV) **115**(3), 211–252 (2015). 10.1007/s11263-015-0816-y
27. Sanh, V., Debut, L., Chaumond, J., Wolf, T.: Distilbert, a distilled version of bert: smaller, faster, cheaper and lighter (2020)
28. Szegedy, C., Vanhoucke, V., Ioffe, S., Shlens, J., Wojna, Z.: Rethinking the inception architecture for computer vision. In: Proceedings of the IEEE Conference on Computer Vision and Pattern Recognition, pp. 2818–2826 (2016)
29. Vaswani, A., et al.: Attention is all you need (2017)
30. Vo, N., et al.: Composing text and image for image retrieval - an empirical odyssey (2018)
31. Wang, W., Xu, Y., Shen, J., Zhu, S.C.: Attentive fashion grammar network for fashion landmark detection and clothing category classification. In: Proceedings of the IEEE Conference on Computer Vision and Pattern Recognition, pp. 4271–4280 (2018)
32. Wu, H., et al.: Fashion IQ: a new dataset towards retrieving images by natural language feedback (2020)
33. Wu, Z., Li, Q., Xia, X.: Multi-timescale forecast of solar irradiance based on multi-task learning and echo state network approaches. IEEE Trans. Ind. Inf. (2020)
34. Zeiler, M.D., Fergus, R.: Visualizing and understanding convolutional networks (2013)

35. Zeng, W., Zhao, M., Gao, Y., Zhang, Z.: Tilegan: category-oriented attention-based high-quality tiled clothes generation from dressed person. Neural Comput. Appl. (2020)

36. Zhang, H., Sun, Y., Liu, L., Wang, X., Li, L., Liu, W.: Clothingout: a category-supervised gan model for clothing segmentation and retrieval. Neural Comput. Appl. **32**, 1–12 (2018)

37. Zhang, Y., Li, X., Lin, M., Chiu, B., Zhao, M.: Deep-recursive residual network for image semantic segmentation. Neural Comput. Appl. (2020)

38. Zhao, M., Liu, J., Zhang, Z., Fan, J.: A scalable sub-graph regularization for efficient content based image retrieval with long-term relevance feedback enhancement. Knowl. Based Syst. **212**, 106505 (2020)

39. Zhao, M., Liu, Y., Li, x., Zhang, Z., Zhang, Y.: An end-to-end framework for clothing collocation based on semantic feature fusion. IEEE Multimedia 1–10 (2020)

40. Zhu, S., Fidler, S., Urtasun, R., Lin, D., Loy, C.C.: Be your own prada: fashion synthesis with structural coherence. In: International Conference on Computer Vision (ICCV), October 2017

41. Zhu, Y., et al.: Aligning books and movies: towards story-like visual explanations by watching movies and reading books (2015)

An Ultra-High Speed Gesture Recognition Algorithm Based on MobileNetV2

Wangpeng He[1($\boxtimes$)], Nannan Liao[1], Wei Liu[1], Jianglei Gong[1,2], Cheng Li[1], and Baolong Guo[1]

[1] Xidian University, Xi'an, China
`{hewp,blguo}@xidian.edu.cn`, `{nnliao,vliu,gongjianglei,`
`licheng812}@stu.xidian.edu.cn`
[2] China Academy of Space Technology, Beijing, China

Abstract. To solve the problem of interference in gesture detection and recognition under complex background, an ultra-high speed gesture recognition method based on a depth model is proposed. Generally, 12.5 frames per second (FPS) can achieve the requirements of real-time detection. This article reaches 2600FPS, which is defined as ultra-high-speed. The proposed algorithm makes up for the defects of the accuracy and robustness in traditional methods, as well as improves the low recognition speed of the general neural network under complex situations. Firstly, a neural network is designed and trained to accurately distinguish three different gestures. Secondly, a pruning and a merging operation is performed on the trained neural network, respectively. Without significantly affecting the detection and recognition results, the network is compressed and the efficiency is improved. Finally, the single-precision floating point data is quantized into integer data to further improve the detection and recognition speed. The experimental results show that the gesture recognition algorithm proposed in this paper can reach 2600FPS under the premise that the accuracy rate is 97.8%.

Keywords: Recognition · Depth model · Neural networks · MobileNet

1 Introduction

Gesture detection [1–7] and recognition is one of the important applications of human-computer interaction. Nowadays gesture recognition has become the focus of computer vision. At present, static gesture recognition mainly includes three steps: separation of gesture contour from the background, extraction of gesture features and classification of gesture. However, the complex background environment, hand posture habits, non-uniform lighting and other factors will have a certain impact on the detection and recognition. Thus, a gesture detection and recognition algorithm with a high recognition rate and time efficiency is of great research importance.

Gesture recognition is generally divided into two categories, traditional methods and convolutional neural network (CNN) based methods. Haar feature [8], clustering algorithm, adaptive boosting (Adaboost) algorithm [9], support vector machines (SVM)

H. Zhang et al. (Eds.): NCAA 2021, CCIS 1449, pp. 590–602, 2021.
https://doi.org/10.1007/978-981-16-5188-5_42

algorithm [10] are often used in traditional methods. Haar is a common operator used to describe features, whereas it is only sensitive to some simple structures, such as edges and line segments. The detection effect of gesture features is not ideal. A clustering algorithm performs as a classification operation that learns the internal structure of data characteristics in the process of training samples, and differentiates the data with the greatest common point into one group, which provides convenience for the next step of data analysis. In general, traditional recognition algorithms have high requirements on the quality of the processed images which shows a high recognition rate in a single background. Once there are interference factors such as complex environment and illumination, the recognition rate will be greatly reduced.

CNN-based deep learning methods are mainly used to classify graphics and detect features. Classical methods include BP (error Back Propagation) algorithm [11], Boltzmann machine [12] and so on. The above algorithms achieve better results for gesture recognition tasks in more complex background scenarios than traditional algorithms, but requires higher training samples, and the recognition speed in complex situations is not desirable, so it is not suitable for some real-time situations.

To sum up, both the two categories have their disadvantages. The speed of the former is fast, but the accuracy and the robustness need to be promoted. On the other hand, CNN-based algorithms have improved the accuracy, but the recognition speed is not ideal due to the structural complexity.

In this paper, a high-precision model based on MobileNetV2 [13–15] is proposed. It is robust to the complex environment and the change of gesture angle that is able to accurately identify the static gesture. In addition, the model fusion and quantization technique can be used to improve the recognition speed by several times at the expense of less than 1% accuracy. Experimental results verify that the optimized gesture recognition algorithm can recognize static gestures accurately and at super high speed.

2 Related Work

MobileNetV2 is typically a lightweight model. It adopts the residual learning module in Residual Neural Network (ResNet) [16] to increase dimension, deeply separate convolution, and reduce the dimension of the input image. Wherein the deep separation convolution is the main structure of the lightweight network. Compared with the conventional convolution operation, it has fewer parameters and lower operation costs. However, deep separation convolution cannot change the number of channels. If the number of channels in the upper layer is small, feature extraction can only be carried out in a low-dimensional space machine, which greatly affects the extraction effect.

To solve this problem, MobileNetV2 adds a 1×1 convolution before deep separation convolution, which alleviates the poor extraction effect in low dimensional space. The second hotspot of the model is Linear Bottlenecks. Considering that the feature extraction of the activation function in low-dimensional space is not as good as that of the Linear one, removing the activation function after the second 1×1 convolution can reduce the feature destruction of the activation function in low-dimensional convolution.

3 The Proposed Method

The workflow of the proposed gesture recognition algorithm is shown in Fig. 1. It can be divided into three parts, the design and training of neural network model, the fusion optimization of neural network model structure and the quantification of the neural network model.

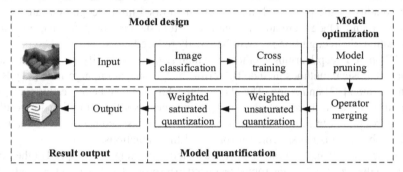

Fig. 1. Workflow of model design

3.1 Improved MobileNetV2

To enhance the recognition rate and speed, the MobileNetV2 network framework is structurally optimized. The improved MobileNetV2 network model is shown in Table 1. The original MobileNetV2 network model is shown in Table 2, where t is the multiple of the internal dimension of the bottleneck layer, c is the dimension of the feature, n is the number of times the bottleneck layer is repeated, and s is the stride of the first convolution of the bottleneck layer units in the network.

Table 1. Model structure of the improved MobileNetV2

Operator	t	c	n	s
Conv2d3 × 3	–	32	1	2
Bottleneck	1	16	1	1
Bottleneck	2	24	1	2
Bottleneck	2	32	1	2
Bottleneck				
Bottleneck	2	64	1	2
Bottleneck	2	96	2	1
Bottleneck	2	160	2	2

(continued)

Table 1. (*continued*)

Operator	t	c	n	s
Bottleneck	2	320	1	1
Conv2d1 × 1	–	1280	1	1
Avgpool/Maxpool	–	–	1	–
FC	–	–	2	–

Table 2. Model structure of the original MobileNetV2

Operator	t	c	n	s
Conv2d	–	32	1	2
Bottleneck	1	16	1	1
Bottleneck	6	24	2	2
Bottleneck	6	32	3	2
Bottleneck	6	64	4	2
Bottleneck	6	96	3	1
Bottleneck	6	160	3	2
Bottleneck	6	320	1	1
Conv2d1 × 1	–	1280	1	1
Avgpool7 × 7	–	–	1	–
Conv2d1 × 1	–	k	–	–

Figure 2 shows the basic Bottleneck. The network layer structure contains 94 layers that are mainly composed of convolution layers, batch normalization layers and nonlinear activation function. The function of the convolution layer is to carry out convolution operations on the input image, which is as same as the operation method of the traditional filter. In the process of analyzing and training the input image, the neural network gradually extracts the features of the gesture image data set from the shallow to the deep for analysis. The basic convolution operation is as follows

$$y(n) = \sum_{i=-\infty}^{\infty} x(i)h(n-i) = x(n) * h(n) \tag{1}$$

where x is the image input by convolution, h is the convolution kernel, and y is the result after convolution. Convolution operation is a basic calculation method in image processing based on deep learning. By updating the parameters of the convolution kernel, the effect of feature extraction on the input image is realized.

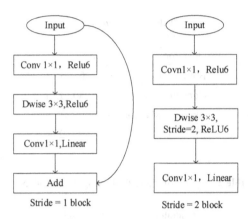

Fig. 2. Advanced MobileNetV2 basic Bottleneck

Relu6 function is transformed based on Relu [17] function, and its function is expressed as follows

$$y(x) = \begin{cases} 0, x \leq 0 \\ x, 0 < x < 6 \\ 6, x \geq 6 \end{cases} \tag{2}$$

where x is the input characteristic information, y is the activation function. This method adopts ReLu6 as the nonlinear activation function, which can maintain the robustness of the system in the case that the accuracy is not ideal.

This method uses nine reversible residual blocks in the improved neural network structure as the main part of the network. In the neural convolutional network, the increase in the number of network layers will cause problems such as vanishing gradient, exploding gradient, and the non-convergence of the later model. The residual block structure can solve the above problems well, so that the number of layers of the deep neural network can reach a very deep level, thereby increasing the accuracy of recognition. In a reversible residual block, the dimension of the inner layer of the block is greater than the dimension of the edge layer of the block. We reduce the dimension of the input feature, expand it, and then reduce it to output. In this way, unnecessary memory usage can be saved during calculation, thereby speeding up recognition.

To further accelerate the speed of image recognition, each reversible residual block adopts a linear bottleneck layer, which can avoid the loss of part of the characteristic information when using a nonlinear activation layer. Secondly, the internal common convolutional layer is improved to a combination of depth separable convolutional layer and point convolutional layer. In this way, the calculation amount can be reduced to $1/K^2$ of the original calculation amount when the convolution kernel of size $K * K$ is used for calculation, thereby speeding up the recognition. In addition, this method adds a point convolution layer as an expansion layer before each depth separable convolution layer. In this way, the number of data channels can be increased and more characteristic information can be obtained. It reduces part of the information lost due to the data passing through the nonlinear layer, increases the expressive ability of the model, and can further improve the accuracy of network recognition.

In this method, add and concat operations are respectively used in the network to perform feature fusion. In the middle part of the neural network, add is used in the tail of each inverted residual block to perform feature fusion. After fusion, the number of channels remains unchanged, which can increase the feature utilization rate of the model. The maximum pooling layer and average pooling layer are added to the tail of the neural network to reduce the size of the model and improve the speed and robustness of the calculation. At this time, concat is used to merge the features of the maximum pooling layer and average pooling layer. After the fusion, the number of channels increases, which can enhance the expression ability of the model.

To avoid the over-fitting problem in the deep neural network, this method uses the dropout layer for regularization in the last part of the neural network. It utilized the fully connected layer for classification to get the result of the neural network prediction. Finally, a three-dimensional vector is an output. These three vectors respectively represent the probability of the three gesture shapes of scissors, rock and cloth obtained by predicting the test image. The object information in the image can be judged by analyzing the output probability.

3.2 Cross-Validation Training

After designing and training the gesture neural network for training, the training set in the data set needs to be input into the network for calculation. The training process uses a 5-fold cross-validation method [18]. The training set is divided into 5 mutually exclusive subsets of the same size, each of which contains 2,000 gesture images, and the number ratio of the three gesture images of rock, scissors and cloth in each subset is close to 1:1:1. Choose any one from the 5 subsets as the validation set during training, and use the remaining four subsets as the training set. By analogy, a total of 5 batches are trained. Each subset is used as a validation set, and each batch is trained for 20 rounds. The cross-validation training method can make full use of the data set, so that the neural network can fully learn the feature information of the image, and effectively avoid the problem of overfitting.

The batches used in the training process are 32, the optimization function is Adam optimizer, the momentum parameters are 0.9, 0.99, and the initial learning rate is 0.01. In each round, the learning rate is decayed purposefully, and the learning rate is attenuated to 0.00001 in the last round. After 180 rounds of training the entire neural network model, the accuracy of the model reached 98.9%, where the confusion matrix is shown in Fig. 3. At this time, the inference speed of the model on the 1080Ti graphics card is 2.3 ms/frame, and the size of the entire model is 24 Mb.

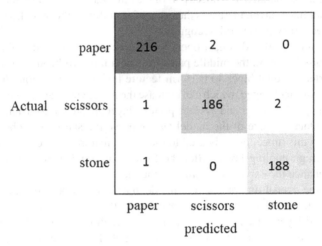

Fig. 3. Confusion matrix of gesture recognition results

3.3 Pruning of the Network Model

The Advanced MobileNetV2 has been able to identify gesture types with high accuracy, and the average frame rate can reach 300 FPS. However, our study found that model compression pruning and operator fusion can greatly improve the operation speed.

The structure of the improved neural network is shown in Table 2, from which it can be seen that the model used in this paper is composed of many identical module structures, among which the main core structure of the model is the reversible convolutional layer structure. With the increase of the number of layers, the number of convolution channels in the reversible convolution structure increases, and the learnable features become more and more abstract. Among them, the number of channels in the whole network changes as 16, 24, 32, 64, 96, 160 and 320. Next, the network is pruned under the condition that the number of channels remains unchanged.

The reversible convolutional layer structure has four variable parameters, which represent the expansion coefficient t within the structure, the number of channels c of the intermediate convolutional network layer, the number of specific channel network structure layers n, and the stride of the intermediate convolutional layer s. The number of channels c is fixed, representing the changing trend of the number of channels of each reversible convolutional layer structure in the entire network system, that is, from the initial 16 input channels to 320 output channels. The stride S of the middle convolutional layer is related to image downsampling. In order to ensure feature learning of different scales, the step size is not changed in the optimization stage. Next, we mainly adjust the other two variables.

The expansion coefficient t represents the channel expansion multiple of the network layer structure. When the expansion coefficient is 1, the number of channels is not expanded. When the expansion coefficient is larger, the characteristic information that the network structure can learn is more in-depth and abstract. The expansion coefficient of the network layer structure designed in the first stage is all 6. In this stage, the expansion coefficient is finally set as 2 after the trade-off test between precision and speed, so that to achieve the trade-off between precision and speed.

The number n of the specific channel network structure layer represents the number of each reversible convolutional layer structure. It can be seen from Table 1 that the number of unoptimized network layers increases from 1 to 4 and then decreases to 1. In this optimization stage, the maximum number of networks is limited to 2, which also follows the structure from high to low, but also removes part similar structure. After the model is pruned, the entire network is more suitable for low-resolution input gesture map information, which can achieve a trade-off between accuracy and speed. After proper pruning of the model, the entire network structure is more compact, and the operation speed can be increased by about two times to reach 1.15 ms/frame without significant loss of accuracy.

3.4 Fusion of Model Operators

After the optimization model in the previous step, the number of layers of the neural network is reduced from 200 to 100. In the entire neural network model framework, there are many 3×3, 1×1 ordinary convolutions and 3×3 group convolutions. These convolution operations contribute more calculations to the entire network.

Wherein, for the ordinary convolution with the size of 3×3, assuming that the height and width of the output feature map are $H_{out} \times W_{out}$, the input dimension is C_{in}, and the output dimension is C_{out}, then the computational amount M_{3*3} contributed by the convolution can be expressed as

$$M_{3\times3} = 3 \times 3 \times C_{in} \times H_{out} \times W_{out} \times C_{out} \tag{3}$$

Similarly, for the ordinary convolution with the size of 1×1, the calculation amount of its contribution is

$$M_{1*1} = C_{in} \times H_{out} \times W_{out} \times C_{out} \tag{4}$$

Group convolution is different from ordinary convolution. The group parameter in the group convolution used in this paper is the same as the number of input channels. Group convolution separates the channels in the feature map and uses different separate convolution kernels to operate. Finally, the processing results are merged. Among them, the amount of calculation required for a packet convolution with a size of 3×3 is:

$$M_{g:3*3} = 3 \times 3 \times H_{out} \times W_{out} \times C \tag{5}$$

where C is the number of channels of input and output. In group convolution, the number of channels of input and output is the same.

As shown in Table 1, a Batch Normalization is added to most of the convolution layers in the whole model framework, that is, the three different convolution layers mentioned above are all connected to the Batch Normalization. The hidden layer information of input and output is standardized in the Batch Normalization layer, so that the activation function of each layer is distributed in a linear interval. The calculation formula of the batch standard layer is as follows

$$X_{bn} = \frac{s(X - m)}{\sqrt{\sigma + \varepsilon}} + b_{bn} \tag{6}$$

where X is the input feature information. m is the mean value of the whole batch feature information. σ is the variance of the whole batch feature information. s and b_{bn} is the parameters learned in the training. ε is an auxiliary number used to prevent overflow of numerical calculations, usually is 0.001. There are 30 Batch Normalization layers in the model optimized in the first step. Next, the Batch Normalization layer immediately following the convolutional layer is optimized and merged with the previous convolutional layer to reduce the amount of computation.

In the actual fusion process, the basic calculation formula of the convolutional layer is

$$X_{conv} = XW + b_{conv} \tag{7}$$

where W is the weight. b_{conv} is the bias and X_{conv} is the output information. In the above formula (6), X_{conv} is used as input, and the final formula is

$$X_{bn} = \frac{s(X - m)}{\sqrt{\sigma + \varepsilon}} X + \frac{s(b_{conv} - m)}{\sqrt{\sigma + \varepsilon}} + b_{bn} \tag{8}$$

$$W'_{conv} = W \frac{s}{\sqrt{\sigma + \varepsilon}} \tag{9}$$

$$b'_{conv} = (b_{conv} - m) \frac{s}{\sqrt{\sigma + \varepsilon}} + b_{bn} \tag{10}$$

where W'_{conv} is the weight information in the fused convolution layer, and the convolution information in the convolution layer absorbs the parameters in the Batch Normalization. b'_{conv} is the bias in the convolutional layer. The W'_{conv} and b'_{conv} have been calculated before the model inference, and the weight information of the convolution in the model has been updated. Therefore, the calculation amount of the convolution layer after fusion is the same as before, while the operation process of batch standardization is omitted.

After the integration of the convolution layer and the Batch Normalization layer, the total number of layers of the whole model decreased from 100 to 72 layers. After the experiment, the running time of the optimized model was shortened from 1.15 ms/frame to 0.76 ms/frame, which shortened 1.5 times, realizing the acceleration of the model.

3.5 Model Quantification

Quantify the model that has been optimized and pruned. The single-precision floating-point weight activation information is matched with the integer value according to the KL divergence. Convert the single-precision floating-point value in the weight to integer data under the premise of keeping the distribution information as complete as possible, thereby improving the speed of the neural network.

Using the neural network's insensitivity to input noise, the weight information of FP32 single-precision floating-point type is quantized into INT8 integer, and the dynamic range of single-precision floating-point type is $-3.4 \times 10^{38} \sim 3.4 \times 10^{38}$, the dynamic range of the integer type is $-128 \sim 127$. Compared with single precision, the dynamic range of integers has extremely low precision and dynamic range, but the corresponding calculation speed can theoretically be increased by 4 times. Experiments prove that it can reach 0.575 ms/frame.

4 Experiment and Analysis

The dataset used in this method is collected from various images containing human's hands. On average, each person collects 1,500 images from different angles. This is shown in Fig. 4.

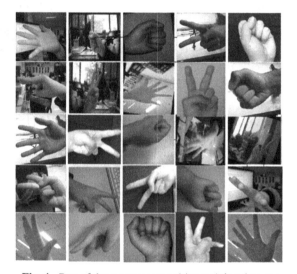

Fig. 4. Part of the gesture recognition training data set

The gesture image dataset contains a total of 15,000 images with the size of 640×640, the images are three-channel color RGB, and the file format is jpg. The images in the dataset are divided into three types of gestures: rock, scissors, and cloth according to the gestures. The ratio of the three types of images is close to 1:1:1.

In practical training period, the image data set needs to be divided into three parts, namely train set, validation set and test set. The train set is input to the neural network for training during the training process. The validation set periodically verifies the rationality of the method during the training process. The test set evaluates the performance of the method when it is completed. Among the total of 15,000 images, 10,000 images are selected as the training set, 1,500 images are selected as the validation set, and the remaining 3,500 images are used as the test set. The entire data distribution ratio is 20:3:7, which is consistent with Deep learning training standards.

The present implementation runs on the Ubuntu-16.04 system of Intel Core i7-7800X, 32 GB memory and GTX 1080TI graphics card. The software platforms are PyCharm, OpenCV and TensorRT, and the three-channel RGB gesture image dataset with resolution is tested.

The improved algorithm of MobileNetV2 proposed in this paper collects and detects rock, paper, scissors gestures made by testers in real-time through a CCD camera. Figure 5 shows part of the detection results. All gestures made by testers randomly can be accurately detected and recognized, and the overall target is just in the target box area.

Fig. 5. Part of the test classification results

Here is a comparison with MobileNetV1 [19], MobilenetV2 [15], GoogleNet [20] and ResNet50 + VGG16 [21], as shown in Table 3. It can be seen from the table that the accuracy of the four methods for simple gesture recognition has reached more than 95%, and the accuracy of the method in this paper has reached 98.7%.

Table 3. Comparison of gesture recognition rate of different models

Model	Accuracy
MobileNetV1	96.2%
MobileNetV2	98.1%
GoogLeNet	95%
ResNet50 + VGG16	97.57%
Advanced MobileNetV2 (ours)	98.7%

On the premise of an average accuracy of 98.7%, most of the frames per second (FPS) transmitted by GPU side can be maintained at 830 FPS, which can meet the requirements of high frame rate static gesture recognition. After model pruning, merging, quantization and other optimization operations, under the same software and hardware conditions, the accuracy drops slightly to 97.8%, but the transmission frame per second can reach about 2600 FPS, that is, ultra-high frame rate static gesture recognition. At the same time, on the CPU side with the same accuracy, the frame rates can reach about 300 FPS and 600 FPS respectively. As shown in Table 4.

Table 4. The accuracy and speed of this algorithm under different conditions

Condition	Accuracy	FPS
GPU	98.7%	830
GPU	97.8%	2600
CPU	98.7%	300
CPU	97.8%	600

5 Conclusion

Aiming at the difficulty of recognizing gestures in complex backgrounds, and the existing algorithms cannot recognize gesture categories at high speed without guaranteeing accuracy, this paper proposes a gesture recognition algorithm based on deep learning. The algorithm first uses the back propagation method and the gradient descent method to update the weights of the neural network initially designed. The internal common convolutional layer is improved to a combination of depth separable convolutional layer and point convolutional layer. Then pruning and merging the overall network to optimize the network model. Finally, the optimized and pruned model is quantified, and the floating-point data is converted into integer data, thus improving the speed of the neural network. Experimental results show that the ultra-high-speed gesture recognition algorithm proposed in this paper can perform ultra-high-speed detection and recognition of static gestures with guaranteed accuracy. On the GPU side, the accuracy rate can reach 97.8% and the speed can reach 2600 FPS.

Acknowledgements. This work was supported by National Natural Science Foundation of China (No. 51805398 and 61972398), Project of Youth Talent Lift Program of Shaanxi University Association for science and technology (No. 20200408).

References

1. Köpüklü, O., Gunduz, A., Kose, N., Rigoll, G.: Real-time hand gesture detection and classification using convolutional neural networks. In: 2019 14th IEEE International Conference on Automatic Face and Gesture Recognition, Lille, France. IEEE (2019)
2. Abdallah, M.B., Kallel, M., Bouhlel, M.S.: An overview of gesture recognition. In: International Conference on Sciences of Electronics, Sousse, Tunisia. IEEE (2012)
3. Wu, C., Xie, J., Zhou, K.: Overview of human-computer interaction technology based on gesture recognition. Comput. Era **2**, 29–32 (2016)
4. Liu, H., Wang, L.: Gesture recognition for human-robot collaboration. A review. Int. J. Ind. Ergon. **68**, 355–367 (2017)
5. Ortega, F.R., Barreto, A.,Rishe, N., Adjouadi, M., Abyarjoo, F.: Poster: real-time gesture detection for multi-touch devices. In: 2013 IEEE Symposium on 3D User Interfaces (3DUI), Orlando, FL, USA. IEEE (2013)
6. Gupta, A., Kumar, Y., Malhotra, S.: Banking security system using hand gesture recognition. In: 2015 International Conference on Recent Developments in Control, Automation and Power Engineering (RDCAPE), Noida, India. IEEE (2015)

7. Lionnie, R., Timotius, I.K., Setyawan, I.: An analysis of edge detection as a feature extractor in a hand gesture recognition system based on nearest neighbor. In: Proceedings of the 2011 International Conference on Electrical Engineering and Informatics, Bandung, Indonesia. IEEE (2011)
8. Park, K.Y., Hwang, S.Y.: An improved Haar-like feature for efficient object detection. Pattern Recogn. Lett. **42**, 148–153 (2014)
9. Zhu, J., Arbor, A., Hastie, T.: Multi-class AdaBoost. Stat. Interface **2**(3), 349–360 (2006)
10. Qin, J., He, Z.S.: A SVM face recognition method based on Gabor-featured key points. In: 2005 International Conference on Machine Learning and Cybernetics, Guangzhou, China, pp. 5144–5149. IEEE (2005)
11. Zhang, W., Li, P.: Temporal spike sequence learning via backpropagation for deep spiking neural networks. In: Advances in Neural Information Processing Systems, vol. 33 (2020)
12. Ackley, D., Hinton, G., Sejnowski, T.: A learning algorithm for Boltzmann machines. Cogn. Sci. **9**(1), 147–169 (1985)
13. Sandler, M., Howard, A., Zhu, M., Zhmoginov, A., Chen, L.: MobileNetV2: inverted residuals and linear bottlenecks. In: CVF Conference on Computer Vision and Pattern Recognition, Salt Lake City, UT, USA (2018)
14. Dong, K., Chengjie, Z., Ruan, Y., Yuzhi, L.: MobileNetV2 model for image classification. In: 2020 2nd International Conference on Information Technology and Computer Application (ITCA), Guangzhou, China. IEEE (2020)
15. Saxen, F., Werner, P., Handrich, S., Othman, E., Al-Hamadi, A.: Face attribute detection with MobileNetV2 and NasNet-mobile. In: 2019 11th International Symposium on Image and Signal Processing and Analysis (ISPA), Dubrovnik, Croatia. IEEE (2019)
16. He, K., Xiangyu Zhang, X., Ren, S., Sun, J.: Deep residual learning for image recognition. In: IEEE Conference on Computer Vision and Pattern Recognition, Las Vegas, NV, USA. IEEE (2016)
17. Hahnloser, R., Sarpeshkar, R., Mahowald, M.A., Douglas, R.J., Seung, H.S.: Digital selection and analogue amplification coexist in a cortex-inspired silicon circuit. Nature **405**, 947–951 (2000)
18. Takada, T., et al.: Internal-external cross-validation helped to evaluate the generalizability of prediction models in large clustered datasets. J. Clin. Epidemiol. **137**, 83–91 (2021)
19. Howard, A.G., et al.: MobileNets: efficient convolutional neural networks for mobile vision applications. In: CVF Conference on Computer Vision and Pattern Recognition (2017)
20. Szegedy, C., et al.: Going deeper with convolutions. In: 2015 IEEE Conference on Computer Vision and Pattern Recognition, Boston, MA, USA. IEEE (2015)
21. Guan, W., Ma, J., Ma, L.: Gesture recognition based on convolution neural network. J. Xi'an Univ. Posts Telecommun. **24**(06), 80–84 (2019)

An Hybrid Model CMR-Color of Automatic Color Matching Prediction for Textiles Dyeing and Printing

Musen Chen[1], Hubert S. Tsang[2,3], Kang T. Tsang[2,3], and Tianyong Hao[1(✉)]

[1] School of Computer Science, South China Normal University, Guangzhou, China
{musen,haoty}@m.scnu.edu.cn
[2] Pacific Textiles Holdings Limited, Hong Kong, China
hubert-tsang@pacific-textiles.com,
kang-tsang@artisantechnologies.cn
[3] Guangzhou Gaozhuan Information Technology Limited, Guangdong, China

Abstract. Automatic color matching is an essential technology for dyeing and printing in the textiles industry to ensure customer quality standards and increase production efficiency. Computer-assisted automatic color matching has played an increasingly important role in textiles dyeing and printing as the cycle time of fashion decreases, with consumers constantly demanding new styles. Machine learning has been widely applied in various fields, however there are still difficulties such as the time-consuming and labor-intensive procedure of manual feature extraction required by conventional machine learning models. For dyeing and printing, the large amount of dyeing recipe data involving dye concentrations, spectra, and substrate materials have made it difficult to build artificial neural network models in complex data fitting. This paper proposes an automatic color matching prediction model, CMR-Color, by incorporating three neural network models including typical CNN, MLP, and ResNet to improve the capability of extracting high-dimensional features from spectral data. It selects the dyes required and respective concentration values of each component in the recipe. Moreover, it uses feature fusion to improve the prediction performance of automatic color matching. The experiment datasets of 72,132 recipes are from a world-class listed company in the textiles industry. The results show that the CMR-Color model achieves the best performance in all three evaluation metrics compared with four state-of-the-art baseline methods, verifying its effectiveness in color matching prediction for textiles dyeing and printing.

Keywords: Textiles dyeing and printing · Color matching · Spectrum · Neural network · MLP · CNN · ResNet

1 Introduction

The size of the global fashion industry is approximately USD$2.5 trillion annually and employs 75 million people worldwide [1]. Textiles are the major component of fashion

© Springer Nature Singapore Pte Ltd. 2021
H. Zhang et al. (Eds.): NCAA 2021, CCIS 1449, pp. 603–618, 2021.
https://doi.org/10.1007/978-981-16-5188-5_43

apparel. WTO data shows that China is responsible for exporting approximately 30% of apparel and 40% of textiles in the world [2], showing the importance of the industry. For fashion brands, the accurate reproduction of colors specified by their designers is critical and determines whether textile mills receive orders. While textiles with inaccurate colors may still be sold to other users, their value is low. Some printing and dyeing enterprises still use backwards production methods that rely largely on human experience and capabilities. The recipe formation process is usually done by a dyeing master who looks at color samples provided by customers and formulates dyeing recipes to achieve customers' color requirements through personal experience. Furthermore, validation of color accuracy relies on quality inspection staffs to have highly color accurate vision, which is tested regularly with tests such as the Farnsworth Munsell 100 Hue Test [3]. These human-centric processes make it difficult to meet the market demand for accuracy, timeliness, and customization [4]. Computer-aided color matching for textiles dyeing and printing is an essential research topic to improve the efficiency and accuracy of color matching and is an important way for textiles enterprises to improve their global competitiveness.

In the textiles dyeing and printing industry, being able to provide a given standard color reference value to automatically predict the most accurate dyeing recipe with associated concentration values of each component in the recipe is vital. The work can be divided into three main steps: 1) analyzing recipe, i.e., determining compositions in a dye recipe based on standard color reference values. 2) loading corresponding spectral data based on dye components and substrate/standard components in the dye recipe. 3) predicting concentration values corresponding to the components in the dye recipe based on spectral data and categorical variables data of "Fiber material", "Dyeing process", and "Substrate delivery". Existing methods of color matching often model the relationship between dyeing recipe and reflectance values of corresponding product mixtures [5], or model relationships between dyeing recipes and corresponding color tristimulus values [6]. However, the automatic dyeing and coloring process is very complex, involving color chemistry [7], optics, and dyeing production issues, such as dyeing time, dyeing temperature, auxiliaries required to increase dye utilization and other factors. In addition, the dyeing process and different effects of light absorption and reflection needed to be considered [8]. Therefore, complex data from the various sources are required to be analyzed in the actual color matching process. The current automatic color matching methods based on tristimulus values can only solve a few automatic dyeing color matching problems and cannot adapt to current intricate automatic printing and color matching environment. Therefore, the above-mentioned common models do not have significant value in the application to actual automatic color matching for textiles dyeing and printing. To sum up, the research of automatic color matching for textiles dyeing and printing faces two main difficulties: 1) How to efficiently and to effectively extract relevant data from a large amount of dyeing recipes with complex relationships between ingredients. 2) How to design an effective model to extract relevant features from complex color matching data to improve the performance of dyeing recipe prediction.

In this paper, a hybrid neural network model, CMR-Color, incorporating typical CNN, MLP, and ResNet is proposed for automatically predicting accurate dyeing recipe for textiles dyeing and printing and concentration values of each component in the recipe. The CMR-Color model applies a divide-and-conquer strategy to process complex data by fusing different models. The ResNet model is used for feature extraction of dye component spectral data and the typical CNN model is for feature extraction of substrate/standard spectral data. After that, categorical variables data of "Fiber material", "Dyeing process", "Substrate delivery" is encoded by deep embedding (Cat2Vec) coding [9] or one-hot coding [10] methods and then are combined into one feature vector represented by feature fusion. Finally, the fused features are used for dyeing recipe prediction to improve the performance of automatic color matching for the textiles dyeing and printing model. Experiment data of 72,132 dyeing recipes are from a large listed company. Through the comparison with existing state-of-the-art baseline methods, the results show that our CMR-Color hybrid model outperforms the baselines in all three evaluation metrics. The comparison demonstrates the effectiveness of the model in automatic color matching for textiles dyeing and printing prediction.

The contributions of this paper are mainly in the following three aspects: 1) two color matching datasets for textiles dyeing and printing are constructed for model training from 72,132 actual dyeing recipes from a large listed company; 2) a hybrid CMR-Color model incorporating multiple neural network models is proposed to extract relevant color features for color matching model improvement; 3) the hybrid model outperforms the state-of-the-art baseline methods through comparison experiments.

2   Related Work

With the rapid development of artificial intelligence, the relevant algorithms and models of artificial intelligence were widely used in different fields. Computer-aided color matching for textiles dyeing and printing has drawn more and more attention with the introduction of artificial intelligence methods. There were three main research directions in the field of computer-aided color matching for textiles dyeing and printing as follows:

Traditional computer-aided color matching and color measurement systems [11–13] were usually built on the basis of Kubelka-Munk optical theory. The representative research was the tristimulus value color matching model system, which calculated the color changes under various light sources to avoid the problem of unqualified color matching caused by light source changes. It was able to quickly correct color recipes to improve color matching efficiency and scientifically managed recipe archives. However, the use of the tristimulus value matching method for color matching required the establishment of a basic database of monochromatic samples, and then formulated a dyeing recipe according to the single constant theory. However, the theory was affected by many factors in actual dyeing and printing production, such as dye mixing, which did not fully follow the principle of additivity. In addition, this method required the preparation of a huge basic database. Even more, the method could not be used in the case of dye replacement or standard material replacement. Therefore, it was difficult to adapt to the current small-batch, fast-paced production needs in the field of printing, dyeing and color matching.

The second research direction was the method of automatic printing and dyeing color matching using conventional machine learning algorithms. Liu et al. [14] established a mathematical model of the chromaticity value and mass ratio of base pigment using a multivariate nonlinear regression method and verified the significant effect of the proposed model. The results showed that spectral curve satisfied the requirement of same colors and spectrum and met the need of camouflage color matching, which provided a solution for the automation and intelligence of camouflage color matching. Chen et al. [15] predicted fabric color by analyzing the relationship between multiple process parameters and dyed fabric color during rolling and dyeing process. This task was viewed as a multidimensional regression problem. A multidimensional support vector regression (M-SVR) model was implemented within a machine learning framework designed for color prediction, and multiple process parameters of the dyeing process were provided to the M-SVR model to predict the dyed fabric color.

The third research direction was an automatic color matching method for textile printing and dyeing based on neural network models. Shen et al. [16] applied back propagation (BP) neural networks for automatic color matching. BP neural networks had reasonable nonlinear mapping capability for complex nonlinear relationships between dyeing recipes and corresponding optical values of fabrics through learning of training data. However, it had problems such as slow convergence speed, large number of hidden layer neurons, and weak network generality. These problems made it encounter greater challenges in the prediction and application of fabric dyeing recipes. Li et al. [17] proposed an improved algorithm based on BP neural networks, through which initial weights, thresholds and learning rates could be determined, reducing the randomness of parameter settings during initial operation of neural networks, accelerating convergence speed, and improving prediction performance. The results denoted that the improved BP algorithm outperformed conventional BP neural network in terms of convergence speed and training accuracy. Rosa et al. [18] used a dataset generated from dyeing experiments to build and train a multilayer perceptron neural network (MLP) to automatically perform color matching. The experiment results verified that the MLP-ANN model partially simulated nonlinear behavior of dyeing process, proving the effectiveness of the MLP model.

3   CMR-Color Fusion Model

This paper proposes a hybrid model CMR-Color based on multi-model fusion to extract relevant features of complex color matching data to increase the accuracy of color reproduction. The task can be converted to the prediction of dyeing recipe components and corresponding concentration values. The model is composed of four parts: a ResNet model, a typical CNN model, a data encoding process, and a MLP model.

For the recipe dye component spectral data, the dye component consists of two-dimensional data with different wavelengths and concentrations of spectral absorption data. Each dye recipe contains various dye components, which increases the complexity of dye component spectral data. In order to express color characteristics of dye component spectral data, this paper applies a ResNet network to extract color features expressed in the spectral data of dye components. The color features of different dye components are extracted by superimposing two-dimensional data of the spectra of multiple dye components in the dye recipe through a multi-channel convolution operation of the ResNet network.

Compared with spectral data of dye components, spectral data of substrate/standard only consists of spectral data at a fixed solubility, so the spectral data of substrate/standard is a sequence of data at different wavelengths along a fixed solubility. A revised CNN model is applied to extract the features of the spectral data and perform a maxpooling operation, which reduces the number of parameters while maintaining main features. Data may contain various numbers of categorical variables, e.g., "Dyeing process" contains 5 categories, "Substrate Delivery" has 96 categories, while "Fiber material" and "Dyeing process" have a relative small number of categories. Therefore, one-hot coding is applied to convert data with normal category numbers into a hot encoding vector, while a deep embedding (Cat2Vec) method is applied to convert data with large category number into an embedding encoding vector.

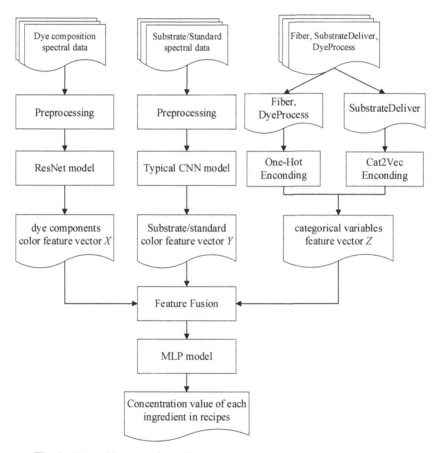

Fig. 1. The architecture of our CMR-Color model for automatic color matching

The architecture of the proposed CMR-Color model is shown in Fig. 1. Given spectral data of dye components in recipes as input to the ResNet model, spectral features of the dye components are captured. The global average pooling layer [19] is applied to reduce feature dimensionality to form a feature vector X. After that, relevant spectral data features of substrate/standard are extracted through the typical CNN model. A global average pooling layer is applied to reduce feature dimensions, thereby forming a feature vector Y. One-hot encoding vector and embedding encoding vector are merged to form a feature vector Z. Finally, all the above features are fused together as a feature vector O, which is input for the MLP model to predict dyeing recipe components and corresponding concentration values.

3.1 Feature Extraction

The typical CNN model is used to extract relevant features from underlying/standard spectral data by left-to-right convolution of input spectral sequence data. In order to use the model to extract features, four main operations are required including convolution, nonlinear transformation, batch normalization, and pooling sampling. After the convolution operation, a nonlinear activation function ReLU and a batch normalization layer [20] are applied. The characteristics of the convolution layer are summarized through a dimensionality reduction operation of the pooling layer. Finally, feature maps are extracted at a higher level, and then all connected to construct a feature matrix. Finally, dimensionality reduction and integration processing are performed through a global average pooling layer to form a feature vector X.

The convolution layer has a convolution process of small-size and learnable weights with a small part of data to generate a feature map. After the data is batch normalized and then input into the activation function, most obtained values fall into the linear region of a nonlinear function, and the derivative is far away from derivative saturation region, avoiding disappearance of the gradient for an accelerated training convergence process.

The BN layer is added to the convolution operation to improve the effect of the model and accelerate model convergence. Therefore, the operation process of the convolution layer includes the processing of the dot product, batch normalization, and the processing of the rectified linear activation function (ReLU). The process is shown in Eqs. (1) and (2).

$$\zeta_h^{(b)} = \text{BN}\left(\sum_{r=1}^{R} \alpha_h^{(b)} \otimes \chi_{(h-1)}^{(r)} + \beta_h^{(b)}\right) \tag{1}$$

$$\zeta_h^{(b)} = \text{ReLU}\left(\zeta_h^{(b)}\right) \tag{2}$$

$\zeta_h^{(b)}$ is the output of the b-th kernel in the h-th convolutional layer. $\chi_{(h-1)}^{(r)}$ is the r-th output of the previous network layer and $\otimes$ represents the convolution operator. $\alpha_h^{(b)}$ and $\beta_h^{(b)}$ represent the b-th kernel of the h-th convolutional layer for weights and deviations. ReLU represents a non-linear activation function, while BN represents a batch normalization process.

A maximum pooling layer is appended to the convolutional layer to avoid overfitting. The layer reduces the complexity and learning time of the network by reducing dimensionality to generalize features of the convolutional layer. The calculation of the maximum pooling layer is shown by Eq. (3).

$$\xi_{h+1}^{(b)} = \max_{(v-1)w < y \leq vw} \left[\zeta_h^{(b)}(y) \right] \tag{3}$$

$\zeta_h^{(b)}(y)$ represents the y-th value in the b-th feature map of the h-th layer, while $\xi_{h+1}^{(b)}$ is the result of the b-th feature map of the $h + 1$-th pooling layer. w is the height of the pooling window.

In this paper, the global average pooling layer (GAP) is applied to each feature map extracted through the typical CNN. GAP is averaged internally for each feature map. It fully considers each part of each feature map, which ensures that it will not be disturbed by one or two specific parts of feature map. Therefore, the ability of the typical CNN model to extract spectral features is improved through the addition of GAP.

3.2 Feature Extraction from Dye Composition Spectral Data

There are a large number of complex dye component spectral data in the color matching data. The ResNet model is used to process these spectral data, and the relevant feature data is extracted to be used as one of the input features of the final MLP model. This paper uses a convolutional layer (CONV), a BN layer and a non-linear activation function ReLU to form a convolutional block M. The basic process of the convolutional block M is as Eq. (4).

$$
\begin{aligned}
y &= CONV(x) \\
s &= BN(y) \\
h &= ReLU(s)
\end{aligned}
\tag{4}
$$

Four different residual networks are built to extract features from the dye component spectral data. The residual network consists of a certain number of residual blocks, which are combined by three convolutional blocks M and a shortcut structure. In forward convolution, each layer of convolution actually extracts only a portion of the data information, therefore the deeper the layer, the more serious the loss of the original data information. This may lead to the phenomenon of under-fitting. The addition of shortcut structure to the residual blocks is equivalent to adding all information of the previous layer of data to each residual block, which retains more original information to a certain extent. This is helpful to enhance the generalization ability and feature extraction ability of the ResNet model.

$$
\begin{aligned}
h_1 &= Block_3^A(x) \\
h_2 &= Block_4^B(h_1) \\
h_3 &= Block_6^C(h_2) \\
h_4 &= Block_3^D(h_3) \\
y &= GAP(h_4)
\end{aligned}
\tag{5}
$$

The processing of dye component spectral data through the residual network is shown in Eq. (5), where $Block_k^m(o)$ denotes the residual network m with k residual block structures, x denotes the dye component spectral data, and GAP denotes the global average pooling layer.

With the introduction of the residual network, the ResNet model avoids the problem of gradient disappearance and network degradation caused by the network depth of the planar network increasing, thereby enhancing the training speed and training effect of the model. The extracted features are enriched by deepening the depth (number of layers) of the model.

3.3 Feature Fusion and Dyeing Recipe Prediction

The typical CNN model captures spectral data characteristic information of the substrate/standard, while the ResNet model can capture the spectral characteristic information of the dye composition. The "Fiber material", "Dyeing process" and "Substrate delivery" in the color matching datasets are categorical variables. They are converted into classification feature information by means of one-hot and Cat2Vec encoding [9]. After that, the feature information of these three parts is fused by a concatenation feature fusion strategy. The concatenation feature fusion strategy is to directly concatenate all the feature vectors with the process shown in Eq. (6).

$$
\begin{aligned}
X &= (X_1, X_2, \ldots, X_p) \\
Y &= (Y_1, Y_2, \ldots, Y_q) \\
Z &= (Z_1, Z_2, \ldots, Z_m) \\
O &= Concatenation\,(X, Y, Z) \\
O &= (X_1, \ldots, X_p, Y_1, \ldots, Y_q, Z_1, \ldots, Z_m)
\end{aligned}
\tag{6}
$$

X represents the feature data vector extracted by the typical CNN model with dimension as p, while Y represents the feature data vector extracted by the ResNet model with dimension is q. Z represents the encoded feature vector of categorical variables data of "Fiber material", "Dyeing process", "Substrate delivery" with the dimension as m. O represents the final data with feature fused. After feature fusion, the obtained features are sent to the MLP model to predict the final result. In the MLP model, there are three different layers: a fully connected layer [21], a batch standardization layer and a dropout layer [22]. In a fully connected neural network, all neurons in each layer are connected to neurons in next layer. In other words, the output of each layer is used as the input of next layer. Each has an activation function and specific weights. The input and output of MLP are shown in Eq. (7).

$$
y = g\left(\sum_{j=1}^{q} k_j^o f\left(\left(\sum_{i=1}^{p} w_{ij} x_i\right) + b_j^h\right) + b^0\right)
\tag{7}
$$

The vectors $x = [x_1, x_2, \ldots, x_p]$. The number of neurons in the hidden layer and the number of neurons in the output layer are q and 4, respectively. The four output neurons correspond to the number of dye components in the recipe. The weight $W = [w_{ij}] (j \in [1, q])$ is a $p*q$ matrix connecting p inputs and q hidden layer nodes. The vector $b = [b_j^h]$ $(j \in [1, q])$ is the offset value of the hidden layer node. The weight $k = [k_j^o] (j \in [1, q])$ is a vector connecting q hidden layer nodes with the output layer. f (*) and g (*) are the activation function ReLU of neurons.

4 Evaluation and Results

4.1 Datasets

The experiment data was real color matching data from the production process of a large listed company in the textiles industry containing more than 300 data tables. After preprocessing, the data was summarized as a new dataset ColorM-A including four parts: dye component spectral data, substrate/standard spectral data, categorical variables data of "Fiber material", "Dyeing process", "Substrate Delivery", and concentration values of each component.

Due to the large amount of data, in order to improve the utilization of the datasets, the following analysis and operations were carried out. 1) First, as a dataset ColorM-A, the quantity of dye components contained in all recipes is analyzed. It was found that 3 types of dyes were contained in 61,300 recipes, which accounted for more than 85% of the total number of dyeing recipes. 2) Count the frequency of use of dye components. In all recipes, there were a total of more than 600 dyes. After excluding some uncommon dyes, the recipes containing the 50 most commonly used dye ingredients is 52,120 groups. 3) Finally, use these 52,120 sets of recipes data as the new color matching dataset ColorM-B. In order to verify the effect of the model and its generalization ability, the two datasets were divided into training datasets and test datasets, with a ratio of 9:1. Tables 1 and 2 show the categories and statistical characteristics of the datasets.

Table 1. The number of categories of the two datasets ColorM-A and ColorM-B

Dataset	#Fiber	#Substrate Delivery	#Dye Process	#Substrate Spectrum	#Standard Spectrum	#Product Spectrum
ColorM-A	5	96	50	70	41,495	760
ColorM-B	4	82	30	61	31,167	414

Table 2. The statistical characteristics of the two datasets ColorM-A and ColorM-B

Dataset	Training dataset	Testing dataset	Total
ColorM-A	64,919	7213	72,132
ColorM-B	46,908	5212	52,120

4.2 Evaluation Metrics

Three metrics were used to evaluate the performance of models including Mean Square Error [23] (MSE), Mean Absolute Error [24] (MAE), and Root Mean Square Error [24] (RMSE). MAE was used to describe the difference between predicted values and true values. The smaller the MAE value, the better a model. MSE calculates square error between predicted values and true values. The RMSE was the square root of the ratio of the square of deviation between predicted values and true values to the number of prediction samples. The Root Mean Square Error was used to calculate the deviation between the predicted value and the true value. RMSE was sensitive to large or small errors in a set of prediction samples, therefore it provides a better representation of the predictive effect of the model. The calculation are as Eqs. (8)–(10), where y_i is true values, f_i is predicted values, and n indicates the number of samples.

$$MAE = \frac{1}{n} \sum_{i=1}^{n} |f_i - y_i| \tag{8}$$

$$MSE = \frac{1}{n} \sum_{i=1}^{n} (f_i - y_i)^2 \tag{9}$$

$$RMSE = \sqrt{\frac{1}{n} \sum_{i=1}^{n} (f_i - y_i)^2} \tag{10}$$

4.3 Settings

The baseline methods of automatic color matching for textile dyeing and printing were derived from two latest application of conventional machine learning models including multiple nonlinear regression [25, 26] and multidimensional support vector machine regression (M-SVR) [15, 27]. Another three baseline models were artificial neural network models including, multilayer perceptron model [6, 18], typical CNN-MLP model and VGG-MLP, in which the latter two models are hybrid models proposed for the ablation experiments of the model CMR-Color hybrid model proposed in this paper. The details of the four baseline models were as follows:

1) Multiple nonlinear regression: There was a nonlinear relationship between dependent variables and independent variables. A multiple nonlinear regression model was usually used for fitting the nonlinear relationship between the spectral data of dyes and the concentration values of dye components
2) Multidimensional support vector machine regression. M-SVR is suitable for prediction of dyeing recipes because it can handle multidimensional data samples and fit non-linear relationships between multiple influencing factors of the dyeing process (including fabric parameters and dyeing recipes) and solubility values through the model.

3) Multilayer perceptron model: Multilayer perceptron (MLP) was a model for color matching prediction. It contains 5 fully connected layers. MLP model can automatically extract solving rules by learning a color matching training dataset. After training, the MLP model can be used to predict the concentration values of the dye recipe and recipe components.

4) typical CNN-MLP model: typical CNN-MLP was a hybrid model proposed to perform ablation experiments on the model CMR-Color hybrid model proposed in this paper. It contains a typical CNN model for feature extraction of dye component spectral data and substrate/standard spectral data, and a MLP model for dyeing recipe prediction. All extracted features were fused into a feature vector representation by a feature fusion method. The fused feature vector was used as the input of a MLP model for predicting dyeing recipe and concentration values of recipe components.

5) VGG-MLP model: VGG-MLP was a hybrid model designed for color matching prediction. It contains a typical CNN model for feature extraction of substrate/standard spectral data, and a VGG model for feature extraction of dye component spectral data. All extracted features are fused into a feature vector representation by a feature fusion method. The fused feature vector was used as the input of a MLP model for predicting dyeing recipe and concentration values of recipe components.

For the parameter settings, the CMR-Color model uses Adam [29] as optimizer, the Mean Square Error function as a loss function, and ReLU as the activation function of each layer. The learning rate, batch size, and dropout rate were set to 8e-5, 36, and 0.2, respectively. L2 regularization was used to reduce model overfitting. The model training was terminated when the loss in period of 10 consecutive periods remains the same or increases. The detailed parameter settings for CMR-Color model was as Table 3.

Table 3. Parameter settings of CMR-Color model

Parameter category	Value
Batch size	36
Optimization	Adam
Learning rate	8e-5
Dropout rate	0.2
Activation function	ReLU
Loss function	MSE with L2 regularization
Epoch	100

4.4 Results

In order to verify the performance of the CMR-Color model, two experiments were carried out in this paper. The first experiment compares the model with all the four baseline methods on the two datasets using the three evaluation metrics. The result is reported in Table 4. On the ColorM-A dataset, the performance of the multiple nonlinear regression model were 0.6511, 0.5705, and 0.8069 in MSE, MAE, and RMSE, respectively. The MLP model had obtained a MSE of 0.1821, a MAE of 0.3017, and a RMSE of 0.4267. Compared with the multiple non-linear regression model, the MLP has achieved 72%, 65%, and 47% improvements on the metrics, respectively. The VGG-MLP model acquired a MSE of 0.0092, a MAE of 0.0678, and a RMSE of 0.0953, improving the MLP model by 94%, 77%, and 76%. The VGG-MLP model was the best performed model among the four baseline models. Our CMR-Color model had achieved a MSE of 0.0075, a MAE of 0.0612 and a RMSE of 0.0866. Compared with the best baseline model VGG-MLP model, the performance of our model had increased by 18%, 10%, and 9% respectively three evaluation metrics. From the results, the CMR-Color model exceeded all baseline models in the all evaluation metrics. The performance of all models on the dataset ColorM-B is better than that on the dataset ColorM-A. The CMR-Color model also outperformed all the baseline models in the three evaluation metrics, indicating the effectiveness of our CMR-Color model of automatic color matching.

Table 4. Results of CMR-Color on printing and dyeing color matching dataset

Dataset	Model	MSE	MAE	RMSE
ColorM-A	Multiple nonlinear regression	0.6511	0.5705	0.8069
	M-SVR	0.5531	0.5258	0.7437
	MLP	0.1821	0.3017	0.4267
	typical CNN-MLP	0.0761	0.1950	0.2758
	VGG-MLP	0.0092	0.0678	0.0953
	CMR-Color	0.0075	0.0612	0.0866
ColorM-B	Multiple nonlinear regression	0.6212	0.5573	0.7881
	M-SVR	0.5242	0.5119	0.7240
	MLP	0.1211	0.2460	0.3479
	typical CNN-MLP	0.0661	0.1817	0.2471
	VGG-MLP	0.0080	0.0636	0.0894
	CMR-Color	0.0063	0.0561	0.0793

The second experiment is to verify the generalization capability of CMR-Color models on the two datasets. After the model training on the training datasets of ColorM-A and ColorM-B, the test experiment was carried out in the test dataset to test the generalization ability of the model. The average values of MSE, MAE, and RMSE on the training dataset of ColorM-A were 0.0063, 0.0584, and 0.0762, respectively, and the average values of MSE, MAE, and RMSE on the test dataset of ColorM-A were 0.0073, 0.0621 and 0.0796. The differences between the results of the CMR-Color model in the training dataset and the test dataset for the dataset ColorM-A were 0.0010, 0.0037, and 0.0034 for the MSE, MAE, and RMSE metrics, respectively. The results show that the gap between the training dataset and the test dataset was within the range of 0.0010, 0.0037, and the gap was within the acceptable range. It shows that the model has a good generalization ability. However, the CMR-Color fusion model trained with the dataset ColorM-A was not as good as the model trained with the dataset ColorM-B in prediction, but the generalization ability was better than the latter. The detailed experiment results are shown in Figs. 2 and 3.

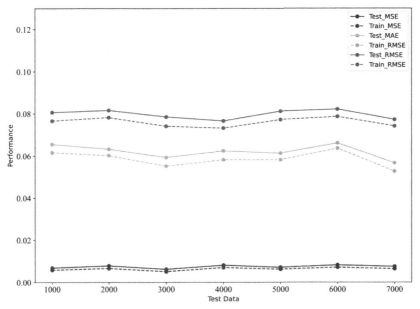

Fig. 2. The performance of model generalization with the increasing of testing data on the dataset ColorM-A

In the recipe data extraction process of the dataset, each recipe consumes a considerable processing time including data loading. To speed up the loading speed, the pre-processed data was saved into files in csv format in advance of training. Experiment results on 100 sets of recipe data show that the average time to load one csv file is 18.02 s. This paper changes the csv files to a pickle format or hdf5 file [30] to improve the IO speed and reduce disk space occupied by the data. Through comparison on the same 100 sets of recipe data, the average time to load one recipe was reduced to 1.22 s. Compared with processing of csv files, the speed has increased by nearly 15 times. At the same time, 16.21 MB of disk space is needed to store data in csv files but just 7.12 MB needed for data in pickle files. Table 5 reported the detailed comparison result on 50 groups and 100 groups of recipe data.

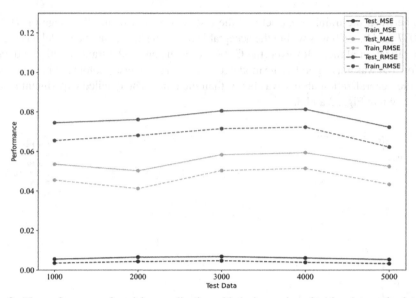

Fig. 3. The performance of model generalization with the increasing of testing data on the dataset ColorM-B

Table 5. The comparison of loading speed and space consumption using CSV, Hdf5 and pickle files

Recipe data	File type	Speed (s)	Disk space Usage (MB)
50 groups	CSV	9.12	16.21
	Hdf5	1.68	3.82
	pickle	0.80	3.53
100 groups	CSV	18.02	32.52
	Hdf5	3.12	7.71
	pickle	1.22	7.12

5   Conclusions

This paper proposed a hybrid model CMR-Color of automatic color matching prediction for textile dyeing and printing. The model was composed of four parts: a ResNet model, a typical CNN model, a data encoding process, and a MLP model. The experiments on 72,132 recipes from a large listed company showed that the CMR-Color model achieved the best performance in all evaluation metrics compared with four state-of-the-art baseline methods, which demonstrated the effectiveness of the model for automatic color matching for textile dyeing and printing. The experiments also presented the efficiency improvement by incorporating an improved file-loading strategy.

References

1. United Nations Economic Commission for Europe: UN Alliance Aims to Put Fashion on Path to Sustainability (2018). https://unece.org/forestry/press/un-alliance-aims-put-fashion-path-sustainability
2. Lu, S.: WTO Reports World Textiles and Apparel Trade in 2019 (2020). https://shenglufashion.com/2020/08/03/wto-reports-world-textiles-and-apparel-trade-in-2019
3. Ghose, S., Parmar, T., Dada, T., Vanathi, M., Sharma, S.: A new computer-based Farnsworth Munsell 100-hue test for evaluation of color vision. Int. Ophthalmol. **34**(4), 747–751 (2014)
4. Convert, R., Schacher, L., Viallier, P.: An expert system for the dyeing recipes determination. J. Intel. Manuf. **11**(2), 145–155 (2000)
5. Furferi, R., Governi, L., Volpe, Y.: Color matching of fabric blends: hybrid Kubelka-Munk + artificial neural network based method. J. Electr. Imag. **25**(6), 061402 (2016)
6. Jawahar, M., Kannan, C.B.N., Manobhai, M.K.: Artificial neural networks for colour prediction in leather dyeing on the basis of a tristimulus system. Colorat. Technol. **131**(1), 48–57 (2015)
7. Christie R.: Colour Chemistry. Royal Society of Chemistry (2014)
8. Chequer, F.M.D., De Oliveira, G.A.R., Ferraz, E.R.A., et al.: Textile dyes: dyeing process and environmental impact. In: Eco-Friendly Textile Dyeing and Finishing, pp. 151–176 (2013)
9. Guo, C., Berkhahn, F.: Entity embeddings of categorical variables (2016). arXiv:1604.06737
10. Zhang, Q., Lee, K., Bao, H., et al.: Category coding with neural network application (2018). arXiv:1805.07927
11. Zhang, B., Li, H.: Research on application for color matching in textile dyeing based on numerical analysis. In: 2008 International Conference on Computer Science and Software Engineering, pp. 357–360. IEEE (2008)
12. Gong, J.H.: Application of computerized color measurement and matching system. Textile Dye. Finish. J. 32–34 (2012)
13. Yin, M., Zhang, B., Deng, X.: Research on reliability analysis in computer color matching for textile dyeing. J. Qingdao Univ. (Eng. Technol. Ed.) 4 (2015)
14. Liu, G., Li, X., Xu, H., et al.: Preliminary application research of regression analysis in camouflage color matching. In: Pacific Rim Laser Damage 2019: Optical Materials for High-Power Lasers. International Society for Optics and Photonics (2019)
15. Chen, Z., Zhou, C., Zhou, Y., Zhu, L., Lu, T., Liu, G.: Multi-dimensional regression for colour prediction in pad dyeing. In: Sun, X., Pan, Z., Bertino, E. (eds.) Cloud Computing and Security. LNCS, vol. 11063, pp. 675–687. Springer, Cham (2018). https://doi.org/10.1007/978-3-030-00006-6_61
16. Shen, J., Zhou, X.: Spectrophotometric colour matching algorithm for top-dyed mélange yarn, based on an artificial neural network. Colorat. Technol. **133**(4), 341–346 (2017)
17. Li, X., Jia, J., Cui, M., et al.: Research on several models of computer color matching for flexographic printing based on improved BP neural network. NIP & digital fabrication conference. Soc. Imag. Sci. Technol. **2018**, 95–98 (2018)
18. Rosa, J.M., Guerhardt, F., Júnior, S.E.R.R.R., et al.: Modeling and Optimization of Reactive Cotton Dyeing Using Response Surface Methodology Combined with Artificial Neural Network (2021)
19. Lin, M., Chen, Q., Yan, S.: Network in network (2013). arXiv:1312.4400
20. Bjorck, J., Gomes, C., Selman, B., et al.: Understanding batch normalization (2018). arXiv:1806.02375
21. Ma, W., Lu, J.: An equivalence of fully connected layer and convolutional layer. (2017). arXiv:1712.01252

22. Baldi, P., Sadowski, P.J.: Understanding dropout. In: Advances in Neural Information Processing Systems, pp. 2814–2822 (2013)
23. Köksoy, O.: Multiresponse robust design: mean square error (MSE) criterion. Appl. Math. Comput. **175**(2), 1716–1729 (2006)
24. Willmott, C.J., Matsuura, K.: Advantages of the mean absolute error (MAE) over the root mean square error (RMSE) in assessing average model performance. Clim. Res. **30**, 79–82 (2005)
25. Zhang, G., Pan, R., Zhou, J., et al.: Spectrophotometric color matching for pre-colored fiber blends based on a hybrid of least squares and grid search method. Text. Res. J. (2021)
26. Moussa, A.: Textile color formulation using linear programming based on Kubelka-Munk and Duncan theories. Color Res. Appl. (2021)
27. Hong, W.T., Jallow, B., Chung, P.E.: Feasibility analysis of dye color modeling in clothing industries with machine learning models. In: 2020 IEEE International Conference on Consumer Electronics-Taiwan (ICCE-Taiwan), pp. 1–2. IEEE (2020)
28. Zhang, Z.: Improved Adam optimizer for deep neural networks. In: 2018 IEEE. ACM 26th International Symposium on Quality of Service (IWQoS), pp. 1–2. IEEE (2018)
29. Nelli, F.: Python Data Analytics. Apress Media, Berkeley (2018)

Obstacle Avoidance Algorithm for Mobile Robot Based on ROS and Machine Vision

Yong Li[1,2]([⊠]) and Yuzhe Liu[1,2]

[1] Chongqing University of Posts and Telecommunications, Chongqing, China
liyong@cqupt.edu.cn
[2] Key Laboratory of Industrial Internet of Things and Network Control, Ministry of Education, Chongqing, China

Abstract. With the robot gradually stepping into our daily life, more and more attention has been paid to the mobile ability of robot, and obstacle avoidance is a key problem. In this paper, the indoor environment is taken as the application scene, and the visual detection and local dynamic obstacle avoidance are studied respectively. Aiming at the shortcomings of the single external sensor lidar's incomplete perception of obstacle information, this paper proposes an obstacle avoidance method based on machine vision for mobile obstacle detection under the ROS operating system. The method is improved based on YOLO-v4 in terms of vision, which can meet the real-time requirements of mobile terminal. Combined with dynamic window approach (DWA), the local obstacle avoidance algorithm is improved. In the process of local obstacle avoidance, visual detection information is integrated to increase the ability of local dynamic obstacle avoidance and improve the performance of robot local obstacle avoidance. Finally, the feasibility and validity of the algorithm are verified in the actual environment.

Keywords: ROS · Visual detection · Dynamic obstacle avoidance · DWA

1 Introduction

With the continuous development of robot technology, robots have gradually entered our life and become an indispensable part of our daily life. And the obstacle avoidance of mobile robot is a core problem to be solved in navigation. Obstacle avoidance of mobile robots is the process of local path planning for unknown obstacles in the map, that is, motion control. The final result of obstacle avoidance is not a trajectory, but a series of control instructions for the robot's motion control. The trajectories obtained after the robot moves according to different control commands are the planned local obstacle avoidance paths.

In the process of obstacle avoidance for mobile robots, obstacle avoidance algorithms can be divided into global obstacle avoidance and local obstacle avoidance according to the degree and change of environmental information. Because there are usually indoor places with dynamic obstacles in the working environment of robots, obstacle avoidance for dynamic obstacles has more practical significance. In this scenario, how to use vision to avoid obstacles for mobile robots is the focus of this paper.

© Springer Nature Singapore Pte Ltd. 2021
H. Zhang et al. (Eds.): NCAA 2021, CCIS 1449, pp. 619–632, 2021.
https://doi.org/10.1007/978-981-16-5188-5_44

2 Visual Detection Algorithm

2.1 Improved Object Detection Algorithm Based on YOLO-v4

The feature extraction network in the object detection algorithm is very important to the detection accuracy and speed of the overall model. The mobile robot needs not only real-time mapping of its surroundings, but also the requirements of positioning, autonomous navigation and obstacle avoidance. These operations require a lot of computational power and occupy a lot of computational resources. Therefore, the detection speed of dynamic obstacles needs to be improved as much as possible while ensuring certain accuracy.

Common single-stage object detection algorithms include RetinaNet, CornerNet, SSD, YOLO and other object detection algorithms. Because the YOLOv4 algorithm achieves the best balance of speed and accuracy in terms of real-time performance and detection accuracy, this paper chooses YOLO-v4 as the visual detection algorithm and improves it so that the improved YOLO-v4 network can ensure accuracy while improving fast detection speed completes real-time detection of mobile obstacles. In order to complete the real-time detection of object detection network on the mobile side of the robot, this paper improves the feature extraction network of YOLO-v4 by referring to the lightweight network structure of MobileNet-v3 [1] and the idea of combining end-to-end and multi-scale features to predict objects. Replace the original CSPDarkNet-53 feature extraction network in YOLO-v4 [2]. The purpose is to ensure the accuracy while running the visual detection algorithm on the mobile side in real time, providing a faster and lighter network to improve the detection performance.

In the original YOLO-v4, the feature map extraction network is CSPDarkNet-53. This network has the problem of complex network structure and deep network layers on the mobile terminal, which cannot meet the needs of real-time detection on the mobile terminal. Therefore, this paper replaces the feature extraction network with a more lightweight MobileNet-v3 network to reduce the overall parameters of the network, thereby reducing the overall network calculations, and improving the propagation capability and memory efficiency of the gradient. There are two different sizes of network structures in the MobileNet-v3 network, MobileNetV3-Small and MobileNetV3-Large [1]. Since MobileNetV3-Large has more identification types and higher accuracy than MobileNetV3-Small, this paper chooses MobileNetV3-Large as the improved feature extraction network of YOLOv-4. The improved overall network structure based on YOLO-v4 is shown in Fig. 1.

The improved feature extraction module of YOLO-v4 is mainly composed of *Bneck* module, which draws on various speed-up ideas in MobileNet-v3 and multi-scale detection ideas in YOLO-v4. The training set picture is input into the improved YOLO-v4 network, and the channel is expanded through a ordinary convolution with a convolution step of 2, then the features are extracted, and finally the downsampling is achieved. When there are multiple *Bneck Blocks*, where n represents the number of *Bneck Blocks*, and s represents the convolution step size. When $s = 1$, only feature extraction is performed; when $s = 2$, downsampling is completed. 1×1 and 3×3 in *Bneck Block* represent the size of the convolution kernel, in order to achieve different scales of feature extraction to increase the field of perception. *RE* and *HS* in *Bneck Block* indicate that the module uses

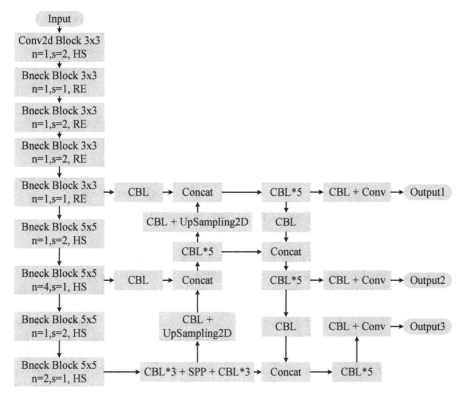

Fig. 1. Improved overall network structure diagram based on YOLO-v4.

Leaky_ReLU activation function or *h-swish* activation function. The detailed structure of the *Bneck Block* is shown in Fig. 2.

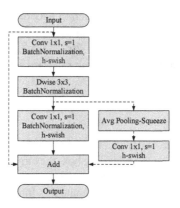

Fig. 2. Bneck block structure.

In Fig. 2, the *Bneck Block* structure is firstly expanded by a 1×1 ordinary convolution layer, and then through the regularization layer and activation function layer. The feature is then extracted through a 3×3 depth separable convolution layer. Finally, a 1×1 ordinary convolution layer is compressed again. The improved structure of CBL module and SPP module in YOLO-v4 network is shown in Fig. 3.

(a) CBL Block   (b) SPP Block

Fig. 3. Structure diagram of CBL and SPP modules in improved YOLO-v4.

The improved YOLO-v4 network uses a ordinary convolution layer for one downsampling and implements four times downsampling operations in the *Bneck Block* structure. The whole feature extraction network has been downsampled 5 times. The network first uniformly adjusts the dimensions of all input pictures to $416 \times 416 \times 3$, and outputs the last three down-sampled feature maps of different scales for multi-scale prediction.

Assuming that there are C types of detected classes, the output dimension of the first feature graph y_1 after 32 times downsampling is $13 \times 13 \times [B \times (Coord + Conf + C)]$. Among them, B is the number of priori boxes, $Coord$ is the number of four parameters of the prediction coordinates, and $Conf$ is the confidence score. There are three priori boxes in each cell of the network for object prediction. Each priori box will get the center coordinate offset (t_x, t_y) of the prediction data, the width and height (t_w, t_h) of the priori box, the confidence of the priori box, and the probability of each category. So each cell needs to have a predicted data of $13 \times 13 \times [3 \times (5 + C)]$. After convolution and upsampling, a new 26×26 feature graph can be obtained from the 13×13 feature graph output from the feature extraction network. The new feature map is merged with the 26×26 feature map of the feature extraction network output. After further feature extraction by convolution module, the output second feature map y_2 is downsampled 16 times and the output dimension is $26 \times 26 \times [3 \times (5 + C)]$. Similarly, the output dimension of the third feature map y_3 is $52 \times 52 \times [3 \times (5 + C)]$ after 8 times the downsampling.

2.2 Loss Function

The loss function of the improved YOLO-v4 is divided into four parts: the center coordinate loss function $Loss_{(x,y)}$ of the bounding box, the target location offset loss function $Loss_{(w,h)}$, the target confidence loss function $Loss_{conf}$, and the target category loss function $Loss_{cls}$. The formula for the center coordinate loss function $Loss_{(x,y)}$ of the bounding box is (1).

$$Loss_{(x,y)} = \lambda_{coord} \sum_{i=0}^{S^2} \sum_{j=0}^{B} \ell_{ij}^{obj} \left[\left(x_i^j - \hat{x}_i^j \right)^2 + \left(y_i^j - \hat{y}_i^j \right)^2 \right] \tag{1}$$

In the formula (1), s^2 means dividing the input picture into $S \times S$ cells, B is the number of bounding boxes in each cell, x_i^j and $\hat{x}_i^j$ are the x-axis coordinate offsets of the predicted and true bounding boxes in the first cell from the upper left corner of the cell, as well as y_i^j and $\hat{y}_i^j$ are the y-axis coordinate offsets of the predicted and true bounding boxes in the first cell from the upper left corner of the cell. ℓ_{ij}^{obj} indicates that there is a measured object in the jth bounding box in the ith cell, and λ_{coord} is the loss balance factor of the bounding box.

The target location offset loss function $Loss_{(w,h)}$ is a weighted sum of the squares of the true value deviation and the prediction value deviation, and its loss function formula is (2).

$$Loss_{(w,h)} = \lambda_{coord} \sum_{i=0}^{S^2} \sum_{j=0}^{B} \ell_{ij}^{obj} \left[\left(\sqrt{w_i^j} - \sqrt{\hat{w}_i^j} \right)^2 + \left(\sqrt{h_i^j} - \sqrt{\hat{h}_i^j} \right)^2 \right] \qquad (2)$$

In the formula (3), w_i^j and h_i^j are the width and height of the predicted bounding box, as well as $\hat{w}_i^j$ and $\hat{h}_i^j$ are the width and height of the true bounding box.

The target confidence loss function $Loss_{conf}$ is a cross-entropy loss function, which consists of two parts: one is the loss when the bounding box contains the measured object, the other is the loss when the bounding box does not contain the measured object. Its overall loss formula is (3).

$$Loss_{conf} = - \sum_{i=0}^{S^2} \sum_{j=0}^{B} \ell_{ij}^{obj} \left[C_i^j \log \left(\hat{C}_i^j \right) + \left(1 - C_i^j \right) \log \left(1 - \hat{C}_i^j \right) \right]$$

$$- \lambda_{noobj} \sum_{i=0}^{S^2} \sum_{j=0}^{B} \ell_{ij}^{noobj} \left[C_i^j \log \left(\hat{C}_i^j \right) + \left(1 - C_i^j \right) \log \left(1 - \hat{C}_i^j \right) \right] \qquad (3)$$

In the formula (4), C_i^j and $\hat{C}_i^j$ are the predictive and true confidence levels in the first cell. ℓ_{ij}^{noobj} indicates that there is no measured object in the jth bounding box in the ith cell. λ_{noobj} is the loss balance factor of confidence.

The target category loss function $Loss_{cls}$ also uses the cross-entropy loss function, and the loss formula is (4).

$$Loss_{cls} = - \sum_{i=0}^{S^2} \sum_{j=0}^{B} \ell_i^{obj} \sum_{c \in classes} \left[p_i^j(c) \log \left(\hat{p}_i^j(c) \right) + \left(1 - p_i^j(c) \right) \log \left(1 - \hat{p}_i^j(c) \right) \right] \qquad (4)$$

In the formula (4), $p_i^j(c)$ and $\hat{p}_i^j(c)$ are the probability of predicting class C and the probability of true class C. ℓ_i^{obj} indicates that there is a measured object in the ith cell.

Thus, the formula of the overall loss function for the improved YOLO-v4 network is (5).

$$Loss = Loss_{(x,y)} + Loss_{(w,h)} + Loss_{conf} + Loss_{cls}$$

$$= \lambda_{coord} \sum_{i=0}^{S^2} \sum_{j=0}^{B} \ell_{ij}^{obj} \left[\left(x_i^j - \hat{x}_i^j \right)^2 + \left(y_i^j - \hat{y}_i^j \right)^2 \right]$$

$$+ \lambda_{coord} \sum_{i=0}^{S^2} \sum_{j=0}^{B} \ell_{ij}^{obj} \left[\left(\sqrt{w_i^j} - \sqrt{\hat{w}_i^j} \right)^2 + \left(\sqrt{h_i^j} - \sqrt{\hat{h}_i^j} \right)^2 \right]$$

$$- \sum_{i=0}^{S^2} \sum_{j=0}^{B} \ell_{ij}^{obj} \left[C_i^j \log\left(\hat{C}_i^j \right) + \left(1 - C_i^j \right) \log\left(1 - \hat{C}_i^j \right) \right] \tag{5}$$

$$- \lambda_{noobj} \sum_{i=0}^{S^2} \sum_{j=0}^{B} \ell_{ij}^{noobj} \left[C_i^j \log\left(\hat{C}_i^j \right) + \left(1 - C_i^j \right) \log\left(1 - \hat{C}_i^j \right) \right]$$

$$- \sum_{i=0}^{S^2} \sum_{j=0}^{B} \ell_i^{obj} \sum_{c \in classes} \left[p_i^j(c) \log\left(\hat{p}_i^j(c) \right) + \left(1 - p_i^j(c) \right) \log\left(1 - \hat{p}_i^j(c) \right) \right]$$

3   Obstacle Avoidance Algorithm for Navigation

3.1   Global Path Planning Algorithm

Global path planning is a global path planned by a mobile robot from its current location to a given target point based on known global map environment information. Common global path planning algorithms include Dijkstra algorithm, A* algorithm, D* algorithm and D* Lite algorithm. Because the D-star Lite algorithm searches backwards in combination with incremental search, it can make good use of node distance information generated in previous iterations to continuously update the optimal path from the current point to the target point in the dynamic barrier map. It can reuse the information of previous search results to achieve efficient search, which greatly reduces the search scope and time, and improves planning efficiency. Therefore, the D-star Lite algorithm is chosen as the global path planning algorithm for mobile robots in this paper.

D-star Lite algorithm is a reverse search global path planning algorithm pro-posed by S. Koenig and M. Likhachev based on LPA-star algorithm. It is also a derivative algorithm of D-star algorithm. The D-star Lite algorithm uses a reverse search method, where the end point is used as the starting point to start the search until the starting point. First, the heuristic values of all nodes in the priority queue are recalculated based on the new starting point location. Second, instead of re-calculating the heuristic values in the queue, a modifier k_m is added to the heuristic values of the new nodes added to the priority queue to represent the overlay of the moving distances of the vehicle or the robot. If obstacles are found in the D-star Lite algorithm, the location of the environment map corresponding to the obstacles is set as the obstacle space, and then the current node is used as the starting point to reschedule a path using the information obtained from previous searches. Not only will the node data for the planned path be updated, but also the traversed nodes obtained from the previous searches will be updated.

A new concept introduced in the D-star Lite algorithm is RHS (right-hand side), which is defined by a formula of (6).

$$rhs(s) = \begin{cases} 0 & , s = s_{goal} \\ \min_{s' \in \text{Pr} \, ed(s)} \left(g\left(s'\right) + c\left(s', s\right) \right) & , s \neq s_{goal} \end{cases} \tag{6}$$

In the formula (6), $rhs(s)$ represents the minimum cost for a node to reach node s from its parent node.

In D-star Lite algorithm, two Key values are needed to determine the priority of a point. The smaller the Key value is, the higher the priority is. The formula is (7).

$$\begin{cases} k_1(s) = \min(g(s), rhs(s)) + h(s, s_{start}) + k_m \\ k_2(s) = \min(g(s), rhs(s)) \end{cases} \tag{7}$$

In the formula (7), k_m is the overlay of the moving distance of a vehicle or a robot. $k_1(s)$ is the smaller value of the $g(s)$ and $rhs(s)$ values of the current node plus the estimated value from the current node to the initial starting point plus k_m. $k_2(s)$ indicates that when the first Key value $k_1(s)$ of the two nodes is equal, the D-star Lite algorithm will prefer the nodes that are close to the end point.

3.2 Obstacle Avoidance Algorithm of Local Path

Obstacle avoidance is a key problem that needs to be solved in the process of mobile robot navigation. Among many local obstacle avoidance algorithms, DWA algorithm is the most widely used. The DWA was proposed by Dieter Fox et al. [5]. This paper chooses the DWA as the local obstacle avoidance algorithm, and finally improves the DWA algorithm with visual detection information to increase the local obstacle avoidance ability for mobile obstacles.

The DWA is mainly based on the kinematics model of the mobile robot to sample the different linear velocity v and angular velocity w in the speed space in real time, and after searching for the optimal speed group in the speed space, it simulates the motion track of the mobile robot in $\triangle t$ time corresponding to the different speed group (v, ω). Finally, an evaluation function is used to evaluate these tracks, and the tracks are further filtered to select the optimal tracks. In this paper, after fusing machine vision, the improved algorithm of DWA is executed as follows:

1. Kinematic model of the robot. Firstly, the kinematics model of mobile robot should be considered. In this paper, two-wheel differential drive is used to control the robot. The formula of kinematic state model is (8).

$$\begin{cases} x(t_n) = x(t_0) + \int_{t_0}^{t_n} \upsilon(t) \cdot \cos \theta(t) dt \\ y(t_n) = y(t_0) + \int_{t_0}^{t_n} \upsilon(t) \cdot \sin \theta(t) dt \\ \theta_t = \theta_t + \omega \cdot \Delta t \end{cases} \tag{8}$$

2. Robot speed sampling. Based on the maximum acceleration and deceleration of the mobile robot, the maximum and minimum speeds that the robot can reach in a single unit of time can be determined [6]. Based on the speed range limitation of the mobile robot, multiple sets of speeds are sampled discretely in the speed space, as shown in Fig. 4.

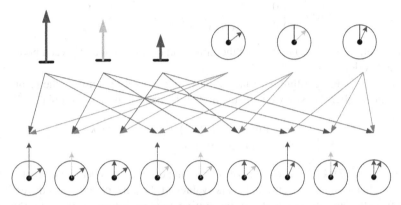

Fig. 4. Sampling at different speed groups.

3. The robot simulates a motion trajectory. The locus of the mobile robot in Δt time is simulated under different speed groups, as shown in Fig. 5.

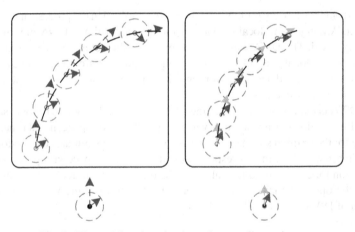

Fig. 5. The mobile robot simulates the sampling trajectory.

4. Trajectory evaluation. After sampling, the robot scores all the trajectories, selects the one with the highest score as the optimal obstacle avoidance trajectory, and sends the speed command corresponding to the trajectory to the STM32 control system through the serial port to drive the robot to perform obstacle avoidance tasks. This paper improves the evaluation function, integrates the visual inspection

information into the evaluation function, and detects in real time whether there are moving obstacles on the simulated motion measurement trajectory corresponding to the current speed group.

5. Real-time detection whether the target point is reached, if yes, stop, otherwise go back to step 2. and repeat the above process until the target point is reached.

Next, the conditions that limit speed are described according to the limitations of the robot and the environment:

1. Based on the maximum and minimum speed of the mobile robot's own performance, the whole speed space search is reduced to a dynamic window [7]. This equation sets the range of linear velocity v and angular velocity w to (9).

$$V_m = \{ \upsilon \in [\upsilon_{\min}, \upsilon_{\max}], \omega \in [\omega_{\min}, \omega_{\max}] \} \tag{9}$$

2. The maximum and minimum acceleration of the robot is limited by the performance of the motor. The equation can set the range of linear velocity v and angular velocity w as (10).

$$V_d = \left\{ (\upsilon, \omega) \middle| \upsilon \in \left[\upsilon_c - \dot{\upsilon}_b \cdot \Delta t, \upsilon_c + \dot{\upsilon}_a \cdot \Delta t \right] \wedge \omega \in \left[\omega_c - \dot{\omega}_b \cdot \Delta t, \omega_c + \dot{\omega}_a \cdot \Delta t \right] \right\} \tag{10}$$

3. Safe distance limits. The mobile robot must stop before hitting an obstacle in the maximum deceleration condition, and there is a range of corresponding speeds. The formula is (11).

$$V_{safe} = \left\{ (\upsilon, \omega) \middle| \upsilon \leq \sqrt{2 \cdot dist(\upsilon, \omega) \cdot \dot{\upsilon}_b} \wedge \omega \leq \sqrt{2 \cdot dist(\upsilon, \omega) \cdot \dot{\omega}_b} \right\} \tag{11}$$

With the above three speed limits, a speed dynamic window will be generated, and the speed space discrete sampling of different speed groups will be performed in this window [12].

In this paper, the DWA algorithm combined with vision can detect whether there are moving obstacles on the simulated motion measurement trajectory in real time, and give a certain weight to the vision, and dynamically determine whether to discard the current trajectory. The modified evaluation function formula is (12).

$$G_{(\upsilon,\omega)} = \sigma(\alpha \cdot head(\upsilon, \omega) + \beta \cdot vel(\upsilon, \omega) + \gamma \cdot det(\upsilon, \omega)) \tag{12}$$

In the formula (12), σ means normalizing the three evaluation functions. α, β, γ are the weight coefficients of each evaluation function. $head(\upsilon, \omega)$ is the evaluation angle function. $vel(\upsilon, \omega)$ is the evaluation speed function. $det(\upsilon, \omega)$ is the evaluation detection function, which is used to evaluate whether a moving obstacle is detected in the current simulated motion trajectory. If a moving obstacle is detected, the trajectory is discarded. Otherwise, set it to a constant ξ.

What's more, each of these items is normalized to smooth the trajectory, and the formula is (13).

$$\begin{cases} normal\_head(i) = \frac{head(i)}{\sum_{i=1}^{n} head(i)} \\ normal\_vel(i) = \frac{vel(i)}{\sum_{i=1}^{n} vel(i)} \\ normal\_det(i) = \frac{det(i)}{\sum_{i=1}^{n} det(i)} \end{cases} \tag{13}$$

Finally, these trajectories are evaluated using the improved evaluation function to select the optimal trajectory. The improved dynamic window execution process is shown in Fig. 6.

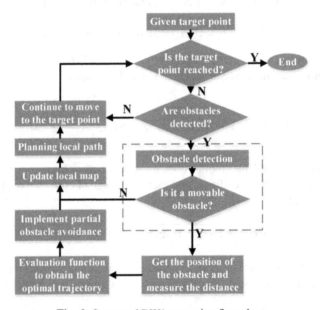

Fig. 6. Improved DWA execution flow chart.

4   Experimental Results and Analysis

The mobile robot verification platform of the experiment is shown in Fig. 7. The robot controller is an industrial computer X30-j1900, which includes lidar sensor, router, Kinect camera sensor, STM32 controller, and stepper motor. The whole robot has a battery life of 7 h, and the maximum operating speed is 0.8 m/s.

The experimental software environment: the operating system is Ubuntu 16.04; the software platform is ROS kinetic 1.12.14. The training dataset is a manually shot local dataset, of which 2,000 are used for the training set and 250 are used for the test set. The network has been trained for 500 rounds, and has undergone 12 different learning rates and optimizer adjustments. The mAP (mean Average Precision) value can be obtained

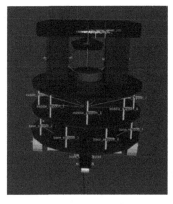

Fig. 7. Two-wheel differential drive robot physical drawing and RViz model drawing.

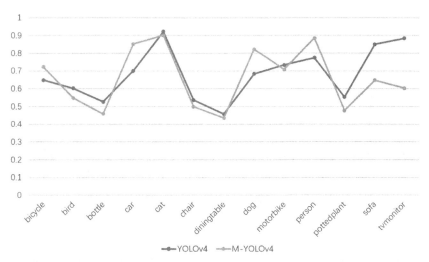

Fig. 8. Comparison of the original YOLO-v4 and the improved YOLO-v4 average precision.

by calculating AP (Average Precision) value for each category in 13 categories. The average precision of each category after calculation is shown in Fig. 8.

The average number of FPS (Frames Per Second) and mAP of the original and improved YOLO-v4 networks are shown in Table 1.

Table 1. Detection data of original and improved YOLO-v4.

Object detection algorithm	mAP	FPS
YOLO-v4	0.682	24
M-YOLO-v4	0.6582	39

It can be seen from Table 1 that although the accuracy of the improved YOLOv4 is about 3% lower than that of the original algorithm, the detection speed is 15 FPS higher. From the above results, it can be seen that the improved YOLOv4 network performance improves the speed performance of visual inspection under the premise of basically ensuring the accuracy, and meets the real-time inspection requirements on mobile robots.

In order to verify the effect of local obstacle avoidance algorithm based on vision and DWA fusion on unknown dynamic obstacles in the environment, the local path planning algorithm will be verified in the actual environment. Firstly, using the global map constructed in advance, the data is visualized in RViz and the target points are given in the map. According to the known information of the map, the global path planner uses D-star Lite algorithm for global path planning, and sends the planned global path to the local path planner.

As shown in Fig. 9, the green arrow is the given target position and pose, and the green line segment is the planned global path.

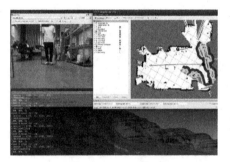 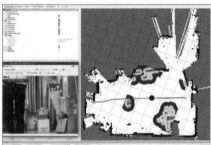

Fig. 9. Global path planning.   **Fig. 10.** Local map update.

The robot immediately plans a global path after the given target point, and the object detection algorithm running in the upper computer also immediately detects the mobile obstacles in the visual window. As shown in Fig. 10, the cyan and purple areas in the figure represent the local cost map generated using the external sensor data of the lidar. In the lower left corner of the RViz visualization interface, the detection results of the host computer after real-time detection by subscribing to the topic published by the Kinect camera of the mobile robot are displayed.

When the moving obstacles in front are detected in real time by the object detection algorithm running in the upper computer, the information of the obstacles is updated in the local cost map. And combined with the visual detection results, the improved DWA algorithm is used for local obstacle avoidance to select the best obstacle avoidance trajectory and control the robot to move.

As shown in Fig. 11, the red line segment is the local optimal obstacle avoidance path planned by the improved DWA algorithm combined with visual information. It can be seen that before the upper computer detects the mobile obstacles, the local path planned by the local path planner is basically consistent with the global path, but after the upper computer detects the mobile obstacles, the improved DWA algorithm can avoid the obstacles with less cost combined with visual information, and complete the local obstacle avoidance with a shorter path faster to return to the global path and continue the navigation task.

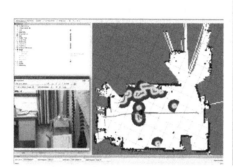

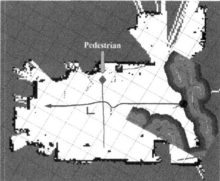

Fig. 11.   Avoiding dynamic obstacles.   **Fig. 12.**   Diagram of experimental results.

The final result of the experiment is shown in Fig. 12, the green trajectory is the actual motion trajectory of the mobile robot, the blue diamond represents the moving obstacle pedestrian, and the red trajectory is the actual motion trajectory of the pedestrian. It can be seen that after receiving the detection results from the upper computer, the improved DWA algorithm combined with the visual information immediately avoided to the left, and adopted the bypass strategy to avoid local obstacles. At this time, after the pedestrian speeds up, the improved DWA algorithm combines with visual detection information to make right turn to avoid pedestrians, and the evaluation function determines that the trajectory can avoid pedestrians at the minimum cost. It effectively reduces the robot's behavior of recovering navigation by rotation, and increases the ability of local obstacle avoidance for mobile obstacles.

5   Conclusion

In this paper, indoor and workshop environments with dynamic obstacles are taken as application scenarios, and the visual detection algorithm and local obstacle avoidance algorithm are studied. In the local obstacle avoidance, the traditional DWA obstacle avoidance algorithm is improved combined with visual information. In the local obstacle avoidance process of the DWA algorithm, the visual detection information of the upper computer is fused to evaluate the simulated trajectory obtained by sampling different speed groups, and the visual information is given a certain weight in the trajectory evaluation function to decide whether to abandon the trajectory and seek other optimal trajectory. Finally, the feasibility and effectiveness of the algorithm are verified in the actual environment. The experimental results show that the improved DWA algorithm combined with vision can assist the mobile robot to complete the obstacle avoidance task through visual detection, and effectively improve the efficiency and success rate of

632 Y. Li and Y. Liu

local obstacle avoidance of mobile robot. The experiments in this paper are all verified in an indoor environment. In the future, we can consider step-by-step outdoor environment for verification and analysis, to further improve the algorithm and consider multiple complex variables and environmental factors, so that it can still achieve the obstacle avoidance task well in the case of external interference.

Acknowledgements. This work was supported by Research and development and application demonstration of key technologies for intelligent manufacturing of robot digital workshop based on the integration of industrial Internet of Things and information physics. Project No. 2017YFE0123000.

References

1. Howard, A., Sandler, M., Chen, B., et al.: Searching for MobileNetV3. In: IEEE/CVF International Conference on Computer Vision (ICCV), pp. 214–220. IEEE, Seoul (2020)
2. Bochkovskiy, A., Wang, C.Y., Liao, H.Y.M.: YOLOv4: optimal speed and accuracy of object detection. Comput. Vis. Pattern Recogn. **28**(5), 72–85 (2020)
3. He, K., Zhang, X., Ren, S., Sun, J.: Deep residual learning for image recognition. In: Proceedings of the IEEE Conference on Computer Vision and Pattern Recognition, pp. 770–778. IEEE, Nevada (2016)
4. Ramachandran, P., Zoph, B., Le, Q.V.: Searching for activation functions. arXiv Preprint **2**(3), 1710–1725 (2017)
5. Fox, D., Burgard, W., Thrun, S.: The dynamic window approach to collision avoidance. IEEE Robot. Autom. Mag. **4**(1), 23–33 (1997)
6. Hong, Z., Chun-Long, S., Zi-Jun, Z., et al.: A modified dynamic window approach to obstacle avoidance combined with fuzzy logic. In: 14th International Symposium on Distributed Computing and Applications for Business Engineering and Science (DCABES), pp. 371–386. IEEE, Guiyang (2016)
7. Ballesteros, J., Urdiales, C., Antonio, B., et al.: A biomimetical dynamic window approach to navigation for collaborative control. IEEE Trans. Human Mach. Syst. **24**(6), 1–11 (2017)
8. Leica, P., Herrera, M., Rosales, C., et al.: Dynamic obstacle avoidance based on time-variation of a potential field for robots formation. In: IEEE Ecuador Technical Chapters Meeting (ETCM), pp. 1–6. IEEE, Cuenca (2018)
9. Kang, W., Yun, S., Kwon, H., et al.: Stable path planning algorithm for avoidance of dynamic obstacles. Annu. IEEE Syst. Conf. Proc. **29**(42), 578–581 (2015)
10. Saranrittichai, P., Niparnan, N., Sudsang, A.: Robust local obstacle avoidance for mobile robot based on dynamic window approach. In: International Conference on Electrical Engineering, pp. 569–575. IEEE, Krabi (2013)
11. Jin, D., Fang, Z., Zeng, J.: A robust autonomous following method for mobile robots in dynamic environments. IEEE Access **36**(99), 12–25 (2020)
12. Yong, L., Yuzhe, L.: Vision-based obstacle avoidance algorithm for mobile robot. In: Chinese Automation Congress (CAC), pp. 1273–1278. IEEE, Shanghai (2020)

A New Total Variation Denoising Algorithm for Piecewise Constant Signals Based on Non-convex Penalty

Donghao Lv[1,2,3,4], Weihua Cao[1,3,4(✉)], Wenkai Hu[1,3,4], and Min Wu[1,3,4]

[1] School of Automation, China University of Geosciences, Wuhan 430074, China
{lvdonghao,weihuacao,wenkaihu,wumin}@cug.edu.cn
[2] School of Information Engineering, Inner Mongolia University of Science and Technology, Baotou 014010, China
[3] Hubei Key Laboratory of Advanced Control and Intelligent Automation for Complex Systems, Wuhan, China
[4] Engineering Research Center of Intelligent Technology for Geo-Exploration, Ministry of Education, Wuhan, China

Abstract. Total variation signal denoising is an effective nonlinear filtering method, which is suitable for the restoration of piecewise constant signals disturbed by white Gaussian noises. Towards efficient denoising of piecewise constant signals, a new total variation denoising algorithm based on an improved non-convex penalty function is proposed in this paper. While ensuring the objective function is convex, a new non-convex penalty is designed. The denoising efficiency is improved by updating the dynamic total variational adjustment in the penalty function to the static adjustment. Experimental results demonstrated that the proposed denoising algorithm improved the denoising efficiency without affecting the denoising effect. The overall performance was shown better than the current excellent denoising algorithm.

Keywords: Denoising algorithm · Total variation · Forward-backward splitting · Piecewise constant signal · White Gaussian noise

1 Introduction

Piecewise constant signals appear in many fields, such as biophysics, geoscience and industrial control [1]. This kind of signals is often destroyed by additional white Gaussian noises that should be restrained in practical applications. Piecewise constant signals can be regarded as special sparse signals [2]. Total variation denoising (TVD) is effective for estimating sparse signals. In the conventional TVD method, the objective function is consisted of data fidelity and penalty terms [3–6]. The discontinuity in noise can be suppressed by TVD methods [7]. Conventional TVD is a l_1-norm regularization. Both the penalty and the objective function are convex, which means the global optimality of the solution is guaranteed [8,9]. However, a conventional TVD algorithm is limited by the

© Springer Nature Singapore Pte Ltd. 2021
H. Zhang et al. (Eds.): NCAA 2021, CCIS 1449, pp. 633–644, 2021.
https://doi.org/10.1007/978-981-16-5188-5_45

underestimation of the amplitudes of discontinuous signals [10]. In recent studies, non-convex penalties perform better reconstruction of the underlying signal [11–14]. Non-convex penalty functions can be designed to restore the sparsity more comprehensively than the convex functions, so as to improve the efficiency of denoising [10,11].

The idea of using non-convex penalty while keeping the objective function convex was originally put forward by Nikolova [15]. Subsequently, the method is called the Convex Non-convex (CNC) method and widely used in time series and image denoising [4,8,11–14]. The denoising effect can be improved by changing the position of the difference matrix in the non-convex penalty function [4]. Through the introduction of intermediate variables and their denoising, the error can be reduced [8,11]. However, the process of these denoising algorithms leads to an increase in the amount of calculation and affects the denoising efficiency. To solve the above problem, a tolerance error total variation denoising (TETVD) algorithm is proposed in this paper, which can improve the denoising efficiency when the noise parameters are unknown. Inspired by the valid results of Moreau-enhanced TVD (MTVD), the algorithm proposed in this paper exploits a non-convex penalty function which can reflect the characteristics of the original signal under the condition of keeping the objective function convex. Based on the TVD model, the calculation of intermediate variables is simplified, and the results of denoising are guaranteed to converge to the optimal solution globally. To demonstrate the effectiveness of the proposed algorithm, this paper verified the denoising accuracy and efficiency with the experimental results, and compared them with the MTVD algorithm proposed in Ref. [11]. The results showed that the proposed algorithm achieved better denoising performance.

The rest of this paper is organized as follows. In Sect. 2, the denoising objective function of piecewise constant signal is given, and the design idea of the penalty function is described. In Sect. 3, the solving process of the denoising objective function is given by theoretical analysis. In Sect. 4, experimental results to verify the accuracy and rapidity of the denoising algorithm are provided. Finally, the work of this paper is summarized in Sect. 5.

2   Problem Statement

Let $y \in \mathbb{R}^N$ be a piecewise constant signal with an additive Gaussian noise $n \in \mathbb{R}^N$, i.e.,

$$y = x + n \qquad (1)$$

where $x \in \mathbb{R}^N$ represents a piecewise constant signal; $\mathbb{R}^N$ denotes the N-dimensional Euclidean space. The objective is to reproduce x from y. This problem can be solved by TVD, which is defined as

$$\text{TVD}(y; \lambda) = \arg \min_{x \in \mathbb{R}^N} \left\{ \frac{\|y - x\|_2^2}{2} + \lambda \|Dx\|_1 \right\} \qquad (2)$$

where $\lambda > 0$ is a regularization parameter, and D is $(N-1) \times N$ matrix

$$D = \begin{bmatrix} -1 & 1 & & & \\ & -1 & 1 & & \\ & & \ddots & \ddots & \\ & & & -1 & 1 \end{bmatrix} \tag{3}$$

The penalty function $\lambda \|Dx\|_1$ in Eq. (2) is convex. It has been confirmed in the literatures that non-convex penalty has a better denoising accuracy [4,8,11–14]. Hence, to promote the denoising performance of piecewise constant signal x from its noisy observation y, the optimization problem with non-convex penalty $\eta(x)$ is formulated as

$$x^* = \arg \min_{x \in \mathbb{R}^N} F_{\lambda \eta(\cdot)}(x), \tag{4}$$

$$= \arg \min_{x \in \mathbb{R}^N} \left\{ \frac{\|y - x\|_2^2}{2} + \lambda \eta(x) \right\} \tag{5}$$

where x^* is the optimal value, $F_{\lambda \eta(\cdot)} : \mathbb{R}^N \to \mathbb{R}$ represents the cost function.

In the subsequent analysis, to improve reproducing precision of x, a new penalty function $\eta(x)$ is designed while keeping $F_{\lambda \eta(\cdot)}$ convex. Then, a faster algorithm is proposed for efficient denoising.

3   Denoising Algorithm

In this section, the non-convex penalty function is constructed for fast iteration. Furthermore, a tolerance error total variation denoising (TETVD) algorithm is designed for the efficient reproduction of piecewise constant signals.

3.1   Design of the Non-convex Penalty Function

The new non-convex penalty is designed by optimizing the calculation of the penalty in MTVD. Using the method in [11], the penalty function $\psi : \mathbb{R}^N \to \mathbb{R}$ of MTVD can be written as

$$\psi(x) = \|Dx\|_1 - \beta \min_{z \in \mathbb{R}^N} \left\{ \frac{\|x - z\|_2^2}{2} + \frac{\|Dz\|_1}{\beta} \right\} \tag{6}$$

where D is the first-order difference matrix in Eq. (3). When $\beta \geq 0$, $\psi(x)$ follows Proposition 5 in Ref. [11], i.e.,

$$0 \leq \psi(x) \leq \|Dx\|_1, \quad \forall x \in \mathbb{R}^N \tag{7}$$

The constrain in Eq. (7) makes sure that the penalty $\psi(x)$ is non-negative. According to Eq. (6), $z \in \mathbb{R}^N$ is the TVD of x. The minimizer z^* is then expressed as

$$z^* = \text{TVD}\left(x; \frac{1}{\beta}\right) = h(x) \tag{8}$$

Substituting (8) into (6), $\psi(x)$ is deduced as

$$\psi(x) = \|Dx\|_1 - \left(\frac{\beta\|x - \text{TVD}(x; \frac{1}{\beta})\|_2^2}{2} + \left\| \text{DTVD}\left(x; \frac{1}{\beta}\right) \right\|_1 \right) \tag{9}$$

$$= \|Dx\|_1 - \left(\frac{\beta\|x - h(x)\|_2^2}{2} + \|Dh(x)\|_1 \right) \tag{10}$$

$$\leq \|Dx\|_1 - \frac{\beta\|x - h(x)\|_2^2}{2} \tag{11}$$

It can be found from Eq. (8) that once x changes, $h(x)$ has to be recalculated, which is computational burdensome. The presence of $h(x)$ increases the calculation in the MTVD algorithm. Hence, the denoising efficiency can be improved by optimizing the calculation of $h(x)$. Since y is the initial value of x in the TVD algorithm, x in $h(x)$ is replaced by y to make $h(x)$ a constant C, i.e.,

$$C = \text{TVD}(y; \frac{1}{\beta}) \tag{12}$$

Then, substituting the constant C into the Eq. (11), the non-convex penalty $\eta : \mathbb{R}^N \to \mathbb{R}$ is defined as

$$\eta(x) = \|Dx\|_1 - \frac{\beta\|x - C\|_2^2}{2} \tag{13}$$

It can be calculated from Eq. (7) and (11) that

$$0 \leq \psi(x) \leq \eta(x) \leq \|Dx\|_1, \quad \forall x \in \mathbb{R}^N \tag{14}$$

According to Eq. (14), in terms of the penalty for large changes in amplitude, the proposed penalty $\eta(x)$ is no greater than that of $\|Dx\|_1$, which reduces the possibility of underestimating the jumping discontinuities.

3.2   Denoising Algorithm Design and Convergence Analysis

$F_{\lambda\eta(\cdot)} : \mathbb{R}^N \to \mathbb{R}$ with $\eta(x)$ as the penalty function can be written as

$$F_{\lambda\eta(\cdot)}(x) = \frac{\|y - x\|_2^2}{2} + \lambda\eta(x) \tag{15}$$

$$= \frac{\|y - x\|_2^2}{2} + \lambda\left(\|Dx\|_1 - \frac{\beta\|x - C\|_2^2}{2} \right) \tag{16}$$

$$= \frac{\|y - x\|_2^2 - \lambda\beta\|x - C\|_2^2}{2} + \lambda\|Dx\|_1 \tag{17}$$

Two terms in Eq. (17) are expressed as

$$f(x) = \frac{\|y - x\|_2^2 - \lambda\beta\|x - C\|_2^2}{2} \tag{18}$$

$$g(x) = \lambda\|Dx\|_1 \tag{19}$$

According to Eq. (17), $F_{\lambda\eta(\cdot)}(x)$ and $f(x)$ are convex if $\beta < \frac{1}{\lambda}$; $g(x)$ is also a convex function if D is the first-order difference matrix (3). Hence, the forward-backward splitting (FBS) algorithm can be used to calculate $\text{TETVD}(y; \lambda)$ [16], which is designed as follows.

TETVD algorithm Given $y \in \mathbb{R}^N$, $\lambda > 0$ and $0 < \beta < \frac{1}{\lambda}$, TETVD is defined as

$$\text{TETVD}(y; \lambda) = \arg \min_{x \in \mathbb{R}^N} F_{\lambda\eta(\cdot)}(x) \tag{20}$$

$$= \arg \min_{x \in \mathbb{R}^N} \left\{ \frac{\|y - x\|_2^2}{2} + \lambda \left(\|Dx\|_1 - \frac{\beta\|x - C\|_2^2}{2} \right) \right\} \tag{21}$$

where C is represented by (12).

The FBS algorithm is given by

$$q^{(k)} = x^{(k)} - \nabla f(x^{(k)}) \tag{22}$$

$$x^{(k+1)} = \arg \min_{x \in \mathbb{R}^N} \left\{ \frac{\|q^{(k)} - x\|_2^2}{2} + g(x) \right\} \tag{23}$$

The iterates $x^{(k)}$ converge to a minimizer of F. The gradient of $f(x^{(k)})$ is given by

$$\nabla f(x^{(k)}) = x^{(k)} - y - \lambda\beta(x^{(k)} - C) \tag{24}$$

From Eqs. (2), (19) and (22)–(24), x^* converges to the following iteration

$$q^{(k)} = y + \lambda\beta(x^{(k)} - C) \tag{25}$$

$$x^{(k+1)} = \text{TVD}(q^{(k)}; \lambda) \tag{26}$$

where the intermediate variable $q^{(k)}$ is consisted of the signals to be denoised and the error between current denoising signal and TVD result. Based on the penalty function of TVD model, as indicated in Eq. (13), l_2-norm of the difference between current iterative value and TVD result is subtracted. $q^{(k)}$ contains the TVD result and the noise information, which is the origin of the name of the TETVD algorithm. With the introduction of intermediate variables, the TVD process is transformed into a constantly updated intermediate variables. The denoising of noisy signals is realized indirectly, which ensures that the proposed TETVD algorithm can estimate the optimal x^* based on the TVD result. On the other hand, the TETVD algorithm contains only one TVD process in each iteration. Compared with the denoising algorithm in Ref. [11], it reduces one TVD calculation in each iteration and shortens the denoising time.

The steps of the proposed TETVD algorithm and the MTVD algorithm in Ref. [11] are given in Algorithms 1 and 2, respectively. Compared with the MTVD algorithm, the TETVD algorithm is more simple and efficient in calculating the intermediate variable $q^{(k)}$ (please refer to Algorithm 1 and Algorithm 2 for the details). Suppose that the time cost for TVD calculation is t_{TVD}. In the iterative part of denoising, the MTVD algorithm needs to execute TVD calculations twice, while the TETVD algorithm executes only one. If the iteration times of both MTVD and TETVD is m, the iteration time cost of MTVD and TETVD is $2mt_{TVD}$ and mt_{TVD}, respectively. Hence, the proposed algorithm increases the denoising efficiency by 50%.

Algorithm 1. TETVD algorithm

Input: $y, \lambda\,(\lambda > 0), \beta\,(0 < \beta < \frac{1}{\lambda})$.
Output: x^*.
1: $k \Leftarrow 1, x^{(k)} \Leftarrow y, C \Leftarrow \mathrm{TVD}(y, \frac{1}{\beta})$;
2: **while** x^k is not convergence **do**
3:     $q^{(k)} \Leftarrow y + \lambda\beta(x^{(k)} - C)$;
4:     $x^{(k+1)} \Leftarrow \mathrm{TVD}(q^{(k)}; \lambda)$;
5:     $k \Leftarrow k + 1$;
6: **end while**
7: $x^* = x^{(k)}$.

Algorithm 2. MTVD algorithm

Input: $y, \lambda\,(\lambda > 0), \beta\,(0 < \beta < \frac{1}{\lambda})$.
Output: x^*.
1: $k \Leftarrow 1, x^{(k)} \Leftarrow 0$;
2: **while** x^k is not convergence **do**
3:     $q^{(k)} \Leftarrow y + \lambda\beta(x^{(k)} - \mathrm{TVD}(x^{(k)}, \frac{1}{\beta}))$;
4:     $x^{(k+1)} \Leftarrow \mathrm{TVD}(q^{(k)}; \lambda)$;
5:     $k \Leftarrow k + 1$;
6: **end while**
7: $x^* = x^{(k)}$.

---

4 Experimental Results

In this section, a series of experimental results are presented to verify the accuracy and rapidity of the proposed TETVD algorithm. The experimental parameters of computer and software are shown in Table 1. To better reflect the performance of the proposed TETVD algorithm, this paper compared it with the MTVD algorithm in Ref. [11], which was one of the existing excellent algorithms. The noises added in experiments (1) and (2) were white Gaussian noises. Experiment (1) was designed to demonstrate the effectiveness of TETVD algorithm through denoising results and denoising efficiency. Experiment (2) was used to reflect the adaptability of TETVD algorithm by processing the noisy signals under different noise parameters and to show that the TETVD algorithm can adapt to the change of noise parameters in a certain extent. The noise parameters of experiment (3) were unknown, and the noisy data came from irreversible electroporation (IRE) experiments. The purpose of experiment (3) was to further verify the effectiveness and advantages of TETVD algorithm through the actual IRE noisy signals, which showed that the proposed TETVD algorithm played a better role in practical IRE application. Experimental results are shown in Figs. 1, 2, 3, 4, 5 and Tables 2, 3, 4.

Table 1. Experimental environment.

CPU	Memory	Operating system	Software
Intel(R) Core(TM) i5-5200U 2.20 GHz	4G	WIN7	MATLAB 2018a

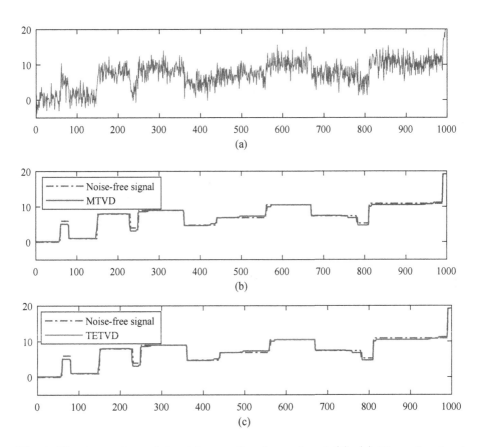

Fig. 1. The comparison of denoising results of experiment (1). (a) The noisy signal ($\sigma = 0.5$); (b) Denoising results using MTVD algorithm; (c) Denoising results using TETVD algorithm.

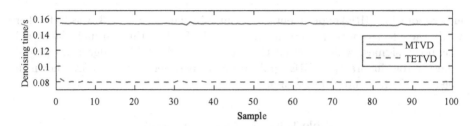

Fig. 2. The denoising time cost of MTVD and TETVD.

Table 2. The data comparison of MTVD and TETVD in experiment (1).

Algorithm	Average error	Max cost time/s	Min cost time/s	Average cost time/s
MTVD	0.7156	0.1556	0.1519	0.1528
TETVD	0.7135	0.0861	0.0797	0.0807

The noisy signal, of which noise standard deviation in experiment (1) is 0.5, is shown in Fig. 1 (a). The results in experiment (1) are shown in Fig. 1, 2 and Table 2. By comparing the denoising effect of MTVD algorithm (see Fig. 1 (b)) with that of TETVD algorithm (see Fig. 1 (c)), it can be found that the denoising accuracy of the TETVD algorithm was improved by 0.29% and the denoising time cost was reduced by 47.19% (see Fig. 2 and Table 2). The experimental results verified that the proposed denoising algorithm could effectively filter the white Gaussian noises in the piecewise constant signal, which not only improved the denoising accuracy, but also greatly improved the denoising efficiency.

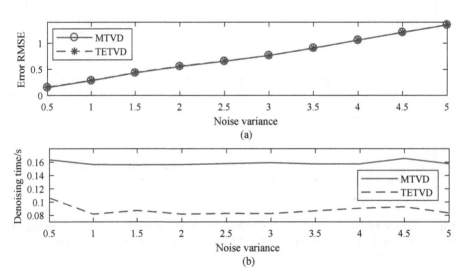

Fig. 3. The statistics of denoising results of experiment (2). (a) The comparison of denoising error (σ varies from 0.5 to 5); (b) The denoising time cost of MTVD and TETVD.

Table 3. The data comparison of MTVD and TETVD in experiment (2).

Algorithm	Average error	Max cost time/s	Min cost time/s	Average cost time/s
MTVD	0.7834	0.1654	0.1559	0.1586
TETVD	0.7804	0.1061	0.0817	0.0876

The results in experiment (2) showed that when the noise standard deviation varied from 0.5 to 5 (see Fig. 3 (a)), compared with the MTVD algorithm, the denoising accuracy of the TETVD algorithm was improved by 0.38% and the denoising efficiency was improved by 44.77% (see Fig. 3 (b) and Table 3). With the change of noise parameters, the denoising efficiency of TETVD algorithm was much faster than that of the MTVD algorithm. The experimental results showed that the proposed TETVD algorithm could better adapt to the change of noise parameters, and the denoising efficiency was not affected by the change of noise parameters.

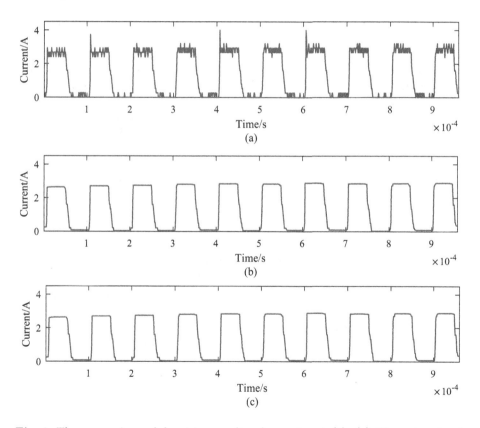

Fig. 4. The comparison of denoising results of experiment (3). (a) The noisy signal obtained from biological experiments; (b) Denoising results using MTVD algorithm; (c) Denoising results using TETVD algorithm.

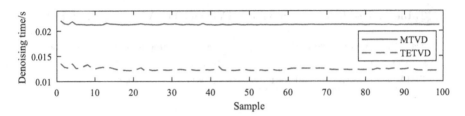

Fig. 5. The denoising time cost of MTVD and TETVD.

Table 4. The denoising time comparison of MTVD and TETVD in experiment (3).

Algorithm	Max cost time/s	Min cost time/s	Average cost time/s
MTVD	0.022	0.0211	0.0213
TETVD	0.0136	0.0121	0.0124

The high voltage step rising edge pulse signals applied by IRE technology can be regarded as piecewise constant signals. Because the derivative in each segment interval is equal, the IRE pulse signals can be regarded as a kind of special sparse signal [1]. The data in experiment (3) came from the tumor current signals in the actual IRE process. It is difficult to obtain noise-free current signals in practical application, so the denoising error curve and statistical results are not given. As can be seen from Fig. 4, 5 and Table 4, the denoising effects of the two algorithms are very similar. However. the denoising efficiency of the TETVD algorithm was 41.78% shorter than that of the MTVD algorithm. The fundamental reasons for the above experimental results lied in the design of the non-convex penalty function $\eta(x)$ in the denoising algorithm and the simplification of the calculation process of intermediate variable $q^{(k)}$.

The design of the penalty under the condition that the objective function is convex can ensure that the denoising results could converge to the optimal solution globally, which is similar to the idea in Ref. [11]. Therefore, comparing the denoising effect of the three groups of experiments, it can be found that the denoising accuracy of MTVD and TETVD is not much different and the denoising effect of TETVD algorithm is slightly improved. In Ref. [11], the dynamic $TVD(x^{(k)}, \frac{1}{\beta})$ process is calculated when solving the intermediate variable $q^{(k)}$. This step is accompanied by each iteration of $q^{(k)}$, which affects the denoising efficiency. In this paper, the dynamic TVD adjustment in the non-convex penalty function is updated to the static adjustment. The intermediate variable is simplified to a calculated first-order function (as shown in Eq. (25)). Hence, the denoising efficiency is improved.

5   Conclusion

To solve the problem of efficient denoising of piecewise constant signals, the TETVD algorithm is proposed to achieve accurate and fast denoising.

Different from the existing algorithms, the TETVD algorithm not only improves the denoising effect, but also greatly improves the denoising efficiency. The TETVD algorithm shows strong adaptability to the change of noise parameters. The experimental results meet the denoising requirements of IRE tumor electrical signals, which is of great practical significance. In the theoretical analysis, it is proved that under the action of the non-convex penalty function designed in this paper, the objective function is always convex. A method for solving the global optimal solution of the convex objective function is given. It is mathematically demonstrated that the objective function proposed in this paper converges to the optimal solution globally. The advantages of the proposed TETVD algorithm are verified by comparing with the MTVD algorithm in Ref. [11]. As a promising future work, the TETVD algorithm in this paper will be further extended to the more generalized adaptive denoising problem for different original signals.

Acknowledgements. This work was supported by the Hubei Province Natural Science Foundation under Grant 2020CFA031, the Inner Mongolia Natural Science Foundation under Grant 2019BS06004, and the National Natural Science Foundation of China under Grants 61773354 and 61903345.

References

1. Little, M.A., Jones, N.S.: Generalized methods and solvers for noise removal from piecewise constant signals: Part I - background theory. Proc. R. Soc. A. **467**(2135), 3088–3114 (2011)
2. Storath, M., Weinmann, A., Demaret, L.: Jump-sparse and sparse recovery using potts functionals. IEEE Trans. Signal Process. **62**(14), 3654–3666 (2014)
3. Condat, L.: A direct algorithm for 1-D total variation denoising. IEEE Signal Process. Lett. **20**(11), 1054–1057 (2013)
4. Du, H., Liu, Y.: Minmax-concave total variation denoising. Signal Image Video P. 12, 1027–1034 (2018)
5. Pan, H., Jing, Z., Qiao, L., Li, M.: Visible and infrared image fusion using l_0-generalized total variation model. Sci. China Inf. Sci. **61**, 049103 (2018)
6. Li, M.: A fast algorithm for color image enhancement with total variation regularization. Sci. China Inf. Sci. 53(9), 1913–1916 (2010)
7. Rudin, L.I., Osher, S., Fatemi, E.: Nonlinear total variation based noise removal algorithms. Physica D: Nonlinear Phenomena **60**(1–4), 259–268 (1992)
8. Lanza, A., Morigi, S., Sgallari, F.: Convex image denoising via nonconvex regularization with parameter selection. J. Math. Imaging Vis. 56(2), 195–220 (2016)
9. Luo, X., Wang, X., Suo, Z., Li, Z.: Efficient InSAR phase noise reduction via total variation regularization. Science China Information Sciences **58**(8), 1–13 (2015). https://doi.org/10.1007/s11432-014-5244-z
10. Selesnick, I., Lanza, A., Morigi, S., Sgallari, F.: Non-convex total variation regularization for convex denoising of signals. J. Math. Imaging Vis. **62**, 825–841 (2020)
11. Selesnick, I.: Total variation denoising via the moreau envelope. IEEE Signal Process. Lett. **24**(2), 216–220 (2017)
12. Zhang, X., Xu, C., Li, M., Sun, X.: Sparse and low-rank coupling image segmentation model via nonconvex regularization. Int. J. Pattern Recog. Artif. Intell. **29**(2), 1555004 (2018)

13. Liu, Y., Du, H., Wang, Z., Mei, W.: Convex MR brain imagereconstruction via nonconvex total variation minimization. Int. J. Imag. Syst. Technol. **28**(4), 246–253 (2018)
14. Yang, J.: An algorithmic review for total variation regularizeddata fitting problems in image processing. Oper. Res. Trans. **21**(4), 69–83 (2017)
15. Nikolova, M., Ng, M.K., Tam, C.: Fast nonconvex nonsmooth minimization methods for image restoration and reconstruction. IEEE Trans. Image Process. **19**(12), 3073–3088 (2010)
16. Bauschke, H.H., Combettes, P.L.: Convex Analysis and Monotone Operator Theory in Hilbert Spaces. Springer, New York (2011). https://doi.org/10.1007/978-1-4419-9467-7

Superpixel Segmentation via Contour Optimized Non-Iterative Clustering

Jianglei Gong[1,2], Nannan Liao[1], Cheng Li[1], Xiaojun Ma[3], Wangpeng He[1(✉)], and Baolong Guo[1]

[1] Xidian University, Xi'an, China
{gongjianglei,nnliao,licheng812}@stu.xidian.edu.cn, {hewp, blguo}@xidian.edu.cn
[2] China Academy of Space Technology, Beijing, China
[3] Qinghai GLI Technology Limited, Xining, China

Abstract. Superpixels intuitively over-segment an image into small partitions with homogeneity. Owing to the superiority of region-level description, it has been widely used in various computer vision applications as a substitute tool for pixels. However, there is still a disharmony between color homogeneity and shape regularity among existing superpixel algorithms, which hinders the performance of the task at hand. This paper introduces a novel Contour Optimized Non-Iterative Clustering (CONIC) superpixel segmentation method. It incorporates contour prior into the non-iterative clustering framework, thus providing a balanced trade-off between segmentation accuracy and visual uniformity. During the joint online assignment and updating step in the conventional Simple Non-Iterative Clustering (SNIC), a subtle feature distance is well-designed to measure the color similarity that considers contour constraint and prevents the boundary pixels from being assigned prematurely. Consequently, superpixels could acquire better visual quality and their boundaries are more consistent with the outlines of objects. Experiments on the Berkeley Segmentation Data Set 500 (BSDS500) verify that CONIC outperforms several state-of-the-art superpixel segmentation algorithms, in terms of both time efficiency and segmentation effects.

Keywords: Superpixels · Image contour · Similarity measurement

1 Introduction

Superpixels commonly partition an image into perceptually homogeneous and spatially connected regions of similar size, as substitutes for pixel-level features in visual analysis. Since introduced by Ren et al [1] in 2003, research on superpixel segmentation increasingly becomes fundamental and popular in image processing and pattern recognition domains. Many advanced computer vision applications are developed on superpixels to achieve more desirable results. Among them are target detection [2], object classification [3], image decomposition [4] and hierarchical representation [5]. In those works, superpixel segmentation performs as an efficient pre-processing step to compute image features and significantly reduces the number of entities in the following steps.

© Springer Nature Singapore Pte Ltd. 2021
H. Zhang et al. (Eds.): NCAA 2021, CCIS 1449, pp. 645–658, 2021.
https://doi.org/10.1007/978-981-16-5188-5_46

The pursuit of excellent superpixels is still a hotspot in this field from its birth to the present. In recent years, a growing number of superpixel algorithms have been proposed to improve the segmentation performance [6]. Generally, several properties are expected for good superpixels, such as accuracy, uniformity, compactness and time efficiency. Many state-of-the-art methods compute an eligibly balanced trade-off between these properties via various techniques [7–12]. Typically, Simple Linear Iterative Clustering (SLIC) [8] acts as an enlightening pioneer to generate desirable superpixels, which has been extended in several latest works [13–21].

However, some drawbacks are exposed in SLIC due to the structure defect by its concise framework [17] in practical applications. The following three deficiencies and shortcomings usually affect the performance. Firstly, it merely relies on local color features and makes a fixed trade-off with spatial distances to enforce the shape regularity [18]. Besides, redundant eigenvalue computations in overlapping local regions are repeated in several iterations [13]. Moreover, split-and-merge post-processing is necessary for region connectivity, which necessarily deteriorates the homogeneity [16].

Aiming at the limitations within SLIC-like methods mentioned above, Achanta et al. [17] proposed Simple Non-Iterative Clustering (SNIC) algorithm in their follow-up works. As the name suggested, SNIC works in a non-iterative manner and removes the limitations of SLIC that iterative label updating processes result in redundant creations of all elements in each restricted region. In SNIC, each pixel is inspected four times at most to calculate the feature distance. It adopts a priority queue to sort the inspected neighboring elements of all seeds, which substantially performs a label expansion process. Once a new label is assigned, the pixel would not be revisited anymore. Consequently, much redundant computation for label updating can be prevented in overlapping local regions. Moreover, since all superpixels are generated by seeds expanding that absorb surrounding pixels, they still maintain the spatial connectivity of homogeneous pixels with the same labels. Therefore, the post-processing is omitted in SNIC.

Another important modification is to generate superpixels whose clustering centroids are evolved using online averaging that thoroughly avoids the iteration. Nevertheless, SNIC adopts a rigid region growing method to generate superpixels, in which a SLIC-like color-spatial feature distance is calculated. Thus it may suffer from the shape compactness that goes against the local homogeneity. As a result, like other SLIC-like algorithms, it sometimes fails to adhere to image contours accurately, especially in complicated texture regions.

Recently, a lot of work has been done on improving the performance of superpixels by various strategies. More subtle distance measurements and cost functions [22], elaborate feature spaces [16], as well as valuable prior information [23] are utilized in many state-of-the-art superpixel generation methods. Among them is gradient or contour prior information, which significantly avoids the crossing of image boundaries when associating a pixel to a superpixel. Giraud et al [18] put forward a novel framework that provides a desirably balanced trade-off among segmentation quality and other characteristics of superpixels. The proposed Superpixels with Contour Adherence using Linear Path (SCALP) takes both regional color feature and contour intensity of all pixels on a linear path from a pixel to a cluster center. Therefore, a joint color-spatial-contour homogeneous measurement has emerged. The resultant superpixels not only show regularity in sizes and shapes but follow regional color homogeneity. Whereas in practice, the additional feature calculations on pixels along the linear path dramatically increase the computational cost, which severely limits its applications.

Consequently, each superpixel algorithm has its superiorities and shortcomings. It is still challenging to seek the potential optimization that provides the best-balanced trade-off for particular applications. Theoretically, a desirable superpixel segmentation algorithm could run sufficiently fast and provide the perfect segments. For example, well adherence to object boundaries or contours, as well as color homogeneity for complicated texture and small size regions. Moreover, for better visual quality, superpixels are expected to be compact, placed regularly and exhibit smooth boundaries [6].

To realize the aforementioned properties together, this paper introduces a new superpixel segmentation method, referred to as Contour Optimized Non-Iterative Clustering (CONIC). Enlightened by the structural properties of SNIC and SCALP, CONIC incorporates contour constraint into the non-iterative clustering (NIC) framework. During the joint online assignment and updating step, a subtle distance measurement is introduced to depict the similarity of a pixel with a cluster. Unlike the empirically fixed factor normalizing color and spatial proximity in many SLIC-like approaches [24], the difference of contour intensity works synthetically with color variation. The proposed measurement globally magnifies the feature distance so as to classify pixels in a more accurate manner, especially in weak boundary and textured regions. It also preserves a moderate spatial constraint that facilitate the visual perception of shape uniformity.

To sum up, by inheriting both the efficiency of the NIC framework and the accuracy of contour-based similarity measurement, the introduced CONIC can generate comparable superpixels with respect to segmentation accuracy and visual effects in a limited computational time, thus performing better in region-based tasks.

2 Related Work

In this section, a binary categorization is adopted to introduce some representative state-of-the-art works. It classifies superpixel algorithms into seed-demand methods and graph-based approaches by the way of superpixel generation [25].

2.1 Seed-Demand Superpixel Segmentation

Seed-demand methods commonly utilize several pre-set seeds to expand superpixels on the image plane with or without prior knowledge. Clustering-based, watershed-based and morphology-based approaches are mainly included in this category.

Clustering-based. These methods usually generate superpixels by grouping pixels from the initialized seeds. Color and spatial information are generally utilized as the regional features. SLIC [8] is considered to be instructive for the following two aspects. First, the joint color-spatial space distance measurement could both control the size and compactness of superpixels. In addition, it localizes the search region for K-means clustering that globally avoids performing redundant distance calculations. Those two properties make SLIC appropriate for deployment and expansion in the follow-up works.

Linear Spectral Clustering (LSC) [15] and Intrinsic Manifold SLIC (IMSLIC) [16] extend SLIC by introducing k-means clustering into elaborately designed distance measurements and feature spaces. LSC applies a weighted k-means method in feature space with higher dimensions by kernel function, which reduces the time complexity of normalized cut (NC) [9] to linear and preserves the global image properties. By computing the geodesic centroidal Voronoi tessellation on a 2-dimensional manifold feature space, IMSLIC makes superpixels sensitive to image content without post-processing to enforce connectivity.

Watershed-based. Superpixels are essentially a special case of an image over-segmentation [1]. Therefore, some marker-controlled watershed transformations can also be classified into superpixel generation methods. Among them are Compact Watershed (CW) [13], Watershed Superpixels (WS) [26] and Waterpixels [27], which select several markers similar to sampling seeds in SLIC. Then the watershed transformation is performed based on the makers and the image gradient. Wherein a spatial constraint is introduced so that provides controllability over the compactness.

Morphology-based. Morphology-based algorithms generate superpixels as evolving outlines starting from initial seeds. In TurboPixels (TP) [7], a level-set-based geometric flow algorithm is adopted to dilate all seeds. It combines a curve evolution model for dilation with a skeletonization process for spatial constraint, thus generating highly regular superpixels. Topology Preserved Superpixel (TPS) [23] partitions an image into superpixels by connecting seeds through several optimal paths vertically and horizontally. A contour prior is necessary for this method since the seed needs to be relocated to the pixel with locally maximal edge magnitudes. On this basis, Dijkstra's algorithm is used to generate the optimal path. Intuitively, TPS can generate topology preserved regular superpixels which are topology preserved.

2.2 Graph-Based Superpixel Segmentation

A graph-based superpixel algorithm generally produces superpixels via a graph model to depict the relationships between adjacent pixels in an image. In this category, graph cut, boundary evolution and energy optimization are three mainstreams [28].

Graph Cut. Normalized Cuts (NC) [9] is a pioneering algorithm used in [1] to partition an image into regular and compact regions. In this method, each pixel is regarded as a node, and then the superpixel generation task is converted into recursively cutting the pixel graph thus minimizing a cost function based on contour and texture information. Entropy Rate Superpixel (ERS) [10] proposes an objective function based on the entropy rate of a random walk on the graph topology. It uses a priority queue to obtain edges to a new graph and calculates the entropy rate from the cut costs on the graph until the connected area reaches the expected number.

Boundary Evolution. Superpixel Lattices (SL) [29] generates superpixels by constructing the vertical and horizontal superpixel boundaries. The optimal paths in both vertical and horizontal are searched within the predefined strips, which are then utilized to split an image and yield superpixels. Superpixels Extracted via Energy-Driven Sampling (SEEDS) [30] generates superpixels by iteratively evolving each initial rectangular region using coarse-to-fine pixel exchanges with neighboring superpixels. It adopts a hill-climbing algorithm to optimize an energy function formed by the histogram features of superpixels.

Energy Optimization. Compact Superpixels (CS) and Constant-Intensity Superpixels (CIS) [31] are two approaches that formulate the superpixel segmentation problem in energy optimization. CS assumes that the input image is intensively covered by half-overlapping square patches of the same size, thus it shows uniform compactness with regular shape and size. CIS assigns each patch the color of the pixel at the center where every single pixel belongs to one of the overlapping patches. By adding a constraint to the energy function, the resultant superpixels have constant intensity. Lazy Random Walk (LRW) [32] converts segmentation into graph partition. The vertex of the graph is the image pixel and the edge is defined on the Gaussian weighting function. It iteratively optimizes superpixels by an energy optimization function based on texture information and object boundaries.

3 Contour Optimized Non-Iterative Clustering

The key idea of the proposed CONIC can be summarized as an improved feature distance that is elaborated to measure the color similarity. It adopts contour constraint to multiply the feature distance of boundary pixels, namely the joint color-spatial-contour measurement. During the non-iterative clustering, the joint feature distance could measure the relationship of a cluster barycenter and unlabeled elements more stably. As a result, CONIC superpixels could acquire better boundary adherence and visual quality.

3.1 Preliminaries on Non-Iterative Clustering

Owing to the non-iterative structure, NIC significantly reduces the computational cost compared with other iteration-needed methods. Since the proposed work combines contour prior with SNIC as a new framework to generate superpixels, the methodology of SNIC framework is presented at the beginning of this section.

- **Step 1.** In an image plane $I = \{I_i\}_{i=1}^{N}$, several pixels are sampled as the incipient seeds $\{s_k\}_{k=1}^{K}$ as well as the cluster barycenters $\{b_k\}_{k=1}^{K}$ with a unique label $L(s_k) = L(b_k) = k$. A small-root priority queue $\mathbf{Q}$ is initialized that always returns the minimum key value while it is not empty.
- **Step 2.** For each seed s_k, the 4-neighboring unlabeled elements $\{I_j\}_{j=1}^{4}$ are inspected in clockwise. The distance $D(I_j, b_k)$ is individually computed as the key value for each element I_j before it is pushed on $\mathbf{Q}$.

$$D(I_j, b_k) = \left\| C(I_j) - C(b_k) \right\|_2^2 + \left\| P(I_j) - P(b_k) \right\|_2^2 \cdot \left(\frac{N_{color}}{N_{spatial}} \right)^2, \qquad (1)$$

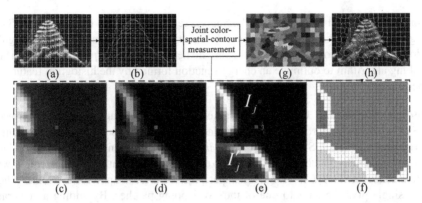

Fig. 1. The principle of CONIC superpixel segmentation. (a-b) Grid sampled seeds distributed in the input image and its contour map (blacker pixels indicate smaller intensities), respectively; (c-d) Zoom-in performance of (a) and (b) in the red rectangle, respectively; (e) Local joint feature distance (whiter pixels indicate greater distances from b_k); (f) Label expansion in the NIC framework; (g) Result of label expansion; (h) Result of superpixel segmentation. The purple dot denotes a cluster barycenter b_k in (c-e).(Color figure online)

where $C()$ is the color feature in 3-channel CIELAB space, $P()$ is the coordinate in 2-dimensional Euclidean space. N_{color} and $N_{spatial}$ are two constants that represent the maximum color and spatial difference within the cluster Ω_k. $\| \ \|_2$ represents the Euclidean distance. Ω_k is expressed as a 5-dimensional feature $F()$, calculated by averaging the joint color-spatial feature $[C(I_i), P(I_i)]$

$$F(\Omega_k) = F(b_k) = \sum_{i \in \Omega_k} [C(I_i), P(I_i)] \Big/ |\Omega_k|, \qquad (2)$$

where $\|$ means the number of pixels in a cluster region.

- **Step 3.** The top-most element I_q in **Q** is popped and assigned a label k which is the same to its seed I_p that previously inspects I_q, i.e., $L(I_q) = L(I_p) = k$.

$$I_q = \arg \min D(I_i, b_k), \ I_i \in \mathbf{Q}, k \in [1, K]. \qquad (3)$$

Then it updates the cluster Ω_k by

$$F(\Omega_k') = F(b_k') = \Big(\sum_{i \in \Omega_k} [C(I_i), P(I_i)] + \big[C(I_q), P(I_q) \big] \Big) / (|\Omega_k| + 1), \qquad (4)$$

where Ω_k' centered at $P(b_k')$ is the updated cluster Ω_k which then absorbs I_q.

- **Step 4.** In the next loop, I_q becomes the new seed of cluster Ω_k, and the 4-neighboring unlabeled elements of I_q are processed similar to in Step 2.
- **Step 5.** Repeat Step 2 to 4 until **Q** is empty.

Notice that an inspected element may not be unique in **Q**. It would be revisited by other seed pixels with different labels, and calculated for more than one distance value. In this case, its final label is decided by the cluster with the minimum distance. A more illustrated procedure can be found in the literature [17] and [33].

3.2 Improved Cluster Distance Measurement

An intuitive bottleneck of the linear clustering framework lies in the trade-off between color consistency and spatial constraint. In other words, as for some SLIC-like super-pixels, the shape regularity and size uniformity preserved by the second term in Eq. (1) sometimes violates the color content in real-world images. As a result, some weak boundaries are difficult to recall, which results in heterogeneous partitions.

Theoretically, the maximum spatial distance $N_{spatial}$ within a cluster is expected to be the sampling step $S = \sqrt{N/K}$. Nevertheless, the maximum color N_{color} is widely different from cluster to cluster and image to image [8]. Aiming at this problem, many SLIC-like methods adopt an empirical constant m as a substitute. In principle, the adherence of superpixel to image boundaries generally decreases with respect to a large m. On the contrary, a small m would lead to irregular superpixels. Consequently, a reasonable value of N_{color} for a balanced trade-off between segmentation accuracy and visual quality is hard to evaluate. To further mitigate that contradiction in the NIC framework, an improved distance measurement is proposed to balance the abovementioned trade-off from a pixel I_j to a cluster barycenter b_k, which is defined as

$$D'(I_j, b_k) = \left(\left\| C(I_j) - C(b_k) \right\|_2^2 + \left\| P(I_j) - P(b_k) \right\|_2^2 \cdot \left(\frac{N_{color}}{N_{spatial}} \right)^2 \right) \cdot N_{contour}, \quad (5)$$

$$N_{contour} = \exp\left(\varepsilon \cdot c(I_j) \right). \quad (6)$$

where $\varepsilon > 0$ balances the influence of the contour prior on the feature distance.

Enlightened by the homogeneous measurement in SCALP, the local contour prior is recast into a variable coefficient. As shown in Eq. (5), the final distance can be adjusted by a joint effort of color, space and contour. Compared with Eq. (1), a new factor $N_{contour} \in [1, \exp(\varepsilon)]$ is introduced to adjust the feature distance from I_j to b_k along with N_{color} and $N_{spatial}$. As shown in Fig. 1c and 1d, if the color of an internal pixel is about the same as its neighboring elements with nearly zero contour intensity, the local region is supposed to be consistently smooth. Wherein the improved feature distance from I_j (blue) to b_k (purple) maintains a low value in Fig. 1e according to Eq. (5). Since the color difference is negligible, the joint distance is mainly adjusted by the spatial term, which eliminates the over-smoothed effect and maintains a regular shape constraint. In addition, $N_{contour} \rightarrow 1$ keeps a stable multiplication of the final $D'(I_j, b_k)$. On the other hand, if I'_j (red) is a boundary pixel with a greater contour intensity, the corresponding $N_{contour}$ increases sharply, resulting in a local maximum value of $D'\left(I'_j, b_k \right)$.

Considering that in the NIC framework, the distance measurement directly determines the feature similarity of a cluster and its neighboring pixels and the priority of label assignment. Therefore, in Fig. 1f, contour pixels with greater distances tend to be assigned in the end, behind the other homogeneous elements. More generally, $N_{contour}$ increases monotonically with the contour intensity in Eq. (6), thus prevents the boundary pixels from being assigned prematurely and guarantees accurate convergence of all clusters. As a result, the outlines of superpixels are more consistent with the object boundary. It is also worth noting that, as a label expansion process, the framework maintains spatial connectivity of the same labels [33]. It indicates that an unlabeled pixel would neither be inspected nor assigned by a cluster if there is a set of continuous contour pixels between them, which further avoids the updating bias of cluster barycenters and misclassification of more pixels.

Figure 2 illustrates a set of visual results that adopts a different kind of feature distances. Both SLIC and SCALP perform on linear iterative clustering framework, while SNIC and the proposed distance measurement work in a non-iterative manner. In Fig. 2b, SCALP calculates the color and contour intensities of all pixels along the linear path. The homogeneous measurement in SCALP could prevent a pixel I'_j to be associated with the cluster centered at b_k in the assignment step. Compared with SLIC based on Eq. (1) in Fig. 2a, the irregularity of the superpixel shape is ameliorated, along with better boundary adherence.

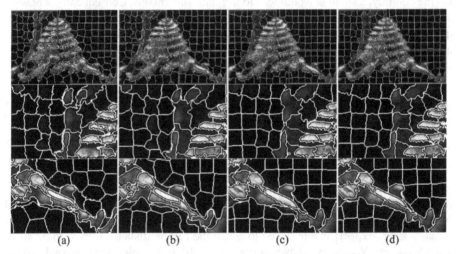

(a)   (b)   (c)   (d)

Fig. 2. Visual results of superpixel segmentation. (a) SLIC; (b) SCALP; (c) SNIC; (d) NIC via the proposed distance measurement. Each segmented image is generated by nearly 200 superpixels, followed by two zoom-in results. See Sect. 4 for more comprehensive evaluations.

Based on conventional color-spatial distance, the proposed measurement achieves a more satisfactory performance. It becomes easier for clusters to classify homogeneous pixels accurately in the NIC framework (Fig. 2d). Accordingly, superpixels in smooth regions maintain the compactness as the initial rectangle. Besides, boundaries are more consistent with the object contours in detailed segments. Furthermore, unlike SCALP that takes all pixels along the linear path into the calculation, the proposed measurement only concerns the feature of the current inspected pixel. In other words, it follows the measurement style of SNIC that inspects pixels individually, so that time efficiency can be guaranteed.

Overall, CONIC inherits both the computation efficiency of the NIC and adherence to contour prior that produces desirable segmentation accuracy. Moreover, it shows a better visual quality that the shape and size of superpixels being consistent and regular. A pseudocode summary of the framework is presented in Algorithm 1.

Algorithm 1: CONIC superpixel segmentation framework

Input: the Lab image I, the expected superpixel number K, the contour intensity map M

Output: the label map L of I

/* Initialization */

initialize cluster seeds $\{s_k\}_{k=1}^{K'}$ by grid sampling at a regular step S.

initialize a priority queue $\mathbf{Q}$ with a small root.

set label $L(I_i) = -1$ for $\{I_i\}_{i=1}^{N}$.

/* Joint assignment and updating */

for each cluster barycenter b_k in $\{b_k\}_{k=1}^{K}$ **do**

    create a vector node $\left[F(b_k), k, D'(s_k, b_k) \right]$.

    push the node on $\mathbf{Q}$ that adopts the distance $D'(\ )$ as the key value for sorting.

end for

while $\mathbf{Q}$ is not empty **do**

    pop the top-most node $\left[F(I_q), k, D'(I_q, b_k) \right]$ corresponding to I_q from $\mathbf{Q}$.

    if I_q is not labeled before **then**

        assign the label of b_k to I_q.

        update the corresponding cluster by Equation (4).

        for each 4-neighboring element I_p of I_q **do**

            if I_p is not labeled before **then**

                push the node $\left[F(I_p), k, D'(I_p, b_k') \right]$ on $\mathbf{Q}$.

            end if

        end for

    end if

end while

return the label map L of I

---

4 Experimental Results and Analysis

In this section, the proposed CONIC is evaluated to verify the superiority. The experiments are performed on the Berkeley Segmentation Data Set 500 (BSDS500) [34], which contains 500 images with the size of 481×321. Since SNIC and SCALP outperform many other state-of-the-art methods such as TPS [7], SLIC [8], WS [26] and ERS [10], the proposed CONIC is only compared with SNIC and SCALP to prove the superiorities. The two references are all based on available code with default parameters, while CONIC is implemented by C/C++ with $\varepsilon = 10$. All methods are executed on an Intel Core i7 4.2 GHz with 16 GB RAM without any parallelization or GPU processing.

4.1 Visual Assessment

Figure 3 illustrates several subjective results for visual analysis of superpixels. Compared with conventional SNIC and SCALP, CONIC exhibits strong shape consistency without apparent misclassification of homogeneous pixels. Besides, it performs stably in both textured regions and smooth background that shows better visual effects. As shown below, CONIC achieves better visual effects from whole to part. Essentially, contour prior is utilized in the distance measurement, which substitutes the rigid color-spatial by a joint color-spatial-contour distance in Eq. (1) in SNIC. As a result, CONIC superpixels ensure boundary adherence and maintain a stably regular shape. Compared with SCALP that also optimizes the distance measure in a similar manner, the spatial constraint is more adaptive to image content and performs better in twig objects as well as textured areas.

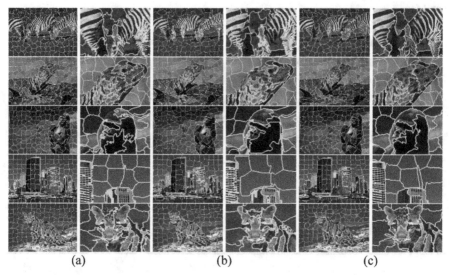

(a)   (b)   (c)

Fig. 3. Visual comparison of segmentation results with 150 expected superpixels. (a) SNIC; (b) SCALP; (c) CONIC. Alternating columns show the corresponding zoom-in performance.

4.2 Metric Evaluation

The performance of CONIC is evaluated quantitatively by two aspects in the field of superpixel segmentation, segmentation quality and superpixel quality. The first category contains Boundary Recall (BR), Boundary Precision (BP) as well as F-Measure to evaluate the boundary recovery, which are used to measure the percentage of the natural boundaries recovered by the superpixel boundaries. Another category includes Undersegmentation Error (UE), Achievable Segmentation Accuracy (ASA) and Compactness (CO), which mainly reflect the effectiveness of superpixels being a pre-processing tool. For these metrics, the greater the value the better, expect for UE.

Figure 4 quantitatively evaluates CONIC compared with SNIC and SCALP via the six metrics mentioned above. From Fig. 3(a) to 3(c), CONIC exhibits much higher BP and F-measure, which means that it can effectively balance the recall and precision in adhering to boundaries. Notice that BR evaluates the degree of ground truth boundaries detected by the superpixels, it does not consider the false detection in theory. Thus CONIC lags behind SNIC and SCALP since there are a large number of boundary pixels in the latter two kinds of irregular superpixels. Theoretically, CONIC pursues strong edge support of superpixels while maintaining the shape regularity, thus achieving desirable results in terms of UE and ASA. Specifically, lower UE means that each superpixel tends to overlap with only one object and avoid straddling over multiple object regions. Besides, higher ASA indicates the performance of superpixels in subsequent is unaffected. Moreover, CONIC also maintains a moderate CO among the three algorithms. CO is another important indicator to assess the visual quality of superpixels. Although CONIC merely exceeds SNIC in Fig. 4(f), it still presents relatively clear and tidy segmentation results. Apart from CO, regularity and smoothness are also crucial in visual assessment, and the superiority of CONIC is shown in Fig. 3(c).

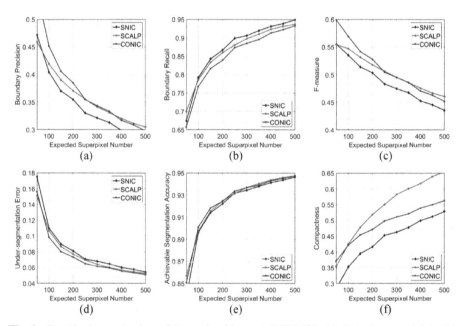

Fig. 4. Quantitative evaluation of three algorithms on BSDS500. (a) Boundary precision; (b) Boundary recall; (c) F-measure; (d) Under-segmentation error; (e) Achievable segmentation accuracy; (f) Compactness. The expected number of superpixels ranges from 50 to 500.

4.3 Running Efficiency

Execution time (ET) is another important assessment item that decides if it is suitable for specific applications. Table 1 shows the execution time of CONIC compared with SNIC and SCALP.

Table 1. Comparison of execution time (milliseconds)

Algorithm	Expected superpixel number									
	50	100	150	200	250	300	350	400	450	500
SNIC	30	31	32	32	33	33	34	34	34	35
SCALP	575	595	609	599	595	566	565	585	549	537
CONIC	19	20	20	21	22	22	23	23	23	24

Benefited from the NIC framework, CONIC could converge efficiently with $O(N)$ time complexity. It suggests that CONIC is the fastest, which runs over 20 times faster than SCALP with respect to a wide range of expected superpixel numbers. Intrinsically, it avoids calculating the additional distance of pixels along the linear path in SCALP and therefore the computation cost is dramatically reduced. In addition, the improved distance measurement achieves a robust and rapid convergence of each cluster in the NIC, without concerning the boundary pixels. Therefore, the neighboring elements can be inspected only once by each seed, which avoids calculating feature distance repeatedly. Consequently, CONIC works 50% faster than conventional SNIC on average.

Moreover, as a plug-and-play role, any effective contour detection method can be directly considered in Fig. 1b (See [34] and references therein for more information). Since the contour intensity can be calculated efficiently offline, the additional time is omitted in this paper.

5 Conclusions

In this paper, a novel superpixel segmentation method termed Contour Optimized Non-Iterative Clustering (CONIC) is presented. By adopting the contour information as the prior information, it provides a balanced trade-off between segmentation accuracy and visual uniformity. The major improvement can be generalized as a subtle similarity measurement for the clustering step that significantly promotes the performance. Experimental results demonstrate that CONIC runs in a limited computational time with state-of-the-art performance on the public dataset.

Future work will focus on several advanced computer vision applications based on the proposed algorithm. For example, since the CONIC superpixels could be more accurate and regular in representing some artificial objects and homogeneous regions, it is more suitable to classify specific features from natural scenes. Besides, it is also available as an efficient tool for supervised land cover classification and object detection in multi-resolution segmentation of remote sensing images.

Acknowledgements. This work was supported by National Natural Science Foundation of China (No.51805398 and 61972398), Project of Youth Talent Lift Program of Shaanxi University Association for science and technology (No.20200408).

References

1. Ren, X., Malik, J.: Learning a classification model for segmentation. In: Proceedings of the International Conference on Computer Vision (ICCV), pp. 10–17. IEEE, Nice (2003)
2. Pappas, O., Achim, A., Bull, D.: Superpixel-level CFAR detectors for ship detection in SAR imagery. IEEE Geosci. Remote Sens. Lett. **15**(9), 1397–1401 (2018)
3. Liu, B., Hu, H., Wang, H., Wang, K., Liu, X., Yu, W.: Superpixel-based classification with an adaptive number of classes for polarimetric SAR images. IEEE Trans. Geosci. Remote Sens. **51**(2), 907–924 (2013)
4. Jin, X., Gu, Y.: Superpixel-based intrinsic image decomposition of hyperspectral images. IEEE Trans. Geosci. Remote Sens. **55**(8), 4285–4295 (2017)
5. Hu, Z., Li, Q., Zou, Q., Zhang, Q., Wu, G.: A bilevel scale-sets model for hierarchical representation of large remote sensing images. IEEE Trans. Geosci. Remote Sens. **54**(12), 7366–7377 (2016)
6. Stutz, D., Hermans, A., Leibe, B.: Superpixels: An evaluation of the state-of-the-art. Comput. Vis. Image Underst. **166**, 1–27 (2018)
7. Levinshtein, A., Stere, A., Kutulakos, K., Fleet, D., Dickinson, S., Siddiqi, K.: Turbopixels: fast superpixels using geometric flows. IEEE Trans. Pattern Anal. Mach. Intell. **31**(12), 2290–2297 (2009)
8. Achanta, R., Shaji, A., Smith, K., Lucchi, A., Fua, P., Susstrunk, S.: SLIC superpixels compared to state-of-the-art superpixel methods. IEEE Trans. Pattern Anal. Mach. Intell. **34**(11), 2274–2282 (2012)
9. Shi, J., Malik, J.: Normalized cuts and image segmentation. IEEE Trans. Pattern Anal. Mach. Intell. **22**(8), 888–905 (2000)
10. Liu, M., Tuzel, O., Ramalingam, S., Chellappa, R.: Entropy rate superpixel segmentation. In: Proceedings of the Conference on Computer Vision and Pattern Recognition (CVPR), pp. 2097–2104. IEEE, Colorado Springs (2011)
11. Vincent, L., Soille, P.: Watersheds in digital spaces: an efficient algorithm based on immersion simulations. IEEE Trans. Pattern Anal. Mach. Intell. **13**(6), 583–598 (1991)
12. Comaniciu, D., Meer, P.: Mean shift: a robust approach toward feature space analysis. IEEE Trans. Pattern Anal. Mach. Intell. **24**(5), 603–619 (2002)
13. Neubert, P., Protzel, P.: Compact watershed and preemptive SLIC: on improving trade-offs of superpixel segmentation algorithms. In: Proceedings of the International Conference on Pattern Recognition (ICPR), pp. 996–1001. IEEE, Stockholm (2014)
14. Zhao, J., Hou, Q., Ren, B., Cheng, M., Rosin, P.: FLIC: Fast linear iterative clustering with active search. In: Proceedings of the AAAI Conference on Artificial Intelligence, pp. 7574–7581. AAAI, New Orleans (2018)
15. Chen, J., Li, Z., Huang, B.: Linear spectral clustering superpixel. IEEE Trans. Image Process. **26**(7), 3317–3330 (2017)
16. Liu, Y., Yu, M., Li, B., He, Y.: Intrinsic manifold SLIC: a simple and efficient method for computing content-sensitive superpixels. IEEE Trans. Pattern Anal. Mach. Intell. **40**(3), 653–666 (2018)
17. Achanta, R., Susstrunk, S.: Superpixels and polygons using simple non-iterative clustering. In: Proceedings of the Conference on Computer Vision and Pattern Recognition (CVPR), pp. 4895–4904. IEEE, Honolulu (2017)

18. Giraud, R., Ta, V., Papadakis, N.: Robust superpixels using color and contour features along linear path. Comput. Vis. Image Underst. **170**, 1–13 (2018)
19. Zou, H., Qin, X., Zhou, S., Ji, K.: A likelihood-based SLIC superpixel algorithm for SAR images using generalized gamma distribution. Sensors **16**(7), 1107 (2016)
20. Lv, N., Chen, C., Qiu, T., Sangaiah, A.K.: Deep learning and superpixel feature extraction based on contractive autoencoder for change detection in SAR images. IEEE Trans. Industr. Inf. **14**(12), 5530–5538 (2018)
21. Yang, S., Yuan, X., Liu, X., Chen, Q.: Superpixel generation for polarimetric SAR using hierarchical energy maximization. Comput. Geosci. **135**, 104395 (2020)
22. Wang, P., Zeng, G., Gan, R., Wang, J., Zha, H.: Structure-sensitive superpixels via geodesic distance. Int. J. Comput. Vision **103**(1), 1–21 (2013)
23. Fu, H., Cao, X., Tang, D., Han, Y., Xu, D.: Regularity preserved superpixels and supervoxels. IEEE Trans. Multimedia **16**(4), 1165–1175 (2014)
24. Li, C., Guo, B., Huang, Z., Gong, J., Han, X., He, W.: GRID: GRID resample by information distribution. Symmetry. **12**(9), 1417 (2020)
25. Gong, Y., Zhou, Y.: Differential evolutionary superpixel segmentation. IEEE Trans. Image Process. **27**(3), 1390–1404 (2018)
26. Hu, Z., Zou, Q., Li, Q.: Watershed superpixel. In: Proceedings of the International Conference on Image Processing (ICIP), pp. 349–353. IEEE, Quebec City (2015)
27. Machairas, V., Faessel, M., Cardenas, D., Chabardes, T., Walter, T., Decencière, E.: Waterpixels. IEEE Trans. Image Process. **24**(11), 3707–3716 (2015)
28. Xiao, X., Zhou, Y., Gong, Y.: Content-adaptive superpixel segmentation. IEEE Trans. Image Process. **27**(6), 2883–2896 (2018)
29. Moore, A., Prince, S., Warrell, J., Mohammed, U., Jones, G.: Superpixel lattices. In: Proceedings of the Conference on Computer Vision and Pattern Recognition (CVPR), pp. 1–8. IEEE, Anchorage (2008)
30. Van den Bergh, M., Boix, X., Roig, G., Van Gool, L.: SEEDS: superpixels extracted via energy-driven sampling. Int. J. Comput. Vision **111**, 298–314 (2015)
31. Veksler, O., Boykov, Y., Mehrani, P.: Superpixels and supervoxels in an energy optimization framework. In: Proceedings of the European Conference on Computer Vision (ECCV), pp. 211–224. Springer, Heraklion (2010). https://doi.org/10.1007/978-3-642-15555-0_16
32. Shen, J., Du, Y., Wang, W., Li, X.: Lazy random walks for superpixel segmentation. IEEE Trans. Image Process. **23**(4), 1451–1462 (2014)
33. Li, C., Guo, B., Wang, G., Zheng, Y., Liu, Y., He, W.: NICE: ssuperpixel segmentation using non-iterative clustering with efficiency. Appl. Sci. **10**(12), 4415 (2020)
34. Arbelaez, P., Maire, M., Fowlkes, C., Malik, J.: Contour detection and hierarchical image segmentation. IEEE Trans. Pattern Anal. Mach. Intell. **33**(5), 898–916 (2011)

Semantic Segmentation via Efficient Attention Augmented Convolutional Networks

Jingjing Cao[1(✉)], Zhengfei Liao[1], and Qiangwei Zhao[2]

[1] Wuhan University of Technology, Wuhan, China
bettycao@whut.edu.cn
[2] Huazhong University of Science and Technology, Wuhan, China

Abstract. Self attention can extract global information by operating on the whole input while convolution layer only operates on a local neighborhood. So concatenating the outputs of convolution and self attention can augment the ability of collecting the contextual information of convolutional networks. However, the complexities of memory and computation of self attention will grow quadratically with the input size, which hinders its applicability on high-resolution images. Thus, we propose the efficient attention augmented convolution module to solve the complexity problem caused by self attention. In this module, there are three branches of operations, which are convolution, efficient attention and column-row attention respectively. Efficient attention has linear complexities with input size by switching the order of matrix multiplication of self attention. Column-row attention is a column attention operation followed by a row attention operation, which is used to collect the spatial information that efficient attention lack of for flattening its input. And the output of this module is the combination of the outputs of these three operations. We replace several convolution layers in fully convolutional networks with this augmentation module and get the efficient attention augmented convolutional networks. Then we test it on PASCAL VOC 2012 semantic segmentation task, and the experimental results show that all the augmented models have improvements on performance compared with those baselines not being augmented.

Keywords: Complexity · Efficient attention · Column-row attention · High-resolution

1 Introduction

Semantic segmentation is one of the fundamental tasks in computer vision, and its goal is to assign all the pixels in an image to different classes thus to segment the image into several regions containing specific semantics. Semantic segmentation has a wide application prospect in the fields of unmanned driving, scene understanding, robot perception, etc. The methods based on convolutional

© Springer Nature Singapore Pte Ltd. 2021
H. Zhang et al. (Eds.): NCAA 2021, CCIS 1449, pp. 659–670, 2021.
https://doi.org/10.1007/978-981-16-5188-5_47

neural networks have made great performance in the application of semantic segmentation. These networks use convolutional layers to extract the semantic information from images. However, the convolutional layer only operates on a local neighborhood of the feature maps, thus missing the global information. This weakness prohibits the convolutional networks to achieve better results in semantic segmentation.

Self-attention [21] can extract global information by operating on all the elements of the input. The core idea of self-attention is to produce a weight matrix by calculating the similarities between the elements and use the matrix to calculate the weighted sum over all the elements. Bello et al. [1] combined self-attention and convolution together, and proposed an module named attention augmented convolution. The module consists of two branches, one uses convolution to operate on the input while another applies self-attention operation, and finally gets the output by concatenating the results from these two branches. This module leads to consistent improvements in image classification and object detection across many different models. However, due to the quadratic memory and computational complexities with respect to the input size of self-attention, this work only applies attention to low-resolution feature maps in later stages of a deep network. And there will be a huge computational cost when applying self-attention on high-resolution images, thus hindering its applicability to resolution-sensitive or resource-hungry tasks.

There are many works trying to overcome these limitations, and one of which [25] proposed an efficient attention mechanism. This mechanism switches the order of matrix multiplication of self attention from $(QK^T)V$ to $Q(K^TV)$ thus changing the complexities from $O(n^2)$ to $O(n)$, for Q, K, V, n the queries, keys, values and input size respectively. So we consider replacing the self-attention in attention augmented convolution with efficient attention to reduce the computational cost. However, efficient attention will flatten the input when applied on feature maps thus damaging the spatial structure of the input. Hence, we use column-row attention to collect spatial information of input which is a column attention followed by a row attention that does not reshape the input. Finally we get the efficient attention augmented convolution module, which has three branches for convolution, efficient attention and column-row attention operations. In this module, we first sum the outputs of efficient attention and column-row attention to obtain the output of attention branches, and by concatenating the outputs of convolution branch and attention branches we get the final result. We use this module to augment fully convolutional networks and test our module on PASCAL VOC 2012 semantic segmentation task. The experimental results show that all the augmented models have improvements on performance compared with those baselines not being augmented. In summary, the main contributions of this paper are two-fold:

– We propose an efficient attention augmented convolution module which combines attention operations and convolution operation together to augment the ability of extracting the contextual information of convolutional networks.

- We use efficient attention and column-row attention in the augmentation module instead of self attention to decrease the quadratic complexities with respect to the input size thus enabling the module to be applied to high-resolution images.

The rest of this paper is organized as follows: In Sect. 2, we introduce the principal research directions of convolutional networks for semantic segmentation and review the related works to decrease the quadratic complexities of self attention. In Sect. 3, we elaborate the mechanism of efficient attention and column-row attention, then the details of efficient attention augmented convolution module are described. We thoroughly evaluate the performance of the proposed module in Sect. 4. Finally, in Sect. 5, conclusions and suggestions for future works are presented.

2 Related Work

2.1 Convolutional Networks for Semantic Segmentation

Convolutional networks have achieved significant performance on image classification task showing its powerful learning ability. And the fully convolutional networks [19] which comes from the image classification networks become the pioneering work to apply convolutional neural networks on semantic segmentation. With the development of deep convolutional neural networks in recent years, the performance on semantic segmentation has gained remarkable improvement. One of the developing directions of semantic segmentation methods is to make the networks extract more global context information to improve the segmentation effect. Chen et al. [2] proposed the atrous convolution for the first time to enlarge the receptive field of filters to merge larger contextual information without increasing the parameters and computational cost. Zhang et al. [24] built the aggregated co-occurrent feature module considering the co-occurrent features between the objects in the images, and improved the segmentation performance by combining the outputs from global average pooling and this module. He et al. [10] proposed an adaptive pyramid context network which can utilize global and local representations to construct the adaptive multi-scale contextual representations, making the prediction for object regions more complete and continuous. Reducing the parameters and computational cost to make the segmentation networks more lightweight is another research direction of semantic segmentation field. Chen et al. [3] applied the depthwise separable convolution to both atrous spatial pyramid pooling and decoder modules, resulting in a faster and stronger encoder-decoder network while reducing the number of parameters and the amount of calculation. He et al. [11] selected MobileNetV2 [18] as the student network when using the student and teacher network on semantic segmentation, and achieved better performance with less parameters. However, collecting pixel-level annotations needed by semantic segmentation is expensive and time-consuming. To alleviate this bottleneck problem, weakly supervised semantic segmentation becomes a research direction of this field. The weakly supervised methods rely on weaker form of annotations such as bounding boxes, scribbles and image-level labels [8] to produce pseudo pixel-level labels. Song et al. [20] proposed a box-driven class-wise masking model and a filling rate guided adaptive loss to make full use of the class-level and region-level supervisions from bounding boxes annotations. Given cheaply obtained scribbles labelings, Vernaza and Chandraker [22] introduced the random-walk label propagation to propagate the sparse labels to unlabeled points thus to learn semantic edges. Fan et al. [6] proposed the cross-image affinity module to use the affinity between images containing the same class to improve the segmentation performance with only image-level labels.

2.2   Works to Decrease the Quadratic Complexities of Self Attention

There exist many works to remedy the drawback of self attention with quadratic complexities in different ways. Dosovitskiy et al. [5] split a high-resolution image into fixed-size patches before attention operation to reduce the input size of this operation. In LambdaNetworks, the lambda layer can transform available contexts into linear functions and apply these functions to each input separately to capture long-range interactions, which bypasses the need for expensive attention maps of self attention, thus enabling its applications to high-resolution images. Child et al. [4] combined atrous self attention and local self attention to get the sparse self attention, which only calculate the similarities between pixels in specific locations thus decreasing the complexities while supporting the long-range coherence. Ho et al. [12] proposed the axial attention which can operate on the input along a specific axis without flattening the input as self attention does, and the global receptive field can be obtained by stacking two axial attention operations along different axes with reasonable memory and computation. Huang et al. [14] proposed a criss-cross attention module for each pixel to extract the contextual information of all the pixels on its criss-cross path, and each pixel can capture the full-image dependencies from all the pixels by taking a further recurrent operation in less computation and memory cost. Inspired by inducing point methods from sparse Gaussian process, Lee et al. [16] introduced an attention scheme which can reduce the computation time of self-attention from quadratic to linear in the number of elements in the input set. Guo et al. [7] used a star-shaped topology to replace the fully-connected structure in self attention, and reduced the complexity from quadratic to linear while preserving capacity to capture both local composition and long-range dependency. Huang et al. [13] factorized the dense affinity matrix in self attention as the product of two sparse affinity matrices related to long spatial interval distances and short spatial interval distances respectively using two successive attention modules thus decreasing the computation and memory complexity substantially. Joutard et al. [15] proposed a new attention module called permutohedral attention module to efficiently capture non-local characteristics of the image which is both memory and computationally efficient. Li et al. [17] formulated the attention mechanism into an expectation-maximization manner and iteratively estimate a much more compact set of bases upon which the attention maps are computed, this method is robust to the variance of input and is also friendly in memory and computation. Shen et al. [25] switched the order of matrix multiplication of attention mechanism from $(QK^T)V$ to $Q(K^TV)$ thus changing the complexities from $O(n^2)$ to $O(n)$, and this efficient attention mechanism is equivalent to self attention but with substantially less memory and computational resource requirements.

3   Method

For the quadratic complexities with input size of self attention, attention augmented convolution module are unable to be applied on high-resolution images which has tens of thousands of pixels. To tackle this problem, we propose the efficient attention augmented convolution module. This module consists of three operations which are convolution, efficient attention and column-row attention respectively. We use the column-row attention operation to extract the spatial information for that efficient attention dosen't take the spatial positions of pixels into consideration. By adding the results of column-row attention and efficient attention together, the efficient attention operation can obtain the spatial information of pixels. And then, the outputs of convolution and two attention operations are concatenated to get the final output of the augmentation module. And we will introduce efficient attention, column-row attention and the augmentation module in detail below.

3.1   Efficient Attention

Given the input feature maps $X \in R^{n \times d}$, self attention first transforms X into Q, K, and V representing queries, keys and values, where $Q \in R^{n \times d_k}$, $K \in R^{n \times d_k}$ and $V \in R^{n \times d_v}$, for n, d, d_k, d_v the input size, depths of input, queries and keys, values respectively. Then self attention does the matrix multiplication characterized by the following equation:

$$O = \rho(QK^T)V \tag{1}$$

And ρ is a normalization function for which the softmax function along each row of the input is a common choice. The left picture in Fig. 1 shows the mechanism of self attention. Self attention first calculates the similarities among all the pixels to get the attention maps S of $n \times n$ size, and each attention map is relative to a pixel. Then S is transformed into a weight matrix by applying softmax normalization along its row. And there will be n weight vectors in the weight matrix which are used to aggregate all the values in V via weighted summation thus obtaining the output of size $n \times d_v$. Both steps of similarity calculation and values aggregation have $O(n^2)$ complexities of memory and computation, thus prohibiting the application of self attention on large inputs.

Efficient attention decreases the complexities from $O(n^2)$ to $O(n)$ by switching the multiplication order of self attention from $(QK^T)V$ to $Q(K^TV)$. The equation of efficient attention mechanism is:

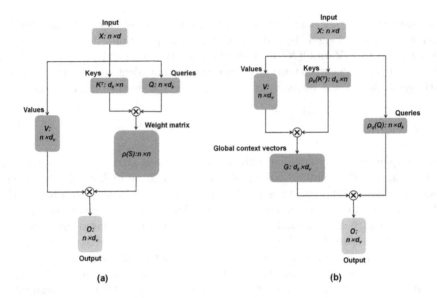

Fig. 1. Comparison of the architectures of self attention and efficient attention.

$$O = \rho_q(Q)(\rho_k(K)^T V) \tag{2}$$

in which ρ_q and ρ_k are normalizers for queries and keys. Softmax functions along the row of queries and along the column of keys are common choices for ρ_q and ρ_k, which make the efficient attention closely approximate the effect of self attention. The K in efficient attention is regarded as d_k global attention maps which correspond to all the pixels, and each of the attention map is relevant to a specific semantic aspect of the entire input. And the attention maps are turned to weight vectors through softmax function, then the vectors are used to aggregate all the values in V via weighted summation to get d_k global contextual vectors G of size $d_k \times d_v$. Finally the efficient attention transforms each query into a set of coefficients, which are used to aggregate all the global context vectors thus obtaining the output feature maps of size $n \times d_v$. So we can see in the right picture in Fig. 1, the steps of contextual vector calculation and contextual vector aggregation only have linear complexities of memory and computation with the input size, thus enabling the efficient attention being applied on high-resolution images.

3.2   Column-Row Attention

For that efficient attention is lack of spatial information of input feature maps, we use column-row attention to collect the spatial information. Column-row attention is a column attention followed by a row attention, which does not flatten the input thus keeping the spatial structure undamaged. Column attention operates on each column of the feature maps while row attention operates on each row.

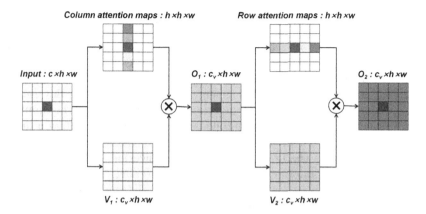

Fig. 2. Illustration of the mechanism of column-row attention. For each pixel (e.g. blue) of the input feature maps, column attention first generates a column attention map which is a weight vector with size h. Then the attention map is used to aggregate the values in the same column in V_1, and we obtain a result in the same location with the pixel of input in O_1. Next row attention takes O_1 as input, and a row attention map will be generated for each pixel (e.g. green), which is used to aggregate the values in V_2. Finally, we get the output of column-row attention O_2. (Color figure online)

Given the input $I \in R^{c \times h \times w}$, column attention first generates Q_1, K_1 and V_1 by applying convolutional layers with 11 filters on I, where $Q_1 \in R^{c_k \times h \times w}$, $K1 \in R^{c_k \times h \times w}$, $V1 \in R^{c_v \times h \times w}$, for h, w, c, c_k, c_v the height, the width, the number of channels of I, Q_1 and K_1, V_1 respectively. For each pixel in Q_1, we can calculate the similarities to the pixels in the same column with this pixel in K_1, and we get the degree of similarity $D \in R^{h \times h \times w}$. By applying a softmax function over the channel dimension of D, we can get the attention maps $A \in R^{h \times h \times w}$, and each attention map is a weight vector with size h. And using the weight vectors to aggregate all the pixels in the same column in V_1, we obtain the output of column attention $O_1 \in R^{c_v \times h \times w}$.

However, column attention only captures the spatial information in each column. To resolve this problem, we apply row attention on the output of column attention to achieve full receptive field. Row attention has the same calculation mechanism with column attention but operates on each row of input. Row attention also generates Q_2, K_2, V_2 with the same number of channels of Q_1, K_1, V_1 in column attention. Since each pixel in O_1 has already aggregated all the values in the same column, aggregating all the pixels in each row in O_1 can harvest full contextual information. So after row attention operation, we can obtain the output O_2 of column-row attention with global contextual information. The mechanism of column-row attention is characterized in Fig. 2.

3.3   Efficient Attention Augmented Convolution Module

The convolution operator lacks of understanding of global contexts for its local operation on input feature maps. Self attention can capture the global information by operating on all the pixels of input, so it is used to augmented the convolution operation in attention augmented convolution module. However, due to the quadratic complexities of memory and computation with the input size, attention augmented convolution module is restricted to low-resolution images. And efficient attention decreases the complexities of self attention from $O(n^2)$ to $O(n)$ by switching the order of matrix multiplication. But efficient attention loses the spatial information of pixels for flattening the feature maps. So we consider using column-row attention to extract the spatial information and then summing the outputs of column-row attention and efficient attention. And we propose the efficient attention augmented convolution module by combining convolution, efficient attention and column-row attention together.

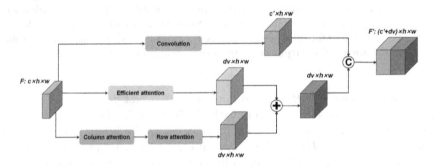

Fig. 3. Diagram of efficient attention augmented convolution module. In this module the input feature maps F will be operated by convolution, efficient attention and column-row attention separately. And c, c', d_v denote the number of channels of input, output of convolution, outputs of attention operations respectively. The spatial size of the feature maps stays unchanged through the calculation process.

The efficient attention augmented convolution module comprises three operations which are convolution, efficient attention and column-row attention respectively. Given the input feature maps $F \in R^{c \times h \times w}$, these three operations are applied on it individually. The convolution operation will keep the spatial size of its output the same with input. Efficient attention will reshape F into $X \in R^{n \times c}$ before subsequent calculations where n equals $h \times w$, and restore its output to the size $d_v \times h \times w$. And column-row attention will output the same number of channels with efficient attention. As in Fig. 3, we first sum the outputs of efficient attention and column-row attention to generate the output of attention operations. And then we concatenate the output of attention operations and the output of convolution along the channel dimension to get the final output feature maps F' of the augmentation module.

4   Experiments

We evaluated the efficient attention augmented convolution module on PAS-CAL VOC 2012 dataset. In this dataset, there are 20 foreground classes and one background class. Following the common practice [23], we used the augmented PASCAL VOC dataset provided by Hariharan et al. [9], in which there are 10582 images for training and 1449 images for validation. We replaced several convolution layers in fully convolutional networks with this augmentation module and get the efficient attention augmented convolutional networks. The experimental results show that all the augmented networks have better performances compared with the baselines. We further did an ablation study, which also validated the utility of the proposed augmentation module. In these experiments, all the models are trained for 100 epochs on 4 NVIDIA TITAN X GPUs with batch size 16.

4.1   Comparison with FCN

The backbone of fully convolutional networks we used is VGG16, and there are 5 convolutional blocks. We replaced the last convolution layer with efficient attention augmented convolution module in the last three convolutional blocks to get the efficient attention augmented convolutional networks. For simplicity, we call the augmented networks as CREA-FCN, where CREA represents column-row attention and efficient attention. As FCN has three network structures called FCN-32s, FCN-16s, and FCN-8s respectively, which can combine feature maps from different convolutional blocks, CREA-FCN also has three different networks which are CREA-FCN-32s, CREA-FCN-16s and CREA-FCN-8s. In the augmentation modules of these CREA-FCN models, the ratio of the channel number of attention output to module output was set to 0.2. Table 1 shows that all the augmented models improve performance compared with the relative baseline, which demonstrates the validity of efficient attention augmented convolution module.

4.2   Ablation Study

We chose FCN-32s as baseline, and conducted thorough experiments to demonstrate the advantage of the efficient attention augmented convolution module. And we also replaced the last convolution layer with augmentation module in the last three convolutional blocks in baseline. The ablation results are shown in Table 2. EA-FCN-32s denotes the network with augmentation module which only combines efficient attention and convolution operation. In CR-FCN-32s, the augmentation module only combines column-row attention and convolution operation. And there is combination of efficient attention and column-row attention in the augmentation module in CREA-32s.

Starting with the baseline, with the efficient attention to collect the global contextual information, the model achieves 0.6% improvement. Replacing the efficient attention with column-row attention, the model improves the performance by 0.8%. This improvement is more than the former for that

Table 1. Results on PASCAL VOC validation set.

Model	Backbone	mIoU
FCN-32s	VGG16	61.2
FCN-16s	VGG16	63.4
FCN-32s	VGG16	65.6
CREA-FCN-32s	VGG16	62.4
CREA-FCN-16s	VGG16	64.5
CREA-FCN-8s	VGG16	66.7

Table 2. The results of ablation study on PASCAL VOC validation set.

Model	mIoU
FCN-32s	61.2
EA-FCN-32s	61.8
CR-FCN-32s	62.0
CREA-32s	62.1
CREA-FCN-32s	62.4

column-row attention can extract the spatial information which is more important to improve the performance of convolutional networks on semantic segmentation. Only combine efficient attention and column-row attention in the augmentation module, the model gets higher score then the above models. And using the efficient attention augmented convolution module, the model achieves the highest mIoU, which surpasses the baseline by 1.2%. All the results validate the utility of the proposed efficient attention augmented convolution module.

5   Conclusion

In this work, we propose the efficient attention augmented convolution module to augment the ability of collecting the contextual information of convolutional networks. This module combines efficient attention, column-row attention and convolution operation together, and has reasonable complexities of memory and computation. Extensive experiments demonstrate the effectiveness of replacing specific convolution layer with this augmentation module.

The problem remained from this work is that the introduction of column-row attention can extract spatial information for efficient attention while increasing the memory complexity and computation complexity of the augmentation module to $O(n\sqrt{n})$. In the future, we will explore a positional encoding method to encode the positional information of pixels to efficient attention, thus to improve the performance of the augmentation module with linear complexities of memory and computation.

References

1. Bello, I., Zoph, B., Vaswani, A., Shlens, J., Le, Q.V.: Attention augmented convolutional networks. arXiv (2019)
2. Chen, L.C., Papandreou, G., Kokkinos, I., Murphy, K., Yuille, A.L.: Deeplab: semantic image segmentation with deep convolutional nets, atrous convolution, and fully connected CRFs. IEEE Trans. Pattern Anal. Mach. Intell. **40**(4), 834–848 (2017)
3. Chen, L.C., Zhu, Y., Papandreou, G., Schroff, F., Adam, H.: Encoder-decoder with atrous separable convolution for semantic image segmentation. arXiv (2018)
4. Child, R., Gray, S., Radford, A., Sutskever, I.: Generating long sequences with sparse transformers. arXiv (2019)
5. Dosovitskiy, A., et al.: An image is worth 16x16 words: transformers for image recognition at scale, pp. 1–21. arXiv (2020)
6. Fan, J., Zhang, Z., Tan, T., Song, C., Xiao, J.: CIAN: cross-image affinity net for weakly supervised semantic segmentation. arXiv (2018)
7. Guo, Q., Qiu, X., Liu, P., Shao, Y., Xue, X., Zhang, Z.: Star-transformer. arXiv preprint arXiv:1902.09113 (2019)
8. Hao, S., Zhou, Y., Guo, Y.: A brief survey on semantic segmentation with deep learning. Neurocomputing **406**, 302–321 (2020)
9. Hariharan, B., Arbeláez, P., Girshick, R., Malik, J.: Simultaneous detection and segmentation. In: Fleet, D., Pajdla, T., Schiele, B., Tuytelaars, T. (eds.) ECCV 2014, Part VII. LNCS, vol. 8695, pp. 297–312. Springer, Cham (2014). https://doi.org/10.1007/978-3-319-10584-0_20
10. He, J., Deng, Z., Zhou, L., Wang, Y., Qiao, Y.: Adaptive pyramid context network for semantic segmentation. In: Proceedings of the IEEE Computer Society Conference on Computer Vision and Pattern Recognition 2019-June, pp. 7511–7520 (2019)
11. He, T., Shen, C., Tian, Z., Gong, D., Sun, C., Yan, Y.: Knowledge adaptation for efficient semantic segmentation, pp. 578–587. arXiv (2019)
12. Ho, J., Kalchbrenner, N., Weissenborn, D., Salimans, T.: Axial attention in multidimensional transformers, pp. 1–11. arXiv (2019)
13. Huang, L., Yuan, Y., Guo, J., Zhang, C., Chen, X., Wang, J.: Interlaced sparse self-attention for semantic segmentation. arXiv preprint arXiv:1907.12273 (2019)
14. Huang, Z., et al.: CCNet: criss-cross attention for semantic segmentation. arXiv (2018)
15. Joutard, S., Dorent, R., Isaac, A., Ourselin, S., Vercauteren, T., Modat, M.: Permutohedral attention module for efficient non-local neural networks. In: Shen, D., et al. (eds.) MICCAI 2019, Part VI. LNCS, vol. 11769, pp. 393–401. Springer, Cham (2019). https://doi.org/10.1007/978-3-030-32226-7_44
16. Lee, J., Lee, Y., Kim, J., Kosiorek, A., Choi, S., Teh, Y.W.: Set transformer: a framework for attention-based permutation-invariant neural networks. In: International Conference on Machine Learning, pp. 3744–3753. PMLR (2019)
17. Li, X., Zhong, Z., Wu, J., Yang, Y., Lin, Z., Liu, H.: Expectation-maximization attention networks for semantic segmentation. In: Proceedings of the IEEE/CVF International Conference on Computer Vision, pp. 9167–9176 (2019)
18. Sandler, M., Howard, A., Zhu, M., Zhmoginov, A., Chen, L.C.: MobileNetV2: inverted residuals and linear bottlenecks, pp. 4510–4520. arXiv (2018)
19. Shelhamer, E., Long, J., Darrell, T.: Fully convolutional networks for semantic segmentation. IEEE Trans. Pattern Anal. Mach. Intell. **39**(4), 640–651 (2017)

20. Song, C., Huang, Y., Ouyang, W., Wang, L.: Box-driven class-wise region masking and filling rate guided loss for weakly supervised semantic segmentation, pp. 3136–3145. arXiv (2019)
21. Vaswani, A., et al.: Attention is all you need. In: Advances in Neural Information Processing Systems, NIPS, December 2017, pp. 5999–6009 (2017)
22. Vernaza, P., Chandraker, M.: Learning random-walk label propagation for weakly-supervised semantic segmentation, pp. 7158–7166. arXiv (2018)
23. Wei, Y., Feng, J., Liang, X., Cheng, M.M., Zhao, Y., Yan, S.: Object region mining with adversarial erasing: a simple classification to semantic segmentation approach. In: Proceedings of the IEEE Conference on Computer Vision and Pattern Recognition, pp. 1568–1576 (2017)
24. Zhang, H., Zhang, H., Wang, C., Xie, J.: Co-occurrent features in semantic segmentation. In: Proceedings of the IEEE Computer Society Conference on Computer Vision and Pattern Recognition, June 2019, pp. 548–557 (2019)
25. Zhuoran, S.S., Mingyuan, Z.Z., Haiyu, Z.Z., Shuai, Y.Y., Hongsheng, L.L.: Efficient attention: attention with linear complexities. arXiv (2018)

Cervical Spondylotic Myelopathy Segmentation Using Shape-Aware U-net

Zhuo Chen[1], Shuqiang Wang[1(✉)], Yong Hu[2], Huiyu Zhou[3], Yanyan Shen[1], and Xiang Li[4]

[1] Shenzhen Institutes of Advanced Technology, Chinese Academy of Sciences, Shenzhen, Guangdong, China
{Zhuo.chen,sq.wang,yy.shen}@siat.ac.cn
[2] Neural Engineering Laboratory, The University of Hong Kong, Hong Kong, China
yhud@hku.hk
[3] United Kingdom University of Leicester, Leicester, UK
[4] The University of Hong Kong-Shenzhen Hosptial, Shenzhen, China
lix7@hku-szh.org
http://leicester.ac.uk

Abstract. Cervical Spondylotic Myelopathy (CSM) is serious cervical spondylosis that can lead to severe disability. To help physicians make diagnoses quickly and efficiently, automatic segmentation methods are urgently needed in clinical practice. Nevertheless, there are great challenges with this task, such as ambiguity of structure boundary and uncertainty of the segmented region. Although some deep learning methods have performed well in medical segmentation tasks, they are not good at processing complex medical images. To solve those problems in automatic medical segmentation, this paper proposes a novel shape-aware segmentation framework for the cervical spondylotic myelopathy segmentation from diffusion tensor imaging (DTI). Specifically, a new shape-aware strategy was adopted that enables backbone networks to simultaneously aggregate both global and local context and efficiently capture long-range dependencies. Extending pyramid pooling with a shape-aware strategy, the shape-aware pyramid pooling module(SAAP) was adopted to integrate multi-scale information and compensate for spatial information loss. This module expands the field of perception and reduces interference in non-lesioned areas. The effectiveness of shape-aware U-net (SAU-net) was evaluated on the cervical spondylotic myelopathy dataset, which consists of 116 patients who underwent surgical decompression and DTI evaluation. The experiment proves that our method can effectively segment CSM lesions.

Keywords: Automatic segmentation method · Shape-aware strategy · SAU-net

1 Introduction

CSM is one of the compression of the spinal cord, accounting for 10%–15% of all cervical spondylotic diseases. This disease may lead to disability and seriously affect

© Springer Nature Singapore Pte Ltd. 2021
H. Zhang et al. (Eds.): NCAA 2021, CCIS 1449, pp. 671–681, 2021.
https://doi.org/10.1007/978-981-16-5188-5_48

the quality of life of patients [1–4]. Diffusion tensor imaging (DTI) has become one of the key diagnostic techniques for CSM analysis [5]. In clinical work, the assessment of a patient's condition requires professional radiologists to manually map the lesion area on DTI images. It is time-consuming and can easily lead to misdiagnosis due to subjective perceptions. Therefore, there is an urgent need for an automatic segmentation method for cervical spondylotic myelopathy in clinical practice. However, it is challenging to obtain accurate segmentation results, because it remains very difficult to get satisfying segmentation for some complex pathological features, which could be extremely small or vary a lot in terms of position, and shape.

CNN continues to make breakthroughs in the application of medical image segmentation [6–12]. For example, U-net [13], DenseUnet [14], 3D U-net [15] are proposed based on symmetrical architectures. These models can combine linked information to efficiently address segmentation tasks. However, the repeated use of fixed-size convolution and single pooling operations limits the field of perception and the efficiency of features [16]. Furthermore, many automatic segmenting methods do not handle complex lesion features well, and these features usually require manual labeling by experienced medical professionals.

Gradient vanishing is a common problem in model training. One of the methods to improve efficiency is to use self-supervised information or non-local modules [17–24]. However, this approach requires the computation of a matrix for each location, and the performance is limited by huge memory. In addition, the pyramid pooling architecture [25–28] and dilated convolution [29–32] are presented to capture multi-scale features and summarizes the overall characteristics of the images. However, the fixed-size square window in the pooling operation limits their flexibility to capture context information.

To address this problem, a novel end-to-end model is proposed, named structure perception U-net. A shape-aware strategy is adopted to enlarge the receptive fields of the model for capturing long-range dependencies and collecting informative contexts. Different from global pooling operations, the shape-aware module (SAM) replaces the square pooling kernels with band shape pooling kernels. More concretely, the SAM consists of a horizontally oriented coding module and a vertically oriented coding module. Furthermore, we adopt this strategy to aggregate both global and local contexts during the encoding phase. The shape-aware strategy was also used to extend the pyramid pooling structure, the new pyramid pooling module enables to deal with the problem of the fuzzy boundaries and the imbalance of class. In a word, we propose an automated segmentation model to segment CSM with the following contributions:

1. A shape-aware module is adopted to capture local context dependencies effectively and prevent irrelevant regions from interfering with label prediction.
2. This shape-aware module is applied to the pyramid pooling module. SAAP module is proposed to connect multi-layer information to better handle the differences in spinal cord location, shape, and size.
3. In the spinal cervical segmentation task, SAU-net obtained better results compared to competing methods.

The rest of the paper is organized as follows. Section 2 discussed related work on the proposed network architecture. Section 3 discussed the specific structure of the proposed SAU-net. Section 4 summarized the results of extensive experiments including an ablation study for the shape-aware module and shape-aware pyramid pooling module. The comparison experiments with advanced methods show that the proposed SAU-net gets a better performance of cervical spondylotic myelopathy segmentation. Finally, Sect. 5 summarized the paper.

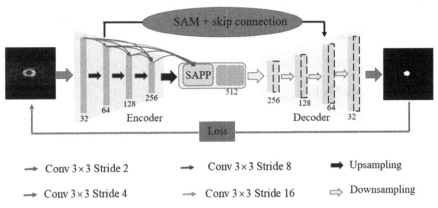

Fig. 1. The details of the SAU-net

2 Relate Work

DCNNs have achieved great success in medical image segmentation in recent years. In particular, U-Net [12] employs an asymmetrical structure, It is one of the popular research directions in the field of medical image segmentation. For instance, Huang et al. [33] proposed a neural network model for multi-organ segmentation, and this model is able to combine multi-domain learning to improve segmentation performance. Metto et al. [34] adopted a new method to segment the femoral condyle cartilage. However, existing models rely on superimposed local feature maps and cannot effectively capture spatial information. To solve this problem, Wang et al. [24] proposed the non-local U-Nets for biomedical image segmentation. This model equipped with flexible global aggregation blocks and had good segmentation performance. Qi et al. [35] proposed a stroke segmentation model named X-net. This method replaced the general convolution with depthwise separable convolution.

Another improvement method is spatial pyramid pooling. This structure integrates the features from different receptive fields through multiple parallel-distributed dilated convolutions to form multi-scale predictions. However, those fixed size sampling operations used in this multi-scale fusion strategy, which limit the receptive fields of the model. In contrast, our proposed shape-aware pyramid pooling module adopts a shape-aware strategy. This module enables the network to enhance the segmentation performance of cervical spondylotic myelopathy.

3 Method

The shape-aware segmentation network is shown in Fig. 1. The structure consists of symmetric encoders and decoders. Skip connections are used between the encoder and decoder. Feature maps of the same scale can be fused to obtain global contextual information of the images. To improve model performance, our proposed shape-aware module (SAM) is appended on skip connections. This module is able to extract the local information of different scales. The SAPP module is proposed to aggregate multi-scale information to better deal with the spinal cord location, shape, size, and boundary confusion issues.

3.1 Shape-Aware Module

When processing objects with irregular shapes, the effectiveness of the average pooling operation could decrease. A large number of irrelevant regions easily affects model performance [36]. To address this problem, we present the shape-aware module (SAM), which replaces the average pooling with two-band shape pooling operations. Two submodules scan the input tensor in both horizontal and vertical directions. This module facilitates capturing information about each location.

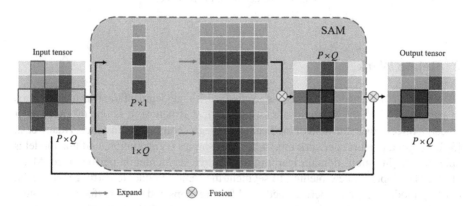

Fig. 2. The details of the Shape-aware Module (SAM).

As illustrated in Fig. 2, two sub-module $(P, 1)$ and $(1, Q)$ are added to the module. Different from the average pooling, the proposed shape sensing module is capable of fusing horizontally encoded information and vertically encoded information. We first feed the input tensor $X \in R^{P \times Q}$ into two sub-modules. The horizontal module and the vertical submodule each consist of a one-dimensional convolution kernel. Thus, the horizontal module output $\beta^P \in R^P$ is calculated as:

$$\beta_i^p = \frac{1}{Q} \sum_{0 \le j < Q} \alpha_{i,j}. \tag{1}$$

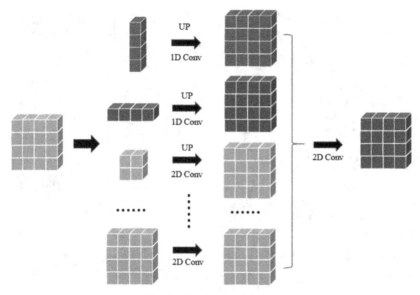

Fig. 3. The details of SAPP.

Similarly, the other output $\beta^q \in R^Q$:

$$\beta_i^p = \frac{1}{P} \sum_{0 \leq j < P} \alpha_{i,j}. \tag{2}$$

To take full advantage of the output of both submodules, we use a softmax layer to sum β_j^q and β_i^p. $\varphi\left(\beta_j^q, \beta_i^p\right)$ denotes the degree of association between position i and position j:

$$\varphi\left(\beta_j^q, \beta_i^p\right) = \frac{exp\left(\beta_j^q, \beta_i^p\right)}{\sum_j^N exp\left(\beta_j^q, \beta_i^p\right)} \tag{3}$$

Finally, we calculate the sum of $\varphi\left(\beta_j^q, \beta_i^p\right)$ and x. The result obtained is the output of SAM.

In the above method, each input tensor is calculated by two sub-modules to obtain the horizontal and vertical position information. By fusing the information in both directions, the output is able to establish the relationship between each position. These properties make the proposed shape-aware module enable to capture of the edge features of the lesion area and reduce the interference of irrelevant areas.

3.2 SAPP Module

The shape-aware strategy is added to the original pyramid module. Specifically, as shown in Fig. 3, we extend pyramid pooling with two sub-module. This module connects and

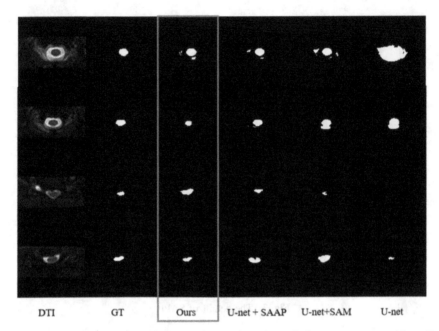

DTI   GT   Ours   U-net + SAAP   U-net+SAM   U-net

Fig. 4. Visualization of ablation experiment on the proposed shape-aware pyramid pooling module and shape-aware module based on CSM dataset.

integrates the feature maps of each sampling layer. In addition, The horizontal and vertical pool layers are added to capture short and long-term dependencies between locations. Two sub-modules compensate for the loss of spatial information due to square pooling. It should be noted that for different feature aggregations, different convolutions strides are required to make the resolution of different features consistent.

Finally, we also add a convolution layer to ensure consistent output size. Thereby, the network can enhance the complementarity of information between different levels by cascading multi-scale features.

4   Evaluation and Results

4.1   Implementation Details

Dataset. The imaging data of cervical spondylotic myelopathy utilized in this experiment were acquired by the University of Hong Kong Shenzhen Hospital. This dataset contains 116 CSM patients' DTI images with cervical spondylotic myelopathy manually labeled masks. Each of the objects is set to $128 \times 128 \times 6$ and each image is sliced into 128×128.

Evaluation Metrics. In this experiment, a 5-fold cross-validation strategy is emplored and a range of evaluation metrics are used to measure the performance of our model, including Dice coefficient (Dic), Intersection over Union (IoU), precision (Pre), and recall (Rec).

$$Dic = \frac{2 \cdot Tp}{2 \cdot Tp + Fn + Fp} \tag{4}$$

$$IoU = \frac{Tp}{Tp + Fn + Fp} \tag{5}$$

$$Pre = \frac{Tp}{Tp + Fp} \tag{6}$$

$$Rec = \frac{Tp}{Tp + Fn} \tag{7}$$

Where Tn, Tp, Fn and Fp refer to the number of true negatives, true positives, false negatives, false positives, respectively.

Implementation. In this paper, our implementation is based on NVIDIA RTX 2080Ti with 11 GB memory and the framework is Pytorch-GPU 1.0. The Adam optimizer is used to minimize the loss function. The same equipment was used for each comparison experiment.

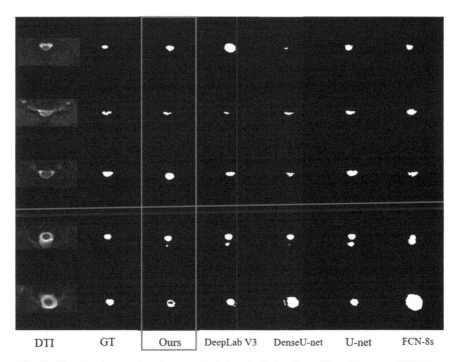

| DTI | GT | Ours | DeepLab V3 | DenseU-net | U-net | FCN-8s |

Fig. 5. Visualization results of our method, DeepLabv3+, DenseUnet, U-net, and FCN-8s.

4.2   Ablation Analysis of SAM and SAAP Module

The shape-aware module is adopted to capture local context information and reduce interference in irrelevant areas. The proposed shape-aware pyramid pooling module aggregates all of the previous features and integrates the feature maps of each sampling layer. To evaluate the performance of the two models, we added SAM and SAAP to the U-net for ablation experiments, respectively. As shown in Table 1, compared to the U-net, we can observe that SAM and SAPP yield better performance in four evaluation metrics (Dic, IoU, precision, and recall). Although there is a decrease in IoU after adding SAM, the higher recall scores in segmentation tasks for cervical spondylotic myelopathy are worthwhile, because we need to make sure all the spines can be detected. Besides Table 1 shows that the SAPP is more effective than SAM. This module performs better with 0.08, 0.0708, and 0.0891 improvements on IoU, precision, and recall, respectively.

The results of the segmentation visualization are shown in Fig. 4. By combining local and non-local operation and multi-scale features, irrelevant and redundant information decreases significantly in the segmentation results. More details of the lesion area are captured with SAM and SAAP. The experimental results show that two proposed modules can help the model to obtain better segmentation performance.

Table 1. Segmentation performance of different backbone networks.

Method	Dice	IoU	Precision	Recall
U-net [13]	0.5783	0.5340	0.5488	0.4070
U-net + SAPP	0.6214	0.5792	0.6471	0.5903
U-net + SAM + SAPP (ours)	0.6614	0.6131	0.6798	0.6586

4.3   Comparison to the Competing Methods

To validate the effectiveness of the proposed method, we compare SAU-net with four state-of-the-art methods, including FCN-8s [37], DenseU-net [14], U-net [13], and DeepLabv3+ [38]. To ensure that the experiments are fair and reasonable, we conduct the experiments in the same equipment environment. It could be clearly observed from Table 2 that our model achieve a better score on the main indicators. SAU-net performs better with 0.1752, 0.2629, 0.1167, and 0.1999 improvements on Dice, IoU, precision, and recall, respectively. Besides, The results of the segmentation visualization of five methods are shown in Fig. 5. Comparison with the other four methods that our proposed SAU-net can segment cervical spondylotic myelopathy very well. Furthermore, our model performs well in handling fuzzy boundaries and the differences in spinal cord location, shape, and size.

Table 2. Comparison with the state-of-the-arts methods on CSM dataset.

Method	Dice	IoU	Pre	Rec
FCN-8s [37]	0.4862	0.3502	0.5631	0.4587
U-net [13]	0.5783	0.5340	0.5488	0.4070
DenseU-net [38]	0.5868	0.5362	0.5719	0.4782
DeepLabv3 [14]	0.5277	0.5016	0.5204	0.4881
SAU-net (ours)	0.6614	0.6131	0.6798	0.6586

5 Conclusion

In this paper, a novel model is presented named SAU-net for cervical spondylotic myelopathy segmentation. This model performs better in the CSM segmentation task. specifically. The proposed SAM can reduce interference from unrelated lesion areas and capture contextual Information effectively. Furthermore, SAPP can deal with the differences in spinal cord location, shape, size, and boundary confusion issues by aggregating multi-scale features. Experiments on the CSM dataset demonstrate that SAU-net could perform better in CSM segmentation tasks.

Acknowledgement. This work is supported by National Natural Science Foundations of China under Grant No. 61872351, International Science and Technology Cooperation Projects of Guangdong under Grant 2019A050510030, Guangdong Science Fund for Distinguished Young Scholars under Grant 2021B1515020019, Shenzhen Key Basic Research Project under Grant No. JCYJ20200109115641762 and Shenzhen Science Fund for Excellent Young Scholars under Grant No. RCYX2020071411464121.

References

1. Shabani, S., Kaushal, M., Budde, M.D., et al.: Diffusion tensor imaging in cervical spondylotic myelopathy: a review. J. Neurosurg. Spine **33**(1), 65–72 (2020)
2. Montgomery, D., Brower, R.: Cervical spondylotic myelopathy. Clinical syndrome and natural history. Orthop. Clin. N. Am. **23**, 487–493 (1992)
3. Wang, S., Hu, Y., Shen, Y., et al.: Classification of diffusion tensor metrics for the diagnosis of a myelopathic cord using machine learning. Int. J. Neural Syst. **28**(02), 1750036 (2018)
4. Wang, S.Q., Li, X., Cui, J.L., et al.: Prediction of myelopathic level in cervical spondylotic myelopathy using diffusion tensor imaging. J. Magn. Reson. Imaging **41**(6), 1682–1688 (2015)
5. Hu, Y., Chan, T.Y., Li, X., et al.: Identify myelopathic cervical spinal cord using diffusion tensor image: a data-driven approach. In: 2015 IEEE International Conference on Digital Signal Processing (DSP), pp. 548–551. IEEE (2015)
6. Long, J., Shelhamer, E., Darrell, T.: Fully convolutional networks for semantic segmentation. In: Proceedings of the IEEE Conference on Computer Vision and Pattern Recognition, pp. 3431–3440 (2015)

7. Lei, B., Xia, Z., Jiang, F., et al.: Skin lesion segmentation via generative adversarial networks with dual discriminators. Med. Image Anal. **64**, 101716 (2020)

8. Wang, S., Shen, Y., Shi, C., et al.: Skeletal maturity recognition using a fully automated system with convolutional neural networks. IEEE Access **6**, 29979–29993 (2018)

9. Li, M., Hu, W., Xie, X., et al.: SACNN: self-attention convolutional neural network for low-dose CT denoising with self-supervised perceptual loss network. IEEE Trans. Med. Imaging **39**(7), 2289–2301 (2020)

10. Cheng, T., Wang, X., Huang, L., Liu, W.: Boundary-preserving mask R-CNN. In: Vedaldi, A., Bischof, H., Brox, T., Frahm, J.-M. (eds.) ECCV 2020. LNCS, vol. 12359, pp. 660–676. Springer, Cham (2020). https://doi.org/10.1007/978-3-030-58568-6_39

11. Li, L., Wu, F., Yang, G., et al.: Atrial scar quantification via multi-scale CNN in the graph-cuts framework. Med. Image Anal. **60**, 101595 (2020)

12. Dolz, J., Gopinath, K., Yuan, J., et al.: HyperDense-Net: a hyper-densely connected CNN for multi-modal image segmentation. IEEE Trans. Med. Imaging **38**(5), 1116–1126 (2018)

13. Ronneberger, O., Fischer, P., Brox, T.: U-net: Convolutional networks for biomedical image segmentation. In: Navab, N., Hornegger, J., Wells, W.M., Frangi, A.F. (eds.) MICCAI 2015. LNCS, vol. 9351, pp. 234–241. Springer, Cham (2015). https://doi.org/10.1007/978-3-319-24574-4_28

14. Li, X., Chen, H., Qi, X., et al.: H-DenseUNet: hybrid densely connected UNet for liver and tumor segmentation from CT volumes. IEEE Trans. Med. Imaging **37**(12), 2663–2674 (2018)

15. Çiçek, Ö., Abdulkadir, A., Lienkamp, S.S., Brox, T., Ronneberger, O.: 3D U-Net: learning dense volumetric segmentation from sparse annotation. In: Ourselin, S., Joskowicz, L., Sabuncu, M.R., Unal, G., Wells, W. (eds.) MICCAI 2016. LNCS, vol. 9901, pp. 424–432. Springer, Cham (2016). https://doi.org/10.1007/978-3-319-46723-8_49

16. Zhao, H., Shi, J., Qi, X., et al.: Pyramid scene parsing network. In: CVPR (2017)

17. Zhou, Z., Rahman Siddiquee, M.M., Tajbakhsh, N., Liang, J.: Unet++: A nested u-net architecture for medical image segmentation. In: Stoyanov, D., et al. (eds.) DLMIA/ML-CDS -2018. LNCS, vol. 11045, pp. 3–11. Springer, Cham (2018). https://doi.org/10.1007/978-3-030-00889-5_1

18. Chen, L.-C., Yang, Y., Wang, J., Xu, W., Yuille, A.L.: Attention to scale: scale-aware semantic image segmentation. In: CVPR (2016)

19. Zhao, H., Jia, J., Koltun, V.: Exploring self-attention for image recognition. In: Proceedings of the IEEE/CVF Conference on Computer Vision and Pattern Recognition, pp. 10076–10085 (2020)

20. Lei, B., Huang, S., Li, H., et al.: Self-co-attention neural network for anatomy segmentation in whole breast ultrasound. Med. Image Anal. **64**, 101753 (2020)

21. Wang, X., Girshick, R., Gupta, A., et al.: Non-local neural networks. In: Proceedings of the IEEE Conference on Computer Vision and Pattern Recognition, pp. 7794–7803 (2018)

22. Zhang, L., Xu, D., Arnab, A., Torr, P.H.S.: Dynamic graph message passing networks. In: CVPR (2020)

23. Oktay, O., Schlemper, J., Folgoc, L.L., et al.: Attention u-net: learning where to look for the pancreas. arXiv preprint arXiv:1804.03999 (2018)

24. Wang, Z., Zou, N., Shen, D., et al.: Non-local U-Nets for biomedical image segmentation. In: Proceedings of the AAAI Conference on Artificial Intelligence, vol. 34, no. 04, pp. 6315–6322 (2020)

25. He, K., Zhang, X., Ren, S., et al.: Spatial pyramid pooling in deep convolutional networks for visual recognition. IEEE Trans. Pattern Anal. Mach. Intell. **37**(9), 1904–1916 (2015)

26. Yang, H., et al.: CLCI-Net: cross-level fusion and context inference networks for lesion segmentation of chronic stroke. In: Shen, D., et al. (eds.) MICCAI 2019. LNCS, vol. 11766, pp. 266–274. Springer, Cham (2019). https://doi.org/10.1007/978-3-030-32248-9_30

27. Chang, J.R., Chen, Y.S.: Pyramid stereo matching network. In: Proceedings of the IEEE Conference on Computer Vision and Pattern Recognition, pp. 5410–5418 (2018)
28. Zhang, H., Patel, V.M.: Densely connected pyramid dehazing network. In: Proceedings of the IEEE Conference on Computer Vision and Pattern Recognition, pp. 3194–3203 (2018)
29. Zhou, L., Zhang, C., Wu, M.: D-linknet: linknet with pretrained encoder and dilated convolution for high resolution satellite imagery road extraction. In: Proceedings of the IEEE Conference on Computer Vision and Pattern Recognition Workshops, pp. 182–186 (2018)
30. Wei, Y., Xiao, H., Shi, H., et al.: Revisiting dilated convolution: a simple approach for weakly- and semi-supervised semantic segmentation. In: Proceedings of the IEEE Conference on Computer Vision and Pattern Recognition, pp. 7268–7277 (2018)
31. Deb, D., Ventura, J.: An aggregated multicolumn dilated convolution network for perspective-free counting. In: Proceedings of the IEEE Conference on Computer Vision and Pattern Recognition Workshops, pp. 195–204 (2018)
32. Mou, L., Chen, L., Cheng, J., et al.: Dense dilated network with probability regularized walk for vessel detection. IEEE Trans. Med. Imaging **39**(5), 1392–1403 (2019)
33. Huang, C., Han, H., Yao, Q., Zhu, S., Zhou, S.K.: 3D U^2-Net: a 3D universal u-net for multi-domain medical image segmentation. In: Shen, D., et al.(eds.) MICCAI 2019. LNCS, vol. 11765, pp. 291–299. Springer, Cham (2019). https://doi.org/10.1007/978-3-030-32245-8_33
34. Dunnhofer, M., Antico, M., Sasazawa, F., et al.: Siam-U-Net: encoder-decoder siamese network for knee cartilage tracking in ultrasound images. Med. Image Anal. **60**, 101631 (2020)
35. Qi, K., Yang, H., Li, C., Liu, Z., Wang, M., Liu, Q., Wang, S.: X-net: brain stroke lesion segmentation based on depthwise separable convolution and long-range dependencies. In: Shen, D., et al. (eds.) MICCAI 2019. LNCS, vol. 11766, pp. 247–255. Springer, Cham (2019). https://doi.org/10.1007/978-3-030-32248-9_28
36. Hou, Q., Zhang, L., Cheng, M.M., et al.: Strip pooling: rethinking spatial pooling for scene parsing. In: Proceedings of the IEEE/CVF Conference on Computer Vision and Pattern Recognition, pp. 4003–4012 (2020)
37. Long, J., Shelhamer, E., Darrell, T.: Fully convolutional networks for semantic segmentation. In: CVPR, pp. 3431–3440 (2015)
38. Chen, L.-C., Zhu, Y., Papandreou, G., Schroff, F., Adam, H.: Encoder-decoder with atrous separable convolution for semantic image segmentation. In: Ferrari, V., Hebert, M., Sminchisescu, C., Weiss, Y. (eds.) ECCV 2018. LNCS, vol. 11211, pp. 833–851. Springer, Cham (2018). https://doi.org/10.1007/978-3-030-01234-2_49

Cloud/Edge/Fog Computing, The Internet of Things/Vehicles (IoT/IoV), and Their System Optimization

An Efficient CSI-Based Pedestrian Monitoring Approach via Single Pair of WiFi Transceivers

Jialai Liu[1], Kai Liu[1], Feiyu Jin[1], Dong Wang[1], Guozhi Yan[1], and Ke Xiao[2(✉)]

[1] College of Computer Science, Chongqing University, Chongqing 400040, China
{jlliu0207,liukai0807,fyjin,snowdong,yanguozhiup}@cqu.edu.cn
[2] College of Computer and Information Science, Chongqing Normal University,
Chongqing 401331, People's Republic of China
xiaoke@cqnu.edu.cn

Abstract. Pedestrian monitoring is a very important issue in many sensitive areas. Traditional technologies mainly include computer vision, infrared imaging, WiFi sniffing, etc. Nevertheless, these technologies cannot simultaneously satisfy low cost, user privacy and high reliability requirements. In view of this, this work aims at proposing a method based on CSI (Channel State Information) to enable pedestrian monitoring by leveraging a single pair of WiFi transceivers, which can work under different temperatures and light conditions as well as in a non-intrusive way. First, we pre-process the raw CSI to sift the interested components. Then, a two-stage clustering method is proposed to counteract the multipath effect, where the CSI pattern for pedestrian activities is learned in the offline phase. During the online phase, a Pedestrian Pass Detection Algorithm (PPDA) is proposed for pass detection. Further, we propose a Pass Direction Recognition Algorithm (PDRA) for direction recognition, by calculating the time of pass Line Of Sight (LOS) and the pass direction indicator. Finally, we implement the system prototype and conduct a series of real-word experiments, and the results conclusively demonstrate the feasibility and efficiency of the proposed methods.

Keywords: CSI · Pedestrian monitoring · Non-intrusive · Performance evaluation

1 Introduction

Pedestrian monitoring is demanded in many application scenarios, such as customer flow analysis [1–3], crowds distribution monitoring [4–7], and sensitive area monitoring [8–10]. It is worth nothing that the demand varies in different scenarios. For examples, user privacy protection is always strengthened in customer flow analysis, whereas for sensitive area monitoring, high reliability in different environmental conditions should be put in a very important place. Moreover, the system cost is another critical factor to be concerned to make it practical.

Traditional technologies for pedestrian monitoring include computer vision [8,11,12], infrared imaging [13,14], WiFi sniffing [1,2,15], etc. Computer vision

© Springer Nature Singapore Pte Ltd. 2021
H. Zhang et al. (Eds.): NCAA 2021, CCIS 1449, pp. 685–700, 2021.
https://doi.org/10.1007/978-981-16-5188-5_49

is widely used due to its simplicity and strong recognizability. However, they suffers from high cost and user privacy issues. Infrared imaging can protect user privacy to a certain extent, but it is vulnerable to ambient environmental change. WiFi sniffing can avoid the above shortages to some extent, but it is an intrusive method, which requires the carrying of portable WiFi device. In recent years, with the convenience of extracting Channel State Information (CSI) from WiFi packets, more and more applications are implemented based on CSI since it contains rich information for environment variations [16–19]. Specifically, with Multiple Input Multiple Output (MIMO) technology, we can arrange multi-links in environment by leveraging a single pair of WiFi transceivers, which makes it possible to recognize human spatial activity.

In this study, we propose a CSI-based approach to enable pedestrian monitoring via a single pair of WiFi transceivers, where the monitoring tasks include pedestrian pass detection and pass direction recognition. According to the Fresnel Zone perception criterion [20], the closer the pedestrian is to the LOS, the greater the degree of impact on CSI will be. On this basis, we learn the pattern offline for pedestrian pass detection. Moreover, for pass direction recognition, we propose a method to calculate the time of passing LOS, and further recognize the direction with multi-link information. In general, this study aims to achieve efficient pedestrian monitoring based on a single pair of WiFi transceivers, which enhances system adaptability and scalability. The main challenges are summarized as follows:

- For pedestrian pass detection, first, due to multipath effect, CSI features may vary a lot in different environments, even with the same experimental settings or the same detection activity, which seriously renders system adaptability. Second, the CSI features will be affected by various kinds of factors, such as walking speed, unrelated activities. Third, perception sensitivity to human activities may change with different links due to Signal Noise Ratio (SNR) and hardware capability alike, increasing the difficulty of collaborative sensing with multi-link.
- For pass direction recognition, direction is a spatial feature which needs multi-link information to identify. First, with limited sensing area for the utilize of only one single pair of WiFi transceivers, CSI features of each link may be affected simultaneously when pedestrian is near to the sensing area, which makes it difficult to design an effective link layout for direction recognition. Second, considering each link may have different perception sensitivities, how to combine all links information to efficiently recognize the direction is also challenging.

To enable efficient pedestrian monitoring and overcome the above challenges, the main contributions of this paper are summarized as follows:

- We present a new system architecture for CSI-based pedestrian monitoring via a single pair of WiFi transceivers. In general, it consists of offline and online phases. During the offline phase, the raw CSI are pre-processed via filtering, carrier selection and compression. Then, a two-stage clustering method is adopted to train the features of each link. Last, the Link Confidence (LC)

for each link is calculated, which measures the perception sensitivity. During the online phase, the online CSI measurements will be pre-processed via filtering, carrier selection and compression once again. Then, a Pedestrian Pass Detection Module (PPDM) is adopted for pass detection, and a Pass Direction Recognition Module (PDRM) is adopted for estimating the moving direction.

- In the offline phase, we propose a two-stage clustering to counteract the multipath effect. In the first stage of clustering, we extract the pre-processed data according to a specific length of time window, and the features mainly include Standard Deviation, Signal Entropy. Considering the static condition, interference, and the probabilistic sharp change in passing LOS, we cluster the features into three categories based on K-means algorithm. According to the results, we define the two clusters which are farther to the origin as active samples. In the second stage of clustering, we first composite consecutive active samples into one example, which represents a pass candidate. After that, we cluster them into two categories using the K-means algorithm based on the features mainly including Signal Entropy, Range, and Absolute Median Difference. Finally, the cluster closer to the origin is viewed as a pass.
- In the online phase, we propose a Pedestrian Pass Detection Algorithm (PPDA) for pedestrian pass detection and a Pass Direction Recognition Algorithm (PDRA) for pass direction recognition via a single pair of WiFi transceivers. Specifically, for pedestrian pass detection, we first select the link with the largest LC as detection link. Then, based on data of detection link, whether there is a pedestrian pass is determined through sequential processes including CSI pre-processing, active sample detection, and pass detection. For pass direction recognition, first, a pre-designed link layout is adopted to confirm the duration of passing through LOS. Then, we estimate the time of passing each LOS based on the duration. Finally, we calculate direction indicator to judge the pass direction.

The remaining of this paper is organized as follows. Section 2 reviews the related work. Section 3 presents the system architecture. Section 4 proposes the algorithms. Section 5 gives performance evaluation, and Sect. 6 summarizes this work.

2   Related Work

Due to the advantage of figure on intelligibility, lots of works are dedicated to achieve pedestrian monitoring based on computer vision. Mang et al. [8] proposed a dynamic graph matching method for pedestrian re-identification, which improved the label estimation process with similarity measurement learned from the intermediate estimated labels, and alleviated the burden in tedious sample labeling. Zhu et at. [12] proposed an efficient pedestrian monitoring method for multiple videos. Based on the distance metrics learned from the training data, it achieved in re-matching or separating the pedestrians in the video.

Considering the unreliability of computer vision in weak light condition, Andres Gomez et al. [13] implemented a CNN-based system by leveraging infrared imaging to enable pedestrians counting. Performance evaluation demonstrated the system not only works in dark environments, but also had a comparable performance to computer vision in bright environments.

Some studies aim to leverage Commercial Off The Shelf (COTS) wireless devices for pedestrian monitoring. Lesani and Miranda-Moreno [1] collected and analyzed the WiFi or Bluetooth packets transmitted by portable device, thereby realizing pedestrian detection and classification. Huang et al. [2] leveraged WiFi sniffer technology to detect the request probes sent by portable WiFi device, then estimated the pedestrian flow based on a probabilistic model.

Due to the advantage of sensitivity for ambient dynamic, CSI has the potential to non-intrusively recognize human activities. Wang et al. [20] used SVM to learn the difference between falling and other activities by extracting features from CSI, thereby realizing fall detection in indoor environments. Qian et al. [17] analyzed the frequency offset caused by pedestrian activity on CSI, and estimated the walking speed and direction to further realize the passive location of pedestrian. Distinguishing from above works, in this study, we propose a two-stage clustering method to counteract multipath effect, and achieve pedestrian monitoring by leveraging a single pair of WiFi transceivers. In this way, we reduce the overhead of system deployment and improve system adaptiveness.

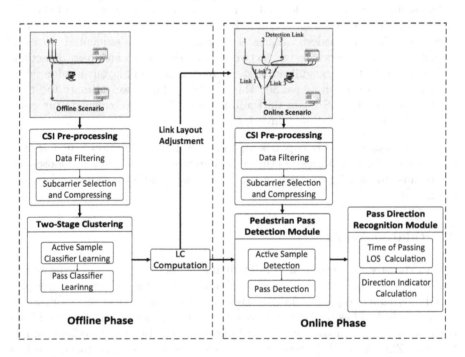

Fig. 1. Workflow of system.

3   System Architecture

In this section, we present a system architecture for CSI-based pedestrian monitoring via a single pair of WiFi Transceivers. As shown in Fig. 1, the system consists of offline phase and online phase.

In the offline phase, we first pre-process the raw CSI including data filtering, subcarrier selection and compression. Then, the pre-processed data is applied for two-stage clustering, where the first stage of clustering is for active sample classifier learning, and the second stage of clustering for pass classifier learning. On this basis, we define and calculate the LC of each link.

In the online phase, we first adjust the link layout, where the geometric parameters could be seen in Subsect. 5.2. We pre-process the raw CSI likewise. Then, we adopt Pedestrian Pass Detection Module (PPDM) to detect whether there is a pass. When a pass is detected, we adopt Pass Direction Recognition Module (PDRM) to judge the pass direction.

4   Proposed Algorithm

4.1   CSI Pre-processing

According to IEEE 802.11 n protocol, Orthogonal Frequency Division Multiplexing (OFDM) is adopted to improve the bandwidth capacity, that is, the data is sliced and then distributed to different subchannels for simultaneous transmission. Therefore, based on intel 5300 NIC and CSI TOOL [16], we can extract 30-dimensional Chanel State Information (CSI) from a packet. As shown in Formula 1, for link l, we denote the CSI with N WiFi packets as H_N^l, and denote the ith subcarrier information as $H_{n,i}^l$, where $1 \leq i \leq 30$. Considering the possible packet loss during WiFi transmission, the linear interpolation is adopted to fill out the missing value in a sequential CSI readings.

$$H_N^l = \left[H_{N,1}^l \ H_{N,2}^l \ \dots \ H_{N,30}^l \right] \tag{1}$$

Data Filtering. According to the Doppler effect in WiFi propagation, the impact of pedestrian pass on CSI mainly concentrates in the low frequency band. After verification by a great amount of experiments, the signal ranges in $[1, 10]$ Hz has a significant reflect on pedestrian pass. Then we select Butterworth filter to get the target signal components, so as to ensure great flatness of the signal in passband.

Subcarrier Selection and Compressing. Since the wireless signal has a frequency-selective fading characteristic for a same environmental change, subcarriers at different frequencies may have utter different performance for pedestrian pass. To get stable features, we select subcarriers with similar performance for analysis by calculating the correlation coefficient between subcarriers. Specifically, for link l with M packets, the correlation coefficient between subcarrier i and j are computed by:

$$coef_{H_{M,i}^l, H_{M,j}^l} = \frac{Cov(H_{M,i}^l, H_{M,j}^l)}{\sqrt{Var(H_{M,i}^l)Var(H_{M,j}^l)}} \tag{2}$$

where $Var(H_{M,i}^l)$ and $Var(H_{M,j}^l)$ are the variance of $H_{M,i}^l$ and $H_{M,j}^l$ respectively, and $Cov(H_{M,i}^l, H_{M,j}^l)$ is the covariance between $H_{M,i}^l$ and $H_{M,j}^l$. We calculate the correlation coefficients between each subcarrier and the rest of the subcarriers, and then select the subcarriers of the top 10 correlation coefficients for analysis. In the experiment, M is set as the number of recording packets in 5 s. Finally, we compress the 10-dimensional data to 1 dimension according to PCA method, and denote the result as $Transf\_H^l$.

4.2   Two-Stage Clustering Method

Although multipath effect can significant expand the communication range for wireless network, it is also the vital factor contributing to the difficulty of constructing a universal propagation model for different environment. Therefore, a CSI-based model usually need to be retrained in a new environment, which incurs laborious manual sample segmentation and labeling tasks. To tackle with above issues and learn the CSI pattern in different environments, we design a two stage clustering method including the active classifier learning and the pass classifier learning. The active sample classifier is used to detect whether there is a human activity happening near the WiFi transceivers, and the pass classifier is to judge the real pass in all detected activities. The training data for two-stage clustering method consists of two kinds of CSI readings. One is recorded when pedestrian is moving through the LOS of WiFi transceivers, and another one is recorded when pedestrian is approaching the LOS.

Active Sample Classifier. In the first stage of clustering, we select a specific length of data segmentation (i.e., the number of recording packets in 0.5 s) for detection, which is denoted as *segment*. To emphasize CSI feature related to the passing pedestrian, certain features including Range, Signal Entropy, and Average Difference are extracted from segments to measure the dispersion degree of CSI. The definitions of Signal Entropy and Average Deviation are shown in Formula 3 and Formula 4, respectively.

Suppose the maximum value of $Transf\_H$ is Max, and the minimum value is Min. We divide range of $[Min, Max]$ into K boxes equally, and then define p_k as the proportion of segment falling into each box. Specifically, the $p_k log_{p_k}$ is defined zero when $p_k = 0$.

$$Signal\ Entropy = \sum_{k=1}^{K} p_k log_{p_k} \tag{3}$$

Since the signal components less 1 Hz have been filtered out, the average value of $Transf\_H$ can be viewed as 0, and suppose *segment* length is N_s, then the *Average Deviation* is defined as follows:

$$Average\ Difference = \frac{1}{N_s} \sum_{i=1}^{N_s} |segment_i| \qquad (4)$$

When the pedestrian walks at a lower speed or completely stopped during the walk, the feature of recorded CSI (especially CSI in the low strength link) are closer to static condition than passing through LOS. To improve the reliability of the proposed method, we use K-means algorithm to cluster the above features into three categories. The two clusters farther from the origin are identified as the active samples, which contain the CSI changes caused by human activity. Therefore, the active sample classifier is designed to detect the true pedestrian pass based on the first stage of clustering results.

Pass Classifier. The second stage of clustering aims to learn a boundary between CSI recorded in the real pass and the CSI recorded in other irrelevant activities. First, we composite the consecutive active samples as an active example in light of the duration of a pass could vary in different conditions. Besides, we discard the examples with the duration less than 1 s, due to they are mainly caused by environmental noise.

After active examples is generated, we divide these examples into two categories, one for the real pass, and the other for irrelevant activity. Due to the fact that the difference between real pass and irrelevant activities mainly reflects on the degree of CSI dynamic change, we extract features including Standard Deviation, Mean Absolute Deviation, Range, Signal Entropy, and Average Difference from active examples. Then, we use K-means algorithm to category the above features into two clusters. The cluster which has a larger Euclidean distance to the origin is regarded as real pass, and the other cluster as irrelevant activity. Finally, the pass classifier is learned based on the results of the second clustering.

4.3 Pedestrian Pass Detection Algorithm

This section introduces a method for pedestrian pass detection through a single pair of WiFi transceivers. According to [16], a single pair of WiFi transceivers with 1 transmitting antenna and 3 receiving antennas (denoted as 1 × 3) could enable a stable communication. Therefore, we deploy the system based on a 1 × 3 communication links, thus there are 3 links available for detection.

Nevertheless, due to SNR and hardware capability, the links in the same wireless network card may have different perception sensitivity. To best use the recording data, Link Confidence (LC) is defined to measure the perception sensitivity of link based on the SNR and hardware capability. On one hand, the impact of SNR is reflected on the distance between the two clusters in the second stage of clustering. That is, a better SNR yields a greater distance between the two clusters. On the other hand, a link with stronger RSSI enables a more stable communication, so we roughly use it to measure the hardware capability. Therefore, we define the LC as follows:

$$LC = \frac{1 - e^{\zeta \cdot \overline{RSSI} \cdot \frac{\|C_{LOS} - C_{near}\|}{C_{near}}}}{1 + e^{\zeta \cdot \overline{RSSI} \cdot \frac{\|C_{LOS} - C_{near}\|}{C_{near}}}} \tag{5}$$

where C_{LOS} and C_{near} represent the farther and nearer centers to the origin in the second stage of clustering. ζ is the adjustment parameter, which is set as 0.01 by default. $\overline{RSSI}$ is the average of RSSI during monitoring. In this way, a larger LC indicates a stronger link perception sensitivity.

According to the above information, in the offline phase, we train active sample classifier and pass classifier, and compute the LC for each link. However, it is observed that the low LC link tends to be vulnerable in monitoring, which could make a negative impact on the result. Therefore, to ensure the effectiveness of the proposed method in multiple scenarios, we select the largest LC link to detect whether there is a pedestrian pass in the online phase.

4.4   Pedestrian Pass Detection Algorithm

Based on the time of pedestrian passing each LOS, the pass direction recognition can be divided into 3 steps. First, we estimate the duration of pedestrian passes through LOS. Then, we calculate the time of passing each LOS during the whole process. Finally, we design an indicator to recognize the pass direction.

Duration of Passing Through LOS Estimation. As noted that, the low LC link tends to be vulnerable in monitoring, causing that it is difficult to split an appropriate duration of passing through LOS. Therefore, we turn to use the largest LC link to estimate an uniform duration of passing through LOS for all links. According to the 1×3 communication link, we first put the largest LC link in the middle, and the other two links aside, as Fig. 2 shows. Then, we adjust the distance between WiFi transceivers and distance between receiving antennas, which are introduced in Subsect. 5.2 in detail. Finally, reviewing the generation mechanism of active example, which should include the conditions of approaching and leaving the LOS, so we view the time range of the active example as the duration of passing through LOS.

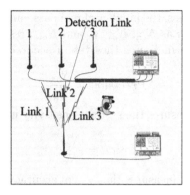

Fig. 2. Link layout

Time of Passing LOS Calculation. According to the observation that the pedestrian approaches is closer to LOS, the greater the degree of CSI changes, we design a method to calculate time of passing LOS t_{LOS} based on the value of $Transf\_H$, which is shown as follows:

$$t_{LOS} = \sum_{i=T_1}^{T_2} \frac{|Transf\_H_i|}{\sum_{i=T_1}^{T_2} |Transf\_H_i|} \cdot t_i \qquad (6)$$

where $Transf\_H_i$ represents the value of $Transf\_H$ at the ith moment. $[T_1, T_2]$ represents the duration of active example. In this way, we can calculate the time of passing each LOS based on the $Transf\_H$ of each link.

Direction Indicator Calculation. Finally, we combine LC and t_{LOS} to efficiently estimate the pass direction $direc\_ind$, which is computed by:

$$direc\_ind = \sum_{l=1}^{3} \sum_{l'=l+1}^{3} \cdot LC^l \cdot LC^{l'} \qquad (7)$$

where $t^{l'}_{LOS}$ and t^{l}_{LOS} represent the time of passing link l' and link l LOS respectively. Particularly, although the online LOS length of edge links change a little compared to the offline phase, we find the LC obtained in the offline phase still works. In the last, if the $direc\_ind$ is positive, it means that the direction is from antenna 1 to antenna 3. Otherwise, the direction is from antenna 3 to antenna 1.

5 Performance Evaluation

5.1 Metrics

In this part, we define *Precision*, *Recall* and *Direc_Acc* to evaluate the system performance. For convenience, we denote the number of correctly detected pass, the number of detected pass, the number of real pass, and the number of correctly recognizing pass direction as N_{cd}, N_d, N_r and N_{dir}, respectively.

For *Precision*, which measures the system accuracy in pass detection, the definition is as follows:

$$Precision = \frac{N_{cd}}{N_d} \qquad (8)$$

For *Recall*, which measures the system sensitivity in pass detection, the definition is as follows:

$$Recall = \frac{N_{cd}}{N_r} \qquad (9)$$

For *Direc_Acc*, which measures the system accuracy in pass direction recognition, the definition is as follows:

$$Direc\_Acc = \frac{N_{dir}}{N_{cd}} \qquad (10)$$

5.2   System Deployment and Parameter Setting

In the offline phase, we have learned the LC, active sample classifier and pass classifier for each link, which enable a simple pedestrian monitoring system. For better performance, some system parameters are still needed to be tuned by more experiments. We conclude the tasks into link layout deployment, least training number exploring, and least transmission frequency confirming.

Link Layout Deployment. According to the Pass Direction Recognition Algorithm (PDRA), we make a strategy to calculate the time of passing each link based on the duration of passing through LOS, which is actually determined by the middle link. The premise of the strategy is that the sensitive area of edge link and middle link has a quite overlap proportion. However, a large overlap proportion will shorten the time interval of passing each LOS, which could be a hinder to direction recognition. Therefore, an effective link layout with appropriate overlap proportion need to be explored.

According to the Fresnel Zone Theory [20], the shape of sensitive area is an ellipse, whose foci correspond to the transmitter and receiver. Hence, the proportion is decided by the distance between WiFi transceivers and the distance between receiving antennas. First, the distance between WiFi transceivers should range in [1, 3] m with the limitation of hardware, and the main energy transmission concentrates the top 8th Fresnel Zone [20]. To avoid the proportion too large or too small, we make a trick of setting the distance between receiving antennas as 0.5 m by default. Then, we changing the overlap proportion by adjusting the distance between the WiFi transceivers.

We set the distance between the WiFi transceivers to 1 m, 1.5 m, 2 m, 2.5 m respectively. For each part, we conduct 200 times of experiment. The *Direc_Acc* result is shown in Fig. 3. According to the result, the best distance between WiFi transceivers is 1.5 m, which is kept as default setting in subsequent experiments.

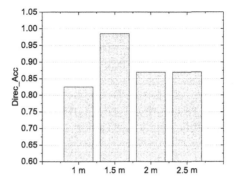

Fig. 3. Distances between WiFi transceivers

Least Training Number Exploring. In the two-stage clustering, we learn both active sample classifier and pass classifier based on K-means algorithm. There is a question about what least size of data set is adequate for training. To explore this issue, we analyze the overall performance of result by gradually changing the training number. We group one time of approaching LOS and one time of passing LOS as one pair, which is set as the increment in each training. The test data set includes 200 times of pass, and the overall performance is shown in Fig. 4. According to the result, it can be seen that the *Recall* keeps stable around 1.00 in the whole training, and the *Precision* become stable when training number reaches 4 pairs, and the *Direc_Acc* become stable when training number reaches 3 pairs. On this basis, we keep the training number as 5 pairs in subsequent experiments.

Least Transmission Frequency Confirming. A high transmission frequency can contribute to the CSI reflects the real environment more clearly. While a higher transmission frequency may put forward higher requirements for hardware and cause a higher energy consume. In this part, we explore the impact

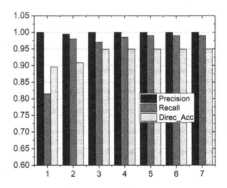

Fig. 4. Different training number

of transmission frequency on the overall performance, and find the least transmission frequency for pedestrian monitoring. We first conduct the experiments 1000 Hz, then get the lower transmission frequency data by down sampling. We conduct 200 times of experiments in total. The overall performance is shown in Fig. 5. According to the result, the Precision and Recall are hardly affected by the transmission frequency, while the *Direc_Acc* keeps a high accuracy (more than 0.95) until the transmission frequency 200 Hz. In subsequent experiments, we keep the transmission frequency 1000 Hz for detail analysis.

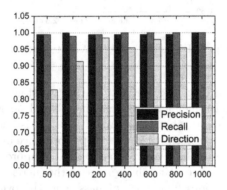

Fig. 5. Different transmission rate (Hz)

5.3   Adaptive Evaluation

With above obtained critical system parameters, a uniformed model is trained for a specific environment. Note that, the training data is collected based on regular conditions, where the volunteer has normal physical parameters, walks at a normal speed, etc.

Different Walking Speeds. First, we evaluate the overall system performance under different walking speeds. According to the Doppler effect of wireless signals, different walking speeds will cause different interference to the signal at the frequency level. Meanwhile it also will cause different duration of passing through LOS. In this set of experiments, the volunteer's speeds are controlled in three intervals, namely, 0.7–0.9 m/s, 1.1–1.3 m/s and 1.5–1.7 m/s, corresponding to slow, normal and fast speeds, respectively. We control the speed by walking a specific distance within a certain duration. Then 200 times of experiment are conducted for each kind of speed. The overall performance is shown in Fig. 6. According to the result, two conclusions are validated corresponding to the above issues. First, the interested signal components still concentrate in the frequency band we selected. Second, the mechanism of compositing consecutive active samples into active example is effective for different duration of passing through LOS.

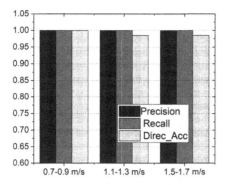

Fig. 6. Different walking speed

Table 1. Information of different volunteers

ID	Weight (Kg)	Height (cm)
male_1	60	170
male_2	65	170
male_3	75	177
female_1	50	155

Different Persons. Then, we evaluate the overall performance for different persons. We recruited four volunteers (3 males and 1 female) to conduct experiments, whose heights and weights are shown in Table 1. Then 50 times of experiment are conducted for each person. The result is shown in Fig. 7. According to result, the overall performance for each person keeps at a high level, which verifies the system has a high adaptivity.

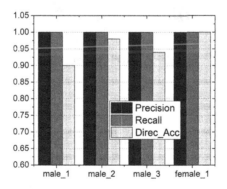

Fig. 7. Different persons

Different Environments. Finally, we test overall performance of the system under different environments. As shown in Fig. 8, we deploy the system in the corridor, warehouse and hall, respectively, which have quite different sizes and physical obstacles, giving totally different signal patterns. As the result shown in Fig. 9, the overall performance in both corridor and warehouse keep at a high level, while it decreases a bit in hall, especially for *Direc_Acc*. We find that the lower SNR and RSSI in hall should responsible for the decrease. Hence, in the situation like hall, we suggest to shorten the distance between WiFi transceivers.

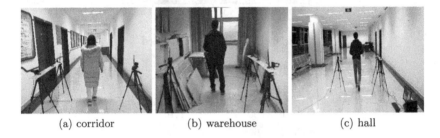

(a) corridor   (b) warehouse   (c) hall

Fig. 8. Different environments

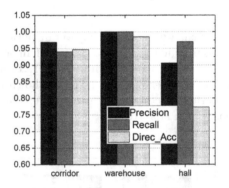

Fig. 9. Different environments

6 Conclusion

This work is dedicated to enhancing the scalability and adaptivity of CSI-based pedestrian monitoring system by leveraging a single pair of WiFi transceivers as well as adopting a low-overhead learning method. First, we proposed a method to pre-process the raw CSI, which includes filtering, subcarrier selection and compressing. Then, due to the multipath effect, the CSI pattern varies in different environments. Therefore, we proposed a two-stage clustering method to counteract the multipath effect. On the basis, we proposed a PPDA and a PDRA to detect whether there is a pass and recognize the pass direction. Finally, we implement the system prototype and conduct a series of real-world experiments. The result conclusively demonstrates the feasibility and effectiveness of the proposed algorithms.

Acknowledgement. This work was supported by the National Natural Science Foundation of China under Grant No. 61872049.

References

1. Lesani, A., Miranda-Moreno, L.: Development and testing of a real-time WiFi-Bluetooth system for pedestrian network monitoring, classification, and data extrapolation. IEEE Trans. Intell. Transp. Syst. **20**(4), 1484–1496 (2018)
2. Huang, B., Mao, G., Qin, Y., Wei, Y.: Pedestrian flow estimation through passive WiFi sensing. IEEE Trans. Mob. Comput. **20**(4), 1529–1542 (2019)
3. Jin, F., et al.: Toward scalable and robust indoor tracking: design, implementation, and evaluation. IEEE Internet Things J. **7**(2), 1192–1204 (2019)
4. Liu, K., et al.: Toward low-overhead fingerprint-based indoor localization via transfer learning: design, implementation, and evaluation. IEEE Trans. Ind. Inform. **14**(3), 898–908 (2018)
5. Zhang, H., Liu, K., Jin, F., Feng, L., Lee, V., Ng, J.: A scalable indoor localization algorithm based on distance fitting and fingerprint mapping in Wi-Fi environments. Neural Comput. Appl. **32**(9), 5131–5145 (2020)
6. Zhang, H., et al.: An annulus local search based localization (ALSL) algorithm in indoor Wi-Fi environments. In: Proceedings of 2018 IEEE International Conference on Ubiquitous Intelligence and Computing (UIC), pp. 887–892. IEEE (2018)
7. Zhang, H., et al.: Dual-band Wi-Fi based indoor localization via stacked denosing autoencoder. In: Proceedings of 2019 IEEE Global Communications Conference (GLOBECOM), pp. 1–6. IEEE (2019)
8. Ye, M., Li, J., Ma, A.J., Zheng, L., Yuen, P.C.: Dynamic graph co-matching for unsupervised video-based person re-identification. IEEE Trans. Image Process. **28**(6), 2976–2990 (2019)
9. Guo, X., Liu, B., Shi, C., Liu, H., Chen, Y., Chuah, M.C.: WiFi-enabled smart human dynamics monitoring. In: Proceedings of the 15th ACM Conference on Embedded Network Sensor Systems, pp. 1–13 (2017)
10. Lin, Y., Gao, Y., Li, B., Dong, W.: Revisiting indoor intrusion detection with WiFi signals: do not panic over a pet!. IEEE Internet Things J. **7**(10), 10437–10449 (2020)
11. Li, D., Zhang, Z., Chen, X., Huang, K.: A richly annotated pedestrian dataset for person retrieval in real surveillance scenarios. IEEE Trans. Image Process. **28**(4), 1575–1590 (2018)
12. Zhu, X., Jing, X.Y., You, X., Zhang, X., Zhang, T.: Video-based person re-identification by simultaneously learning intra-video and inter-video distance metrics. IEEE Trans. Image Process. **27**(11), 5683–5695 (2018)
13. Gomez, A., Conti, F., Benini, L.: Thermal image-based CNN's for ultra-low power people recognition. In: Proceedings of the 15th ACM International Conference on Computing Frontiers (CF), pp. 326–331 (2018)
14. Liu, Q., Lu, X., He, Z., Zhang, C., Chen, W.S.: Deep convolutional neural networks for thermal infrared object tracking. Knowl.-Based Syst. **134**, 189–198 (2017)

15. Fukuzaki, Y., Mochizuki, M., Murao, K., Nishio, N.: Statistical analysis of actual number of pedestrians for Wi-Fi packet-based pedestrian flow sensing. In: Proceedings of the 2015 ACM International Conference on Ubiquitous Computing (UbiComp), pp. 1519–1526 (2015)
16. Qian, K., Wu, C., Yang, Z., Liu, Y., Jamieson, K.: Widar: decimeter-level passive tracking via velocity monitoring with commodity Wi-Fi. In: Proceedings of the 18th ACM International Symposium on Mobile Ad Hoc Networking and Computing (MobiHoc), pp. 1–10 (2017)
17. Qian, K., Wu, C., Zhang, Y., Zhang, G., Yang, Z., Liu, Y.: Widar2.0: passive human tracking with a single Wi-Fi link. In: Proceedings of the 16th Annual International Conference on Mobile Systems, Applications, and Services (MobiSys), pp. 350–361 (2018)
18. Qian, K., Wu, C., Zhou, Z., Zheng, Y., Yang, Z., Liu, Y.: Inferring motion direction using commodity Wi-Fi for interactive exergames. In: Proceedings of the 2017 Conference on Human Factors in Computing Systems (CHI), pp. 1961–1972 (2017)
19. Ali, K., Liu, A.X., Wang, W., Shahzad, M.: Keystroke recognition using WiFi signals. In: Proceedings of the 21st Annual International Conference on Mobile Computing and Networking (MobiCom), pp. 90–102 (2015)
20. Wang, Y., Wu, K., Ni, L.M.: Wifall: device-free fall detection by wireless networks. IEEE Trans. Mob. Comput. **16**(2), 581–594 (2016)

Optimal Path Planning for Unmanned Vehicles Using Improved Ant Colony Optimization Algorithm

Hongchang Deng[1] and Jing Zhu[1,2]($\boxtimes$) (ID)

[1] College of Automation Engineering, Nanjing University of Aeronautics and Astronautics, Jiangsu 211100, China
drzhujing@nuaa.edu.cn
[2] Institute of Systems Engineering, Macau University of Science and Technology, Macau, China

Abstract. To prevent the locally optimal problem and slow convergence problem of unmanned vehicles (UVs) path planning, an improved ant colony algorithm is proposed by using a dynamic pheromone volatility coefficient. The best path is searched by selecting the appropriate pheromone volatility coefficient in ant colony algorithm, which has better searching ability, and converges to the optimal value quickly. The experimental results are illustrated to compare with other improved ant colony optimization algorithms to verify the effectiveness and efficiency of our proposed path planning method for UVs.

Keywords: Path planning · Ant colony optimization · Unmanned vehicle

1 Introduction

Path planning refers to find the best path from the beginning to the end in a specific environment under the premise of optimizing one or several performance indicators, and in other cases, it also refers to find the best path to accomplish reconnaissance, search and other tasks. There are many applications of path planning, including the movement of robot in industry, the reconnaissance and search task of unmanned aerial vehicles (UAVs) and unmanned vehicles (UVs) in military field, the movement of scavenging robot in the smart home, and so on. The methods of path planning on UAVs and UVs are various. In [1], the receding-horizon path planning method is proposed to realize positioning and autonomous search functions of manned aircraft with the use of multi-step planning for systems with limited sensor footprints. Coverage path planning, an energy-aware path planning algorithm, is mentioned in [2], in which the path covering all target points or other requirements is searched with little energy consumed in UVs. The collaborative path planning algorithm for target tracking is developed in [3], which makes use of dynamic occupied grids, Bayesian filters, just name a few, to enable the tracking movement of UAVs and UVs in urban environments. Although path planning has been studied for a long time, there are still some problems. For example, scholars only consider geometric constraints but do not pay attention to the characteristics and

© Springer Nature Singapore Pte Ltd. 2021
H. Zhang et al. (Eds.): NCAA 2021, CCIS 1449, pp. 701–714, 2021.
https://doi.org/10.1007/978-981-16-5188-5_50

practical significance of UVs and UAVs. The convergence speed and optimization result in path planning will also affect the application degree of the algorithm. And swarm intelligence bionic algorithms have achieved good results in this respect.

Up to today, scholars have developed sorts of advanced path planning algorithms on the basis of traditional optimization algorithms, including A* algorithm [4, 5], roadmap algorithm (RA) [6, 7], cell decomposition method (CD) [8, 9], artificial potential field method (APF) [10, 11], to name but a few. However, with the change of search environment, the expansion of search space, and the passage of time, the computational cost and the demand of storage space of the classical traditional path planning algorithm will increase geometrically. To this end, researchers proposed swarm intelligence optimization algorithms, including the ant colony optimization algorithm (ACO) [12], neural network [13, 14], genetic algorithm (GA) [15, 16], cuckoo algorithm [15, 17], particle swarm optimization (PSO) [16, 18], and artificial bee colony algorithm (ABC) [19, 20], etc. ACO is a heuristic random search algorithm proposed in the 1990s [12]. When an ant colony is searching for some food, the pheromone [21] on the path will affect the ant's choice of path, and eventually form the best path from the nest to the food. However, ACO also has some obstacles when applied to path planning. For example, a small pheromone volatilization coefficient will reduce the randomness of the algorithm's search, while a large one will reduce the convergence speed. In addition, the convergence rate of ACO is slow and local best results are easy to appear. Therefore, international scholars have also improved ACO for these problems. In [22], the authors used ACO for UAV path planning while also meeting the requirement of obstacle avoidance. But when the number of obstacles is too large or the complexity is relatively large, the performance of the algorithm proposed by [22] will decrease. In [23], the idea of fuzzy logic (FL) is applied to ACO, using the rank-based ant system and virtual path length to realize the path planning of UVs. However, the calculation time of this method needs to be further reduced. Liu Guoliang and others [24] used ACO to design a UAV location-assignment method in the problem of multi-UAV formation path planning, and then adopted a new strategy to select the next target node to find the globally best path. However, the improved ant colony algorithm in [24] has not been tested in other application environments. Green Ant (G-Ant) [25] not only considers the path length of the vehicle but also considers the energy consumed during the driving of the vehicle in the path planning of the unmanned ground vehicle (UGV). But the route found by the green ants is not necessarily the path with the shortest energy consumption. In [26], authors proposed and designed a dynamic viewable method based on the local environment model, a new rule of ant colony state transfer, and a reverse eccentric expansion method to improve ACO to realize the unmanned surface vehicle (USV) in the static position and dynamic state. Know the path planning in the environment to avoid collisions. In [27], ACO was used to draw a digital map of the drone's mission environment, and a mathematical model of the drone's horizontal and vertical flight trajectory was established to simulate the flight trajectory of the drone's mission. We can see from the above description that scholars have improved ACO through various means, allowing ACO to show better performance in path planning and be applied in more fields. However, the research of path planning algorithms is still in the stage of solving problems such as convergence speed, local optimization, unmanned vehicle modeling, dynamic environment, and path planning in emergencies. In addition, It should also consider the actual performance of the research object to improve the practicality of the algorithm.

The variation of pheromone volatilization coefficient is rarely considered in ACO algorithms. An improved ant colony method is proposed to change the pheromone volatilization coefficient. As such, the convergence speed is enhanced and the local optimum phenomena is largely avoided. We set up the search space by the Cartesian coordinate system, other than the raster map. The pheromone volatility coefficient changes along with the iteration times. In the beginning of the search, we use a relatively large pheromone volatilization coefficient. Afterwards, in the middle and late stages of a search, the pheromone volatilization coefficient turns to be small, to improve the searching accuracy.

The rest of this paper is organized as follows. Section 2 introduces the classical ant colony optimization algorithm and its application in path planning. Section 3 addresses the main results of this paper, including task environment modeling, improvement of pheromone volatilization coefficient, and the flow of improving ant colony optimization algorithm. Section 4 exhibits the comparison of experimental simulation with other UV path planning methods. Finally, Sect. 5 concludes the whole paper.

2 Path Planning Using ACO Algorithm

2.1 Classical Ant Colony Optimization Algorithm

In the biological world, when ants search for food [12, 28, 29], they secrete pheromones along the path that they traveled, as such clues are left for the ants behind them. Therefore, after a period of time, through the evaporation and accumulation of pheromones, a path with the largest pheromones from the ant nest to the object will be formed, which is also the optimal path. Ant colony algorithm uses artificial ants to simulate this process. Each artificial ant is placed at the starting point, and then the artificial ant independently selects the next target point according to the pheromone residue, path and heuristic information after evaporation. At time t, the probability $p_{ij}^k(t)$ of ant k moving from target i to target j is.

$$
p_{ij}^k(t) = \begin{cases} \dfrac{[\tau_{ij}(t)]^\alpha \cdot [\eta_{ij}(t)]^\beta}{\sum_{S \in J_k(i)} [\tau_{is}(t)]^\alpha \cdot [\eta_{is}(t)]^\beta}, & j \in J_k(i) \\ 0, & otherwise \end{cases} \tag{1}
$$

where, α and β represent the relative importance of pheromones and heuristic factors, respectively; τ_{ij} is the amount of pheromone between target points i and j; η_{ij} is the heuristic information, representing the expectation extent of ants from the target point i to j, and $\eta_{ij} = 1/d_{ij}$, where d_{ij} is the distance between i and j. $J_k(i) = \{1, 2, ..., n\}$ is the set of target points that ant k is allowed to choose in the next step;$tabu_k$ records the current target point that ant k has passed. When the path cost from target i to target j decreases, the state transition probability of the road segment will increase. Therefore, when the ant chooses the next moving target, it will be more inclined to choose target j.

When all ants traverse n targets once, the pheromone quantity on each path should be updated according to (2).

$$\tau_{ij}(t+n) = (1-\rho) \cdot \tau_{ij}(t) + \Delta\tau_{ij} \tag{2}$$

where, ρ represents pheromone volatility coefficient; $\Delta\tau_{ij}$ represents the pheromone increment between i and j in this iteration, which can be obtained as.

$$\Delta\tau_{ij} = \sum_{k=1}^{m} \Delta\tau_{ij}^{k} \tag{3}$$

where, $\Delta\tau_{ij}^{k}$ represents the amount of pheromone left between i and j by the k ant in this iteration. If the ant does not pass through two points i and j, t is equal to zero. $\Delta\tau_{ij}^{k}$ can be expressed by.

$$\Delta\tau_{ij}^{k} = \begin{cases} \frac{Q}{L_k}, & \text{when ant k passes i and j in this iteration} \\ 0, & \text{otherwise} \end{cases} \tag{4}$$

where, Q is the positive constant, and L_k represents the length of the path traveled by the k ant in this iteration.

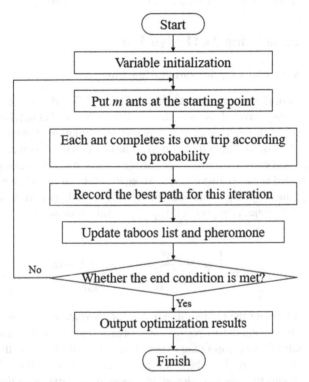

Fig. 1. Flow chart of basic ant colony optimization algorithm

The flow chart of the basic ACO is shown in Fig. 1. The process of path planning based on the basic ACO is briefly described as follows. In the initial time, the number of search targets n, the number of ants m, the importance factor α of pheromone, the importance factor β of heuristic information, the volatility coefficient ρ, pheromone slight Q, the initial iteration number *iter* and the maximum allowable iteration number $iter_{max}$ are set. The target distance matrix, pheromone matrix, path distance matrix, optimal path recording matrix of each generation, and optimal path length recording vector of each generation are established. Then put the ants on the starting point of the driverless car. The ant chooses the next search target according to the target selection probability formula (1), and updates the ant taboo. When all the targets are visited and the ant returns to the starting position, the ant's search ends. Then the next ant searches until all the ants have finished the search. At this point, an iteration is completed, and the best path of the iteration is recorded. Then, according to formula (2) to formula (4), the pheromone on each path is updated, and the tabu list is cleared before the next iteration. The algorithm finds the best path before the end of iteration. So far, the basic ant colony algorithm has completed the whole optimization process.

2.2 Application of Basic Ant Colony Optimization Algorithms

ACO is essentially a parallel algorithm with a positive feedback mechanism and strong robustness. It has many applications, including traveling salesman problem (TSP), optimal tree problem, integer programming problem, general continuous optimization problem, vehicle routing problem (VRP), etc. Figure 2 shows the result of simple obstacle avoidance path planning for robots using the basic ant colony algorithm.

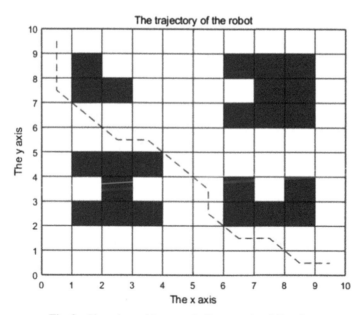

Fig. 2. Obstacle avoidance path diagram of mobile robot

In Fig. 2, the black area represents the obstacle, the white area represents the passable area, and the black dotted line refers to the moving trajectory of robot. In this simple experiment, the robot mobile environment is constructed as a 10*10 grid map. In the grid map, obstacles like "concave" or "L" will appear. This kind of obstacle is likely to lead artificial ants into a deadlock state, thus reducing the number of ants participating in the search and affecting the final search results. Therefore, we consider a completion method to solve the ant deadlock problem.

3   Path Planning Using Improved ACO Algorithm

3.1   Task Environment Modeling

There are many kinds of search environment modeling in path planning, such as Cartesian coordinate system, raster map, probability path diagram, and so on. In the common raster maps, if ants encounter "concave" and "L" obstacles in the search process, ants are prone to the deadlock phenomenon, which affects the optimality of search results. Therefore, in view of the shortcomings of grid map, we use the Cartesian coordinate system to model the search environment, and represents the task points in the form of coordinates. The environment modeling is shown in Fig. 3.

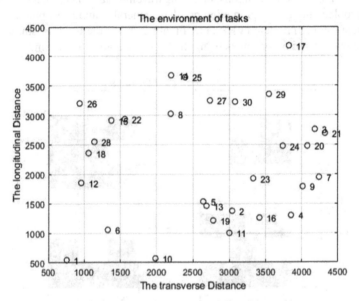

Fig. 3. Search environment modeling schematic

According to the task point coordinates to be searched, the task environment is constructed as a plane Cartesian coordinate system of (4500–500) * (4500–500), as depicted in Fig. 3. The X-axis and Y-axis in the figure represent the transverse distances and longitudinal distances between any two task points respectively, in meters. The task point coordinates are composed of the two, and each task point is labeled, as shown in the black circle in Fig. 3. Treat the driverless car as a particle, search all mission points in the environment map and return to the starting point.

As for the deadlock phenomenon of ants in the grid map, we consider a fence method to solve this problem. In the process of driving, UVs often encounter obstacles of various shapes. We consider using straight line segments to enclose the obstacle into a polygon, as shown in Fig. 4. The black areas represent obstacles, and the black dotted line segments are straight line segments surrounding the obstacle. To avoid affecting the optimization results, we should make the area of the polygon as small as possible, and avoid "concave"-shaped and "L"-shaped edges. In this way, in the process of ant search, deadlock phenomenon can be effectively avoided, and the optimization accuracy is improved as well.

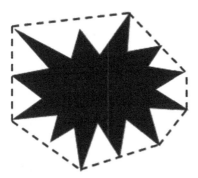

Fig. 4. Diagram of obstacle handling

3.2 Improvement of Pheromone Volatilization Coefficient

The pheromone volatilization coefficient of the classical ACO is a small constant. As such, when using the basic ACO for path search, the residual pheromone amount in the search after the initial pheromone volatilization is large. For the next iteration ants with a larger impact on target selection, they are more inclined to choose the path of the pheromone, consequently leading to the reduction of search range and search randomness. Thus, the locally optimal solution is made. To solve the issues of slow convergence and local optimal in classical ACO, we change the pheromone volatilization coefficient in this paper. The improved expression of the pheromone volatilization coefficient is.

$$\rho(iter) = \begin{cases} \left(1 - \frac{iter}{iter_{max}}\right)\rho(iter - 1), & if \ iter\langle\left[\frac{iter_{max}}{b}\right] and \ \rho\rangle\rho_{min} \\ \rho_{min}, & otherwise \end{cases} \tag{5}$$

where *iter* represents the current number of iterations and $iter_{max}$ represents the maximum number of iterations; ρ_{min} represents the minimum pheromone volatility coefficient. Parameter of b is an adjustable positive parameter with a value range of 3 to $\sqrt{iter_{max}}$, and the specific value of b is determined according to the maximum number of iterations.

In (5), the pheromone volatility coefficient varies with iterations. With the increase of iteration, $\rho(iter)$ decreases from large to small until it decreases to the minimum value. In this improvement, the parameter of b is used to divide the whole iteration process into two parts. In the early part of the iteration, $\rho(iter)$ varies with iterations; the second part is the middle and late part of the iteration, and the pheromone volatilization coefficient takes its minimum value. The value range of parameter b is determined according to the maximum number of iterations, and the maximum value is $\sqrt{iter_{max}}$. When the value of $\frac{iter_{max}}{b}$ is not an integer, let $[\frac{iter_{max}}{b}]$ be the integer that is less than or equal to $\frac{iter_{max}}{b}$ and close to $\frac{iter_{max}}{b}$.

3.3 The Flow of Improved Ant Colony Algorithm

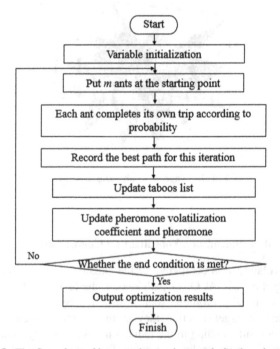

Fig. 5. The flow chart of improved ant colony optimization algorithm

The flow chart of the improved ant colony algorithm is shown in Fig. 5. The process of path planning realized by the improved ACO is briefly described as follows: at the initial time, the number of search targets n, the number of ants m, the importance factor of pheromone α, the importance factor of heuristic information β, the minimum value of pheromone volatility coefficient ρ_{min}, the initial value of pheromone volatility coefficient ρ, the light value of pheromone Q, the initial number of iterations *iter* and the maximum allowable number of iterations $iter_{max}$ were set. The target distance matrix, pheromone matrix, path distance matrix, optimal path recording matrix of each generation, and optimal path length recording vector of each generation are established. Then put the ants on the starting point of the driverless car. The ant chooses the next search target according to the target selection probability formula (1), and updates the ant taboo. When all the targets are visited and the ant returns to the starting position, the ant's search ends. Then the next ant searches until all the ants have finished the search. At this point, an iteration is completed, and the best path of the iteration is recorded. Firstly, the pheromone fluctuation coefficient is updated according to formula (5), and then the pheromone on each path is updated to formula (4) according to the global pheromone update formula (2), and the next iteration is started after the tabu list is cleared. The algorithm finds the best path before the end of iteration.

4 The Experimental Results

To illustrate the effectiveness of the improved algorithm proposed in this paper and to improve the convergence speed of the algorithm, this section uses MATLAB software to conduct experimental verification. We compare it with the basic ACO and other improved ACO based on regulating pheromone volatility [30–33]. The basic idea of an adaptive ant colony algorithm is: after each iteration, the current optimal solution is obtained and retained. When the issue scale becomes large, because of the existence of ρ, the pheromones of paths that have never been searched gradually dwindle or even disappear. Thus, this will reduce the globality of the algorithm. When ρ is too large, the probability of the previously searched path being selected here is very high. And this will also affect the globality of the algorithm. Therefore, it is necessary to adaptively change the value of ρ. The adaptive formula is shown in (6).

$$\rho(t) = \begin{cases} 0.95\rho(t-1), & \text{If } 0.95\rho(t-1) \geq \rho_{min} \\ \rho_{min}, & \text{Otherwise} \end{cases} \tag{6}$$

To simplify the experiment, the analysis and experimental simulation are carried out based on a two-dimensional plane. The initial parameters of the algorithm are as follows: the number of search targets $n = 30$; the number of ants $m = 50$; pheromone importance factor $\alpha = 1$; heuristic information importance factor $\beta = 5$; pheromone intensity $Q = 100$; the minimum value of pheromone volatilization coefficient $\rho_{min} = 0.1$. The maximum number of iterations allowed is $iter_{max} = 100$. Figures 6, 7 and 8 show the optimal path obtained by the basic ACO, improved ACO and adaptive ACO, respectively. Figure 9 shows the convergence curve comparison of these methods and

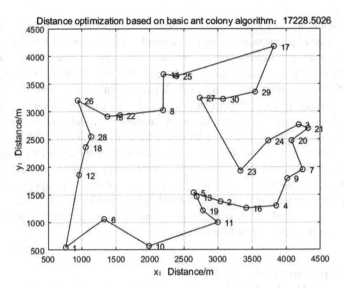

Fig. 6. Path results of basic ant colony optimization algorithm

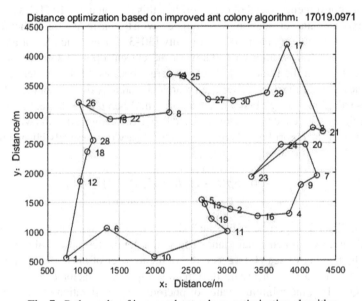

Fig. 7. Path results of improved ant colony optimization algorithm

those in [31–33]. It can be seen from Fig. 9 that the proposed improved ACO algorithm has the highest convergence speed among all. The path length comparisons are as shown in Table 1, from which we can find that our proposed result has the shortest path length, as well.

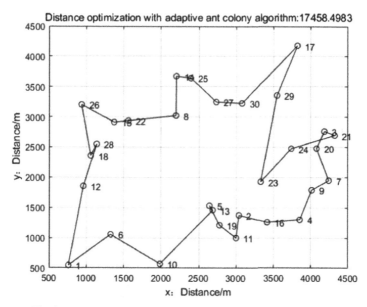

Fig. 8. Path results of adaptive ant colony optimization algorithm

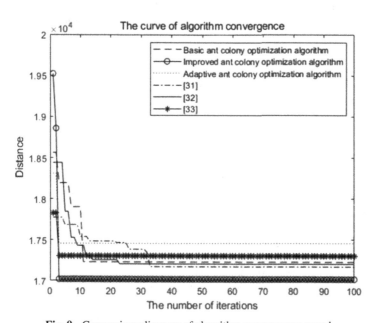

Fig. 9. Comparison diagram of algorithm convergence speed

Table 1. The path length of the experimental results

The algorithm name	The path length of the search results
Basic ant colony algorithm	17228.5206 m
Improved ant colony algorithm	**17019.0971 m**
Adaptive ant colony algorithm	17458.4983 m
Reference [31]	17171.1176 m
Reference [32]	17204.7807 m
Reference [33]	17301.4208 m

5 Conclusions

Ant colony algorithm is widely used in path planning, whereas, there still are unsolved problems, such as slow convergence speed, local optimization in real applications. To this end, this paper proposes an improved ACO algorithm on UV path planning with high convergence speed and global optimization ability by using a time-varying pheromone volatilization coefficient. The iterative process consists of two parts. In the beginning paragraph, the pheromone volatilization coefficient decreases from a large value along with iteration times. In the second part, the pheromone volatilization coefficient remains at a small value and gradually reduced. There is still a lot of room for improvement. In our next work, we shall consider the constraints of the actual working environment and the performance of UV itself to enhance the applicability of the ACO algorithm.

Acknowledgements. This work was fund by the Science and Technology Development Fund, Macau SAR (File no. 0050/2020/A1).

References

1. Tisdale, J., Kim, Z., Hedrick, J.K..: Autonomous UAV path planning and estimation. IEEE Robot. Autom. Mag. **16**(2), 35–42 (2009)
2. Di Franco, C., Buttazzo, G.: Energy-aware coverage path planning of UAVs. In: 2015 IEEE International Conference on Autonomous Robot Systems and Competitions, pp. 111–117. IEEE, Vila Real (2015)
3. Yu, H., Meier, K., Argyle, M., Beard, R.W.: Cooperative path planning for target tracking in urban environments using unmanned air and ground vehicles. IEEE/ASME Trans. Mechatron. **20**(2), 541–552 (2015)
4. Yang, R., Cheng, L.: Path planning of restaurant service robot based on a-star algorithms with updated weights. In: 2019 12th International Symposium on Computational Intelligence and Design (ISCID), pp. 292–295. IEEE, Hangzhou (2019)
5. Zhang, Z., Tang, C., Li, Y.: Penetration path planning of stealthy UAV based on improved sparse a-star algorithm. In: 2020 IEEE 3rd International Conference on Electronic Information and Communication Technology (ICEICT), pp. 388–392. IEEE, Shenzhen (2020)

6. Cao, Y., Han, Y., Chen, J., Liu, X., Zhang, Z., Zhang, K.: A tractor formation coverage path planning method based on rotating calipers and probabilistic roadmaps algorithm. In: 2019 IEEE International Conference on Unmanned Systems and Artificial Intelligence (ICUSAI), pp. 125–130. IEEE, Xi'an (2019)

7. Ravankar, A.A., Ravankar, A., Emaru, T., Kobayashi, Y.: HPPRM: hybrid potential based probabilistic roadmap algorithm for improved dynamic path planning of mobile robots. IEEE Access **8**, 221743–221766 (2020)

8. Gonzalez, R., Kloetzer, M., Mahulea, C.: Comparative study of trajectories resulted from cell decomposition path planning approaches. In: 2017 21th International Conference on System Theory, Control and Computing (ICSTCC), pp. 49–54. IEEE, Sinaia (2017)

9. Lupascu, M., Hustiu, S., Burlacu, A., Kloetzer, M.: Path planning for autonomous drones using 3D rectangular cuboid decomposition. In: 2019 23rd International Conference on System Theory, Control and Computing (ICSTCC), pp. 119–124. IEEE, Sinaia (2019)

10. Chen, M., Zhang, Q., Hou, L.: Improved artificial potential field method for dynamic target path planning in LBS. In: 2018 Chinese Control and Decision Conference (CCDC), pp. 2710–2714. IEEE, Shenyang (2018)

11. Chen, Z., Xu, B.: AGV path planning based on improved artificial potential field method. In: 2021 IEEE International Conference on Power Electronics, Computer Applications (ICPECA), pp. 32–37. IEEE, Shenyang (2021)

12. Dorigo, M., Maniezzo, V., Colorni, A.: Ant system: optimization by a colony of cooperating agents. IEEE Trans. Syst. Man Cybern. -Part B (Cybern.) **26**(1), 29–41 (1996)

13. Luo, M., Hou, X., Yang, J.: Multi-robot one-target 3D path planning based on improved bioinspired neural network. In: 2019 16th International Computer Conference on Wavelet Active Media Technology and Information Processing, pp. 410–413. IEEE, Chengdu (2019)

14. Wang, J., Chi, W., Li, C., Wang, C., Meng, M.Q.-H.: Neural RRT*: learning-based optimal path planning. IEEE Trans. Autom. Sci. Eng. **17**(4), 1748–1758 (2020)

15. Wang, J., Shang, X., Guo, T., Zhou, J., Jia, S., Wang, C.: Optimal path planning based on hybrid genetic-cuckoo search algorithm. In: 2019 6th International Conference on Systems and Informatics (ICSAI), pp. 165–169. IEEE, Shanghai (2019)

16. Tong, Y., Zhong, M., Li, J., Li, D., Wang, Y.: Research on intelligent welding robot path optimization based on GA and PSO algorithms. IEEE Access **6**, 65397–65404 (2018)

17. Wang, W., Tao, Q., Cao, Y., Wang, X., Zhang, X.: Robot time-optimal trajectory planning based on improved cuckoo search algorithm. IEEE Access **8**, 86923–86933 (2020)

18. Liu, X., Gu, Q., Yang, C.: Path planning of multi-cruise missile based on particle swarm optimization. In: 2019 International Conference on Sensing, Diagnostics, Prognostics, and Control (SDPC), pp. 910–912. IEEE, Beijing (2019)

19. Li, X., Huang, Y., Zhou, Y., Zhu, X.: Robot path planning using improved artificial bee colony algorithm. In: 2018 IEEE 3rd Advanced Information Technology, Electronic and Automation Control Conference (IAEAC), pp. 603–607. IEEE, Chongqing (2018)

20. Tian, G., Zhang, L., Bai, X., Wang, B.: Real-time dynamic track planning of multi-UAV formation based on improved artificial bee colony algorithm. In: 2018 37th Chinese Control Conference (CCC), pp. 10055–10060. IEEE, Wuhan (2018)

21. Bonabeau, E., Dorigo, M., Theraulaz, G.: Inspiration for optimization from social insect behave. Nature **406**(6), 39–42 (2000)

22. Chen, J., Ye, F., Jiang, T.: Path planning under obstacle-avoidance constraints based on ant colony optimization algorithm. In: 2017 IEEE 17th International Conference on Communication Technology (ICCT), pp. 1434–1438. IEEE, Chengdu (2017)

23. Song, Q., Zhao, Q., Wang, S., Liu, Q., Chen, X.: Dynamic path planning for unmanned vehicles based on fuzzy logic and improved ant colony optimization. IEEE Access **8**, 62107–62115 (2020)

24. Liu, G., Wang, X., Liu, B., Wei, C., Li, J.: Path planning for multi-rotors UAVs formation based on ant colony algorithm. In: 2019 International Conference on Intelligent Computing, Automation and Systems (ICICAS), pp. 520–525. IEEE, Chongqing (2019)
25. Jabbarpour, M.R., Zarrabi, H., Jung, J.J., Kim, P.: A green ant-based method for path planning of unmanned ground vehicles. IEEE Access **5**, 1820–1832 (2017)
26. Wang, H., Guo, F., Yao, H., He, S., Xu, X.: Collision avoidance planning method of USV based on improved ant colony optimization algorithm. IEEE Access **7**, 52964–52975 (2019)
27. Li, Z., Han, R.: Unmanned aerial vehicle three-dimensional trajectory planning based on ant colony algorithm. In: 2018 37th Chinese Control Conference (CCC), pp. 9992–9995. IEEE, Wuhan (2018)
28. Kumar, P., Dwivedi, R., Tyagi, V.: Fuzzy ant colony optimization based energy efficient routing for mixed wireless sensor network. In: 2019 International Conference on Issues and Challenges in Intelligent Computing Techniques (ICICT), pp. 1–7. IEEE, Ghaziabad (2019)
29. Khaled, A., Farid, K.: Mobile robot path planning using an improved ant colony optimization. Int. J. Adv. Robot. Syst. **15**(3), 1–7 (2018)
30. Gambardella, L.M., Dorigo, M.: Solving symmetric asymmetric TSPs by ant colonies. In: Proceedings of the IEEE Conference on Evolutionary Computation, pp. 622–627. IEEE, Nagoya (1996)
31. Liu, T., Yin, Y., Yang, X.: Research on logistics distribution routes optimization based on ACO. In: 2020 5th International Conference on Information Science, Computer Technology and Transportation (ISCTT), pp. 641–644. IEEE, Shenyang (2020)
32. Liu, Y., Hou, Z., Tan, Y., Liu, H., Song, C.: Research on multi-AGVs path planning and coordination mechanism. IEEE Access **8**, 213345-213356 (2020)
33. Li, J., Zhang, J.: Global path planning of unmanned boat based on improved ant colony algorithm. In: 2021 4th International Conference on Electron Device and Mechanical Engineering (ICEDME), pp. 176–179. IEEE, Guangzhou (2021)

Spreading Dynamics, Forecasting, and Other Intelligent Techniques Against Coronavirus Disease (COVID-19)

Daily PM2.5 Forecasting Using Graph Convolutional Networks Based on Human Migration

Choujun Zhan, Wei Jiang$^{(\boxtimes)}$, Qiaoling Zhen, Haoran Hu, and Wei Yuan

School of Electrical and Computer Engineering, Nanfang College,
Guangzhou 510970, China

Abstract. Most existing deep learning methods for air pollution concentration forecasting mainly focus on temporal characteristics of air pollutants. However, the spatial characteristics of air pollution concentration are closely related between nearby cities. In this study, we construct Target-city Graphs (TCG) to reveal the features of air pollutants between cities by using intercity migration networks. Then, we develop Graph Convolutional Neural Networks (GCN) and Graph Attention Networks (GAT) with Sum Aggregation (Sum-agg) and Mean Aggregation (Mean-agg) functions to forecast daily PM2.5 concentration time series based on TCG graph representing. The experimental results indicate that the GAT with Sum aggregation performs the best in forecasting PM2.5 while considering the intercity migration data.

Keywords: Air pollution · PM2.5 Forecasting · Graph Representing · Graph Neural Network · Intercity Migration network · Graph Attention Networks

1 Introduction

Air pollution is a critical environmental issue seriously influencing human outdoor activities and health [1]. With the development of Deep Learning (DL), researchers adopted Deep Neural Networks (DNN) to forecast the concentration of air pollutants, such as PM2.5 and PM10 [2–5], or predicting greenhouse gas CO_2 [6]. Previous studies focus on the temporal characteristic of air pollutants, which utilize Recurrent Neural Networks (RNN) to capture the historical features in time series [6,7], or signal decomposition method, such as Wavelet Decomposition (WD), to decompose air pollutants time series for further analysis [8].

However, the spatial characteristic is also a significant feature for improving the predictive power of machine learning methods. One way is to transit the spatial characteristic into graph representing. Then, prediction models based on graph representation can be proposed to predict time series, such as wind power [9] and traffic system [10,11]. The structure of the graph is different from

© Springer Nature Singapore Pte Ltd. 2021
H. Zhang et al. (Eds.): NCAA 2021, CCIS 1449, pp. 717–727, 2021.
https://doi.org/10.1007/978-981-16-5188-5_51

conventional data structures such as image and signal and can represent the complex distortion relationship of data on a non-Euclidean plane. To solve graph representing tasks, graph classification and regression problem, Scarselli *et al.* first proposed the Graph Neural Network (GNN) [12]. Then, Kipf *et al.* proposed and summarized the Graph Convolutional Neural Network (GCN), which is an advanced GNN by using spectral or spatial convolutional processing [13]. Based on GCN, Velivckovic *et al.* proposed a Graph Attention Network (GAT) which further captures the features of edge in graph [14].

In recent years, due to the development of GNNs, many studies utilized GNNs to forecast air pollution. For instance, novel GCNs combining RNN to capture the dynamic properties of fine-grained and long-term dependencies of PM2.5 [15,16]. Besides, a study considers dynamic wind-field to build a graph (network) for PM2.5 forecasting using GCNs [17]. These researches pay attention to the factors which influence the air pollution concentration and then build a graph (network) that depends on these factors. Moreover, Wang *et al.* propose an Attentive Temporal Graph Convolutional Network (ATGCN) to capture the relationship between different locations to predict air quality of urban stations [18]; namely, the graph is based on the features of different air quality observation stations.

In this study, combining the intercity migration data in China, we propose a novel graph representation called Target-city graph (TCG). This graph data structure reflects the relationships of air pollution between cities and the impact of migration on air pollution. Besides, graph representation can supplement the insufficient information of daily data by aggregating the information of neighbor nodes. In addition, we develop GCNs to forecast daily PM2.5 concentration based on TCG and obtain a better result while using the migration data using GAT model.

The rest of this study goes as follows: In Sect. 2, we describe the adopted air pollution dataset, migration dataset and introduce the study area. In Sect. 3, we present the Target-city graph (TCG) graph representing, Graph Convolutional Neural Network (GCN) and Graph Attention Network (GAT) with 2 aggregation functions. Section 4 also presents the experimental results of the models, including GCN-Sum, GCN-Mean, GAT-Sum, GAT-Mean and BPNN. The conclusion is given in Sect. 5.

2   Datasets and Study Area

2.1   Air Pollution Data

The air pollution dataset is provided by China's Ministry of Environmental Protection (MEP, from https://www.aqistudy.cn). This dataset consists two parts of data: one of which is daily air pollutant concentration data, including PM2.5, PM10, CO, NO_2, SO_2 and O_3; the other is meteorological data, including temperature, humidity and wind level. Each type of data in a city is the average value of different observation stations in the same city. Here, the air pollutants

PM10, CO, NO_2, SO_2, O_3, the rank of air quality in cities of China, temperature, humidity and wind level, these 9 indicators are using as features which input into prediction models.

2.2 AutoNavi Migration Data

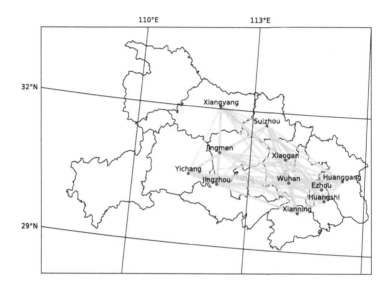

Fig. 1. The migration network in Hubei province

AutoNavi Big Data (trp.autonavi.com/home.html) provides the migration network dataset in each province of China. The migration dataset consists of the migration routes from cities to cities in a province, and each migration route has a specific volume of migrations, which is denoted by the AutoNavi migration index (AMI). In detail, AMI reflects the daily migration population from city to city. In this study, the migration data in Hubei province is adopted. According to the AutoNavi migration data, it can be established a migration network which is shown in the Fig. 1.

2.3 Study Area

In this study, we focus on forecasting air pollution and considering the migration network in Hubei province, China. We utilize the AutoNavi migration data and the air pollution dataset in 11 cities located in Hubei province, namely, Suizhou, Ezhou, Xianning, Jingzhou, Jingmen, Xiaogan, Wuhan, Yichang, Xiangyang, Huangshi, and Huanggang. The selected time range of these two datasets is from December 1st, 2019, to November 29th, 2020.

3   Methodologies

3.1   Graph Representing

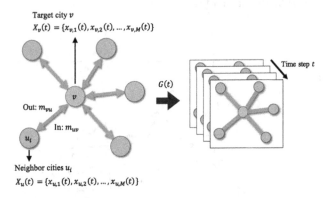

Fig. 2. Target-city Graph (TCG) Representing

According to the migration network of Hubei, the air pollution data and meteorological data of cities in Hubei province, we can define a Target-city Graph (TCG) which reflects the air pollution considering intercity migration. TCG is a directed graph, denoted as $G(\mathcal{V}, \mathcal{E}, \mathcal{M})$, where $\mathcal{V}$ represents nodes (cities) in the graph $\{v, u_i\} \in \mathcal{V}$. Here, v is target city and u_i is neighbor city; the number of nodes is $|\mathcal{V}| = N$; $\mathcal{E}$ is the edge and $\{vu_i, u_iv, vv\} \in \mathcal{E}$; $\mathcal{M}$ is the weight of the edge composed of the AutoNavi migration index, divided into incoming migration index m_{uv} and outgoing migration index m_{vu}; the structure of TCG is shown in Fig. 2.

Note that a TCG is composed of target city (orange node) and neighbor city (blue node). The target city with a feature set composed of air pollution time series feature $X_v(t)$ on day t, where $X_v(t) = \{x_{v,1}(t), x_{v,2}(t), \ldots, x_{v,M}(t)\}$, $X_v(t) \in \mathbb{R}^{M \times 1}$; similarly, each neighbor city also has an air pollution feature set $X_u(t) = \{x_{u,1}(t), x_{u,2}(t), \ldots, x_{u,M}(t)\}$, $X_u(t) \in \mathbb{R}^{M \times 1}$.

Then, TCGs on different days t consists of TCG time series $G(t)$. In this study, we use TCG as the input data of a sample, and then combine the PM2.5 concentration $y(t+1)$ of target city on the day $t+1$, then a supervised learning mapping relationship $\{G(t), y(t+1)\}$ is obtained. The purpose is to use the TCG on the day t to predict the PM2.5 concentration of the target city one-day ahead $t+1$. TCG can use the air pollution and meteorological features of the target city to predict PM2.5 concentration based on the migration index (edge weight) of neighbor cities.

3.2   Graph Convolutional Network

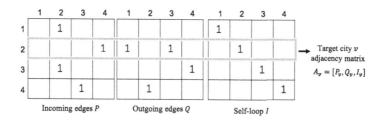

Fig. 3. Target city adjacency matrix

The adopted Graph Convolutional Neural Network (GCN) in this research is the spatial GCN proposed by Kipf *et al.* [13]. In this study, PM2.5 concentration forecasting utilizing TCGs actually belongs to the regression of the node-task. The spatial node-task GCN mainly consists of two main parts. The first part is the aggregation function, with the TCG graph presentation based on the feature set $X_v(t)$ of target city v and the feature set $X_u(t)$ of its neighbor u. The aggregation function can be defined as:

$$a_v = agg(X_v(t), X_u(t)) \tag{1}$$

where $agg(\cdot)$ is the aggregation function and a_v refers to the output of target city v from aggregation function.

The second part of GCN is update function. A Fully-connected Neural Network (FNN) are used as update function in this study, which can defined as follows:

$$o_v = \sigma(W_f a_v) \tag{2}$$

where $\sigma(\cdot)$ is an FNN with a nonlinear activation function, and W_f is the parameter matrix in FNN. Here, we utilize the ReLU function as the activation function of FNN.

In detail, there are 2 aggregation function are used in this study, which proposed by Hamilon *et al.* [19]. The aggregation function $agg(\cdot)$ can further develop 2 types of aggregation functions: Sum Aggregation (Sum-agg, Eq. (3)) and Mean Aggregation (Mean-Agg, Eq. (4)).

$$a_v = \sum_{u \in N[v]} w_u X_u(t) + w_v X_v(t), \tag{3}$$

$$a_v = \frac{1}{N}[\sum_{u \in N[v]} w_u X_u(t) + w_v X_v(t)], \tag{4}$$

where w_u is the weighted coefficient.

In order to denote the aggregation function for directed graph, we use the adjacent matrix $A_v \in \mathbb{R}^{1 \times 3N}$ (Eq. (5)) based on the research [20]. The adjacent matrix A_v of target city v consists of three parts, indegree adjacent matrix $P_v \in \mathbb{R}^{1 \times N}$, outdegree adjacent matrix $Q_v \in \mathbb{R}^{1 \times N}$, and self-loop matrix $I_v \in \mathbb{R}^{1 \times N}$, which shown in Fig. 3.

$$A_v = \begin{cases} 1 \text{ if } \{vu_i, u_iv, vv\} \in E, \\ 0 \text{ otherwise.} \end{cases} \tag{5}$$

Moreover, we define the indegree matrix $D_{\text{in}} \in \mathbb{R}^{N \times N}$ and outdegree matrix $D_{\text{out}} \in \mathbb{R}^{N \times N}$ for the normalization processing of graph aggregation. D_{in} and is diagonal matrix with the sum of degrees (Eq.(6)):

$$D_{\text{in}} = \begin{bmatrix} d(v_1) & 0 & \cdots & 0 \\ 0 & d(v_2) & \cdots & 0 \\ \vdots & \vdots & \ddots & \vdots \\ 0 & 0 & \cdots & d(v_n) \end{bmatrix} \tag{6}$$

where the $d(\cdot)$ is the sum of the degrees at node v. We can define the global degree matrix $D \in \mathbb{R}^{N \times 3N}$, where $D = [D_{\text{in}}, D_{\text{out}}, I]$. Then, we can denote the normalized matrix calculation of Sum-agg in Eq. (7) and Mean-agg in Eq. (8).

$$a_v = (D^{-\frac{1}{2}})^T A_v D^{-\frac{1}{2}} H_v W, \tag{7}$$

$$a_v = \frac{1}{N}[(D^{-\frac{1}{2}})^T A_v D^{-\frac{1}{2}} H_v W], \tag{8}$$

where the $H_v = [X_{u,1}(t), X_{u,2}(t), \ldots, X_{u,N-1}(t), X_v(t)] \in \mathbb{R}^{M \times N}$ is the matrix of features in neighbor city features ($X_{u,i}(t)$) and target city features is $X_v(t)$. Here, we have $D_{in} = D_{out}$, as the number of incoming and outgoing edges of a city are the same. Based on Sum-agg and Mean-agg, we develop 2 GCNs which are nominated as GCN-Sum and GCN-Mean.

3.3   Graph Attention Network

In aggregation operation, some neighboring cities are insignificant for predicting the PM2.5 concentration of the target city. Therefore, the aggregation operation should focus on aggregating the important neighbor cities to avoid noise information from those insignificant nodes. The Graph Attention Network (GAT) [14] proposed by Velivckovic et al. can decide whether to aggregate the information of a neighbor city according to the attention correlation coefficient α.

In this study, we define the incoming and outgoing attention correlation coefficients α_{vu}, α_{uv}, which is derived from the features of the weight of the directed edge m_{vu} and m_{uv} in TCG. The calculation of outgoing attention coefficient α_{uv} is as follows:

$$\alpha_{vu} = \frac{\exp(m_{vu})}{\sum_{k \in N[v]} \exp(m_{vk})}, \tag{9}$$

where the m_{vu} is the outgoing migration index between target city and neighbor city and k are the other neighbor cities except neighbor u. Similarly, the incoming attention coefficient α_{uv} can be calculated by the incoming migration index m_{uv}.

Based on the attention coefficient α, the aggregation function can be rewritten as follows:

$$a_v = agg(X_v(t), X_u(t), \alpha_{uv}, \alpha_{vu}), \qquad (10)$$

Then, Sum-agg and Mean-agg of GAT can be defined as Eq. (11) and Eq. (12):

$$a_v = \sum_{u \in N[v]} (a_{vu} + a_{uv}) w_u X_u(t) + w_v X_v(t), \qquad (11)$$

$$a_v = \frac{1}{N} [\sum_{u \in N[v]} (a_{vu} + a_{uv}) w_u X_u(t) + w_v X_v(t)], \qquad (12)$$

In conclusion, we can develop 2 GATs which are GAT-Sum and GAT-Mean with different 2 aggregation functions.

4 Experimental Result

4.1 Experimental Settings

The proposed models GCN-Sum, GCN-Mean, GAT-Sum, GAT-Mean are utilized to forecast the PM2.5 concentration time series based on the TCG consists of the AutoNavi migration and the air pollution information in each city. The time range of the dataset is from December 1st, 2019, to November 29th, 2020, 365 days (samples) in total. 70% of the data set, that is from December 1st, 2019 to August 10th, 2020, is utilized as the training set, and the rest 30%, that is from August 11th, 2020 to November 29th, 2020, is adopted as the test set.

Note that the size of the experimental dataset in this study is small and the structure of the above-mentioned models with the number of neurons are small scale. Consequently, we added the Back Propagation Neural Network (BPNN) as the baseline model. We find the best hyper-parameters of each model by grid searching, and then each GCN model trains 4000 times and BPNN trains 800 times to verify the stability, which is equivalent to a total of 22000 models. Furthermore, these models add the L2 regularization in the Mean Square Error (MSE) loss function in the optimization operation. Based on the predicted PM2.5 $f(t + 1)$ and observed PM2.5 $y(t + 1)$, the loss function with L2 regularization is as follows:

$$l(w) = \frac{1}{n} \sum_{i=1}^{n} (f_i(t + 1) - y_i(t + 1))^2 + \lambda \sum_{j=1}^{M} w_j^2 \qquad (13)$$

where the $l(w)$ is the loss which depends on the parameter w of the model; $\lambda \sum_{j=1}^{M} w_j^2$ is the L2 regularization item with L2 parameter λ. Here, the L2 parameter is also selected by grid searching. Finally, all the parameters setting details of each model are presented in Table 1.

Table 1. Hyper-parameter configurations of each model

Model	Neuron	Learning Rate	L2	Running times
BPNN	54	0.01	0.001	800
GCN-Mean	48	0.0001	0.1	4000
GCN-Sum	56	0.0001	0.001	4000
GAT-Mean	56	0.001	0.1	4000
GAT-Sum	56	0.001	0.001	4000

4.2 Evolution Criteria

We used four common evaluation criteria for regression tasks in the processes of training and testing, which are MSE, RMSE, MAE, and R^2. The calculation methods of these four evaluation criteria can be calculated from the Eq. (14) to Eq. (17), where $f(t+1)$ is the predicted output of PM2.5 concentration by models, $y(t+1)$ is the observed PM2.5 concentration. For MSE, MAE, and RMSE, the smaller they are, the better result is. The range of R^2 is $(-\infty, 1]$, then when R^2 is closer to 1 means a better forecasting results.

– Mean Square Error (MSE):

$$MSE = \frac{1}{n}\sum_{i=1}^{n}(f_i(t+1) - y_i(t+1))^2 \tag{14}$$

– Root Mean Square Error(RMSE):

$$RMSE = \sqrt{MSE} = \sqrt{\frac{1}{n}\sum_{i=1}^{n}(f_i(t+1) - y_i(t+1))^2} \tag{15}$$

– Mean Absolute Error (MAE):

$$MAE = \frac{1}{n}\sum_{i=1}^{n}|f_i(t+1) - y_i(t+1)| \tag{16}$$

– R Square (R^2):

$$R^2 = 1 - \frac{\sum(f(t+1) - y(t+1))^2}{\sum(f(t+1) - \bar{y}(t+1))^2} \tag{17}$$

where the $\bar{y}(t+1)$ is the average of observed values.

4.3 Forecasting Results

In this study, we adopt cities Ezhou, Xianning, Jingmen, and Wuhan as illustrative examples and utilize four different GCNs and BPNN to predict the PM2.5

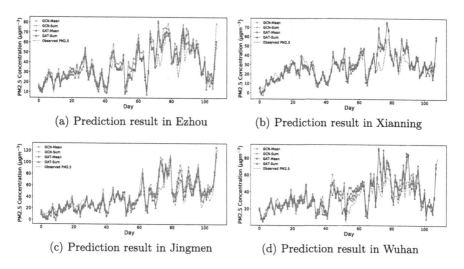

(a) Prediction result in Ezhou   (b) Prediction result in Xianning

(c) Prediction result in Jingmen   (d) Prediction result in Wuhan

Fig. 4. Prediction results in cities (Color figure online)

concentration of the adopted cities. The prediction results of the four adopted cities are shown in Fig. 4, the red dotted lines in Fig. 4 represent the observed PM2.5 concentration, and the yellow lines stand for the GCN-Mean model prediction, the gray lines refer for the prediction result of the GCN-Sum model, the brown lines are the prediction result of the GAT-Mean model, and the blue represents the prediction result of the GAT-Sum model.

In detail, Figure 4(a), 4(b), and 4(c), show that the GAT-Sum model obtains the best performance, and the worst model is GCN-Mean, which means the prediction performance of GAT-Sum is the best while predicting datasets in 3 cities of Ezhou, Xianning, and Jingmen. In addition, Fig. 4(d) shows that the prediction performance of the GCN-Sum model is the best for Wuhan.

In order to detailedly observe the performance of different models in different datasets, the average evaluation results of 4 GCN models test 16000 times and BPNN tests 800 times are shown in Table 2. Among the evaluation results of the Ezhou, Xianning, and Jingmen datasets, 4 evaluation criteria of the GAT-Sum model are all the best.

In detail, the MSE, RMSE, MAE, and R^2 of GAT-Sum for prediction air quality in Ezhou are 46.7773, 6.8034, 4.9661, and 0.8212, respectively. Additionally, the R^2 is higher 0.02 to the result of the GCN-Sum model, which ranks second. Besides, the MSE, RMSE, MAE and R^2 of using GAT-Sum to predict the air quality in Xianning are 45.6052, 6.7229, 4.9067, and 0.7702, respectively. Moreover, the MSE, RMSE, MAE, and R^2 of using GAT-Sum to predict the Jingmen dataset are 60.9353, 7.6678, 5.4397, and 0.7646, respectively. In the predicted results of the Wuhan dataset, the four evaluation criteria results of the GCN-Sum model are the best, among which the MSE, RMSE, R^2 are 70.7920 8.2768, and 0.6943, respectively. Additionally, the R^2 of GCN-Sum is only about 0.01 higher than the R^2 of GAT-Sum. In the evaluation results of all models predicting the Wuhan dataset, MSE is higher than 70, and R^2 is not up to 0.7.

Table 2. Evaluation Results in Cities

Model	Ezhou				Xianning			
	MSE	RMSE	MAE	R^2	MSE	RMSE	MAE	R^2
BPNN	177.9978	13.3499	10.5221	0.0162	177.7044	13.3327	10.5012	0.0163
GCN-Avg	71.9266	8.4756	5.9657	0.7230	72.4489	8.5070	5.9385	0.6275
GCN-Sum	50.9000	7.0728	4.9761	0.8066	50.1582	7.0372	4.9188	0.7466
GAT-Avg	53.6160	7.2880	5.0605	0.7955	56.3243	7.4752	5.1084	0.70585
GAT-Sum	**46.7773**	**6.8034**	**4.9661**	**0.8212**	**45.6052**	**6.7229**	**4.9067**	**0.7702**
Model	Jingmen				Wuhan			
	MSE	RMSE	MAE	R^2	MSE	RMSE	MAE	R^2
BPNN	178.1118	13.3279	10.5169	0.0199	178.2537	13.3227	10.4986	0.0168
GCN-Avg	107.8953	10.1417	7.0639	0.5943	104.9011	10.0579	6.9512	0.5579
GCN-Sum	69.1988	8.1471	5.6065	0.7357	**70.7920**	**8.2768**	**5.6300**	**0.6943**
GAT-Avg	79.5287	8.7147	5.9972	0.6964	90.0416	9.2204	6.2872	0.6795
GAT-Sum	**60.9353**	**7.6678**	**5.4397**	**0.7646**	71.3412	8.2771	5.7577	0.6801

5   Conclusion

In this study, we build a graph representing the data structure called Target-city Graph (TCG) by connecting the air pollution between cities while using migration networks. Then, we develop four models based on Graph Convolution Networks (GCN) and Graph Attention Networks (GAT), and utilize Sum aggregation and Mean aggregation functions to forecast daily PM2.5 concentration. For GCN-Sum and GCN-Mean, they only aggregate the features of air pollutants and ignore the migration index between cities. For GAT-Sum and GAT-Mean, they utilize the migration index between cities as the attention coefficient of GAT while aggregating. The experimental results indicate that the GAT-Sum model performs the best in three of four datasets, which means the migration data can improve the predictive power. Moreover, the performances of the Sum-agg models, which are better than the Mean-agg models.

Acknowledgment. This work was supported by Science and Technology Program of Guangzhou, China (201904010224), Natural Science Foundation of Guangdong Province, China (2020A1515010761), and National Science Foundation of China Project 72004174.

References

1. Massey, D., Masih, J., Kulshrestha, A., Habil, M., Taneja, A.: Indoor/outdoor relationship of fine particles less than 2.5 μm (PM2. 5) in residential homes locations in central Indian region. Build. Environ. **44**(10), 2037–2045 (2009)
2. Mahajan, S., Chen, L.-J., Tsai, T.-C.: An empirical study of pm2. 5 forecasting using neural network. In: Proceedings of the 2017 IEEE SmartWorld, Ubiquitous Intelligence & Computing, Advanced & Trusted Computed, Scalable Computing & Communications, Cloud & Big Data Computing, Internet of People and Smart City Innovation (SmartWorld/SCALCOM/UIC/ATC/CBDCom/IOP/SCI), pp. 1–7. IEEE (2017)

3. Biancofiore, F., et al.: Recursive neural network model for analysis and forecast of PM10 and PM2. 5. Atmos. Pollut. Res. **8**(4), 652–659 (2017)
4. Zhu, H., Lu, X.: The prediction of PM2. 5 value based on ARMA and improved BP neural network model. In: 2016 International Conference on Intelligent Networking and Collaborative Systems (INCoS), pp. 515–517. IEEE (2016)
5. Voukantsis, D., Karatzas, K., Kukkonen, J., Räsänen, T., Karppinen, A., Kolehmainen, M.: Intercomparison of air quality data using principal component analysis, and forecasting of PM10 and PM2. 5 concentrations using artificial neural networks, in Thessaloniki and Helsinki. Sci. Total Environ. **409**(7), 1266–1276 (2011)
6. Chen, Z., Ye, X., Huang, P.: Estimating carbon dioxide (CO2) emissions from reservoirs using artificial neural networks. Water **10**(1), 26 (2018)
7. Tao, Q., Liu, F., Li, Y., Sidorov, D.: Air pollution forecasting using a deep learning model based on 1D convnets and bidirectional GRU. IEEE Access **7**, 76690–76698 (2019)
8. Cheng, Y., Zhang, H., Liu, Z., Chen, L., Wang, P.: Hybrid algorithm for short-term forecasting of PM2. 5 in China. Atmos. Environ. **200**, 264–279 (2019)
9. Zhang, H., Liu, Y., Yan, J., Han, S., Li, L., Long, Q.: Improved deep mixture density network for regional wind power probabilistic forecasting. IEEE Trans. Power Syst. **35**(4), 2549–2560 (2020)
10. Zhu, J., Song, Y., Zhao, L., Li, H.: A3T-GCN: attention temporal graph convolutional network for traffic forecasting. arXiv preprint arXiv:2006.11583 (2020)
11. Byeonghyeop, Yu., Lee, Y., Sohn, K.: Forecasting road traffic speeds by considering area-wide spatio-temporal dependencies based on a graph convolutional neural network (GCN). Transp. Res. Part C: Emerg. Technol. **114**, 189–204 (2020)
12. Scarselli, F., Gori, M., Tsoi, A.C., Hagenbuchner, M., Monfardini, G.: The graph neural network model. IEEE Trans. Neural Netw. **20**(1), 61–80 (2008)
13. Kipf, T.N., Welling, M.: Semi-supervised classification with graph convolutional networks. arXiv preprint arXiv:1609.02907 (2016)
14. Veličković, P., Cucurull, G., Casanova, A., Romero, A., Lio, P., Bengio, Y.: Graph attention networks. arXiv preprint arXiv:1710.10903 (2017)
15. Wang, S., Li, Y., Zhang, J., Meng, Q., Meng, L., Gao, F.: PM2. 5-GNN: a domain knowledge enhanced graph neural network for PM2. 5 forecasting. In: Proceedings of the 28th International Conference on Advances in Geographic Information Systems, pp. 163–166 (2020)
16. Qi, Y., Li, Q., Karimian, H., Liu, D.: A hybrid model for spatiotemporal forecasting of PM2. 5 based on graph convolutional neural network and long short-term memory. Sci. Total Environ. **664**, 1–10 (2019)
17. Zhou, H., Zhang, F., Du, Z., Liu, R.: Forecasting PM2. 5 using hybrid graph convolution-based model considering dynamic wind-field to offer the benefit of spatial interpretability. Environ. Pollut. **273**, 116473 (2021)
18. Wang, C., Zhu, Y., Zang, T., Liu, H., Yu, J.: Modeling inter-station relationships with attentive temporal graph convolutional network for air quality prediction. In: Proceedings of the 14th ACM International Conference on Web Search and Data Mining, pp. 616–634 (2021)
19. Hamilton, W.L., Ying, R., Leskovec, J.: Inductive representation learning on large graphs. arXiv preprint arXiv:1706.02216 (2017)
20. Li, Y., Tarlow, D., Brockschmidt, M., Zemel, R.: Gated graph sequence neural networks. arXiv preprint arXiv:1511.05493 (2015)

A Novel Approach to Ship Operational Risk Analysis Based on D-S Evidence Theory

Tao Liu[1], Yuanzi Zhou[1]([✉]), Junzhong Bao[1], Xizhao Wang[2], and Pengfei Zhang[3]

[1] Navigation College, Dalian Maritime University, Dalian 116026, China
baojunzhong@dlmu.edu.cn
[2] China Ship Scientific Research Center, Wuxi 214082, China
wangxizhao@cssrc.com.cn
[3] School of Maritime Science and Engineering, Solent University, Southampton SO140YN, UK
pengfei.zhang@solent.ac.uk

Abstract. In view of the complex environment in which risk analysis of ship accidents is carried out, and the uncertainty and ambiguity of experts' judgements in risk analysis, this paper proposes a risk analysis method based on intuitionistic fuzzy linguistic set and D-S evidence theory. Intuitionistic fuzzy entropy is applied to determine the weight of each criterion, and then the risk value of m for each attribute is aggregated based on D-S evidence theory. In terms of expert information aggregation, expert weights are firstly obtained based on evidence distance and fuzzy entropy, and then experts' judgements for attributes are merged via D-S theory to yield the risk ranking of each attribute. Finally, a cruise ship collision scenario is provided as a case to verify the rationality and effectiveness of the proposed method. The result validates that D-S evidence theory is an efficient tool for ship risk analysis.

Keywords: D-S evidence theory · Intuitionistic fuzzy linguistic variables · Ship risk analysis

1 Introduction

As the size of large ships such as cruise ships increases, greater losses may be caused in the event of heavy casualties, requiring a strengthening supervision and risk management [1]. Many serious accidents of serious consequences such as fire, collision, grounding and so on, have taken place on cruise ships over the last few decades [2]. Pagiaziti et al. [3] proposed a quantitative risk model for the damage stability associated with collision and grounding accidents of passenger ships. Stefanidis et al. [4] noted that passenger ships needed to constantly review and update their modeling techniques and regulations in order to evacuate large passenger ships safely and efficiently in emergency situations and dangerous environmental conditions. Ruponen et al. [5] proposed an automatic breach assessment method using level sensor measurement data to analyze the extent of the damage. Spyrou et al. [6] proposed a risk model for assessing passenger ship fire safety during the design stage, combining the probability of ignition, the reliability

© Springer Nature Singapore Pte Ltd. 2021
H. Zhang et al. (Eds.): NCAA 2021, CCIS 1449, pp. 728–741, 2021.
https://doi.org/10.1007/978-981-16-5188-5_52

of the installed suppression system, and the prediction of losses in the event of fire growth. Vanem and Skjong [7] analyzed the risks related to passenger ship collisions and landings, concluding that evacuation performance should be improved so as to reduce the risk of passenger ship collisions and landings.

The lack of historical data is a huge challenge when conducting risk assessment for cruise ships. To compromise the shortage of prior probability of accidents, as a usual approach in risk analysis, a panel of experts are convened to provide judgement on risk factors. In addition, experts' preferences are often presented in the form of qualitative information, which is best represented by fuzzy values. Intuitionistic fuzzy sets (IFS) were introduced as a means of extending a fuzzy conventional set by Atanassov [8]. Ship risk assessment often involves uncertain or fuzzy information such as expert's judgement. Intuitionistic fuzzy linguistic set is a theory suitable for processing such information.

This paper introduces Dempster–Shafer (D-S) evidence theory to integrate experts' information. D-S evidence theory can integrate multiple subjects, such as multiple people's predictions, different sensors' data, different classifiers' outputs. It has the following advantages: it can deal with the uncertainty caused by randomness and by fuzziness; it does not require prior information and conditional probability density; and it shows a great deal of flexibility in its ability to distinguish between 'not knowing' and 'uncertain'. D-S evidence theory thus has a wide range of applications in the field of ship risk assessment. Li et al. [9] put forward an approach to vessel collision risk assessment based on D-S evidence theory. Talavera et al. [10] analyzed the information contained in a known distribution of vessel traffic on a waterway under the framework of the Dempster-Shafer theory. Certa et al. [11] proposed the D-S theory of evidence as a proper mathematical framework to deal with the epistemic uncertainty which often affects expert opinions on risk parameters' occurrence, severity and detection and was then applied to the propulsion system of a fishing vessel operating in Sicily.

This paper's main contributions include: First, an intuitionistic fuzzy linguistic set is used to convert expert judgement into intuitionistic fuzzy numbers to quantify the fuzziness and hesitancy of expert evaluation information. Secondly, the Jousselme distance and fuzzy entropy are combined to handle the conflict of evidence in order to determine the expert weight. Thirdly, the multi-expert weighted evidences are aggregated according to D-S rules, which verifies the effectiveness of D-S evidence theory in ship operational risk analysis.

The remainder of this paper proceeds as follows. Section 2 explains some basic concepts and definitions about intuitionistic fuzzy variables, and D-S evidence theory. Section 3 illustrates the study's flowchart and calculation process, and discusses the risk level ranking of three stages of cruise ship operation. Finally, Sect. 4 presents the study's conclusion and suggests future work.

2 Methodology

Considering that experts' judgements may vary due to their diverse experiences and expertise, this study applies the intuitionistic fuzzy set to express and fuse their judgements in accordance with evidence theory.

2.1 Entropy Weight Method

The entropy weight method is an objective weighting method, which depends on the discreteness of the data itself. This section introduces three methods of weighting: intuitive fuzzy entropy, Jousselme distance and fuzzy entropy.

Intuitive Fuzzy Entropy. For any intuitionistic fuzzy number, the entropy of the intuitionistic fuzzy number can be calculated by Eqs. (1)–(4) [12]:

The expert's intuitionistic fuzzy entropy E_i^y regarding an attribute o_i is:

$$E_i^y = \sum_{j=1}^{n} \lambda_j e_{ij}^y \tag{1}$$

Where the expert's intuitionistic fuzzy entropy e_{ij}^y in reference to the attribute o_i in the alternative x_j. λ_j is the weight of an alternative x_j and is equal for each alternative.

$$\lambda_j = \frac{1}{n}(j = 1, 2, \cdots n) \tag{2}$$

$$\sum_{j=1}^{n} \lambda_j = 1 \tag{3}$$

$$E_i^y = \frac{1}{n}\sum_{j=1}^{n} e_{ij}^y = \frac{1}{n}\sum_{j=1}^{n} \frac{1 - |\mu_{ij}^y - v_{ij}^y|^2 + (\pi_{ij}^y)^2}{2} \tag{4}$$

The expert weight of an attribute o_i is yielded by Eq. (5):

$$w_i^y = \frac{1 - E_i^y}{\sum\limits_{i=1}^{m}\left(1 - E_i^y\right)}(i = 1, 2, \cdots, m) \tag{5}$$

The expert weight matrix W^y of the attribute set $\{o_i | i = 1, 2, \cdots, m\}$ is denoted as Eq. (6):

$$W^y = \left[w_1^y, w_2^y, \cdots w_m^y\right]^T \tag{6}$$

Jousselme Distance and Fuzzy Entropy. In group decision-making, the experts' weights should be assigned. Bao et al. [13] adopted the optimal combination weighting method based on square sums of distance to calculate the attribute weights. This study proposes a new evidence fusion method based on Jousselme distance and fuzzy theory. Experimental results show that this method can effectively reduce the role of evidence with large uncertainty in fusion and solve fusion paradox problems, while providing very good fusion process convergence and recognition accuracy [14].

Jousselme Distance. Suppose m_1 and m_2 are two mass functions on the recognition frame, then the distance between them is obtained by Eq. (7):

$$d(m_1, m_2) = \sqrt{\frac{1}{2}(\vec{m_1} - \vec{m_2})^T \underline{\underline{D}}(\vec{m_1} - \vec{m_2})} \tag{7}$$

$\vec{m_1}$ and $\vec{m_2}$ are vectors derived from evidence m_1 and m_2. The elements of $\underline{\underline{D}}$ can be expressed as Eq. (8):

$$\underline{\underline{D}} = \frac{|\theta_1 \cap \theta_2|}{|\theta_1 \cup \theta_2|}, \ (\theta_1, \theta_2 \in \Theta) \tag{8}$$

From this, the distance matrix Q between each piece of evidence can be obtained by Eq. (9):

$$Q = \begin{bmatrix} 0 & d_{12} & \cdots & d_{1l} \\ d_{21} & 0 & \cdots & d_{2l} \\ \vdots & \vdots & \ddots & \vdots \\ d_{l1} & d_{l2} & \cdots & 0 \end{bmatrix} \tag{9}$$

According to Eq. (9), the similarity between the evidences (y th and z th expert's) can be calculated by Eq. (10):

$$sim(y, z) = 1 - d_{yz} \tag{10}$$

Obtain the evidence similarity matrix S by Eq. (11):

$$S = \begin{bmatrix} 1 & 1 - d_{12} & \cdots & 1 - d_{1l} \\ 1 - d_{21} & 1 & \cdots & 1 - d_{2l} \\ \vdots & \vdots & \ddots & \vdots \\ 1 - d_{l1} & 1 - d_{l2} & \cdots & 1 \end{bmatrix} \tag{11}$$

Calculate the degree of support of the y th evidence given by other evidence as the credibility of the evidence which is denoted in Eq. (12):

$$Sup(m_y) = \sum_{z=1, z\neq z}^{l} sim(y, z), y = 1, 2, \cdots l \tag{12}$$

Normalize the evidence's credibility, and obtain the weight of the evidence by Eq. (13):

$$\sigma_y = \frac{Sup(m_y)}{\sum\limits_{y=1}^{l} Sup(m_y)} \tag{13}$$

Fuzzy Entropy. Given the identification frame $\Theta = \{\theta_1, \theta_2, \cdots, \theta_n\}$, if the probability of each element in Θ is equal, then $BetP_{m_y}(\theta_j)$ is obtained by Eq. (14) [15]:

$$BetP_{m_y}(\theta_j) = \sum_{\theta_j \subseteq O, O \in \Theta} \frac{m_y(O)}{|O|} \tag{14}$$

$BetP_{m_y}(\theta_j)$ is the Pignistic probability of θ_j under the basic trust assignment $m_y, |O|$ represents the number of elements contained in O.

The corresponding entropy value is yielded by Eq. (15):

$$H(m_y) = - \sum_{j=1, \theta \in \Theta}^{n} (BetP_{m_y}(\theta_j) \log_2 (BetP_{m_y}(\theta_j) + (1 - BetP_{m_y}(\theta_j)) \log_2 (1 - BetP_{m_y}(\theta_j)))$$

(15)

The evidence weight is calculated by Eq. (16):

$$\rho_y = \frac{\exp(-\alpha \cdot H(m_y))}{\sum_{y=1}^{l} \exp(-\alpha \cdot H(m_y))}$$

(16)

The selection of parameter α in Eq. (16) mainly depends on an experiential value, herein α is set as six [14].

Obtain Evidence Weights Based on Both Jousselme Distance and Fuzzy Entropy. Combine the evidence weight σ_y based on Jousselme distance and the evidence weight ρ_y based on fuzzy entropy to obtain a new evidence weight β_y.

First, calculate the relative credibility of the evidence m_y by Eqs. (17) and (18):

$$Cred(m_y) = \sigma_y \times \rho_y^{-\Delta\sigma_y}$$

(17)

$$\Delta\sigma_y = \sigma_y - \frac{1}{l} \sum_{y=1}^{l} \sigma_y$$

(18)

Normalize $Cred(m_i)$ to get the modified weight coefficient β_y by Eq. (19):

$$\beta_y = \frac{Cred(m_y)}{\sum_{y=1}^{l} Cred(m_y)}$$

(19)

According to the weight obtained (Eq. 19), the evidence is weighted and modified by Eq. (20):

$$m_{MAE}(\theta_j) = \sum_{y=1}^{l} \beta_y \times m_y(\theta_j), \forall \theta_j \in \Theta$$

(20)

The modified $m_{MAE}(\theta_j)$ are fused to yield the ranking of risk level for each alternative in Sect. 2.3.

2.2 Intuitionistic Fuzzy Set

For a multi-attribute decision-making problem, an expert set $P = \{P_1, P_2, \cdots P_l\}$, composed of l experts, an alternative set $X = \{x_1, x_2, \cdots x_n\}$ composed of n alternatives, and a set of attributes $O = \{o_1, o_2, \cdots o_m\}$ composed of m attributes under each alternative are constructed. Assuming that the judgement of the expert P_y on the alternative x_j with respect to the attribute o_i can be expressed as the intuitionistic fuzzy number $g_{ij}^y = \left\langle \mu_{ij}^y, v_{ij}^y \right\rangle$, then the decision matrix G^y of y th expert's intuitionistic fuzzy set can be obtained by Eq. (21) [16]:

$$
G^y = \begin{bmatrix}
\left\langle \mu_{11}^y, v_{11}^y \right\rangle & \left\langle \mu_{12}^y, v_{12}^y \right\rangle & \cdots & \left\langle \mu_{1n}^y, v_{1n}^y \right\rangle \\
\left\langle \mu_{21}^y, v_{21}^y \right\rangle & \left\langle \mu_{22}^y, v_{22}^y \right\rangle & \cdots & \left\langle \mu_{2n}^y, v_{2n}^y \right\rangle \\
\vdots & \vdots & \vdots & \vdots \\
\left\langle \mu_{m1}^y, v_{m1}^y \right\rangle & \left\langle \mu_{m2}^y, v_{m2}^y \right\rangle & \cdots & \left\langle \mu_{mn}^y, v_{mn}^y \right\rangle
\end{bmatrix}
\tag{21}
$$

According to the definition of the mass function of evidence theory, the intuitionistic fuzzy number in the intuitionistic fuzzy set vector can be expressed as the mass function on the recognition frame Θ, and its mass function m_i^y satisfies the following conditions denoted in Eq. (22):

$$
m_i^y = \begin{cases}
m_i^y(x_j) = \dfrac{\mu_{ij}^y}{\sum\limits_{j=1}^{n}(1-v_{ij}^y)} \\
m_i^y(\Theta) = 1 - \sum\limits_{j=1}^{n} m_i^y(x_j) \\
m_i^y(\varphi) = 0
\end{cases}
\tag{22}
$$

According to the weight of an expert on the attribute set, the mass function is then modified by Eq. (23):

$$
\hat{m}_i^y = \begin{cases}
\hat{m}_i^y(x_j) = \dfrac{w_i^y}{w_{max}^y} m_i^y(x_j) \\
\hat{m}_i^y(\Theta) = 1 - \sum\limits_{j=1}^{n} \hat{m}_i^y(x_j) \\
\hat{m}_i^y(\varphi) = 0
\end{cases}
\tag{23}
$$

The adjusted values of mass function of the attribute set are aggregated via the D-S evidence theory to obtain the mass function value of the alternative set, denoted as m^y. The resulting expert's mass function matrix of the alternative set is obtained by the Eq. (24):

$$
m^y = \left[m^y(x_1), m^y(x_2) \cdots m^y(x_n), m^y(\Theta) \right]
\tag{24}
$$

2.3 D-S Evidence Theory

Identification Framework. For a decision-making problem, the recognition frame is represented by Θ. The elements in Θ should meet the condition of mutual exclusion, and the answer can only take one element in Θ at any time.

Basic Probability Assignment (m) Function. $2^{\Theta} \rightarrow [0, 1]$ is the basic probability assignment function of the recognition framework, namely the mass function, which satisfies the following conditions: $m(\varphi) = 0$, $\sum_{A \subseteq \Theta} m(A) = 1$. $m(A)$ is the basic probability of A which represents the degree of belief in the hypothesis set A.

Belief Function. The belief function is also called the reliability function. The formula of the belief function based on the basic probability assignment function in the recognition framework Θ is $Bel(A) = \sum_{B \subseteq A} m(B), \forall A \subseteq \Theta$. The degree of belief $Bel(A)$ is the total probability for all B. Based on the definition of the belief function and the probability assignment function, the following conclusions can be drawn: $Bel(\varphi) = m(\varphi) = 0$, $Bel(\Theta) = \sum_{B \subseteq \Theta} m(B) = 1$.

Dempster's Rule of Combination. Assume that $Bel_1, Bel_2, \cdots Bel_n$ are belief functions within the same recognition framework. $m_1, m_2, \cdots m_n$ are their corresponding mass functions. According to the D-S synthesis rule, the mass function of A after the fusion of n evidences can be obtained by Eqs. (25) and (26):

$$(m_1 \oplus m_2 \oplus \ldots \oplus m_n)(A) = \begin{cases} \dfrac{1}{K} \displaystyle\sum_{A_1 \cap A_2 \cap \cdots A_n = A} m_1(A_1) \cdot m_2(A_2) \cdots m_n(A_n), A \neq \varphi \\ 0, A = \varphi \end{cases}$$

(25)

$$K = \sum_{A_1 \cap \ldots \cap A_n \neq \varphi} m_1(A_1) \cdot m_2(A_2) \ldots m_n(A_n) = 1 - \sum_{A_1 \cap \cdots \cap A_n = \varphi} m_1(A_1) \cdot m_2(A_2) \cdots m_n(A_n)$$

(26)

Where $m_1 \oplus m_2 \oplus \cdots \oplus m_n$ is the orthogonal sum and K is the normalized constant representing the degree of conflict between evidences.

3 Case Study

In this section, the risk level of cruise ship operation is analyzed for collision accidents in three scenarios including operating in congested waters, sea cruising and when docking. Thirty-five experts are invited to evaluate the possibility of accident occurrence and severity of consequences using intuitionistic fuzzy linguistic variables.

Step 1 Constructing Evaluation Criteria for Attributes
The FSA report [17, 18] draws the FN curve diagrams of four types of accidents: collision, grounding, contact and fire. It is concluded that collisions are accidents with low

frequency but with serious consequences and risk control measures should be taken. When operating in congested waters (narrow channels), cruise ships are affected by the surrounding navigation environment and its maneuverability is limited, resulting in potential risk of collision. During the stage at sea cruising, collision accidents can be caused by external environmental factors, crew members' misjudgment of the situation and their operational errors. Also, when docking, cruise ships may collide with service vessels. Hence, there are risks of collision in all three operational stages but with different possibilities of accidents. This study takes the cruise ship sailing in the waters of the Pearl River estuary in southern China as its topic of research. To rank the levels of risk of collision, firstly, this paper develops a questionnaire to survey experts' judgements on cruise ship operation risk. This questionnaire including basic information of experts (position, professional title, educational background, sea service experience, type and size of ships worked on) are distributed to thirty-five experts who are invited to contribute their preferences on risk attributes.

The operational stages in congested waters (x_1), the sea cruising (x_2), and the docking (x_3) are considered high-risk stages of collision accidents, so this paper defines the possibility of occurrence (o_1) and severity of consequences (o_2) as two risk attributes. The evaluation criteria are constructed as per a source [19] for experts' judgements (see Table 1). The entropy weight method is applied for evaluating confidence of each expert in making the judgement [20], finally ten experts' judgements are selected as evidences to rank the levels of risk.

Table 1. Rating for likelihood and severity related IFNs.

Linguistic terms	IFNs	Frequency	Impact
Extremely low (EL)	(0.10,0.90)	Remote=Might occur once in a life time	Negligible (Injury not requiring first aid, no cosmetic vessel damage, no environmental impact, no missed voyages)
Low (L)	(030,0.60)	Occassional=Might occur once every five years	Minor (Injury requiring first aid, cosmetic vessel damage, no environmental impact, no missed voyages)
Medium low (ML)	(0.50,0.50)	Likely=Might occur once every season	Significant (Injury requiring more than first aid, vessel damage, some environmental damage, a few missed voyages or a financial loss)
High (H)	(0.70,0.20)	Probable=Might occur monthly	Critical (Severe injury, major vessel damage, major environmental damage, missed voyages)

(continued)

Table 1. (*continued*)

Linguistic terms	IFNs	Frequency	Impact
Extremely high (EH)	(0.90,0.10)	Frequent=Might occur weekly or daily	Catastrophic (Loss of life, loss of vessel, extreme environmental impact)

Step 2 Converting Evaluation Values into m Values (Tables 2 and 3)

Table 2. Intuitive fuzzy judgement of risk attributes.

Expert (P_k)	Attribute (o_i)	Congested waters	Cruising at sea	Docking
P_1	o_1	(0.10,0.90)	(0.10,0.90)	(0.10,0.90)
	o_2	(0.30,0.60)	(0.10,0.90)	(0.30,0.60)
P_2	o_1	(0.10,0.90)	(0.10,0.90)	(0.30,0.60)
	o_2	(0.50,0.50)	(0.50,0.50)	(0.50,0.50)
...	...	...	...	...
P_9	o_1	(0.50,0.50)	(0.30,0.60)	(0.70,0.20)
	o_2	(0.30,0.60)	(0.50,0.50)	(0.30,0.60)
P_{10}	o_1	(0.30,0.60)	(0.10,0.9)	(0.30,0.60)
	o_2	(0.30,0.60)	(0.10,0.90)	(0.30,0.60)

Table 3. The values of m for risk attributes.

Expert (P_k)	Attribute (o_i)	$m_i^k(x_1)$	$m_i^k(x_2)$	$m_i^k(x_3)$	$m_i^k(\Theta)$
P_1	o_1	0.333	0.333	0.333	0.001
	o_2	0.333	0.111	0.333	0.223
P_2	o_1	0.167	0.167	0.500	0.166
	o_2	0.333	0.333	0.333	0.001
...	...	...	...	...	...
P_9	o_1	0.294	0.176	0.412	0.118
	o_2	0.231	0.385	0.231	0.153
P_{10}	o_1	0.333	0.111	0.333	0.223
	o_2	0.333	0.111	0.333	0.223

Step 3 Calculating the Entropy Weight of Each Attribute and Modifying the m Value (Table 4)

The expert weight vectors for attribute o_i are presented in below.

$$W^1 = \{w_1^1, w_2^1\} = \{0.564, 0.436\} \quad W^6 = \{w_1^6, w_2^6\} = \{0.500, 0.500\}$$
$$W^2 = \{w_1^2, w_2^2\} = \{0.593, 0.407\} \quad W^7 = \{w_1^7, w_2^7\} = \{0.500, 0.500\}$$
$$W^3 = \{w_1^3, w_2^3\} = \{0.621, 0.379\} \quad W^8 = \{w_1^8, w_2^8\} = \{0.529, 0.471\}$$
$$W^4 = \{w_1^4, w_2^4\} = \{0.535, 0.465\} \quad W^9 = \{w_1^9, w_2^9\} = \{0.512, 0.488\}$$
$$W^5 = \{w_1^5, w_2^5\} = \{0.505, 0.495\} \quad W^{10} = \{w_1^{10}, w_2^{10}\} = \{0.500, 0.500\}$$

Table 4. m values modified by the attribute weight.

Expert (P_k)	Attribute (o_i)	$m_i^k(x_1)$	$m_i^k(x_2)$	$m_i^k(x_3)$	$m_i^k(\Theta)$
P_1	o_1	0.333	0.333	0.333	0.001
	o_2	0.257	0.086	0.257	0.400
P_2	o_1	0.167	0.167	0.500	0.166
	o_2	0.229	0.229	0.229	0.313
...	...	...	...	...	...
P_9	o_1	0.294	0.176	0.412	0.118
	o_2	0.220	0.367	0.220	0.193
P_{10}	o_1	0.333	0.111	0.333	0.223
	o_2	0.333	0.111	0.333	0.223

Step 4 Generating m Values of Experts' Judgements

The m value of experts' judgements are presented in Table 5.

Table 5. m values of experts' judgements integrated with D-S evidence theory.

Expert (P_k)	$m(x_1)$	$m(x_2)$	$m(x_3)$	$m(\Theta)$
P_1	0.3648	0.2697	0.3648	0.0007
P_2	0.2080	0.2080	0.5000	0.0841
...	...	...	...	...
P_9	0.2900	0.2792	0.3860	0.0448
P_{10}	0.4115	0.0981	0.4115	0.0789

Step 5 Obtaining Aggregated Experts' Weights and Further Modifying the m Values of Experts' Judgements

Jousselme distance matrix Q is presented in below.

$$Q = \begin{bmatrix} 0 & 0.1565 & 0.0549 & 0.2136 & 0.3145 & 0.0794 & 0.2185 & 0.1927 & 0.0582 & 0.1339 \\ 0.1565 & 0 & 0.1753 & 0.3547 & 0.4341 & 0.1688 & 0.3495 & 0.3411 & 0.1125 & 0.1751 \\ 0.0549 & 0.1753 & 0 & 0.2225 & 0.2700 & 0.0573 & 0.1865 & 0.1779 & 0.0641 & 0.1865 \\ 0.2136 & 0.3547 & 0.2225 & 0 & 0.2787 & 0.2175 & 0.1616 & 0.0977 & 0.2586 & 0.2393 \\ 0.3145 & 0.4341 & 0.2700 & 0.2787 & 0 & 0.2756 & 0.1274 & 0.1873 & 0.3278 & 0.4281 \\ 0.0794 & 0.1688 & 0.0573 & 0.2175 & 0.2756 & 0 & 0.1814 & 0.1830 & 0.0669 & 0.1814 \\ 0.2185 & 0.3495 & 0.1865 & 0.1616 & 0.1274 & 0.1814 & 0 & 0.0777 & 0.2404 & 0.3134 \\ 0.1927 & 0.3411 & 0.1779 & 0.0977 & 0.1873 & 0.1830 & 0.0777 & 0 & 0.2314 & 0.2710 \\ 0.0582 & 0.1125 & 0.0641 & 0.2586 & 0.3278 & 0.0669 & 0.2404 & 0.2314 & 0 & 0.1559 \\ 0.1339 & 0.1751 & 0.1865 & 0.2393 & 0.4281 & 0.1814 & 0.3134 & 0.2710 & 0.1559 & 0 \end{bmatrix}$$

Similarity between evidences:

$$S = \begin{bmatrix} 1 & 0.8435 & 0.9451 & 0.7864 & 0.6855 & 0.9206 & 0.7815 & 0.8073 & 0.9418 & 0.8661 \\ 0.8435 & 1 & 0.8247 & 0.6453 & 0.5659 & 0.8312 & 0.6505 & 0.6589 & 0.8875 & 0.8249 \\ 0.9451 & 0.8247 & 1 & 0.7775 & 0.7300 & 0.9427 & 0.8135 & 0.8221 & 0.9359 & 0.8135 \\ 0.7864 & 0.6453 & 0.7775 & 1 & 0.7213 & 0.7825 & 0.8384 & 0.9023 & 0.7414 & 0.7607 \\ 0.6855 & 0.5659 & 0.7300 & 0.7213 & 1 & 0.7244 & 0.8726 & 0.8127 & 0.6722 & 0.5719 \\ 0.9206 & 0.8312 & 0.9427 & 0.7825 & 0.7244 & 1 & 0.8186 & 0.8170 & 0.9331 & 0.8186 \\ 0.7815 & 0.6505 & 0.8135 & 0.8384 & 0.8726 & 0.8186 & 1 & 0.9223 & 0.7596 & 0.6866 \\ 0.8073 & 0.6589 & 0.8221 & 0.9023 & 0.8127 & 0.8170 & 0.9223 & 1 & 0.7686 & 0.7290 \\ 0.9418 & 0.8875 & 0.9359 & 0.7414 & 0.6722 & 0.9331 & 0.7596 & 0.7686 & 1 & 0.8441 \\ 0.8661 & 0.8249 & 0.8135 & 0.7607 & 0.5719 & 0.8186 & 0.6866 & 0.7290 & 0.8441 & 1 \end{bmatrix}$$

Credibility:

$Sup(m_1) = 7.5778, Sup(m_2) = 6.7324, Sup(m_3) = 7.6050, Sup(m_4) = 6.9558, Sup(m_5) = 6.3565$
$Sup(m_6) = 7.5887, Sup(m_7) = 7.1436, Sup(m_8) = 7.2402, sup(m_9) = 7.4842, Sup(m_{10}) = 6.9154$

Weight σ_y:

$$\sigma_1 = 0.1058, \sigma_2 = 0.0940, \sigma_3 = 0.1062, \sigma_4 = 0.0971, \sigma_5 = 0.0888$$
$$\sigma_6 = 0.1060, \sigma_7 = 0.0998, \sigma_8 = 0.1011, \sigma_9 = 0.1045, \sigma_{10} = 0.0966$$

Experts' Pignistic probabilities of three alternatives are yielded respectively by Eq. (14), as is shown in Table 6.

Table 6. Experts' Pignistic probabilities

Expert (P_k)	$BetP_{m_k}(x_1)$	$BetP_{m_k}(x_2)$	$BetP_{m_k}(x_3)$
P_1	0.3650	0.2699	0.3650
P_2	0.2360	0.2360	0.5280
...	...	...	...
P_9	0.3049	0.2941	0.4009
P_{10}	0.4378	0.1244	0.4378

Fuzzy entropy:

$$H(m_1) = 2.7349, H(m_2) = 2.5745, H(m_3) = 2.7549, H(m_4) = 2.4485, H(m_5) = 2.1953$$
$$H(m_6) = 2.7549, H(m_7) = 2.5195, H(m_8) = 2.5375, H(m_9) = 2.7327, H(m_{10}) = 2.5195$$

Weight ρ_y:

$$\rho_1 = 0.0208, \rho_2 = 0.0545, \rho_3 = 0.0185, \rho_4 = 0.1161, \rho_5 = 0.5306$$
$$\rho_6 = 0.0185, \rho_7 = 0.0759, \rho_8 = 0.0681, \rho_9 = 0.0211, \rho_{10} = 0.0759$$

Relative credibility:

$$\mathrm{Cred}(m_1) = 0.1082, Cred(m_2) = 0.0924, Cred(m_3) = 0.1089, Cred(m_4) = 0.0965, Cerd(m_5) = 0.0882$$
$$Cred(m_6) = 0.1086, Cred(m_7) = 0.0997, Cred(m_8) = 0.1014, Cred(m_9) = 0.1063, Cred(m_{10}) = 0.0958$$

Normalized weight coefficient:

$$\beta_1 = 0.1076, \beta_2 = 0.0918, \beta_3 = 0.1083, \beta_4 = 0.0959, \beta_5 = 0.0877$$
$$\beta_6 = 0.1080, \beta_7 = 0.0991, \beta_8 = 0.1008, \beta_9 = 0.1057, \beta_{10} = 0.0952$$

Weighted modifications to the evidence:

$$m_{MAE}(x_1) = 0.3728, \ m_{MAE}(x_2) = 0.3044, \ m_{MAE}(x_3) = 0.2735, \ m_{MAE}(\Theta) = 0.0493$$

Step 6 Generating the m Value of Each Stage by Aggregating the Modified m Values of Each Expert

$$m(x_1) = 0.8070, m(x_2) = 0.1377, m(x_3) = 0.0552, m(\Theta) = 0.0001$$

Step 7 Ranking the Levels of Risk for Three Operational Stages
The following risk rankings are yielded in below.

$$x_1 \succ x_2 \succ x_3$$

In this study, the advantages of the proposed approach seem apparent. Firstly, to mitigate the uncertainty of evidences collected in this study, the authors of the paper apply intuitionistic fuzzy entropy to yield the attribute weight. The larger the entropy value, the greater the uncertainty of the intuitionistic fuzzy number and the less the weight of such attribute [21]. Secondly, D-S evidence theory can fuse uncertain information when there is no prior probability, eliminate the information uncertainty well and make full use of the evidence of multisource information to improve assessment accuracy [22].

4 Conclusion

In this paper, a method combining intuitionistic fuzzy linguistic sets and D-S evidence theory is proposed. Taking collision accidents as an example, this study analyzes cruise ship operation risk levels in congested waters, sea cruising and docking. Through information fusion, it is concluded that the risk of collision accidents between ships in congested waters is the greatest. This approach can not only be applied to risk analysis for cruise ship operation, but also to handling other problems with uncertain information in ship risk analysis, including the estimation of accident frequency. This will be the focus of the next study.

References

1. Allianz Global Corporate & Specialty (AGCS): Safety and Shipping Review 2020. AGCS, Munich (2020)
2. Lois, P., Wang, J., Wall, A., Ruxton, T.: Formal safety assessment of cruise ships. Tour. Manage. **25**(1), 93–109 (2004)
3. Pagiaziti, A., Maliaga, E., Eliopoulou, E., Zaraphonitis, G., Hamann, R.: Statistics of collision, grounding and contact accidents of passenger and container ships. In: Proceedings of the 5th International Symposium on Ship Operations, Management and Economics (SOME), Athens, Greece, pp. 28–29. (2015)
4. Stefanidis, F., Boulougouris, E., Vassalos, D.: Modern trends in ship evacuation. In: Proceedings of Sustainable and Safe Passenger Ships (2020)
5. Ruponen, P., Pulkkinen, A., Laaksonen, J.: A method for breach assessment onboard a damaged passenger ship. Appl. Ocean Res. **64**, 236–248 (2017)
6. Spyrou, K.J., Koromila, I.A.: A risk model of passenger ship fire safety and its application. Reliab. Eng. Syst. Saf. **200**, 106937 (2020)
7. Vanem, E., Skjong, R.: Collision and grounding of passenger ships-risk assessment and emergency evacuations. In: Proceedings of the 3rd International Conference on Collision and Grounding of Ships (ICCGS), vol. 195, p. 202. (2004)
8. Atanassov, K.T.: Intuitionistic fuzzy sets. Fuzz. Sets Syst. **4120**(1), 87–96 (1986)
9. Li, B., Pang, F.W.: An approach of vessel collision risk assessment based on the D-S evidence theory. Ocean Eng. **74**, 16–21 (2013)
10. Talavera, A., Aguasca, R., Galván, B., Cacereño, A.: Application of Dempster-Shafer theory for the quantification and propagation of the uncertainty caused by the use of AIS data. Reliab. Eng. Syst. Saf. **111**, 95–105 (2013)
11. Certa, A., Hopps, F., Inghilleri, R., La Fata, C.M.: A Dempster-Shafer Theory-based approach to the Failure Mode, Effects and Criticality Analysis (FMECA) under epistemic uncertainty: application to the propulsion system of a fishing vessel. Reliab. Eng. Syst. Saf. **159**, 69–79 (2017)
12. Wang, L.: Multi-criteria group decision making method based on improved intuitionistic fuzzy entropy and information integration operator. Inf. Contr. **49**(2), 219–224+232 (2020)
13. Bao, J., Zhou, Y., Li, R.: Competitive advantage assessment for container shipping liners using a novel hybrid method with intuitionistic fuzzy linguistic variables. Neural Comput. Appl. (2021). https://doi.org/10.1007/s00521-021-05718-z
14. Hou, X., Cai, B., Jin, W., Duan, W.: A new weighted evidence fusion algorithm based on evidence distance and fuzzy entropy theory. J. Guangxi Normal Univ. (Nat. Sci. Ed.) **33**(1), 45–51 (2015)
15. Li, C., Zhou, Y., Zhang, C.: A new evidence conflict measurement method combined conflict coefficient K and pignistic probability distance. J. Air Force Eng. Univ. (Nat. Sci. Ed.) **17**(2), 91–97 (2016)
16. Chen, Y., Cai, Z., Zhang, Z., Xiang, H.: Method for group decision-making information integration based on evidence theory and intuitionistic fuzzy set. Syst. Eng. Electron. **37**(3), 594–598 (2015)
17. International Maritime Organization (IMO): FIRESAFE I and II Studies – FSA on Fires on Ro-Ro Decks of Passenger Ships. MSC 101/17. IMO, London (2019)
18. IMO: FSA-Cruise ships Details of the Formal Safety Assessment. IMO, London (2008)
19. Yazdi, M.: Risk assessment based on novel intuitionistic fuzzy-hybrid-modified TOPSIS approach. Saf. Sci. **110**, 438–448 (2018)
20. Zhao, D., Li, C., Wang, Q., Yuan, J.: Comprehensive evaluation of national electric power development based on cloud model and entropy method and TOPSIS: a case study in 11 countries. J. Clean. Prod. **277**, 123190 (2021)

21. Wu, J., Wang, L., Li, L.: 2-Dimensional interval neutrosophic linguistic numbers and their utilization in group decision making. In: Zhang, H., Zhang, Z., Wu, Z., Hao, T. (eds.) NCAA 2020. CCIS, vol. 1265, pp. 234–246. Springer, Singapore (2020). https://doi.org/10.1007/978-981-15-7670-6_20
22. Gong, Y., Su, X., Qian, H., Yang, N.: Research on fault diagnosis methods for the reactor coolant system of nuclear power plant based on D-S evidence theory. Ann. Nucl. Energy **112**, 395–399 (2018)

Short-Term Building Load Forecast Based on Patch Learning with Long Short-Term Memory Network and Support Vector Regression

Zhaohui Dan, Bo Wang$^{(\boxtimes)}$, Huijin Fan, and Lei Liu

Key Laboratory of Ministry of Education for Image Processing and Intelligent Control, Artificial Intelligence and Automation School, Huazhong University of Science and Technology, 430074 Wuhan, China
wb8517@hust.edu.cn

Abstract. This paper proposes a novel short-term building load forecasting approach under the framework of patch learning, a novel data-driven model that aggregates a global model and several patch models to further reduce forecasting errors. A PL-LSTM-SVR model is hereby employed to address such a time-series based forecasting problem, where the long short-term memory network is considered as the global model and the support vector regression is selected as the patch model. To obtain satisfying performances, an infinity norm measurement is selected to evaluate load forecasting errors and identify patch locations. Furthermore, a genetic algorithm with elitist preservation strategy is introduced for hyperparameter tuning. The performances of the proposed PL-LSTM-SVR model are tested and verified on two different data sets, and compared with four advanced building load forecasting models on several common metrics.

Keywords: Patch learning · Long short-term memory · Support vector regression · Time series forecasting · Elitist genetic algorithm

1 Introduction

1.1 Background and Motivation

The buildings and buildings construction sectors combined are responsible for over one-third of global final energy consumption and nearly 40% of total direct and indirect CO_2 emissions in 2020 [10]. Besides, the energy consumed in the buildings sector will grow by almost 40% (1.0% p.a.) by 2050 [3]. That is why there has been an significant and increasing emphasis in building energy efficiency worldwide [1,14,17].

Building load forecasting is the basis for effective building energy-saving design and retrofitting. It is generally classified into (1) long-term forecast, (2) medium-term forecast, and (3) short-term forecast [16]. Among them, the short-term load

H. Zhang et al. (Eds.): NCAA 2021, CCIS 1449, pp. 742–756, 2021.
https://doi.org/10.1007/978-981-16-5188-5_53

forecast (STLF) contributes to two purposes. One is the real-time control of building energy systems, including demand response, demand management, charging/discharging energy storage units, and energy transactions [6]. The other is for generation dispatch and demand curtailments in a microgrid [5,6].

However, non-stationary, non-linear, and multi-seasonality characteristics of building load data as well as factors like weather, building context and occupancy, etc. [19] may lead into large local errors in STLF, and then make the smooth and normal operation of the building energy system and the microgrid challenging.

1.2   Literature Review

Common methods for STLF mainly include (1) physical models, (2) hybrid methods [7], and (3) data-driven methods. Physical models can explain the heat transfer mechanism though, lots of on-site information is required and the modeling is time-consuming [20]. Hybrid methods perform better in accuracy and computational efficiency. But there are still problems coming with physical models [20]. By contrast, data-driven methods are concerned for its ease of use, practicability, adaptability and high forecasting accuracy [23]. Besides, they can work on available data like historical load data, etc. via smart meters without on-site information.

Data-driven models have obtained widespread attention in the field of STLF. Specifically, recurrent models like LSTM is capable of identifying the trend over time without additional time tags or features. Specifically, [19] employs LSTM networks with improved sine cosine optimization algorithm. An robust short-term electrical load forecasting framework is proposed in [6] with nine different hybrids of recurrent neural networks and clustering are explored and delivering 20%–45% improvement in accuracy. Besides, [8] investigates the usefulness of advanced recurrent neural network based strategies for building energy predictions. The SVR model is another main algorithm in STLF for its excellent generalization capability with high forecasting accuracy even on a small training set. A novel vector field-based support vector regression method is proposed in [28], which achieves better performance than commonly used methods in accuracy, robustness, and generalization. A weighted SVR model with nu-SVR and epsilon-SVR is developed in [13], which yields higher accuracy with the differential evolution (DE) algorithm as hyperparameter optimization. In addition, an improved ensemble model is proposed in [22]. Two cases demonstrates that this model achieves better performance, regarding accuracy, robustness, and generalization. [15] develops a new ensemble model which combines least squares support vector regression (LSSVR), and the radial basis function neural network (RBFNN) and incorporates symbiotic organism search (SOS) as hyperparameters optimization. As the accuracy requirements of building load forecasting increase, both ANN and ARIMA are generally used as benchmark models to compare with new models [11,13,21,24].

Most of the data-driven algorithms introduced above mainly focus on global forecasting performance where large local errors are ignored. However, in practice, large local errors may bring challenges. Specifically, the units of a distributed energy system are generally designed according to the normal environment. Under a low load condition, problems like excessive exhaust temperature, reduced efficiency, and accelerated carbon deposits, etc. will occur. A energy storage system is generally used to avoid the low load condition. However, if there were large local errors (assume that the forecast is high) in the building load forecast, the energy storage system might not to be activated in time and the distributed energy system would be in the low load condition for hours. Therefore, in the STLF field, forecasting models like patch learning (PL) which pays attention to large local errors are worthy to be introduced and explored.

Patch learning (PL) [25] is a novel idea for improving model performance. As summarized in [25], before the PL is proposed, the performance of a data-driven model is generally strengthened from depth (e.g. deep network [12]), width (e.g. a multi-layer perceptron network with more nodes [2]), non-linearity (e.g. a support vector regression with the radial basis function kernel [18]), and ensemble learning [29], etc. Differently, the idea behind PL is that the overall model performance is improved through the reduction of large local errors. Under the framework of PL, multiple single models are connected in both parallel and series [25]. First, an initial global model is trained on the training set. Then, patches where large local errors occur will be identified. For each patch, a specifically designed patch model is trained and applied to cope with the large local error. Furthermore, the effectiveness of the novel PL framework is verified in [25] on five different regression experiments. However, the application of PL in the field of time series forecasting remains to be explored.

In addition to the model structure, the performance of a data-driven model is sensitive to hyperparameters as well. Since the parameter tuning of a data-driven model is generally non-analytic, grid search is widely used in the hyperparameter optimization of simple models. Nevertheless, for complex models, the enumeration method may cause large computational load. By contrast, the intelligent algorithm is a relatively suitable alternative [4,13,15,19,21,26,27]. Genetic algorithm (GA) [9] is a wildly attentional intelligent method for optimization, imitating the biological evolution process. However, the genes in GA are not absolutely independent of each other. The good combination may be destroyed by a direct crossover. In this way, the excellent genes cannot be inherited continuously. Yet, the elitist genetic algorithm (EGA) can prevent this weakness by copying the best individuals to the next generation without crossover.

1.3 Novelty and Contributions

This paper proposes a novel data-driven model, namely PL-LSTM-SVR for short-term building load forecasting under the patch learning framework based on time series data. To be specific, the LSTM model is selected as the global model for its excellent ability in time series forecasting tasks without additional features. The SVR model is employed as a patch model for its effective non-linear mapping ability on a small training set [27]. Since accuracy metrics with averaging operation focus on global forecasting accuracy and may ignore large local errors, an L-infinity norm measurement is introduced to locate large local errors, for the sake of accurate and reliable forecasting. Furthermore, the EGA is introduced for the hyperparameter optimization of the global model, and the grid search method is applied to the patch model. Additionally, a comprehensive evaluation is applied on the performance of the proposed PL-LSTM-SVR model. Specifically, simulations based on two different building load data sets are employed to evaluate the accuracy, robustness, and generalization performances of the proposed approach, to verify its superiority. In general, the major contributions are summarized as the following:

(1) The application of PL is extended to the field of STLF on time series data for the first time;
(2) The L-infinity norm is employed instead of sum of squared errors (SSE) to measure forecasting errors and identify patch locations, for better evaluation of the performances;
(3) The EGA and the grid search method are introduced for the hyperparameter optimization of the global model and the patch model respectively.
(4) The accuracy, robustness, and generalization performance of the PL-LSTM-SVR are verified based on two different data set.

The rest of this paper is organized as follows. The proposed PL-LSTM-SVR based STLF will be presented in detail in Sect. 2. Case studies for model performances based on two different data sets will be provided in Sect. 3. The conclusion will be shown in Sect. 4.

2   PL-LSTM-SVR Based Load Forecasting

2.1   STLF Problem Formulation

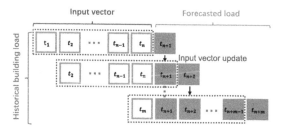

Fig. 1. Sliding window

For STLF based on time series data, data sets should be formulated into the supervised learning sample pattern. Time series single-step forecasting is realized in the form of sliding window, as shown in Fig. 1. The hollow squares represent the historical building load data, while the solid squares represent forecasted load. The first n timestamps of time series load which is framed by the dotted box, is the input vector for the forecasting of the $n + 1$ th timestamp:

$$l_{t_{n+1}} = Forecast(x_{t_1}, ..., x_{t_n}) \qquad (1)$$

Where l_t and x_t denote the forecasted load and the input load at time t, respectively. n denotes the length of the input vector. Next, as the input window slides to the right, $t_{t_{n+1}}$ is included in the input sequence, and x_{t_1} is excluded. The mathematical description is:

$$l_{t_{n+2}} = Forecast(x_{t_2}, ..., x_{t_{n+1}}) \qquad (2)$$

The above process is repeated until the STLF is completed.

2.2   Patch Learning Framework

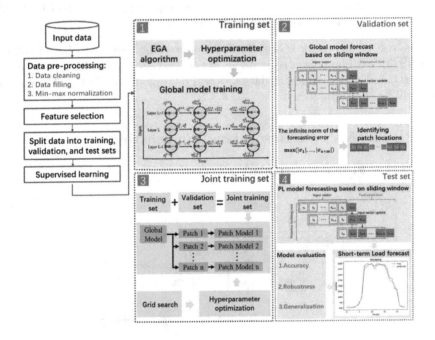

Fig. 2. Research outline

As shown in Fig. 2, the patch learning framework consists of five parts, including data preparation, global model training, identifying patch locations, patch models training, and short-term load forecasting.

The real data collected usually contains missing or noisy data, therefore, data cleaning and data filling are required. Besides, the min-max normalization and feature selection are included. Then, the preprocessed data will be divided into training data, validation data and test data in proportion, and converted into supervised learning samples in the way of sliding window.

Subsequently, as shown in the dotted box one, based on the prepared training data set, the EGA is employed for the hyperparameter optimization of the global model. Then the global model will be trained with the optimized hyperparameters.

For the dotted box two, based on the forecasted load of the trained global model on validation set, patches will be identified. Besides, the infinity norm is used as the indicator for identifying patch locations. Here, the validation set is between the training set and the test set on time series, and it has the same length as the test set. Therefore, the patches can be identified in advance on the validation set.

In box three, the initial training set and the validation set are spliced into a joint training set for the training of patch models. Furthermore, the grid search method is applied for the hyperparameter optimization of patch models.

Finally, the experiments for model performance (i.e. accuracy, robustness, and generalization performance) of the proposed PL-LSTM-SVR model will be provided.

2.3   Global Model

There are several different LSTM network architectures, and the stacked LSTM is selected as the global model for its simplicity and effectiveness. The global model structure is shown in Fig. 3, which is composed of four neural network layers. Specifically, one input layer, two hidden layers composed of stacked LSTM networks, and one perceptron network layer.

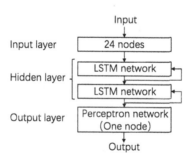

Fig. 3. Global model structure

Based on experience and trial-and-error, the performance of the LSTM model is sensitive to parameters and the hyperparameter optimization is necessary. However, for a deep model, the training process is relatively time-consuming. Therefore, an effective optimization algorithm, EGA, is introduced to search for the best parameter combination.

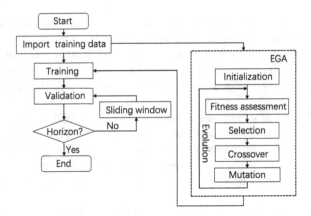

Fig. 4. Global model flowchart

The algorithm flowchart of the global model improved by EGA is presented in Fig. 4. Previously, a training set in the form of supervised learning samples is supposed to be prepared. Then, the EGA will search for the best parameter combination in the way of evolutionary iteration (including initialization, fitness assessment, selection, crossover, and mutation). The forecasting accuracy is considered as the fitness function in fitness assessment. The hyperparameter optimization process is followed by the training of the global model with the optimized parameters. Next, the global model will be forward-validated on the validation set. During this period, the model input vector will continue to be updated in the form of a sliding window. Finally, the forecasted load on the validation set will be stored and applied to the identifying of patch locations.

2.4   Identifying Patch Locations

As introduced in Sect. 2.2, the validation set of the global model has the same length as the test set and is connected in time series. In this way, the patches in the test set can be identified on the validation set in advance. The detailed process is demonstrated in Fig. 5. First, the maximum local error is located and indexed based on the infinity norm of the forecasting error. Then the patch is complemented to a preset length like in Fig. 6. Next, according to the previously saved patch index, the last patch is removed from the forecasted load. Then, the above process is repeated on the remaining forecasted load until all the patches are obtained. Furthermore, there are two ways suggested in [25] to determine the optimal number of patch models, called early stopping and regularization, respectively. A method similar to early stopping is adopted here. Specifically, the historical building load data is splitted into a training set and a validation set. Then, different PL-LSTM-SVR models with different number of patches are trained on the training set, and their performances on the validation set are monitored. The one with the best validation performance is chosen as the final PL-LSTM-SVR model.

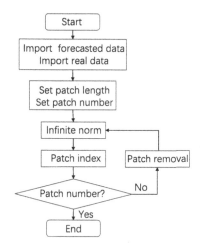

Fig. 5. Identifying patch locations

Fig. 6. The patch diagram

2.5 Patch Model

The algorithm flowchart of the patch model based on SVR is displayed in Fig. 7. For each patch model, compared with Fig. 4, there are only two differences. One is that the training set of a patch model is depending on both its patch location and the forecasted load of the global model on the test set. Specifically, as for time series forecasting, the training set of a patch model ought to be connected to its test set (i.e. the patch) in time series. However, the patches are usually discretely distributed within the horizon, and not linked to the known historical data (i.e. the joint training set formed by the training set and the validation set). Therefore, part of the forecasted load of global model is applied to complete training sets of patch models. The second difference is about the hyperparameter optimization. Grid search method is introduced for patch models. The above hyperparameter optimization and training process will be repeated until all patch models are trained.

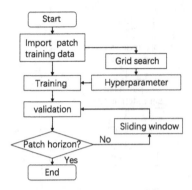

Fig. 7. Patch model flowchart

3 Case Study

3.1 Data Description

Data Set I. Obtained from the OpenEI website, data set I contains electricity load profile of an office building in Alaska, Anchorage, USA. This data set consists of the annual power consumption with a resolution of one minute in 2004, presenting obvious seasonal and periodic characteristics. The processed data set I has the resolution of one hour.

Data Set II. Data set II includes data collected by smart meters of an commercial building in Shanghai, China. Dirty data and missing data is inevitably introduced. Therefore, data preprocessing is required. The processed data set II is composed of building electricity load with a resolution of one hour from July to August in 2020, showing stable periodic characteristics.

3.2 Setup

Data Pre-processing

Data Cleaning. For reasons like the abnormal working status of meters, non-numerical value or infinite value is brought into the collected data. Here, the outliers are marked and deleted, and the vacancies caused by data deletion will be filled later.

Data Filling. According to the periodic characteristics of the building load data, missing data will be supplemented by data from the last period.

Data Segmentation. Both data sets I and II are segmented into training set, validation set, and test set, respectively. For data set I, the training set is from 00:00 on July 3, 2020 to 00:00 on August 16, 2020, the validation set is from 00:00 on August 16, 2020 to 00:00 on August 18, 2020, and the test set is from 00:00

on August 18, 2020 to 00:00 on August 20, 2020. For data set II, the training set is from 00:00 on June 17, 2004 to 00:00 on August 9, 2004, the validation set is from 00:00 on August 9, 2004 to 00:00 on August 11, 2004, and the test set is from 00:00 on August 11, 2004 to 00:00 on August 13, 2004.

Normalization. The min-max normalization method is introduced. Data normalization is beneficial to both the speed of gradient descent optimization and the improvement of accuracy.

3.3   Result and Discussions

The experiments designed for the evaluation of the accuracy, robustness, and generalization performance of the proposed PL-LSTM-SVR model will be carried out based on data set I and data set II, respectively. On this basis, four advanced building load forecasting algorithms, namely LSTM, SVR, random forest (RF), and gradient boosting decision tree (GBDT) are introduced for comparison.

Accuracy. The model accuracy experiment is a quantitative evaluation of the forecasting accuracy on the training set. A variety of metrics for accuracy are introduced, including R^2, MAE, RMSE, MAPE, and CVRMSE.

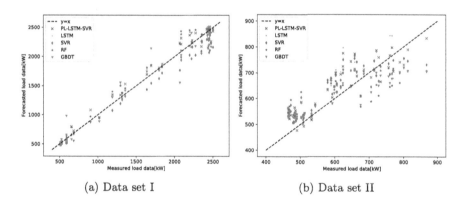

(a) Data set I   (b) Data set II

Fig. 8. The fitting results of building load forecasting on training set

The fitting results between the forecasted load and the measured load for each model is showed in Fig. 8. The scatter is distributed on both sides of the baseline. The PL-LSTM-SVR model fits better than the others, with R^2 equal to 0.99 and 0.72 for data set I and data set II, respectively. The R^2 of LSTM, SVR, RF, and GBDT are 0.98, 0.96, 0.98, and 0.96, respectively, on data set I. For data set II, the R^2 are 0.66, 0.68, 0.59, and 0.70, respectively. The relative error distribution of all models on two data sets are demonstrated in Fig. 9. The proposed PL-LSTM-SVR performs higher accuracy than the other models, with

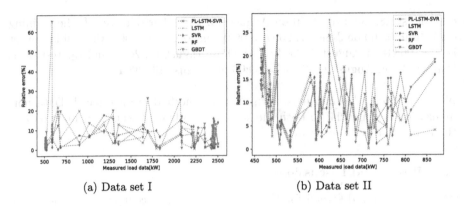

(a) Data set I   (b) Data set II

Fig. 9. The relative error of building load forecasting on training set

Table 1. Accuracy metrics

		PL-LSTM-SVR	LSTM	SVR	RF	GBDT
Data set I	R^2	0.99	0.98	0.96	0.98	0.96
	MAE (kW)	68.62	77.96	111.52	68.81	105.22
	RMSE (kW)	93.35	107.15	153.5	106.39	162.94
	MAPE (%)	5.15	5.74	6.32	5.3	7.63
	CVRMSE (%)	6.33	7.26	10.41	7.21	11.05
Data set II	R^2	0.72	0.66	0.68	0.59	0.7
	MAE (kW)	51.38	57.09	57.03	62.78	53.71
	RMSE (kW)	60.93	67.29	65.32	73.67	63.37
	MAPE (%)	8.8	9.8	9.57	10.47	8.81
	CVRMSE (%)	10.01	11.06	10.74	12.11	10.42

accuracy improvement being about 2.91%–48.16% for data set I and 0.11%–18.98% for data set II. As shown, the error of both the PL-LSTM-SVR model and the RF model are the smallest compared to the remaining models on data set I. Besides, for load forecasting above 1250kW which accounted for a relatively large proportion, the error of the PL-LSTM-SVR model is smaller than that of the RF model. The Table 1 displays four error metrics as well as R^2. For the PL-LSTM-SVR model, the MAE, RMSE, MAPE, and CVRMSE are 68.62, 93.35, 5.15%, and 6.33% respectively, on data set I, and 51.38, 60.93, 8.8%, and 10.01%, respectively, on data set II. In general, all four metrics on both data sets illustrate that the proposed PL-LSTM-SVR model achieves the best accuracy level compared to other advanced forecsting models.

Robustness. The data collected for building load forecasting may deviate from reality for various reasons like monitoring system failure, instrument damage, and sudden unit shutdown, etc. The ability to maintain acceptable forecasting performance under interference is gradually focused. Gaussian white noise is added to the input load of the test set to the robustness evaluation. Specifically, the proportion of the added noise in the input load increases from 20% to 80%. The variation of R^2 with different noise proportion is applied to indicate the robustness performance. Figure 10 shows that there is a downward trend for R^2 as the noise proportion increases, especially on data set II. For the PL-LSTM-SVR model, the R^2 changes from 0.9592 to 0.9588 on data set I, and from 0.872 to 0.845 on data set II. The SVR model results in the worst performance, which means SVR is sensitive to noise. As for the attenuation rate, the performances of the PL-LSTM-SVR, RF and LSTM are the best, especially on data set I. The R^2 of RF and LSTM are only changed from 0.9597 to 0.9596 and from 0.9415 to 0.9388, respectively on data set I. Although RF performs better than PL-LSTM-SVR on data set I, the difference is subtle. In addition, PL-LSTM-SVR is significantly more robust than other models including RF on data set II.

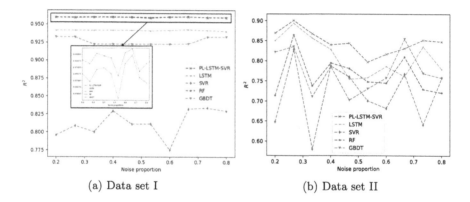

(a) Data set I   (b) Data set II

Fig. 10. Robustness performance comparison

Generalization. Generalization performance refers to the capacity of a model to forecaste load beyond the training set. This experiment is performed on the test set. According to Fig. 11, the generalization error fluctuation of the PL-LSTM-SVR is the smallest, with accuracy improvement up to 6.91% on data set I and 1.89%-7.02% on data set II. Table 2 reveals the generalization performance of all four models. The MAE, RMSE, MAPE, and CVRMSE of the PL-LSTM-SVR model are 110.18, 146.44, 8.6%, and 10.53%, respectively, on data set I, and 59.19, 68.06, 5.94%, and 10.51%, respectively, on data set II. For data set I, LSTM, RF, and GBDT have lower MAPE than PL-LSTM-SVR though, PL-LSTM-SVR performs better on other metrics. Similarly on data set II, the SVR model performs better than PL-LSTMLSVR on MAE, yet worse on the other metrics. In general, the PL-LSTM-SVR model shows better generalization performance compared to the other four models.

Table 2. Generalization metrics

Data set	Metrics	PL-LSTM-SVR	LSTM	SVR	RF	GBDT
Data set I	R^2	0.96	0.93	0.75	0.96	0.94
	MAE (kW)	110.18	120.63	254.78	110.71	120.89
	RMSE (kW)	146.44	178.44	367.9	177.6	182.6
	MAPE (%)	8.6	8.59	15.51	6.43	7.44
	CVRMSE (%)	10.53	12.83	26.46	12.77	13.13
Data set II	R^2	0.8	0.77	0.79	0.76	0.73
	MAE (kW)	59.19	62.5	57.28	63.77	61.91
	RMSE (kW)	68.06	72.97	68.9	74.56	78.26
	MAPE (%)	9.54	10.21	9.72	10.15	9.55
	CVRMSE (%)	10.51	11.27	10.64	11.51	12.09

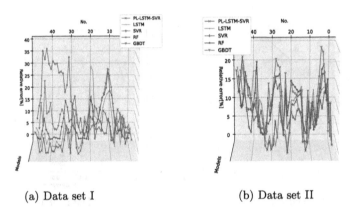

(a) Data set I   (b) Data set II

Fig. 11. Generalization performance comparison

4   Conclusion

In this paper, a PL-LSTM-SVR approach for short-term building load fore-casting is proposed, under the framework of patch learning. The LSTM network, which is employed as the global model, and the SVR algorithm, which is employed as the patch model, are combined both in series and parallel. Comparing with the standard PL, some revisions are introduced for the time series forecasting problem. For the patch locations identification, the infinity norm measurements are employed instead of SSE, and the patch models are updated via a joint training set adopted from both the global model training data and patch model validation data. In addition, EGA and grid search method are employed for the hyperparameter tuning for global model and patch models, respectively. In the end, case studies on two different data sets are developed with four other advanced building load forecasting models considering accuracy, robustness, and generalization performance. The experiments results show that the PL-LSTM-SVR model achieves better performance in accuracy, robustness and generalization than any of the other four models. The proposed PL-LSTM-SVR model can enrich data-driven model alternatives of short-term building load forecasting and explore the application of patch learning in the field of time series forecasting.

Acknowledgement. This research is supported by the National Nature Science Foundation of China [grant numbers 61803162].

References

1. Baldwin, A.N., Loveday, D.L., Li, B., Murray, M., Yu, W.: A research agenda for the retrofitting of residential buildings in china - a case study. Energy Policy **113**, 41–51 (2018). https://doi.org/10.1016/j.enpol.2017.10.056
2. Bishop, C.M.: Neural Networks for Pattern Recognition. Oxford University Press, New York (1995)
3. BP: bp energy outlook: 2020 edition (2020)
4. Bui, D.K., Nguyen, T.N., Ngo, T.D., Nguyen-Xuan, H.: An artificial neural network (ANN) expert system enhanced with the electromagnetism-based firefly algorithm (EFA) for predicting the energy consumption in buildings. Energy **190**, 116370 (2020). https://doi.org/10.1016/j.energy.2019.116370
5. Chaouachi, A., Kamel, R.M., Andoulsi, R., Nagasaka, K.: Multiobjective intelligent energy management for a microgrid. IEEE Trans. Industr. Electron. **60**(4), 1688–1699 (2013). https://doi.org/10.1109/TIE.2012.2188873
6. Chitalia, G., Pipattanasomporn, M., Garg, V., Rahman, S.: Robust short-term electrical load forecasting framework for commercial buildings using deep recurrent neural networks. Appl. Energy **278**, 115–410 (2020). https://doi.org/10.1016/j.apenergy.2020.115410
7. Dong, B., Li, Z., Rahman, S.M., Vega, R.: A hybrid model approach for forecasting future residential electricity consumption. Energy Build. **117**, 341–351 (2016). https://doi.org/10.1016/j.enbuild.2015.09.033
8. Fan, C., Wang, J., Gang, W., Li, S.: Assessment of deep recurrent neural network-based strategies for short-term building energy predictions. Appl. Energy **236**, 700–710 (2019). https://doi.org/10.1016/j.apenergy.2018.12.004
9. Holland, J.H.: An introductory analysis with applications to biology, control, and artificial intelligence. In: Adaptation in Natural and Artificial Systems. University of Michigan Press, Ann Arbor (1975)
10. IEA: Buildings (2020)
11. Kim, Y., Gu Son, H., Kim, S.: Short term electricity load forecasting for institutional buildings. Energy Rep. **5**, 1270–1280 (2019). https://doi.org/10.1016/j.egyr.2019.08.086
12. LeCun, Y., Bengio, Y., Hinton, G.: Deep learning. Nature (2015). https://doi.org/10.1038/nature14539
13. Li, K., Xie, X., Xue, W., Dai, X., Chen, X., Yang, X.: A hybrid teaching-learning artificial neural network for building electrical energy consumption prediction. Energy Build. **174**, 323–334 (2018). https://doi.org/10.1016/j.enbuild.2018.06.017
14. Liu, G., Li, X., Tan, Y., Zhang, G.: Building green retrofit in China: policies, barriers and recommendations. Energy Policy **139**, 111356 (2020). https://doi.org/10.1016/j.enpol.2020.111356

15. Massaoudi, M., Refaat, S.S., Chihi, I., Trabelsi, M., Oueslati, F.S., Abu-Rub, H.: A novel stacked generalization ensemble-based hybrid LGBM-XGB-MLP model for short-term load forecasting. Energy **214**, 118874 (2021). https://doi.org/10.1016/j.energy.2020.118874

16. Mat Daut, M.A., Hassan, M.Y., Abdullah, H., Rahman, H.A., Abdullah, M.P., Hussin, F.: Building electrical energy consumption forecasting analysis using conventional and artificial intelligence methods: a review. Renew. Sustain. Energy Rev. **70**, 1108–1118 (2017). https://doi.org/10.1016/j.rser.2016.12.015

17. Rosenow, J., Cowart, R., Bayer, E., Fabbri, M.: Assessing the European union's energy efficiency policy: will the winter package deliver on 'efficiency first'? Energy Res. Soc. Sci. **26**, 72–79 (2017). https://doi.org/10.1016/j.erss.2017.01.022

18. Smola, A.J., Schlkopf, B.: A tutorial on support vector regression. Stat. Comput. **14**(3), 199–222 (2004)

19. Somu, N., Gauthama Raman, M.R., Ramamritham, K.: A hybrid model for building energy consumption forecasting using long short term memory networks. Appl. Energy **261**, 114131 (2020). https://doi.org/10.1016/j.apenergy.2019.114131

20. Sun, Y., Haghighat, F., Fung, B.C.: A review of the-state-of-the-art in data-driven approaches for building energy prediction. Energy Build. **221**, 110022 (2020). https://doi.org/10.1016/j.enbuild.2020.110022

21. Tran, D.H., Luong, D.L., Chou, J.S.: Nature-inspired metaheuristic ensemble model for forecasting energy consumption in residential buildings. Energy **191**, 116552 (2020). https://doi.org/10.1016/j.energy.2019.116552

22. Wang, R., Lu, S., Feng, W.: A novel improved model for building energy consumption prediction based on model integration. Appl. Energy **262**, 114561 (2020). https://doi.org/10.1016/j.apenergy.2020.114561

23. Wang, Z., Wang, Y., Zeng, R., Srinivasan, R.S., Ahrentzen, S.: Random forest based hourly building energy prediction. Energy Build. **171**, 11–25 (2018). https://doi.org/10.1016/j.enbuild.2018.04.008

24. Wen, L., Zhou, K., Yang, S.: Load demand forecasting of residential buildings using a deep learning model. Electr. Power Syst. Res. **179**, 106073 (2020). https://doi.org/10.1016/j.epsr.2019.106073

25. Wu, D., Mendel, J.M.: Patch learning. IEEE Trans. Fuzzy Syst. **28**(9), 1996–2008 (2020)

26. Yuan, Z., Wang, W., Wang, H., Mizzi, S.: Combination of cuckoo search and wavelet neural network for midterm building energy forecast. Energy **202**, 117728 (2020). https://doi.org/10.1016/j.energy.2020.117728

27. Zhang, F., Deb, C., Lee, S.E., Yang, J., Shah, K.W.: Time series forecasting for building energy consumption using weighted support vector regression with differential evolution optimization technique. Energy Build. **126**, 94–103 (2016). https://doi.org/10.1016/j.enbuild.2016.05.028

28. Zhong, H., Wang, J., Jia, H., Mu, Y., Lv, S.: Vector field-based support vector regression for building energy consumption prediction. Appl. Energy **242**, 403–414 (2019). https://doi.org/10.1016/j.apenergy.2019.03.078

29. Zhou, Z.H.: Ensemble Methods: Foundations and Algorithms. CRC Press (2012). https://doi.org/10.1201/b12207

Empirical Mode Decomposition Based Deep Neural Networks for AQI Forecasting

Wei Jiang, Yuxia Fu, Fabing Lin, Jing Liu, and Choujun Zhan[✉]

School of Electrical and Computer Engineering, Nanfang College Guangzhou, Guangzhou 510970, China

Abstract. The Air Quality Index (AQI) is a significant indicator that can intuitively reflect the levels of air pollution. Accurate forecasting of AQI will help governments control air pollution problems and prevent citizens from a smoggy environment. In this research, we propose a general hybrid model for short-term AQI forecasting. First, we adopt the Empirical Mode Decomposition (EMD) method to decompose historical AQI time series for extracting decomposed components as features. Then, the decomposed components of AQI and the concentration of other air pollutants, such as PM2.5, PM10 and etc., are utilized as input features to train 2 parallel 1D Convolutional neural networks (1DCNN). Finally, the output of the 1DCNN is adopted as input features for train a Long short-term memory (LSTM) network. Experimental based on datasets from 2 observation stations demonstrated that the proposed hybrid model performs the best results.

Keywords: Prediction modeling · Deep learning · Air quality · Time series forecasting

1 Introduction

With the development and progress of industrial civilization, mankind is facing many environmental crises: global warming, hazardous waste, depletion of resources, air pollution and etc. Millions of people die every year from diseases caused by exposure to outdoor air pollution [1,2]. China, developing rapidly in the past 20 years, has become increasingly serious about air pollution [3]. The Air Quality Index (AQI) is considered criteria that can evaluate air quality pollution [4]. Additionally, AQI is also an important indicator for reflecting and evaluating air quality. AQI is derived from six main pollutants: fine particulate matter (PM2.5), ozone (O_3), sulfur dioxide (SO_2), inhalable particulate matter (PM10), nitrogen dioxide (NO_2) and carbon monoxide (CO).

AQI (ranged in size from 0 to 500) measures the overall quality of air. Based on AQI, air quality can be divided into 6 classes, including good, moderate, light pollution, moderate pollution, heavy pollution and severe pollution. The AQI level provides a good reference for people's outdoor activities [5]. The lower

© Springer Nature Singapore Pte Ltd. 2021
H. Zhang et al. (Eds.): NCAA 2021, CCIS 1449, pp. 757–769, 2021.
https://doi.org/10.1007/978-981-16-5188-5_54

the level, the better the air quality, while the higher the level, the larger the value, the worse the air quality. Being able to predict the air pollution index is very important for people's outdoor activities. Therefore, a good method for forecasting AQI can help people prevent the harm caused by a smoggy environment [6].

During the past decade, plenty of researchers adopted Machine Learning (ML) and Deep Learning (DL) approaches to predict the concentration of air pollutants, such as PM2.5 and PM10 [7–10]. Previous studies indicated that DL approaches perform well in time series forecasting. Liu *et al.* adopted classical Machine Learning algorithms, including SVM and Random Forest (RF), to forecast AQI time series [11]. Similarly, SVM is also adopted to forecast AQI time series in Mexico [12]. A new approach based on neural networks and optimal stochastic variables is developed for AQI forecasting [13]. In [14], an improved model based on LSTM and a full-connected neural network is developed for air quality forecasting. A Kalman Filter-based LSTM model is also developed for AQI forecasting [15]. Other researchers also developed different ML methods for AQI prediction [16,17].

In most realistic scenarios, classical machine learning methods can not provide good performance in predicting complicated time series, especially in some complicated nonlinear systems, such as wind speed [18] and rainfall [19]. Therefore, a hybrid model is always required in the task of time series forecasting. In [20], a hybrid model based on 1DCNN and Binary Gated Recurrent Unit (BGRU) is proposed for PM2.5 forecasting. Another way to construct a hybrid model is to combine a signal decomposition algorithm with historical data and a DL or ML model, such as a hybrid model [21] based on Wavelet Decomposition (WD) for short-term PM2.5 forecasting. Empirical Mode Decomposition (EMD) is a popular method for decomposing time series to extract the information of features [22]. In this study, we adopt both ways to construct a hybrid model based on EMD, 1D-CNN and LSTM. Furthermore, many studies have tried to discretize the continuous value, turn the regression task into a classification task [19,23,24], which performed a good result. Here, we also discretize the AQI time series and predict the AQI level.

The rest of this study goes as follows: In Sect. 2, we present the EMD algorithm, 1D-Convolutional layer and the proposed hybrid model. In Sect. 3, we describe the adopted dataset and conduct feature engineering. Section 3 also presents the experimental results of the proposed model and the comparative models, including 1DCNN, LSTM, CLSTM, EMD-1DCNN, EMD-LSTM, and EMD-CLSTM. The conclusion and future work is given in Sect. 4.

2   Methodologies

2.1   Empirical Mode Decomposition

Empirical Mode Decomposition (EMD), proposed by Huang *et al.* in 1996 [25], is an effective approach for decomposing signals based on Hilbert Huang transform

(HHT). Different from Fourier transform and wavelet transform, HHT decomposes signal by relying on the time scale features of the signal itself. Hence, EMD is suitable for analyzing non-linear and non-stationary signals. EMD will decompose the signal into several Intrinsic Mode Functions (IMFs).

In this study, we utilize EMD to decompose the historical AQI series $Y(t)$, to achieve a new part of features. Here, we define the $Y(t) = \{y(t), y(t-1), y(t-2), ..., y(t-n)\}$, where $n = 23$. Historical data is strictly used to avoid leaking feature information. The procedure is shown in Algorithm 1, and the main steps of EMD are as follows:

1. Initialize the given historical 24-h AQI series $Y(t)$ as the first signal $Y_0(t)$, namely, $Y_0(t) = Y(t)$, and settle the number of decomposed IMFs $k = 10$;
2. Link all the maximal points n_{max} in $Y_0(t)$ to form an upper envelope curve $u_0(t)$ and all the minimal points n_{min} to be a lower envelope curve $l_0(t-q)$;
3. Compute the mean envelope curve by Eq. (1), and then calculate the difference $d_0(t)$ between the $Y_0(t)$ and $m_0(t)$ by Eq. (2).

$$m_0(t) = \frac{1}{2}(u_0(t) + l_0(t)), \tag{1}$$

$$d_0(t) = Y_0(t) - m_0(t). \tag{2}$$

4. The $d_0(t)$ should satisfies with 2 requirements:
   a) For $d_0(t)$, the number of extremum n_e and the number of zero-crossings n_z have to satisfy with Eq. (3);

$$(n_z - 1) \leq n_e \leq (n_z + 1). \tag{3}$$

   b) Both averages of n_{max} and n_{min} equal to 0.
   Consider it as the first IMF $F_0(t) = d_0(t)$ when $d_0(t)$ is satisfied, if it not satisfies, then repeat the step 2 to 4 ;
5. Then, after obtaining the $F_0(t)$, repeat step 1 to 5 based on $F_0(t)$ to generate other IMFs. Finally, we will obtain several IMFs $F_0(t), F_1(t), F_2(t), ..., F_K(t)$, where $F_i(t) = \{f_i(t), f_i(t-1), f_i(t-2), ..., f_i(t-n)\}, n = 23$.

2.2   1D Convolutional Neural Network

1D (Dimension) Convolutional Neural Network (1DCNN), a kind of neural network, is able to extract the feature of 1 dimensional signals and widely utilized for dealing with word and time series. In this work, 1DCNN utilizes a 1D convolution kernel to process the historical 24 h AQI series $F(t)$ and air pollutants $X(t)$ in the convolution operation. The kernel focus to extract features instead of 24-hour time step while convoluting. Then, after the 1D convolution operation, the max pooling operation is used for generating the maximum values among columns extracted from the input features. The entire 1D convolution and max pooling operations are maintaining the length of 24-h time interval.

Algorithm 1. Empirical Mode Decomposition

Input: historical 24 hours AQI series $Y(t) = \{y(t), y(t-1), y(t-3), ..., y(t-n)\}$, where $n = 23$;

Output: IMFs $F_0(t), F_1(t), F_2(t), ..., F_k(t)$;

Initialization:

Set the AQI series $Y(t)$ as the first signal $Y_0(t)$;

Set the number of IMFs $k = 10$;

The zero crossings number is n_z.

1: **for** $i = 1$ to k **do**

2:    link all maximal and minimal points n_{max} and n_{min} of $Y_0(t)$, and $n_e = n_{max} + n_{min}$;

3:    Connect all n_{max} and n_{min} to be an upper envelope curve $u_0(t)$ and a lower envelope curve $l_0(t)$;

4:    $m_0(t) = \frac{1}{2}(u_0(t) + l_0(t))$

5:    $d_0(t) = Y_0(t) - m_0(t)$

6:    **if** $[(n_z - 1) \le n_e \le (n_z + 1)$ & $avg(n_{max}) + avg(n_{min}) = 0]$ **then**

7:        $F_i(t) = d_0(t)$;

8:        $y_0 = F_i(t)$;

9:    **end if**

10: **end for**

11: **return** IMFs $F_0(t), F_1(t), F_2(t), ..., F_k(t)$, where $F_i(t) = \{f_i(t), f_i(t-1), f_i(t-2), ..., f_i(t-n)\}, n = 23$.

In details, assume that the inputted feature set $F(t)$ or $X(t)$ with the size $(n+1) \times m$, where the $(n+1)$ is the length of time step and m is the number of features. Then, the original size of feature set $m \times (n+1)$ converts to $(n+1) \times c$, where the c is the number of new features after 1D convolution operation. Finally, the size of feature set after max pooling is $(n+1) \times p$, where p is the number of new features after max pooling.

2.3   The Proposed EMD-Hybrid Model

The proposed EMD-hybrid Neural Network is based on the 1DCNNs and LSTMs. The flowchart of the proposed model is shown in Fig. 1 and 2. The one-hour ahead predicted AQI ($y(t+1)$) are utilized as label while training the model. Additionally, the predicted AQI $Y(t+1)$ in each sample is discretized as 6 classes $c_1(t+1), c_2(t+1), ..., c_6(t+1)$ (details in Sect. 3.1).

In details, the proposed model consists of three parts. Part 1 adopts the EMD (Algorithm 1) to decompose historical 24 h AQI time series ($Y(t)$) into IMFs ($F(t)$) (shown in Eq. (5)). Then, the IMFs and historical air pollutant features $X(t)$ (shown in Eq. (4), including PM2.5, PM10, CO, SO_2, NO_2), are input to 1DCNNs and pooling layers (Part 2). The outputs from max pooling layers are combined and reshaped as new features. In part 3, new features from pooling layers input into LSTMs. Which provide the recombined results. Finally, we obtain the ultimate classification result by a Softmax function from Eq. (6), where p_i is the probability of classes, o are outputs from the last layer.

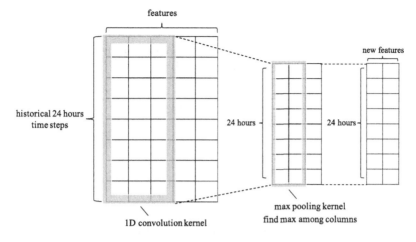

Fig. 1. The procedure of 1D convolution

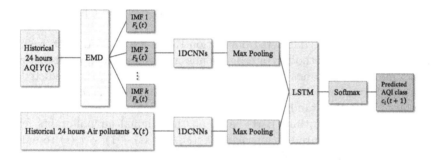

Fig. 2. The structure of EMD-hybrid model

$$X(t) = \begin{bmatrix} x_1(t) & x_2(t) & \dots & x_m(t) \\ x_1(t-1) & x_2(t-1) & \dots & x_m(t-1) \\ \vdots & \vdots & \ddots & \vdots \\ x_1(t-n) & x_2(t-n) & \dots & x_m(t-n) \end{bmatrix} \qquad (4)$$

$$F(t) = \begin{bmatrix} f_1(t) & f_2(t) & \dots & f_k(t) \\ f_1(t-1) & f_2(t-1) & \dots & f_k(t-1) \\ \vdots & \vdots & \ddots & \vdots \\ f_1(t-n) & f_2(t-n) & \dots & f_k(t-n) \end{bmatrix} \qquad (5)$$

$$p_i = \frac{exp(o_i)}{\sum_j exp(o_j)}. \qquad (6)$$

The error between outputted probabilities p_i and true classes $c_i(t+1)$ are computed with the Cross Entropy function Eq. (7). Moreover, the regularization item $\lambda \sum_{i=1}^{M} w_j^2$ is added, where the λ is the parameter of L_2. Here, we found that when $\lambda = 0.001$, the method provides a better result.

$$l(w) = -\sum_{i=1}^{k} c_i(t+1) \ln(p_i(t+1)) + \lambda \sum_{j=1}^{M} w_j^2. \tag{7}$$

3   Experimental Results

3.1   Dataset and Preprocessing

The adopted dataset in this study is provided by China National Environmental Monitoring Centre (CNEMC), from May 17, 2014 to June 10, 2019, including hourly Air Quality Index (AQI) and hourly indicators of 6 air pollutants: PM2.5, PM10, SO_2, NO_2, CO, O_3. In this study, we mainly adopt 2 air quality observation stations 1350A and 1128A from Guangzhou city and Changchun city as illustrative examples.

We preprocess the 2 datasets from station 1350A and 1128A. First, we utilize linear interpolation method to interpolate missing values. Then, we discretize the dataset into one-hour ahead predicted AQI series. In details, the predicted AQI series $y(t+1)$ can be divide into 6 classes, $\{c_1(t+1), c_2(t+1), \ldots, c_6(t+1)\}$ (shown in Table 1) with the standard of the Ministry of Ecology and Environment of the China [26]. In the third part, based on the original air pollutants feature $x_i(t)$ we utilize 3 feature enhancements $x_i^2(t), ln(x_i(t)+1), \sqrt{x_i(t)}$ to enhance air pollutant features. Finally, these features are standardized.

Table 1. AQI levels standard

Level class	Range	Notation
Excellent	$0 < Y(t) \le 50$	$c_1(t)$
Good	$50 < Y(t) \le 100$	$c_2(t)$
Lightly Polluted	$100 < Y(t) \le 150$	$c_3(t)$
Moderately Polluted	$150 < Y(t) \le 200$	$c_4(t)$
Heavily Polluted	$200 < Y(t) \le 300$	$c_5(t)$
Severely Polluted	$300 < Y(t)$	$c_6(t)$

3.2   Evolution Criteria

A multi-classification task can be considered as multiple binary classifications, the confusion matrix of multi-classification task can be defined as Table 2, compare the prediction AQI class $p_i(t+1)$ with the true AQI class $c_i(t+1)$ and

Table 2. Confusion matrix

Confusion matrix	Prediction					
	0	1	2	3	4	5
True 0	T_0^0	F_0^1	F_0^2	F_0^3	F_0^4	F_0^5
1	F_1^0	T_1^1	F_1^2	F_1^3	F_1^4	F_1^5
2	F_2^0	F_2^1	T_2^2	F_2^3	F_2^4	F_2^5
3	F_3^0	F_3^1	F_3^2	T_3^3	F_3^4	P_3^5
4	F_4^0	F_4^1	F_4^2	F_4^3	T_4^4	F_4^5
5	F_5^0	F_5^1	F_5^2	F_5^3	F_5^4	T_5^5

judge whether the prediction is true or false. The T_i^j stands for true predictions, F_i^j is a false prediction, and i, j represents actual AQI and the predicted AQI.

Based on confusion matrix, 4 criteria are adopted to evaluate different predictive methods.

1. Accuracy: This indicator stands for the rate of true predictions T in all prediction samples. The formula of Accuracy is defined as:

$$Accuracy = \frac{T}{T + F}. \tag{8}$$

2. macro-Precision: Precision is the proportion of the target classes in the evaluation of the captured classes, and then average the Precision from each class sample to obtain macro-Precision.

$$macro\text{-}Precision = \frac{1}{n} \sum_{k=0}^{n} \frac{T_k^k}{\sum_i F_i^k + T_k^k}. \tag{9}$$

3. Recall: Recall-rate means that recalling the percentage of target classes from the focus range, then average the Recall of each sample to obtain macro-Recall.

$$macro\text{-}Recall = \frac{1}{n} \sum_{k=0}^{n} \frac{T_k^k}{\sum_j F_k^j + T_k^k}. \tag{10}$$

4. macro-F1: F1-Measure is the synthesis of Precision and Recall, which is the score of weighted F-Measure, and the weight α is 1. Then, we also average F1 measure to obtain the macro-F1.

$$macro\text{-}F1 = \frac{1}{n} \sum_{k=0}^{n} \frac{(\alpha^2 + 1)T_k^k}{\sum_i F_i^k + \sum_j F_k^j + 2T_k^k}, (\alpha = 1). \tag{11}$$

3.3 Comparative Models

In this study, we adopt several comparative models to compare with the performance of the proposed model. Figure 3 shows the 2 training feature sets, IMFs

$F(t)$ of historical AQI series and historical air pollutants $X(t)$, and 3 comparative models. Then, we can utilize different feature set to different models, which
means each model may have 2 different choices of feature sets. For instance,
we input historical air pollutant features to 1DCNNs. Otherwise, if we input
IMFs to 1DCNNs, then the model is called EMD-1DCNN because we adopted
the EMD in this model. Finally, we compose 6 combination models: 1DCNN,
LSTM, CLSTM, EMD-1DCNN, EMD-LSTM, EMD-CLSTM, the information
of these models is shown in Table 3.

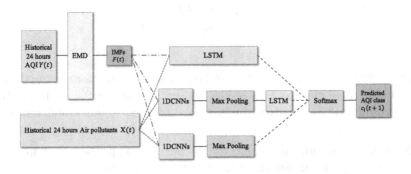

Fig. 3. The combinations of comparative models

Table 3. Comparative models

Model name	Feature set	Model combination
1DCNN	Historical air pollutants	1DCNNs + Max Pooling
LSTM	Historical air pollutants	LSTM
CLSTM	Historical air pollutants	1DCNNs + LSTM
EMD-1DCNN	Historical IMFs	EMD + 1DCNNs + Max Pooling
EMD-LSTM	Historical IMFs	EMD + LSTM
EMD-CLSTM	Historical IMFs	EMD + 1DCNNs + Max Pooling + LSTM

3.4 Forecasting Results

To study and test the ability of the models to forecast AQI levels, we adopt 2
datasets recorded by two observation stations (1350A in Guangzhou and 1128A
in Changchun). For each case, the dataset has been prepossessed and divided into
two subsets: training set (70% records) and testing set (30% records). In order
to assess the performance of the proposed technique (EMD-hybrid), we adopted
6 comparative models to evaluate the results. We employed 1DCNN, LSTM,
CLSTM, EMD-1DCNN, and EMD-LSTM, EMD-CLSTM). For each model, we
utilized grid searching to find the best hyper-parameters (shown in Table 4).

Table 4. Parameter configurations of models

Model	Basic settings		Learning rate	Dropout	L2
	Hidden layer	Neuron			
1DCNN	2	24,24	0.01	0	0.001
LSTM	3	128,128,128	0.01	0.2	0.001
CLSTM	2+3	24*2,128*3	0.01	0.2	0.001
EMD-1DCNN	2	24,24	0.01	0	0.001
EMD-LSTM	3	128,128,128	0.01	0.2	0.001
EMD-CLSTM	2+3	24*2,128*3	0.01	0.2	0.001
EMD-hybrid (Proposed)	2+2+3	24*2,24*2,128*3	0.01	0.2	0.001

In this study, each model trains 50 times, which means we totally train 2,000 different models. Then, the average value of the 4 evaluation criteria are shown in Table 5. Figure 4 shows the mean value and 95% CI of the 4 criteria of the 7 different methods.

Table 5. Evaluation scores of models in each dataset

Model	Guangzhou 1350A				Changchun 1128A			
	Accuracy	Precision	Recall	F1	Accuracy	Precision	Recall	F1
1DCNN	0.8765	0.7291	0.5841	0.6339	0.8363	0.6836	0.6415	0.6557
LSTM	0.8768	0.7146	0.5937	0.6268	0.8390	**0.7195**	0.6655	0.6805
CLSTM	0.8755	0.7430	0.6190	0.6544	0.8345	0.6940	0.6694	0.6758
EMD-1DCNN	0.7443	0.5741	0.6741	0.6008	0.5991	0.4273	0.5715	0.4503
EMD-LSTM	0.8280	0.6943	0.7357	0.6970	0.7133	0.6459	0.6359	0.6177
EMD-CLSTM	0.8169	0.7225	**0.7671**	0.7312	0.7971	0.6989	0.7168	0.7004
EMD-hybrid	**0.8790**	**0.7794**	0.7617	**0.7537**	**0.8528**	0.7040	**0.7441**	**0.7207**

The experimental results indicate that the proposed EMD-hybrid model performs 6 best scores out of 56 scores (4 criteria per dataset of 7 different methods). We record all the evaluation results of each model after 50 times tests, and then calculate the average values of these results. Table 5 shows the average evaluation results of each model in 2 observation stations.

In Table 5, the prediction results of dataset from station 1350A (Guangzhou), the average results of 3 scores accuracy, precision, recall are the highest. The average accuracy score is 0.8790, precision score is 0.7794 and F1 score is 0.7537. The prediction results of dataset from station 1128 (Changchun), also performs the 3 highest scores, accuracy, recall and F1 score, the accuracy score is 0.8528, recall score is 0.7441 and F1 score is 0.7207.

The models utilize the EMD algorithm and IMFs feature set perform the highest recall and F1 scores in the datasets from station 1350A. The recall scores of EMD-CLSTM and EMD-LSTM models are 0.7671 (highest) and 0.7312. The recall and F1 scores of EMD-CLSTM model are higher than other models, except the proposed model. However, the accuracy and precision of EMD-based models are not high, which means if only input historical IMFs to the model, the performances are not accurate. The model combining historical IMFs and historical air pollutants can obtain an accurate result and perform high recall and F1 scores.

These results are summarized in Fig. 4, the thin black bars on the color bars stand for 95% CI. In Fig. 4(a) and Fig. 4(b), the proposed model (blue bar) is the most accurate model in all cases, the 95% CI results of the proposed model are stable in each score of each dataset from stations.

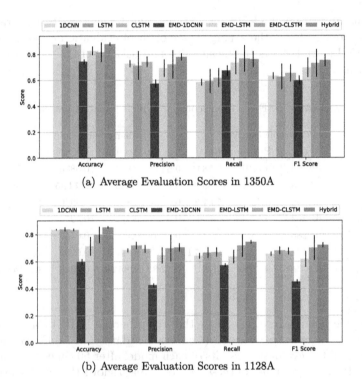

(a) Average Evaluation Scores in 1350A

(b) Average Evaluation Scores in 1128A

Fig. 4. Average evaluation scores in different cases. Different bar with different color stands for different results of models. Pink, red, orange, yellow, gray, cyan and blue are the results of 1DCNN, LSTM, CLSTM, EMD-1DCNN, EMD-LSTM, EMD-CLSTM and the proposed model. The black thin bar stands for 95% CI. (Color figure online)

4   Conclusion

Air Quality Index (AQI) forecasting is an essential issue in air pollution problem solving, attracting lots of attention. In this paper, we propose a novel EMD-hybrid model for AQI classes forecasting based on Empirical Mode Decomposition (EMD), 1D Convolution Neural Network (1DCNN) and Long Short-term Memory Neural Network (LSTM). To examine the ability of the proposed EMD-hybrid model, 2 datasets recorded from 2 cities of China, which are Changchun and Guangzhou, are adopted to predict one-hour ahead AQI classes.

Above all, the datasets are preprocessed with a series of data preprocessing procedures: interpolation, feature enhancement, and standardization; the predicted AQI is discretized into 6 classes. Then, in the experimental results, compared with 6 comparative models including 1DCNN, LSTM, CLSTM, EMD-1DCNN, EMD-LSTM, and EMD-CLSTM, the proposed EMD-hybrid model can achieve a better forecasting performance with the maximum of accuracy score, precision score and F1 score in Guangzhou case, and the maximum of accuracy, recall and F1 scores in Changchun case.

In future work, air pollution prediction based on deep learning algorithms using more correlated features like weather conditions, human activities, wind speed and direction will be researched for more complex air pollution forecasting. Besides, we will adopt and compare more different decomposing algorithms in the model for air pollution time series prediction.

Acknowledgments. This work was supported by Natural Science Foundation of Guangdong Province, China (2020A1515010761), Science and Technology Program of Guangzhou, China (201904010224), and National Science Foundation of China Project 72004174.

References

1. Lee, B.-J., Kim, B., Lee, K.: Air pollution exposure and cardiovascular disease. Toxicol. Res. **30**(2), 71–75 (2014). https://doi.org/10.5487/TR.2014.30.2.071
2. Cohen, A.J., et al.: Estimates and 25-year trends of the global burden of disease attributable to ambient air pollution: an analysis of data from the global burden of diseases study 2015. Lancet **389**(10082), 1907–1918 (2017)
3. Xing, Y.-F., Xu, Y.-H., Shi, M.-H., Lian, Y.-X.: The impact of PM2. 5 on the human respiratory system. J. Thorac. Dis. **8**(1), E69 (2016)
4. Nigam, S., Rao, B.P.S., Kumar, N., Mhaisalkar, V.A.: Air quality index-a comparative study for assessing the status of air quality. Res. J. Eng. Technol. **6**(2), 267–274 (2015)
5. Massey, D., Masih, J., Kulshrestha, A., Habil, M., Taneja, A.: Indoor/outdoor relationship of fine particles less than 2.5 μm (PM2. 5) in residential homes locations in central Indian region. Build. Environ. **44**(10), 2037–2045 (2009)
6. Pearce, D.: Economic valuation and health damage from air pollution in the developing world. Energy Policy **24**(7), 627–630 (1996)

7. Mahajan, S., Chen, L.-J., Tsai, T.-C.: An empirical study of PM2. 5 forecasting using neural network. In: Proceedings of the 2017 IEEE SmartWorld, Ubiquitous Intelligence & Computing, Advanced & Trusted Computed, Scalable Computing & Communications, Cloud & Big Data Computing, Internet of People and Smart City Innovation (SmartWorld/SCALCOM/UIC/ATC/CBDCom/IOP/SCI), pp. 1–7. IEEE (2017)

8. Biancofiore, F., et al.: Recursive neural network model for analysis and forecast of PM10 and PM2. 5. Atmos. Pollut. Res. **8**(4), 652–659 (2017)

9. Zhu, H., Lu, X.: The prediction of PM2. 5 value based on ARMA and improved BP neural network model. In: Proceedings of the 2016 International Conference on Intelligent Networking and Collaborative Systems (INCoS), pp. 515–517. IEEE (2016)

10. Voukantsis, D., Karatzas, K., Kukkonen, J., Räsänen, T., Karppinen, A., Kolehmainen, M.: Intercomparison of air quality data using principal component analysis, and forecasting of PM10 and PM2. 5 concentrations using artificial neural networks, in Thessaloniki and Helsinki. Sci. Total Environ. **409**(7), 1266–1276 (2011)

11. Liu, H., Li, Q., Dongbing, Yu., Yu, G.: Air quality index and air pollutant concentration prediction based on machine learning algorithms. Appl. Sci. **9**(19), 4069 (2019)

12. Sotomayor-Olmedo, A., Aceves-Fernández, M.A., Gorrostieta-Hurtado, E., Pedraza-Ortega, C., Ramos-Arreguín, J.M., Emilio Vargas-Soto, J.: Forecast urban air pollution in Mexico City by using support vector machines: a kernel performance approach (2013)

13. Russo, A., Raischel, F., Lind, P.G.: Air quality prediction using optimal neural networks with stochastic variables. Atmos. Environ. **79**, 822–830 (2013)

14. Ao, D., Cui, Z., Gu, D.: Hybrid model of air quality prediction using k-means clustering and deep neural network. In: 2019 Chinese Control Conference (CCC), pp. 8416–8421. IEEE (2019)

15. Song, X., Huang, J., Song, D.: Air quality prediction based on LSTM-Kalman model. In: Proceedings of the 2019 IEEE 8th Joint International Information Technology and Artificial Intelligence Conference (ITAIC), pp. 695–699. IEEE (2019)

16. Zou, Z., Cai, T., Cao, K.: An urban big data-based air quality index prediction: a case study of routes planning for outdoor activities in Beijing. Environ. Plann. B: Urban Anal. City Sci. (2019). https://doi.org/10.1177/2399808319862292

17. Zhenghua, W., Zhihui, T.: Prediction of air quality index based on improved neural network. In: Proceedings of the 2017 International Conference on Computer Systems, Electronics and Control (ICCSEC), pp. 200–204. IEEE (2017)

18. Chen, J., Zeng, G.-Q., Zhou, W., Wei, D., Kang-Di, L.: Wind speed forecasting using nonlinear-learning ensemble of deep learning time series prediction and extremal optimization. Energy Convers. Manage. **165**, 681–695 (2018)

19. Zhan, C., Wu, F., Wu, Z., Tse Chi, K.: Daily rainfall data construction and application to weather prediction. In: Proceedings of the 2019 IEEE International Symposium on Circuits and Systems (ISCAS), pp. 1–5. IEEE (2019)

20. Tao, Q., Liu, F., Li, Y., Sidorov, D.: Air pollution forecasting using a deep learning model based on 1D convnets and bidirectional GRU. IEEE Access **7**, 76690–76698 (2019)

21. Cheng, Y., Zhang, H., Liu, Z., Chen, L., Wang, P.: Hybrid algorithm for short-term forecasting of PM2. 5 in China. Atmos. Environ. **200**, 264–279 (2019)

22. Zhu, S., Lian, X., Liu, H., Jianming, H., Wang, Y., Che, J.: Daily air quality index forecasting with hybrid models: a case in China. Environ. Pollut. **231**, 1232–1244 (2017)
23. Chen, Z., Ye, X., Huang, P.: Estimating carbon dioxide (CO2) emissions from reservoirs using artificial neural networks. Water **10**(1), 26 (2018)
24. Shaohua, X., Li, J., Liu, K., Lu, W.: A parallel GRU recurrent network model and its application to multi-channel time-varying signal classification. IEEE Access **7**, 118739–118748 (2019)
25. Huang, N.E., et al.: The empirical mode decomposition and the Hilbert spectrum for nonlinear and non-stationary time series analysis. Proc. R. Soc. Lond. Seri. A: Math. Phys. Eng. Sci. **454**(1971), 903–995 (1998)
26. MEP China. Technical regulation on ambient air quality index (on trial)(hj633-2012). China Environmental Science Press, Beijing, China (2012)

Author Index

Printed in the United States
by Baker & Taylor Publisher Services